T0233887

Lecture Notes in Computer Science 11928

More information about this series at http://www.springer.com/series/7410

Joseph K. Liu · Xinyi Huang (Eds.)

Network and System Security

13th International Conference, NSS 2019
Sapporo, Japan, December 15–18, 2019
Proceedings

 Springer

Editors
Joseph K. Liu
Monash University
Clayton, VIC, Australia

Xinyi Huang
Fujian Normal University
Fuzhou, China

Preface

This volume contains the papers presented at the 13th International Conference on Network and System Security (NSS 2019) held in Sapporo, Japan, during December 15–18, 2019.

There were 89 submissions. Each submission was reviewed by at least 2, and on the average 2.8, Program Committee members. The committee decided to accept 36 full papers and 7 short papers. The program also included 4 invited papers to cover the hottest areas in cybersecurity.

We would like to thank our general chairs Chunhua Su, Jun Shao, Hiroaki Kikuchi, and Zhe Liu; our publication chairs Weizhi Meng and Thomas Tan; our web chair Yu Wang; the local organization team; and all the Program Committee members for their support to this conference. Without their tremendous effort, we could not have organized the conference successfully.

Finally, we also thank the University of Aizu and Zhejiang Gongshang University for their full support in organizing NSS 2019.

December 2019

Joseph K. Liu
Xinyi Huang

ISSN 0302-9743   ISSN 1611-3349   (electronic)
Lecture Notes in Computer Science
ISBN 978-3-030-36937-8   ISBN 978-3-030-36938-5   (eBook)
https://doi.org/10.1007/978-3-030-36938-5

LNCS Sublibrary: SL4 – Security and Cryptology

This Springer imprint is published by the registered company Springer Nature Switzerland AG
The registered company address is: Gewerbestrasse 11, 6330 Cham, Switzerland

Organization

Program Committee

Man Ho Au	The Hong Kong Polytechnic University, Hong Kong, China
Joonsang Baek	University of Wollongong, Australia
Zubair Baig	Deakin University, Australia
Chao Chen	Swinburne University of Technology, Australia
Fei Chen	Shenzhen University, China
Jiageng Chen	Central China Normal University, China
Xiaofeng Chen	Xidian University, China
Cheng-Kang Chu	Huawei, Singapore
Hui Cui	Murdoch University, Australia
Chunpeng Ge	Nanjing University of Aeronautics and Astronautics, China
Xinyi Huang	Fujian Normal University, China
Julian Jang-Jaccard	Massey University, New Zealand
Veronika Kuchta	Monash University, Australia
Miroslaw Kutylowski	Wrocław University of Science and Technology, Poland
Junzuo Lai	Jinan University, China
Li Li	Monash University, Australia
Kaitai Liang	University of Surrey, UK
Joseph Liu	Monash University, Australia
Shengli Liu	Shanghai Jiao Tong University, China
Jiqiang Lu	Beihang University, China
Rongxing Lu	University of New Brunswick, Canada
Xiapu Luo	The Hong Kong Polytechnic University, Hong Kong, China
Siqi Ma	CSIRO, Australia
Weizhi Meng	Technical University of Denmark, Denmark
Kazuhiko Minematsu	NEC Corporation, Japan
Chris Mitchell	Royal Holloway University of London, UK
Ruben Rios	University of Malaga, Spain
Jun Shao	Zhejiang Gongshang University, China
Chunhua Su	University of Aizu, Japan
Shi-Feng Sun	Monash University, Australia
Shamik Sural	Indian Institute of Technology, India
Willy Susilo	University of Wollongong, Australia
Ding Wang	Peking University, China
Hua Wang	Victoria University, Australia

Yu Wang	Guangzhou University, China
Ian Welch	Victoria University of Wellington, New Zealand
Ste en Wendzel	University of Applied Sciences, Worms and Fraunhofer FKIE, Germany
Qianhong Wu	Beihang University, China
Toshihiro Yamauchi	Okayama University, Japan
Guomin Yang	University of Wollongong, Australia
Yanjiang Yang	Huawei, Singapore
Wun-She Yap	Universiti Tunku Abdul Rahman, Malaysia
Jiangshan Yu	Monash University, Australia
Yong Yu	Shaanxi Normal University, China
Tsz Hon Yuen	The University of Hong Kong, Hong Kong, China
Lu Zhou	University of Aizu, Japan

Additional Reviewers

Al-Shaboti, Mohammed
Cui, Handong
Cui, Nan
Dai, Pingsuang
Enkhtaivan, Batnyam
Feng, Hanwen
Geeraerts, Gilles
Haseeb, Junaid
Isshiki, Toshiyuki
Li, Wanpeng
Li, Yiming
Li, Zengpeng
Liu, Mengjiang
Lu, Alex
Ma, Xinshu

Pan, Jing
Praitheeshan, Purathani
Qin, Xianrui
Shen, Jun
Sui, Zhimei
Tang, Wenyi
Wang, Hao
Wang, Jianfeng
Wang, Mingming
Wang, Shenqing
Wang, Yunling
Wu, Mingli
Yang, Hao
Zhang, Xiaoyu
Zhao, Liangrong

Contents

x   Contents

Short Papers

Invited Papers

Measuring Security of Symmetric Encryption Schemes Against On-the-Fly Side-Channel Key-Recovery Attacks

Bagus Santoso[1]([⊠]), Yasutada Oohama[1], and Chunhua Su[2]

[1] University of Electro-Communications, Tokyo, Japan
{santoso.bagus,oohama}@uec.ac.jp
[2] University of Aizu, Aizuwakamatsu, Japan
chsu@u-aizu.ac.jp

Abstract. In this paper, we propose a framework to analyze the security of symmetric encryption schemes against an adversary which attempts to recover the secret key by mounting side-channel attacks. In our adversarial side-channel model, the adversary is allowed to eavesdrop the public communication channel to obtain the ciphertexts and to collect on-the-fly some information about the secret keys of the scheme via measurement of certain physical phenomenon induced by the physical device, when the device is running the encryption process. Based on our framework, we derive the maximum success probability of the adversary to recover the secret keys. Our analysis does not assume any computation or storage limitation on the adversary and uses the bandwidths of the public communication channel and side-channel as the parameters. Hence, our results apply even in the case of quantum adversaries. Though in our framework the adversary does not have full control of the physical device, our framework is entirely independent of the type of physical phenomenon observed by the adversary and also of the method used by the adversary, which is interesting in its own right.

Keywords: Side-channel · One-helper source coding system · Mutual information

1 Introduction

Background and Motivation. There has been a tremendous rise in the deployment of small computing devices as parts of a computer network, e.g., internet of things (IoT), cyber-physical system (CPS). The merits and impacts of such network have been explored and well advertised. However, since small computing devices are usually lacking of protection on their own, the vulnerability of one device may affect the whole network. In order to guarantee the security of the whole network, we need to protect the devices connected to the network from two ways of attacks, i.e., the attacks from software side and the ones from the hardware or physical side. Especially, it is a challenging task to protect small devices

© Springer Nature Switzerland AG 2019
J. K. Liu and X. Huang (Eds.): NSS 2019, LNCS 11928, pp. 3–17, 2019.
https://doi.org/10.1007/978-3-030-36938-5_1

against physical attacks if they are scattered on certain location such as in a wireless sensor network (WSN). It is very costly to provide security surveillance for each device in such situation, and it is also very costly to put each device in a certain case strong enough against any tampering or observation from outside. Hence, one can consider that a small device implementing a cryptographic algorithm in such network is vulnerable to an adversary which attempts to collect information about secret keys or data stored in the device by probing physical phenomenon which are generated during the execution of cryptographic process.

Research Question. In this paper, we are focusing on devices which are implementing symmetric encryption schemes. We are considering an adversary which not only listens to the public communication channel and obtains the ciphertexts, but also attempts to extract the secret key stored in the device via *side-channel*, i.e., measurable physical phenomenon which are generated during the execution of encryption process. Physical phenomenon such as electro-magnetic (EM) radiation, power consumption, or response timing which are generated during the process of encryption may correlated to the value of the keys and/or plaintext used in the process and thus, by measuring those, one may obtain some additional information about the secret keys. Our main question is that: *"How much is the maximum success probability of such adversary to reveal the secret key, if we know the amount of information the adversary can extract from the side-channel?"*

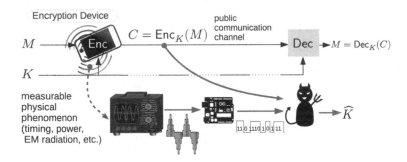

Fig. 1. On-the-fly side-channel key-recovery attack

Scope of Our Research

On-the-Fly Side-Channel Key-Recovery Attacks. The attacks the adversary can mount differ depending on how much an adversary has access to the physical device where the encryption scheme is deployed/implemented. In this research, we are focusing on the adversary who has no direct physical access to the device but can obtain the ciphertexts sent via the public communication channel and also to probe and measure the physical phenomenon generated by the encryption device during the process of encryption *on-the-fly*. And the goal of the adversary is to recover the secret key used by the encryption device. We call this model as *on-the-fly side-channel key-recovery attack*, or simply *n-the-fly side-channel attack*. We show the adversarial model diagram in Fig. 1. An adversary who has a more (physical) access to the physical device may perform side-channel attacks on the device offline, i.e., the adversary runs the encryption device on its own chosen plaintexts and obtains the corresponding ciphertexts while also measures the generated physical phenomenon. While the security against offline side-channel attacks is desirable, in this paper, we will put our focus on the on-the-fly side-channel attacks and put the offline side-channel attacks on hold as future research.

Generic Analysis of Side-Channel Attacks. In practical world, the success of an adversary on learning some secret information from the side-channel is greatly influenced by the type of physical phenomenon probed by the adversary and the sensitivity of the measurement device owned by the adversary. However, in the framework we use in this research, we can treat the type of the physical phenomenon probed by the adversary and the method used by the adversary to measure the phenomenon as a *black-box*, since we derive our results based on only the maximum amount of information the adversary can extract from the measurement. In short, our analysis results are robust and generic, in the sense that they can apply to any kind of side-channel adversary.

Overview of Our Methodology

In this paper, we are utilizing one-helper source coding system introduced by Ahlswede and Körner in [2] as the main tool for our analysis. In this system, two sources X and Y are encoded at two separate nodes into $\phi(X)$ and $\varphi(Y)$ respectively. Then, $\phi(X)$ and $\varphi(Y)$ are sent via communication channel to a sink node, in where an estimator/decoder function ψ generates an estimation $\widehat{X}$ of X based on $\phi(X)$ and $\varphi(Y)$. The system is illustrated in Fig. 2.

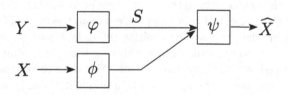

Fig. 2. One-helper system

As we will explain in later sections in this paper, we can treat the decoder ψ to represent the adversary which tries to obtain information about X from $\varphi(Y)$ and $\phi(X)$. We can treat X as the secret key, Y as the encryption scheme's plaintext and secret key pair and φ as the symmetric encryption scheme. And we can treat $\phi(X)$ as the entire process of probing the leaked information about X via side-channel and encoding the information into format or codes which the adversary can decode or process. First, we derive new upper-bounds on the success probability of decoder ψ in above system and then, we apply those upper bound to obtain the upper-bound of the success probability of the adversary on recovering the secret keys by mounting on-the-fly side-channel attack.

Related Works. The relation between the upper-bound of success decoding probability and the secrecy has been explored in the literature [11,13]. The upper-bound proposed in [13] is proven based on the assumption that the probability distribution of X and $\varphi(Y)$ are uniform and independent. And the upper-bound proposed in [11] is proven based on the assumption that the probability distribution of X is a uniform distribution. We are interested on deriving new upper-bounds without any assumption on the distribution of the sources. In this paper, we prove a couple of new upper-bounds without restricting the distribution of the sources. Our first bound is based on a certain variational distance and the second bound is based on mutual information.

Several theoretical models analyzing the security of a cryptographic system against side-channel attacks have been proposed in the literature. However, most of the existing works are applicable only for specific characteristics of the leaked physical information. For example, Brier et al. [4] and Coron et al. [5] propose a statistical model for side-channel attacks using the information from power consumption and the running time, whereas Agrawal et al. [1] propose a statistical model for side-channel attacks using electromagnetic (EM) radiations. A more general model for side-channel attacks is proposed by Köpf et al. [8] and Backes et al. [3], but they are heavily dependent upon implementation on certain specific devices. Micali et al. [9] propose a very general security model to capture the side-channel attacks, but they fail to offer any hint of how to build a concrete countermeasure against the side-channel attacks.

One of the close existing models to ours is the framework for analyzing side-channel attacks proposed by Standaert et al. [12]. However, the authors of [12] are focusing more on how to estimate the leakage function which represents the signals leaked by the device during the encryption process. Another model that is similar to ours in the sense that it is independent from the type of leaked physical information is the model proposed by Chérisey et al. However, their focus is more on how to model the noises which appear during the measurement of physical phenomenon induced by the encrypting device. We can treat the models shown in [6,7,12] as the complements of our model. In a nutshell, those models in [6,7,12] provide us: *the amount of information about secret keys a side-channel adversary can obtain via measurement*. Whereas, our model provides us: *the (total) success probability of an adversary to reveal the secret key using information from both public communication channel and side-channel, given the maximum amount of information it can obtain via measurement.*

2   Preliminaries

Let X and Y be two correlated discrete random variables representing two correlated sources. Let $\mathcal{X}$ and $\mathcal{Y}$ be discrete sets which are countably infinite and let X and Y take values from $\mathcal{X}$ and $\mathcal{Y}$ respectively. Now, consider a one-helper system which consists of:

- two encoders: $\phi : \mathcal{X} \to \mathcal{M}$ and $\varphi : \mathcal{Y} \to \mathcal{L}$, and
- an estimator/decoder $\psi : \mathcal{M} \times \mathcal{L} \to \mathcal{X}$.

Let consider the following system. Sources $X \in \mathcal{X}$ and $Y \in \mathcal{Y}$ are encoded separately into $\phi(X) \in \mathcal{M}$ and $\varphi(Y) \in \mathcal{L}$ respectively. Then, the estimator/decoder ψ generates an estimation $\widehat{X} \in \mathcal{X}$ of X based on $\phi(X)$ and $\varphi(Y)$. Let random variable S denote $\varphi(Y)$. Note that we have the following Markov's chain: $X \leftrightarrow Y \leftrightarrow S$.

Definition 1 (Success Decoding Probability). *Let $\phi : \mathcal{X} \to \mathcal{M}$, $\varphi : \mathcal{Y} \to \mathcal{L}$ be the encoders and $\psi : \mathcal{M} \times \mathcal{L} \to \mathcal{X}$ be the estimator/decoder in the system described above (Fig. 2). We define the following.*

$$P_c(\phi, \varphi, \psi | p_{XY}) := \Pr\left[\psi(\phi(X), \varphi(Y)) = X\right],$$

where (X, Y) takes values from $\mathcal{X} \times \mathcal{Y}$ according to a probability distribution p_{XY} which can be written as follows:

$$p_{XY} := \{p_{XY}(x, y)\}_{(x,y) \in \mathcal{X} \times \mathcal{Y}}.$$

We define the maximum success decoding probability as follows.

$$P_{c,\max}(p_{XY}) := \max_{\phi, \varphi, \psi} P_c(\phi, \varphi, \psi | p_{XY}).$$

The following proposition is shown and proven in Oohama [10]. For the sake of convenience, we rewrite the original proposition as follows.

Proposition 1 (Oohama [10]). *Let (X, Y) take values from $\mathcal{X} \times \mathcal{Y}$ according to a probability distribution p_{XY}. For any $\eta > 0$, the following holds.*

$$P_{c,\max}(p_{XY}) \leq p_{SX}\left\{ \log |\mathcal{M}| \geq \log \frac{1}{p_{X|S}(X|S)} - \eta \right\} + 2^{-\eta}. \tag{1}$$

3   Upper-Bounds of Success Decoding Probability

Here we state our results on deriving upper-bounds of success decoding probability. Our results are derived based on Proposition 1. The first result is the following proposition.

Proposition 2. *Let (X, Y) take values from $X \times Y$ according to a probability distribution p_{XY}. For any $\phi : X \to M$, $\varphi : Y \to L$, $\psi : M \times L \to X$ and any $\eta, \upsilon > 0$, the following holds.*

$$P_c(\phi, \varphi, \psi | p_{XY}) \leq p_{SX} \left\{ |p_{X|S}(X|S) - p_X(X)| \geq \frac{1}{2^\eta |M|} - \frac{1}{2^{\eta+\upsilon}} \right\}$$
$$+ p_X \left\{ p_X(X) > \frac{1}{2^{\eta+\upsilon}} \right\} + 2^{-\eta}.$$

Based on Proposition 2, we derive Theorems 1 and 2.

Theorem 1. *Let (X, Y) take values from $X \times Y$ according to a probability distribution p_{XY}. For any $\phi : X \to M$, $\varphi : Y \to L$, $\psi : M \times L \to X$, $\upsilon \in [\log(|M| + 1), \log \frac{1}{p_{max}})$, the following holds.*

$$P_c(\phi, \varphi, \psi | p_{XY}) \leq 2^\upsilon p_{max} + \frac{|M|}{p_{max}} \times \mathbb{E}_{SX} \left[|p_{X|S}(X|S) - p_X(X)| \right],$$

where $p_{max} := \max_{x \in X} p_X(x)$.

From Theorem 1, we obtain the following corollary.

Corollary 1. *Let (X, Y) take values from $X \times Y$ according to a probability distribution p_{XY}. For any $\upsilon \in [\log(|M| + 1), \log \frac{1}{p_{max}})$, the following holds.*

$$P_c(\phi, \varphi, \psi | p_{XY}) \leq 2^\upsilon p_{max} + |M| \times \sum_{\substack{x \in X \\ s \in L}} |p_X(x) - p_{X|S}(x|s)|, \qquad (2)$$

where $p_{max} := \max_{x \in X} p_X(x)$.

Theorem 2. *Let (X, Y) take values from $X \times Y$ according to a probability distribution p_{XY}. For any For any $\phi : X \to M$, $\varphi : Y \to L$, $\psi : M \times L \to X$, $\upsilon \in [\log(|M| + 1) + 2, \log \frac{1}{p_{max}})$, the following holds.*

$$P_c(\phi, \varphi, \psi | p_{XY}) < 2^{\upsilon+1} p_{max} + \frac{|L|}{(2^\upsilon - |M|) p_{max}} \times \sum_{\substack{x \in X \\ s \in L}} |p_{SX}(s, x) - p_S(s) p_X(x)|, \quad (3)$$

where $p_{max} := \max_{x \in X} p_X(x)$.

By applying Pinsker's inequality into the second term of Eq. (3) we obtain as follows.

Corollary 2. *Let (X, Y) take values from $X \times Y$ according to a probability distribution p_{XY}. For any For any $\phi : X \to M$, $\varphi : Y \to L$, $\psi : M \times L \to X$, $\upsilon \in [\log(|M| + 1), \log \frac{1}{p_{max}})$, the following holds.*

$$P_c(\phi, \varphi, \psi | p_{XY}) < 2^{\upsilon+1} p_{max} + \frac{|L|}{(2^\upsilon - |M|) p_{max}} \times \sqrt{2 \ln 2 \times I(X; S)}, \qquad (4)$$

where $p_{max} := \max_{x \in X} p_X(x)$.

Remark 1. Oohama [10] has derived a tighter upper-bound based on mutual information. However, several claims in the proof of the corresponding theorem have been left unproven.

4 Proof of the Main Results

In this section we will show the proof of theorems and corollaries presented in the previous section.

4.1 Proof of Proposition 2

First, we can rewrite Eq. (1) in Proposition 1 as follows.

$$P_{c,\max}(p_{XY}) \le p_{SX}\left\{\log|\mathcal{M}| \ge \log\frac{1}{p_{X|S}(X|S)} - \eta\right\} + 2^{-\eta}$$

$$\le p_{SX}\left\{\log|\mathcal{M}| + \eta \ge \log\frac{1}{p_{X|S}(X|S)}\right\} + 2^{-\eta}$$

$$\le p_{SX}\left\{2^\eta\,|\mathcal{M}| \ge \frac{1}{p_{X|S}(X|S)}\right\} + 2^{-\eta}$$

$$\le p_{SX}\left\{p_{X|S}(X|S) \ge \frac{1}{2^\eta\,|\mathcal{M}|}\right\} + 2^{-\eta}. \tag{5}$$

First, let us find the upper-bound of the probability $p_{SX}\left\{p_{X|S}(X|S) \ge \frac{1}{2^\eta|\mathcal{M}|}\right\}$ in Eq. (5).

$$p_{SX}\left\{p_{X|S}(X|S) \ge \frac{1}{2^\eta\,|\mathcal{M}|}\right\}$$

$$= p_{SX}\left\{\left(p_{X|S}(X|S) \ge \frac{1}{2^\eta\,|\mathcal{M}|}\right)\bigwedge\left(p_X(X) - p_{X|S}(X|S) > \frac{1}{2^{\eta+\upsilon}} - \frac{1}{2^\eta\,|\mathcal{M}|}\right)\right\}$$

$$+ p_{SX}\left\{\left(p_{X|S}(X|S) \ge \frac{1}{2^\eta\,|\mathcal{M}|}\right)\bigwedge\left(p_X(X) - p_{X|S}(X|S) \le \frac{1}{2^{\eta+\upsilon}} - \frac{1}{2^\eta\,|\mathcal{M}|}\right)\right\}$$

$$\overset{(a)}{\le} p_X\left\{p_X(X) > \frac{1}{2^{\eta+\upsilon}}\right\} + p_{SX}\left\{p_{X|S}(X|S) - p_X(X) \ge \frac{1}{2^\eta\,|\mathcal{M}|} - \frac{1}{2^{\eta+\upsilon}}\right\}$$

$$+ p_{SX}\left\{p_{X|S}(X|S) - p_X(X) \ge \frac{1}{2^\eta\,|\mathcal{M}|} - \frac{1}{2^{\eta+\upsilon}}\right\}$$

$$\overset{(b)}{\le} p_X\left\{p_X(X) > \frac{1}{2^{\eta+\upsilon}}\right\} + p_{SX}\left\{|p_{X|S}(X|S) - p_X(X)| \ge \frac{1}{2^\eta\,|\mathcal{M}|} - \frac{1}{2^{\eta+\upsilon}}\right\}. \tag{6}$$

It is easy to see that the transformation (*a*) above holds based on the following Lemma 1. The proof is shown in Appendix A.

Lemma 1. *For any random variable $A \in \mathcal{A}$, functions $f : \mathcal{A} \to \mathbb{R}, g : \mathcal{A} \to \mathbb{R}$, and real numbers $u, v \in \mathbb{R}$, the followings holds.*

$$p_A \{(f(A) \geqq u) \wedge (g(A) > v)\} \geqq p_A \{f(A) + g(A) > u + v\}. \tag{7}$$

It is also easy to see that the transformation (b) above holds based on the following Lemma 2. The proof is shown in Appendix B.

Lemma 2. *For any random variable $A \in \mathcal{A}$, functions $f : \mathcal{A} \to \mathbb{R}$, and a positive $u \in \mathbb{R}$, the following holds.*

$$p_A \{f(A) \geqq u\} \leqq p_A \{|f(A)| \geqq u\}.$$

This ends the proof of Proposition 2. □

4.2   Proof of Theorem 1

We prove Theorem 1 by continuing the proof of Proposition 2. Based on the assumption that $2^v \geqq |\mathcal{M}| + 1$, using Markov inequality on the second term of Eq. (6), we have the followings.

$$
\begin{aligned}
p_{SX} &\left\{ \left| p_{X|S}(X|S) - p_X(X) \right| \geqq \frac{1}{2^\eta |\mathcal{M}|} - \frac{1}{2^{\eta+v}} \right\} \\
&\leqq \frac{1}{2^{-\eta}(|\mathcal{M}|^{-1} - 2^{-v})} \mathbb{E}_{SX} \left[\left| p_{X|S}(X|S) - p_X(X) \right| \right] \\
&= \frac{|\mathcal{M}| 2^{\eta+v}}{2^v - |\mathcal{M}|} \mathbb{E}_{SX} \left[\left| p_{X|S}(X|S) - p_X(X) \right| \right] \\
&\overset{(a)}{\leqq} |\mathcal{M}| 2^{\eta+v} \mathbb{E}_{SX} \left[\left| p_{X|S}(X|S) - p_X(X) \right| \right],
\end{aligned}
\tag{8}
$$

where the transformation (a) holds since $2^v \geqq |\mathcal{M}| + 1$.

Now, let us set $2^{\eta+v} = \frac{1}{p_{\max}}$. Thus, for any $x \in \mathcal{X}$, it is impossible to have $p_X(x) > \frac{1}{2^{\eta+v}} = p_{\max}$. Applying this and Eq. (8) into Eq. (6), we can further upper-bound Eq. (5) as follows.

$$p_{SX} \left\{ p_{X|S}(X|S) \geqq \frac{1}{2^\eta |\mathcal{M}|} \right\} + 2^{-\eta} \leqq 2^v p_{\max} + \frac{|\mathcal{M}|}{p_{\max}} \mathbb{E}_{SX} \left[\left| p_{X|S}(X|S) - p_X(X) \right| \right]. \tag{9}$$

This ends the proof of Theorem 1. □

4.3 Proof of Corollary 1

We proof Corollary 1 by continuing the proof of Theorem 1. We can rewrite the second term of Eq. (9) as follows.

$$\frac{|M|}{p_{max}} \mathbb{E}_{SX}\left[|p_{X|S}(X|S) - p_X(X)|\right] = \frac{|M|}{p_{max}} \sum_{x \in X, s \in \mathcal{L}} p(s,x)|p_{X|S}(X|S) - p_X(X)|$$

$$= |M| \sum_{x \in X, s \in \mathcal{L}} \frac{1}{p_{max}} p(s,x)|p_{X|S}(X|S) - p_X(X)|$$

$$\leq |M| \sum_{x \in X, s \in \mathcal{L}} |p_{X|S}(X|S) - p_X(X)|.$$

The transformation to the last inequality holds since $p(s,x) = p(s|x)p(x) \leq p(x) \leq p_{max}$ holds. This ends the proof of Corollary 1. □

4.4 Proof of Theorem 2

Similar to the proof of Theorem 1, we start from rewriting the second term in Eq. (6) in the proof of Proposition 2.

$$p_{SX}\left\{|p_{X|S}(X|S) - p_X(X)| \geq \frac{1}{2^\eta |M|} - \frac{1}{2^{\eta+v}}\right\}$$

$$= p_{SX}\left\{\left(|p_{X|S}(X|S) - p_X(X)| \geq \frac{1}{2^\eta |M|} - \frac{1}{2^{\eta+v}}\right) \bigwedge \left(p_S(S) \geq \frac{1}{2^\eta|\mathcal{L}|}\right)\right\}$$

$$+ p_{SX}\left\{\left(|p_{X|S}(X|S) - p_X(X)| \geq \frac{1}{2^\eta |M|} - \frac{1}{2^{\eta+v}}\right) \bigwedge \left(p_S(S) < \frac{1}{2^\eta|\mathcal{L}|}\right)\right\}$$

$$\overset{(a)}{\leq} p_{SX}\left\{|p_{SX}(S,X) - p_X(X)p_S(S)| \geq \frac{1}{2^{2\eta}|\mathcal{L}|}\left(\frac{1}{|M|} - \frac{1}{2^v}\right)\right\}$$

$$+ p_S\left\{p_S(S) < \frac{1}{2^\eta|\mathcal{L}|}\right\} \tag{10}$$

It is easy to see that the transformation (a) holds based on the following Lemma 3. Note that $|p_{X|S}(X|S) - p_X(X)| \geq 0$ holds and since $2^v \geq |M| + 1$ holds, $\frac{1}{2^\eta|M|} - \frac{1}{2^{\eta+v}} \geq 0$ holds. The proof is shown in Appendix C.

Lemma 3. *For any random variable $A \in \mathcal{A}$, functions $f : \mathcal{A} \to \mathbb{R}_{\geq 0}, g : \mathcal{A} \to \mathbb{R}_{\geq 0}$, and real numbers $u, v \geq 0$, the followings holds.*

$$p_A\left\{f(A)g(A) \geq uv\right\} \geq p_A\left\{(f(A) \geq u) \wedge (g(A) \geq v)\right\}. \tag{11}$$

Now, let us focus on the first term in Eq. (10). Remind again that $|p_{X|S}(X|S) - p_X(X)| \geq 0$ holds and $\frac{1}{|M|} - \frac{1}{2^v} \geq 0$ holds thanks to $2^v \geq |M| + 1$. Thus, we can ply Markov's inequality and obtain as follows.

$$p_{SX}\left\{|p_{SX}(S,X) - p_X(X)p_S(S)| \geq \frac{1}{2^{2\eta}|\mathcal{L}|}\left(\frac{1}{|\mathcal{M}|} - \frac{1}{2^v}\right)\right\}$$

$$\leqq \frac{2^{\eta}2^{\eta+v}|\mathcal{M}||\mathcal{L}|}{(2^v - |\mathcal{M}|)}\mathbb{E}_{SX}\left\{|p_{SX}(S,X) - p_X(X)p_S(S)|\right\}. \tag{12}$$

Now, let us set $2^{\eta+v} = \frac{1}{p_{\max}}$. Thus, we obtain as follows.

$$\text{Eq. (12)} = \frac{|\mathcal{M}||\mathcal{L}|}{2^v\left(2^v - |\mathcal{M}|\right)p_{\max}^2}$$
$$\times \mathbb{E}_{SX}\left\{|p_{SX}(S,X) - p_X(X)p_S(S)|\right\}$$
$$\stackrel{(a)}{\leqq} \frac{|\mathcal{L}|}{(2^v - |\mathcal{M}|)p_{\max}^2} \times \sum_{\substack{x \in X \\ s \in \mathcal{L}}} p(s,x)\,|p_{SX}(S,X) - p_X(X)p_S(S)|$$
$$\stackrel{(b)}{\leqq} \frac{|\mathcal{L}|}{(2^v - |\mathcal{M}|)p_{\max}} \times \sum_{\substack{x \in X \\ s \in \mathcal{L}}} |p_{SX}(S,X) - p_X(X)p_S(S)|. \tag{13}$$

Transformation (a) holds since $2^v \geq |\mathcal{M}| + 1$. And transformation (b) holds since for all s, x, $p(s,x) \leqq p_{\max}$.

Now, let us focus on the second term of Eq. (10). First, let define the following set.

$$\mathcal{B} := \left\{s : p_S(s) < \frac{1}{2^{\eta}|\mathcal{L}|}\right\}$$

Since $\mathcal{B} \subsetneq \mathcal{L}$, we obtain the followings.

$$p_S\left\{p_S(S) < \frac{1}{2^{\eta}|\mathcal{L}|}\right\} = \sum_{s \in \mathcal{B}} p_S(s) < \frac{|\mathcal{B}|}{2^{\eta}|\mathcal{L}|} < \frac{1}{2^{\eta}} = 2^v p_{\max}. \tag{14}$$

Combining Eqs. (14) and (13) into Eq. (10) and apply it into Eq. (6), we obtain the Eq. (3). This ends the proof of Theorem 2. $\qquad\square$

5   Application to Security Against On-the-Fly Side-Channel Attacks

In this section, we show the application of our main results to the analysis of security against on-the-fly side-channel key-recovery attacks. We also discuss the intuitive meaning of the derived upper-bound of the success probability of the adversary.

We let the decoder ψ represent the decoder used by adversary $\mathcal{A}$ who launches on-the-fly side-channel attacks. We let X represent the cryptographic secret key

K, φ represent a cryptosystem and ϕ represent a channel which "leaks" the side-information of the key to the adversary $\mathcal{A}$. Thus, here S represents the ciphertext C. The inputs to the cryptosystem are represented by Y. W.l.o.g., we assume that Y contains the plaintext M and the secret key K. Note that Theorem 2 does not assume any relation between X and Y. This means that Theorem 2 and all its corollaries will still apply even when X and Y are correlated to each other. For the sake of simplicity, we define $p_{MK} := p_{XY}$ and let $\mathcal{Y}$ define the domain of $M\|K$, where "$a\|b$" represents the sequential concatenation of string a and string b (Fig. 3).

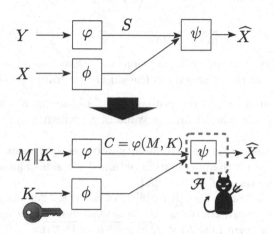

Fig. 3. Application to on-the-fly side-channel adversary model

It should be noted that here we do not put any assumption on ϕ other than ϕ is a mapping from $\mathcal{X}$ onto $\mathcal{M}$. The size of the image of the map ϕ, i.e., $|\mathcal{M}|$, represents the output of the best encoding scheme the adversary $\mathcal{A}$ can apply to the raw physical data/signals it collects from the devices to convert them into symbols $\mathcal{A}$ can process. Note that this formulation allows the case where the adversary $\mathcal{A}$ uses stochastic encoding scheme.

Remark 2. In this paper we assume that the decoder ψ used by adversary $\mathcal{A}$ is deterministic. However, this does not limit our result to only deterministic adversary, since the upper-bound of the correct probability of deterministic decoders are also the upper-bound of the correct probability of stochastic ones.

We can rewrite the Corollary 2 to fit our scenario as the following corollary.

Corollary 3. *Let $(K, M\|K)$ take values from $\mathcal{X} \times \mathcal{Y}$ according to a probability distribution p_{MK}. For any For any $\phi : \mathcal{K} \to \mathcal{M}$, $\varphi : \mathcal{Y} \to \mathcal{L}$, $\psi : \mathcal{M} \times \mathcal{L} \to \mathcal{K}$, $v \in [\log(|\mathcal{M}| + 1), \log \frac{1}{p_{\max}})$, the following holds.*

$$\mathrm{P}_c(\phi, \varphi, \psi | p_{MK}) < 2^{v+1} p_{\max} + \frac{|\mathcal{L}|}{(2^v - |\mathcal{M}|) p_{\max}} \times \sqrt{2 \ln 2 \times I(K; \varphi(M, K))}, \quad (15)$$

where $p_{\max} := \max\limits_{k \in \mathcal{X}} p_K(k)$. In particular, by setting $v := \log(|\mathcal{M}| + 1)$, we obtain the following.

$$P_c(\phi, \varphi, \psi | p_{MK}) < 2(|\mathcal{M}| + 1)p_{\max} + |\mathcal{L}|p_{\max} \times \sqrt{2 \ln 2 \times I(K; \varphi(M, K))}. \quad (16)$$

In order to understand the concrete meaning of Corollary 3, let us consider the case where the secret keys are chosen according to uniform distribution, i.e., $p_{\max} = 1/|\mathcal{X}|$. Hence, we can rewrite the Eq. (15) as follows.

$$P_c(\phi, \varphi, \psi | p_{MK}) < 2\frac{|\mathcal{M}| + 1}{|\mathcal{X}|} + \frac{|\mathcal{L}|}{|\mathcal{X}|}\sqrt{2 \ln 2 \times I(K; \varphi(M, K))}$$

$$= \frac{1}{|\mathcal{X}|} + \frac{2|\mathcal{M}| + 1}{|\mathcal{X}|} + \frac{|\mathcal{L}|}{|\mathcal{X}|}\sqrt{2 \ln 2 \times I(K; \varphi(M, K))}. \quad (17)$$

In informal way, the above inequation says that the upper-bound of the success probability of the adversary is the sum of several upper-bounds:

(1) The upper-bound of success probability of obtaining K via pure *random* guess (brute force search) on the value of K, which is represented by the term $1/|\mathcal{X}|$.
(2) The upper-bound of success probability of correctly guessing/obtaining the secret key based on the information obtained via side-channel which is represented by the term $(2|\mathcal{M}| + 1)/|\mathcal{X}|$.
(3) The upper-bound of success probability of correctly guessing/the secret key based on the ciphertexts obtained via public communication channel, represented by the term $|\mathcal{L}|/|\mathcal{X}| \times \sqrt{2 \ln 2 \times I(K; \varphi(M, K))}$.

Discussion. Recall that the size of $|\mathcal{M}|$ represents the maximum amount of information the adversary $\mathcal{A}$ can get via side-channel. Equation (17) clearly shows that the larger $|\mathcal{M}|$ is, the larger the upper-bound of adversary's success probability is. In general, $|\mathcal{M}|$ must be smaller than $|\mathcal{X}|$, as the adversary usually gets noisy data from the measurement. One can express $(2|\mathcal{M}| + 1)/|\mathcal{X}|$ as $1/(|\mathcal{X}|/(2|\mathcal{M}| + 1) = 1/O(|\mathcal{X}|/|\mathcal{M}|)$. We consider that it is interesting to see that the term $O(|\mathcal{X}|/|\mathcal{M}|)$ appears here. Assume that each symbol in $\mathcal{M}$ represents a subset of symbols in $\mathcal{X}$ such that the size of any subset is the same. This means that when K is chosen according to the uniform distribution, the best strategy that $\mathcal{A}$ can use to recover the secret key K from the result of measurement, i.e., $\phi(K) \in \mathcal{M}$, is simply to always pick one value of from $|\mathcal{X}|/|\mathcal{M}|$ possible values randomly according to uniform distribution. However, one may notice that our upper-bound is actually larger than $|\mathcal{M}|/|\mathcal{X}|$, i.e., $(2|\mathcal{M}| + 1)/|\mathcal{X}|$. This means that there might be another way to obtain a tighter upper-bound.

A similar argument can be applied also to the third term in Eq. (17), i.e., $|\mathcal{L}|/|\mathcal{X}| \times \sqrt{2 \ln 2 \times I(K; \varphi(M, K))}$, which corresponds to the success probability of $\mathcal{A}$ obtains the secret key K via the ciphertext $\varphi(M, K)$. It is interesting to see that the mutual information $I(K; \varphi(M, K))$ appears here. Intuitively, this indicates that if we can keep $I(K; \varphi(M, K))$ small enough, then we can reduce the success probability of adversary $\mathcal{A}$.

Acknowledgments. Bagus Santoso is supported by JSPS Kiban (C) 18K11292 and together with Yasutada Oohama, are supported by JSPS Kiban (B) 18H01438. Chunhua Su is supported by JSPS Kiban (B) 18H03240 and JSPS Kiban(C) 18K11298.

A Proof of Lemma 1

Let us define the followings.

$$W(A) = \begin{cases} 1 & \text{if } f(A)g(A) \geq uv, \\ 0 & \text{otherwise.} \end{cases}$$

$$U(A) = \begin{cases} 1 & \text{if } f(A) \geq u, \\ 0 & \text{otherwise.} \end{cases} \qquad V(A) = \begin{cases} 1 & \text{if } g(A) \geq v, \\ 0 & \text{otherwise.} \end{cases}$$

Now, let us rewrite Eq. (11).

$$
\begin{aligned}
p_A&(W(A) = 1) \\
&= p_A\left\{(W(A) = 1) \wedge (U(A) = 1) \wedge (V(A) = 1)\right\} \\
&\quad + p_A\left\{(W(A) = 1) \wedge \overline{((U(A) = 1) \wedge (V(A) = 1))}\right\} \\
&\geq p_A\left\{(W(A) = 1) \wedge (U(A) = 1) \wedge (V(A) = 1)\right\} \\
&= p_A\left\{(U(A) = 1) \wedge (V(A) = 1)\right\}.
\end{aligned}
$$

The last transformation is due to the fact that if $f(A) = u + \alpha$ and $g(A) = v + \beta$ hold for some $\alpha, \beta \geq 0$, then automatically $f(A)g(A) = (u + \alpha)(v + \beta) \geq uv + \alpha\beta + \alpha v + \beta u$ holds, since $\alpha\beta, \alpha v, \beta u \geq 0$. This ends the proof. $\qquad\square$

B Proof of Lemma 2

Let us define the following set.

$$S := \{\alpha \in \mathcal{A} : f(\alpha) \geq 0\}$$

Thus, we have as follows.

$$
\begin{aligned}
p_A&\{|f(A)| \geq u\} \\
&= p_A\{(|f(A)| \geq u) \wedge (A \in S)\} + p_A\{(|f(A)| \geq u) \wedge (A \in \mathcal{A}\backslash S)\} \\
&\overset{(a)}{\geq} p_A\{(f(A) \geq u) \wedge (A \in S)\} + p_A\{(f(A) \geq u) \wedge (A \in \mathcal{A}\backslash S)\} \\
&= p_A\{f(A) \geq u\}.
\end{aligned}
$$

The transformation (a) is due to the facts that:

- since $u > 0$, if $A \in \mathcal{A}\backslash S$, it is impossible to have $f(A) \geq u$,
- and if $A \in S$, $|f(A)| = f(A)$ by definition of S.

This ends the proof. $\qquad\square$

C   Proof of Lemma 3

Let us define the followings.

$$W(A) = \begin{cases} 1 & \text{if } f(A) + g(A) > u + v, \\ 0 & \text{otherwise.} \end{cases}$$

$$U(A) = \begin{cases} 1 & \text{if } f(A) \geq u, \\ 0 & \text{otherwise.} \end{cases} \qquad V(A) = \begin{cases} 1 & \text{if } g(A) > v, \\ 0 & \text{otherwise.} \end{cases}$$

Now, let us rewrite Eq. (7).

$$\begin{aligned} p_A(W(A) = 1) &= p_A\{(W(A) = 1) \wedge (U(A) = 1) \wedge (V(A) = 1)\} \\ &\quad + p_A\left\{(W(A) = 1) \wedge (\overline{(U(A) = 1) \wedge (V(A) = 1)})\right\} \\ &\geq p_A\{(W(A) = 1) \wedge (U(A) = 1) \wedge (V(A) = 1)\} \\ &= p_A\{(U(A) = 1) \wedge (V(A) = 1)\}. \end{aligned}$$

The last transformation is due to the fact that if $f(A) = u + \alpha$ and $g(A) = v + \beta$ hold for some $\alpha \geq 0$ and $\beta > 0$, then automatically $f(A) + g(A) = u + v + (\alpha + \beta) > u + v$ holds. This ends the proof.   □

References

1. Agrawal, D., Archambeault, B., Rao, J.R., Rohatgi, P.: The EM side—channel(s). In: Kaliski, B.S., Koç, K., Paar, C. (eds.) CHES 2002. LNCS, vol. 2523, pp. 29–45. Springer, Heidelberg (2003). https://doi.org/10.1007/3-540-36400-5_4
2. Ahlswede, R., Körner, J.: Source coding with side information and a converse for the degraded broadcast channel. IEEE Trans. Inf. Theory **21**(6), 629–637 (1975)
3. Backes, M., Köpf, B.: Formally bounding the side-channel leakage in unknown-message attacks. In: Jajodia, S., Lopez, J. (eds.) ESORICS 2008. LNCS, vol. 5283, pp. 517–532. Springer, Heidelberg (2008). https://doi.org/10.1007/978-3-540-88313-5_33
4. Brier, E., Clavier, C., Olivier, F.: Correlation power analysis with a leakage model. In: Joye, M., Quisquater, J.-J. (eds.) CHES 2004. LNCS, vol. 3156, pp. 16–29. Springer, Heidelberg (2004). https://doi.org/10.1007/978-3-540-28632-5_2
5. Coron, J., Naccache, D., Kocher, P.C.: Statistics and secret leakage. ACM Trans. Embed. Comput. Syst. **3**(3), 492–508 (2004)
6. de Chérisey, E., Guilley, S., Rioul, O., Piantanida, P.: Best information is most successful mutual information and success rate in side-channel analysis. IACR Trans. Cryptogr. Hardw. Embed. Syst. **2019**(2), 49–79 (2019). https://doi.org/10.13154/tches.v2019.i2.49-79
7. de Chérisey, E., Guilley, S., Rioul, O., Piantanida, P.: An information-theoretic model for side-channel attacks in embedded hardware. In: ISIT 2019 (2019)

8. Köpf, B., Basin, D.A.: An information-theoretic model for adaptive side-channel attacks. In: ACM Conference on Computer and Communications Security, pp. 286–296. ACM (2007)
9. Micali, S., Reyzin, L.: Physically observable cryptography. In: Naor, M. (ed.) TCC 2004. LNCS, vol. 2951, pp. 278–296. Springer, Heidelberg (2004). https://doi.org/10.1007/978-3-540-24638-1_16
10. Oohama, Y.: On a relationship between the correct probability of estimation from correlated data and mutual information. IEICE Trans. Fundam. Electron. Commun. Comput. Sci. **101–A**(12), 2205–2209 (2018). https://doi.org/10.1587/transfun.E101.A.2205
11. Santoso, B., Oohama, Y.: Information theoretic security for Shannon cipher system under side-channel attacks [†]. Entropy **21**(5), 469 (2019). https://doi.org/10.3390/e21050469
12. Standaert, F.-X., Malkin, T.G., Yung, M.: A unified framework for the analysis of side-channel key recovery attacks. In: Joux, A. (ed.) EUROCRYPT 2009. LNCS, vol. 5479, pp. 443–461. Springer, Heidelberg (2009). https://doi.org/10.1007/978-3-642-01001-9_26
13. Wyrembelski, R.F., Wiese, M., Boche, H.: Strong secrecy in bidirectional broadcast channels with confidential messages. IEEE Trans. Inf. Forensics Secur. **8**(2), 324–334 (2013)

Unsupervised Insider Detection Through Neural Feature Learning and Model Optimisation

Liu Liu[1], Chao Chen[1(✉)], Jun Zhang[1], Olivier De Vel[2], and Yang Xiang[1]

[1] School of Software and Electrical Engineering, Swinburne University of Technology, Hawthorn, VIC 3122, Australia
chaochen@swin.edu.au
[2] Department of Defence, Defence Science and Technology Group, Edinburgh, SA 5111, Australia

Abstract. The insider threat is a significant security concern for both organizations and government sectors. Traditional machine learning-based insider threat detection approaches usually rely on domain focused feature engineering, which is expensive and impractical. In this paper, we propose an autoencoder-based approach aiming to automatically learn the discriminative features of the insider behaviours, thus alleviating security experts from tedious inspection tasks. Specifically, a Word2vec model is trained with a corpus transformed from various security logs to generate event representations. Instead of manually selecting Word2vec model parameters, we develop an autoencoder-based "parameter tuner" for the model to produce an optimal feature set. Then, the detection is undertaken by examining the reconstruction error of an autoencoder for each transformed event using the Carnegie Mellon University (CMU) CERT Programs insider threat database. Experimental results demonstrate that our proposed approach could achieve an extremely low false-positive rate (FPR) with all malicious events identified.

Keywords: Insider threats · Data analytics · Deep autoencoder · Cyber security

1 Introduction

Insider threats are caused by people who reside within an organisation, which can result in irreparable damages and significant financial loss to the victim organisation [25]. According to the 2018 Clearswift Insider Threat Index (CITI) Annual Report [7], most security incidents are attributed to malicious insiders. Thus, it is critical to develop effective and efficient means to protect organisations from insider threats.

Supported by the Defence Science and Technology (DST) Group, Department of Defence, Australia.

© Springer Nature Switzerland AG 2019
J. K. Liu and X. Huang (Eds.): NSS 2019, LNCS 11928, pp. 18–36, 2019.
https://doi.org/10.1007/978-3-030-36938-5_2

Effective Insider threat detection can be challenging. Firstly, insiders are granted privileged, having accesses behind security mechanisms, which causes their malicious behaviours to be hard to detect. Insiders with direct organisational network access can help them obtain security policy knowledge. Therefore, they can evade detection by purposely covering their malicious actions. Secondly, modern IT infrastructure is becoming increasingly complex, generating a large amount of audit data which often overwhelms the few malicious insider footprints [24]. Furthermore, an insider attack may quietly persist for a long time, during which each malicious action is taken intermittently, resulting in weaker indicators of compromise (IoC). Hence, manual insider detection tasks can be time-consuming, labor-intensive and ineffective.

The existing insider threat detection approaches mainly rely on the domain knowledge provided by security experts [25]. The first type of approach is rule- or signature-based, which encodes each known attack vector precisely as a pre-determined rule. Any behaviour is labelled anomalous if it matches one or more rule [17,26,28]. This approach is generally good at detecting known insider attacks as long as proper domain knowledge is provided by security experts. However, rule-based approaches fail to deal with unknown or previously unseen insider attacks. The second approach uses statistical and machine learning based techniques [26,31,36]. Compared with rule-based approaches, less domain knowledge is required for statistical and machine learning approaches when extracting features, and they are often capable of detecting unknown insider attacks. However, the statistical and machine learning-based methods are not suitable to analyse multiple types of audit data when just one statistical or machine learning algorithm is applied. In this case, an additional mechanism may be required to orchestrate the alerts generated from multiple sub-detectors, resulting in relatively high deployment and engineering costs. More recently, deep learning algorithms have been applied to detect malicious insiders [16,24,32] which, due to the algorithms' inherent ability to represent and learn features, can often conduct a one-off analysis of various audit data with almost no domain knowledge involved.

Currently, deep learning based approaches tend to extract features from the frequency of activities [16,24]. For example, in our previous work [24], we concatenated the hourly frequencies of various activity occurrences in a specific type of security log into a feature vector that represents a user's daily behaviour. In that work, an autoencoder was trained with a feature set for each type of security log. Reconstruction errors that measure the distance between an original feature vector and the vector reconstructed from the trained autoencoder were employed for identifying unusual feature vectors leading to potentially abnormal behaviours. In total, there were four autoencoders trained using the *http*, *file*, *device* and *logon* logs, respectively. The reconstructed errors resulting from different security logs were averaged over the number of users and a final decision was made if a user generated a high averaged reconstruction error in any given day. Obviously, the previous work did not taken full advantage of all the available information of security log of different types. To overcome this, additional feature engineering tasks may be required to incorporate more feature sets, which come from different types of security logs. For example, the approach proposed in [4] extracted features based on insider attack scenarios, which introduces various features derived from the scenarios. However, in this case, domain knowledge becomes critical for providing information about insider attack scenarios, which is not generally available in practical applications. As a result, in this paper, we attempt to combine a Word2vec model with an autoencoder-based architecture to remove the dependency of the domain knowledge [27]. That is, different types of security logs are transformed into distributed representations of words (i.e. word embedding) generated by the Word2vec model. As such, text information coming from a variety of security logs can be utilized to form a more meaningful context, possibly revealing clues of malicious behaviours. Hence, the feature sets are generated by averaging the vectors of distributed representations from the context of events. We then apply other similar autoencoder detector to perform the detection.

The contributions of this paper are summarised as follows:

- A new insider threat detection approach is proposed, which can automatically learn the features and optimise the model.
- Based on the Word2vec model, we can utilize the text information from multiple types of security logs, providing a richer base for the autoencoder to learn from.
- Through the proposed approach, the final decision making does not need any additional orchestration or scoring mechanisms, while achieving a low FPR of less than 1%.

The rest of this paper is organised as follows: Sect. 2 presents related literature. Next, the autoencoder based approach is detailed in Sect. 3. Section 4 presents the results from the numerical experiments, along with a comparative study. Finally, Sect. 5 concludes this paper.

2   Related Work

In this section, we review the existing insider threat detection approaches that are closely related to our work. In general, these approaches can be roughly categorised as signature-based and anomaly-based [17, 26, 28]. A signature-based approach often establishes a set of signatures (rules) that describe the known insider attack vectors to undertake the detection [17, 26, 28]. The anomaly-based approaches detect insider threats from anomaly detection which usually rely on statistical machine learning [5, 9, 16, 21, 22, 26, 30, 35, 37] or deep learning algorithms [4, 23, 24, 32].

Maloof et al. developed a system named ELICIT [26] to analyse information events converted from low-level network traffic and relevant contextual information. Several detectors were built with hand-coded rules and statistical algorithms such as density estimation for detecting a range of specific scenarios. Similarly, in the approach proposed by Nguyen et al. [28], two behavioural rule sets were generated using daily accesses to files and directories for each user and each process, respectively. An alert is triggered once a process forking a child or executing a program that is not on the authorised list, or a process' execution that is largely unmatched with the known process trees. In addition, Hanley *et al.* presented an efficient rule-based approach for detecting data exfiltration-related insider attacks as an adjunct to a security information and event management (SIEM) platform, Splunk [17]. A number of searches are executed across human resource records, email history and Active Directory (AD) logs, to examine whether a user is breaking predefined rules such as transmitting a large amount of data to recipients who are not on an authorised list. All of these signature-based approaches can be effective against their targeted malicious behaviours. However, the quality of the rules is essentially determined by the domain knowledge provided by security experts. Furthermore, the major limitation of signature-based approaches is that they are not able to deal with unknown attacks with which the predefined rules do not comply.

The anomaly-based approaches detect insider threats by either modelling the audit data with a statistical method or training a model with the extracted features using a machine learning algorithm. A typical example is the Beehive system [35], which obtains 15 features for a total of 35,000 hosts on a daily basis from a wide range of security logs. Then, the PCA and k-means clustering algorithms are applied to undertake the detection. This approach largely reduces the reliance on the domain knowledge, in which only a few security policy based features that require domain knowledge. Furthermore, some deep learning based approaches have been proposed [4,23,24,32], which require little domain knowledge. In particular, both Tuor's and Liu's approaches [24,32] leverage the frequency of activities to extract features from various security logs. Tuor's approach then implements insider threat detection by using a recurrent neutral network (RNN), whereas Liu's approach focuses on unsupervised learning in which a deep autoencoder is trained for detecting anomalous events by examining the reconstruction error. Although there is little reliance on specific domain knowledge, the deep learning based approaches extract features empirically and this may impact on the overall performance of the detector.

3   New Unsupervised Insider Detection Approach

This section details the proposed insider threat detection approach. As illustrated in Fig. 1, this approach comprises three major components: *log2corpus*, *feature extraction* and *insider threat detection*. Firstly, the *log2corpus* component transforms the security logs into a Word2vec trainable corpus following the '4W' sentence template [23]. Such a corpus retains key information extracted from the raw security logs and, no matter the type of the security log, the format is identical, providing a unified standard for generating corpus. This component is also the key that enables the proposed approach works with various types of security logs. The feature extraction process is still required in the proposed approach, which is undertaken by the second component *feature extraction*. However, unlike

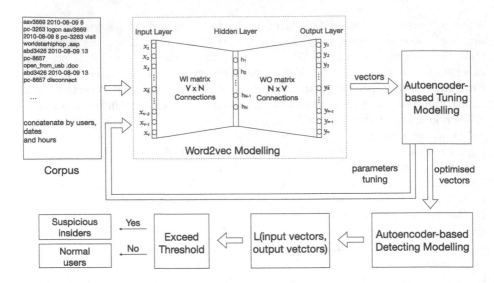

Fig. 1. Flowchart of the proposed approach

conventional approaches that depend on domain knowledge, the *feature extraction* component takes advantage of the resulting distributed representation of the words (i.e., the word embeddings) from the Word2vec model to construct features from text. Then, an autoencoder model is trained with the feature set for detecting malicious events. If any feature yields a large reconstruction error, the corresponding event is labelled as suspicious. A user who is associated with multiple suspicious events will be labelled as a malicious insider. The above detection is realised with the *insider threat detection* component.

3.1 Transforming Security Logs into Corpus

In this paper, the audit data sources are the same as the ones mentioned in [24], namely *http*, *file*, *device* and *logon* logs. These security logs are commonly available in an organisation, which are important data for detecting malicious insiders [8,10,23,25,31,35].

Although security logs exist in a text format, compared to natural languages, they lack natural linguistic properties because: (1) paragraph and sentence structures do not explicitly exist in a security log, (2) the existence of a large number of duplicate entries break the paragraph and sentence into inconsistent structures which may not strictly follow the syntax, and (3) redundant attributes introduce noise into a security log, undermining the lexical relations between words. Thus, in order to ensure that the distributed representation equally reflects the context of a word, we need to pre-process the security logs. We achieve this using the concept of a '4W' sentence template [23]. The template (see Table 1) is designed to extract key information from security logs and reconstruct the linguistic properties. For example, given an event drawn from a *http* log:

Table 1. The '4W' sentence template

Template	Word(s)	Description
who	**user**	user's unique ID
when	**date**	date extracted from timestamp
	hour	hour extracted from timestamp
where	**pc**	computer's unique ID, i.e. hostname
what	**activity**	download, upload, copy, delete and etc.
	content	separately defined

```
{W1B6-H3IT50UV-3446USEM},04/25/2011 06:29:31,
BMN3207,PC-9138,http://feedburn.com/Bobby_Robson
/dodgin/HFF_Arj_Vebafvqrfubyvqnlf1049160149.html, WWW Visit
```

we extract the information **user** = BMN3207, **date** = 20110425, **hour** = 6, **pc** = PC-9138, **activity** = Visit and **content** = .html to populate the 4W sentence template, resulting in the **text** = "BMN3207 20110425 6 PC-9138 Visit .html". Once events are transformed into text fragments for all the security logs, they are combined into a corpus, such as

```
aav3669 2010-08-09 8 pc-3263 visit
worldstarhiphop .asp aav3669 2010-08-09
10 pc-3263 visit meetup .aspx aav3669
2010-08-09 11 pc-3263 visit newsmax
.aspx aav3669 2010-08-09 12 pc-3263
visit fbcdn .asp aav3669 2010-08-09
13 pc-3263 visit tigerdirect .htm
...
```

3.2 Feature Learning Through Word Embedding

As previously mentioned, the rule-based approach relies on domain knowledge to characterise the behaviour of a malicious insider. Such a reliance not only incurs expensive research and development cost, but also loses the ability to detect unknown attacks. The statistical/machine learning approaches require less domain knowledge. However, in some cases, domain knowledge is still required to extract features that are related to particular behaviours. In contrast, current deep learning based approaches often employ frequency-based features, which requires little or no domain knowledge.

Particularly, the approach proposed by Tuor *et al.* [32] creates a feature vector which is consisted of 408 activities over 24 h (*e.g.*, daily) for one user. The vector is then combined with another six categorical values, yielding a 414-dimensional feature vector. In our previous work [24], the feature vector is constructed by concatenating hourly counts of activities for each day. No domain knowledge is required for extracting features in this case. However, the feature set seems to be very empirical, and its effectiveness is not controllable in practice. Therefore, in this paper, we propose an automatic way to extract features. The features are constructed via word embeddings obtained from Word2vec and the best parameters of Word2vec are tuned by minimising the loss of an autoencoder.

The 4W sentence template is used to extracted several keywords in terms of each of raw event, then combining each transformed event into a corpus feeding into a Word2vec model. The trained word2vec model will produce a vector representation with a fixed dimension for each keyword. This allows the semantic meanings of words to be preserved in vector representations. When the word vectors are generated according to each event, then averaged them as the feature vector. In this case, the length of the feature vector is equal to the parameter *vector_size* used for training the Word2vec model. Except for *vector_size*, training a Word2vec model also requires two parameters *window* and *epoch* which specify the size of the neighbouring *window* and the maximal number of iterations, respectively. For the autoencoder training, we employ the mean squared error as the loss function to minimize. The parameter settings for the Word2vec model is chosen during the autoencoder's training. Naturally, the minimal loss indicates that the trained autoencoder best fits the data and, therefore, resulting in the optimal parameters settings for Word2vec model. The tested parameters are detailed in Sect. 4.

3.3   Autoencoder-Based Insider Threat Detection

In this subsection, we introduce our approach for anomaly-based insider threat detection. In terms of anomaly detection [3], a baseline model is firstly established for representing users normal behaviours. Then, the baseline model will be compared to a user's behaviour model. Any significantly deviation in behaviour will be labelled as anomalous. As introduced in the previous subsection, the feature set is constructed by transforming raw security logs into identically formatted texts, training a Word2vec model, and then averaging word vectors for each transformed event. Thus, each feature vector corresponds to a particular behaviour by a user. An autoencoder is then trained with the feature set, where the key assumption is that training data represents only normal behaviours. Therefore, each feature vector can be reconstructed with a small error using the trained autoencoder. While a user is generating many events across different security logs, the detector will invoke the trained autoencoder to examine each of the corresponding feature vectors associated with the user. The final decision is made if a user has a number of suspicious feature vectors (events) that is higher than a given threshold. The fundamental concepts of an autoencoder are presented below.

The autoencoder is a neural network that learns in an unsupervised manner. Typically, an optimal autoencoder model is trained by minimising the cost function:

$$\phi, \psi = \arg\min_{\phi,\psi} \|X - (\psi \circ \phi)X\|^2$$

where ϕ and ψ represent the encoder and decoder respectively, and

$$\phi : \mathcal{X} \to \mathcal{F}$$

$$\psi : \mathcal{F} \to \mathcal{X}$$

The simplest form of an encoder is composed of only one hidden neural network layer which can be expressed as

$$\mathbf{z} = \sigma(\mathbf{W}\mathbf{x} + \mathbf{b})$$

where $\mathbf{z}, \mathbf{z} \in \mathbb{R}^p = \mathcal{F}$ is an image referred to as a code or latent variable, σ is the activation function (e.g., rectified linear unit (ReLU), sigmoid and tanh function), $\mathbf{W}$ is a weight maxtrix, $\mathbf{b}$ is a bias vector, and $\mathbf{x}, \mathbf{x} \in \mathbb{R}^d = \mathcal{X}$. $\mathbf{W}\mathbf{x} + \mathbf{b}$ is also called an affine transformation. Inversely, an encoder attempts to reconstruct the original input $\mathbf{x}$ as $\mathbf{x}'$, subject to the following expression

$$\mathbf{x}' = \sigma'(\mathbf{W}'\mathbf{z} + \mathbf{b}')$$

where σ', $\mathbf{W}'$ and $\mathbf{b}'$ correspond to σ, $\mathbf{W}$ and $\mathbf{b}$ but they may differ between decoder and encoder. Based on the above equations, the cost function can be rewritten as a reconstruction error, for example

$$\mathcal{L}(\mathbf{x}, \mathbf{x}') = \|\mathbf{x} - \mathbf{x}'\|^2 = \|\mathbf{x} - \sigma'(\mathbf{W}'(\sigma(\mathbf{W}\mathbf{x} + \mathbf{b})) + \mathbf{b}')\|^2$$

where the $l2$-norm (i.e., the squared error or Euclidean distance) is adopted. Other measures such as the Cosine distance, Mahalanobis Distance and Kullback-Leibler (KL) divergence can also be used [19].

When constructing a multi-layer autoencoder, it increases the number of hidden layers, which in theory can yield a better feature representation with each hidden layer being scaled to a manageable magnitude. Namely, the encoder will be extended as

$$\phi(\mathbf{x}) = (\phi^{(n)} \circ \cdots \phi^{(k)} \circ \cdots \phi^{(2)} \circ \phi^{(1)})\mathbf{x}$$

where n represents the number of hidden layers and each $\phi^{(k)}$ is of the following form

$$\mathbf{z}^{(\mathbf{k})} = \sigma^{(k)}(\mathbf{W}^{(k)}\mathbf{x} + \mathbf{b}^{(k)})$$

Similarly, the decoder can be written as

$$\psi(\mathbf{z}) = (\psi^{(n)} \circ \cdots \psi^{(k)} \circ \cdots \psi^{(2)} \circ \psi^{(1)})\mathbf{z}$$

where $\psi^{(k)}$ is aligned with

$$\mathbf{x}'^{(\mathbf{k})} = \sigma'^{(k)}(\mathbf{W}'^{(k)}\mathbf{z} + \mathbf{b}'^{(k)})$$

The loss of the autoencoder is a key metric for the proposed approach, such that the parameters *vector_size*, *window* and *epoch* can be determined for training the Word2vec model. Once the autoencoder is trained with the feature set resulting from the Word2vec model, insider threat detection can be undertaken. As mentioned before, we assume that the training data is one-class (i.e., normal events only). Theoretically, reconstructing a feature vector with the autoencoder should lead to only a small error, which is a measure of the distance between an original vector and its reconstructed vector. As the autoencoder is a neural network, its architecture and parameters will impact the performance [15]. Accordingly, the following aspects need to be considered (1) the number of layers including input and output layers, (2) the number of hidden units for each layer and the selection of the activation function, and (3) the construction of the loss function. Section 4 will describe how the autoencode is constructed and its parameters determined. Assuming that a reconstructed error is expressed as $\mathcal{L}$, the detection can be realised when

$$\mathcal{L}(\mathbf{x}, \mathbf{x}') \geq threshold$$

where $\mathcal{L}(\mathbf{x}, \mathbf{x}')$ is the reconstruction error between the original feature vector $\mathbf{x}$ and its reconstructed vector $\mathbf{x}'$ based on the autoencoder model. In practice, however, it is difficult to choose an appropriate threshold, especially when the data is large. Alternatively, we apply the top-k recommendation algorithm [12] to generate only the top-k anomalous feature vectors. In other words, the detector calculates the reconstruction errors for all the feature vectors, sorts the reconstruction errors in descending order, and reports only the top k ones.

In addition, we set the detection to be conducted on a weekly basis. That is, once the security logs are collected for a given week, the detection process starts using the *text2corpus* component mentioned in [23]. When the Word2vec model and the autoencoder are trained with optimal parameters, it can detect suspicious events among all security logs.

4   Numerical Experiments

Numerical experiments are undertaken with the Carnegie Mellon University (CMU) CERT Program's insider threat database v6.2 [14]. Training the corpus with Word2vec is implemented with Gensim [29], and the autoencoder-based detector is implemented using the Python deep learning library Keras [6] with a Tensorflow [1] backend. The following subsections present the details of the experimental dataset, the experiment setting and experimental evaluation.

4.1   Experimental Dataset

The CMU insider threat database was created by simulating a large-scale organisation's daily operations [14,20]. The database contains the daily activities of 4000 users across an organisation during one and a half years, which is approximately 200 GB in size. There are three categories in the dataset, namely the host data, network data and contextual data. These data allow the construction of a security posture of the organisation's intranet. Aside the psychometric and decoy data which provide some contextual information, the rest of the data are all security logs. These include *http*, *device*, *file* and *logon* logs. For generating the database content, security experts designed and executed a range of insider

Table 2. Ground truth of the experimental dataset for the malicious user ACM2278. (N.B.: Date format is month/day/year hh:mm:ss.)

Week	User	Date	Log type	PC
Week 1 20100816–20100822	ACM2278	08/18/2010 21:47:42	logon	PC-8431
		08/18/2010 22:59:20	*device*	PC-8431
		08/19/2010 01:34:19	*file*	PC-8431
		08/19/2010 01:37:20	*file*	PC-8431
		08/19/2010 01:38:10	*file*	PC-8431
		08/19/2010 01:46:04	*file*	PC-8431
		08/19/2010 05:23:05	*device*	PC-8431
		08/19/2010 06:10:59	*logon*	PC-8431
		08/19/2010 01:34:19	*http*	PC-8431
		08/19/2010 01:37:20	*http*	PC-8431
		08/19/2010 01:38:10	*http*	PC-8431
		08/19/2010 01:46:04	*http*	PC-8431
Week 2 20100823–20100829	ACM2278	08/24/2010 01:02:58	logon	PC-8431
		08/24/2010 03:24:16	*device*	PC-8431
		08/24/2010 03:34:21	*file*	PC-8431
		08/24/2010 03:43:48	*file*	PC-8431
		08/24/2010 03:48:51	*file*	PC-8431
		08/24/2010 04:15:32	*device*	PC-8431
		08/24/2010 04:20:39	*logon*	PC-8431
		08/24/2010 03:34:21	*http*	PC-8431
		08/24/2010 03:43:48	*http*	PC-8431
		08/24/2010 03:48:51	*http*	PC-8431

attacks that represent various attacker intentions, targets and associated attack vectors.

Processing the original 200 GB dataset needed an excessive amount of computing resources to maintain the processing time at a manageable level (*e.g.*, a couple of hours). Therefore, to conduct the experiments, we chose two weeks of data generated by 500 users. A malicious user 'ACM2278', who has undertaken the most representative insider attacks during the two weeks selected, is among the 500 users. Although in our experiments, we chose to conduct the detection on a weekly basis owing to limited computational resources, the proposed approach can be adapted to various time intervals as, for example, fortnightly or a daily. Table 2 shows the ground truth of the experimental dataset for the malicious user ACM2278. In total, there are twelve malicious events during the week from 16/Aug/2010 to 22/Aug/2010 and ten malicious events between 23/Aug/2010 to 29/Aug/2010.

Table 3. Losses for different sets of parameters in the Word2vec model

Word2vec parameters	Week 1's autoencoder loss	Week 2's autoencoder loss
window: 5, *epoch*: 5, *vector_size*: 50	1.2197	1.2347
window: 5, *epoch*: 5, *vector_size*: 100	0.8771	1.0340
window: 5, *epoch*: 5, *vector_size*: 200	0.7739	0.8520
window: 5, *epoch*: 5, *vector_size*: 300	0.7474	0.7251
window: 5, *epoch*: 5, *vector_size*: 400	0.7204	0.7552
window: 5, *epoch*: 5, *vector_size*: 500	0.6826	0.6973
window: 5, *epoch*: 10, *vector_size*: 50	1.2716	1.3187
window: 5, *epoch*: 10, *vector_size*: 100	1.0010	1.0901
window: 5, *epoch*: 10, *vector_size*: 200	0.7608	0.7508
window: 5, *epoch*: 10, *vector_size*: 300	0.7107	0.7376
window: 5, *epoch*: 10, *vector_size*: 400	0.7010	0.6973
window: 5, *epoch*: 10, *vector_size*: 500	0.7018	0.7142
window: 10, *epoch*: 5, *vector_size*: 50	1.1476	1.1302
window: 10, *epoch*: 5, *vector_size*: 100	0.7551	0.7999
window: 10, *epoch*: 5, *vector_size*: 200	0.7146	0.7287
window: 10, *epoch*: 5, *vector_size*: 300	0.7068	0.7040
window: 10, *epoch*: 5, *vector_size*: 400	0.6965	0.7576
window: 10, *epoch*: 5, *vector_size*: 500	0.7288	0.7133
window: 10, *epoch*: 10, *vector_size*: 50	0.9208	1.7029
window: 10, *epoch*: 10, *vector_size*: 100	0.7407	1.1105
window: 10, *epoch*: 10, *vector_size*: 200	0.7149	0.7976
window: 10, *epoch*: 10, *vector_size*: 300	0.7067	0.7497
window: 10, *epoch*: 10, *vector_size*: 400	0.6997	0.7296
window: 10, *epoch*: 10, *vector_size*: 500	0.7208	0.7414
window: 10, *epoch*: 20, *vector_size*: 50	1.0129	1.4001
window: 10, *epoch*: 20, *vector_size*: 100	0.8695	1.2004
window: 10, *epoch*: 20, *vector_size*: 200	0.7201	0.7207
window: 10, *epoch*: 20, *vector_size*: 300	0.6803	0.6822
window: 10, *epoch*: 20, *vector_size*: 400	0.7220	0.6822
window: 10, *epoch*: 20, *vector_size*: 500	0.6787	0.7139
window: 10, *epoch*: 30, *vector_size*: 100	0.6833	0.8882
window: 10, *epoch*: 40, *vector_size*: 100	0.8361	1.1759
window: 10, *epoch*: 30, *vector_size*: 300	0.7259	0.7992
window: 10, *epoch*: 40, *vector_size*: 300	0.7167	0.7197
window: 10, *epoch*: 30, *vector_size*: 400	0.6945	0.8569
window: 10, *epoch*: 40, *vector_size*: 400	0.6937	0.7418

4.2   Experimental Setting

As previously mentioned, there are three parameters to be set when training a Word2vec model, namely *window* size, *epoch*, *vector_size*. We select the skip-gram model and hierarchical softmax as activation function, which previously have been proven effective in dealing with security logs [23]. The autoencoder architecture consists of three layers, which should be sufficiently large [13]. The number of hidden units for the three layers are specified as $\frac{vector\_size}{2}$, $\frac{vector\_size}{4}$, $\frac{vector\_size}{8}$, respectively, where the number of each layer's hidden units halves the preceding layer's number. The setting of the other parameters is the same as used in our previous work [24]. Table 3 lists the losses for the different parameters used for training the Word2ec model. As seen in the table, for the 1st week, the best autoencoder setting is achieved when '*window* = 10, *epoch* = 20 and *vector_size* = 500', which is consistent with the results from [23]. However, for the 2nd week, the minimal loss occurs with '*window* = 10, *epoch* = 20 and *vector_size* = 300'. This difference suggests that the Word2vec's parameters needs to be tuned for different week's data, rather than fix a constant set of parameters empirically. On the other hand, it also suggests that the proposed approach is flexible and adapts to variations in the insider threat data.

When the features have been generated using the optimal Word2vec model, they are used as inputs for training the autoencoder. Subsequently, the detector will compute the reconstruction error for each feature vector based on the trained autoencoder. In fact, reconstruction error is a distance metric between the original feature vector and its reconstructed vector, which can be defined with various distance metrics. In our experiments, we implement two of the most commonly-used distance metrics: Euclidean distance and Kullback-Leibler (KL) divergence.

4.3   Experimental Results

In the previous subsection, Table 3 summarised the sets of Word2vec's parameters and the corresponding losses obtained for the autoencoder for the two weeks from 16/Aug/2010 to 22/Aug/2010 (Week 1) and 23/Aug/2010 to 29/Aug/2010 (Week 2). Firstly, for each experiment, we chose the two sets of parameters which resulted in the smallest losses, in order to demonstrate the best performance for the proposed approach. Secondly, two inferior sets of parameters which led to relatively large losses were selected to undertake comparative experiment. This will show that the performance is highly dependent on the parameters of the Word2vec model. Table 4 shows the sets of parameters selected for the following experiments, where the two 'good' and 'bad' sets of parameters were selected for each week.

Table 4. Selected parameters of the Word2vec model

Word2vec parameters	Week 1's autoencoder loss	Week 2's autoencoder loss
window: 10, *epoch*: 20, *vector_size*: 300	0.6803	
window: 10, *epoch*: 20, *vector_size*: 500	0.6787	
window: 5, *epoch*: 5, *vector_size*: 50	1.2197	
window: 10, *epoch*: 40, *vector_size*: 100	0.8361	
window: 10, *epoch*: 20, *vector_size*: 300		0.6822
window: 10, *epoch*: 20, *vector_size*: 400		0.6822
window: 5, *epoch*: 5, *vector_size*: 50		1.2347
window: 10, *epoch*: 30, *vector_size*: 100		0.8882

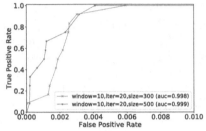 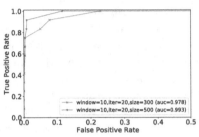

(a) Results from the 'good' autoencoder (Note: the scale of False Positive Rate is 0.00 - 0.01)

(b) Results from the 'bad' autoencoder model (Note: the scale of False Positive Rate is 0.00 - 0.50)

Fig. 2. The ROC curve for Week 1 (16/Aug/2010 to 22/Aug/2010)

The autoencoders trained with the feature set resulted from the above four sets of parameters are applied to detect the suspicious events. Figures 2(a) and (b) present the RoC curves illustrating the results from 'good' and 'bad' sets of parameters respectively for Week 1, where the Euclidean distance is employed as the metric for reconstruction error. Figure 2(a) suggests that the proposed approach can detect all malicious events (i.e., TPR = 1.0) with FPRs as low as 0.59% and 0.41% with two sets of parameter settings, respectively. Meanwhile, it demonstrates that when the other settings are the same, a larger value of *vector_size* yields better performance on the dataset. In contrast, as illustrated in Fig. 2(b), the FPRs are lifted up to 22.84% and 11.61% respectively for detecting all malicious events, which are significantly worse than the former ones. Figures 3(a) and (b) present the RoC curves for the data from Week 2. They have shown a similar result with the Week 1. Particularly, the 'good' parameters of the Word2vec model can reach a TPR of 1 with FPRs of 0.67% and 0.72%, respectively in Fig. 3(a). However, the other set of parameters result in the FPRs of 23.22% and 11.20%, as shown in Fig. 3(b).

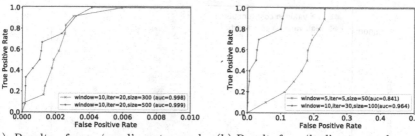

(a) Results from 'good' autoencoder (Note: the scale of False Positive Rate is 0.01)

(b) Results from 'bad' autoencoder model (Note: the scale of False Positive Rate is 0.50)

Fig. 3. The ROC curve for Week 2 (23/Aug/2010 to 29/Aug/2010)

Figures 4 and 5 present a comparison regarding the computed workload for security analysts under the 'good' and 'bad' sets of parameter settings. According to Fig. 4, security analysts need to investigate 25k to 50k events to identify the malicious ones if the parameters are not properly selected. While in an ideal case they only need to investigate less than 1.5k events. Figure 5 illustrates the results from the data of Week 2. Similar to the situation depicted in Week 1, approximately 1.5k events need to be investigated when the parameter settings of the Word2vec model and the autoencoder are both properly optimized.

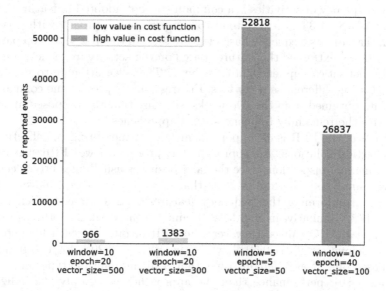

Fig. 4. No. of reported suspicious events in different model structures for Week 1 (16/Aug/2010 to 22/Aug/2010)

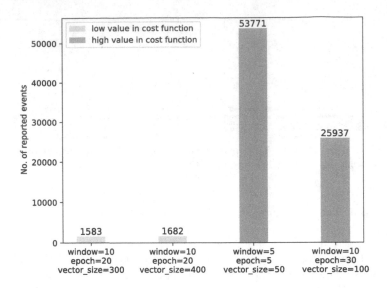

Fig. 5. No. of reported suspicious events in different model structures for Week 2 (23/Aug/2010 to 29/Aug/2010)

4.4 Results Analysis and Comparison

In this subsection, the proposed approach are compared with other existing studies. Since frequency of activities is a common concept adopted in feature extraction [2,11,16,18,24,33,34], we intend to compare our approach with a typical approach that adopts frequency based feature sets. In the first set of comparative experiments, we extracted the features based on the activity frequency, counting how many activities happened in each hour. Then, we attempt to create the feature set using different security logs. Figures 6 and 7 present the comparisons for the data obtained from the two weeks, showing that the proposed approach outperforms the remaining frequency-based approaches.

In practice, the FPR is an important metric for measuring the effectiveness of the detection solutions. An approach that produces lower FPR can reduce efforts for manual inspection, since the false positives usually need to be checked by security analysts. The results show that our approach can achieve an FPR of 0.67%, outperforming the frequency feature-based approach which has an FPR of 3.16%. Similarly, in the data obtained from Week 2, both approaches achieve similar AUC values. However, the FPR of our approach for detecting all the malicious events is 0.59%, while the FPR is 3.20% for the frequency feature-based one. It also demonstrates that utilizing multiple types of security log obtain better performance than the approaches using only the individual feature set.

We also compared our approach with the previous work [23]. We specify the parameters ($window = 10$, $epoch = 20$, $vector\_size = 300$) the same as [23] for training the Word2vec model. Then, we tested a range of thresholds (i.e., τ),

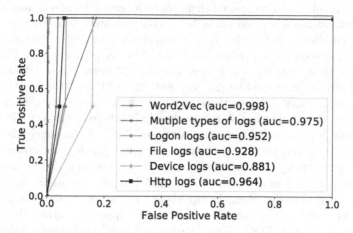

Fig. 6. The comparison with frequency-based feature extraction in Week 1 (16/Aug/2010–22/Aug/2010)

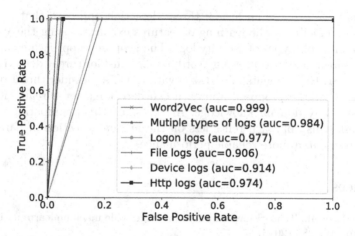

Fig. 7. The comparison with frequency-based feature extraction in Week 2 (23/Aug/2010–29/Aug/2010)

Table 5. The comparison with manual model selection

Time period	Cost for finding all malicious events				
	Automatic model tuning	Manual model tuning			
		$\tau = 0.3$	$\tau = 0.5$	$\tau = 0.7$	$\tau = 0.9$
20100816–20100822	1583	N/A	656	863	961
20100823–20100829	966	N/A	517	866	1014

recorded the results, and compared them with the result from our automatically chosen Word2vec model. Table 5 details the comparison, where 'cost' is the metric to find all malicious events. In other words, the cost indicates the total number of events which need to be further investigated by security experts. The results from Week 1 show that our method reported 1583 events as suspicious events needed to be investigated, while [23] only output less than 1000 events (ranging from 656 to 961 under different thresholds) which require further investigation. However, if the threshold was 0.3, the method in [23] failed to detect all malicious insider events. Similar results were achieved in Week 2. Although the manual model tuning achieved better results with the some particular parameters, the unstable outputs brought more risks to cause malicious events to be missed. For example, choosing 0.3 as a threshold, the model missed the malicious events in both weeks. Additionally, when the threshold tau was set to 0.9, the number of further investigated events exceeded that in our approach (automatically tuned parameters) in Week 2. Thus, the new approach provides better reliability.

5   Conclusion

In this paper, we propose an insider threat detection approach that applies an autoencoder to facilitate the learning of features extracted using the Word2vec model from multiple types of security logs. The proposed approach comprises of automated feature extraction using Word2vec and insider threat detection using an autoencoder. Experiments undertaken with the CMU insider threat database demonstrate that the proposed approach can detect insider threats effectively without using any domain knowledge. At the same time, comparing with the existing work, this approach relies less on the manual selection of parameters, and could result in a more reliable performance.

References

1. Abadi, M., et al.: TensorFlow: a system for large-scale machine learning. In: OSDI 2016, pp. 265–283 (2016)
2. Böse, B., Avasarala, B., Tirthapura, S., Chung, Y.Y., Steiner, D.: Detecting insider threats using radish: a system for real-time anomaly detection in heterogeneous data streams. IEEE Syst. J. **11**(2), 471–482 (2017)
3. Chandola, V., Banerjee, A., Kumar, V.: Anomaly detection: a survey. ACM Comput. Surv. (CSUR) **41**(3), 15 (2009)
4. Chattopadhyay, P., Wang, L., Tan, Y.P.: Scenario-based insider threat detection from cyber activities. IEEE Trans. Comput. Soc. Syst. **5**(3), 660–675 (2018)
5. Chen, X., et al.: Android HIV: a study of repackaging malware for evading machine-learning detection. IEEE Trans. Inf. Forensics Secur. **15**(1), 987–1001 (2020)
6. Chollet, F., et al.: Keras (2015). https://keras.io
7. Clearswift: clearswift insider threat index 2018 (2018). https://www.clearswift.com/about-us/pr/press-releases/cybersecurity-incidents-insider-threat-falls-uk-and-germany-post-gdpr. Accessed August 2019

8. Collins, M.: Common sense guide to mitigating insider threats. Technical report, Carnegie-Mellon University, Pittsburgh, PA, United States (2016)
9. Coulter, R., Han, Q.L., Pan, L., Zhang, J., Xiang, Y.: Data driven cyber security in perspective - intelligent traffic analysis. IEEE Trans. Cybern. https://doi.org/10.1109/TCYB.2019.2940940
10. Coulter, R., Pan, L.: Intelligent agents defending for an IoT world: a review. Comput. Secur. **73**, 439–458 (2018)
11. Coulter, R., Pan, L., Zhang, J., Xiang, Y.: A visualization-based analysis on classifying Android malware. In: Chen, X., Huang, X., Zhang, J. (eds.) ML4CS 2019. LNCS, vol. 11806, pp. 304–319. Springer, Cham (2019). https://doi.org/10.1007/978-3-030-30619-9_22
12. Deshpande, M., Karypis, G.: Item-based top-n recommendation algorithms. ACM Trans. Inf. Syst. (TOIS) **22**(1), 143–177 (2004)
13. Gao, X., Ichise, R.: Adjusting word embeddings by deep neural networks. In: ICAART (2), pp. 398–406 (2017)
14. Glasser, J., Lindauer, B.: Bridging the gap: a pragmatic approach to generating insider threat data. In: 2013 IEEE Security and Privacy Workshops, pp. 98–104. IEEE (2013)
15. Goodfellow, I., Bengio, Y., Courville, A., Bengio, Y.: Deep Learning, vol. 1. MIT Press, Cambridge (2016)
16. Haidar, D., Gaber, M.M.: Adaptive one-class ensemble-based anomaly detection: an application to insider threats. In: 2018 International Joint Conference on Neural Networks (IJCNN), pp. 1–9. IEEE (2018)
17. Hanley, M., Montelibano, J.: Insider threat control: using centralized logging to detect data exfiltration near insider termination. Technical report, Software Engineering Institute, Carnegie-Mellon University, Pittsburgh, PA (2011)
18. Jiang, J., Wen, S., Yu, S., Xiang, Y., Zhou, W.: Identifying propagation sources in networks: state-of-the-art and comparative studies. IEEE Commun. Surv. Tutor. **10**(1), 465–481 (2017)
19. Knorr, E.M., Ng, R.T., Tucakov, V.: Distance-based outliers: algorithms and applications. VLDB J.-Int. J. Very Large Data Bases **8**(3–4), 237–253 (2000)
20. Lindauer, B., Glasser, J., Rosen, M., Wallnau, K.C., ExactData, L.: Generating test data for insider threat detectors. JoWUA **5**(2), 80–94 (2014)
21. Liu, A., Martin, C., Hetherington, T., Matzner, S.: A comparison of system call feature representations for insider threat detection. In: Proceedings from the Sixth Annual IEEE SMC Information Assurance Workshop, pp. 340–347. IEEE (2005)
22. Liu, A., Martin, C.E., Hetherington, T., Matzner, S.: AI lessons learned from experiments in insider threat detection. In: AAAI Spring Symposium: What Went Wrong and Why: Lessons from AI Research and Applications, pp. 49–55 (2006)
23. Liu, L., Chen, C., Zhang, J., De Vel, O., Xiang, Y.: Insider threat identification using the simultaneous neural learning of multi-source logs. In: Submitted to IEEE Access (2019)
24. Liu, L., De Vel, O., Chen, C., Zhang, J., Xiang, Y.: Anomaly-based insider threat detection using deep autoencoders. In: 2018 IEEE International Conference on Data Mining Workshops (ICDMW), pp. 39–48. IEEE (2018)
25. Liu, L., De Vel, O., Han, Q.L., Zhang, J., Xiang, Y.: Detecting and preventing cyber insider threats: a survey. IEEE Commun. Surv. Tutor. **20**(2), 1397–1417 (2018)

26. Maloof, M.A., Stephens, G.D.: ELICIT: a system for detecting insiders who violate need-to-know. In: Kruegel, C., Lippmann, R., Clark, A. (eds.) RAID 2007. LNCS, vol. 4637, pp. 146–166. Springer, Heidelberg (2007). https://doi.org/10.1007/978-3-540-74320-0_8
27. Mikolov, T., Sutskever, I., Chen, K., Corrado, G.S., Dean, J.: Distributed representations of words and phrases and their compositionality. In: Advances in Neural Information Processing Systems, pp. 3111–3119 (2013)
28. Nguyen, N., Reiher, P., Kuenning, G.H.: Detecting insider threats by monitoring system call activity. In: 2003 IEEE Systems, Man and Cybernetics Society Information Assurance Workshop, pp. 45–52. IEEE (2003)
29. Řehůřek, R., Sojka, P.: Software framework for topic modelling with large corpora. In: Proceedings of the LREC 2010 Workshop on New Challenges for NLP Frameworks, pp. 45–50. ELRA, Valletta, May 2010
30. Sun, N., Zhang, J., Rimba, P., Gao, S., Zhang, L.Y., Xiang, Y.: Data-driven cybersecurity incident prediction: a survey. IEEE Commun. Surv. Tutor. **21**(2), 1744–1772 (2019)
31. Ted, E., et al.: Detecting insider threats in a real corporate database of computer usage activity. In: Proceedings of the 19th ACM SIGKDD International Conference on Knowledge Discovery and Data Mining, pp. 1393–1401. ACM (2013)
32. Tuor, A., Kaplan, S., Hutchinson, B., Nichols, N., Robinson, S.: Deep learning for unsupervised insider threat detection in structured cybersecurity data streams. In: Workshops at the Thirty-First AAAI Conference on Artificial Intelligence (2017)
33. Wen, S., Haghighi, M.S., Chen, C., Xiang, Y., Zhou, W., Jia, W.: A sword with two edges: propagation studies on both positive and negative information in online social networks. IEEE Trans. Comput. **64**(3), 640–653 (2015)
34. Wu, T., Wen, S., Xiang, Y., Zhou, W.: Twitter spam detection: survey of new approaches and comparative study. Comput. Secur. **76**, 265–284 (2018)
35. Yen, T.F., et al.: Beehive: large-scale log analysis for detecting suspicious activity in enterprise networks. In: Proceedings of the 29th Annual Computer Security Applications Conference, pp. 199–208. ACM (2013)
36. Young, W.T., Goldberg, H.G., Memory, A., Sartain, J.F., Senator, T.E.: Use of domain knowledge to detect insider threats in computer activities. In: Security and Privacy Workshops (SPW), pp. 60–67. IEEE (2013)
37. Zhang, J., Xiang, Y., Wang, Y., Zhou, W., Xiang, Y., Guan, Y.: Network traffic classification using correlation information. IEEE Trans. Parallel Distrib. Syst. **24**(1), 104–117 (2013)

Dynamic Searchable Symmetric Encryption with Forward and Backward Privacy: A Survey

Qingqing Gan[1], Cong Zuo[2,3], Jianfeng Wang[4(✉)], Shi-Feng Sun[2,3], and Xiaoming Wang[1]

[1] Department of Computer Science, Jinan University, Guangzhou 510632, China
gan_qingqing@foxmail.com, twxm@jnu.edu.cn
[2] Faculty of Information Technology, Monash University, Clayton 3168, Australia
{cong.zuo1,shifeng.sun}@monash.edu
[3] Data61, CSIRO, Melbourne, Sydney, Australia
[4] State Key Laboratory of Integrated Service Networks (ISN),
Xidian University, Xi'an 710071, China
jfwang@xidian.edu.cn

Abstract. Searchable symmetric encryption (SSE) has been proposed that enables the clients to outsource their private encrypted data onto the cloud server and later the data can be searched with limited information leakage. However, existing surveys have not covered most recent advances on SSE technique. To fill the gap, we make a survey on state-of-the-art representative SSE schemes in cloud environment. We mainly focus on dynamic SSE schemes with forward and backward privacy, two vital security elements to maintain query privacy during data update operations. Specifically, we discuss about SSE protocols based on query expressiveness, including single keyword search, conjunctive keyword search, range search, disjunctive keyword search and verifiable search. Finally, through comparison on query expressiveness, security and efficiency, we demonstrate the strengths and weaknesses of the existing SSE protocols.

Keywords: Cloud storage · Cloud security · Searchable symmetric encryption · Forward privacy · Backward privacy

1 Introduction

Cloud computing becomes an ideal computing infrastructure to provide the shared configurable computing resources. In cloud computing model, individuals or enterprises can outsource their own data onto the cloud server and enjoy the on-demand utilization cloud services, greatly cutting down the local storage and computation cost. Since the data are remotely stored on the cloud server, the data owners lose full control with their sensitive data. In order to protect data privacy, the data owners choose to encrypt their data before uploading to the

© Springer Nature Switzerland AG 2019
J. K. Liu and X. Huang (Eds.): NSS 2019, LNCS 11928, pp. 37–52, 2019.
https://doi.org/10.1007/978-3-030-36938-5_3

cloud. Unfortunately, the encryption mechanism hinder the high-quality applications such as keyword search. A trivial method is to download and decrypt all the ciphertexts to execute the plaintext keyword search. However, this solution tends to be inefficient because of the large amount of communication overhead. How to realize secure and efficient keyword search over the encrypted database becomes an urgent problem.

Searchable symmetric encryption (SSE) emerges as a promising cryptographic tool that can achieve both privacy-preserving and searchability. Specifically, SSE allows data owners to encrypt their data and outsource the encrypted database to the cloud server, later the cloud server can perform the search operations over the ciphertexts when receiving the search queries. The first practical SSE scheme was introduced by Song et al. [38], where sequential scanning technique is adopted to achieve search operation. Soon afterward, several SSE protocols (such as [8,11,16,27,31,33,37,41,46]) are proposed to enrich the query expressiveness, as well as improving security and performance requirements.

Generally, the above solutions mainly consider the static database setting, where the encrypted database cannot be modified once the encrypted database has been built. In practice, the encrypted database requires updates, such as insertion, modification and deletion. Therefore, dynamic SSE schemes are proposed to support data update operations, such as schemes [7,22,43,61]. However, these dynamic SSE schemes are exposed to security issues. For instance, inserting a new document might leak whether the document contains a keyword that was previously searched. That's to say, the adversary can inject a small number of files to the server and analyze whether the search queries match the injected files. Such a leakage can bring heavy impact on the client's query privacy. To address the above issue, SSE protocols with forward and backward privacy (see [1,4,6,19,34,39,40,47,49,62]) are proposed to against the privacy threats when update happens.

In order to overview the existing SSE techniques, several comprehensive surveys on SSE were proposed (such as [12,17,18,35,48,57]). For example, Wang et al. [48] provided a survey on SSE protocols in terms of different functionalities and analyzed these SSE approaches by efficiency and security comparison. Poh et al. [35] presented a detailed overview on the structures, properties, efficiency and security of state-of-the-art SSE schemes. However, these above surveys have not analyzed most recent SSE schemes with enhanced security in dynamic setting. To fill the research gap, we present a comprehensive review on several meaningful SSE schemes with forward and backward privacy in cloud storage. By comparing the functionality, security and efficiency, we point out the advantages and disadvantages of the state-of-the-art SSE schemes.

1.1 Our Contribution

In this article, we study several existing SSE schemes with forward and backward privacy and classify these protocols based on different functionalities. The main contribution can be summarised as follows:

– We first give out a brief description for searchable symmetric encryption (SSE) and then analyze the forward and backward privacy, two demanding security features for dynamic SSE schemes.
– Several recent dynamic SSE schemes with forward and backward privacy for single keyword search are analyzed. Then we extend the query functionalities to conjunctive keyword search, range search and disjunctive keyword search. Finally, SSE protocols with verifiable search are discussed.
– Comparisons of existing SSE schemes are presented, including the query expressiveness, search efficiency and security, which outline the similarities and differences of the representative SSE solutions.

1.2 Organization

The rest of the paper is organized as follows. In Sect. 2, we give out the background knowledge of SSE primitive. Section 3 analyzes the definition of forward and backward privacy in dynamic SSE schemes. Section 4 focuses on previous works on single keyword search. In Sect. 5, we discuss existing works on rich queries, including conjunctive queries, range queries and disjunctive queries. Section 6 presents the analysis and comparison on verifiable SSE constructions. Finally, the conclusion and future work are given out in Sect. 7.

2   Searchable Symmetric Encryption

2.1   Architecture of SSE

An SSE scheme contains three entities: data owner, cloud server and data user. The architecture of SSE is illustrated in Fig. 1.

– **Data Owner.** A data owner, the owner of the data, first uses his or her secret key to encrypt the document into ciphertext for data privacy protection. In order to search the data efficiently, the data owner also encrypts each keyword to create an index. Then the data owner combines all the ciphertexts and indexes to build an encrypted searchable database and uploads the encrypted database to the cloud server. Later, if the data owner would like to share the data with a group of users, he or she will send the secret keys via a secure channel to the data users.
– **Cloud Server.** A cloud server offers storage and search operation on the encrypted database. When receiving a search query from a data user, the cloud server executes the search for the documents containing the particular keyword by matching the encrypted index. Then the search results will send back to the data user.
– **Data User.** A data user is an entity who has access to the outsourced data. If the data user requires some documents containing a desired keyword, he or she will use the secret key to generate a search query embedded with the search keyword. Then the data user submits the query to the cloud server. After receiving the search result from the cloud server, the data user can decrypt the ciphertexts with the secret key and obtain the corresponding documents.

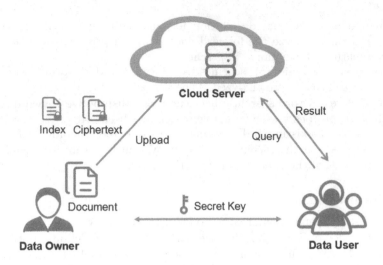

Fig. 1. Architecture of SSE

2.2 Definition of SSE

An SSE scheme includes a polynomial-time algorithm and an interactive protocol as follows.

– $Setup(1^\lambda, DB)$: Run by the data owner, the Setup algorithm inputs a security parameter λ and a database DB that is consisted of a list of document identifiers and keywords, and outputs the secret key sk and an encrypted database EDB. The data owner outsources EDB to the cloud server and sends sk to the data user by a secure channel.

– $Search(sk, q, EDB)$: The search protocol is run between the data user and the cloud server by an interactive manner. The data user inputs the secret key sk and the search query q that contains the search keyword. The cloud server inputs EDB to perform the search operations. At the end of the protocol, the data user outputs the search result which matches the search query and the cloud server outputs nothing.

2.3 Privacy Requirements of SSE

For security consideration, an SSE scheme should satisfy some properties to guarantee the data privacy. Thus we classify the privacy requirements into five main items: index privacy, document privacy, query privacy, search pattern privacy, access pattern privacy. These security requirements should be guaranteed for SSE constructions, and the specific descriptions are shown in Table 1.

Table 1. Privacy requirements and descriptions

Privacy requirement	Description
Index privacy	The index should not reveal any information of the keyword to the cloud server or the adversary
Document privacy	The confidentiality of the documents stored in the cloud should be maintained
Query privacy	The adversary cannot obtain any information about the underlying keyword in the search query
Search pattern privacy	Any information should not be revealed about whether two search results contain the same keyword
Access pattern privacy	The adversary should not be aware of any extra information about underlying documents from the search results

2.4 Security Models of SSE

To analyze the privacy requirements in SSE solutions, we discuss some major security models in the literature. Song et al. [38] defined the security of the first SSE scheme as indistinguishable against chosen plaintext attacks (IND-CPA), that guarantee the server cannot obtain anything about the underlying plaintext from the ciphertext.

To enhance the security of SSE, Goh [16] proposed the security model called indistinguishable against chosen keyword attacks (IND-CKA), to prevent an adversary from learning the contents of the document when given the encrypted index. A slightly stronger security model named IND2-CKA was also introduced by Goh, which makes the indexes from two documents in different size be indistinguishable. Later, Curtmola et al. [11] introduced a non-adaptive IND-CKA1 model and an adaptive IND-CKA2 model, respectively. Both models have considered the security between the submitted query and the search results from previous search operations.

3 Dynamic SSE

To meet the requirement of data dynamism, dynamic SSE was introduced [7,22] that can achieve both search and update operations. However, extra leakage information has been involved during the data addition and data deletion process. For example, the adversary can analyze whether a newly added or deleted document includes previously search keywords. One of the malicious attacks is called file-injection attacks proposed by Zhang et al. [59], that can expose search queries by inserting several target documents to the database. To settle the above leakages, two security requirements, forward and backward privacy, were first taken into account by Stefanov et al. [40].

3.1   Forward Privacy of Dynamic SSE

Forward privacy was informally defined in scheme [40], which was focused on the privacy preserving for the database and the previous search queries during update process. To be specific, forward privacy is defined to ensure that the database updating does not reveal any information about the newly added documents that match the previous search tokens.

Suppose op denotes the update operation, ind denotes the identifier of the document, and w denotes the keywords. Similar to schemes [4,60], the formal definition of forward privacy is shown as follows:

Definition 1. *An $\mathcal{L}$-adaptively-secure dynamic SSE scheme is forward private if the update leakage function $\mathcal{L}_{Update}(q_i) = (i, op_i, ind_i)$, where $q_i = (ind_i, w_i, op_i)$ is an update query.*

In the dynamic SSE protocols, if the forward privacy is not guaranteed, the cloud server can maintain all the earlier search queries and verify whether these queries match the update document. If the verification get through, the cloud server learns that the newly added file contains the specific keyword embedded in the search queries. Furthermore, with an file-injection attack, the cloud server can obtain the relationship between the keyword and the search query, greatly impacting the security of SSE applications. Therefore, forward privacy is quite essential in dynamic SSE schemes, and various forward private SSE solutions have been proposed.

3.2   Backward Privacy of Dynamic SSE

Backward privacy was first considered in [40] and Bost et al. [6] gave out the formal definition for this new security notion. At a high level, backward privacy protect the database privacy when updates happen during the search queries. In a dynamic SSE scheme, backward privacy means that any information about the file identifiers should not revealed from a search query when the document is added before and deleted later.

More formally, backward privacy is categorised into three types: backward privacy with insertion pattern, backward privacy with update pattern and weak backward privacy. Let $q_i = (ind_i, w_i, op_i)$ represents an update query, $TimeDB_{w_i}$ represents the list of documents containing keyword w_i at current time, a_{w_i} represents the number of times that inserted documents containing w_i, $Updates_{w_i}$ represents the list of time stamps for the updates on w_i, and $DelHist_{w_i}$ represents the deletion history for w_i. Similar to scheme [6], the detailed definitions of backward privacy are shown as follows:

Definition 2. *An $\mathcal{L}$-adaptively-secure dynamic SSE scheme is backward private with insertion pattern (Type I) if the update leakage function $\mathcal{L}_{Update}(q_i) = (i, op_i)$, and the search leakage function $\mathcal{L}_{Search}(w_i) = (TimeDB_{w_i}, a_{w_i})$.*

Definition 3. *An $\mathcal{L}$-adaptively-secure dynamic SSE scheme is backward private with update pattern (Type II) if the update leakage function $\mathcal{L}_{Update}(q_i) = (i, op_i, w_i)$, and the search leakage function $\mathcal{L}_{Search}(w_i) = (TimeDB_{w_i}, Updates_{w_i})$.*

Definition 4. *An $\mathcal{L}$-adaptively-secure dynamic SSE scheme is weak backward private (Type III) if the update leakage function $\mathcal{L}_{Update}(q_i) = (i, op_i, w_i)$, and the search leakage function $\mathcal{L}_{Search}(w_i) = (TimeDB_{w_i}, DelHist_{w_i})$.*

For the above three levels of backward privacy, Type I is the strongest level and most secure, while Type III is relatively weak and least secure. It is noticeable that all these types can ensure the basic security requirement of preserving the identifiers of the documents containing keyword w and that were deleted before the search query for w.

4   SSE Schemes on Single Keyword Search

For SSE schemes with single keyword search, they can be categorised into two types: SSE schemes on sequential scan and SSE schemes on secure index. Thus several previous works have been proposed in [11,16,21,38]. However, when update operations are required on the encrypted data, many traditional SSE schemes are exposed to privacy threats. For example, the adversary injects some new documents onto the encrypted database, thus obtaining privacy information from the submitted query. This attack is also known as file-injection attack, one of the most common security attacks that various existing dynamic SSE protocols suffer from. To resist the above attack, Stefanov et al. [40] designed a dynamic SSE protocol with forward privacy based on oblivious RAM (ORAM). Bost [4] constructed a new forward private SSE scheme, called $\Sigma o\varphi o\varsigma$, that achieves optimal computation complexity of search and update. The main technique is based on trapdoor permutation and the location of the newly inserted file is unlinkable to the search token.

In 2017, Bost et al. [6] formally defined the notion of backward privacy and gave out several SSE protocols satisfying forward privacy and different types of backward privacy. Yoneyama et al. [54] proposed another dynamic SSE solution with forward privacy, which tends to be secure against malicious server. Based on the algebraic pseudo-random function (PRF), this solution can combine each index and keyword with a tag, and then store the tag and the encrypted index for update procedure.

Since the scheme [54] relied on public key cryptography and had I/O inefficiency problem, Song et al. [39] presented two novel SSE solutions, named FAST and FASTIO, realizing forward privacy with symmetric key primitives. Specifically, their schemes utilize a classic data structure called singly linked list and each update operation can be regarded as a node in the singly linked list. With the current key and state, the server can calculate the previous state, but cannot predict about future keys or states. Therefore, the forward privacy has been maintained in their schemes. Sun et al. [42] proposed a single-keyword SSE

Table 2. Comparison with existing SSE schemes with single keyword search

Schemes	FS	BS	Search efficiency	Update efficiency
Kurosawa et al. [26]	×	×	$O(d)$	$O(u \cdot d)$
Stefanov et al. [40]	✓	×	$O\left(min\begin{pmatrix} a_w + log(N) \\ r \cdot log^3(N) \end{pmatrix}\right)$	$O(u \cdot log^2(N))$
Bost et al. [5]	✓	×	$O\left(min\begin{pmatrix} a_w + log^2(N) \\ r \cdot log^3(N) \end{pmatrix}\right)$	$O(log^2(N))$
Bost [4]	✓	×	$O(a_w)$	$O(1)$
Yoneyama et al. [54]	✓	×	$O(a_w)$	$O(1)$
Bost et al. [6] (Fides)	✓	Type II	$O(a_w)$	$O(1)$
Bost et al. [6] (Janus)	✓	Type III	$O(r + b_w)$	$O(1)$
Song et al. [39]	✓	×	$O(a_w)$	$O(1)$
Sun et al. [42]	✓	Type III	$O(r + b_w)$	$O(1)$
Chamani et al. [9] (Orion)	✓	Type I	$O(r \cdot log^2(N))$	$O(log^2(N))$
Chamani et al. [9] (Horus)	✓	Type III	$O(r \cdot log(b_w) \cdot log(N))$	$O(log^2(N))$
Amjad et al. [1] (Fort)	✓	Type I	$O(r + \sum_{\forall w} b_w)$	$O(log^2(N))$
Amjad et al. [1] (Bunker-B)	✓	Type II	$O(a_w)$	$O(1)$
Zuo et al. [63] (FB-DSSE)	✓	Type I$^-$	$O(a_w)$	$O(1)$

scheme with forward and backward privacy by adopting symmetric puncturable encryption, realizing both secure and efficient search over scalable database.

To optimize the search time in previous SSE solutions, Chamani et al. [9] also constructed three new SSE protocols achieving three level of backward privacy. The oblivious map (OMAP), Path-ORAM and PRF are adopted in their constructions to guarantee different kinds of backward privacy. Li et al. [28] enhanced the security definition of forward privacy to "forward search privacy", and then designed an efficient SSE scheme based on hidden pointer technique, satisfying with the new security requirement. Subsequently, a number of SSE protocols (such as [1,5,10,34,42,49]) on single keyword search with forward and backward privacy were designed, trying to seek out a better balance between security property and search efficiency.

Recently, Zuo et al. [63] presented a novel dynamic SSE named FB-DSSE, achieving both forward and backward privacy based on symmetric encryption with homomorphic addition and bitmap index. Most importantly, this scheme first defined Type I$^-$ for backward privacy, a new type ensuring somewhat stronger backward privacy that does not leak the insertion time of matching files. And their scheme only costs constant interaction between the user and the server, greatly saving communication overhead. By leveraging the data splitting technique, FB-DSSE is extended to multi-block environment (named MB-FB-DSSE), which is suitable and efficient for the large-scale data search and update operations.

Table 2 demonstrates the comparison results of several existing representative SSE schemes with support for single keyword search. Note that, FS is short for forward privacy; BS is short for backward privacy; d represents the number of documents; u represents the number of updated keyword-document pairs; r represents the size of the result; N represents the number of keyword-document pairs; a_w represents the number of times for the queried keyword w that was inserted to the database previously; b_w represents the number of deleted documents that containing keyword w.

5   SSE Schemes on Rich Queries

5.1   Conjunctive Queries

Conjunctive keyword search allows the client to query multiple keywords, namely, the returned documents in the search results contain all these queried keywords. This function can be achieved by trivially invoking single keyword search for each queried keyword separately and calculate the intersection over the search results. However, such a method may lead to inefficiency issues or extra leakages.

In 2013, Cash et al. [8] put forward the first sublinear SSE scheme, called Oblivious Cross-Tags (OXT), that achieves conjunctive keyword search and general Boolean queries. Their solution finds out a tradeoff between efficiency and security by defining the leakage functions. Then Cash et al. [7] implemented SSE protocols in dynamic setting and their constructions show high efficiency when dealing with large-scale database. Sun et al. [41] proposed a secure and efficient multi-client SSE scheme supporting Boolean queries. Based on RSA function, their proposed protocol realizes non-interaction between the data owner and the client. Furthermore, the technique of attribute-based encryption is embedded into their scheme to achieve fine-grained access control on the cloud data.

Lai et al. [27] constructed a new SSE protocol with support for conjunctive queries, named Hidden Cross-tags (HXT), enhancing the privacy-preserving while maintaining the search efficiency. By employing hidden vector encryption and bloom filter, their protocol can prevent the keyword pair result pattern leakage during the conjunctive search procedure. So far, a variety of SSE solutions with conjunctive queries were proposed, such as schemes [3,19,23,52,58].

5.2   Range Queries

Range query is another important search capability in SSE construction. An SSE protocol with range queries can return all the documents or records within the requested range, which is quite useful in practical cloud storage. For example, A high school teacher would like to obtain all the records satisfying $80 \leq SCORE \leq 89$ in the exam or the company plans to analyze the income distribution within the range [5,000, 15,000]. Thus range query acts as a vital role to achieve the above requests. In order to achieve high efficiency and less leakage, various SSE schemes with range queries have been proposed.

Faber et al. [14] constructed an SSE protocol supporting for range queries, which can be treated as functional extension of the OXT protocol [8]. Moreover,

Table 3. Comparison with existing SSE schemes with rich queries

Schemes	Dynamism	Query type	Security	Index size	Search efficiency
Cash et al. [8]	×	Conjunctive	IND-CKA2	$O(d+n)$	$O(l)$
Cash et al. [7]	✓	Conjunctive	IND-CKA2	$O(d+n)$	$O(l)$
Lai et al. [27]	×	Conjunctive	IND-CKA2	$O(d+n)$	$O(l)$
Hu et al. [19]	✓	Conjunctive	FS	$O(d+n)$	$O(l)$
Faber et al. [14]	✓	Range	IND-CKA2	$O(d+n)$	$O(l)$
Zuo et al. [62] (Sec. 4.3)	✓	Range	FS	$O(d+n)$	$O(a_w)$
Zuo et al. [62] (Sec. 4.4)	✓	Range	BS	$O(d+n)$	$O(a_w)$
Tahir et al. [44]	×	Disjunctive	IND-CKA2	$O(d \cdot n)$	$O(m \cdot log(d))$
Du et al. [13]	✓	Disjunctive	FS	$O(d \cdot t)$	$O(d)$
Wu et al. [51] (Sec. 5)	×	Disjunctive	IND-CKA2	$O(d \cdot n)$	$O(m \cdot r \cdot log(d))$

their scheme can deal with scalable database as well as additional features like data dynamism. Zuo et al. [62] built two dynamic SSE schemes with support for range queries. The first scheme is based on a new designed binary tree and trapdoor permutation equipped with forward privacy to resist file-injection attacks. While the second one adopts the Paillier encryption and can support backward privacy with limited numbers of files. Both the proposed schemes with range search are proved secure in the random oracle model. Other related schemes (for instance, schemes [3, 30, 45, 50, 53, 56]) also focused on the SSE with range queries.

5.3 Disjunctive Queries

Disjunctive query is one form of Boolean query, returning search results that contain at least one keyword among the requested query, which is different to conjunctive query. Kim et al. [24] presented an SSE scheme based on fully homomorphic encryption (FHE) with support for disjunctive queries. However, their scheme only considers the efficiency, without any detailed security analysis. Based on the probabilistic bucket-encrypting index structure, Du et al. [13] designed a novel forward-private SSE solution on disjunctive queries. Their solution has well solved the trade-off issue between privacy and search efficiency.

Recently, Yuan et al. [55] investigated a secure multi-client conjunctive SSE scheme and extended this scheme to support disjunctive query. Their construction is mainly based on a distributed index framework and allows parallel search operations among numerous servers. Wu et al. [51] proposed an efficient and secure SSE protocol on disjunctive queries, named VBT-2, which is the first scheme enabling both single-round communication and sublinear search efficiency. More research on disjunctive queries can be found in [8, 13, 20, 44, 58].

Table 3 compares the most recent SSE schemes with query expressiveness, in terms of functionality, security and efficiency. Note that n represents the number of keywords; l represents the number of files containing w_1; m represents the number of terms in a conjunctive query; t represents the number of buckets.

Table 4. Comparison with existing verifiable SSE schemes

Schemes	Dynamism	Query type	Verifiablity	Security	Verify efficiency
Azraoui et al. [2]	×	Conjunctive	Public	IND-CKA2	$O(m)$
Sun et al. [43]	√	Conjunctive	Public/Private	UC-CKA2	$O(m + r)$
Bost et al. [5]	√	Single	Private	FS	$O(r)$
Yoneyama et al. [54]	√	Single	Private	FS	$O(r)$
Wang et al. [46]	×	Conjunctive	Private	IND-CKA2	$O(k)$
Zhu et al. [61]	√	Boolean	Private	IND-CKA2	$O(log(n))$
Miao et al. [31]	×	Conjunctive	Public/Private	IND-CKA2	$O(l)$
Soleimanian et al. [37]	×	Boolean	Public	IND-CKA2	$O(l \cdot m)$
Ogata et al. [33]	×	Single	Private	IND-CKA2	$O(r)$
Zhang et al. [60]	√	Single	Private	FS	$O(r)$

6   Verifiable SSE Schemes

In most SSE schemes, the cloud server is defined as semi-trusted, while in practice, the cloud server may be malicious and may return the incorrect or incomplete search results. Thus a verification mechanism is necessary to check the search result and detect the potential misbehaviors. Verifiable keyword search enables the client to verify the search results returned by the cloud server, including correctness and completeness verification. The first verifiable SSE protocol was proposed by Kurosawa and Ohtaki [25] and soon afterwards, they extended their verifiable SSE to support dynamic operations in scheme [26]. However, both schemes brought heavy cost on computation and storage aspects.

Sun et al. [43] investigated an efficient verifiable SSE scheme with support for conjunctive keyword search and data dynamic. Relied on bilinear-map accumulator and collision-resistant accumulation tree, the verification solution proposed in their scheme can be either publicly or privately verifiable. Bost et al. [5] proposed the first verifiable dynamic SSE with forward privacy based on verifiable hash tables. This research also defines the lower bounds on the computational complexity for search and update operations.

Later, Wang et al. [46] designed a verifiable SSE scheme with conjunctive keyword search suited for large encrypted database. Their protocol is inspired from the scheme [41] and employs bilinear-map accumulators to achieve the search result verification, even when the search result is returned as empty. However, their scheme has expensive computation cost since the bilinear pairings are required. Besides, the verification process for the non-membership cannot be completed in a batch method and needs to be calculated one by one, which incurs heavy computation cost on the data user side.

Recently, Soleimanian et al. [37] proposed two publicly verifiable SSE schemes for single and Boolean keyword search respectively. Their schemes achieve high efficiency with less computational overhead by leveraging simple and fast cryptographic components, such as pseudo-random functions and digital signatures.

However, the communication complexity in the first scheme is linear to the number of documents, while the second scheme brings too much leakage to the cloud server. Miao et al. [31] constructed two SSE protocols with verifiability based on the enhanced vector commitment and bloom filter. The basic one can support single keyword search while the extended one can support conjunctive keyword search.

Later, Zhang et al. [60] presented another efficient verifiable SSE scheme with forward privacy by introducing multiset hash functions, realizing correctness and completeness verifiablity for the search result. What's more, their scheme can achieve optimized search and update efficiency compared with related schemes. Several other proposed SSE solutions also support verifiability, such as [2, 15, 29, 32, 33, 36, 54, 61].

For better description, a comparison of verifiable SSE schemes is given in Table 4. Note that, k represents the number of selected identifiers for verification where $k \leq l$, since a sample checking method is adopted in [46].

7   Conclusion and Future Work

This paper first revisited the notion of SSE and then discussed two promising security properties of SSE schemes as forward and backward privacy. Then various existing SSE protocols with different functions were discussed, including single keyword search, conjunctive keyword search, range search, disjunctive keyword search and verifiable search. As for the future work, we consider four main directions as follows:

– As we know, most previous dynamic SSE schemes have not considered forward or backward privacy. For existing SSE solutions, some can only achieve weak backward privacy. Therefore, in the future, how to construct SSE protocols with strong forward and backward privacy can be treated as one of the vital research directions.
– Improving search performance is another direction for future work, especially to deal with the search requests over large-scale cloud data.
– We seek for SSE approaches with support for various query functionalities, such as ranked keyword search, fuzzy keyword search and similarity search with forward and backward privacy.
– Applying forward or backward privacy requirement to other cryptographic primitives can also be treated as one future direction to enhance the cloud security one step further.

Acknowledgment. This work was supported by the National Natural Science Foundation of China (Nos. 61702401 and 61902315), the Fundamental Research Funds for the Central Universities (No. XJS17053).

References

1. Amjad, G., Kamara, S., Moataz, T.: Forward and backward private searchable encryption with SGX. In: Proceedings of the 12th European Workshop on Systems Security, p. 4. ACM (2019)

2. Azraoui, M., Elkhiyaoui, K., Önen, M., Molva, R.: Publicly verifiable conjunctive keyword search in outsourced databases. In: 2015 IEEE Conference on Communications and Network Security (CNS), pp. 619–627. IEEE (2015)
3. Boneh, D., Waters, B.: Conjunctive, subset, and range queries on encrypted data. In: Vadhan, S.P. (ed.) TCC 2007. LNCS, vol. 4392, pp. 535–554. Springer, Heidelberg (2007). https://doi.org/10.1007/978-3-540-70936-7_29
4. Bost, R.: Σοφος: forward secure searchable encryption. In: Proceedings of the 2016 ACM SIGSAC Conference on Computer and Communications Security, pp. 1143–1154. ACM (2016)
5. Bost, R., Fouque, P.A., Pointcheval, D.: Verifiable dynamic symmetric searchable encryption: optimality and forward security. IACR Cryptology ePrint Archive, vol. 2016, p. 62 (2016)
6. Bost, R., Minaud, B., Ohrimenko, O.: Forward and backward private searchable encryption from constrained cryptographic primitives. In: Proceedings of the 2017 ACM SIGSAC Conference on Computer and Communications Security, pp. 1465–1482. ACM (2017)
7. Cash, D., et al.: Dynamic searchable encryption in very-large databases: data structures and implementation. In: NDSS, vol. 14, pp. 23–26. Citeseer (2014)
8. Cash, D., Jarecki, S., Jutla, C., Krawczyk, H., Roşu, M.-C., Steiner, M.: Highly-scalable searchable symmetric encryption with support for boolean queries. In: Canetti, R., Garay, J.A. (eds.) CRYPTO 2013. LNCS, vol. 8042, pp. 353–373. Springer, Heidelberg (2013). https://doi.org/10.1007/978-3-642-40041-4_20
9. Chamani, G.J., Papadopoulos, D., Papamanthou, C., Jalili, R.: New constructions for forward and backward private symmetric searchable encryption. In: Proceedings of the 2018 ACM SIGSAC Conference on Computer and Communications Security, pp. 1038–1055. ACM (2018)
10. Cui, S., Song, X., Asghar, M.R., Galbraith, S.D., Russello, G.: Privacy-preserving searchable databases with controllable leakage. arXiv preprint arXiv:1909.11624 (2019)
11. Curtmola, R., Garay, J., Kamara, S., Ostrovsky, R.: Searchable symmetric encryption: improved definitions and efficient constructions. In: Proceedings of the 13th ACM Conference on Computer and Communications Security, pp. 79–88. ACM (2006)
12. Dowsley, R., Michalas, A., Nagel, M., Paladi, N.: A survey on design and implementation of protected searchable data in the cloud. Comput. Sci. Rev. 26, 17–30 (2017)
13. Du, M., Wang, Q., He, M., Weng, J.: Privacy-preserving indexing and query processing for secure dynamic cloud storage. IEEE Trans. Inf. Forensics Secur. 13(9), 2320–2332 (2018)
14. Faber, S., Jarecki, S., Krawczyk, H., Nguyen, Q., Rosu, M., Steiner, M.: Rich queries on encrypted data: beyond exact matches. In: Pernul, G., Ryan, P.Y.A., Weippl, E. (eds.) ESORICS 2015. LNCS, vol. 9327, pp. 123–145. Springer, Cham (2015). https://doi.org/10.1007/978-3-319-24177-7_7
15. Ge, X., et al.: Towards achieving keyword search over dynamic encrypted cloud data with symmetric-key based verification. IEEE Trans. Dependable Secure Comput. PP(99), 1 (2019)
16. Goh, E.J., et al.: Secure indexes. IACR Cryptology ePrint Archive, vol. 2003, p. 216 (2003)
17. Han, F., Qin, J., Hu, J.: Secure searches in the cloud: a survey. Future Gener. Comput. Syst. 62, 66–75 (2016)

18. Handa, R., Krishna, C.R., Aggarwal, N.: Searchable encryption: a survey on privacy-preserving search schemes on encrypted outsourced data. Concurrency Comput. Pract. Experience **31**(17), e5201 (2019)
19. Hu, C., et al.: Forward secure conjunctive-keyword searchable encryption. IEEE Access **7**, 35035–35048 (2019)
20. Kamara, S., Moataz, T.: Boolean searchable symmetric encryption with worst-case sub-linear complexity. In: Coron, J.-S., Nielsen, J.B. (eds.) EUROCRYPT 2017. LNCS, vol. 10212, pp. 94–124. Springer, Cham (2017). https://doi.org/10.1007/978-3-319-56617-7_4
21. Kamara, S., Papamanthou, C.: Parallel and Dynamic searchable symmetric encryption. In: Sadeghi, A.-R. (ed.) FC 2013. LNCS, vol. 7859, pp. 258–274. Springer, Heidelberg (2013). https://doi.org/10.1007/978-3-642-39884-1_22
22. Kamara, S., Papamanthou, C., Roeder, T.: Dynamic searchable symmetric encryption. In: Proceedings of the 2012 ACM Conference on Computer and Communications Security, pp. 965–976. ACM (2012)
23. Kerschbaum, F., Tueno, A.: An efficiently searchable encrypted data structure for range queries. arXiv preprint arXiv:1709.09314 (2017)
24. Kim, M., Lee, H.T., Ling, S., Wang, H.: On the efficiency of fhe-based private queries. IEEE Trans. Dependable Secure Comput. **15**(2), 357–363 (2018). https://doi.org/10.1109/TDSC.2016.2568182
25. Kurosawa, K., Ohtaki, Y.: UC-Secure Searchable Symmetric Encryption. In: Keromytis, A.D. (ed.) FC 2012. LNCS, vol. 7397, pp. 285–298. Springer, Heidelberg (2012). https://doi.org/10.1007/978-3-642-32946-3_21
26. Kurosawa, K., Ohtaki, Y.: How to update documents *Verifiably* in searchable symmetric encryption. In: Abdalla, M., Nita-Rotaru, C., Dahab, R. (eds.) CANS 2013. LNCS, vol. 8257, pp. 309–328. Springer, Cham (2013). https://doi.org/10.1007/978-3-319-02937-5_17
27. Lai, S., et al.: Result pattern hiding searchable encryption for conjunctive queries. In: Proceedings of the 2018 ACM SIGSAC Conference on Computer and Communications Security, pp. 745–762. ACM (2018)
28. Li, J., et al.: Searchable symmetric encryption with forward search privacy. IEEE Trans. Dependable Secure Comput. (2019). https://doi.org/10.1109/TDSC.2019.2894411
29. Liu, X., Yang, G., Mu, Y., Deng, R.: Multi-user verifiable searchable symmetric encryption for cloud storage. IEEE Trans. Dependable Secure Comput. (2018). https://doi.org/10.1109/TDSC.2018.2876831
30. Loh, R., Zuo, C., Liu, J.K., Sun, S.-F.: A multi-client DSSE scheme supporting range queries. In: Guo, F., Huang, X., Yung, M. (eds.) Inscrypt 2018. LNCS, vol. 11449, pp. 289–307. Springer, Cham (2019). https://doi.org/10.1007/978-3-030-14234-6_16
31. Miao, M., Wang, J., Wen, S., Ma, J.: Publicly verifiable database scheme with efficient keyword search. Inform. Sci. **475**, 18–28 (2019)
32. Najafi, A., Javadi, H.H.S., Bayat, M.: Verifiable ranked search over encrypted data with forward and backward privacy. Future Gener. Comput. Syst. **101**, 410–419 (2019)
33. Ogata, W., Kurosawa, K.: No-dictionary searchable symmetric encryption. IEICE Trans. Fundam. Electron. Commun. Comput. Sci. **102**(1), 114–124 (2019)
34. Ozmen, M.O., Hoang, T., Yavuz, A.A.: Forward-private dynamic searchable symmetric encryption with efficient search. In: 2018 IEEE International Conference on Communications (ICC), pp. 1–6. IEEE (2018)

35. Poh, G.S., Chin, J.J., Yau, W.C., Choo, K.K.R., Mohamad, M.S.: Searchable symmetric encryption: designs and challenges. ACM Comput. Surv. (CSUR) **50**(3), 40 (2017)
36. Shao, J., Lu, R., Guan, Y., Wei, G.: Achieve efficient and verifiable conjunctive and fuzzy queries over encrypted data in cloud. IEEE Trans. Serv. Comput. (2019). https://doi.org/10.1109/TSC.2019.2924372
37. Soleimanian, A., Khazaei, S.: Publicly verifiable searchable symmetric encryption based on efficient cryptographic components. Des. Codes Crypt. **87**(1), 123–147 (2019)
38. Song, D.X., Wagner, D., Perrig, A.: Practical techniques for searches on encrypted data. In: Proceeding 2000 IEEE Symposium on Security and Privacy, S&P 2000, pp. 44–55. IEEE (2000)
39. Song, X., Dong, C., Yuan, D., Xu, Q., Zhao, M.: Forward private searchable symmetric encryption with optimized i/o efficiency. IEEE Trans. Dependable Secure Comput. (2018). https://doi.org/10.1109/TDSC.2018.2822294
40. Stefanov, E., Papamanthou, C., Shi, E.: Practical dynamic searchable encryption with small leakage. In: NDSS, vol. 71, pp. 72–75 (2014)
41. Sun, S.-F., Liu, J.K., Sakzad, A., Steinfeld, R., Yuen, T.H.: An efficient non-interactive multi-client searchable encryption with support for boolean queries. In: Askoxylakis, I., Ioannidis, S., Katsikas, S., Meadows, C. (eds.) ESORICS 2016. LNCS, vol. 9878, pp. 154–172. Springer, Cham (2016). https://doi.org/10.1007/978-3-319-45744-4_8
42. Sun, S.F., et al.: Practical backward-secure searchable encryption from symmetric puncturable encryption. In: Proceedings of the 2018 ACM SIGSAC Conference on Computer and Communications Security, pp. 763–780. ACM (2018)
43. Sun, W., Liu, X., Lou, W., Hou, Y.T., Li, H.: Catch you if you lie to me: efficient verifiable conjunctive keyword search over large dynamic encrypted cloud data. In: 2015 IEEE Conference on Computer Communications (INFOCOM), pp. 2110–2118. IEEE (2015)
44. Tahir, S., Steponkus, L., Ruj, S., Rajarajan, M., Sajjad, A.: A parallelized disjunctive query based searchable encryption scheme for big data. Future Generation Computer Systems (2018, in press). https://doi.org/10.1016/j.future.2018.05.048
45. Wang, J., Chow, S.S.M.: Forward and backward-secure range-searchable symmetric encryption. IACR Cryptology ePrint Archive, vol. 2019, p. 497 (2019)
46. Wang, J., Chen, X., Sun, S.-F., Liu, J.K., Au, M.H., Zhan, Z.-H.: Towards efficient verifiable conjunctive keyword search for large encrypted database. In: Lopez, J., Zhou, J., Soriano, M. (eds.) ESORICS 2018. LNCS, vol. 11099, pp. 83–100. Springer, Cham (2018). https://doi.org/10.1007/978-3-319-98989-1_5
47. Wang, Q., Guo, Y., Huang, H., Jia, X.: Multi-user forward secure dynamic searchable symmetric encryption. In: Au, M.H., et al. (eds.) NSS 2018. LNCS, vol. 11058, pp. 125–140. Springer, Cham (2018). https://doi.org/10.1007/978-3-030-02744-5_9
48. Wang, Y., Wang, J., Chen, X.: Secure searchable encryption: a survey. J. Commun. Inf. Netw. **1**(4), 52–65 (2016)
49. Wei, Y., Lv, S., Guo, X., Liu, Z., Huang, Y., Li, B.: FSSE: forward secure searchable encryption with keyed-block chains. Inf. Sci. **500**, 113–126 (2019). https://doi.org/10.1016/j.ins.2019.05.059
50. Wu, S., Li, Q., Li, G., Yuan, D., Yuan, X., Wang, C.: ServeDB: secure, verifiable, and efficient range queries on outsourced database. In: 2019 IEEE 35th International Conference on Data Engineering (ICDE), pp. 626–637. IEEE (2019)

51. Wu, Z., Li, K., Li, K., Wang, J.: Fast boolean queries with minimized leakage for encrypted databases in cloud computing. IEEE Access **7**, 49418–49431 (2019). https://doi.org/10.1109/ACCESS.2019.2910457

52. Wu, Z., Li, K.: Vbtree: forward secure conjunctive queries over encrypted data for cloud computing. In: Very Large Data Bases, vol. 28, no. 1, pp. 25–46 (2019)

53. Xu, C., Zhang, C., Xu, J.: vchain: Enabling verifiable boolean range queries over Blockchain databases. In: Proceedings of the 2019 International Conference on Management of Data, pp. 141–158. ACM (2019)

54. Yoneyama, K., Kimura, S.: Verifiable and forward secure dynamic searchable symmetric encryption with storage efficiency. In: Qing, S., Mitchell, C., Chen, L., Liu, D. (eds.) ICICS 2017. LNCS, vol. 10631, pp. 489–501. Springer, Cham (2018). https://doi.org/10.1007/978-3-319-89500-0_42

55. Yuan, X., Yuan, X., Zhang, Y., Li, B., Wang, C.: Enabling encrypted boolean queries in geographically distributed databases. IEEE Trans. Parallel Distrib. Syst. 1–1 (2019). https://doi.org/10.1109/TPDS.2019.2940945

56. Yuan, X., Guo, Y., Wang, X., Wang, C., Li, B., Jia, X.: EncKV: an encrypted key-value store with rich queries. In: Proceedings of the 2017 ACM on Asia Conference on Computer and Communications Security, pp. 423–435. ACM (2017)

57. Zhang, R., Xue, R., Liu, L.: Searchable encryption for healthcare clouds: a survey. IEEE Trans. Serv. Comput. **11**(6), 978–996 (2017)

58. Zhang, Y., Li, Y., Wang, Y.: Conjunctive and disjunctive keyword search over encrypted mobile cloud data in public key system. Mob. Inf. Syst. **2018**, 1–11 (2018)

59. Zhang, Y., Katz, J., Papamanthou, C.: All your queries are belong to us: the power of file-injection attacks on searchable encryption. In: 25th {USENIX} Security Symposium ({USENIX} Security 16), pp. 707–720 (2016)

60. Zhang, Z., Wang, J., Wang, Y., Su, Y., Chen, X.: Towards efficient verifiable forward secure searchable symmetric encryption. In: Sako, K., Schneider, S., Ryan, P.Y.A. (eds.) ESORICS 2019. LNCS, vol. 11736, pp. 304–321. Springer, Cham (2019). https://doi.org/10.1007/978-3-030-29962-0_15

61. Zhu, J., Li, Q., Wang, C., Yuan, X., Wang, Q., Ren, K.: Enabling generic, verifiable, and secure data search in cloud services. IEEE Trans. Parallel Distrib. Syst. **29**(8), 1721–1735 (2018)

62. Zuo, C., Sun, S.-F., Liu, J.K., Shao, J., Pieprzyk, J.: Dynamic searchable symmetric encryption schemes supporting range queries with forward (and backward) security. In: Lopez, J., Zhou, J., Soriano, M. (eds.) ESORICS 2018. LNCS, vol. 11099, pp. 228–246. Springer, Cham (2018). https://doi.org/10.1007/978-3-319-98989-1_12

63. Zuo, C., Sun, S.-F., Liu, J.K., Shao, J., Pieprzyk, J.: Dynamic searchable symmetric encryption with forward and stronger backward privacy. In: Sako, K., Schneider, S., Ryan, P.Y.A. (eds.) ESORICS 2019. LNCS, vol. 11736, pp. 283–303. Springer, Cham (2019). https://doi.org/10.1007/978-3-030-29962-0_14

A Graph Database-Based Approach to Analyze Network Log Files

Lars Diederichsen[1], Kim-Kwang Raymond Choo[2(✉)], and Nhien-An Le-Khac[3]

[1] German Federal Police, Potsdam, Germany
lars.diederichsen@protonmail.com, lars.diederichsen@gmx.de
[2] University of Texas at San Antonio, San Antonio, USA
raymond.choo@fulbrightmail.org
[3] School of Computer Science, University College Dublin, Dublin, Ireland
an.lekhac@ucd.ie

Abstract. Network log files from different sources often need to be analyzed in order to facilitate a more accurate assessment of the cyber threat severity. For example, using command line tools, any log file can be reviewed only in isolation. While using a log management system allows for searching across different log files, the relationship(s) between different network activities may not be easy to establish from the analysis of these different log files. We can use relational databases to establish these relationships, for example using complex database queries involving multiple join operations to link the tables. In recent years, there has been a trend of using graph databases to manage data for semantic queries (e.g. importing a fixed amount of log data for subsequent analysis). Hence, in this paper, we propose a new approach to analyze network log files, by using the graph database. Specifically, we posit the importance of constantly monitoring log files for new entries for immediate processed and analysis, and their results imported into the graph database. To facilitate the evaluation of our proposed approach, we use the Zeek network security monitor system to produce log files from monitored network traffic in real-time. We then explain how graph databases can be used to analyze network log files in near-real time within a network security-monitoring environment. Findings from our research demonstrate the utility of graph data in analyzing log data.

Keywords: Network log analysis · Graph database · Real-time analysis · Network security

1 Introduction

Network security monitoring (NSM) is one of several widely used approaches in information security operation centers (SOC), where network traffic is monitored, logged and analyzed in real-time in order to detect any kind of malicious behavior within the network [1]. There is a broad range of network intrusion detection systems that can be applied within a NSM environment, such as reputation-based detection systems (attempt

© Springer Nature Switzerland AG 2019
J. K. Liu and X. Huang (Eds.): NSS 2019, LNCS 11928, pp. 53–73, 2019.
https://doi.org/10.1007/978-3-030-36938-5_4

to detect connections from a protected network to IP addresses and hosts on the Internet that have shown malicious actions in the past). Another category is signature-based detection systems (IDS) like Snort [11, 12] or Suricata [13], which analyze network packets for specific patterns [10]. A more sophisticated category is the security incident and event management systems (SIEM), which allows for the correlation and aggregation of detected events.

These different NSM categories require different extent of resources and have different capabilities [4]. For example, a signature-based IDS displays a limited amount of data related to a particular alert message [10]. First, it stores the content and metadata of the network traffic packet that led to the alert, as well as storing metadata of the rule triggering the alert. Thus, while analyzing an alert, one can only determine the exact trigger. It is clear that such an approach does not yield the necessary information required in order to assess the severity of the threat and formulate an appropriate mitigation strategy. A more comprehensive analysis is required, for example by analyzing log files created by different networking components like web proxies, routers, and so on. A number of commercial NSM systems also produce log files that may inform an investigation and/or risk mitigation strategy. For example, the Zeek NSM system [14] (Zeek was formerly known as Bro [7] and hereinafter referred to only as Zeek) produces various log files of different Internet protocols. Since every log file includes different data, they need to be examined separately. Thus, an analysis of the log files requires time and manpower commitment, in order to better understand the context of the IDS alert. This necessitates the design of system or tool to automate the connection of data from different log files. We posit the importance of a graph database in such a context. Specifically, converting log data into nodes and relationships of a graph database could give different insights on how the data interrelates. We also note that graph databases have been utilized in many different areas, ranging from social network analysis to routing analysis to product recommendation in electronic and mobile commerce to medical research, and so forth [9].

Therefore, in this paper we examine the feasibility of modeling and using a graph database for performing log file analysis within an NSM environment in real-time. In a NSM environment, creating log files is an ongoing process. For example, whenever an event occurs on the network, a log record is created by some devices or systems. Therefore, one has to constantly monitor for new log data and to process any new log data immediately. Due to the volume, variety, and velocity of data in such log files and other relevant information, real-time collection and analysis of log files is challenging, in practice. Specifically, in this paper we focus on the following challenge:

1. How do we integrate information from heterogeneous information sources to facilitate the identification of relationships between various network traffic entities in a real-time logging NSM environment?

Hence, in this paper we demonstrate how we can use a data graph to semantically represent log file data correctly. Then, we present a method to transfer log data into a graph database in a real-time NSM environment. We show that using a set (or sets) of queries, we can retrieve information from the modelled data graph to facilitate the analysis and validation of a particular event at a glance, and/or find network traffic anomalies (potential indicator(s) for a network intrusion).

The rest of this paper is structured as follows. Section 2 reviews related work in the literature. We describe and evaluate our proposed approach in Sects. 3 and 4, respectively. Finally, Sect. 5 concludes this research.

2 Related Work

Although graph databases have been studied and applied in different disciplines [9], there have been limited attempts to utilize graph databases for network analysis. Schindler [15], for example, proposed an approach based on graph databases to analyze log data for detecting advanced persistent threat attacks. Specifically, he used graph databases to model cyber-attacks based on the kill chain model [16] and analyze log data using support vector machine (SVM) techniques. Djanali et al. [17] used graph clustering to create IDS rules from HTTP logs. Neise [4] has a similar approach for detecting network intrusions, based on data graph-based log file analysis. The author extracted and transformed data from various log files created by Zeek and stored them in a Neo4j graph database, focusing only on the analysis of previously gathered packet captures. The author also emphasized on the importance of near real-time analysis.

Unlike these aforementioned approaches, we focus on the usage of network traffic data, such as those processed by Zeek, in a real-time NSM environment, as we argue that using previously gathered packet captures that can only display network traffic of a small and limited timeframe is not as useful in understanding the threat landscape. Rather, we monitor log files for new entries, and any new detected entry will be extracted, transformed and stored into the graph database in near real-time. We also note that the data graph model used by Neise [4] does not appear to be sufficiently detailed. The use of only one node per log entry may be sufficient for an overall consideration, but it is too generic if one wants to have a more detailed insight into the relationship between different entities. In other words, the graph's potential in representing interdependencies between entities is not maximized. In our work, a separate data graph model is proposed for each Zeek log file used. Those data graph models are then connected with each other where possible to bring the necessary depth into relationship details.

3 Proposed Approach

In this section, we will explain how log files are prepared prior to describing our approach of modelling network log files using graph databases.

3.1 Log File Preparation

As a use case, we will focus on the usage of the conn.log, the dns.log, and the http.log created by Zeek. However, in practice our proposed approach can be used on any log files. As explained earlier, log files have to be monitored for new data entries that need to be processed.

3.1.1 Monitoring the Logs

The monitoring of the log files has to ensure that no log data entry will remain undetected and log rotation is handled properly. The usage of the Linux built-in command tail with the option "−F" is one of several ways to monitor log files. The tail command displays, by default, the last ten lines of a file. Using the option "F" causes the tail to output attached data as the log file grows. It also tracks the observed file by its name by periodically opening the file to verify if it has been deleted and re-created. Any log rotation will be handled by this behavior.

3.1.2 Parsing and Importing Logs

Every new recognized log data will be converted into a Python dictionary for further processing. This log data dictionary will then be used as parameter for a function that creates nodes and relationships from the extracted log data to model a data graph and import it into a Neo4j graph database [5]. Using the third-party Python library Py2neo2 [8], the nodes and relationships that build the graph will be created. Afterwards, the graph data will be imported into Neo4j. We also need to consider the following features in log files when creating the data graphs:

- Timestamp from each log record needs to be converted and stored in human-readable format, split into date and time.
- Value of *conn.log*'s conn_state value needs to be converted and stored in human-readable format.
- Value of *conn.log*'s history value needs to be converted and stored in human-readable-format.
- If the *dns.log*'s answers value contains more than one value, it will be split into IP addresses and/or host domains. Each will be later assigned to a separate node.
- The referrer value from the http.log will also be connected with the corresponding URI node, as well as the Referrer node from that referring connection graph.

3.2 Log File Modelling for conn.log

The conn.log file is used for tracking and logging of general information regarding TCP, UDP and ICMP traffic. The logged information can be interpreted using flow semantics, with information about the involved host computers and further metadata of the connection. The following represents a full record of Zeek's *conn.log* file. The red numbers are used for referencing to equivalent fields (Fig. 1).

[1]1481941838.417565 [2]C2qCzf4J6MLlRnwF9e [3]172.16.2.96 [4]64812 [5]224.0.0.252 [6]5355 [7]udp
[8]dns [9]0.101830 [10]54 [11]0 [12]S0 [13]. [14]. [15]0 [16]ShA [17]2 [18]110
[19]0 [20]0 [21](empty).

Fig. 1. Example of a record of conn.log (Color figure online)

More details on these fields are described in Appendix A. The evaluation of the information that can be derived from Zeek's conn.log to identify entities and relationships resulted in the following proposed graph model (Fig. 2).

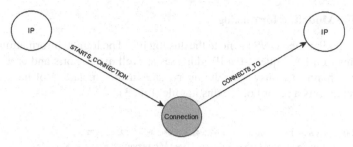

Fig. 2. Graph data model for conn.log: An example

The proposed conn.log graph consists of two different entity types that are represented by three nodes. The nodes are labeled as connection or IP. The "Connection" node represents the connection itself and contains most of the connection's metadata. An "IP" node represents the source host as well as the destination host computer, and contains the relevant IP address as a single property (Table 1).

Table 1. Nodes and their properties of conn.log graph data model

Name of node	Property name
Connection	ts, duration, uid, service, proto, orig_bytes, resp_bytes, orig_ip_bytes, resp_ip_bytes, tunnel_parents, missed_bytes, local_orig, local_resp, orig_pkts, resp_pkts, conn_state, history
IP	Ip

The nodes are interconnected by two different relationships. The "IP" representing the source host has a relationship "STARTS_CONNECTION" with the "Connection".

This relationship is directed from the IP node to the Connection node and contains the source port of the connection as a property. The "Connection" node has a relationship "CONNECTS_TO" with the "IP" node representing the destination host. This relationship contains the destination host's port as a property and is directed from the Connection node to the IP node (Table 2).

Table 2. Relationships of conn.log graph data model

Relationship	Property	Relationship from -> to
STARTS_CONNECTION	port	IP -> Connection
CONNECTS_TO	port	Connection -> IP

3.3 Log File Modeling for dns.log

Zeek writes all identified DNS traffic to the dns.log file. The logged information includes the timestamp of a DNS query, the IP addresses as well as the ports and protocol used, the queried domain, the answer to the query, and further metadata of the query. The following represents a record of the dns.log file (Fig. 3).

^{1}1481942844.665111 ^{2}CzoGu82M0OtQs2Kv4a^{3}172.16.2.96 ^{4}52794 ^{5}172.16.2.1 ^{6}53 ^{7}udp ^{8}26543 ^{9}0.144302 ^{10}google.com ^{11}1 ^{12}C_INTERNET ^{13}1 ^{14}A ^{15}0 ^{16}NOERROR ^{17}F ^{18}F ^{19}T ^{20}T ^{21}0 ^{22}216.58.202.14^{23}5.000000 ^{24}F

Fig. 3. Example of a record of dns.log

More details on these fields are described in Appendix B. The evaluation of a dns.log entry identified three different entity types to use as nodes. The fact that a log record in the conn.log, which is identified to be a DNS connection (the *conn.log*'s "service" key has "dns" as value in it) usually has the same unique identifier like the corresponding *dns.log*'s record, provides an opportunity to link both graphs together. Therefore, a fourth entity type could be identified. The identified entities are labelled as follows (i) DNS; (ii) IP; (iii) Host; (iv) Connection.

Modelling a data graph using these entities resulted in the following proposed graph (Fig. 4).

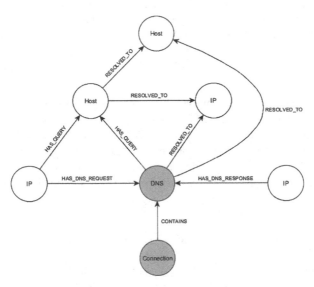

Fig. 4. Graph data model for dns.log

A "DNS" node that represents the DNS connection itself and contains most of the metadata of this connection. Similar to the conn.log data graph, two "IP" nodes represent a host computer and store the IP addresses in a single property. Additionally, an "IP" node will also be created for any IP address inside the query answer. A "Host" node represents a domain name containing it as a single property. In the graph, one "Host" will represent the queried Internet domain name. For any possible domain name from the query answer, an additional "Host" node will be created. The "Connection" node will represent the connection from the conn.log data graph that has the same "uid" value as the "DNS". In this way, the dns.log data graph is linked to the corresponding conn.log data graph.

The dns.log data graph interconnects the nodes via not less than six relationships.

The corresponding "Connection" node has a directed connection to the "DNS" node using the relationship "CONTAINS". The "IP" node representing the source host of the connection has a relationship "HAS_DNS_REQUEST" directed to the "DNS" node.

Both, the "IP" node and the "DNS" node have a propertyless relationship "HAS_QUERY" directed to the "Host" node that represents the queried domain. The "IP" node that represents the response host of this connection has a propertyless relationship directed to the "DNS" node that is named "HAS_DNS_RESPONSE". The last relationship in this graph is named "RESOLVED_TO". This is used to connect the "DNS" node with the "Host" or "IP" nodes resulting from the DNS query answer and has the corresponding time-to-live value as a property. It is also used to connect the "Host" node of the queried host with the "Host" or "IP" nodes from the DNS query answer and has the timestamp of the connection as a property (Tables 3 and 4).

This way, the graph can be easily queried for the time a host has been resolved to a specific IP address or another domain.

Table 3. Nodes and their properties of dns.log graph data model

Name of node	Property Name
DNS	ts, trans_id, uid, rtt, proto, qtype, qtypye_name, qclass, qclass_name, aa, tc, rd, ra, z
IP	ip
Host	host

Table 4. Relationships of dns.log graph data model

Relationship	Property	Relationship from -> to
HAS_QUERY	–	DNS -> Host
	–	IP -> Host
RESOLVED_TO	ttl	DNS -> Host
	ttl	DNS -> IP
	ts	Host -> Host
	ts	Host -> IP
CONTAINS	–	Connection -> DNS
HAS_DNS_REQUEST	–	IP -> DNS
HAS_DNS_RESPONSE	–	IP -> DNS

3.4 Log File Modelling for http.log

Zeek writes HTTP request and response pairs and all relevant metadata together to a single record to the http.log file. The following represents an exemplary record of the http.log file (Fig. 5).

[1]1481941849.586397 [2]CeXruB4EHUes3ZpLEg [3]172.16.2.96 [4]49157 [5]187.33.238.74 [6]80 [7]1
[8]GET [9]www.msftncsi.com [10]/ncsi.txt [11]. [12]1.1 [13]Microsoft NCSI [14]0 [15]14
[16]200 [17]OK [18]. [19]. [20](empty)[21] [22]. [23]. [24]. [25]. [26].
[27]F3gzej2YMBnmnVl6p9[28]. [29]text/plain

Fig. 5. Example of a record of http.log

More details on these fields are described in Appendix C. On the basis of the given information, the evaluation of the http.log data resulted in a proposed data graph that includes seven different entity types represented by not less than eight nodes (Fig. 6).

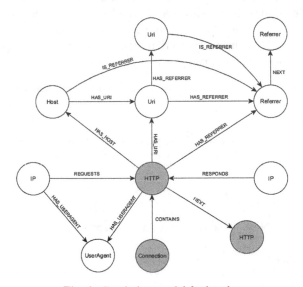

Fig. 6. Graph data model for http.log

A "HTTP" node represents the HTTP connection itself and includes most of the metadata of the connection.

Equally to the aforementioned graphs, the "IP" nodes represent host computers and contain the IP address as their single property. Similarly, to the DNS graph, the "Connection" node represents the connection from the conn.log data graph that has the same *uid* value as the "HTTP" node. In this way, the http.log data graph can be linked together with the corresponding conn.log data graph. The "Host" node represents the requested domain name. The "Uri" node represents the Uri from the http.log. The "Referrer" node represents the *http.log*'s referrer value. The user agent value from the http.log is represented by the "UserAgent".

The http.log data graph interconnects the nodes by using nine different relationships labels. All relationships used in this graph do not contain any property. Most relationships are labelled straightforward to indicate the end node. Some eponymous relationships are used to connect different nodes. For instance, the relationship "NEXT" is used to represent temporal order for both, "Referrer" nodes and "HTTP" nodes. The temporal order for "HTTP" nodes represents the trans_depth value of the log file and thus indicates the pipelined depth into the connection of the complete request/response transaction. Connecting "Referrer" nodes in a temporal order gives the opportunity to reproduce the sequence of referrers. The following table shows the used relationship of the http.log graph and their direction (Table 5).

Table 5. Relationships of http.log graph data model

Relationship	Relationship from -> to
CONTAINS	Connection -> HTTP
HAS_USERAGENT	HTTP -> UserAgent
	IP -> UserAgent
HAS_HOST	HTTP -> Host
HAS_URI	HTTP -> Uri
	Host -> Uri
HAS_REFERRER	HTTP -> Referrer
	Uri -> Referrer
	Uri -> Uri
IS_REFERRER	Host -> Referrer
	Uri -> Referrer
REQUESTS	IP -> HTTP
RESPONDS	IP -> HTTP
NEXT	HTTP -> HTTP
	Referrer -> Referrer

3.5 Indexes and Constraints

Neo4j is capable of index-free adjacency. Nevertheless, it features indexing to find start points for graph traversals quicker. Furthermore, Neo4j helps enforcing data integrity with the use of constraints that can be applied to nodes as well as to relationships. Unique property constraints ensure that property values are unique for all nodes with a given label. The use of constraints automatically creates an index on the given node and property [15].

In the proposed graph data model, unique constraints will be used for most of the nodes. The uniqueness assures that only one node will always represent the same entity. The following table shows the constraints that are used to guarantee unique nodes based on the corresponding property (Table 6).

Table 6. Constraints used for uniqueness

Node	Unique property
Connection	uid
IP	ip
Host	host
UserAgent	useragent
Referrer	referrer

In addition to the constraints, three indexes will be used for the proposed graph data model.

Since DNS and HTTP connections can have multiple log entries and thus multiple nodes with the same *uid*, using a constraint for uniqueness for these nodes would result in errors. These can be prevented by only using indexes on the *uid* of these nodes. An Uri node is expected to belong to just one host. If there is an identical URI (e.g. index.html) belonging to another host, it also shall be represented by another node. For this reason, the usage of a unique constraint for Uri nodes was abandoned and an index on the Uri was created instead.

4 Evaluation Setup and Findings

We simulate the traffic of a network that could be monitored to evaluate the utility of our proposed approach described in Sect. 3.

The evaluations were performed using a virtual machine using Oracle VirtualBox, Version 5.0.40. The virtual machine was set up with the following specifics:

- Ubuntu Server 16.04.2 LTS, 2 CPU's, 10 GB RAM, Zeek version 2.5-76, Neo4j version 3.2, and a network adapter for internal network.
- The host computer to the virtual machine was a Lenovo ThinkPad T530 with Intel Core i7 CPU, 16 GB RAM and Ubuntu 16.04 LTS as operating system

To simulate network traffic, several packet capture files were replayed in real-time, by using the Linux tool *tcpreplay*. *Tcpreplay* replays the traffic of a given packet capture file by sending its content packet-by-packet over a given network interface in the stored time interval. Zeek then monitored this simulated network traffic.

4.1 Importing Log Data

Various packet capture files were used for simulating network traffic to test the created Python scripts. These capture files included the *pcap* files of week 1 of the 1999 DARPA Intrusion Detection Evaluation Data Set (DARPA) [2] and the maccdc2012_00000.pcap [6] from the 2012 Mid-Atlantic Collegiate Cyber Defense Competition (MACCDC) [3]. The MACCDC capture was used to allow us to compare the output with the results of the prior work from Neise [4]. The DARPA files include network traffic of a 24 h/day. Thus, replaying these files also took 24 h. While replaying the DARPA packet capture files, no issue with processing speed was detected, which implies the potential of (near) real-time analysis. Every file was also replayed using 4x the speed. Even with the multiplied replay speed, no issue could be detected and this suggested the possibility of having (near) real-time analysis.

Although a short delay (approximately up to 2–3 min) between data logging and ingesting it into Neo4j could be observed a couple of times, the delay was always quickly caught up to as soon as network traffic decreased.

The replay of the MACCDC file revealed the limitations of how we imported data into the graph database. In this file, 8,635,943 packets with 935,501,635 bytes were sent in almost 71 min over the network. After replaying this file, it occurred that only about 130.000 out of almost 4.000.000 graphs were processed and stored in Neo4j. Almost all 15,000 DNS graphs were processed. About 18,000 of nearly 76,000 HTTP graphs (around 42%) were processed and only a little more that 97,000 out of almost 3,900,000. Connection graphs (around 2.5%) were created. A near-real time analysis of the HTTP graphs and Connection graphs was not feasible with this result. Only the DNS graphs could be analyzed almost in real-time. After a number of tests replaying with different speed settings, it could be validated that importing the data was too slow in this case. The final outcome was that processing the log files from the MACCDC file and writing the data to Neo4j took almost 40 h. Thus, to evaluate the speed of writing data into the graph database, the following experiments were performed.

To assure a uniform flow of log data, DARPA's "outside.tcpdump" of week 1's Friday was analyzed with Zeek prior the experiments. The resulted log files were used as the experiment's baseline. The number of log entries per log file is shown in Table 7.

Table 7. Number of log entries

Log file	Number of log entries
conn.log	39931
dns.log	6843
http.log	59398

To import the log files' data, the code of the particular Python scripts used had to be changed. Instead of monitoring the log files for new entries using the Linux command tail, the files were imported completely and read line by line to be processed.

The experiments were performed with different storage sizes of the database to find out how the writing performance relates to the number of nodes and relationships in the graph database. The expectation was that there should be no real measurable decrease of performance with a growing database. Therefore, after completing the replay of DARPA's week 1 files, the changed Python scripts were started for ten minutes to process the above mentioned prepared log files. During the process, the number of created Connection nodes, DNS nodes, and HTTP nodes was then queried every 60 s.

These nodes indicate the number of processed log entries from the given log file. By calculating the average number of created nodes, the writing speed for every given log file could by assessed realistically. These numbers were also compared to numbers taken randomly during the normal monitoring process and could be confirmed as valid values.

The experiments revealed that the conn.py script created 1620 Connection nodes per minute on average. The number of nodes and relationships already stored in the database had no significant effect on the writing performance. The dns.py script created usually between 600 and 700 DNS nodes per minute with 639 nodes on average. The http.py script created 267 HTTP nodes on average.

Here, a significant decrease in performance was demonstrable in relation to the number of nodes and relationships in the database. With a load of 289,000 nodes and 1,489,000 relationships, the http.py script created 336 HTTP nodes on average. After day 5 of the DARPA files and with 1,553,000 nodes and 7,555,000 relationships already stored in the database, only 200 HTTP nodes were created on average (Fig. 7).

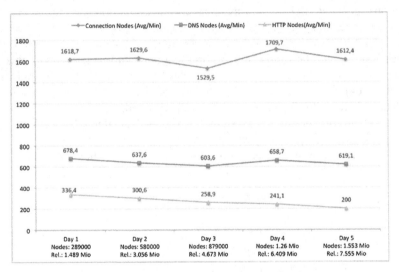

Fig. 7. Average numbers of created nodes

The constant numbers in created Connection nodes result from the size of the created graph with only three nodes and two relationships. The lower but overall constant number of DNS nodes result from the higher number of created nodes and relationships compared to the conn.log graph on the one hand. On the other hand, a dns.log graph is imported in four small transactions instead of one complete transaction in order to prevent transient errors. The same holds true for the way the http.py script writes a HTTP graph to the database. The even lower numbers of created HTTP nodes result from the complexity of the graph data model. Not only has the graph to be created for the given log data. It also queries the database for a Host node and its associated Uri node to create the IS_REFERRER and HAS_REFERRER relationships. The significant loss of writing performance is most likely connected with the growing number of http.log graphs in conjunction with the number of nodes per graph and their complex interconnections among each other.

The disk memory that was used for storing the data is negligible as expected. After replaying the DARPA files, the database comprised 1,553,000 nodes, 7,555,000 relationships, and more than 7,500,000 properties. This number of data required about 795 MB of disk space, which is more than 3.5 times the disk space of 216 MB that Zeek's created log files used.

Issues While Importing Data: Using an index for the uri value in Uri nodes may raised an error. This happened when the value of an URI was longer than 32,766 bytes, which is the maximum supported length of an indexed property value in Neo4j. Since a length of more than 32,766 bytes is not a normal length for an URI, it should be considered how to handle this issue.

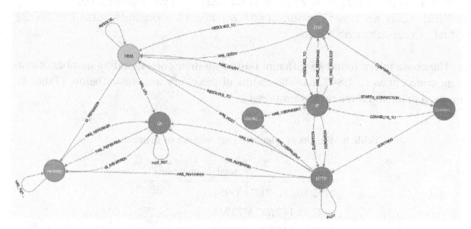

Fig. 8. Interconnected graph data model

The approach for monitoring and processing the different log files was to handle the files separately. Every log file should be processed on its own to ensure a modular structure, where data graphs can be added or removed at will. Thus, there was no identified requirement to create a new file or database that would collect the output of every log file and that also had to be monitored. The major advantage seen in this approach was the opportunity to add or remove log files at will without further changes to any code. However, monitoring and processing the log files separately means that there are multiple processes trying to insert data into Neo4j at the same time. Since Neo4 J is using an ACID consistency model to ensure that data is safe and consistently stored, two operations cannot be processed on the same node at the same time. Hence, whenever two transactions tried to use the same node, the latter transaction raised a TransientError due to a locked client that blocked the execution of that transaction. This behavior was noted at random times without any apparent pattern and independently of the database's size. In other tests, the error was not raised at all, neither using a new database nor a heavily populated one. Therefore, to counter the problem and to shorten the time needed to perform transactions, the import of dns.log and http.log data was split up into smaller transactions.

4.2 Querying the Database

Having a populated graph database, the graphs can now be analyzed. Figure 8 shows Neo4j's graphic representation of the data graph's schema. The analysis took place while replaying and monitoring DARPA's Week's 1 Thursday files with a speed multiplier of four. The following queries were executed, while the database was populated with about 1,055,000 nodes, 5,439,000 relationships and 8,435,000 property entries.

4.2.1 Querying the Connection Graph

The following query finds the hosts of the network that are responsible for the highest number of recorded outgoing connections so far:

```
MATCH (i:IP)-[sc:STARTS_CONNECTION]->(c:Connection)
RETURN i.ip as host, count(sc) as total_connections ORDER BY
total_connections DESC
```

The above query found 45 different hosts with their corresponding number of outgoing connections in 1,847 ms. The results of the query are shown below (Table 8), truncated to the top three results for brevity.

Table 8. Results of query for total number of connections

"host"	"total_connections"
"172.16.112.100"	39988
"172.16.117.52"	22924
"172.16.115.87"	18864

The above query only returns the number of outbound connections. To find out if the hosts with the most connections also produce the highest volume of outgoing traffic, the query only needs to be slightly modified to the following:

```
MATCH (i:IP)-[sc:STARTS_CONNECTION]->(c:Connection)
RETURN i.ip as host,
sum(toInteger(c.orig_ip_bytes)) as sent_bytes
ORDER BY sent_bytes DESC
```

As expected, the query found 45 hosts with their corresponding number of sent_bytes. The following results were returned in 3,181 ms (Table 9). Again, the results are truncated for brevity.

A comparison of both query results demonstrates that the number of outgoing connections and the number of bytes sent by a host do not necessarily correlate. In fact, the host that has by far the highest volume of sent bytes has only 1,052 outgoing connections.

Table 9. Results of query for total number of sent bytes

"host"	"total_connections"
"172.16.112.100"	39988
"172.16.117.52"	22924
"172.16.115.87"	18864

4.2.2 Querying the DNS Graph

The following query searches for the top domains queried for a given day (here: 26th July 2017):

```
MATCH(d:DNS{date: "2017-07-26"})-[hq:HAS_QUERY]-> (h:Host)
RETURN DISTINCT h.host as dns_query, COUNT(hq) AS total ORDER
BY total DESC
```

With the usage of additional human readable date and time in the graph, writing queries is easier for an analyst since it is unnecessary to either calculate or convert the original timestamps first. The query above found 2,469 records and returned the results after 849 ms.

Knowing which domains have been resolved to IP addresses in the past is a valuable opportunity to reduce the time needed for validating IDS alerts. The following query searches the graph for domains that have been resolved to the given IP address.

```
MATCH(i:IP{ip: "206.132.25.37"}) <-[:RESOLVED_TO]-(h:Host)
RETURN h.host
```

The query was completed after 4 ms and showed the only result "discuss. washingtonpost.com".

Querying the HTTP Graph: One strength of graph database is - without any doubt - the representation of social networks. Finding the friend of a friend's friend is an easy task for a graph database. This strength can be figuratively used to reproduce the reason how or why a user called a specific website by examining which domain was the referrer and who was the referrer of the referrer and so on. The following query searches the graph for paths of referrers beginning with the website http://www.usatoday.com/sports/sfront. htm as first referrer. Then, it splits the path into every single node and returns the next referring domain.

```
MATCH p=(ref:Referrer)-[:HAS_REFERRER*]->(r:Referrer)
WHERE ref.referrer= "http://www.usatoday.com/sports/sfront.htm" AND r.referrer="-"
UNWIND nodes(p) as refs
RETURN DISTINCT refs.referrer
```

The results of the query were returned in 5 ms and revealed a path of four entries.

4.3 Using the Graph Database for IDS Alert Validation

As stated in the introduction, an IDS alert only shows data concerning the network packet that triggered the alarm. Thus, we have implemented a small experimental web application called BroNeo, to provide a quick overview of the situation that led to the alarm and to expedite the alert validation. BroNeo uses five parameters; the IP addresses and ports of the source and destination hosts and the timestamp of the IDS alert that is to be examined. These parameters are sufficient for querying the graph database to provide the necessary information about what has happened. BroNeo provides the information gathered from the corresponding conn.log, which is extended by aggregations concerning the given hosts. These aggregations include each host's number of incoming and outgoing connections as well as their total number of sent and received bytes. To assess the situation even better and quickly recognize which domain belongs to the IP addresses, the graph model allows for showing of all domains whose IP address have been resolved.

```
MATCH (i:IP {ip:{sourceip}}) < -[:RESOLVED_TO]-(host:Host)
WITH host
OPTIONAL MATCH (host)-[:RESOLVED_TO]-> (alias:Host)
RETURN   collect(distinct   host.host)   +   collect(distinct
alias.host) as source_host
```

BroNeo additionally can provide the full HTTP Request/Response stream of the connection in chronological order. The following query searches for the needed data and part of its output is shown in Fig. 9.

```
MATCH (orig:IP {ip:{sip}})-[sc:STARTS_CONNECTION {port:{spt}}] -> (c:Connection)-
[ct:CONNECTS_TO {port:{dpt}}] ->(resp:IP {ip:{dip}})
WITH c
OPTIONAL MATCH (c)-[:CONTAINS]->(http)
WITH http
OPTIONAL MATCH (uri:Uri)<-[:HAS_URI]-(http)-[:HAS_HOST] ->(host:Host),(http)-
[:HAS_REFERRER]->(ref:Referrer),
(ua)<-[:HAS_USERAGENT]-(http)
RETURN http, ua.user_agent as user_agent, host.host AS host, uri.uri AS Uri, ref.referrer AS
referrer
ORDER BY http.trans_depth
```

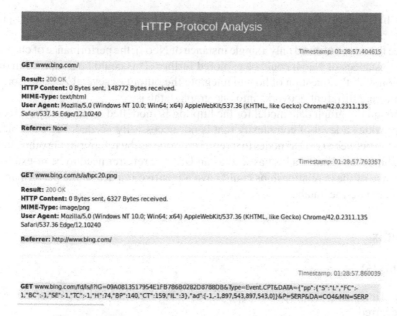

Fig. 9. BroNeo – Displayed data of HTTP protocol analysis

5 Conclusion and Future Work

In this paper, we demonstrated the potential of using a graph database for log file analysis in a NSM environment in near-real time. There are, however, a number of areas that our proposed approach can be improved. For example, our developed code was sufficient in the monitoring of a network with 45 users, but its utility in a larger scale, real-world network has not been evaluated. For example, to be able to monitor larger networks, the developed code needs to be optimized. Different approaches of monitoring and processing the log files or importing the data into the graph database in near real-time should also be examined.

From a log file analysis point of view, using a graph database allows any log data to be easily displayed, for example related data from different log files could be found with simple queries, and the sequence of referrers could be found with a single, simple query. Through this, a malicious cyber activity can be easily reconstructed, for example how a host computer was led to a website that automatically downloaded malware (in a drive-by download). With the knowledge of this path, the graph database could then be simply queried for other hosts that are linked to the same path or at least parts of the same path. This also helps to reduce the time required to analyze such cases.

While using graph databases to analyze log file opens up new possibilities to gain different insights into correlation of log data, there is a need to extend our work to include different log files into the graph database. Zeek, for instance, creates many more log files that are definitely of investigative and forensic interest. Examples include Zeek's ssh.log, ssl.log, and files.log (the latter log stores the MD5 and SHA1 value of every file seen in the network). Values from the additional log files could be checked automatically with services like Virustotal.com, and their results could then be integrated into the graph. The integration of third-party tools should also be part of future research.

Since this paper utilized only a single instance of Neo4j, the performance of clustering multiple instances of Neo4j could be explored further. This could be examined in direct connection with the question of how to integrate the output of several Zeek sensors that are monitoring different networks into one graph database.

Although the graph data model for the http.log is modelled semantically correct, its design provides a level of complexity that is not necessarily needed. For example, the relationship between two Uri nodes that represents one as the referrer of the other and the relationships that identify a host as well as an Uri as a referrer need to be re-examined. The absence of these relationships could have a positive impact on the performance of writing data into the database.

Appendix

A. cnn.log [5]

(1)   ts: Timestamp that represents the time when the first packet of the connection occurred,
(2)   uid: Unique Identifier (UID) for the connection,
(3)   id.orig_h: IP address of source host,
(4)   id.orig_p: Source port,
(5)   id.resp_h: IP address of destination host,
(6)   id.resp_p: Destination port,
(7)   proto: Transport layer protocol,
(8)   service: Identification of an application protocol,
(9)   duration: Duration of the connection in seconds,
(10) orig_bytes: Number of payload bytes the originator sent,
(11) resp_bytes: Number of payload bytes the responder sent,
(12) conn_state: Summary of the connection state. 3
(13) local_orig: Connection is originated locally
(14) local_resp: Connection is responded locally
(15) missed_bytes: Indicates the number of missed bytes and represents packet loss
(16) history: State history of connections.4
(17) orig_pkts: Number of packets that the originator sent,
(18) orig_ip_bytes: Number of IP level bytes that the originator sent (this is taken from the IP total length header field),
(19) resp_pkts: Number of packets that the responder sent,
(20) resp_ip_bytes: Number of IP level bytes that the responder sent,
(21) tunnel_parents: If this connection was over a recognized tunnel, this indicated UID values for any encapsulating parent connection used over the lifetime of this inner connection.

B. dns.log [5]

(1)   ts: Timestamp that represents the earliest time at which the DNS protocol message over the associated connection is observed,

(2)   uid: UID of the connection over which DNS messages are being transferred,

(3)   id.orig_h: IP address of source host,

(4)   id.orig_p: Source port,

(5)   id_resp_h: IP address of destination host,

(6)   id.resp_p: Destination port,

(7)   proto: Transport layer protocol,

(8)   trans_id: A 16-bit identifier that is assigned by the program that generated the DNS query and that is also used in responses to match up replies to outstanding queries,

(9)   rtt: Round trip time for the query response, indicating the delay between the moment that the request was seen until the answer has started,

(10)   query: Domain name that is the subject of the DNS query,

(11)   qclass: QCLASS value specifying the class of the query,

(12)   qclass_name: Descriptive name for the class of the query,

(13)   qtype: QTYPE value specifying the type of the query,

(14)   qtype_name: Descriptive name for the type of the query,

(15)   rcode: Response Code value in DNS response messages,

(16)   rcode_name: Descriptive name for the response code value,

(17)   AA: Authoritative Answer bit for response messages,

(18)   TC: Truncation bit that specifies whether the message was truncated,

(19)   RD: Recursion Desired bit that indicates in a request message whether the client wants recursive service for this query,

(20)   RA: Recursion Available bit that indicates in a response message that the server supports recursive queries,

(21)   Z: A reserved field that is usually "0" in queries and responses,

(22)   answers: Set of resolved IP addresses and domains in the query answer,

(23)   TTLs: shows the caching intervals of the associated resources described in the query answer,

(24)   rejected: Rejected bit indicated whether the server rejected the DNS query.

C. http.log [5]

(1)   ts: Timestamp for when the request happened

(2)   uid: UID for the connection,

(3)   id.orig_h: IP address of source host,

(4)   id.orig_p: Source port,

(5)   id.resp_h: IP address of destination host,

(6)   id.resp_p: Destination port,

(7)   trans_depth: Number representing the pipelined depth into the connection of this request/response transaction,

(8)   method: Method used in the HTTP request (i.e. GET, POST, etc.),

(9)   host: HTTP Host header value,
(10) uri: URI used in the request,
(11) referrer: HTTP "referer" header,
(12) version: Version portion of the HTTP request,
(13) user_agent: HTTP User-Agent header value,
(14) request_body_len: Uncompressed content size of the data transferred from the client in bytes,
(15) response_body_len: Uncompressed content size of the data transferred from the server in bytes,
(16) status_code: HTTP status code returned by the server,
(17) status_msg: Human-readable HTTP status message,
(18) info_code: Reply code returned by the server,
(19) info_msg: Human-readable reply message,
(20) tags: Tags that are a set of indicators of various attributes discovered and related to a particular request/response pair.
(21) username: HTTP Basic Authentication user name (if found),
(22) password: HTTP Basic Authentication password (if found),
(23) proxied: All of the headers that may indicate if the request was proxied,
(24) orig_fuids: List of unique file IDs6 in the request,
(25) orig_filenames: List of filenames in the request,
(26) orig_mime_types: MIME types for request objects,
(27) resp_fuids: List of FUIDs in the response,
(28) resp_filenames: List of filenames in the response,
(29) resp_mime_types: MIME types for response objects.

References

1. Bejtlich, R.: The practice of network security monitoring: understanding incident detection and response. No Starch Press (2013)
2. MIT Lincoln Laboratory. DARPA Intrusion Detection Evaluation. http://www.ll.mit.edu/ideval/data/1999data.html. Accessed 4 June 2017
3. National CyberWatch Center. MACCDC—Home of National CyberWatch Mid Atlantic CCDC (2017). https://www.maccdc.org. Accessed 27 July 2017
4. Neise, P.: Intrusion Detection Through Relationship Analysis. SANS Institute InfoSec Reading Room (2016). https://www.sans.org/reading-room/whitepapers/detection/intrusion-detection-relationship-analysis-37352. Accessed 18 March 2017
5. Neo4j. Neo4j, the world's leading graph database. https://neo4j.com/. Accessed 21 Aug 2017
6. Netresec. PCAP files from the US National CyberWatch Mid-Atlantic Collegiate Cyber Defense Competition (MACCDC) (2017). https://www.netresec.com/?page=MACCDC. Accessed 20 Apr 2017
7. Paxson, V.: Bro: a system for detecting network intruders in real-time. Comput. Netw. **31**(23), 2435–2463 (1999)
8. Py2neo. The py2neo v3 Handbook. http://py2neo.org/v3/. Accessed 11 Mar 2017
9. Robinson, I., Webber, J., Eirfrem, E.: Graph Databases - New Opportunities for Connected Data, 2nd edn. O'Reilly Media Inc., Sebastpol (2015)

10. Sanders, C., Smith, J.: Applied Network Security Monitoring: Collection, Detection, and Analysis. Elsevier (2013)
11. Roesch, M.: Snort: lightweight intrusion detection for networks. In: Lisa, vol. 99, no. 1, pp. 229–238, November 1999
12. Snort - Network Intrusion Detection & Prevention System. http://www.snort.org/. Accessed 21 Aug 2017
13. Suricata. Suricata—Open Source IDS/IPS/NSM engine. https://suricata-ids.org/. Accessed 21 Aug 2017
14. Zeek.org. The Zeek Network Security Monitor. https://www.bro.org. Accessed 15 Jan 2019
15. Schindler, T.: Anomaly detection in log data using graph databases and machine learning to defend advanced persistent threats. In: Gesellschaft für Informatik e.V. (Hrsg.) Informatik 2017. Lecture Notes in Informatics (LNI). Gesellschaft für Informatik, Bonn (2017)
16. Uetz, R., Benthin, L., Hemminghaus, C., Krebs, S., Yilmaz, T.: BREACH: a framework for the simulation of cyber attacks on company's networks. In: Digital Forensics Research Conference Europe (Poster) (2017)
17. Djanali, S., et al.: Coro: graph-based automatic intrusion detection system signature generator for evoting protection. J. Theor. Appl. Inf. Technol. **81**(3), 535–546 (2015)

Full Papers

A Privacy-Enhancing Framework
for Internet of Things Services

Lukas Malina[1]([✉]), Gautam Srivastava[2,3], Petr Dzurenda[1], Jan Hajny[1],
and Sara Ricci[1]

[1] Department of Telecommunications, Brno University of Technology,
Brno, Czech Republic
{malina,dzurenda,hajny,ricci}@feec.vutbr.cz
[2] Department of Mathematics and Computer Science, Brandon University,
270 18th Street, Brandon R7A 6A9, Canada
srivastavag@brandonu.ca
[3] Research Center for Interneural Computing, China Medical University,
Taichung 40402, Taiwan, Republic of China

Abstract. The world has seen an influx of connected devices through
both smart devices and smart cities, paving the path forward for the
Internet of Things (IoT). These emerging intelligent infrastructures and
applications based on IoT can be beneficial to users only if essential private and secure features are assured. However, with constrained devices
being the norm in IoT, security and privacy are often minimized. In
this paper, we first categorize various existing privacy-enhancing technologies (PETs) and assessment of their suitability for privacy-requiring
services within IoT. We also categorize potential privacy risks, threats,
and leakages related to various IoT use cases. Furthermore, we propose
a simple novel privacy-preserving framework based on a set of suitable
privacy-enhancing technologies in order to maintain security and privacy within IoT services. Our study can serve as a baseline of privacy-
by-design strategies applicable to IoT based services, with a particular
focus on smart things, such as safety equipment.

Keywords: Authentication · Cryptography · Evaluation ·
Identification · Internet of Things · Privacy · Privacy-enhancing
technologies · Security · Safety

1 Introduction

Emerging Intelligent Infrastructures (II) that interconnect various IoT applications and services are meant to provide convenience to people, open new benefits
to society, and benefit our environment. There are many IoT applications and
use cases that are either already implemented or are in varying research stages
heading towards potential implementation. The general overview of IoT environments and applicable scenarios are depicted in Fig. 1.

© Springer Nature Switzerland AG 2019
J. K. Liu and X. Huang (Eds.): NSS 2019, LNCS 11928, pp. 77–97, 2019.
https://doi.org/10.1007/978-3-030-36938-5_5

Fig. 1. The IoT environment and application areas.

Nevertheless, connected objects, sensors and digital systems around people's lives form a large intelligent network that can serve as a medium for the leakage of personal data [27,61,63]. It is essential during the design and application stages of intelligent networks to include privacy protection into incoming infrastructures and IoT applications. Engineers, practitioners, and researchers can develop various privacy protection principles, technologies or Privacy by Design (PbD) strategies. PbD is a term for a multifaceted concept which involves various technological and organizational components, implementing privacy, and data protection principles. In [18], Hoepman proposes eight privacy design strategies, divided into 2 categories, namely data-oriented (1–4) and process-oriented (5–8). The strategies are briefly described as follows:

1. **Minimize:** processed personal data should be constrained to the minimal amount.
2. **Hide:** personal data and their interrelationships (linkability) should be protected or not public.
3. **Separate:** personal data should be processed in a distributed way.
4. **Aggregate** (Abstract): limit as much as possible the detail in which personal data is processed, aggregating data in the highest level.
5. **Inform:** data subjects should be informed whenever their personal data is processed.
6. **Control:** data subjects should be provided control over the processing of their personal data.
7. **Enforce:** processing personal data should be committed in a privacy-friendly way, and should be adequately enforced.
8. **Demonstrate:** the system should able to demonstrate compliance with the privacy policy and any applicable legal requirements.

Many PbD strategies can be solved by privacy protection techniques called Privacy-Enhancing Technologies (PETs). PETs are based on the principles of data minimization, anonymization, pseudonymization, and data protection that allow users to protect their privacy and their personally identifiable information (PII).

The European Union Agency for Network and Information Security (ENISA) has been active in PETs for many years by collaborating closely with privacy experts from academia and industry. ENISA defines PETs as the broader range of technologies that are designed for supporting privacy and data protection. The ENISA report given in [8] provides a fundamental inventory of the existing approaches and privacy design strategies and the technical building blocks of various degree of maturity from research and development in general ICT. The report [8] distinguishes the following basic privacy techniques:

- **Authentication** (e.g. privacy features of authentication protocols);
- **Attribute-based credentials**;
- **Secure private communications**;
- **Communications anonymity and pseudonymity**;
- **Privacy in databases**:
  - Respondent privacy: statistical disclosure control;
  - Owner privacy: privacy-preserving data mining;
  - User privacy: private information retrieval;
- **Storage privacy**;
- **Privacy-preserving computations**;
- **Transparency-enhancing techniques**;
- **Intervenability-enhancing techniques**.

In this paper, we focus on privacy-preserving techniques that can be deployed in IoT based services.

1.1 Privacy in Standards and Regulations

Privacy protection is already an important part of EU regulations and international standards. In 2011, the ISO organization released the ISO/IEC 29100:2011 Privacy Framework Standard that aims at the protection of PII from the beginning of data collection, data usage, data storage to final data destruction. The standard presents 11 principles:

1. consent and choice
2. purpose legitimacy and specification
3. collection limitation
4. data minimization
5. use, retention, and disclosure limitation
6. accuracy and quality
7. openness, transparency, and notice
8. individual participation and access
9. accountability
10. information security
11. privacy compliance

The general data protection regulation (GDPR) replaced the Data Protection Directive 95/46/EC in 2018 [57]. The GDPR covers most basic data security and privacy principles by Article 5 that includes lawfulness, fairness, transparency, purpose limitation, data minimization, accuracy, storage limitation, integrity and confidentiality, and accountability. In addition, the GDPR is stricter in various privacy aspects such as consent, right to be forgotten and privacy (and data protection) by design and by default that is mentioned in Article 25. Hence, privacy-preserving IoT applications and services are required also by the above-mentioned regulations.

1.2   Privacy in IoT Applications and Communication Model

In general, a common IoT communication model consists of several entities such as users, service providers, and third parties. It is also defined by several processes, such as data sensing, interaction, collection, and presentation. Ziegeldorf *et al.* present an IoT model with 4 different IoT entities [64]. Those entities are smart things (IoT sensors, actuators), services (backends), subjects (humans who receive data and/or produce/send data), and infrastructures (including network sub-entities based communication technologies). They also introduce 5 different IoT data flows: interaction, presentation, collection, dissemination and processing.

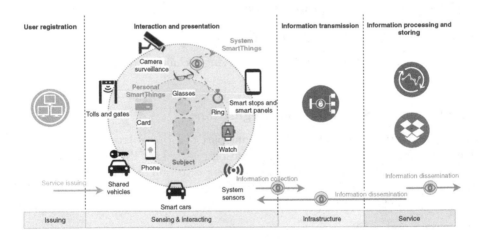

Fig. 2. The IoT communication model and privacy breaches.

Figure 2 depicts our view of an IoT model and potential privacy breaches that are marked with eye icons. The human interaction with proximity and vicinity IoT smart things (sensors, interfaces) may lead to several privacy threats and leakages that have to be mitigated. The list of privacy issues is presented in detail in Sect. 4.

In this paper, we aim at privacy-required IoT applications and privacy issues in IoT. We also provide an assessment of technical-based PETs in various IoT applications. Based on the results of our categorization and assessment, we propose a novel general framework that should address potential privacy leakages and threats within data processes in various IoT scenarios. Our framework enhances traditional privacy-preserving models (e.g. Hoepman's eight privacy design strategies [18]) by concrete steps and privacy-preserving technical countermeasures suited for private and secure IoT services.

The rest of the paper is organized as follows. In Sect. 2 we describe the state-of-the-art. We follow this in Sect. 3 by exploring specific use cases of IoT where users have or may experience privacy issues. Section 4 presents privacy issues in IoT. Next, in Sect. 5 we deal with the categorization and assessment of PETs in IoT. Section 6 presents our proposal of a general privacy-preserving framework for IoT. Lastly, we give some concluding remarks in Sect. 7.

2 State of the Art

There are plenty of interesting studies and survey papers focusing on security and privacy in IoT [23,29,41,42,48]. Furthermore, there are surveys and study papers that focus solely on privacy in IoT. Some examples are given in [6,22,25, 36,44,45].

Seliem et al. review existing research and propose solutions to rising privacy concerns from a multiple viewpoint to identify the risks and mitigations in [44]. The authors provide an evaluation of privacy issues and concerns in IoT systems due to resource constraints. They also describe IoT solutions that embrace a variety of privacy concerns such as identification, tracking, monitoring, and profiling. Sen et al. deal with differences between privacy and security in [45]. The authors present 11 general approaches and techniques that are being used to fulfill privacy requirements. Nevertheless, their analysis and classification models are not very deep. Vasilomanolakis et al. provide comparative analysis of four IoT architectures. Those are IoT-A, BeTaaS, OpenIoT, and IoT@Work [55]. The authors compare the general security requirements and four privacy features (data privacy, anonymity, pseudonymity, unlinkability) of the IoT architectures. The paper concludes stating that IoT-A and IoT@Work provide some privacy protection but privacy and identity management requirements should be balanced. Furthermore, Li et al. review the state-of-the-art principles of privacy laws as well as the architectures for IoT and the representative PETs [22]. The authors demonstrate how privacy legislation maps to privacy principles which in turn drive the design of privacy-enhancing technologies. The authors consider 4 layers such as the perception layer (data sensing), networking layer (data transaction), middleware layer (data storage and processing) and application layer (data presentation and usage), and they classify and analyze PETs by these layers. In [6], Cha et al. survey 120 papers focusing on the solutions of PETs in IoT. Authors classify PETs in IoT into 7 research domains:

- Control Over Data
- Enforcement
- Anonymization or Pseudonymization
- Personal Data Protection
- Anonymous Authorization
- Partial Data Disclosure
- Holistic Privacy Preservation

Furthermore, the authors conduct 15 privacy principles from GDPR and ISO/IEC 29100:2011, and link the principles with PETs papers and present some future directions of advanced technologies. The classification of 120 privacy-oriented IoT papers shows that 28% of papers are dedicated to building and home automation, 13% for e-healthcare, 13% for smart cities, 9% for wearables, 8% for automotive, 2% smart manufacturing and 27% are general oriented. In our study, we categorize and present concrete privacy-required IoT applications in Sect. 3.

The above noted surveys provide comprehensive literature reviews about the PETs including several classifications but there are a lack of basic guidelines for a privacy-by-design implementation of privacy-requiring IoT applications and concrete PETs recommendations.

3   Privacy-Requiring IoT Applications and Use Cases

With the new conveniences promised by IoT comes new privacy and security vulnerabilities. In an area where often times the devices involved are constrained and as such do not have the capabilities of running high powered security protection, we see definitive vulnerabilities. In this section, we will explore some specific use cases of IoT where users have or may experience privacy issues in no particular order.

In late 2015, two security researchers were able to show that over 68,000 medical device systems were exposed online, and that 12,000 of them belonged to one healthcare organization [35]. The major concern with this discovery was that these devices were connected to the Internet through computers running very old versions of Windows XP, a version of the OS which is known to have lots of exploitable vulnerabilities. This version of Windows although dated is still to this day part of many legacy systems worldwide, adding to the future privacy threats to IoT devices connected to such systems. These devices were discovered by using Shodan, a search engine that can find IoT devices online that are connected to the internet. These are easy to hack via brute-force attacks and using hard-coded logins. During their research, the two experts found anesthesia equipment, cardiology devices, nuclear medical systems, infusion systems, pacemakers, magnetic resonance imaging (MRI) scanners, and other devices all via simple Shodan queries. Although not yet ever reported, there is a chance that hackers gaining access to medical devices may change settings to these devices which could cause physical harm to someone connected to such a device.

For smart home IoT, one well documented attack is the Fingerprint and Timing based Snooping (FATS) attack presented by Srinivasan *et al.* in [50]. The FATS attack involves activity detection, room classification, sensor classification, and activity recognition from Wi-Fi traffic metadata from a sensor network deployed in the home the precursor to today's smart home IoT devices. The FATS attack relies on wireless network traffic instead of observations from a last-mile Internet service provider or other adversary located on a Wide Area Network (WAN). The FATS attack demonstrates that traffic analysis attacks in the style of FATS are as effective for the current generation of consumer IoT devices as they were for sensor networks ten years ago.

In another significant real-world attack, a recent article in Forbes magazine highlighted research by Noam Rotem and Ran Locar at vpnMentor, who exposed a Chinese company called Orvibo, which runs an IoT management platform. They showed that their database was easily accessible through direct connection to it, exposing openly user logs which contained 2 billion records including user passwords, account reset codes, payment information and even some "smart" camera recorded conversations. Below is a list of data that was available through this ground-breaking breach.

- Email addresses
- Passwords
- Account reset codes
- Precise Geolocation
- IP Address
- Username (ID)
- Family name

This specific breach pinpoints the type of data can be available through unsecured IoT devices or networks.

Consider another IoT use case involving assisted living, were we consider senior citizens who appreciate living independently as summarized in [16]. In this scenario, a number of unobtrusive sensors screen their vital signs and deliver information to the cloud for fast access by family members and third parties such as doctors, and health care providers. There are two levels of privacy issues here, one dealing with senior citizen medical information and the other with their personal data. Combining IoT devices for monitoring vitals and storage mechanisms like cloud storage can present a new domain of issues trying to integrate constrained devices (IoT) with the unconstrained (cloud storage).

Important social challenges stem from the necessity to adapt Smart City services to the specific characteristics of every user [60]. A service deployed in a Smart City may have many configurations options, depending on user expectations and preferences; the knowledge of these preferences usually means the success or failure of a service. In order to adapt a service to the specific user's preferences, it is necessary to know them, and this is basically done based on a characterization of that specific user. Nevertheless, a complete characterization of user preferences and behavior can be considered as a personal threat, so the great societal challenge for this, and for any service requiring user characterization, is to assure user's privacy and security. Thus, in order to achieve user consent, trust in, and acceptance of Smart Cities, integration of security and privacy preserving mechanisms must be a key concern of future research. The overall priority must be to establish user confidence in the upcoming technologies, as otherwise users will hesitate to accept the services provided by Smart Cities.

In the near future autonomous vehicles will be commonplace [21,59]. In the meantime, the development of Internet of Vehicles (IoV) is ongoing where a myriad of sensors, devices and controllers are attached to vehicles in an effort to allow for autonomous control. It is quite significant to design a privacy mechanism which ensures that collection of IoV Big Data is trusted and not tampered with. There is a huge risk of fraudulent messages injected by a malicious vehicle that could easily endanger the whole traffic system(s) or could potentially employ the entire network to pursue any dangerous activity for its own wicked benefits.

Finally, in [49], Solanas et al. discuss the notions of Smart Health (s-Health), as the synergy between mobile health and smart cities. Although s-Health might help to mitigate many health related issues, its ability to gather unprecedented amounts of information could endanger the privacy of citizens. In the context of s-Health, the information gathered is often rather personal. From the data, it would be possible to infer citizens' habits, their social status, and even their religion. All these variables are very sensitive, and when they are combined with health information, the result is even more delicate. This s-Health scenarios are also very related to smart safety systems where protective equipment (such as helmets, glasses or hazmat suites) is being monitored and traced.

We summarize our findings listing areas of IoT, some concrete applications, and the privacy concerns in Table 1. The privacy concerns used match the list from [13], where Finn et al. identify 7 privacy concerns, defined as follows:

- **Privacy of person:** encompasses the right to keep body functions and body characteristics private.
- **Privacy of behaviour and action:** this concept includes sensitive issues such as sexual preferences and habits, political activities and religious practices.
- **Privacy of communication:** aims to avoid the interception of communications, including mail interception, the use of bugs, directional microphones, telephone or wireless communication interception or recording and access to e-mail messages.
- **Privacy of data and image:** includes concerns about making sure that individuals' data is not automatically available.
- **Privacy of thoughts and feelings.** People have a right not to share their thoughts or feelings.
- **Privacy of location and space:** individuals have the right to move about in public or semi-public space without being identified.
- **Privacy of association:** says that people have a right to associate with whomever they wish, without being monitored.

Table 1. IoT areas with the example of applications and privacy concerns [13]

IoT area	Application	Privacy concerns
Healthcare IoT	Geniatech, Cycore	Data, person
Internet of underwater things	WFS Tech	Communication
Smart home	Orvibo	Data, location
Smart cities	Cisco	Communication, location data
IoT blockchain implementations	Helium	Personal, data
Internet of vehicles	RideLogic	Action, image

4 Categorization of Privacy Issues: Threats, Leakages and Attacks in an IoT Environment

In this section, we categorize privacy issues and present brief descriptions, potential prevention approaches and compromised IoT areas. Security attacks and privacy threats in IoT have been analyzed in various studies [2,6,33,64]. Lopez *et al.* detect 3 IoT privacy problems: user privacy, content privacy and context privacy [25]. Furthermore, there have been seven privacy threat categories for IoT given in [6,64]. Our analysis presents 12 privacy issues divided into 3 classes:

- privacy **threats:** this class represents the weaknesses and flaws of IoT services and systems that could be misused by other system entities and/or lead to leakages and attacks,
- privacy **leakages:** this class represents more serious problems and flaws that can directly breach user privacy and/or can be misused by passive and active attackers,
- privacy **attacks:** this class represents issues that are intentionally performed by passive and active attackers in order to break user privacy and misuse the observed information for criminal activities.

We categorize general privacy protection and prevention approaches as follows:

- *Data minimization:* limiting data collection to only necessary information.
- *Data anonymization:* encrypting, modifying or removing personal information in such a way that the data can no longer be used to identify a natural person.
- *Data security:* the process of protecting data from unauthorized access and data corruption.
- *Data control:* monitoring and controlling the data by defining policies.
- *Identity management:* policies and technologies for ensuring that the proper users have access to technology resources.
- *Secure communication:* communication protocol that allow people sharing information with the appropriate confidentiality, source authentication, and data integrity protection.
- *User awareness/informed consent transparency:* users give their consents about data usage and they are aware which data are processed.

In Table 2, we describe privacy issues, general prevention approaches and link the issues with target IoT area and services. To be noted, that some more complex attacks can be performed by the combination of several privacy leakages and threats.

5   Categorization of Privacy-Enhancing Technologies for Internet of Things

In this section, we present and categorize privacy-enhancing technologies. We focus on PETs that can be

- implemented in devices,
- used as applications (user side),
- applied in networks,
- applied in data storage, cloud and back-end servers.

PETs may provide these basic privacy features:

- (P1) *anonymity:* user is not identifiable as the source of data (user is indistinguishable).
- (P2) *pseudonymity:* user is identifiable only to system parties (issuers), trades off between anonymity and accountability.
- (P3) *unlinkability:* actions of the same user cannot be linked together, and all sessions are mutually unlinkable.
- (P4) *untracebility:* user's credentials and/or actions cannot be tracked by system parties (issuers).
- (P5) *revocation:* a dedicated system party is able to remove person or its credential from the system.
- (P6) *data privacy:* stored and/or released information do not expose undesired properties, e.g. identities, user's vital data etc.

Further, PETs combine privacy features with common security features such as:

- (S1) *data confidentiality:* sensitive data are protected against eavesdropping and exposing by encryption techniques.
- (S2) *data authenticity and integrity:* data are protected against their lost or modification by the unauthorized entities.
- (S3) *authentication:* proof that a connection is established with an authenticated entity or access to services is granted only to authenticated entity.
- (S4) *non-repudiation:* proof that a data is signed by a certain entity (entity cannot deny this action).
- (S5) *accountability:* a user should have specific responsibilities.

As above, privacy (P1–P6) and security (S1–S5) features are only basic and common. Table 3 presents PETs categorized into 6 processes (data authenticity, user authentication, communication, computation/data processing, data storing and data dissemination), and provides a brief description of PETs, their privacy

Table 2. Categorization of Privacy Threats, Leakages, Attacks with Prevention Approaches and Affected IoT Areas

Privacy issue (threat/ leakage/ attack)	Description	Prevention approaches	IoT areas
Data over-collection threat	Unaware and/or superabundant collection of personal data	*Data minimization, data anonymization*	All IoT areas with data collection
Linkage threat	Disclosing unexpected results by different systems can lead to linkage of personal data by data correlation	*Data minimization, data anonymization, user awareness/informed consent transparency*	All IoT areas with data collection and dissemination
Identification threat	Associating a user identity with personal data, e.g., name, address, gender, physical signatures (voice, face)	*Data anonymization, identity management, data security*	All IoT areas with data collection and dissemination
Lifecycle transitions leakage	Leaking personal data from devices and systems in their lifecycle that are not under their control or by changing the ownership of smart things	*Data control, identity management, data security*	Smart cities, smart homes, IoV
Privacy-violating interactions and presentation leakage	Conveying and presenting private information through a public medium (voice, video screens) that leads to disclosure of user private information to an Unwanted audience	*Data anonymization, user awareness/informed consent transparency*	Health care, smart cities
Localization leakage	Undesirable determining of a person's location by Global Positioning System (GPS) coordinates, IP addresses, latency, or cell phone location	*Data anonymization, data control*	Health care, IoV, smart cities
Behavioral leakage	Undesirable determining and recording a person's behavior through space and time	*Data anonymization, data control*	IoV, smart cities, smart homes, smart grid
Tracking attack	Attackers can determine and record a person's movement through time and space (based on localization or behavioral leakages and user identification), e.g., data exploitation by criminals for robberies/kidnapping	*Data anonymization, data minimization, data control*	IoV, smart cities, smart homes
Profiling attack	Attackers can compile and analyze information about users in order to infer their personal interests by correlation With their profiles and data, e.g. exposing a target's life pattern, unsolicited personalized e-commerce, blackmailing	*Data minimization, data anonymization*	Health care, smart cities, IoV, smart grid

(continued)

Table 2. (*continued*)

Privacy issue (threat/ leakage/ attack)	Description	Prevention approaches	IoT areas
Inventory attack	Attackers can send various query requests to the object and analyze the related responses in order to collect Special interests of users, e.g., unauthorized detection of health issues, burglaries, industrial espionage	*Data control, identity management, data security*	Health care, IoV, smart industry, IoT device exchanging
Eavesdropping Attack	Attackers can observe and eavesdrop communication in order to directly get private information and/or notification about a user's presence, i.e. detection some encrypted communications	*Data security, secure communication*	All IoT areas with data collection and dissemination
Identity-theft Attack	Attackers can steal user identity (credentials) and misuse his/her services, and/or harm his/her reputation	*Data security, identity management*	IoV, smart cities, healthcare, smart industry

and security features and standards and/or examples of references for existed IoT implementations or the PET's consideration in IoT. Mentioned technologies may conduct and represent many various schemes that have different properties. Furthermore, this analysis for simplicity does not involve advanced and special features, e.g. malleability, no framing, transparency, and intervenability, which can be found in the special variants of PET schemes.

In addition, it is assumed that well-established techniques already provide principally native features such as soundness, correctness, unforgeability, completeness etc. Suitable and matured PETs for IoT applications are integrated into our proposed framework in the following Sect. 6.

6   Privacy-Preserving Framework for Internet of Things

In this section, we propose a general privacy-preserving framework for an IoT communication model. Our proposed novel framework is mainly based on general security and privacy requirements of IoT applications and potential privacy issues in IoT based services. The general concept of the proposed framework is depicted in Fig. 3. The framework contains 4 initial processes, 6 privacy-preserving data procedures, and 4 general post-processes. The privacy preserving data procedures are mainly focused on embedding the PETs in IoT services (e.g. access control in smart cities/smart buildings, IoV data exchanging etc.). These framework processes can be applied linearly in time. Furthermore, we recommend suitable types of PETs in order to solve concrete privacy-issues in each detected area and aspect in the general IoT model.

Table 3. Categorization of Technical-based Privacy-enhancing Technologies and IoT-related References

Process	Technology name	Description	Privacy and security features	Standards and/or the examples of IoT-related references
Data authenticity	Blind Signatures (BS)	BS enable signers to disguise the content of a signed message	P3–P4, P6, S2, S4	[ISO/IEC 18370], [34,58]
	Group Signatures (GS)	GS offers privacy-preserving properties for signers who sign the messages on behalf of the group	P2–P5, S2–S4	[ISO/IEC 20008], [10,12,15,31]
	Ring Signatures (RS)	RS offers similar privacy-preserving properties as GS. It is computationally infeasible to determine which group members' keys were used to produce the signature	P2–P5, S2–S4	[9,11,54]
User authentication	Attribute-Based Credentials (ABC)	ABC enable entities (users) to anonymously or pseudo-anonymously prove the possession of various personal attributes in order to get access to services. The solutions are often based on anonymous credentials and zero-knowledge protocols	P2–P6, S2–S5	ISO/IEC 27551 [1,4,37,46]
	Anonymous and Pseudonymous Authentication (A&PA)	A&PA enable entities (users) to anonymously or pseudo-anonymously authenticate in ICT systems. The authentication protocols have specific privacy features.	P1–P4, S3	[ISO/IEC 20009], [ISO/IEC 29191], [7]
Communication	Onion Routing (OR)	Anonymous networks like Tor rely on passing through multiple nodes with a layer of encryption added at each node	P1, P3, P4, S1, S2	[3,17]
	Encrypted Communication (EC)	EC enables basic privacy protection of transmitted data against external observers. Methods are usually based on basic encryption, DTLS, VPNs, PGP, email encryption and so on	P6, S1–S4	[39], [30]
	Mix-networks (MixNets)	MixNets transport data via multiple relays with certain delays and cover traffic to mask statistical leaks that could trace messages	P2	[51]
	Proxies and Crowds (P& C)	P& C approaches use intermediaries (proxy servers) in order to hide data senders. With Crowds a user is join a crowd and uses services anonymously	P1, P2	[43]

(continued)

Table 3. (*continued*)

Process	Technology name	Description	Privacy and security features	Standards and/or the examples of IoT-related references
Computation	Homomorphic Encryption (HE)	HE allows the performing of selected operations on encrypted data	P6, S1, S2	[28,47]
	Polymorphic Encryption and Pseudonymisation (PE& P)	PE& P provides the security and privacy infrastructure for big data analytics	P2, P6, S1	[56]
	Multiparty Computations (MC)	MC enables several parties to jointly compute a function over their inputs, while at the same time keeping these inputs private	P6, S5	[32,52]
	Searchable Encryption (SE)	SE allows the performing of predefined searches on encrypted data located on untrusted third party without the need to decrypt	P6, S1, S2	[26]
	Attribute-Based Encryption (ABE)	ABE is public-key encryption techniques in which user's secret key and the ciphertext are dependent upon attributes. The attributes can be represented by geographic location, user's age and account level (premium, standard, basic) in case of streaming services. Only a user with specific attributes can decrypt the ciphertext	P6, S1, S2, S5	[19,38]
Data Storing	Statistical Disclosure Control (SDC)	SDC techniques include tabular data protection, queryable database protection, microdata protection, etc. The goal is storing data (i.e., data set, data base or tabular) that preserve their statistical validity while protecting the privacy of each data subject	P6, S5	[24,62]
	Data Splitting (DS)	DS means partitioning a data set into fragments in such a way that the fragment considered in isolation is no longer sensitive. Each fragment is then stored in a different site	P6	[20]
Data Dissemination	Differential Privacy (DP)	DP releases information that contains nothing about an individual while contains useful information about a population	P6	[40]
	Syntactic Anonymization Techniques (SAT)	SAT merges general techniques to remove, suppress or generalize identifying information from data (images, text, voice, video, etc.), the de-identification methods (such as k-anonymity) under low-privacy requirements and location privacy methods by obfuscation and cloaking	P1, P2, P6	[40,53]

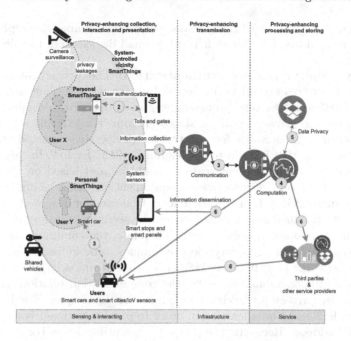

Fig. 3. The proposed privacy-preserving framework for IoT environment.

Before employing concrete PETs into an IoT application, initial Privacy-by-Design strategies and procedures must be set and performed in order to be in line with privacy standards and principles, i.e., ISO/IEC 29100:2011, [18,57]. The *initial processes* of the framework are defined as follows:

- **System Definition:** Define data flaws and data procedures for the concrete IoT application/system.
- **Privacy Analysis:** Analyze the privacy breaches and issues in the concrete IoT application/system.
- **Data Definition:** Define concrete datasets, user's vital and sensitive data that should be protected and set limitation.
- **Legal Definition:** Set and ensure purpose legitimacy, consents and information strategies in according to regulations and laws.

Then, the *technical processes* should be set and ensured by employing PETs in these 6 privacy-preserving data procedures:

1. **Privacy-preserving Information Collection:** The collection of data including some user-specific parameters (user location, user consumption, etc.) should ensure user privacy and data authenticity. Employing anonymous/ pseudonymous digital signatures such as digital group signatures (GS) should provide data authenticity, non-repudiation and also hide users as sources of data in the group of members. This approach provides k-anonymity where k is the number of all members. The implementation of short (few KBs)

group signatures (e.g. [10,12,31]) that need several asymmetric cryptographic operations could be feasible in IoT using small devices (i.e. mobiles, micro-controllers).

2. **Privacy-preserving User Authentication:** The privacy of users who access IoT services should be protected by privacy-preserving user authentication. ABC seems as very promising approach due to the support of various security and privacy features. Moreover, some efficient ABC schemes (e.g. [5,14,46]) are also suitable for constrained devices (e.g. existed smartcard implementation) that is point to the readiness of ABC for IoT. In case of smart safety systems, the user identification should be also based on PETs/ABC schemes and the verification of safety equipment can be done anonymously.

3. **Privacy-preserving Communication:** Collected and sensed data from vicinity and personal smart things should be securely transferred via a network infrastructure to a service area. Therefore, the communication should be protected by standard encryption techniques suitable for IoT and heterogeneous networks (e.g. DTLS, wolfSSL). In case of uploading or exchanging sensitive and anonymous user data, the communication relations should be protected by privacy-preserving communication techniques based on onion routing, MixNets or broadcasting in order to provide source privacy, i.e. hide source IP address. Recently, the paper [3] has utilized the Tor Network for IoT. Moreover, anonymous digital signatures and GS can be used to ensure data authenticity and integrity without leaking the identity of a sender.

4. **Privacy-preserving Computation:** The back-end servers of IoT services or cloud infrastructures should perform privacy-preserving data processing. For privacy-preserving computation, there are many possible techniques and privacy-preserving options, such as HE, SW, ABE, MC, and PE&P. Using techniques such as homomorphic encryption is possible to perform some data analysis and keep data private for owners. Nonetheless, HE and SE methods could be less applicable to performance-constrained client nodes (see results in [47]). Therefore, these heavy computation operations should be performed at powerful back-end servers or clouds. On the other hand, fine-grained access control on encrypted outsourced data can be realized by ABE schemes. The work [19] shows the results of ABE on small devices with promising efficiency in terms of processing time and energy consumption.

5. **Privacy-preserving Data Storing:** A service area should store only necessary data in a privacy-preserving way. There are several SDC techniques (microdata protection, etc.) that enable users to store data and protect their privacy. These approaches lead to data minimization. Also, the data should be secured by standard methods (e.g. storage encryption). The implementation of SDC techniques should not be problematic on most IoT platforms and storages but data minimization should be done in a reasonable way without losing the important data for an analysis.

6. **Privacy-preserving Data Dissemination:** The results of data processing that are disseminated and presented back to users or to third parties should not contain any vital and/or private information about concrete users. The

combination of presentation rules and data minimization strategies should be employed in order to keep user privacy.

After embedding PETs into data procedures, *post-processes* for sustainability and general management must be followed:

- **Evaluation:** The final application/service should be evaluated whether PETs and technical processes mitigate privacy and security issues.
- **Control:** The functionality of concrete privacy-preserving data procedures should be constantly controlled.
- **Monitoring:** The data visibility and transparency in the system should be ensured.
- **Compliance:** The compliance with the current regulations and laws should be checked, and the system should be able to demonstrate this.

7 Conclusion

This paper focuses on privacy protection in Intelligent Infrastructures and IoT applications. In this work, we detected privacy-requiring IoT applications, and analyzed and categorized various privacy issues and privacy-enhancing technologies from the perspective of IoT. Based on the analyzed privacy breaches in IoT and privacy-enhancing technologies divided into 6 categories, a general framework was proposed that consists of 8 general processes and 6 technical privacy-preserving procedures. The presented framework should serve as a guideline for establishing privacy-preserving IoT applications and systems in line with privacy-by-design concepts. The particular applications that will benefit from the framework the most are identification systems, access control systems, smart safety systems, smart-grids and health care.

Acknowledgment. This paper is supported by the Ministry of Industry and Trade grant # FV20354, the TACR project TL02000398 and European Union's Horizon 2020 research and innovation programme under grant agreement No 830892, project SPARTA. For the research, infrastructure of the SIX Center supported by National Sustainability Program under grant LO1401 was used.

References

1. Alpár, G., et al.: New directions in IoT privacy using attribute-based authentication: position paper (2016)
2. Atamli, A.W., Martin, A.: Threat-based security analysis for the internet of things. In: International Workshop on Secure Internet of Things, pp. 35–43. IEEE (2014)
3. Baumann, F.W., Odefey, U., Hudert, S., Falkenthal, M., Breitenbücher, U.: Utilising the tor network for IoT addressing and connectivity. In: Proceedings of the 8th International Conference on Cloud Computing and Services Science (CLOSER 2018), pp. 27–34. SciTePress, March 2018

4. Bernal Bernabe, J., Hernandez-Ramos, J.L., Skarmeta Gomez, A.F.: Holistic privacy-preserving identity management system for the internet of things. Mob. Inf. Syst. **2017**, 6384186:1 (2017)
5. Camenisch, J., Drijvers, M., Dzurenda, P., Hajny, J.: Fast keyed-verification anonymous credentials on standard smart cards. In: Dhillon, G., Karlsson, F., Hedström, K., Zúquete, A. (eds.) SEC 2019. IAICT, vol. 562, pp. 286–298. Springer, Cham (2019). https://doi.org/10.1007/978-3-030-22312-0_20
6. Cha, S.C., Hsu, T.Y., Xiang, Y., Yeh, K.H.: Privacy enhancing technologies in the internet of things: perspectives and challenges. IEEE Internet Things J. **6**, 2159–2187 (2018)
7. Chatzigiannakis, I., Vitaletti, A., Pyrgelis, A.: A privacy-preserving smart parking system using an IoT elliptic curve based security platform. Comput. Commun. **89**, 165–177 (2016)
8. Danezis, G., et al.: Privacy and data protection by design-from policy to engineering. arXiv preprint arXiv:1501.03726 (2015)
9. Debnath, A., Singaravelu, P., Verma, S.: Privacy in wireless sensor networks using ring signature. J. King Saud Univ.-Comput. Inf. Sci. **26**(2), 228–236 (2014)
10. Derler, D., Slamanig, D.: Highly-efficient fully-anonymous dynamic group signatures. In: Proceedings of the 2018 on Asia Conference on Computer and Communications Security, pp. 551–565. ACM (2018)
11. Dwivedi, A.D., Srivastava, G., Dhar, S., Singh, R.: A decentralized privacy-preserving healthcare blockchain for IoT. Sensors **19**(2), 326 (2019)
12. Emura, K., Hayashi, T.: A light-weight group signature scheme with time-token dependent linking. In: Güneysu, T., Leander, G., Moradi, A. (eds.) LightSec 2015. LNCS, vol. 9542, pp. 37–57. Springer, Cham (2016). https://doi.org/10.1007/978-3-319-29078-2_3
13. Finn, R.L., Wright, D., Friedewald, M.: Seven types of privacy. In: Gutwirth, S., Leenes, R., de Hert, P., Poullet, Y. (eds.) European Data Protection: Coming of Age, pp. 3–32. Springer, Heidelberg (2013). https://doi.org/10.1007/978-94-007-5170-5_1
14. Hajny, J., Dzurenda, P., Malina, L.: Attribute-based credentials with cryptographic collusion prevention. Secur. Commun. Netw. **8**(18), 3836–3846 (2015)
15. He, D., Chen, C., Bu, J., Chan, S., Zhang, Y., Guizani, M.: Secure service provision in smart grid communications. IEEE Commun. Mag. **50**(8), 53–61 (2012)
16. Henze, M., Hermerschmidt, L., Kerpen, D., Häußling, R., Rumpe, B., Wehrle, K.: User-driven privacy enforcement for cloud-based services in the internet of things. In: 2014 International Conference on Future Internet of Things and Cloud, pp. 191–196. IEEE (2014)
17. Hoang, N.P., Pishva, D.: A TOR-based anonymous communication approach to secure smart home appliances. In: 2015 17th International Conference on Advanced Communication Technology (ICACT), pp. 517–525. IEEE (2015)
18. Hoepman, J.-H.: Privacy design strategies. In: Cuppens-Boulahia, N., Cuppens, F., Jajodia, S., Abou El Kalam, A., Sans, T. (eds.) SEC 2014. IAICT, vol. 428, pp. 446–459. Springer, Heidelberg (2014). https://doi.org/10.1007/978-3-642-55415-5_38
19. Jahan, M., Seneviratne, S., Chu, B., Seneviratne, A., Jha, S.: Privacy preserving data access scheme for IoT devices. In: 2017 IEEE 16th International Symposium on Network Computing and Applications (NCA), pp. 1–10. IEEE (2017)
20. Kelarev, A.V., Yi, X., Cui, H., Rylands, L.J., Jelinek, H.F.: A survey of state-of-the-art methods for securing medical databases. AIMS Med. Sci. **5**(1), 1–22 (2018)

21. Kong, Q., Lu, R., Ma, M., Bao, H.: A privacy-preserving sensory data sharing scheme in internet of vehicles. Futur. Gener. Comput. Syst. **92**, 644–655 (2019)
22. Li, C., Palanisamy, B.: Privacy in internet of things: from principles to technologies. IEEE Internet Things J. **6**(1), 488–505 (2019)
23. Lin, J., Yu, W., Zhang, N., Yang, X., Zhang, H., Zhao, W.: A survey on internet of things: architecture, enabling technologies, security and privacy, and applications. IEEE Internet Things J. **4**(5), 1125–1142 (2017)
24. Liu, F., Li, T.: A clustering-anonymity privacy-preserving method for wearable IoT devices. Secur. Commun. Netw. **2018**, 1–8 (2018)
25. Lopez, J., Rios, R., Bao, F., Wang, G.: Evolving privacy: from sensors to the internet of things. Future Gener. Comput. Syst. **75**, 46–57 (2017)
26. Ma, M., He, D., Kumar, N., Choo, K.K.R., Chen, J.: Certificateless searchable public key encryption scheme for industrial internet of things. IEEE Trans. Ind. Inform. **14**(2), 759–767 (2017)
27. Ma, Y., Wu, Y., Li, J., Ge, J.: APCN: a scalable architecture for balancing accountability and privacy in large-scale content-based networks. Inf. Sci. (2019)
28. Mai, V., Khalil, I.: Design and implementation of a secure cloud-based billing model for smart meters as an internet of things using homomorphic cryptography. Future Gener. Comput. Syst. **72**, 327–338 (2017)
29. Malina, L., Hajny, J., Fujdiak, R., Hosek, J.: On perspective of security and privacy-preserving solutions in the internet of things. Comput. Netw. **102**, 83–95 (2016)
30. Malina, L., Srivastava, G., Dzurenda, P., Hajny, J., Fujdiak, R.: A secure publish/subscribe protocol for internet of things. In: Proceedings of the ARES 2019. ACM (2019)
31. Malina, L., Vives-Guasch, A., Castellà-Roca, J., Viejo, A., Hajny, J.: Efficient group signatures for privacy-preserving vehicular networks. Telecommun. Syst. **58**(4), 293–311 (2015)
32. von Maltitz, M., Carle, G.: Leveraging secure multiparty computation in the internet of things. arXiv preprint arXiv:1806.02144 (2018)
33. Medaglia, C.M., Serbanati, A.: An overview of privacy and security issues in the internet of things. The Internet of Things, pp. 389–395. Springer, New York (2010). https://doi.org/10.1007/978-1-4419-1674-7_38
34. Nieto, A., Rios, R., Lopez, J.: Digital witness and privacy in IoT: anonymous witnessing approach. In: 2017 IEEE Trustcom/BigDataSE/ICESS, pp. 642–649. IEEE (2017)
35. Patton, M., Gross, E., Chinn, R., Forbis, S., Walker, L., Chen, H.: Uninvited connections: a study of vulnerable devices on the internet of things (IoT). In: IEEE Joint Intelligence and Security Informatics Conference, pp. 232–235. IEEE (2014)
36. Porambage, P., Ylianttila, M., Schmitt, C., Kumar, P., Gurtov, A., Vasilakos, A.V.: The quest for privacy in the internet of things. IEEE Cloud Comput. **3**(2), 36–45 (2016)
37. Put, A., De Decker, B.: Attribute-based privacy-friendly access control with context. In: Obaidat, M.S. (ed.) ICETE 2016. CCIS, vol. 764, pp. 291–315. Springer, Cham (2017). https://doi.org/10.1007/978-3-319-67876-4_14
38. Ramos, J.L.H., Bernabé, J.B., Skarmeta, A.F.: Towards privacy-preserving data sharing in smart environments. In: Eighth International Conference on Innovative Mobile and Internet Services in Ubiquitous Computing, pp. 334–339. IEEE (2014)
39. Raza, S., Trabalza, D., Voigt, T.: 6LoWPAN compressed DTLS for CoAP. In: 2012 IEEE 8th International Conference on Distributed Computing in Sensor Systems, pp. 287–289. IEEE (2012)

40. Gómez Rodríguez, C.R., Barrantes S., E.G.: Using differential privacy for the internet of things. In: Lehmann, A., Whitehouse, D., Fischer-Hübner, S., Fritsch, L., Raab, C. (eds.) Privacy and Identity 2016. IAICT, vol. 498, pp. 201–211. Springer, Cham (2016). https://doi.org/10.1007/978-3-319-55783-0_14

41. Rodriguez, J.D.P., Schreckling, D., Posegga, J.: Addressing data-centric security requirements for IoT-based systems. In: 2016 International Workshop on Secure Internet of Things (SIoT), pp. 1–10. IEEE (2016)

42. Roman, R., Zhou, J., Lopez, J.: On the features and challenges of security and privacy in distributed internet of things. Comput. Netw. **57**(10), 2266–2279 (2013)

43. Rothenpieler, P., Altakrouri, B., Kleine, O., Ruge, L.: Distributed crowd-sensing infrastructure for personalized dynamic IoT spaces. In: Proceedings of the First International Conference on IoT in Urban Space, pp. 90–92. ICST (Institute for Computer Sciences, Social-Informatics and Telecommunications Engineering) (2014)

44. Seliem, M., Elgazzar, K., Khalil, K.: Towards privacy preserving IoT environments: a survey. Wireless Communications and Mobile Computing 2018 (2018)

45. Sen, A.A.A., Eassa, F.A., Jambi, K., Yamin, M.: Preserving privacy in internet of things: a survey. Int. J. Inf. Technol. **10**(2), 189–200 (2018)

46. Sene, I., Ciss, A.A., Niang, O.: I2PA: an efficient abc for IoT. Cryptography **3**(2), 16 (2019)

47. Shafagh, H., Hithnawi, A., Droescher, A., Duquennoy, S., Hu, W.: Talos: encrypted query processing for the internet of things. In: Proceedings of the 13th ACM Conference on Embedded Networked Sensor Systems, pp. 197–210. ACM (2015)

48. Sicari, S., Rizzardi, A., Grieco, L.A., Coen-Porisini, A.: Security, privacy and trust in internet of things: the road ahead. Comput. Netw. **76**, 146–164 (2015)

49. Solanas, A., et al.: Smart health: a context-aware health paradigm within smart cities. IEEE Commun. Mag. **52**(8), 74–81 (2014)

50. Srinivasan, V., Stankovic, J., Whitehouse, K.: Protecting your daily in-home activity information from a wireless snooping attack. In: Proceedings of the 10th International Conference on Ubiquitous Computing, pp. 202–211. ACM (2008)

51. Staudemeyer, R.C., Pöhls, H.C., Wójcik, M.: The road to privacy in IoT: beyond encryption and signatures, towards unobservable communication. In: 2018 IEEE 19th International Symposium on A World of Wireless, Mobile and Multimedia Networks (WoWMoM), pp. 14–20. IEEE (2018)

52. Tso, R., Alelaiwi, A., Rahman, S.M.M., Wu, M.E., Hossain, M.S.: Privacy-preserving data communication through secure multi-party computation in health-care sensor cloud. J. Signal Process. Syst. **89**(1), 51–59 (2017)

53. Ullah, I., Shah, M.A., Wahid, A., Mehmood, A., Song, H.: ESOT: a new privacy model for preserving location privacy in internet of things. Telecommun. Syst. **67**(4), 553–575 (2018)

54. Vance, N., Zhang, D.Y., Zhang, Y., Wang, D.: Privacy-aware edge computing in social sensing applications using ring signatures. In: IEEE 24th International Conference on Parallel and Distributed Systems (ICPADS), pp. 755–762. IEEE (2018)

55. Vasilomanolakis, E., Daubert, J., Luthra, M., Gazis, V., Wiesmaier, A., Kikiras, P.: On the security and privacy of internet of things architectures and systems. In: Proceedings of SIoT, pp. 49–57. IEEE (2015)

56. Verheul, E.R., Jacobs, B., Meijer, C., Hildebrandt, M., de Ruiter, J.: Polymorphic encryption and pseudonymisation for personalised healthcare. IACR Cryptology ePrint Archive 2016/411 (2016)

57. Voigt, P., Von dem Bussche, A.: The EU General Data Protection Regulation (GDPR) A Practical Guide, 1st edn. Springer International Publishing, Cham (2017). https://doi.org/10.1007/978-3-319-57959-7
58. Wang, X., Jiang, J., Zhao, S., Bai, L.: A fair blind signature scheme to revoke malicious vehicles in vanets. Comput. Mater. Contin. **58**(1), 249–262 (2019)
59. Xu, W., et al.: Internet of vehicles in big data era. IEEE/CAA J. Autom. Sin. **5**(1), 19–35 (2017)
60. Yang, Y., Wu, L., Yin, G., Li, L., Zhao, H.: A survey on security and privacy issues in internet-of-things. IEEE Internet Things J. **4**(5), 1250–1258 (2017)
61. Yao, Z., Ge, J., Wu, Y., Jian, L.: A privacy preserved and credible network protocol. J. Parallel Distrib. Comput. (2019)
62. Yavari, A., Panah, A.S., Georgakopoulos, D., Jayaraman, P.P., van Schyndel, R.: Scalable role-based data disclosure control for the internet of things. In: 2017 IEEE 37th International Conference on Distributed Computing Systems (ICDCS), pp. 2226–2233. IEEE (2017)
63. Zhou, R., Zhang, X., Wang, X., Yang, G., Wang, H., Wu, Y.: Privacy-preserving data search with fine-grained dynamic search right management in fog-assisted internet of things. Inf. Sci. **491**, 251–264 (2019)
64. Ziegeldorf, J.H., Morchon, O.G., Wehrle, K.: Privacy in the internet of things: threats and challenges. Secur. Commun. Netw. **7**(12), 2728–2742 (2014)

Using Audio Characteristics for Mobile Device Authentication

Matthew Dekker and Vimal Kumar[✉]

University of Waikato, Hamilton 3240, New Zealand
matthewtdekker@gmail.com, vkumar@waikato.ac.nz

Abstract. This work attempts to use the innate manufacturing defects in hardware components as identification characteristics for mobile phones. Different components of mobile phones related to I/O operations, such as sensors, were assessed for suitability. From this process, efforts were focused on using both the phone's speaker and microphone in combination to generate samples containing hardware defects which could then be classified. In our approach, a known audio was played using a cellphone's speakers and recorded using the same device's speaker, creating an audio sample. Multiple different groups of samples were taken to test the impact of certain variables on the sample accuracy. The collected samples then had their frequency responses extracted and classified. Different classifiers were used to classify samples with some configurations of classifiers and sample groups achieving over 99.9% accuracy. The results presented in this paper indicate that the manufacturing defects in speakers and microphones could potentially be used for the purposes of device identification.

Keywords: Mobile devices · Authentication · Fingerprinting · Speaker · Microphone · Naive Bayes · Random Forest · Sequential minimal optimisation

1 Introduction

Mobile phones are common personal devices that are ubiquitous with modern life and tend to be carried everywhere by their owner. Their commonality in daily life has given rise to their use in identification schemes such as payment authorisation [14] and other important activities. Yet, they have seen limited use in activities that require a high level of security, such as access control systems. One reason for their rarity in these areas is due to the risk posed by a remote attacker being able to extract and duplicate the software credentials from such a highly connected device. Software based solutions to this problem are inherently risky due to mobile phones having a large attack surface where a single exploit chain could allow an attacker to compromise a device and gain access to a controlled area. In this scenario, a hardware based authentication credential could allow mobile phones to be used for access control while remaining inaccessible to a

© Springer Nature Switzerland AG 2019
J. K. Liu and X. Huang (Eds.): NSS 2019, LNCS 11928, pp. 98–113, 2019.
https://doi.org/10.1007/978-3-030-36938-5_6

remote attacker that has gained access to the device. This research focuses on finding the physical layer characteristics of a device that could meet this goal and be used to accurately identify a device as part of an access control system.

2 Background

The characteristics used for identification, including for access control, generally fall into three groups. These are known as authentication factors and can be summarised as: something a user has; something that a user knows; or something that a user is [13]. These factors form the basis for the existing techniques and systems that are used in access control. Card readers test what someone has, passwords prompts and pin pads test what someone knows, and biometric readers test what someone is. When an access control system is setup it can use one or more of these factors.

Mobile phones are used by over two thirds of the world's population [11] and tend to be used as an analogue for their user as they are generally only used by one person. Our fundamental premise is that they can be used as one of the factors of authentication. For mobile phones to be useful in access control they need to have benefits and risks equivalent to current methods. Since the mobile phone would be a test of what the user has; it is directly comparable to swipe cards and similarly styled access tokens. One of the main benefits of these tokens is that when properly configured, they require an attacker to obtain near physical access to the card to successfully attack it [12]. The networked design of smartphones makes this characteristic difficult to replicate using current methods and consequently discourages the use of software based credentials as they could be stolen by a remote attacker and cloned onto an unauthorised device.

One way to get around these issues is to use the physical hardware of the device to generate valid authentication credentials. While an attacker could potentially remotely clone software, they would have difficulty remotely profiling, and then replicating, the hardware characteristics. A successful way to bypass this issue is through the use of Hardware Security Modules (HSM) which store the sensitive authentication credentials in a way that prevents their duplication from software. While useful, HSMs add cost to each phone they are built into and cheaper devices are unlikely to include them. Further to this, attacks against HSMs are possible, meaning it may still be possible to clone data from them.

3 Literature Review

While there are many parts to a mobile phone, only certain components are useful for generating a fingerprint. These broadly fall into two main categories: sensors, and radio transceivers. In this context, sensors are mobile components which gather information from the surrounding environment and digitise it for use by the device, and radio transceivers are components that use radio frequencies to wirelessly interact with other devices or the environment. Mobile phones today support a number of sensors such as *accelerometer, gyroscope, magnetometer, GPS etc.*. An extensive list of the sensors generally found on Android devices can be found in [9]. Common radio transceivers on mobile phones support radio communication standards such as *Bluetooth, IEEE 802.11, NFC, etc.*. For a component to be useful for fingerprinting it needs to:

- Interact with the physical world by either having externally measurable outputs or by recording information from the environment.
- Be common in devices so the fingerprinting technique is broadly applicable.
- Have minimal reliance on other hardware components for generating output or recording information.

Both sensors and radio transceivers generally meet this criteria however, sensors are the focus for this work. Sensors are strong candidates for identifiable physical characteristics as, by definition, they interact with the device's environment and tend to meet the other criteria listed above. In addition to this they are often cheaply produced and contain tiny discrepancies which prevent them from capturing a perfect recording of their environment. These discrepancies may be unique between components in certain conditions and can potentially be used for fingerprinting.

In [5], the accelerometer was shown to be accessible to web applications through javascript without triggering permission requests, thus allowing for remote fingerprinting of a device. This work involved continuously polling the accelerometer while the device was in a stationary position. After enough values had been obtained, the device will be turned over to finish polling and finally the fingerprint will be calculated. Their results found that they were able to uniquely identify 8.3% of 3600 devices just from the collected accelerometer readings, which rose to 53% when the accelerometer readings were paired with User-Agent strings. [15] also fingerprints the accelerometer but does so by using the vibration feature of the device to provide a known stimulus and improve the accuracy of the fingerprint. The system was able to achieve 99% accuracy when presented with data from a known device. [17] looks at how the accelerometer can be used as a second factor. In this experiment, the system is trained by gathering accelerometer readings while the device is vibrating for predefined amounts of time. Work done in [5,15] and [17] showed that the accelerometer could be used as a fingerprinting mechanism to differentiate between a large sample size of devices. The ubiquity of gyroscopes in mobile phones makes them a potential source for identification characteristics too. However as pointed out in [5] the gyroscope requires constant angular velocity rotation at different speeds to perform fingerprinting, which is difficult even in lab conditions. Despite this challenge, [16] looked specifically at using the gyroscope to fingerprint a device. This method involved measuring the output of the gyroscope while the phone was vibrating with a known pattern for 10 s. From this data, the author tested various classification methods and was able to obtain an identification accuracy of 87.5%. In [4], the magnetometer was used for fingerprinting. The authors designed a low cost system which allowed them to stimulate the magnetometer. [3] also looked at fingerprinting a device using a similar technique. Their focus was on testing how portable the fingerprint was when different sound cards were used. GPS fingerprinting has phased in and out of viability as the technology behind it has changed. It has recently been shown to be a viable fingerprinting method in certain applications but is not useful for access control due to the technology being inaccurate when indoors.

A thorough summary of techniques using camera that are applicable to mobile phones has been collected by the authors of [2]. Fingerprinting a camera is equivalent to image source identification and normally involves interaction from a user to generate and transfer an image on request. However, our opinion is that this level of interaction is undesirable for an access control system.

3.1 Audio Component Fingerprinting

In a similar fashion to the previous sections, both the microphone and speaker systems of a device are subject to minor hardware discrepancies which affect their performance in measurable ways.

Authors in [6] generated 65 distinct tones spread out across the range of frequencies that are commonly supported by speaker systems. By playing these tones through a speaker, the resulting sounds could then be measured to look for frequencies that had a distorted amplitude, otherwise known as the frequency response. An ideal speaker should have a flat frequency response across the majority of the frequencies it supports meaning this ideal can be used as a baseline when playing a known audio file. The classification method had over 80% accuracy when tested using speakers in a range of devices. The work in, [5] also looked at fingerprinting using the speaker and microphone on a phone. For these tests they played a range of frequencies through the phone's speaker then used the phone's microphone to record the result. This combination meant that the resulting data represented the combined distortions from both the microphone and speaker. The authors found that they were able to use the data from this process to identify devices in the vast majority of instances. They also found that the surface the phone was resting on and the audio characteristics of the environment around the phone impacted the successful classification of a known device. Since using both the speaker and microphone on a device creates a closed loop system, no external hardware is needed for data collection, making the method flexible and opens up a range of applications for the technique. In our work we use the same setup as in [5] to illustrate that the microphone and the speaker system can be used for authentication with a high degree of accuracy.

4   Hypothesis and Approach

To summarize, our hypothesis is that *individual components in a device contain benign manufacturing variances that are observable in their output and are unique to each device. Further, these variances can be measured and used for device authentication.*

Specifically, we aim to capture audio characteristics from the device by playing a known sound through the device's speaker and simultaneously recording the played sound through the device's microphone. Audio characteristics such as the frequency response are then extracted from the recording and classified. If there are any observable defects in the samples it is hoped that they are unique to the device, reliable, and suitably complex to allow for the originating device to be identified from a pool of known devices.

There are three main stages in our approach. First, the data is gathered in a controlled manner that prevents the inclusion of unwanted variables. Second, the collected data is processed to extract the audio characteristics and stored in a format that is compatible with the classifier. Finally, the processed data is classified to determine if the extracted characteristics are useful for identification. Figure 1 shows a high level view of this process.

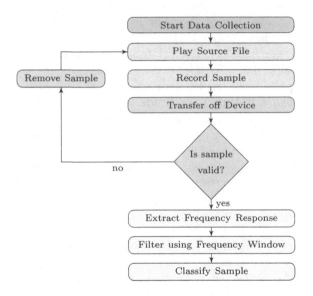

Fig. 1. Overview of the approach

5   Testing Conditions and Considerations

The following conditions were used to ensure that all samples met a common standard and the tests had the greatest chance of success. Where possible variables were controlled or eliminated from the testing process.

5.1   Source Audio Files

The source files are used to define the baseline testing conditions of each test. Some parts of these files are constants across all tests while others change based on the current test. The constants in all samples are:

- **File type** - All source files used the *wav* file format.
- **Sampling rate** - All source files had a sample rate of 44.1 kHz. 44.1 kHz was chosen as it allows for all desired frequencies to be captured.
- **Audio Prefix and Suffix** - 0.5 s of silence was added to the start and end of each source file to ensure that that start and end of the desired frequency range is recorded properly.

Test data was collected by modifying the following parts of the audio files:

- **Frequency range** - Each source file contained frequencies across a given range. The ranges spanned from as low as 1 kHz to the entire tested range. The total frequency range used across all source files was 0.2 kHz–20 kHz. However, the lower bound of 400 Hz was used for the majority of tests.
- **Frequency stepping** - The interval between frequency steps across the tested frequency range. A step of 50 could result in the following sequence: 100 Hz 150 Hz 200 Hz.
- **Play time** - The length of time in seconds that each frequency is played.
- **File length** - Not explicitly set, but varies based on the other factors.
- **File Size** - Not explicitly set, but varies based on the other factors.

Each source file was generated using audacity V2.0.5. The files were generated from a clean project, had 0.5 s of silence added and then each frequency was manually added through the "Tone Generator" tool with the Sine waveform and an amplitude of 0.8. After adding all of the frequencies in the range 0.5 s of silence was added to the end of the file and then exported with the type "WAV (Microsoft) signed 16 bit PCM".

5.2   Data Collection

The data collection process involved using a custom Android application loaded onto each of the 20 devices we used to record samples. 19 of the devices were mobile phones while 1 was a tablet. 15 out of the 20 devices were different models and 5 were the same make and model (LG Nexus 5). Measures were taken to ensure that the samples were all collected under similar conditions. Once collected the samples were manually inspected to ensure the collection process hadn't resulted in any malformations. Any malformed samples were discarded and replaced with new samples from the same device. For each of the main tests 20 samples were taken from each device.

5.3   App Process

The Android application ensured that the data collection process could be tightly controlled and meet the requirements without introducing unexpected behaviours. The application would simultaneously play a source file through the device's speaker and record the sample via the device's microphone. Once the source file had finished playing the recording stopped and saved the captured audio to the device's file system. This process was repeated until enough samples had been collected from a source file and then moved on to the next source file. Where possible the collected sample audio files were saved with the same attributes as the source files to prevent the loss or distortion of the audio characteristics. The following attributes were matched:

- **File type** - Samples were also stored in the *wav* file format.
- **Sampling rate** - 44.1 kHz was also used in the microphone output.
- **Audio encoding** - The audio encoding of the samples was also 16 bit PCM.

5.4   Manual Review of Samples

Each file was manually inspected to check for malformations such as recording issues or external interference on the samples. For this, the raw amplitude was plotted against the length of the file and visualised as a graph. Visualising the data like this allowed for a quick inspection process that highlighted any anomalous dips or spikes in audio volume that characterised a malformed or otherwise undesirable sample. In an effort to reduce the bias of this process, the sample's frequency response was not extracted for inspection. This type of inspection is inherently subjective but some guidelines were followed. A file was excluded if it contained any of the following features:

- Large, one off spikes not present in other samples.
- A sizeable difference in length to the source file.
- Missing sections of the sample as seen in Fig. 2
- High levels of sound during the silent prefix or suffix.

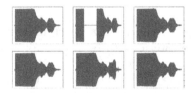

Fig. 2. The top middle sample is missing a section of the sample and would be excluded by the manual inspection process. The rest of the samples are valid.

6   Data Processing

The raw samples from the devices were processed to extract the audio characteristics and converted to a format that could be read by the classifier.

6.1 Frequency Extraction Using FFT

After reading the sample into memory, the script would run the entire sample through a Fast Fourier Transform *(fft)* to extract the frequency components present in the sample. After experimenting with the Rectangle, Blackman, Hamming, and Hanning windows, the Rectangle window was chosen because it doesn't distort the frequencies represented. Due to their nature, other windows flattened the frequency responses near the start and end of the range. The *fft* used was from the NumPy package [7] and specifically designed for real input [8]. This implementation of the *fft* outputs complex values which are then converted to absolute values using the in-built python function abs(x).

6.2 Frequency Filtering

After the frequencies were extracted from the sample the results were filtered. The filtering process takes a list of frequencies in the source file and looks for frequencies that are within a set number of Hz of any of the known frequencies. For example, with a frequency window of 1 Hz and the known frequencies 100 Hz and 200 Hz the filter would output all values within the ranges 99 Hz–101 Hz and 199 Hz–201 Hz. The rest of the values would be removed. The filtering windows used were: [*None, 0.5 Hz, 1 Hz, 5 Hz, 10 Hz, 20 Hz*].

6.3 Writing to ARFF Files and Training Samples

After filtering the frequencies, the data was written to the appropriate *arff* file using the liac-arff (V2.3.1) [1] package. During this process, the Python script also split the samples into training and testing files. We initially used 5 training samples and 15 testing samples but we later changed this to iterate over every option from 3–10 training samples with the remaining used for testing.

The files used for training or testing were randomly chosen. Once chosen the samples kept their designation (training or testing) across all filtering windows. Each iteration to split the training data operated independently meaning that the random selection of samples for training and testing was not carried over, i.e. For the same device and experiment, a different selection of samples would be used for 3 training samples and 4 training samples within a test.

6.4 Classification

After the data had been processed it was fed into the classifiers. We verified that all expected files had been generated by the processor before continuing. The software WEKA [10] was used for classification. WEKA was used since it supports a wide range of machine learning algorithms. For a classifier to be useful it needed to be able to classify a distinct class (the device) given the data provided (the extracted frequencies). Out of the many classifiers that WEKA offers, it was decided to use Naive Bayes *(nb)*, Random Forest *(rf)*, and Sequential Minimal Optimization *(smo)*. The default settings in WEKA were used for the classifiers and could likely be improved with further research.

7   Data Collection

We collected three different groups of data for classification. We began by collecting data for the original targeted frequency ranges, then for the ultrasound frequency range and then collected data for iteration testing. These are explained below in the section.

7.1   Targeted Frequency Range Tests

This data was collected to test the classification accuracy given a range of controlled variants. The source files were chosen so that most of them covered a frequency range of around 2 kHz and the total frequency range across the files was 400 Hz–10 kHz. The frequency step for these tests was fixed at 50 Hz. In an effort to find a lower bound that would result in low classification accuracy, the length of time each frequency was played varied between 0.1 s, 0.2 s, and 0.5 s depending on the test. Finally, a set of tests that covered the entire 400 Hz–10 kHz range were also included. While the size of these tests made classification difficult, it was thought that the larger frequency range could result in a unique, composite characteristic for identification. In total there were 18 tests with 20 samples being collected from each of the 20 devices for each test.

7.2   Ultrasonic Frequency Tests

We then collected data for experimentation in the ultrasound frequency (*uf*) range. These tests followed a similar testing process to the Targeted Frequency Range Tests but focused on the 18 kHz–20 kHz frequency range. The *uf* is preferable for several reasons. From a technical perspective the *uf* may be easier to isolate from background noise than frequencies in the audible spectrum, and from a usability standpoint it is preferable to use frequencies that won't annoy the user. To further improve usability the 0.5 s play time was removed from this stage, leaving only the shorter times and an even shorter 1 kHz frequency range was used for some tests. These changes resulted in tests that were only around 3 s in length, including the 1 s of silence at the start and end of the file. In total 6 tests were collected during this stage.

Dirty tests of the ultrasonic source files were added alongside the standard test environment in order to assess the performance of these tests in a more realistic environment. Dirty testing involved conducting the same Ultrasonic Frequency Tests in the same room and environment, but with added background noise. Background noise was simulated by the author talking, playing music, opening and closing doors, eating, and interacting with other objects.

7.3   Iteration Testing

Finally, we focused on trying to improve the classification rates for devices that likely share similar audio characteristics. It was hypothesised that devices of the same make and model would contain the same audio components and be more difficult to identify than devices of different makes and models. This hypothesis was supported by some of the early results and was feared to worsen when extrapolated out to larger sets of devices of the same make and model. One suggestion for countering this was that repeatedly playing a sample through the device it originated from would strengthen the audio characteristics and improve the classification accuracy of similar devices. This is the basis of iteration testing.

For these tests a smaller set of devices was used. Instead of all of the devices available, only the 5 LG Nexus 5 devices were used for this stage. Each device had new samples collected from a curated set of tests in addition to the samples gathered from standard testing of the devices. These initial samples formed the first iteration. The samples from the first iteration were then used as source files and played again through the corresponding device, forming the second iteration. This was repeated until the fifth iteration had been collected from each device. As with the other tests, 20 samples were collected from each device for each test. Each sample was then iterated over, resulting in 20 final output samples.

Results from this section are discussed later.

8   Results

The processing and classification stages generated a large amount of data points with over 21000 individual results. In this section we present the results of our experiments. Unless stated otherwise, the grouping used is of the standard tests.

The classification performance shown in Fig. 3 was extremely good with all three classification algorithms able to achieve over 93% accuracy in the standard tests. The dirty and iteration tests performed objectively worse than the standard tests, however, their degraded performance was conditional and could be brought back up near the results obtained through standard testing.

Directly comparing the classification algorithms showed that *rf* and *smo* performed the best with neither algorithm dropping below 99% classification accuracy. *nb* performed worse, dropping as low as 93.29% accuracy but still obtaining over 98% accuracy with 8 samples.

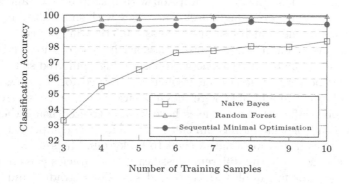

Fig. 3. Comparison of classification algorithms during standard testing.

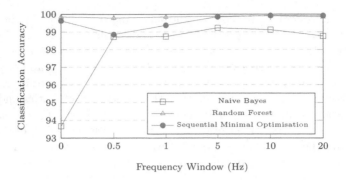

Fig. 4. Comparison of Classification Algorithms at different frequency windows using 8 training samples. A filtering window of 0 Hz represents no filtering.

The best classification accuracy was achieved by *rf* with 9 training samples where only 22 out of 36954 samples were misclassified, giving a 99.94% classification accuracy. *nb* with 3 training samples performed the worst where 3834 out of 57114 samples were misclassified for 93.29% classification accuracy.

These results indicate that across a large frequency range the audio components definitely impart characteristics on their output that can be used for identification.

Observed Trends in Classification Performance: The results from the standard tests showed some interesting trends. One such trend is observable in the classification accuracy for each frequency window, as shown in Fig. 4.

We can see how the classification algorithms perform when given various amounts of data. It can be seen that, *rf* performed the best out of all three but also showed that it is accurate with both very tight filtering windows (0.5 Hz) and unfiltered data. The high classification accuracy across this spectrum suggests that internally, *rf* is identifying the device characteristics to implicitly filter out the background noise. *smo* also performed well but showed that it needed a wider filtering window (5 Hz) to achieve the same level of accuracy as *rf* but could maintain high levels of accuracy after that point. *nb* performed the worst and the results suggested that accuracy drops off with both too much and too little data. Being able to achieve a high level of accuracy with small filtering windows makes these techniques much less intensive as a 0.5 Hz windows can result in a few hundred data points being fed into a classifier instead of thousands.

Figure 5 shows the accuracy of *nb* when classifying unfiltered samples where the only difference is how long each frequency is played for. Playing each frequency for a longer amount of time results in a larger sample file which contains more data points after the frequencies have been extracted using the *fft*. The implication of this is that *nb* has difficulty identifying the component's characteristics and gives disproportionate weight to background noise.

We can also see how the different classification accuracies are impacted by the number of training samples. Both *rf* and *smo* saw a gradual improvement

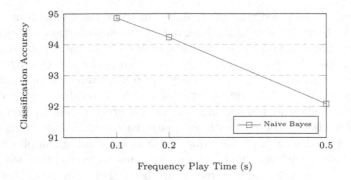

Fig. 5. Naive Bayes classification accuracy in samples vs different frequency play times.

in accuracy with more samples, both algorithms were able to achieve over 99% accuracy with just 3 training samples as seen in Fig. 3. This is significant as only using 3 samples for training provides very little information to build profiles of the devices and requires the classifier to classify 17 unknown samples from each device. Both algorithms had a clear increase in classification accuracy at 4 samples with no or only minor improvements as the number of training samples increased further. Unlike the other algorithms, *nb* showed large improvements as the number of training samples increased and seemed to be continuing that trend, suggesting that with enough training samples it may be possible for *nb* to achieve similar levels of accuracy to the other algorithms.

Classification Performance with Dirty Samples: While the results from the standard tests were positive, they utilised samples that were recorded in highly desirable, and likely unrealistic, conditions. The dirty tests were captured in an environment that was more indicative of real-world conditions. The results from the dirty tests however were also very positive. Figure 6 shows how the classification algorithms performed when presented with this data.

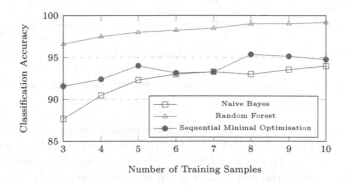

Fig. 6. Comparison of classification algorithms using data from dirty tests

The results from the dirty tests matched many of the trends from the standard tests with *rf* performing the best out of the classification algorithms and the results improving with more training samples. Unlike the standard tests, the dirty tests proved to be a challenge for *smo* which performed closer to *nb* than to *rf*. *smo* also showed a similar tendency for gradual improvements in classification accuracy as more training samples were added, but had higher volatility. *rf* performed the best and maintained at least 2% greater classification accuracy over the other classification algorithms at any given number of training samples. The trend of *rf* having higher accuracy with more training samples was more distinct and along with *nb*, maintained a trend that suggested that with greater than 10 training samples the accuracy could be further improved. This reduced accuracy was expected as some of the devices were unable to operate in the *uf* range where the dirty testing was performed. These devices then effectively had a frequency response of 0 after filtering had been applied and were indistinguishable from each other. Newer devices were more likely to properly support the *uf* range suggesting that this accuracy may improve as devices improve.

Classification Performance with Similar Devices: Two hypotheses were posed during this research. First, a pool of devices of the same make and model would be more difficult to classify than a pool of disparate devices. Second, the distortions in samples could be increased by replaying the captured sample back through the device. We tested both of these hypotheses by applying the iterative tests to a pool of 5 LG Nexus 5 devices. Figures 7 and 8 show the aggregate classification accuracy from each iteration using 8 and 3 training samples.

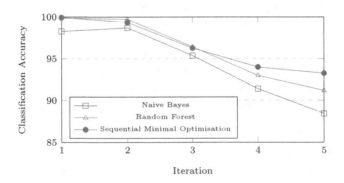

Fig. 7. Comparison of classification accuracy at each iteration using 8 training samples

Both Figs. 7 and 8 start off with very high classification accuracy that reduces with each iteration, suggesting that both of the presented hypotheses are wrong, but these results aren't quite as damning as they first seem. The reported results were aggregated from the results of a given number of iterations meaning that any poor performances could drastically reduce the aggregate accuracy. In this case it was noted that high numbers of training samples reduced the classification

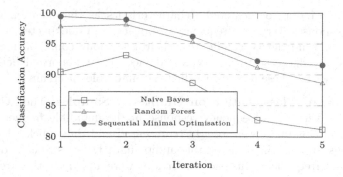

Fig. 8. Comparison of classification accuracy at each iteration using 3 training samples

accuracy, possibly due to the defect characteristics being similar. Additionally, we found that most of the misclassifications occurred in the inaudible frequency range and each iteration of the samples drastically reduced the classification accuracy for these tests, dragging down each iteration's average.

To work around these points, the aggregation was rerun using results from 3 training samples and the tests involving the inaudible frequency range were excluded. This resulted in the data shown in Fig. 9. We can see that while classification accuracy is still high at the first iteration, there is still room for improvement and applying multiple iterations to the sample was able to do exactly that in some cases. *nb* benefited the most from the iterative process with a positive trend in accuracy. The other classification algorithms had either minor or no improvement in accuracy over the iterations.

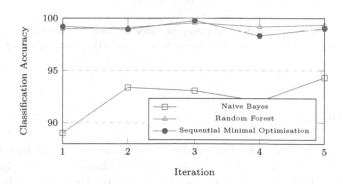

Fig. 9. Iteration Sample Accuracy - Using 3 training samples and excluding tests that include frequencies in the inaudible frequency range.

On the whole, the iterative testing was inconclusive. Aspects of the results were promising but a larger pool of devices is needed to prove or disprove either hypothesis. It's also likely that the LG Nexus 5 devices are poor candidates for this type of test due to their audio characteristics as they contain very high frequency responses, very low frequency responses, and unexpected distortions. While they're valid device candidates, their behaviour could be more representative of an edge case than a typical device. Their abnormal behaviour is exemplified by how these devices handled the inaudible spectrum.

Performance of Classification on Unfiltered Samples: The LG Nexus 5 devices had a very weak frequency response in the inaudible frequency range. Frequencies in this range were poorly represented and thus quickly lost during the iterations until minimal discernible audio characteristics remained near the original target frequencies. Instead, distortions were added at other frequencies. This lack of features near the original frequencies resulted in poor classification accuracy for samples that were filtered using a frequency window but moderate - high classification accuracy when the samples were unfiltered. Figure 10 shows the classification accuracy at each frequency window using data collected from 5th iteration tests in the inaudible frequency range.

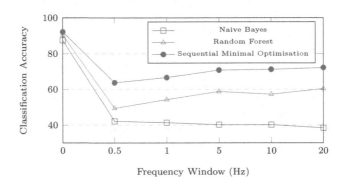

Fig. 10. Classification algorithms at different filtering windows for 5th iteration tests in the inaudible frequency range. A filtering window of 0 Hz represents no filtering.

9 Conclusion

Our hypothesis was that physical hardware components contain tiny manufacturing variations that could be used for authentication in mobile phones. We used a combination of a speaker and a microphone for testing this and our results as outlined in this paper look promising. We used three different classifiers for testing the hypothesis. The results show that all classifiers were able to achieve high levels of accuracy when trying to identify samples from a known pool of devices, however *rf* worked better in most cases than the other two. In some configurations, classification of samples taken from a pool of 20 devices was over 99.9% accurate. It was also found that certain types of tests may be able to accurately identify devices of the same make and model or perform well given a level of background noise.

While the results are encouraging, in future we would work with a larger pool of devices on further research challenges such as using a mixed frequency sample such as a music file for authentication, testing on more devices of the same make and model and reducing the total end to end time to make this a viable authentication factor on a mobile phone.

References

1. liac-arff 2.3.1. https://pypi.org/project/liac-arff/
2. Baldini, G., Steri, G.: A survey of techniques for the identification of mobile phones using the physical fingerprints of the built-in components. IEEE Commun. Surv. Tutorials **19**(3), 1761–1789 (2017)
3. Baldini, G., Steri, G., Amerini, I., Caldelli, R.: The identification of mobile phones through the fingerprints of their built-in magnetometer: an analysis of the portability of the fingerprints. In: 2017 International Carnahan Conference on Security Technology (ICCST), pp. 1–6. IEEE (2017)
4. Baldini, G., Steri, G., Giuliani, R., Kyovtorov, V.: Mobile phone identification through the built-in magnetometers. arXiv preprint arXiv:1701.07676 (2017)
5. Bojinov, H., Michalevsky, Y., Nakibly, G., Boneh, D.: Mobile device identification via sensor fingerprinting (2014)
6. Clarkson, W.B.: Breaking assumptions: distinguishing between seemingly identical items using cheap sensors. Ph.D. thesis, Princeton University (2012)
7. Developers N: Numpy. https://www.numpy.org/
8. Developers N numpy.fft.rfft. https://docs.scipy.org/doc/numpy/reference/generated/numpy.fft.rfft.html
9. Google: Android 8.1 compatibility definition (2017). https://source.android.com/compatibility/8.1/android-8.1-cdd.pdf
10. Hall, M., Frank, E., Holmes, G., Pfahringer, B., Reutemann, P., Witten, I.H.: The weka data mining software: an update. ACM SIGKDD Explor. Newslett. **11**(1), 10–18 (2009)
11. Intelligence G: Global mobile trends 2017 (2017). https://www.gsma.com/globalmobiletrends/
12. Khattab, A., Jeddi, Z., Amini, E., Bayoumi, M.: RFID security threats and basic solutions. RFID Security. ACSP, pp. 27–41. Springer, Cham (2017). https://doi.org/10.1007/978-3-319-47545-5_2
13. Ometov, A., Bezzateev, S., Mäkitalo, N., Andreev, S., Mikkonen, T., Koucheryavy, Y.: Multi-factor authentication: a survey. Cryptography **2**(1), 1 (2018)
14. Profis, S.: Everything you need to know about NFC and mobile payments (2014). https://www.cnet.com/how-to/how-nfc-works-and-mobile-payments/
15. Sanorita, D., Nirupam, R., Wenyuan, X., Romit, R.C., Srihari, N.: Accelprint: imperfections of accelerometers make smartphones trackable. In: Proceedings of the 21st Annual Network and Distributed System Security Symposium (2014)
16. Tahaei, M.: Gyrovib: Sensor-based smartphone identification
17. Van Goethem, T., Scheepers, W., Preuveneers, D., Joosen, W.: Accelerometer-based device fingerprinting for multi-factor mobile authentication. In: Caballero, J., Bodden, E., Athanasopoulos, E. (eds.) ESSoS 2016. LNCS, vol. 9639, pp. 106–121. Springer, Cham (2016). https://doi.org/10.1007/978-3-319-30806-7_7

Ethereum Analysis via Node Clustering

Hanyi Sun, Na Ruan$^{(\boxtimes)}$, and Hanqing Liu

Department of Computer Science and Engineering, Shanghai Jiao Tong University,
Shanghai, China
naruan@cs.sjtu.edu.cn

Abstract. As an open source public blockchain with the capabilities
of running smart contract, Ethereum provides decentralized Ethernet
virtual machines to handle peer-to-peer contracts through its dedicated
cryptocurrency Ether. And as the second largest blockchain, the amount
of transaction data in Ethereum grows fast. Analysis of these data can
help researchers better understand Ethereum and find attackers among
the users. However, the analysis of Ethereum data at the present stage
is mostly based on the statistical characteristics of Ethereum nodes and
lacks analysis of the transaction behavior between them. In this paper,
we apply machine learning in Ethereum analysis for the first time and
cluster users and smart contract into groups by using transaction information in existing blocks. The clustering results are analyzed by using
the identity information of the available Ethereum users and smart contracts. Based on the clustering results, we propose a new way of user
identity discrimination and malicious user detection.

Keywords: Blockchain · Ethereum · Network embedding

1 Introduction

As the second largest blockchain platform, Ethereum [1] has had a market
value of nearly 20 billion since its inception in 2015. Different from traditional
blockchain like Bitcoin [2], Ethereum is an emerging blockchain platform in
which users can create smart contracts. This feature makes the data structure of
Ethereum more complicated compared with other blockchains. A smart contract
is a contract implemented in code that can be executed automatically after its
creation [3]. In Ethereum, transactions between users are mainly done through
direct Ether trading and invocation to smart contracts.

In previous Ethereum studies, researchers focused on the statistical characteristics of Ethereum nodes and lacks analysis of the trading behavior between
them [4]. Therefore, based on the work of predecessors, this study focuses on
the cluster of Ethereum nodes and analysis of the clustering result. Specifically,
the Ether trading between users and users in Ethereum, the creation of smart
contracts and the invocation of smart contracts were studied. The clustering
algorithm of machine learning was applied for the first time in Ethereum data

© Springer Nature Switzerland AG 2019
J. K. Liu and X. Huang (Eds.): NSS 2019, LNCS 11928, pp. 114–129, 2019.
https://doi.org/10.1007/978-3-030-36938-5_7

analysis. Based on the clustering results of experiment, we propose a new way of user identity discrimination and malicious user detection.

There are two types of accounts in Ethereum, external owned accounts (EOAs) and smart contract accounts. The EOAs represent the Ethereum users in the form of a hash value, and the smart contract accounts represent smart contracts in Ethereum. In this paper, we mainly foucs on three types of transaction relationships between EOAs and smart contract accounts, including Ether transactions between external owned accounts, smart contract creation between external owned accounts and smart contract account, and smart contract invocation between external owned accounts and smart contract accounts. The two different accounts types and three different transaction relationship types form the heterogeneous network of Ethereum.

For the feasibility of the experiment, we only used part of Ethereum transaction data due to huge amount of them. Among these data, we filter the three transaction types and two account types which form a Ethereum heterogeneous network. We learn about the eigenvector representation of the account nodes in Ethereum based on the heterogeneous network. And clustering algorithms are used to cluster the nodes eigenvector representation into groups. In the analysis of the clustering results, we got some interesting observations and findings. For example, the clustering results shows that the nodes in Ethereum have obvious clustering trend and there are some clusters led by nodes with known identities. By collecting the identity information about nodes in Ethereum, we can predict the identity of the clusters to which these nodes belong including exchange market and attackers. Moreover, we propose a new way of user identity discrimination and malicious user detection based on the clustering results. Although there are some methods for malicious user detection, they are only applicable to those nodes with large degree. In this paper, our new method use the nodes with known identities to predict the identity of other nodes in the clustering results. On generality, our method could be more adapted to the specificity of Ethereum.

The main contributions of this paper are as follows:

- In our research, this paper applies clustering algorithm in the analysis of Ethereum for the first time. We collect and filter the transactions from Ethereum blocks and cluster the accounts nodes included in them.
- We use node embedding algorithm to calculate the eigenvector representation for the external owned account nodes and smart contract account nodes in the Ethereum. Based on the eigenvector, we cluster those nodes into groups and visualize the clustering results.
- We obtain some new observations by the analysis of clustering result which makes us have a better understanding of Ethereum.
- We propose a new way of malicious user detection based on the clustering result and the nodes whose identities is already known.

The rest of paper is organized as follows. In Sect. 2 we introduce the background of our paper, including Ethereum and the machine learning algorithm we used. In Sect. 3, we introduce our system model. In Sect. 4, we analyze the clustering results and propose a new way of user identity discrimination and malicious user detection. We conclude the paper in Sect. 5.

2   Background

Ethereum is the second largest blockchain and has a market value of nearly 20 billion since its inception. And it has its own cryptocurrency Ether which can be traded or used to pay for smart contract operations. Different from traditional blockchain with currency trading as the main function, users in Ethereum can develop more complex functions by developing smart contracts. These smart contracts run according to the established code, and can be called by users in Ethereum after deployment [5]. Meanwhile, user have to pay some fees to perform the operation when calling smart contracts. There some research of user relationships in Bitcoin [6–9], but they are not suitable for the case of Ethereum due to the difference in structure.

2.1   Accounts and Transactions

The accounts in Ethereum has two types, external owned accounts (EOAs) and smart contract accounts.

External owned accounts represent accounts that belongs to external owner of Ethereum, and each external owned account has its own Ether balance. The owner of the external owned account can transfer information from his or her external owned account by creating and signing a transaction. If the owner's external balance is sufficient to cover the cost of the transaction, the transaction is valid. Then the originator account will deduct the corresponding Ether amount, and the recipient account will receive the amount. In addition to direct Ether trading between external owned accounts, Ether can also be traded by calling a smart contract and the transaction deduction is determined by the code written in advance within the smart contract.

The smart contract account represents the smart contract deployed in Ethereum which controlled by the code written in advance. Each smart contract account stores the hash value of the smart contract code. In the case of a invocation, the smart contract account receives a transaction message and activate the smart contract code stored in it, which allows it to read and write to the internal storage or send other messages such as creating another smart contract.

The various activities of Ethereum's external owned and smart contract accounts are realized through transactions which are packaged into blocks and then broadcast to the entire Ethereum network. A transaction is a message that is sent from one account to another. Transactions can contain binary data called payload and Ether coins. If the target account contains code, the code will execute, and payload is the input data. If the target account is a zero account, the transaction will create a new smart contract. And each transaction in Ethereum contains the sender's signature, the recipient and the number of Ethers sent.

At the same time, based on different transaction types, Ethereum's transaction information also contains several other types, such as gas, gasprice and other optional data items used as smart contract execution fees.

Due to the features of blockchain, different activities in Ethereum will form transactions such as Ether trading transactions, smart contract creation and smart contract invocation. At the same time, these transactions are packaged into blocks and spread throughout the Ethereum network.

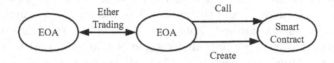

Fig. 1. Three transaction types in Ethereum

As shown in Fig. 1, we mainly focus three different trading relationships between external owned accounts and smart contract accounts:

- Direct Ether trading transactions between EOAs.
- One EOA creates a smart contract account. The external owned account firstly writes the code of the smart contract, and uploads the smart contract to the Ethereum by paying a certain amount of Ether.
- One EOA calls a smart contract account. Once a smart contract account is uploaded to the Ethereum, the users in the Ethereum can call the smart contract and realize the trading activity through the code logic in it.

In Ethereum, the Ether transaction may be done by calling a smart contract. In this case, we treat it as both smart contract invocation and Ether trading transaction in this paper.

2.2   Method of Node Embedding

In Ethereum, there are two different accounts types and three different transaction relationship types between them which form a heterogeneous network. SO in this paper, we learn from Metapath2vec [10] as the eigenvector representation learning method.

In the previous application, Metapath2vec mainly solved the problem of learning the eigenvector representation of scholars and conferences in the academic network. The main idea of Metapath2vec is to use the meta-path to guide the random walk [11] acquisition path in the academic network and learn these paths. Suppose there are three different nodes in the academic network, scholars, papers and venues. Meanwhile there are two different relationships papers written by authors and these papers are published on venues. The idea of Metapath2vec is to guide the way of random walks through a meta-path, A-P-C-P-A.

Fig. 2. Meta-Path in academic networks

As shown in Fig. 2, in the academic network we first select an author A and then randomly walk to a paper P written by the author A and the venue V which the paper published at. Then randomly walk to another paper P which published at this conference and the author A of the paper. By analogy, a path of author-paper-venue is formed. This Meta-Path guides random walks in the academic network, forming many different paths that preserve the concept of "word context". After that, each path obtained by random walk is considered as a sentence, the node is considered as a word and the adjacent nodes in the path are regarded as contexts. Then these paths are learned by using the skip-gram model [12]. In this way, the eigenvector representation of the nodes in the academic network can be obtained. There are two different nodes and three different relationships in the Ethereum network which is similar to academic networks. In this paper, we learn the eigenvector representation of the nodes in Ethereum with reference to the idea of Metapath2vec.

3   System Model

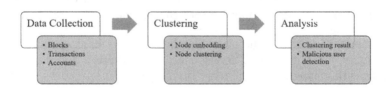

Fig. 3. Our system model with three phases

As shown in Fig. 3, our model can be divided into three phases: Data Collection, Clustering and Analysis. Data Collection collects the block data we used. Clustering part contains Node Embedding and Node Clustering. Node Emmbedding learns the eigenvector representation of the nodes in Ethereum. Node Clustering presents the clustering results and visualize [13] them. The Analysis part will analyze the clustering results and give some new opinions.

3.1   Data Collection

The dataset of Ethereum blocks we used is from previous works of others [4]. We choose the first 10 millions of transactions and detect the three main activities, Ether trading, smart contract creation and smart contract invocation included in them. At the same time, in order to ensure the validity of the analysis, we only pay attention to the transactions confirmed in the Ethereum block, and do not consider the transactions that failed for various reasons.

Among the transactions in the block, the types of transactions we need are only Ether trading, smart contract creation and smart contract invocation. In order to extract the required transaction types from the block data, we observed that the three behavior patterns in the transaction are related to the main trading activities we are concerned with.

- The Create behavior corresponds to the creation of a smart contract.
- The Call behavior corresponds to the invocation of a smart contract.
- When the number of Ethers in the transaction is greater than 0, the two accounts in transaction have made a Ether trading.

By detecting these three behaviors in the transaction, we filter out the three types of transactions and classify them. At the same time, we exclude four types of transactions that are unrelated to the three main activities. One is that the transaction between external owned accounts but the number of Ether traded is 0. The second is the transaction in which the number of gas in the smart contract that supports the contract is 0, which means the smart contract cannot run. The third type is the Ether trading transaction between accounts which fail for various reasons. The fourth is a transaction that fails when an external owned account creates a smart contract account.

By eliminating invalid transactions and classifying and counting the selected transactions, the Table 1 is obtained.

Table 1. Number of transactions

Transaction type	Number
Ether trading transaction	**8913083**
Smart contract creation	**119347**
Smart contract invocation	**1924918**

As can be seen from Table 1, the number of Ether trading transactions is 8,913,083. The proportion of Ether trading transactions in Ethereum exceeds the sum of smart contract creation and smart contract invocation. It can be known that ether trading occupy the vast majority of transactions in Ethereum. At the same time, the smart contract creation is the least of the three types of transactions and only has a number of 119,347. Therefore, in the analysis part, we will pay more attention to the type of Ether trading transaction in Ethereum.

The number of accounts we get from the selected transactions are shown in Table 2. Based on the transactions data, we obtained 406,774 external owned account addresses and 119,347 smart contract account addresses, a total of 526,121 account addresses. There are more account addresses in Ethereum, but

Table 2. Number of accounts

Account type	Number
External owned account	**406774**
Smart contract account	**119347**
Total	**526121**

we only consider the account addresses obtained from the transactions. In other word, for other external owned accounts in Ethereum that have never made any Ether trading transactions, smart contract creation and smart contract invocation, we do not consider them in our analysis. It can be seen that the number smart contract account is as same as the number of transactions of smart contract creation. At the same time, we observed that there are a few external owned accounts which included in many transactions have play a very important role in the trading of Ethereum. Therefore, we will give more weight to these important nodes in the node emmbedding part.

3.2 Node Embedding

Before node clustering, we need to learn the eigenvector representation of the nodes in Ethereum. In the network we built, there are two types of nodes external owned accounts and smart contract accounts. And there are three types of relationships between the two types of nodes, Ether trading transactions between external owned accounts, smart contract creation and smart contract invocation between external owned accounts and smart contract accounts. In order to learn the eigenvector representation of the nodes in the Ethereum network, we have improved the idea based on Metapath2vec.

An important problem when learning the eigenvectors of nodes in network is how to transform the structure of network into the form which skip-gram model can handle. To solve this problem, Metapath2vec capture the semantic and structural correlations between different types of nodes by using meta-path-based random walks to generate paths.

In our experiments, we used the idea of improved Metapath2vec by using a mixed meta-path to guide the generation of random paths. Since external owned accounts is the main body of Ethereum, we consider the following scenarios such as both two external owend accounts have Ether trading transactions with another account, or both external owned accounts have called a same smart contract or an external owned account have called a smart contract created by another external account. In these cases, we believe that these accounts may belong to the same category or have similarities. So we use the following mixed meta-path to guide the process of random walks to generate paths and use these paths to learn the eigenvector representation of the nodes.

As shown in Fig. 4, external owned accounts are expressed by node U, smart contract accounts are expressed by SC and the transactions are represented by a

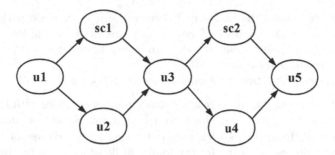

Fig. 4. Meta-path in Ethereum

line between nodes. In order to generate a path, we first select an external owned account node *u1* and then randomly walk to an external owned account node *u2* or smart contract account node *sc1* that has had a transaction relationship with it. After that, it randomly walk to another external owned account node *u3* which has a transaction relationship with the node obtained before. Then through this node, it continues to find a next external owned account node or smart contract account node. And so on, then it can walk randomly to get a fixed length path, which saves the context of the account nodes in the Ethereum network.

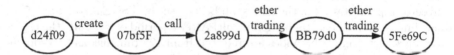

Fig. 5. A sample path in Ethereum

Figure 5 shows part of a sample path generated by randomly walk, actual accounts are represented by the node with the first six digits of their account addresses. In this path, d24f09, 2a899d, BB79d0 and 5Fe69C represent four external owned account nodes, and 07bf5F represents a smart contract account node. The lines between them represent the different types of relationships including contract creation, contract invocation and Ether trading. 2a899d calls smart contract account 07bf5F which is created by d24f09, so we can think that these two nodes d24f09 and 2a899d are closely related. At the same time, 2a899d and 5Fe69C may have a close relationship because they both have Ether trading with BB79d0.

In order to save the relationship between nodes in Ethereum network as much as possible by random walks, the specific settings of our experiment are as follows:

– Set the path length of the random walk to 100 during the random walk.

- Calculate the degree the nodes in Ethereum. For each node with a degree greater than 30, the number of paths that are randomly moved from this node as starting point is set to 300. For other nodes, the path with those node as starting point is set to 100.
- Set the eigenvector representation dimension of the nodes to 128.

In Sect. 3.1, we found that there are a small number of nodes with large accessibility have a very important influence on Ethereum. So we set more random paths which start from nodes with larger degrees. In the course of the experiment, we get millions of paths by randomly walk which save the information in Ethereum network. Then we input those paths into the skip-gram model for training and get the eigenvector representation of each node in 128 dimensions. We visualize and cluster the eigenvectors of these nodes and then analysis the clustering result.

3.3 Node Clustering

For the analysis of the node eigenvectors obtained by node embedding, we first reduce their dimensions and visualize them. T-distributed stochastic neighbor embedding abbreviated as TSNE is a machine learning algorithm used for dimensional reduction. And it is a nonlinear dimensionality reduction algorithm, which is very suitable for high-dimensional data dimensionality reduction to 2D or 3D for visualization.

First, we use the PCA dimensionality reduction algorithm [14] to initialize the eigenvector representation of the nodes, and then use the TSNE algorithm [15] to reduce dimension of the initialization result. After a period of training, the eigenvector representation of the nodes are reduced from 128 dimensions to 3 dimensions. Then we visualize the eigenvector of nodes after the dimension reduction.

In Fig. 6, each blue point represents an external owned account node or a smart contract account node in Ethereum. And the nodes in the figure are represented by three-dimensional vectors. It can be seen from the figure that after the dimensional reduction by the TSNE dimensionality reduction algorithm, the eigenvectors of the nodes show obvious clustering trends, and the boundaries between the clusters are also obvious. Based on the eigenvectors after dimension reduction, we cluster the nodes in Ethereum.

Since we have a large number of nodes and no fixed number of clusters, we have adopted the Birch algorithm that works better on larger data sets in the clustering of nodes. The Birch algorithm is an algorithm based on hierarchical clustering. It adopts a tree structure to perform fast clustering and has a good effect on large data sets. The clustering algorithm shows great results on our dataset.

Some important parameters of the Birch are as follows:

- threshold: we set the value to 0.6
- branching_factor: due to the large number of nodes, we set it to 100
- n_clusters: with no prior knowledge, we set it to None
- compute_labels: the default is True

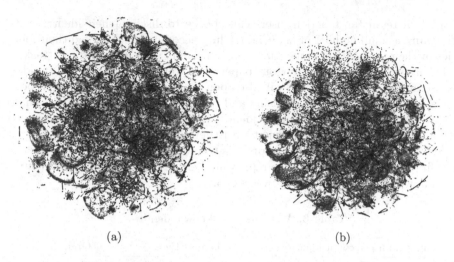

(a)   (b)

Fig. 6. Eigenvector visualization (Color figure online)

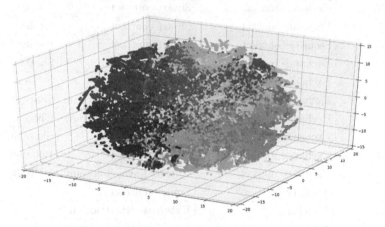

Fig. 7. Clustering result (Color figure online)

As shown in Fig. 7, we visualize the 3-dimension eigenvector of nodes in Ethereum. In Fig. 7, each colored point represents an external owned account node or a smart contract account node in Ethereum. And we distinguish the nodes in different clusters with different colors. There are many different clusters in the clustering result. In the Analysis Section, we will analyze the clustering results of the nodes and give our opinions.

4   Analysis

4.1   Nodes with Known Identity

Access to users' real identities in Ethereum is extremely difficult because users in Ethereum only need hash strings of addresses to make transactions. However, in the Ethereum tag function, users can choose to disclose their identities. In Ethereum, a small number of financial trading accounts has disclosed their identities in their tags. At the same time, some accounts were identified as attackers by Ethereum users or some previous papers due to malicious behavior. In addition, some real-life social groups will also open their Ethereum addresses on social media networks for use in fundraising and other purposes. Through these channels, we can get a small amount of identity information about external owned accounts and smart contract accounts in Ethereum.

Since the Ethereum account address is too long, we only list the shortest of their first six digits in the table to represent their address. Some of the accounts with known identities are shown in Table 3.

Table 3. Accounts with known identities

Account addr	Account identity	Account type	Organization
70faa2	Exchange market	External owned account	ShapeShift
209c47	Exchange market	Smart contract	Poloniex
fa5227	Exchange market	Smart contract	Kraken
aa1a6e	Security contract	Smart contract	ReplaySafe
1c39ba	Exchange market	Smart contract	ShapesShift
e94b04	Exchange market	Smart contract	Bittrex
9e6316	Exchange market	External owned account	ShapeShift
96fc45	Exchange market	External owned account	Changelly
9bcb07	Exchange market	Smart contract	ShapeShift
b42b20	Exchange market	Smart contract	Poloniex
42da8a	Exchange market	External owned account	YUNBI
7c2021	Attacker	Smart contract	/
3898d7	Attacker	External owned account	/
8b3b3b	Attacker	External owned account	/
29dfaa	Attacker	External owned account	/
bb9bc2	Fundraising organization	Smart contract	DAO
a74476	Exchange market	Smart contract	Golem

In Table 3, the first column represents the abbreviation of account addresses and the second column represents the known identity of the account address including exchange market, attacker and so on. The third column in the table represents the account type, including external owned account and smart contract account. The fourth column indicates the real organization to which the account address belongs.

As can be seen from the table, the nodes with known identities are mostly exchange markets which play important roles for Ethereum transactions, or attacker account addresses that are harmful to Ethereum. The accessibility of these nodes is generally high, and their identity information will be an important reference for the analysis in clustering results.

4.2   Clustering Result Analysis

In Sect. 3, we clustered the nodes vectors. Since the number of nodes in our experiment is more than 500,000, the number of clusters in the clustering result is also large. For effective analysis, we selected the top ten clusters for analysis.

Table 4. Some known accounts

Cluster ID	Number of nodes
4	14710
12	14060
29	13798
24	13597
15	13431
19	13173
9	12794
10	12215
3	11521
17	9047

In Table 4, There are some of these clusters containing nodes with known identities:

- Among the known identity nodes, there are four account addresses 70faa2, 1c39ba, 9e6316, and 9bcb07 who belong to the cluster 4. In Table 3, all four account addresses belong to the exchange market organization ShapeShift. And it can be speculated that the nodes in the cluster are mostly related to the exchange market ShapeShift.
- Similarly, it can be speculated that cluster 12 is dominated by another exchange market, Poloniex. Account addresses b42b20 and 209c47 are both in this cluster, and they belong to exchange market Poloniex according to Table 3.
- At the same time, we observed that two of the four known attackers, 3898d7 and 29dfaa belong to cluster 17. It can be speculated that the nodes in this cluster may be related to malicious attack nodes.

Among the clusters of clustering results, we find that several well-known exchange markets are the core of several large clusters. At the same time, we also found a cluster that is suspected to be related to malicious users. Among the four attacker-related account addresses of known identities, two account addresses of attackers exist in this cluster. Based on this cluster, we propose a new way for malicious user detection.

4.3   Malicious User Detection

There are already some works in malicious user analysis [16] in blockchain. However, the complexity of Ethereum structure makes these methods inadequate. We propose a more extensive and convenient malicious user detection strategy for Ethereum based on our experimental results.

In Table 3, we list four nodes associated with the attackers, and two of them 3878d7 and 29dfaa are in a same cluster. In the previous Ethereum activities, due to the large number of spam smart contracts creation (these smart contracts are usually similar in code and rarely have been called since their creation), the two nodes were identified as malicious users who manufacture junk smart contracts to consume the storage space of Ethereum. Base on the nodes with known identities, we propose a strategie for the detection of malicious users in Ethereum.

Our malicious user detection method is based on the vector space distance of the nodes. Based on the clustering results, the main steps are as follows:

- Given the known malicious users a1 and a2 and their cluster T.
- Mark the two nodes as malicious nodes, and then calculate the distance of all the nodes in the cluster T from a1 and a2 respectively.
- Select the n points closest to a1 to form N1 and the n points closest to a2 to form N2. The intersection of the two sets is taken, and the nodes in the intersection are marked as potentially malicious users.
- Find out all the marked potentially malicious users to form set A. Then do the same for every two node in A.
- The method will iterate t times to mark possible malicious users in the cluster.

In the actual analysis, we mark the two known nodes 3988d7 and 29dfaa in cluster 17 as malicious user nodes. At the same time, set n to 200 and iterate the entire detection strategy twice. By analysis of the nodes included in the obtained potentially malicious users set A, we find a node 40525a has similar malicious user behavior.

Part of the transactions of the external owned account 40525a is shown in Fig. 8. We look up all the transactions made by the node account 40525a in Ethereum and find that the node currently creates 2,504 smart contracts. We detected the smart contract created by the account and found that the smart contract code created by it is same. It proves that the node is not a developer of smart contracts but a malicious user node like the previous two external owned account nodes who consumes Ethereum's storage space by creating a large number of identical and unattended smart contract. Since the frequency and number of smart contracts created by this node is not as obvious as the previous two smart contracts, the node has not been identified as an attacker by the Ethereum Community Forum or other papers about Ethereum. But according to our analysis, this node has a great possibility of being a malicious user.

In this way, we can quickly find potential attackers without having to check the accounts in the entire Ethereum.

From		To	Value	[Txn Fee]
0x40525ac2fe3befe...	OUT	Contract Creation	0 Ether	0.00586
0x40525ac2fe3befe...	OUT	Contract Creation	0 Ether	0.00686
0x40525ac2fe3befe...	OUT	Contract Creation	0 Ether	0.00586
0x40525ac2fe3befe...	OUT	Contract Creation	0 Ether	0.00588
0x40525ac2fe3befe...	OUT	Contract Creation	0 Ether	0.00586
0x40525ac2fe3befe...	OUT	0xdf4ce5547129c55...	0 Ether	0.0290000145
0x40525ac2fe3befe...	OUT	0xd8509212d1464d...	0 Ether	0.0290000145
0x40525ac2fe3befe...	OUT	Contract Creation	0 Ether	0.00586
0x40525ac2fe3befe...	OUT	0xd8509212d1464d...	0 Ether	0.0290000145
0x40525ac2fe3befe...	OUT	0x1e621321e99f3d6...	0 Ether	0.0290000145
0x40525ac2fe3befe...	OUT	0xd8509212d1464d...	0 Ether	0.0290000145
0x40525ac2fe3befe...	OUT	0x6428ce12a1b6aa...	0 Ether	0.029668154334
0x40525ac2fe3befe...	OUT	Contract Creation	0 Ether	0.00586
0x40525ac2fe3befe...	OUT	0x1e621321e99f3d6...	0 Ether	0.0290000145
0x40525ac2fe3befe...	OUT	Contract Creation	0 Ether	0.00586
0x40525ac2fe3befe...	OUT	0xdf4ce5547129c55...	0 Ether	0.0290000145
0x40525ac2fe3befe...	OUT	0xdf4ce5547129c55...	0 Ether	0.0290000145

Fig. 8. Suspected malicious behavior

5 Related Work

In recent years, there are some studies in Ethereum Analysis. Researchers have adopted different methods such as graph analysis and complex networks modeling framework.

Chen et al. conducted the first systematic study on Ethereum [4]. They applied graph analysis to characterize the three main activities on Ethereum, Ether transaction, smart contract creation and smart contracts invocation. They devised a new way to collect the transaction data and construct three graph from the data to make analysis. In their next work, they designed a systematic data exploration framework with high-fidelity for Ethereum [17].

Ferretti et al. employed the modeling techniques of the complex network in Ethereum analysis [18]. They represented the flow of transactions happened in the blockchain as a network, where nodes are the Ethereum accounts. It has been observed that the wider the network, the greater the likelihood of a hub in the network, which means that some nodes in the blockchain are more mobile. It also can be seen how the use of blockchains changes over time.

6 Conclusion

In this paper, we analyze the behavior of users in Ethereum by using the method of node embedding and node clustering. We filter out the transactions and addresses of accounts related to the three transaction types from Ethereum blocks. Then we construct the Ethereum network to learn the eigenvectors of the account nodes based on the filtered data. And we cluster the eigenvectors of the account nodes in Ethereum. The clustering result is analyzed and draw some new opinions. At the same time, it also proves the clusterability of account nodes in Ethereum. We propose a malicious user detection method based on clustering results and the nodes with known identities. In the future work, we will continue the research and detect potential malicious users through our method and verify them.

Acknowledgments. This work is supported by: Chinese National Research Fund (NSFC) No. 61702330.

References

1. Wood, G.: Ethereum: a secure decentralised generalised transaction ledger. Ethereum Project yellow paper **151**, 1–32 (2014)
2. Nakamoto, S.: Bitcoin: a peer-to-peer electronic cash system (2008)
3. Buterin, V.: A next-generation smart contract and decentralized application platform. white paper (2014)
4. Chen, T., Zhu, Y., Li, Z., et al.: Understanding Ethereum via graph analysis. In: IEEE INFOCOM 2018-IEEE Conference on Computer Communications, pp. 1484–1492. IEEE (2018)
5. Bartoletti, M., Pompianu, L.: An empirical analysis of smart contracts: platforms, applications, and design patterns. In: Brenner, M., et al. (eds.) FC 2017. LNCS, vol. 10323, pp. 494–509. Springer, Cham (2017). https://doi.org/10.1007/978-3-319-70278-0_31
6. Meiklejohn, S., Pomarole, M., Jordan, G., et al.: A fistful of bitcoins: characterizing payments among men with no names. In: Proceedings of the 2013 Conference on Internet Measurement Conference, pp. 127–140. ACM (2013)
7. Zhao, C., Guan, Y.: A graph-based investigation of bitcoin transactions. In: Peterson, G., Shenoi, S. (eds.) DigitalForensics 2015. IAICT, vol. 462, pp. 79–95. Springer, Cham (2015). https://doi.org/10.1007/978-3-319-24123-4_5
8. Maesa, D.D.F., Marino, A., Ricci, L.: An analysis of the bitcoin users graph: inferring unusual behaviours. In: Cherifi, H., Gaito, S., Quattrociocchi, W., Sala, A. (eds.) Complex Networks & Their Applications V. COMPLEX NETWORKS 2016. Studies in Computational Intelligence, vol. 693, pp. 749–760. Springer, Cham (2017). https://doi.org/10.1007/978-3-319-50901-3_59
9. Reid, F., Harrigan, M.: An analysis of anonymity in the bitcoin system. In: Altshuler, Y., Elovici, Y., Cremers, A., Aharony, N., Pentland, A. (eds.) Security and Privacy in Social Networks, pp. 197–223. Springer, New York (2013). https://doi.org/10.1007/978-1-4614-4139-7_10
10. Dong, Y., Chawla, N.V., Swami, A.: Metapath2vec: scalable representation learning for heterogeneous networks. In: Proceedings of the 23rd ACM SIGKDD International Conference on Knowledge Discovery and Data Mining, pp. 135–144. ACM (2017)
11. Perozzi, B., Al-Rfou, R., Skiena, S.: Deepwalk: online learning of social representations. In: Proceedings of the 20th ACM SIGKDD International Conference on Knowledge Discovery and Data Mining, pp. 701–710. ACM (2014)

12. Mikolov, T., Sutskever, I., Chen, K., et al.: Distributed representations of words and phrases and their compositionality. In: Advances in Neural Information Processing Systems, pp. 3111–3119 (2013)

13. Smilkov, D., Thorat, N., Nicholson, C., et al.: Embedding projector: interactive visualization and interpretation of embeddings. arXiv preprint arXiv:1611.05469 (2016)

14. Jolliffe, I.: Principal Component Analysis. Springer, Heidelberg (2011). https://doi.org/10.1007/978-1-4757-1904-8

15. Maaten, L., Hinton, G.: Visualizing data using t-SNE. J. Mach. Learn. Res. **9**, 2579–2605 (2008)

16. Liu, H., Ruan, N., Du, R., et al.: On the strategy and behavior of bitcoin mining with N-attackers. In: Proceedings of the 2018 on Asia Conference on Computer and Communications Security, pp. 357–368. ACM (2018)

17. Chen, T., Li, Z., Zhang, Y., et al.: DataEther: data exploration framework for Ethereum. In: Proceedings of the 39th IEEE International Conference on Distributed Computing Systems (2019)

18. Ferretti, S., D'Angelo, G.: On the Ethereum blockchain structure: a complex networks theory perspective. Pract. Exp. Concurrency Comput., e5493 (2019)

19. Bok. https://www.bokconsulting.com.au/blog/ethereum-network-attackers-ip-address-is-traceable/. Accessed 25 Oct 2016

20. Latetot. https://www.reddit.com/r/ethereum/comments/55rd3j/attacker_is_gearing_up_again_for_new_spam_deluge/. Accessed Nov 2016

Strong Known Related-Key Attacks and the Security of ECDSA

Tsz Hon Yuen$^{(\boxtimes)}$ and Siu-Ming Yiu

The University of Hong Kong, Pok Fu Lam, Hong Kong
{thyuen,smyiu}@cs.hku.hk

Abstract. The classical related-key attack (RKA) model fails to capture some real world systems that introduce related secret keys by design. In some blockchain applications, public keys are generated in a way that the corresponding secret keys are additively related. The difference between two secret keys are known to some third parties. In this paper, we propose the *Strong Known Related-Key Attack* (Strong KRKA) model to capture this scenario.

ECDSA has long been considered to be inferior to Schnorr signature in terms of security, in sprite of its popularity in the standardization and real world usage. In this paper we show that Schnorr signature is not secure in the Strong KRKA model. In contrast, the security of ECDSA in the Strong KRKA model can be reduced to the unforgeability of ECDSA under chosen message attack. This theoretical result gives a different view of the relative security level of ECDSA and Schnorr, since ECDSA was developed in 1992.

Keywords: Related-key attack · ECDSA · Schnorr signature · Blockchain

1 Introduction

The related-key attack (RKA) model captures real world attacks like tampering or fault injection attack. For the case of public key cryptosystem [1], it considers the security of encryption or signature with respect to a single public key. The encryption or verification algorithms is run by taking the original public key as the input. The RKA model mainly considers the attacks happened during the *run time* of the decryption or signing algorithms.

In this paper, we consider the case that related secret key is deliberately introduced to public key cryptosystem during the *design phase*. In this case, a pair of related secret keys correspond to a pair of related public keys. The relationship between secret keys is known to the adversary. As a result, the security of encryption or signature has to be considered with respect to multiple public keys. Looking ahead, we will introduce a new security model to capture this kind of public key cryptosystem. This security model is inspired by the non-hardened key derivation in Bitcoin Improvement Protocol (BIP) 32 and Bitcoin's stealth address.

© Springer Nature Switzerland AG 2019
J. K. Liu and X. Huang (Eds.): NSS 2019, LNCS 11928, pp. 130–145, 2019.
https://doi.org/10.1007/978-3-030-36938-5_8

BIP 32 Non-hardened Key Derivation. BIP 32 describes hierarchical deterministic wallet (HD wallet). A child key can be derived from a parent key. Suppose the parent secret key is x_0 and the parent public key is $X_0 = g^{x_0}$. There is also a *chain code* for the parent key c_0, which is a 32 bytes extended information about the key. Then to derive a non-hardened child key with index i, it computes

$$S = \mathsf{HMAC} - \mathsf{SHA512}_{c_0}(X_0 || i),$$

where c_0 is used as the key of the hash function. Denote s_L as the first 32 bytes of S and s_R as the last 32 bytes of S. The child secret key $x_1 = x_0 + s_L$, the child public key $X_1 = X_0 \cdot g^{s_L}$ and the child chain code is $c_1 = s_R$.

The problem of using the standard Schnorr signature with BIP 32 non-hardened child key is that a signature from X_0 can be computed from a signature of X_1 (or vice versa). Note that the computation of s_L does not include secret key. If the chain code c_0 and the child index i is known, the adversary can compute s_L. If (R, z) is a valid Schnorr signature for X_0 (such that $g^z = RX_0^c$), then $(R, z + cs_L)$ is also a valid signature for X_1:

$$g^{z+cs_L} = RX_0^c g^{cs_L} = Rg^{c(x_0+s_L)} = RX_1^c,$$

where $c = H(R, m)$ for some message m. On the other hand, there is no known attack for ECDSA in this setting.

Bitcoin's stealth address also has a similar structure of related secret key. However, the related secret key is generated by two parties in a transaction. Details of stealth address will be discussed in Sect. 6.2. We will show the potential problem of using Schnorr signature with BIP 118 in Sect. 6.3.

1.1 Modelling Related-Key by Design

In our previous example, related-key in BIP 32 is used for digital signatures. For the ease of presentation, we mainly focus on the related-key of digital signature in this paper. In the classical RKA security model for signature [1], the adversary wins the security game if he can output a valid signature with respect to a challenge public key pk. The adversary can query the signing oracle on a message m and a function ϕ of the secret key sk (e.g., ask for a signature signed by $\phi(sk) = sk + \Delta$, where Δ is a constant chosen by the adversary).

Result 1: Strong Known RKA Model Captures Real Attack in Blockchain. In this paper, we require the following changes to the RKA security model:

1. Assume that the public key is computed from the secret key by a one-way function $\mathcal{T}$, i.e., $pk = \mathcal{T}(1^\lambda, sk)$, λ is the security parameter. Then the signing oracle on a message m_i and a function ϕ_i returns a valid signature σ_i signed by $\phi(sk_i)$; and a related public key $pk_i = \mathcal{T}(1^\lambda, \phi(sk_i))$. The adversary wins by outputting a valid signature with respect to any pk_i. This variant is called the Strong RKA security in [1].

Table 1. Difference between security models in this paper.

	(Chosen) Related Key Attack	Known Related Key Attack
Single public key	RKA [1]	KRKA
Multiple public keys	Strong RKA [1]	Strong KRKA

2. The related-key function ϕ is only known by the adversary but not chosen by the adversary. It is similar to the difference between the chosen message attack and the known message attack in digital signature. We call this variant as Known RKA (KRKA) security.

By combining the Strong RKA with Known RKA model, the Strong KRKA captures the security of signatures signed by secret keys derived by BIP 32. It is because (1) the adversary can ask for valid signatures signed by different parent and child keys and will try to forge any one of the corresponding public keys (Strong RKA), and (2) the adversary only knows that the parent and child keys are differed by s_L which is the output of a hash function, but the adversary cannot set s_L to arbitrary value (KRKA).

Since there are two modifications to the classical RKA security model, we have 4 possible security models, as shown in Table 1. Interestingly, it is mention in [1] that there is no known application-relevant attack by the Strong RKA model. In this paper, we give a concrete example that a combination of Strong RKA model and KRKA model is useful to capture the security of BIP 32 non-hardened key derivation (and stealth address). BIP 32 is widely used as HD wallet for Bitcoin as well as other cryptocurrencies, such as Ethereum.

1.2 ECDSA and Schnorr Signature in Strong KRKA Model

Our new Strong KRKA model gives us a rather suprising result on the security of ECDSA and Schnorr signature. In short, we show that Schnorr signature is not secure in the Strong KRKA model. On the other hand, we can reduce the Strong KRKA security of ECDSA to the existential unforgeability against chosen message attack (EUF-CMA) of ECDSA.

There are many discussion about whether Schnorr signature or ECDSA is a better digital signature scheme in practice. The EUF-CMA of Schnorr signature is well-understood for years [10]. On the other hand, ECDSA is known to be malleable: if (s, t) is a ECDSA signature on a message m, then $(-s, t)$, is also a valid signature on m. Therefore ECDSA is not strongly unforgeable against chosen message attack (SUF-CMA). The ECDSA malleability is one of the causes of transaction malleability in the Bitcoin system, and a number of related attacks are found [4]. Comparatively, Schnorr signature is SUF-CMA secure [8].

Many people considers that Schnorr signature is more secure than (or at least as secure as) ECDSA. The only issue hindering the use of Schnorr signature is the patent problem. Since the expiry of the patent in 2008, there are calls to change ECDSA to Schnorr signature in various systems. For example, some developers and researchers suggest to use Schnorr signature to replace ECDSA in Bitcoin. The Schnorr signature also allows batch verification and can be easily converted to multi-signatures or threshold signatures. The ETSI specification [5] mentioned a number of advantages of using (EC-)Schnorr over ECDSA, including simpler signing algorithm, easier implementation of hash function, and Schnorr's security in the random oracle model. The Schnorr signature has no identified technical drawback compared to ECDSA in [5].

Result 2: Schnorr Signature is Not as Secure as ECDSA in the Strong Known RKA Model. It is commonly believed that Schnorr signature is more secure than ECDSA. For example, Schnorr signature is strongly unforgeable [8] but ECDSA is not. For Schnorr signature, the EUF-CMA is reduced to the discrete logarithm (DL) problem in the random oracle model [10]. The EUF-CMA security of ECDSA is reduced to the DL problem in the generic group model [2,3,12], or in the bijective random oracle model [6].

It is known that both Schnorr signature and ECDSA are not EUF-CMA secure in the RKA model (known as the EUF-CM-RKA security) [9]. In this paper, we will show that the Strong Known RKA model is just enough to differentiate between Schnorr signature and ECDSA. We will demonstrate that Schnorr signature is not EUF-CM-sKRKA secure. Other the other hand, ECDSA does not have the same weakness. In fact, we are able to show that (EC)DSA is EUF-CM-sKRKA secure in the random oracle model if (EC)DSA is EUF-CMA secure. To the best of the authors' knowledge, it is the first proof that (EC)DSA is potentially more secure than Schnorr signature in a model which is weaker than some well-established security model.

2   Backgrounds

Schnorr signature, DSA and ECDSA are the most well-known discrete logarithm (DL)-based digital signature schemes. DSA and ECDSA are commonly used in various standards even though no rigorous security proofs were given when these standards are set. On the other hand, the security of the Schnorr signature is well-known under the random oracle model [10]. However, the Schnorr signature remained patented until 2008 and hence its usage is relatively limited in the industry [5].

Schnorr Signature [11]. In a group $\mathbb{G}$ of prime order q with generator g, a signing key x coincides with exponent, a verification key $X = g^x$, a signature on a message m is (c, s), where:

$$c = H(g^r, m), \quad s = r + cx \mod q,$$

r is a random element randomly chosen from the exponent space and H is a collision resistant hash function that maps into the exponent space. Verification works by firstly recovering $g^r = g^s / X^c$ and then checking if $c = H(g^r, m)$.

(EC)DSA. DSA was firstly specified by NIST. ECDSA was proposed in 1992 in response to the NIST request. Both DSA and ECDSA use an extra *conversion*

Table 2. Comparing ECDSA and Schnorr signature. ROM stands for random oracle model and BRO stands for bijective random oracle model.

	EUF-CMA	MU-EUF-CMA	SUF-CMA	EUF-CM-RKA	EUF-CM-sKRKA
Schnorr signature	$\checkmark$ (ROM [10])	$\checkmark$ (ROM [8])	$\checkmark$ (ROM [8])	$\times$ [9]	$\times$ (this paper)
ECDSA	$\checkmark$ (BRO [6]/ generic group model [2,3,12])	$\checkmark$ (generic group model [7])	$\times$	$\times$ [9]	$\checkmark$ (reduce to EUF-CMA in ROM, this paper)

function f to map group elements into the exponent space $\mathbb{Z}_q$. An (EC)DSA signature on a message m is (s, t), where:

$$t = f(g^r), \quad s = (H(m) + xt)/r \mod q.$$

Verification works by firstly recovering $g^r = (g^{H(m)} X^t)^{1/s}$ and then checking if $t = f(g^r)$. For DSA defined in a prime-order subgroup of the multiplicative group of some prime field $GF(p)$, the conversion function f is define as $A \mapsto (A \mod p) \mod q$. For ECDSA, it is defined on elliptic curves over some finite field $\mathbb{F} = GF(p^n)$ and its group elements are points $(x, y) \in \mathbb{F} \times \mathbb{F}$. The conversion function f for ECDSA is the mapping $A \mapsto A.x \mod q$, where $A.x$ denotes the encoding of the x-coordinate of A as an integer.

ECDSA vs Schnorr signature is shown in Table 2. For Schnorr signature, the existential unforgeability against chosen message attack (EUF-CMA) is reduced to the DL problem in the random oracle model [10]. The formal security of ECDSA is less studied than that of Schnorr signature. The EUF-CMA security of ECDSA is reduced to the DL problem in the generic group model [2,3,12], or in the bijective random oracle model [6].

   The security of Schnorr signature in the multi-user setting is shown in [8]. The multi-user EUF-CMA security (MU-EUF-CMA) of ECDSA is shown in [7] using the generic group model.

3 Preliminaries

3.1 Notations

For a finite set $\mathbb{A}$, we use the symbol $a \leftarrow_s \mathbb{A}$ as the random sampling according to the uniform distribution. We also use $\leftarrow_s$ for assignments from randomized algorithms and $\leftarrow$ for deterministic algorithms. For any function $F : \mathbb{A} \to \mathbb{B}$, we write $\mathrm{Dom}(F)$ as the domain of F and $\mathrm{Rng}(F)$ as the range of F.

   Let $\mathbb{G}$ be a cyclic group of prime order q, with generator g. Suppose $x \leftarrow_s \mathbb{Z}_q^*$. The discrete logarithm (DL) assumption is that given (g, g^x), no probabilistic polynomial time algorithm can output x.

3.2 Signature Schemes

A signature scheme consists of three algorithms:

- KeyGen: On input a security parameter 1^λ, it outputs a signing key sk and a verification key pk.
- Sign: On input a signing key sk and a message m, it outputs a signature σ or the failure indicator $\perp$.
- Verify: On input a verification key pk, a message m and a signature σ, it outputs 1 for acceptance or 0 for rejection.

A signature scheme is correct if for all $(\text{sk}, \text{pk}) \leftarrow_s \text{KeyGen}(1^\lambda)$ and all m in the message space, $\text{Verify}(\text{pk}, m, \text{Sign}(\text{sk}, m)) = 1$.

Unforgeability. The existential unforgeability under chosen message (EUF-CMA) game is defined in Algorithm 1. The game is executed with an adversary $\mathcal{A}$ by running INIT first and its output are the inputs to $\mathcal{A}$. Next, the Sign oracle queries of $\mathcal{A}$ are answered by the corresponding procedures. Finally, $\mathcal{A}$ calls FIN and terminates. Whenever the stop command is invoked, its argument is considered as the output of the game. We define the advantage of an adversary in the Game as the probability that the game outputs 1.

Algorithm 1. Game EUF-CMA.

```
1  Procedure INIT(1^λ):                9  Procedure FIN(m*, σ*):
2  |  (sk, pk) ←_s KeyGen(1^λ);        10  |  if m* ∈ L then
3  |  L ← ∅;                           11  |  |_ stop with 0;
4  |_ return pk;                       12  |  if Verify(pk, m*, σ*) = 0 then
5  Procedure SIGN(m_i):                13  |  |_ stop with 0;
6  |  σ_i ←_s Sign(sk, m_i);           14  |_ stop with 1;
7  |  L ← L ∪ {m_i}};
8  |_ return σ_i;
```

Definition 1. *A signature scheme is (t, q_s, ϵ)-secure under the EUF-CMA if there is no adversary running in time t, with q_s queries to the signing oracle, has advantage larger than ϵ.*

4 RKA Security Model

The related-key attack (RKA) model is intended to capture real world attacks like tampering or fault injection attack. For example, an adversary manipulates a hardware-stored secret key by electromagnetic radiation and obtains the signature signed by the manipulated secret key.

4.1   RKA and Strong RKA Models

RKA is formalized as a security game that also allows an adversary to obtain signatures for modified keys. Denote the secret key space as $\mathcal{S}$. Thus, an adversary is allowed to query related-key deriving (RKD) functions $\phi_i : \mathcal{S} \to \mathcal{S}$ as well as messages to the signing oracle. We say that Φ is a class of RKD functions. For example, denote $\Phi^+ = \{\phi_i(x) = x + b_i : b_i \in \mathcal{S}\}$, $\Phi^* = \{\phi_i(x) = x * a_i : a_i \in \mathcal{S}\}$ and $\Phi^{\mathsf{aff}} = \{\phi_i(x) = a_i x + b_i : a_i, b_i \in \mathcal{S}\}$.

Φ-**EUF-CM-RKA.** [1] We recall existential unforgeability under chosen message and (chosen) RKA defined by RKD function class Φ. This security model of Φ-EUF-CM-RKA is formalized by Algorithm 2.

Algorithm 2. Game Φ-EUF-CM-RKA.

---

1 **Procedure** INIT(1^λ):
2 $\quad$ Same as EUF-CMA;

3 **Procedure** SIGN(m_i, ϕ_i):
4 $\quad$ **if** $\phi_i \notin \{\Phi \cup identity\ map\}$ **then**
5 $\quad\quad$ return $\perp$;

6 $\quad$ $\sigma_i \leftarrow_s \mathsf{Sign}(\phi_i(\mathsf{sk}), m_i)$;
7 $\quad$ **if** ϕ_i *is identity map* **then**
8 $\quad\quad$ $\mathbb{L} \leftarrow \mathbb{L} \cup \{m_i\}$;

9 $\quad$ return σ_i;

10 **Procedure** FIN(m^*, σ^*):
11 $\quad$ Same as EUF-CMA;

Φ-**EUF-CM-sRKA.** [1] Bellare *et al.* extends the RKA security for *separable* signature. *Separable* signature means that for any $(\mathsf{sk}, \mathsf{pk}) \leftarrow \mathsf{KeyGen}(1^\lambda)$, there exists a deterministic algorithm $\mathcal{T}$ such that $\mathsf{pk}' \leftarrow \mathcal{T}(1^\lambda, \mathsf{sk})$ and the distribution of pk is indistinguishable to pk'. This security model of Φ-EUF-CM-sRKA (Strong RKA) is formalized by Algorithm 3. The difference with the standard RKA model is highlighted.

Definition 2. *A signature scheme is (t, q_s, ϵ)-secure under the Φ-EUF-CM-RKA (resp. Φ-EUF-CM-sRKA) if there is no adversary running in time t, with q_s queries to the signing oracle, has advantage larger than ϵ in Game Φ-EUF-CM-RKA (resp. Φ-EUF-CM-sRKA).*

4.2   (Strong) Known-RKA Security

We give the new security model of existential unforgeability under chosen message and known RKA defined by RKD function class Φ. Recall the difference between the known message attack (KMA) and CMA for signature is that the adversary only knows the message-signature pairs in KMA, while the adversary is able to specify the message for the signing oracle in CMA. In the new known

---

Algorithm 3. Game Φ-EUF-CM-sRKA.

1	**Procedure** INIT(1^λ):	10	**Procedure** FIN(i^*, m^*, σ^*) :
2	$\quad$ Same as EUF-CMA;	11	$\quad$ **if** $(\mathsf{pk}_{i^*}, m^*) \in \mathbb{L}$ **then**
3	**Procedure** SIGN(m_i, ϕ_i):	12	$\quad\quad$ stop with 0;
4	$\quad$ **if** $\phi_i \notin \{\Phi \cup identity\ map\}$ **then**	13	$\quad$ **if** Verify($\mathsf{pk}_{i^*}, m^*, \sigma^*$) $= 0$ **then**
5	$\quad\quad$ return $\perp$;	14	$\quad\quad$ stop with 0;
6	$\quad$ $\sigma_i \leftarrow_s \mathsf{Sign}(\phi_i(\mathsf{sk}), m_i)$;	15	$\quad$ stop with 1;
7	$\quad$ $\mathsf{pk}_i \leftarrow \mathcal{T}(1^\lambda, \phi_i(\mathsf{sk}))$;		
8	$\quad$ $\mathbb{L} \leftarrow \mathbb{L} \cup \{(\mathsf{pk}_i, m_i)\}$;		
9	$\quad$ return $(\mathsf{pk}_i, \sigma_i)$;		

RKA model, the adversary only knows the RKD functions that he can query for the signing oracle (yet the adversary can still choose the message). It is weaker than the classical RKA model, in which the adversary can set the RKD functions to any function in Φ.

This security model of Φ-EUF-CM-KRKA is formalized by Algorithm 4. The difference with the standard RKA model is highlighted.

Algorithm 4. Game Φ-EUF-CM-KRKA.

1	**Procedure** INIT(1^λ):	10	**Procedure** SIGN($m_i,\ j$):
2	$\quad$ $(\mathsf{sk}, \mathsf{pk}) \leftarrow_s \mathsf{KeyGen}(1^\lambda)$;	11	$\quad$ **if** $j \notin [0, q_s]$ **then**
3	$\quad$ $\mathbb{L} \leftarrow \emptyset$;	12	$\quad\quad$ return $\perp$;
4	$\quad$ $\phi_0 \leftarrow identity\ map$;	13	$\quad$ $\sigma_i \leftarrow_s \mathsf{Sign}(\phi_j(\mathsf{sk}), m_i)$;
5	$\quad$ $\mathbb{S} \leftarrow \{\phi_0\}$;	14	$\quad$ **if** $j = 0$ **then**
6	$\quad$ **for** $j \leftarrow 1$ **to** q_s **do**	15	$\quad\quad$ $\mathbb{L} \leftarrow \mathbb{L} \cup \{m_i\}$;
7	$\quad\quad$ $\phi_j \leftarrow_s \Phi$;	16	$\quad$ return σ_i;
8	$\quad\quad$ $\mathbb{S} \leftarrow \mathbb{S} \cup \{\phi_j\}$;	17	**Procedure** FIN(m^*, σ^*):
9	$\quad$ return pk, $\mathbb{S}$;	18	$\quad$ Same as EUF-CMA;

Finally, we give the combined security model of Strong Known RKA model formalized by Algorithm 5. The difference with the standard RKA model is highlighted.

Definition 3. *A signature scheme is (t, q_s, ϵ)-secure under the Φ-EUF-CM-KRKA (resp. Φ-EUF-CM-sKRKA) if there is no adversary running in time t, with q_s queries to the signing oracle, has advantage larger than ϵ in Game Φ-EUF-CM-KRKA (resp. Φ-EUF-CM-sKRKA).*

Algorithm 5. Game Φ-EUF-CM-sKRKA.

1 **Procedure** INIT(1^λ):
2     $(\mathsf{sk}, \mathsf{pk}) \leftarrow_s \mathsf{KeyGen}(1^\lambda)$;
3     $\mathbb{L} \leftarrow \emptyset$;
4     $\phi_0 \leftarrow$ identity map ;
5     $\mathbb{S} \leftarrow \{\phi_0\}$;
6   **for** $j \leftarrow 1$ **to** q_s **do**
7        $\phi_j \leftarrow_s \Phi$;
8        $\mathbb{S} \leftarrow \mathbb{S} \cup \{\phi_j\}$;
9   return pk, $\mathbb{S}$;

10 **Procedure** SIGN(m_i, j):
11   **if** $j \notin [0, q_s]$ **then**
12   return $\bot$;
13     $\sigma_i \leftarrow_s \mathsf{Sign}(\phi_j(\mathsf{sk}), m_i)$;
14     $\mathsf{pk}_i \leftarrow \mathcal{T}(1^\lambda, \phi_j(\mathsf{sk}))$;
15     $\mathbb{L} \leftarrow \mathbb{L} \cup \{(\mathsf{pk}_i, m_i)\}$;
16   return $(\mathsf{pk}_i, \sigma_i)$;

17 **Procedure** FIN(i^*, m^*, σ^*) :
18   **if** $(\mathsf{pk}_{i^*}, m^*) \in \mathbb{L}$ **then**
19   stop with 0;
20   **if** $\mathsf{Verify}(\mathsf{pk}_{i^*}, m^*, \sigma^*) = 0$ **then**
21   stop with 0;
22   stop with 1;

4.3 Relationship Between Models

We summarize the relationship between different security models in Table 3 with EUF-CMA. We also include the strong unforgeability (SUF-CMF) and multi-user security (MU-EUF-CMA) for completeness.

According to the definition of the security models, it is obvious that the RKA model is stronger than KRKA model (chosen relation vs. known relation). Similarly, the Strong RKA model is stronger than Strong KRKA model.

On the other hand, the Strong RKA model is stronger than the RKA model (forgery on multiple public keys vs. forgery on a single public key). Similarly, the Strong KRKA model is stronger than KRKA model.

There is no straightforward relationship between the RKA model and the Strong KRKA model. It is known that ECDSA is not RKA secure [9]. In the next section, we will show that ECDSA is secure in the Strong KRKA model if ECDSA is EUF-CMA secure. We leave the relationship between the RKA model and the Strong KRKA model as an interesting open problem.

Table 3. Relationship between different security models. Model A $\Rightarrow$ Model B means that Model A is weaker than Model B. Model A $\rightarrow$ Model B means that there exists a scheme secure in Model A but not secure in Model B. The grey box indicates the major work of this paper.

EUF-CM-sRKA $\Longleftarrow$ EUF-CM-sKRKA   MU-EUF-CMA

$\Uparrow$ $\nearrow$ $\Uparrow$ $\Uparrow$

EUF-CM-RKA $\Longleftarrow$ EUF-CM-KRKA $\Longleftarrow$ EUF-CMA $\Longrightarrow$ SUF-CMA

5   Security of Schnorr Signature and ECDSA

It is known that both Schnorr signature and DSA are not secure in the Φ^{aff}-EUF-CM-RKA model [9]. It is straightforward to see that ECDSA is also not secure in the Φ^{aff}-EUF-CM-RKA model. In this section, we show that (EC)DSA is secure against our Strong Known RKA Model, but Schnorr signature is not. Therefore, it gives an important separation between the security between these two schemes.

5.1   Insecurity of Schnorr Signature in (Strong) KRKA Model

We show that the Schnorr signature scheme is not Known RKA secure with respect to additive functions by providing a simple and efficient attack. This additive relation between secret keys is realistic in the real world, such as BIP 32. In later section, we will also show that by using stealth address in Bitcoin, multiple secret keys of the same user are related additively.

According to the security model, an adversary $\mathcal{A}$ is given $\delta_1, \ldots, \delta_n$ such that $\phi_i(\mathsf{sk}) = \mathsf{sk} + \delta_i$ for $i \in [1, n]$. Then $\mathcal{A}$ queries the RKA signing oracle with input (m^*, ϕ_1) for some random message m^*. The oracle returns the signature (z, c) such that:
$$R = g^z g^{-c(\mathsf{sk}+\delta_1)}, \quad c = H(R, m^*).$$
Then $\mathcal{A}$ returns $(z - c\delta_1, c)$ as an forgery for the message m^*. Hence Schnorr signature scheme is not Known RKA secure. By similar argument, we can see that Schnorr signature is not Strong KRKA secure.

5.2   Security of (EC)DSA in Strong KRKA Model

We first show that the Φ^{aff}-EUF-CM-sKRKA security of (EC)DSA can be reduced to the EUF-CMA security, under the ROM model. The KRKA security of (EC)DSA follows from the Strong KRKA security.

Security of Φ^{aff}-EUF-CM-sKRKA. We prove that (EC)DSA is secure in the Φ^{aff}-EUF-CM-sKRKA model. The class of additive RKD functions Φ^{aff} captures the case that the secret keys are linearly related, e.g., $\phi(\mathsf{sk}) = a \cdot \mathsf{sk} + b$ for some $a, b \in \mathbb{Z}_q$. Therefore, the Φ^{aff}-EUF-CM-sKRKA model already captures the attacks in the Φ^+-EUF-CM-sKRKA model.

The proof differs from the proof of EUF-CMA in [6] in a few ways. Firstly, the simulation of the signing oracle is modified to capture the signature with respect to the class of RKD functions Φ^{aff}. Secondly, the extraction of secret key in the proof of EUF-CMA in [6] uses the simulation transcript of a past signing oracle query, and it requires the collision resistant property of the hash function H. However, the same argument no longer holds if the past signing oracle query includes RKD functions. The collision resistant property is not enough. We discover that the security can be shown alternatively if we use the random oracle model for H. As a result, we also have to add the relevant simulation of the random oracle model and make sure that it is consistent with the rest of the proof.

Algorithm 6. Game 0 is the Φ^{aff}-EUF-CM-sKRKA for (EC)DSA, in the random oracle model.

1 **Procedure** INIT:	28 **Procedure** RO(m):
2 $\quad$ pick $H : \{0,1\}^* \to \mathbb{Z}_q$;	29 $\quad$ return $H(m)$;
3 $\quad x \leftarrow_s \mathbb{Z}_q^*; X \leftarrow g^x$;	30 **Procedure** FIN($i^*, m^*, (s^*, t^*)$):
4 $\quad \mathbb{L} \leftarrow \emptyset$;	31 $\quad$ if $(\mathsf{pk}_{i^*}, m^*) \in \mathbb{L}$ then
5 $\quad a_0 \leftarrow 1, b_0 \leftarrow 0$;	32 $\quad\quad$ stop with 0;
6 $\quad \mathbb{S} \leftarrow \{(a_0, b_0)\}$;	33 $\quad$ if $s^* = 0$ or $t^* = 0$ then
7 $\quad$ for $j \leftarrow 1$ to q_s do	34 $\quad\quad$ stop with 0;
8 $\quad\quad \phi_j(x) := a_j x + b_j \leftarrow_s \Phi^{\mathrm{aff}}$;	35 $\quad h^* \leftarrow H(m^*)$;
9 $\quad\quad \mathbb{S} \leftarrow \mathbb{S} \cup \{(a_j, b_j)\}$;	36 $\quad U^* \leftarrow g^{h^*}(X^{a_{i^*}} g^{b_{i^*}})^{t^*}$ // $i^* \in [0, q_s]$
10 $\quad$ return $X, \mathbb{S}$;	37 $\quad$ if $U^* = 1$ then
11 **Procedure** SIGN(m_i, j):	38 $\quad\quad$ stop with 0;
12 $\quad r_i \leftarrow_s \mathbb{Z}_q; R_i \leftarrow g^{r_i}$;	39 $\quad R^* \leftarrow (U^*)^{1/s^*}$;
13 $\quad$ if $R_i = 1$ then	40 $\quad$ if $t^* \neq f(R^*)$ then
14 $\quad\quad$ return $\bot$;	41 $\quad\quad$ stop with 0;
15 $\quad t_i \leftarrow f(R_i)$;	42 $\quad$ stop with 1;
16 $\quad$ if $t_i = 0$ then	
17 $\quad\quad$ return $\bot$;	
18 $\quad h_i \leftarrow H(m_i)$;	
19 $\quad \mathsf{sk}_i \leftarrow a_j x + b_j$ // $j \in [0, q_s]$	
20 $\quad \mathsf{pk}_i \leftarrow g^{\mathsf{sk}_i}$;	
21 $\quad u_i \leftarrow h_i + \mathsf{sk}_i t_i$;	
22 $\quad$ if $u_i = 0$ then	
23 $\quad\quad$ return $\bot$;	
24 $\quad s_i \leftarrow u_i / r_i$;	
25 $\quad \sigma_i \leftarrow (s_i, t_i)$;	
26 $\quad \mathbb{L} \leftarrow \mathbb{L} \cup \{(\mathsf{pk}_i, m_i)\}$;	
27 $\quad$ return $(\mathsf{pk}_i, \sigma_i)$;	

Theorem 1. *Let $\mathcal{A}$ be an adversary that (τ, q_s, ϵ)-breaks the Φ^{aff}-EUF-CM-sKRKA security of (EC)DSA, with q_H random oracle queries. Then, there exists an adversary $\mathcal{A}_{\mathrm{CMA}}$ that $(\tau_{\mathrm{CMA}}, q_s, \epsilon_{\mathrm{CMA}})$-breaks the EUF-CMA security of (EC)DSA, where:*

$$\epsilon \leq (q_s + 1)(\epsilon_{\mathrm{CMA}} + \frac{q_s q_H}{q}), \quad \tau_{\mathrm{CMA}} = \tau + O(q_s)\tau_e,$$

where τ_e is the time of exponentiation in $\mathbb{G}$.

Proof. The security is shown by a game-hopping proof. We define $\mathrm{Adv}_{\mathcal{A}_i}(1^\lambda)$ as the advantage of the adversary $\mathcal{A}$ in Game i, with security parameter λ. We omit the security parameter for simplicity.

- **Game 0** in Algorithm 6 gives the complete EUF-CM-sKRKA for (EC)DSA. The random oracle is provided by RO. Therefore, $\epsilon = \mathrm{Adv}_{\mathcal{A}_0}$.
- **Game 1** in Algorithm 7 is modified from Game 0 that the hash function H is now replaced by sampling. By the random oracle model, we have $\mathrm{Adv}_{\mathcal{A}_0} = \mathrm{Adv}_{\mathcal{A}_1}$.

Algorithm 7. Game 1 is the same as Game 0 except the Procedure INIT and RO (highlighted in gray box).

---

1 Procedure INIT:

2 $\quad H^O \leftarrow \emptyset$;

3 $\quad x \leftarrow_s \mathbb{Z}_q^*; X \leftarrow g^x$;

4 $\quad \mathbb{L} \leftarrow \emptyset$;

5 $\quad a_0 \leftarrow 1, b_0 \leftarrow 0$;

6 $\quad \mathbb{S} \leftarrow \{(a_0, b_0)\}$;

7 $\quad$ **for** $j \leftarrow 1$ **to** q_s **do**

8 $\qquad \phi_j(x) := a_j x + b_j \leftarrow_s \Phi^{\text{aff}}$;

9 $\qquad \mathbb{S} \leftarrow \mathbb{S} \cup \{(a_j, b_j)\}$;

10 $\quad$ **return** $X, \mathbb{S}$;

11 Procedure RO(m):

$\quad$ **if** $(m, h) \in H^O$ **then**
$\quad \quad$ **return** h;
$\quad h \leftarrow_s \mathbb{Z}_q \backslash \text{Rng}(H^O)$;
$\quad H^O \leftarrow H^O \cup \{(m, h)\}$;

12

13 $\quad$ **return** h;

- Finally, Algorithm 8 shows how to build an adversary $\mathcal{A}_{\text{CMA}}$ to break the EUF-CMA security of (EC)DSA, by running as the challenger of Game 1 and making use of the output from $\mathcal{A}_1$. $\mathcal{A}_{\text{CMA}}$ uses the output of INIT$_{\text{CMA}}$ from its challenger (of the EUF-CMA security) to simulate the challenger of Game 1 in line 9. This change is indistinguishable to $\mathcal{A}_1$. The SIGN procedure in Algorithm 8 is simulated by using the signing oracle output from the challenger of the EUF-CMA security. Finally, the validation of the output from $\mathcal{A}_1$ is same as except line 38, 39 and 51. We want to show that $\text{Adv}_{\mathcal{A}_1} \leq (q_s + 1)(\text{Adv}_{\mathcal{A}_{\text{CMA}}} + q_s q_H / q)$.

We can see that the signing oracle output is correct by running the verification of (s_i, t_i) against the related key pk_j:

$$g^{r_i} = g^{\frac{H(m_i)}{s_i}} (X^{a_j} g^{b_j})^{\frac{t_i}{s_i}} = g^{\frac{a_{j*} H(m_i)}{s' a_j}} (X^{a_j} g^{b_j})^{\frac{a_{j*} t_i}{s' a_j}}$$

$$= g^{\frac{(a_{j*} b_j) t_i + a_{j*} H(m_i)}{s' a_j}} (X^{a_{j*}})^{\frac{t_i}{s'}} = g^{\frac{(a_{j*} b_j - a_j b_{j*}) t_i + a_{j*} H(m_i)}{s' a_j}} (X^{a_{j*}} g^{b_{j*}})^{\frac{t_i}{s'}}$$

$$= g^{\frac{H(m'_i)}{s'}} (X^{a_{j*}} g^{b_{j*}})^{\frac{t'}{s'}} = g^{\frac{H(m'_i)}{s'}} X'^{\frac{t'}{s'}} = g^{r'}.$$

Then we have $f(g^{r_i}) = f(g^{r'}) = t' = t_i$. Hence (s_i, t_i) is a valid signature with respect to pk_i.

When $\mathcal{A}_1$ outputs a valid forgery $(i^*, m^*, (s^*, t^*))$, line 51 of Algorithm 8 is reached if $i^* = j^*$. It happens with probability $\frac{1}{q_s + 1}$. By the checking of line 40, m^* was not queried to SIGN$_{\text{CMA}}$ in line 15. If m^* was also not queried to SIGN$_{\text{CMA}}$ in line 20, then $\mathcal{A}_{\text{CMA}}$ wins by line 51.

We now show that m^* was not queried to SIGN$_{\text{CMA}}$ in line 20. Observe that in line 19, m'_i is randomly chosen from the message space and it is not given to the $\mathcal{A}_1$. $\mathcal{A}_1$ can only calculate $H(m'_i)$ as in line 21. By the random oracle model, $\mathcal{A}_1$ cannot find some m'_i and use it as m^* with probability more than $\frac{q_s q_H}{q}$. Therefore, we have $\text{Adv}_{\mathcal{A}_1} \leq (q_s + 1)(\epsilon_{\text{CMA}} + q_s q_H / q)$.

Algorithm 8. The construction of adversary $\mathcal{A}_{\text{CMA}}$ against EUF-CMA, using the adversary $\mathcal{A}_1$ for Game 1. (Interaction with the challenger of EUF-CMA is highlighted in the gray box).

---

1 **Procedure** $\text{INIT}(1^\lambda)$:
2    $H^O \leftarrow \emptyset, \mathbb{L} \leftarrow \emptyset$;
3    $j^* \leftarrow_s [0, q_s]$;
4    $a_0 \leftarrow 1, b_0 \leftarrow 0$;
5    $\mathbb{S} \leftarrow \{(a_0, b_0)\}$;
6   **for** $j \leftarrow 1$ **to** q_s **do**
7      $\phi_j(x) := a_j x + b_j \leftarrow_s \Phi^{\text{aff}}$;
8      $\mathbb{S} \leftarrow \mathbb{S} \cup \{(a_j, b_j)\}$;
9    $X' \leftarrow \text{INIT}_{\text{CMA}}(1^\lambda)$;
10    $X \leftarrow (X' g^{-b_{j^*}})^{1/a_{j^*}}$;
11   **return** $X, \mathbb{S}$;
12 **Procedure** $\text{SIGN}(m_i, j)$:
13   **if** $j = j^*$ **then**
14      $\text{pk}_i \leftarrow X'$;
15      $\sigma_i \leftarrow \text{SIGN}_{\text{CMA}}(m_i)$;
16   **else**
17   isNewH $\leftarrow$ false;
18   **while** isNewH $=$ false **do**
19        $m_i' \leftarrow_s \mathcal{M}$;
20        $(s', t') \leftarrow \text{SIGN}_{\text{CMA}}(m_i')$;
21        $h_i \leftarrow \frac{(a_{j^*} b_j - a_j b_{j^*}) t_i + a_{j^*} H(m_i)}{a_j}$;
22   **if** $(\cdot, h_i) \notin H^O$ **then**
23          $H^O \leftarrow H^O \cup \{(m_i', h_i)\}$;
24   isNewH $\leftarrow$ true;
25      $t_i \leftarrow t'$;
26      $s_i \leftarrow \frac{s' a_j}{a_{j^*}}$;
27      $\text{pk}_i \leftarrow X^{a_j} g^{b_j}$;
28      $\sigma_i \leftarrow (s_i, t_i)$;
29    $\mathbb{L} \leftarrow \mathbb{L} \cup \{(\text{pk}_i, m_i)\}$;
30   **return** (pk_i, σ_i);

31 **Procedure** $\text{RO}(m)$:
32   **if** $(m, h) \in H^O$ **then**
33   **return** h;
34    $h \leftarrow_s \mathbb{Z}_q \backslash \text{Rng}(H^O)$;
35    $H^O \leftarrow H^O \cup \{(m, h)\}$;
36   **return** h;
37 **Procedure** $\text{FIN}(i^*, m^*, (s^*, t^*))$:
38   **if** $i^* \neq j^*$ **then**
39   stop with 0;
   // $\text{pk}_{i^*} = \text{pk}_{j^*} = X'$
40   **if** $(\text{pk}_{i^*}, m^*) \in \mathbb{L}$ **then**
41   stop with 0;
42   **if** $s^* = 0$ *or* $t^* = 0$ **then**
43   stop with 0;
44    $h^* \leftarrow H(m^*)$;
45    $U^* \leftarrow g^{h^*} X'^{t^*}$;
46   **if** $U^* = 1$ **then**
47   stop with 0;
48    $R^* \leftarrow (U^*)^{1/s^*}$;
49   **if** $t^* \neq f(R^*)$ **then**
50   stop with 0;
51   run $\text{FIN}_{\text{CMA}}(m^*, (s^*, t^*))$;

To conclude, we have $\epsilon \leq (q_s + 1)(\epsilon_{\text{CMA}} + q_s q_H/q)$. Finally, the running time is dominated by $O(q_s)$ exponentiation in the signing oracle queries. $\square$

The security of (EC)DSA under the EUF-CMA attack can be reduced to the DL problem in the bijective random oracle model [6] or in the generic group model [2,3,12].

6 Strong KRKA Attack in the Bitcoin System

The Strong KRKA security model not only captures the tampering attack, it can also be used to capture the security of some variants in Bitcoin system, such as BIP 32 non-hardened key derivation and *stealth address*. Combining with the result of the previous section, ECDSA is secure with the use of these Bitcoin variants, while the standard Schnorr signature is not secure.

6.1 BIP 32 Non-hardened Key Derivation

BIP 32 describes how a hierarchical deterministic wallet (HD wallet) generate keys from a single seed. We have described how non-hardened secret keys are derived in Sect. 1 according to BIP 32. Every parent secret key is linearly related to its child secret key by design. Therefore, all non-hardened secret keys derived in BIP 32 are linearly related. Note that the adversary can only know the difference between secret keys, but he cannot set it to arbitrary value by the security of the HMAC-SHA512 function.

BIP 32 standardizes the key generation process in HD wallet and it does not consider what message to be signed with these keys. Strong KRKA attack is dangerous in the setting that the message to be signed is not related to the signer public key/address.

6.2 Stealth Address

The idea of stealth address was firstly proposed in a Bitcoin forum[1]. It allows the recipient to remain anonymous, even after sharing his stealth address. The most common version of stealth address was proposed by CryptoNote in 2013[2]. Stealth address was implemented for Bitcoin and is widely used as a cornerstone to many anonymous cryptocurrencies, such as Monero.

The stealth address is described as follows. Suppose that the recipient Bob has a long term secret key $(a, b) \in \mathbb{Z}_p^2$ and public key $(A = g^a, B = g^b) \in \mathbb{G}^2$. The sender Alice picks a random number $r \leftarrow_s \mathbb{Z}_q$ and puts $R = g^r$ in the transaction. The one-time recipient address is (the hash of) $Y = A \cdot g^{H'(B^r)}$, where $H' : \mathbb{G} \to \mathbb{Z}_q$ is a collision resistant hash function. Bob can use b (which is known as the viewing key) to check if he is the intended recipient of the transaction with (R, Y) by checking if $Y = A \cdot g^{H'(R^b)}$. Bob's one-time secret key corresponding to Y is $a + H(R^b)$.

Related-Key Attack for Stealth Address. If Alice sends some Bitcoin to Bob in two different transactions, then Bob's one-time secret keys are $y_1 = a + H(R_1^b)$ and $y_2 = a + H(R_2^b)$ respectively. Therefore, y_1 and y_2 are linearly related: $\delta = y_1 - y_2 = H(R_1^b) - H(R_2^b)$. If the Bitcoin system uses the Schnorr signature, there is potential attack when Bob uses y_2 to output (z, c) for a

---

[1] https://bitcointalk.org/index.php?topic=5965.0.
[2] CryptoNote v 2.0 Whitepaper. https://cryptonote.org/whitepaper.pdf.

message m. In this case, Alice with the knowledge of $\delta = H(B^{r_1}) - H(B^{r_2})$, can output a signature $(z' = z + c\delta, c)$ for the same message m. We can see that it is a valid signature for Y_1:

$$g^{z'} = g^{z+c\delta} = (RY_2^c) \cdot g^{c\delta} = Rg^{y_2c+c\delta} = RY_1^c, \quad c = H(R, m).$$

This attack can be launched simply by the knowledge of the difference δ of the two secret keys. This attack is captured in the Strong KRKA model, by signing oracle queries with the addition function.

Note that for the case of stealth address, the adversary can only know the difference δ, but he cannot set δ to arbitrary value since $\delta = H(B^{r_1}) - H(B^{r_2})$. He cannot find such r_1 and r_2 satisfying this relation, assuming the pseudo-randomness of the output of H. Therefore, the attack is precisely captured by the Strong KRKA model, but not the classical RKA model.

We have shown that ECDSA is secure in the Strong KRKA model for affine functions. Therefore, ECDSA is not affected by the use of stealth address. There is potential threat of using stealth address with standard Schnorr signature.

6.3   BIP 118 SIGHASH_NOINPUT

We note that in the normal use case of Bitcoin transaction with BIP 32 key/stealth address, the signer's address (=hash of his public key) is included in the message. The Strong KRKA attack on the standard Schnorr signature does not apply to this use case. However, we cannot guarantee what message will be signed in the future update of the Bitcoin protocol.

BIP 118 is useful for building Lightning Network channels to increase the scalability of Bitcoin system and to enable micropayment over Bitcoin. In particular, a new signing flag SIGHASH_NOINPUT is proposed, such that the signature does not commit to any of the inputs. All fields related to the input address/sequence/outpoint are replaced with string of 0s. Therefore, using standard Schnorr signature with BIP 32 non-hardened key/stealth address and BIP 118 SIGHASH_NOINPUT are insecure.

7   Conclusion

In this paper, we showed that, for the first time, ECDSA is potentially more secure than the standard Schnorr signature in the Strong Known RKA model. The Strong Known RKA model captures the attack on BIP 32 and stealth address in Bitcoin and other cryptocurrencies. Therefore if Schnorr signature or other DL-type signatures (including multi-signatures, aggregate signatures, threshold signatures, etc.) are proposed in the blockchain system, it is highly recommended to evaluate their Strong Known RKA security.

Acknowledgment. This project is partially supported by the grant of the University of Hong Kong (Project No. 201901159007), and the CRF grant (CityU: C1008-16G) of the Government of HKSAR, Hong Kong.

References

1. Bellare, M., Cash, D., Miller, R.: Cryptography secure against related-key attacks and tampering. In: Lee, D.H., Wang, X. (eds.) ASIACRYPT 2011. LNCS, vol. 7073, pp. 486–503. Springer, Heidelberg (2011). https://doi.org/10.1007/978-3-642-25385-0_26
2. Brown, D.R.L.: Generic groups, collision resistance, and ECDSA. Des. Codes Cryptography **35**(1), 119–152 (2005)
3. Brown, D.R.L.: On the provable security of ECDSA. In: Blake, I.F., Seroussi, G., Smart, N.P. (eds.) Advances in Elliptic Curve Cryptography. London Mathematical Society Lecture Note Series, pp. 21–40. Cambridge University Press, Cambridge (2005)
4. Decker, C., Wattenhofer, R.: Bitcoin transaction malleability and MtGox. In: Kutyłowski, M., Vaidya, J. (eds.) ESORICS 2014. LNCS, vol. 8713, pp. 313–326. Springer, Cham (2014). https://doi.org/10.1007/978-3-319-11212-1_18
5. ETSI: Electronic signatures and infrastructures (ESI); cryptographic suites. ETSI Technical Specification 119 312 (v1.2.1) (2017)
6. Fersch, M., Kiltz, E., Poettering, B.: On the provable security of (EC)DSA signatures. In: Weippl, E.R., Katzenbeisser, S., Kruegel, C., Myers, A.C., Halevi, S. (eds.) CCS 2016, pp. 1651–1662. ACM (2016)
7. Galbraith, S.D., Malone-Lee, J., Smart, N.P.: Public key signatures in the multi-user setting. Inf. Process. Lett. **83**(5), 263–266 (2002)
8. Kiltz, E., Masny, D., Pan, J.: Optimal security proofs for signatures from identification schemes. In: Robshaw, M., Katz, J. (eds.) CRYPTO 2016. LNCS, vol. 9815, pp. 33–61. Springer, Heidelberg (2016). https://doi.org/10.1007/978-3-662-53008-5_2
9. Morita, H., Schuldt, J.C.N., Matsuda, T., Hanaoka, G., Iwata, T.: On the security of the Schnorr signature scheme and DSA against related-key attacks. In: Kwon, S., Yun, A. (eds.) ICISC 2015. LNCS, vol. 9558, pp. 20–35. Springer, Cham (2016). https://doi.org/10.1007/978-3-319-30840-1_2
10. Pointcheval, D., Stern, J.: Security proofs for signature schemes. In: Maurer, U. (ed.) EUROCRYPT 1996. LNCS, vol. 1070, pp. 387–398. Springer, Heidelberg (1996). https://doi.org/10.1007/3-540-68339-9_33
11. Schnorr, C.P.: Efficient identification and signatures for smart cards. In: Brassard, G. (ed.) CRYPTO 1989. LNCS, vol. 435, pp. 239–252. Springer, New York (1990). https://doi.org/10.1007/0-387-34805-0_22
12. Stern, J., Pointcheval, D., Malone-Lee, J., Smart, N.P.: Flaws in applying proof methodologies to signature schemes. In: Yung, M. (ed.) CRYPTO 2002. LNCS, vol. 2442, pp. 93–110. Springer, Heidelberg (2002). https://doi.org/10.1007/3-540-45708-9_7

Threat Assessment of Enterprise Applications via Graphical Modelling

Manjunath Bilur, Anugrah Gari, and R. K. Shyamasundar[✉]

Department of Computer Science and Engineering, Indian Institute of Technology,
Bombay, India
manjunathbilur@gmail.com, anugrahgari106@gmail.com,
shyamasundar@gmail.com

Abstract. Cyber resiliency has been a very challenging engineering research. There have been several case studies done to assess cyber resiliency of enterprise business application through application of attack graphs. The challenge of automation lies in extracting from a general business enterprise system, the distinct layers like asset layer, service layer, business process task layer etc., so that the task dependencies together with formal vulnerability specification can be integrated to arrive at attack graphs. In this paper, we develop a model for threat analysis of an enterprise from a set of given vulnerabilities in various layers of the business process. Starting from the business process model (BPMN) of the given enterprise, we first obtain its' task dependency graph, we obtain the hierarchical dependency graph consisting of asset-, service- and business process-layer. From the graphical dependency graph and the vulnerability specifications we obtain a logical specification of vulnerability/threat propagation for deriving multi step multi stage attacks using MulVAL (MulVAL: http://people.cs.ksu.edu/xou/argus/software/mulval.).

The attack graph generated from MulVAL, is imported into the graphical DB, Neo4J so that an online/real-time flexible analysis of vulnerability/threat propagation can be done. We further demonstrate how with additional inputs, it is possible to realize risk analysis of the system. Thus, our integrated model has made threat analysis both re-configurable and scalable. We illustrate the application of our approach to enterprise systems and the power of graphical modeling for the analysis of threat assessments of business enterprise applications. This in turn allows the use of various mitigation techniques for controlling the propagation of threats/vulnerabilities.

Keywords: BPMN · Attack and dependence graph · Vulnerabilities · Threat assessment

1 Introduction

Threat is an unavoidable evil which persists and grows exponentially with the increase in easy reach of computing base for the common man. The security of

© Springer Nature Switzerland AG 2019
J. K. Liu and X. Huang (Eds.): NSS 2019, LNCS 11928, pp. 146–166, 2019.
https://doi.org/10.1007/978-3-030-36938-5_9

the new age network in which information flows at wire speed is an important demand for service providers and administrators for handling ever evolving conflicts against adversaries. Due deliberations to address the security issues with respect to particular software, vulnerability, and application in isolation is in vogue since several years. Today an attacker can infiltrate a well guarded network through multi-step, multistage attacks. The attacker can use numerous vulnerabilities present at various stages as a stepping stone to the next level. A hierarchical and proactive threat mitigation and vigilance is an indispensable demand.

Several approaches have been proposed for analyzing attacks using various concepts like logic trees [11,12], cyber threat trees [3,10], fault trees [6], attack trees [15] etc. Abstractly, an attack tree is essentially an AND-OR tree. The name attack tree was first proposed by Salter et al. [14]. Attack trees cover a complete canvas of tree-based notions used for threat modelling, Weiss [18] and Amoroso [3] have proposed tree based approaches to analyze security of systems. Threat modelling using attack graphs is explored in [13]. Schneier [15,16], articulates the use of Attack trees to model and analyze threats in digital platforms. Further, several metrics to quantify attack paths or resources required for the attacker have been explored in [17]; metrics are usually based on probability, CVSS or dependency etc. One of the broad guidelines in security is that the system should be built such that the ROI does not payoff for adversaries. Various techniques to understand and classify high impact paths have also been suggested and attack trees [15,17] stands out as the best bet for attack modelling for modern multistep and multistage vulnerable systems.

The root of the attack tree is in essence the node that abstracts the main security threat that the attacker would try to reach. From the root, the tree is branched out to child nodes that depict sub-attacks. The branching is carried out till attacks cannot be further broken down into sub-attacks. The branching may be an "AND" or an "OR" branch. Last level child nodes that cannot further be broken down are called leaf (Fact) nodes. Keinzle and Wulf [2] have covered a wide spectrum of modelling using attack trees. Several researchers have envisaged various templates and patterns of generating and applying the attack tree concept [4,5,15,17].

Several attack graph software applications are available both free and commercial. One of the most widely available tool is: MulVAL (Multihost Multistage Vulnerability Analysis) [11]. MulVAL is a Datalog based modeling language for various elements in vulnerability analysis like bug specification, configuration description, reasoning rules, operating-system permissions and privilege model, etc. In a sense, the formal Datalog specification leverages existing vulnerability-database and scanning tools by expressing their output in Datalog. Once such a specification is captured by the user, the attack graph generation corresponds to executing the Datalog program. Usage of MulVAL for threat assessment has been explored in [1,4,11,17].

A recent manual case study [4] illustrates derivation of risk assessment through interconnected attack graphs and entity dependency graphs. The authors demonstrate the use of additional rules specific to application for threat assessment and further arrive at an impact assessment of an application based on CVSS scores pertaining to vulnerability of the application as envisaged by NIST. The main aim of our paper is to provide a computational framework, where threat analysis/risk assessment can be interactively analyzed through visualization and *cypher* queries using graphical databases like Neo4J.

In [1], a mathematical analysis has been explored through a case study for impact assessment by a probabilistic modelling of the attack graph impact on the dependency graph.

In this paper, we describe an integrated computational model and a framework for vulnerabilities/risk analysis by building attack tress using nuances of task graph, dependency graph, logical analysis of vulnerabilities, probabilistic analysis and graphical database. We start from the BPMN model of the given enterprise application, generating task dependencies, from which a logical propagation of vulnerabilities is realized through MulVAL after generation of interaction rules among the tasks and the vulnerabilities in the system. The attack graph generated by MulVAL is pipelined to a graph DB, Neo4J for real-time/flexible analysis of attacks as well as risk analysis. Threat analysis/risk assessment can be flexibly analyzed through visualization and *cypher* queries on Neo4J. We illustrate various aspects of the model and the framework. In summary, our computational framework leads to a security knowledge base that can be effectively used by security experts and system administrators to enhance the quality and cost of enterprise network security management.

Rest of the paper is organized as follows: Sect. 2 provides a brief background for business models (BPMN), vulnerability specifications (CVSS), attack graph generation system (MulVAL) and graphic DB (Neo4J); it also describes a running example used for illustration in the sequel. Section 3 describes our approach of arriving at task dependencies, consolidated input generation for MulVAL for attack graph generation. Section 4 discusses how the attack graph generated by the MulVAL is exported to a graphical DB, Neo4J for realizing a spectrum of threat assessments via *Cypher* queries. The paper concludes with Sect. 5.

2   Background

In this section, we provide a brief overview of various concepts and tools in our approach like BPMN, CVSS, MulVAL and Neo4j. We further describe a running example used for illustration.

2.1   Business Model Architecture and BPMN

Any business process is dependent on various sub modules that can be analyzed as sub layers known as abstraction layers. The main layers are: Asset layer, Service layer and Business Process task layer. Asset layer mainly deals with disks and hardware that support the business process. Service layer consists of services like database services, web servers, application servers that run several services like shopping service, booking service, payment service, RBAC services. At the top, the business process layer would list all the tasks that make the complete business process.

The dependency graph is to be derived based on the overall logic of inter-dependence among all layers. It is evident that a service at service layer may depend on more functions in addition to those provided by the Asset layer. At the business process layer, one task may depend on other task/tasks for completion of the process.

One of well-known notations for business process modelling is the BPMN model [9]. It clearly portrays the understanding of all players, flow of proce-dures, options available, interactions among different entities of the application etc. We use BPMN for modelling for business enterprises for extracting vari-ous task dependencies and for mapping the logical architecture to the physical architecture.

2.2 Common Vulnerability Scoring System (CVSS)

This is an open framework that has unique standardized scoring system. This acts as a benchmark and is useful for any organization. It has three groups: Base, Temporal and Environmental. The numerical score is between 0–10. These scores are provided by National Vulnerability Database (NVD). The score indi-cates the usefulness of that vulnerability to the attacker in terms of its ease of exploit-ability and the impact it is going to have on integrity, availability and confidentiality. More the value, the better it is for the attacker. So a good attacker would look for high value vulnerabilities in the system.

Base: The constant basic characteristics of a vulnerability
Temporal: The characteristics that change on time but not on environment
Environment: Characteristics that are specific to particular environment

We use CVSS to derive an assessment of vulnerability propagation.

2.3 MulVAL [11]

MulVAL stands for "Multi-host, Multi-stage Vulnerability Analysis Language". It is a software research tool, providing a framework for modeling the interaction of software bugs with system and network configurations. MulVAL uses Data-log as its modeling language. For a proper assessment, the Datalog specification should capture host configuration, network configuration, principals, vulnerabil-ity, task definition, access controls etc.

Interaction Rules: The reasoning engine consists of a collection of Datalog rules that captures the operating system behavior and the interaction of various com-ponents in the network. These are rules defining how and what paths are available to the attacker in multistage and multi path attack. It starts with what would be the final occurrence that is followed by all those that aid in achieving these. It forms the logical specification by which MulVAL generates the attack graph correspondingly. For details, the reader is referred to [11]. We use MulVAL for generating attack trees.

2.4   Graph DB - Neo4j

The ease of storage and modelling the business model to assess threat impact in real time that can scale is an important factor for the use of graph DB Neo4j. It depicts connected as well as semi structured data using graphs. It allows us to retrieve any information from models by using *Cypher* Queries. Cypher Query Language (CQL) is available to do any transactions on the database. No complex joins are required for information retrieval. Some of the different clauses in *Cypher* queries are:-

Read Clauses: [MATCH, WHERE, START, LOAD CSV]
Write Clauses: [CREATE, MERGE, SET, DELETE, REMOVE, FOREACH, CREATE, UNIQUE]
General Clauses: [RETURN, ORDER BY, LIMIT, SKIP, WITH, UNWIND, UNION, CALL]

For further details, the reader is referred to [7,8]. We use Neo4j for flexible real-time analysis of attack graphs.

2.5   Running Example

Here, we describe a business application that will be used for illustration in the sequel. BPMN model for our running example is shown in Fig. 1 along with functions of various tasks given below:

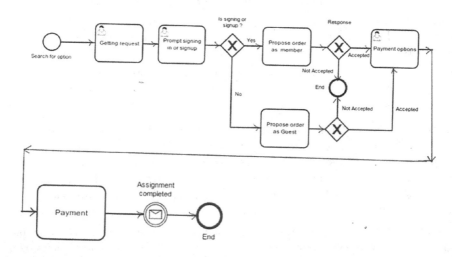

Fig. 1. BPMN model for business process under consideration

Task *T1*: Search for options (start of the application)
Task *T2*: Selecting an option

Task *T3*: Prompt for signing in or signing up
Task *T4*: If signed in, place order as a member
Task *T5*: If not signed in, place order as a guest
Task *T6*: Payment done via UPI, Net Banking, debit/credit card
Task *T7*: Prompt payment confirmation message

Vulnerabilities in Our Running Example. For illustration, we assume that our payment gateway has five vulnerabilities. The detailed attributes along with its impact score (Base Score) etc., is shown in Table 1.

Table 1. Vulnerability information

Vulnerability	CVSS score	Exploited result
CVE-2016-9962	6.4	Container escape
CVE-2016-3697	7.8	Privilege escalation
CVE-2018-15514	8.8	Privilege escalation
CVE-2018-2844	8.8	Virtual machine escape
CVE-2016-0777	6.5	Privilege escalation

HW/SW Architecture. For the running example, we use the HW/SW architecture as shown in Fig. 2.

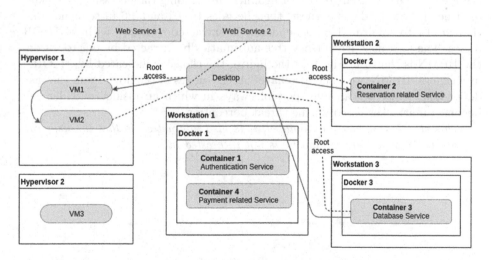

Fig. 2. Software architecture for the model under consideration

3 Modelling Threat Assessment of Business Applications: Our Approach

Given the logical and physical architectures of the business enterprise application, a major step in assessing is to arrive at a possible attack graph that depicts the way attacks/vulnerabilities can propagate resulting in attacks. In this section, we describe how the dependencies of various tasks along with vulnerabilities are integrated to generate an input with which the attack graph is generated by MulVAL that provides a basis for tracing out possible propagation of attacks/vulnerabilities in the business enterprise.

3.1 Generation of Attack Graphs

This is one of the complex tasks that involves the generation of a graphical model that will show dependencies among various tasks and services taking into account the deployed HW/SW configuration along with their possible vulnerabilities. Such a graphical model enables us to arrive at possible propagation/exploitation of the expected vulnerabilities.

Step 1: Derivation of task flow graph and task dependency tree: The task graph for the BPMN depicted in Fig. 1 is shown in Fig. 3. To trace possible attack/threat propagation in the system, we first extract possible logical dependencies of the tasks. For instance, from the task graph, we can observe that after initiation of the business process, T1 is executed followed by T2 and T3 in sequence. After T3, there are two options with the attacker either to login-if-member else continue as-guest. If logged-in, then the sequence of the path is T4 followed by T6 and then go to T7 to confirm after doing the necessary payment, or if he chooses to do as a guest, then he goes to T5 and T6 in sequence and then to T7 to confirm. This dependency is extracted as a tree with AND/OR nodes. The task flow dependency tree automatically extracted by our tool from the BPMN is shown in Fig. 4; in the figure, the choice is indicated by "T_OR"; in a general BPMN, we could also have "AND" nodes in the flow. From the task dependency tree, we can infer possible ways in which an insider/outsider can become an attacker based on the threat perception.

This step is completely automated; it is also interactive so that the user can remove those dependencies that he is not interested in.

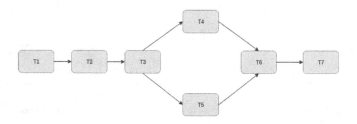

Fig. 3. Task flow graph

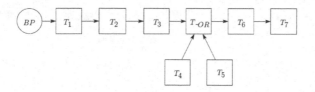

Fig. 4. Logical task dependency tree

Step 2a: Derive Asset, Service, Business layer and their dependency graph: Having derived the logical dependencies, we need to map the dependencies to physical system architecture over which the business enterprise will be deployed. For the running example, let us assume that the system architecture available for deployment is as shown in Fig. 2. From the task flow graph and task dependency trees, we need to arrive at the physical network architecture for each of the tasks with details of hardware/software along with their respective vulnerabilities. The mapping is to be done by the actual system designed for the task. From the logical/physical architectures shown in Figs. 4 and 2 respectively, we obtain an integrated representation of the asset layer, service layer and the business process layer for the business application and the dependencies. For the running example, such a hierarchical layer is depicted in Fig. 5; one can observe that T1(Business Process Layer) is dependent on web1(Service layer) that is hosted on VM1 running in Hypervisor1(Asset Layer). The graph depicts all possible dependencies.

Step 2b: Generation of input configuration File for MulVAL: From the dependencies, we can extract the information needed for MulVAL. The input (input.P) file for analysis to MulVAL contains **attackerLocated()**- the starting point of the attack, **attackerGoal()** is the final goal of the attack; the fact nodes capture the dependencies in the business application model. Needless to say, the precision of the output depends on the precision of the input. Thus, the Datalog input to MulVAL should be as precise as possible. Various information captured in the input is detailed below. The Fact Nodes are generated from the hierarchical graph (which already depicts all possible dependencies). This is augmented with the knowledge of the impact of vulnerabilities based on the users' knowledge; the latter is classified into (1) derived nodes – user with the knowledge declares an inference from a set of fact nodes based on the impact of vulnerabilities, and (2) interaction rules: capture the impact of the vulnerabilities and its flow based on the dependencies. These are illustrated below.

1. **Fact Nodes:** This is the classic MulVAL input that extracts the relations among system components deployed, network information, access controls, vulnerabilities, tasks and their logical dependencies of the system (essentially the hierarchical dependencies derived in the previous step) in the Datalog style. For the running example, this is depicted in Fig. 5. The information is captured as Datalog facts. Additional fact nodes may need to be added by the administrator to depict the complete business transaction flow. In the

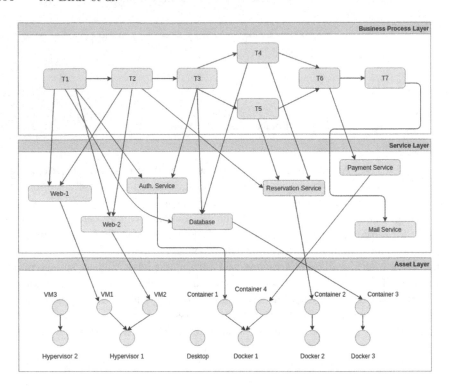

Fig. 5. Dependency graph among all three layers

running example, the following node needs to be added as it provides the flow of dependency from end-to-end:

nodeImpact(business_process, flow, t1, t2, t3, t_or, t6, t7).

For the running example, part of initial standard input (input.P) generated for MulVAL is shown in Fig. 6. The interpretation of rules are given below:

(a) **attackGoal(nodeImpact(business_process))**:
    nodeImpact(business_process) is the derived node for which it is assumed that if an attacker for the given enterprise business application with the deployed architecture with all the known vulnerabilities, access rights and actual deployment configuration can reach this node. The attacker would be able to reach this node through a combination of a subset of these facts. The goal can be changed to any node to check for anticipated vulnerability to any desired depth in the network and can be used to harden and curb any information loss or compromise the system.

(b) **iaasHostInfo(iaas, hypervisor, kvmd, kvm),**
    deploymentInfo(docker1, workstation1, dockerd, docker)
    These are fact nodes (leaf Nodes) that describe the actual deployment of software and hardware used to accomplish the business mission. These are the basic building facts that can be checked if the faulty deployment is assisting the attacker to reach the attack goal.

```
/*attackGoal(execCode(_, _)).*/
attackGoal(nodeImpact(business_process)).

attackerLocated(internet).



/* iaas */
iaasHostInfo(iaas, hypervisor1, kvmd, kvm).
iaasHostInfo(iaas, hypervisor2, kvmd, kvm).

iaasGuestInfo(iaas, vm1, hypervisor1, kvmd, kvm).
iaasGuestInfo(iaas, vm2, hypervisor2, kvmd, kvm).
iaasGuestInfo(iaas, vm3, hypervisor2, kvmd, kvm).

/* docker */
deploymentInfo(docker1, workstation1, dockerd, docker).
deploymentInfo(docker2, workstation2, dockerd, docker).
deploymentInfo(docker3, workstation3, dockerd, docker).

containerInfo(docker1, container3, workstation1, dockerd, docker).
containerInfo(docker2, container4, workstation2, dockerd, docker).
containerInfo(docker3, container2, workstation3, dockerd, docker).
containerInfo(docker3, container1, workstation3, dockerd, docker).
```

Fig. 6. Input.P for MulVAL for the application

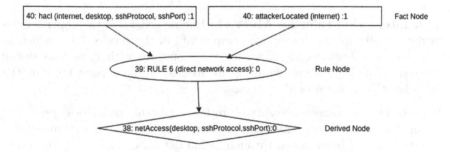

Fig. 7. An attack tree illustration via derived node

2. **Derived Nodes**: Using a set of fact nodes, the user can describe inference of attack/vulnerability propagation. Several derived rules need to be introduced using the fact nodes indicating the possible inference by the user. Figure 7 illustrates the way a derived node is arrived at.
3. **Rule Nodes**: Create all possible rules (meant in the Datalog sense; rules are numbered) over and above the default/standard rule nodes, as it captures the

way the attack/vulnerability gets propagated down the goal. This requires a thorough understanding of rules/nodes, processes, and tasks and their dependencies as well as an understanding of hardware/software architecture. Such an introduction is illustrated below:

(a) *execCode(Container3, root):*
    It indicates that the attacker has got root privilege on Container3 and can execute any arbitrary code.

(b) *vulExists(workstation2, 'CVE-2016-9962', dockerd, localExploit, vmEscalation):*
    It indicates that above mentioned vulnerability(defined by CVE id whose details can be obtained from NIST website) is present in workstation2 through dockerd daemon which can be locally exploited giving raise to vmEscalation.

(c) *containerInfo(docker3, container3, workstation3, dockerd, docker):*
    It indicates that container3 is in docker3 which is in workstation3.

(d) *deploymentInfo(docker3, workstation3, dockerd, docker):*
    It indicates that dockerd daemon running docker3 is running in workstation3.

(e) From the above, the following rule is introduced.
    interaction_rule((execCode(workstation3,docker):-
    vulExists(workstation3, 'CVE-2016-9962', dockerd, localExploit, vmEscalation),
    containerInfo(docker3, container3, workstation3, dockerd, docker),
    deploymentInfo(docker3, workstation3, dockerd, docker),
    execCode(container3,root)),
    rule_desc('Container Escalation',0.4)).

Step 3: Interaction rules for MulVAL: Having generated the dependencies of hardware/software on the service components in the service layer which in turn impacts the business layer, we need to come up with rules that define propagation of vulnerabilities resulting in attacks at the service layer or the business layer. This consists of two steps:

1. Map the known vulnerability/attack to the applicable nodes of dependency graph. This is done by extracting the known hardware/software vulnerabilities (these could be obtained through global databases like CVSS and other vulnerability databases) in the physical/logical architecture after appropriate probing/mapping of the software; further, vulnerabilities could be classified as possible or imposible based on underlying access controls enforced in the system.

2. Once the possible vulnerabilities are assigned to the appropriate nodes of the dependency graph, we need to extract the possible ways these vulnerabilities can cause an attack or propagate an attack using the dependencies in the graph, as rules in the form of Datalog rules.
   For instance, consider the interaction among T1, web-1 and VM1 shown in Fig. 5. Suppose the attacker has reached VM1 (corresponding to desktop). Let

```
interaction_rule((nodeImpact(database, container1):-
    networkServiceInfo(container1, sshd, sshProtocol, sshPort, ssh),
    execCode(container1, root)),
        rule_desc('An impacted child task affects a Process',0.9)
    ).

interaction_rule((execCode(vm2,root)):-
    iaasGuestInfo(iaas, vm2, hypervisor2, kvmd, kvm)
    execCode(hypervisor2, kvm)),
        rule_desc('An impacted child task affects a Process',0.7)
    ).

interaction_rule((execCode(hypervisor2, kvm)):-
    iaasGuestInfo(iaas, vm2, hypervisor2, kvmd, kvm),
    iaasHostInfo(iaas, hypervisor2, kvmd, kvm),
    vulExists(hypervisor2, 'CVE-2016-6258', kvmd, localExploit, vmEscalation),)),
        rule_desc('An impacted child task affects a Process',0.7)
    ).

interaction_rule((execCode(workstation3,docker):-
    vulExists(workstation3, 'CVE-2014-3499', dockerd, localExploit, vmEscalation),
    containerInfo(docker3, container2, workstation3, dockerd, docker),
    deploymentInfo(docker3, workstation3, dockerd, docker),)),
        rule_desc('An impacted child task affects a Process',0.7)
    ).


derived(nodeImpact(business_process)).
derived(nodeImpact(t_and)).
derived(nodeImpact(t_or)).
derived(nodeImpact(t_flow)).
```

Fig. 8. Interaction Rules for the application

us assume VM1 has a vulnerability that allows the attacker to execute any code in VM1 with superuser privilege. Now, web-1 that is dependent on VM1 suffers and hence T1 gets compromised. This is captured as a Datalog rule. For the running example, using the CVSS vulnerabilities shown in Table 1, the interaction rules generated in this manner, as per the dependencies, are shown in Fig. 8.

- Note that the "interaction_rule" in Fig. 8 is a meta keyword and not part of Datalog rule (that keyword is used for our system).
- Interpretation of one of the rules in Fig. 8 is as follows: if attacker gets root privilege to execute any arbitrary code on Hyperuser2 where kvm daemon is running and presence of fact node iaasGuestInfo(iaas, vm2, hypervisor2, kvmd, kvm) will result in attacker gaining root privilege in VM2 to execute any arbitrary code. The rule_desc is defining the complete rule and stating what is the outcome with metric value to depict severity.

Better the effort in introducing the set of rules, better will be the attack graph from MulVAL.

Step 4: Attack Graph generation: Now the input.P can be fed as input and the attack tree can be generated as output from MulVAL.

- MulVAL generates attackgraph.eps (Attack tree graph), vertices.csv (nodes in the attack tree), attackgraph.txt (relations among nodes in the attack tree) for the corresponding Input.P file. One can directly see attack graph or convert using eps to pdf online converter. The attack graph generated is shown in Fig. 9.

The attack graph is in .eps format and the complete listing of all nodes that forms part of the attack tree is in vertices.csv file. The graph generated by MulVAL for the running example is shown in Fig. 9. It is the overall attack graph as generated by MulVAL for the given input of the business application. The graph can be traced from any leaf node till attackGoal(nodeImpact(business_process)) is reached. But for an attacker these can be traced from the point of injection like existence of vulnerability in the system.

4   Analysis and Assessment of Threats

While the attack graph has a wealth of information, it can be observed that threat analysis with respect to vulnerabilities like propagation, shortest path for reaching a certain asset etc, is quite difficult as the graph is in .eps format. For this reason, the attack graph is imported into graph DB, Neo4J, so that analysis can be done in a variety of ways.

After exporting attackgraph.txt (attack graph) and vertices.csv (node listing) into graph DB (Neo4J), we would be in a position to do variety of analysis including a visualization of the attack trees for fragments of attack graph.

Consider fragments of the attack graph imported into Neo4J as follows:

- relations.csv (Fig. 12): This table is captured from the attack graph generated by MulVAL engine; it described the tree structure in logical form as parent and child. Its' many to many relations, is the result of complex attack graph.
- vertices.csv (Fig. 13): This table is generated by MulVAL engine itself as VER-TICES.CSV on successful execution. Node Ids are those which are assigned by MulVAL and are unique to each node. The NodeDetails represent the node name along with its dependencies. NodeType describes the type of Node, indicating whether it is Leaf Node (Basic Node)/Fact Node, AND Node (Rule Node that is applied on leaf or derived nodes for further progress of attack tree) and OR Node (an outcome of application of rule on fact nodes).

The attack tree generated by the Neo4J corresponding to the above information is shown in Fig. 10. In the figure, different color of nodes are used to differentiate types of nodes. In the diagram, purple color represents *Fact node*, maroon color represents *Rule node* and Yellow color represents *Derived node*.

It is easy to see that vulnerability propagation resulting in threats can be captured through reachability; realized through varieties of *Cypher* queries. This is illustrated in the following section.

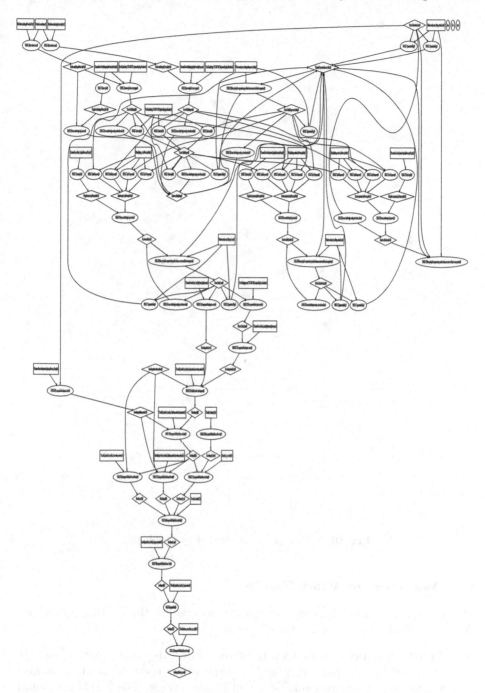

Fig. 9. Attack graph generated by MulVAL

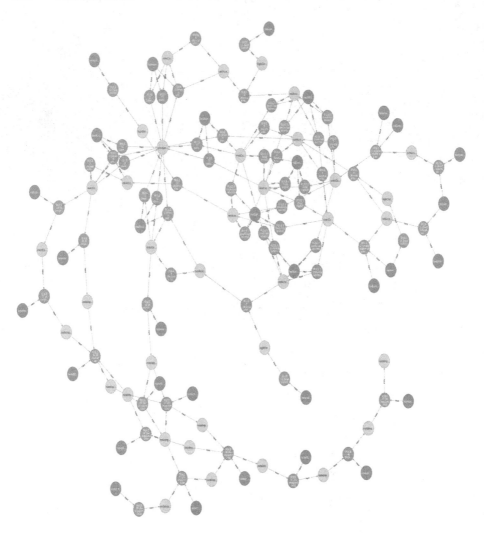

Fig. 10. Attack graph generated by graph DB

4.1 Assessment of Attack Graphs

Having the attack graph on hand, we can extract possible threats through cypher queries; typical queries are illustrated below:

- **All paths from one node to any other node**: All possible paths available to attacker from a particular node at any other node or Goal. This also suggests paths that are available for an insider attack. The Neo4J command say up to 20 paths from node 36 to node 1 is shown in Fig. 14.

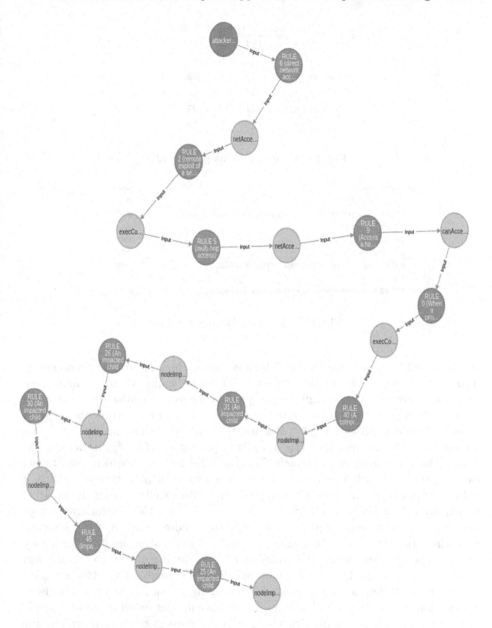

Fig. 11. Shortest path from attacker to Goal in graph DB

The above query can be interpreted as follows: check up to twenty paths originating from Node whose id is 26 to Node id 1 (in our case Node id:1 is attackGoal). The output paths are all displayed graphically. The shortest/longest among all these can be further classified for analysis. In Fig. 11, we have described

1	Child	Parent
2	14	11
3	13	14
4	17	18
5	22	19
6	21	22
7	25	26

Fig. 12. Relations.csv as per Neo4J

1	Node	NodeDetails	NodeType
2	1	nodeImpact(business_process)	OR
3	2	RULE 25 (An impacted child task affects an Process)	AND
4	3	nodeImpact(t7)	OR
5	4	RULE 42 (impacted child)	AND
6	5	nodeImpact(web2,vm2)	OR
7	6	RULE 35 (A compromised host impacts a service)	AND
8	7	execCode(vm2,root)	OR
9	8	RULE 41 (A compromised host impacts its guests)	AND

Fig. 13. vertices.csv as per Neo4J

shortest path between two Nodes. The path shows how an attacker who enters into system where vulnerability exists (Leaf Node) and carries out multi-step multi-stage attack on the complete enterprise business application as the attacker satisfies the required rule conditions, progresses. We can observe how the attacker from leaf node is progressing by meeting the rule conditions at each step and finally is able to compromise the complete application. The figure depicts the starting node in purple color (attackerLocated(internet)) from which the attacker exploits rule 6, which is a direct access to network on http through which it gains network access into the system. Then the vulnerability allows the attacker to exploit rule 2 i.e. attacker gains remote access into the network with root privilege. So the attacker gets root privilege to execute code any arbitrary code and which the attacker further uses to carry out multi-step, multi-stage attack due to dependencies among the nodes and keeps gaining ability to execute any arbitrary code at all levels with root privilege. Thereafter the attacker gains enough rights to impact any independent nodes like Task 2 in the main business application. The attacker builds upon this to have impact on all nodes and finally impact the main business application. The figure depicts the above explanation in a graphical structure. These are paths that an attacker located anywhere in the Internet can use vulnerable injection points to ingress and step wise progress.

- **Shortest, longest or K-length paths from one node to another**: Aids in identifying shortest or other paths an attacker has, on reaching a particular node to any other node – leading to estimate min/max resources required by an attacker to damage.

```
MATCH (p:Node{id:26}),(n:Node{id:1}),
path=((p)-[*1..20]->(n))
return path
```

Fig. 14. Neo4J cypher query for up to 20 paths

4.2   Bottleneck or Intersection Nodes

Identification bottlenecks aids the admin to identify where network hardening is required thereby isolating the attacker with acceptable vulnerabilities within the system. Based on threat perception, invest only in addressing that vulnerability which allows an outsider to gain entry to critical levels of system.

4.3   Impact Calculation on a Path for Security Metrics

CVSS score for a vulnerability is an internationally accepted metric for given security threat in a system. It is constantly verified and updated for correctness. The score indicates the threat due to vulnerability. The same metric can be used to identify the max and min impact path in the attack graph. The metric values can be assigned to the vulnerable fact nodes and values can be propagated. Impact calculation logic is as follows:

$$\text{Node Impact Score } (N_i) = \frac{CVSS\ Base\ score\ for\ Vulnerability}{10}$$

For two node N_1 and N_2 as input:

AND Node   : Impact Score $= N_1 \times N_2$
OR Node   : Impact Score $= N_1 + N_2 - N_1 \times N_2$
$(N_1 \text{ OR } N_2) \text{ AND } N_3$: Impact Score $= (N_1 + N_2 - N_1 \times N_2) \times N_3$

Based on the impact and vulnerabilities, it becomes easy to decide on which vulnerability patching would meet sufficiently the security requirement.

4.4   Metric Based Evaluations

The system can capture various metric evaluations including probability based assessments; this is illustrated below:

- All leaf nodes are given a random probability between 0 and 1 (both excluded). However, the network admin is free to allot any probability to the node being compromised based on the average observation of the network.
- Further progression of the probability from leaf to root is realized as follows:

      AND Node   New Probability=Min (All incoming Probability)
      OR Node   New Probability=Max (All incoming Probability)

- The leaf with max probability indicates the most likely point of attack. From this, we can find the shortest path upto the main Goal along with probabilistic assessments.

The same model can be used to do assessment with respect to:

- **Detectability**: The ability of the attacker being detected due to monitors by assigning appropriate values.
- **Cost**: The overall cost that would be required for an attacker to commit actions to achieve a target.
- **Technical Skill**: The technical skill required to progress into network till goal is reached by the attacker. The skill may be approximated by some metric assigned to nodes.

The model is flexible enough to model network hardening based on **Green, Yellow and Red Zone**. This is possible by collecting all shortest paths from vulnerable nodes/intersection points that are identified as demarcation boundaries for zones. The model can be extended to multi-business processes where the same underlying asset/service layer supports more than one business process, where the attacker can exploit vulnerabilities of one stage to attack on another.

4.5   General Strategy for Threat Analysis

Iterate the steps described earlier based on the assessment by the user, till the intended level of security is reached.

The information about the attack graph generated by MulVAL is captured in Neo4J so that varieties of queries called *Cypher* queries can be asked. The attack graph generated from Neo4J for the attack graph shown in Fig. 9 is shown in Fig. 10. From such a graph we can *Cyper*-query for varieties of threats/attacks.

In our model, the logical data and relationships are imported to Neo4J with appropriate headers. One can do any kind of assessment by assigning necessary metrics as appropriate and firing cypher queries. Our platform can do assessment likes (a) CVSS score based, (b) Probability based, (c) Zone based (Green - Acceptable, Yellow- Danger, Red-Immediate action required), and (d) extendable to detectability, cost for attacker, technical skill required by attacker to carry out multi-step attacks, etc.

Nco4J allows any number of attributes and carry out assessment on the graph in real time assisting the administrator to take corrective steps.

Illustration of Analysis of a Particular Threat Scenario: Vulnerabilities that aid the attacker to gain access are CVE-2016-0777, CVE-2016-3697 and CVE-2018-15514 present in the Desktop that has root access to Hypervisor-1 and Workstation-2 and Workstation-3. CVE-2016-9962 is a vulnerability that is part of docker and aids the attacker in ability to move out of container. The vulnerability that allows attacker to open virtual machine is CVE-2018-2844 which is part of VM kernel.

The attacker can exploit both web and ssh vulnerability on the desktop that has root access to VM1. On accessing VM1, the attacker can bypass isolation between VM1 and Hypervisor-1, by exploiting the vulnerability in the kernel – the attacker can now access VM2 and execute any arbitrary code as it hosts web service-2. Once web service is compromised, any service dependent on it gets affected. As the desktop has root access to Container-2 and Container-3, the attacker gets privilege to execute any code in database/reservation service – damaging the services.

5   Conclusions

In this paper, we have demonstrated how integration of various tools that enable us to arrive at a spectrum of threat analysis/risk analysis for a business enterprise application. It starts with a BPMN model and generates all the dependencies from which a complete information about the HW/SW architecture of the application is obtained. Now using the databases of vulnerabilities in various, HW/SW and service components of the application, we arrive at a logical specification for MulVAL that generates an attack graph for the system. As the attack graph is not easily amenable for flexible assessment, we pipeline into Neo4J using which it becomes flexible to do a variety of threat/risk analysis as well as other applicable metric based threat/risk assessment on the system. While there have been several case studies, there is no methodology supporting a computational platform that enables end-to-end analysis. It entails semi-automation of the whole threat assessment in which validation from admin or user is sought at regular intervals which is quite appropriate. This ensures speedy assessment, avoiding human error factors and enables the cross-checking of automation at various levels, thus reducing false negatives/positives as much as possible. Being pro-active, our approach can be used for prevention of attacks. The model is highly scalable and up-gradable to meet most of enterprise business applications in vogue. The attacker can be tracked at each level as he progresses from leaf node to main goal. For better management, we can also classify users as they reach various threat levels into color code schemes like (a) **Red**: Severe threat to system, on attacker reaching depth greater than 70%, (b) **Yellow**: Medium level threat to system, on attacker reaching depth 50% and (c) **Green**: Low level threat to system, on attacker reaching depth 10%. Based on color code scheme the administrator can track the attacker and take a call on network hardening.

To sum up, our platform can be effectively used (through queries) to gather information for hardening, impact recovery recommendations or self healing solutions as well as admin-based assessment of the system.

References

1. Albanese, M., Jajodia, S.: A graphical model to assess the impact of multi-step attacks. J. Defense Model. Simul. **15**(1), 79–93 (2018)
2. AMENAZA: attack tree modelling (2019). http://www.amenaza.com/documents. php

3. Amoroso, E.G.: Fundamentals of Computer Security Technology. Prentice-Hall Inc., Upper Saddle River (1994)
4. Cao, C., Yuan, L.P., Singhal, A., Liu, P., Sun, X., Zhu, S.: Assessing attack impact on business processes by interconnecting attack graphs and entity dependency graphs. In: 32nd Annual IFIP WG 11.3 Conference, DBSec 2018, Bergamo, Italy, 16–18 July 2018, pp. 330–348 (2018)
5. Jajodia, S., Noel, S., Kalapa, P., Albanese, M., Williams, J.: Cauldron: Mission-centric cyber situational awareness with defense in depth. In: Proceedings of IEEE Military Communications Conference MILCOM, pp. 1339–1344, November 2011
6. Kumar, R., Stoelinga, M.: Quantitative security and safety analysis with attack-fault trees. In: Proceedings of the 18th IEEE International Symposium on High Assurance Systems Engineering (HASE 2017), HASE, pp. 25–32. IEEE (2017)
7. Neo4J: Neo4J: The leading graphical database (2019). https://neo4j.com/
8. Neo4J: Tutorial (2019). https://www.tutorialspoint.com/neo4j/neo4j_tutorial.pdf
9. OMG: BPMN: Business Process Model and Notation. https://www.omg.org/spec/BPMN/2.0/About-BPMN/
10. Ongsakorn, P., Turney, K., Thornton, M., Nair, S., Szygenda, S., Manikas, T.: Cyber threat trees for large system threat cataloging and analysis, pp. 610–615
11. Ou, X., Govindavajhala, S., Appel, A.W.: MulVAL: a logic-based network security analyzer. In: Proceedings of 14th USENIX Security Symposium, SSYM 2005, vol. 14 (2005)
12. Poolsapassit, N., Ray, I.: Investigating computer attacks using attack trees. In: Craiger, P., Shenoi, S. (eds.) DigitalForensics 2007. ITIFIP, vol. 242, pp. 331–343. Springer, New York (2007). https://doi.org/10.1007/978-0-387-73742-3_23
13. Saini, V., Duan, Q., Paruchuri, V.: Threat modeling using attack trees. J. Comput. Sci. Coll. 23(4), 124–131 (2008)
14. Salter, C., Saydjari, O., Schneier, B., Wallner, J.: Towards a secure system engineering methodology (1998)
15. Schneier, B.: Attack trees. Dr. Dobb's J. 24, 21–29 (1999)
16. Schneier, B.: Secrets and Lies: Digital Security in a Networked World (2004)
17. Wang, L., Noel, S., Jajodia, S.: Minimum-cost network hardening using attack graphs. Comput. Commun. 29, 3812–3824 (2006)
18. Weiss, J.D.: A system security engineering process. In: 14th Annual NCSC/NIST National Computer Security Conference (1991)

A Blockchain-Based IoT Data Management System for Secure and Scalable Data Sharing

Yawei Wang[1], Chenxu Wang[1,2]([✉]), Xiapu Luo[3], Kaixiang Zhang[4],
and Huizhong Li[4]

[1] School of Software Engineering, Xi'an Jiaotong University, Xi'an, China
wangyawei@stu.xjtu.edu.cn
[2] MoE Key Lab of INNS, Xi'an Jiaotong University, Xi'an, China
cxwang@mail.xjtu.edu.cn
[3] Department of Computing, Hong Kong Polytechnic University, Hong Kong, China
luoxiapu@gmail.com
[4] WeBank Co., Ltd., Shenzhen, China
{kxzhang,wheatli}@webank.com

Abstract. At present, the centralized architecture for the Internet of Things (IoT) data management faces the risks of data leakage, single-point failure, and vulnerability to malicious attacks. Recently, many researchers and security analysts are focusing on the blockchain technology to solve the security and privacy issues of the IoT data management. However, current blockchain technologies are unable to meet the highly concurrent IoT data transactions and the fast expansion of IoT devices due to the decentralized architecture. Moreover, there is a lack of useful solutions for effective data sharing between public and private networks, and networks with different services (e.g., smart grid and intelligent transportation). In this paper, we propose a decentralized data access model for IoT data storage and sharing based on the FISCO-BCOS blockchain. In the model, we divide the IoT devices that handle different services into different set-chains. These set-chains share data with each other through an elaborate access control model. Experimental results show that the proposed model fits the characteristics of the IoT data management, guaranteeing the privacy and security requirements with better scalability. Our model can be used as a solution for smart cities.

Keywords: Blockchain · IoT · Data management · Access control

1 Introduction

Traditional IoT models typically consist of a centralized data center that manages and processes data collected from hundreds of thousands of connected devices. However, the number of IoT devices has reached an unprecedented

© Springer Nature Switzerland AG 2019
J. K. Liu and X. Huang (Eds.): NSS 2019, LNCS 11928, pp. 167–184, 2019.
https://doi.org/10.1007/978-3-030-36938-5_10

scale, and the cost of centralized services persistently increases. At the same time, IoT devices are vulnerable to malicious attacks and infections [1,2]. Traditional IoT models have not been capable of meeting the growing demands of the IoT ecosystem, which includes multiple homogeneous and heterogeneous subnetworks. For example, some smart traffic networks of multiple streets can be regarded as a homogeneous network because these devices have similar business logics. However, the IoT devices for smart health-care or smart home constitute a heterogeneous network because their business logics are different. Both homogeneous and heterogeneous networks require to efficiently share data with each other to provide more valuable service.

Researches and practices have taken the advance of the blockchain technology to solve the pain points in the IoT data management. Makhdoom *et al.* [3] analyzed the difficulties and prospects of combining blockchains with IoT. They believe that the main difficulty lies in the fact that IoT devices are growing too fast, and the performance of the current blockchain architectures are still not up to the requirements of high concurrency. Yi *et al.* [4] conducted preliminary researches on some classic and newly developed consensus algorithms. They suggested that Ethermint implemented by Tendermint is a good choice for the IoT platform. However, their proposal does not solve the problem of the increasing expansion with IoT devices. Sun *et al.* [5] introduced an Ethereum-based rich-thin-clients solution to the problems caused by limited resources of IoT devices when adopting mining mechanisms of blockchain in IoT scenarios. Ali *et al.* [6] proposed to combine Ethereum sidechains with the InterPlanetary File System (IPFS) to protect IoT data privacy. However, these proposals face the low performance of the Ethereum network. Besides, it requires transaction fees and has poor scalability. Dorri *et al.* [7] proposed a blockchain-based smart home framework and analyzed its security. However, their proposal only handles the IoT devices for the same business, ignoring the hybrid characteristics of IoT services. In summary, the existing solutions propose to use public chains such as Ethereum to solve the security and privacy issues in the IoT data management. However, some features of the public blockchains are not suitable for dealing with IoT transactions, such as high transaction latency, high transaction costs, lack of scalability, and poor handling capability of hybrid networks.

In this paper, we implement an access control model of parallel set-chains based on the FISCO-BCOS blockchain architecture [8]. As shown in Fig. 1, we build a route chain which acts as the main chain to manage multiple set-chains. Multiple sidechains are built as set-chains which run in parallel. We develop a routing scheme to link set chains to the route chain and arrange IoT devices from different organizations or for different service types to different set chains. The route chain performs the authentication management of IoT devices. It categorizes the IoT devices into different set chains according to their device properties and service types. Set chains are sub-IoT-networks which handle a variety of business logics in parallel, and isolate the services from each other. They share data through the predefined access control policies which are implemented as smart contracts running on the route chain.

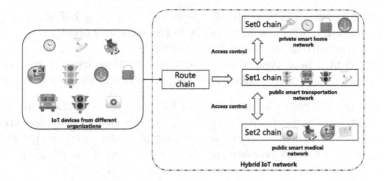

Fig. 1. A parallel chain architecture for hybrid IoT networks

There are several challenges associated with integrating the blockchain technology to the IoT networks. One of the challenges is the privacy issue of the IoT blockchain. We propose a data-sharing model which employs two layers of access control to ensure privacy and security. At the authentication level, we generate a device certificate for each device, and the device needs to verify that the certificate is complete when entering the network. Thus, other devices cannot access the data from this device without authentication. At the data level, we customize and generate a smart contract for each device to control the access for its data when the device is registering. This guarantees that the data is shared with the requester under the device's customized access control. We also use smart contracts to reduce the high cost of collaboration for agents and prevent individuals from being attacked.

Another challenge is the limited resources of the IoT devices to store large amounts of data. Existing data storage and management systems generally adopt centralized cloud services, which exposes users' data to the risk of being leaked. To solve this problem, we use the IPFS [9] for data storage in an immutable way. An IoT device packages the data, uploads it to IPFS, and logs the returned hash value. The returned hash values are then sent to the route chain, which is responsible to route different device requests to different set chains. We deployed routing contracts on the route chain. As mentioned earlier, we divide the devices into different set chains according to information such as organizations and service types of the IoT device. The routing contract records the paths of devices and distributes their transactions to the eligible set chain. In summary, we make the following contributions:

- Based on the FISCO parallel chain architecture, we built a distributed management framework in the context of IoT data sharing and management.
- We design a data access control protocol for IoT data privacy protection in the interaction between different set chains. This access control model is more suitable for decentralized systems.

- We introduced the IPFS as the decentralized storage of IoT data. It solves the problems of limited resources of the IoT devices and possible data leakage caused by the current centralized cloud services.
- We implement a prototype of our model and evaluate its performance with experiments. The results validate the effectiveness and efficiency of our model.

The rest of this paper is organized as follows. Section 2 shows the review of relevant literature. Section 3 presents an overview of the proposed architecture. Section 4 shows the distributed access control model. Section 5 presents the conducted experiments to evaluate the effectiveness and efficiency of the model. Section 6 concludes the work.

2   Related Work

2.1   Blockchain-Based IoT Data Management

The combination of blockchain and IoT has attracted the most attention recently. Due to the lack of an IoT-centric consensus protocol, the existing blockchain system cannot meet the requirements of the IoT in terms of transaction delay and scalability. Many solutions have been proposed to solve these problems.

Sagirlar et al. [10] took the first step towards the goal by designing Hybrid-IoT, a hybrid blockchain architecture for IoT. In Hybrid-IoT, subgroups of IoT devices form POW blockchains, referred to as POW sub-blockchains. The connections among the POW sub-blockchains employ a BFT inter-connector framework, such as Polkadot or Cosmos. Our sub-chain uses the BFT consensus algorithm and performs better in terms of throughput and transaction latency. Li et al. [11] used the blockchain system to design an identity authentication mechanism and a data protection mechanism for IoT devices. Compared with their proposed system, our advantage is that owners of IoT devices can customize their access control policies and have more autonomy. Alphand et al. [12] proposed IoTChain, which is a combination of OSCAR architecture and ACE authorization framework. IoTChain provides an end-to-end solution for securely authorized access to IoT resources. In the system they propose, the data is stored by the server, and we use IPFS to store the data. Our models have lower storage costs and higher data privacy, preventing problems such as single points of failure on the server.

There are also several practices to integrate the IoT with blockchain. IOTA [13] is the first open-source distributed ledger that is being built to power the future of the IoT with feeless microtransactions and data integrity for machines. By solving the inefficiencies of the Blockchain, IOTA utilizes the Tangle (Directed Acyclic Graph) structure to bridge the missing link for the Internet of Everything and Web 3.0. Compared to traditional blocks, IOTA's distributed ledger does not include transactions that are grouped and stored in a sequential chain. Moreover, without the need for monetary rewards, IOTA is not limited to transactional value settlements. It is possible to store information within Tangle transactions securely or even spread more significant amounts of data across multiple bundled or linked transactions. This structure also enables high scalability of transactions. The more activity in 'the Tangle', the faster transactions can be confirmed. However, IOTA does not currently support smart contracts. Thus there is a lack of proper ways to achieve fine-grained access control. Plasma [14] is proposed for incentivized and enforced the execution of smart contracts which is scalable to a significant amount of state updates per second (potentially billions), enabling the blockchain to be able to represent a significant amount of decentralized financial applications worldwide. These smart contracts are incentivized to continue operation autonomously via network transaction fees, which is ultimately reliant upon the underlying blockchain to enforce transactional state transitions.

IoTeX [15] solves the problems of low scalability and high operating costs by introducing the token economy into the IoT. In short, IoTeX is the next generation of IoT-based blockchain platform with high scalability, privacy, isolation, and exploitability for incubating new IoT applications and ecosystems. IoTeX uses a faster consensus algorithm (RDPoS) designed for IoT and can support millions of nodes with instant finality, low latency. IoTeX pulls states off the root chain to further boost privacy, scalability, and interoperability. The ADEPT [16] IoT system is a decentralized IoT using blockchain technology created by IBM and Samsung. The full name of ADEPT is Autonomous Decentralized Peer-to-Peer Telemetry, which is designed to provide the best security for transactions. The system is based on three protocols: Blockchain, BitTorrent, and TeleHash. ADEPT uses Ethereum, a smart contract-based system that enables devices connected to it to communicate securely and efficiently with complex business logic. ADEPT is a complete user-centric IoT platform similar to IOTA Tangle. IOTA uses a distributed database model called Tangle (DAG), which is technically superior to blockchain in terms of scalability and feasibility of micropayments.

In summary, we propose an IoT data management architecture, which takes the advantages of parallel chains to solve the scalability issue in the blockchain. We also employ the IPFS system for IoT data storage to solve the resource-limitation problem in IoT devices.

2.2 Blockchain Architecture Analysis in the IoT Scenario

At present, the problems faced by the IoT data management systems mainly include central server failure, single point of failure, the infeasibility of fine-grained data sharing, and lack of privacy. The blockchain techniques have some natural features such as decentralized architecture, fault tolerance, and cryptographic security, to solve these problems. There are currently a large number of blockchain platforms, including Bitcoin [17], Ethereum [18], Hyperledger-Fabric [19], IOTA [13], and FISCO-BCOS [8]. The mainstream consensus algorithms include Proof of Work (POW), Proof of Stack (POS), Practice Byzantine Fault Tolerant (PBFT), and IOTA (Tangle). We compare and analyze the functionality, security, and applicability of these mainstream blockchain systems and consensus algorithms in the IoT environment. There are four requirements for a blockchain platform used for IoT considering the main performance.

First, the blockchain platform should provide a hybrid network. The solution of the existing blockchain combined with IoT applies to the homogeneous network (the same network that handles the service with a similar logic). With the development of the IoT, the blockchain platform is required to provide a hybrid network to solve the problem of many heterogeneous networks like smart cities. Hybrid networks enable these heterogeneous sub-networks to be isolated at the transaction level and shared at the data level to better serve smart cities.

Second, fast transaction confirmation is an important reference factor for the IoT environment, which requires the blockchain to reach consensus without forking. Only BFT-based consensus algorithms satisfy this requirement.

Third, the ideal blockchain system should not need transaction fees. Considering that the IoT network needs to process millions of transactions every day, and the number of devices increases persistently, the number of transactions is continuing to rise.

Fourth, the blockchain system is required to have good scalability. Faced with the rapid growth of IoT devices, the blockchain system needs to handle more and more business. The IoT systems have put forward higher capacity and scalability requirements, and the single-chain architecture will always encounter software architecture or hardware resources. The system characteristics of the blockchain determine that adding nodes in the blockchain will only enhance the system's fault tolerance and increase the participants' credit endorsement without improving performance.

Table 1 shows the comparison of several leading blockchain platforms. A comprehensive analysis indicates that FISCO-BCOS is more suitable for the IoT environment. FISCO-BCOS [8] is an open-sourced, cross-industry, and secure blockchain platform developed and rebuilt based on Ethereum [18]. FISCO-BCOS supports open consortium chain applications, supports multi-chain, and cross-chain communication. It removes the concept of tokens to improve operational efficiency and reduce business costs without relying on token issuance. FISCO-BCOS retains the gas control logic of the smart contract engine to ensure computing security. The practical Byzantine fault-tolerant (PBFT) [20] algorithm and the Raft algorithm [21] perform better than other algorithms in terms of throughput. Both FISCO-BCOS and Hyperledger-Fabric use a practical Byzantine fault-tolerant algorithm. However, FISCO-BCOS allows multiple blockchains to run concurrently. Therefore, the throughput of the FISCO-BCOS blockchain is higher than Hyperledger-Fabric. FISCO-BCOS uses high-intensity algorithms to encrypt the blocks, transactions, and data stored on the hard disk. The keys are managed independently to ensure data security and extend the EVM instruction set. FISCO-BCOS introduces the CNS (Contract Name Service) mechanism to name and address smart contracts to simplify the management of contracts by business developers. According to the above analysis, we choose FISCO-BCOS as the underlying blockchain for our model.

3   Model

3.1   Overview

In this paper, we propose a blockchain-based IoT network architecture for data management. Figure 2 presents the architecture of the framework which consists of three parts, including applications, FISCO-BCOS, and IPFS. The workflow of the proposed system is as follows: First, users provide the necessary device information of an IoT device for identity authentication to join in the network. Second, according to the identity authentication provided by the IoT device, the route chain assigns the IoT device into different set chains. The network ID of the attached set chain is returned to the application. Third, the application collects the data generated by the IoT device. It packages and uploads the encrypted data to the IPFS for data storage. Finally, the application sends the returned file-hash-values to the corresponding set chain for data index storage. It is worth noting that only data indexes (IPFS file-hashes) rather than the raw data are stored on the blockchain, which significantly reduces the storage cost of the blockchain system. Moreover, our applications interact with the corresponding set chain directly for data indexes storage without the routing of the route chain, which significantly reduces the burden of the route chain.

Table 1. Comparison of leading blockchain systems

Features	Bitcoin	Ethereum	Hyperledger-Fabric	IoTA	FISCO
Consensus	POW	POW, POS	PBFT	Coordinator	PBFT
Consensus finality	×	×	√	×	√
Blockchain forks	√	√	×	√	×
Run smart contracts	×	√	√	×	√
Fee less	×	×	√	×	√
Scalable	×	×	×	√	√
TX throughput (TPS)	7	8–9	Thousands	7–12	Thousands

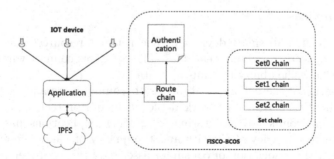

Fig. 2. The overall architecture of the model

Figure 3 presents the network topology. In our model, an IoT device interacts with the application and communicates with the nodes of the route chain.

Through this process, device registration, data upload, and download are completed. After the IoT device is registered, it will be distributed to the corresponding set chain. The route chain records the path information of each IoT device. When the data of the IoT device needs to be uploaded or downloaded, the route chain communicates with the corresponding set chain nodes according to the path of the recorded IoT device.

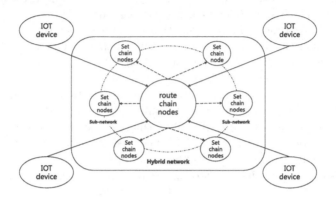

Fig. 3. Network topology

We deploy a smart contract on the route chain to manage IoT devices. This smart contract is responsible for distributing the newly added IoT devices to the corresponding set chain and recording the path of the device (can be regarded as a routing table). On the other hand, a smart contract deletes the device's path information when a device fails to work due to a change in location or device damage. We also deploy different smart contracts on the set chains, and we use the smart contracts to control access to data so that IoT devices belonging to different set chains can access and share data with each other.

3.2   IoT Devices

IoT devices include all smart devices with constraint resources such as smart TVs, smart speakers, toys, and wearables. These devices connect wirelessly to a network and have the ability to transmit data.

The scenarios of the IoT applications are becoming more and more diverse. The government's intelligent network deployed in fire protection, street lighting, cycling, environmental monitoring, and other applications has improved the management efficiency of the city and the quality of life of the citizens. At the same time, the association of consumer asset data (water meters, electricity meters, home security, vehicles, etc.) provides consumers with a more convenient life. To maximize the utility of these devices, it is important to allow these devices to access the data generated by others for coordination. At the same time, it is critical to protect the privacy of users.

An application client is primarily responsible for three tasks. First, it collects data from an IoT device. Second, it packages and uploads the collected data to IPFS. The returned file hash value is recorded and encrypted. Third, it sends a transaction request to the route chain and returns the query result. Applications run on moderate personal computers or edge devices with high computational performance, where data can either be analyzed locally or sent to the IPFS for storage and shared through the Blockchain network.

3.3   FISCO-BCOS Blockchain

As shown in Fig. 1, our model includes two types of blockchains, namely the route chain and set chains. IoT devices of different organizations are divided into corresponding set chains through the route chain. The set chains are isolated from each other, processing transactions in parallel.

The Route Chain: The route chain has three tasks. First, it completes the device's identity authentication. While IoT drives the digitization of various industries, it also brings new security challenges. The tools used to attack the IoT devices are becoming more advanced, and the threshold for attacking technology is getting lower. At the same time, there is a lack of supervision of the IoT. To solve this problem, we carry out strict identity authentication for IoT devices and introduce arbitration nodes to supervise the IoT. In our model, the route chain is responsible for identity authentication. IoT devices need to provide the necessary information to generate a certificate for authentication. The information includes device ID, serial number, organization, service type, and network ID. The identity authentication process is shown in Fig. 4. We run three types of nodes on the route chain, namely: organization nodes which are operated by different organizations; arbitration nodes which are operated by the government and other regulatory parts; deposit nodes which are operated by trusted

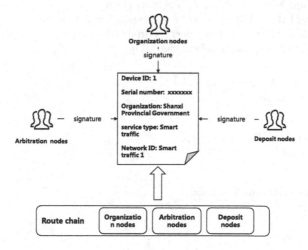

Fig. 4. Identity authentication

third-party depositories. All three types of nodes on the route chain have to sign the certificate of an IoT device and store the signed certificate on the chain. To verify the identity of the device, we examine whether the three types of nodes have correctly signed the signature by checking their public keys.

Second, the route chain distributes the IoT devices into different set chains according to their organizations, service types, and network IDs. Since there may be multiple sub-networks under the same service type (e.g., smart traffic may include multiple street networks), we introduce the field of Network ID to identify the subnets. That is, each service type may have multiple networks, and we use network ID to differentiate them. As shown in Fig. 1, signal light devices belong to smart traffic in terms of service types. However, the lights at different streets may be assigned with different network IDs. We divide these devices into different set chains based on these parameters. Each set chain only processes the transactions of a limited number of devices and thus maintains high performance.

As shown in Algorithm 1, we use Map in the smart contract to record the path information of the IoT device and deploy the smart contract on the route chain. $Map1$ is a nested Map. The first key is the service type field, the second key is the network ID field, and the value is the set chain ID field. $Map2$ records the device ID information of each chain deployment. The key is the set chain ID field, and the value is the IoT device ID field. We initialize $Map1$ based on

---

Algorithm 1. Assign IoT devices on the route chain

    Input: $IoTID, cert, servicetype, netID$
    Output: $chainID$
1 **Initialize**$Map1$,Map2;
2 **if** $cert \neq null$ **then**
3   **if** $Map1[servicetype] \neq null$ **then**
4   **if** $Map1[servicetype][netID] \neq null$ **then**
5   Add the IoT device to the corresponding set chain;
6            $chainID = Map1[servicetype][netID]$;
7            $IoTID$ append to $Map2[chainID]$;
8   **else**
9   Network ID does not exist;
10   goto final;
11   **else**
12   Service type does not exist;
13   goto final;
14 **else**
15   IoT device certificate is invalid;
16   goto final;
17 **final** ;
18 **return** $chainID$;

---

the service type and network ID provided by the hybrid network and initialize *Map*2 to null. The input parameter *IoTID* is the ID of the IoT device, *cert* is the device certificate of the IoT, *servicetype* is the service type of the IoT device (smart home, smart traffic, etc.), and *netID* is the ID of the network to which the IoT device belongs(differentiate between different networks in the same service type). The output parameter *chainID* is the ID of the set chain where the IoT device is located.

Third, the route chain is responsible for access control of data sharing. It accepts the application's transaction requests and distributes the transactions to different set chains in which the data of the IoT device is processed. The set chain handles the specified transaction. We deploy a routing contract on the route chain that records the information for each set chain and the path of an IoT device to set chains, which is analogous to a routing table. Each transaction gets the corresponding device path through the smart contract.

The Set Chains: With the development of the IoT, there is a growing need for hybrid networks to solve the problems of many heterogeneous scenarios such as smart cities and smart homes. Hybrid networks enable these heterogeneous subnetworks to be isolated at the transaction level and shared at the data level to provide better services.

In our model, each set chain represents a specific IoT network. For example, in a smart city scenario, the first set chain can be used to process smart home devices. The second set chain handles devices such as smart meters, and the third chain handles devices for smart medical. Each set chain executes a specific business scenario. We have designed an access control strategy to allow IoT devices on different set chains to store and access data. As shown in Fig. 1, the route chain and multiple set chains form a multi-chain parallel architecture that provides distributed access control for hybrid IoTs.

When a new subnetwork needs to be added to the hybrid network, we can easily add a set chain to handle transactions in the new network. As the number of sub-networks increases, the transaction volume will increase sharply to reach the performance bottleneck of a single blockchain. Then we can quickly add a new set chain to alleviate the pressure of the current blockchain network. We record all nodes of the new blockchain to the routing smart contract and redeploy them by the system administrator. When the service starts initialization, the nodes are started to generate a new blockchain. We can only add new devices to the new blockchain. But we cannot port old devices to the new blockchain. The parallel multi-chain architecture is analogous to the sub-tables in the database, or the sub-SET model in the Internet service. In theory, as long as sufficient resources are invested, there is no upper limit of traffic volume.

3.4   Data Storage

The IoT, as it exists today, is a distributed network of intelligent objects with software and data management being provided by centralized third-party entities. In this mode, data storage and privacy protection have become a concern for users. On the one hand, IoT devices have limited storage resources and cannot support the growing IoT data. On the other hand, the existing IoT data management model mostly uses centralized cloud services. In this mode, the user must fully trust the third party and delegate the data to the cloud service provider. However, the user data is exposed to the problem of leakage, and the user's privacy is not guaranteed. In our model, we use blockchain and peer-to-peer data storage to implement IoT data privacy, where each device has full access to their own data without having to trust any third-party entities to manage IoT software or data.

To solve these problems, our model employs IPFS as the file storage system. It solves the problem that the device is limited in storage resources while enhances the privacy of data. IPFS (Interplanetary File System) aims to be a completely decentralized Internet file system [9]. IPFS files are content-addressed and are identified by their hashes. IPFS can protect data privacy and solves the problem of limited storage resources of IoT devices. Therefore, We employ IPFS as the file storage and sharing platform.

4   Access Control Strategy

4.1   Traditional Access Control Strategy

Traditional access control models include Discretionary Access Control (DAC), Mandatory Access Control (MAC), and Role-Based Access Control (RBAC). However, they all have shortcomings such as too large subject authority, complicated management work, and lack of flexibility.

Discretionary Access Control (DAC) means that the user has the right to access the objects (files, data tables, etc.) created by itself, and can grant the access of other users to these objects, and reclaim the access rights from the users who grant the rights. The disadvantage of this model is that the authority of the subjects is too high and may leak information. When the number of users is large, and the amount of management data is large, the access control list will be vast and difficult to maintain.

Mandatory Access Control (MAC) is an access method for systems to force the subject to obey the access control policy. It uses the read up and write down to ensure the integrity of the data and uses the read down and write up to ensure the confidentiality of the data. The shortcomings are mainly to achieve a large workload, inconvenient management, and inflexibility. It emphasizes confidentiality too much, does not have a strong ability to work on the system continuously, and lacks consideration of the manageability of authorization.

4.2   Distributed Access Control Strategy

In this paper, we make some changes based on Role-Based Access Control (RBAC) and propose an access control model that is more suitable for distributed systems. Traditional RBAC models require a centralized mechanism to be responsible for role partitioning and rights management, which is not suitable for decentralized systems. In our access control model, we have decentralized data management rights. The user divided the roles and customized their own access control strategies.

We implemented two layers of access control. The first layer checks the certificate of the devices to determine if a device has permission to enter the network. The second layer is the customized access control by the IoT device when registering the device on the route chain. A smart contract implements the access policies. We deploy the device's smart contract on the set chain where the data of the device is located. The route chain stores the smart contract's address and device ID to provide routing for data storage and query.

Currently, we offer two customized access strategies, namely the fee mode and the token mode. The fee mode means that the device specifies the amount of fees that other devices need to pay to access its data. Other devices or applications need to pay the specified amount of fees before they can get the hash value of the data. This mode satisfies the scenarios that users want to share their data for economic benefits. The token mode means that users generate random keys as tokens for their devices. The token owners can send their tokens to other involving parts in a proper manner, e.g., giving the token face to face. Other users can access the data once they get the tokens. We implement the access strategies through smart contracts. In the fee mode, the smart contract checks the balance of user accounts and controls the entire transaction process. Users can also recharge their accounts with smart contracts. The smart contract process is shown in the table Smart contract. In the token mode, the smart contract checks whether the token provided by the user is correct, and then issues the data hash value if it is correct. Otherwise it rejects the request. In the future, we will continue to enrich the access strategies.

We define two types of transactions in the smart contract for access control. One is storage transaction, which is responsible for storing the hash values of IPFS files in the smart contract. The other is query transaction, which is responsible for accessing data generated by other devices.

Storage Transaction: We exploit the Map structure for data storage in the smart contract, the key is the timestamp of the data uploaded, and the value is the hash value returned by IPFS. When storing data in a blockchain, the device provides its own device ID, certificate, and parameters for storage transaction to the set chain. The storage transaction includes the incoming timestamp and the hash value of the data as parameters to store the data in the Map.

Query Transaction: As we mentioned before, we offer two customizable access control strategies, one is fee mode, and the other is token mode. When an application wants to assess the data of a certain device, it needs to provide to the route chain the certificate, the ID of the device they want to access, and the access mode (fee or token). After the route chain verifies the certificate, the route chain queries the smart contract address of the accessed device according to the accessed device ID. Then the route chain calls the smart contract in the corresponding set chain by sending a query transaction to the corresponding address. In the fee method, the user needs to pay a proper amount of fees. After that, it provides a timestamp to get the data. In the token method, a query transaction has to carry the token and a timestamp to get the data. The flow chart of the data query is shown in Fig. 5.

5   Experiments

We implement a prototype of the proposed model. We deployed four blockchains (including one route chain and three set-chains) based on FISCO-BCOS, with two nodes deployed on each chain. We used three types of cloud servers as experimental environments, namely 4G memory and four cores, 2G memory and two cores, 1G memory and one core. Besides, we tested the upload speed of IPFS in an 8G 8cores, 2 MB bandwidth environment. The operating system is Ubuntu 16.04 TLS. In the following experiments, we evaluate the performance of the system by examining the metrics of throughput, latency, and resource consumption such as memory and CPU.

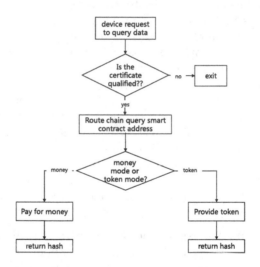

Fig. 5. Flowchart of data query

5.1   Throughput and Latency

In this experiment, we test the throughput and latency by varying the send rates under different configuration environments. The results for the 2G memory and two cores environment are presented in Table 2. As we increase the send rate, the max latency also increases. The average throughput reaches 201 tps. We also test our system in other resource configuration environments. In the 2G memory and one core environment, the average throughput is 115 tps. When we increase the number of CPUs in the system, the performance increases, and the total time decreases. In the 4G memory and four cores environment, the throughput reaches 236 tps.

Table 2. Throughput and latency in the 2G memory and two cores environment

Test	Send rate	Total time	Min latency	Max latency	Throughput
1	100 tps	0.524 s	0.006 s	0.040 s	100 tps
2	300 tps	1.472 s	0.005 s	0.087 s	203 tps
3	500 tps	2.440 s	0.017 s	0.109 s	204 tps
4	1000 tps	5.104 s	0.006 s	0.119 s	196 tps

5.2 Resource Consumption

We also test the memory and CPU usage of the system. Figure 6a to c show the CUP consumption. Figure 6d presents the memory consumption. In the one core environment, when the send rate is 1000 tps, the system CPU consumption reaches 90%, which is close to the system bottleneck. When the send rate is 1000 tps, the CPU consumption in the two core environment reaches 51%, and the CPU consumption in the four core environment is 30%, which is far from the system bottleneck. When the transmission rate is 1000 tps, the 2G memory consumption reaches 70%, the 4G memory consumption is 49%, and the system does not reach its bottleneck.

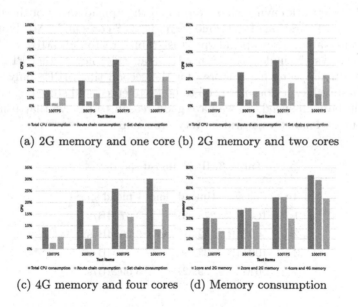

(a) 2G memory and one core (b) 2G memory and two cores

(c) 4G memory and four cores   (d) Memory consumption

Fig. 6. Resource consumption

5.3   Scalability Analysis and Deployment Considerations

As shown in Fig. 6, the set chains consume far more resources than the route chain. When we add more set chains, the growth rate of resources consumed by the route chain is not very large. This is the basis for our model to have good scalability. In the four cores and 4G memory environment, the CPU consumption of the routing chain is only 8.42% when the send rate is 1000 tps, which shows that our model has a lot of room for expansion. This is the basis for the excellent scalability of our model.

The experimental results show that the system performs well in terms of throughput and latency. As the amount of transactions increases, the set chain that handles a specific transaction consumes more resources, while the route chain responsible for transaction distribution consumes fewer resources. We can also continue to add multiple set chains on this basis to improve the scalability of the system. Under the condition of 4 cores and 4G memory, the CPU utilization rate of processing 1000 transactions is 30.25%, and the memory usage rate is 49.8%. We believe that the throughput of the model can be further improved if more resource is available.

5.4   IPFS Storage Efficiency

In the public network environment, we tested the upload speed of the IPFS file system. The configuration of the cloud server is 8G 8 cores and 2 MB bandwidth. As seen from Table 3, the upload speed is stable at around 5MB/s. The more IPFS storage system nodes, the higher the read efficiency of the IPFS storage system. When the same file is stored for the second time, IPFS only needs to judge its hash value. It does not need to be fragmented and stored again, so the storage will be high-speed. So we have good reason to believe that using IPFS for distributed cloud storage will be very promising.

Table 3. IPFS upload speeds

Test	File size	Upload time	Upload speed
1	1G	278.08 s	3.67 MB/s
2	500 MB	152.3 s	3.28 MB/s
3	100 MB	23.6 s	4.24 MB/s
4	50 M	9.82 s	5.09 MB/s

6   Conclusion

In this paper, we take the advance of the FISCO-BCOS blockchain as the underlying blockchain to manage the data in the IoT. Based on FISCO-BCOS, we built a distributed access model in the IoT environment. Our model is flexible to adapt to the requirements of different IoT scenarios, such as smart homes, smart cities, etc. The model sets different processing operations for data with different degrees of privacy and allows fine-grained control access. We use IPFS as a file storage system to further enhance the privacy of data and reduce the storage resource consumption of IoT devices. Finally, we implement a prototype of the model and conduct extensive experiments to evaluate the efficiency and effectiveness. Experimental results show that our model performs well in terms of transaction latency, throughput, and scalability.

Acknowledgment. The research presented in this paper is supported in part by National Natural Science Foundation (No. 61602370, 61672026, 61772411, U1736205), Postdoctoral Foundation (No. 201659M2806, 2018T111066), Fundamental Research Funds for the Central Universities (No. 1191320006), Shaanxi Postdoctoral Foundation, Project JCYJ20170816100819428 supported by SZSTI, CCF-NSFOCUS KunPeng Research Fund (No. CCF-NSFOCUS 2018006), CCF-Tencent WeBank Funding (No. CCF-Webank RAGR20180101) and Huawei HIRP Funding (No. HIRPO2018081501475).

References

1. Kouicem, D.E., Bouabdallah, A., Lakhlef, H.: Internet of Things security: a top-down survey. Comput. Netw. **141**, 199–221 (2018)
2. Vikas, B.O.: Internet of Things (IoT): a survey on privacy issues and security. Int. J. Sci. Res. Sci. Eng. Technol. **1**(3), 168–173 (2015)
3. Makhdoom, I., Abolhasan, M., Ni, W.: Blockchain for IoT: the challenges and away forward. In: Proceedings of the 15th International Joint Conference on e-Business and Telecommunications Volume 2: SECRYPT. INSTICC (2018)
4. Yi, H., Wei, F.: Research on a suitable blockchain for IoT platform. In: Patnaik, S., Jain, V. (eds.) Recent Developments in Intelligent Computing, Communication and Devices. AISC, vol. 752, pp. 1063–1072. Springer, Singapore (2019). https://doi.org/10.1007/978-981-10-8944-2_123
5. Sun, H., Hua, S., Zhou, E., Pi, B., Sun, J., Yamashita, K.: Using ethereum blockchain in Internet of Things: a solution for electric vehicle battery refueling. In: Chen, S., Wang, H., Zhang, L.-J. (eds.) ICBC 2018. LNCS, vol. 10974, pp. 3–17. Springer, Cham (2018). https://doi.org/10.1007/978-3-319-94478-4_1
6. Ali, M.S., Dolui, K., Antonelli, F.: IoT data privacy via blockchains and IPFs. In: Proceedings of the Seventh International Conference on the Internet of Things, p. 14. ACM (2017)
7. Dorri, A., Kanhere, S.S., Jurdak, R., Gauravaram, P.: Blockchain for IoT security and privacy: the case study of a smart home. In: 2017 IEEE International Conference on Pervasive Computing and Communications Workshops (PerCom workshops), pp. 618–623. IEEE (2017)
8. Fisco bcos. https://github.com/FISCO-BCOS/
9. IPFs. https://ipfs.io/
10. Sagirlar, G., Carminati, B., Ferrari, E., Sheehan, J.D., Ragnoli, E.: Hybrid-IoT: hybrid blockchain architecture for Internet of Things-pow sub-blockchains. In: 2018 IEEE International Conference on Internet of Things (iThings), pp. 1007–1016. IEEE (2018)

11. Li, D., Peng, W., Deng, W., Gai, F.: A blockchain-based authentication and security mechanism for IoT. In: 2018 27th International Conference on Computer Communication and Networks (ICCCN), pp. 1–6. IEEE (2018)
12. Alphand, O., Amoretti, M., Claeys, T., et al.: IoTchain: a blockchain security architecture for the Internet of Things. In: 2018 IEEE Wireless Communications and Networking Conference (WCNC), pp. 1–6. IEEE (2018)
13. Iota. https://www.iota.org/
14. Plasma. https://plasma.io/
15. Iotex. https://iotex.io/
16. Panikkar, S., Nair, S., Brody, P., Pureswaran, V.: IBM Adept: an IoT practitioner perspective-Draft Copy for Advance Review (2015)
17. Nakamoto, S., et al.: Bitcoin: a peer-to-peer electronic cash system (2008)
18. Ethereum. https://www.ethereum.org/
19. Hyperledger fabric. https://www.hyperledger.org/
20. Castro, M., Liskov, B., et al.: Practical byzantine fault tolerance. In: OSDI, vol. 99, pp. 173–186 (1999)
21. Ongaro, D., Ousterhout, J.: In search of an understandable consensus algorithm. In: 2014 {USENIX} Annual Technical Conference ({USENIX}{ATC} 14), pp. 305–319 (2014)

Towards Secure Open Banking Architecture: An Evaluation with OWASP

Deina Kellezi[1], Christian Boegelund[1], and Weizhi Meng[1,2(✉)]

[1] Department of Applied Mathematics and Computer Science,
Technical University of Denmark, Lyngby, Denmark
weme@dtu.dk
[2] Department of Computer Science, Guangzhou University, Guangzhou, China

Abstract. The European Union passed the PSD2 regulation in 2015, which gives ownership of bank accounts to the private person owning it. As a result, the term *Open Banking*, allowing third party providers and developers access to bank APIs, has emerged, welcoming a myriad of innovative solutions for the financial sector. However, multiple cyber security issues arise from exposing bank data to third party providers through an API. In this work, we propose an architectural model that ensures clear separation of concern and easy integration with Nordea's Open Banking APIs (sandbox version), and a technological stack, consisting of the micro-framework Flask, the cloud application platform Heroku and persistent data storage layer (using Postgres). We analyze the web application's security threats, and determine whether or not the technological frame provides adequate security protection, by leveraging the OWASP Top 10 list of the Ten Most Critical Web Application Security Risks. Our results can support future developers and industries working on web applications for Open Banking towards security improvement by choosing the right frameworks and considering the most important vulnerabilities, as well as contributing to the documentation and development of Nordea's APIs.

Keywords: Web security · Open Banking API · OWASP · Threat and risk · PSD2 regulation · Secure architecture

1 Introduction

The financial sector is transforming radically. Technological innovations arise due to new regulations, demanding banks to develop APIs that enables the following two features: (1) Access to bank account information; and (2) Triggering of transactions between different accounts.

Nordea, one of the largest banks in the Nordics, released the first version of their Open Banking API in January 2019. As one of few banks, they also released a sandbox version that allows possible third party providers to use the API in

© Springer Nature Switzerland AG 2019
J. K. Liu and X. Huang (Eds.): NSS 2019, LNCS 11928, pp. 185–198, 2019.
https://doi.org/10.1007/978-3-030-36938-5_11

a test environment. Online banking applications are one of the most lucrative targets for attacks. Many have been mitigated through Nordea's own protocols, such as the production APIs requiring a multiple step authentication through nemID when signing up. However, breaking into an application, by gaining access to a user's password, can give intruders direct access to triggering transactions. The application security itself, on a range of different areas such as data storage, injections and communication, should therefore be considered very important to mitigate during development, as this can easily result in breaches.

Up to 3300 developers are currently registered as developers on Nordea Open Banking, and only one product has been realized so far. The adoption of Open Banking exposes data to more actors than ever before, especially new companies and startups, and therefore also an enlargement of the security risks that the financial industry is facing, with existing risks being increased and new risks being introduced [7]. Moreover, the threat becomes higher when leveraging applications on a web platform, with possibly insecure protocols that might not be possible on a desktop or phone application.

Due to the complicated process of obtaining a financial license to use actual production data, in this work, we delimit the problem by using only the sandbox version to develop the solution of triggering transactions based on habits, and to model the possible threats. In particular, we first identify the background of the technology stack needed to support development of a deployed web application, with a persistent data storage layer and a high level of security. We also define the system architecture as well as how it will communicate with the API. We then use the OWASP Top 10 list of the Ten Most Critical Web Application Security Risks methodology to study the possible threats and its risk levels. Our contributions in this paper can be summarized as follows.

- We propose a system architecture of the web application in practice, in collaborating with Nordea Open Banking.
- We identify relevant potential attacks on our system, and analyze the risk by considering the OWASP Top 10 list. We also provide insights on how to mitigate them accordingly.

The remainder of this article is structured as follows: Sect. 2 clarifies the important background information of the Flask framework and Nordea's Open Banking API. In Sect. 3, we present the proposed web application architecture of secure Open Banking. Section 4 evaluates our proposed architecture by leveraging the OWASP Top 10 list. Section 5 introduces the related work, and Sect. 6 summarizes our work with future directions.

2   Background

The micro-framework for web development, Flask (for Python), will be used to develop the application. Flask mitigates many security threats by default, supplemented by a number of renowned third-party extensions and packages from authenticated by the Flask community, and is customize-able to a great extend.

It is also provides out of the box abstraction layers for communicating with the popular object relational database Postgres and the cloud application platform Heroku for deployment.

2.1 The Flask Framework

A Flask application is initialized by creating an application instance through the Flask class with the application package as argument. The web server then passes all received requests from clients, in this case web browsers, to this application instance. The logic is handled using the Web Server Gateway Interface (WSGI) as protocol, constantly awaiting requests. The framework is compliment with the WSGI server standard [8].

The application instance also needs to know which part of the logic needs to run for each URL requested. This is done through a mapping of URLs to the Python functions handling the logic associated with a URL. This association between URL, and the function handling it, is called a route, defined by the @package.route decorator. The return value of the function is the response that the client receives in the form of a template or a redirect.

2.2 Cloud Application Platform

Heroku is one of the first and largest Platform as a Service (PaaS) provider with their Cloud Application Platform. The developer can deploy an application to Heroku using Git to first clone the source code from the developer branch and then push the application to the Heroku Git server. The command automatically triggers the installation, configuration and deployment of the application. The platform uses units of computing, dynos, to measure usage of the service and perform different tasks on the server. It also provides a large number of plugins and addons for databases, email support, and many other services. Heroku supports Postgres [6] databases as an add-on, created and configured through the command line client.

2.3 Database Management

Flask puts no restriction on what database packages can be used and supports a number of different database abstraction layer packages. The web application will run on the Postgres database engine supported by the ORM, SQLAlchemy. This is based on the following evaluation on a number of different criteria:

- **Easy usage:** Using a database abstraction layer (object-relational mappers ORMs) such as SQLAlchemy provides transparent conversion of high-level object-oriented operations into low-level database instructions, compared to writing raw SQL statements [16].
- **Performance:** ORM conversions can result in a small performance penalty, yet the productivity gain far outweighs the performance degradation. The few outlying queries that degrade the performance can be subsidized by raw SQL statements.

- **Portability:** The application platform of choice, Heroku, supports a number of different database engine choices, the most popular and extensible being Postgres and MySQL [2].
- **Integration:** Flask includes several package designed to handle ORMs, such as Flask-SQLAlchemy [17], which includes engine-specific commands to handle connection.

2.4   The Nordea Open Banking APIs

The Nordea APIs provide access to a number of different endpoints in order to facilitate the connection to the accounts of the user. Some API endpoints must be used in order to authenticate the user before changing the data, while other endpoints involve a number of side effects, e.g. changing the balance on the accounts [3]. In the following, we will go through a list of the relevant endpoints, the most crucial being:

- **Access Authorization.** To leverage the functionality of the API, the `Client ID` and `Client Secret` must be obtained. The values can be retrieved by creating a project on the Nordea Open Banking website. The `Client ID` and `Client Secret` are parameters which are configured to the Client, and they are never exposed to the actual application user. Once the account has been approved, we must obtain an access token in order to gain access to the API.
- **Account Information Services.** The API of Account Information includes the possibility to check the contents of the different sample accounts in the sandbox version. We can create new accounts, delete accounts and add funds to said accounts. This can be done by sending a request to the `Accounts` endpoint [3].
- **Payment Initialization Services.** The Payment Initialization API provides functionality to create payments directly in the API, moving funds from one account to another [3].

3   Our Proposed Web Application Architecture

3.1   The Architecture

In order to define the architecture, we present a model based on the Model-View-Controller architecture (MVC) specifically adjusted for web development as proposed by Dragos-Paul Pop and Adam Altar [11]. They found that developers often combine HTML code with server side programming languages during web development to create dynamic web pages and applications, and this leads to highly entangled and unmaintainable code. With an MVC pattern, it is possible to prevent cluttering by separating the three overall parts of a web application. The model also proposes how to handle the API integration through an abstraction layer and include it in the MVC.

- **Model:** A persistent data storage layer through a data centre or database.
- **Controller:** The HTTP requests triggered by user actions and general routing of different sub-pages.
- **View:** The HTML code and mark-up languages in the templates rendered to the user as a result of a request.

These three main components will be built through a modular approach, using blueprints as recommended by Flask.

Figure 1 presents the proposed diagram for the adjusted MVC, further adjusted to include supplementary components for interacting with the API. This model allows us to further propose how this fits into the Flask Framework and an effective abstraction layer integration with the API.

The Model. Presented as blue in the figure and shows the modelling of the data objects and relationships. This is the direct representation of the schema in the database. Whenever the SQLAlchemy methods, either querying, updating or deleting data, are called on the defined data objects in the model, the database is updated accordingly. This also provides simpler commands for establishing connections to Postgres through the URL of the database as handled by the controller.

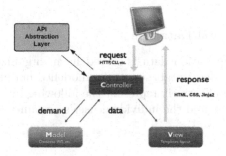

Fig. 1. MVC architecture for web application. (Color figure online)

The Controller. Presented as green in the figure and shows the controller separated into three blueprints:

- `auth_controller`: Rendering the pages responsible for signing up and authenticating users logging in.
- `main_controller`: Rendering the pages of the specific user session, containing URLs for creating habits, checking off habits that are completed, overview over habits, overview over accounts and settings. This is restricted to authenticated users only.
- `admin_controller`: Rendering the pages of the administration page included for demonstration purposes that allows to test the different API functionality. This is restricted to users with admin rights only.

The blueprints provide a clearer separation of the different states in the application. This separation could done through application dispatching, ie. creating multiple application objects, however, this would require separate configurations for each of the objects and management at the server level (WSGI). Blueprints instead support the possibility of separation at the Flask application level, ensuring the same application and object configurations across all controllers, and most importantly the same API access. This means that a Blueprint object works similarly to a Flask application object, but is not an actual application as it is a blueprint of how to construct or extend the application at runtime [1]. When binding a function with the decorator @auth.route, the blueprint will record the intention of registering the associated function from the auth package blueprint on the application object. It will also prefix the name of the blueprint (given to the Blueprint constructor) auth to the function.

The View. Presented as orange in the figure and shows the inheritance hierarchy of the templates that primarily consist of HTML and CSS, built upon a number of frameworks. The inheritance is supported by the Jinja2 Template Engine, offered by Flask, enabling all templates to inherit from a base design, as well as register onto their specific controller through the aforementioned blueprints. This also allows dynamic rendering of values provided as argument to the templates when rendered [1].

3.2   Object Relational Database

Ensuring that the application data is stored in an organized and secure way requires a database model. Databases can be modelled in different ways, and we need a model that can effectively represent the following information: Users, the individual user's habits, and the individual user's accounts. This constitutes an object relational database [18].

API Abstraction Layer. We present two supplementary API and Parser classes to the MVC model. These classes work as abstraction layers for easing communicating with the APIs and filtering out unnecessary data for the application. The purpose is to avoid interacting directly with the API and therefore avoiding unnecessary complexities and errors by encapsulating complex requests in methods and handling responses accordingly.

The user's bank and account information can be retrieved directly through the Account Information Services API as a JSON response. The calls to retrieve this response is separated into several methods in the Parser class. The response is first separated into a list object as a field in the Parser, and then indexed to extract the needed information. It also consists of different conversion methods to convert different account representations, as well as methods to hash and check account numbers. The API class contains the methods handling the Payment Initialization Service API, hence triggering transactions between the bank accounts, called whenever habits have been checked off. Through the fields of the API class we were also able to keep the access token saved across web pages without having to re-instantiate it. Both classes are created as instances for the controller.

Platform Architecture. In order for the application to be deployed in production mode, we propose a platform hosted on the cloud application platform, Heroku [2], with the database connected through Heroku's Postgres add-on.

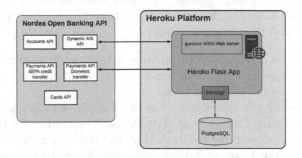

Fig. 2. Platform architecture.

Figure 2 shows the architecture of the platform the application is deployed onto. The Flask application itself is as described run through a WSGI server during development. The application will therefore need to be configured to run through HTTP/HTTPS Server instead to run outside of local host. We propose Gunicorn, a WSGI HTTP server, as recommended by Heroku [5]. The application will send the ORM statements to the database through the database driver psycopg2, the most popular for the Python language.

4 Evaluation of Attacks Against Application Integrating with Open Banking API

Methodology. The methodology for applying the OWASP Top 10 list, to the described application and its architecture, entails systematically going through the list from most critical to least critical threat. The OWASP methodology provides a threat modelling method for categorizing the threats in six different areas, that might result in the weighing of threats to change:

Four of these areas are pre-determined in the model and have been the basis of the top 10 ranking in the first place. The categorizations for each element in the list can be viewed from the OWASP documentation [13,14]. However, observing the two areas, Threat Agents and Business Impact, these areas impact how critical a given threat is. If the Threat Agent and/or Business Impact has a low threat level, then the threat can quickly become irrelevant. OWASP provides a comprehensive model for calculating the risk factor of Threat Agents and Business Impacts [15].

However, the limitations imposed by using the sandbox version means that we have a non-existing user base, lacking business context and problems that arise as a result of using the sandbox that prevent testing some of the factors. It can therefore be difficult to reach feasible estimates of both Threat Agents and Business Impact. The Threat Agents will therefore simply be assumed high across all areas, since the financial industry is generally a critical target due to the possibility of financial rewards. The Business Impact estimation needs to include factors like financial damage, reputation damage, non-compliance and privacy violation, data that requires an actual business context. We therefore conduct simple estimates of Business Impact, based on factors that are critical for the end user and their bank accounts:

1. **Low:** Security is compromised in areas not containing sensitive data, areas that do not trigger unintentional transactions, or attempt attacks that does not affect the application in any way.
2. **Medium:** Security is compromised such that the attacker gains access to sensitive data in the form of bank data or habits stored in the database.
3. **High:** Security is compromised such that the attacker gains access to functionality using the Payment Initialization Service and can trigger unintentional transactions, leading to either small, substantial or large financial consequences.

Each threat area in the top 10 list will be addressed, with an emphasis on the areas that are estimated as highly for the Business Impact.

4.1   Applying OWASP to the Application Ensuring Secure Integration with the API

Injection and XSS, Threat Agents: 3, Business Impact: 1. We propose a critical approach to user input to prevent injection. A number of tests should be made:

– Input should be filtered
– Output should be escaped by filtering input

All input fields from the user should be filtered from code-like plain text or injecting raw SQL statements into the database. Submitting unfiltered input into the database can result in a large exposure to SQL injections. This can be detrimental to the privacy of the data; potentially allowing an attacker access to view the bank information of the user. No further measures need to be proactively taken to prevent injections. ORM SQLAlchemy automatically filters the input of the user, and the Flask framework automatically escapes output when inserting values into templates, mitigating threats such as JavaScript injection or similar.

Broken Authentication - Threat Agents: 3, Business Impact: 3. We propose a number of actions to mitigate broken authentication, as it is one of the most critical threats against the application and the API:

- A set of criteria for the user credentials at sign up
- Preventing that passwords are saved in plain text
- Using multi-factor authentication during either sign-up and/or login
- A user should only be allowed to enter URLs that they are authenticated to enter

The user is required to provide a user name and password at sign-up. Most application nowadays provide the possibility of signing up through email. This is so the company is able to authenticate and send information through a mail integration. The user name should therefore be a valid email, so we are able to perform multi-factor authentication by sending a confirmation email to the address. The Flask-Mail extension provides a simple interface to set up SMTP with your Flask application and to send messages directly from the controller. We also require the to be at least 10 characters long, include both lowercase and uppercase letters, numbers as well as a special sign. Most password breaches happen as a result of weak password criteria, and setting up a number of requirements for the password is therefore an easy and very effective ways of preventing broken authentication.

The authentication can also be broken by gaining access to the database and extracting the plain text version of the password. Therefore only the hashed version of the password is stored in the database. The bcrypt hashing algorithm, combined with salting, is one of the most effective ways to permit brute force attacks. A salt with a length of 12 characters will result in millions of different combinations, making it almost impossible for an attacker to decode. It does have a larger penalty on the time complexity compared to other hashing algorithms. However, we are willing to make this trade-off.

The Flask-Login extension provides user session management for Flask and allows us to restrict views through a simple decorator to only authenticated users. The Flask framework therefore provides an easy way of restricting specific URLs.

Sensitive Data Exposure - Threat Agents: 3, Business Impact: 3. We propose only storing the most important data in the database for the application to run. The remaining data will be exposed during run time from the API response, retrieved by the API abstraction layer. The information stored in the database includes a hashed version of the account number, and the name of the account. The rest of the information of that specific account can be retrieved at run time by checking the hashed account number against all the user's accounts in the API. The idea is to keep as much information as possible from an attacker that gains access to the database without compromising functionality.

XML External Entities - Threat Agents: 3, Business Impact: 1. The application accepts no uploads or XML and therefore, an attack of this nature has no Business Impact. It is therefore not relevant to address.

Broken Access Control - Threat Agents: 3, Business Impact: 3. We propose ensuring that the functionality of the application is only exposed to the specific user logged in. The user is able to check off a number of habits and actions, resulting in automatically transfer funds. It is therefore necessary to ensure that it is not possible to gain access to this POST request from other sources. For instance, including the current user ID in the POST request to the URL, would enable an attacker access from the outside, since the request could easily be faked. Thus, the only to ensure that the it is in fact the logged in user performing the check off, is to check the user owning the habit up against the user that is currently in the session. If an attacker is not allowed to check off a habit, but attempts to do it anyway, they are redirected to an error page. We also log the attempt in our logging system. This allows us to have an overview of potential security issues and discover possible threat agents.

In order to further strengthen the application, we have implemented protection against Cross-Site Request Forgery (CSRF) with the Flask package `CSRFProtect`. This is done by adding a hidden field to all forms. This results in the user having to fill out the form on the website in order to have their request accepted, thus creating a defence against a myriad of automatic scripts. As an additional security measure, CSRF also requires a secret key to sign the token.

Security Misconfiguration - Threat Agents: 3, Business Impact: 2. Misconfiguration can have a number of different sources that can bring distrust to the application, some of which include:

- Revealed stack traces or overly informative error messages
- Improperly configured permissions
- Incorrect values for security settings across servers, frameworks, libraries or databases

We propose using large parts of the security packages and settings offered by the different parts of the technical stack. Flask provides a number of ways to handle custom error messages to the user to prevent showing stack traces or overly informative error messages to users. We propose a combination of the following. Message Flashing, that can be included in the templates, making it possible to record a custom message at the end of a request and access it in the next request and only next request. The Python logging package also provides the possibility of printing custom messages and stack traces to the console, limiting the information from showing specific request methods and URLs. However, in 2014, Flask eliminated error and stack traces from application running in production mode[1], so it is no longer necessary to create custom error messages.

For mitigating improperly configured permissions, the cloud service provider of choice does not allow open default sharing permissions to the Internet or other users. This ensures that sensitive data stored within cloud storage is not accessed wrongfully. Heroku PaaS is a large service provider and regular audits are performed to ensure that permission breaches does not occur. Lastly, the included

---

[1] https://github.com/pallets/flask/issues/1082.

Flask packages provide a number of security settings. One example is the Flask LoginManager package, from which it is possible to choose from different levels (none, basic or strong) of security against user session tampering. The latter ensures that Flask-Login keeps track of the client IP address as well as browser agent during browsing. If a change is detected, the user will automatically be logged out.

Components with Known Vulnerabilities - Threat Agents: 3, Business Impact: 3. The components we use have no major known vulnerabilities. The Flask framework is one of the most popular Python micro-frameworks and therefore has a number of requirements to ensure adequate security. Moreover, the wide community of developers and contributors ensure that measures are taken to maintain this security level by frequently updating the most popular and renowned packages. The Postgres database [6] is also addressed at several levels:

- Database file protection. All files stored within the database are protected from reading by any account other than the Postgres superuser account.
- Connections from a client to the database server are, by default, allowed only via a local Unix socket, not via TCP/IP sockets.
- Client connections can be restricted by IP address.
- Client connections may be authenticated vi other external packages.
- Each user in Postgres is assigned a username and password.
- Users may be assigned to groups, and table access may be restricted, for instance through admin privileges.

Furthermore, as mentioned previously, there are currently problems with the deployment of the application to Heroku PaaS. Heroku is not known to have any known vulnerabilities itself. However, the server routinely crashes in production mode with no useful error messages when enforcing HTTPS on Heroku. We suspect that this is caused by problems with the TLS Layer, with error messages that stem from Nordea's Open Banking API. Hence we suspect that the errors stem from how the API handles the TLS Layer in the sandbox version. This imposes a high risk for the packages sent between the application and the API to be intersected. However, no sufficient documentation explains how to mitigate this issue in Nordea's documentation.

Insufficient Logging and Monitoring - Threat Agents: 3, Business Impact: 2. As mentioned previously, whenever a user attempts to check off the habit, or perform any other actions in the application, of another user, it is added to the log. The log is handled through a logging package offered by the Python library. We propose also including logging for IP addresses and alarm whenever a user is logged in from a different country.

Discussion. Applying the OWASP Top 10 Threats and Risk Modelling Framework to the application shows that it can mitigate a large part of the most critical threats to the application. The threats posed by Broken Authentication, the most critical in terms of Business Impact, is now largely protected from breaches that could result in the user losing account funds. The same applies for Sensitive Data Exposure and Broken Access Control that were also categorized as very critical threats. However, the OWASP framework also exploited that the components with known vulnerabilities posed a high threat to the application. Specifically Nordea's APIs. The problems with the TLS Layer in Nordea's Open Banking API force us to use HTTP in production mode to avoid the routinely crashes occurring with HTTPS. This means that the packages sent from the API to the application are encrypted. Packages that can contain access tokens, client IDs or secret keys that might give access to Nordea's infrastructure. This vulnerability is impossible to handle without more documentation of the API, since it does not stem from the application itself.

5   Related Work

The previous work carried out on web applications integrating with Open Banking APIs is limited, and practically non-existing using the technical stack described in this paper. This is due to two reasons such as:

- The novelty of most of the interfaces, including Nordea's APIs
- The requirements of developers need to be approved by national financial authorities for using the APIs in production

These factors has delimited the pool of possible researchers to only a few authorized third-parties or those using the sandbox version. No official paper has dived into integrating with Nordea's Open Banking API as a third party provider, nor proposed a model for a architectural model or stack that secures bank account information and transaction functionality in a web application. Nevertheless, a lot of work has generally been done in the field of web application security overall, including several models to identify, analyze and mitigate possible security breaches under a cyber attack. One example is a study on in the field of web application security vulnerabilities detection, that conducts a security analysis and threat modelling based on the OWASP Top 10 list and Threat Modelling [12].

The sandbox version of the Nordea Open Banking API was officially released during the beginning of the project in January 2019. During the attempt to generate the `access_token` for establishing connection before beginning the development of the application, the error codes were limited to generic server errors. The limited sample codes and lacking documentation on possible error codes made it difficult to correct. In order to find a solution, we conducted a simulation with the API simulation tool named Postman [4]. The connection was successful, the code in Postman worked and did not return any error codes. This led to the conclusion that something was wrong with our implementation of the

API calls. To understand the difference between the HTTP-packages, the difference between them were negligible. We contacted the senior software architect of Nordea Open Banking. The support team tried to assist us in making the API work and assess the possible errors made through logging of their own servers. Ultimately, they did not succeed in resolving the issue. The origin of the error was later found: The redirect URI, a crucial part of the OAuth^2 2.0-process was set to an incorrect value. We decided to contribute to the community of developers using the Nordea Open Banking API by creating a pull request[3]. At the moment, the samle code only works with version 2 of the API, while the API has been updated to version 3 since then. to contribute to the wider community of developers using the Nordea Open Banking API.

6   Conclusion and Future Work

In this work, we systematically proposed and described a technical stack and architectural model to ensure a web application that could integrate easily with Nordea's Open Banking API in a secure manner. This was used as input to the OWASP Top 10 Threats and threat modelling methodology to identify the most prevalent threats to the application data and, indirectly, the functionality of the APIs. The OWASP recommendations were used to prevent these attacks by taking adequate security methods to the most critical areas. The results showed that many of these security measures were either handled automatically by the components offered by the technical stack, or were easily preventable through included packages of the Flask Framework. However, it also shows that the application faces a high risk due to the compromising handling of the TLS Layer in the API, causing the production server to routinely crash when using HTTPS These risks may propagate upwards in the architecture, resulting in high risks for the user's account data and funds. Since the server records show that the errors stem from the API itself, it is most likely not due to the choices of any of the cloud application platform, packages, libraries, database or frameworks. The results also show that creating an API Abstraction Layer eases communication with the API during development, and that it can be implemented as a modification to the MVC for web applications.

For future work, we intend to contact the support team of the API to gain more information on the handling of the TLS Layer, information that is currently lacking in the sandbox documentation. This may lead to one more contribution to the documentation, other than the pull-request made to the Open Banking Team code samples [9,10]. We could also consider applying other popular threat models to the application in attempt to find other vulnerabilities not detected by the use of OWASP.

Acknowledgments. Weizhi Meng was partially supported by H2020-SU-ICT-03-2018: CyberSec4Europe with No. 830929, and National Natural Science Foundation of China (No. 61802077).

---

[2] OAuth is one of the leading protocols within authentication.

[3] The PR can be seen here: https://github.com/NordeaOB/examples/pull/7.

References

1. Grinberg, M.: Flask Web Development: Developing Web Applications with Python. OReilly, California (2014)
2. Heroku Dev Center (2018). https://devcenter.heroku.com/categories/reference
3. Nordea Open Banking Team (2019). https://developer.nordeaopenbanking.com/app/documentation?api=Accounts%20API
4. Post Learning Center. https://learning.getpostman.com/docs/postman/api_documentation/intro_to_api_documentation/s
5. Heroku Dev Center (2019). https://devcenter.heroku.com/articles/heroku-postgresql. Documentation
6. The PostgreSQL Global Development Group (1996–2019). https://www.postgresql.org/docs/12/index.html
7. Kiljan, S., Simoens, K., Cock, D.D., van Eekelen, M.C.J.D., Vranken, H.P.E.: A survey of authentication and communications security in online banking. ACM Comput. Surv. **49**(4), 61:1–61:35 (2017)
8. Pallets Team: Flask's Documentation. http://flask.pocoo.org/docs/1.0/
9. Rogaway, P., Shrimpton, T.: Cryptographic hash-function basics: definitions, implications, and separations for preimage resistance, second-preimage resistance, and collision resistance. In: Roy, B., Meier, W. (eds.) FSE 2004. LNCS, vol. 3017, pp. 371–388. Springer, Heidelberg (2004). https://doi.org/10.1007/978-3-540-25937-4_24
10. Niels, P., David, M.: A future adaptable password scheme. The OpenBSD Project (1999)
11. Dragos-Paul, P., Adam, A.: Designing an MVC model for rapid web application development. Procedia Eng. **69**, 1172–1179 (2014)
12. Sajjad, R., Mamoona, H., Bushra, H., Ansar A., Muhammad, A., Kamil, I.: Web application security vulnerabilities detection approaches: a systematic mapping study. IEEE (2015)
13. The OWASP Foundation: OWASP top 10 - the ten most critical web application security risks. Release notes (2013)
14. The OWASP Foundation: Top 10 List (2017). https://www.owasp.org/index.php/Category:OWASP_Top_Ten_2017_Project. Documentation
15. The OWASP Foundation: Risk Rating Methodology (2017). https://www.owasp.org/index.php/OWASP_Risk_Rating_Methodology. Documentation
16. The SQLAlchemy authors and contributors (2019). https://docs.sqlalchemy.org/en/13/. Documentation
17. Pallets Team (2010). https://flask-sqlalchemy.palletsprojects.com/en/2.x/. Flask-SQLAlchemy Documentation
18. IBM Informix (2011). https://www.ibm.com/support/knowledgecenter/hu/SSGU8G_11.50.0/com.ibm.gsg.doc/ids_gsg_416.htm

OutGene: Detecting Undefined Network Attacks with Time Stretching and Genetic Zooms

Luís Dias[1,2]($\boxtimes$) (iD), Hélder Reia[1,2], Rui Neves[3] (iD), and Miguel Correia[2] (iD)

[1] CINAMIL, Academia Militar, Instituto Universitário Militar, Lisbon, Portugal
{dias.lfxcm,reia.hf}@mail.exercito.pt
[2] INESC-ID, Instituto Superior Técnico, Lisbon, Portugal
[3] Instituto de Telecomunicações, Instituto Superior Técnico, Lisbon, Portugal
{rui.neves,miguel.p.correia}@tecnico.ulisboa.pt

Abstract. The paper presents OutGene, an approach for streaming detection of malicious activity without previous knowledge about attacks or training data. OutGene uses clustering to aggregate hosts with similar behavior. To assist human analysts on pinpointing malicious clusters, we introduce the notion of *genetic zoom*, that consists in using a genetic algorithm to identify the features that are more relevant to characterize a cluster. Adversaries are often able to circumvent attack detection based on machine learning by executing attacks at a low pace, below the thresholds used. To detect such stealth attacks, we introduce the notion of *time stretching*. The idea is to analyze the stream of events in different time-windows, so that we can identify attacks independently of the pace they are performed. We evaluated OutGene experimentally with a recent publicly available dataset and with a dataset obtained at a large military infrastructure. Both genetic zoom and time stretching have been found to be useful, and high values of recall and accuracy were obtained.

Keywords: Time stretching · Genetic zooms · Intrusion detection · Security analytics

1 Introduction

The exponential growth of data and of its value makes data assets mission-critical to many organizations [38]. The increasing occurrence of cybercrime and, generically, of cyberattacks [8], raises the need for better methods of protecting computers and the information they store, process and transmit. This objective

This research was supported by national funds through Fundação para a Ciência e Tecnologia (FCT) with reference UID/CEC/50021/2019 (INESC-ID), by the Portuguese Army (CINAMIL), and by the European Commission under grant agreement number 830892 (SPARTA). We warmly thank prof. Victor Lobo for feedback on a previous version of this work.

J. K. Liu and X. Huang (Eds.): NSS 2019, LNCS 11928, pp. 199–220, 2019.
https://doi.org/10.1007/978-3-030-36938-5_12

is challenging as, for example, the average time a company takes to detect certain attacks, Advanced Persistent Threats (APTs), is about 100 days [32].

Intrusion Detection Systems (IDS) have been proposed as an attempt to deal with this increasing number of attacks, that often manage to elude existing protections [11,12]. Most IDSs are either *signature-based* (search for known attack patterns) or *anomaly-based* (detect deviations from baseline behavior), but both approaches have limitations: knowledge about attack patterns tends to be incomplete, as new attacks and attack variants are constantly appearing [43]; and anomaly-based detection requires clean training data, i.e., data of normal operation without attacks, to train the IDS, which is hard to obtain in systems in production. Moreover, anomaly-based IDSs have to discover attacks hidden among what may be a huge amount of data representing normal behavior [58]. IDSs can also be classified as network-based (that inspect communication data) or host-based (that inspect host activity). Finally, IDSs can be classified as online (detect intrusions in runtime) and offline (detect intrusions later, when decided by someone). This paper is about *online network-based intrusion detection*.

Machine learning (ML) approaches for intrusion detection have been receiving much attention [4,5,13,20,29,58]. Handling high volumes of security-relevant data is unfeasible for humans, so ML techniques can come to assistance. An example approach are the above-mentioned anomaly-based IDSs, with their drawbacks [4]. A more recent ML approach to intrusion detection uses *clustering and/or outlier detection* to identify entities – typically users or hosts – that have an anomalous behavior [7,18,40,55,56]. To be precise, the approach does not detect intrusions, but anomalies that have to be further diagnosed as intrusions or some other sort of anomaly. This approach is interesting because it does not require knowledge about attacks (signatures/rules) or clean training data. However, it brings in two difficulties. First, a human analyst has to inspect the outliers or suspect clusters, which is a non-trivial task, although it is also necessary in anomaly-based detection and even signature-based detection (although in this latter case the attack is already labelled with a class). Second, attackers can often circumvent ML-based attack detection by executing attacks – e.g., port scanning – at a low pace, below the thresholds used.

We present OUTGENE, a network intrusion detection approach that detects attacks that are undefined (no signatures) without clean training data. This contrasts to both signature-based detection, that needs attack signatures, and anomaly-based detection, that needs clean training data. OUTGENE does clustering of hosts with similar behavior and detects ouliers, leveraging the assumption that hosts that are doing attacks behave in a way that is distinguishable from the others. OUTGENE does online, *streaming*, attack detection, i.e., it does detection continuously, not by processing bulk data sporadically.

OUTGENE solves the two difficulties mentioned above. First, to assist human analysts on pinpointing malicious clusters, we introduce the notion of *genetic zoom*. The idea is to use a genetic algorithm to identify the best subset of features that provides the same clustering output as the full set of features. For example, genetic zoom might say that out of 26 features, only a certain subset of 8 features is relevant to obtain the clusters. Examples of such features might be the number of ports used by an entity and the number of ports contacted by an entity. It is much easier to understand what was the malicious behavior by inspecting the values of 8 features instead of 26.

Second, to detect *stealth attacks* that try to pass below the radar of the detection scheme, we introduce the notion of *time stretching*. The idea is to analyse the stream of events in different time-windows, at different time scales, so that we can detect attacks independently of the pace at which they are executed (e.g., a slow network scan). For example, an attack may be detected if we analyse traffic at the scale of one hour, but not at the scale of one day or one minute.

We implemented the proposed approach as a system that we also designate OutGene. This system is based on a set of large-scale data processing and storage packages. Incoming data, e.g., network flow data, is consumed by Apache Kafka [28], that stores it using the Hadoop Distributed File System (HDFS) [42]. The first is used to decouple processing from data producers and the former as long-term storage and checkpoint location (for the aggregation process). Apache Spark [34] consumes data incoming from Kafka and does most of the analysis.

Much research in machine learning-based intrusion detection uses synthetic datasets [4]. Instead, we aim that OutGene works in real settings so we evaluated it using real network data from two real-world networks: one dataset that is publicly available [50] and another from an administrative network of a large military infrastructure that we collected for this work. Moreover, we emulated stealth attacks, which may pass unnoticed by traditional detection systems, to evaluate our approach on such attacks. The obtained results in both datasets reveal that there are significant improvements by analyzing different time-windows as well as by having outlier explanation provided by *genetic zoom*. The use of real network data was challenging due to data noise, lack of full context, and lack of labels. Nevertheless, high values of recall and accuracy were obtained with the military network dataset (near 1).

The main contributions are: (1) a practical approach for online detection of network attacks that uses clustering and outlier detection to avoid the need of knowledge about attacks and clean training data, implemented and tested with real-data datasets; (2) the genetic zoom mechanism, which uses a genetic algorithm to help the human analyst; (3) the time stretching mechanism, that analyses traffic in different time frames, in order to detect stealth attacks.

2   OutGene Approach Overview

OutGene does not rely on knowledge about what is bad behavior as in signature-based methods, or what is good behavior, as in typical anomaly detection. Hence, our approach does not use supervised learning that needs training data, nor rules or thresholds, which can be easily circumvented by attackers or are sensitive to new systems deployed in a network.

Inspired by [7,18,56], OutGene uses unsupervised learning, more specifically, a clustering algorithm to group entities with similar behaviors. The term *entity* designates something that is identified by an IP address: typically a host but there are other possibilities, like a network behind NAT [45]. Furthermore, OUTGENE uses feature selection jointly with clustering to obtain a better description (i.e., the most relevant features) of anomalous groups (i.e., of small clusters). The main goal of the developed work is to extract useful information to detect and characterize cyberattacks from *streaming* data, without information of previous patterns. Since most of the used features are count-based (e.g., count of bytes sent), the approach does time-based aggregation of the events in real time through incremental aggregation [24].

OUTGENE aims to *detect attacks* and *select the relevant features* to: classify them by performing clustering to extract information from network flows (that we will designate *netflow* as it is typically Netflow data [10], although it may also be extracted from raw packet data) using *generic features* that are considered relevant in the scope of security; provide improved insight on outliers using *genetic zoom*, a genetic algorithm to search for the *specific features* that characterizes outliers (i.e., small clusters) in our set of data; do detection using *time stretching*, i.e., repeating the previous steps on different time-windows. By doing this, it is possible to get more knowledge about the data and apply this knowledge to classify and label specific behaviors.

The approach is divided in two phases. The *pre-runtime phase* consists in exploratory data analysis to prepare the *runtime phase*, when OUTGENE continuously processes data to detect attacks. They are explained in detail next.

Pre-runtime Phase. The pre-runtime phase is executed before the system is deployed to define generic feature extraction and normalization (see Fig. 1). This phase consists in exploratory data analysis techniques and can be detailed in three steps: the definition of the normalization of the data, to transform the data so that we know what parameters to normalize to make all data consistent; the feature selection, to know which features are going to be extracted to characterize the available data, as well as the time periods (to aggregate time-windows) to extract the features; the definition of how the features are extracted, given the kind of data considered.

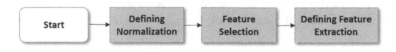

Fig. 1. Flowchart of the pre-runtime phase

Runtime Phase. The runtime phase corresponds to detection in normal operation (see Fig. 2). The stream of data that is processed contains the traffic flows that are collected (e.g., by routers) and passed to OUTGENE. The processing starts by generic feature extraction and normalization. The extracted features are given

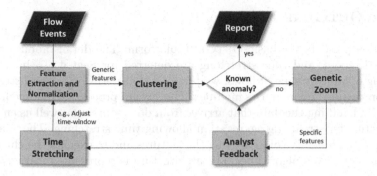

Fig. 2. Flowchart of the runtime phase (notice the *genetic zoom* and *time stretching* processes, respectively on the right and bottom-left)

as input to the clustering algorithm which groups entities (typically hosts) with similar behavior.

If clustering produces outliers, there are two options. If this kind of outlier/anomaly has been observed before, which is the typical case in cruise speed, it can simply be reported. Otherwise, manual intervention by a human analyst is required, which is inevitable when the possibility of unknown attacks is considered.

The purpose of *genetic zoom* is to assist the human analyst on diagnosing malicious clusters (among the outliers only). The idea is to use a *genetic algorithm* [17] to identify the features that are more relevant to characterize a cluster. The genetic algorithm is used to understand which features are important to identify an entity as belonging to that cluster. Moreover, it helps understanding which features better characterize the data in general, discarding features that are less important, i.e., that do not change the clusters that are obtained, at a certain iteration of the loop. The pre-runtime phase involves defining features that are potentially useful to pinpoint outliers. However, not all of these features may be relevant at each iteration of the loop in runtime. Hence, choosing a subset of the original features with the genetic algorithm will lead to better knowledge of the anomaly.

The second mechanism we introduce is *time stretching*. Figure 2 shows a single loop in which features are passed to clustering, then clusters are diagnosed automatically or, in some cases, manually. However, in reality there are several loops executed in parallel processing flows corresponding to several time-windows (e.g., 10 min, 30 min, 1 h, 4 h, 8 h, 1 day), leveraging incremental aggregation. Hence, OutGene is not limited to bulk processing of large data corresponding to long periods. This processing in different time-windows is what we designate time stretching and what allows detecting both conspicuous attacks quickly (e.g., DDoS) and stealth attacks (e.g., slow port scan).

3   The OutGene Platform

This section presents the basic OutGene platform. The details about cluster-ing, genetic zoom, and time stretching are deferred for Sect. 4. To handle the processing of large volume of flows, we propose a platform based on distributed stream processing and analytics modules. The stream processing module has the objective of handling the data that arrives from data sources, as well as enabling checkpointing for streaming aggregation allowing time stretching. The analytics module has the objective of extracting the features and to execute the clustering and the genetic zoom algorithms. The architecture is represented in Fig. 3).

Stream Processing Module. The stream processing module decouples data streams from the analytics module. To do so, the Apache Kafka [28] framework and HDFS [42] were used. Apache Kafka is a distributed streaming platform, with capabilities to publish and subscribe streams of records, similar to a mes-sage queue or enterprise messaging system; To accomplish this, Kafka stores streams of records in categories called topics in a fault-tolerant way. A topic is a category or feed name to which records are published. Topics in Kafka are always multi-subscriber, that is, a topic can have zero, one, or more consumers that sub-scribe to the data written to it. Kafka topics are divided in partitions. Partitions allow us to parallelize a topic by splitting the data in that particular topic across the multiple servers. In order to guarantee the correct operation of the brokers (servers), a broker manager is needed. This service can be implemented with the Apache Zookeeper coordination service [23]. For the experiments we created a Kafka topic with replication factor 3 (i.e., all data is replicated in 3 nodes), where the data streams corresponding to netflow data were inserted. Regarding HDFS, its main role is to store checkpoints (for the aggregation process) as explained later, although it might also be used for long-term storage.

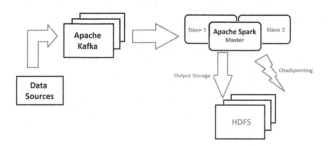

Fig. 3. System architecture

Analytics Module. The analytics module is where all the computation is made. To implement it, the Apache Spark framework was used as a Kafka consumer. Apache Spark is a distributed and highly scalable in-memory data analytics system with four main submodules: Spark SQL, Spark Streaming, MLlib and GraphX. For OutGene, only the Spark Streaming and MLlib modules are necessary. The Spark MLlib module is able to run advanced data analysis algorithms in a scalable way. In its core, Apache Spark provides the runtime for in-memory massive parallel data processing, and different parallel machine learning libraries are running on top of it. Apache Spark distributes tasks over multiple computer nodes (i.e., worker nodes), although even on a single node it can spill data to disk avoiding the main memory bottleneck [27]. Regarding Spark Streaming, it is able to process continuous streams of data in real time, with the functionality of checkpointing and windowing. Later we explain how it is used. Every Spark application consists on a driver program that runs the main function and executes various parallel operations in a cluster. The main abstraction Spark provides is the *resilient distributed dataset* (RDD), which is a collection of elements—similar to an array—partitioned across the nodes of the cluster that can be operated on in parallel. It is possible to ask Spark to persist RDDs in memory, allowing them to be reused efficiently across parallel operations.

4   OutGene Approach Instantiation

The OutGene approach can be instantiated in different ways. An instantiation entails four aspects: feature extraction, clustering, feature selection with a genetic algorithm (i.e., genetic zoom), and online mode processing of different time-windows (i.e., time stretching). We present each of the aspects next.

4.1   Feature Extraction

Selecting the features to use is a crucial step, because they provide the symptoms that allow distinguishing normal traffic from attacks. The Spark transformations and operations needed to perform feature extraction can be divided in three steps: (1) a *Map* transformation, to group pairs of values; (2) the *CountByValue* operation for features that count the frequency of an occurrence (e.g., number of connections made); (3) the *reduceByKey* operation, to remove the repeated values by summing the values for each entity (e.g., a computer, IP, user).

The selected features were extracted from network flows. The choice of such data to implement OutGene was based on good results in related work [21,40, 44]. A set of 26 features was used, split in two groups: the first half are features about the source computer (i.e., the source IP address) and the other half are about the destination computer (destination IP address). The first half features are shown in Table 1. The other 13 features are similar (e.g., DConn connections received, and DPSum packets received). In the table, it is clear that only four application-layer protocols are considered explicitly in the features: HTTP, IRC, SMTP, and SSH. We selected these protocols based on the literature, instead of selecting a larger range (not trivial as there are around 1000 well-known ports plus 10000 reserved ports) or selecting the ports used in the datasets (which would be a form of bias). We decided to stick to what the literature says is meaningful and observe the results, which were quite positive (Sect. 5.3). Features are extracted for a given time-window (e.g., 10 min, 1 h, 1 day).

Table 1. Features extracted for a source IP

Feature	Description
SConn	Number of connections made
SPus	Number of ports used in source
SPcon	Number of ports contacted by a source
SPsum	Sum of packets sent by a source
SP80t	Sum of packets sent by a source to port 80 (HTTP)
SP80f	Sum of packets sent by a source from port 80 (HTTP)
SP194t	Sum of packets sent by a source to port 194 (IRC)
SP194f	Sum of packets sent by a source from port 194 (IRC)
SP25t	Sum of packets sent by a source to port 25 (SMTP)
SP25f	Sum of packets sent by a source from port 25 (SMTP)
SP22t	Sum of packets sent by a source to port 22 (SSH)
SP22f	Sum of packets sent by a source from port 22 (SSH)
SBytes	Sum of bytes sent by a source

4.2   Clustering Algorithm

Our approach aims to differentiate well-behaved from misbehaving entities, so the clustering algorithm has to separate entities with different behavior, being different behavior expressed by different values of features. From the clustering algorithms available in Apache Spark MLlib, we have chosen *K-means* [31] for two reasons: (1) it splits data points into a predefined number of clusters $\mathcal{K}$, which is important to force the appearance of small clusters with outliers; (2) K-means is known to be a good option when the number of samples is large (e.g., more than 10,000), which is our case.

K-means works iteratively, assigning each data point to one of $\mathcal{K}$ groups based on the distance to the group's centroid. The distance metric used is often the Euclidean distance, which is also the one we used in practice. At the end, data points with similar features are in the same cluster. The output of this algorithm is the number of the cluster to which each entity belongs to, and the central point (centroid) of each cluster.

The features have to be normalized using min-max normalization before clustering is performed. Interestingly we also did experiments with logarithmic normalization, but the detection results were much worse, as this form of normalization mitigates the differences between outliers and normal behavior.

4.3   Genetic Zoom

The genetic zoom mechanism is based on a *genetic algorithm* [17]. The goal is to find the best subset of features that provides the same clustering output as generic features (i.e., initial clustering). The genetic zoom scheme is based on a wrapper model [3] that iteratively (1) selects subsets of features and (2) evaluates clustering quality using the selected subset (see Fig. 4). Given that an exhaustive search of the $2^{\mathcal{D}}$ possible feature subsets (where $\mathcal{D}$ is the number of generic features) is intractable for high dimensionality, we choose as search strategy a genetic algorithm to provide a near-optimal response, by selecting a acceptable subset of features (i.e., the fitness function output stabilizes). Notice that the analyzed clusters are only the outliers, that are more likely to be the entities with misbehavior. The analyst either reports known anomalies or searches for new ones.

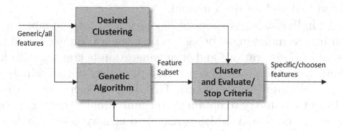

Fig. 4. The wrapper model for feature selection

Genetic algorithms entail four concepts: gene, individual, population, and generation. A gene is a property that characterizes an individual. An individual is a candidate solution to the problem that one wants to solve with the algorithm. An individual is characterized by a set of genes. A population is a set of individuals, which can be modified from generation to generation. A generation is a new population, inheriting individuals from previous populations or modifying them (e.g., with operators such as crossover and mutation).

In this work, 26 genes were used, corresponding to the 26 features. Since we want to reduce the number of features, each gene can have the value 1 or 0 corresponding to a feature being active or not for that individual. The *zoom* consists in reducing the number of active features/genes (number of 1s in the individual's array of features) to a number $\mathcal{F}$ lower than 26. $\mathcal{F}$ will be the lowest possible as long as there is an individual (i.e., set of features) that reproduces the same outliers as the clustering with all the features.

The selection of individuals used to breed a new generation is made using a fitness function. We use maximizing fitness function to get higher value possible (details below). The fitness function does the following:

1. Reduce the number of genes/features that are active (i.e., set to '1') to $\mathcal{F}$;
2. Re-execute the clustering algorithm with the selected features;

3. Only if the same outliers (i.e., clusters with one entity) are present, calculate the similarity between new output and initial clustering using the rand index adjusted for chance [22];
4. The similarity score is returned (a value between 0 and 1).

After getting this evaluation, the best individuals (the ones that obtained highest similarity score) are selected for the next generation. To create a new population, two operators are used: crossover and mutation. The crossover operator requires two individuals that came from the previous generation, called the parents, and the offspring is created by exchanging genes of parents among themselves until the crossover point is reached. After the crossover operator is executed, the mutation operator is applied. Mutation is applied to a new offspring formed to change their genes given a low random probability. It occurs to maintain diversity within the population and prevent premature convergence. Both the crossover and mutation operator use functions that shuffle the attributes of the input individual and return a mutant.

In this work individuals have a set of 26 genes (i.e., total number of features). A population has $\mathcal{N}$ individuals, being the first generation generated randomly. There is a total of $\mathcal{G}$ generations and each generation is created with half of the best individuals from the previous generation plus a set of individuals generated with crossover and mutation operations. This way, we keep our best individuals and mutate from them to try to obtain better individuals. In the experiments we have used $\mathcal{N} = 32$ and $\mathcal{G} = 40$ which revealed to achieve good results efficiently.

The genetic algorithm was implemented using an evolutionary algorithm framework – the Distributed Evolutionary Algorithms in Python (DEAP) [16] –, as OUTGENE was mostly implemented in Python. DEAP is a recent evolutionary computation framework for rapid prototyping and testing of ideas, seeking to make algorithms explicit and data structures transparent. The genetic algorithm can be fully configured through DEAP by configuring the fitness function and the existing operators. The configurations made were based on the GENITOR scheme [52]: when selecting the individuals for a new generation, the best individuals of the previous generation are kept.

4.4 Time Stretching

OUTGENE analyses data on different time-windows, what we call time stretching, to allow detecting stealth attacks. For that purpose we leverage the concept of *incremental aggregation*, which consists in executing aggregate functions (e.g., count or sum) continuously over streams of data [24]. The aggregate functions are used to calculate the values of the features.

To avoid the effort of executing the aggregate functions several times in parallel, we execute them on a *base time-window* of duration $\mathcal{B}$. In practice we considered $\mathcal{B} = 10$ min. Then, for the larger time-windows, OUTGENE simply executes the aggregate functions over the results obtained for $\mathcal{B}$. For example, whenever base time-window number i finishes, the system calculates the features not only for $\mathcal{B}_i$ of 10 min, but also for the time-window of 30 min using the results of the last 3 last base time-windows $(\mathcal{B}_{i-2}, \mathcal{B}_{i-1}, \mathcal{B}_i)$. The same idea is applied for the larger time-windows.

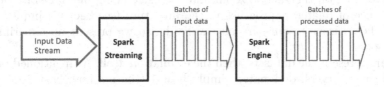

Fig. 5. Spark streaming process

Time stretching has been instantiated leveraging the incremental aggregation supported by the Spark Streaming module. This module works as shown in Fig. 5, receiving live input data streams and dividing the data into mini batches. The mini batches are then processed, by the clustering algorithm in OUTGENE.

The operations supported by Spark Streaming are similar to those of Apache Spark, but with a time parameter that has to be defined. For feature extraction, the main operation used was *reduceByKeyandWindow*, that is similar to *reduceByKey* (used in batch mode) but with two more parameters: window length, the total duration of the window, and sliding interval, the interval at which the window operation is performed. As shown in Fig. 6, every time the window slides over a source data stream (DStream), the source RDDs that fall within the window are combined and operated upon to produce the RDDs of the windowed DStream.

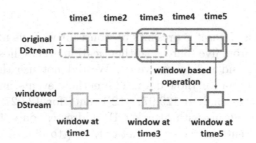

Fig. 6. Spark streaming window operations (adapted from [1])

For the experiments we set up an HDFS directory to store Apache Spark streaming information (checkpointing) necessary for window aggregation. Apart from the checkpointing data, the outputted data (extracted features and clustering results) was also saved on a HDFS directory to keep the progress registered.

5   Experimental Evaluation

This section presents the experimental evaluation of the OUTGENE instance we created, focused on the genetic zoom and time stretching mechanisms. Despite the existence of related approaches in the literature (see Sect. 6), implementations of those closer to ours are not available, so we present no experimental comparisons.

We first present the datasets, then the evaluation itself. As mentioned before, we used three servers, designated simply host 1 (the master), host 2 and host 3 (slaves). All software components were installed in the three servers: Kafka, Spark, Zookeeper, HDFS, and our own code.

5.1   Dataset Characterization

We used two datasets in the experimental evaluation: netflow events from the Los Alamos National Laboratory (LANL) corporate network [25,26], and netflow events that we obtained at a large military infrastructure. The information about the datasets is summarized in Table 2.

Table 2. Summary of the dataset characteristics

Dataset	Size	Num. events	Num. hosts
LANL	1.1 GB (compressed)	129,977,412	12,027
Military	160 GB		5,500

LANL Dataset. This dataset represents 58 consecutive days of pseudonymized event data collected from five sources: authentication events, hosts process start/ stop, DNS, netflow, and red team events. We did not use the whole dataset but only the redteam and netflow data. The netflow events have 1.1 GB when compressed and correspond to 129,977,412 events for 12,027 computers. The red team events provide us with attacker IP addresses, only 4, that we use to identify malicious events in the other dataset, i.e., to obtain ground truth for the evaluation. The dataset comes in text files. Each line of the netflow event files contains a timestamp (an epoch time starting at 0), connection duration, source computer, source port, destination computer, destination port, protocol, packet count, and byte count. The well-known ports (e.g., 80 and 443) are not pseudonymized, only the IP addresses. A few sample lines of data are:

```
1,9,C3090,N10471,C3420,N46,6,3,144
1,9,C3538,N2600,C3371,N46,6,3,144
2,0,C4316,N10199,C5030,443,6,2,92
```

Military Network Dataset. This dataset was obtained from the Security Information and Event Management (SIEM) system [6] in production in that network, which collects Netflow events from internal routers. Collecting these flows can give us insights of eventual misbehavior of internal entities, undetected by deployed security systems. The dataset corresponds to a full month, with approximately 5,500 computers and 160 GB of size. As shown in Table 3, we emulated 4 stealth/slow attacks (e.g., probing) at different pace to evaluate OutGene, and provide us with detailed ground truth. We also emulated a noisy attack (high volume of data exfiltrated to an unexpected destination). The main reasons for the chosen emulated attacks were: (1) to be able to evaluate our time stretching analysis; and (2) to have attacks that are unnoticed by traditional protection systems.

Table 3. Attacks in the military network dataset

SrcIP	DstIP	Attack
S1	D1	Stealth/slow port scan: 1-to-1 - every port (5 s pace for 1 day)
S2	/24 net	Stealth/slow port scan: one to many - every port (1 s pace for 1 day)
S3	D3	Stealth dictionary attack: SSH auth requests (with 2 min interval for half day)
S4	D4	Stealth dictionary attack: SSH auth requests (with 30 s interval for 20 min)
S5	D5	Data exfiltration: unusual volume of data sent to one entity (1.5 GB in 7 min)

5.2 Detection with Genetic Zoom

This section evaluates OutGene's genetic zoom mechanism. As mentioned before, genetic zoom allows the analyst to understand what are the relevant features for OutGene's decisions (i.e., attack detection after initial clustering). We considered a 24 h subset of the LANL dataset in which the attacker with pseudonym IP address C17693 generated many events. We designate the subset *attday*. Notice that no data is available about what attacks were performed by the attacker.

Table 4 shows the clusters obtained for *attday*. We considered the number of clusters $\mathcal{K} = 15$. This value should not be too large or several clusters would represent similar behavior, or too small or there would be no small clusters with outliers. In practice, experience is needed to define the value and obtain good results, but values in the range of 15 to 20 tend to provide good results. As we expected, there are large clusters (2 in this case), and small clusters (13), as observed in the table. Our focus is on clusters having 1 entity. Typically, small clusters correspond either to machines with different yet legitimate behaviour (e.g., web server, web proxy, etc.) or to misbehaving entities. The other clusters might be interesting but without contextual information it is difficult to draw conclusions.

The output of the genetic algorithm (Table 5) shows that there were 8 important features: number of different ports used, number of different ports contacted,

Table 4. Clustering results for day *attday* (LANL dataset)

Initial clustering															
Cluster number	0	10	1	12	9	5	7	3	6	13	4	11	14	2	8
Number of entities	7078	660	12	10	9	6	4	2	2	2	2	1	1	1	1
Clustering after genetic zoom															
Cluster number	0	7	14	5	3	1	11	2	13	10	6	9	12	8	4
Number of entities	7080	646	24	14	7	6	4	2	2	1	1	1	1	1	1

Table 5. Output of genetic algorithm (LANL dataset)

```
-- End of (successful) evolution --
Best allOfFame individual is [0,1,1,0,1,0,1,0,0,0,0,1,0,0,0,0,1,1,0,0,0,0,0,0,1,0], (0.9309)
```

sum of packets sent to port 80, sum of packets sent to port 194, sum of packets sent from port 22, sum of packets received, sum of packets received to port 80, and sum of packets received form port 22. Hence, all the oultiers obtained in the initial clustering are also obtained by redoing the clustering with this subset of features (bottom of the table). The results are 93% similar.

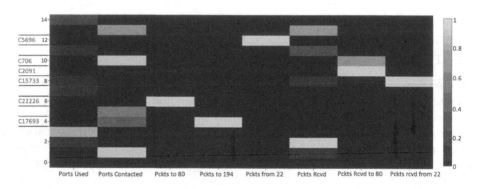

Fig. 7. Heatmap of features vs. clusters after genetic zoom at *attday*, with clusters with a single IP address identified on the left (LANL dataset)

To help understanding the meaning of the small clusters, Fig. 7 shows a heatmap for the clustering after genetic zoom was applied. The 8 features are at the bottom of the figure (x-axis) and the 15 clusters on the left (y-axis), whereas the color represents the value of each feature for each cluster. In the figure it is possible to observe that the outliers are those with higher values in certain features. IP C17693 (cluster 4) is the known attacker, who contacted many different ports (possibly doing a port scan) and was the only IP contacting port 194. The IP C706 (cluster 10) received several packets to port 80 and contacted several ports, which indicates it corresponds to a webserver, so it is normal behavior. The IP C2091 (cluster 9), also received several packets to port 80, but unlike the previous, it has not contacted several ports, which seems suspicious. The IP C22226 (cluster 6) have high number of packets sent to port 80 which seems suspicious. The IP C5696 (cluster 12) sent several packets from port 22, which may indicate it is a server suffering an attack, or is just one server being accessed by network administrator. The IP C15733 (cluster 8) has several packets received from port 22, which may indicate it is accessing IP C5696.

We did a similar exercise with the military network dataset and the 5 attacks we injected (Table 3). The main features identified for each attack were:

- *slow port scan 1-to-1:* SPcon, SP194t, SP25t
- *slow port scan 1-to-/24-net:* SPcon, SP194t, SP25t
- *stealth dictionary attack SSH 2 min:* SP22t
- *stealth dictionary attack SSH 30 sec.:* SP22t
- *data exfiltration:* SBytes

In summary, instead of having to extract information from the values of all the 26 features, by using the genetic zoom mechanism the analyst understands which subset of features is relevant to differentiate the clusters. In the LANL dataset case, we have limited knowledge about the computers, but we could still extract some information by inspecting the values of these 8 features and identify the red team IP address. That IP was isolated in a cluster, contacted many ports and sent several packets to port 194. In the military network dataset we have more information about both the attacks and the machines, so we can conclude that the mechanism is indeed useful.

5.3 Detection with Time Stretching

To evaluate time stretching, we used the military dataset with the attacks we injected (Table 3). We ran OutGene and compared results on time-windows from 10 min to 24 h, as shown in Table 6. The table is divided in two parts, which show the results in the detection of either attackers or victims. To allow the visualization of the time stretching capabilities, the results are shown for each time-window. Also, clusters are indicated by cluster ranking (the smallest cluster has the highest rank, 1st) and the cluster size in percentage (entities within cluster divided by the total number of entities). Moreover, for each attack, we bolded the time-window were the attack was better detected, i.e., more clearly observable. Next, we provide an interpretation of the table's content.

Regarding attack detection, in the case of both *slow port scans* running for almost a day, OutGene achieved excellent results in every time windows. The attacker was completely isolated in every case. Concerning the detection of the *stealth dictionary attack* to the SSH service of half a day and 2 min intervals, one can observe that the attack is detected (i.e., appears in the highest ranks) starting only from the 4 h time-window, which is expectable as this is the slowest attack. On the contrary, for a similar attack with a highest pace (30 s), the best result is achieved in smaller time windows (starting from 10 min). In both cases we

Table 6. Time stretching evaluation (military network dataset)

Attack detected	Cluster rank/% machines in cluster for each time-window					Comments
	10 min	1 h	4 h	8 h	1 day	
Slow port scan 1-to-1 5 s	1st/0.05%	1st/0.04%	1st/0.04%	1st/0.03%	1st/0.02%	Attacker was detected in every window
Slow port scan1-to-/24-net 1 s	1st/0.09%	1st/0.07%	1st/0.06%	1st/0.05%	1st/0.03%	Attacker was detected in every window
Stealth dict. attack SSH – 2 min	9th/30%	7th/8%	1st/0.04%	1st/0.03%	1st/0.02%	Attacker detected in bigger windows
Stealth dict. attack SSH – 30 s	1st/0.05%	1st/0.04%	1st/0.03%	1st/0.03%	8th/4.1%	Attacker detected in smaller windows
Data exfiltration out of office time	1st/0.12%	4th/0.35%	6th/1.44%	9th/6.4%	11th/7.5%	Attacker in smaller clusters for smaller windows
Detected victim of	Cluster rank/% machines in cluster for each time-window					Comments
	10 min	1 h	4 h	8 h	1 day	
Slow port scan 1-to-1 5 s	1st/0.05%	1st/0.04%	1st/0.04%	1st/0.03%	1st/0.02%	Victim was detected in every window
Slow port scan 1-to-/24-net 1 s	–	–	–	6th/2%	5th/1.7%	Victims in /24 net grouped in same cluster
Stealth dict. attack SSH – 2 min	7th/0.42%	6th/0.4%	5th/0.34%	2th/0.04%	1th/0.02%	Victim is a server that changes cluster
Stealth dict. attack SSH – 30 s	1st/0.8%	1st/0.04%	6nd/0.43%	6th/0.20%	4th/13%	Victim is a server that changes cluster
Data exfiltration out of office time	1st/0.12%	3th/0.28%	4th/0.5%	6th/1.8%	7th/4.1%	Victim in smaller clusters for smaller windows

verified that the suspicious entity is indeed an attacker, not a normal computer with different behavior (e.g., a server). Similarly, for the *data exfiltration attack* where an attacker collects data into a staging point of the internal network, the best results are obtained in the smallest time-window, as the attack took only a few minutes. To conclude, concerning attacker detection, we remark that when analysing time-windows without any trace of emulated attacks, all the machines used to emulate attacks were not in suspicions clusters (e.g., were in the larger cluster).

In relation to victim detection, in the case of *slow port scan* 1-to-1, we can observe that the victim is always in the top ranked clusters. Regarding the slow port scan (1-to-/24-net), there are several victims, as they are all the computers in a /24 subnet. With the smaller time-windows they are scattered in several clusters, but for the larger (8 h, 1 day) they become more concentrated in smaller, higher rank, clusters (6th/2% and 5th/1.7%). Concerning the *stealth dictionary attacks*, having contextual information, we know the victim is a server and usually belongs to small clusters. The only suspicion is the fact that the server moves between clusters and gets in top ranked clusters. Finally, concerning *data exfiltration*, we observe exactly the same behaviour as explained for attack detection (previous paragraph). Besides these emulated attacks, some machines with suspicious behavior have been found and their IPs given to the security team for further investigation.

These results can render values for recall/true positive rate (TPR), accuracy (ACC), and fall-out/false positive rate (FPR), shown in Table 7. Given the usual definitions of true/false positive (right/wrong alarms, TP/FP) and true/false negative (right/wrong no-alarms, TN/FN), we have the usual definitions for the three metrics: TPR = TP/(TP+FN); ACC = (TP+TN)/(TP+TN+FP+FN); FPR = FP/(TN+FP). We count as an alarm a cluster with a single IP. All time-windows in the table include attacks and are assumed to include a single attack each. On average each time-window had 2880 entities. The columns are self explanatory and the main results are on the three columns on the right. As we can observe, the TPR and accuracy are quite high, whereas the FPR is low as desirable (all metrics have values between 0 and 1). The bottom row shows that in (almost) all the windows there was a false alarm, i.e., one cluster with a single computer (a server).

In summary, we can conclude that the time stretching mechanism allows detecting attacks independently of their pace.

Table 7. Performance evaluation (military network dataset)

Attack	Num. alerts	Best time-window	TPR	ACC	FPR (%)
Slow port scan 1-to-1 5 s	3	1 day	1.00	0.99	0.04
Slow port scan 1-to-/24-net 1 s	4	1 day	1.00	0.99	0.10
Stealth dict. attack SSH 2 min	4	1 day	1.00	0.99	0.10
Stealth dict. attack SSH 30 s	3	10 min	1.00	0.99	0.07
Data exfiltration	3	10 min	1.00	0.98	0.07
Clean traffic	1				0.03

6 Related Work

Several surveys offer an extensive review regarding the use of ML techniques in the cybersecurity domain [4,5,20,58]. The first work in this category is apparently due to Lee and Stolfo, who used a supervised ML scheme to detect attacks [29]. Most research in the area used datasets that date back to 1999 and that do not represent the actual cybersecurity landscape nor the difficulty in processing noisy data of real world systems [30,39,54,57].

Most intrusion detection research focus on *signature-based* detection to detect known attacks, or *anomaly-based* detection that typically learns a model of what is considered normal and detects deviations from that model. The first is unable to detect unknown attacks; the former can detect them but at the cost of high false positive rates. OUTGENE does not need knowledge about what is good or bad behavior, although it assumes that attacks are rare and exhibit distinctive behavior. Hence, when analyzing previous work, we focused our research on experiments using unsupervised learning methods and using real data at large-scale.

Yen et al. [56] proposed Beehive, one of the first systems exploring the challenges of big data security analytics for real-world log data, using clustering to identify outliers. The main drawback is that processing is done on a daily basis and there is no feature selection method for interpretability. Gonçalves et al. [18] and Sacramento et al. [40] proposed semi-automatic cluster labeling and the implementation of feature extraction using MapReduce framework. The relevant limitations are the same as Beehive's. Veeramachaneni et al. [51] use an ensemble of outlier detection methods and introduces log stream ingestion using window aggregation for efficient feature extraction, although they focus on web logs. The problem of outlier explanation remains. A few other works use related approaches [7,33,37,47,55].

The previous works rely on batch and mini-batch processing, hence, it is worth mentioning some recent works that do stream analysis, although they rely on knowledge of what good behavior is: Cinque et al. use entropy to infer deviations from a baseline [9]; DeepLog is inspired in natural language processing and interprets logs as elements of a sequence that follows grammar rules [14]; Kitsune uses an ensemble of neural networks called autoencoders to collectively differentiate between normal and abnormal traffic patterns [36].

In what concerns feature selection for clustering, [15] and [3] provide a good overview of several methods. Our choice for the use of a genetic algorithm was inspired in [35,46], as well as in its success in finance [19] or in simulating attackers' efforts to evade classifiers [53].

Although OUTGENE was evaluated with examples of SSH brute forcing, port scan and data exfiltration attacks to illustrate the capabilities offered by time stretching, it was not designed to detect specific attacks. However, we mention some works regarding stealth/slow attacks detection. In what concerns detection of SSH dictionary attacks [48,49] or data exfiltration [33], most works rely on count based features (e.g., count of auth failures). In every case, it is necessary to define thresholds/baselines that can be circumvented. For instance, the popular tool Fail2ban [2], with the default configuration, bans IPs that make 5 failed login attempts over a 10 min period. Hence, a smart attacker would never exceed 4 login attempts in each 10 min period. Furthermore, he could use different source IPs to perform the attack. Satoh et al. [41] highlight the existence of atypical inter-arrival times between an auth-packet and the next. This feature can be derived from single flows of the SSH protocol. Since this is also a misuse-based method, a malicious user can circumvent it emulating a normal connection by manipulating the sending rate of the packets.

None of the related works in the literature provides mechanisms similar or equivalent to genetic zoom and time stretching.

7   Conclusion

We developed OutGene, an unsupervised learning approach for network intrusion detection, that detects attacks that are undefined (no signatures) without clean training data. It performs clustering of hosts with similar behavior and detects outliers, with the assumption that attackers behave differently from the majority. OutGene advances the state of the art with the genetic zoom and time stretching mechanisms. We show that it is useful to detect attacks in real network data.

References

1. Apache Spark documentation. https://spark.apache.org/. Accessed 22 Apr 2019
2. Fail2ban. https://www.fail2ban.org. Accessed 22 Apr 2019
3. Alelyani, S., Tang, J., Liu, H.: Feature selection for clustering: a review. Data Clustering **29**, 110–121 (2013)
4. Bhuyan, M., Bhattacharyya, D., Kalita, J.: Network anomaly detection: methods, systems and tools. IEEE Commun. Surv. Tutorials **6**(1), 303–336 (2014)
5. Buczak, A., Guven, E.: A survey of data mining and machine learning methods for cyber security intrusion detection. IEEE Commun. Surv. Tutorials **18**(2), 1153–1176 (2016)
6. Cárdenas, A., Manadhata, P., Rajan, S.: Big data analytics for security intelligence. Cloud Secur. Alliance, 10–11 (2013)
7. Casas, P., Mazel, J., Owezarski, P.: Unsupervised network intrusion detection systems: detecting the unknown without knowledge. Comput. Commun. **35**(7), 772–783 (2012)
8. CheckPoint: 2018 security report: Welcome to the future of cyber security (2018)
9. Cinque, M., Corte, R.D., Pecchia, A.: Entropy-based security analytics: measurements from a critical information system. In: 2017 47th Annual IEEE/IFIP International Conference on Dependable Systems and Networks, pp. 379–390, June 2017
10. Claise, B.: Cisco systems netflow services export version 9. Technical report, RFC 3954. IETF RFC 3954 (2004)
11. Debar, H., Dacier, M., Wespi, A.: Towards a taxonomy of intrusion detection systems. Comput. Netw. **31**(8), 805–822 (1999)
12. Denning, D.E., Neumann, P.G.: Requirements and model for IDES: a real-time intrusion detection expert system. Technical report, Computer Science Laboratory, SRI International, Menlo Park, CA (1985)
13. Dias, L.F., Correia, M.: Big data analytics for intrusion detection: an overview. In: Handbook of Research on Machine and Deep Learning Applications for Cyber Security, pp. 292–316. IGI Global (2020)
14. Du, M., Li, F., Zheng, G., Srikumar, V.: DeepLog: anomaly detection and diagnosis from system logs through deep learning. In: ACM SIGSAC Conference on Computer and Communications Security (2017)
15. Dy, J.G., Brodley, C.E.: Feature selection for unsupervised learning. J. Mach. Learn. Res. **5**, 845–889 (2004)
16. Fortin, F.A., Rainville, F.M.D., Gardner, M.A., Parizeau, M., Gagné, C.: Deap: evolutionary algorithms made easy. J. Mach. Learn. Res. **13**, 2171–2175 (2012)
17. Goldberg, D.E., Holland, J.H.: Genetic algorithms and machine learning. Mach. Learn. **3**(2), 95–99 (1988)

18. Gonçalves, D., Bota, J., Correia, M.: Big data analytics for detecting host misbehavior in large logs. In: Proceedings of the 14th IEEE International Conference on Trust, Security and Privacy in Computing and Communications (2015)
19. Gorgulho, A., Neves, R., Horta, N.: Applying a GA kernel on optimizing technical analysis rules for stock picking and portfolio composition. Expert Syst. Appl. **38**(11), 14072–14085 (2011)
20. Habeeb, R.A.A., Nasaruddin, F., Gani, A., Hashem, I.A.T., Ahmed, E., Imran, M.: Real-time big data processing for anomaly detection: a survey. Int. J. Inf. Manage. **45**, 289–307 (2018)
21. Hellemons, L., Hendriks, L., Hofstede, R., Sperotto, A., Sadre, R., Pras, A.: SSHCure: a flow-based SSH intrusion detection system. In: Sadre, R., Novotný, J., Čeleda, P., Waldburger, M., Stiller, B. (eds.) AIMS 2012. LNCS, vol. 7279, pp. 86–97. Springer, Heidelberg (2012). https://doi.org/10.1007/978-3-642-30633-4_11
22. Hubert, L., Arabie, P.: Comparing partitions. J. Classif. **2**(1), 193–218 (1985)
23. Hunt, P., Konar, M., Junqueira, F., Reed, B.: Zookeeper: wait-free coordination for internet-scale systems. In: USENIX Annual Technical Conference (2010)
24. Jin, C., Carbonell, J.: Incremental aggregation on multiple continuous queries. In: Esposito, F., Raś, Z.W., Malerba, D., Semeraro, G. (eds.) ISMIS 2006. LNCS (LNAI), vol. 4203, pp. 167–177. Springer, Heidelberg (2006). https://doi.org/10.1007/11875604_20
25. Kent, A.D.: Comprehensive. Multi-Source Cyber-Security Events, Los Alamos National Laboratory (2015)
26. Kent, A.D.: Cyber security data sources for dynamic network research. Dyn. Netw. Cyber-Secur. **1**, 37–65 (2016)
27. Kienzler, R.: Mastering Apache Spark 2.x: Scalable Analytics Faster than Ever. Packt Publishing, Birmingham (2017)
28. Kreps, J., Narkhede, N., Rao, J., et al.: Kafka: a distributed messaging system for log processing. In: Proceedings of NetDB, pp. 1–7 (2011)
29. Lee, W., Stolfo, S.: Data mining approaches for intrusion detection. In: Proceedings of the 7th USENIX Security Symposium, January 1998
30. Leung, K., Leckie, C.: Unsupervised anomaly detection in network intrusion detection using clusters. In: Proceedings of the 28th Australasian Conference on Computer Science, pp. 333–342 (2005)
31. MacQueen, J.B.: Some methods for classification and analysis of multivariate observations. In: Proceedings of 5th Berkeley Symposium on Mathematical Statistics and Probability, pp. 281–297 (1967)
32. Mandiant: Special report, M-TRENDS 2018 (2018)
33. Marchetti, M., Pierazzi, F., Colajanni, M., Guido, A.: Analysis of high volumes of network traffic for advanced persistent threat detection. Comput. Netw. **109**, 127–141 (2016)
34. Meng, X., et al.: MLlib: machine learning in apache spark. J. Mach. Learn. Res. **17**(1), 1235–1241 (2016)
35. Middlemiss, M., Dick, G.: Feature selection of intrusion detection data using a hybrid genetic algorithm/KNN approach. In: Design and Application of Hybrid Intelligent Systems, pp. 519–527. IOS Press (2003)
36. Mirsky, Y., Doitshman, T., Elovici, Y., Shabtai, A.: Kitsune: an ensemble of autoencoders for online network intrusion detection. In: Proceedings of the Network and Distributed System Security Symposium (2018)

37. Osada, G., Omote, K., Nishide, T.: Network intrusion detection based on semi-supervised variational auto-encoder. In: Foley, S.N., Gollmann, D., Snekkenes, E. (eds.) ESORICS 2017. LNCS, vol. 10493, pp. 344–361. Springer, Cham (2017). https://doi.org/10.1007/978-3-319-66399-9_19
38. OTA: Cyber incident & breach trends report (2018)
39. Otey, M.E., Ghoting, A., Parthasarathy, S.: Fast distributed outlier detection in mixed-attribute data sets. Data Min. Knowl. Discov. **12**(2–3), 203–228 (2006)
40. Sacramento, L., Medeiros, I., Bota, J., Correia, M.: Flowhacker: detecting unknown network attacks in big traffic data using network flows. In: 17th IEEE International Conference on Trust, Security and Privacy in Computing and Communications, pp. 567–572 (2018)
41. Satoh, A., Nakamura, Y., Ikenaga, T.: A flow-based detection method for stealthy dictionary attacks against secure shell. J. Inf. Secur. Appl. **21**, 31–41 (2015)
42. Shvachko, K., Kuang, H., Radia, S., Chansler, R.: The Hadoop distributed file system. In: IEEE 26th Symposium on Mass Storage Systems and Technologies, pp. 1–10 (2010)
43. Sommer, R., Paxson, V.: Outside the closed world: on using machine learning for network intrusion detection. In: Proceedings of the 30th IEEE Symposium on Security and Privacy, pp. 305–316 (2010)
44. Sperotto, A., Schaffrath, G., Sadre, R., Morariu, C., Pras, A., Stiller, B.: An overview of IP flow-based intrusion detection. IEEE Commun. Surv. Tutorials **12**(3), 343–356 (2010)
45. Srisuresh, P., Holdrege, M.: IP network address translator (NAT) terminology and considerations. IETF Request for Comments: RFC 2663, August 1999
46. Stein, G., Chen, B., Wu, A.S., Hua, K.A.: Decision tree classifier for network intrusion detection with GA-based feature selection. In: Proceedings of the 43rd ACM Annual Southeast Regional Conference, vol. 2, pp. 136–141 (2005)
47. Stergiopoulos, G., Talavari, A., Bitsikas, E., Gritzalis, D.: Automatic detection of various malicious traffic using side channel features on TCP packets. In: Lopez, J., Zhou, J., Soriano, M. (eds.) ESORICS 2018. LNCS, vol. 11098, pp. 346–362. Springer, Cham (2018). https://doi.org/10.1007/978-3-319-99073-6_17
48. Su, Y.N., Chung, G.H., Wu, B.J.: Developing the upgrade detection and defense system of SSH dictionary-attack for multi-platform environment. iBusiness **3**(01), 65 (2011)
49. Thames, J.L., Abler, R., Keeling, D.: A distributed active response architecture for preventing SSH dictionary attacks. In: IEEE Southeastcon, pp. 84–89 (2008)
50. Turcotte, M.J.M., Kent, A.D., Hash, C.: Unified Host and Network Data Set, chap. 1, pp. 1–22, November 2018
51. Veeramachaneni, K., Arnaldo, I., Cuesta-Infante, A., Korrapati, V., Bassias, C., Li, K.: AI^2: training a big data machine to defend. In: Proceedings of the 2nd IEEE International Conference on Big Data Security on Cloud (2016)
52. Whitley, D.: The GENITOR algorithm and selection pressure. In: Proceedings of the 3rd International Conference on Genetic Algorithms, pp. 116–121 (1989)
53. Xu, W., Qi, Y., Evans, D.: Automatically evading classifiers. In: Proceedings of the 2016 Network and Distributed Systems Symposium (2016)
54. Yamanishi, K., Takeuchi, J.I., Williams, G., Milne, P.: On-line unsupervised outlier detection using finite mixtures with discounting learning algorithms. Data Min. Knowl. Discov. **8**(3), 275–300 (2004)
55. Yen, T.F.: Detecting stealthy malware using behavioral features in network traffic. Ph.D. thesis, Carnegie Mellon University Department of Electrical and Computer Engineering (2011)

56. Yen, T.F., et al.: Beehive: large-scale log analysis for detecting suspicious activity in enterprise networks. In: Proceedings of the 29th ACM Annual Computer Security Applications Conference (2013)
57. Zhang, J., Zulkernine, M.: Anomaly based network intrusion detection with unsupervised outlier detection. In: 2006 IEEE International Conference on Communications, vol. 5, pp. 2388–2393 (2006)
58. Zuech, R., Khoshgofthaar, T., Wald, R.: Intrusion detection and big heterogeneous data: a survey. J. Big Data 2, 90–107 (2015)

OVERSCAN: OAuth 2.0 Scanner
for Missing Parameters

Karin Sumongkayothin[✉], Pakpoom Rachtrachoo, Arnuphap Yupuech,
and Kasidit Siriporn

Faculty of Information and Communication Technology,
Mahidol University, Salaya, Thailand
`karin.sum@mahidol.ac.th`,
`{pakpoom.rac,arnuphap.yup,kasidit.sir}@student.mahidol.ac.th`

Abstract. The websites are developed rapidly and wildly used by people around the world. The main reason is the increase of the immense number of internet users, which results in the security control of accessing sensitive information is necessary. The authorization server as the one security aspect which controls the access permission to the system. Many authentication protocols were proposed to meet these functional requirements. The open-standard authorization (OAuth) protocol is one of the well-known solutions widely used. However, many developers still misuse this protocol, which can cause security breaches. This paper proposes a tool named *OVERSCAN*, which is an OAuth2.0 scanner for misused or missing parameters. The experiments of using OVERSCAN have been conducted over 45 samples supporting OAuth2.0 protocol. The results show that 84.4% of samples lack significant parameters which can cause security problems.

Keywords: OAuth · Vulnerability scanner · Network protocol security

1 Introduction

The growth of internet user has been dramatically increasing since it was introduced in the last few decades. To achieve the information security preservation, the access grant over the particular information is necessary. The authorization is the process to determine the user access levels. Many mechanisms can serve the authorization flow, and one of them is Open Authorization (OAuth). OAuth is an authorization framework which is wildly used to grant access permission through a trusted third-party service. Even though the framework is officially provided under RFC [7], the incorrect OAuth implementation still exists until the present. The inaccurate implementation such as missing some particular OAuth parameters or HTTP headers may prompt security concerns such as stealing sensitive information, gaining the illegal access, and identity theft [4,13]. The OAuth2.0 framework defines the role of components as:

- Resource Owner: the user who delegate access to his protected information.

© Springer Nature Switzerland AG 2019
J. K. Liu and X. Huang (Eds.): NSS 2019, LNCS 11928, pp. 221–233, 2019.
https://doi.org/10.1007/978-3-030-36938-5_13

- Client (aka. Relying Party): the service API or application which asks for permission to access the *resource owner*'s protected information.
- User agent: the intermediary that is used by the *resource owner* to interact with the *client*.
- Authorization server (aka. Identity Provider): the server which grants the scoped access to the *client* to access the protected information on behalf of *resource owner*.
- Protected resource server: the server that holds the protected information which can be accessed by using provided grant from the *authentication server*.

The framework supports many *grant types* which each type has a different flow to able access the protected resource. However, the most commonly used are *implicit* and *authorization code* grant type. The difference between the two mentioned grant types are as illustrated in Figs. 1 and 2.

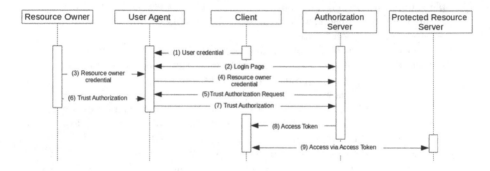

Fig. 1. Implicit grant flow

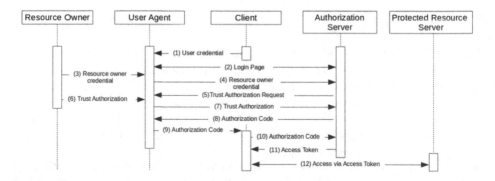

Fig. 2. Authorization code grant flow

The clear difference between implicit and authorization code grant is how the client acquis the access token. In implicit grant type, the client directly receives access token after the resource owner confirming the trust authorization (step (7) and (8) of Fig. 1). In authorization code grant type, the *authorization code* (aka. code) is sent back to the user agent before passing on to the client (step (8) of Fig. 2). The client then exchanges the code with the access token that was created by the authorization server (step (9) of Fig. 2). Although the implicit grant is clearly better in the term of performance, authentication code grant is recommended when requiring higher security.

In this paper, we propose the tool named OVERSCAN, which is the scanner for the OAuth2.0 vulnerabilities focusing on the web application. It was implemented with the JAVA language as the Burpsuit[1] extension which covers the vulnerabilities listed in the RFC6819 [10].

1.1 Related Work

The OAuth2.0 framework [7] was introduced as the guideline for implementing the flow to delegate access to the unauthorized client. It was classified as a double-redirection protocol [5] since it redirects the request back and forth between client and authorization server through the user-agent application. The first redirection is when the client sends the redirects URI to make the user agent forwards its request to the authorization server. The second redirection takes place after confirming the trust authorization message. The response message is redirected to the client or authorization server depending on the grant type is being used. Since the flow consists of redirections, the security flaws may exist if it is not well-implemented. OAuth 2.0 Threat Model and Security Considerations [10] was published to provide the additional security considerations in OAuth 2.0. It shows the possible security flaws in OAuth flow under incorrect parameter configurations.

Pai et al. [12] proposed the formal method based on knowledge flow analysis [14] to verify the security of OAuth2.0 protocol. As a result, it emphasizes the existence of a security flaw in OAuth client credentials flow. Chari et al. [3] presented another security analysis method by using Universal Composability Security Framework [2]. The universal composability paradigm can guarantee the strong security properties of the protocol, although it was used as a component of an arbitrary system. Their analysis was focused on OAuth2.0 authorization code flow. It shows the necessity of using the SSL like functionality to protect the communication channel between the client and the authorization server. They also show that the session identifier does not need to be decided in advance, which can mitigate the possibility of the attacks such as the session hijacking or session swapping. Feng and Sathiamoorthy [15] introduced the method to analyze the vulnerability of the OAuth 2.0 framework using an attacker model. The attacker model consists of four modules representing the type of attacks which are monitoring attack, replay attack, phishing attack, and impersonation attack. Their experiment was conducted focusing on the data transmission of the user-agent & authorization server, and user-agent & client. The results show

---

[1] https://portswigger.net/burp.

that the OAuth2.0 framework is susceptible to such simple attacks as cross-site request forgery attack, replaying attack, and network traffic interception. The root cause is that the framework did not explicitly define which component affects the security of the protocol. For example, there were no recommendations of using TLS to protect the callback endpoints, enforcing process to ensure the security of the client, nor limiting of multiple uses of authorization code.

In analytical terms of practical usage, Argyriou et al. [1] studied the possible mechanism causing the flaws in the OAuth 2.0 framework. Because the framework does not clearly define the formal standard of communication primitive between the user-agent and the client; the authentication method, therefore, depends on the decision of the developer. The analysis was done by investigating the communication between the resource owner and the authorization server based on the OAuth 2.0 framework. It shows that the misconfiguration in implicit grant flow and authorization code flow may lead to many security flaws such as cross-site request forgery, session wrapping, and mixing redirect end-point. The [6,8] reiterated that the security issues of the OAuth 2.0 flow were caused by the implementation, not from the framework. They also stated that missing or incorrect using some significant parameters such as a state-parameter or X-FRAME-OPTIONS in HTTP header, will cause the security risk.

Zhou et al. [16] implemented the tool named SSOScan for verifying the communication characteristics of the application using Facebook Single Sign-On APIs. It automatically identifies the risks that occur during the authentication process. SSOScan can detect four vulnerabilities which are access token misuse, signed requests misuse, app_secret parameter leakage, and user OAuth credential leakage. The vulnerability analysis proceeds in two ways consisting of the simulation attack for checking the access token and signed request misused, and passive monitoring to identify the credential leakage. As a result, 20.3% of websites using Facebook SSO are vulnerable, where users are unable to login due to 2.3% implementation error. Another OAuth2.0 testing tool, OAuthGuard, was proposed by Li et al. [9]. This tool focuses on analyzing the vulnerabilities of web application utilizing Google Sign-in. By scanning 137 sample sites using OAuthGuard, it shows that 40.9% of samples have at least one serious vulnerability, where 9.5% have an insecure implementation.

Unlike the existing tools, OVERSCAN is designed to compatible with any web application supporting OAuth 2.0. It serves as the free extension of Burp Suite Community Edition[2] to identify the possible threats caused by insecure implementation.

1.2   Contribution and Paper Organization

The most vulnerabilities in OAuth services caused by a faulty client design as has been stated in [6]. Since the client is an application, it is somewhat unmanageable and hard to identify the configuration. Fortunately, the information sent back

---

[2] https://portswigger.net/.

and forth between the client and authorization server must be through the user-agent. It allows to intercept and investigate the information at this point.

In this paper, we propose the OAuth 2.0 vulnerability scanner named OVER-SCAN. It works as a proxy which will intercept the incoming and outgoing packets of the internet browser. It focuses on identifying the missing significant parameter and HTTP header, which lead to the security issue. The main contributions of this paper are:

- Propose new scanning tool, OVERSCAN which works nicely to any clients and authorization servers.
- Describe the conceptual design and implementation of OVERSCAN.
- Conduct the experiments over 25 websites on vary authorization servers (45 scannings in total) to identify the possible missing parameters that cause of weak security.

The rest of the paper is organized as follows. In Sect. 2, we provide an overview of OVERSCAN design and construction. Then the misused parameter and related vulnerabilities, that can be identified by OVERSCAN are described in Sect. 3. We deliver the analysis and results of the experiment conducted on the sample web applications in Sect. 4. We give a discussion of OVERSCAN limitation in Sect. 5. We conclude the paper in Sect. 6.

2 Design and Construction Overview of OVERSCAN

OVERSCAN is designed in the purpose of analyzing data transmitted through the web browser during the access-token request process. Therefore, capturing the information that is sent in and out across the browser is necessary for the operation. This section we describe the details of OVERSCAN design and implementation.

From the objective to analyze the OAuth traffic to discover the vulnerability, we implement OVERSCAN as the free extension of a Burp Suite Community Edition. Burp Suite Community Edition (in short Burp) is the free graphical interception proxy which can capture all requests and responses between the browser and target applications. It allows the user to extend the Burp's functionality by adding the additional code called the *extension*. The traffic pass through the browser will be intercepted by Burp then checked by OVERSCAN for the possible security issue. OVERSCAN operation consists of four phases as illustrated in Fig. 3.

2.1 Traffic Classification

OVERSCAN will retrieve all traffic captured by Burp and then proceed the classification as of Fig. 2. It first checks whether the traffic is request or response and then classifies whether it is under OAuth protocol or not. Only OAuth related message will be highlighted and sent to scan for vulnerabilities. OVER-SCAN supports investigating the vulnerability that may occur during implicit or

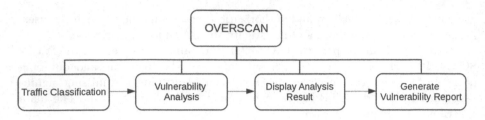

Fig. 3. OVERSCAN operation

authorization grant request. To distinct these two requests from the other messages, the parameter *response_type* must be observed. It will contain the value *"token"* when it is implicit grant request while *"code"* for the authorization code grant request (Fig. 4).

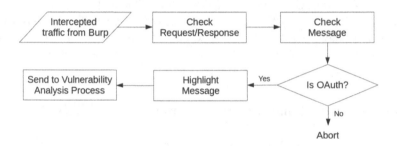

Fig. 4. OVERSCAN traffic classification

2.2 Vulnerability Analysis

What is used to verify for vulnerabilities consists of two parts: OAuth missing parameter and missing secure parameter in HTTP headers. The target message is checked based on the countermeasure methods mentioned in RFC6819. Then the scanning results will be passed to display by Burp as Fig. 5. The details of missing parameters and supported vulnerabilities can be found in Sect. 3.

2.3 Display Analysis Result

OVERSCAN highlights and adds the comment to the vulnerable OAuth traffic displayed in Burp Proxy HTTP History. The highlight color is according to the severity levels defined by the Common Vulnerability Scoring System (CVSS)[3]. The severity can be categorized into three levels: High (Orange), Medium (Yellow), and None (Green). The example of the display result is as shown in the Fig. 6.

---

[3] https://www.first.org/cvss/v3.0/specification-document.

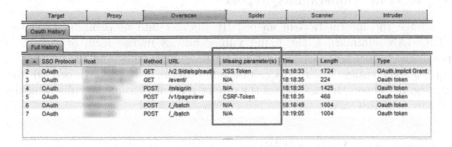

# ▲	SSO Protocol	Host	Method	URL	Missing parameter(s)	Time	Length	Type
2	OAuth		GET	/v2.9/dialog/oauth	XSS Token	18:18:33	1724	OAuth Implicit Grant
3	OAuth		GET	/event/	N/A	18:18:35	224	Oauth token
4	OAuth		POST	/m/signin	N/A	18:18:35	1425	Oauth token
5	OAuth		POST	/v1/pageview	CSRF-Token	18:18:35	468	Oauth token
6	OAuth		POST	/_/batch	N/A	18:18:49	1004	Oauth token
7	OAuth		POST	/_/batch	N/A	18:19:05	1004	Oauth token

Fig. 5. Vulnerability analysis results

#	Host	Method	URL	Comment	▼ Params	Edited	Status	Length
87		GET	/v2.9/dialog/oauth?client_id=5...	XSS Token	✓		302	1724
79		POST	/_/batch	N/A	✓		200	1004
93		POST	/m/signin	N/A	✓		200	1425
113		POST	/_/batch	N/A	✓		200	1004
95		POST	/v1/pageview	CSRF-Token	✓		200	468
73	https://collector-medium.lightste...	POST	/api/v0/reports		✓		200	431
75	https://collector-medium.lightste...	OPTIONS	/api/v0/reports				200	270
76	https://collector-medium.lightste...	POST	/api/v0/reports		✓		200	431

Fig. 6. Display analysis results (Color figure online)

Host Name	URL	Missing Parameter (s)	Severity Level	Grant type
		CSRF-Token	8.8	---
		XSS Token	6.1	Implicit Grant (Warning)

Implicit Grant Warning:
The implicit grant type has used for mobile application and web application, which does not guarantee user data security. This type is a simple grant that can be used by public clients. By the server will immediately return the access token without having to do authorization code, therefore, the disclosure of Token to users and other applications on the user's device. In general, it is not recommended to use Implicit Grant type, Oauth 2.0 will recommend using authorization code with Proof Key for Code Exchange (PKCE) instead of using implicit flow.

Fig. 7. Vulnerability report

2.4   Generate Vulnerability Report

To arrange the information in an orderly manner and more understandable, OVERSCAN summarizes the found vulnerabilities in the form of document report. The report will give the details of the vulnerability and the suggestion to migrate the issues. The report can be generated in either HTML or PDF format. Figure 7 shows the example of the report generated from the vulnerabilities found by OVERSCAN.

3   Supported Vulnerabilities

Parametric usage methods are particularly relevant to OAuth protocol security. Missing some parameters may result in allowing the adversary to obtain the credential information. The list of parameters supported by OVERSCAN for security checking is as according to Table 2.

Table 1. List of parameters for security checking

Missing parameter	Possible threat	Severity level
X-CSRFToken	– CSRF attack against redirect URL (Authentication code & Implicit grant)	8.8 High (CVSS 3.0)
State-Parameter	– CSRF attack against redirect URI (Authorization code & Implicit grant) – DoS using manufactured authorization "codes"	7.8 High (CVSS 3.0)
Redirect_URI (HTTPS for redirect URI)	– Authorization code phishing – User session impersonation	6.1 Medium (CVSS 3.0)
X-XSS-Protection	– Authorization codes can be stolen through vulnerable client	6.1 Medium (CVSS 3.0)
X-Content-Type-Options	– Authorization codes can be stolen through vulnerable Client	6.1 Medium (CVSS 3.0)
X-Frame Options	– Clickjacking attack against authorization	4.7 Medium (CVSS 3.0)

3.1   X-CSRFToken

X-CSRFToken is an HTTP token to against Cross-Site Request Forgery (CSRF) attack. It is also known as CSRF-Token. This token is a large random unique number which is unpredictable for each authentication request. It is associated with the HTTP header to ensure the validity of the source of information.

3.2   State Parameter

State Parameter is the parameter preserving the state information of authentication procedures which allows the user to restore the previous state of the application. It is also useful for CSRF attack mitigation on the redirection endpoint. The value of this parameter is unique and non-guessable, which will be generated during the initial request. To validate the response, the recipient must confirm that the state-parameter of request and response message must be the same value. Since OAuth was classified as double-redirection protocol, it is susceptible to the CSRF attack without state parameter.

Another benefit of using state parameter is Denial of Service (DoS) mitigation. The attack scenario is when the attacker floods the valid URIs with a random authorization code to the client. Generally, the client will forward all the received messages to the authorization server. Due to a large number of HTTPS connections, it can cause the server out of service. However, when the state parameter is implemented; the client will drop the message containing the invalid state parameter. The attacker needs the right state parameter in order to successfully attack, which results in decreased attack effectiveness.

3.3   Redirect_URI

Redirect_URI is a parameter to change the direction of the traffic to the next endpoint of the flow. The URI of all endpoints should be integrated the SSL/TLS protection (HTTPS) to prevent authorization code phishing and user session impersonation.

3.4   X-XSS-Protection

They also stated that missing or X-XSS-Protection is a parameter in the HTTP response header that stops pages from loading when cross-site scripting (XSS) attacks are detected. This vulnerability affects when the attacker discovers the XSS flaw in the client. The attacker can inject the script (e.g. Javascript) then lures the user to send the request containing the malicious redirect URI. Since the redirect URI includes a malicious script, the attacker can steal the authorization code or access token from the user. By the fact that using pre-configured redirect URI instead of a dynamic one may solve this issue, it cannot guarantee that every server will follow this configuration. By using X-XSS-Protection parameter, we can make sure that the malicious script will not be loaded. There are four ways to configure X-XSS-Protection parameter, which are:

- **X-XSS-Protectoin: 0:** disable XSS protection.
- **X-XSS-Protectoin: 1:** enable XSS protection and the browser sanitizes the page if cross-site scipt was detected.
- **X-XSS-Protectoin: 1; mode = block:** enable XSS protection and the browser prevents the page form rendering if cross-site scipt was detected.
- **X-XSS-Protectoin: 1; report = ⟨report-uri⟩:** enable XSS protection and the browser sanitizes the page and sends the report to defined URI.

3.5   X-Content-Type-Options

Another solution to mitigate the impact of XSS attacks rather than X-XSS-Protection is to use X-Content-Type-Options parameter. X-Content-Type-Options is the element in HTTP header which can prevent the MIME sniffing for sending XSS attack by the attacker. MIME Sniffing is the feature that the web browser uses to examine the downloaded asset content to determine the file format. However, MIME Sniffing can cause a security issue when the attacker disguises an HTML file as a valid file type. It allows the attacker to successfully bypassing the protection to upload the malicious code to the server. It can cause an XSS attack when the web browser renders the malicious HTML file. To mitigate the attack, providing X-Content-Type-Options with *nosniff* option will disable MINE Sniffing functionality. By disabling MINE Sniffing functionality, the web browser will no longer analyze the received content.

3.6   X-Frame Options

As mentioned in [10], Clickjacking is one of the malicious methods to let the attacker steals the user's authentication credentials. The malicious site may construct transparent iFrame with an invisible button wrapping around the significant locations (e.g Authorize button). Once the user clicks on that location, he did click the hidden button then sends the user's credentials to the attacker. X-Frame Options is the security element in HTTP header, which provides the feature of Clickjacking prevention. X-Frame Options can contain three values, which are:

- **DENY:** disable the loading of the page in a frame.
- **SAMEORIGIN:** allows the page to be loaded in a frame on the same origin as the page itself.
- **ALLOW-FROM** ⟨uri⟩: allows the page to be loaded only in a frame on the specific URI.

4   Experimental Analysis

The experiment was conducted over 45 samples of web application supporting an OAuth 2.0 protocol. The sample group consists of the local and international websites that use the service from the different OAuth authorization servers: Facebook, Google, and other servers. In this experiment, we focus on examining two aspects: the grant type used and the missing parameters that may cause a security weakness. We found that 42% out of the samples still use Implicit grant type to delegate the user access right. The numbers are high even though using the implicit grant type was reported as causing the security susceptible [11]. In the aspect of using the security-related parameters, the experimental yield the result as Fig. 8. The most parameter that was missing from the sample group is X-XSS-Protection, accounting for 48.9% of the total samples. The second highest of missing parameters obtained from the experiment is X-Content-Type-Options, representing 42.2%. Next is X-Frame Options, which accounts for 37.8% of the total. The remaining three are X-CSRFTOKEN, State Parameter and Redirect_URI which represent 15.6%, 11.1% and 2.2%, respectively. Interestingly, the top three missing parameters are the secure parameter used in the HTTP header, which X-Frame Options is one of them. It was specified by [7] that is necessary for the security of the OAuth application. Nonetheless, there are over 37% of websites from the experiment that does not use this parameter. Furthermore, one of the experimental results shows that the redirection endpoint does not support SSL/TLS, which may lead to serious security flaws such as the session hijacking.

By the fact that some samples are free of the missing parameter, while some have more than one. Figure 9 demonstrates the number of samples containing a different number of missing parameters. More than 50% of samples contain one to two missing parameters necessary for security purposes, and only 13.3% possess all the parameters that we have considered.

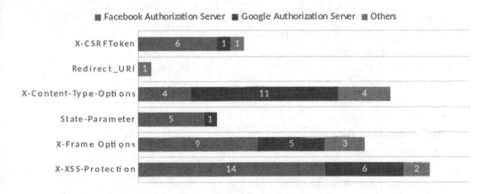

Fig. 8. Missing parameter

5   Features and Limitations

OVERSCAN was designed to compatible with a variety of authorization servers that support OAuth 2.0 protocol. It provides the abilities to determine the vulnerability, which possibly occurs during OAuth authentication flow via the parameters missing from the transmitted message. Table 2 shows the comparison of the supporting features with the other two OAuth vulnerability scanners: SSOSCAN and OAuthGuard.

Although OVERSCAN supports most of the vulnerabilities detected by the other two scanners, it cannot analyze the message directly sent between the client and authorization server. Since it uses Burp as the host for the operations, it can only intercept the message sent through the web browser. Therefore, it impossible for OVERSCAN to verify the security flaws happening after the beginning of

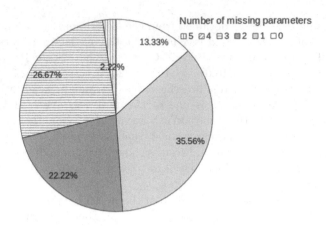

Fig. 9. Number of samples which have 0 to 5 missing parameters

Table 2. Comparison of supported features

Supported feature	OAuthGuard	SSOScan	OVERSCAN
Support a wide range of identity providers			✓
Stand alone application	✓	✓	
Identify OAuth grant type			✓
Protection	✓		
Instant warning message	✓	✓	
Generate technical report	✓		✓
CSRF vulnerability detection	✓		✓
Impersonation attack detection	✓		✓
ClickJacking attack detection			✓
Unsafe redirect URI detection	✓	✓	✓
Client secret leakage detection		✓	
Authorization code leakage detection	✓	✓	✓

the Access Token exchange process. Aside from that, OVERSCAN is unable to support protection and instant warning inline with the above reasons. Instead of giving the instant warning message when anomalies were found, OVERSCAN will summarize them in the readable technical report.

6   Conclusion

OVERSCAN is the anomaly detector which aims for identifying the missing significant security parameters used during the OAuth 2.0 grant request process. It can determine missing parameters which result in threats such as CSRF attack, confidential data leakage, and session stealing. As the experimental results of using OVERSCAN over 45 samples, only 15.56% are free of missing parameter.

The parameter which most frequently missing is XSS protection while insecure Redirect URI is the least.

References

1. Argyriou, M., Dragoni, N., Spognardi, A.: Security flows in OAuth 2.0 framework: a case study. In: Tonetta, S., Schoitsch, E., Bitsch, F. (eds.) SAFECOMP 2017. LNCS, vol. 10489, pp. 396–406. Springer, Cham (2017). https://doi.org/10.1007/978-3-319-66284-8_33
2. Canetti, R.: Universally composable security: a new paradigm for cryptographic protocols, vol. 2000, pp. 136–145, November 2001. https://doi.org/10.1109/SFCS.2001.959888
3. Chari, S., Jutla, C.S., Roy, A.: Universally composable security analysis of OAuth v2.0. IACR Cryptology ePrint Archive, vol. 2011, p. 526, January 2011
4. Chen, E.Y., Pei, Y., Chen, S., Tian, Y., Kotcher, R., Tague, P.: OAuth demystified for mobile application developers. In: Proceedings of the 2014 ACM SIGSAC Conference on Computer and Communications Security, CCS 2014, pp. 892–903. ACM, New York (2014). https://doi.org/10.1145/2660267.2660323http://doi.acm.org/10.1145/2660267.2660323
5. Corella, F., Lewison, K.P.: Security analysis of double redirection protocols (2011)
6. Ferry, E., O'Raw, J., Curran, K.: Security evaluation of the OAuth 2.0 framework. Inf. Comput. Secur. **23**, 73–101 (2015). https://doi.org/10.1108/ICS-12-2013-0089
7. Hardt, D.: The OAuth 2.0 authorization framework. RFC 6749, RFC Editor, October 2012. http://www.rfc-editor.org/rfc/rfc6749.txt
8. Li, W., Mitchell, C.J.: Security issues in OAuth 2.0 SSO implementations. In: Chow, S.S.M., Camenisch, J., Hui, L.C.K., Yiu, S.M. (eds.) ISC 2014. LNCS, vol. 8783, pp. 529–541. Springer, Cham (2014). https://doi.org/10.1007/978-3-319-13257-0_34
9. Li, W., Mitchell, C.J., Chen, T.: OAuthguard: protecting user security and privacy with OAuth 2.0 and OpenID connect. arXiv abs/1901.08960 (2019)
10. Lodderstedt, T., McGloin, M., Hunt, P.: OAuth 2.0 threat model and security considerations. RFC 6819, RFC Editor, January 2013
11. Lodderstedt, T., Bradley, J., Labunets, A., Fett, D.: OAuth 2.0 security best current practice. Internet-Draft draft-ietf-oauth-security-topics-09, IETF Secretariat, November 2018. http://www.ietf.org/internet-drafts/draft-ietf-oauth-security-topics-09.txt
12. Pai, S., Sharma, Y., Kumar, S., Pai, R.M., Singh, S.: Formal verification of OAuth 2.0 using alloy framework. In: 2011 International Conference on Communication Systems and Network Technologies, pp. 655–659, June 2011. https://doi.org/10.1109/CSNT.2011.141
13. Richer, J., Sanso, A.: OAuth 2 in Action. Manning Publications, New York (2017)
14. Torlak, E., van Dijk, M., Gassend, B., Jackson, D., Devadas, S.: Knowledge flow analysis for security protocols. CoRR abs/cs/0605109 (2006). http://arxiv.org/abs/cs/0605109
15. Yang, F., Manoharan, S.: A security analysis of the OAuth protocol. In: IEEE Pacific Rim Conference on Communications, Computers and Signal Processing (PACRIM), pp. 271–276, August 2013. https://doi.org/10.1109/PACRIM.2013.6625487
16. Zhou, Y., Evans, D.: SSOScan: automated testing of web applications for single sign-on vulnerabilities, August 2014

LaT-Voting: Traceable Anonymous E-Voting on Blockchain

Peng Li and Junzuo Lai[✉]

Jinan University, Guangzhou, China
penglijnu@gmail.com, laijunzuo@gmail.com

Abstract. In order to achieve anonymous voting, various cryptographic techniques are usually leveraged to avoid privacy leakage. However, traditional e-voting systems are excessively dependent on a centralized platform for publishing voting activity and storing ballots, which cannot ensure the security against tampering. Recently, numerous solutions based on blockchain are proposed to eliminate this threat. Nevertheless, these schemes are not applicable for wide adoption owing to the inefficiency in detecting double-voting. Meanwhile, there are no novel manners can both trace back to a malicious voter who voted twice, and discover his real identity simultaneously. Therefore, to settle the two aforementioned issues effectively, the first blockchain-based anonymous and traceable decentralized voting scheme called LaT-Voting is proposed in this paper. To better coordinate the conflict relationship between anonymity and accountability, we propose a new notion called *prefix-based linkable-and-traceable anonymous authentication*, which (i) achieves the authentication process without disclosing user privacy; (ii) provides a practical linkability to rapidly link two messages originated from a user; (iii) realizes a subtle traceability to track the user who authenticated twice.

Keywords: E-voting · Blockchain · Anonymous authentication · Linkability · Traceability

1 Introduction

Over the past decades, voting plays a critical role for people to exercise their power in modern society since its generation. As a problem-solving approach, it provides a straightforward and convenient way to make a decision according to a number of opinions especially when there are multiple choices. It ranges from boardroom voting, classroom voting and national election, etc. Traditional paper voting suffers from low efficiency, high cost and unintentional errors, thus it has gradually been replaced by electronic voting (e-voting) system which owns outstanding advantages and meets the development trend in modern society.

E-voting generally means the transmission and collection of people's suffrages by means of an electronic manner [1], which has obtained considerable concerns and interests as one of the most intractable cryptographic protocol problems [2].

© Springer Nature Switzerland AG 2019
J. K. Liu and X. Huang (Eds.): NSS 2019, LNCS 11928, pp. 234–254, 2019.
https://doi.org/10.1007/978-3-030-36938-5_14

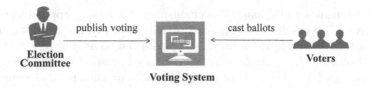

Fig. 1. Traditional e-voting system.

A typical e-voting model consists of three roles as illustrated in Fig. 1, i.e., an election committee, voters and a centralized voting system. An election committee publishes an election activity which usually includes multiple candidates through the centralized system. A large number of voters who have an eligible identity could cast ballots through the centralized voting system, while the election committee will then finish the ballot counting. A centralized voting system acts as a bulletin board to broadcast voting activity and collect all the ballots, which actually plays a role as a centralized database. Different cryptographic techniques have been proposed to establish e-voting systems, such as mix-net [3], blind signature [4], homomorphic encryption [5], group signature [6], ring signature [7], etc.

It is well known that reducing dependency of a centralized platform is desired in practice. However, in Fig. 1, a centralized platform unavoidably faces all the weaknesses of single point of failure. In contrast, the emerging blockchain technology provides a distributed, transparent and immutable ledger that ensures the transparency and reliability. The ledger is maintained by a group of nodes in a P2P network, and is verified by the whole network on the basis of a designated consensus protocol. This guarantees the realiable transmission through an untrusted network environment. More interestingly, the smart contract on top of blockchain can be automatically and securely executed, and will faithfully deal with all the message transmissions and perform related computations. Hence, blockchain can improve the transparency and ensure immutability in voting together with smart contract.

Despite of the limitation of the centralized model, e-voting schemes are subject to other unavoidable challenges. Firstly, traditional e-voting systems are so vulnerable to be tampered with, thus, it is naturally to be suspicious of the trustworthiness of the voting result. Secondly, users' sensitive information may be stored on the voting system together with the corresponding votes, which will raise the risk of privacy leakage. More importantly, double-voting is always unavoidable in most voting schemes, but there is no high-efficiency operations to check whether it happens. Last but not least, if a malicious voter casts twice, effective ways are needed to trace back to this voter without the cooperation of other parties.

There have been numerous researches to address these above mentioned challenges. Distributed architecture is designed to address single point of failure [8], but the blockchain technology not only realizes distributed storage but also maintains a immutable ledger to avoid data modification in a decentralized way.

Encryption schemes and signature mechanisms are generally applied to preserve voter's privacy. To check the double-casting while achieving anonymity, linkable group signature [6] and linkable ring signature [9] can be used as tools to link any two ballots sent by an identical voter, but they need considerable exponent calculations which are inefficient to implement linkability quickly. Furthermore, to find out who casts twice, Tracing-by-Linking group signature [10], linkable threshold ring signature [7], traceable ring signature [11] can realize the function of traceability. However, these related implementations are impractical since these schemes involve complicated constructions and massive computations. In order to track a misbehaving voter, the group manager in the general group signature schemes is capable of opening all members' signatures [12] while increasing the risk of privacy breach. Other related threshold schemes in [13] and [14] can trace a ballot and its owner, but they need to introduce additional trusted parties to join in.

Until now, none of the existing researches has resolved all of the above mentioned issues simultaneously. Therefore, our work is motivated to design and achieve a decentralized e-voting with security, anonimity, linkability, traceability in a concise and efficient manner. To fulfill this task, we have to address three challenges: design a rapid method to link two ballots voted by the same voter, coordinate the conflict relationship between anonymity and accountability. Accordingly, we investigate an effective manner for not only rapidly detecting double-casting, but also grasping the double-voted voter and exposing his identity. To achieve the rapid linkability, we choose the innovative trick of common-prefix in [15] to reach this goal. We also realize the public traceability based on [16] so as to further reveal the double-voted voter's identity without any trusted authority.

Our Contributions. In this paper, we propose the blockchain-based anonymous and traceable decentralized voting scheme called LaT-Voting, which ensures the ballots confidentiality and voter anonymity while achieving stronger accountability. Specifically,

(1) We design and construct a blockchain-based decentralized e-voting scheme, which is not dependent on any central third party to complete voting process. It ensures the security of ballot content by supporting a distributed way to store encrypted ballots. Moreover, the immutable ledger of blockchain acts as a secure and tamper-resistant database so that to avoid data modification.

(2) To achieve the speedy linkability while better coordinating the anonymity and accountability, we propose a concrete scheme called prefix-based linkable-and-traceable anonymous authentication, which realizes authentication without any privacy disclosing, and provides a practical linkability to rapidly link two authenticated messages sent from an identical user. More importantly, the public traceability is implemented to track the misbehaving user who authenticated twice or more. Particularly, it is anonymous if a user authenticates once, since anyone cannot tell one's identity from the authentication transcript. However, the linkability and public traceability

are activated as long as two messages authenticated by a same key, everyone can link the two messages and expose the user's identity.

(3) We design the voting scheme on top of blockchain, and illustrate the voting process by smart contract. Smart contract is used for collecting ballots and verifying their validity, and exposing the double-voted voters. In addition, we provide the security analysis of our proposed voting scheme.

The remainder of the paper is organized as follows. The related work is present in Sect. 2, and in Sect. 3 we will give the essential preliminaries. We describe the system model in Sect. 4, and propose the concrete voting scheme together with the linkable-and-traceable anonymous authentication in Sect. 5. Next, we will give the correctness and security of LaT-Voting in Sect. 6, and analysis the evaluation results in Sect. 7. Finally, we summarize our research work of this paper in Sect. 8.

2 Related Work

Researching on e-voting has gained considerable attention and interest with the swift development of the Internet. We review some representative works.

Centralized Voting. Numerous e-voting systems are usually carried out in a centralized manner. The essential processes of voting, like ballots collection and ballots tallying, are executed and managed by the role of authority, such as the system administrator or the group manager, which may make the privacy in danger. The centralized services are involved in the execution of voting protocol in [17] and [18], but [17] can keep voters in anonymity and [18] distributes trust to different authorities. In addition, a centralized platform is normally used to store voting data, which is easily attacked by malicious adversaries and will be subject to the trouble of single point of failure and privacy disclosure. Helios in [19] and the protocol in [20] are both implemented with a web-based bulletin board that enables anyone to observe the dynamic process in the voting, but it usually suffers from privacy disclosure and the awkward issue of single point of failure.

Distributed Voting. There are several studies on the distributed voting schemes. [21] considers a distributed asynchronous system to realize the ballot collection in every server. [22] introduces a distributed architecture for web-based voting, which distributes the task of collecting ballots over multiple servers to reduce the opportunity of the single failure in tallying. [23] designs a distributed architecture for allowing to vote at any voting station, [24] implements a distributed processing architecture to process ballots over several web servers. [25] presents a distributed voting system with a fully asynchronous ballot collection subsystem which includes a number of nodes to provide immediate assurance that the ballot is recorded as the voter cast. Although the researches in [21–25] aim to convert the treatment to a distributed fashion in e-voting, their schemes are actually dependent on a centralized system to offer services, which is inconsistent with our purpose to devise a decentralized e-voting protocol.

Decentralized Voting. There are also various researches concentrated on designing voting protocols without relying the role of authority or a central platform. The typical self-tallying (such as [2,26,27]) protocol achieves that the process of voting is carried out by the voters themselves without the involvement of other parties, which provides stronger privacy protection and supports the dispute-freeness. But the drawback of this kind of protocol is that it requires all the voters must join in the voting. Unfortunately, even a single one that deviates from the protocol will result in the failure of tallying. Therefore, it is not suitable for large scale voting due to its non-scalability.

Blockchain-Based Voting. [28] realizes a self-tallying voting using Bitcoin, the ballots are not required to be encrypted, but with the help of a commitment process which chooses a randomness to hide the real value of the ballot and needs the sum of all the random numbers is zero. [29] also implements a self-tallying voting on blockchain through designing a two-round protocol. However, [28,29] only support two candidates, even though they are decentralized via taking advantage of the self-tallying. [30] is a decentralized voting which supports self-tallying and multiple candidates. In addition, [31] establishes a platform-independent voting system to eliminate the limitations on the number of voters and candidates, [32] attempts to remove the role of any trusted party by using blockchain, but both of them only make the ballots to be secret. The above mentioned researches are limited to their specific requirements, but our work focus on holding the anonymity while keeping the accountability.

Traceable Voting. In order to preserve privacy, typical e-voting systems usually reveal the feature of untraceability [21,33–35] that separates the relevancy between the ballot and its owner. Mixnet [35], DC-net [33,36], blind signature [37] and ring signature [38] make it possible to attain untraceability, but the double-casting becomes an intractable issue needs to be worked out. It is necessary to balance privacy and accountability so as to prevent from abusing the anonymity. Linkable group signature in [6] and linkable ring signature in [1,9] have been suggested to be used in constructing e-voting system, but it can only verify whether two valid signatures are from the same signer. However, the two kinds of signature schemes make linking-and-tracing come true in [10] and [7]. But both the ring signature and group signature schemes are not succinct to reach the goal of traceability. Similarly, traceable ring signature [11] could be applied to voting, which realizes the public traceability that can track the public key of the owner who signed two signatures, but massive computation and complex operations are involved. In addition, [13] introduces revocable anonymity to voting, which can recover the identity of the voter, yet it must rely on the coordination with other parities. [14] constructs a complex voting protocol which satisfies the anonymity and traceability simultaneously, but only allowing the administrator to track the ballot and locate the voter with the help of other trusted parties. The above mentioned studies are constrained to accomplish the public traceability while holding the anonymity. By comparison, our scheme provides a subtle protocol with anonymity and public traceability in e-voting for the purpose of avoiding anonymity misuse and holding accountability.

3   Preliminaries

3.1   Blockchain

Blockchain is a distributed, transparent and immutable ledger that consists of a large number of transactions which are recorded in blocks. Each block involves a certain number of transactions and a hash of the previous block, and is generated according to a predefined consensus protocol. Numerous blocks in sequence connect to a chain which we called blockchain. Blockchain offers a distributed manner to keep a consistent replicate and avoid data tampering by rewarding miners for jointly maintaining the blockchain network.

In general, blockchain can be regarded as a public ledger. The data that will be recorded on the blockchain is sent to the blockchain network in the form of a transaction, which is signed and sent by the user. After the transaction is broadcast to the whole network, it will be verified and packed into a block together with other transactions, these transactions will be written into the blockchain after the block is confirmed. On the other hand, it is visible to view all the data transmissions for the public, thus, anyone is available to check the validity of all the transactions.

A blockchain address is a randomly generated anonymous address by computing a hash of the public key. Thus, the address acts as a pseudoym to hide user's identity. A transaction should be signed by the corresponding secret key, no one can send a transaction through a random address without the corresponding secret key.

3.2   Smart Contract

A smart contract can be considered as a self-executing computer program [29] which transfers the running processes into executable codes as a legal agreement. The necessary fairness and credibility can be ensured directly through the automated execution of contract code. The reason that it cannot be widely applied to represent its intelligence before is mainly due to the lack of a secure and decentralized development environment [8]. However, in the blockchain distributed network, each node updates the duplicate locally based on the current execution result after runing the smart contract. Blockchain has the possibility of providing a trustworthy and decentralized mode to accelerate its exploitation. Currently, smart contracts are designed as multiple kinds of reliable and decentralized applications while offering fair and secure services to avoid dishonesty, downtime and tampering.

3.3   zk-SNARK

Zero-knowledge proof is a delicate cryptographic protocol, which enables a prover to generate a proof and convince the verifier that he indeed knows a secret without leaking any additional knowledge of the secret. In voting protocols, zero-knowledge proof is widely employed to guarantee the operations are not deviated from the required rules. In this paper, we exploit the zk-SNARK [39] to accomplish the specific proof for a NP-language $\mathcal{L} = \{x | \exists w, s.t., C(x, w) = 1\}$ [15], where x is a statement, w is a witness for x, and C is a boolean circuit. Informally, zk-SNARK is made of three algorithms:

- KeyGen$(1^\lambda, C) \longrightarrow (pk, vk)$. The KeyGen algorithm inputs a security parameter 1^λ and a circuit C, and outputs a proving key pk and a verification key vk. Both of the keys are public parameters.
- Prover$(pk, x, w) \longrightarrow \pi$. The Prover algorithm inputs the proving key pk, a statement x, and a witness w. It outputs a proof π.
- Verifier$(vk, x, \pi) \longrightarrow 0/1$. The Verifier algorithm inputs the verification key vk, the statement x, and the corresponding proof π. It outputs 1 if π is a valid attestation for $x \in \mathcal{L}$.

Informally, the zk-SNARK satisfies the following properties.

- *Completeness.* A prover can generate a proof such that it can be passed through the verification by the verifier with probability 1.
- *Soundness.* No polynomial-time adversary is capable of forging a valid attestation that can be accepted by the verifier with non-negligible probability.
- *Efficiency.* The randomized algorithms run in time polynomial in the sizes of the corresponding input.
- *Zero-knowledge.* The procedure only reveals the statement rather than any secret.
- *Proof of knowledge.* If the verifier accepts a statement from a prover, there is a polynomial-time extractor who can generate a valid witness when giving oracle access to the prover.

4   System Model

4.1   Entities

As shown in Fig. 2, four entities are involved in the voting protocol, namely, the certificate authority, the election committee, voter and the smart contract.

- *Certificate Authority*, identified by CA, is mainly to certify and manage the user's identity, and issues a related certificate to the user.
- *Election Committee*, identified by EC, is the organizer of voting, whose task is to post a voting activity and compute the election result.
- *Voter*, identified by V_i, is the participant who has the right to cast a ballot before deadline.
- *Smart Contract*, identified by SC, is designed primarily for collecting and verifying ballots, detecting double-voting and tracing the double-voted voters.

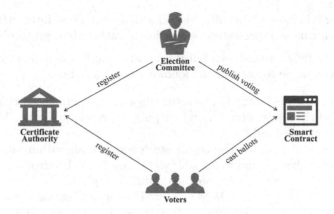

Fig. 2. The system model of LaT-Voting.

4.2 Requirements

Our LaT-Voting scheme requires the following properties.

- *Privacy:* The content of ballot is kept secret from the public, except the role who performs the tallying.
- *Anonymity:* The voter should be kept anonymous when casting a ballot, and no one can link a ballot to a voter.
- *Unforgeability:* No one can forge user's identity to generate a ballot, and anyone can test whether a ballot is generated correctly.
- *Public verifiability:* Any party should be convinced that all ballots have been counted when tallying, and the final election result can be verified.
- *Traceability:* Double-voted behavior can be detected by seeking the linkability of two ballots. Any voter who voted twice will be discovered and his identity will be tracked and exposed.

5 Traceable Anonymous E-Voting

In this section, we will firstly present the new notion, called prefix-based linkable-and-traceable anonymous authentication, to support an anonymous yet accountable requirement, and then describe how our decentralized e-voting scheme works so as to ensure security, anonymity, linkability and traceability. The voting protocol is tested on an open blockchain.

5.1 Prefix-Based Linkable-and-Traceable Anonymous Authentication

The prefix-based linkable-and-traceable anonymous authentication can be built on any certificate generation procedure, and therefore we can construct it as other existing schemes. Meanwhile, we prefer to design a non-interactive authentication which can be represented as algorithms rather than protocols.

Syntax. Formally, a prefix-based linkable-and-traceable anonymous authentication (PLTAA) scheme consists of the following six algorithms.

- Setup(1^λ) $\longrightarrow$ (MPK, MSK). The setup algorithm is a function that takes as input a security parameter 1^λ, and outputs a master public key MPK and a master secret key MSK.
- CertGen(pk, MSK) $\longrightarrow$ σ. The certificate generation algorithm takes as input a user's public key pk and the master secret key MSK. It outputs a certificate σ that can validate the corresponding public key pk.
- Auth($m = m_l \| m_r, pk, sk, \sigma$, MPK) $\longrightarrow$ π. The authentication algorithm takes as input a message m that has a left part m_l (i.e. a prefix) and a right part m_r, the user's public key pk and secret key sk, the certificate σ, and the master public key MPK. It outputs an authentication token π on the message m to show that the user who created the message m indeed has the secret key corresponding to a valid certificate.
- Verify(m, π, MPK) $\longrightarrow$ 1/0. The verification algorithm takes as input a message m, an authentication token π and the master public key MPK. It outputs 1 or 0 to decide whether the proof is valid or not.
- Link(m_1, m_2, π_1, π_2) $\longrightarrow$ 1/0. The link algorithm takes as input two messages m_1, m_2 and their corresponding authentication tokens π_1, π_2. It outputs 1 if m_1 and m_2 have a common prefix with a fixed length; otherwise, it outputs 0.
- Trace(π_1, π_2) $\longrightarrow$ pk. The trace algorithm takes as input the two authentication tokens π_1, π_2 corresponding to the linked two messages. It outputs the traced public key pk, which points to the user who authenticates two messages having a common prefix.

Correctness. Correctness of PLTAA scheme must satisfy:

- *Verification correctness.* Authentication tokens generated according to specification will successfully pass the verification by Verify.
- *Linking correctness.* If two messages sharing a common prefix are authenticated by a user, they can certainly be linked by Link.
- *Tracing correctness.* If two messages are linked, the same originator who authenticated them will be traced by Trace.

Notions of Security. Security of PLTAA schemes has four aspects: unforgeability, anonymity, linkability and accountability.

Unforgeability. Unforgeability for PLTAA schemes is defined as the following game between the Challenger $\mathcal{C}$ and the Adversary $\mathcal{A}$.

1. $\mathcal{A}$ creates a master key pair (MPK, MSK).
2. $\mathcal{A}$ performs the certificate generation process with $\mathcal{C}$. When $\mathcal{C}$ submits a public keys pk to $\mathcal{A}$, $\mathcal{A}$ returns a certificates σ to $\mathcal{C}$.

3. $\mathcal{A}$ randomly chooses q message $m_1, \ldots, m_q$ and asks $\mathcal{C}$ to authenticate them. $\mathcal{C}$ produces and outputs the corresponding authentication tokens $\pi_1, \ldots, \pi_q$.
4. $\mathcal{A}$ selects a message m and creates the corresponding π, and outputs (m, π).

$\mathcal{A}$ wins if:

1. $\mathsf{Verify}(m, \pi, \mathsf{MPK}) = 1$;
2. $m \in \{m_1, \ldots, m_q\}$.

We denote by

$$\mathbf{Adv}_{\mathcal{A}}^{Unfo}(\lambda) = \Pr[\mathcal{A} \; wins \; the \; game].$$

Definition 1 (Unforgeability). *A PLTAA scheme is unforgeable, if for all PPT adversary $\mathcal{A}$, $\mathbf{Adv}_{\mathcal{A}}^{Unfo}(\lambda)$ is negligible.*

Anonymity. Anonymity for PLTAA schemes is defined as the following game between the Challenger $\mathcal{C}$ and the Adversary $\mathcal{A}$.

1. $\mathcal{A}$ creates a master key pair $(\mathsf{MPK}, \mathsf{MSK})$.
2. $\mathcal{A}$ performs the certificate generation process with $\mathcal{C}$. When $\mathcal{C}$ submits two public keys pk_1, pk_2 to $\mathcal{A}$, $\mathcal{A}$ returns the corresponding certificates σ_1, σ_2 to $\mathcal{C}$.
3. $\mathcal{A}$ chooses a messages m and asks $\mathcal{C}$ to authenticate it. $\mathcal{C}$ randomly picks $b \in \{1, 2\}$, uses (pk_b, sk_b, σ_b) to authenticate m, and sends the newly generated authentication token π_b to $\mathcal{A}$.
4. After receiving π_b, $\mathcal{A}$ outputs the guess b'.

$\mathcal{A}$ wins if $b' = b$. We denote by

$$\mathbf{Adv}_{\mathcal{A}}^{Anon}(\lambda) = \left| \Pr[\mathcal{A} \; wins \; the \; game] - \frac{1}{2} \right|.$$

Definition 2 (Anonymity). *A PLTAA scheme is anonymous, if for all PPT adversary $\mathcal{A}$, $\mathbf{Adv}_{\mathcal{A}}^{Anon}(\lambda)$ is negligible.*

Linkability. Linkability for PLTAA schemes is defined as the following game between the Challenger $\mathcal{C}$ and the Adversary $\mathcal{A}$.

1. $\mathcal{C}$ creates a master key pair $(\mathsf{MPK}, \mathsf{MSK})$ and gives $\mathcal{A}$ the master public key MPK.
2. $\mathcal{C}$ performs the certificate generation process with $\mathcal{A}$. When $\mathcal{A}$ submits a public key pk to $\mathcal{C}$, $\mathcal{C}$ returns a certificate σ to $\mathcal{A}$.
3. $\mathcal{C}$ chooses two messages $m_l||m_1, m_l||m_2$ sharing a common prefix m_l to $\mathcal{A}$, and asks $\mathcal{A}$ to authenticate them. $\mathcal{A}$ creates the corresponding authentication tokens π_1, π_2, and outputs $(m_l||m_1, \pi_1), (m_l||m_2, \pi_2)$.

$\mathcal{A}$ wins if:

1. Verify($m_l||m_i, \pi_i, \mathsf{MPK}$) = 1 for $i = 1, 2$;
2. Link($m_l||m_1, m_l||m_2, \pi_1, \pi_2$) = 0.

We denote by

$$\mathbf{Adv}_{\mathcal{A}}^{Link}(\lambda) = \Pr[\mathcal{A} \ wins \ the \ game].$$

Definition 3 (Linkability). *A PLTAA scheme is linkable, if for all PPT adversary $\mathcal{A}$, $\mathbf{Adv}_{\mathcal{A}}^{Link}(\lambda)$ is negligible.*

Accountability. Accountability for PLTAA schemes is defined as the following game between the Challenger $\mathcal{C}$ and the Adversary $\mathcal{A}$.

1. $\mathcal{C}$ creates a master key pair (MPK, MSK) and gives $\mathcal{A}$ the master public key MPK.
2. $\mathcal{C}$ performs the certificate generation process with $\mathcal{A}$. When $\mathcal{A}$ submits a public key pk to $\mathcal{C}$, $\mathcal{C}$ returns a certificate σ to $\mathcal{A}$.
3. $\mathcal{C}$ chooses two messages $m_l||m_1, m_l||m_2$ sharing a common prefix m_l to $\mathcal{A}$, and asks $\mathcal{A}$ to authenticate them. $\mathcal{A}$ creates the corresponding authentication tokens π_1, π_2, and outputs $(m_l||m_1, \pi_1), (m_l||m_2, \pi_2)$.

$\mathcal{A}$ wins if:

1. Verify($m_l||m_i, \pi_i, \mathsf{MPK}$) = 1 for $i = 1, 2$;
2. Link($m_l||m_1, m_l||m_2, \pi_1, \pi_2$) = 1;
3. Trace(π_1, π_2) = pk', but $pk' \neq pk$; or, Trace(π_1, π_2) = $\bot$.

We denote by

$$\mathbf{Adv}_{\mathcal{A}}^{Acco}(\lambda) = \Pr[\mathcal{A} \ wins \ the \ game].$$

Definition 4 (Accountability). *A PLTAA scheme is accountable, if for all PPT adversary $\mathcal{A}$, $\mathbf{Adv}_{\mathcal{A}}^{Acco}(\lambda)$ is negligible.*

Construction. We proceed to construct such a PLTAA scheme. Similar to other anonymous authentication schemes, we also utilize the zero-knowledge proof technique to achieve anonymity. Specifically, we apply zk-SNARK to obtain an efficient construction. Since the assurance contributing to linkability-and-traceability is the prefix, consequently, we will exploit it to support an anonymous-yet-accountable requirement. In a nutshell, the authentication process creates a linking tag committed to the prefix and the user's secret key. To satisfy the requirement of accountability, we will also provide a tracing tag which will be used for tracking.

Let S = (S.Setup, S.Sign, S.Verify) be a signature scheme, Z = (Z.Setup, Z.Prover, Z.Verifier) be the zk-SNARK protocol. Also, assume $\mathcal{H} : \{0,1\}^* \longrightarrow \{0,1\}^n$ represents a secure hash function, the public function F : $pk = F(sk)$ denotes a key-pair verification algorithm. The PLTAA scheme is as follows.

- Setup(1^λ). The setup algorithm first invokes S.Setup(1^λ) to create a signing key msk and a verification key mpk, and calls Z.Setup(1^λ) to obtain the public parameters PP for zk-SNARK. The public parameters are MPK $=$ $(\mathcal{H}, mpk, \text{PP})$, the master secret key is MSK $= (msk)$.
- CertGen(pk_i, MSK). The certificate generation algorithm calls S.Sign(m, msk) to compute a signature σ_i on a public key pk_i, and outputs σ_i.
- Auth($p||m_r, pk_i, sk_i, \sigma_i$, MPK). On input a message $p||m_r$ including a prefix p, the authentication algorithm dose the following:
  1. Compute a linking tag $t_1 = \mathcal{H}(p, sk_i)$ and a tracing tag $t_2 = \mathcal{H}(p, pk_i, sk_i) + m_r \cdot sk_i$.
  2. Let $x = (p||m_r, \text{MPK})$ be the common knowledge, $w = (pk_i, sk_i, \sigma_i)$ be the private witness. Call key-pair verification algorithm $pk = \text{F}(sk)$, certificate verification algorithm S.Verify(mpk, m, σ) for the language

$$\mathcal{L} = \{t_1, t_2, x = (p||m_r, \text{MPK})|\ \exists w = (pk_i, sk_i, \sigma_i), s.t.,$$
$$pk_i = \text{F}(sk_i) \wedge \text{S.Verify}(pk_i, \sigma_i, mpk) = 1 \wedge$$
$$t_1 = \mathcal{H}(p, sk_i) \wedge t_2 = \mathcal{H}(p, pk_i, sk_i) + m_r \cdot sk_i\},$$

   where the function F is to confirm if the two keys correspond to a public-secret key pair, the S.Verify algorithm is used for checking whether σ_i is a valid certificate. Next, call zk-SNARK proving algorithm Z.Prover(x, w, PP) to produce a proof η related to the statement $x \in \mathcal{L}$.
  3. At last, the algorithm outputs an authentication token $\pi = (t_1, t_2, \eta)$.
- Verify($p||m_r, \pi$, MPK). The verification algorithm invokes Z.Verifier(x, π, PP), and outputs 0 or 1 for invalid or valid, respectively.
- Link(m_1, m_2, π_1, π_2). Let $\pi_1 = (t_1^1, t_2^1, \eta_1)$, $\pi_2 = (t_1^2, t_2^2, \eta_2)$, the link algorithm checks whether t_1^1 in π_1 equals to t_1^2 in π_2. If $t_1^1 = t_1^2$, it outputs 1 for linked; otherwise, it outputs 0.
- Trace(π_1, π_2). If $t_1^1 = t_1^2$, the trace algorithm computes a derived secret key sk_i and calls the function F to calculate the corresponding public key $pk_i = \text{F}(sk_i)$ pointing to the user i.

The correctness and security theorems are given in Appendix A.

5.2   The LaT-Voting Protocol

Now we prepare to describe a general protocol for a type of voting scheme with traceability back to malicious voters who voted twice or more in a voting activity. Notice that we let each user generate a distinct blockchain address for a voting activity, namely, each user has a unique address, which is regarded as a simple solution to achieve anonymity in the blockchain network. And on the basis of this protocol, we can also extend it to additional voting schemes by appending an incentive mechanism to reward honest participants.

The workflow of LaT-Voting is depicted as follows.

(1) Each participant should register at CA to obtain a certificate. Then, they can post a voting activity or cast a ballot.

(2) EC prepares to post a voting activity. After the voting is announced, each voter is allowed to join in.

(3) When receiving the notification of voting, each voter can cast a ballot before deadline.

(4) SC verifies every ballot and picks out all double-voted ballots. Then EC calculates the election result according to the valid ballots.

(5) SC tracks the identities of double-voted voters according to the linked ballots.

The whole process of our LaT-Voting protocol is shown in Fig. 3, more details are described as follows.

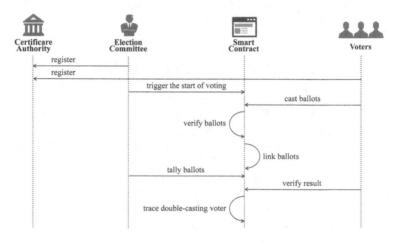

Fig. 3. The process of LaT-Voting.

Register. CA calls S.Setup to create the signing key pair (mpk, msk). EC generates his key pair (pk_{EC}, sk_{EC}), and registers at CA to get a certificate σ_{EC}. Similarly, V_i also creates his key pair (pk_i, sk_i), and registers at CA to get a certificate σ_i. This registration process is normally done offline only once for each user by calling S.Sign algorithm.

Publish. Before starting a voting activity, EC should create a new blockchain account address α_{EC}, a key pair (epk, esk) that is only for this activity, and the epk will be used for voters to encrypt their own votes. EC prepares the related parameters Param containing a unique voting activity serial number Num, a list of k candidates (each one corresponds to a unique identifier ID_j), the public parameters MPK (i.e. a hash function $\mathcal{H}$, CA's public key mpk, the SNARK's public parameters PP), the encryption key epk, the deadline t, the tally mechanism T, and an authentication token π_{EC} on Num and α_{EC}. π_{EC} can be created through calling Auth algorithm, i.e.,

$$\pi_{EC} = \mathsf{Auth}(Num\|\alpha_{EC}, pk_{EC}, sk_{EC}, \sigma_{EC}, \mathsf{MPK}).$$

Then EC codes a voting smart contract SC which contains all above public parameters for this voting activity. After successfully compiling the contract SC, he puts the code of SC into a transaction, and sends the newly constructed transaction into the blockchain network through the previously generated address α_{EC}.

Cast. Once a new generated block includes the above transaction in blockchain, everyone could retrieve the transaction and the contract SC. Voters first check if the address α_{EC} corresponds to the one in contract SC, and test the validity of contract SC. Then, V_i starts to create his one-time anonymous blockchain address α_i, then encrypts his ballot with the public key epk to produce a corresponding encrypted ballot C_i.

Additionally, V_i invokes Auth algorithm to attach an authentication token

$$\pi_i = \mathsf{Auth}(Num || C_i, pk_i, sk_i, \sigma_i, \mathsf{MPK}).$$

Finally, V_i puts (C_i, π_i) into a transaction and sends them to the blockchain network using the one-time address α_i before the deadline.

Tally. SC runs $\mathsf{Verify}(Num || C_i, \pi_i, \mathsf{MPK})$ to check the validity of π_i. If π_i is valid, SC will proceed to run $\mathsf{Link}(C_i, C_*, \pi_i, \pi_*)$ for each ballot and its authentication token. C_* is the verified ballot which has passed through the Verify algorithm, π_* is the corresponding authentication token. This operation ensures that C_i is the first and valid submission from an eligible voter. Yet for any unauthenticated or double-voted ballot, the contract will drop it.

Finally, SC picks out all the valid votes till the deadline. Then EC will retrieve them, encrypt and calculate the election result $r = (r_1, \ldots, r_k)$. EC publishes r together with a corresponding zero knowledge proof π_{result} to prove the process is properly executed. Concretely, π_{result} is for the NP-language

$$\mathcal{L}_r = \{\mathsf{Param}, C^*, r \,|\, \exists esk, s.t., epk = \mathsf{F}(esk) \wedge B_i = \mathsf{Dec}(esk, C_i) \\ \wedge_{j=1}^{k} r_j = \mathsf{T}(ID_j; B_1, \ldots, B_n)\},$$

where C^* contains all the valid ballots in tallying, B_i indicates the plaintext of the encrypted ballot C_i, r represents the final voting result for k candidates, the Dec algorithm is to decrypt each encrypted ballot, r_j is the sum of ballots of each candidate, T denotes a tallying mechanism for all the candidates. And the secret key esk acts as the witness to establish an effective attestation.

At last, EC puts the result r and the corresponding proof π_{result} into a transaction, and sends it to the blockchain network using his address α_{EC}. After a new block containing r and π_{result} is appended to the blockchain, each one can verify the correctness of the election result.

Trace. If a voter casts two ballots C_i and C_i', there will be two authenticated tokens π_i and π_i' containing two distinct tracing tags. Specifically,

$$t_2 = \mathcal{H}(Num, pk_i, sk_i) + C_i \cdot sk_i,$$

$$t_2' = \mathcal{H}(Num, pk_i, sk_i) + C_i' \cdot sk_i.$$

Since the encrypted vote is randomly generated even though it encrypts a same value, thus C_i and C_i' are different. Consequently, the secret key of the double-voted voter can be easily derived by calling Trace algorithm, i.e.

$$sk_i = \frac{t_2 - t_2'}{C_i - C_i'}.$$

Then SC can locate this voter according to the public key $pk_i = \mathsf{F}(sk_i)$.

6　Correctness and Security Analysis

6.1　Correctness Analysis

The correctness is satisfied by the public verifiability which is provided by the cryptographic schemes and the blockchain platform. The cryptographic schemes achieve: (i) the certificate generated by S.Sign can be verified by S.Verify, (ii) the key pair can be verified by the function F; (iii) the proof created by Z.Prover can be verified by Z.Verifier; (iv) the linking-and-tracing correctness can be ensured by our PLTAA scheme. In addition, the blockchain platform serves as a decentralized public bulletin which contains the overall ballots from all the qualified voters. Meanwhile, the blockchain also ensures the consistent execution of all the transactions, which makes all the mining nodes mutually maintain an identical distributed ledger that contains the overall transactions mentioned above. And any inconsistency that causes an error would lead to the rejection of the transaction. It means that all the voters can be convinced that each ballot on the blockchain will be checked and verified by all the mining nodes, and any invalid ballot in the transaction will be refused to be appended to the ledger unless an adversary takes control of a certain percentage of compromised nodes in the blockchain network.

6.2　Security Features of the LaT-Voting Protocol

- *Privacy:* The ballots stored on the blockchain are in the form of ciphertext, which are encrypted by the key epk, and only the corresponding key esk could decrypt them. It realizes the ballot confidentiality that only EC with the esk other than anyone can calculate the final election result, and the ballot information is unknown to other parities.
- *Anonymity:* Every voter casts his ballot using a randomly generated one-time address α_i which prevents an adversary from linking a voter through his multiple addresses that have ever been involved in various transactions. Meantime, each authentication token $\pi_i = (t_1, t_2, \eta)$ created by Auth has two hash values $\mathcal{H}(Num, sk_i)$, $\mathcal{H}(Num, pk_i, sk_i)$ that can be considered as random numbers without revealing voter's any information, which realizes the anonymity based on our PLTAA scheme.

- *Unforgeability:* No one can forge a linking tag $t_1 = \mathcal{H}(Num, sk_i)$ in his authentication token such that it will be linked with another linking tag which is not generated by him. That is to say, an adversary cannot fake other voters' identities to cast a ballot. It is guaranteed by the unforgeability feature of our PLTAA scheme. Consequently, an adversary cannot forge a ballot in the name of a voter or fabricate an authentication token to track the voter's identity.
- *Public verifiability:* The whole process of voting is presented as a series of transactions, and stored as multiple blocks in a distributed ledger. Due to the openness and verifiability of the blockchain platform, the public have the right to verify whether all the ballots are recorded on the blockchain and the related authentication token are correctly generated, and check the validity of the final election result. In other words, it ensures the truthfulness in a transparent and verifiable fashion.
- *Traceability:* We fully capitalize on the PLTAA scheme so as to establish the linkability in a novel manner. It can rapidly detect whether there exists two messages authenticated by a same voter according to $\mathcal{H}(Num, sk_i)$, thus it is impossible for an adversary to authenticate two messages without being linked. Besides only linking the two ballots when double casting happens, on the contrary, we further try to infer his real identity based on the submitted information, even though he did that anonymously. Therefore, PLTAA scheme also provides an innovative strategy for tracking back to the double-casting voter who indeed submitted two authenticated ballots according to the tracing tag $t_2 = H(Num, pk_i, sk_i) + C_i \cdot sk_i$. Hence, as long as any two valid ballots corresponding to an identical voter, our solution could make his identity to be forcibly disclosed to the public in an ingenious way so as to enable the double voting can be avoided.

7   Conclusion

We present the LaT-Voting, a blockchain-based anonymous and traceable decentralized voting protocol, which provides novel privacy protection against disclosing personal identity information, and a practical linkability to rapidly link two ballots sent from the same voter. Moreover, to relieve the tension between anonymity and accountability, we achieve a subtle traceability to track the participant who is double-voted. We put forward a new notion called linkable-and-traceable anonymous authentication to meet the anonymous yet accountability requirement. A specific construction of this scheme is proposed, and it shows the usability and compatibility to the voting protocol and the blockchain infrastructure. We further list the security features of our voting protocol.

A   Correctness and Security Theorems

We outline the correctness and security theorems for the construction of our PLTAA scheme.

Correctness. Given a key pair (pk, sk) and a prefix p, we assume that the certificate σ is the output of S.Sign(sk, MPK), the authentication token $\pi = (t_1, t_2, \eta)$ is the output of Auth$(p||m, pk, sk, \sigma, \mathsf{MPK})$. We depict three types of correctness in turn.

1. Assume a statement $x = (p||m_r, \mathsf{MPK})$, a witness $w = (pk, sk, \sigma)$. Since $\sigma = \mathsf{S.Sign}(sk, \mathsf{MPK})$, we have S.Verify$(pk, \sigma, \mathsf{MPK}) = 1$ by the correctness of signature scheme S. Since sk exactly corresponds to pk such that $pk = \mathsf{F}(sk)$, the correctness is ensured by the function F. Since $\eta = \mathsf{Z.Prover}(x, w, \mathsf{PP})$, we have Z.Verifier$(x, \pi, \mathsf{PP}) = 1$ by the correctness of algorithm Z. Thus, the *verification correctness* is ensured.
2. Let $\mathcal{H}$ denote a secure hash function, $p||m_1$, $p||m_2$ be two messages with a common prefix p. Assume π_1, π_2 are the corresponding authentication tokens, we can achieve the *linking correctness*. If Verify$(p||m_i, \pi_i, \mathsf{MPK}) = 1$ for $i = 1, 2$. Since $t_1 = \mathcal{H}(p, sk)$, there must be the same value of $\mathcal{H}(p, sk)$ in π_1, π_2 such that the two messages are linked by the correctness of the hash function $\mathcal{H}$.
3. Meanwhile, the *tracing correctness* is also similar. If Verify$(m_i, \pi_i, \mathsf{MPK}) = 1$ for $i = 1, 2$; Link$(m_1, m_2, \pi_1, \pi_2) = 1$. Since $t_2 = \mathcal{H}(p, pk, sk) + m \cdot sk$, thus, π_1, π_2 have the same value of $\mathcal{H}(p, pk, sk)$ due to the correctness of the hash function $\mathcal{H}$, and the remaining part of t_2 will be used for inferring the public key pk.

Security. We list the security theorems in the following aspects.

Theorem 1 (Unforgeability). *A PLTAA scheme is unforgeable under the random oracle model.*

Proof. We require any uncertified attacker cannot forge one's identity to authenticate a message due to the lack of a secret key which corresponds to a public key and a certificate. Assume a user with (pk, sk) obtains a certificate σ. For a message $p||m$, the user calls Auth to produce an authentication token $\pi = (t_1, t_2, \eta)$, which will be successfully verified by invoking Verify. For the authentication token π, it consists two hash values and one proof, which is the only transcript that can be seen by the attacker. The two hash values are computed by $\mathcal{H}(p, sk)$ and $\mathcal{H}(p, pk, sk)$. In order to forge a valid authentication on $p||m$, the attacker needs to obtain the secret key sk that can be extracted from randon oracle queries. Therefore, even an adversary obtains the pk and σ, there is no way to forge a π' using a forged sk' such that it can pass the verification without the corresponding sk.

Theorem 2 (Anonymity). *A PLTAA scheme is anonymous under the random oracle model.*

Proof. We require that the attacker cannot tell the user after he got the authentication transcript. Assume a user with (pk, sk) obtains a certificate σ and create an authentication token $\pi = (t_1, t_2, \eta)$ on the message $p||m$. But t_1, t_2 in the authentication transcript can be viewed as random values, which are unable to discover one's sk. That is to say, none can recognize the difference between $\mathcal{H}(p, sk)$, $\mathcal{H}(p, pk, sk) + m \cdot sk$ and a random value.

Theorem 3 (Linkability). *A PLTAA scheme is linkable under the random oracle model.*

Proof. The linkability is ensured by generating the tag t_1 in Auth. An attacker with (pk, sk) chooses two message $p\|m_1$, $p\|m_2$ sharing a common prefix p, invokes Auth to authenticate them and obtains π_1, π_2. Apparently, π_1, π_2 will pass verification by calling Verify. However, $\mathcal{H}(p, sk)$ in tag t_1 of the authenticate transcript makes all messages authenticated by using an identical sk to be linked, i.e., $p\|m_1$ and $p\|m_2$ will be linked.

Theorem 4 (Accountability). *A PLTAA scheme is accountable under the random oracle model.*

Proof. The accountability is achieved by creating the tag t_2 in Auth. An attacker with (pk, sk) chooses two message $p\|m_1$, $p\|m_2$ sharing a common prefix p, calls Auth to authenticate them and obtains the corresponding authentication tokens π_1, π_2. Apparently, π_1, π_2 will pass verification by calling Verify, and m_1, m_2 will be linked by calling Link. However, π_1, π_2 will get the same value of $\mathcal{H}(p, pk, sk)$ in tag t_2 if using the same (pk, sk). Accordingly, the pk is exposed with the help of the rest part of tag t_2, i.e., $m_i \cdot sk$ for $i = 1, 2$.

Summarizing the above aspects, we have:

Theorem 5 (Security). *A PLTAA scheme is secure provided the discrete logarithm problem is difficult under the random oracle model.*

References

1. Chow, S.S.M., Liu, J.K., Wong, D.S.: Robust receipt-free election system with ballot secrecy and verifiability. In: NDSS, vol. 8, pp. 81–94 (2008)
2. Kiayias, A., Yung, M.: Self-tallying elections and perfect ballot secrecy. In: Naccache, D., Paillier, P. (eds.) PKC 2002. LNCS, vol. 2274, pp. 141–158. Springer, Heidelberg (2002). https://doi.org/10.1007/3-540-45664-3_10
3. Lee, B., Boyd, C., Dawson, E., Kim, K., Yang, J., Yoo, S.: Providing receipt-freeness in mixnet-based voting protocols. In: Lim, J.-I., Lee, D.-H. (eds.) ICISC 2003. LNCS, vol. 2971, pp. 245–258. Springer, Heidelberg (2004). https://doi.org/10.1007/978-3-540-24691-6_19
4. Abe, M.: A secure three-move blind signature scheme for polynomially many signatures. In: Pfitzmann, B. (ed.) EUROCRYPT 2001. LNCS, vol. 2045, pp. 136–151. Springer, Heidelberg (2001). https://doi.org/10.1007/3-540-44987-6_9
5. Hirt, M., Sako, K.: Efficient receipt-free voting based on homomorphic encryption. In: Preneel, B. (ed.) EUROCRYPT 2000. LNCS, vol. 1807, pp. 539–556. Springer, Heidelberg (2000). https://doi.org/10.1007/3-540-45539-6_38

6. Liu, J.K., Wei, V.K., Wong, D.S.: Linkable spontaneous anonymous group signature for Ad Hoc groups. In: Wang, H., Pieprzyk, J., Varadharajan, V. (eds.) ACISP 2004. LNCS, vol. 3108, pp. 325–335. Springer, Heidelberg (2004). https://doi.org/10.1007/978-3-540-27800-9_28

7. Tsang, P.P., Wei, V.K., Chan, T.K., Au, M.H., Liu, J.K., Wong, D.S.: Separable linkable threshold ring signatures. In: Canteaut, A., Viswanathan, K. (eds.) INDOCRYPT 2004. LNCS, vol. 3348, pp. 384–398. Springer, Heidelberg (2004). https://doi.org/10.1007/978-3-540-30556-9_30

8. Li, M., et al.: Crowdbc: a blockchain-based decentralized framework for crowdsourcing. IEEE Trans. Parallel Distrib. Syst. 30(6), 1251–1266 (2018)

9. Tsang, P.P., Wei, V.K.: Short linkable ring signatures for E-Voting, E-Cash and attestation. In: Deng, R.H., Bao, F., Pang, H.H., Zhou, J. (eds.) ISPEC 2005. LNCS, vol. 3439, pp. 48–60. Springer, Heidelberg (2005). https://doi.org/10.1007/978-3-540-31979-5_5

10. Wei, V.K.: Tracing-by-linking group signatures. In: Zhou, J., Lopez, J., Deng, R.H., Bao, F. (eds.) ISC 2005. LNCS, vol. 3650, pp. 149–163. Springer, Heidelberg (2005). https://doi.org/10.1007/11556992_11

11. Fujisaki, E., Suzuki, K.: Traceable ring signature. In: Okamoto, T., Wang, X. (eds.) PKC 2007. LNCS, vol. 4450, pp. 181–200. Springer, Heidelberg (2007). https://doi.org/10.1007/978-3-540-71677-8_13

12. Kiayias, A., Tsiounis, Y., Yung, M.: Traceable signatures. In: Cachin, C., Camenisch, J.L. (eds.) EUROCRYPT 2004. LNCS, vol. 3027, pp. 571–589. Springer, Heidelberg (2004). https://doi.org/10.1007/978-3-540-24676-3_34

13. Smart, M., Ritter, E.: Remote electronic voting with revocable anonymity. In: Prakash, A., Sen Gupta, I. (eds.) ICISS 2009. LNCS, vol. 5905, pp. 39–54. Springer, Heidelberg (2009). https://doi.org/10.1007/978-3-642-10772-6_5

14. Ling, L., Liao, J.: Anonymous electronic voting protocol with traceability. In: 2011 International Conference for Internet Technology and Secured Transactions, pp. 59–66. IEEE (2011)

15. Lu, Y., Tang, Q., Wang, G.: Zebralancer: private and anonymous crowdsourcing system atop open blockchain. In: 2018 IEEE 38th International Conference on Distributed Computing Systems (ICDCS), pp. 853–865. IEEE (2018)

16. Hinterwälder, Gesine, Zenger, Christian T., Baldimtsi, Foteini, Lysyanskaya, Anna, Paar, Christof, Burleson, Wayne P.: Efficient E-Cash in practice: NFC-based payments for public transportation systems. In: De Cristofaro, Emiliano, Wright, Matthew (eds.) PETS 2013. LNCS, vol. 7981, pp. 40–59. Springer, Heidelberg (2013). https://doi.org/10.1007/978-3-642-39077-7_3

17. Malina, L., Smrz, J., Hajny, J., Vrba, K.: Secure electronic voting based on group signatures. In: 2015 38th International Conference on Telecommunications and Signal Processing (TSP), pp. 6–10. IEEE (2015)

18. Moran, T., Naor, M.: Split-ballot voting: everlasting privacy with distributed trust. ACM Trans. Inf. Syst. Secur. (TISSEC) 13(2), 16:1–16:43 (2010)

19. Adida, B.: Helios: Web-based open-audit voting. USENIX security symposium 17, 335–348 (2008)

20. Culnane, C., Schneider, S.: A peered bulletin board for robust use in verifiable voting systems. In: 2014 IEEE 27th Computer Security Foundations Symposium, pp. 169–183. IEEE (2014)

21. Dini, G.: A secure and available electronic voting service for a large-scale distributed system. Future Gener. Comput. Syst. 19(1), 69–85 (2003)

22. Burton, C., Karunasekera, S., Harwood, A., Stanley, D., Ioannou, I.: A distributed network architecture for robust internet voting systems. In: Wimmer, M.A., Traunmüller, R., Grönlund, Å., Andersen, K.V. (eds.) EGOV 2005. LNCS, vol. 3591, pp. 300–308. Springer, Heidelberg (2005). https://doi.org/10.1007/11545156_29

23. Gibson, J.P., Lallet, E., Raffy, J.-L.: Engineering a distributed e-voting system architecture: meeting critical requirements. In: Giese, H. (ed.) ISARCS 2010. LNCS, vol. 6150, pp. 89–108. Springer, Heidelberg (2010). https://doi.org/10.1007/978-3-642-13556-9_6

24. Kyrillidis, L., Cobourne, S., Mayes, K., Dong, S., Markantonakis, K.: Distributed e-voting using the smart card web server. In: 2012 7th International Conference on Risks and Security of Internet and Systems (CRiSIS), pp. 1–8. IEEE (2012)

25. Chondros, N., et al.: D-demos: a distributed, end-to-end verifiable, internet voting system. In: 2016 IEEE 36th International Conference on Distributed Computing Systems (ICDCS), pp. 711–720. IEEE (2016)

26. Groth, J.: Efficient maximal privacy in boardroom voting and anonymous broadcast. In: Juels, A. (ed.) FC 2004. LNCS, vol. 3110, pp. 90–104. Springer, Heidelberg (2004). https://doi.org/10.1007/978-3-540-27809-2_10

27. Hao, F., Ryan, P.Y., Zieliński, P.: Anonymous voting by two-round public discussion. IET Inf. Secur. 4(2), 62–67 (2010)

28. Zhao, Z., Chan, T.-H.H.: How to vote privately using bitcoin. In: Qing, S., Okamoto, E., Kim, K., Liu, D. (eds.) ICICS 2015. LNCS, vol. 9543, pp. 82–96. Springer, Cham (2016). https://doi.org/10.1007/978-3-319-29814-6_8

29. McCorry, P., Shahandashti, S.F., Hao, F.: A smart contract for boardroom voting with maximum voter privacy. In: Kiayias, A. (ed.) FC 2017. LNCS, vol. 10322, pp. 357–375. Springer, Cham (2017). https://doi.org/10.1007/978-3-319-70972-7_20

30. Yang, X., Yi, X., Nepal, S., Han, F.: Decentralized voting: a self-tallying voting system using a smart contract on the ethereum blockchain. In: Hacid, H., Cellary, W., Wang, H., Paik, H.-Y., Zhou, R. (eds.) WISE 2018. LNCS, vol. 11233, pp. 18–35. Springer, Cham (2018). https://doi.org/10.1007/978-3-030-02922-7_2

31. Yu, B., et al.: Platform-independent secure blockchain-based voting system. In: Chen, L., Manulis, M., Schneider, S. (eds.) ISC 2018. LNCS, vol. 11060, pp. 369–386. Springer, Cham (2018). https://doi.org/10.1007/978-3-319-99136-8_20

32. Zhang, W., et al.: A privacy-preserving voting protocol on blockchain. In: 2018 IEEE 11th International Conference on Cloud Computing (CLOUD), pp. 401–408. IEEE (2018)

33. Sampigethaya, K., Poovendran, R.: A framework and taxonomy for comparison of electronic voting schemes. Comput. Secur. 25(2), 137–153 (2006)

34. Cooke, R., Anane, R.: A service-oriented architecture for robust e-voting. SOCA 6(3), 249–266 (2012)

35. Li, H., Kankanala, A.R., Zou, X.: A taxonomy and comparison of remote voting schemes. In: 2014 23rd International Conference on Computer Communication and Networks (ICCCN), pp. 1–8. IEEE (2014)

36. Chaum, D.: The dining cryptographers problem: unconditional sender and recipient untraceability. J. Cryptology 1(1), 65–75 (1988)

37. Pan, H., Hou, E.S.H., Ansari, N.: An e-voting system that ensures voter confidentiality and voting accuracy. In: Proceedings of IEEE International Conference on Communications, pp. 825–829. IEEE (2012)

38. Zhang, F., Kim, K.: ID-based blind signature and ring signature from pairings. In: Zheng, Y. (ed.) ASIACRYPT 2002. LNCS, vol. 2501, pp. 533–547. Springer, Heidelberg (2002). https://doi.org/10.1007/3-540-36178-2_33
39. Ben-Sasson, E., Chiesa, A., Genkin, D., Tromer, E., Virza, M.: SNARKs for C: verifying program executions succinctly and in zero knowledge. In: Canetti, R., Garay, J.A. (eds.) CRYPTO 2013. LNCS, vol. 8043, pp. 90–108. Springer, Heidelberg (2013). https://doi.org/10.1007/978-3-642-40084-1_6

Distributed Secure Storage System Based on Blockchain and TPA

Huili Wang[1,2], Wenping Ma[1], Haibin Zheng[3(✉)], and Qianhong Wu[4]

[1] State Key Laboratory of Integrated Services Networks, Xidian University,
Xi'an 710071, People's Republic of China
wpma@mail.xidian.edu.cn
[2] China Electronics Standardization Institute, Beijing, China
wanghuili@cesi.cn
[3] School of Electronic and Information Engineering, Beihang University,
Beijing, China
zhenghaibin29@buaa.edu.cn
[4] School of Cyber Science and Technology, Beihang University, Beijing, China
qianhong.wu@buaa.edu.cn

Abstract. With the rapid development of cloud computing technology, more and more users save a large amount of data in cloud storage. In addition to meeting the performance requirements, how to ensure the integrity of these data has become a hot topic for academic research in recent years. Provable data possession (PDP) based on trusted party auditor (TPA) is an important method to solve this problem. Decentralized storage based on blockchain technology, which has emerged in recent years, can well realize the proof of data possession. But it can't seamlessly interface with high-performance cloud storage. In this paper, we propose a PDP model based on blockchain and TPA (BT-PDP). On this basis, a distributed secure file system (FS) is implemented to realize a BT-PDP proof of massive electronic data.

Keywords: PDP · Blockchain · TPA · Distributed filesystem

1 Introduction

With the development of information technology, the data produced by people is too much to manage and maintain. Moreover, there is an increasing need for people to frequently access local data in different places with the development of mobile communication and mobile computing, which further increases the management cost and professional requirements of maintaining local data. In order to solve this problem, the data era with cloud computing as the main technology and data outsourcing as the main feature has entered people's daily life. Under this trend, the propose and development of cloud storage [12] provide people with a large number of convenient, ubiquitous external data storage services.

For data outsourced to cloud storage providers, the data integrity must be firstly guaranteed. Multiple requirements for data integrity verification of outsourced storage were first proposed by Francesc et al. [13]. In response to these

© Springer Nature Switzerland AG 2019
J. K. Liu and X. Huang (Eds.): NSS 2019, LNCS 11928, pp. 255–271, 2019.
https://doi.org/10.1007/978-3-030-36938-5_15

requirements, Ateniese et al. [2] proposed the first static data possession proof scheme to ensure the integrity of files on untrusted storage servers. However, the PDP did not address the issue of consistency of multiple copies, nor did it consider the issue of ownership time proof. After that, the MB-PMDDP proposed by Barsoum et al. [3] is used to solve dynamic data updates and the ID-DPDP proposed by Wang [18] is used to solve the problem of data storage on different cloud servers. Neither of them gave a clear answer to the proof of ownership time, nor did them have a relevant research on the credibility of the trusted party auditor (TPA). Shacham et al. [14] formally proposed proof of retrievability (PoR). Tan et al. [16] systematically studied the integrity of cloud storage from the perspective of provable data integrity (PDI) and looked forward to research directions, including multipath methods, privacy protection methods, dynamic data, and proof of cross-cloud data integrity. Integrating domestic and foreign cloud data integrity proof mechanisms, existing research, whether it is POR, PDI or PDP, mainly focuses on the technical solutions proposed from the perspective of cloud server provider (CSP). However, there is a lack of complete technical solutions for the proof of ownership time and the credibility of the TPA itself.

The emergence of blockchain, a decentralized typical technology, provides a potential solution to the above problems. The blockchain is a distributed database architecture that has gradually emerged with the increasing popularity of digital currencies such as bitcoin [11] and ethereum [19]. Blockchain has the nature characteristics of decentralization and data non-tamperability. Compared with cloud storage system in the current criticized central server environment, the blockchain system in distributed environment can better solve the user data security risk problem. Firstly, the consensus mechanism of the whole network authentication makes all nodes in the network mutually restrict and cooperate with each other to maintain the security and stability of the distributed storage system. Secondly, the anonymous protection measures for participants in blockchain and the reward mechanism during block generation can further stimulate the behaviour of the outsourced data storage service providers to store services. In addition, the non-tampering characteristics of the data on the blockchain prevents malicious nodes from seeking improper benefits by tampering with transaction records. This provides a safe and reliable basis for the deposit of transaction records between users and nodes. This shows that blockchain technology can serve as the underlying platform for distributed storage systems, providing a scalable space for data storage systems in terms of data security and integrity verification.

Our Contribution

Committed to addressing the contradiction between the security privacy requirements of users' outsourced data and the interests of data storage service providers, the contributions of this work can be summarized as follows.

- Combined with blockchain and trusted third-party auditing techniques, we propose a new system architecture of PDP model based on block chain and TPA, called BT-PDP.
- We research the technology of provable data possession (PDP) to provide data security storage and data integrity verification services, making users remotely control fragmented and decentralized offshore data as they control local data in a distributed environment.
- We transform existing blockchain and TPA technologies, providing effective consensus incentive mechanism and third-party audit mechanism to realize the PDP proof of massive electronic data.

2 Related Work

Ateniese et al. [2] proposed provable data possession (PDP), which publicly verifies the integrity of data. It is suitable for application environments such as cloud storage. This scheme proposes a public verification method, but the calculation of the RSA modular exponential operation used in generating evidence is very expensive and does not support the dynamic operation of the data. The proof of retrievability (PoR), which was formally proposed by Shacham et al. [14], can restore slightly corrupted data by using the sentinel mechanism while verifying data integrity. But the initialization process of the scheme requires introducing data fault-tolerant pre-processing, so it is also difficult to implement dynamic operations such as data modification, insertion, and deletion. In 2017, Yan et al. [20] proposed a remote data possession checking (RDPC) based on the homomorphic hash function, which can safely resist forgery attacks and alternative attacks. In the same year, Tian et al. [17] proposed to use a dynamic hash table to store the freshness information of the data block. The generation of data block freshness information in the scheme does not include the sequence number of the data block, so there is no need to recalculate a large number of data block labels after the data block dynamic operation, which improves the performance of the data dynamic operation. Li et al. [9] proposed a flexible multi-copy based data integrity verification scheme that computes labels based on vector dot product instead of exponential operations. For each copy of the index, only one verification tag needs to be generated, which used for the owner of the data to verify the integrity of the copy.

There have been some work to implement data possession proof schemes in the context of distributed blockchain. Burstcoin [5] uses the proof of space (PoSpace) as a consensus to prove that nodes need to pay a large amount of hard disk space to store data in a specific order, and then prove it through the directed acyclic graph and the merkle tree to the verify nodes. However, these nodes some store meaningless bytes, which causes a lot of space waste. If some meaningful content such as user files and encrypted data can be stored, it can be used to establish a network resource sharing community. Based on this thought, in 2017, Protocol Lab [10] proposed proof of spacetime (PoSt) in Filecoin's official technical documents, which proved the result through recursive on the timeline can reduce the malicious node to launch the witch attack and external attack. In 2018, the emerging distributed storage network Genaro [6] improved the file fingerprint-based sentinel proof of retrievability (SPoR) scheme proposed in [8], changing the original single file fingerprint to random and multiple choices. It holds better features to prevent retrospective proof of being replayed by malicious nodes, and more granular file fingerprints for incentive mechanism.

Blaze [4] proposed the encrypted file system of Unix system in 1993, which is used to solve the problem of transparent encryption of files. However, the distributed file system was not widely used at that time. Adya [1] presented the FARSITE file system to solve data security issues in an untrusted environment at the OSDI conference in 2002. eCryptfs [7] designed from the stacked file system of Cryptfs by Zadok et al. [21] is to construct a general encrypted file system, which can be docked with various disk file systems and combined with existing distributed file systems. But this scheme not only fails to solve the problem of file integrity verification, but also has poor performance. Shu [15] proposed a stacked file system of shield in 2014, similar to ecryptfs, which mainly addresses the confidentiality of cloud data. It does not propose a system solution to data integrity issues, nor does it combine with the PDP mechanism. As for the combination with TPA, there are no related applications and academic research until now.

3   System Model and Design Objectives

3.1   System Model

The BT-PDP model based on blockchain and TPA is a decentralized network composed of users, storage providers, blockchain and TPA. Each node on the network can be either a user who has proven demand for data possession in the Internet or a relatively large node, such as a storage provider. And the network also includes blockchain network and independent TPA. Blockchain network manages transactions between users and storage providers, and TPA connects with the judiciary. The system model is shown in Fig. 1.

Blockchain: A storage provider in Blockchain network gains revenue by providing storage to users, while users request to store the data by submitting PDP applications to the blockchain network. The overall process is performed by the blockchain network between users and storage providers. After the storage provider receives the application and saves the data, it needs to provide POSt proof to the blockchain to ensure the correct storage of the data. At the same time, the non-tamperable nature of blockchain can also play a role in regulating storage behavior.

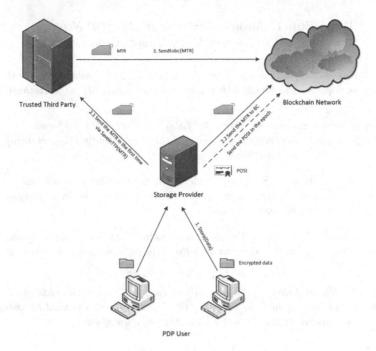

Fig. 1. System model

TPA: At present, the judicial system for electronic data processing mechanism is not complete. Therefore, TPA is introduced into the model. Under this system, TPA can be implemented by a notary institution. It is a specific node in blockchain storage network. It can be a node with super computing power and huge storage space.

Storage Provider: A larger node in the BT-PDP network that connects file system. It provides storage space to blockchain network, and waits for the transaction to be established to gain revenue. Each storage provider maintains its own storage space, which reduces the burden on the entire network and increases the stability of storage to a certain extent.

User: An entity with PDP proof requirement. Save the data in the location provided by the Storage Provider and check the integrity of the data at any time. When necessary, relevant judicial evidence can be provided through TPA.

There are some protocols between them, these protocols are shown in Definition 1.

Definition 1. *Involved Protocols in BT-PDP Network
(Store, Challenge, Get, Manage, Update)*

$Store(Data) \rightarrow digitalstamp$: *User executes the Store protocol to submit the storage request, and finally obtains the corresponding file: digitalstamp.*

$Challenge(digitalstamp) \rightarrow$ ("true", "false") : *User/TPA performs Challenge protocol to check the integrity of the corresponding digitalstamp data, and returns a boolean value.*

$Get(Space) \rightarrow Award$: *Storage provider executes the Get protocol and submits its own storage space information Space to the network. Finally get encrypted file data and award reward.*

$Manage(Data)$: *Executed by the blockchain network to match the available storage space saved on the network with the data information submitted by the user.*

$Update(alg, digitalstamp_{old}) \rightarrow digitalstamp_{new}$: *If the user needs to change the encryption mode of the data, the Update protocol is used to update the electronic stamp of the data to ensure the security of data.*

3.2 Design Objectives

Improvement of Existing PDP Model. The existing PDP scheme does not apply timestamp to the whole data proof. Assuming the scenario that the ownership of knowledge is owned by A, B first does the PDP. When intellectual property problems arise, even if A proves first and B proves later, it is still impossible to prove the fact that ownership is A. Therefore, it is necessary to store the time proof provided by the service provider to improve the PDP model. The timestamp service can provide a proof that it creates a timestamp tag to indicate that a data exists at a particular point in time. The validity of PDP scheme can be further guaranteed by generating a unique proof with unique timestamp and combining the characteristics of blockchain.

Centralized Requirements. Through judicial appraisal, notarization or third-party certification, PDP proof can play a more effective role in the judicial process. The centralized approach is also more in line with the national judicial system.

PDP Proof of Massive Data. Existing blockchain technology has a bottleneck in transaction performance, which can only achieves the confirmation of thousands of transaction records per second. The natural horizontal scalability of TPA centers is needed to meet the high concurrency needs. In the distributed storage environment, the PDP proof of tens of thousands of files per second is undoubtedly a huge challenge. In addition, if the storage can be realized without changing the user's usage habits of the storage interface, it is possible to solve the PDP proof of massive data while utilizing the high performance of the distributed file system.

4   System Implementation

4.1   System Architecture

There is a decentralized network in the BT-PDP model. Each node on the network can be either an existing single user or a relatively large node, such as a storage provider. Each storage provider can be rewarded not only by providing storage space to other users on the blockchain, but also by PDP proof, to constitute a purely distributed storage network. Due to the natural non-tamperable modification of blockchain, PDP proof of electronic data can be easily realized from a technical point of view. However, under the non-regulatory mechanism, the enforceability of electronic data is poor, so TPA is introduced into the model. TPA can be implemented by a notary organization, which is a specific node in the blockchain storage network with super computing power and large storage space. It is easy to realize PDP proof of massive electronic data on this node. The file system designed in this paper is implemented to meet such requirements. The overall BT-PDP system architecture is shown in Fig. 2.

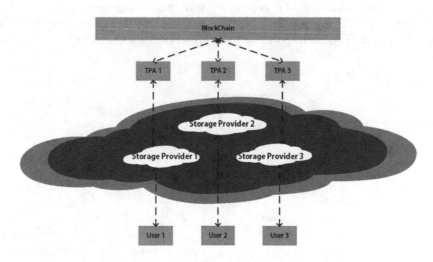

Fig. 2. BT-PDP system architecture

The implementation of each sub-module in the BT-PDP model is described in detail below.

4.2   Implementation of TPA

In the network provided by users and storage providers, there will be data piracy and illegal tampering. When user saves the data to the storage provider, the storer calculates $\{HMAC_i\}_{(1<i<s)}$ by $HMAC(File)$, constructs merkle tree MT according to the calculation $HMAC_i$, and finally verifies $HMAC_R = (HMAC_{left} \mid HMAC_{right})$ and sends $HMAC_R$ to TPA. TPA then calculates $\{HMAC_i\}_{(1<i<t)}$ by $HMAC(h_i)$ based on received hash h_i within a specified time $t \in (t_1, t_2)$, and constructs MT according to the calculation $HMAC_i$, and finally saved $HMAC_R$ in the blockchain for public auditing. (see Algorithm 5)

TPA saves hash values sent by users to form a PDP database for later user to verify data. There is a time server in TPA to ensure the accuracy of the preservation time. TPA records the time stamp of the current time stamp from the NTP server at the time point when the complete data is received, as the real preservation time of the data.

TPA provides authentication services to user through the challenge protocol. If the user needs to re-verify the files, they make a request to the TPA.

Data Preservation. Users store data to storage providers through $Store(Data)$. In the process of storage, the storage provider calculates the hash value $HMAC_i$ of the data through $HMAC(File)$ and sends it to the main node after the calculation is completed. The main node communicates with TPA and blockchain. TPA and blockchain receive the hash value of the data, and save the hash value according to the set time interval (see Algorithm 4). TPA constructs the corresponding MT generating root hash value and saves it to the PDP database of TPA to form a blockchain to ensure the third-party verification mechanism. The corresponding data preservation architecture is shown in Fig. 3.

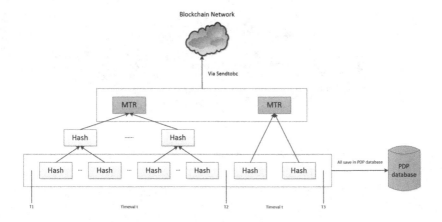

Fig. 3. Data preservation architecture

Data Validation. Users send data validation applications to TTP through the challenge (see Definition 2 for application structure). According to the electronic stamp, find the corresponding digitalstamp in the PDP database and save the time. Meanwhile, the encryption algorithm are assumed to be MD5. If it exists, TTP calculates the corresponding hash value h_i according to $HMAC(File)$, and then calculates the dstamp through $Gen\_dstamp(h_i, MD5)$ (see Algorithm 1) to match the digital-stamp. If success, return the proof. (see Algorithm 6)

Definition 2. *Request Structure*

The prove of PDP: Hash value

Time : The server receive the PDP request

ALG : *Hash algorithm*

Update Preservation. If the hash algorithm is decoded, the user can apply for an updaten. Users send update preservation application via $Update(alg, dstamp)$ (assuming alg is the sha128 algorithm at this time). TPA receives the application and gets the current time t_1 through NTP server and uses $Gen\_dstamp(dstamp_{old}, SHA128)$ to calculate $dstamp_{new}$, and then updated the corresponding data in the PDP database. (see Algorithm 7)

Supervision Mechanism of TPA. The TPA differentiates the received hash value $\{HMAC_i\}_{(1<i<s)}$ according to a certain time $t \in (t_1, t_2)$ and constructs MT with all hash value $\{HMAC_i\}_{(s_1<i<s_2)}$ of the same time period to get $HMAC_R$. TPA only saves the hash value of the file and sends the calculated root hash value to the blockchain. If TPA is not trusted, we monitor whether TPA itself has tampering behavior through the decentralization of blockchain. And through this mechanism, we can reduce the amount of data sent to the blockchain and ensure the efficiency of the blockchain. The cost of efficiency is memory consumption. For example, assuming that TPA receives 1 million hash values (SHA128) in one second, the size of memory required is 1.58 GB. The TPA audit process is shown in Fig. 4.

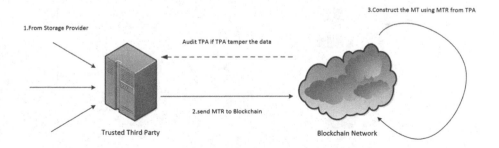

Fig. 4. TPA audit process

4.3   Blockchain

Using the non-tamperable properties of the blockchain, we construct a distributed storage network based on blockchain. Storage providers in the network generate revenue by providing storage to users through $Get(space)$, while users submit PDP applications to the network to store data through $Store(Data)$. The whole process is carried out by the network through $Manage(Data)$ to users and storage providers. After the storage provider receives the application, it saves the data and provides POSt proof to the network through $HMAC(Data)$, which also realizes PDP proof of the data. In order to further ensure the security of transactions, TPA is saved in blockchain as transaction records through $HMAC(h_i)$ and $hash_{trade}$, then publicized throughout the network. The whole process is shown in Fig. 5.

Large Node. In order to solve the problem of massive PDP proof, there are bound to be some nodes with higher performance, that is, large nodes. These nodes must use a distributed secure file system to improve the performance of the nodes. Due to the high performance of the large nodes, it can also be used as a mining machine. In addition, the large node communicates with the TPA through a separate host to ensure the efficiency of entire PDP system.

Proof of Spacetime (POSt). Since the data needs to be stored at the storage for a period of time, the storage certificate provided for the first time is not sufficient to explain that the data is still safely stored at the storage provider after a period of time. So the storage provider needs to provide the proof of

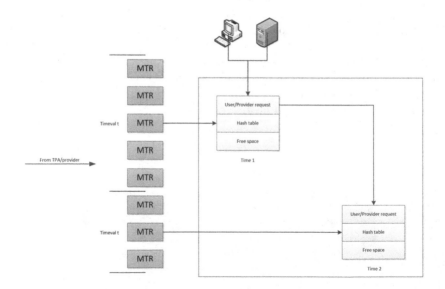

Fig. 5. Process of TPA auditing by BlockChain

space time, that is, the storage provider needs to continuously provide POSt for a period of time to ensure the validity of the PDP.

TPA Interface. The first time a user saves data, it needs to be saved in TPA. After that, it only needs to be saved in the blockchain and does not need to pass the TPA. When PDP proof is needed in the future, the hash value h_i in the document will be extracted by the judiciary according to a certain legal process and the technical system of blockchain. Then calculates the $HMAC(File)$ for the original file, and compared with the extracted data h_i to provide judicial proof of the data according to the results submitted by the user.

4.4   Distributed Secure File System

Since BT-PDP is a completely decentralized network, the performance of the network is limited by the nodes in the network. Therefore, we introduce large nodes to ensure the efficiency of the whole system under massive PDP requests. In order to ensure the efficiency of whole network, node must have a higher data storage efficiency, so we introduce a distributed secure file system at the node to achieve this purpose.

System Architecture. Users save and verify files by file system, and seamlessly combine the file system with disk file system by virtual filesystem switch (VFS) mechanism of linux. The file system is stacked on the disk file system, so that the data stored in the disk file system will be encrypted and processed by the integrity of the file system, making the data stored on the disk encrypted and file integrity information is saved. Not only disk file system, but also distributed file system can be supported by our secure file system. This series of operations is transparent to the user. The mechanism principle of distributed secure file system is shown in Fig. 6.

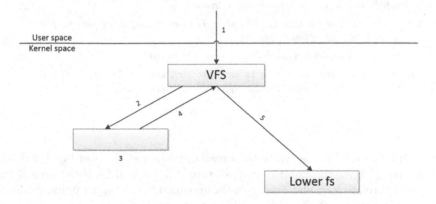

Fig. 6. Mechanism principle of distributed secure file system

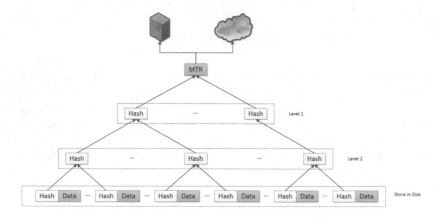

Fig. 7. The structure of the entire MT

System Initialization. When the file system is created, the system initializes according to the initial password or public key password pair specified by the user who mounts the file system. When the file system is mounted again, the mounted user is authenticated. (see Algorithm 3)

Encryption Processing. Distributed secure file system can store a large amount of data with high fault tolerance and throughput. Aiming at the problem of data privacy protection in VFS system, we propose an encryption processing scheme that supports data read-write operation in cloud, which achieves data storage persistence and easy reading. The definition of the encrypted information structure is as follows.

Definition 3. *Crypto_info Structure*

---

crypto_blkcipher : encryption algorithm used to store encrypted data, such as aes, twofish and other encryption algorithms

crypto_hash : hash algorithm used to store key-related information, such as md5, sha128 and other hash algorithms

hmac_tfm : hash algorithm used to preserve file integrity

hmac_table : hash algorithm used to save the structure of the entire MT (Fig. 7), in case to calculate the file $HMAC_{root}$ next time

---

Read Operation: The user initiates a read operation at the user layer and falls into the kernel layer through the read system. File system finds the underlying file system through VFS and reads out the specified file, at which point the file is encrypted. VFS gives the encrypted file content to file system. File system reads the content $\{File_i\}_{(1<i<s)}$ and $File_i = (HMAC_i + File_enc)$ according to the

information stored in root. Then obtains the initial key key_{enc} by crypto-hash according to $key_{enc} = Hash(key_{user})$ (see Algorithm 2), and then combined key_{enc} with tfm to get $\{File_p\}_{(1<p<s)}$ by running $tfm.Decrypt_{key_{enc}}(File_{enc})$. At this point, the decryption of the contents is completed, then sends $File_{plain}$ to VFS.

Write Operation: The user initiates a write operation at the user layer and falls into the kernel layer through the write system. File system finds the underlying file system through VFS and reads out the specified file, at which point the file is encrypted. VFS gives the encrypted file content to file system. The VFS finds the file system and delivers the data written by user to the file system. The file system name obtains the initial key key_{enc} by crypto-hash according to $key_{enc} = Hash(key_{user})$ (see Algorithm 2), and then combines key_{enc} with tfm to get $File_{enc}$ by running $tfm.Encrypt_{key_{enc}}(D)$. After encryption, equally divides the file content $File_{enc}$ into several blocks $\{File_{enc_i}\}_{(1<i<s)}$, re-forms $File_i = \{HMAC(File_{enc_i}) + File_{enc_i}\}$, and form MT by each part $HMAC(File_{enc_i})$ to ensure file integrity. File system finds the corresponding underlying disk file system through VFS, and sends $\{File_i\}_{(1<i<s)}$ to VFS, which is handed over to the underlying file system to flush the contents to disk.

5   System Analysis

5.1   Security

The user can set a password through transparent encryption processing of the file system VFS, and transmit it to the storage provider after local encryption and integrity processing. Since the storage provider cannot know the user's password and the data at the storage provider is in the form of ciphertext, the user's data is secure. In addition, the user can check the integrity of the data through the TPA from time to time, which further ensuring the security of the file.

5.2   Advantages of Decentralization

Decentralization indicates that any node in the network can provide corresponding services, so that every node in the network may store data that attackers are interested in. For the attacker, it is difficult to find the target data, which guarantees the security of the data to a certain extent. Furthermore, because the users of the whole network can participate in providing storage services, the data is more scattered than centralized storage, and the loss is smaller when a single node fails.

5.3   TPA Comply with Relevant Laws

As a technical means, TPA can be connected with the judiciary. However, the traditional judicial subjects have no ability to preserve electronic evidence, such as courts and notaries. Based on this situation, we introduce third-party preservation to supplement this deficiency. As long as we ensure that the preservation technology and the preservation process are credible, the result will be effective.

6 Performance

The existing blockchain's tps processing can't reach a million levels, it's actually tens of thousands of levels. But cloud storage can reach millions of processing per second in extreme cases. TPA is a centralized structure that not only maintains high concurrency, but also scales horizontally with the performance of cloud storage. Since the TPA performs the delay operation, that is, the hash value in the interval is regarded as arriving at the same time, so the concurrency of the blockchain is greatly reduced when the MT_{root} entering the blockchain.

7 Algorithm Description

According to the system implementation architecture of the above BT-PDP model, we present the algorithm of each module in this section.

Algorithm 1. Gen_dstamp

Input: $Hash$: The hash of PDP file; ALG : Hash Algorithm
Output: $digitalstamp$: The prove of PDP file
 1: Get current time $Time_{prove}$ via NTP server
 2: $Hash_{org} = Hash + Time_{prove}$
 3: $Hash_{final} = ALG(Hash_{org})$
 4: Save $Hash_{final}, ALG, Time_{prove}$ in digitalstamp
 5: **return** digitalstamp

Algorithm 2. Keygen implement

Input: $User_{passphrase}$:User use this to mount filesystem; Alg:Decide which hash algorithm generate key;
Output: User Encryption Key,Key_{user}
 1: generate $salt$ random number;
 2: combine $User_{passphrase}$ with $salt$ to generate the Key_{start}
 3: **for** i = 1 to 65536 **do**
 4:     generate Key_{user} via $Alg(Key_{start})$;
 5:     $Key_{start} = Key_{user}$;
 6: **end for**
 7: insert Key_{user} to key list L;
 8: **return** Key_{user}

Algorithm 3. User login

Input: *Passphrase*: User use this to mount filesystem;
Output: "Ture" or "False"
1: generate userkey Key_{user} via $Keygen(passphrase)$;
2: for each key Key in key list L
3:     if Key_{user} matched Key
4:         return "Ture";
5:     return "False";

Algorithm 4. TTP protocol

1: **while** In a period of time t **do**
2:     TTP receives the user's verification request and obtains a *dstamp*;
3:     TTP obtains $Hash_{file}$, T_{prove} and Alg_{hash} through *dstamp*;
4:     TTP calculates $Hash_t$ by $Alg_{Hash}(Hash_{file} + T_{prove})$;
5:     **if** If $Hash_t$ in the PDP database **then**
6:         TTP provides user with a proof (Definition 2) that meets legal requirements;
7:     **else**
8:         Prompt user that file not saved
9:     **end if**
10: **end while**

Algorithm 5. TTP protocol

1: **while** In a period of time t **do**
2:     TTP receives the hash $\{hash_i\}_1 < i < s$ from the storage node;
3:     Construct MT for the hash value received in time t, and get $Hash_{root}$;
4:     Send $Hash_{root}$ to the blockchain;
5: **end while**

Algorithm 6. PDP protocol

Input: *digitalstamp* : The prove of PDP file;
Output: "True" , "False";
1: Extract $Hash,Time$ from *digitalstamp*;
2: Search $Hash$ in PDP Database and get corresponding $Time_{record}$;
3: **if** Can not find $Hash$ **then**
4:     return False;
5: **end if**
6: **if** $Time == Time_{record}$ **then**
7:     return True;
8: **end if**
9: **return** False

Algorithm 7. Update protocol

Input: ALG : New hash algorithm;$digitalstamp_{old}$: The prove of PDP file;
Output: $digitalstamp_{new}$;
  1: Extract $Hash$ from $digitalstamp_{old}$;
  2: Get current time $Time_{prove}$ via NTP server;
  3: $Hash_{org} = Hash + Time_{prove}$;
  4: $Hash_{final} = ALG(Hash_{org})$;
  5: Save $Hash_{final}, ALG, Time_{prove}$ in $digitalstamp_{new}$;
  6: Delete $digitalstamp_{old}$;
  7: **return** $digitalstamp_{new}$;

8   Conclusion

Based on blockchain and TPA technology, this paper proposed the system framework of BT-PDP. It designed the formal model of BT-PDP, and solved the contradiction between the security privacy requirements of user data storage and the interests of data storage providers. This model transforms existing blockchain and TPA technology, provides an effective consensus incentive mechanism and a third-party audit mechanism, realizes PDP proof of massive electronic data, and finally forms a secure, reliable and efficient distributed data storage system.

Acknowledgements. This paper is supported by the National Key R&D Program of China through project H1943050901, by the Natural Science Foundation of China through projects 61972019, 61932011, 61772538.

References

1. Adya, A., et al.: FARSITE: federated, available, and reliable storage for an incompletely trusted environment. ACM SIGOPS Oper. Syst. Rev. **36**(SI), 1–14 (2002)
2. Ateniese, G., et al.: Provable data possession at untrusted stores. In: Proceedings of the 14th ACM Conference on Computer and Communications Security, pp. 598–609. ACM (2007)
3. Barsoum, A.F., Hasan, M.A.: Provable multicopy dynamic data possession in cloud computing systems. IEEE Trans. Inf. Forensics Secur. **10**(3), 485–497 (2014)
4. Blaze, M.: A cryptographic file system for UNIX. In: Proceedings of the 1st ACM Conference on Computer and Communications Security, pp. 9–16. ACM (1993)
5. Dziembowski, S., Faust, S., Kolmogorov, V., Pietrzak, K.: Proofs of space. In: Gennaro, R., Robshaw, M. (eds.) CRYPTO 2015. LNCS, vol. 9216, pp. 585–605. Springer, Heidelberg (2015). https://doi.org/10.1007/978-3-662-48000-7_29
6. Genaro, N., Torija, A., Ramos-Ridao, A., Requena, I., Ruiz, D., Zamorano, M.: A neural network based model for urban noise prediction. J. Acoust. Soc. Am. **128**(4), 1738–1746 (2010)
7. Halcrow, M.: eCryptfs: a stacked cryptographic filesystem. Linux J. **2007**(156), 2 (2007)
8. Juels, A., Kaliski Jr, B.S.: PORs: proofs of retrievability for large files. In: Proceedings of the 14th ACM Conference on Computer and Communications Security, pp. 584–597. ACM (2007)

9. Li, L., Yang, Y., Wu, Z.: FMR-PDP: flexible multiple-replica provable data possession in cloud storage. In: 2017 IEEE Symposium on Computers and Communications (ISCC), pp. 1115–1121. IEEE (2017)
10. Moran, T., Orlov, I.: Proofs of space-time and rational proofs of storage. IACR Cryptology ePrint Archive 2016/35 (2016)
11. Nakamoto, S., et al.: Bitcoin: a peer-to-peer electronic cash system (2008)
12. Schmuck, F.B., Haskin, R.L.: GPFS: a shared-disk file system for large computing clusters. In: FAST, vol. 2 (2002)
13. Sebé, F., Domingo-Ferrer, J., Martinez-Balleste, A., Deswarte, Y., Quisquater, J.J.: Efficient remote data possession checking in critical information infrastructures. IEEE Trans. Knowl. Data Eng. **20**(8), 1034–1038 (2008)
14. Shacham, H., Waters, B.: Compact proofs of retrievability. In: Pieprzyk, J. (ed.) ASIACRYPT 2008. LNCS, vol. 5350, pp. 90–107. Springer, Heidelberg (2008). https://doi.org/10.1007/978-3-540-89255-7_7
15. Shu, J., Shen, Z., Xue, W.: Shield: a stackable secure storage system for file sharing in public storage. J. Parallel Distrib. Comput. **74**(9), 2872–2883 (2014)
16. Tan, S., Jia, Y., Han, W.H., et al.: Research and development of provable data integrity in cloud storage. Chin. J. Comput. **38**(1), 164–177 (2015)
17. Tian, H., et al.: Dynamic-hash-table based public auditing for secure cloud storage. IEEE Trans. Serv. Comput. **10**(5), 701–714 (2015)
18. Wang, H.: Identity-based distributed provable data possession in multicloud storage. IEEE Trans. Serv. Comput. **8**(2), 328–340 (2014)
19. Wood, G., et al.: Ethereum: a secure decentralised generalised transaction ledger. Ethereum Proj. Yellow Pap. **151**(2014), 1–32 (2014)
20. Yan, H., Li, J., Han, J., Zhang, Y.: A novel efficient remote data possession checking protocol in cloud storage. IEEE Trans. Inf. Forensics Secur. **12**(1), 78–88 (2016)
21. Zadok, E., Badulescu, I., Shender, A.: Cryptfs: a stackable Vnode level encryption file system. Technical report, Technical report CUCS-021-98, Computer Science Department, Columbia University (1998)

SSHTDNS: A Secure, Scalable and High-Throughput Domain Name System via Blockchain Technique

Zhentian Xiong[1], Zoe L. Jiang[1,2(✉)], Shuqiang Yang[1,2], Xuan Wang[1,2], and Junbin Fang[3]

[1] School of Computer Science and Technology, Harbin Institute of Technology, Shenzhen, Shenzhen 518055, China
xiongzhentian@stu.hit.edu.cn, zoeljiang@hit.edu.cn, Sqyang9999@126.com, wangxuan@cs.hitsz.edu.cn
[2] Pengcheng Laboratory, Shenzhen 518055, China
[3] Jinan University, Guangzhou 510000, China
junbinfang@foxmail.com

Abstract. Domain name system is an important infrastructure of the Internet, which is responsible for mapping domain name to IP address. However, it is facing serious security threats due to its distributed structure with a center. Blockchain has received extensive attention due to its decentralized, secure and trusted characteristics since the existence of Bitcoin. In this paper, we propose a new domain name system based on blockchain techniques called SSHTDNS. The form of consortium chain is adopted in SSHTDNS to guarantee the management of Top-Level Domain names, and linkable ring signature technique is used for identity anonymity and voting fairness of these consortium nodes. Multi-chain structure is designed with sharding protocol to enhance the scalability and throughput of the system. In addition, SSHTDNS allows nodes to use index databases outside the chain to speed up domain name resolution and verification. A combination of these techniques enables a secure, scalable and high-throughput domain name system.

Keywords: DNS · Consortium chain · Multi-chain · Sharding protocol · Linkable ring signature

1 Introduction

Domain Name System (DNS) is an important infrastructure of the Internet, which maps memorable domain names to the numerical IP address, giving people easier access to the Internet [1,2]. Currently, DNS is distributed structure with

This research is supported by National Natural Science Foundation of China (No. 61872109), Basic Research Project of Shenzhen, China (No. JCYJ20180507183624136), Guangdong Key R&D Program (No. 2019B010136001).

a dispatch center, the Internet Corporation for Assigned Names and Numbers (ICANN), who is responsible for scheduling and managing the system. Current DNS is vulnerable to DDoS attack, cache poisoning, vanishing risk, blinding risk and so on. According to Global DNS Threat Report 2018, 77% organizations have suffered at least one DNS attack in 2018. Although many researchers have proposed solutions, such as DNSSEC [3], which guarantees data integrity and reliability through signature and hash techniques, but the DNS still exists serious centralization risks. Once ICANN is attacked or controlled by hacker, it will cause problems of single point of failure and power abuse, which can be a serious hazard to the entire domain name system.

Blockchain seems like a solution due to its decentralization, security and credibility. Bitcoin is one of the most famous Blockchain projects, and was proposed by Satoshi Nakamoto in 2009 [4]. People extracted the underlying technique of Bitcoin and named Blockchain. Blockchain is a trusted distributed database that stores records in chronological order, and the blockchain protocol maintains the distributed database in a decentralized network. According to its different read and write permissions and the degree of centralization, blockchain can be divided into public chain, consortium chain and private chain, which are more and more centralized. Bitcoin is the representative of Blockchain 1.0, while Ethereum is the representative of Blockchain 2.0, it combines Blockchain 1.0 with smart contract [15] to provide a platform for developers to deploy Decentralized Applications (DAPP), which greatly expands the function of the blockchain. Namecoin is the first blockchain-based domain name system [5], while facing serious security threats. Blockstack is the first naming system which operates directly on top of the Bitcoin blockchain [6], while performance is limited by the Bitcoin. Also there are several schemes such as Nebulis [7] and ConsortiumDNS [8]. However, the scalability and throughput in these projects cannot satisfy the domain name service, which will be discussed in detail in Sect. 2.

This paper proposes a secure, scalable, high-throughput domain name system called SSHTDNS. The most important domain name in current DNS is the Top-Level Domain (TLD), which includes three categories: general Top-Level Domain (gTLD) such as *com* and *org*, country-code Top-Level Domain (ccTLD) such as *us* and *cn*, and infrastructure Top-Level Domain *arpa* [16]. In order to reduce the degree of centralization and manage TLD better, SSHTDNS considers adopting consortium chain. Each country maintains several consortium nodes (Consortium nodes are applied, built and maintained by each country. The specific allocation is determined by the international organization, which will not be discussed in this paper), and all nodes can form a consortium to manage the Chain. The application to register a TLD need to be decided by the consortium's fair vote. SSHTDNS uses linkable ring signature scheme to ensure anonymity and fairness during the voting process. To enhance the scalability of the system, SSHTDNS adopts multi-chain structure, a main chain and multiple subchains. The main chain records operations on TLD, and each subchain records other operations under TLD such as register, logout and cession, which also conforms to the hierarchical structure of the current DNS. To increase the throughput of the system and avoid the centralized problem on subchains caused by too few participating nodes, SSHTDNS uses sharding protocol [17–19] to uniformly and randomly partition the nodes into smaller committees, each of them processes records on a subchain independently. The sharding protocol increases the blockchain's throughput with the computational power of the network. There are three types of nodes in SSHTDNS: consortium nodes, ordinary nodes and light nodes. Light nodes can store only the main chain and part of subchains to provide domain name resolution services, which can reduce the storage load of nodes and increase the quantity of nodes to provide domain name service. In addition, we can use key-value database outside the blockchain for storing index to speed up the domain name resolution and verification.

The rest of this paper consists of the following sections. Section 2 gives an introduction on other DNS projects based on blockchain techniques. Section 3 describes the design of SSHTDNS in detail, the workflow of nodes, and the used cryptographic technique. Section 4 analyzes the characteristics of SSHTDNS. Section 5 makes a conclusion to this work.

2   Related Work

In this part, we firstly introduce the early DNS and some improvements to its security issues, then introduce and analysis several DNS projects based on blockchain techniques: Namecoin, Blockstack, Nebulis and ConsortiumDNS.

2.1   Early DNS

Domain name system was designed primarily for academic and military purposes in the early Internet, and the designers never anticipated the Internet could be world widely adopted in the future. Therefore they did not consider the security of the system. As a result it is fundamentally vulnerable. With the widespread use of DNS, solutions to improve system security have also been gradually proposed. In the 1990s, the IETF Domain Name System Security Working Group proposed the DNS Security Extension Protocol (DNSSEC) [9] to enhance security of DNS infrastructure, which provides end-to-end data authenticity and integrity protection. Then, Atenises proposed a scheme that can provide data confidentiality and defend against replay attacks by using symmetric encryption technique [11]. Wilkinson used the indirect routing technique of SCOLD key components to defend against DDoS attacks [26]. Fetzer utilized SSL protocol to enhance the trustworthiness of the infrastructure [27] in 2005. Fanglu Guo imported cookies to detect DNS spoofing attacks [10]. However, none of them have addressed the problems of centralization.

2.2   Namecoin

Namecoin [5] is the first case that combines domain name service and blockchain techniques. It is a fork of Bitcoin with modifications, so Namecoin and Bitcoin share the most functionalities and mechanisms such as Proof of Work (PoW) [4,12], they use the same math problem for mining, miners can mine in both systems without consuming double computing power, but this may cause security risks. Namecoin uses *.bit* as its TLD name, which means all of current domain names can be migrated with *.bit* added, such as *.com.bit*. But Namecoin uses PoW as its consensus mechanism, which means it is easy to suffer from 51% attack due to its insufficient computing power. Despite this, Namecoin still has significant value on the way to improve the domain name services.

2.3 Blockstack and Nebulis

Blockstack [6] is the first domain name system which operates directly on top of the system of Bitcoin. Consider the security issue on Namecoin, Blockstack migrates the domain name system to the Bitcoin System, which can resist the 51% power attack by taking advantage of Bitcoin's sufficient power. In the meantime, Bitcoin nodes cannot be conscious of the existence of Blockstack by layering blockchains and using virtual chain technique, the downside is the performance of Blockstack is limited by the Bitcoin. Nebulis [7] is a platform that is similar to Blockstack, it is a global distributed directory to replace the existing domain name system, the difference between them is that Nebulis uses IPFS [13] as a replacement for HTTP and utilizes Ethereum [14] to provide domain name service, which is also limited by the performance of Ethereum.

2.4 ConsortiumDNS

ConsortiumDNS [8] proposes a new domain name service based on the form of consortium chain. ConsortiumDNS divides the network nodes into query nodes and miner nodes, and the system is designed to be three-layer structure with a supernumerary external storage. In the meantime, ConsortiumDNS builds index for blocks and records to accelerate the DNS resolution process. Different from the fully public chain structure adopted by Namecoin and Blockstack, the consortium chain structure adopted by ConsortiumDNS is more conductive to permission management, which can reduce the digital crimes on domain names. However, ConsortiumDNS has poor scalability for the chain structure and low throughput for operating domain name application.

3   SSHTDNS

In this part, we present SSHTDNS. The first part mainly describes the designed structure of the chain in SSHTDNS. The second part introduces the workflow of the nodes, and the last part introduces the linkable ring signature technique.

3.1 SSHTDNS Chain Structure

Blockchain can be divided into three types: public chain, consortium chain and private chain. Public chain is completely decentralized, and anyone can participate in the whole process and enjoy same right. Private chain is centralized, and mostly used inside an organization and opened to individual persons or entities. Consortium chain owns multiple centers and is often used to form an alliance between multiple organizations to manage the blockchain. Consortium chain has a good balance between decentralization and permission management. TLD often represents a country or institution, such as us, uk, gov, org. In view of the importance and particularity of TLD, our scheme SSHTDNS utilizes the structure of consortium chain to manage these TLD names. Nodes in the consortium chain often play different roles, and there are three types of nodes in SSHTDNS, all nodes are identified by their own public key.

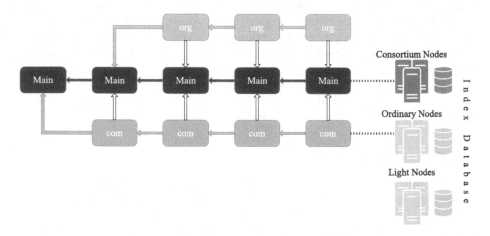

Fig. 1. Structure of SSHTDNS

- *Consortium Nodes.* As we have mentioned before, the consortium nodes are selected by international organization and maintained by the countries, all of them form an alliance to manage the entire system. The consortium nodes are mainly responsible for requests on the TLD, scheduling the ordinary nodes, generating parameters of the system and generating blocks on the main chain after the consensus process, which generally do not provide domain name resolution services.
- *Ordinary Nodes.* Ordinary node is also called full node, and any participant can become a full node as long as they have deploying complete information of the system. After completing the node identity establishment process in Step 2 of Subsect. 3.2, ordinary nodes can participate in the block generation process on a certain subchain in sharding protocol, and they can provide the most complete domain name service such as domain name resolution, registration request under TLD and so on.

- *Light Nodes.* As time goes by, the blockchain system will become heavier and heavier, the Bitcoin system has exceeded 200 GB up to now [25], which has already imposed requirements on the deployment nodes' storage capacity. Any participant can become a light node and only store the main chain and part of subchains. They cannot participate in the block generation process, and only provide partial domain name resolution services. More participating nodes in the system can provide domain name resolution services better.

Most blockchain projects are currently single-chain structures, which is not scalable. Then SSHTDNS considers a multi-chain structure. As shown in Fig. 1, SSHTDNS owns a main chain with multiple subchains. The main chain is responsible for storing a small amount of important information: operations on TLDs and hash values of all subchains in the same block height, while each subchain is responsible for storing all operations under each specific TLD such as *com* or *org*, and all of the subchains maintain the same block height with the main chain. Subchains can be extended and abandoned legally. Now assume that international organizations elect multiple consortium nodes, which establish a full connection to form an alliance. When an organization wants to register a .*com* TLD name, it needs to be voted by the consortium nodes to decide whether to allow it. Linkable ring signature will be used to protect anonymity of the voters and fairness during the voting process, which will be introduced in detail in the Subsect. 3.3. If the application is allowed, the applicant is the owner of the domain name, and the domain name and the owner's public key will be written to the blockchain. As for ordinary nodes, they will be assigned to different subchains randomly by sharding protocol. Nodes in the same shard will also establish a full connection, which will form an ordinary committee to verify the legitimacy of the requests. If there is a request that someone applies to register *google.com*, then the committee needs to verify whether the request has been signed correctly by the *com* TLD owner and the domain name have not been registered by others. If the request is logout or transferring to someone, then the committee needs to verify whether it has been signed correctly by the owner. Sharding protocol will be discussed in detail in the Subsect. 3.2. As we can see on the right side of Fig. 1, nodes can utilize an external index database outside the blockchain to store indexes, thus speeding up the domain name resolution. Take the key-value database Redis as an example, it can process 100,000 read and write requests per second. The subchain identifier and block height in each record of the database can be used to quickly locate the block where it belongs and verify the correctness of the parsing results. For a case where a domain name corresponds to multiple IP addresses, the database can randomly return different IP address to achieve load balancing as the current DNS does.

Since the main chain and subchains play different roles, their respective block structures are different. Table 1 shows the block structure of subchains. Block head includes *com*-subchain identifier, timestamp, block height, previous hash, merkle root of the block body, version number and other important information. Block body records all of the operations under a specific TLD such as *com*: registered, logout, update or transfer to someone. *Sig* is the signature algorithm,

SK_0 is the secret key of the previous domain name owner, (PK_1, SK_1) is the public-private key pair of the legal applicant(owner), IP', PK' are respectively updated IP address and public key. Table 2 shows the block structure of the main chain, which is mostly similar to the subchain's block structure. However, the block body includes two parts, one is the hash value of all records in the same period on each subchains, and the other is the various operations on the TLD names. It is worth noting that the registration of TLD requires to record all the signatures of the consortium nodes that agree to this application. And the block head needs to record the Merkle roots of the two parts.

Table 1. Block structure of *.com* subchain

Block	.com Identifier	Timestamp	Block height
	Previous hash	Merkle root	Version number
Head	Other information		
Block	**Operations under .com subchain:**		
	Registered: $Sig_{SK_0}(DomainName - IP - PK_1)$		
Body	**Logout:** $Sig_{SK_1}(DomainName - IP - PK_1)$		
	Transfer/Update: $Sig_{SK_1}(DomainName - IP' - PK')$		

Table 2. Block structure of the main chain

Block	Mainchain identifier	Timestamp	Block height
	Previous hash	Version number	Other information
Head	Merkle root of TLD	Merkle root of subchains	
	Hash Values of all of the subchains		
Block	**Operations on TLD names:**		
	Registered: $Sig_{SK_i}(TLD - IP - PK_1)$		
Body	**Logout:** $Sig_{SK_1}(TLD - IP - PK_1)$		
	Transfer/Update: $Sig_{SK_1}(TLD - IP' - PK')$		

3.2 SSHTDNS Node Workflow

The previous subsection describes the multi-chain structure of SSHTDNS, operations in different TLD can be handled separately, and there are three types of nodes, this part will explain how to uniformly and safely partitions the ordinary nodes into smaller groups to handle operations on different TLDs independently, called sharding protocol. Sharding protocol makes it possible to increase SSHTDNS's throughput almost linearly with the computational power of the network, a certain proportion of byzantine adversaries can be tolerated in the meantime, the chart of node workflow is shown in Fig. 2.

The main idea of sharding protocol is to uniformly partition the computing power. The sharding protocol introduces the concept of periods, and divides all nodes into smaller committees in one period. Each committee owns N members, and can independently process a part of the operations set called shard. Then, SSHTDNS can process more requests in the same amount of time, and the whole operations on a subchain can be divided into one or more shards. All of the consortium nodes form a consortium committee, which is responsible for collecting and verifying the consensus results of all ordinary committees, running byzantine fault tolerance algorithm, forming a final consensus results and broadcasting it. Other ordinary nodes receive the final consensus results, verify the results, and record it on the main chain and corresponding subchains. In each period, the node workflow consists of the following steps:

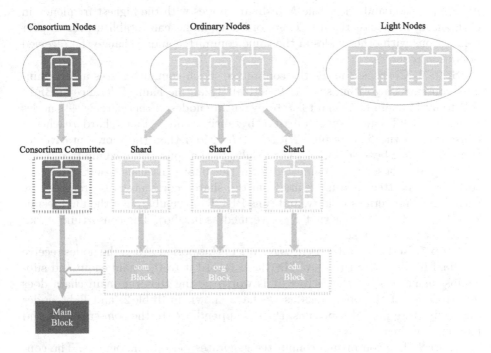

Fig. 2. Node workflow

Step 1. Ordinary Nodes collect the operation requests from the last period.
Step 2. Ordinary Nodes establish their identities. Each ordinary node locally calculates to get the identity of participating sharding protocol. They choose their public key PK and IP address, which can be used for subsequent authentication and communication. They also use the public random string generated by the consortium committee in the last period as the randomness of this round. D is the difficulty value set by the system. By continuously doing the PoW, ordinary node finds a *nonce* to satisfy the following formula yields a valid identity.

The solution of PoW allows other nodes to verify and accept their identities, while avoiding Sybil Attacks [20].

$$H(randomness||IP||PK||nonce) < D \tag{1}$$

Step 3. Nodes form committee. Ordinary nodes will be assigned to different committees randomly according to their established identities, such as he last k bits of their own hash value if there were 2^k committees.

Step 4. Nodes establish full connections with other nodes belonging to the same committee. After completing the identity establishment process, the ordinary nodes send their established identities to the consortium nodes. Each consortium node independently verifies the validity of these identities and collects N members in each shard. Then the consortium committee internally makes a union operation and selects the N ordinary nodes with the highest frequency in each shard, broadcast the list. Then, ordinary nodes can establish peer-to-peer connections with other nodes in the same committee and exchange the received operation requests.

Step 5. Consensus inside the committee. Each committee uses a deterministic consensus algorithm such as Practical Byzantine Fault Tolerance (PBFT) [21] to avoid chain forks and tolerate byzantine nodes, if there are $3f + 1$ nodes in total, PBFT can tolerate up to f byzantine nodes. Each shard reaches a consensus on the final results: $R_1, R_2, ..., R_N$, and then the representatives of committee members broadcast their results to the consortium committee.

Step 6. Consortium committee form the final consensus result. The consortium committee collects results from the shard representatives processed by each shard and verifies validity, and runs PBFT internally to get the final result: $R = \{R_2, ...R_N\}$ (Assume that R_1 is verified as invalid). The consortium nodes broadcast the final result R.

Step 7. Nodes record consensus results in this period. All of the nodes receive the final result and verify its validity, and record it to the main chain and subchains maintained by themselves. It is worth noting that the main chain does not store all of the operations as we have shown in Table 2, and light nodes may only store partial subchains, then it appends R_2 to the *com*-subchain and ignores other results.

Step 8. The consortium committee generates period randomness. The consortium nodes run a XOR scheme to generate a secure public random string that will be used in next period PoW.

3.3   Linkable Ring Signature

When applying to register a TLD name, the organization firstly initiates a registration request to a consortium node which becomes the proxy consortium node of the applicant. And the proxy consortium node sends the request to the consortium committee, then the consortium nodes vote after the request is audited. Only when the number of consents reaches a certain percentage, the registration is allowed, and the organization will be assigned a subchain. In order to ensure the fairness of the voting process and the anonymity of voting nodes, SSHTDNS utilizes Linkable Ring Signature (LRS) during the voting process.

In order to realize that a member on behalf of the entire group to sign message anonymously, Chaum proposed group signature in 1991 [22]. However, group signature has central administrator. Rivest et al. proposed ring signature without center administrator in 2001 [23], where any member can use his private key to sign message without the consent of other members. LRS [24] is one of the ring signatures with linkability, i.e. anyone can make a good judge of whether signatures are signed by the same group member. In other words, each user can only vote once anonymously per vote. Next, we will introduce the standard model of LRS.

Linkable Ring Signature. A linkable ring Signature scheme is a tuple $(Init, Sign, Verify, Link)$.

- $Init$. Assume there are n users in the consortium committee, a group members' public key list $PK = \{PK_1, PK_2, ..., PK_n\}$, a secret key list $SK = \{SK_1, SK_2, ..., SK_n\}$, and a message needs to be signed $m \in \{0, 1\}^*$. The anonymous signer owns public-private key pair $\{PK_i, SK_i\}, (1 \leq i \leq n)$.
- $Sign$. Take the public keys of all group members PK, the secret key of the signer SK_i and the message m as input, output a linkable ring signature σ.
- $Verify$. Take the public keys of all group members PK, a message m and a signature σ as input, output either 1 or 0 for valid or invalid.
- $Link$. Take two signature σ and σ' as input, output nothing if one or two signatures are invalid, otherwise output either 1 or 0 for linked or unlinked.

Correctness. A LRS scheme is correct if both $Verify$ and $Link$ output 1 for all PK, SK, i, m, m', i.e.

$$Verify(PK, m, Sign(PK, SK_i, m)) = 1$$
$$Link(Sign(PK, SK_i, m), Sign(PK, SK_i, m')) = 1 \tag{2}$$

Property. A LRS scheme owns the following properties:

- $Unforgeable$. It is computationally difficult for anyone other than a legitimate signer to forge a signature.
- $Anonymous$. The probability of anyone who wants to know who is the real signer will not exceed the probability of guessing.
- $Linkable$. Anyone can detect if two valid signatures were signed by the same group member.

LRS can implement anonymous voting, while Blockchain is not anonymous. Its address is just pseudonyms [32], especially for the consortium nodes, whose addresses are known to all of the nodes. When the node sends out the voting result, it exposes the voter. So we can use a public account to issue the voting results. The proxy consortium node publishes the public account's public-private key pair (pk, sk) that has been encrypted by consortium nodes' public keys, as shown in Table 3. Then all of the consortium nodes can decrypt the public voting account by their own secret key. Of course, the public account will have some restrictions, such as login time and login times.

Table 3. Public voting account sharing

$Enc_{PK_1}(pk)$	$Enc_{PK_1}(sk)$
$Enc_{PK_2}(pk)$	$Enc_{PK_2}(sk)$
...	...
$Enc_{PK_{n-1}}(pk)$	$Enc_{PK_{n-1}}(sk)$
$Enc_{PK_n}(pk)$	$Enc_{PK_n}(sk)$

4   Discussion and Analysis

Compared to the current domain name resolution system in Fig. 3, the new domain name system SSHTDNS reconstructed in this paper has the following properties.

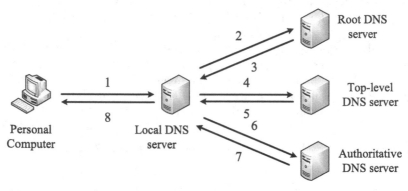

1.Request to resolve *www.google.com*
2.Initiate a request to the Root DNS server if the Local DNS server does not have a corresponding cache
3.Return the *com* Top-level DNS server IP address: IP1
4.Initiate a request to the *com* Top-level DNS server
5.Return the *google.com* Authoritative DNS server IP address: IP2
6.Initiate a request to the *google.com* Authoritative DNS server
7.Return the IP address of *www.google.com* : IP3
8.Local DNS server sends IP3 to the personal computer

Fig. 3. Domain name resolution system

4.1   Advantages

Security. In the early domain name system, security issues were not considered in the system, which was vulnerable to various attacks. Until the promulgation of RFC2535 DNSSEC, which implements data source verification, data integrity verification through digital signature and hash algorithm. Although the security of DNS was gradually taken seriously, it still exists various security threats, such as DDoS attack, vanishing risks, blinding risks and so on [28].

- **DNS cache poisoning.** The current domain name system uses name caching to improve the efficiency of domain name resolution. However, the resolution process is based on the connection-less and unreliable protocol, UDP, and usually does not have any authentication mechanism. Therefore, attackers can exploit the vulnerabilities that the caching mechanism performs no check on the data, and trick the name server into caching virtual resource records with a large lifetime to deceive customers. In SSHTDNS, blockchain has the characteristic of data tamper-proof, nodes can quickly verify the correctness of the data with the properties of Merkle Tree and hash chains. The cache data in the index database can be guaranteed by periodically replaying the data in the blockchain.
- **DDoS attack.** Distributed Denial of Service (DDoS) is a kind of attack that the attacker manipulates a large number of BotNet [29] to exploit various system requests to exhaust the system's network resources, then the attacked facility cannot provide normal services for legitimate users. As we can see in Fig. 3, all of the resolution requests will be assigned to the server that owns a definite address step by step. Even though the domain name server might be a cluster of machines, they may still be vulnerable to DDoS attack. If the attacked server is root domain name server or TLD name server, it will have a major impact on a country or organization. In SSHTDNS, the consortium nodes are only responsible for the registration and logout requests of the TLD, and generally do not provide domain name resolution. When applicant launches a request to the consortium node outside the chain, the consortium node will act as a proxy to issue the request to the consortium committee. Therefore, malicious nodes will not have the opportunity to initiate a large-scale invalid request on the chain. In addition, consortium nodes need to verify the validity of the ordinary nodes' identities in the sharding protocol, the consortium nodes can establish a blacklist cache and refuse to accept their requests. Also, the PBFT consensus algorithm used internally by the committee allows a small number of nodes to crash. As for DDoS attack on ordinary nodes, it will not have a major impact on the system running.
- **Computing power attack.** Part of the current blockchain systems are vulnerable to 51% power attack. The main reason is that they utilize the probabilistic consensus algorithm such as PoW. When the attacker gathers more than half of the system's computing power, they can rewrite the previous blocks or even completely control the system. SSHTDNS utilizes PoW as a means of preventing sybil attack, and uses PBFT, a deterministic consensus algorithm, as the main consensus mechanism. PBFT can tolerate no more than $1/3$ of Byzantine nodes, while ordinary nodes may be malicious in the PoW of sharding protocol. We Can control the proportion of Byzantine nodes by controlling the security parameters and the shard size [17].

An event that occurs less than $2^{-\lambda}$ is considered negligible, for a given security parameter λ. We assume that the public random string generated in the previous period has good randomness, then we have: For every sufficiently large integer $n' \geq n_0$: among the first n' identities created, at most $n'/3 - 1$ are controlled by the adversary.

Proof. If all nodes start at the same time, and the computing power ratio controlled by the adversary in the all ordinary nodes is f. Now, let X_i be an indicator random variable which takes value 1 if the ith identity is generated by the honest. Let $X = \sum_{i=1}^{n'} X_i$, and X follows a binomial distribution:

$$Pr[X \le 2n'/3] = \sum_{k=0}^{2n'/3} Pr[X = k] = \sum_{k=0}^{2n'/3} \binom{k}{n'} f^{n'-k}(1-f)^k \qquad (3)$$

This probability decreases exponentially in n'. Given λ, we can find n_0 such that $Pr[X \le 2n'/3] \le 2^{-\lambda}, \forall n' \ge n_0$. The shard size N is at least n_0 to ensure that the proportion of Byzantine nodes in a shard will not exceed $1/3$. For $f = 1/4$, if $N = 600$, then something bad happens is one in a million, if $N = 100$, the probability is four thousandths.

- **Vanishing risk.** Vanishing risk is proposed by Fang [28], where the authorized domain name is maliciously deleted by hackers. Based on the current domain name resolution system in Fig. 3, we take a gTLD as an example. If TLD *com* is deleted from the root DNS servers, users cannot access to the TLD and its sub-domain names, and the *com* branch collapses. SSHTDNS records important TLD on the main chain. Once the domain name registration is successful, the applicant controls the power. The request can be considered effective only when it has been signed by the domain owner's private key. Thus the risk of vanishing can be well avoided.
- **Blinding risk.** Blinding risk is also proposed by Fang [28], where the domain name server is controlled by hackers and refuses to provide resolution for a local DNS server in a specific scope. For example, the root DNS server and its images in Fig. 3 refuse to provide resolution of TLD name for users in a certain region, then the users cannot get domain name information normally. However, there is no such risk in SSHTDNS. All nodes can have complete domain name information if they want, or they can send resolution requests to multiple nodes even if they do not have a complete copy.

Scalability. The scalability here refers to the structural scalability of the chain. SSHTDNS is designed as a main chain with multiple sub-chains. The main chain only needs to store the fingerprints of all the data in subchains. In theory, the number of sub-chains can be infinitely expanded as long as the application is legal. As time goes by, more and more domain names under different TLDs need to be processed by the system, and the system can be expanded by attaching more sub-chains to the main chain. In addition, a sub-chain records the registration and logout of the domain names under the fixed TLD. If there are too many registration-delete pairs in a sub-chain, it will store lots of useless information. Then the TLD owner can apply to the consortium committee to re-open a sub-chain under the same TLD and give up the old one after migrating its useful information, which can purify the system.

High-Throughput. Throughput refers to the maximum rate at which the blockchain can process requests. The current blockchain system's throughput is generally not satisfactory. Take Bitcoin as an example, all nodes in the system are competing for the same batch of transactions, so the system can only process 3–7 transactions per second [30]. However, SSHTDNS utilizes a sharding protocol to achieve high throughput. It uniformly partitions the network nodes into smaller committee, and each committee can process requests within one shard independently. Therefore, the process is parallelism, and the throughput of the system is almost linear with the system's computing power.

Assume there are n processors, and they form 2^k committees, each of them has N members. Now the question is similar to the extended coupon collector problem [33] where there are 2^k types of coupon in some urn, and we need to calculate the number of draws to collect N copies of each coupon. It has been shown in [34] that the expected number of PoW solution E is:

$$
\begin{aligned}
E &= 2^k \log 2^k + (N-1)2^k \log\log 2^k + O(2^k) \\
&= k\frac{n}{N} + n\log k - \frac{n}{N}\log k + O(\frac{n}{N})
\end{aligned}
\tag{4}
$$

If $N < k$, we can achieve $O(n/\log n)$ scalability in throughput. If $N > k$, we have $kn/N < n$ or $E = O(n\log k)$ given that $k < N$. Since $n = N2^k$, we have $E = O(n\log\log n)$, thus the $O(n/\log\log n)$ scalability in throughput. The latter is more practical since N must be of a few hundreds to provide security guarantee.

Besides, [34] also shows that if N is large enough, E is asymptotically $O(N2^k)$. It means we can achieve high-throughput in linear scalability if the committee size is chosen properly, [17] has proved that $N > 24\ln(2^k)$ can satisfy the needs by using Chernoff bound.

Anonymity. Each country maintains several consortium nodes and all of nodes form a consortium committee. The consortium committee often needs to vote on major decisions. In order to ensure fairness during the voting process, SSHTDNS adopts linkable ring signature technique, which allows group members to verify the validity of the vote, but does not know the voter. Besides, the public voting account can solve the problem of pseudonym. Such design can ensure identity anonymity and reduce retaliatory votes.

4.2 Problems

Although the system we designed has the above advantages, there still remains some problems. For example, SSHTDNS uses index databases outside the chain to speed up the efficiency of domain name resolution. However, it causes redundant storage of data, which will increase the storage load of nodes. In addition, the private key in SSHTDNS is of high importance. To solve this problem, we can decompose the signature key into multiple sub-keys, and each organization custody a sub-key in the country. The signature of consortium nodes can be executed only when the number of participating sub-keys reaches a certain range, the pivotal technique used is secret sharing [31].

5   Conclusion

In order to solve the various security problems and centralized risks in the current DNS, this paper considers using decentralized, secure and trusted blockchain technique to reconstruct the domain name system. This paper uses the form of consortium chain, and utilizes multi-chain structure combined with sharding protocol, linkable ring signature technique. SSHTDNS, a new domain name system is proposed, which is secure, scalable in structure, high-throughput with good anonymity, trusted response, low storage requirements. In the future, it is better to reduce the redundant storage of nodes and improve the efficiency of the linkable ring signature algorithm.

References

1. Mockapetris, P.: Rfc 1034: Domain names: concepts and facilitie (2003). https://tools.ietf.org/html/rfc1034
2. Mockapetris, P.: Rfc 1035: Domain names: implementation and specification (2004). http://www.ietf.org/rfc/rfc1035.txt
3. Weiler, S., Blacka, D.: Clarifications and implementation notes for DNS security (DNSSEC) (2013). https://tools.ietf.org/html/rfc6840
4. Nakamoto, S.: Bitcoin: A peer-to-peer electronic cash system (2009). bitcoin.org
5. Namecoin (2011). https://Namecoin.info
6. Muneeb, A., Nelson, J., Shea, R., et al.: Block stack: a global naming and storage system secured by block chains. In: 2016 USENIX Annual Technical Conference (USENIX ATC 16), pp. 181–194 (2016)
7. Nebulis (2016). https://www.nebulis.io/
8. Wang, X., Li, K., Li, H., Li, Y., Liang, Z.: ConsortiumDNS: a distributed domain name service based on consortium chain. In: 2017 IEEE 19th International Conference on High Performance Computing and Communications; IEEE 15th International Conference on Smart City, Bangkok, pp. 617–620 (2017)
9. Eastlake, D.: RFC 2535: Domain Name System Security Extensions (1999). https://tools.ietf.org/html/rfc2535 (1999)
10. Guo, F., Chen, J., Chiueh, T.: Spoof detection for preventing DoS attacks against DNS servers. In: Proceedings of the 26th IEEE International Conference on Distributed Computing Systems, Lisboa, Portugal, pp. 37–37 (2006)
11. Ateniese, G., Mangard, S.: A new approach to DNS security (DNSSEC). In: The 8th-ACM Conference on Computer and Communications Security, pp. 86–95 (2001)
12. Jakobsson, M., Juels, A.: Proofs of work and bread pudding protocols. Secure Information Networks, pp. 258–272 (1999)
13. Benet, J.: PFS - Content Addressed, Versioned, P2P File System. Technical report, Protocol Labs (2014)
14. Buterin, V.: A next generation smart contract & decentralized application platform (2015). https://www.ethereum.org/pdfs/EthereumWhitePaper.pdf/
15. Nick, S.: Formalizing and securing relationships on public networks (1997). https://ojphi.org/ojs/index.php/fm/article/view/548/469
16. Wikipedia contributors. Top-Level Domain (2018). https://en.wikipedia.org/w/index.php?title=Top-level_domain&oldid=872277589

17. Luu, L., Narayanan, V., Zheng, C., Baweja, K., Gilbert, S., Saxena, P.: A secure sharding protocol for open Blockchains. In: The 2016 ACM SIGSAC Conference on Computer and Communications Security (CCS '16), pp. 17–30 (2016)
18. Kokoris-Kogias, E., Jovanovic, P., Gasser, L., Gailly, N., Syta, E., Ford, B.: OmniLedger: a secure, scale-out, decentralized ledger via sharding. In: 2018 IEEE Symposium on Security and Privacy (S&P), pp. 19–34 (2018)
19. Mahdi, Z., Movahedi, M., Raykova, M.: RapidChain: scaling Blockchain via full sharding. In: The 2018 ACM SIGSAC Conference on Computer and Communications Security (CCS 2018), pp. 931–948 (2018)
20. Douceur. J.R.: The sybil attack. In: The 1st International Workshop on Peer-to-Peer Systems (IPTPS), pp. 251–260(2002)
21. Castro, M., Liskov, B.: Practical byzantine fault tolerance. In: The Third Symposium on Operating Systems Design and Implementation, pp. 173–186 (1999)
22. Chaum, D., van Heyst, E.: Group signatures. In: Workshop on the Theory and Application of of Cryptographic Techniques, pp. 257–265 (1991)
23. Rivest, R.L., Shamir, A., Tauman, Y.: How to leak a secret. In: International Conference on the Theory & Application of Cryptology & Information Security, pp. 552–565 (2001)
24. Liu, J.K., Wei, V.K., Wong, D.S.: Linkable spontaneous anonymous group signature for ad hoc groups. In: Australasian Conference on Information Security and Privacy (ACISP 2004), pp. 325–335 (2004)
25. Baron, C.: The Statistics Portal (2019). https://www.statista.com/statistics/647523/worldwide-bitcoin-blockchain-size/
26. Wilkinson, D., Chow, C.E., Cai, Y.: Enhanced secure dynamic DNS update with indirect route. In: IEEE Information Assurance Workshop, pp. 335–341 (2004)
27. Fetzer, C., Pfeifer, G., Jim, T.: Enhancing DNS security using the SSL trust infrastructure. In: The 10th IEEE International Workshop on Object-oriented Real-time Dependable Systems (WORDS 2005), pp. 21–28 (2005)
28. Fang, B.: Country autonomous root domain name resolution architecture from the perfective of country cyber sovereignty. Inf. Secur. Commun. Priv. 2014(12), 35–38 (2014)
29. Du, Y., Cui, X.: Botnet and its inspiration. China Data Commun. 5, 9–13 (2005)
30. Wikipedia contributors. Bitcoin: Scalability (2017). https://en:bitcoin:it/wiki/Scalability
31. Jarecki, S., Kiayias, A., Krawczyk, H., et al.: Highly-efficient and composable password-protected secret sharing (or: how to protect your bitcoin wallet online). In: 2016 IEEE European Symposium on Security and Privacy (EuroS&P), Saarbrucken, pp. 276–291 (2016)
32. Sasson, E.B., et al.: Zerocash: decentralized anonymous payments from bitcoin. In: The 2014 IEEE Symposium on Security and Privacy (S&P), pp. 459–474 (2014)
33. Wikipedia. Coupon collector's problem (2018). https://en.wikipedia.org/wiki/Couponcollector'sproblem
34. Newman, D.J.: The double dixie cup problem. Am. Math. Monthly 67(1), 58–61 (1960)

A Practical Dynamic Enhanced BFT Protocol

Feng Shen, Yu Long$^{(\boxtimes)}$, Zhen Liu$^{(\boxtimes)}$, Zhiqiang Liu$^{(\boxtimes)}$, Hongyang Liu, Dawu Gu$^{(\boxtimes)}$, and Ning Liu$^{(\boxtimes)}$

School of Electronic Information and Electrical Engineering,
Shanghai Jiao Tong University, Shanghai, China
{shenfeng2017,longyu,liuzhen,ilu_zq,LiuHongyang,dwgu,ningliu}@sjtu.edu.cn

Abstract. Emerging as a distributed system maintaining a public ledger via consensus protocol, blockchain technology is showing its great potential in various scenarios such as supply chain, financial industry, internet of things (IoT), etc. Among kinds of consensus protocols, Byzantine Fault Tolerance (BFT) protocols are playing an important part in the design of the blockchain system. Most BFT protocols, however, are static with no support for a dynamic property (i.e. nodes can join/leave a working system) and lack mechanisms to punish faulty nodes, which highly limit their wider adoption in the practical settings. This paper presents a dynamic enhanced BFT (DEBFT) protocol that is designed to support dynamic property and faulty nodes punishment. Based on HoneyBadger BFT, DEBFT employs Dynamic Threshold Identity-based Encryption and Distributed Key Generation to enable changes of the consensus group without reconfiguring the whole system, besides, evaluation metrics are also introduced to evaluate consensus nodes and clear faulty ones out of the system.

Keywords: Blockchain · Consensus · Dynamic property · BFT protocols

1 Introduction

The emergence of Bitcoin in 2008 [18] opened up the era of blockchain technology, which is an ingenious innovation that realizes consensus among distributed nodes by combining P2P network, distributed database, consensus protocol, cryptography, game theory and so on. Serving as a distributed ledger maintained by multiple participants, blockchain has shown its great potential in cryptocurrencies, financial industry, internet of things (IoT) and many other scenarios.

Blockchain can be classified into permissionless and permissioned ones according to entry limitation for network nodes. In a permissionless blockchain such as Bitcoin and Ethereum [21], anyone can join the system without a specific identity, whereas in a permissioned setting, every node maintaining the public ledger has an identity, and this identity is known to any other nodes in the system

© Springer Nature Switzerland AG 2019
J. K. Liu and X. Huang (Eds.): NSS 2019, LNCS 11928, pp. 288–304, 2019.
https://doi.org/10.1007/978-3-030-36938-5_17

even though they may not trust each other. With the development of blockchain technology, permissioned blockchain is gaining more and more attraction within business and financial fields for its efficiency and controllability.

In the design of blockchain, the consensus mechanism is a core part to reach an agreement on the global ledger. In traditional distributed systems like database and file system, Byzantine Fault Tolerance (BFT) protocols have been intensively studied. Normally, BFT protocols run among a fixed set of consensus nodes, and can finally reach deterministic consensus and high efficiency with the tolerance of less than 1/3 malicious nodes. Due to these merits, BFT protocols especially PBFT [8] and its derivatives [4,19] are widely deployed to construct consensus mechanisms in permissioned blockchain systems, e.g. Hyperledger Fabric [1], Tendermint [13] et al.

1.1 Research on BFT Protocols

Classical BFT protocols need a leader to lead the consensus process, and it will be replaced if it is found faulty. PBFT [8] proposed in 1999 is a typical BFT protocol of such a case, and it is the first practical BFT protocol that works under weak synchronous network assumption. Later works extend PBFT to simplify the design and reduce the cost, e.g. Zyzzyva [12] proposed in 2007 allows clients to adopt proposals from the leader optimistically and solve the inconsistency if needed. However, the main problem for BFT protocols with a leader is its vulnerability when suffering DoS attacks [16].

Some leaderless BFT protocols have been constructed in the face of DoS attacks. HoneyBadger BFT [16] is the first practical asynchronous BFT protocol without a leader. It combines threshold encryption with an efficient realization of Asynchronous Common Subset (ACS), together with a random selection method for proposals. With these in hand, the communication cost of HoneyBadger BFT is greatly reduced. In 2018, Duan et al. [9] extended HoneyBadger BFT to BEAT by replacing its cryptography components. And BEAT provides different versions for various scenarios. Hashgraph [3] is another leaderless BFT protocol that takes advantage of a kind of gossip about gossip design to realize virtue voting, as a result, it saves much communication overhead.

Besides the single consensus scheme, BFT protocols are also introduced together with other consensus protocols to achieve better performance. Typical blockchain schemes including Byzcoin [11], RapidChain [22], Elastico [15] et al. combine proof-of-work (PoW) with BFT to achieve both security and efficiency. Apart from them, Cosmos [14] combines delegated proof-of-stack (DPoS) with BFT under the same consideration.

All BFT protocols listed above, however, can only support static setting in which network nodes are fixed, and they can not support dynamically changes of the consensus group without reconfiguring the whole system. Indeed, the change of consensus group for a permissioned blockchain system is of necessity in business and financial fields, and without support for dynamic property, the reconfiguration process may be burdensome and costly. On the other hand, how to detect inactive or even malicious nodes is also of great importance, but it is not referred in most BFT protocols. Based on these observations, we carry out this work to build an enhanced BFT protocol atop HoneyBadger BFT, and a comparison among related BFT protocols is shown in Table 1.

Table 1. Comparation among typical BFT protocols

BFT protocols	Optimal Comm. Compl	Worst Comm. Compl	Dynamic property	DoS resilience
PBFT	$O(N^2)$	∞	No	No
HoneyBadger BFT	$O(N)$	$O(N)$	No	Yes
BEAT	$O(N)$	$O(N)$	No	Yes
This work	$O(N)$	$O(N)$	Yes	Yes

Comm. Compl means Communication Complexity

1.2 Our Contribution

- We propose a new dynamic enhanced BFT (DEBFT) protocol under leaderless setting with $O(N)$ communication complexity, which allows consensus nodes to dynamically join and leave the network.
- We design Join and Quit protocol, providing detailed protocol procedures as well as data structures of relevant messages types. By Join and Quit protocol, DEBFT allows a consensus node to join or leave the consensus group without reconfiguring the whole system.
- We describe the metrics to assess the behavior of a consensus node, and design Clear protocol to clear malicious or inactive consensus nodes out of the system to maintain its long-term benign work.
- We analyze key properties of the DEBFT, including *dynamic property, fairness, agreement, and total order.*

1.3 Paper Organization

The rest of this paper is organized as follows. We start by introducing the system module (Sect. 2). After that, the overview of HoneyBadger BFT is described (Sect. 3), as well as the building blocks of this work (Sect. 4). Next, we give the detailed protocol design (Sect. 5) and its security analysis (Sect. 6), then we conclude the paper (Sect. 7).

2 System Module

Participants Definition. There are three kinds of participants in this system: client, dealer, and consensus node (noted as node in the following context for simplification). Here we depict their roles in our protocol.

- Clients generate transaction requests and broadcast them to all nodes. Clients will also gather feedback from nodes. Enough signatures from different nodes on one transaction denote it has been output as a consensus result.
- Dealer represents a trusted party providing validity check for nodes. Hence it is responsible for the initialization of the system and leads the dynamic joining process of nodes.
- Nodes are validated by the dealer before joining the system. They will receive transactions from clients, then execute the protocol together to get the consensus result that decides which transactions should be output.

Timing Assumption. The system works under a partially synchronous network assumption [10]. For all nodes computation proceeds in synchronized rounds and messages are received by their recipients within some specified time bound. We assume that the nodes are equipped with synchronized clocks to guarantee this round synchronization. In our system, there exists an adversary. In every round of communication, the adversary can wait for the messages of the uncorrupted nodes to arrive, then decide on his computation and communication strategy for that round. The adversary can still ensure that his messages delivered to the honest nodes on time. Therefore we should always assume the worst case that the adversary speaks last in every communication round.

Security Module. Assuming that there exists an adversary willing to prevent the system from making consensus or to subvert the system, here gives the definition of its ability.

The adversary can completely control up to t corrupted nodes, and t satisfies $3t + 1 \leq n$ where n is the total number of consensus nodes. The controlled nodes are called faulty nodes standing on the opposite of honest nodes which totally obey the protocol. Faulty nodes can choose arbitrary malicious actions, including not responding, sending conflicting messages to different nodes, corrupting other nodes and so on.

3 Reviewing HoneyBadger BFT

HoneyBadger BFT is the first practical asynchronous BFT protocol. Clients in the network will send their transaction requests to all nodes, and nodes execute the BFT protocol in consecutive rounds. At the beginning of a round every node will raise its proposal and at the end of this round a common subset of proposals will be output as the consensus result. Figure 1 shows the basic working procedures. Next we will depict main components applied in HoneyBadger BFT.

3.1 Protocol Components

HoneyBadger BFT mainly consists of two components: threshold encryption and Asynchronous Common Subset (ACS). In every round, each node chooses a set of transactions as its proposal and encrypts it through threshold encryption scheme, then submits the ciphertext as input to ACS module and a common subset of these ciphertexts will be output. At last the subset will be decrypted still by threshold encryption scheme to get final consensus results.

HoneyBadger BFT uses the threshold encryption scheme TPKE from Baek and Zheng [2]. In the design of TKPE, to decrypt the ciphertext, at least $t + 1$ nodes need to get their decryption shares separately and combine them together. This design ensures that the adversary controlling less than t faulty nodes can not get the plaintext without the help of honest nodes. As TPKE is secure under the adaptive chosen ciphertext attack, its application in HoneyBadger BFT helps to realize censorship resilience property which prevents the adversary from delaying honest client requests on purpose. ACS is the main module to reach consensus among nodes. As Fig. 1 shows, it consists of Reliable Broadcast (RBC) module and Binary Agreement (BA) module. In HoneyBadger BFT, RBC module from Cachin and Tessaro [7] is used to transmit the proposal of each node to all other nodes. BA module from Mostéfaoui [17] is used to decide on a bit vector indicating which proposals should be output as the consensus result.

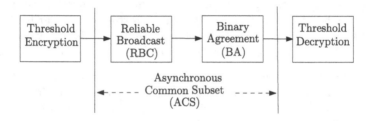

Fig. 1. HoneyBadger BFT

3.2 Protocol Security Properties

On a high level HoneyBadger BFT satisfies below properties [16]:

- (Agreement) If any correct node includes transaction tx into its consensus result, then every correct node includes tx into its consensus result.
- (Total Order) If one correct node has output the sequence of transactions $\langle tx_0, tx_1, \ldots tx_j \rangle$ and another has output $\langle tx'_0, tx'_1, \ldots tx'_j \rangle$, then $tx_i = tx'_i$ for $i \leq min(j, j')$.
- (Censorship Resilience) If a transaction tx is input to $n - t$ correct nodes, then it is eventually output by every correct node. Intuitively this means the adversary cannot prevent a transaction from being output as a consensus result.

3.3 Limitations of HoneyBadger BFT

As the first practical asynchronous BFT protocol which guarantees both liveness and safety, HoneyBadger BFT has abundant application scenarios like banks and financial institutions. It is especially suitable for permissioned blockchain applications, where a fixed number of nodes are authorized to enter the system.

However, HoneyBadger BFT is a traditional static BFT protocol which means that it could not support a consensus node to join or leave the consensus group without reconfiguring the whole system. On the other hand, there may exist malicious or inactive nodes in the system, and the current protocol lacks the function to detect these faulty nodes to exclude them from the system, this may hamper the long-term benign working of the system.

Considering above limitations, this paper focuses on the dynamic property and clear function of BFT protocol. Through the application of cryptography components introduced in Sect. 4, together with rational protocol procedure, we construct the new protocol DEBFT which is based on HoneyBader BFT.

4 Building Blocks

This section describes several cryptography components applied in our work. We will separately show their functions and details.

Dynamic Threshold Identity-Based Encryption (DTIBE). The threshold encryption scheme TPKE [2] in HoneyBadger BFT can only set the threshold parameter and define the consensus group during the configuration phase. We utilize the dynamic threshold identity-based (DTIBE) scheme from Susilo et al. [20] for its dynamic property, where after the initialization of the system, a sender can dynamically select the set of recipients as well as dynamically set the threshold t upon the creation of ciphertext. This character meets the need of joining and quitting of members in a working consensus system. Figure 2 shows the details.

DTIBE Scheme

A DTIBE scheme is comprised of the following five steps.

– **DTIBE.Setup($1^\lambda, N$) → (MPK, SK)**

• Takes the security parameter 1^λ and the maximum network node number N as input, the setup algorithm outputs (MPK, SK), where MK is the master public key and SK is the master secret key.

– **DTIBE.Gen(ID, MPK, SK) → d_{ID}**

• Takes as input an identity ID and the master key pair (MPK, SK), the key generation algorithm outputs a private key of ID, which is denoted by d_{ID}.

– **DTIBE.Enc($ID_1, ID_2, \ldots, ID_n, t, M, MPK$) → CT**

• Takes as input a set of identities $ID_1, ID_2, \ldots, ID_n$, a threshold number t, a message M and the master public key MPK, where $n \leq N$ and $\lfloor (n-1)/3 \rfloor \leq t \leq n$, the encryption algorithm outputs a ciphertext, which is denoted by CT.

– **DTIBE.ShareDec(CT, d_{ID}, MPK) → S_{ID} or $\perp$**

• Takes as input a ciphertext CT for ($ID_1, ID_2, \ldots, ID_n, t$), a private key d_{ID} of identity ID and the master public key MPK, the decryption algorithm outputs a decryption share denoted by S_{ID} or $\perp$.

– **DTIBE.Combine($CT, S_{ID_1}{}', S_{ID_2}{}', \ldots, S_{ID_n}{}', MPK$) → M or $\perp$**

• Takes as input a ciphertext CT for ($ID_1, ID_2, \ldots, ID_n, t$), at least t decryption shares $S_{ID_1}{}', S_{ID_2}{}', \ldots, S_{ID_n}{}'$ and the master public key MPK, the combination algorithm outputs the message M or $\perp$.

Fig. 2. The algorithm procedure of DTIBE

Distributed Key Generation (DKG). HoneyBadger BFT uses BA to decide on a bit vector representing the proposals to be output. Its BA scheme uses the Boldyreva's pairing-based threshold signature scheme [5] as a randomizer to build the common coin which can not support changes of consensus group flexibly. In this work we use the Distributed Key Generation (DKG) scheme from Gennaro et al. [10] to generate randomness and the updated BA is represented as $\widetilde{BA}$ in our work. To distinguish from the primitive ACS in HoneyBadger BFT, we define the combination of RBC and $\widetilde{BA}$ as Round Common Subset (RCS) in our scheme. Figure 3 shows the details to generate randomness by the DKG scheme.

---

the Common Coin Based on DKG

DKG allows a set of n parties to jointly generate a pair of public and private keys according to the distribution defined by the underlying cryptosystem.

For discrete log based schemes, DKG amounts to generating a secret sharing of a random, uniformly distributed value x and making public the value $y = g^x$. Hence we use this as a randomizer to build the common coin in $\widetilde{BA}$ protocol.

Assuming there are n nodes labeled from P_1 to P_n, each node has identities of all other nodes and each node can not be fabricated. The public parameter is node number n and faulty node number t which works as a threshold and satisfies $\lfloor (n-1)/3 \rfloor \le t \le n$.

– ***Generating x :***
- Each player P_i performs a $Pedersen - VSS$ of a random value z_i as a dealer.
- Each player verifies the values, then builds the set of non-disqualified players $QUAL$.
- The distributed secret value x is not explicitly computed by any party, but it equals $x = \sum_{i \in QUAL} z_i mod\ q$.

– ***Extracting*** $y = g^x \bmod p$
- Each player $i \in QUAL$ exposes $y_i = g^{z_i} \bmod p$ via Feldman VSS.
- After verification, each player computes $y = \prod_{i \in QUAL} y_i$.

– ***Generating randomness***
- Get $Value = h(y)$ via a hash function $h()$.

Fig. 3. The common coin based on DKG

Boneh-Boyen Short Signature Scheme. In Sect. 2, we assume the identity of a node can not be fabricated. For this purpose, a node needs to transmit kinds of messages to other nodes with its signature. In this work this is ensured by using the Boneh-Boyen short signature scheme [6], and its main procedures are shown in Fig. 4.

Boneh-Boyen Signature Scheme

– *Key Generation* :
- $KeyGen(k) \rightarrow (SIG_{pk_i}, SIG_{sk_i})$. k stands for the security parameter. SIG_{sk_i} is used for a node to generate signature and SIG_{pk_i} is used by other nodes to check the validity of its signature.

– *Signature Generation* :
- $SigGen(m, SIG_{sk_i}) \rightarrow \delta$. m is the message to be signed and δ stands for the output signature.

– *Signature Verification* :
- $SigVerify(\delta, SIG_{pk_i}) \rightarrow 1 \ or \ 0$. Other nodes verify whether δ and SIG_{pk_i} matches. If it is a valid signature output 1 otherwise output 0.

Fig. 4. Boneh-Boyen signature scheme

5   Protocol Design

This chapter provides the detailed description of our dynamic enhanced BFT protocol DEBFT, including the initialization phase, regular consensus procedure and Join/Quit/Clear protocols for specific functions.

5.1   System Initialization

As mention in Sect. 3, there exist clients, a dealer, and consensus nodes in the system. In our system, D_{trust} represents the trusted dealer. N is the possible maximal number of nodes. n is the current number of nodes. Let P_i represents the ith node in the system, where $i \in \{1, 2, \cdots, n\}$. t is the maximal number of faulty nodes, which satisfies $t = \lfloor (n-1)/3 \rfloor$.

Before the system begins to work, each node P_i with identity ID_i will generate its signature key pair (SIG_{pk_i}, SIG_{sk_i}) by the Boneh-Boyen signature scheme. SIG_{pk_i} is the public key of node P_i, and SIG_{sk_i} is its secret key to generate signature. D_{trust} verifies whether each node P_i should join the consensus group, then executes the $DTIBE.Setup$ algorithm and broadcasts master public key MPK to all valid nodes in network. D_{trust} will generate and send the secret key d_{ID_i} for node P_i via the $DTIBE.Gen$ algorithm. The public information of node P_i can be represented by a pair (ID_i, SIG_{pk_i}) which is signed and bound by the D_{trust}.

5.2   Regular Consensus Procedure

This part depicts the whole process for transactions to be confirmed. The consensus protocol proceeds in consecutive rounds. Assuming the current round is numbered as r, each node generates its proposal then the consensus protocol executes among all nodes. Finally the consensus result of round r is a common subset of the proposals. Figure 5 gives an intuitive representation of the whole procedure, detail steps are as follows.

– **step 1: Batch Selection**

- Clients send requests to all nodes, and each node P_i stores enough requests in a local FIFO queue buf_i. There is a properly set parameter B representing the batch size. P_i randomly selects B/n elements from the first B elements of buf_i.

– **step 2: Threshold Encryption**

- P_i chooses the decryption set and uses the $DTIBE.Enc$ algorithm to encrypt the elements selected in step 1, and gets ciphertext v_i as output.

– **step 3: Agreement on Ciphertexts**

- $RCS[r]$ is responsible for generating the common subset of proposals for round r. In this phase n nodes run $RCS[r]$ together, and each node P_i passes v_i as input to it. $RCS[r]$ consists of n reliable broadcast instances $\{RBC_i\}_n$ to disseminate the n proposals and n binary agreement instances $\{\widetilde{BA_i}\}_n$ to collect votes for the n proposals. Here node P_i is the sender of RBC_i and $\widetilde{BA_i}$ decides whether its proposal will be accepted. Detailed process is listed as follows.

- v_i is the input of RBC_i, and RBC_i will disseminate it to all other nodes.
- For node P_i, upon delivery of v_j from RBC_j, if input has not yet been provided to $\widetilde{BA_j}$, then provide input 1 to $\widetilde{BA_j}$. as referred previously DKG scheme is used to generate randomness during the process of $\widetilde{BA_j}$.
- Upon delivery of value 1 from at least $n - t$ instances of $\widetilde{BA}$, provide input 0 to each instance of $\widetilde{BA}$ that has not yet been provided input.
- Once all instances of $\widetilde{BA}$ have completed, get output from $RCS[r]$: an agreement on a common subset $\{v_j\}_{j \in S}$, where $S \subset [1 \ldots n]$ containing all indexes of each $\widetilde{BA}$ that delivered 1.

– **step 4: Threshold Decryption**

- Each node P_i uses $DTIBE.ShareDec$ to calculate its decryption shares for $v_j, j \in S$.
- Each node P_i multicasts the shares to all other nodes.
- For each element in $\{v_j\}_{j \in S}$, node P_i waits until receiving at least $t + 1$ valid shares, then uses $DTIBE.Combine$ to get the plaintext $\{y_j\}_{j \in S}$.
- Let $\{block\}_r = sorted(\cup y_j), j \in S$, such that $\{block\}_r$ is sorted in a canonical order (e.g., lexicographically).
- P_i updates buf_i and gets ready for round $r + 1$.

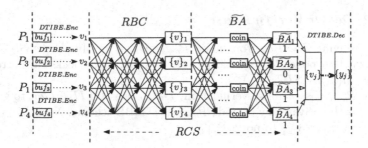

Fig. 5. Regular consensus procedure

5.3 Join Protocol

Join protocol is designed to allow a new node to join the network without stopping and reconfiguring the whole system.

Assuming there already exist n nodes in the system, a new node numbered as $n+1$ is willing to join the system, which satisfies $n+1 \leq N$. The protocol process is shown in Fig. 6 and we show the details as follows.

– **step** 1: *Join Request Phase*

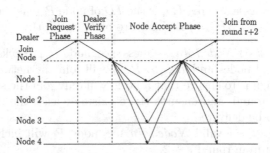

Fig. 6. Join protocol

- Node P_{n+1} invokes *KeyGen* of Boneh-Boyen signature scheme to generate its key pairs $(SIG_{pk_{n+1}}, SIG_{sk_{n+1}})$.
- Node P_{n+1} sends *JoinReq* to D_{trust}.

$$JoinReq = ((Join, SUB_{n+1}, SIG_{pk_{n+1}}, ID_{n+1}), SigGen(h(m), SIG_{sk_{n+1}})) \quad (1)$$

Join is a message type. SUB_{n+1} is the materials submitted by P_{n+1} to be verified by D_{trust}. $SIG_{pk_{n+1}}$ is the public key of node P_{n+1}. ID_{n+1} is the ID of P_{n+1}. $h(m)$ is the hash of the concatenation of the information above, and this applies to all $h(m)$ in the following description. $SigGen(h(m), SIG_{sk_{n+1}})$ is the signature of P_{n+1} on $h(m)$.

– *step* 2: *Dealer Verify Phase*

- After receiving *JoinReq* from node P_{n+1}, D_{trust} firstly checks SUB_{n+1} to verify whether node P_{n+1} should join the system, then checks the correctness of $SigGen(h(m), SIG_{sk_{n+1}})$.
- If node P_{n+1} passes above verification, D_{trust} uses *DTIBE.Gen* to generate $d_{ID_{n+1}}$ as the private key of node P_{n+1} in DTIBE scheme. Next D_{trust} sends *JoinAcc* with $d_{ID_{n+1}}$ to node P_{n+1}.

$$JoinAcc = ((Accept, JoinReq), SigGen(h(m), SIG_{sk_{D_{trust}}})) \qquad (2)$$

Accept is a message type. $SigGen(h(m), SIG_{sk_{D_{trust}}})$ is the signature of D_{trust} on $h(m)$.

– *step* 3: *Node Accept Phase*

- After receiving *JoinAcc*, Node P_{n+1} broadcasts *JoinAcc* to all nodes.
- For each node $P_i, i \in (1, \ldots, n)$, after receiving *JoinAcc* from node P_{n+1}, if the signature of D_{trust} is valid then replies *NodeJoinAcc* to node P_{n+1}.

$$NodeJoinAcc = ((JoinConf, ID_{n+1}, ID_i, r), SigGen(h(m), SIG_{sk_i})) \quad (3)$$

JoinConf is a message type. ID_i is the ID of node P_i. r is the current round number. $SigGen(h(m), SIG_{sk_i})$ is signature of P_i on $h(m)$.

- After receiving $2t+1$ *NodeJoinAcc* messages, node P_{n+1} packages and broadcasts them to all nodes and D_{trust}. P_{n+1} will join the network from round $r + 2$. This design is to ensure that a node will only join the system from the beginning of a round, and ensures there exists at least the time of a round for messages to be delivered.
- After receiving $2t + 1$ valid *NodeJoinAcc*, node P_i will include node P_{n+1} into the system from round $r + 2$.

5.4   Quit Protocol

Quit protocol is designed to allow a node to quit from the network without stopping and reconfiguring the whole system. When a node $P_k, k \in (1, \ldots n)$ wants to leave the network, The protocol process is shown in Fig. 7 and below gives the details.

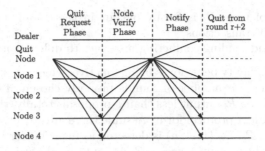

Fig. 7. Quit protocol

- *step* 1: ***Quit Request Phase***

- Node P_k broadcasts *QuitReq* to all nodes in the system.

$$QuitReq = ((Quit, ID_k, SIG_{pk_k}), SigGen(h(m), SIG_{sk_k})) \quad (4)$$

Quit is a message type. ID_k is the identity of P_k and SIG_{pk_k} is its public key. $SigGen(h(m), SIG_{sk_k})$ is signature of node P_k on $h(m)$.

- *step* 2: ***Node Verify Phase***

- For each node $P_i, i \in (1, \ldots, n)$ in the system, after receiving *QuitReq* from node P_k, if the signature is valid replies *NodeQuitAcc* to node P_k.

$$NodeQuitAcc = ((QuitConf, ID_k, ID_i, r), SigGen(h(m), SIG_{sk_i})) \quad (5)$$

QuitConf is a message type. ID_i is the identity of node P_i. r is the current round number. $SigGen(h(m), SIG_{sk_i})$ is the signature of P_i on $h(m)$.

- *step* 3: ***Notify Phase***

- After receiving $2t + 1$ *NodeQuitAcc* messages, node P_k packages and broadcasts them to all nodes and D_{trust}. P_k will quit from the network from round $r + 2$.
- After receiving the $2t + 1$ valid *NodeQuitAcc* message, node P_i will exclude node P_k from the network from round $r + 2$.

5.5 Clear Protocol

Clear protocol is design to exclude malicious or inactive nodes from consensus group. Before depicting details of Clear protocol, we describe how to evaluate actions of nodes to find faulty ones.

Firstly consider malicious behavior, if node P_i detects malicious behavior of node P_j, it will invoke Clear protocol at once. Generally, malicious behavior includes below items:

– The proposal of node P_j is finally output in the common subset, while it contains invalid transactions.
– Node P_j is found sending conflicting messages to different nodes.

Another kind of faulty behavior is being inactive, which needs to be measured properly. Assuming w is number of rounds properly chosen, if during the most recent w rounds, node P_j output less than p proposals totally, then other honest nodes can invoke Clear protocol for it. Assume there already exist n nodes in the system and a node $P_s, s \in (1, \ldots n)$ is detected as malicious or inactive. To keep the liveness and robust of the system, P_s needs to be cleared from the network. The protocol process is shown in Fig. 8 and the details is given as follows.

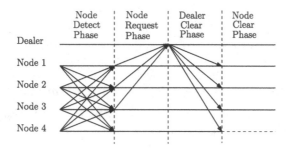

Fig. 8. Clear protocol

– *step 1: **Node Detect Phase***

• Each node P_i evaluates actions of all nodes during consensus processes, and will note some nodes as inactive or malicious.

– *step 2: **Node Request Phase***

• If node P_i considers node P_s as malicious or inactive, it will send message $Clear Req$ to D_{trust}.

$$ClearReq = ((Clear, ID_s, ID_i), SigGen(h(m), SIG_{sk_i})) \qquad (6)$$

$Clear$ is a message type. ID_s is the identity of the node to be cleared. ID_i is the identity of P_i. $SigGen(h(m), SIG_{sk_i})$ is signature of P_i on $h(m)$.

– *step 3: **Dealer Clear Phase***

• If D_{trust} has received $ClearReq$ about ID_s from more than t different nodes, it will broadcast $ClearAcc$ to the whole network and add P_s into its blacklist.

$$ClearAcc = ((Clr, ID_s), SigGen(h(m), SIG_{sk_{D_{trust}}})) \qquad (7)$$

Clr is a message type. $SigGen(h(m), SIG_{sk_{D_{trust}}})$ is signature of D_{trust} on $h(m)$.

- *step* 4: *Node Clear Phase*

- After receiving *ClearAcc* about ID_s from D_{trust}, node P_i will immediately clear P_s from its view of the network, and add it into its local blacklist.

6   Security and Performance

In this section, we will analyze several properties of the new scheme, including dynamic property, censorship resilience, agreement, and total order. We also show the performance and further consideration of DEBFT protocol.

6.1   Dynamic Property

Theorem 1. *In an already working system, requests from nodes to join or leave the consensus group will finally take effect if and only if they are valid.*

Proof. When a new node wants to join the system, the dealer will verify its request and sign if it is valid. Since the dealer is assumed to be reliable, nodes can trust the messages sent by the dealer with valid signatures. Next current consensus nodes will send *NodeJoinAcc* messages representing their acceptance. Later when every honest node receives *NodeJoinAcc* from $2t + 1$ nodes it can ensure at least $t + 1$ honest nodes has accepted this new node. This stands for the acceptance of the consensus group and every honest node will finally include the new node into the consensus group.

When a node currently in the consensus group wants to leave the system, it will broadcast *QuitReq* to all other nodes with its signature which cannot be fabricated. Other nodes will send *NodeQuitAcc* and finally receive at least $2t+1$ *NodeQuitAcc* from other nodes. This quorum contains at least $t+1$ honest nodes representing the acceptance of the consensus group and finally all honest nodes will exclude this node from the consensus group.

Since the dealer provides validation for new nodes, the sybil attack cannot take effect. And an honest node will only quit from the network by sending *QuitReq* by itself because its signature cannot be fabricated. In a word, only valid requests will finally take effect.

Theorem 2. *The system could clear malicious and inactive nodes timely and correctly.*

Proof. Through communication among nodes during the consensus process, malicious actions of faulty nodes could be detected by honest nodes, and inactive nodes could be detected through statistical results collected in recent rounds. All honest nodes will sponsor *Clear* protocol to exclude the malicious or inactive nodes from the system, and the dealer will receive enough signatures for a faulty node and process to clear it. On the other hand, the adversary could not attack an honest node to exclude it from the system, since the threshold is $t + 1$ and there are at most t malicious nodes.

6.2   Normal Consensus Properties

Theorem 3. *The system satisfies censorship resilience property.*

Proof. Due to DTIBE scheme applied in the protocol, at any time a node specifies the decryption set and a threshold t according to its view of all nodes. DTIBE scheme ensures the input to RCS protocol is secure under the adaptive chosen ciphertext attack, which can avoid the adversary from early getting the content of proposals and deliberately delaying a specific request. DKG scheme is adopted to generate randomness in $\widehat{BA}$ and it can effectively avoid any bias on randomness. These properties together guarantee that the final consensus result will not be manipulated by the adversary. Now let T be the size of requests previously input to any correct node before request m, since in every round, the number of committed requests has the same order with batch size B, then m will be committed within $O(T/B + \lambda)$ epochs except with negligible probability, where λ is a security parameter.

Theorem 4. *The system satisfies agreement property.*

Proof. For the property of DKG all honest nodes in the system will generate the same unbiased randomness, which is resistant to the attack of $t+1$ faulty nodes. Hence RCS protocol guarantees that in each round r a common subset will be output. If any honest nodes output request m, then m must be the plaintext of one component in the common subset of $RCS[r]$. According to the robustness of DTIBE scheme, every honest node will give their shares to decrypt the ciphertext to get request m, and m will finally be the output of all honest nodes.

Theorem 5. *The system satisfies the total order property.*

Proof. Firstly, since the system works in consecutive rounds, the consensus results of different rounds have an order. When considering the output requests in the same round, there exists an public ordering method(e.g., lexicographically), as a result all honest nodes will output requests in the same order.

The main consensus procedure of this new protocol inherits from HoneyBadger BFT, as a result DEBFT inherits the merits of its communication complexity which is $O(N)$, detail proof is shown in [16].

6.3   Further Consideration

As defined in Sect. 2, DEBFT protocol works under a partial synchronous network. Compared to the asynchronous network assumption, this limitation is due to the work environment of DKG scheme applied in $\widehat{BA}$ [10]. It has been proved that the DKG scheme can safely work under a partially synchronous communication module. To extend DEBFT to asynchronous environment, we should find a way to generate randomness resistant to t malicious nodes under asynchronous assumption in a dynamic changing group. When still using DKG scheme, this can be solved by specifying the $QUAL$ set before the beginning of a round, and one solution is to generate $QUAL$ set from previous consensus result. This aspect could be further researched.

7 Conclusion

In this paper, we have proposed a practical dynamic enhanced BFT protocol. While reserving the merits of HoneyBadger BFT, through the combination of two appropriate cryptography components and rational protocol design, we realized dynamic joining and quitting functions for nodes and function to clear faulty nodes for the system. Analysis of several properties is given. It is believed that this new protocol has a wide range of application scenarios.

Acknowledgement. We would like to thank the anonymous reviewers for their helpful feedback. The authors are supported by the National Natural Science Foundation of China (Grant No. 61572318, 61932014, 61672347, 61672339), and the Shanghai Science and Technology Innovation Fund (Grant No. 19511101400).

References

1. Androulaki, E., et al.: Hyperledger fabric: a distributed operating system for permissioned blockchains. In: Proceedings of the Thirteenth EuroSys Conference, p. 30. ACM (2018)
2. Baek, J., Zheng, Y.: Simple and efficient threshold cryptosystem from the gap Diffie-Hellman group. In: 2003 Proceedings of the Global Telecommunications Conference, GLOBECOM 2003, San Francisco, CA, USA, 1–5 December 2003, pp. 1491–1495 (2003). https://doi.org/10.1109/GLOCOM.2003.1258486
3. Baird, L.: The swirlds hashgraph consensus algorithm: fair, fast, byzantine fault tolerance. Swirlds Technical report SWIRLDS-TR-2016-01 (2016)
4. Bessani, A.N., Sousa, J., Alchieri, E.A.P.: State machine replication for the masses with BFT-SMART. In: 44th Annual IEEE/IFIP International Conference on Dependable Systems and Networks, DSN 2014, Atlanta, GA, USA, 23–26 June 2014, pp. 355–362 (2014). https://doi.org/10.1109/DSN.2014.43
5. Boldyreva, A.: Threshold signatures, multisignatures and blind signatures based on the Gap-Diffie-Hellman-group signature scheme. In: Desmedt, Y.G. (ed.) PKC 2003. LNCS, vol. 2567, pp. 31–46. Springer, Heidelberg (2003). https://doi.org/10.1007/3-540-36288-6_3
6. Boneh, D., Boyen, X.: Short signatures without random oracles and the SDH assumption in bilinear groups. J. Cryptol. **21**(2), 149–177 (2008). https://doi.org/10.1007/s00145-007-9005-7
7. Bracha, G.: Asynchronous Byzantine agreement protocols. Inf. Comput. **75**(2), 130–143 (1987)
8. Castro, M., Liskov, B., et al.: Practical Byzantine fault tolerance. In: OSDI 1999, pp. 173–186 (1999)
9. Duan, S., Reiter, M.K., Zhang, H.: BEAT: asynchronous BFT made practical. In: Proceedings of the 2018 ACM SIGSAC Conference on Computer and Communications Security, pp. 2028–2041. ACM (2018)
10. Gennaro, R., Jarecki, S., Krawczyk, H., Rabin, T.: Secure distributed key generation for discrete-log based cryptosystems. J. Cryptol. **20**(1), 51–83 (2007). https://doi.org/10.1007/s00145-006-0347-3

11. Kokoris-Kogias, E., Jovanovic, P., Gailly, N., Khoffi, I., Gasser, L., Ford, B.: Enhancing bitcoin security and performance with strong consistency via collective signing. In: 25th USENIX Security Symposium, USENIX Security 2016, Austin, TX, USA, 10–12 August 2016, pp. 279–296 (2016). https://www.usenix.org/conference/usenixsecurity16/technical-sessions/presentation/kogias

12. Kotla, R., Alvisi, L., Dahlin, M., Clement, A., Wong, E.L.: Zyzzyva: speculative byzantine fault tolerance. ACM Trans. Comput. Syst. **27**(4), 7:1–7:39 (2009). https://doi.org/10.1145/1658357.1658358

13. Kwon, J.: Tendermint: consensus without mining (2014). http://tendermint.com/docs/tendermint.pdf

14. Kwon, J., Buchman, E.: Cosmos: a network of distributed ledgers (2016). https://cosmos.network/whitepaper

15. Luu, L., Narayanan, V., Zheng, C., Baweja, K., Gilbert, S., Saxena, P.: A secure sharding protocol for open blockchains. In: Proceedings of the 2016 ACM SIGSAC Conference on Computer and Communications Security, pp. 17–30. ACM (2016)

16. Miller, A., Xia, Y., Croman, K., Shi, E., Song, D.: The honey badger of BFT protocols. In: Proceedings of the 2016 ACM SIGSAC Conference on Computer and Communications Security, Vienna, Austria, 24–28 October 2016, pp. 31–42 (2016). https://doi.org/10.1145/2976749.2978399

17. Mostéfaoui, A., Hamouma, M., Raynal, M.: Signature-free asynchronous byzantine consensus with $t < n/3$ and $o(n^2)$ messages. In: ACM Symposium on Principles of Distributed Computing, PODC 2014, Paris, France, 15–18 July 2014, pp. 2–9 (2014). https://doi.org/10.1145/2611462.2611468

18. Nakamoto, S.: Bitcoin: a peer-to-peer electronic cash system (2008). www.bitcoin.org

19. Sousa, J., Bessani, A.: Separating the WHEAT from the chaff: an empirical design for geo-replicated state machines. In: 34th IEEE Symposium on Reliable Distributed Systems, SRDS 2015, Montreal, QC, Canada, 28 September–1 October 2015, pp. 146–155 (2015). https://doi.org/10.1109/SRDS.2015.40

20. Susilo, W., Guo, F., Mu, Y.: Efficient dynamic threshold identity-based encryption with constant-size ciphertext. Theor. Comput. Sci. **609**, 49–59 (2016). https://doi.org/10.1016/j.tcs.2015.09.006

21. Wood, G.: Ethereum: A secure decentralised generalised transaction ledger. Ethereum project yellow paper, vol. 151, pp. 1–32 (2014)

22. Zamani, M., Movahedi, M., Raykova, M.: RapidChain: scaling blockchain via full sharding. In: Proceedings of the 2018 ACM SIGSAC Conference on Computer and Communications Security, CCS 2018, Toronto, ON, Canada, 15–19 October 2018, pp. 931–948 (2018). https://doi.org/10.1145/3243734.3243853

Pre-adjustment Based Anti-collusion Mechanism for Audio Signals

Juan Zhao$^{(\boxtimes)}$ ⓘ, Tianrui Zongⓘ, Yong Xiangⓘ, Longxiang Gaoⓘ, and Gleb Beliakovⓘ

Deakin University, Burwood, Melbourne, VIC 3125, Australia
{zhaojua,tianrui.zong,yong.xiang,longxiang.gao,
gleb.beliakov}@deakin.edu.au

Abstract. Collusion attack is considered as one of the most popular and challenging attacks for audio signals, which violates the copyright seriously. Conventional methods cannot cope with the hybrid attack which consists of collusion attack and other attacks. In this paper, we propose a pre-adjustment process (PAP) based mechanism to tackle it by destroying the perceptual quality of the colluded signal, which removes the motivation of traitors to implement collusion attack. We transform the host audio signal into DCT domain and segment the DCT coefficients into blocks. Then the DCT coefficients are modified according to a pre-designed adjustment matrix (AM) to generate the PAP signal. When multiple PAP signals are averaged to generate the colluded signal, the energy of certain frequency bands in the colluded signal will be eliminated or reduced, which degrades the perceptual quality of the colluded signal greatly. The proposed method can withstand not only collusion attack but also hybrid attacks. It is also secure, as the secret keys used in PAP will not be passed to the receiver. By combining the proposed method with other leading-edge watermarking algorithms, its performance on copyright protection can be further improved. Theoretical analysis and experimental results show the superiority of the proposed mechanism.

Keywords: Audio watermarking · Collusion attack · Desynchronization attacks · Perceptual quality degradation

1 Introduction

Nowadays the rapid development of digital communication and multimedia processing technology has made the modification and distribution of the multimedia files much easier, which leads to piracy issues, such as copyright infringement. One of the popular copyright protection technologies is digital watermarking, which embeds the copyright information, such as logo, ID number and signature, into the multimedia content. The embedded information can be detected

This work was supported in part by the Australian Research Council under grant LP170100458.

or extracted from the multimedia files for copyright protection purposes when necessary. Digital watermarking is applicable to image [1–3], audio [4–6] and video [7–9]. In this paper, we focus on audio signals.

Collusion attack is to make the embedded copyright information not detectable by merging multiple audio files into one file. Independent fingerprinting [10] is one category in digital watermarking which aims to tackle collusion attack. In independent fingerprinting, the copyright information as well as the identity information of the user, such as ID number and signature, is coded into a unique fingerprint sequence. The fingerprint sequence will be used to generate the fingerprinted audio signal which contains the identity information of the corresponding authorized user. By keeping the fingerprint sequences orthogonal, it is possible to identify the traitors who involved in a collusion attack using the spread spectrum (SS) based algorithm [11]. In [12], Wang et al. employed the independent and identically distributed (iid) Gaussian noise as fingerprint sequences and analyzed the anti-collusion performance of the SS based scheme under maximum and the threshold detector.

The collusion attack not only can be applied alone, but also can be applied with other attacks such as desynchronization attacks, which is referred as hybrid attack in this paper. Although the independent fingerprint algorithms can resist collusion attack to some extent, they have little robustness against the hybrid attack, such as collusion-desynchronization hybrid attack.

The desynchronization attack breaks the alignment between the embedder and the receiver, which can make the embedded copyright information not detectable. Common desynchronization attacks include cropping, jittering and time scaling. Recently some research outcomes have been carried out to cope with desynchronization attacks. Arnaud et al. proposed an audio watermarking method against desynchronization attack [13] based on finding geometric features as synchronization positions. In [14], the mean value of the third-level DWT coefficients is employed as global characteristic to tackle desynchronization attack. Liu et al. [15] achieved the robustness against desynchronization attacks by embedding synchronization bits into their constructed residual of the frequency-domain coefficients logarithmic mean (FDLM) feature. Although the above-mentioned robust watermark algorithms are effective against desynchronization attacks, none of them can handle collusion attack.

Mathematically a collusion attack can be modeled as a multiple-input-single-output (MISO) system. Completely retrieving all of the original audio signals involved in a collusion attack from one colluded signal is theoretically not possible in a MISO system. Therefore, different from the conventional anti-collusion methods which aim at tracing the traitors, in this paper we propose a pre-adjustment process (PAP) based anti-collusion mechanism which aims to destroy the perceptual quality of the colluded signal. To achieve this, we first transform the host signal into DCT domain and segment the DCT coefficients into blocks. The DCT coefficients will then be modified according to an adjustment sequence to generate the PAP signal. The adjustment sequence is unique for each PAP signal. If multiple PAP signals are averaged to generate a colluded signal, the energy of certain low frequency bands in the colluded signal will be reduced greatly, even eliminated, which will destroy the perceptual quality of the colluded signal. The proposed method is effective to not only collusion attack but also hybrid attacks, as common attacks have little impact on the energy eliminating process caused by PAP. The performance of the proposed method can be further improved by combining with leading-edge robust watermarking algorithms.

The reminder of this paper is organized as follows. Section 2 illustrates the proposed PAP. The advantages and robustness of PAP are demonstrated in Sect. 3. Section 4 shows the performance when the proposed PAP is applied with the state-of-art robust audio watermarking method. Finally, Sect. 5 concludes the paper.

2   The Proposed PAP

2.1   Motivation

As mentioned in Sect. 1, the conventional anti-collusion methods can be hardly implemented in real-world applications due to their limitations. In this paper, we focus on degrading the perceptual quality of the colluded signal. We design the PAP to achieve this, which can be formulated as

$$H'(k) = [H_1(k) \cdot A(1), \ H_2(k) \cdot A(2), \ldots, \ H_N(k) \cdot A(M)], \tag{1}$$

where $H_i(k)$ is the ith block of the selected DCT coefficients, $i = 1, \ 2, \ldots, M$, $H'(k)$ is the modified DCT coefficients, $A(i)$ is the adjustment factor which takes value of -1 or 1, and M is the total number of the segments. Figure 1 demonstrates the process in Eq. (1). From Fig. 1 we observe that once a colluded signal is generated by averaging H and H', the energy of the 2nd and the 3rd DCT frequency blocks in the colluded signal will be eliminated, which will greatly degrade the perceptual quality of the colluded signal. The traitors will lose the motivation of implementing collusion attack if the commercial value of the colluded signal is removed because of the severe perceptual quality degradation. Figure 2 illustrates the process of the proposed PAP based anti-collusion mechanism. Firstly, the host audio signal x will be processed by PAP. Secondly, robust watermarking technology will be applied on the PAP signal for copyright protection enhancement. Finally, the embedded copyright information can be detected or extracted for copyright protection purposes.

2.2   DCT Transform and Segmentation

Assume the host audio signal is x with length L_x. Since we aim to eliminate the energy of certain frequency bands in the colluded copy, we first transform x into DCT domain by [16]

$$X(k) = l(k) \sum_{n=0}^{L_x-1} x(n)\cos\frac{\pi(2n+1)k}{2L_x}, \tag{2}$$

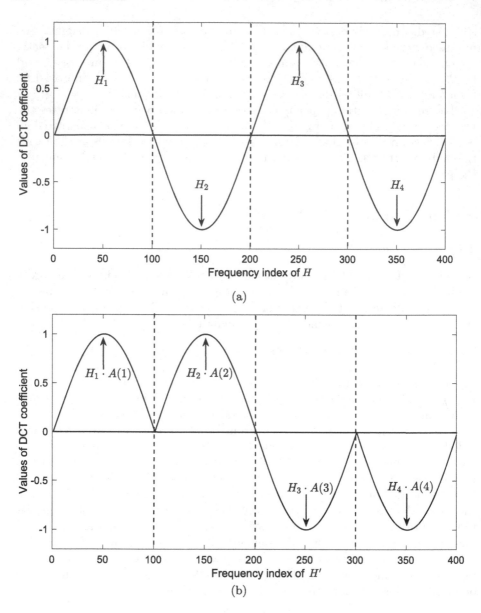

Fig. 1. The DCT coefficients of the host signal and the PAP signal when $A(1) = 1$, $A(2) = -1$, $A(3) = -1$, and $A(4) = 1$. (a) Host signal H. (b) PAP signal H'.

where $X(k)$ is the kth DCT coefficient of x, $k = 1, 2, \ldots, L_x - 1$, and

$$l(k) = \begin{cases} \frac{1}{\sqrt{L_x}}, & \text{if } k = 0; \\ \frac{2}{\sqrt{L_x}}, & \text{otherwise.} \end{cases} \quad (3)$$

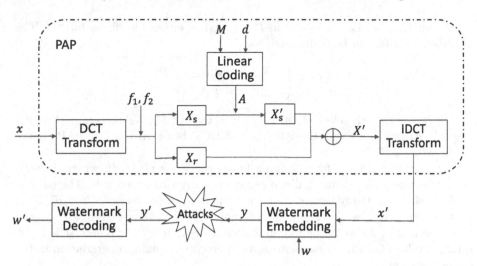

Fig. 2. The flow chart of the PAP based anti-collusion mechanism.

The human auditory system (HAS) is more sensitive to low-frequency components [17]. Therefore, in the proposed PAP we only modify the low-frequency components of the host signal x. Denote f_1 as the lower boundary of the frequency band used in PAP. The upper boundary of the selected frequency band can be calculated as

$$f_2 = f_1 + M \cdot L_s - 1, \tag{4}$$

where M and L_s are both positive integers and will be introduced later in this section. Then the selected frequency band X_s can be expressed as

$$X_s = [X(f_1),\ X(f_1+1),\dots,\ X(f_2)]. \tag{5}$$

Denote the frequency components which are not selected as X_r. X_r can be calculated as

$$X_r = X \setminus X_s. \tag{6}$$

Finally, we segment X_s into M blocks with equal length L_s, which can be expressed as

$$X_s = [X_{s,1},\ X_{s,2},\dots,\ X_{s,M}], \tag{7}$$

where $X_{s,i}$, $i = 1,\ 2,\dots,\ M$, is the ith block in X_s.

2.3   Adjustment Matrix (AM) Generation

From Eq. (1) we can see that the adjustment factors are needed to modify the selected DCT coefficients X_s. In this section, we design an adjustment matrix (AM) to generate the adjustment factors for each PAP signal. Denote the AM as P with size $M \times N_c$, where N_c is the total number of the PAP signals required by the application. Each element in P is coded by either bit "0" or bit "1". The modification rule can be formulated as

$$X'_{j,i} = \begin{cases} -X_{s,i}, & \text{if } P(i,j) = 0; \\ X_{s,i}, & \text{if } P(i,j) = 1, \end{cases} \tag{8}$$

where $X'_{j,i}$ is the ith selected DCT block in the jth PAP signal, and $P(i,j)$ is the adjustment factor for the ith selected DCT block in the jth PAP signal, $i \in [1, M]$, $j \in [1, N_c]$.

To generate AM, we first design a linear codebook $C(M, d)$, where d represents the minimum hamming distance between any two codewords. Then P can be formed by randomly taking N_c codewords from the codebook $C(M, d)$. Note that M and d are two determining factors for N_c. For example, if $d = 1$, N_c can reach up to 2^M; if $d = 2$, the maximum value of N_c is 2^{M-1}. When M is fixed, a larger value of d will cause more severe perceptual quality degradation in the colluded signal.

As mentioned in Eq. (1), the adjustment factor should take value of -1 or 1. In order to meet this requirement, we update P to generate the final AM by

$$P(i,j) = 2 \cdot P(i,j) - 1, \tag{9}$$

where $i = 1, 2, \ldots, M$, $j = 1, 2, \ldots, N_c$.

2.4   Adjustment and IDCT Transform

Denote the adjustment sequence for the jth PAP signal as A_j with size $M \times 1$, $j \in [1, N_c]$. Then P can be expressed as

$$P = [A_1, A_2, ..., A_{N_c}]. \tag{10}$$

Similar to Eq. (1), the selected DCT coefficients of the jth PAP signal can be calculated by applying A_j to X_s, which can be formulated as

$$X'_{s,j} = [X_{s,1} \cdot A_j(1), X_{s,2} \cdot A_j(2), \ldots, X_{s,M} \cdot A_j(M)], \tag{11}$$

where $A_j(i)$, $i = 1, 2, \ldots, M$, is the adjustment factor for the ith block in the jth PAP signal, and $X'_{s,j}$ is the modified selected DCT coefficients of the jth PAP signal.

Then the DCT coefficients of the jth PAP signal X'_j can be obtained by combining $X'_{s,j}$ with X_r via

$$X'_j = X'_{s,j} \cup X_r. \tag{12}$$

Finally the jth PAP signal x'_j can be generated by

$$x'_j = \text{IDCT}(X'_j), \tag{13}$$

where $\text{IDCT}(\cdot)$ is the inverse DCT operator.

3   The Effectiveness of PAP

In this section, we will first discuss the security level of the proposed PAP. Then we will show the excellent perceptual quality of the PAP signal by simulation results. We will also analyze the resistance of the proposed PAP against collusion attack both theoretically and experimentally. Among collusion attacks, averaging attack [18] is one of the most popular attack where the traitors share the risk of getting caught equally. Therefore, in this paper we focus on the averaging attack. Figure 3 illustrates the general model of the averaging attack. The averaging attack can be applied alone, which is referred as averaging-alone attack in this paper, and can be applied with other attacks as well, which is referred as hybrid attacks in this paper.

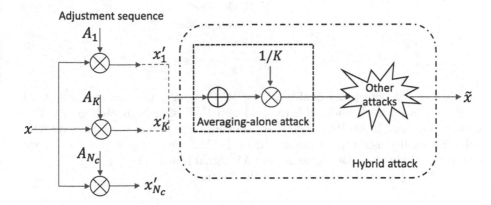

Fig. 3. The general model of the averaging attack.

3.1   Security

The proposed PAP aims to degrade the perceptual quality of the colluded signal by eliminating the energy of certain frequency bands in the colluded signal. Therefore, the security level of the proposed PAP is measured by the difficulty of recovering the eliminated energy. To recover the energy, the traitors need the knowledge of the secret keys, such as f_1, M, L_s, and P. However, the proposed PAP requires neither detection nor decoding stage at the receiver end, which blocks the traitors' access to these secret keys. Therefore, the proposed PAP is secure.

3.2   Perceptual Quality Evaluation of the PAP Signals

To make sure the distortion caused by the proposed PAP is imperceptible, we adopt the widely used perceptual evaluation of audio quality (PEAQ) algorithm [19] to measure the perceptual quality of the PAP signals. The PEAQ algorithm returns a mark named objective difference grade (ODG), which ranges from -4 to 0. The larger ODG value, the better perceptual quality. According to [20], when the ODG value is greater than -1, the distortion is imperceptible; when the ODG value is less than -3, the distortion is annoying.

We randomly chose 40 mono-channel audio clips from 4 different genres (see Table 1) as the host audio signals for testing. Each signal has a duration of 60 seconds, the sample rate of 44.1 kHz, and the resolution of 16 bits.

Table 1. Host signals used in the simulations

Host signals	Genres
$x_1 \sim x_{10}$	Folk music
$x_{11} \sim x_{20}$	Rock music
$x_{21} \sim x_{30}$	Classic music
$x_{31} \sim x_{40}$	Pop music

To test the perceptual quality of the PAP signals, we randomly select 20 PAP signals for each audio clip to yield 200 PAP signals in each genre. The ODG values for all 800 PAP signals are shown in Fig. 4, and the averaged ODG value for each music type is calculated in Table 2. From Fig. 4 and Table 2 we can observe that the ODG value of the PAP signal is around -0.4, which implies the excellent perceptual quality of the PAP signal.

Table 2. Averaged ODG values for 4 types of music adjusted by the proposed PAP

Host signals	Averaged ODG
$x_1 \sim x_{10}$	-0.4882
$x_{11} \sim x_{20}$	-0.4447
$x_{21} \sim x_{30}$	-0.3287
$x_{31} \sim x_{40}$	-0.4281

3.3 PAP Against Averaging-Alone Attack

Since the proposed PAP aims to degrade the perceptual quality of the colluded signal by reducing or even eliminating the energy of certain frequency bands in the colluded signal, in this section we first theoretically introduce the mechanism to reduce the energy of the colluded signal in the frequency domain. Assume a colluded signal $\tilde{x}$ is generated by PAP signal x'_a and PAP signal x'_b via

$$\tilde{x} = \frac{x'_a + x'_b}{2}. \tag{14}$$

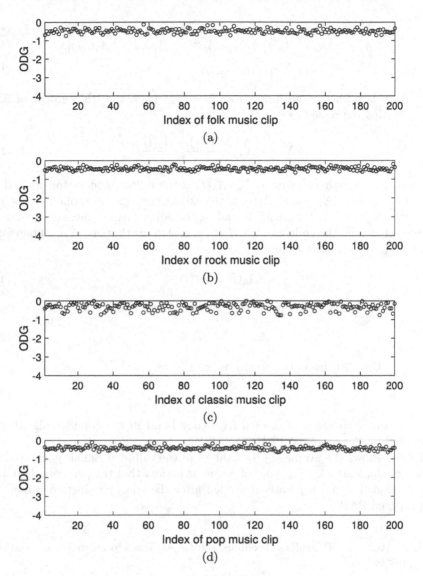

Fig. 4. The ODG values for 4 types of music after PAP. (a) $x_1 \sim x_{10}$: folk music. (b) $x_{11} \sim x_{20}$: rock music. (c) $x_{21} \sim x_{30}$: classic music. (d) $x_{31} \sim x_{40}$: pop music.

Following Eqs. (2)–(5), we can obtain the selected DCT coefficients of x'_a, x'_b and $\tilde{x}$ as $X'_{s,a}$, $X'_{s,b}$ and $\tilde{X}_s$, respectively. Using Eqs. (7) and (11) we can have the segmented $X'_{s,a}$, $X'_{s,b}$, and $\tilde{X}_s$ as

$$X'_{s,a} = [X_{s,1} \cdot A_a(1),\ X_{s,2} \cdot A_a(2), \ldots,\ X_{s,M} \cdot A_a(M)], \tag{15}$$

$$X'_{s,b} = [X_{s,1} \cdot A_b(1),\ X_{s,2} \cdot A_b(2), \ldots,\ X_{s,M} \cdot A_b(M)], \tag{16}$$

$$\tilde{X}_s = [\tilde{X}_{s,1},\ \tilde{X}_{s,2}, \ldots,\ \tilde{X}_{s,M}]. \tag{17}$$

Since DCT is a linear transform, from Eqs. (14)–(17), the ith segment of $\tilde{X}_{s,i}$ can be further expressed as

$$\tilde{X}_{s,i} = X_{s,i} \cdot \frac{A_a(i) + A_b(i)}{2}, \tag{18}$$

where $X_{s,i}$ is the ith segment in X_s, $A_a(i)$ is the adjustment factor applied to the ith segment of $X'_{s,a}$, and $A_b(i)$ is the adjustment factor applied to the ith segment of $X'_{s,b}$, $i = 1, 2, \ldots, M$. Recalling the adjustment sequences A_a and A_b are extracted from the codebook $C(M, d)$, it is obvious that $A_a \neq A_b$. Therefore, exist $i \in [1, M]$ which satisfies

$$A_a(i) \neq A_b(i). \tag{19}$$

Since A_a and A_b can only take values of -1 or 1, we can obtain

$$A_a(i) + A_b(i) = 0. \tag{20}$$

Substitute Eqs. (20) into (18), finally we can have

$$\tilde{X}_{s,i} = 0, \tag{21}$$

which means the energy of the ith frequency band in the colluded signal $\tilde{x}$ is eliminated by the proposed PAP.

Table 3 shows the averaged ODG values of the colluded signals generated by averaging-alone attack for 4 types of music. It is clear that the perceptual quality of the colluded signal is greatly degraded after the energy reduction caused by the proposed PAP.

Table 3. Averaged ODG values of colluded signals generated by averaging-alone attack for 4 types of music

Host signals	Averaged ODG
$x_1 \sim x_{10}$	-3.5067
$x_{11} \sim x_{20}$	-3.5534
$x_{21} \sim x_{30}$	-3.5603
$x_{31} \sim x_{40}$	-3.6231

3.4 PAP Against Hybrid Attacks

Since the proposed PAP resists averaging attack by energy reduction, the resilience of the proposed PAP against hybrid attacks can be measured by how much energy can be recovered by the hybrid attacks, which can be estimated by ODG values. A lower ODG value implies that the energy recovered by the hybrid attacks is less. The robustness of the PAP against hybrid attacks will be demonstrated by experimental results.

As common attacks can be categorized into signal processing attacks and desynchronization attacks, in this section we classify the hybrid attacks into averaging-signal-processing attacks and averaging-desynchronization attacks.

Averaging-Signal-Processing Attacks. Common signal processing attacks include noise addition, amplitude scaling, low-pass filtering and compression. Table 4 shows the averaged ODG values for the colluded signal generated by averaging-signal-processing attacks. We can observe that the proposed PAP is resilient to averaging-signal-processing attacks as the ODG values are all below -3.5.

Low-pass filtering, MP3 compression and AAC compression attacks mainly focus on reducing the energy of the high-frequency components of the signal. Since the proposed PAP is implemented on the selected low-frequency coefficients, it is robust to 8kHz low-pass filtering attack, 128 bits MP3 compression and 128 bits AAC compression.

The effect of Gaussian noise addition spreads on the entire frequency band. It cannot recover the energy reduced by the proposed PAP in certain frequency bands. Therefore, the proposed PAP is resistant to Gaussian noise addition with SNR 30 dB.

Amplitude scaling attack can modify the energy of the entire audio signal. However, it is not possible to recover the eliminated energy by amplitude scaling. Table 4 shows the resistance of the proposed PAP against 90% amplitude scaling attack.

Table 4. Averaged ODG values for the colluded signal generated by averaging-signal-processing attacks

Attacks		Averaged ODG			
		Folk music	Rock music	Classic music	Pop music
Low-pass filtering	8 kHz	−3.5256	−3.5286	−3.5394	−3.6646
Gaussian noise (SNR)	30 dB	−3.7241	−3.6214	−3.6262	−3.5804
MP3	128 kps	−3.5286	−3.6869	−3.6967	−3.5672
AAC	128 kps	−3.6809	−3.6485	−3.6802	−3.5524
Amplitude scaling	90%	−3.6423	−3.6275	−3.6586	−3.5689

Averaging-Desynchronization Attacks. Common desynchronization attacks include cropping, jittering and time scaling. By applying desynchronization attacks on the averaged signal, the alignment between the embedder and the decoder will be destroyed. However, the proposed PAP does not require a decoding or detecting process. Therefore, destroying the synchronization will not affect the proposed PAP. Besides, the misalignment caused by desynchronization attacks cannot recover the reduced energy, which means the proposed PAP is effective against desynchronization attacks.

Table 5 shows the averaged ODG values for the colluded signal generated by averaging-desynchronization attacks. It is clear that the proposed PAP is robust to cropping attack at rate 5%, 10% and 50%, jittering attack at rate 1%, 5% and 10%, and 95%, 99%, 101% and 105% time scaling.

Table 5. Averaged ODG values for the colluded signal generated by averaging-desynchronization attacks

Attacks		Averaged ODG			
		Folk music	Rock music	Classic music	Pop music
Cropping	5%	−3.6265	−3.5412	−3.5246	−3.6869
	10%	−3.5458	−3.5542	−3.6632	−3.5648
	50%	−3.7162	−3.6485	−3.7254	−3.7023
Jittering	1%	−3.5624	−3.6152	−3.6852	−3.6145
	5%	−3.6654	−3.7022	−3.7015	−3.6502
	10%	−3.6821	−3.7036	−3.6689	−3.7259
Time scaling	95%	−3.6726	−3.5968	−3.6945	−3.6674
	99%	−3.5912	−3.6820	−3.5978	−3.5524
	101%	−3.5648	−3.5987	−3.5649	−3.5816
	105%	−3.5649	−3.6948	−3.7155	−3.6564

4   PAP with Robust Digital Watermarking

As mentioned in Sect. 1, the SS based conventional anti-collusion algorithms cannot tackle hybrid attacks, especially averaging-desynchronization attacks. This is because SS based algorithms require perfect synchronization between the embedder and the receiver. Once the synchronization is destroyed, the SS based algorithms can neither trace the traitors nor protect the copyright. However, when combined with leading-edge robust watermarking technologies, the proposed PAP can resist both collusion attacks and other common attacks.

In this section, we combine the proposed PAP with the robust watermarking algorithm proposed in [15] and compare the performance with the conventional anti-collusion algorithm proposed in [12] under common signal processing and desynchronization attacks. The embedding rate is set to 10 bps. The ODG values for the signal watermarked by [12] and the signal watermarked by [15] with PAP are −1.08 and −0.91, respectively. The robustness against attacks is measured by bit error rate (BER). Smaller BER means better robustness against attacks.

Table 6 shows the performance of both method in [12] and method in [15] with PAP against common attacks. It is obvious that the conventional anti-collusion algorithm proposed in [12] cannot withstand desynchronization attacks, while the proposed PAP combined with the robust watermarking technology proposed in [15] shows excellent robustness against both signal processing attacks and desynchronization attacks.

Table 6. BER (%) for method in [12] and the proposed PAP with method in [15] under common signal processing attacks and desynchronization attacks

Attacks		Method in [12]	PAP with [15]
Low-pass filtering	8 kHz	12	5
Gaussian noise (SNR)	30 dB	1	4
MP3	128 kps	48	3
AAC	128 kps	3	1
Amplitude scaling	90%	11	0
Cropping	5%	47	0
	10%	51	0
	50%	53	0
Jittering	1%	45	1
	5%	47	1
	10%	49	2
Time scaling	95%	48	2
	99%	50	1
	101%	49	1
	105%	51	2

5   Conclusion

In this paper, we propose a PAP based anti-collusion mechanism for audio signals. Different from the conventional anti-collusion methods, we cope with collusion attack by degrading the perceptual quality of the colluded signal. By modifying the DCT coefficients of the host signal using the pre-designed AM, the energy of certain frequency bands in the colluded signal will be reduced or eliminated, which will significantly degrade the perceptual quality of the colluded signal. The advantages and robustness of the proposed PAP are demonstrated by both theoretical analysis and experimental results. When combined with robust watermarking algorithms, the proposed PAP can outperform the conventional anti-collusion methods by a large margin.

References

1. Wang, X., Wu, J., Niu, P.: A new digital image watermarking algorithm resilient to desynchronization attacks. IEEE Trans. Inf. Forensics Secur. **2**(4), 655–663 (2007)
2. Nezhadarya, E., Wang, Z.-J., Ward, R.-K.: Robust image watermarking based on multiscale gradient direction quantization. IEEE Trans. Inf. Forensics Secur. **6**(4), 1200–1213 (2011)
3. Fang, H., Zhang, W., Zhou, H., Cui, H., Yu, N.: Screen-shooting resilient watermarking. IEEE Trans. Inf. Forensics Secur. **14**(6), 1403–1418 (2018)
4. Xiang, Y., Natgunanathan, I., Peng, D., Zhou, W., Yu, S.: A dual-channel time-spread echo method for audio watermarking. IEEE Trans. Inf. Forensics Secur. **7**(2), 383–392 (2011)
5. Xiang, Y., Natgunanathan, I., Guo, S., Zhou, W., Nahavandi, S.: Patchwork-based audio watermarking method robust to de-synchronization attacks. IEEE/ACM Trans. Audio Speech Lang. Process. **22**(9), 1413–1423 (2014)
6. Su, Z., Zhang, G., Yue, F., Chang, L., Jiang, J., Yao, X.: SNR-constrained heuristics for optimizing the scaling parameter of robust audio watermarking. IEEE Trans. Multimed. **20**(10), 2631–2644 (2018)
7. Asikuzzaman, M., Alam, M.-J., Lambert, A.-J., Pickering, M.-R.: Robust DT CWT-based DIBR 3D video watermarking using chrominance embedding. IEEE Trans. Multimed. **18**(9), 1733–1748 (2016)
8. Joshi, A.M., Gupta, S., Girdhar, M., Agarwal, P., Sarker, R.: Combined DWT–DCT-based video watermarking algorithm using arnold transform technique. In: Satapathy, S.C., Bhateja, V., Joshi, A. (eds.) Proceedings of the International Conference on Data Engineering and Communication Technology. AISC, vol. 468, pp. 455–463. Springer, Singapore (2017). https://doi.org/10.1007/978-981-10-1675-2_45
9. Mareen, H., Praeter, J.-D., Wallendael, G.-V., Lambert, P.: A novel video watermarking approach based on implicit distortions. IEEE Trans. Consum. Electron. **64**(3), 250–258 (2018)
10. Wu, M., Trappe, W., Wang, Z.-J., Liu, K.-R.: Collusion-resistant fingerprinting for multimedia. IEEE Signal Process. Mag. **21**(2), 15–27 (2004)
11. Cox, I.-J., Kilian, J., Leighton, F.-T., Shamoon, T.: Secure spread spectrum watermarking for multimedia. IEEE Trans. Image Process. **6**(12), 1673–1687 (1997)
12. Wang, Z.-J., Wu, M., Zhao, H.-V., Trappe, W., Liu, K.-R.: Anti-collusion forensics of multimedia fingerprinting using orthogonal modulation. IEEE Trans. Image Process. **14**(6), 804–821 (2005)
13. Dessein, A., Cont, A.: An information-geometric approach to real-time audio segmentation. IEEE Signal Process. Lett. **20**(4), 331–334 (2013)
14. Jiang, W., Huang, X., Quan, Y.: Audio watermarking algorithm against synchronization attacks using global characteristics and adaptive frame division. Signal Process. **162**, 153–160 (2019)
15. Liu, Z., Huang, Y., Huang, J.: Patchwork-based audio watermarking robust against de-synchronization and recapturing attacks. IEEE Trans. Inf. Forensics Secur. **14**(5), 1171–1180 (2019)

16. Wu, J.-L., Shin, J.: Discrete cosine transform in error control coding. IEEE Trans. Commun. **43**(5), 1857–1861 (1995)
17. Fallahpour, M., Megías, D.: Secure logarithmic audio watermarking scheme based on the human auditory system. Multimed. Syst. **20**(2), 155–164 (2014)
18. Cheng, M., Miao, Y.: On anti-collusion codes and detection algorithms for multimedia fingerprinting. IEEE Trans. Inf. Theory **57**(7), 4843–4851 (2011)
19. Thiede, T., et al.: PEAQ-the ITU standard for objective measurement of perceived audio quality. IEEE Trans. Inf. Theory **48**(1/2), 3–29 (2000)
20. Bhat, V., Sengupta, I., Das, A.: An audio watermarking scheme using singular value decomposition and dither-modulation quantization. Multimed. Tools Appl. **52**(2–3), 369–383 (2011)

Detecting Intruders by User File Access Patterns

Shou-Hsuan S. Huang, Zechun Cao$^{(\boxtimes)}$, Calvin E. Raines, Mai N. Yang,
and Camille Simon

University of Houston, Houston, TX 77204, USA
shuang@cs.uh.com, zcao3@uh.edu

Abstract. Our society is facing a growing threat from data breaches where confidential information is stolen from computer servers. In order to steal data, hackers must first gain entry into the targeted systems. Commercial off-the-shelf intrusion detection systems are unable to defend against the intruders effectively. This research uses cyber behavior analytics to study and report how anomalies compare to normal behavior. In this paper, we present methods based on machine learning algorithms to detect intruders based on the file access patterns within a user file directory. We proposed a set of behavioral features of the user's file access patterns in a file system. We validate the effectiveness of the features by conducting experiments on an existing file system dataset with four classification algorithms. To limit the false alarms, we trained and tested the classifiers by optimizing the performance within the lower range of the false positive rate. The results from our experiments show that our approach was able to detect intruders with a 0.94 F1 score and false positive rate of less than 3%.

Keywords: Intrusion detection · Cybersecurity · Cyber behavior analytics · File accessing pattern · Machine learning

1 Introduction

One purpose of computer security is to limit information access to a certain authorized group of people. Although current computer security methodology keeps out some intruders, it does not deter the most persistent ones. Through backdoors, brute force, or with stolen credentials, intruders can gain access to valuable data and abilities normally reserved for trusted individuals. Once inside, intruders can create a multitude of problems. They could install malware, deface websites or delete documents. These actions would visibly affect the system, requiring damage control or likely an audit. In 2014, the U.S. Office of Personnel Management [20] lost the personal information of millions of people. These individuals were put at risk of blackmail or identity theft. More recently, Equifax disclosed that a massive data breach in 2017 may have impacted 143 million consumers, which is nearly 44% of the US population. In this incident, attackers got their hands on names, SSN, birth date, addresses, some driver license numbers, and about 209,000 credit card numbers, causing the impact of this breach to last for years to come [24]. In both instances, data theft put many people at risk and damaged the reputations of the organizations stolen from. For these reasons, designing an effective

© Springer Nature Switzerland AG 2019
J. K. Liu and X. Huang (Eds.): NSS 2019, LNCS 11928, pp. 320–335, 2019.
https://doi.org/10.1007/978-3-030-36938-5_19

intrusion detection system (IDS) that is capable of quickly raising alarms to security breaches is extremely important.

However, many of the existing IDSs do not provide enough protection as we experience an increasing number of data breaches. Some of the existing IDSs are adopting the misuse-based detecting approach, such as network IDSs Snort and Bro [36]. They rely on pre-defined signatures to identify known attacks. The main problem with this approach is that it fails to properly detect unknown threats because the high number of new vulnerabilities that are discovered every day are not available to the experts for analysis and inclusion in the signature database. Additionally, detecting attacks based on prior knowledge often fails to develop effective signatures as there are usually numerous ways to exploit the same vulnerability [36]. As a result, the misuse-based approach raises too many false alarms by including as many attack signatures as possible, while some attacks can easily evade detection by a slight variance. Additionally, more and more attacks are launched by insiders who are abusing their privileges. The misuse-based IDS cannot detect the attack from an insider, because the intruder can deliberately avoid attacking against vulnerabilities that have been previously exploited.

In this paper, we hypothesize that the deviation of the intruder's cyber behavior from the normal one can be used to detect attempted malicious exploitations. For example, an intruder possessing valid admin credentials is not going to alert existing security systems while logging into the system. Since the objective of the intruders is to scan the data, identify the information of value to them, and quickly exfiltrate the data, the behavior of the intruders will be different from that of the normal users. Differences in intruders' behavior caused by their malicious nature leave traces that can be used for detection. Desiring the ability to detect intruders based on their behavior, we propose an approach that describes the user's behavior through effective features. The objective of this research is to use the differences in the behavioral features in detecting intruders.

As the computer system has been more and more involved in activities in our lives, the file becomes an essential carrier of important and sensitive information, which is often the ultimate target of intruders. Since the file system is the permanent place to store all the files of the host, any malicious execution intended to steal information or damage a host will eventually set its sight upon the file system [31]. Therefore, in this paper, we propose a new intrusion detection approach that uses behavioral features to detect intruders in the file system.

The remainder of this paper is organized as follows. In Sect. 2, we will discuss the existing research on behavior modeling and intrusion detection. Section 3 will expand on presenting and evaluating our behavioral features in modeling user behavior in the file system. In Sect. 4, we will build multiple classifiers with selected features to validate our hypothesis that the user's behavioral difference is sufficient to identify the intruders. Lastly, we will conclude our paper with a summary of our contribution and briefly mention how our approach may be able to further improve intrusion detection in Sect. 5.

2   Related Work

In one of the earliest researches about IDS, Anderson [2] described that audit trails contain valuable information and could be utilized for the purpose of misuse detection by identifying the anomaly. The proposed misuse-based detecting approach focuses on modeling what is normal, instead of what is anomalous. Since then, we have seen research [12, 22] following this direction with success to a certain extent. But the misuse-based approach is prone to generate many false alarms. Additionally, it has always been a difficult task for researchers to know what to monitor in the system [36]. In an attempt to model normal behavior, Denning [11] presented a host-based IDS that is capable of detecting anomaly by computing statistics (login frequency, password fails, etc.) of system events. Javitz et al. [17] later developed a system called IDES, which issues alerts by comparing the new event's parameters to the thresholds established in the statistical models built on past events, such as a set number of mean values, standard deviations, etc.

In comparison to the host-based IDS, researchers have also studied network-based IDS that detects anomalies by monitoring network packets. Based on existing research [34], many intruders route their SSH connections through a series of computers to make backtracing more difficult. This results in a slower response time, which can be used in stepping-stone intrusion detection. Yang et al. [34] used a clustering-partitioning algorithm to calculate round-trip times of send/echo packet pairs in the network. In doing so they could successfully determine if an intruder was routing their traffic through multiple hosts. Similarly, Kuo et al. [21] proposed an algorithm based on association rule mining to detect stepping-stone SSH attacks. These works focused on detecting intruders by monitoring network activities and shown robustness even under certain types of evasion techniques.

There is relatively little work has been completed in detecting intrusion to the file system. Stolfo et al. [31] developed a File Wrapper Anomaly Detector (FWRAP) which monitors the file system and extracted static features, such as user ID, current directory, file name, etc. from the records. Then Probabilistic Anomaly Detection (PAD) algorithm was applied to detect abnormal processes. However, this approach did not utilize dynamic features and occupied system memory with a large number of files. Other file system intrusion detection methods, such as honeyfiles [35] and decoy documents [4], had proven to be effective under certain assumptions. But there are many limitations, for example, it is expensive to deploy bait files in every user's computer, and the false alarms are overwhelming for the users who are searching intensively in their daily tasks.

We realize that many related studies to our work are attempting to solve masquerader detection problems. Unlike intrusion attack, masquerade attack is a class of attacks in which a user of a system poses as, or assumes the identity of another legitimate user [28]. To detect a masquerader by behavior, existing research tried to model user's cyber behavior based on various information, for example, operating system command [30, 33], mouse usage [26], keyboard usage [19], etc. As Schonlau et al. [30] being the pioneer to design a dataset in an attempt to detect masqueraders, their dataset (SEA) recorded a series of UNIX commands for each user. Although this dataset was widely utilized, it had the limitations of being restricted to UNIX commands and a lack of real "intrusion" behavior. Recently, Camina et al. [7, 8] focused on file system objects and proposed a new feature abstraction model called locality to characterize users and detect masqueraders. Compared to the action-based approach, their locality-based features showed better performance in capturing user behavior for masquerader detection. In summary, although the research in modeling user's cyber behavior is prolific, there is very limited research has been conducted in the behavior-based intrusion detection method.

3 Modeling User Behavior in File System

Since the file system is often the endpoint of the intrusion chain, it is important to provide protection to it. Therefore, we set the focus of this paper on detecting malicious behavior in the file system. Our working hypothesis is that the intruders behave differently compared to normal users due to their malicious nature. To capture such behavioral differences, we need to define features to model users' behavior in the file system. In this section, we will present in detail how our behavioral features are designed and computed based on the file access logs. We will then evaluate their effectiveness in detecting intruders in a file system dataset extracted from the public repository.

3.1 Behavioral Feature Space in File Access

To profile the user's behavior in the file system, one should continuously monitor the events generated by the system. These events are usually triggered by the OS, applications or users' actions, containing file system objects access history. Modern system logging tools, such as audit [6] in the Windows system, are able to record not only the file system objects that have been accessed, e.g. files and directories, but also the timing information for each record. Without loss of generality, we assume the logs recorded by the system during a time span t can be denoted by a segment of consecutive access entries $s = e_1, e_2, \ldots, e_n$. Each entry e_i, $(1 \leq i \leq n)$ in s describes an access record in the file system with a timestamp. Note that we partition the logs into segments based on the time window of length t because it is not feasible to profile behavior by a single access entry. The behavioral feature space in the file system can be denoted as F, from which another higher dimensional feature space F' can be mapped by a function ϕ

$$\phi(F) \to F'. \tag{1}$$

A user's behavior in the file system can be viewed as how the file system objects are accessed during a period of time. Thus, we consider temporal and spatial features are essential in deriving other feature spaces by function ϕ. We now propose three basic temporal- and spatial-based features in the behavioral feature space F.

- $time(e_i)$: Timestamp in seconds since the system epoch of an entry e_i logged by the system.
- $file(e_i)$: The file accessed by entry e_i. In the file system log, it is typically represented by the file ID or name of the accessed file.
- $path(e_i)$: Full access path of the file identified by $file(e_i)$. In a tree-structured file system, $path(e_i)$ provides spatial information for the entry e_i.

We expect other behavioral features can be mapped from the feature space F in order to model various behaviors in the file system.

3.2   File Access Behavioral Features

In this section, we introduce two sets of behavioral features that can be mapped from F to detect intruders in the file system. Recall that given a sequence of events $s = e_1, e_2, \ldots, e_n$ during a time window of length t, let $\|s\| = n$ be the size of the file system log segment. The behavioral feature space F can be defined as

$$F = \{time(e_i), file(e_i), path(e_i)\}. \tag{2}$$

Non-frequency-Based Feature Set. These features derived from F give the overall measures of the users within a given time window of length t. Note that the features in this set are intuitively designed aiming to identify the difference in the intruder's behavior from the normal ones.

Entries Per Second (EPS). EPS is the number of log entries within a one-second period. We define

$$EPS = \frac{\|s\|}{time(e_n) - time(e_1)}, \tag{3}$$

where $\|s\|$ denotes the size of the log segment, which is the number of recorded entries of log within the segment. EPS measures how quickly entries are created, which gives an idea of how quickly files are being accessed. A normal user would assumedly spend ample time on a single file, while an intruder would move through many files quickly.

Fraction Unique Path (FUP). This feature shows how many of the paths in the sequence are distinct, measures the diversity of the accessed file. FUP is defined as

$$FUP = \frac{\|\{path(e_i)\}\|}{\|s\|}. \tag{4}$$

A normal user would likely use the same paths repeatedly, but an intruder would rarely use the same path twice.

Fraction Unique Location (FUL). This feature more accurately represents repeated use of the same file. We define FUL as

$$FUL = \frac{\|\{file(e_i)\}\|}{\|s\|}. \tag{5}$$

Different files necessarily have different paths, but two paths may end up in the same file because of the shortcuts. Again, a normal user would be expected to end up at the same file often, but an intruder would access many different files.

Fraction Multiway (FM). This metric combines FUP and FUL. The number of unique files is necessarily smaller than the number of unique paths, thus we have $FM \leq 1$. The smaller FM is, the more often different chosen paths ended at the same location. FM is defined as

$$FM = \frac{\|\{file(e_i)\}\|}{\|\{path(e_i)\}\|}. \tag{6}$$

A normal user should have a favorite way of getting to a known file. An intruder doing an uninformed search would find the same file in every path it can be found.

Fraction Single Path (FSP). FSP measures how many of the paths were only used once in the given sequence of entries. We have FSP as

$$FSP = \frac{\|\{e_i : path(e_i) \neq path(e_j) \forall i \neq j\}\|}{\|\{path(e_i)\}\|}. \tag{7}$$

Intruders don't need to repeatedly revisit files. In contrast, a normal user would likely use the same path multiple times.

Average Location Time (ALT). ALT averages the difference in time between the first and last entry of each unique location in the given sequence of entries. Let $L = \{file(e_i)\}$, for $k \in L$, let $k_{first} = e_x$: $file(e_x) = k \neq file(e_y) \forall y < x$, and $k_{last} = e_z$: $file(e_z) = k \neq file(e_y) \forall y > z$. Then,

$$ALT = \frac{\sum_L time(k_{last}) - time(k_{first})}{\|L\|}. \tag{8}$$

A normal user might return to a file previously used a few minutes later, while an intruder would avoid looking at the same file over time.

Average Consecutive Time (ACT). ACT measures how long on average a user is working on the same file. The denominator reduces sequence s by removing entries whose path is the same as the previous entry. ACT is defined as

$$ACT = \frac{time(e_n) - time(e_1) + 1}{\|\{e_i : path(e_i) \neq path(e_{i-1})\}\|}. \tag{9}$$

A normal user would be expected to spend longer on a single file than an intruder would.

Average Consecutive Repetitions (ACR). Instead of looking at how much time a user spends before changing files, ACR looks at how many entries are created in succession before moving. Therefore,

$$ACR = \frac{\|s\|}{\|\{e_i : path(e_i) \neq path(e_{i-1})\}\|}. \tag{10}$$

A user repeatedly saving their work would create multiple consecutive entries, while an intruder should do very few actions on a single file.

Average Depth (AD). AD provides the average number of depths in s. We have AD as

$$AD = \frac{\sum_{e_i} (\|path(e_i)\| - 1)}{\|s\|}, \tag{11}$$

where $\|path(e_i)\| - 1$ is the number of directories in an entry's path, which is equivalent to the depth. A normal user would likely use shortcuts or put their files in easy to access locations, while an intruder doing a depth-first search would reach the deepest parts of a file system.

Average Movement Distance (AMD). AMD calculates how many steps the user moves from one entry to its next on average. We define AMD as

$$AMD = \frac{\sum_{e_i} \| path(e_i) \neq path(e_{i-1}) \|}{\| s \|}, \tag{12}$$

where the numerator calculates the distance between two entries. It does so by summing how many different directories or locations there are between two consecutive entries. For example, if event entry 0/1/3/7 is followed by 0/1/2/9/12, the distance would be 5. This signifies moving from $7 \to 3$, $3 \to 1$, $1 \to 2$, $2 \to 9$, and $9 \to 12$: a total of five steps. A normal user would jump to a very different area when deciding to work on a different task. An intruder, in contrast, would simply check the nearest file.

Frequency-based Feature Set. Comparing to the features proposed above, which are the overall metrics relative to the time window, frequency-based features profile user's behavior based on defined events' frequencies. The event is defined by feature function m, by which intruders and normal users are likely to have different measures. We expect the following 6 features functions to capture the differences in file access patterns.

File Visit Duration (FVD). For each new file accessed that was different than the file that was previously accessed, FVD is measured as the total duration of the user's access time. Thus we have,

$$m(FVD) = \big(time(e_j) - time(e_i) + 1 \big), \tag{13}$$

where $i < j$, $e_i = e_j$, $e_{i-1} \neq e_i$ and $e_{j+1} \neq e_j$. The idea in designing this feature is that we expect normal users have a bigger portion of the files that have long access time, while the majority of the files accessed by intruders only being accessed briefly.

Change in Depth Per Second (CDPS). Given a one-second sequence of entries $e_1, e_2, \ldots, e_n$, feature CDPS measures the largest depth difference in the sequence as

$$m(CDPS) = (max(\| path(e_i) \| - 1) - min(\| path(e_i) \| - 1)), \tag{14}$$

where $\| path(e_i) \| - 1$ is the entry's path as we described in feature AD previously. Following a similar intuition with FVD, we expect intruders to be more active in searching for valuable information. Consequently, large changes in depth occur more frequently than in normal users.

Change in Files Per Minute (CFPM). We measure the number of file switches within pairs of consecutive entries during the time window of one minute. Assume we have a one-minute sequence $e_1, e_2, \ldots, e_n$, CFPM is computed as in below

$$m(CFPM) = (\| file(e_i) \neq file(e_{i+1}) \|). \tag{15}$$

In this feature, we expect to see fewer file location switches within one minute for normal users, who are performing their daily tasks.

Change in Files Per Second (CFPS). Following the similar idea of CFPM, we shorten the time window to one second in CFPS. For automated file system activities, such as searching, batch operations, etc. it is common to generate numerous location switches within one second. We skip the formula of CFPS here due to its similarity with CFPM.

Number of Times Each File Visited (NTFV). For each unique file in a sequence $e_1, e_2, \ldots, e_n$, NTFV is computed by counting the number of visits for each unique file. Note that we count consecutive entries that are accessing the same file as one visit. To formally define NTFV, we first define the equivalence condition $e_i \equiv e_j$ if $file(e_i) = file(e_j)$ and $file(e_i) \neq file(e_k) \forall 1 \leq i < k < j \leq n$. Based on the equivalence condition, the entries sequence can be partitioned into disjoint sets $G = \{g_1, g_2, \ldots, g_m\}$. For any equivalent classes set $g_z \in G$, we can compute NTFV as in below

$$m(NTFV) = (\|g_z\|). \tag{16}$$

Unlike feature ALT describes how long a user spends time on each file, NTFV focuses on the access frequency of each file. We expect that normal users may visit some files repeatedly, but intruders are less likely to do so.

Changes in Depth in Consecutive Entries (CDCE). For each pair of consecutive entries that are different, we measure the depths difference between entries. Assume we have a sequence of entries $e_1, e_2, \ldots, e_n$, CDCE is computed by the following formula

$$m(CDCE) = (\|\|path(e_i)\| - \|path(e_{i+1})\|\|) \forall e_i \neq e_{i+1}. \tag{17}$$

We simplified the CDCE in Eq. 17 because it computes the difference between depths.

With the 6 feature functions defined above, we have a sequence of measures $m_1, m_2, \ldots, m_n$ for a given block of entries. By applying a predefined threshold value v, threshold-based frequency $f(v)$ can be computed by the formula below

$$f(v) = \frac{\|\{i \mid m_i \geq v\}\|}{n}, (1 \leq i \leq n). \tag{18}$$

Derived from the behavioral feature space F, we have presented the definitions of 16 behavioral features in order to distinguish the access patterns of the normal users and the intruders. Next, we will evaluate the proposed features with the existing Windows file system logs dataset for their effectiveness in detecting intruders.

3.3 Feature Evaluation

Most of the prior behavior modeling research was intended to solve the masquerader detection problem. Among them, Camina et al. [6] focused on the Windows file system and used the native Windows event logger to record data on each user over five to ten weeks of working days. The normal logs were preprocessed to filter for actions on user objects only, as opposed to system or application objects. The logs were then sanitized for confidentiality. This dataset was named WUIL [6], stands for Windows-Users and -Intruder simulations Logs, aimed to generate more faithful normal-attack patterns by simulating data exfiltration attacks on the users' machines. By the time we obtained the dataset, the WUIL dataset has been updated to contain a set of normal activity from 76 users and three types of simulated attacker logs for each of the users. The users were volunteers of varying ages, positions, and computer familiarity. Windows system users were chosen because of their abundance. The attacks were restricted to five minutes each, and each of the three attack logs was simulated with a different method.

While each dataset had its weaknesses, the WUIL dataset overcame many pitfalls of its predecessors. It did not use the one-versus-the-others approach found in the SEA [30] dataset. It had the attack and normal data collected from the same machine, which is suitable for intrusion detection analysis. For these reasons, we decide to use the WUIL dataset in this paper to evaluate our intrusion detection method. A few log entries from the WUIL dataset are shown in Table 1. The dataset contains 6 columns of information: entry number, date, clock time, seconds since 12:00 AM on January 1st, 2011 (SS11), depth, and path.

Table 1. Sample entries from the WUIL repository

Entry	Date	Clock Time	SS11	Depth	Path
70	14/02/2012	12:50:59 p.m.	35405459	5	0/1/2/7/15/12
71	14/02/2012	12:50:59 p.m.	35405459	5	0/1/2/7/15/12
72	14/02/2012	12:51:01 p.m.	35405461	4	0/1/2/7/17
73	14/02/2012	12:51:01 p.m.	35405461	4	0/1/2/7/17
74	14/02/2012	12:51:01 p.m.	35405461	4	0/1/2/7/12

The entry number is an indexing element and thus is not very informative for our experiments. SS11 column provides an easy-to-use reckoning of time, such that both date and clock time columns could be derived from SS11. For this reason, we refer to SS11 for the timestamps of the log entries. Depth measures how many levels in the directory of an accessed file's path, e.g., 0/1/3/9/14 has a depth of four. Depth was used in Camina et al.'s original experimentation [6] and was also used by the authors to break user activity into tasks [9]. In this paper, we decide to use the path column for our experiments because depth could be easily derived from the path.

Since the intruders' logs were simulated as five minutes of the malicious activities, it is important to have a comparable size in normal users' data. To achieve this, the normal log entries are split into distinct five-minute blocks, discarding those that aren't suitably active. A block is considered inactive if it contains a gap lasting more than two minutes. To keep as many normal blocks as possible, the first entry after a gap lasts longer than two minutes starts a new block. This could potentially result in a block that lasts merely over three minutes. Therefore, we discarded the blocks that last four minutes or less to ensure they span a comparable length of time with intruders. Reducing the entire log entries down to these active time blocks throws out a sizable amount of normal data, but this is necessary as the intruders' logs included in the dataset are highly active and time-restricted. If all of the inactive blocks had been kept, the normal data would have been overwhelmed by inactivity, which introduces noise into our experiment. To create a balanced dataset with both classes, we only use the first three five-minute blocks extracted from the normal users. Consequently, the resulting experiment dataset contains 442 data blocks, in which 220 blocks are from normal users, the rest of them are from intruders.

Table 2. Behavioral features ranked by permutation importance

Behavioral Feature	Expected		Importance
	Normal	Intruder	
Change in Files Per Second (CFPS)	Low	High	60.98
Change in Files Per Minute (CFPM)	Low	High	39.45
Average Consecutive Time (ACT)	High	Low	36.84
Entries Per Second (EPS)	Low	High	34.23
Change in Depth Per Second (CDPS)	Low	High	33.96
Average Depth (AD)	Low	High	29.56
Average Movement Distance (AMD)	High	Low	25.66
Fraction Unique Path (FUP)	≈ 0	≈ 1	23.81
Average Location Time (ALT)	High	Low	21.99
Fraction Unique Location (FUL)	≈ 0	≈ 1	21.19
Average Consecutive Repetitions (ACR)	High	Low	21.05
Fraction Single Path (FSP)	≈ 0	≈ 1	17.66
Fraction Multiway (FM)	≈ 1	< 1	16.25
File Visit Duration (FVD)	High	Low	16.08
Number of Times Each File Visited (NTFV)	High	Low	14.58
Change in Depth in Consecutive Entries (CDCE)	Low	High	11.14

We argue that intrusion detection is a binary classification problem between intruders and normal users. To evaluate the effectiveness of the behavioral features in classification models, we compute features' permutation importance by the experiment dataset. The permutation importance is an intuitive, model-agnostic method to estimate the feature importance for classifier and regression models [1]. The procedure to compute permutation importance is straightforward: we take a classification model that is fit to the dataset, and measure its predictive accuracy as baseline performance; for each feature, we then permute its values in the dataset, and compute the decreased performance after permutation; the feature's importance can be computed as the difference with the baseline performance. If a feature with high importance value shows a large performance decrease after permutation, the indicates a strong influence on the classification model, while an irrelevant feature has the value close to 0. In Table 2, we list all 16 behavioral features with our intuitive expectations for their ranges and ranked by the permutation importance with the Random Forest (RF) model.

For the classification problem of intrusion detection, Table 2 shows that our features are all influential, but not all the features equally contribute to the classification performance. The design similarity in CFPS and CFPM results in a high correlation coefficient of 0.76 between these two features. To our surprise, both of them are the top 2 important features to the classification performance, with CFPS has far more superior importance value than the rest of the group. In Sect. 4, we will select a subset of the features to train the classifiers, and evaluate their performances in detecting intruders in the dataset.

4 Experiments and Results

Our experiments attempt to validate our working hypothesis, that the proposed features can capture the behavior difference to detect intruders in the file system. In this section, we select and use behavioral features with four classification algorithms, namely Decision Tree (DT), Random Forest (RF), Support Vector Machine (SVM) and Neural Network (NN) with the dataset extracted from the WUIL repository. We evaluate their performances by a metric that is customized for the intrusion detection problem.

4.1 Performance Measure

One way to analyze the classification performance is by plotting the classifier's Receiver Operating Characteristic (ROC) curves [25]. The ROC curve evaluates the classification performance in a two-dimensional space. It can be understood as the relation of the ratios of the correctly identified positive samples (true positive rate, TPR) and the incorrectly classified negative samples (false positive rate, FPR) at various threshold settings. One of the frequently used metrics extracted from the ROC curve is the value of area under the entire curve, commonly denoted as AUC. With a correctly chosen threshold, a two-class classifier has an AUC value of 1 achieves perfect accuracy, and the classifier that predicts the class at random has an AUC value of 0.5.

In general, acquiring a classifier with large AUC value is desirable, one of the major drawbacks of relying on the AUC metric, however, is that it summarizes the entire curve, including regions that may not be relevant to the security problems (e.g. the regions with high FPR) [23]. Comparing to other classification applications, IDS has much lower tolerance on the false alarm. Dealing with false alarm is not only extremely time- and labor-intensive, but also decreases the chance of a system administrator to capture the real alarms fired by the intruders, which makes the system essentially useless. To remedy this limitation, the Partial Area Under the Curve (pAUC) [18] can be used as a summary index of detecting accuracy over a range of FPR that is of security interest, i.e.

$$pAUC(t_0) = \int_0^{t_0} ROC(t)dt, \tag{19}$$

where $[0, t_0]$ is the range of interest that needs to be specified before using the pAUC metric. In our experiments, we particularly focus on reducing FPR instead of treating TPR and FPR as equally important. In the training process of our experiments, we specify

$t_0 = 0.05$, which means we train and optimize the classifiers by maximizing the pAUC value within the range of 0–5% in FPR.

Although the pAUC value provides an overall evaluation of the classification performance within the range of interest, we need a set of metrics to describe a classifier's performance provided a chosen classification threshold. Accuracy is not an ideal indicator because, in a real organization, the number of normal users is several orders of magnitude greater than the intruders. Hence, all the accuracy values are close to 1 and these results prevent capturing the true effectiveness of a classifier. On the contrary, the F1 score combines precision and recall into a single value, in which the precision indicates how much a given approach is likely to provide a correct result, and recall is used to measure the detection rate. F1 score reaches its best value at 1 with perfect precision and recall, and the worst possible value at 0.

4.2 Feature Selection

Whereas permutation importance is generally considered as an efficient technique that works well in practice, we should not select the features by directly referring to the ranking. In fact, one drawback of the permutation importance is that the importance of correlated features may be overestimated [32]. To reduce the effect of the correlation on the importance measure, e.g. highly correlated features CFPS and CFPM, the Recursive Feature Elimination (RFE) algorithm should be used to make the feature selection [14]. RFE algorithm is inspired by [16] and implemented in this paper with the random forest algorithm. In RFE, features are eliminated iteratively to examine the classifier's performance change. The algorithm is recursive as it updates the ranking based on features' importance after each iteration, then the least important feature is eliminated until no further features remain [14]. Applying the RFE in our experiments eliminated feature CDCE, and achieved the best classification performance with the remaining 15 features. Therefore, we use this 15-feature dataset to train and evaluate the classifiers in the rest of this section.

4.3 Experimental Settings

All our experiments in this paper are conducted with R. For all 442 samples in the dataset, 80% of them are for training and 20% are reserved for testing. We employ the 10-fold cross-validation approach, enabled by R's *caret* package, to train the classifiers. In the training process, parameters are chosen by maximizing the classifier's pAUC(0.05) value. Then the performance is evaluated by applying the classifiers to the testing dataset. DT is based on the decision tree algorithm [5, 27, 29]. In this experiment, we used the *rpart* package of R to implement the recursive partitioning procedure in growing the decision tree. Using the *rpart* package allows the training function to use Gini Index-based measurement [3] in performing recursive partitioning for modeling. Comparing to DT, an RF classifier contains many decision trees, each of which is constructed by instances with randomly sampled features and produces a response when a set of predictor values are given as input [10, 15]. We construct the RF classifier by using R's *randomforest* package. Existing researches indicate that SVM-based algorithms show noticeable performance gains in anomaly detection system [13, 28,

37] over other machine learning algorithms. In our experiments, we evaluate the SVM classifier by *R*'s package *e1071* with different kernels and report the best performance results from the linear kernel. In the NN classifier, the outcome values come from the input data passing through the multiple successive neural network layers in between. Each layer learns a specific feature of input data and contributes to the final decision. We select a three-layer neural network with the backpropagation algorithm, in which the hyperparameters of the network are optimized by the grid search process to maximize the pAUC(0.05) value. We implemented the NN classifier by the *mxnet* package in *R*, which is a powerful tool to construct and customize the state-of-art deep learning models.

4.4 Experimental Results

Figure 1 plots four ROC curves by applying the classifiers to the testing dataset. We removed the data points that have TPR lower than 70% on the y-axis from the graph, to reduce the redundancy and improve the readability. The x-axis denotes the FPR in percentage, is in the logarithm scale to set the focus on the range of interest of 0–5%.

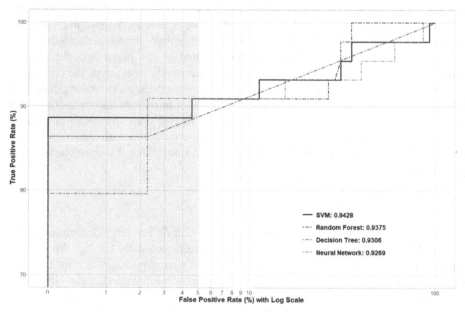

Fig. 1. Comparison of the ROC curves with partial AUC ($\leq$5%).

As we can see in Fig. 1, classifiers perform differently by varying FPR on the x-axis. The RF has a higher true positive rate than other classifiers with higher FPR, however, SVM has the edge if only 2% FPR or less is allowed. In Fig. 1, pAUC(0.05) value is computed by measuring the size of the region under the ROC curve with FPR smaller or equal than 5%. Although the NN classifier has the lowest pAUC(0.05) value of 0.9269, it reaches the highest true positive rate at the 3% FPR mark. In order to compare four classifiers with the same FPR upper bound, we summarize their best performances respect to 5%, 3% and 1% FPR.

Table 3. Performance of four classifiers with different FPR tolerance values

	DT			RF			SVM			NN		
	5%	3%	1%	5%	3%	1%	5%	3%	1%	5%	3%	1%
Precision	1.000	1.000	1.000	0.952	0.975	1.000	0.952	1.000	1.000	0.976	0.976	1.000
Recall	0.864	0.864	0.864	0.909	0.886	0.864	0.909	0.886	0.886	0.909	0.909	0.795
F1 Score	0.927	0.927	0.927	0.930	0.929	0.927	0.930	0.940	0.940	0.941	0.941	0.886

In Table 3, with every FPR upper bound value evaluated, we list the precision, recall and F1 score for each classifier. We notice that DT retains the same performance for all three upper bound values. This is due to its sparse threshold data points on the ROC curve, and the best performance is achieved at the point where FPR is 0. For the FPR upper bound values of 3% and 5%, the NN classifier performs the best with the highest F1 scores of 0.941. However, SVM surpasses all other classifiers in the F1 score with a 1% FPR upper bound value. These findings from Table 3 are coherent with what we observed in Fig. 1, and validate our hypothesis that the proposed behavioral features are effective in discovering different behaviors to detect intruders in the dataset.

5 Conclusion

In this paper, we hypothesize that intruders have different cyber behavior patterns compared to that of the normal users in a system, which can then be used to detect intrusions. Instead of focusing on local and static features as in existing research, we described a behavior-based model that can be used to detect intruders based on the user file access patterns. The result of our experiments is very encouraging. It supported our hypothesis that normal user behavior in a file system is significantly different from the intruder's, and our proposed behavioral-based model is effective in detecting such behavior deviation with an F1 score of 0.94 and false positive rate upper bound of 3%.

Future work will focus on exploring other possible behavioral features in order to further improve performance. We plan to explore more temporal and spatial features of the time series, including the access order of the file system objects, elapse time before revisiting the same file, etc. Although our method shows a high detection rate with the dataset extracted from the WUIL repository, we are interested in validating this approach with other types of the dataset to further validate this work.

Acknowledgment. We would like to thank Raúl Monroy for creating and sharing the WUIL dataset [6]. This work was supported in part by the National Science Foundation (NSF) under grants NSF-1659755, NSF-1433817, and NSF-1356705.

References

1. Altmann, A., Tolosi, L., Sander, O., Lengauer, T.: Permutation importance: a corrected feature importance measure. Bioinformatics **26**(10), 1340–1347 (2010). ISSN 1460-2059, 1367–4803, p. 395
2. Anderson, J.P.: Computer security threat monitoring and surveillance. Technical report, James P. Anderson Company, Fort Washington, Pennsylvania (1980)
3. Atkinson, E.J., Therneau, T.M.: An Introduction to Recursive Partitioning Using the Rpart Routines. Mayo Foundation, Rochester (2000)
4. Bowen, B.M., Hershkop, S., Keromytis, A.D., Stolfo, S.J.: Baiting inside attackers using decoy documents. In: Chen, Y., Dimitriou, T.D., Zhou, J. (eds.) SecureComm 2009. LNICST, vol. 19, pp. 51–70. Springer, Heidelberg (2009). https://doi.org/10.1007/978-3-642-05284-2_4
5. Breiman, L., Friedman, J.H., Olshen, R.A., Stone, C.J.: Classification and Regression Trees. Wadsworth & Brooks, Monterey (1984)
6. Camiña, J.B., Hernández-Gracidas, C., Monroy, R., Trejo, L.: The Windows-users and-intruder simulations logs dataset (WUIL): an experimental framework for masquerade detection mechanisms. Expert Syst. Appl. **41**, 919–930 (2014)
7. Camiña, J.B., Monroy, R., Trejo, L.A., Medina-Perez, M.A.: Temporal and spatial locality: an abstraction for masquerade detection. IEEE Trans. Inf. Forensics Secur. **11**(9), 2036–2051 (2016)
8. Camiña, B., Monroy, R., Trejo, L.A., Sánchez, E.: Towards building a masquerade detection method based on user file system navigation. In: Batyrshin, I., Sidorov, G. (eds.) MICAI 2011. LNCS (LNAI), vol. 7094, pp. 174–186. Springer, Heidelberg (2011). https://doi.org/10.1007/978-3-642-25324-9_15
9. Camiña, J.B., Rodríguez, J., Monroy, R.: Towards a masquerade detection system based on user's tasks. In: Stavrou, A., Bos, H., Portokalidis, G. (eds.) RAID 2014. LNCS, vol. 8688, pp. 447–465. Springer, Cham (2014). https://doi.org/10.1007/978-3-319-11379-1_22
10. Chen, Y.W., Lin, C.J.: Combining SVMs with various feature selection strategies. In: Guyon, I., Nikravesh, M., Gunn, S., Zadeh, L.A. (eds.) Feature Extraction. STUDFUZZ, vol. 207, pp. 315–324. Springer, Berlin (2006). https://doi.org/10.1007/978-3-540-35488-8_13
11. Denning, D.E.: An intrusion-detection model. IEEE Trans. Softw. Eng. **13**(SE-2), 222–232 (1987)
12. D'haeseleer, P., Forrest, S., Helman, P.: An immunological approach to change detection: algorithms, analysis, and implications. In: IEEE Symposium on Security and Privacy (1996)
13. Eskin, E., Arnold, A., Prerau, M., Portnoy, L., Stolfo, S.: A geometric framework for unsupervised anomaly detection. In: Barbará, D., Jajodia, S. (eds.) Applications of Data Mining in Computer Security. ADIS, vol. 6, pp. 77–101. Springer, Boston, MA (2002). https://doi.org/10.1007/978-1-4615-0953-0_4
14. Gregorutti, B., Michel, B., Saint-Pierre, P.: Correlation and variable importance in random forests. Stat. Comput. **27**(3), 659–678 (2017)
15. Gupta, B., Rawat, A., Jain, A., Arora, A., Dhami, N.: Analysis of various decision tree algorithms for classification in data mining. Int. J. Comput. Appl. **163**(8), 15–19 (2017)
16. Guyon, I., Weston, J., Barnhill, S., Vapnik, V.: Gene selection for cancer classification using support vector machines. Mach. Learn. **46**, 389–422 (2002)
17. Javitz, H.S., Valdes, A.: The SRI IDES statistical anomaly detector. In: Proceedings of IEEE Computer Society Symposium on Research in Security and Privacy, Oakland, CA, USA, pp. 316–326 (1991)
18. Jiang, Y., Metz, C.E., Nishikawa, R.M.: A receiver operating characteristic partial area index for highly sensitive diagnostic tests. Radiology **201**(3), 745–750 (1996)

19. Killourhy, K., Maxion, R.: Why did my detector do *That*?! In: Jha, S., Sommer, R., Kreibich, C. (eds.) RAID 2010. LNCS, vol. 6307, pp. 256–276. Springer, Heidelberg (2010). https://doi.org/10.1007/978-3-642-15512-3_14

20. Koerner, B.I.: Inside the cyberattack that shocked the US government, October 2016. https://www.wired.com/2016/10/inside-cyberattack-shocked-us-government/. Accessed 21 Mar 2018

21. Kuo, Y., Huang, S.S.: Detecting stepping-stone connection using association rule mining. In: Proceedings of International Conference on Availability, Reliability, and Security, Fukuoka, pp. 90–97 (2009)

22. Lunt, T.F.: A survey of intrusion detection techniques. Comput. Secur. **12**, 405–418 (1993)

23. Ma, H., Bandos, A.I., Gur, D.: On the use of partial area under the ROC curve for comparison of two diagnostic tests. Biometrical J. **57**, 304–320 (2015)

24. Newman, L.H.: How to protect yourself from that massive Equifax breach, September 2017. https://www.wired.com/story/how-to-protect-yourself-from-that-massive-equifax-breach/. Accessed 21 Mar 2018 (2017)

25. Provost, F., Fawcett, T., Kohavi, R.: The case against accuracy estimation for comparing induction algorithms. In: Proceedings of the Fifteenth International Conference on Machine Learning, pp. 445–453 (1998)

26. Pusara, M., Brodley, C.E.: User re-authentication via mouse movements. In: Proceedings of ACM Workshop on Visualization and Data Mining Computer Security (VizSEC/DMSEC), pp. 1–8 (2004)

27. Quinlan, J.R.: Introduction of decision trees. Mach. Learn. **1**(1), 81–106 (1986)

28. Salem, M.B., Stolfo, S.J.: Modeling user search behavior for masquerade detection. In: Sommer, R., Balzarotti, D., Maier, G. (eds.) RAID 2011. LNCS, vol. 6961, pp. 181–200. Springer, Heidelberg (2011). https://doi.org/10.1007/978-3-642-23644-0_10

29. Salzberg, S.L.: C4.5: programs for machine learning by J. Ross Quinlan. Morgan Kaufmann Publishers, Inc., 1993. Mach. Learn. **16**(3), 235–240 (1994)

30. Schonlau, M., DuMouchel, W., Ju, W.-H., Karr, A.F., Theus, M., Vardi, Y.: Computer intrusion: detecting masquerades. Statistic. Science **16**(1), 58–74 (2001)

31. Stolfo, S.J., Hershkop, S., Bui, L.H., Ferster, R., Wang, K.: Anomaly detection in computer security and an application to file system accesses. In: Hacid, M.-S., Murray, N.V., Raś, Z.W., Tsumoto, S. (eds.) ISMIS 2005. LNCS (LNAI), vol. 3488, pp. 14–28. Springer, Heidelberg (2005). https://doi.org/10.1007/11425274_2

32. Strobl, C., Boulesteix, A.L., Kneib, T., Augustin, T., Zeileis, A.: Conditional variable importance for random forests. BMC Bioinf. **9**(1), 307 (2008)

33. Wu, H., Huang, S.S.: User behavior analysis in masquerade detection using principal component analysis. In: Proceedings of 8th International Conference on Intelligent Systems Design and Applications (ISDA), pp. 201–206 (2008)

34. Yang, J., Huang, S.S.: Mining TCP/IP packets to detect stepping-stone intrusion. Comput. Secur. **26**(7), 479–484 (2007)

35. Yuill, J., Zappe, M., Denning, D., Feer, F.: Honeyfiles: deceptive files for intrusion detection. In: Proceedings of the 5th Annual IEEE SMC Information Assurance Workshop (IAW 2004), pp. 116–122 (2004)

36. Zanero, S.: Behavioral intrusion detection. In: Aykanat, C., Dayar, T., Körpeoğlu, İ. (eds.) ISCIS 2004. LNCS, vol. 3280, pp. 657–666. Springer, Heidelberg (2004). https://doi.org/10.1007/978-3-540-30182-0_66

37. Zhang, F., Wang, Y., Wang, H.: Gradient correlation: are ensemble classifiers more robust against evasion attacks in practical settings? In: Hacid, H., Cellary, W., Wang, H., Paik, H.-Y., Zhou, R. (eds.) WISE 2018. LNCS, vol. 11233, pp. 96–110. Springer, Cham (2018). https://doi.org/10.1007/978-3-030-02922-7_7

Blockchain-Enabled Privacy-Preserving Internet of Vehicles: Decentralized and Reputation-Based Network Architecture

Xinshu Ma, Chunpeng Ge, and Zhe Liu[✉]

College of Computer Science and Technology, Nanjing University of Aeronautics
and Astronautics, Nanjing, China
maxinshusu@gmail.com,{gecp,zhe.liu}@nuaa.edu.cn

Abstract. With the rapid growth of the transportation systems, the
Internet of Vehicles (IoV) has evolved as a new theme in both industry
and academia from traditional vehicular ad hoc networks (VANETs).
However, the multi-sources and multi-domain information disseminated
over the network has brought huge security issues for the communications
in the IoV system. In this paper, we present a lightweight blockchain-
based framework for IoV to meet the requirements of security, privacy
and high availability. We propose a novel hierarchical data sharing framework where two types of sub-blockchain are formed allowing for flexible
access control. In addition, we propose a reconfigured blockchain structure to acclimatize itself to the vehicular network which is composed of a
number of lightweight and low-energy IoT devices. Moreover, we design
a lightweight reputation-based consensus algorithm with a multi-weight
reputation evaluation mechanism to prevent internal collusion of network
nodes. Based on the proposed architecture, security analysis is illustrated
to show the security and privacy of the proposed framework.

Keywords: Blockchain · IoV · Privacy preserving · Data sharing

1 Introduction

The concept of Internet of Vehicles (IoV), one of the revolutions driven by Internet of Things (IoT), to attain the vision of "smart vehicles, has evolved from the
conventional Vehicle Adhoc Networks (VANETs) where the limited capacity for
handling all the information that is aggregated by numerous vehicles and other
actuators (such as sensors and mobile devices) in their vicinity has become the
most primary problem with the sustainable growth of the number of connected
vehicles [10,16,20,30]. A recent report conducted by a renowned organization
revealed that the number of cars sold worldwide is expected to 0.5 billion by the
end of 2019 [26], and it's projected that we will have 2 billion motorized vehicles
including cars, trucks, and buses by 2030 [6]. Such growth has opened a conspic-
uously challenging but lucrative market for both industry and academia [20].

© Springer Nature Switzerland AG 2019
J. K. Liu and X. Huang (Eds.): NSS 2019, LNCS 11928, pp. 336–351, 2019.
https://doi.org/10.1007/978-3-030-36938-5_20

The IoV is defined as a comprehensive platform integrating IoT technology with the intelligent transportation systems (ITSs), which could support multi-fold functions such as dynamic information services, intelligent traffic control, intelligent vehicle management [17]. The IoV is anticipated to cope with the in-depth intelligent integration of human, vehicles, things (such as sensors) and the environment, boost the efficiency of transportation, and improve the quality of municipal services to make humans content with their vehicles [10,16,30].

However, as IoV involves the myriad of different participants such as numerous vehicles, various sensors, passengers, drivers, Road Side Units (RSUs), cloud servers, etc., it is a challenging issue to realize data sharing and ensure the interoperability in the context of IoV. Namely, the multi-domain and multi-sources data disseminated among the vehicular network usually contains some sensitive information (such as vehicle identification, personalization information, and navigation information) [10], and thus participants are unwilling to share information with each other owing to a sizable lack of trust on each part. Hence, it is of extraordinary significance to ensure the security and privacy of data sharing and support mitigating techniques to the malicious attacks.

Recently, the Blockchain technology, the core technology of Bitcoin [24] and other cryptocurrencies [8], is being considered as a powerful tool for enabling trusted interactions between various devices in a decentralized way. The integration of blockchain technology with IoV has drawn increasing attentions of a large number of researchers and developers, the reasons are fourfold: (*i*) blockchain is an immutable, replicated and tamper-evident distributed ledger and thus enables IoV to conduct *audits*; (*ii*) it adopts multiple cryptographic algorithms to protect the *security and privacy* of the information; (*iii*) it could achieve a *rough consensus* based on designated distributed consensus algorithm where nodes do not need to confide in each other [14]. Despite all these advantages stemming from blockchain, some challenges might emerge during integrating IoV with existing blockchain technology such as high resource consumption and high memory overhead.

With this in mind, in this paper, we present a lightweight blockchain to meet the requirements of IoV to cope with the data sharing problem aforementioned. The main contributions of this paper are summarized as follows:

1. A hierarchical structure is adopted to optimize the resource consumption and provide flexible access control and two kinds of blockchains *IntraChain* and *InterChain* are employed in the intra-vehicular network and inter-vehicular network both of which are reconstructed to mitigate the devices' pressure of storage and calculation.

2. A novel consensus protocol akin to Delegated Proof of Stake (DPoS) [1] is proposed in the intervehicular network to reach an agreement with the aggregated data and manage the fluctuation of reputation values of each node among IoV.

3. We show that our proposed blockchain-enabled decentralized framework for IoV is secure by throughly analyzing its security with respect to the adversary model.

The paper is organized as follows. Section 2 reviews the related works in the literature. Section 3 presents the system model, adversary model of the new architecture. Section 4 illustrates the methodology behind the proposed blockchain-based IoV framework. Section 5 presents the detailed working mechanism of two chains, especially the novel reputation-based consensus algorithm. Section 6.1 elaborates the security analysis. Ultimately, Sect. 7 concludes the paper.

2   Related Work

2.1   IoV Security

In IoV, heterogeneity and the large number of vehicles increases the security requirements for the communication and data sharing. A demonstration [11] at Black Hat cybersecurity conference showed how to control a Jeep Cherokee on the move via some softwares, which shows the potential risks on the road for IoV. Compared to IoT security which has been studied by numerous previous survey works comprehensively, IoV security is less studied but is analogical to IoT security to some extent. Thus a number of security solutions developed for IoT could also be implemented in IoV. Porambage et al. [25] introduces a pervasive authentication protocol for the resource limited wireless sensor networks (WSNs). Sharaf et al. [27] proposed a novel scheme for authentication procedure in IoT by generating a unique fingerprint for each device. Zhang et al. [33] proposed a method to measure and defend against DDoS attack over IoT network. Some works focusing on the privacy-preserving approaches when the devices transmitting sensitive data via the untrusted channel. Yao et al. [32] proposed an anonymous privacy-preserving data reporting mechanism for IoT applications. The secure communication schemes for vehicular networks has been studied in several previous works [13,34].

2.2   Blockchain for IoV

With the advances in networking technologies, embedded processors, and artificial intelligence, the trend of harnessing the blockchain technology to create a decentralized, secure and efficient IoV network is increasingly inexorable. Yang et al. [31] proposed a decentralized trust management mechanism based on blockchain for IoV, employing a joint Proof of Work and Proof of Stake consensus algorithm to reach an agreement about the trust level of each devices. Liu et al. [22] proposed an adaptive electric vehicle participation mechanism in smart grid platform using blockchain to minimize the charging cost of electric vehicles. Gao et al. [15] proposed a blockchain-based payment scheme for vehicles to protect the privacy of the user information during the data sharing process. Jiang et al. [19] proposed a distributed IoV network architecture where several types of nodes are defined and several sub-blockchain networks are formed. Kang et al. [21] proposed an optimizing consensus management mechanism using reputation-based voting scheme and contract theory to ensure the security and traceability of data sharing in IoV. Sharma [28] presented an energy-efficient transaction model for the blockchain-enabled IoV using distributed clustering-mechanism based on stochastic volatility model to reduce the burden of processing transactions on each device.

3 Problem Definition

3.1 System Model

As shown in Fig. 2, a decentralized, secure, and privacy-preserving communication framework for the vehicular networks mainly contains multiple vehicles, multiple RSUs (e.g., traffic lights, toll station, gas station, among others), multiple infrastructures (e.g., transport station, cloud computing platform) multiple humans and personal devices (e.g., cell phones), and all the sensors along with actuators within the vehicle. The heterogeneous network architecture of IoV consists of five types of vehicular communications: Vehicle-to-Vehicle (V2V), Vehicle-to-RSU (V2R), Vehicle-to-Personal devices (V2P), Vehicle-to-Sensors (V2S), and Vehicles-to-Infrastructure (V2I), as shown in Fig. 1. We simplify the complex system into two two-level fundamental paradigms:

1. *Intra-vehicular network layer:* including the connections between all the sensors, actuators, and personal devices within the individual vehicle, i.e., V2S and V2R;
2. *Inter-vehicular network layer:* including the information exchange among vehicles, RSUs, and infrastructures, i.e., V2V, V2R, and V2I.

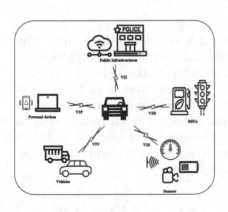

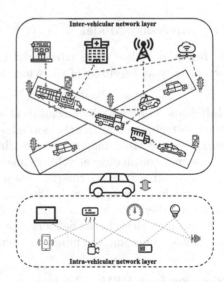

Fig. 1.   Fig. 2.

Note that different type of the aforementioned communications over IoV are enabled utilizing different wireless access technologies (WATs) (such as IEEE Wireless Access in Vehicular Environments (WAVE), GSM, LTE, WiFi, bluetooth, among others), to ensure the seamless connections between all actors. The responsibility of each actor in our framework is listed as follows:

- RSUs: Based on the relatively high data processing and data storage capacity, RSUs take charge of major computing and storage tasks. Namely, RSUs serve as the full nodes in the conventional Bitcoin network storing the latest version of the entire blockchain, and as the important force for the block generation and reputation consensus. Besides, they ought to monitor the traffic conditions, disseminate the valuable information immediately, and supervise the vehicles operations via collecting and analyzing its behaviors.
- Vehicles: Each vehicle need to interact with other vehicles, RSUs, and infrastructures via sending/responding information to tune with the changing circumstances. Beyond that, vehicles should rate the trust level of other vehicles/RSUs as the feedback of the service quality and broadcast the rating message to the network to reach an agreement via a certain algorithm. Note that vehicles have the same right to compete for the mining task allowing an increase of its own reputation value.
- Sensors and Actuators: They are responsible to control the movement of vehicles, gather vehicle situations data such as fuel consumption and car diagnostics, and aggregate environmental data (e.g., temperature, weather conditions, etc.), and report the emergency event to the vehicle when necessary.
- Cloud Server: It is mainly in charge of cloud backup of the blockchain data and other information storage.

3.2   Adversary Model

We briefly overview three adversarial cases aiming to destroy the availability, data privacy and security of the whole vehicular system:

Malicious Vehicles. It is contingent that a few vehicles are manipulated by attackers trying to interfere the normal operation of the whole system. This could bring about severe damages via increasing the traffic crashes and even fatalities. We assume the malicious vehicles mainly destroy the system in three ways: (i) broadcasting false information, packet dropping, packet selective forwarding, e.g., spreading the signal of traffic congestion when the ahead road is clear to make the other vehicles take a detour. (ii) Generating unfair reputation values to the other vehicles in the network to damage their reputation and thus acquire the chance to become the miner to alter block content.

Compromised RSUs. Analogically, RSUs placed along the road are more susceptible to be compromised by attackers and thus they are assumed as semi-trusted. Since all of the RSUs perform as the full node responsible for storing all blocks in the blockchain, it would be catastrophic if most of RSUs are under the malicious control. Nevertheless, it is impracticable for the attackers to launch a large-scale intrusion attack due to the limited ability. Thus, we assume that the attack could compromise a few RSUs (i.e., tampering the block content and generating new blocks) within a certain period of time.

DoS/DDoS Attack. The object is to prevent some or all legitimate requests/information from being responded/acquired, by sending a mass of requests to the target device causing its computational resources unavailable [9]. Either external device or the individual device within IoV might be manipulated to initiate this attack and we only assume the latter case in our framework.

4 Methodology

In this section, we briefly introduce the fundamental methodology of our design—blockchain technology, system architecture of the decentralized IoV framework, and the reconfigured blockchain structure tailored for vehicular communication systems.

4.1 Architecture Overview

In this paper, we explore how the blockchain technology could be applied in the vehicular network. As mentioned above, a hierarchical network model is proposed which is illustrated in Fig. 2. Accordingly, *IntraChain* and *InterChain*, these two types of blockchain are adopted to process different transactions and information in *Intra-vehicular network* and *Inter-vehicular network* respectively.

IntraChain. Smart sensors, actuators of individual vehicle, and user's personal phones/computers are located within the *Intra-vehicle network* tier and are centrally managed by vehicular central controller (i.e., local miner). In each vehicle, there exists a local private blockchain named *IntraChain* which keeps tracks of interactions within the vehicle and sticks to a certain policy list for the internal access control and external access control management. Due to the sensitivity of the interaction information inside the vehicle, the encryption algorithm is involved in the internal communications. Each transaction initiated by the "things" should be tagged with the requester ID and requestee ID that is assigned by the controller at the initialization stage. The central controller each received transaction in accordance with the policy list set by the vehicle's owner.

Besides the block header, the block body contains a number of transactions collected by the local miner within a certain period of time. Since the communication traffic of the intra-vehicular network is not high, it is rational to store the block data in the vehicle locally and all of the transactions are chained together as an immutable ledger. Therefore, all the information related to the present and past conditions of the vehicle (including speed, direction, location, lane, the number of passengers, etc.) will be well preserved, which could be considered as the black-box data in case of emergency.

InterChain. Multiple vehicles, and RSUs constitute an *Inter-vehicular network* layer along with public infrastructures (cloud server). All the vehicles want to receive the information from the other vehicles/RSUs, even by accessing the sensors of the neighboring vehicles. Each vehicle in the network could act as either a requester collecting data or a provider sharing its own data while on the road. Since each node even RSUs in the network might perform compliantly or disobediently, it is anticipated that each node could enjoy qualified services. Therefore, a reputation evaluation mechanism is needed to improve the stability and availability of the entire system. It is worth noting that nodes (vehicles or RSUs) might transform the performance between normal and abnormal just as in the real world situations.

We adopt the *InterChain* as a public ledger which records the interactions among *Inter-vehicular network* and the reputation value of each actor, allowing accident prevention, autonomous decision making, and data auditing. However, some compromised and malicious nodes might provide incorrect feedback to the former service aiming to decrease the service quality and stability of the network. Thus a novel consensus algorithm based on the fusion of the average reputation value is necessary. Due to the constrained resources of the vehicles, only block headers are saved locally which is similar to the Simplified Payment Verification (SVP) nodes in the Bitcoin. Conversely, the RSUs must have a copy of the full *InterChain*, thus every transaction and block that has ever taken place must be saved and upload the data to the cloud server periodically.

4.2 Reconstructed Blockchain Constitution

Considering IoV is composed of resource-constrained and low-energy devices, it is irrational to require these devices to possess equal computational power to the miners in the conventional blockchain network, which makes the task of supporting distributed storage and security quite challenging. Thus, in our proposed framework, a reconstructed blockchain architecture is proposed for *InterChain*.

Block Detail. The structure of a reformatory block, akin to Bitcoin, consists of the block header and the block body. The block header, detailed in Table 1, is composed of the current block header's hash, previous block header's hash, root of the reputation tree, policy list, a timestamp, and root of the transaction tree. Here, the item of reputation tree is added into block and the root of the tree is recorded by block header. As shown in Fig. 3, we utilize the modified Merkle Patricia Trie structure to record the reputation values, where only modified data is stored in the new block, efficiently reducing the burden of memory.

Accordingly, the block body is composed of the reputation tree and transactions tree. The reputation value of each vehicle and RSU will be recalculated once the acts in suspicious ways, such as querying privacy data against the access policy which is stored in the block header generated by the administrator, and creating or relaying the invalid blocks or transactions. And the details of reputation evaluation scheme are elaborated in Sect. 5.2. It should be noted that a cryptographically authenticated data structure—modified Merkle Patricia Trie (MPT) applied in Ethereum [29] is adopted to store the reputation value of each UAV as depicted in Fig. 3, which could quickly and efficiently identify data that has changed without having to retrieve over all the data in order to make the comparison.

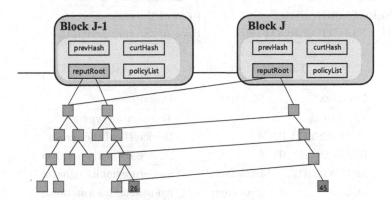

Fig. 3. Example of the modified Merkle Patricia Trie structure for recording the reputation values. Two blocks B_{J-1} and B_J containing two reputation trees, it is shown that the reputation value 26 was changed to 45 in the latter block B_J. Specifically, only the modified data would be stored in the new block and the unmodified data would be linked to the new root without duplication, efficiently reducing the request of memory compared to the original Merkle Tree which is adopted in Bitcoin [24].

Transaction Detail. As for defining transactions, inspired from [12], communications between vehicles, RSUs and the cloud server among the whole system are formatted as transactions. Owing to the constrained storage space of vehicles, a micro-size transaction structure is proposed as shown in Table 2. The detail information of a transaction includes the transaction type's IDs of the requester and requestee (similar to the addresses in the blockchain), the signature of the requester (i.e., sender) and the additional data if necessary. It is worth noting that the length of the additional data is variable ranging from 0 to 1024 bits.

Transaction Handling. Due to that various weighting factor is embraced into the proposed reputation evaluation algorithm, we define a set of operations to be recorded as transactions with different weighting factors. We briefly elaborate six kinds of transactions as follows:

- **Interest.** The requester initiates *Interest* to query specific information from a number of neighboring vehicles/RSUs or one appointed actor.
- **Reply.** The vehicle/RSU reply to the *Interest* transaction with the additional information.
- **Report.** The vehicle/RSU actively publishes the latest information (related to the road conditions, weather report, etc.).

Table 1. Composition of a block

Contents	Size(bit)	Description
BLOCK_HASH	80	Hash value of current block header
PREV_HASH	80	Hash value of previous block header
TIMESTAMP	24	Unix timestamp of the block
REPUTATION_ROOT	80	Root of the reputation tree
TRANSACTION_ROOT	80	Root of the transaction tree

Table 2. Composition of a transaction

Contents	Size(bit)	Description
TX_TYPE	4	Transaction type
REQUESTER_ID	8	Device ID of the sender
REQUESTEE_ID	8	Device ID of the receiver
SIGNATURE	1024/2048	Signature/multi-signature
DATA	Maximum 1024	Additional information

- **Rating.** The vehicle/RSU sends the feedback via this transaction after dealing with the specific devices utilizing the reputation evaluation scheme.
- **Alert.** The vehicle/RSU creates an *Alert* transaction to sound a warning once it finds itself under a certain kind of attack thus other nodes could perform corresponding actions towards different attacks.
- **Help.** The vehicle/RSU generates such transaction as an emergency call which will be disseminated with the highest priority in order to contact the services (such as police, family, etc.).

Periodically Memory Release. With the continuous operation of the vehicular system, there is no doubt that the blockchain distributed ledger would become increasingly larger. Considering the restricted memory space of RSUs, freeing up memory at a frequency of every 12 h is sufficient for recycling the memory space. Namely, the distributed ledger of blockchain in the proposed framework needs to be baked up to the cloud server and the physical memory of RSUs is released periodically.

5   Detailed Mechanism of the InterChain

In this section, we elaborate in detail of the working mechanism of our proposed *InterChain* framework which consists mainly of reputation evaluation scheme and the consensus algorithm.

5.1   Data Processing

Each node (vehicles and RSUs) in the network is assigned a pair of public key and private key as mentioned at the initiate stage. The unique ID of each node is derived from its own public key to ensure the anonymity of the framework. All the nodes receiving the transactions need to verify data integrity and consistency via checking if two *digests* match with each other. The transaction is relayed to the neighbors or replied with specific data if validation passes with certain probability $\mathcal{P}$ generalized from the sender's reputation value. Otherwise, the received transaction is considered as false and not transmitted if it lacks data integrity. Thus, all devices need to perform the hash function and digital signature before sending messages. It is worth noting that Keccak [4,5], a high-performance hash function in both code size and cycle count [3,23] compared to other lightweight hash functions (such as Quark [2], PHOTON [18], and SPONGENT [7]), is adopted to generate a *message digest*. To reduce memory usage, the 160-bit output is truncated to 80-bit which saves a mount of space.

5.2   Reputation Evaluation Scheme

Individual Reputation Calculation. The proposed framework maintains a trust rating for each node based on activities it has performed harnessing the reputation evaluation scheme. Generally, each node is initialized with a fixed reputation value 100 which could be decreased for performing malicious/incredible actions or increased for correctly performing *Alert* and mining task.

Each node in the network evaluate the reputation of other nodes based on the direct historical interactions with them. Considering the characteristics of different transactions, the weighting factor W of each transaction is embraced into the evaluation scheme. Beside, since the timeliness of data should also be considered into out algorithm, we evaluate each record at time t. At time t, the evaluation result $R_{u,v}(t)$ of node v generated by node u from the direct observation is calculate via:

$$R_{u,v}(t) = \sum_{i=1}^{C(u,v,t)} \sigma(t,i) \cdot Q(v,i) \cdot W(v,i) / \sum_{i=1}^{C(u,v,t)} W(v,i) \qquad (1)$$

where $C(u,v,t)$ denotes the interaction count of all the transactions between u and v before the specific time t; $Q(v,i)$ represents the quality evaluation of the ith transaction with node v; and $W(v,i)$ represents the significance factor of the ith transaction with node v.

Besides, $\sigma(t,i)$ is proposed as the perish coefficient depicting the timeliness of the ith service. Let $t(i)$ represents the time of ith transaction and we have

$$\sigma(t,i) = 1/(t(i) - t), \qquad (2)$$

which shows that the decay of the service quality is inversely proportional to the transaction time length.

Reputation Fusion. The miner might receive conflicting reputation values about one specific node. In the proposed framework, weighted reputation fusion is utilized on these ratings to obtain a relatively objective result. Let $R(t_0)$ denote the set of all reputation values last time at t_0, $R_v(t)$ denote the new calculated reputation value of node v at time t, and $\mathcal{R}_v$ denote the latest aggregated reputation values of node v. At first, we abandon the highest reputation value and the lowest reputation value from the aggregated data set R as follows:

$$\mathcal{R}_v^* = \mathcal{R}_v \not\subset \{\max(\mathcal{R}_v), \min(R)_v\}. \tag{3}$$

Then, the weighted average reputation value of node v is calculated via:

$$R_v(t) = \sum_{i=1}^{N} \frac{R_i(t_0)}{\sum_{j=1}^{N} R_j(t_0)} \cdot R_{(i,v)}(t), \tag{4}$$

where $R_{i,v}(t) \in \mathcal{R}_v^*$ and N denotes the number of rating transactions received by the miner.

5.3 Consensus Protocol

The consensus algorithm, which ought to be automatically executed by each node (vehicles and RSUs), is presented in this section, involving the regulations of committee selection and block generation.

Committee Selection. To relieve the burden of the IoV devices, we adopt the core idea of DPoS electing the committee via certain voting methods where block are generated in turn instead of Proof of Work algorithm that requires lots of computational resources to solve a complex mathematical challenge. Considering the actual situation of IoV system, we propose a hybrid scheme combining *Strategy 1* with *Strategy 2* to select miners.

Strategy 1: Randomly Selected RSU as Miner. Based on the premise that the majority of RSUs are trusted and the computational ability is comparably strong, it is rational to randomly assign a RSU to act as the miner responsible for collecting all the transactions, verifying transactions, and managing the changes of reputation values, to mitigate the computation load of vehicles.

Strategy 2: Voted Vehicle/RSU as Miner. In this case, members of committee are selected by their reputation value R and only top 15% of nodes (both vehicles and RSUs) could become the candidates. Then, a group of k active miners (three fifths of the miner candidates) are voted among committee and each of them takes turn to generate blocks within a certain time slot. Formally, the re-election of the committee is triggered by any omitting of block generation or forks in blockchain ledger.

Strategy 3: Hybrid Miner Selection. It's obvious that both *Strategy 1* and *Strategy 2* have their advantages. Herein, we consider nodes density and network connectivity into our consensus algorithm to propose a hybrid selection strategy by taking advantages of both methods. When the network is unstable and few vehicles are enabled for connection, or the node density is lower than a threshold such as in the middle of the night, *Randomly Selected RSU as Miner* is employed to provide a stable and available service. Otherwise (e.g., in the rush hour), *Voted Vehicle/RSU as Miner* is utilized to get a relatively high-quality service. Based on the observation, different strategies are employed in different situations.

Block Generation. If the rate of block generation is slow, the size of block will be quite large due to the accumulative transactions over time, which could cause the communication delay or slow down the transmission rate. Otherwise, extremely frequent mining could become the computation burden for each node. Consequently, the suitable block generation rate is significant for the proposed framework. We propose two strategies in our model.

Generating Block by Fixed Size. Each block is generated with the same size limit, for example, each block including the same number of verified transactions. Thus, the time slot between two blocks is fluctuant. Let α denote the time interval of mining process, β denote the designated block size, t_0 represent the time period that periodically releases the memory (cf. Sect. 4.2), and Δ represent the average allocated size of storage space in RSUs. We have the following constraint:

$$\beta \cdot floor(\frac{t_0}{\alpha}) \leq \Delta, \tag{5}$$

where $floor(\cdot)$ represents rounding down to the nearest integer.

Generating Block by Fixed Time. Each block is created at a fixed time interval which requires the mining task to be rotated at the same frequency. The next new round of mining process starts instantly after the generation of the previous block. It is adjustable that the stipulating of the time period between two rounds of block generation owing to the diverse communication requirements of different tasks. We have the following constraint:

$$\beta' \cdot floor(\frac{t_0}{\alpha'}) \leq \Delta, \tag{6}$$

Clearly, both Eqs. 5 and 6 ensure that all collected data in the blockchain could be well stored in each devices before next round of memory release.

6   Performance Analysis and Evaluation

6.1   Security Analysis

Scenario of Malicious Vehicles. As mentioned before, a malicious vehicle might damage the availability of the whole system in two methods. Broadcasting fake information which might cause traffic accidents could be defended by the novel reputation evaluation scheme. It mainly because the activities of each devices in the network are being evaluated to build a trust rating scheme and the receiver accepts or drops the message according to the reputation value of the vehicle. Thus, those fake information and unfair reputation report messages could be blocked with high probability.

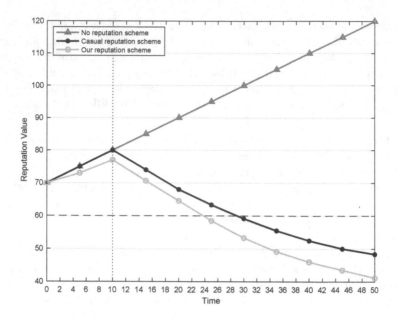

Fig. 4. Reputation fluctuation of a malicious node

Scenario of Compromised RSUs. In the proposed framework, it is supposed that only a fraction of RSUs might be compromised in a given period of time. Once the RSU is compromised, the saved data (i.e., blocks) might be deleted or modified and the RSU could tamper the reputation value when generating the new blocks. However, the same version of the latest blockchain stored in all the RSUs among the whole network according to the fundamental principle of the blockchain technology. Thus there always exits more than half of RSUs compliant to the basic rules and consensus algorithms such that the compromised RSU is prone to be recognized via the detection of deviant behaviors and kicked out of the system using vote transaction in order to prevent it from serving the malicious activities. In addition, the compromised RSUs also might fabricate and spread fake information. However, the reputation value of RSU should also be evaluated by the same scheme with other vehicles, so the vehicles would give a low credit grade if they do not satisfied with the service provided.

Scenario of DoS/DDoS Attacks. In our system, the reputation evaluation scheme allows to reduce the probability of being undermined by DoS/DDoS attack due to that a sender sending the same message within a certain time will be flagged via setting reputation value to zero and the message initiated by it would not be relayed by the neighbor nodes. Overall, each node among the system could supervise the packet flows and send alert transaction to warn the neighbor vehicles to ban all the access permissions of the malicious node.

6.2   Simulation Results and Analysis

We create a simple instantiation of the proposed consensus algorithm based on the reputation evaluation schema utilizing MATLAB tool. We observe the changes of a malicious node's reputation value in three scenarios, including (1) no reputation scheme, which is equivalent to the case that all the reputation values linearly increase by the time; (2) random rating reputation scheme where the individual reputation value is rated casually without the aforementioned equations listed in Sect. 5.2, and (3) our proposed reputation evaluation scheme.

As shown in Fig. 4, the changing trends for different cases are in an opposite way. The reputation value of the compromised node in the first case indicates an linear increment with time while the rest cases show a steep decline below the threshold ($R = 60$). Specially, the reputation value in our solution decreases faster than in case two, owing to that timeliness, service weighting factors and the history reputation of the rater are all taken into consideration in our solution. Thus the accuracy and security of the reputation evaluation in vehicular networks could be guaranteed.

7   Conclusion

In this paper, we investigate a blockchain-based decentralized data sharing framework in vehicular networks. Considering the inherent hierarchical architecture of IoV, a hierarchical blockchain-based data sharing framework is proposed where two types of sub-blockchain networks (intra-vehicular network and inter-vehicular network) are formed allowing for flexible access control and reduced data storage consumption. Additionally, a reconstructed blockchain structure is illustrated to acclimatize itself to the vehicular network which is composed of a number of lightweight and low-energy IoT devices. Besides, we also design a reputation-based consensus scheme which is akin to the core idea of DPoS consensus algorithm but a multi-weight reputation evaluation mechanism is utilized to prevent internal collusion of network nodes. Based on the proposed architecture, security analysis is illustrated to show the security, privacy-preserving of the proposed framework.

Acknowledgment. This work was supported by the National Natural Science Foundation of China (Grant No. 61802180, 61702236, 61872181), the Natural Science Foundation of Jiangsu Province (Grant No. BK20180421), the National Cryptography Development Fund (Grant No. MMJJ20180105), the Fundamental Research Funds for the Central Universities (Grant No. NE2018106).

References

1. Dpos description on bitshares. http://docs.bitshares.org/bitshares/dpos.html
2. Aumasson, J.-P., Henzen, L., Meier, W., Naya-Plasencia, M.: QUARK: a lightweight hash. In: Mangard, S., Standaert, F.-X. (eds.) CHES 2010. LNCS, vol. 6225, pp. 1–15. Springer, Heidelberg (2010). https://doi.org/10.1007/978-3-642-15031-9_1

3. Balasch, J., et al.: Compact implementation and performance evaluation of hash functions in ATtiny devices. In: Mangard, S. (ed.) CARDIS 2012. LNCS, vol. 7771, pp. 158–172. Springer, Heidelberg (2013). https://doi.org/10.1007/978-3-642-37288-9_11
4. Bertoni, G., Daemen, J., Peeters, M., Van Assche, G.: Keccak specifications. Submission to NIST (Round 2), pp. 320–337 (2009)
5. Bertoni, G., Daemen, J., Peeters, M., Van Assche, G.: Keccak sponge function family main document. Submission to NIST (Round 2), vol. 3, no. 30 (2009)
6. Bill, L.: Is our planet ready for 2 billion cars? http://alert-conservation.org/issues-research-highlights/2016/5/8/are-you-ready-for-a-planet-with-2-billion-cars-hg583. Accessed 19 Dec 2017
7. Bogdanov, A., Knežević, M., Leander, G., Toz, D., Varıcı, K., Verbauwhede, I.: SPONGENT: a lightweight hash function. In: Preneel, B., Takagi, T. (eds.) CHES 2011. LNCS, vol. 6917, pp. 312–325. Springer, Heidelberg (2011). https://doi.org/10.1007/978-3-642-23951-9_21
8. Bonneau, J., Miller, A., Clark, J., Narayanan, A., Kroll, J.A., Felten, E.W.: Sok: research perspectives and challenges for bitcoin and cryptocurrencies. In: 2015 IEEE Symposium on Security and Privacy, pp. 104–121. IEEE (2015)
9. Chen, J., Feng, Z., Wen, J.Y., Liu, B., Sha, L.: A container-based dos attack-resilient control framework for real-time UAV systems. In: 2019 Design, Automation & Test in Europe Conference & Exhibition (DATE), pp. 1222–1227. IEEE (2019)
10. Contreras-Castillo, J., Zeadally, S., Guerrero-Ibañez, J.A.: Internet of vehicles: architecture, protocols, and security. IEEE IoT J. 5(5), 3701–3709 (2017)
11. Danny, Y.: Hackers demonstrate how to take control of cars. In: Proceedings of Black Hat Security Conference, Las Vegas, NV, USA, p. 834. Black Hat (2015)
12. Dorri, A., Kanhere, S.S., Jurdak, R., Gauravaram, P.: Blockchain for IoT security and privacy: the case study of a smart home. In: 2017 IEEE International Conference on Pervasive Computing and Communications Workshops (PerCom Workshops), pp. 618–623. IEEE (2017)
13. Emara, K., Woerndl, W., Schlichter, J.: On evaluation of location privacy preserving schemes for vanet safety applications. Comput. Commun. 63, 11–23 (2015)
14. Castelló Ferrer, E.: The blockchain: a new framework for robotic swarm systems. In: Arai, K., Bhatia, R., Kapoor, S. (eds.) FTC 2018. AISC, vol. 881, pp. 1037–1058. Springer, Cham (2019). https://doi.org/10.1007/978-3-030-02683-7_77
15. Gao, F., Zhu, L., Shen, M., Sharif, K., Wan, Z., Ren, K.: A blockchain-based privacy-preserving payment mechanism for vehicle-to-grid networks. IEEE Netw. 32(6), 184–192 (2018)
16. Gerla, M., Lee, E.K., Pau, G., Lee, U.: Internet of vehicles: from intelligent grid to autonomous cars and vehicular clouds. In: 2014 IEEE World Forum on Internet of Things (WF-IoT), pp. 241–246. IEEE (2014)
17. Guerrero-Ibanez, J.A., Zeadally, S., Contreras-Castillo, J.: Integration challenges of intelligent transportation systems with connected vehicle, cloud computing, and Internet of Things technologies. IEEE Wirel. Commun. 22(6), 122–128 (2015)
18. Guo, J., Peyrin, T., Poschmann, A.: The PHOTON family of lightweight hash functions. In: Rogaway, P. (ed.) CRYPTO 2011. LNCS, vol. 6841, pp. 222–239. Springer, Heidelberg (2011). https://doi.org/10.1007/978-3-642-22792-9_13
19. Jiang, T., Fang, H., Wang, H.: Blockchain-based internet of vehicles: Distributed network architecture and performance analysis. IEEE IoT J. (2018)
20. Kaiwartya, O., et al.: Internet of vehicles: motivation, layered architecture, network model, challenges, and future aspects. IEEE Access 4, 5356–5373 (2016)

21. Kang, J., Xiong, Z., Niyato, D., Ye, D., Kim, D.I., Zhao, J.: Toward secure blockchain-enabled internet of vehicles: optimizing consensus management using reputation and contract theory. IEEE Trans. Veh. Technol. **68**(3), 2906–2920 (2019)

22. Liu, C., Chai, K.K., Zhang, X., Lau, E.T., Chen, Y.: Adaptive blockchain-based electric vehicle participation scheme in smart grid platform. IEEE Access **6**, 25657–25665 (2018)

23. Meuser, T., Schmidt, L., Wiesmaier, A.: Comparing lightweight hash functions-PHOTON & quark (2015)

24. Nakamoto, S., et al.: Bitcoin: a peer-to-peer electronic cash system (2008)

25. Porambage, P., Schmitt, C., Kumar, P., Gurtov, A., Ylianttila, M.: PAuthKey: a pervasive authentication protocol and key establishment scheme for wireless sensor networks in distributed IoT applications. Int. J. Distrib. Sens. Netw. **10**(7), 357430 (2014)

26. Scotiabank, S.: Number of cars sold worldwide from 1990 to 2019 (in million units). https://www.statista.com/statistics/200002/international-car-sales-since-1990/. Accessed 22 Aug 2019

27. Sharaf-Dabbagh, Y., Saad, W.: On the authentication of devices in the Internet of Things. In: 2016 IEEE 17th International Symposium on A World of Wireless, Mobile and Multimedia Networks (WoWMoM), pp. 1–3. IEEE (2016)

28. Sharma, V.: An energy-efficient transaction model for the blockchain-enabled internet of vehicles (IoV). IEEE Commun. Lett. **23**(2), 246–249 (2018)

29. Wood, G., et al.: Ethereum: a secure decentralised generalised transaction ledger. Ethereum Project Yellow Paper **151**(2014), 1–32 (2014)

30. Yang, F., Wang, S., Li, J., Liu, Z., Sun, Q.: An overview of internet of vehicles. China Commun. **11**(10), 1–15 (2014)

31. Yang, Z., Yang, K., Lei, L., Zheng, K., Leung, V.C.: Blockchain-based decentralized trust management in vehicular networks. IEEE IoT J. **6**(2), 1495–1505 (2018)

32. Yao, Y., Yang, L.T., Xiong, N.N.: Anonymity-based privacy-preserving data reporting for participatory sensing. IEEE IoT J. **2**(5), 381–390 (2015)

33. Zhang, C., Green, R.: Communication security in internet of thing: preventive measure and avoid DDoS attack over IoT network. In: Proceedings of the 18th Symposium on Communications & Networking, pp. 8–15. Society for Computer Simulation International (2015)

34. Zhang, L., Wu, Q., Qin, B., Domingo-Ferrer, J., Liu, B.: Practical secure and privacy-preserving scheme for value-added applications in vanets. Comput. Commun. **71**, 50–60 (2015)

Privacy Preserving Machine Learning with Limited Information Leakage

Wenyi Tang[1], Bo Qin[1], Suyun Zhao[1]([✉]), Boning Zhao[1], Yunzhi Xue[2], and Hong Chen[1]

[1] Renmin University of China, Beijing, China
zhaosuyun@ruc.edu.cn
[2] Institution of Software, Chinese Academy of Sciences, Beijing, China

Abstract. Machine learning is now playing important roles in daily lives, however, the privacy leakages are increasingly getting serious in the meantime. Current solutions to the privacy issues in machine learning, like differential privacy or homomorphic encryption either could only be applied to some specific scenarios or bring huge modification to the model construction, not to mention massive efficiency loss. In this paper, we consider addressing the privacy issue in machine learning from another perspective, without modification to models or severe efficiency loss. We proposed a straightforward privacy preserving machine learning scheme, training machine learning models directly over encrypted data. Ideally, this scheme could provide privacy protection to both training data and test data. We gave it a try by applying order preserving encryption (OPE) to the scheme. We discussed the possibility of using OPE to reveal the order information confidentially for model training. Several OPE algorithms were chosen to utilize the proposed method. Finally, comprehensive experiments were deployed on both synthetic and real datasets. The experiments on real datasets show that the learning performance of several well-known classifiers on before and after encryption changes slightly. The experiments on synthetic datasets show the classifier performance could be ranked according to fidelity and reliability.

Keywords: Machine learninig · Privacy preserving · Order preserving encryption

1 Introduction

Machine learning has become a major component of numerous applications. Companies and organizations use machine learning algorithms as essential components of their service, and sometimes the model training itself is another kind of service. Generally, the generalization ability of the trained model depends on the quantity and quality of the training data. Therefore, to provide better service, a mass of original data are collected for model training, which brings serious privacy leakage in practice.

ⓒ Springer Nature Switzerland AG 2019
J. K. Liu and X. Huang (Eds.): NSS 2019, LNCS 11928, pp. 352–370, 2019.
https://doi.org/10.1007/978-3-030-36938-5_21

The privacy issue in machine learning has been considered by academic community and government for a long time. With the European Union announcing the General Data Protection Regulation (GDPR), people started paying more attention to privacy protection.

The first try is anonymity, which includes deleting some real information, perturbing the original data or other ways, whereas these anonymity methods were turned out to be not safe enough in the Netflix prize challenge [4], in which the users' private information were extracted by differential attacks even all sensitive information were removed. To protect against such attacks, differential privacy has been carefully studied for providing the strongest privacy protection, as well as a framework to quantify the privacy loss [12]. It limits the probability of extracting individual information from an aggregated database, focusing on preserving privacy from public data. However, typical differential privacy machine learning frameworks do not protect the data itself, which means they either do not share the data [1] or only add noise in the specific procedure [24]. Such specialty makes the differential privacy framework could not fit in the service provider scenario arbitrarily. Moreover, if the dataset itself is private, the differential framework could be unapplicable as well.

Another perspective is preserving the privacy through data confidentially, which is mostly implemented by using some cryptographic primitives like Homomorphic Encryption (HE) and Secure Multiparty Computation (SMC). Compared with differential privacy solutions, the cryptography-based solutions are more intuitive. In fact, it is remarkably challenging to locate what kind of information is 'private' and selectively preserve such information from being revealed from a large dataset. Therefore, the cryptographic frameworks could provide more reliable security guarantee, which may have great prospect. However, current cryptography-based schemes are often caught in trouble for 2 main reasons: 1. they bring huge modification to target models; 2. the frequent parameter sharing brings extra interaction load to model training. Such reasons are stumbling blocks to the cryptography-based privacy preserving machine learning using in service providing.

For supervised learning, the algorithm tries to discover the relationship between a feature vector and a label to construct a classifier. Generally, the data would be preprocessed before being fitted into the model. Common preprocess methods include min-max normalization, z-score normalization. Such preprocess methods inevitably change the values of the feature vectors, which indicates the precise data are not necessary for the learning procedure of a classifier and only some information contained in the dataset is critical for learning. If we can selectively expose such information instead of private data itself, it would be a great solution for privacy preserving machine learning applications. Therefore, consider a straightforward idea: is it possible to train models over encrypted data and still obtain similar result? We believe it is possible for the developing of property preserving encryption.

The notion of property preserving encryption [23] allows anyone to check a property on plaintexts by running a public test over the corresponding cipher-texts, suggesting that selective and secure exposure of critical information is possible. In fact, the homomorphic encryption systems could be regarded as a property preserving encryption, which preserve the property of polynomial cal-culation. The property considered in this paper is *order information* and the method to reveal order information safely is OPE. It is a functional encryption scheme developed for efficient encrypted data query. Therefore, the ciphertext of OPE implicitly holds some distribution information of the original data, which is likely to be learnable, and if it is, with its cryptographic level security property, OPE could be a great choice in privacy preserving machine learning.

In this paper, we propose a simple and universal used model to consider the privacy protection, machine learning over encrypted data, which achieves two major purposes:

1. the data used in model training is private;
2. the fully trained model is private.

Along with OPE, these purposes could be achieved easily and efficiently. The considered model is a high-level one so that it could be applied to many scenarios. This model also presents an open issue in privacy preserving data mining: how much information contained in dataset is enough to train a model? And how do we securely dispose such information without any privacy loss?

The main contribution of this paper contains:

- we firstly consider to use the limited information leakage of the dataset to perform privacy-preserving model training;
- we firstly combine OPE with machine learning, and analyze the information leakage of OPE to show that it may fit in current machine learning models;
- we use special criteria to assess how an OPE algorithm is appropriate for model training, and choose 3 typical implementations of OPE to evaluate.

The rest of this paper is organized as follows. Section 2 presents the recent work about OPE and privacy preserving machine learning. Section 3 gives a general view and security analysis of our model. Section 4 discusses the reveal-ing of order information by order preserving information, and why the model training could be performed over OPE ciphertexts. Section 5 comprehensively demonstrates and analyzes the experimental results of our methods. In Sect. 6 we conclude this paper.

2 Related Work

We firstly review some work of Order-Preserving Encryption, then we review the progress in privacy preserving machine learning.

2.1   Order-Preserving Encryption

OPE provides efficient range query over ciphertext, which is usually used for building secure database. Several methods have been proposed, such schemes hold great practical value in practice. The first OPE [2] was proposed in 2004, which is based on bucket partitioning and was proven insecure sooner. In 2016, Boneh et al. proposed the notion of Order-Revealing Encryption [7], which introduces an extra public evaluation algorithm to perform comparison instead of revealing order information directly in numeric field. Current researches about OPE fall into two categories, the stateful solutions and the stateless solutions. The stateful solutions require the algorithm along with an extra state parameter, which represents the current state of all ciphertext and changes the pre-existing ciphertext while the state parameter changes [25] [16]. Such methods are not appropriate for the proposed purpose since the updating of ciphertext invalidates the fully-trained models. A more reasonable choice is stateless solutions, which does not require prior changes for existing ciphertext. To increase security, some stateless solutions like [5,6,17] are based on s partition, and they were designed to be non-deterministic encryptions, meaning that the same plaintext might be encrypted into different ciphertext for frequency hiding. Chenette et al. presented another kind of solution [9]. They treated plaintext as fixed-length binary string, and every ciphertext bit was the modular value of a encrypted result produced by a symmetric encryption (like AES) with prefix sub-plaintext string of the corresponding plaintext bit. The procedure of comparing two ciphertexts was actually finding the first different bit (most significant different bit).

2.2   Privacy Preserving Machine Learning

There were two groups of researchers ([3,18]) putted forward the notion of privacy preserving data mining (PPDM) in the same year of 2000, after that, a mount of different methods were applied to meet the need in data mining or machine learning. Differential privacy based methods were widely studied and was usually applied to public data training, which could prevent personal data from being extracted. Researchers from Google Brain introduced the differential privacy into non-convex objectives deep neural networks with noisy stochastic gradient descent (SGD), and proposed moments accountant to track precise privacy loss in model training [1]. They then proposed another strategy, using an ensemble of teachers trained on disjoint subsets of sensitive data to label the public data [24], so that the non-sensitive knowledge could be transferred to the student model. Reza Shokri and Vitaly Shmatikov presented distributed SGD and designed a system for collaborative deep learning among multiple participants [26]. The participants would firstly train their own model on private data, and then selectively shared model parameters with differential privacy, which brought attractive trade-off between utility and privacy. Meng et al. addressed the problem of privacy-preserving social recommendation under personalized privacy settings with differential privacy [20].

Apart from differential privacy, other frameworks combining several cryptographic primitives were proposed to deal with different private part of machine learning. Homomorphic encryption and secure multi-party computation are the most widely used primitives to build PPDM schemes.

The first fully homomorphic encryption scheme [13] was proposed in 2009. Since then numerous researches have been done in improving the efficiency of HE schemes so that it would be applied in practical. Secure multi-party computation was firstly introduced in 1982 [27], which also suffered limitation in efficiency. Ideally, secure multi-party computation enables jointly computing a function from the private inputs of each party, who would not have to reveal such inputs to others, so that the privacy is preserved. Many progresses have been made in decades, and now SMC and HE have been used to construct various machine learning models. The basic idea of such solutions is replacing the arithmetic operation in models with homomorphic/SMC ones, so that the computation could be executed over encrypted data. In [8], the authors extracted some basic operations in the model computing as building blocks, applying several homomorphic cryptosystems to implement and constructed classifiers over encrypted data, which could be applied to build multiple models. Another group of researchers also presented a privacy preserving ridge regression system combining HE and garbled circuits [22]. CryptoNets [14] was another significant work, which used HE to apply neural networks to encrypted data, which brought high throughput. After that MiniONN [19] was proposed in 2017, which presented a framework to transfer a well-trained model into an obvious version by using several SMC protocols. Payman Mohassel and Yupeng Zhang proposed a two-server model with SMC protocols for linear regression, logistic regression and neural network training, which achieved great efficiency [21].

3   Scheme Description

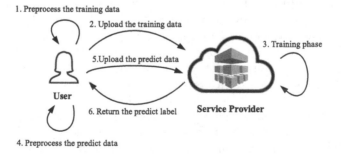

Fig. 1. Dataflow of proposed scheme

3.1   Scheme Overview

Our scheme is quite straightforward – applying any model training procedure directly to the OPE-encrypted data set. Figure 1 shows a general data flow of our scheme. The key component of the scheme is the preprocess procedure in step 1 and 4 from Fig. 1, which contains:

- the metadata of the raw dataset should be erased;
- the labels for classification should be replaced by meaningless identifiers;
- the name of features should be substituted by meaningless strings.
- encrypt every feature with OPE independently (vertical encryption).

Encryption are applied feature by feature independently, which is referenced from the common normalization methods such as min-max normalization and z-score normalization, since the OPE could be treated as another kind of 'normalization'.

As a result, 2 parts of data are protected in this architecture: one is the data from step 1 in Fig. 1, which are some historical data or pre-existing data with tagged labels (for supervised learning); the other is the data in step 4, which could be new data generated recently, and needs to be imported to the trained model for predictions. Therefore the scheme could achieve both privacy preserving training and classification.

3.2   Security Analysis

We define the adversary model first. It is clear, without regard to the transmission failure in network, the only possible leakage in the scheme is the service provider. Therefore, in this paper, we consider the service provider as *Honest but Curious*, which means the service provider would execute the protocol correctly, meanwhile, tries to extract private information from the uploaded data. In the worst case, the service provider may be attacked and comprised, as a result, the service provider would become only *Curious*, with the attacker having complete access to the data and trained model.

Considering the adversary model defined before, the possible leakage points are the transmission procedure and service provider, therefore, the solution is cryptographic level protection. In this case, the minimum level of the processed data is resisting cipher-only attack (COA security) since we protect privacy by preserving data confidentiality. It is true that COA security is a rather weak security model, whereas in this particular situation, the servers in the proposed model are unable to obtain any other information other than ciphertext, the privacy could be preserved by the data confidentiality that COA security provides. According to the formal definition of COA security, the attacker could not retrieve any information of the plaintext from the ciphertext, which could be considered an ideal situation of privacy protection. If the encryption algorithm is COA security, as long as the security parameters remain confidential, neither service provider nor the attacker could retrieve meaningful plaintext from the uploaded data. The encryption procedure also brings native access control to the trained model because the raw data has to be encrypted as the training data did, otherwise the fitting and prediction would make no sense.

Note that even the order preserving encryption is a practical and efficient method in some database, but it is also a risky one in privacy preserving. On one hand, it has been proven that database protected by order preserving encryption is highly possible to be attacked with some auxiliary information [11, 15], so it is important that the released data does not carry any information that may lead to privacy leakage (as described in step 1 and 4). On the other hand, Some particular kinds of data are suggested to avoid using order preserving encryptions. For example, a typical image is a matrix of several pixel points, each point consists of values of three color channel (RGB). The value of each color channel ranges from 0 to 255. For a dataset of images, it is very likely that every possible values of a color channel would appear multiple times. If we deal such data with naive order preserving mapping, the processed data would be very much likely to be themselves, which turns out to be in vain. So, for a dense and bespread feature dataset, it is suggested to avoid using order preserving mapping (at least deterministic order preserving) for privacy preserving purpose.

4   Learning with OPE Ciphertexts

In this section, we give a brief introduction about OPE and discuss the different way to reveal order information.

4.1   Order Preserving Encryption

As the name implies, the order information indicates the comparison relationship in a certain range. The formal definition is given below, for any mapping function $F : D \rightarrow R$, in which D denotes domain and R denotes range, we say F is an order preserving mapping if:

$$\forall x_i, x_j \in D, \; if \; x_i < x_j, \; then \; F(x_i) < F(x_j)$$

For example, a list with 5 values (2, 5, 23, 0, 13), a function that maps these values into (2, 3, 5, 1, 4) is an order preserving mapping. Note that equality relationship is not mentioned in the definition because, for confidentiality concern, a much more secure choice of order preserving function is order preserving encryption, which applies different ways of handling equal elements in different cryptographic algorithms. The equality-handling methods roughly divide into two types: deterministic and non-deterministic. The deterministic algorithms encrypt one plaintext to a certain ciphertext, no matter how many times the same plaintext appears. In such methods, the revealed information contains not only order, but also frequency. The non-deterministic algorithms, on the contrast, encrypt one plaintext to several different ciphertext if the plaintext appears multiple times, which makes such algorithms one-to-many mapping functions. Note that since the comparison relationship between two unequal values still holds, all possible ciphertext of one plaintext e.g. $x_i \in (x_i - 1, x_i + 1)$ lie within a limited range e.g. $(F(x_i - 1), F(x_i + 1))$.

4.2   Model Training over OPE Ciphertexts

We discuss the principle of model training over OPE ciphertexts from two perspectives.

Information Preserved by OPE. In information theory, information entropy is a concept describing the average rate at which information is produced by a stochastic source of data. For a dataset D with $|Y|$ different classes, the information entropy of is computed as:

$$Ent(D) = -\sum_{k=1}^{|Y|} p_k \log_2 p_k$$

in which p_k represents the frequency of the k_{th} sample. In our vertical encryption, it is clear that $Ent(D)$ remains invariant after encrypted by deterministic OPE. When it comes to non-deterministic OPE, randomness would be involved. Ideally, the distribution of non-deterministic OPE ciphertexts is closed to uniform, which leads to that every ciphertexts would only appear once, making the dataset barely contains information entropy. This is a similar situation to dealing with continuously distributed values. In such cases, the common solution is to discretize the continuous feature values using bi-partition technique, which would get an approximate result of the plaintext result, making the entropy of ciphertexts closer to the original one.

Model Training over Data. From a high level perspective, all of the machine learning models can be divided into two categories based on whether they assume the data obeys a specific distribution or not – parametric models and non-parametric models.

Parametric models, such as linear regression, logistic regress, would assume all the data come from a specific distribution first, then search the whole parametric space of the distribution to find the best match for the given training set. For the OPE ciphertext data, the marginal distribution of ciphertext could be regarded as asymmetric strech or compress of the original marginal distribution, which means the best position in parametric space would be altered. However, the universal distribution would remain mostly invariant, which means the same model may still be functional over ciphertexts.

Non-parametric models, such as decision tree, naive bayes, k-nearest neighbor and so on, would try to find a best match in the training data, since they do not assume the distribution of data, they may sometimes obtain generalization ability to the data that never appear in training set. The non-parametric models works with only one requirement: the data could be ranked, which perfectly fits the property of OPE. Theoretically, the model training could work on ciphertexts as well as on plaintexts.

5   Evaluation

In this section, we firstly describe some configuration of our experiments, including the OPE we choose to evaluate, the datasets and machine learning models we tested, and the special criteria we use to evaluate the performance of different models over specific OPE algorithm. Then we give comprehensive demonstration and analysis to results of our experimental results.

5.1   Experiments Configuration

OPE Algorithms. We give brief introductions to the OPE algorithms evaluated in our experiment, for more details about each algorithm, please refer to the cited paper.

OPEA [17] is a non-deterministic OPE based on cipher space division. OPEA would firstly discretize the integer s into sequential-partitions randomly, in which the interval between two adjacent partitions are non-empty. Then for a specific integer plaintext value b, it would be encrypted to a random integer in partition $[L_b, U_b]$, where the L_b and U_b denote the lower bound and upper bound of the b_{th} partition. Therefore, OPEA is an one-to-many mapping encryption (Fig. 2).

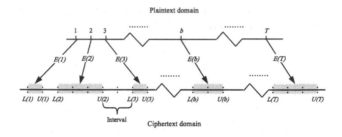

Fig. 2. The one-to-many mapping in OPEA

Hypergeometric OPE [5] is also a cipher space division-based OPE. Different with OPEA, it uses a pseudo random function to divide the ciphertext space according to hypergeometric distribution, and mapping the same plaintext to one ciphertext. The authors notice that an order preserving function f from $[M]$ to $[N]$ corresponds to a unique M-out-of-N random sequence without repetition (the right-hand of 1), which indicates that the generation of an OPF could be considered as an experiment of x success (random draws for which the object drawn has a specified feature) in y draws, without replacement, from a finite population of size M contains exactly N objects with such feature (Hypergeometric distribution). The equality of both probabilities means the generation of an OPE could be accomplished by recursively calling a pseudo Hypergeometric sample algorithm with secret key. And this is exactly how the Hypergeometric OPE scheme was constructed. For more details about Hypergeometric OPE, please refer to [5].

$$Pr[f(x) \leqq y < f(x+1) : f \leftarrow OPF_{[M],[N]}] = \frac{\binom{y}{x}\binom{N-y}{M-x}}{\binom{N}{M}} \qquad (1)$$

mOPE [25] is a sort tree-based OPE which leaks no more information than order. In the original scheme, the encryption procedure is designed with 2 parts: one is building a binary sort tree upon the plaintexts, and tagging each left branch with "0", right branch with "1", then generates encode for every node by concating all bits on the path from the root to the current location in the tree, padding it with postfix "1...0" to fixed length. The other part is generating semantically secure ciphertext using common symmetric encryption scheme. As shown in Fig. 3, by transforming the fixed length binary codes into decimal form, the numbers preserve the order information of all plaintext, such that the user could request range query using ordered encode and gets the semantically secure ciphertexts. In our scenario, the symmetric encryption could be omitted, and we also do not consider the situation that the mOPE tree needs to be balanced. We simply use all existed plaintexts to build the mOPE tree and then partitioning the training and testing sets.

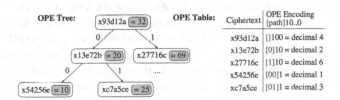

Fig. 3. Overview of mOPE

We also involve AES algorithm as a comparison, and to avoid decimal overflow, we reduce the length of AES ciphertexts by module 2^{16}. As for the parameter settings for OPE, OPEA use random number generator ranges from 0 to 999, ciphertext space of Hypergeometric OPE is limited in $(0, 2^{31} - 1)$, mOPE does not require parameter setting.

Datasets and Models. We deploy 2 groups of experiments to evaluate the performance of the mentioned OPEs fitting in the proposed model, using several datasets for different purposes. The first one is the Wisconsin Diagnostic Breast Cancer dataset (WDBC) from UCI Machine Learning Repository [10], which is used to test the compatibility of different machine learning models over the encrypted data. The other group with randomly generated datasets are used to assess the impact of some extreme cases, in which the expecting learning accuracy is not significantly better than random guess. We limit the upper bound of the learning accuracy by change the number of the classes, which ranges from 2 to 7 (corresponding to D2–D7). Both the features and labels are generated randomly. The details about these datasets are listed in Table 1. All the datasets are splitted by 75% & 25% as training set and testing set respectively. The data could be retrieved on https://github.com/Tomfortemp/tested-data.

Table 1. Information of the datasets

Group	Data name	Records	Features	Classes
WDBC	D1	569	30	2
Randomly synthetic	D2–7	2000	100	2–7

We also consider some generally-used machine learning models including: linear regression, logistic regression, k-nearest neighbor, support vector machine, naive bayes, decision tree, random forest and gradient boost decision tree. All the models are implemented by using the scikit-learn library with all parameters set as default.

Special Criteria. Most previous work consider the training accuracy as crucial and only evaluation indicator. The experiments were usually tested over some widely applied dataset, achieving highly learning accuracy for most models. However, for some datasets resulting in lower learning accuracy, accuracy might be a misguidance. Some models may obtain the frequency distribution as a minimum margin of learning accuracy, even with cross-validation, the new coming data may still cause the plaintexts-trained model and the ciphertexts-trained model to produce quite another answers since they are different in inner logic, making it less meaningless in accuracy value as well as less convincing in learnability. Therefore, we propose Match Rate (MR) to evaluate the fidelity of the ciphertext-trained model, which is defined as the proportion of records on which the plaintext-trained model and the ciphertext-trained model produce the same prediction in a testing set.

5.2 Demonstration and Analysis

The OPE algorithms we choose to evaluate preserve some iconic properties of typical OPE ciphertexts. Firstly, all of three algorithms reveal the arithmetic order information directly on integer field, which is friendly to the current machine learning models. The learning algorithms could execute on the ciphertexts without any changes, which is quite different from other cryptography-based solutions. Secondly, the distribution properties of three OPE ciphertexts vary from each other. Hypergeometric OPE maps the plaintexts into a larger ciphertext space, acting like a random order preserving function, with the frequency information still remains. OPEA ciphertexts look like a uniform distribution on ciphertext space, with almost no duplicated records. mOPE ciphertexts are more 'tighter' compared with others, with the frequency information preserves as well.

Group 1. In the first group of experiments we take a quick glance over the proposed model, which is shown in Fig. 4 and Table 2. Compared with plaintexts-trained model, the ciphertext-trained models perfectly preserve the learning accuracy no matter which OPE is applied. It is also showed in the result that the fidelity level of model remains pretty high in all models.

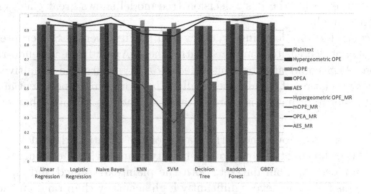

Fig. 4. Experiment on group 1

Table 2. Results of WDBC dataset

Models	Raw accuracy	Hypergeometric		mOPE		OPEA		AES	
		Acc	MR	Acc	MR	Acc	MR	Acc	MR
Linear regression	0.94	0.94	0.98	0.96	0.94	0.94	0.98	0.60	0.63
Logistic regression	0.923	0.959	0.940	0.947	0.929	0.929	0.935	0.586	0.615
Naive bayes	0.929	0.941	0.988	0.947	0.947	0.941	0.988	0.592	0.615
KNN	0.929	0.917	0.881	0.970	0.923	0.923	0.876	0.527	0.526
SVM	0.893	0.911	0.863	0.953	0.917	0.911	0.862	0.361	0.266
Decision tree	0.929	0.929	0.976	0.929	0.988	0.929	0.976	0.550	0.562
GBDT	0.947	0.947	1.0	0.947	1.0	0.953	0.94	0.604	0.597

Non-Tree-Based Models. For the non-tree-based models tested in this paper (including logistic regression, knn, naive bayes, and svm), even though different models achieve different accuracy, the ciphertext-trained models still have similar performance with the plaintexts-trained models. The great performance in high MR and low accuracy difference shows that, these models are able to produce highly similar learning results relying on only the information that OPE algorithms provide. The causes of such performance might due to that these models concern the changing properties of data rather than precise data. It may also be connected with the impact from randomness introduced by OPEA to the generalization ability of models. The match rate of KNN and SVM are slightly lower than others, which may indicates that OPE encryption may influence the decision making of both models. We will take a closer look in the experiments of Group 2.

Tree-Based Models and Boosting. As is well-known, tree-based models are easily get overfitting, which is also considered as unstable models – with little changes on data comes great changes over the trained models. The tree-based models we evaluated, even for the basic decision tree model shows great effect on both accuracy and fidelity.

As a control group, learning accuracy and fidelity over AES-encrypted data show significant decreasing compared with others. Apart from a pseudo-random projection, AES could also be considered as a cryptographic primitive which leaks only the relation of equality vertically. Therefore, this experiment also indicates that order information is more suitable in machine learning than equality.

Group 2. Figure 5 shows the performance of the mentioned models over our synthetic data, showing the how models' fidelity change with the accuracy declining. With uniform random dataset, both the plaintext-trained and ciphertext-trained models fail to achieve significantly high accuracy than random choosing.

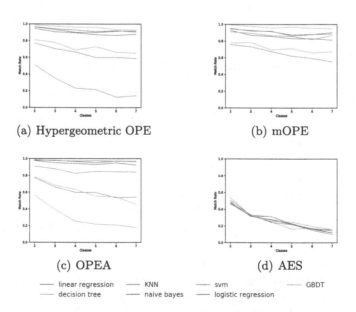

Fig. 5. MR curves on experiments of the second group

We repeated the training for several times and concluded that the average accuracy of every model were approximately close to $1/2, 1/3...1/7$. There are mainly 2 possible reasons: for almost uncorrelated datasets, the models could at least learn the frequency distribution to keep the accuracy above prescribed minimum; even in extremely low accuracy situations, the OPE could still keep the reliability of the plaintexts-trained models.

According to the trend of MR curves, the reliability and fidelity over OPE-processed data depend on different models and different OPE algorithms. As analyzed before, the tree-based models show extremely volatile, because decision tree model is easy to get overfitting, which explains its poor effect over OPEA ciphertexts. The reason why the accuracy difference stay low in both models due to the prescribed minimum learning accuracy, so, for multi-class problems, the decision tree are not good choice to perform privacy preserving machine learning over OPEA encrypted data. With weaker classifiers assembled, boosting can improve such performance to a certain extent. The former stated non-tree-based models remain stable, MR tend to flatten out with the increasing of classes. Logistic regression and linear regression perform well over every OPE algorithms, which show great compatibility to the machine learning over OPE encrypted data. KNN and SVM are both models that make decisions based on distance. Take euclidean distance as example, the process of OPE changes a record position in the whole feature space, however, since the order information is preserved, the relative position between each record is roughly preserved, which makes such models could obtain similar result over OPE ciphertexts. For tree-based models, the fluctuations in MR should due to the structural change of trees and overfitting by the OPE encryption. Therefore, the aggregation and boosting could make some improvement since they increase the stability and generalization ability of models. On one hand the experiments show that boosting brings better performance to simple tree models, it also indicates that the boosting models are more suitable to fit encrypted data on the other hand.

The performance of various models is usually affected by the datasets. So, for datasets that most machine learning models could achieve high accuracy, it would obtain highly reliable training result no matter what model was chosen to train over encrypted data. For other datasets, if the various models perform closely in accuracy, one should also take the reliability into consideration when deciding which model to choose. Even if the tree-based models show slightly advance in accuracy, they also tend to produce unreliable results.

5.3 Efficiency

The proposed method is quite different from the most popular homomorphic-based or secure multi-party computation based solutions. Instead of changing the construction of machine learning models to adapt the properties of homomorphic ciphertext, we choose to reveal the important information that contained in the data itself confidentially, so that the models could learn similarly to the plaintexts-trained models. The proposed method treat all of the applied models as black boxes, therefore it does not involve interactive load like homomorphic-based or SMC-based solutions. Theoretically, the extra load of the proposed model comes from 2 aspects: one is the time consumed by the encryption procedure of the training datasets, the other is the extra model training time over encrypted datasets compared with that over the raw datasets.

Table 3. Time consumption of encryption

Procedure	AES	Hypergeometric	OPEA	mOPE
KeyGeneration	–	–	$O(n)$	$O(nlogn)$
Encryption	$O(1)$	$O(logM)$	$O(1)$	$O(logn)$

Encryption Load. Compared to common symmetric encryption algorithms like AES, it is fairly to say that most order-preserving encryption schemes are not so efficient. Because in most cases, the OPE considers the whole state of a dataset in encryption procedure, which is more complicate than common symmetric encryption. In our model, the datasets is encrypted with OPE vertically, which means for each feature, OPE is applied to all of values of n instances. For Hypergeometric OPE, once the ciphertext space is determined, the encryption algorithm would recursively call a pseudo-Hypergeometric sample function to run a binary search over the ciphertext space, so the average time complexity is $O(logM)$ (M is the size of ciphertext space). For OPEA, the KeyGeneration procedure consumes a linear time complexity with the size of ciphertext space M. The encryption after the KeyGeneration is quite efficient since such procedure is an indexed sequential search, which is a constant level of time complexity. For mOPE, the encryption procedure relies on the balancing binary search tree built upon all n values in a feature, which consumes a $O(nlogn)$ time complexity. After the tree has been built, the encryption of each plaintext is a binary search over the built tree which consumes $O(logn)$. The time-consuming results are listed in Table 3, with both theoretical analysis and empirical results. We also give the AES time-consuming data as a comparison. Note that even the time consuming of the encryption scheme is significant, we still consider it worthwhile since it brings enhancements to the security level of the outsourced data. Furthermore, the large batch of encryption over the dataset is actually an one-time-consumption. When the model was fully trained, the data in actual use are much less. Table 3 shows the encryption average time load for encrypting 1000 plaintext. Hypergeometric OPE and AES use a random string as secret key, so the key generation procedure for these 2 schemes are omitted. OPEA needs to pre-divide the whole ciphertext space by generating a series of random numbers as secret key. mOPE needs to rank all the plaintext into a binary balanced sort tree as secret key. So key generation procedure for these 2 schemes are considered.

Training Load. The other load is caused by the ciphertext expansion invoked by OPE encryption. In fact, in our experiments, only OPEA and Hypergeometric OPE would bring ciphertext expansion for sure. As for mOPE, there is no clear relationship between the size of original data and the length of the final encode.

Table 4. Expansion of ciphertext

OPE	D1	D7–12
Raw data	124 KB	585 KB
Hypergeometric OPE	219 KB	1.6 MB
mOPE	115 KB	719 KB
OPEA	190 KB	1.3 MB
AES	139 KB	1.2 MB

Table 4 shows the expansion of the datasets in our experiments. Note that for data length consideration, we compress the ciphertexts of AES encryption by modulo each one with 2^{16} to avoid float overflow. Mostly, how much the ciphertext expands mainly depends on the possible range of plaintext value in linear dependency, which is obviously superior that the exponential expansion of homomorphic encryption. Besides, in training phase, usually the data would be preprocessed before fitting into the models. In other word, the extra load in training is negligible. Without the extra interactive load, the proposed method achieves much better efficiency.

6 Conclusion

This work applies a well-known functional encryption to machine learning applications. In our simple scheme, the data privacy could be protected by OPE under only COA security notion in cryptography. As a result, once the data is released after encrypted by OPE, the training procedure is completely non-interactive and supports private prediction based on the natural 'access control' of an encryption algorithm, which means. Furthermore, in evaluation, we proposed an extra criteria to evaluate whether a certain data processing scheme fits the privacy preserving machine learning framework or not, which has potential to be applied to more encryption schemes. Compared with the evaluation methods applied before, our proposal is more rigorous and pays more attention to the fidelity of the ciphertext-trained model, which is a critical factor of producing reliable predictions. Three order preserving encryption schemes were applied to the model, plentiful of experiments suggest that, with only the information OPE reveals, most machine learning models are able to obtain knowledge as much as those from raw data. We also evaluated the efficiency of our scheme. Experiments show that the time consumption of our scheme mainly increases in the initial encryption, while bringing negligible overhead in model training and using, which distinguishes our schemes from most cryptography-based schemes. We believe this scheme could be a new direction of privacy protection in machine learning. This work is also a potential solution to the open issues proposed in this paper.

Acknowledgment. This paper is supported by the National Key Research & Develop Program of China through project 2017YFB1400700, 2017YFB0802500, 2018YFB1004401 and 2016YFB1000702, by the Natural Science Foundation of China through project 61772538, 61672083, 61370190, 61532021, 61472429, 61772536, 61772537, 61732006, 61702522, 91646203 and 61402029, by the National Cryptography Development Fund through project MMJJ20170106.

References

1. Abadi, M., et al.: Deep learning with differential privacy. In: Weippl, E.R., Katzenbeisser, S., Kruegel, C., Myers, A.C., Halevi, S. (eds.) Proceedings of the 2016 ACM SIGSAC Conference on Computer and Communications Security, Vienna, Austria, 24–28 October 2016, pp. 308–318. ACM (2016). https://doi.org/10.1145/2976749.2978318, http://doi.acm.org/10.1145/2976749.2978318
2. Agrawal, R., Kiernan, J., Srikant, R., Xu, Y.: Order-preserving encryption for numeric data. In: Weikum, G., König, A.C., Deßloch, S. (eds.) Proceedings of the ACM SIGMOD International Conference on Management of Data, Paris, France, 13–18 June 2004, pp. 563–574. ACM (2004). https://doi.org/10.1145/1007568.1007632, http://doi.acm.org/10.1145/1007568.1007632
3. Agrawal, R., Srikant, R.: Privacy-preserving data mining. In: Chen, W., Naughton, J.F., Bernstein, P.A. (eds.) Proceedings of the 2000 ACM SIGMOD International Conference on Management of Data, 16–18 May 2000, Dallas, Texas, USA, pp. 439–450. ACM (2000). https://doi.org/10.1145/342009.335438, http://doi.acm.org/10.1145/342009.335438
4. Bell, R.M., Koren, Y.: Lessons from the Netflix prize challenge. SIGKDD Explor. **9**(2), 75–79 (2007). https://doi.org/10.1145/1345448.1345465. http://doi.acm.org/10.1145/1345448.1345465
5. Boldyreva, A., Chenette, N., Lee, Y., O'Neill, A.: Order-preserving symmetric encryption. In: Joux, A. (ed.) EUROCRYPT 2009. LNCS, vol. 5479, pp. 224–241. Springer, Heidelberg (2009). https://doi.org/10.1007/978-3-642-01001-9_13
6. Boldyreva, A., Chenette, N., O'Neill, A.: Order-preserving encryption revisited: improved security analysis and alternative solutions. In: Rogaway, P. (ed.) CRYPTO 2011. LNCS, vol. 6841, pp. 578–595. Springer, Heidelberg (2011). https://doi.org/10.1007/978-3-642-22792-9_33
7. Boneh, D., Lewi, K., Raykova, M., Sahai, A., Zhandry, M., Zimmerman, J.: Semantically secure order-revealing encryption: multi-input functional encryption without obfuscation. In: Oswald, E., Fischlin, M. (eds.) EUROCRYPT 2015. LNCS, vol. 9057, pp. 563–594. Springer, Heidelberg (2015). https://doi.org/10.1007/978-3-662-46803-6_19
8. Bost, R., Popa, R.A., Tu, S., Goldwasser, S.: Machine learning classification over encrypted data. In: 22nd Annual Network and Distributed System Security Symposium, NDSS 2015, San Diego, California, USA, 8–11 February 2015. The Internet Society (2015). https://www.ndss-symposium.org/ndss2015/machine-learning-classification-over-encrypted-data

9. Chenette, N., Lewi, K., Weis, S.A., Wu, D.J.: Practical order-revealing encryption with limited leakage. In: Peyrin, T. (ed.) FSE 2016. LNCS, vol. 9783, pp. 474–493. Springer, Heidelberg (2016). https://doi.org/10.1007/978-3-662-52993-5_24

10. Dua, D., Graff, C.: UCI machine learning repository (2017). http://archive.ics.uci.edu/ml

11. Durak, F.B., DuBuisson, T.M., Cash, D.: What else is revealed by order-revealing encryption? In: Weippl, E.R., Katzenbeisser, S., Kruegel, C., Myers, A.C., Halevi, S. (eds.) Proceedings of the 2016 ACM SIGSAC Conference on Computer and Communications Security, Vienna, Austria, 24–28 October 2016, pp. 1155–1166. ACM (2016). https://doi.org/10.1145/2976749.2978379

12. Dwork, C.: Differential privacy: a survey of results. In: Agrawal, M., Du, D., Duan, Z., Li, A. (eds.) TAMC 2008. LNCS, vol. 4978, pp. 1–19. Springer, Heidelberg (2008). https://doi.org/10.1007/978-3-540-79228-4_1

13. Gentry, C.: Fully homomorphic encryption using ideal lattices. In: Mitzenmacher, M. (ed.) Proceedings of the 41st Annual ACM Symposium on Theory of Computing, STOC 2009, Bethesda, MD, USA, 31 May–2 June, 2009, pp. 169–178. ACM (2009). https://doi.org/10.1145/1536414.1536440, http://doi.acm.org/10.1145/1536414.1536440

14. Gilad-Bachrach, R., Dowlin, N., Laine, K., Lauter, K.E., Naehrig, M., Wernsing, J.: CryptoNets: applying neural networks to encrypted data with high throughput and accuracy. In: Balcan, M., Weinberger, K.Q. (eds.) Proceedings of the 33nd International Conference on Machine Learning, ICML 2016, New York City, NY, USA, 19–24 June 2016. JMLR Workshop and Conference Proceedings, vol. 48, pp. 201–210 (2016). JMLR.org, http://jmlr.org/proceedings/papers/v48/gilad-bachrach16.html

15. Grubbs, P., Sekniqi, K., Bindschaedler, V., Naveed, M., Ristenpart, T.: Leakage-abuse attacks against order-revealing encryption. In: 2017 IEEE Symposium on Security and Privacy, SP 2017, San Jose, CA, USA, 22–26 May 2017, pp. 655–672. IEEE Computer Society (2017). https://doi.org/10.1109/SP.2017.44

16. Kerschbaum, F.: Frequency-hiding order-preserving encryption. In: Ray, I., Li, N., Kruegel, C. (eds.) Proceedings of the 22nd ACM SIGSAC Conference on Computer and Communications Security, Denver, CO, USA, 12–16 October 2015, pp. 656–667. ACM (2015). https://doi.org/10.1145/2810103.2813629

17. Li, Y.-N., Wu, Q., Tang, W., Qin, B., Wang, Q., Miao, M.: Outsourcing encrypted excel files. In: Liu, J.K., Samarati, P. (eds.) ISPEC 2017. LNCS, vol. 10701, pp. 506–524. Springer, Cham (2017). https://doi.org/10.1007/978-3-319-72359-4_30

18. Lindell, Y., Pinkas, B.: Privacy preserving data mining. In: Bellare, M. (ed.) CRYPTO 2000. LNCS, vol. 1880, pp. 36–54. Springer, Heidelberg (2000). https://doi.org/10.1007/3-540-44598-6_3

19. Liu, J., Juuti, M., Lu, Y., Asokan, N.: Oblivious neural network predictions via MiniONN transformations. In: Thuraisingham, B.M., Evans, D., Malkin, T., Xu, D. (eds.) Proceedings of the 2017 ACM SIGSAC Conference on Computer and Communications Security, CCS 2017, Dallas, TX, USA, 30 October–03 November 2017, pp. 619–631. ACM (2017). https://doi.org/10.1145/3133956.3134056

20. Meng, X., et al.: Personalized privacy-preserving social recommendation. In: McIlraith, S.A., Weinberger, K.Q. (eds.) Proceedings of the Thirty-Second AAAI Conference on Artificial Intelligence, New Orleans, Louisiana, USA, 2–7 February 2018. AAAI Press (2018). https://www.aaai.org/ocs/index.php/AAAI/AAAI18/paper/view/16768

21. Mohassel, P., Zhang, Y.: SecureML: a system for scalable privacy-preserving machine learning. In: 2017 IEEE Symposium on Security and Privacy, SP 2017, San Jose, CA, USA, 22–26 May 2017, pp. 19–38. IEEE Computer Society (2017). https://doi.org/10.1109/SP.2017.12

22. Nikolaenko, V., Weinsberg, U., Ioannidis, S., Joye, M., Boneh, D., Taft, N.: Privacy-preserving ridge regression on hundreds of millions of records. In: 2013 IEEE Symposium on Security and Privacy, SP 2013, Berkeley, CA, USA, 19–22 May 2013, pp. 334–348. IEEE Computer Society (2013). https://doi.org/10.1109/SP.2013.30

23. Pandey, O., Rouselakis, Y.: Property preserving symmetric encryption. In: Pointcheval, D., Johansson, T. (eds.) EUROCRYPT 2012. LNCS, vol. 7237, pp. 375–391. Springer, Heidelberg (2012). https://doi.org/10.1007/978-3-642-29011-4_23

24. Papernot, N., Abadi, M., Erlingsson, Ú., Goodfellow, I.J., Talwar, K.: Semi-supervised knowledge transfer for deep learning from private training data. CoRR abs/1610.05755 (2016). http://arxiv.org/abs/1610.05755

25. Popa, R.A., Li, F.H., Zeldovich, N.: An ideal-security protocol for order-preserving encoding. In: 2013 IEEE Symposium on Security and Privacy, SP 2013, Berkeley, CA, USA, 19–22 May 2013, pp. 463–477. IEEE Computer Society (2013). https://doi.org/10.1109/SP.2013.38

26. Shokri, R., Shmatikov, V.: Privacy-preserving deep learning. In: Ray, I., Li, N., Kruegel, C. (eds.) Proceedings of the 22nd ACM SIGSAC Conference on Computer and Communications Security, Denver, CO, USA, 12–16 October 2015, pp. 1310–1321. ACM (2015). https://doi.org/10.1145/2810103.2813687, http://doi.acm.org/10.1145/2810103.2813687

27. Yao, A.C.: Protocols for secure computations (extended abstract). In: 23rd Annual Symposium on Foundations of Computer Science, Chicago, Illinois, USA, 3–5 November 1982, pp. 160–164. IEEE Computer Society (1982). https://doi.org/10.1109/SFCS.1982.38

Blockchain Based Owner-Controlled Secure Software Updates for Resource-Constrained IoT

Gabriel Jerome Solomon[1], Peng Zhang[2], Yuhong Liu[1(✉)], and Rachael Brooks[1]

[1] Santa Clara University, Santa Clara, CA 95053, USA
{gsolomon,yliu,rbrooks}@scu.edu
[2] College of Electronic and Information Engineering, Shenzhen University,
Shenzhen 518060, China
zhangp@szu.edu.cn
https://www.scu.edu, https://www.szu.edu.cn

Abstract. With a large number of connected Internet of Things (IoT) devices deployed across the world, they have become popular targets of malicious attacks raising great security challenges. Many manufacturers are making great efforts to keep the software on these devices up-to-date to protect the security of these IoT devices. However, the software update process itself may also be manipulated by attackers, such as roll-back attack and replay message attack. Cryptography based solutions may effectively defend against such attacks. However, as many IoT devices are resource-constrained devices, they cannot afford the high resource requirements and heavy computation overhead caused by Cryptography based security solutions.

To protect secure software update for resource-constrained IoT devices, in this paper, we propose a security design and protocol for owner-controlled software updates for IoT devices through blockchain. The introduction of blockchain technology cannot only effectively secure the distribution of software updates for multiple manufacturers with high-availability, improved security, and reduced cost; but also provide a payment platform to facilitate financial transactions between IoT manufacturers and owners.

Keywords: Blockchain · Internet of Things · Software updates · Security · Confidentiality · Integrity · Availability

1 Introduction

Every device will soon be connected to the Internet. The Internet of Things (IoT) market is projected to climb to 1.3 billion dollars by 2026 [1]. Business Insider projects that more than 64 billion IoT devices will be installed in 2025 [2], more than 8 times the United Nation's projects of the world's population [3]. The tremendous amount of IoT devices, however, have raised various security risks.

© Springer Nature Switzerland AG 2019
J. K. Liu and X. Huang (Eds.): NSS 2019, LNCS 11928, pp. 371–386, 2019.
https://doi.org/10.1007/978-3-030-36938-5_22

For example, personal information security and confidentiality are now both given and sometimes stripped away from us by the devices we use. Personal and financial information can be leaked from devices. The Mirai attack demonstrates that thousands of IoT devices can be leveraged to perform botnet DDoS attacks and render services inaccessible [4,5].

The most critical component of our devices is the software that runs on them. Nevertheless, the software has access to our information and the ability to govern, send, receive, and control it. Software itself can be insecure [6]. In addition, the configuration settings, parameters, and access control on devices are also set by so-called "firmware" software. All forms of software are updated. Thus, the confidentiality, integrity, and availability of the software update process itself is key to information security.

However, software updates themselves is an important security threat against IoT devices [7]. The software update process can expose IoT devices to intentionally malicious and unintentionally insecure software. Moreover, simply the prevention of software updates (DDoS attacks) or users not updating devices (due to low availability) can create vulnerabilities. Attacks against IoT devices software updates can come in several forms, such as roll-back (or forward) attacks, replay message attacks, malicious node attacks, man-in-the-middle attacks, Sybil attacks, and denial of service (DoS) attacks [8,9].

Manufacturers currently update IoT devices by a client-server model. The client is the IoT device and the server is controlled by the manufacturer and hosts a repository of versions of binary software updates. As the number of devices grows, this model requires increasing resources from the manufacturers. In addition to this, important updates may not be available due to high loads on the server when updates are published by a manufacturer.

More importantly, although cryptography-based solutions can effectively protect the confidentiality and integrity of the software updates, most resource-constrained IoT devices cannot afford the high resource requirements and heavy computation overhead caused by such solutions.

In this work, we propose to address the security of IoT software updates by introducing a blockchain platform. A blockchain-based digital currency named Bitcoin [10] was first introduced by Satoshi Nakamoto in 2008, which relies on blockchain to secure transactions without a centralized trusted third party. The decentralized nodes that participate in the chain validate transactions by confirming a block in a linked-list style of connections that links blocks by using a SHA256 hash [11]. Since there is no trusted third-party, all transactions are announced on a public ledger that can verify the transactions and the order of the transactions to prevent double-spending.

In this paper we design a distribution framework for software updates for resource-constrained IoT devices that provide confidentiality, integrity, and availability.

Our major contributions are summarized as follows:

- We propose a secure owner-controlled software update framework for resource-constrained IoT devices that provides high-availability and improved security. In particular, we propose to store the software update files through cloud servers to ensure high-availability. More importantly, blockchain technologies are introduced to handle manufacturer authentication as well as secure distributions of the key to the software update files. To protect the integrity and confidentiality of the software update files, these files are encrypted and stored at remote cloud servers. The keys to these files are first encrypted by the corresponding IoT owners' public keys and then posted to the blockchain. Furthermore, the inclusion of software versions in the encrypted posts on the blockchain can effectively protect the proposed framework against roll-back/forward attacks.

- The proposed framework is particularly designed to reduce the costs for resource-constrained IoT devices. Specifically, IoT owners are introduced to help manage multiple IoT devices centrally to avoid communication overhead for each IoT devices. More importantly, different from existing studies that directly employ IoT devices as the blockchain nodes, we propose to use third party blockchain network to help the secure distribution of software updates, which can significantly reduce the resource and energy requirements for resource-constrained IoT devices and make the proposed framework practical.
- The proposed framework also supports an integrated and auditable payment solution through blockchain, which ensures trustworthy transactions between manufacturers and IoT device owners.

The rest of the paper is organized as follows: Sect. 2 introduces the state-of-the-art research and the research gap related to software updates. Section 3 discusses the problems and weaknesses of current software update distribution models. Section 4 defines and introduces the proposed solution and cryptosystems incorporated within it. Section 5 is our security analysis including evaluation against common IoT attacks. The paper finishes with a description of notable features, a conclusion, and description of future research.

2 Related Work

In this section, we discuss existing attacks and their relationship to previous research. We then state the pros and cons of several groups of existing studies and how they inspire or relate to our proposed framework.

2.1 Attacks Against IoT Devices

There are various common attacks against IoT devices that can impact software updates or be allowed through malicious software updates. The roll-back attack [12] attempts to downgrade software to an older version. This downgrade would mean a move to insecure older firmware or software that leads to vulnerabilities and other open doors for malicious activities by the attacker. The replay message attack [8] replays a valid message to the IoT device. Repeatedly replaying this valid message can delay resource-constrained IoT devices and drain limited IoT compute resources. The malicious node attack [13] of IoT devices can alter the update or attempt to provide it's own update to another IoT device within the local network. The Sybil attack [14] is about impersonation. Sybil attacks can provide malicious updates as it impersonates the owner or other services for the IoT device. The DoS attacks [15] can be used to leverage many IoT devices as bots to deny services by inundating the services with network traffic. Attacks against IoT devices have been significant and caused a lot of harm. There are also good examples of what can be done when IoT devices are compromised and used to impact other services. The Mirai [5,16] botnet attack globally impacted the internet. Malware [17] on vending machines impacted a university. A 5-year-old OpenSSL Heartbleed security flaw still infects over 200,000 IoT devices running outdated software [18]. The need to keep IoT devices software updated is critical.

2.2 IoT Blockchain Software Update Related Research

With regard to software update and device configuration with blockchain-based research, there have been several research directions that range from management of device configuration settings, firmwire updates, to full software updates.

The authors of [19] present a blockchain-based method for firmware updates that supports a "pull" technique where the IoT device is part of the blockchain nodes and also participates in peer-to-peer delivery. While this work effectively delivers firmware, it does not provide a solution for resource-constrained IoT devices that are not computationally powerful enough to participate in the blockchain network. Zhao, et al. propose a secure and privacy-preserving software update framework [20] that uses blockchain technologies to guarantee proof-of-delivery to IoT devices. Zhao's technique leverages a smart-contract where the manufacturer provides an incentive to the transmission nodes to deliver the software update. Leiba et al. [21] bring forward a blockchain-based network where distribution nodes are incentivized to deliver software updates and receive a payment from the manufacturer for proof-of-delivery. The authors of [22] propose a blockchain solution with lower cost proof-of-work for scheduled block creation for IoT implementation and control of IoT device configurations.

Boudguiga et al. [23] use blockchain to address availability and liveness for IoT software updates. The work brings forth two novel ideas of innocuous nodes that verify payload updates and IoT devices that can cache updates and deliver them to other IoT devices with less connectivity. However, the involvement of IoT devices as the blockchain nodes generates extra overhead for IoT devices and is therefore not suitable for the resource-constrained scenario. In addition to the delivery of the payload software updates, there are other factors to consider like how to account for multiple version of binaries and their storage. The authors of a blockchain-based solution [24] improve on previous research by accounting for multiple versions of binaries and storing of the binaries into the routers closer to the IoT devices. This work does not provide participation incentive for the blockchain nodes nor the ability for payment through smart contract.

On the one hand, these works motivate our usage of smart contracts to provide the financial model payment to the manufacturer's and incentives for payload node participation. We propose the use of Etherium's Solidity based smart contracts as they provide a Turing-complete smart contract solution. On the other hand, however, these studies do not particularly handle the integrity and confidentiality of the software updates, which is one of the novelties of our work.

2.3   Using IoT Devices as Blockchain Nodes

Some existing researches implement blockchain node functions directly on IoT devices for various purposes. Different solutions are proposed to reduce the overhead. For example, Samaniego and Deters [25] propose the virtualization of IoT components to edge computing to conserve power. Their analysis shows improved performance of software configuration information and ability to update devices by offloading this work from the devices. The authors of [26] implement blockchain to secure IoT device operations and data in a smart home scenario. To improve the performance, the computationally heavy proof-of-work has been replaced by a trust-based system. However, the proposed system depends on a secure home network and a computationally fast "home miner" within the framework. IOTA blockchain technology provides a "Tangle" [27] directed acyclic graph (DAG) that presents a robust and secure method for IoT devices to participate in blockchain transactions with a much lower computational proof-of-work than that of most blockchain technologies. Samaniego and Jamsrandor [28] evaluated the performance of hosting blockchain for IoT and demonstrated the improved latency performance in the fog versus the cloud. They concluded blockchain as not being suitable to host on resource-constrained IoT devices.

Although great efforts have been made to reduce the overhead of blockchain, at current stage, it is still not practical to utilize resource-constrained IoT devices as blockchain nodes. Therefore, in this work, we propose to construct the blockchain network through third party computing nodes. Moreover, to protect software update files from being compromised by malicious blockchain nodes, the software update files are encrypted and stored separately at the remote cloud server, and the keys to these files are encrypted by the IoT owner's public key before posting to the blockchain. The details of the proposed framework will be discussed in Sect. 4.

3   Problem Statement

The motivation of this research comes from the large number of IoT devices without any standardized or secure means of updating the software. Also, the current client-server model of updating the software on IoT devices is insufficient for scaling and creates unnecessary cost and burden upon the manufacturer and the IoT devices.

The traditional client-server model of software does not scale as the number of devices grows. The availability deteriorates further when software that is component-based requires components of software coming from multiple manufacturers to be delivered to a single type of IoT device. The untimely or slow updates of a device can lead impatient owners to cancel updates before they are complete. So, high availability is critical to IoT devices security.

This is further complicated by the need for manufacturers to update IoT devices using both "push" and "pull" software update methodologies depending on the economic software licensing models. "push" models are software updates that manufacturers may wish to get on devices at no or low cost to the user. "pull" models are those in which the client is willing to pay for the update.

Whether the update is component-based, pull, or push model, devices with outdated versions of software pose security risks. Besides, the traditional client-server model is prone to a malicious server and other impersonation related attacks and is a single source of failure for the delivery of the update to devices.

While current research attempts to address software updates using blockchain technology, none of the previous models include the owner's involvement in the decision making process and provides support for the software licensing models.

The goal of our proposed framework is to provide confidentiality, integrity, and availability while also giving control to the owner. In particular, the framework design aims to support the "pull" software update technique with incentives for a node's participation in the network. In addition, it should reduce the computational and resource costs for resource-constrained IoT devices.

4 Proposed Solution

We chose to mainly focus on the "pull" economic model. The "push" economic model is a perfunctory functional extension of our design. For example, in the "push" model the smart contract would be between the manufacturer who pays a fee to the blockchain nodes for delivery of the software update. The owner would not be charged a fee.

The use of blockchain allows manufacturers to both collect payment and also provide an incentive to the blockchain network for software update delivery through the smart contract.

Although this is not the focus of this research, our solution is also compatible with other techniques that prevent software piracy [29,30] once it is received by the owners.

In addition to benefiting the users with quick and highly available software updates, our framework handles multiple versions of the software update by caching the binaries to cloud data storage and providing reliable and audit friendly public ledger of device updates through blockchain. The public ledger can be used as an auditing record for both manufacturers and owners of IoT devices.

4.1 Terminology

Table 1 describes the notation we use through this paper. The manufacturer of IoT device d_{il} is indicated by m_i. b_j indicates the software update binary that will ultimately be sent from the manufacturer m_i to the device d_{il}. The header h_i is the "manifest" or "header" portion of the binary b_j that describes its version, size, and other manufacturer or device specification information. The payload delivery nodes p_k make up the nodes of the blockchain. The owner o_l represents that owners computer or mobile device (typically a smart phone) where the human owner monitors and manages her IoT devices.

Table 1. Terminology and definitions

Object	Notation	Definition
Manufacturer	$M = \{m_1, m_2, ..., m_n\}$ where $m_i \in M, i \in Z^+, n \geq 1$	The company, vendor, or business that manufacture and produce the IoT device. The manufacturers range is size from large to small and may or may not be independent of each other
Software update	$B = \{b_1, b_2, ..., b_n\}$ where $b_j \in B, j \in Z^+, n \geq 1$	Software update payload (often a binary file) that is transferred to the device
Header	h_j is part of b_j	First n-bytes of the software update b_j that contains information on the manufacturer, version, and other meta-data related to the software release
Blockchain payload nodes	$P = \{p_1, p_2, ..., p_n\}$ where $p_k \in P, k \in Z^+, n \geq 1$	Payload nodes in the blockchain service update requests and are paid a fee for hosting and serving the payload binary. These nodes detect and verify the software update version. They maintain the block chain public ledger. They are paid a fee for their services
Transaction	T_{x_j} where $j \in Z^+$	Transaction record j in the public ledger of the blockchain specifying a specific software update transaction
Owner	$O = \{o_1, o_2, ..., o_n\}$ where $o_l \in O, l \in Z^+, n \geq 1$	The individual/person who owns and/or manages 1, 2, ..., n IoT devices
IoT device	$D = \{d_{11}, d_{12}, ..., d_{n1}, d_{nm}\}$ where $d_{il} \in D, i \in Z^+, l \in Z^+, n \geq 1, m \geq 1$ with $i \in \{manufacturers\}$ and $l \in \{owners\}$	An IoT device ranging from a smart-light bulb, smart-TV, phone, to an IoT device in a vehicle. The set of devices are explicitly heterogeneous and resource-constrained
Cloud data storage	C	Cloud data storage that holds encrypted binary software update files b_j

4.2 Design

In our framework, these are the primary roles and responsibilities (Fig. 1):

- Manufacturer m_i: Posts new updates to the blockchain and delivers the software update to the cloud data storage.

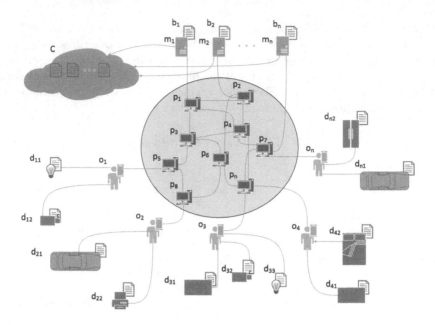

Fig. 1. Framework design

- payload node p_k: Verifies the validity of the update and delivers the update keys to the IOT devices that it services.
- Owner o_l: Approves updates, pay fees to satisfy the smart contract, decrypt keys, and downloads and decrypts software updates.
- Device d_{il} Downloads the software update b_j from it's owner o_l.

Our blockchain and cloud data server are shared across all manufacturers. In other words, the proposed framework is not a per-manufacturer construct. This allows payload nodes to participate in an active economy and service multiple companies and increase resource availability for all. In addition, component-based software updates can occur between manufacturers. A device's software can be updated by multiple manufacturers from the same payload delivery node. Sharing the blockchain also increases its security to several known attacks [31, 32] as the length of the blockchain will grow more rapidly with more nodes participating.

A copy of the blockchain's public ledger is held by each p_k node. A copy of the payload binary b_j is stored in cloud data storage C.

The blockchain model provides a public ledger which can be leveraged by manufacturers to audit software installations across their devices while also maintaining user privacy. In addition, manufactuer and owner concerns over compliance with software licensing agreements can be more easily maintained.

Furthermore, our model seeks to standardize update information by categorizing updates for easy owner review and approval. Updates have specific manifest information for the type of software update {security, bug fixes, features} which allow owners to easily review updates for approval or denial. The owners can be made easily aware of all the software versions they own and that are installed on various IoT devices. For businesses that own IoT devices operating in the "pull" software model, the business can more easily manage software expenses via owner approval.

From the security point of view, our design handles verification of the software version and manufacturer. Moreover, the process by which we handle device and manufacturer public and private keys prevents incorrect or malicious updates. Through this mechanism, we also defend against rollback attacks on IoT devices.

4.3 Key Distribution, Encryption, and Decryption Process

We begin by explaining the structure and tools for our algorithm. We first define our asymmetric and symmetric cryptosystems with key generation, encryption, and decryption functions as follows:

1. $Asymmetric = \{KeyGen_a(\lambda), E_a(\chi, k), D_a(c, k)\}$
2. $Symmetric = \{KeyGen_s(\lambda), E_s(\chi, k), D_s(c, k)\}$
   where λ is the security parameter, χ is the message (the software update b_j or other binary data), c is the encrypted message, and k is a key.

We also define UID as a universal identifier to a unique software version release from a manufacturer. $\{UID = url\|version\}$. url is a valid URI [33] typically of the form https://www.manufacturer.com/* and $version$ follow the unique version numbering scheme of the specific manufacturer.

In particular, the key setup distribution, encryption, and decryption steps are as follows:

Key Setup. The manufacturer m_i runs $KeyGen_a(\lambda)$ to generate a public key PK_{m_i} and private key SK_{m_i} pair. The owner o_l also generates a public key and private key pair. The key pair for m_i is (PK_{m_i}, SK_{m_i}). The key pair for o_l is (PK_{o_l}, SK_{o_l}). The owner and manufacturer are now set up to communicate.

Encryption of the Payload Binary. m_i runs $KeyGen_s(\lambda)$ for the payload binary to generate k_{b_j}. The payload data b_j is then encrypted using $E_s(b_j, k_{b_j})$.

Uploading Software Update to Cloud. The software update $E_s(b_j, k_{b_j})$ is uploaded to the cloud C. The size of the software update is often larger than the block size available in the blockchain. Thus, the encrypted update is sent to a cloud database.

Uploading of Key to Blockchain. m_i creates h_{Eb_j} which is a SHA-3 [34] cryptographic hash for the encrypted binary. To simplify our description, we define and let the software update message be defined as um where $um = \{UID\|h_{Eb_j}\|E_a(k_{b_j}, PK_{o_l})\}$. The um is signed using ECDSA [35]. The signed um is notated as σ. Both the um and σ are uploaded to the blockchain.

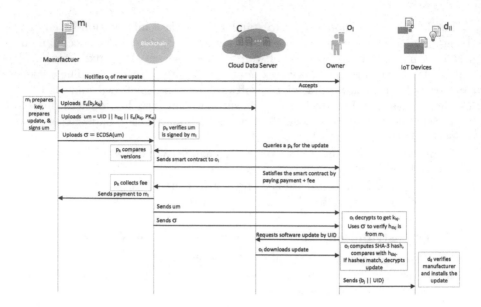

Fig. 2. Software update process

4.4 Contents of the Block

In our block, we store the following itemized contents. These first three items make up the *um*.

- UID - Unique identifier of the update which is used by p_k as an identifier to compare versions
- h_{Eb_j} - Hash of the encrypted binary which is stored on the cloud
- $E_a(k_{b_j}, PK_{o_l})$ - the encrypted key which can be used by o_l to decrypt the binary
- σ - signature of the *um* for delivery to owner o_l

4.5 Distribution and Download of the Update

In this section, we will discuss the distribution of the smart contract, delivery of the software update, and it's final installation on the target IoT device as shown in Fig. 2.

Satisfying the Smart Contract. p_k sends the smart contract to o_l. o_l satisfies the smart contract by paying p_k the cost of the software plus a fee for delivery. p_k takes its fee and sends the payment to m_i.

Setup of Software Update for Delivery to the Owner. p_k sends the signature σ and software update message *um* to o_l. The encrypted software update $E_s(b_j, k_{b_j})$ is downloaded from cloud data store C to the owner o_l.

Downloading the Update to the IoT Device. The owner o_l verifies the *um* is signed by m_i using σ. Then, the owner o_l decrypts the payload binary key k_{b_j} using it's private key SK_{o_l}. $k_{b_j} \leftarrow D_a(E_a(k_{b_j}, PK_{o_l}), SK_{o_l})$. The owner then downloads $E_s(b_j, k_{b_j})$ from the cloud C using the UID. The owner computes the hash h'_1 for $E_s(b_j, k_{b_j})$ and compares it to h_{Eb_j}. If the hashes match then the owner can proceed to decrypt the update. The owner o_l decrypts the payload binary by performing $b_j \leftarrow D_s(E_s(b_j, k_{b_j}), k_{b_j})$.

Installation of the Update. The owner sends the update $b_j \| UID$ to the device d_{il}. The device then verifies the manufacturer matches it's own manufacturer UID by reading the manifest of b_j and it's own on-device manufacturer information. If the manufacturer information matches, then the device installs the software update.

It should be noted that this installation methodology assumes that the owner and devices are part of a secure network thus preventing man-in-the-middle attacks between owner and IoT devices.

5 Security Analysis

In this section, we analyze our framework's security against several common IoT attacks.

5.1 Software Update Integrity and Manufacturer Authentication

The integrity of the software comes from the immutable blockchain ledger, the software update's encryption, and the ECDSA signed SHA-3 cryptographic hash.

The blockchain node p_k verifies that the signature σ is from manufacturer m_i using m_i's public key. p_k then computes a SHA-3 hash h'_2 of $E_s(b_j, k_{b_j})$ and compares h_{Eb_j}. The transaction T_x is then posted to the blockchain and added to the public ledger as a verified immutable software update that is available for download and not been tampered with by attackers.

The blockchain ensures the security and successful delivery of the software update to a device's owner while the encryption of the update itself prevents tampering. The cryptographic hash ensures that the update itself has not been modified during transmission or by a malicious payload node.

The manufacturer is authenticated by blockchain node p_k. Before installing the software update, the blockchain checks all components of the UID (certificate, url, version).

5.2 Defense of Common IoT Attacks

There have been a wide variety of IoT attacks. Our framework is resilient to the common IoT attacks, as shown in Table 2, due to our guarantee of software delivery and the use of blockchain techniques.

In addition, since the owner controls whether the IoT device is updated or not, the owner is able to potentially prevent situations in which the most recent software update makes their device less secure.

Moreover, the owners may prefer to thoroughly test a software update in their environment before using it on all of their IoT devices. For example, a large farming company that deploys a manufacturer's IoT devices for harvesting farmland may choose to not update all of their devices until one of their smaller farms have tested the update in production for a full season. Deploying software without owner control may potentially expose the farming company to unnecessary financial loss if they are in the middle of harvesting season where millions of dollars are at risk. In other words, the security of the software update itself is not the only risk for IoT devices and for their owners. Some companies choose to run older versions of software until a slower or non-critical point in their business cycle. Our solution allows for this flexibility and control.

Table 2. Common IoT attacks

Attack	Description	Security by
Roll-back (or forward) attack	An attack that attempts to roll an IoT devices backward (or forward) to a insecure version of the software	Protection by checking of encrypted manifest version information
Replay Message Attack	If Eve resends a software update to the IoT device, the device could be exposed to attacks	This is prevented through our framework's use of ECDSA
Malicious updates	A manufacturer or payload delivery node joins the blockchain intending to provide malicious updates by either altering a manufacturer's update or providing its own update	Malicious manufacturer can be prevented by the proposed authentication process. By blockchain, malicious nodes would need to be the majority of nodes
Attacks against Software Confidentiality	Malicious blockchain nodes aim to learn the content of software update files	The software update files are encrypted and stored separately at remote cloud servers. In addition, the key to the software files are encrypted by the IoT owners' public keys
Sybil attack	51% attack to provide malicious updates to IoT devices	Due to our incentivization of payload nodes we expect participation, the longer length of the blockchain will make these attacks difficult
DoS (Denial of Service)	Using IoT devices as a botnet to attack other systems	Minimized due to security of updates. Our framework prevents these types of attacks from being likely since IoT software will be updated and less prone to becoming part of a botnet

6   Feature Comparisons

Our framework also has several advantages over other existing frameworks that improve security considerations as seen in Table 3. First, the proposed off-chain storage of the software binary files avoid limited block data size by reducing the size of the data stored on the blockchain. The computational and financial costs with storing data in a block or smart contract is also a factor. For example, Etherium [36] charges gas for data to be stored in a smart contract.

In addition, the low computational complexity of many IoT devices is a challenge for security solutions that require complex mathematical computations to provide the security. With the wide range of IoT device computational power, our solution provides a multi-level approach where the manufacturer m_i, blockchain payload nodes p_k, and the o_l owner handle most of the computational complexity simplifying the number of computations on the IoT devices. Through this method, we are able to provide security for resource-constrained IoT devices.

Our usage of smart contract is to both incentivize the blockchain payload nodes p_k to participate and the owners of IoT devices to pay the manufacturer m_i for the software update itself. This methodology allows the use of a "pull" software delivery model which allows owner control when updates occur and also improves integrity of the software update for IoT devices by the blockchain.

Peer-to-peer file sharing systems such as Bit-Torrent-style storage solutions, InterPlanetary File System (IPFS), or DHT [19], or can be used instead of cloud server as long as high-availability and performance is maintained. Off-chain storage allows for file sizes large enough to store software updates while on-chain solutions do not. Even if the software update is small in size and can fit on-chain, since it is part of the block chain the data also be unnecessarily duplicated at every blockchain node.

Table 3. Research comparison

Framework	Integrity of software update	On-chain or off-chain availability*	IoT computational complexity	Smart contract*	Owner-controlled
Boudguiga et al. [23]	Yes	On-chain	High	No	No
Lee et al. [19]	Yes	On-chain	High	No	No
Leiba et al. [21]	Yes	Off-chain	High	Yes	No
Yohan et al. [24]	Yes	Off-chain	Low	No	No
Zhao et al. [20]	Yes	On-chain	Low	Yes	No
Proposed framework	Yes	Off-chain	Low	Yes	Yes

*Smart Contracts that are used to incentivize payload nodes and/or provide payment to a manufacturer.

7   Conclusion and Future Work

In this paper, our blockchain-based solution secures the software updates for resource-constrained IoT devices. Our framework leverages the high availability of the cloud in concert with the high security and immutability of blockchain based transactions to provide both confidentiality, integrity, and availability for IoT software updates. We introduced owner approval of updates and a smart contract based system that allows owners to pay for and control updates. Our system also has the advantage of providing an audit-able ledger of software updates for both the owner and the manufacturer. In addition, our framework is device agnostic.

Our next steps include the implementation of generalized smart contracts for both push and pull methodologies. We intend to examine the potential parallelism of the framework. We also have an interest in investigating replacement and caching strategies for expiring updates and how that can interface with an immutable blockchain framework. Another related future direction of this research is investigation and prevention of common undesired side effects of software updates such as data corruption or other factors that could tamper with the integrity of the device's operation itself.

Acknowledgment. This work was supported by the National Natural Science Foundation of China (61702342) and the Science and Technology Innovation Projects of Shenzhen, China (JCYJ20170302151321095).

References

1. Global internet of things (IoT) market size and forecast to 2026, June 2019
2. Newman. IoT report: how internet of things technology growth is reaching mainstream companies and consumers, January 2019
3. United Nations. World population prospects 2019 data booklet, June 2019
4. Kolias, C., Kambourakis, G., Stavrou, A., Voas, J.: DDoS in the IoT: mirai and other botnets. Computer **50**(7), 80–84 (2017)
5. Newman. What we know about Friday's massive east coast internet outage, October 2016
6. McGraw, G.: Software security. IEEE Secur. Priv. **2**(2), 80–83 (2004)
7. Ronen, E., Shamir, A., Weingarten, A.-O., O'Flynn, C.: IoT goes nuclear: creating a ZigBee chain reaction. In: 2017 IEEE Symposium on Security and Privacy (SP), pp. 195–212. IEEE (2017)
8. Nawir, M., Amir, A., Yaakob, N., Lynn, O.B.: Internet of things (IoT): taxonomy of security attacks. In: 2016 3rd International Conference on Electronic Design (ICED), pp. 321–326. IEEE (2016)
9. Zhang, C., Green, R.: Communication security in internet of thing: preventive measure and avoid DDoS attack over IoT network. In: Proceedings of the 18th Symposium on Communications & Networking, pp. 8–15. Society for Computer Simulation International (2015)
10. Nakamoto, S., et al.: Bitcoin: a peer-to-peer electronic cash system (2008)
11. Bider, D., Baushke, M.: SHA-2 data integrity verification for the secure shell (SSH) transport layer protocol. Technical report (2012)

12. Krejčí, R., Hujňák, O., Švepeš, M.: Security survey of the IoT wireless protocols. In: 2017 25th Telecommunication Forum (TELFOR), pp. 1–4. IEEE (2017)
13. Pongle, P., Chavan, G.: A survey: attacks on RPL and 6LoWPAN in IoT. In: 2015 International Conference on Pervasive Computing (ICPC), pp. 1–6. IEEE (2015)
14. Zhang, K., Liang, X., Rongxing, L., Shen, X.: Sybil attacks and their defenses in the internet of things. IEEE Internet Things J. 1(5), 372–383 (2014)
15. Alsaadi, E., Tubaishat, A.: Internet of things: features, challenges, and vulnerabilities. Int. J. Adv. Comput. Sci. Inf. Technol. 4(1), 1–13 (2015)
16. Newman, L.H.: The botnet that broke the internet isn't going away. Wired, December 2016
17. Smith. University attacked by its own vending machines, smart light bulbs & 5,000 IoT devices, 12 February 2017
18. Smith. Heartbleed still affects 200,000 devices: Shodan, 12 February 2017
19. Lee, B., Lee, J.-H.: Blockchain-based secure firmware update for embedded devices in an internet of things environment. J. Supercomput. 73(3), 1152–1167 (2017)
20. Zhao, Y., Liu, Y., Yu, Y., Li, Y.: Blockchain based privacy-preserving software updates with proof-of-delivery for internet of things. arXiv preprint arXiv:1902.03712 (2019)
21. Leiba, O., Yitzchak, Y., Bitton, R., Nadler, A., Shabtai, A.: Incentivized delivery network of IoT software updates based on trustless proof-of-distribution. In: 2018 IEEE European Symposium on Security and Privacy Workshops (EuroS&PW), pp. 29–39. IEEE (2018)
22. Huh, S., Cho, S., Kim, S.: Managing IoT devices using blockchain platform. In: 2017 19th International Conference on Advanced Communication Technology (ICACT), pp. 464–467. IEEE (2017)
23. Boudguiga, A., et al.: Towards better availability and accountability for IoT updates by means of a blockchain. In: 2017 IEEE European Symposium on Security and Privacy Workshops (EuroS&PW), pp. 50–58. IEEE (2017)
24. Yohan, A., Lo, N.-W., Achawapong, S.: Blockchain-based firmware update framework for internet-of-things environment. In: Proceedings of the International Conference on Information and Knowledge Engineering (IKE), pp. 151–155. The Steering Committee of The World Congress in Computer Science, Computer... (2018)
25. Samaniego, M., Deters, R.: Using blockchain to push software-defined IoT components onto edge hosts. In: Proceedings of the International Conference on Big Data and Advanced Wireless Technologies, p. 58. ACM (2016)
26. Dorri, A., Kanhere, S.S., Jurdak, R., Gauravaram, P.: Blockchain for IoT security and privacy: the case study of a smart home. In: 2017 IEEE International Conference on Pervasive Computing and Communications Workshops (PerCom Workshops), pp. 618–623. IEEE (2017)
27. Popov, S.: The tangle. cit. on, p. 131 (2016)
28. Samaniego, M., Deters, R.: Blockchain as a service for IoT. In: 2016 IEEE International Conference on Internet of Things (iThings) and IEEE Green Computing and Communications (GreenCom) and IEEE Cyber, Physical and Social Computing (CPSCom) and IEEE Smart Data (SmartData), pp. 433–436. IEEE (2016)
29. Conner, K.R., Rumelt, R.P.: Software piracy: an analysis of protection strategies. Manag. Sci. 37(2), 125–139 (1991)
30. Givon, M., Mahajan, V., Muller, E.: Software piracy: estimation of lost sales and the impact on software diffusion. J. Mark. 59(1), 29–37 (1995)
31. Heilman, E., Kendler, A., Zohar, A., Goldberg, S.: Eclipse attacks on Bitcoin's peer-to-peer network. In: 24th {USENIX} Security Symposium ({USENIX} Security 2015), pp. 129–144 (2015)

32. Eyal, I., Sirer, E.G.: Majority is not enough: Bitcoin mining is vulnerable. Commun. ACM **61**(7), 95–102 (2018)
33. Duerst, M., Suignard, M.: RFC 3987: internationalized resource identifiers (IRIS). IETF, January 2005
34. Bertoni, G., Daemen, J., Peeters, M., Van Assche, G.: Keccak specifications. Submission to NIST (round 2), pp. 320–337 (2009)
35. Johnson, D., Menezes, A., Vanstone, S.: The elliptic curve digital signature algorithm (ECDSA). Int. J. Inf. Secur. **1**(1), 36–63 (2001)
36. Wood, G.: Ethereum: a secure decentralised generalised transaction ledger. Ethereum Proj. Yellow Pap. **151**, 1–32 (2014)

Sequential Aggregate MACs
with Detecting Functionality Revisited

Shingo Sato[1(✉)], Shoichi Hirose[3], and Junji Shikata[1,2]

[1] Graduate School of Environment and Information Sciences,
Yokohama National University, Yokohama, Japan
`sato-shingo-cz@ynu.jp`, `shikata-junji-rb@ynu.ac.jp`
[2] Institute of Advanced Sciences, Yokohama National University, Yokohama, Japan
[3] Faculty of Engineering, University of Fukui, Fukui, Japan
`hrs_shch@u-fukui.ac.jp`

Abstract. We revisit sequential aggregate message authentication codes with detecting functionality (SAMDs) where aggregation is a keyless procedure. SAMDs enable us to compress multiple MAC-tags into a shorter aggregate tag and to identify invalid messages or invalid positions of messages once the aggregate tag is regarded as invalid. Therefore, the SAMD is an extended model from aggregate message authentication codes (AMACs) and sequential AMACs. In this paper, we propose a refined model of SAMDs: we classify SAMD into two types, SAMD-MOBT and SAMD-MOAT, and formalize security notions along with each model of SAMDs. Furthermore, we present generic constructions of SAMD-MOBT and SAMD-MOAT from any MAC, a cryptographic hash function, and a disjunct matrix. Our results show that SAMD-MOAT is more convenient than SAMD-MOBT, however it is more difficult to construct SAMD-MOAT that meets all the security notions defined in this paper. These results clarify suitable applications of SAMDs by taking into account both convenience and achievable security levels.

Keywords: Message authentication · MAC · Aggregate MAC ·
Sequential aggregate MAC

1 Introduction

1.1 Background and Related Work

The message authentication code (MAC) is a fundamental and important primitive in cryptography. The aggregate MAC (AMAC) is a scheme that can compress multiple MAC-tags into a single shorter tag called an aggregate tag. The AMAC enables us to verify validity of multiple messages by using the shorter aggregate tag, and AMACs are useful in the case where a lot of senders (e.g., devices) transmit their local messages to a receiver, since the total amount of size of MAC-tags is drastically reduced. Katz and Lindell [6] gave the model and security formalization of AMACs and proposed a simple construction of

© Springer Nature Switzerland AG 2019
J. K. Liu and X. Huang (Eds.): NSS 2019, LNCS 11928, pp. 387–407, 2019.
https://doi.org/10.1007/978-3-030-36938-5_23

AMACs by using exclusive-or of MAC-tags. However, it is impossible to detect invalid messages once the aggregate tag is regarded as invalid. Therefore, Hirose and Shikata [5] proposed AMAC schemes having functionality of both compressing multiple MAC-tags and identifying invalid messages, which we call AMADs (AMACs with detecting functionality). They proposed the model and security formalization for AMADs, and proposed a construction of AMADs by using disjunct matrices. In those AMACs or AMADs, the aggregate process of compressing multiple MAC-tags is a keyless procedure, but there are other related works (e.g., [8]) where the aggregate process needs a secret key.

Sequential aggregate MACs (SAMACs) have been studied as another line of research for compressing multiple MAC-tags. SAMACs enable us to verify not only validity of multiple messages but also validity of a sequential order of messages with functionality of compressing multiple MAC-tags. SAMACs would be useful in applications such as IoT networks and mobile ad-hoc networks (MANET) since the amount of data-size transmitted in networks can be reduced. Eikemeier et al. [3] formalized the model and security for SAMACs. They also introduced history-freeness which is a property that a new aggregate tag depends only on a local message of each sender and the prior aggregate tag, and they proposed history-free SAMAC schemes. Ma and Tsudik [7] gave a construction by using collision-resistant hash functions for SAMACs with forward security, however, they did not give a security proof of their SAMAC. Hirose and Kuwakado [4] proposed another construction of SAMACs with forward security and showed its security proof. In those SAMACs the aggregate process needs a secret key, while Sato et al. [9] proposed SAMACs with keyless aggregate process.

As extension of SAMACs, Sato et al. [10] proposed SAMACs with detecting functionality (SAMDs) that have the following functionalities: (i) compressing MAC-tags into a shorter aggregate tag; and (ii) identifying invalid messages or invalid positions of messages once the aggregate tag is regarded as invalid. They also showed its application to long data transmission by data-partitioning with a shorter tag compared to the normal technique where the long data requires the total amount of the MAC-tags on all the partitioned messages. In general, such an identifying mechanism of SAMDs is more complicated than that of AMADs, since SAMDs additionally need to detect wrong positions of message-components. Hence, it is interesting to develop SAMDs having an efficient identifying mechanism. Unfortunately, the SAMD scheme in [10] does not guarantee the unforgeability for the sequence of valid message/tag pairs (see Appendix A), which may be brought by complicatedness of security of SAMDs. However, the underlying idea of construction of the identifying mechanism in SAMDs of [10] by using disjunct matrices was quite new and interesting. The purpose of this paper is to propose a refined model and security formalization of SAMDs and to provide constructions of SAMDs by further developing the technique in [10].

1.2   Our Contribution

We revisit SAMDs where the aggregation procedure is keyless, and propose a refined model of SAMDs. Specifically, we classify SAMD into two types,

SAMD-MOBT (SAMD having message-order before tagging) and SAMD-MOAT (SAMD having message-order after tagging), and we propose and formalize security notions along with each model of SAMDs. Furthermore, we present generic constructions of SAMD-MOBT and SAMD-MOAT. More specifically, the contribution of this paper is as follows.

We propose a model of SAMD-MOBT and formalize its security notions, unforgeability, message-identifiability, and order-identifiability in Sect. 3. In this model, message-order is given beforehand and shared with senders; each sender generates a MAC-tag according to the message-order in parallel; and then, an aggregate tag is generated with keyless aggregation. We also present a generic construction called HSAMD_1 from any MAC, a cryptographic hash function, and a disjunct matrix. As a result, we prove that HSAMD_1 meets all the security notions mentioned above in the random oracle model, if the underlying MAC meets pseudorandomness.

Similarly, in Sect. 4, we propose a model of SAMD-MOAT and formalize its security notions as well. In this model, after each sender generates a MAC-tag on an individual message in parallel, message-order is given; and then, an aggregate tag is generated based on the message-order and all the MAC-tags with keyless aggregation. Since each MAC-tag is generated independently of the message-order in this model, it is even possible to generate sequential aggregate tags from MAC-tags without changing the formats or inputs for the underlying MAC function. In this sense, SAMD-MOAT is more convenient than SAMD-MOBT, however we will see that it is more difficult to construct SAMD-MOAT that meets all the security notions defined in this paper. We present a generic construction called HSAMD_2 from any MAC, a cryptographic hash function, and a disjunct matrix. As a result, we prove that HSAMD_2 meets unforgeability, message-identifiability, and a weak version of order-identifiability, if the underlying MAC meets pseudorandomness.

2   Preliminaries

In this paper, we use the following notation. For a positive integer n, let $[n] := \{1, 2, \ldots, n\}$. If we write a *negligible* function $\varepsilon : \mathbb{N} \rightarrow [0, 1]$, it means that $\varepsilon(\lambda) < 1/g(\lambda)$ holds for any polynomial g and a sufficiently large integer λ. We describe $\{x_i\}_{i \in [n]} := \{x_1, x_2, \ldots, x_n\}$ as a set of values x_i for $i \in [n]$, and $(x_i)_{i \in [n]} := (x_1, x_2, \ldots, x_n)$ as a sequence of values x_i for $i \in [n]$. For a set S, a subset $X \subset S$, and elements $x_1, \ldots, x_n \in S$ that some are in X and the others are in $\bar{X}$ (i.e., $S \backslash X$), let $(x_i)_{i \in [n] \wedge x_i \in \bar{X}}$ be the sequence of elements which are in $\bar{X}$. We denote a polynomial in n by $\mathrm{poly}(n)$. Probabilistic polynomial time is abbreviated as PPT.

2.1   Message Authentication Code (MAC)

A MAC scheme consists of three polynomial-time algorithms (KGen, Tag, Vrfy) as follows, where $\mathcal{K}$ is a key-space, $\mathcal{M}$ is a message-space, and $\mathcal{T}$ is a tag-space.

- k ← KGen(1^λ): KGen is a randomized algorithm which, on input a security parameter λ, outputs a secret key k ∈ $\mathcal{K}$.
- t ← Tag(k, m): Tag is a deterministic algorithm which, on input a secret key k and a message m ∈ $\mathcal{M}$, outputs a tag t ∈ $\mathcal{T}$.
- 1/0 ← Vrfy(k, m, t): Vrfy is a deterministic algorithm which, on input a secret key k, a message m, and a tag t, outputs 1 (acceptance) or 0 (rejection).

It is required that MAC schemes (KGen, Tag, Vrfy) meet correctness in the following way: For all k ← KGen(1^λ) and all m ∈ $\mathcal{M}$, we have 1 ← Vrfy(k, m, Tag(k, m)).

We next define security notions of MACs: Unforgeability against chosen message attacks (called UF-CMA security) and pseudorandomness.

A MAC scheme MAC = (KGen, Tag, Vrfy) meets UF-CMA security, if for any PPT adversary A against MAC, $Adv_{\mathsf{MAC,A}}^{\mathrm{uf}}(\lambda) := \Pr[\text{A wins}]$ is negligible, where [A wins] is the event that A wins in the following game:

Setup: k ← KGen(1^λ) and $\mathcal{L}_{\mathsf{Tag}}$ ← ∅.
Tagging: Given a message query m ∈ $\mathcal{M}$, tagging oracle $\mathsf{Tag}_k(\cdot)$ returns t ← Tag(k, m) and sets $\mathcal{L}_{\mathsf{Tag}}$ ← $\mathcal{L}_{\mathsf{Tag}}$ ∪ {m}. The number of queries submitted by A is at most Q = poly(λ).
Output: A outputs a forgery (m^*, t*). A wins if 1 ← Vrfy(k, m^*, t*) and $m^* \notin \mathcal{L}_{\mathsf{Tag}}$ hold.

A MAC scheme MAC = (KGen, Tag, Vrfy) meets **pseudorandomness** if for any PPT algorithm D, the following advantage is negligible:

$$Adv_{\mathsf{MAC,D}}^{\mathrm{pr}}(\lambda) := \left| \Pr[\mathsf{D}^{\mathsf{Tag}_k(\cdot)}(1^\lambda) = 1] - \Pr[\mathsf{D}^{f(\cdot)}(1^\lambda) = 1] \right|.$$

Here, D is given an oracle either $\mathsf{Tag}_k(\cdot)$ or $f(\cdot)$ and determines which oracle is given; $\mathsf{Tag}_k(\cdot)$ is the tagging oracle which, on input m ∈ $\mathcal{M}$, returns t = Tag(k, m); and $f(\cdot)$ is an oracle which, on input m ∈ $\mathcal{M}$, returns $f(m)$ for a random function $f : \mathcal{M} \to \mathcal{T}$.

2.2   Disjunct Matrices and Non-adaptive Group Testing

A disjunct matrix (or cover-free family) is well studied in combinatorics and bioinformatics, and it is defined as follows: For vectors $\boldsymbol{v} = (v_1, \ldots, v_n)$ and $\boldsymbol{v}' = (v_1', \ldots, v_n')$ in $\{0,1\}^n$, $\boldsymbol{v} \preceq \boldsymbol{v}'$ if $v_i \leq v_i'$ for every $i \in [n]$.

Definition 1 (d-disjunct matrix). *A $\{0,1\}$-matrix $\boldsymbol{G}$ is a d-disjunct matrix if any d columns of $\boldsymbol{G}$ do not cover any other column of $\boldsymbol{G}$. Here, d columns $\boldsymbol{g}_{j_1}, \boldsymbol{g}_{j_2}, \ldots, \boldsymbol{g}_{j_d}$ are said to cover a column $\boldsymbol{g}$ if $\boldsymbol{g} \preceq \boldsymbol{g}_{j_1} \vee \boldsymbol{g}_{j_2} \vee \cdots \vee \boldsymbol{g}_{j_d}$ where $\vee$ is the component-wise (logical) sum.*

For a $u \times N$ d-disjunct matrix $\boldsymbol{G} = (g_{i,j})$ and every $i \in [u]$, $I(\boldsymbol{G}, i)$ is the set of j $(1 \leq j \leq N)$ such that $g_{i,j} = 1$. We use this notation later in this paper.

Group testing (e.g., see [2] for the survey) is a method to specify some special items called *defectives* among many whole items with a small number of tests than the trivial individual testing for each item. Suppose that there are totally N items of which there are at most d defectives. In this paper, we focus on non-adaptive group testing in which we need to know d beforehand and we need to select all the subsets of N items to be tested without knowing the results of other tests. This type of testing is typically designed by providing a $u \times N$ d-disjunct matrix, where u is the number of tests, since it efficiently detects all the defectives by the following simple procedure:

1. $J \leftarrow \{id_1, id_2 \ldots, id_N\}$, namely, J is initially the whole set consisting of all IDs of the items.
2. For all $i = 1, 2, \ldots, u$, do the following: For each $i \in [u]$, if the result of the i-th test is negative, then $J \leftarrow J \backslash \{id_{i,1}, id_{i,2}, \ldots, id_{i,w_i}\}$, where $\{id_{i,1}, id_{i,2}, \ldots, id_{i,w_i}\}$ is a set of all IDs involved in the i-th test.
3. Output J

We note that the output J includes all the defectives which can be easily seen by the property of d-disjunct matrices.

3 SAMD Having Message-Order Before Tagging

We consider a model and security of SAMDs having message-order before tagging which we call *SAMD-MOBT*. In this model, message-order is given beforehand and shared with senders; each sender generates a MAC-tag according to the message-order in parallel; and then, an aggregate tag is generated without secret key (i.e., keyless aggregation).

3.1 Model and Security of SAMD-MOBT

An SAMD-MOBT scheme consists of five polynomial-time algorithms (KGen, Tag, Vrfy, DSeqAgg, DSAVrfy) as follows: N is the number of senders, $\mathcal{ID} = \{id_i\}_{i \in [N]}$ is an ID-space, $\mathcal{K}$ is a key-space, $\mathcal{M}$ is a message-space, $\mathcal{T}$ is a tag-space, and $\mathcal{T}_{agg}$ is an aggregate tag-space.
$\mathcal{S} := \{(id_{\ell_1}, id_{\ell_2}, \ldots, id_{\ell_N}) \mid id_{\ell_i} \neq id_{\ell_j}$ for any distinct$i, j \in [N]\}$ denotes the set of all sequences of distinct IDs with length N: In the following, a sequence is fixed before executing Tag algorithm.

- $k_{id} \leftarrow$ KGen(1^λ, id): KGen is a randomized algorithm which, on input a security parameter 1^λ and an ID id $\in \mathcal{ID}$, outputs a secret key $k_{id} \in \mathcal{K}$.
- $t \leftarrow$ Tag(k_{id}, i, m): Tag is a deterministic algorithm which, on input a secret key k_{id}, information on message-order $i \in [N]$, and a message $m \in \mathcal{M}$, outputs a tag $t \in \mathcal{T}$.
- $1/0 \leftarrow$ Vrfy(k_{id}, i, m, t): Vrfy is a deterministic algorithm which, on input a secret key k_{id}, an order information $i \in [N]$, a message $m \in \mathcal{M}$, and a tag $t \in \mathcal{T}$, outputs 1 (acceptance) or 0 (rejection).
- $\tau \leftarrow$ DSeqAgg(T): DSeqAgg is a deterministic algorithm which, on input a sequence of tags $T = ((id_{\ell_i}, t_i))_{i \in [N]}$ such that $(id_{\ell_1}, \ldots, id_{\ell_N}) \in \mathcal{S}$, outputs a tuple of sequential aggregate tags $\tau \in \mathcal{T}_{agg}$.

- $J/\bot \leftarrow \mathsf{DSAVrfy}(K, M, \tau)$: $\mathsf{DSAVrfy}$ is a deterministic algorithm which, on input a set of key/ID pairs $K = \{(\mathsf{k}_{\mathsf{id}_i}, \mathsf{id}_i)\}_{i \in [N]}$, a sequence of ID/message pairs $((\mathsf{id}_{\ell_i}, m_i))_{i \in [N]}$ for any $(\mathsf{id}_{\ell_1}, \dots, \mathsf{id}_{\ell_N}) \in \mathcal{S}$, and an aggregate tag τ, outputs a list J or an error message $\bot$, where J is a list consisting of IDs whose messages are invalid or their order is invalid.

In the above definition, we note that the number of participating senders is fixed, namely always N as in the model in [5, 10].

We require that the following condition of correctness holds:

- For all $\mathsf{id} \in \mathcal{ID}$, all $\mathsf{k}_{\mathsf{id}} \leftarrow \mathsf{KGen}(1^\lambda, \mathsf{id})$, all $m \in \mathcal{M}$, and all $i \in [N]$, we have $1 \leftarrow \mathsf{Vrfy}(\mathsf{k}_{\mathsf{id}}, i, m, \mathsf{Tag}(\mathsf{k}_{\mathsf{id}}, i, m))$.
- For all $\mathsf{id} \in \mathcal{ID}$, all $\mathsf{k}_{\mathsf{id}} \leftarrow \mathsf{KGen}(1^\lambda, \mathsf{id})$, and all $M = ((m_i, \mathsf{id}_{\ell_i}))_{i \in [N]}$ such that $(\mathsf{id}_{\ell_i})_{i \in [N]} \in \mathcal{S}$, we have $\emptyset \leftarrow \mathsf{DSAVrfy}(K, M, \tau)$, where $K = \{(\mathsf{k}_{\mathsf{id}_i}, \mathsf{id}_i)\}_{i \in [N]}$ and $\tau \leftarrow \mathsf{DSeqAgg}(((\mathsf{id}_{\ell_i}, \mathsf{Tag}(\mathsf{k}_{\mathsf{id}_{\ell_i}}, i, m_i)))_{i \in [N]})$.

As security of SAMD-MOBT, we define $\mathsf{aggUF\text{-}CMA}$ security and identifiability along with our model.

Definition 2 (aggUF-CMA security). *Let d be a positive integer. An SAMD-MOBT scheme $\mathsf{SAMD} = (\mathsf{KGen}, \mathsf{Tag}, \mathsf{Vrfy}, \mathsf{DSeqAgg}, \mathsf{DSAVrfy})$ meets d-aggUF-CMA security if for any PPT adversary A against SAMD, the advantage $Adv^{\mathsf{agg\text{-}uf}}_{\mathsf{SAMD},\mathsf{A}}(\lambda) := \Pr[\mathsf{A}\ wins]$ is negligible. $[\mathsf{A}\ wins]$ is the event that A wins in the following game:*

Setup: $\mathsf{k}_{\mathsf{id}_i} \leftarrow \mathsf{KGen}(1^\lambda, \mathsf{id}_i)$ *for all* $i \in [N]$, $K \leftarrow \{(\mathsf{k}_{\mathsf{id}_i}, \mathsf{id}_i)\}_{i \in [N]}$, *and* $\mathcal{L}_{\mathsf{SA}} \leftarrow \emptyset$.

Tagging: *Given the j-th ID/message sequence $M^{(j)} = ((\mathsf{id}_i^{(j)}, m_i^{(j)}))_{i \in [N]}$ such that $(\mathsf{id}_1^{(j)}, \dots, \mathsf{id}_N^{(j)}) \in \mathcal{S}$, aggregate tagging oracle $\mathsf{DSATag}_K(\cdot)$ does the following:*

1. $t_i^{(j)} \leftarrow \mathsf{Tag}(\mathsf{k}_{\mathsf{id}_i^{(j)}}, i, m_i^{(j)})$ *for all* $i \in [N]$.

2. Output $\tau^{(j)} \leftarrow \mathsf{DSeqAgg}(((\mathsf{id}_i^{(j)}, t_i^{(j)}))_{i \in [N]})$.

3. Set $\mathcal{L}_{\mathsf{SA}} \leftarrow \mathcal{L}_{\mathsf{SA}} \cup \{M^{(j)}\}$.

The number of queries which A submits to the aggregate tagging oracle is at most $Q = \mathrm{poly}(\lambda)$.

Output: A *outputs* $M^* = ((\mathsf{id}_{\ell_i^*}, m_i^*))_{i \in [N]}$ *and* τ^* *such that* $(\mathsf{id}_{\ell_i^*})_{i \in [N]} \in \mathcal{S}$. *Compute* $J \leftarrow \mathsf{DSAVrfy}(K, M^*, \tau^*)$. A *wins if it holds that* $J \neq \bot$, $|J| \leq d$, *and* $((i, \mathsf{id}_{\ell_i^*}, m_i^*))_{i \in [N] \wedge \mathsf{id}_{\ell_i^*} \in J} \neq ((i, \hat{\mathsf{id}}_i, \hat{m}_i))_{i \in [N] \wedge \hat{\mathsf{id}}_i \in J}$ *for any* $((\hat{\mathsf{id}}_i, \hat{m}_i))_{i \in [N]} \in \mathcal{L}_{\mathsf{SA}}$. *Namely, A wins if the output J of $\mathsf{DSAVrfy}$ is not an error message, the number of IDs id with (i, m, t) such that $0 \leftarrow \mathsf{Vrfy}(\mathsf{k}_{\mathsf{id}}, i, m, t)$ is at most d, and the messages or positions of valid IDs $\mathsf{id} \notin J$ are substituted.*

As an example of forgeries by an adversary, we can consider the following: If an ID/message query is $((\mathsf{id}_1, m_1), (\mathsf{id}_2, m_2), (\mathsf{id}_3, m_3), \dots, (\mathsf{id}_N, m_N))$, an aggregate tag on $((\mathsf{id}_2, m_2'), (\mathsf{id}_1, m_1), (\mathsf{id}_3, m_3), \dots, (\mathsf{id}_N, m_N))$ is a valid forgery for $J = \{\mathsf{id}_2\}$ since the order of id_1 is changed.

Concerning identifiability, we define two notions, message-identifiability and order-identifiability. Message-identifiability guarantees validity of each message-component, and does not always guarantee the order of message-components. On the other hand, order-identifiability guarantees that the order of message-components is correct under the assumption that each message-component is valid. Therefore, by taking into account both notions, a verifier can check validity of not only message-components but also the order of them.

First, we formalize message-identifiability. This is the same definition of the identifiability for group-testing aggregate MACs in [5], and this is reasonable since the identifiability in [5] just focuses on detecting invalid message/tag pairs themselves. Specifically, message-identifiability is defined by two notions, completeness and soundness. Informally, completeness guarantees that no adversary can make a verifier regard valid message/tag pairs as invalid ones. On the other hand, soundness guarantees that no adversary can make a verifier regard invalid message/tag pairs as valid ones.

Definition 3 (Message-Identifiability). *Let d be a positive integer. An SAMD-MOBT scheme* SAMD $=$ (KGen, Tag, Vrfy, DSeqAgg, DSAVrfy) *meets d-message-identifiability if it satisfies d-message-completeness and d-message-soundness that are defined as follows. Let A be a PPT adversary against* SAMD, *and we consider the following game:*

Setup: $k_{id_i} \leftarrow$ KGen$(1^\lambda, id_i)$ *for all* $i \in [N]$, *and* $K \leftarrow \{(k_{id_i}, id_i)\}_{i \in [N]}$.
Tagging: *For a given triplet of IDs, order-information, and messages* (id_{ℓ_i}, i, m_i), *tagging oracle* Tag$_K(\cdot)$ *returns* $t_i \leftarrow$ Tag$(k_{id_{\ell_i}}, i, m_i)$. *The number of queries which* A *submits is at most* $Q = \text{poly}(\lambda)$.
Output: A *outputs* $((id_{\ell_i^*}, m_i^*, t_i^*))_{i \in [N]}$. *Compute* $J \leftarrow$ DSAVrfy(K, M^*, τ^*), *where* $M^* \leftarrow ((id_{\ell_i^*}, m_i^*))_{i \in [N]}$ *and* $\tau^* \leftarrow$ DSeqAgg$(((id_{\ell_i^*}, t_i^*))_{i \in [N]})$.

- *Completeness:* SAMD *meets d-message-completeness if for any PPT adversary* A, *the advantage* $Adv_{\text{SAMD,A}}^{\text{m-ident-c}}(\lambda)$ *is negligible.* $Adv_{\text{SAMD,A}}^{\text{m-ident-c}}(\lambda)$ *is the probability that* $|J| \leq d$ *and* $J \cap \{id_{\ell_i^*} \mid 1 \leftarrow$ Vrfy$(k_{id_{\ell_i^*}}, i, m_i^*, t_i^*), 1 \leq i \leq N\} \neq \emptyset$ *hold.*
- *Soundness:* SAMD *meets d-message-soundness if for any PPT adversary* A, *the advantage* $Adv_{\text{SAMD,A}}^{\text{m-ident-s}}(\lambda)$ *is negligible, where* $Adv_{\text{SAMD,A}}^{\text{m-ident-s}}(\lambda)$ *is the probability that* $|J| \leq d$ *and* $\{id_{\ell_i^*} \mid 0 \leftarrow$ Vrfy$(k_{id_{\ell_i^*}}, i, m_i^*, t_i^*), 1 \leq i \leq N\} \backslash J \neq \emptyset$ *hold.*

Second, we define order-identifiability. The notion of order-identifiability is defined under the assumption that message-identifiability is met, namely, provided that each component of message/tag pair is valid, the security of order-identifiability is meaningful. This notion discusses whether the order of message-components is valid or not, since substitution of message-components is guaranteed by message-identifiability. In the same way as message-identifiability, completeness and soundness are defined for order-identifiability: Completeness prevents a verifier from regarding the correct order of sequential messages as wrong one; Soundness prevents a verifier from regarding the wrong order of sequential messages as correct one.

Definition 4 (Order-Identifiability). *Let* d *be a positive integer. An SAMD-MOBT scheme* SAMD $=$ (KGen, Tag, Vrfy, DSeqAgg, DSAVrfy) *meets* d-*order-identifiability if it satisfies* d-*order-completeness and* d-*order-soundness defined as follows. Let* A *be a PPT adversary against* SAMD, *and we consider the following game:*

Setup: $\mathsf{k}_{\mathsf{id}_i} \leftarrow \mathsf{KGen}(1^\lambda, \mathsf{id}_i)$ *for all* $i \in [N]$, $K \leftarrow \{(\mathsf{k}_{\mathsf{id}_i}, \mathsf{id}_i)\}_{i \in [N]}$, *and* $\mathcal{L}_{\mathrm{SA}} \leftarrow \emptyset$.

Tagging: *Given the* j-*th ID/message sequence* $M^{(j)} = ((\mathsf{id}_i^{(j)}, m_i^{(j)}))_{i \in [N]}$ *such that* $(\mathsf{id}_1^{(j)}, \ldots, \mathsf{id}_N^{(j)}) \in \mathcal{S}$, *aggregate tagging oracle* $\mathsf{DSATag}_K(\cdot)$ *does the following:*

   1. $\mathsf{t}_i^{(j)} \leftarrow \mathsf{Tag}(\mathsf{k}_{\mathsf{id}_i^{(j)}}, i, m_i^{(j)})$ *for all* $i \in [N]$.

   2. $\tau^{(j)} \leftarrow \mathsf{DSeqAgg}(((\mathsf{id}_i^{(j)}, \mathsf{t}_i^{(j)}))_{i \in [N]})$.

   3. Output $(\mathsf{t}_1^{(j)}, \ldots, \mathsf{t}_N^{(j)}, \tau^{(j)})$, *and set* $\mathcal{L}_{\mathrm{SA}} \leftarrow \mathcal{L}_{\mathrm{SA}} \cup \{M^{(j)}\}$.
   The number of queries which A *submits to the aggregate tagging oracle is at most* $Q = \mathrm{poly}(\lambda)$.

Output: A *outputs* $((\mathsf{id}_{\ell_i^*}, m_i^*, \mathsf{t}_i^*))_{i \in [N]}$ *such that* $((\mathsf{id}_{\ell_i^*}, m_i^*))_{i \in [N]} \notin \mathcal{L}_{\mathrm{SA}}$ *and there exists the* q-*th sequence query satisfying* $\{(\mathsf{id}_{\ell_i^*}, m_i^*)\}_{i \in [N]} = \{(\mathsf{id}_i^{(q)}, m_i^{(q)})\}_{i \in [N]}$. *Then, compute* $J \leftarrow \mathsf{DSAVrfy}(K, ((\mathsf{id}_{\ell_i^*}, m_i^*))_{i \in [N]}, \tau^*)$, *where* $\tau^* \leftarrow \mathsf{DSeqAgg}(((\mathsf{id}_{\ell_i^*}, \mathsf{t}_i^*))_{i \in [N]})$.

- *Completeness:* SAMD *meets* d-*order-completeness if for any PPT adversary* A, *the advantage* $Adv_{\mathrm{SAMD,A}}^{\mathrm{o\text{-}ident\text{-}c}}(\lambda)$ *is negligible.* $Adv_{\mathrm{SAMD,A}}^{\mathrm{o\text{-}ident\text{-}c}}(\lambda)$ *is defined as the probability that* $|J| \leq d$ *and* $J \cap \{\mathsf{id}_{\ell_i^*} \mid (i, \mathsf{id}_{\ell_i^*}, m_i^*) \in \{(i, \mathsf{id}_i^{(j)}, m_i^{(j)})\}_{j \in [Q]}, 1 \leftarrow \mathsf{Vrfy}(\mathsf{k}_{\mathsf{id}_{\ell_i^*}}, i, m_i^*, \mathsf{t}_i^*), 1 \leq i \leq N\} \neq \emptyset$ *hold.*
- *Soundness:* SAMD *meets* d-*order-soundness if for any PPT adversary* A, *the advantage* $Adv_{\mathrm{SAMD,A}}^{\mathrm{o\text{-}ident\text{-}s}}(\lambda)$ *is negligible, where* $Adv_{\mathrm{SAMD,A}}^{\mathrm{o\text{-}ident\text{-}s}}(\lambda)$ *is defined as the probability that* $|J| \leq d$ *and* $\{\mathsf{id}_{\ell_i^*} \mid (i, \mathsf{id}_{\ell_i^*}, m_i^*) \notin \{(i, \mathsf{id}_i^{(j)}, m_i^{(j)})\}_{j \in [Q]}, 1 \leftarrow \mathsf{Vrfy}(\mathsf{k}_{\mathsf{id}_{\ell_i^*}}, i, m_i^*, \mathsf{t}_i^*), 1 \leq i \leq N\} \backslash J \neq \emptyset$ *hold.*

As mentioned before, order-identifiability is formalized under the assumption that message-identifiability is met. So, in the both definitions of order-completeness and order-soundness, the success condition of adversaries includes the condition $1 \leftarrow \mathsf{Vrfy}(\mathsf{k}_{\mathsf{id}_{\ell_i^*}}, i, m_i^*, \mathsf{t}_i^*)$, which means that message/tag pairs are not substituted before aggregation.

3.2   Construction of SAMD-MOBT

We propose a construction called HSAMD$_1$ for SAMD-MOBT. The idea behind this construction is that, before aggregation, each sender generates a MAC-tag not only on its local message but also on a position of the message in a sequence of messages. By this, we can prevent the attacks of changing the order so that its validity is guaranteed by security of the underlying MACs.

In addition, an aggregator generates an aggregate tag on received MAC-tags and a counter. The counter is a one-time value kept by an aggregator and updated after sending an aggregate tag. By including a counter, we can prevent exchanging subsequences in queried ID/message sequences by the following reason: Any (outside) adversary has to know MAC-tags in order to generate an aggregate tag on a new counter and a new sequence. However, it is difficult for him/her to know MAC-tags from the pseudorandomness of MACs and the assumption of random oracles.

To construct HSAMD_1, we use the following parameters and primitives based on a security parameter λ: Let $N = \mathrm{poly}(\lambda)$ be the number of senders, $\mathsf{MAC} = (\mathsf{MAC.KGen}, \mathsf{MAC.Tag}, \mathsf{MAC.Vrfy})$ be a MAC scheme, $\boldsymbol{G} \in \{0,1\}^{u \times N}$ be a d-disjunct matrix, $H : \{0,1\}^* \to \mathcal{T}$ be a random oracle, $\mathsf{count} \leftarrow 1$ be a counter which is kept by an aggregator and updated after an aggregate tag is sent, and $\mathsf{count}_{ver} \leftarrow 1$ be a counter which is kept by a verifier.

$\mathsf{HSAMD}_1 = (\mathsf{KGen}, \mathsf{Tag}, \mathsf{Vrfy}, \mathsf{DSeqAgg}, \mathsf{DSAVrfy})$ is given as follows:

- $\mathsf{k}_{\mathsf{id}} \leftarrow \mathsf{KGen}(1^\lambda, \mathsf{id})$: Output a key $\mathsf{k}_{\mathsf{id}} \leftarrow \mathsf{MAC.KGen}(1^\lambda)$ for an ID id.
- $t \leftarrow \mathsf{Tag}(\mathsf{k}_{\mathsf{id}}, i, m)$: Output a tag $t_i \leftarrow \mathsf{MAC.Tag}(\mathsf{k}_{\mathsf{id}}, i\|m)$.
- $1/0 \leftarrow \mathsf{Vrfy}(\mathsf{k}_{\mathsf{id}}, i, m, t)$: Output $b \leftarrow \mathsf{MAC.Vrfy}(\mathsf{k}_{\mathsf{id}}, i\|m, t) \in \{0,1\}$.
- $\tau \leftarrow \mathsf{DSeqAgg}(T)$: For $T = ((\mathsf{id}_{\ell_1}, t_1), \ldots, (\mathsf{id}_{\ell_N}, t_N))$, do the following:
  1. For an ID-string $\mathbf{s} = (\mathsf{id}_{\ell_1}, \ldots, \mathsf{id}_{\ell_N}) \in \mathcal{S}$ and $I(\boldsymbol{G}, i) = \{i_1, i_2, \ldots, i_k\}$, we define a string $\mathbf{s}(\boldsymbol{G}, i) := (\mathsf{id}_{\ell_{i_1}}, \mathsf{id}_{\ell_{i_2}}, \ldots, \mathsf{id}_{\ell_{i_k}})$ consisting of IDs keeping the order of $\mathbf{s}$. Then, for every $i \in [u]$, compute $\tau_i \leftarrow H(\mathsf{count}, t_{i_1}, \ldots, t_{i_k})$.
  2. Output $\tau := (\mathsf{count}, (\tau_i)_{i \in [u]})$ and set $\mathsf{count} \leftarrow \mathsf{count} + 1$.
- $J/\perp \leftarrow \mathsf{DSAVrfy}(K, M, \tau)$: The verification for $M = ((\mathsf{id}_{\ell_i}, m_i))_{i \in [N]}$ and $\tau = (\mathsf{count}, (\tau_i)_{i \in [u]})$ is as follows:
  1. Output $\perp$ if $\mathsf{count} \neq \mathsf{count}_{ver}$.
  2. $J \leftarrow \{\mathsf{id}_{\ell_i}\}_{i \in [N]}$.
  3. For $i \in [u]$, do the following: $J \leftarrow J \backslash \{\mathsf{id}_{\ell_j}\}$ for all $j \in \{i_1, \ldots, i_k\}$ if
  $$\tau_i = H(\mathsf{count}, t_{i_1}, \ldots, t_{i_k}) \text{ holds, where } \left(\mathsf{id}_{\ell_{i_1}}, \ldots, \mathsf{id}_{\ell_{i_k}}\right) = \mathbf{s}(\boldsymbol{G}, i) \text{ and}$$
  $$(t_{i_1}, \ldots, t_{i_k}) = \left(\mathsf{Tag}\left(\mathsf{k}_{\mathsf{id}_{\ell_{i_1}}}, i_1\|m_{i_1}\right), \ldots, \mathsf{Tag}\left(\mathsf{k}_{\mathsf{id}_{\ell_{i_k}}}, i_k\|m_{i_k}\right)\right).$$
  4. Output J and set $\mathsf{count}_{ver} \leftarrow \mathsf{count}_{ver} + 1$.

Theorems 1 and 2 below show security of HSAMD_1.

Theorem 1 (Unforgeability). *Suppose that the number of IDs whose messages or their positions in sequential messages are invalid is at most d. If MAC meets pseudorandomness and $\boldsymbol{G}$ is a d-disjunct matrix, the resulting HSAMD_1 meets d-aggUF-CMA security in the random oracle model.*

Theorem 2 (Identifiability). *Suppose that the number of IDs whose messages or their positions in sequential messages are invalid is at most d. Then, we have the following in the random oracle model: (i) If $\boldsymbol{G}$ is a d-disjunct matrix, HSAMD_1 meets d-message-identifiability; (ii) If $\boldsymbol{G}$ is a d-disjunct matrix and MAC meets UF-CMA security, HSAMD_1 meets d-order-identifiability.*

We provide security proofs of Theorems 1 and 2 in which A is a PPT adversary against HSAMD_1. Let n be the bit-length of MAC-tags and a counter, Q_h be the number of queries issued to the random oracle $H(\cdot)$, Q_t be the number of queries issued to $\mathsf{DSATag}_K(\cdot)$, and $\mathcal{L}_H$ be the list of query/answer pairs submitted to $H(\cdot)$.

Proof of Theorem 1. We prove that HSAMD_1 meets d-$\mathsf{aggUF\text{-}CMA}$ security. We consider the following events:

- [Coll]: The event that A finds a collision of the random oracle $H(\cdot)$.
- [Change]: The event that A changes the orders of valid ID/message pairs for a queried sequence. For example, for a queried $((\mathsf{id}_1, m_1), (\mathsf{id}_2, m_2), (\mathsf{id}_3, m_3), \ldots, (\mathsf{id}_N, m_N))$, A generates a forgery on $((\mathsf{id}_2, m_2), (\mathsf{id}_1, m_1), (\mathsf{id}_3, m_3), \ldots, (\mathsf{id}_N, m_N))$.
- [Combine]: The event that A makes a forgery by combining subsequences in queried ID/message sequences. For example, for two queried sequences

$$((\mathsf{id}_1, m_1), \ldots, (\mathsf{id}_{N/2}, m_{N/2}), (\mathsf{id}_{N/2+1}, m_{N/2+1}), \ldots, (\mathsf{id}_N, m_N)) \text{ and}$$
$$((\mathsf{id}_1, m_1'), \ldots, (\mathsf{id}_{N/2}, m_{N/2}'), (\mathsf{id}_{N/2+1}, m_{N/2+1}'), \ldots, (\mathsf{id}_N, m_N')),$$

the adversary may generate a forgery on $((\mathsf{id}_1, m_1), \ldots, (\mathsf{id}_{N/2}, m_{N/2}), (\mathsf{id}_{N/2+1}, m_{N/2+1}'), \ldots, (\mathsf{id}_N, m_N'))$.
- [Forge]: The event that A makes forgeries of the underlying MACs.

Notice that a counter count is used to prevent the event [Combine].
Then, we have

$$Adv_{\mathsf{HSAMD}_1, \mathsf{A}}^{\mathsf{agg\text{-}uf}}(\lambda) \leq \Pr[\mathsf{Coll}] + \Pr[\mathsf{Change} \mid \overline{\mathsf{Coll}}]$$
$$+ \Pr[\mathsf{Combine} \mid \overline{\mathsf{Change}} \wedge \overline{\mathsf{Coll}}]$$
$$+ \Pr[\mathsf{Forge} \mid \overline{\mathsf{Combine}} \wedge \overline{\mathsf{Change}} \wedge \overline{\mathsf{Coll}}].$$

We consider the event [Coll]. We construct a PPT algorithm B breaking the collision-resistance of $H(\cdot)$ as follows: It generates keys for all IDs and simulates $\mathsf{DSATag}_K(\cdot)$. When A outputs (M^*, τ^*), where $M^* = ((\mathsf{id}_{\ell_i^*}, m_i^*))_{i \in [N]}$ and $\tau^* = (\mathsf{count}^*, (\tau_1^*, \ldots, \tau_N^*))$, then B computes $J \leftarrow \mathsf{DSAVrfy}(K, M^*, \tau^*)$ and finds a pair $((\mathsf{count}', \mathsf{t}_1', \ldots, \mathsf{t}_{k'}'), \tau_i^*) \in \mathcal{L}_H$ such that $\tau_i^* = H(\mathsf{count}^*, \mathsf{t}_{i_1}^*, \ldots, \mathsf{t}_{i_k}^*)$ and $(\mathsf{count}^*, \mathsf{t}_{i_1}^*, \ldots, \mathsf{t}_{i_k}^*) \neq (\mathsf{count}', \mathsf{t}_1', \ldots, \mathsf{t}_{k'}')$, where $\mathsf{t}_{i_j}^* \leftarrow \mathsf{Tag}(\mathsf{k}_{\mathsf{id}_{\ell_j^*}}, m_j^*)$ for each $j \in [k]$. Finally, it outputs the pair $((\mathsf{count}^*, \mathsf{t}_{i_1}^*, \ldots, \mathsf{t}_{i_k}^*), (\mathsf{count}', \mathsf{t}_1', \ldots, \mathsf{t}_{k'}'))$. Then, $\Pr[\mathsf{Coll}] \leq (Q_h + uQ_t)^2 / 2^{n+1}$ holds since the number of queries submitted to $H(\cdot)$ is at most $(Q_h + uQ_t)$.

As for [Change $\mid \overline{\mathsf{Coll}}$], A outputs a forgery by exchanging orders of ID/message pairs without making any forgeries of MACs. By using the adversary A, we construct a PPT algorithm D breaking the pseudorandomness of a MAC scheme, as follows:

Setup: Given the oracle $\mathsf{Tag}(\cdot)$ in the pseudorandomness game, do the following:
- $\mathsf{k}_{\mathsf{id}_i} \leftarrow \mathsf{KGen}(1^\lambda, \mathsf{id}_i)$ for all $i \in [N]$, and $K \leftarrow \{(\mathsf{k}_{\mathsf{id}_i}, \mathsf{id}_i)\}_{i \in [N]}$.
- $\mathsf{id}^* \xleftarrow{U} \{\mathsf{id}_i\}_{i \in [N]}$, $\mathcal{L}_{\mathsf{SA}} \leftarrow \emptyset$, $\mathcal{L}_H \leftarrow \emptyset$, and $\mathsf{count} \leftarrow 1$.

- Simulate the random oracle $H(\mathsf{count}, t_{i_1}, \ldots, t_{i_k})$ as follows:
  1. If there exists a pair $((\mathsf{count}, t_{i_1}, \ldots, t_{i_k}), \tau_i) \in \mathcal{L}_H$, return τ_i.
  2. Otherwise, return $\tau_i \xleftarrow{U} \mathcal{T}$ and set
     $\mathcal{L}_H \leftarrow \mathcal{L}_H \cup \{((\mathsf{count}, t_{i_1}, \ldots, t_{i_k}), \tau_i)\}$.

Tagging: For the j-th query $M^{(j)} = ((\mathsf{id}_i^{(j)}, m_i^{(j)}))_{i \in [N]}$ to $\mathsf{DSATag}_K(\cdot)$, do the following:

1. For all $i \in [N]$, let $t_i^{(j)} := \mathsf{Tag}(i \| m_i^{(j)})$ if $\mathsf{id}_i^{(j)} = \mathsf{id}^*$, and compute $t_i^{(j)} \leftarrow \mathsf{MAC.Tag}(\mathsf{k}_{\mathsf{id}_i^{(j)}}, i \| m_i^{(j)})$ if $\mathsf{id}_i^{(j)} \neq \mathsf{id}^*$.
2. Return $(\mathsf{count}, (\tau_i^{(j)})_{i \in [u]}) \leftarrow \mathsf{DSeqAgg}((\mathsf{id}_i^{(j)}, t_i^{(j)})_{i \in [N]})$.
3. $\mathsf{count} \leftarrow \mathsf{count} + 1$ and $\mathcal{L}_{\mathsf{SA}} \leftarrow \mathcal{L}_{\mathsf{SA}} \cup \{M^{(j)}\}$.

Output: When A outputs an ID/message sequence $M^* = ((\mathsf{id}_{\ell_i^*}, m_i^*))_{i \in [N]}$ and an aggregate tag $\tau^* = (\mathsf{count}^*, (\tau_i^*)_{i \in [u]})$, do the following:

1. Let v be the order of id^* in M^*.
2. $t_i^* \leftarrow \mathsf{MAC.Tag}(\mathsf{k}_{\mathsf{id}_{\ell_i^*}}, i \| m_i^*)$ for all $i \in [N] \backslash \{v\}$, and $t_v^* \leftarrow \mathsf{Tag}(v \| m_v^*)$.
3. Find $((\mathsf{count}^*, t_{i_1}^*, \ldots, t_{i_k}^*), \tau_i^*) \in \mathcal{L}_H$ including t_v^*.
4. Abort this game if there does not exist such a pair.
5. $J \leftarrow \mathsf{DSAVrfy}(K, M^*, \tau^*)$. (then, note that id^* is valid.)
6. Output 1 if the success condition of A holds. Output 0 otherwise.

We analyze the above algorithm D. If A knows MAC-tags for aggregate tags received from $\mathsf{DSATag}_K(\cdot)$, it can generate a valid forgery swapped the orders of messages. And, the probability that A outputs a valid forgery without querying to $H(\cdot)$ is at most 2^{-n}. Hence, the success probability is at least $N^{-1}(\Pr[\mathsf{Change} \mid \overline{\mathsf{Coll}}] - 2^{-n})$.

Regarding $[\mathsf{Combine} \mid \overline{\mathsf{Change}} \wedge \overline{\mathsf{Coll}}]$, A outputs a forgery by combining subsequences in queried sequences without changing orders of messages. In order to generate a valid forgery, A needs to know MAC-tags generated by $\mathsf{DSATag}_K(\cdot)$ again. Notice that a counter value count prevents any adversary from generating a forgery by selecting aggregate tags on subsequences in queried sequences. Thus, a PPT algorithm D$'$ breaking the **pseudorandomness** of MACs is constructed in the same way as the algorithm D, and the success probability of D$'$ is at least $N^{-1}(\Pr[\mathsf{Combine} \mid \overline{\mathsf{Change}} \wedge \overline{\mathsf{Coll}}] - 2^{-n})$.

If $[\mathsf{Forge} \mid \overline{\mathsf{Combine}} \wedge \overline{\mathsf{Change}} \wedge \overline{\mathsf{Coll}}]$ happens, A makes a valid forgery for the underlying MACs. By using A, we construct a PPT algorithm F breaking UF-CMA security, in the same was as the above one D except for the process of **Output** phase as follows: Given $M^* = ((\mathsf{id}_{\ell_i^*}, m_i^*))_{i \in [N]}$ and $\tau^* = (\mathsf{count}^*, (\tau_i^*)_{i \in [u]})$ from A, do the following:

1. Let v be the order of id^* in M^*.
2. $t_i^* \leftarrow \mathsf{MAC.Tag}(\mathsf{k}_{\mathsf{id}_{\ell_i^*}}, i \| m_i^*)$ for all $i \in [N] \backslash \{v\}$.
3. Find $((\mathsf{count}^*, t_{i_1}^*, \ldots, t_{i_k}^*), \tau_i^*) \in \mathcal{L}_H$ including $i_j = v$. ($j \in [k]$)
4. Abort if there does not exist such a pair or $v \| m_v$ has been submitted to the given oracle $\mathsf{Tag}(\cdot)$.
5. $J \leftarrow \mathsf{DSAVrfy}(K, M^*, \tau^*)$. (then, id^* is valid.)
6. Output $(v \| m_v^*, t_v^*)$ if the success condition of A holds. Abort otherwise.

We analyze the output of F. If A generates a forgery of MACs, it submits this tag to $H(\cdot)$ with overwhelming probability. Thus, F can find the targeted MAC-tag from $\mathcal{L}_H$. The probability that A outputs the valid forgery in aggUF-CMA game without querying $H(\cdot)$ is at most 2^{-n}. The success probability is at least $N^{-1}(\Pr[\mathsf{Forge} \mid \overline{\mathsf{Combine}} \wedge \overline{\mathsf{Change}} \wedge \overline{\mathsf{Coll}}] - 2^{-n})$.

From the discussion above, we obtain

$$Adv^{\text{agg-uf}}_{\mathsf{HSAMD}_1,\mathsf{A}}(\lambda) \leq 2N \cdot Adv^{\text{pr}}_{\mathsf{MAC},\mathsf{D}}(\lambda) + N \cdot Adv^{\text{uf}}_{\mathsf{MAC},\mathsf{F}}(\lambda)$$

$$+\frac{(Q_h + uQ_t)^2}{2^{n+1}} + \frac{3}{2^n}$$

$$\leq 3N \cdot Adv^{\text{pr}}_{\mathsf{MAC},\mathsf{D}}(\lambda) + \frac{(Q_h + uQ_t)^2}{2^{n+1}} + \frac{N+3}{2^n}.$$

Note that $Adv^{\text{uf}}_{\mathsf{MAC}}(\lambda) \leq Adv^{\text{pr}}_{\mathsf{MAC},\mathsf{D}}(\lambda) + 2^{-n}$ from Proposition 2.7 in [1]. Therefore, the proof is completed.

Proof of Theorem 2. We show HSAMD_1 meets d-message-identifiability. Regarding d-message-completeness, all valid messages are regarded as valid ones from the property of d-disjunct matrices. As for d-message-soundness, we show that HSAMD_1 meets this security from the collision-resistance of $H(\cdot)$ and the property of d-disjunct matrices. A PPT algorithm B which finds a collision of $H(\cdot)$ is constructed as follows: It generates keys of all IDs and simulates tagging oracle. When A outputs $((m_i^*, \mathsf{id}_{\ell_i^*}, t_i^*))_{i \in [N]}$, B computes $J \leftarrow \mathsf{DSAVrfy}(K, M^*, \tau^*)$, where $M^* \leftarrow ((m_i^*, \mathsf{id}_{\ell_i^*}))_{i \in [N]}$ and $\tau^* = (\mathsf{count}^*, (\tau_i^*)_{i \in [u]}) \leftarrow \mathsf{DSeqAgg}$ $(((\mathsf{id}_{\ell_i^*}, t_i^*))_{i \in [N]})$. Then, it checks whether there exists $\mathsf{id}_{\ell_v^*}$ such that $t_v^* \neq \mathsf{MAC.Tag}(\mathsf{k}_{\mathsf{id}_{\ell_v^*}}, v \| m_v^*)$ and $\tau_i^* = H(\mathsf{count}^*, t_{i_1}', \cdots, t_{i_{k'}}')$ including $i_j = v$ ($j \in [k']$), where for $j \in [k']$, $t_{i_j}' = \mathsf{MAC.Tag}(\mathsf{k}_{\mathsf{id}_{i_j}}, i_j \| m_{i_j}^*)$. If so, B outputs $(\mathsf{count}^*, t_{i_1}', \ldots, t_{i_{k'}}')$ and $(\mathsf{count}^*, t_{i_1}^*, \ldots, t_{i_k}^*)$. Then, $(\mathsf{count}^*, t_{i_1}', \cdots, t_{i_{k'}}') \neq (\mathsf{count}^*, t_{i_1}^*, \cdots, t_{i_k}^*)$ holds from $t_v^* \neq \mathsf{MAC.Tag}(\mathsf{k}_{\mathsf{id}_{\ell_v^*}}, v \| m_v^*)$. Thus, B outputs a collision of $H(\cdot)$. We have $Adv^{\text{m-ident-s}}_{\mathsf{HSAMD}_1,\mathsf{A}}(\lambda) \leq Q_h^2/2^{n+1}$ since the number of queries submitted to $H(\cdot)$ is at most Q_h.

Next, we consider d-order-identifiability of HSAMD_1. d-order-completeness is obviously met from the property of d-disjunct matrices and the correctness of MACs. As for d-order-soundness, A finds a collision of $H(\cdot)$ or breaks the UF-CMA security of the underlying MACs. The probability that A breaks the collision-resistance of $H(\cdot)$ is at most $(Q_h + uQ_t)^2/2^{n+1}$. As for the event of making a forgery of MACs, we construct a PPT adversary F breaking UF-CMA security of MACs as follows:

Setup: Given the oracle $\mathsf{Tag}(\cdot)$ in UF-CMA game, do the following:
- $\mathsf{k}_{\mathsf{id}_i} \leftarrow \mathsf{KGen}(1^\lambda, \mathsf{id}_i)$ for all $i \in [N]$ and $K \leftarrow \{(\mathsf{k}_{\mathsf{id}_i}, \mathsf{id}_i)\}_{i \in [N]}$.
- $\mathsf{id}^* \overset{U}{\leftarrow} \{\mathsf{id}_i\}_{i \in [N]}$, $\mathcal{L}_{\mathsf{SA}} \leftarrow \emptyset, \mathcal{L}_H \leftarrow \emptyset$ and $\mathsf{count} \leftarrow 1$.
- Simulate the random oracle $H(\mathsf{count}, t_{i_1}, \ldots, t_{i_k})$ as follows:
  1. If there exists a pair $((\mathsf{count}, t_{i_1}, \ldots, t_{i_k}), \tau_i) \in \mathcal{L}_H$, return τ_i.
  2. Otherwise, return $\tau_i \overset{U}{\leftarrow} T$ and set
     $\mathcal{L}_H \leftarrow \mathcal{L}_H \cup \{((\mathsf{count}, t_{i_1}, \ldots, t_{i_k}), \tau_i)\}$.

Tagging: For the j-th query $M^{(j)} = ((\mathsf{id}_i^{(j)}, m_i^{(j)}))_{i \in [N]}$ to $\mathsf{DSATag}_K(\cdot)$, do the following:

1. For all $i \in [N]$, let $t_i^{(j)} := \mathsf{Tag}(i\|m_i^{(j)})$ if $\mathsf{id}_i^{(j)} = \mathsf{id}^*$, and compute $\mathsf{t}_i^{(j)} \leftarrow$ $\mathsf{MAC.Tag}(\mathsf{k}_{\mathsf{id}_i^{(j)}}, i\|m_i^{(j)})$ if $\mathsf{id}_i^{(j)} \neq \mathsf{id}^*$.

2. Return $(\mathsf{t}_i^{(j)})_{i \in [N]}$ and $\tau^{(j)} \leftarrow \mathsf{DSeqAgg}\left(((\mathsf{id}_i^{(j)}, \mathsf{t}_i^{(j)}))_{i \in [N]}\right)$.

3. $\mathsf{count} \leftarrow \mathsf{count} + 1$ and $\mathcal{L}_{\mathsf{SA}} \leftarrow \mathcal{L}_{\mathsf{SA}} \cup \{M^{(j)}\}$.

Output: When A outputs $((\mathsf{id}_{\ell_i^*}, m_i^*, \mathsf{t}_i^*))_{i \in [N]}$, do the following:

1. Find the q-th query satisfying $\{(\mathsf{id}_{\ell_i^*}, m_i^*)\}_{i \in [N]} = \{(\mathsf{id}_i^{(q)}, m_i^{(q)})\}_{i \in [N]}$ ($q \in [Q_t]$). Abort this game if there does not exist such a query.

2. Let v be the order of id^*.

3. Find $((\mathsf{count}^*, \mathsf{t}_{i_1}^*, \ldots, \mathsf{t}_{i_k}^*), \tau_i^*) \in \mathcal{L}_H$ including $i_j = v$ ($j \in [k]$).

4. Abort if there does not exist such a pair.

5. Output the pair $(v\|m_v^*, \mathsf{t}_v^*)$ if $(v, \mathsf{id}^*, m_v^*) \notin \{(v, \mathsf{id}_v^{(j)}, m_v^{(j)})\}_{j \in [Q_t]}$ holds. Abort otherwise.

F simulates the environment of A completely. If for the output of A, $(v, \mathsf{id}^*, m_v^*) \notin \{(v, \mathsf{id}_v^{(j)}, m_v^{(j)})\}_{j \in [Q_t]}$ holds, $v\|m_v^*$ has never been queried to $\mathsf{DSATag}_K(\cdot)$. Hence, if $(v\|m_v^*, \mathsf{t}_v^*)$ is valid, the output is a valid forgery in UF-CMA game. In this case, the success probability of A is at most $N \cdot Adv_{\mathsf{MAC},\mathsf{F}}^{\mathsf{uf}}(\lambda) + 2^{-n}$. Therefore, we obtain $Adv_{\mathsf{HSAMD}_1,\mathsf{A}}^{\mathsf{o\text{-}ident\text{-}s}}(\lambda) \leq N \cdot Adv_{\mathsf{MAC},\mathsf{F}}^{\mathsf{uf}}(\lambda) + (Q_h + uQ_t)^2/2^{n+1} + 2^{-n}$.

From the above discussion, the proof is completed.

4   SAMD Having Message-Order After Tagging

We consider a model and security of SAMDs having message-order after tagging which we call *SAMD-MOAT*. In this model, after each sender generates a MAC-tag on an individual message in parallel, message-order is given; and then, an aggregate tag is generated from message-order and all the MAC-tags without a secret key (i.e., keyless aggregation). Note that in this model, it is possible to aggregate MAC-tags whenever message-order is given to an aggregation node (or aggregator). In this sense, SAMD-MOAT is more convenient than SAMD-MOBT.

4.1   Model and Security of SAMD-MOAT

An SAMD-MOAT scheme consists of five polynomial-time algorithms (KGen, Tag, Vrfy, DSeqAgg, DSAVrfy) as follows: The symbols N, $\mathcal{ID}$, $\mathcal{K}$, $\mathcal{M}$, $\mathcal{T}$, $\mathcal{T}_{agg}$, and $\mathcal{S}$ are the same as those in SAMD-MOBT; and a sequence is given after executing Tag algorithm.

– $\mathsf{k}_{\mathsf{id}} \leftarrow \mathsf{KGen}(1^\lambda, \mathsf{id})$: KGen is a randomized algorithm which, on input a security parameter 1^λ and an ID $\mathsf{id} \in \mathcal{ID}$, outputs a secret key $\mathsf{k}_{\mathsf{id}} \in \mathcal{K}$.

- t ← Tag(k_{id}, m): Tag is a deterministic algorithm which, on input a secret key k_{id} and a message m, outputs a tag t ∈ $\mathcal{T}$.
- 1/0 ← Vrfy(k_{id}, m, t): Vrfy is a deterministic algorithm which, on input a secret key k_{id}, a message m ∈ $\mathcal{M}$, and a tag t, outputs 1 or 0.
- τ ← DSeqAgg(T): DSeqAgg is a deterministic algorithm which, on input a sequence of tags $T = ((id_{\ell_i}, t_i))_{i \in [N]}$ such that $(id_{\ell_1}, \ldots, id_{\ell_N}) \in \mathcal{S}$, outputs a tuple of sequential aggregate tags $\tau \in \mathcal{T}_{agg}$.
- $J/\bot$ ← DSAVrfy(K, M, τ): DSAVrfy is a deterministic algorithm which, on input a set of key/ID pairs $K = \{(k_{id_i}, id_i)\}_{i \in [N]}$, a sequence of ID/message pairs $((id_{\ell_i}, m_i))_{i \in [N]}$ for any $(id_{\ell_1}, \ldots, id_{\ell_N}) \in \mathcal{S}$, and an aggregate tag τ, outputs a list J or an error message $\bot$, where J is a list consisting of IDs whose messages are invalid or their order is invalid.

We require that the following condition (i.e., correctness) holds:

- For all id ∈ $\mathcal{ID}$, all k_{id} ← KGen(1^λ, id) and all m ∈ $\mathcal{M}$, we have 1 ← Vrfy(k_{id}, m, Tag(k_{id}, m)).
- For all id ∈ $\mathcal{ID}$, all k_{id} ← KGen(1^λ, id) and all $M = ((id_{\ell_i}, m_i))_{i \in [N]}$ such that $(id_{\ell_i})_{i \in [N]} \in \mathcal{S}$, we have $\emptyset$ ← DSAVrfy(K, M, τ), where $K = \{(k_{id_i}, id_i)\}_{i \in [N]}$ and τ ← DSeqAgg$(((id_{\ell_i}, \text{Tag}(k_{id_{\ell_i}}, m_i)))_{i \in [N]})$.

As security of SAMD-MOAT, the notions of aggUF-CMA security, message-identifiability, and order-identifiability are formalized along with the model of SAMD-MOAT in a similar way as those of SAMD-MOBT. In addition, we define the weaker notion of order-soundness, which is called weak-order-soundness.

Definition 5 (aggUF-CMA security). *Let d be a positive integer. An SAMD-MOAT scheme* SAMD = (KGen, Tag, Vrfy, DSeqAgg, DSAVrfy) *meets d-aggUF-CMA security if for any PPT adversary A against* SAMD*, the advantage* $Adv^{agg\text{-}uf}_{SAMD,A}(\lambda) := \Pr[A \text{ wins}]$ *is negligible. [A wins] is the event that A wins in the following game:*

Setup: k_{id_i} ← KGen(1^λ, id_i) *for all* $i \in [N]$, K ← $\{(k_{id_i}, id_i)\}_{i \in [N]}$, *and* $\mathcal{L}_{SA}$ ← $\emptyset$.

Tagging: *Given the j-th ID/message sequence* $M^{(j)} = ((id_i^{(j)}, m_i^{(j)}))_{i \in [N]}$ *such that* $(id_1^{(j)}, \ldots, id_N^{(j)}) \in \mathcal{S}$, *aggregate tagging oracle* DSATag$_K(\cdot)$ *does the following:*

  1. $t_i^{(j)}$ ← Tag($k_{id_i^{(j)}}$, $m_i^{(j)}$) *for all* $i \in [N]$.
  2. *Output* $\tau^{(j)}$ ← DSeqAgg$(((id_i^{(j)}, t_i^{(j)}))_{i \in [N]})$,
  3. *Set* $\mathcal{L}_{SA}$ ← $\mathcal{L}_{SA} \cup \{M^{(j)}\}$.

  The number of queries which A submits to DSATag$_K(\cdot)$ *is at most* $Q = $ poly(λ).

Output: *A outputs* $M^* = ((id_{\ell_i^*}, m_i^*))_{i \in [N]}$ *and* τ^* *such that* $(id_{\ell_i^*})_{i \in [N]} \in \mathcal{S}$. *Compute* J ← DSAVrfy(K, M^*, τ^*). *A wins if it holds that* $J \neq \bot$, $|J| \leq d$, *and* $((i, id_{\ell_i^*}, m_i^*))_{i \in [N] \wedge id_{\ell_i^*} \in J} \neq ((i, \hat{id}_i, \hat{m}_i))_{i \in [N] \wedge \hat{id}_i \in J}$ *for any* $((id_i, \hat{m}_i))_{i \in [N]} \in \mathcal{L}_{SA}$ *hold.*

Definition 6 (Message-Identifiability). *Let d be a positive integer. An SAMD-MOAT scheme* SAMD $=$ (KGen, Tag, Vrfy, DSeqAgg, DSAVrfy) *meets d-message-identifiability if it meets d-message-completeness and d-message-soundness that are defined as follows. Let* A *be a PPT adversary against* SAMD, *and we consider the following game:*

Setup: $k_{id_i} \leftarrow$ KGen$(1^\lambda, id_i)$ *for all* $i \in [N]$, *and* $K \leftarrow \{(k_{id_i}, id_i)\}_{i \in [N]}$.

Tagging: *Given an ID/message pair* (id_{ℓ_i}, m_i), *tagging oracle* Tag$_K(\cdot)$ *returns* $t_i \leftarrow$ Tag(k_{id_i}, m_i). *The number of queries which* A *submits is at most* $Q =$ poly(λ).

Output: A *outputs* $((m_i^*, id_{\ell_i^*}, t_i^*))_{i \in [N]}$. *Compute* $J \leftarrow$ DSAVrfy(K, M^*, τ^*), *where* $M^* \leftarrow ((id_{\ell_i^*}, m_i^*))_{i \in [N]}$ *and* $\tau^* \leftarrow$ DSeqAgg$(((id_{\ell_i^*}, t_i^*))_{i \in [N]})$.

- *Completeness:* SAMD *meets d-message-completeness if for any PPT adversary* A, *the advantage* $Adv_{SAMD,A}^{m\text{-}ident\text{-}c}(\lambda)$ *is negligible.* $Adv_{SAMD,A}^{m\text{-}ident\text{-}c}(\lambda)$ *is the probability that* $|J| \le d$ *and* $J \cap \{id_{\ell_i^*} \mid 1 \leftarrow$ Vrfy$(k_{id_{\ell_i^*}}, m_i^*, t_i^*), 1 \le i \le N\} \ne \emptyset$ *hold.*
- *Soundness:* SAMD *meets d-message-soundness if for any PPT adversary* A, *the advantage* $Adv_{SAMD,A}^{m\text{-}ident\text{-}s}(\lambda)$ *is negligible, where* $Adv_{SAMD,A}^{m\text{-}ident\text{-}s}(\lambda)$ *is the probability that* $|J| \le d$ *and* $\{id_{\ell_i^*} \mid 0 \leftarrow$ Vrfy$(k_{id_{\ell_i^*}}, m_i^*, t_i^*), 1 \le i \le N\} \backslash J \ne \emptyset$ *hold.*

Definition 7 (Order-Identifiability). *Let d be a positive integer. An SAMD-MOAT scheme* SAMD $=$ (KGen, Tag, Vrfy, DSeqAgg, DSAVrfy) *meets d-order-identifiability if it satisfies d-order-completeness and d-order-soundness defined as follows. Let* A *be a PPT adversary against* SAMD, *and we consider the following game:*

Setup: $k_{id_i} \leftarrow$ KGen$(1^\lambda, id_i)$ *for all* $i \subset [N]$, $K \leftarrow \{(k_{id_i}, id_i)\}_{i \in [N]}$, *and* $\mathcal{L}_{SA} \leftarrow \emptyset$.

Tagging: *Given the j-th ID/message sequence* $M^{(j)} = ((id_i^{(j)}, m_i^{(j)}))_{i \in [N]}$ *such that* $(id_1^{(j)}, \ldots, id_N^{(j)}) \in \mathcal{S}$, *aggregate tagging oracle* DSATag$_K(\cdot)$ *does the following:*

1. $t_i^{(j)} \leftarrow$ Tag$(k_{id_i^{(j)}}, m_i^{(j)})$ *for all* $i \in [N]$.
2. $\tau^{(j)} \leftarrow$ DSeqAgg$(((id_i^{(j)}, t_i^{(j)}))_{i \in [N]})$.
3. *Output* $(t_1^{(j)}, \ldots, t_N^{(j)}, \tau^{(j)})$, *and set* $\mathcal{L}_{SA} \leftarrow \mathcal{L}_{SA} \cup \{M^{(j)}\}$.

The number of queries which A *submits to tagging oracle is at most* $Q =$ poly(λ).

Output: A *outputs* $((id_{\ell_i^*}, m_i^*, t_i^*))_{i \in [N]}$ *such that* $((id_{\ell_i^*}, m_i^*))_{i \in [N]} \notin \mathcal{L}_{SA}$ *and there exists the q-th sequence query satisfying* $\{(id_{\ell_i^*}, m_i^*)\}_{i \in [N]} = \{(id_i^{(q)}, m_i^{(q)})\}_{i \in [N]}$. *Then, compute* $J \leftarrow$ DSAVrfy$(K, ((id_{\ell_i^*}, m_i^*))_{i \in [N]}, \tau^*)$, *where* $\tau^* \leftarrow$ DSeqAgg$(((id_{\ell_i^*}, t_i^*))_{i \in [N]})$.

- *Completeness:* SAMD *meets d-order-completeness if for any PPT adversary* A, *the advantage* $Adv_{SAMD,A}^{o\text{-}ident\text{-}c}(\lambda)$ *is negligible.* $Adv_{SAMD,A}^{o\text{-}ident\text{-}c}(\lambda)$ *is defined as the probability that* $|J| \le d$ *and* $J \cap \{id_{\ell_i^*} \mid (i, id_{\ell_i^*}, m_i^*) \in \{(i, id_i^{(j)}, m_i^{(j)})\}_{j \in [Q]}, 1 \leftarrow$ Vrfy$(k_{\ell_i^*}, m_i^*, t_i^*), 1 \le i \le N\} \ne \emptyset$ *hold.*

- *Soundness:* SAMD *meets d-order-soundness if for any PPT adversary* A, *the advantage* $Adv_{\mathsf{SAMD},A}^{\text{o-ident-s}}(\lambda)$ *is negligible, where* $Adv_{\mathsf{SAMD},A}^{\text{o-ident-s}}(\lambda)$ *is defined as the probability that* $|J| \leq d$ *and* $\{id_{\ell_i^*} \mid (i, id_{\ell_i^*}, m_i^*) \notin \{(i, id_i^{(j)}, m_i^{(j)})\}_{j \in [Q]}, 1 \leftarrow \mathsf{Vrfy}(k_{\ell_i^*}, m_i^*, t_i^*), 1 \leq i \leq N\} \backslash J \neq \emptyset$ *hold.*

In addition, we define d-weak-order-soundness in the same way as d-order-soundness except that in the d-weak-order-soundness game, $\mathsf{DSATag}_K(\cdot)$ just returns an aggregate tag $\tau^{(j)}$ while in d-order-soundness game, it returns MAC-tags and an aggregate tag $(t_1^{(j)}, \ldots, t_N^{(j)}, \tau^{(j)})$.

The following proposition states a relationship between d-aggUF-CMA security and d-weak-order-soundness.

Proposition 1. *If an SAMD-MOAT scheme meets d-aggUF-CMA security, it also meets d-weak-order-soundness.*

Proof. Let A be a PPT adversary breaking d-weak-order-soundness. We construct a PPT algorithm B breaking d-aggUF-CMA security as follows: B is given the tagging oracle in d-aggUF-CMA security game. When A submits message sequence, it issues this to the given oracle and returns the response. When A outputs $((id_{\ell_i^*}, m_i^*, t_i^*))_{i \in [N]}$, it computes $\tau^* \leftarrow \mathsf{DSeqAgg}(((id_{\ell_i^*}, t_i^*))_{i \in [N]})$ and outputs $((id_{\ell_i^*}, m_i^*))_{i \in [N]}$ and τ^*. If A breaks d-weak-order-soundness, B also breaks d-aggUF-CMA security. This is because the output in d-weak-order-soundness game can be viewed as a forgery which is generated by exchanging message-orders in d-aggUF-CMA game. Hence, we complete the proof.

4.2   Construction of SAMD-MOAT

We construct an SAMD-MOAT scheme HSAMD_2. The difference between HSAMD_1 and HSAMD_2 is as follows: In HSAMD_2, each sender does not need to generate a MAC-tag on the order information of local messages while in HSAMD_1, each sender has to include the order information as a part of a message in generating a MAC-tag. However, HSAMD_2 does not meet order-soundness because the relation between messages and orders is not guaranteed while in HSAMD_1, the relation is guaranteed by the underlying MACs. Even though HSAMD_2 does not guarantee order-soundness, a verifier can detect IDs whose local messages or order information are invalid (see Proposition 1).

To construct HSAMD_2, we use the following parameters and primitives based on a security parameter λ: Let $N = \mathsf{poly}(\lambda)$ be the number of senders, $\mathsf{MAC} = (\mathsf{MAC.KGen}, \mathsf{MAC.Tag}, \mathsf{MAC.Vrfy})$ be a MAC scheme, $G \in \{0,1\}^{u \times N}$ be a d-disjunct matrix, $H : \{0,1\}^* \to \mathcal{T}$ be a random oracle, $\mathsf{count} \leftarrow 1$ be a counter which is kept by an aggregator and updated after an aggregate tag is sent, and $\mathsf{count}_{ver} \leftarrow 1$ be a counter which is kept by a verifier.

$\mathsf{HSAMD}_2 = (\mathsf{KGen}, \mathsf{Tag}, \mathsf{Vrfy}, \mathsf{DSeqAgg}, \mathsf{DSAVrfy})$ is given as follows:

- $k_{id} \leftarrow \mathsf{KGen}(1^\lambda, id)$: Output a key $k_{id} \leftarrow \mathsf{MAC.KGen}(1^\lambda)$ for an ID id.
- $t \leftarrow \mathsf{Tag}(k_{id}, m)$: Output a tag $t \leftarrow \mathsf{MAC.Tag}(k_{id}, m)$.

- $1/0 \leftarrow \mathsf{Vrfy}(\mathsf{k_{id}}, m, \mathsf{t})$: Output $b \leftarrow \mathsf{MAC.Vrfy}(\mathsf{k_{id}}, m, \mathsf{t}) \in \{0, 1\}$.
- $\tau \leftarrow \mathsf{DSeqAgg}(T)$: For $T = ((\mathsf{id}_{\ell_1}, \mathsf{t}_1), \ldots, (\mathsf{id}_{\ell_N}, \mathsf{t}_N))$, do the following:
  1. For all $i \in [u]$, $\tau_i \leftarrow H(\mathsf{count}, (i_1, \mathsf{t}_{i_1}), (i_2, \mathsf{t}_{i_2}), \ldots, (i_k, \mathsf{t}_{i_k}))$, where $I(G, i) = \{i_1, i_2, \ldots, i_k\}$.
  2. Output $\tau = (\mathsf{count}, (\tau_i)_{i \in [u]})$ and set $\mathsf{count} \leftarrow \mathsf{count} + 1$.
- $J/\bot \leftarrow \mathsf{DSAVrfy}(K, M, \tau)$: The verification for $M = ((m_i, \mathsf{id}_{\ell_i}))_{i \in [N]}$ and $\tau = (\mathsf{count}, (\tau_i)_{i \in [u]})$ is as follows:
  1. Output $\bot$ if $\mathsf{count} \neq \mathsf{count}_{ver}$.
  2. $J \leftarrow \{\mathsf{id}_i\}_{i \in [N]}$.
  3. For $i \in [u]$, do the following: $J \leftarrow J \backslash \{\mathsf{id}_{\ell_j}\}$ for all $j \in \{i_1, \ldots, i_k\}$ if $\tau_i = H(\mathsf{count}, (i_1, \mathsf{t}_{i_1}), \ldots, (i_k, \mathsf{t}_{i_k}))$ holds, where $(\mathsf{id}_{\ell_{i_1}}, \ldots, \mathsf{id}_{\ell_{i_k}}) = \mathbf{s}(G, i)$ and $\mathsf{t}_{i_1} = \mathsf{Tag}(\mathsf{k}_{\mathsf{id}_{\ell_{i_1}}}, m_{i_1}), \ldots, \mathsf{t}_{i_k} = \mathsf{Tag}(\mathsf{k}_{\mathsf{id}_{\ell_{i_k}}}, m_{i_k})$.
  4. Output J and set $\mathsf{count}_{ver} \leftarrow \mathsf{count}_{ver} + 1$.

We can show the security of the above construction (see Theorems 3 and 4 below). The proofs are provided in Appendix B: The proofs can be given in a similar way as those of Theorems 1 and 2 but more complicated than those due to the model of SAMD-MOAT.

Theorem 3 (Unforgeability). *Suppose that the number of IDs whose messages or their positions in sequential messages are invalid is at most d. If MAC meets pseudorandomness and G is a d-disjunct matrix, then, the resulting SAMD-MOAT scheme HSAMD$_2$ satisfies d-aggUF-CMA security in the random oracle model.*

Theorem 4 (Identifiability). *Suppose that the number of IDs whose messages or their positions in sequential messages are invalid is at most d. Then, we have the following in the random oracle model: (i) If G is a d-disjunct matrix, HSAMD$_2$ meets d-message-identifiability; (ii) If G is a d-disjunct matrix and MAC meets pseudorandomness, HSAMD$_2$ meets d-order-completeness and d-weak-order-soundness.*

5   Conclusion

In this paper, we proposed a refined model and security formalization of SAMDs where aggregation is a keyless procedure: There were two types of SAMDs, SAMD-MOBT and SAMD-MOAT. In each model, we provided a generic construction from any MACs, a cryptographic hash function, and a disjunct matrix. Our construction of SAMD-MOBT satisfied all the security formalizations, while our construction of SAMD-MOAT met all the security formalizations except order-soundness but satisfied weak-order-soundness. This means that constructing fully secure SAMD-MOAT is more difficult than that of SAMD-MOBT, while SAMD-MOAT is more convenient than SAMD-MOBT since the aggregate process can be executed anytime in SAMD-MOAT. Our results clarify suitable applications of SAMDs by taking into account both convenience and achievable security levels. For instance, the model of SAMDs in [10] is very close to that of SAMD-MOAT, but the application considered in [10] (i.e., sending long data by data-partitioning) can be realized by our model SAMD-MOBT with high security level.

Acknowledgements. The authors would like to thank anonymous referees for their helpful comments. This research was conducted under a contract of Research and Development for Expansion of Radio Wave Resources funded by the Ministry of Internal Affairs and Communications, Japan.

Appendix A: Cryptanalysis of [9] and [10]

Regarding sequential aggregate message authentication codes (SAMACs) with keyless aggregation, the hash-based SAMAC scheme in [9,10] which we call HSAMAC was constructed. The authors claim that if the underlying MAC scheme meets pseudorandomness, then HSAMAC satisfies aggUF-CMA security. However, there exists a counterexample that HSAMAC is broken in the aggUF-CMA game [9,10] due to the corrupt setting even though the underlying MAC scheme meets pseudorandomness. In this setting, an adversary can issue some IDs to a corrupt oracle and get the corresponding secret keys before accessing a tagging oracle. The attack is as follows: An adversary obtains a secret key k_{id} by submitting a query id to the corrupt oracle, submits a message-sequence query $(\ldots, m, \ldots)$ to the tagging oracle, and receives an aggregate tag τ. Then, he/she computes a MAC-tag t on the message m included in the queried sequence and finds a collision m' such that $t = Tag(k, m')$. The adversary submits an aggregate tag τ and a message sequence replaced m by m'. Notice that although HSAMAC may not be broken by this attack if the underlying MAC is NMAC/HMAC, the claim in [9,10] is not correct in the sense that HSAMAC obtained from any pseudorandom MAC does not always fulfill the security.

However, it should be noted that HSAMAC meets aggUF-CMA security without the corrupt setting. The security proof without the corrupt setting can be provided in a similar way as [9,10] without considering the corrupt oracle. In addition, its application to data-partitioning considered in [9,10] is still valid, since we do not need to consider the corrupt setting in this application.

As for SAMD schemes, the hash-based scheme was proposed in [10] and we call it HSAMD. This scheme meets the unforgeability defined in [10]. However, in the case where A outputs a forgery including some invalid message/tag pairs, HSAMD does not guarantee that the order of valid message/tag pairs is unchanged. This type of attacks will be possible by using the attacking technique for HSAMAC mentioned above.

Appendix B: Proofs of Theorems 3 and 4

We provide security proofs of Theorems 3 and 4 in which A is a PPT adversary against HSAMD$_2$. Let n be the bit-length of MAC-tags, Q_h be the number of queries issued to the random oracle $H(\cdot)$, Q_t be the number of queries issued to the tagging oracle, and $\mathcal{L}_H$ be the list of query/answer pairs submitted to $H(\cdot)$.

Proof of Theorem 3. We prove that $\mathsf{HSAMD_2}$ meets d-$\mathsf{aggUF\text{-}CMA}$ security. In the same way as the proof of Theorem 1, we consider the following events:

- [Coll]: The event that A finds a collision of the random oracle $H(\cdot)$.
- [Change]: The event that A changes the orders of valid ID/message pairs for a queried message sequence.
- [Combine]: The event that A makes a forgery by combining subsequences in queried ID/message sequences.
- [Forge]: The event that A makes forgeries of the underlying MACs.

Then, we have

$$Adv^{\text{agg-uf}}_{\mathsf{HSAMD_2},A}(\lambda) \leq \Pr[\text{Coll}] + \Pr[\text{Change} \mid \overline{\text{Coll}}]$$
$$+ \Pr[\text{Combine} \mid \overline{\text{Change}} \wedge \overline{\text{Coll}}]$$
$$+ \Pr[\text{Forge} \mid \overline{\text{Combine}} \wedge \overline{\text{Change}} \wedge \overline{\text{Coll}}].$$

We consider the event [Coll]. It is possible to construct a PPT algorithm breaking the collision-resistance of the random oracle and get $\Pr[\text{Coll}] \leq \frac{(Q_h + uQ_t)^2}{2^{n+1}}$ since the number of queries submitted to the random oracle is at most $(Q_h + uQ_t)$.

We consider [Change $\mid \overline{\text{Coll}}$]. If A knows MAC-tags, it is possible to swap orders for a queried message sequence. Namely, A can generate any order swapping forgery (or valid sequence forgery). Thus, we show that if the underlying MACs meet pseudorandomness, the probability that those events happen is negligible. We construct a PPT algorithm D breaking pseudorandomness as follows:

Setup: Given the tagging oracle $\mathsf{Tag}(\cdot)$ in pseudorandomness game, do the following:
- $k_{\mathsf{id}_i} \leftarrow \mathsf{KGen}(1^\lambda, \mathsf{id}_i)$ for all $i \in [N]$ and $K \leftarrow \{(k_{\mathsf{id}_i}, \mathsf{id}_i)\}_{i \in [N]}$.
- $\mathsf{id}^* \xleftarrow{U} \{\mathsf{id}_i\}_{i \in [N]}$, $\mathcal{L}_{\mathsf{SA}} \leftarrow \emptyset$, $\mathcal{L}_H \leftarrow \emptyset$, and count $\leftarrow 1$.
- Simulate the random oracle $H(\text{count}, (i_1, \mathsf{t}_{i_1}), \ldots, (i_k, \mathsf{t}_{i_k}))$:
  1. If $((\text{count}, (i_1, \mathsf{t}_{i_1}), \ldots, (i_k, \mathsf{t}_{i_k})), \tau_i) \in \mathcal{L}_H$ holds, return τ_i.
  2. Otherwise, return $\tau_i \xleftarrow{U} \mathcal{T}$ and set
     $\mathcal{L}_H \leftarrow \mathcal{L}_H \cup \{((\text{count}, (i_1, \mathsf{t}_{i_1}), \ldots, (i_k, \mathsf{t}_{i_k})), \tau_i)\}$.

Tagging: For each query $M^{(j)} = ((\mathsf{id}_i^{(j)}, m_i^{(j)}))_{i \in [N]}$ to $\mathsf{DSATag}_K(\cdot)$, do the following:
1. For all $i \in [N]$, do the following:
   - If $\mathsf{id}_i^{(j)} = \mathsf{id}^*$, $\mathsf{t}_i^{(j)} \leftarrow \mathsf{Tag}(m_i^{(j)})$.
   - If $\mathsf{id}_i^{(j)} \neq \mathsf{id}^*$, $\mathsf{t}_i^{(j)} \leftarrow \mathsf{MAC.Tag}(k_{\mathsf{id}_i^{(j)}}, m_i^{(j)})$.
2. Return $(\text{count}, (\tau_i^{(j)})_{i \in [u]}) \leftarrow \mathsf{DSeqAgg}(((\mathsf{id}_i^{(j)}, \mathsf{t}_i^{(j)}))_{i \in [N]})$ to A.
3. Set $\mathcal{L}_{\mathsf{SA}} \leftarrow \mathcal{L}_{\mathsf{SA}} \cup \{M^{(j)}\}$.

Output: When A outputs an ID/message sequence $M^* = ((\mathsf{id}_{\ell_i^*}, m_i^*))_{i \in [N]}$ and an aggregate tag $\tau^* = (\mathsf{count}^*, (\tau_i^*)_{i \in [u]})$, do the following:

1. Let v be the order of id^* in M^*.
2. $\mathsf{t}_i^* \leftarrow \mathsf{MAC.Tag}(\mathsf{k}_{\mathsf{id}_{\ell_i^*}}, m_i^*)$ for all $i \in [N] \backslash \{v\}$, and $\mathsf{t}_v^* \leftarrow \mathsf{Tag}(m_v^*)$.
3. Find $((\mathsf{count}^*, (i_1, \mathsf{t}_{i_1}^*), \ldots, (i_k, \mathsf{t}_{i_k}^*)), \tau_i^*) \in \mathcal{L}_H$ including t_v^*.
4. Abort this game if there does not exist such a pair.
5. $J \leftarrow \mathsf{DSAVrfy}(K, M^*, \tau^*)$. (note that id^* is valid since it is included in $\mathcal{L}_H$.)
6. Output 1 if $J \neq \perp$, $|J| \leq d$, and $((i, \mathsf{id}_{\ell_i^*}, m_i^*))_{i \in [N] \wedge \mathsf{id}_{\ell_i^*} \notin J} \neq ((i, \bar{\mathsf{id}}_i, \bar{m}_i))_{i \in [N] \wedge \bar{\mathsf{id}}_i \notin J}$ for all $((\bar{\mathsf{id}}_i, \bar{m}_i))_{i \in [N]} \in \mathcal{L}_{\mathsf{SA}}$. Output 0 otherwise.

D simulates the view of A. If A submits the valid MAC-tag of the target ID, D can find it from $\mathcal{L}_H$. Besides, the probability that A wins without querying the tag is at most 2^{-n}. Thus, the success probability of these algorithms is at least $N^{-1}(\mathrm{Pr}[\mathsf{Change} \mid \overline{\mathsf{Coll}}] - 2^{-n})$.

As for $[\mathsf{Combine} \mid \overline{\mathsf{Change}} \wedge \overline{\mathsf{Coll}}]$, we can apply the same discussion as $[\mathsf{Change} \mid \overline{\mathsf{Coll}}]$ since it is possible to generate any forgery by using MAC-tags if these tags are known. So, we can construct a PPT algorithm breaking the pseudorandomness of MACs in the same way as D with at least success probability $N^{-1}(\mathrm{Pr}[\mathsf{Combine} \mid \overline{\mathsf{Change}} \wedge \overline{\mathsf{Coll}}] - 2^{-n})$.

Regarding $[\mathsf{Forge} \mid \overline{\mathsf{Combine}} \wedge \overline{\mathsf{Change}} \wedge \overline{\mathsf{Coll}}]$, we construct a PPT algorithm F breaking the UF-CMA security of MACs. This algorithm is the same as D except that when A outputs $M^* = ((\mathsf{id}_{\ell_i^*}, m_i^*))_{i \in [N]}$ and $\tau^* = (\mathsf{count}^*, (\tau_i^*)_{i \in [u]})$, do the following:

1. Let v be the order of id^* in M^*.
2. $t_i^* \leftarrow \mathsf{MAC.Tag}(\mathsf{k}_{\mathsf{id}_{\ell_i^*}}, m_i^*)$ for all $i \in [N] \backslash \{v\}$.
3. Find a pair $((\mathsf{count}^*, (i_1, \mathsf{t}_{i_1}^*), \ldots, (i_k, \mathsf{t}_{i_k}^*)), \tau_i^*) \in \mathcal{L}_H$ including $i_j = v$. ($j \in [k]$)
4. Abort if there does not exist such a pair or m_v has been submitted to the given oracle $\mathsf{Tag}(\cdot)$.
5. $J \leftarrow \mathsf{DSAVrfy}(K, M^*, \tau^*)$. (assume that id^* is valid.)
6. Output (m_v^*, t_v^*) if $J \neq \perp$, $|J| \leq d$, and $((i, \mathsf{id}_{\ell_i^*}, m_i^*))_{i \in [N] \wedge \mathsf{id}_{\ell_i^*} \notin J} \neq ((i, \bar{\mathsf{id}}_i, \bar{m}_i))_{i \in [N] \wedge \bar{\mathsf{id}}_i \notin J}$ for all $((\bar{\mathsf{id}}_i, \bar{m}_i))_{i \in [N]} \in \mathcal{L}_{\mathsf{SA}}$. Abort this game otherwise.

The output of F is a valid forgery of a MAC. If A wins in the security game without submitting MAC-tags to $H(\cdot)$, the abort event happens in **Output** phase. The probability that this abort event happens is at most 2^{-n}. Hence, the success probability of F is at least $N^{-1}(\mathrm{Pr}[\mathsf{Forge} \mid \overline{\mathsf{Combine}} \wedge \overline{\mathsf{Change}} \wedge \overline{\mathsf{Coll}}] - 2^{-n})$.

From the discussion above, we obtain

$$Adv_{\mathsf{HSAMD}_2, \mathsf{A}}^{\mathsf{agg\text{-}uf}}(\lambda) \leq 3N \cdot Adv_{\mathsf{MAC}, \mathsf{D}}^{\mathsf{pr}}(\lambda) + \frac{(Q_h + uQ_t)^2}{2^{n+1}} + \frac{N+3}{2^n}.$$

Therefore, the proof is completed.

Proof of Theorem 4. $\mathsf{HSAMD_2}$ satisfies both of d-message-completeness and d-message-soundness in the same way as the proof of Theorem 2. That is, it meets d-message-completeness from the property of d-disjunct matrices and soundness from d-disjunct matrices and the collision-resistance of the random oracle.

We consider d-order-completeness and d-weak-order-soundness. From the property of d-disjunct matrices and the correctness of MACs, $\mathsf{HSAMD_2}$ meets d-order-completeness. And, it also meets d-weak-order-soundness from Proposition 1 and Theorem 3. Therefore, the proof is completed.

References

1. Bellare, M., Kilian, J., Rogaway, P.: The security of the cipher block chaining message authentication code. J. Comput. Syst. Sci. **61**(3), 362–399 (2000)
2. Du, D.Z., Hwang, F.K.: Combinatorial Group Testing and Its Applications. Series on Applied Mathematics, 2nd edn, vol. 12. World Scientific (2000)
3. Eikemeier, O., et al.: History-free aggregate message authentication codes. In: Garay, J.A., De Prisco, R. (eds.) SCN 2010. LNCS, vol. 6280, pp. 309–328. Springer, Heidelberg (2010). https://doi.org/10.1007/978-3-642-15317-4_20
4. Hirose, S., Kuwakado, H.: Forward-secure sequential aggregate message authentication revisited. In: Chow, S.S.M., Liu, J.K., Hui, L.C.K., Yiu, S.M. (eds.) ProvSec 2014. LNCS, vol. 8782, pp. 87–102. Springer, Cham (2014). https://doi.org/10.1007/978-3-319-12475-9_7
5. Hirose, S., Shikata, J.: Non-adaptive group-testing aggregate MAC scheme. In: Su, C., Kikuchi, H. (eds.) ISPEC 2018. LNCS, vol. 11125, pp. 357–372. Springer, Cham (2018). https://doi.org/10.1007/978-3-319-99807-7_22
6. Katz, J., Lindell, A.Y.: Aggregate message authentication codes. In: Malkin, T. (ed.) CT-RSA 2008. LNCS, vol. 4964, pp. 155–169. Springer, Heidelberg (2008). https://doi.org/10.1007/978-3-540-79263-5_10
7. Ma, D., Tsudik, G.: Extended abstract: forward-secure sequential aggregate authentication. In: IEEE Symposium on Security and Privacy, pp. 86–91. IEEE Computer Society (2007)
8. Minematsu, K.: Efficient message authentication codes with combinatorial group testing. In: Pernul, G., Ryan, P.Y.A., Weippl, E. (eds.) ESORICS 2015. LNCS, vol. 9326, pp. 185–202. Springer, Cham (2015). https://doi.org/10.1007/978-3-319-24174-6_10
9. Sato, S., Hirose, S., Shikata, J.: Generic construction of sequential aggregate MACs from any MACs. In: Baek, J., Susilo, W., Kim, J. (eds.) ProvSec 2018. LNCS, vol. 11192, pp. 295–312. Springer, Cham (2018). https://doi.org/10.1007/978-3-030-01446-9_17
10. Sato, S., Hirose, S., Shikata, J.: Sequential aggregate MACs from any MACs: aggregation and detecting functionality. J. Internet Serv. Inf. Secur. **9**(1), 2–23 (2019)

A Novel Approach for Traffic Anomaly Detection in Power Distributed Control System and Substation System

Li Zhang[1], Zhuo Lv[2], Xuesong Zhang[3]($\boxtimes$), Cen Chen[2], Nuannuan Li[2], Yidong Li[1], and Wei Wang[1] (iD)

[1] Beijing Key Laboratory of Security and Privacy in Intelligent Transportation,
Beijing Jiaotong University, Beijing 100044, China
{17120445,ydli,wangwei1}@bjtu.edu.cn
[2] State Grid Henan Electric Power Research Institute, Zhengzhou 450052, China
zhuanzhuan2325@sina.com, 1020065011@qq.com, 18339231859@163.com
[3] National Computer Network Emergency Response Technical Team/Coordination
Center of China, Beijing, China
zhang-xue-song@163.com

Abstract. Industrial Control Systems (ICS) are the critical infrastructures of power grids. It is very important to monitor and control industrial equipment through the networks. Most ICSs currently used in smart grid contain IT key equipment and communication technologies to implement the communication and logic control functions. However, unlike traditional IT network traffic, these power-related industrial control systems have variety of proprietary protocols. Obviously, in typical complex systems the manually intensive processing of data is costly and sub-optimal. In this paper, we propose an novel traffic anomaly detection model for power ICS based on Multi-Head attention (MHA) method, in which the collected raw traffic was converted into the form of matrix. The MHA and Convolutional Neural Network (CNN) model were used to classify traffic data. We replace the traditional feature extraction and rule making process with an acceptable computational cost. The effectiveness of our approach is demonstrated by experiments on two real world power ICS testbeds: a power generation simulation platform based on a distributed control system (DCS) and a substation slave station. Comparing with some classical machine learning algorithms and Convolutional Neural Networks, the experimental results show that our MHA model outperforms the CNN-based and classical machine learning detection models with an accuracy rate of 99.86%.

Keywords: Power distributed control system · Anomaly detection · Traffic classification

1 Introduction

The Industrial Control Systems (ICS) is critical infrastructures for monitoring and controlling of various industrial processes and equipment. These systems

© Springer Nature Switzerland AG 2019
J. K. Liu and X. Huang (Eds.): NSS 2019, LNCS 11928, pp. 408–417, 2019.
https://doi.org/10.1007/978-3-030-36938-5_24

play an important role in all types of critical infrastructure assets such as power generation, transmission and distribution facilities. However, on the one hand, with the development of technology and the increasing demand for services, traditional security methods usually isolated the ICS from other systems and networks [19]. On the other hand, modern Information and Communication Technologies have integrated into ICSs. With the introduction of new technologies, some security hazards in modern communication technology have been brought into the ICSs. Researchers have paid a lot of attention in anomaly detection with network traffic for traditional IT network systems. Unlike traditional IT systems, the network environment on which ICSs implemented is not complicated. The number of communication nodes, device network configuration, and data size are often fixed. The research mentioned above basically needs to extract specific features or formulate rules for detecting and filtering based on log files or traffic data of the control system.

Most existing intrusion detection methods with network traffic employed in ICSs are signature-based. In this work, an innovative anomaly detection model, named Multi-Head Attend (MHA) model is proposed, which can abandon the cumbersome and complex neural network structure, and at the same time it can be explainable. Most importantly, we do not have to spend much effort in extracting features and rules. After converting network traffic to a matrix, we will extract valid detection features through resource on the computation. Although Convolutional Neural Networks have high performance in this field, it would hope to find some high-latitude relationships between traffic data and be able to display them intuitively. It is desirable that the model can explain why abnormal traffic can be detected. The extensive experimental results demonstrate the effectiveness of our MHA models. It achieves the detection accuracy as 99.86% and F-score of over 0.99 with the data set.

Our contributions can be summarized as follows.

1. We propose MHA detection model that effectively detects anomalous behavior in real power generation and substation traffic. It has the ability to explore hidden features to detect unknown behavior.
2. We conduct experiments with real power generation distributed control system and intelligent substation system. In this work we consider the network security problem of the industrial control system through the network traffic, and obtain good results from above scenarios.

The rest of this paper is organized as follows. We review related work in Sect. 2. Section 3 introduces MHA detection method. Section 4 describes the data sets and experiments. We illustrate the evaluation of MHA model in Sect. 5. Section 6 concludes this paper.

2   Literature Review

The issue of ICS security has been receiving widespread attentions. There exist several ICS anomaly detection methods, such as device-based, process-based, program-based and network-based detection. The device-based detection mainly adapts the fingerprinting technique for detecting malicious devices. Formby et al. [2] proposed several approaches for creating fingerprints tailored for devices in the ICS context, and primarily use the message response time and operation time measurements. The process-based detection methods emphasized more on the physical process variables, such as sensor readings, actuator states and the mathematical relationships between them. Feng et al. [1] proposed a framework that is designed to systematically generate invariant rules from information contained within ICS operational data logs, using a combination of several machine learning and data mining techniques.

The focus of this paper is the network-based detection methods which reveal anomalies by investigating the network traffic like header, payload, sequence of messages and other information through the ICS network traffic. Kravchik et al. [5] applied the proposed method by using a variety of deep neural network architectures including different variants of convolutional and recurrent networks. Applying representation learning approach to malware traffic classification using raw traffic data, Wang et al. [17] proposed a malware traffic classification method using convolutional neural network by taking traffic data as images. In our previsous work, we used machine learning methods to detect anomalies [8–11,13,14] or malware [6,12,15,16,18] based on network traffic or on static features of applications.

Network traffic is sequential, and correlation exists between raw traffic, which is especially prominent in industrial control systems traffic environment. In order to well perform the inspection tasks, we need to find a method considering not only the traffic features, but also the relationships of raw traffic. We got inspiration from the paper published by Google in arxiv in June 2017, Vaswani et al. [7] proposed a network structure called "Transformer" based on the attention mechanism for the machine translation problem in Natural Language Processing (NLP). They use this method to effectively extract the multidimensional relationship between word vectors, thus better implementing the work of text translation. In this work, we design the attention mechanism to complete the anomaly detection task of industrial network traffic.

3   Method

The transformer model was proposed by Google Brain [7], which uses stacked self-attention and point-wise, fully connected layer to process the inputs and outputs. Our goal is to build a more accurate and efficient detection model by extracting and acquiring multi-dimensional traffic relationships and characteristics. We adopt the multi-head attention architecture to capture the multi-dimensional features from the traffic context. The anomaly detection model we proposed is mainly composed of two parts. One is to use multi-head attention layer to obtain the multi-dimensional characteristic relationship between each packet from traffic cluster. The second is a fully connected layers for classification. In this paper, we only use full connection to complete binary classification task. The structure of this model is shown in Fig. 1. The model not only has high training and detection efficiency, but also has higher detection accuracy than the classical machine learning and deep learning algorithms.

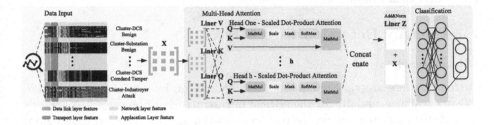

Fig. 1. The structure of MHA detection model.

We regard the traffic cluster having n packets as the embedded vector. In this way we can get an input sequence $(x_1, \ldots, x_n)$ and each packet is like a encoded word vector. After the processing of scaled dot-product attention layer we will get a sequence of continuous representation $z = (z_1, \ldots, z_n)$. Given z, we apply global average pooling and fully connected layer to classify. The input consists of three parts as Queries, Keys and Values, the dimension of queries and keys d_k, and the values of dimension d_v. After compute the dot products of the query with all keys, we divide each by $\sqrt{d_k}$ and apply the softmax function to obtain the weights on the values. When compute the attention function, we pick the cluster of traffic into a matrix Q. The keys and values also use the same matrix but named K and V, we call this method as Self Attention. The matrix of outputs is computed like this:

$$Attention\,(Q, K, V) = softmax\left(\frac{QK^T}{\sqrt{d_k}}\right) V \qquad (1)$$

where $Q \in R^{n*d_k}, K \in R^{n*d_k}, V \in R^{n*d_v}$. We can explain it from each vector.

In practice, we adapt the Multi-Head Attention model that is the perfection of attention mechanism. It is actually simple. The model maps Q, K and V through the parameter matrix $W^{Q,K,V}$. It makes the model jointly attend to information from different representation subspace at different traffic packets. We expect the model be able to capture the implied features between packets and even clusters through raw traffic. We perform the attention function with d_n-dimensional keys, values and queries. The multi-head attention performs linearly project the queries, keys and values h times with different, learned linear projections to d_k, d_k and d_v dimensions respectively.

$$MultiHead(Q, K, V) = ZW^O$$
$$Z = Concat(head_1, \ldots, head_h) \qquad (2)$$
$$\text{where } head_i = Attention(QW_i^{\ Q}, KW_i^{\ K}, VW_i^{\ V})$$

The projections are parameter matrices $W_i{}^Q \in R^{d_n*d_k}$, $W_i{}^K \in R^{d_n*d_k}$, $W_i{}^V \in R^{d_n*d_v}$ and $W_i{}^O \in R^{d_v*d_n}$. In this work, we employ $n = 28$ as the packet number of a traffic cluster and $h = 8$ parallel attention layers or heads. The size of each head is 64.

4   Anomaly Detection with MHA

4.1   Dataset

Currently, there are very few public data sources on industrial control system network traffic, especially for the critical infrastructures of power grids. It needs to be stated that although we use real industrial equipment, we need to recognize that the scale of the system are smaller than production environment. Although the data set is small, it reflect the characteristics of the industrial network. The original objective is to combine the characteristics of the industrial control network environment to find better anomaly detection methods. The dataset contains three types of benign traffic about DCS and substation equipment at normal operation traffic, in which the substation traffic is composed of two parts: the station control layer and the process layer. The detail information is shown in Table 1.

Table 1. The detailed information of 9 kinds of traffic

Name	Type	Number of packets	Details
DCSBEN	Benign	1192358	Benign DCS traffic
SCLBEN	Benign	284110	Benign Substation control layer traffic
SPLBEN	Benign	15227	Benign Substation process layer traffic
DCSARP	Malicious	5616	ARP spoofing on DCS
DCSDOS	Malicious	1887101	Dos Attack on DCS
DCSSNIF	Malicious	8542	Nmap sniffing on DCS
DCSTAM	Malicious	21930	Command tamper on DCS
SCLI	Malicious	64094	IndustRoyer virus attack on substation control layer
SPLI	Malicious	2212	IndustRoyer virus attack on substation process layer

4.2   Data Preparation

Data preparation aims to convert raw traffic format by PCAP to model input data. It includes these steps: traffic format, traffic cleaning, cluster generation and numpy data conversion.

1. Traffic Format. In this step we will load the initial data formated with PCAP. Then we use Scapy to analyze and process these original data. We hope to get two kinds of data. One contains all traffic layer information and the other just contains the payload of the packet.
2. Traffic Cleaning. The data we want to use is the real-time traffic of industrial control system. When deploying the traffic sniffer, it is inevitable to generate some noise traffic. To ensure the accuracy of data, we filter out these interference traffic.

3. Cluster Generation. This step trims all packets to uniform length. If the packet length is longer than 128 bytes, it would be trimmed to 128 bytes, and if it is less than 128 bytes, the 0×00 would be appended until satisfied the limit. The continuous traffic packet will be filled in 3584 bytes. It means that every 28 trimmed packets will generate a $28 * 128$ bytes matrix.
4. Numpy Processed Data Conversion. In this step we convert all the data into a numpy array and store it effectively. This will greatly facilitate our work afterwards.

Experimental data collection consists all layer of traffic, including 3 types of benign and 6 types of malicious traffic. About 417676 traffic data were used to generate 14917 different traffic cluster in total.

4.3 Experimental Setup

We conduct experiments with deep learning models and other machine learning models. All the experiments are conducted in the same circumstance with the same data set. We use Keras, a high-level neural networks API based on TensorFlow [3].

Parameter and Structure. After data pre-processing, we get a $28 * 128$ size matrix. We used the Adam optimizer [4] with learning rate $= 0.001$, $\beta_1 = 0.9, \beta_2 = 0.999$, and $\epsilon = 1e^{-08}$. After attention layer we implement a global average pooling layer to get 512 feature maps which are the most optimal features for classification and one fully connected layer is behind. The activation of convolutional layer is Relu and a fully connected layer is Softmax.

A variety of classical structures of convolution neural networks (LeNet, simple VGG, simple AlexNet) were used to conduct classification experiments. The first convolution layer of LeNet model performs a convolution operation with 6 kernels of size 5 * 5. The result of the first Conv2D layer are 6 feature maps of size 28 * 128. There is a 2 * 2 max pooling operation in first pooling layer followed the first Conv2D layer. 6 feature maps with size of 14 * 64 were got after processing. The kernel size of second Conv2D layer is 5 * 5, and the second maxpooling layer is still 2 * 2. For each convolutional layer, we apply Relu to achieve scale invariance. Finally, we adopt fully connected layers to aggregate the features learned form the pooling layer and the last convolutional layer to do classification.

We compare the traditional methods with our proposed method and use scikit-learn packages to complete the experiments. These methods use the same data set and include SVM, Decision Tree, Random Forest (RF). The max depth of decision tree and random forest is 5, and the estimators of random forest is 10.

5   Results

Table 2. Detection results

Method name	ACC	Precision	Recall	F1-Score	Time(s)
MHA	**0.998**	0.9996	0.9996	**0.998**	19.615
CNN-LeNet	0.950	0.9510	0.9500	0.949	19.360
CNN-sVGG	0.989	0.9893	0.9899	0.989	94.229
CNN-sAlexNet	0.955	0.9601	0.9531	0.955	23.220
SVM-rbf	0.962	0.9640	0.9614	0.962	405.92
SVM-linear	0.983	0.9842	0.9836	0.983	198.99
DT	0.952	0.9560	0.9500	0.951	4.967
RF	0.956	0.9598	0.9553	0.956	4.099

The results of the experiments based on the real DCS and substation system data set are illustrated in Table 2. Four evaluation metrics, accuracy (ACC), precision (PRE), recall and F-score (F1), were used to evaluate the overall performance of a classifier:

$$ACC = \frac{TP + TN}{TP + FP + FN + TN} \tag{3}$$

$$Precision = \frac{TP}{(TP + FP)} \tag{4}$$

$$Recall = \frac{TP}{TP + FN} \tag{5}$$

$$F - score = \frac{2 * Precision * Recall}{Precision + Recall} \tag{6}$$

We evaluate the detection results through the result of prediction. For malicious clusters, false positive (FP) is the number of instances incorrectly classified as benign. Likewise, for benign traffic cluster, if the predict result is very close to 1, the cluster is considered as malicious, which is False Negative (FN). The rest values are correspondingly divided into True Positive (TP) and True Negative (TN).

Table 2 shows that the attention model provides the highest accuracy and F-score than other methods, indicating that the attention model is more effective and more suitable for industrial network traffic environment. The relationship and deeper features between the control network traffic achieved by the MHA model mainly through continuously optimizing the multi-dimensional linear variation feature matrix. CNN-based models need to have deeper and more complex network structures or have more training rounds to support if it wants to expand the model's receptive field to obtain deep features to achieve higher detection accuracy.

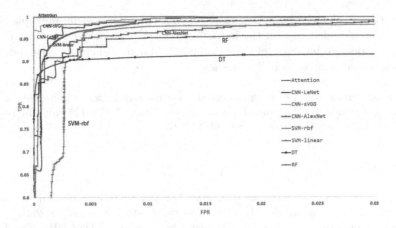

Fig. 2. ROC curves based on MHA, CNN based and machine learning model.

Receiver Operating Characteristic (ROC) curves for the methods are shown in Fig. 2. Attention performs more efficiently than the other classifiers with small FPR. Among these methods, the proposed method Performs the best. It is obvious that the different CNN and SVM structure have different performance. The sVGG achieves better accuracy and F-score than LeNet and sAlexNet. Compared with the sVGG, the accuracy with the Attention model is improved by 1.1%. However, the processing time of sVGG is long, which takes 74.61 s more than Attention model. The RBF kernel based SVM not only has lower accuracy, but also requires more training time. The linear SVM's training time is 198.99 s that is longer than attention model, and the accuracy rate is also lower 0.11. In summary, the detection accuracy of the MHA method is higher in current data set than in other methods, and has certain advantages in time and computational efficiency.

6 Conclusion

In this paper, we collected and analyzed network traffic of control systems in power generation and substation environments. We not only consider to use convolutional neural networks to detect anomaly traffic information from images converted by raw traffic, but also we hoped that the relationship between the cluster traffic can be extracted through the model as the basis for detecting and classification. The complex network structure can be simplified to improve the calculation speed and detection efficiency. Inspired by characteristics of network traffic in ICS, we propose MHA models for the detection of anomalies, which considers the traffic relationships in ICS with attention mechanism. This model provides a new way for power ICS traffic anomaly detection. The extensive experimental results show that MHA model is effective and has advantages over other mentioned machine learning and CNN-based models.

In future work, we plan to improve our model by supporting multiple classification. We will also expand the industrial control network traffic scenarios, so that the model can have better detection performance and can be more adaptive in a wide scope related to ICS scenarios.

Acknowledgements. The work reported in this paper was supported in part by Natural Science Foundation of China, under Grant U1736114, and in part by CNCERT/CC, under Grant number K19GY500020.

References

1. Feng, C., Palleti, V.R., Mathur, A., Chana, D.: A systematic framework to generate invariants for anomaly detection in industrial control systems. In: 26th Annual Network and Distributed System Security Symposium, NDSS 2019, San Diego, California, USA, 24–27 February 2019. The Internet Society (2019)
2. Formby, D., Srinivasan, P., Leonard, A., Rogers, J., Beyah, R.A.: Who's in control of your control system? device fingerprinting for cyber-physical systems. In: 23rd Annual Network and Distributed System Security Symposium, NDSS 2016, San Diego, California, USA, 21–24 February 2016. The Internet Society (2016)
3. Group, K.: Keras: the python deep learning library. http://keras.io/
4. Kingma, D.P., Ba, J.: Adam: a method for stochastic optimization (2015)
5. Kravchik, M., Shabtai, A.: Detecting cyber attacks in industrial control systems using convolutional neural networks. In: Lie, D., Mannan, M. (eds.) Proceedings of the 2018 Workshop on Cyber-Physical Systems Security and PrivaCy, CPS-SPC@CCS 2018, Toronto, ON, Canada, 19 October 2018, pp. 72–83. ACM (2018)
6. Liu, X., Liu, J., Wang, W., He, Y., Zhang, X.: Discovering and understanding android sensor usage behaviors with data flow analysis. World Wide Web **21**(1), 105–126 (2018)
7. Vaswani, A., et al.: Attention is all you need. In: Guyon, I., et al. (eds.) Advances in Neural Information Processing Systems 30: Annual Conference on Neural Information Processing Systems 2017, 4–9 December 2017, Long Beach, CA, USA, pp. 6000–6010 (2017)
8. Wang, W., Battiti, R.: Identifying intrusions in computer networks with principal component analysis. In: Proceedings of the The First International Conference on Availability, Reliability and Security, ARES 2006, 20–22 April 2006, Vienna, Austria, pp. 270–279 (2006)
9. Wang, W., Guan, X., Zhang, X.: Processing of massive audit data streams for real-time anomaly intrusion detection. Comput. Commun. **31**(1), 58–72 (2008)
10. Wang, W., Guan, X., Zhang, X., Yang, L.: Profiling program behavior for anomaly intrusion detection based on the transition and frequency property of computer audit data. Comput. Secur. **25**(7), 539–550 (2006)
11. Wang, W., Guyet, T., Quiniou, R., Cordier, M., Masseglia, F., Zhang, X.: Autonomic intrusion detection: adaptively detecting anomalies over unlabeled audit data streams in computer networks. Knowl.-Based Syst. **70**, 103–117 (2014)
12. Wang, W., Li, Y., Wang, X., Liu, J., Zhang, X.: Detecting android malicious apps and categorizing benign apps with ensemble of classifiers. Future Gener. Comp. Syst. **78**, 987–994 (2018)
13. Wang, W., Liu, J., Pitsilis, G., Zhang, X.: Abstracting massive data for lightweight intrusion detection in computer networks. Inf. Sci. **433–434**, 417–430 (2018)

14. Wang, W., Shang, Y., He, Y., Li, Y., Liu, J.: Botmark: automated botnet detection with hybrid analysis of flow-based and graph-based traffic behaviors. Inf. Sci. **511**, 284–296 (2020)
15. Wang, W., Wang, X., Feng, D., Liu, J., Han, Z., Zhang, X.: Exploring permission-induced risk in android applications for malicious application detection. IEEE Trans. Inf. Forensics Secur. **9**(11), 1869–1882 (2014)
16. Wang, W., et al.: Constructing features for detecting android malicious applications: Issues, taxonomy and directions. IEEE Access **7**, 67602–67631 (2019)
17. Wang, W., Zhu, M., Zeng, X., Ye, X., Sheng, Y.: Malware traffic classification using convolutional neural network for representation learning, pp. 712–717 (2017)
18. Wang, X., Wang, W., He, Y., Liu, J., Han, Z., Zhang, X.: Characterizing android apps' behavior for effective detection of malapps at large scale. Future Gener. Comp. Syst. **75**, 30–45 (2017)
19. Yang, J., Zhou, C., Yang, S., Xu, H., Hu, B.: Anomaly detection based on zone partition for security protection of industrial cyber-physical systems. IEEE Trans. Ind. Electron. **65**(5), 4257–4267 (2018)

EEG-Based Person Authentication with Variational Universal Background Model

Huyen Tran[1], Dat Tran[1(✉)], Wanli Ma[1], and Phuoc Nguyen[2]

[1] Faculty of Science and Technology, University of Canberra, Canberra, Australia
{huyen.tran,dat.tran,wanli.ma}@canberra.edu.au
[2] A2I2, Deakin University, Waurn Ponds, Australia
phuoc.nguyen@deakin.edu.au

Abstract. Silent speech is a convenient and natural way for person authentication as users can imagine speaking their password instead of typing it. However there are inherent noises and complex variations in EEG signals making it difficult to capture correct information and model uncertainty. We propose an EEG-based person authentication framework based on a variational inference framework to learn a simple latent representation for complex data. A variational universal background model is created by pooling the latent models of all users. A likelihood ratio of user claimed model to the background model is constructed for testing whether the claim is valid. Extensive experiments on three datasets show the advantages of our proposed framework.

1 Introduction

Electroencephalography (EEG) is the electrophysiological method of using electrodes to record the electrical activities, which is generated by the brain. The brain wave signals of each individual is unique and can be used for biometric identification, therefore they have been used widely for the verification tasks. While the signals (aka EEG signals) can be recorded using invasive sensors in clinical environment, the researchers typically do that non-invasively from the electrodes placed on the scalp surface. EEG provides rich information about brain activities. They carry the physiology characteristics of individual as well as convey the information in changing mental activities and even in person's mood. Regardless of having plentiful information, EEG signals are well known for their low signal to noise ratio. EEG signals are weak as their main source is synchronous activity of cortical neurons and it is characterized by small signal amplitudes. Additionally, the signals would be weakened by the thickness of the skull when using non-invasive device. There are several factors, which lead to the noisy of the signal such as the sensor imperfection, the device placements, the recording procedures. All these factors add variations to the signals and make them difficult to be modeled. Therefore, in order to extract useful information from EEG signals, one should consider the methods that could capture those variations.

© Springer Nature Switzerland AG 2019
J. K. Liu and X. Huang (Eds.): NSS 2019, LNCS 11928, pp. 418–432, 2019.
https://doi.org/10.1007/978-3-030-36938-5_25

Because of generalization property and ability to handle high dimensional input, support vector machine (SVM) method was used for EEG-based person verification in [9]. However, due to the complexity in the data, SVM does not scale well to big data. Deep learning methods can scale linearly to data and have been introduced to model EEG signals [2,6,14]. With the popularity of consumer EEG devices, now EEG signals can be collected feasibly in a non-laboratory environment. Therefore, it is promising to use deep learning to model the increasing data.

In this paper, we used EEG signals of imagined speech for person authentication. Silent speech is a convenient and natural way as users can imagine speaking their password instead of typing it. However, there are many variations involving in silent speaking because of the differences in speed, rhythm, mood, etc. Thus, a capable method is necessarily to capture those variations. We used Variational Autoencoder method (VAE) as a framework [5] to develop a Variational Universal Background Model (UBM) for EEG-base user authentication. A latent Gaussian Mixture (GM) was used to model each user latent vector, then all the user GMs were pooled together to create a UBM for score normalization purposes. With the introduction of the latent GM, however, the minimization objective becomes difficult. Therefore, we derived an approximation objective which is an upper bound to the target objective. We carried extensive experiments on three datasets: (1) the MNIST dataset for testing our model; (2) the imagined speech dataset which is the main application of our method; and (3) the motor imagery dataset.

2 Preliminaries

We summarize likelihood ratio test, Gaussian Mixture Models, and Variational Auto Encoder in the following sections. These form the basic for our methods.

2.1 Likelihood Ratio Test

We build on the statistical hypothesis testing framework for EEG-based person authentication. Hypothesis testing tests whether a data point satisfies a target hypothesis or not. It amounts to calculating the likelihood ratio between the likelihood of a data point x coming from the target hypothesis H_0, the claimed identity, versus the likelihood of that data point coming from a null hypothesis H_1. If this ratio exceeds some chosen threshold the data point is said to satisfy the target hypothesis [13]:

$$s(x) = \frac{p(x|H_0)}{p(x|H_1)} \begin{cases} \geq \tau & \text{accept} \\ < \tau & \text{reject} \end{cases}$$

where τ is the chosen threshold.

Mathematically, we use a statistical model θ_u to represent H_0, θ_{bg} to represent the alternative hypothesis H_1, we have the likelihood ratio statistic in logarithm domain:

$$s(x) = \log p(x|\theta_u) - \log p(x|\theta_{bg})$$

2.2　Gaussian Mixture Models (GMM)

Let denote a set of EEG signals from one user as $X = \{x_1 \ldots x_T\} = \{x_t\}_{t=1}^T$, where $x_t \in \mathbb{R}^D$ with D is the number of features.

A Gaussian Mixture Model (GMM) is a model that comprise of K Gaussians, which can be a representation for a set of a feature vectors. In GMM, we assume that all feature vectors are independent. Given θ the set of parameters of the GMM, the likelihood of a set of T feature vectors is:

$$P(X|\theta) = \prod_{t=1}^{T} P(x_t|\theta) \tag{1}$$

$$P(x_t|\theta) = \sum_{k=1}^{K} w_k \mathcal{N}(x_t|\mu_k, \Sigma_k) \tag{2}$$

$$\theta = \{w_k, \mu_k, \Sigma_k\}_{k=1}^{K} \tag{3}$$

where $\mathcal{N}(x|\mu_k, \Sigma_k)$ is the kth Gaussian distribution, which has D dimension, with mean μ_k and diagonal covariance matrix Σ_k ($k = \{1, K\}$). w_k is the weight of this Gaussian with $\Sigma_{k=1}^{K} w_k = 1$ and $\forall k : w_k \geq 0$

2.3　Variational Auto Encoder (VAE)

A data point $x \in \mathcal{X} \subset \mathbb{R}^n$ is assumed to be generated by a low dimensional latent variable $z \in \mathcal{Z} \subset \mathbb{R}^m$, where $m \ll n$. The distribution of x can be complex, but we can assume z has a simple distribution, i.e. $\mathcal{N}(0, I)$. We use a neural network to map from z to x. The generative process for a data point x is as follows, suppose the distribution of x is Bernoulli and z is Normal:

$$z \sim \mathcal{N}(0, I)$$
$$\mu = \text{decoder}(z)$$
$$x \sim Bern(\mu)$$

where decoder(z) is a neural network mapping $z \in \mathcal{Z}$ to the mean parameter of the Bernoulli distribution of x.

On the other hand, we will find out which latent z is mapped to a given data point x. This attributes to computing the posterior of z given x, $p(z|x; \theta)$. By Bayes rule, we have:

$$p(z|x) = \frac{p(x|z; \theta)p(z)}{Z} \tag{4}$$

where $Z = \int p(x|z; \theta)p(z)dz$ is the normalization constant.

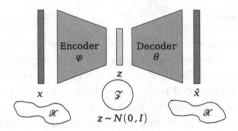

Fig. 1. Variational Auto Encoder architecture.

The normalization term Z requires integration over z which is intractable. To overcome this we can use an approximate distribution $q(z|x;\phi)$, such as $\mathcal{N}(\mu,\sigma^2 I)$ for approximating the posterior. The classic way is to use mean field approximation, however a preferred modern way is to use amortized variational method to distribute the cost of estimating the parameters of q over all data [5]. We use a neural network to map x to the mean and variance parameters of this q distribution, see Fig. 1:

$$x \sim p_{\text{data}}(x)$$
$$(\mu,\sigma^2) = \text{encoder}(x)$$
$$z \sim \mathcal{N}(\mu,\sigma^2 I)$$

The objective is minimizing the Kullback-Leibler distance between the true posterior $p(z|x)$ and the variational posterior $q(z|x)$.

$$\min_{(\theta,\phi)} D_{KL}\left(q(z|x;\phi)\|p(z|x;\theta)\right) \tag{5}$$

where (θ,ϕ) are parameters of the decoder and the encoder networks parameterizing these distributions, and $p(z|x;\theta)$ is calculated as in Eq. 4. In practice, instead of $p(z|x;\theta)$, we use an unnormalized version $p(x,z;\theta) = p(z|x;\theta)Z$. The objective becomes:

$$\underset{(\theta,\phi)}{\text{argmin}}\, D_{KL}\left(q(z|x;\phi)\|p(x,z;\theta)\right) \equiv \underset{(\theta,\phi)}{\text{argmax}} -D_{KL}\left(q(z|x;\phi)\|p(x,z;\theta)\right) \tag{6}$$

The objective is called ELBO and can be written as follows:

$$\begin{aligned}
\text{ELBO}(\theta,\phi,x) &= -D_{KL}\left(q(z|x;\phi)\|p(x,z;\theta)\right)\\
&= -\mathbb{E}_{q(z|x;\phi)} \log \frac{q(z|x;\phi)}{p(x,z;\theta)} \tag{7}\\
&= -\mathbb{E}_{q(z|x;\phi)} \log \frac{q(z|x;\phi)}{p(z)p(x|z;\theta)}\\
&= -D_{KL}(q(z|x;\phi)\|p(z)) + \mathbb{E}_{q(z|x;\phi)}p(x|z;\theta) \tag{8}
\end{aligned}$$

Reparameterization trick [5] is used together with the objective (8) for training.

2.4 Related Works

Universal background model provides the basic for the statistical hypothesis testing framework for speaker verification [12]. The maximum a posteriori is a point estimate of the posterior of the user distribution [7]. The combination of SVM and UBM was introduced in [9]. Some recent works [11,16] are also based on SVM. These frameworks model directly the feature vectors as opposed to ours, which used a latent variational representation for modeling the complex variation in the observed data, thanks to the powerful function approximation ability by neural networks. Some recent works also used generative models for augmenting EEG datasets [1] or for classification [4].

3 Methods

3.1 Mixture of Gaussians Prior

We use a Gaussian Mixture (GM) prior for modeling each user in the z space, and call this Variational Gaussian Mixture model (VGM). The reason is that user data can have a complex distribution due to diverse variations in the choice of data representation, collecting process, or noises from sensors. Therefore using a single model would not be expressive enough to account for the level of diversity needed in the latent space for the target task. The prior for each user u is:

$$p_u(z; \gamma_u) = \sum_{k=1}^{K} \alpha_k \mathcal{N}(z|\mu_k, \sigma_k^2 I) \tag{9}$$

where K is the number of components, $\gamma_u = (\alpha_k, \mu_k, \sigma_k^2)$ is the parameter for the mixing weight, mean and variance of each component Gaussian for the user u.

For the posterior, we can also use a mixture of Gaussians. In that case, the encoder would need to parameterize the parameters of the component means, variances and mixing weights, which resembles a mixture density network [3]. For simplicity, we use a single Gaussian for modeling the posterior. This choice can be justified by the view that each data point of the user is one variant and comes from just one of the component Gaussian, only the whole user data set would make up a mixture model.

Training would update these parameters for each user separately, while the VAE encoder and decoder are trained jointly for all users.

The training objective for each user u is similar to Eq. 8 but with the additional parameter γ_u since the prior is no longer $\mathcal{N}(0, I)$:

$$\text{ELBO}_u(\theta, \phi, \gamma_u, x) = -D_{KL}(q(z|x; \phi)\|p(z; \gamma_u)) + \mathbb{E}_{q(z|x;\phi)} p(x|z; \theta) \tag{10}$$

However the KL distance between the prior mixture distribution $p_u(z; \gamma_u)$ and the posterior single Gaussian distribution need an approximation, which is presented in the next section.

The objective for all user data is the mean of all user's ELBO:

$$\text{ELBO}(\theta, \phi) = \frac{1}{|\mathcal{U}|} \sum_{u \in \mathcal{U}} \mathbb{E}_{x \sim p_{data}(X_u)} \text{ELBO}_u(\theta, \phi, \gamma_u, x) \tag{11}$$

where $\mathcal{U}$ is the index set of all users, $p_{data}(X_u)$ is the data distribution of user u. The framework is trained end-to-end using stochastic gradient descent.

3.2 Kullback-Leibler (KL) Divergence Between a Gaussian Distribution and a Gaussian Mixture

We derive the necessary Propositions 1 and 2 for calculating a close form variational upper bound of the Kullback-Leibler divergence between a posterior approximation and its GM prior. The details of the proofs can be found in the supplemental material.

Proposition 1. *Let $f(x) = \mathcal{N}(x; \mu_f, \Sigma_f)$ and $g(x) = \mathcal{N}(x; \mu_g, \Sigma_g)$ be two Gaussian distributions in $\mathbb{R}^n$. The Kullback-Leibler (KL) divergence between $f(x)$ and $g(x)$ is:*

$$D_{KL}(f(x)\|g(x)) = -\frac{n}{2} \log \left(\frac{\det \Sigma_f}{\det \Sigma_g} \right) - \frac{n}{2}$$
$$+ \frac{1}{2}\text{trace}\left(\Sigma_f \Sigma_g^{-1} \right) + \frac{1}{2}(\mu_f - \mu_g)\Sigma_g^{-1}(\mu_f - \mu_g)^T . \square \tag{12}$$

Proposition 2. *The variational upper bound of the Kullback-Leibler divergence between a unimodal distribution $f(x)$ and a mixture model $g(x) = \sum_k \alpha_k g_k(x)$ is:*

$$D_{KL}(f(x)\|g(x)) \leq D_{var}(f(x)\|g(x)) \overset{\text{def}}{=} -\log \sum_k \alpha_k \exp\left(-D_{KL}(f(x)\|g_k(x))\right) . \square \tag{13}$$

3.3 Hypothesis Testing for Variational Posterior

The hypothesis testing in our model is as follows. Given a test data point x and a claimed identity u, we can compute the variational posterior distribution $q_\phi(z|x) = \mathcal{N}(z|\mu_x, \sigma_x^2)$ for this x. We simply use the posterior mean $z_x = \mu_x$ for computing the likelihood ratio. The likelihood ratio test is as follows:

$$\text{score}(x, u) = \frac{p(z_x|H_1)}{p(z_x|H_0)} = \frac{p(z_x|\theta_u)}{p(z_x|\theta_{bg})} > \tau \tag{14}$$

where H_1 is the hypothesis the user vector u comes from the model θ_u and the null hypothesis H_0 is that the user vector u comes from the background model θ_{bg}.

The score can then be compared with a chosen threshold τ for the accept/reject decision [15].

3.4 Universal Background Model

A large mixture model is constructed by combining the mixture models of all subjects, except for the target subject, $p(z_x|\theta_{\text{bg}}) = \frac{1}{B}\sum_{b=1}^{B}p(z_x|\theta_b)$, where B is the number of subjects. We employ three different versions for scoring a test vector x:

$$\text{score1}(x, u) = \log p(z_x|\theta_u) \tag{15}$$

$$\text{score2}(x, u) = \log p(z_x|\theta_u) - \log \frac{1}{B}\sum_{b=1}^{B}p(z_x|\theta_b) \tag{16}$$

$$\text{score3}(x, u) = \log p(z_x|\theta_u) - \log \max_b p(z_x|\theta_b) \tag{17}$$

where Eq. 15 is without background normalization, while Eqs. 16 and 17 are with background normalization.

4 Experiments

4.1 Datasets

We use three datasets for our experiments, namely MNIST, EEG imagined speech, and BCI motor imagery datasets.

The MNIST dataset consists of handwriting digits ranging from 0 to 9. There 60,000 images for training and 10,000 for testing.

The imagined speech dataset [8] contains EEG signals of fifteen subjects, which were recorded while they were doing tasks of silently speaking different words in their mind without making any noises or moving any muscles. All subjects were healthy and at the ages between 22 to 32 years old. The system of 64 channels was used to collect signals. Each participant needed to complete at least one of the following four imagined speech tasks:

- Vowels: /a/, /i/ and /u/.
- Short words: "in", "out" and "up".
- Long words: "cooperate" and "independent".
- Short and long words: "in" and "cooperate".

There are 100 trials for each sound or word in a session of experiment, each trial lasts for 5 s. The raw data were recorded at 1000 Hz, and the published dataset had been preprocessed to remove any artifacts and down sample to 256 Hz. Therefore, each trial has dimension of $64 \times 5 \times 256$ (81920). That is significantly large compared to the size of the dataset, and it could not be used as a feature of our model, so it was necessarily to decrease the dimension of the data points. First, we downed sample to 128 Hz, then used Fast Fourier Transform to convert the EEG signals to the representation in the frequency domain up to 64 Hz.

Next, we computed the powers of five common EEG frequency bands Delta (up to 4 Hz), Theta (4–8 Hz), Alpha (8–15 Hz), Beta (15–32 Hz) and Gamma ($\geq$32 Hz). Thus, we obtained a feature vector of size 64 × 5 for each trial in the experiment. In this dataset, the training and testing sets are not separated, so we randomly split trials into two sets, 4/5 of the trials for training and 1/5 of them for testing.

The motor imagery dataset [10] consists of EEG data from 15 healthy subjects aged between 22 and 40 years. The subjects were measured in two sessions on two different days, within a week. We only use motor imagination data in this experiment. There are six movement types: elbow flexion/extension, forearm supination/pronation and hand open/close; all with the right upper limb.

4.2 Experiment Settings

We used Gaussian and Gaussian mixture model (GMM) as two baselines and compared them to VAE, VGM with scoring Eqs. 15, and their UBM variants with scoring Eq. 16 or 17. Each model was trained on the training data of each individual. Then the background model for the null hypothesis is constructed by pooling the models of all other users. The background model score is computed as either the average score over all individual models, Eq. 16, or the maximum, Eq. 17, whichever is better.

The parameters of Gaussian are mean and covariance. The parameters of GMM are means, covariances and mixing weights of the mixture. The parameters of VAE are weights of encoder and decoder networks. The parameters of VGM are also weights of encoder and decoder networks plus the prior's means and covariances. The encoder and decoder are 3-layer MLP with hidden size 500. The output layer of the encoder parameterizes the mean and variance of each Gaussian component, while the output layer of the decoder parameterizes the mean of the Bernoulli distribution. We used Adam optimizer with learning rate 0.001, batchsize 20, and trained until convergence.

4.3 Experimental Results

The performance measures are DET curve, Area Under Curve (AUC) and Equal Error Rate (EER).

MNIST. Table 1 compares the performance of different methods. The figures shows that when using UBM all of the methods perform better compare with without using UBM. The variational methods, i.e. VAE and VGM, is outperform the baselines as resulting in higher AUC and lower EER in both models with and without UBM. For UBM version of all models, all scores improve by 1.4 to 4.7% on average, with the highest AUC at 98.6% by VGM method.

Table 1. MNIST dataset test AUC and EER of different methods.

	Without UBM		With UBM	
	AUC	EER	AUC	EER
Gaussian	61.9 ± 7.4	38.1 ± 7.4	62.6 ± 7.8	37.5 ± 7.7
GMM	66.8 ± 10.1	33.3 ± 10.1	71.5 ± 13.6	28.9 ± 13.6
VAE	76.9 ± 7.7	28.7 ± 6.3	80.1 ± 8.4	26.7 ± 6.8
VGM	97.2 ± 2.1	7.9 ± 4.0	98.6 ± 1.3	5.3 ± 2.9

Table 2 shows that the number of latent Z dimension has effect on the performance of the variational methods. Both VAE and VGM perform better when the number of latent dimension is increased. While VAE only slightly improve the performance over the increasing the dimension, the VGM yield considerably better when increasing latent dimensions from 20 to 40. However, it vaguely increase with 100 dimensions. It suggest that the latent with 40 dimensions is effective in our experiment. The using of UBM model once again enhance the performance of both methods.

Table 2. MNIST dataset test AUC scores of VAE and VGM at different number of Z dimensions.

	Z dimensions	Without UBM		With UBM	
		AUC	EER	AUC	EER
VAE	20	75.3 ± 11.7	29.7 ± 8.9	77.9 ± 13.0	28.5 ± 9.9
	40	75.5 ± 10.4	24.9 ± 12.4	77.8 ± 11.8	28.2 ± 9.2
	100	76.9 ± 7.7	28.7 ± 6.3	80.1 ± 8.4	26.7 ± 6.8
VGM	20	91.1 ± 7.0	14.8 ± 7.9	93.1 ± 6.8	12.8 ± 7.6
	40	96.7 ± 2.0	8.5 ± 3.8	98.3 ± 1.1	5.8 ± 2.6
	100	97.2 ± 2.1	7.9 ± 4.0	98.6 ± 1.3	5.3 ± 2.9

As our proposed methods show the promising results on MNIST dataset, the investigation of person authentication on the imagined speech dataset was carried out.

Imagined Speech Dataset. Table 3 shows similar advantages of the proposed method on the imagined speech dataset. It can be seen that VAE and VGM models, while share similar performances, are better than the baselines. It is noticeable that UBM score normalization dramatically improves all methods, over 91% AUC. The VGM has highest mean AUC score, at 95.3%.

Table 3. Imagined speech dataset test AUC and EER of different methods.

	Without UBM		With UBM	
	AUC	EER	AUC	EER
Gaussian	60.2 ± 22.4	36.0 ± 20.6	91.8 ± 18.3	7.9 ± 18.0
GMM	78.0 ± 26.0	19.7 ± 23.7	91.7 ± 18.2	7.9 ± 17.9
VAE	84.6 ± 29.6	10.6 ± 19.6	93.5 ± 13.8	5.5 ± 13.4
VGM	84.5 ± 29.8	8.9 ± 15.9	95.3 ± 14.3	5.7 ± 14.5

Table 4 shows the effect of different Z dimensions. It illustrates that the best number of latent dimensions for VAE is 100 while it is 40 for VGM. The reason could be that the latent GMM is very flexible and requires only a small latent size of 40. Higher dimension makes it worse at test time.

Table 4. Imagined speech dataset test AUC scores of VAE and VGM at different Z dimensions.

	Z dimensions	Without UBM		With UBM	
		AUC	EER	AUC	EER
VAE	20	85.2 ± 25.3	11.6 ± 19.5	92.9 ± 14.5	6.0 ± 13.9
	40	84.1 ± 29.8	10.8 ± 19.6	91.9 ± 16.5	7.1 ± 16.0
	100	84.6 ± 29.6	10.6 ± 19.6	93.5 ± 13.8	5.5 ± 13.4
VGM	20	75.9 ± 33.4	13.3 ± 17.5	93.8 ± 15.3	6.5 ± 15.7
	40	84.5 ± 29.8	8.9 ± 15.9	95.3 ± 14.3	5.7 ± 14.5
	100	84.4 ± 27.7	9.0 ± 16.1	93.8 ± 15.1	6.3 ± 15.3

Figure 2 compares the DET curves of all methods, where the VGM+UBM has highest performance.

Motor Imagery Dataset. Finally, we study the performance of our method on an additional EEG dataset, the motor imagery dataset, in Table 5. We do cross validation and the best parameters are used and the results are reported. We used similar settings as in the imagined speech dataset. Overall, this dataset is harder than the imagined speech dataset and the MNIST dataset. We observe a similar trend in performance among the method. The Gaussian method has lowest AUC score, followed by GMM, VAE, and VGM. UBM models also improve the performance, by 3.5% for Gaussian, 6.5% for GMM, 3.6% for VAE, and 4.5% for VGM. The highest AUC score is 75.7% by VGM method.

Table 5. Motor imagery dataset test AUC and EER of different methods.

	Without UBM		With UBM	
	AUC	EER	AUC	EER
Gaussian	58.7 ± 8.5	41.8 ± 8.4	62.2 ± 11.6	38.8 ± 11.3
GMM	68.1 ± 14.0	32.2 ± 14.3	74.6 ± 17.2	25.8 ± 17.4
VAE	68.3 ± 18.5	28.5 ± 13.1	71.9 ± 24.6	24.3 ± 18.2
VGM	71.2 ± 17.1	26.2 ± 12.8	75.7 ± 20.8	22.6 ± 16.3

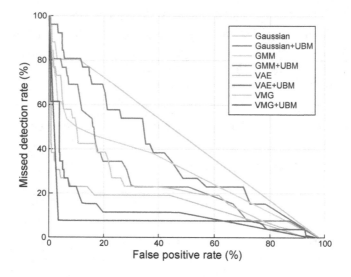

Fig. 2. DET curves comparisons on test data between methods.

5   Conclusion

We have developed a novel framework for EEG-based authentication with variational universal mixture model. The complex data distribution for every user was pooled to a universal background model for score normalization. We provided a proof of the lower bound objective for optimization, concerning the complexity involving the latent mixture prior. Extensive experiments are performed on three datasets, e.g. MNIST dataset, imagined speech dataset, and motor imagery dataset. Experimental results showed that our methods have better performance than the baselines and demonstrated the effectiveness of our method.

A   Appendix

A.1   KL Divergence Derivations

We state the first proposition without proof.

Proposition 3. *Let $f(x) = \mathcal{N}(x; \mu_f, \Sigma_f)$ and $g(x) = \mathcal{N}(x; \mu_g, \Sigma_g)$ be two Gaussian distributions in $\mathbb{R}^n$. The Kullback-Leibler (KL) divergence between $f(x)$ and $g(x)$ is:*

$$D_{KL}(f(x)\|g(x)) = -\frac{n}{2}\log\left(\frac{\det\Sigma_f}{\det\Sigma_g}\right) - \frac{n}{2}$$

$$+ \frac{1}{2}\text{trace}\left(\Sigma_f\Sigma_g^{-1}\right) + \frac{1}{2}(\mu_f - \mu_g)\Sigma_g^{-1}(\mu_f - \mu_g)^T$$

The following proposition provides the basis for the training objective of our proposed VGM model.

Proposition 4. *The variational upper bound of the Kullback-Leibler divergence between a unimodal distribution $f(x)$ and a mixture model $g(x) = \sum_k \alpha_k g_k(x)$ is:*

$$D_{KL}(f(x)\|g(x)) \leq -\log\sum_k \alpha_k \exp\left(-D_k\right)$$

where $D_k = \int f(x)\log\frac{f(x)}{g_k(x)}dx$ is the KL divergence between $f(x)$ and $g_k(x)$, the unimodal component distribution of the mixture $g(x)$.

Proof. We have

$$D_{KL}(f(x)\|g(x)) = \int f(x)\log\frac{f(x)}{g(x)}dx = \int f(x)\log f(x)dx - \int f(x)\log g(x)dx \tag{18}$$

$$= L_f - L_g \tag{19}$$

where $L_f = \int f(x)\log f(x)dx$ and $L_g = \int f(x)\log\sum_k \alpha_k g_k(x)dx$, and the index k runs from 1 to K.

We will use variational method to lower bound L_g. Let us introduce variational variables $a_1, \ldots, a_K$, with $\sum_k a_k = 1$, $a_k > 0$, $k = 1, \ldots, K$,

$$L_g = \int f(x)\log\sum_k a_k\frac{\alpha_k g(x)}{a_k}dx \tag{20}$$

$$\geq \int f(x)\sum_k a_k\log\frac{\alpha_k g_k(x)}{a_k}dx = L'_g \tag{21}$$

where we use Jenssen inequality in Eq. 21. We want to find the a_k that maximizes this lower bound. Since Eq. 21 is concave in each a_k it has a global maximum. Let take partial derivative of L'_g w.r.t. each a_k then set it to zero and let us denote $D_k = D_{KL}(f(x)\|g_k(x))$ for brevity:

$$\frac{\partial L_g'}{\partial a_k} = 0 = \int f(x) \left(\log \frac{\alpha_k g_k(x)}{a_k} + a_k(-\frac{1}{a_k}) \right) dx \tag{22}$$

$$0 = \int f(x) \left(\log \alpha_k + \log g_k(x) - \log a_k - 1 \right) dx \tag{23}$$

$$\log a_k = \int f(x) \left(\log \alpha_k + \log g_k(x) - \log f(x) + \log f(x) - 1 \right) dx \tag{24}$$

$$\log a_k = \log \alpha_k - D_k + \int f(x) \left(\log f(x) - 1 \right) dx \tag{25}$$

$$a_k = \frac{\alpha_k \exp(-D_k)}{\exp \left(\int f(x) \left(1 - \log f(x) \right) dx \right)} \tag{26}$$

$$\sum_{k=1}^{K} a_k = 1 = \frac{\sum_k \alpha_k \exp(-D_k)}{\exp \left(\int f(x) \left(1 - \log f(x) \right) dx \right)} \tag{27}$$

$$\exp\left(\int f(x) \left(1 - \log f(x) \right) dx \right) = \sum_k \alpha_k \exp(-D_k) \tag{28}$$

where we have used $\int f(x)dx = 1$ in Eq. 24.
From Eq. 26 and Eq. 28 we have:

$$a_k = \frac{\alpha_k \exp(-D_k)}{Z} \tag{29}$$

$$\text{where } Z = \sum_{k=1}^{K} \alpha_k \exp(-D_k) \tag{30}$$

Plug L_g' in Eq. 21 into Eq. 18:

$$D_{KL}(f(x)\|g(x)) = L_f - L_g$$
$$\leq L_f - L_g'$$
$$= \int f(x) \log f(x) dx - \int f(x) \sum_k a_k \log \frac{\alpha_k g_k(x)}{a_k} dx$$
$$= \int f(x) \left[\log f(x) - \sum_k a_k \log \frac{\alpha_k g_k(x)}{a_k} \right] dx$$
$$= \int f(x) \left[\log f(x) - \sum_k a_k \log \frac{g_k(x)Z}{\exp(-D_{KLk})} \right] dx \tag{31}$$
$$= -\log Z + \int f(x) \left[\log f(x) - \sum_k a_k \log \frac{g_k(x)}{\exp(-D_k)} \right] dx \tag{32}$$
$$= -\log Z + A \tag{33}$$

where we substituted $a_k = \frac{\alpha_k \exp(-D_k)}{Z}$ in Eq. 31 and move $\log Z$ out of the integral in Eq. 32.

We will show that $A = 0$:

$$A = \int f(x) \left[\log f(x) - \sum_k a_k \log \frac{g_k(x)}{\exp(-D_k)} \right] dx$$

$$= \int f(x) \left[\sum_k a_k \log f(x) - \sum_k a_k \log \frac{g_k(x)}{\exp(-D_k)} \right] dx$$

$$= \sum_k a_k \left[\int f(x) (\log f(x) - \log g_k(x)) \right] dx - D_k$$

$$= \sum_k a_k D_k - D_k$$

$$= 0$$

where we again used the facts that $\int f(x)dx = 1$ and $\sum_k a_k = 1$.
We have shown that $D_{KL}(f(x) \| g(x)) \leq L_f - L'_g = -\log Z$. ∎

References

1. Abdelfattah, S.M., Abdelrahman, G.M., Wang, M.: Augmenting the size of EEG datasets using generative adversarial networks. In: 2018 International Joint Conference on Neural Networks (IJCNN), pp. 1–6. IEEE (2018)
2. Bashivan, P., Rish, I., Yeasin, M., Codella, N.: Learning representations from EEG with deep recurrent-convolutional neural networks. arXiv preprint arXiv:1511.06448 (2015)
3. Bishop, C.M.: Mixture Density Networks (1994)
4. Dai, M., Zhong, D., Na, R., Wang, S., Zhang, S.: EEG classification of motor imagery using a novel deep learning framework. Sensors **19**(3), 551 (2019)
5. Kingma, D.P., Welling, M.: Auto-encoding variational bayes. arXiv preprint arXiv:1312.6114 (2013)
6. Lawhern, V.J., Solon, A.J., Waytowich, N.R., Gordon, S.M., Hung, C.P., Lance, B.J.: EEGNet: a compact convolutional neural network for eeg-based brain-computer interfaces. J. Neural Eng. **15**(5), 056013 (2018)
7. Marcel, S., del R Millán, J.: Person authentication using brainwaves (EEG) and maximum a posteriori model adaptation. IEEE Trans. Pattern Anal. Mach. Intell. **29**(4), 743–752 (2007)
8. Nguyen, C.H., Karavas, G.K., Artemiadis, P.: Inferring imagined speech using EEG signals: a new approach using riemannian manifold features. J. Neural Eng. **15**(1), 016002 (2017)
9. Nguyen, P., Tran, D., Le, T., Huang, X., Ma, W.: EEG-based person verification using multi-sphere SVDD and UBM. In: Pei, J., Tseng, V.S., Cao, L., Motoda, H., Xu, G. (eds.) PAKDD 2013, Part I. LNCS (LNAI), vol. 7818, pp. 289–300. Springer, Heidelberg (2013). https://doi.org/10.1007/978-3-642-37453-1_24
10. Ofner, P., Schwarz, A., Pereira, J., Müller-Putz, G.R.: Upper limb movements can be decoded from the time-domain of low-frequency EEG. PloS one **12**(8), e0182578 (2017)
11. Pham, T., Ma, W., Tran, D., Nguyen, P., Phung, D.: Multi-factor EEG-based user authentication. In: 2014 International Joint Conference on Neural Networks (IJCNN), pp. 4029–4034. IEEE (2014)

12. Reynolds, D.A.: Comparison of background normalization methods for text-independent speaker verification. In: Fifth European Conference on Speech Communication and Technology (1997)
13. Reynolds, D.A., Quatieri, T.F., Dunn, R.B.: Speaker verification using adapted gaussian mixture models. Digit. Signal Process. **10**(1–3), 19–41 (2000)
14. Schirrmeister, R.T., et al.: Deep learning with convolutional neural networks for EEG decoding and visualization. Hum. Brain Mapp. **38**(11), 5391–5420 (2017)
15. Tran, D.T.: Fuzzy approaches to speech and speaker recognition. Ph.D. thesis, University of Canberra (2000)
16. Tran, N., Tran, D., Liu, S., Ma, W., Pham, T.: EEG-based person authentication system in different brain states. In: 2019 9th International IEEE/EMBS Conference on Neural Engineering (NER), pp. 1050–1053. IEEE (2019)

An Efficient Vulnerability Detection Model for Ethereum Smart Contracts

Jingjing Song[1,2], Haiwu He[3,4(✉)], Zhuo Lv[5], Chunhua Su[6], Guangquan Xu[7], and Wei Wang[1,2,8]

[1] Beijing Key Laboratory of Security and Privacy in Intelligent Transportation, Beijing Jiaotong University, 3 Shangyuancun, Beijing 100044, China
{17120479,wangwei1}@bjtu.edu.cn
[2] School of Computer and Information Technology, Beijing Jiaotong University, 3 Shangyuancun, Beijing 100044, China
[3] Shandong Computer Science Center (National Supercomputer Center in Jinan), Shandong Provincial Key Laboratory of Computer Networks, Qilu University of Technology (Shandong Academy of Sciences), Jinan, China
hehw@sdas.org
[4] iExec Blockchain Tech, Lyon, France
[5] State Grid Henan Electric Power Research Institute, Zhengzhou 450052, China
zhuanzhuan2325@sina.com
[6] University of Aizu, Aizu-Wakamatsu, Fukushima Prefecture, Japan
chsu@u-aizu.ac.jp
[7] Tianjin University, Tianjin 300350, China
losin@tju.edu.cn
[8] Division of Computer, Electrical and Mathematical Sciences & Engineering (CEMSE), King Abdullah University of Science and Technology (KAUST), Thuwal 23955-6900, Saudi Arabia

Abstract. Smart contracts are decentralized applications running on the blockchain to meet various practical scenario demands. The increasing number of security events regarding smart contracts have led to huge pecuniary losses and destroyed the ecological stability of contract layer on the blockchain. Faced with the increasing quantity of contracts, it is an emerging issue to effectively and efficiently detect vulnerabilities in smart contracts. Existing methods of detecting vulnerabilities in smart contracts like Oyente mainly employ symbolic execution. This method is very time-consuming, as the symbolic execution requires the exploration of all executable paths in a contract. In this work, we propose an efficient model for the detection of vulnerabilities in Ethereum smart contracts with machine learning techniques. The model is able to effectively and fast detect vulnerabilities based on the patterns learned from training samples. Our model is evaluated on 49502 real-world smart contracts and the results verify its effectiveness and efficiency.

Keywords: Blockchain · Smart contracts · Vulnerability detection

© Springer Nature Switzerland AG 2019
J. K. Liu and X. Huang (Eds.): NSS 2019, LNCS 11928, pp. 433–442, 2019.
https://doi.org/10.1007/978-3-030-36938-5_26

1   Introduction

The concept of smart contract was first proposed by Nick Szabo in 1990s. Nevertheless, at that time, the exploration only stayed at theoretical level due to the lack of trusted execution environment. Since 2009, with the emergence of blockchain technology that was first applied in Bitcoin [19], a reliable execution environment has been offered to smart contracts. The remote point-to-point value delivery can be realized without any trusted third party through the blockchain. However, as Bitcoin system is not Turing-complete, it is unable to handle complex business logic via smart contracts.

Inspired by Bitcoin, Vitalik Buterin developed Ethereum in 2013 [9]. Ethereum is an open-source distributed computing platform and operating system based on blockchain, which features smart contracts. To meet more business scenario demands, Ethereum provides a Turing-complete Ethereum Virtual Machine (EVM) [5] that enables developers to deploy decentralized applications (Dapps) on it. Dapps are also called smart contracts. Blockchain as a newly developed technology is vulnerable [16] in terms of lacking of regulations and programmable characteristics. These vulnerabilities can be easily exploited, resulting in big losses.

Based upon mainstream vulnerability detection methods, such as symbolic execution, formal verification with F* framework and K framework, and symbolic analysis, some tools have been released publicly. For example, Oyente [18] and Securify [22] take about 28 or 18 s to detect vulnerabilities in each contract, respectively. We can see that prior tools are very time-consuming and unsuitable for batch vulnerability detection, as these tools mainly employ symbolic execution or symbolic analysis that requires the exploration of all executable paths in a contract or analysis of dependency graphs of the contract. In this work, we propose a model in the aim to improve the efficiency of vulnerabilities detection in smart contracts on the premise of ensuring accuracy of the detection based on machine learning techniques.

Our contributions are summarized as follows.

- To better characterize features of smart contracts, we collect 49502 real-world smart contracts from Ethereum official website [1]. We further extract 1619-dimension bigram features from simplified operation codes to construct a feature space.
- The model is proven to be time-saving and suitable for batch detection of vulnerabilities in smart contracts. We run the model on real contracts and the predictive recall and precision of the model reach over 96%. In addition, the detection time of the model is about 4 s per contract.

The remainder of this paper is organized as follows. Related work is summarized in Sect. 2. Section 3 provides the description of the data, features and models. Experiments and results are presented in Sect. 4. Concluding remarks follow in Sect. 5.

2 Related Work

There are related works on vulnerabilities detection in smart contracts. The issue of smart contracts security has draw public attentions [2]. Grishchenko et al. [10] defined formal semantics for contracts source codes with F* framework. These semantics were executable, but not fully automated. Then Tsankov et al. [22] proposed an automated security tool named Securify that is only for attributes that can be proved or disproved by checking simple attributes. Bhargavan et al. [12] provided a strategy to verify contracts through putting source codes and bytecodes into an existing verification system. The prototype of ZEUS [14] claimed that it was a sound analyzer with zero false negatives by translating contracts to LLVM framework. Jiang et al. [13] provided a novel fuzzer named ContractFuzzer to test Ethereum smart contracts whether they are vulnerable or not. Due to random generation of test Oracle, the system could not cover all paths [4,11]. Some vulnerability types were defined in [7,15,20]. In our previous work, we detect malware or anomalies with static [17,27–29] or dynamic analysis [23,25] or with network traffic [23,24,26].

3 The Detection Model

As described in Fig. 1, the model is constructed with six steps. First, verified smart contracts are collected from Ethereum official website. Second, source codes are transformed into operation codes (opcode), and then operation codes are simplified. Third, we extract 1619-dimension bigram features from simplified opcodes and label contracts with six types of vulnerabilities. Next we employ One vs. Rest (OvR) algorithm for multi-label classification, where C_1, C_2, C_3, C_4, C_5 and C_6 correspond to Integer Overflow vulnerability (Overflow), Integer Underflow vulnerability (Underflow), Transaction-Ordering Dependence (TOD), Callstack Depth Attack vulnerability (Callstack), Timestamp Dependency (Timestamp) and Reentrancy vulnerability (Reentrancy). For balanced examples like C_1 vs. The Rest or C_2 vs. The Rest, we can classify them directly. For the remaining four types of vulnerabilities, we need to employ sampling algorithms to balance them before classification because of class imbalance. Lastly, we construct models on the balanced training sets.

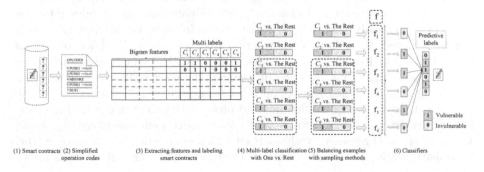

(1) Smart contracts (2) Simplified operation codes   (3) Extracting features and labeling smart contracts   (4) Multi-label classification with One vs. Rest (5) Balancing examples with sampling methods   (6) Classifiers

Fig. 1. The process of training models

3.1   Data Sets, Labels and Feature Space

We collect about $50K$ smart contracts with source codes from Ethereum official website, where smart contracts has been verified before September 2018. The data sets contain contracts with six types of vulnerabilities. The data is described in Table 1. For TOD, Callstack, Timestamp and Reentrancy vulnerabilities, the ratios of negative to positive examples are quite imbalanced, even up to 100:1, where negative examples are in the majority class and positive examples are in the minority class without exception. So the data sets are considered to be class-imbalance. Note that our data sets are open-source and our access to the data sets are legitimate.

Table 1. The description of data sets

Number	Overflow	Underflow	TOD	Callstack	Timestamp	Reentrancy
This type	22128	9699	1436	192	477	100
The rest	27374	39803	48066	49310	49025	49402
Total	49502	49502	49502	49502	49502	49502

We employ an authoritative tool named Oyente to label all contracts, and each contract is with six labels. Then we manually check the correctness of labels. The labels are independent from each other in each type of vulnerability. For instance, an example with the multi-label vector like [1 0 1 0 0 0] demonstrates that it has the first and the third vulnerabilities and an example with [0 0 0 0 0 0] has no vulnerability, theoretically.

We adopt n-gram algorithm for feature extraction. N-Gram refers to n words that appear continuously in text. Specially, bigram is exceptional situations of n-gram, where n is 2. Finally, We take bigrams as features in this paper. According to our statistics, the opcode length of each contract is about 4364 on average and there are more than 100 opcodes in total. So directly using n-gram algorithm to extract features may lead to the curse of dimensionality caused by excessive number of features.

In order to reduce the dimension of the features, we simplify opcodes by dislodging the operands and classifying functionally similar opcodes into one category. Specifically, each PUSH instruction is followed by an operand, which can be removed. For BLOCK information instructions, a simplified opcode is acted as the substitution for six opcodes, which have the same impact on Timestamp vulnerability. Thus after the processing, there are only about 50 opcodes remaining. The simplified rules of opcodes are described in Table 2.

Each distinct bigram is a feature and ultimately we extract 1619-dimension features, which can be used to identify vulnerabilities effectively. We construct a feature space (FS) where each contract has its corresponding feature vector. Each feature value in a feature vector is calculated from the ratio of the number

Table 2. The simplification rules

Substitutes	Original opcodes
MATH	ADD MUL SUB DIV SDIV SMOD MOD ADDMOD MULMOD
CONSTANT1	BLOCKHASH TIMESTAMP NUMBER DIFFICULTY GASLIMIT
CONSTANT2	ADDRESS ORIGIN CALLER
COMPARISON	LT GT SLT SGT
LOGIC_OP	AND OR XOR NOT
DUP	DUP1-DUP16

of each bigram to the number of bigrams occurred in the contract. The feature space (FS) and f_{ij} is defined in Eq. 1.

$$FS = \begin{pmatrix} f_{11} & f_{12} & \cdots & \cdots & f_{1,1619} \\ f_{21} & f_{22} & \cdots & \cdots & f_{2,1619} \\ \vdots & \vdots & \vdots & \vdots & \vdots \\ f_{i1} & \cdots & f_{ij} & \cdots & f_{i,1619} \\ \vdots & \vdots & \vdots & \vdots & \vdots \end{pmatrix} , \quad f_{ij} = \frac{n_{i,c_j}}{n_{all,c_j}} \tag{1}$$

where f_{ij} is the feature frequency of the ith bigram in the jth contract, a decimal number between 0 and 1. We define n_{i,c_j} as the number of the ith bigram occurrences in the jth contract and define n_{all,c_j} as the sum of all bigram occurrences in the same contract. Note that if a bigram feature does not appear in the contract, the corresponding f_{ij} is 0.

3.2 Training Set

Normally, training sets consist of 70% examples randomly selected from data sets in supervised classification. Nevertheless, in this work, the training sets are imbalanced because classification categories are not roughly equally represented. To tackle this problem successfully, we take a measure to diminish the class-imbalance impact. So we adopt Synthetic Minority Oversampling Technique (SMOTE) [6] to extend the number of minority class to be similar to that of the majority class. SMOTE is an oversampling technique, interpolating between the minority class to generate extra ones.

3.3 Classification Algorithms

The multi-label classification task is realized by splitting, that is, dividing a multi-label classification task into several binary classification tasks. The classification results of these binary classifiers are integrated to provide the final results of multi-label classification. We adopt One vs. Rest (OvR) strategy to fulfill multi-label classification. In this work, the main idea of OvR is to train three binary classifiers in the condition of taking one category as positive class and the other categories as negative class. In the process of training, if the example is predicted to be positive in some of the six categories, and thus the corresponding labels would be 1, which means the example has vulnerabilities in these categories. Based on the feature space and labels of training set, we employ Random Forest (RF) [3] to develop the model to detect vulnerabilities in smart contracts. We also adopt Support Vector Machine (SVM) [21] and k-Nearest Neighbor (KNN) [8] for comparison.

3.4   Test Set

70% of data sets have used as training set, and if the remaining 30% is used as test sets directly, the results of classification may not objective on imbalanced test sets. It is essential to balance the test sets without interfering the authenticity of samples. In order to balance the test set, we adopt random sampling method to select samples from $15K$ real-world smart contracts. For four vulnerabilities, namely, TOD, Callstack, Timestamp and Reentrancy, we randomly select samples from the majority class, and the number of samples which are selected from the majority class is five times as many as the number of the minority class. Then we combine the samples selected from the majority class and all samples of the minority class to form test sets. The test sets contain enough samples without fictitious samples. So the test sets of our experiment are authentic, effective and representative.

4   Results

We conduct extensive experiments aiming to compare the performance of three multi-label classifiers. F1-score, Micro-F1, Macro-F1 are used to measure the performance of the classifiers. F1-score is a measure used to evaluate binary classifiers and it is defined as $F1 - score = (2 \times P \times R)/(P + R)$. Micro-F1 and Macro-F1 are measurements used to evaluate multi-label classification. When calculating Micro-F1, the value is susceptible to the classification results of categories with many samples. When calculating Macro-F1, the weights of each category are equal regardless of the number of samples in each category. And they are defined in the following Equations.

$$micro-F1 = \frac{2 \times \frac{TP}{TP+FP} \times \frac{TP}{TP+FN}}{\frac{TP}{TP+FP} + \frac{TP}{TP+FN}}, \quad macro-F1 = \frac{2 \times \frac{1}{n}\sum_{i=1}^{n} P_i \times \frac{1}{n}\sum_{i=1}^{n} R_i}{\frac{1}{n}\sum_{i=1}^{n} P_i + \frac{1}{n}\sum_{i=1}^{n} R_i} \quad (2)$$

In Table 3, RF classifier produces higher F1-score values than SVM classifier and KNN classifier in each binary classification task. The predictive Micro-F1 value and Macro-F1 value of RF multi-label classifier are the highest among three classifiers, and they all reach over 93%. Micro-F1 value is larger than Macro-F1 value, because the number of test samples for both Overflow and Underflow vulnerabilities are large and F1-score values to these two categories are high, so Micro-F1 value is bias to high value. Thus we choose RF classifier as our model.

Table 3. The detection performance comparison of three classifiers trained by training sets balanced with SMOTE

	F1-score						Micro-F1	Macro-F1
	Overflow	Underflow	TOD	Callstack	Timestamp	Reentrancy		
RF	**0.98**	**0.98**	**0.94**	**0.91**	**0.92**	**0.90**	**0.9698**	**0.9303**
SVM	0.97	0.97	0.92	0.92	0.91	0.91	0.9618	0.9268
KNN	0.97	0.97	0.92	0.90	0.91	0.91	0.9558	0.9237

Receiver Operating Characteristic (ROC) curves is used to measure the model performance by trading off relative costs of True Positive Rate (TPR) and False Positive Rate (FPR) where $TPR = TP/(TP + FN)$ and $FPR = FP/(TN + FP)$. On ROC curve, FPR is represented as X-axis and TPR is represented as Y-axis. Theoretically, the ideal point would be $(0, 1)$, which means all positive samples and negative samples are classified correctly, respectively. Thus the point closer to top left indicates that classification results are better. The ROC curves of our model are shown in Fig. 2.

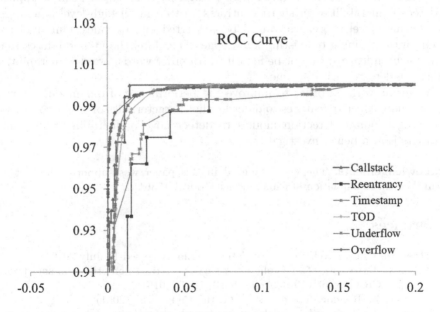

Fig. 2. The ROC curves of our model

Approximate $3K$ real-world smart contracts are detected by the model. According to the statistics, as shown in Table 4, our model spends about 4 s in detecting per contract, which is much faster than Oyente that takes about 28 s to detect vulnerabilities per contract.

Table 4. The comparison in detection time

	Our model	Oyente
Times (seconds)	4.07	28.50

5   Concluding Remarks

In order to secure the contract layer on Ethereum and to purify Dapps markets, in this work, we propose a model for effectively and efficiently detecting six types of vulnerabilities of smart contracts based on extracted static characteristics. We employ three supervised ensemble classification algorithms, namely, RF, SVM and KNN to conduct comparative experiments and finally e select RF classifier as our model. The experimental results demonstrate the effectiveness and efficiency of the model. First, the bigram features extracted from simplified opcodes represent static features of contracts. Second, the model is appropriate for rapid batch detection of vulnerabilities in smart contracts, and its detection speed is about 4 s on a smart contract on average. Finally, the model is reliable with the predictive Micro-F1 and Macro-F1 over 93%. The model can be applied to detect vulnerabilities in smart contracts written in all high-level languages, because high-level languages can all be converted into opcodes. Our model is based on the training of existing knowledge. Therefore, the vulnerabilities that have not been learned cannot be identified. In order words, novel vulnerabilities cannot be detected with our model.

In future work, in order to improve the performance of our model, we will explore more effective features to describe the characteristics of smart contracts. Designing anomaly detection models to detect novel vulnerabilities in smart contracts is also being investigated.

Acknowledgements. The work reported in this paper was supported in part by Natural Science Foundation of China, under Grant U1736114.

References

1. Ethereum Official Website. https://etherscan.io. Accessed 14 July 2019
2. Atzei, N., Bartoletti, M., Cimoli, T.: A survey of attacks on ethereum smart contracts. IACR Cryptol. ePrint Arch. **2016**, 1007 (2016)
3. Breiman, L.: Random forests. Mach. Learn. **45**(1), 5–32 (2001)
4. Brent, L., et al.: Vandal: a scalable security analysis framework for smart contracts. arXiv preprint. arXiv:1809.03981 (2018)
5. Buterin, V., et al.: A next-generation smart contract and decentralized application platform. White Pap. **3**, 37 (2014)
6. Chawla, N.V., Bowyer, K.W., Hall, L.O., Kegelmeyer, W.P.: SMOTE: synthetic minority over-sampling technique. J. Artif. Intell. Res. **16**, 321–357 (2002)
7. Chen, T., et al.: Towards saving money in using smart contracts. In: 2018 IEEE/ACM 40th International Conference on Software Engineering: New Ideas and Emerging Technologies Results (ICSE-NIER), pp. 81–84. IEEE (2018)

8. Cover, T.M., Hart, P., et al.: Nearest neighbor pattern classification. IEEE Trans. Inf. Theory **13**(1), 21–27 (1967)
9. Dannen, C.: Introducing Ethereum and Solidity. Springer, Berlin (2017). https://doi.org/10.1007/978-1-4842-2535-6
10. Grishchenko, I., Maffei, M., Schneidewind, C.: A semantic framework for the security analysis of Ethereum smart contracts. In: Bauer, L., Küsters, R. (eds.) POST 2018. LNCS, vol. 10804, pp. 243–269. Springer, Cham (2018). https://doi.org/10.1007/978-3-319-89722-6_10
11. He, N., Wu, L., Wang, H., Guo, Y., Jiang, X.: Characterizing code clones in the Ethereum smart contract ecosystem. arXiv preprint. arXiv:1905.00272 (2019)
12. Hildenbrandt, E., et al.: KEVM: a complete formal semantics of the Ethereum virtual machine. In: 2018 IEEE 31st Computer Security Foundations Symposium (CSF), pp. 204–217. IEEE (2018)
13. Jiang, B., Liu, Y., Chan, W.: ContractFuzzer: fuzzing smart contracts for vulnerability detection. In: Proceedings of the 33rd ACM/IEEE International Conference on Automated Software Engineering, pp. 259–269. ACM (2018)
14. Kalra, S., Goel, S., Dhawan, M., Sharma, S.: ZEUS: analyzing safety of smart contracts. In: NDSS (2018)
15. Li, X., Jiang, P., Chen, T., Luo, X., Wen, Q.: A survey on the security of blockchain systems. Future Gener. Comput. Syst. (2017)
16. Lin, I.C., Liao, T.C.: A survey of blockchain security issues and challenges. IJ Netw. Secur. **19**(5), 653–659 (2017)
17. Liu, X., Liu, J., Zhu, S., Wang, W., Zhang, X.: Privacy risk analysis and mitigation of analytics libraries in the android ecosystem. IEEE Trans. Mobile Comput. (2019)
18. Luu, L., Chu, D.H., Olickel, H., Saxena, P., Hobor, A.: Making smart contracts smarter. In: Proceedings of the 2016 ACM SIGSAC Conference on Computer and Communications Security, pp. 254–269. ACM (2016)
19. Nakamoto, S., et al.: Bitcoin: a peer-to-peer electronic cash system (2008)
20. Praitheeshan, P., Pan, L., Yu, J., Liu, J., Doss, R.: Security analysis methods on Ethereum smart contract vulnerabilities: a survey. arXiv preprint. arXiv:1908.08605 (2019)
21. Suykens, J.A., Vandewalle, J.: Least squares support vector machine classifiers. Neural Process. Lett. **9**(3), 293–300 (1999)
22. Tsankov, P., Dan, A., Drachsler-Cohen, D., Gervais, A., Buenzli, F., Vechev, M.: Securify: practical security analysis of smart contracts. In: Proceedings of the 2018 ACM SIGSAC Conference on Computer and Communications Security, pp. 67–82. ACM (2018)
23. Wang, W., Guan, X., Zhang, X.: Processing of massive audit data streams for real-time anomaly intrusion detection. Comput. Commun. **31**(1), 58–72 (2008). https://doi.org/10.1016/j.comcom.2007.10.010
24. Wang, W., Guyet, T., Quiniou, R., Cordier, M., Masseglia, F., Zhang, X.: Autonomic intrusion detection: adaptively detecting anomalies over unlabeled audit data streams in computer networks. Knowl.-Based Syst. **70**, 103–117 (2014)
25. Wang, W., Li, Y., Wang, X., Liu, J., Zhang, X.: Detecting android malicious apps and categorizing benign apps with ensemble of classifiers. Future Gener. Comput. Syst. **78**, 987–994 (2018)
26. Wang, W., Shang, Y., He, Y., Li, Y., Liu, J.: BotMark: automated botnet detection with hybrid analysis of flow-based and graph-based traffic behaviors. Inf. Sci. **511**, 284–296 (2020)

27. Wang, W., Wang, X., Feng, D., Liu, J., Han, Z., Zhang, X.: Exploring permission-induced risk in android applications for malicious application detection. IEEE Trans. Inf. Forensics Secur. **9**(11), 1869–1882 (2014)
28. Wang, W., Zhao, M., Wang, J.: Effective android malware detection with a hybrid model based on deep autoencoder and convolutional neural network. J. Ambient Intell. Humaniz. Comput. **10**(8), 3035–3043 (2019)
29. Wang, X., Wang, W., He, Y., Liu, J., Han, Z., Zhang, X.: Characterizing android apps' behavior for effective detection of malapps at large scale. Future Gener. Comput. Syst. **75**, 30–45 (2017)

A Comparative Study on Network Traffic Clustering

Yang Liu[✉], Hanxiao Xue, Guocheng Wei, Lisu Wu, and Yu Wang

School of Computer Science, Guangzhou University, Guangzhou 510006, China
{yang_liu,hxue,weiguocheng,wulisu}@e.gzhu.edu.cn, yuwang@gzhu.edu.cn

Abstract. Accurate network traffic classification is vital to the areas of network security. There are many applications using dynamic ports and encryption to avoid detection, so previous methods such as port number and payload-based classification exist some shortfalls. An alternative approach is to use Machine learning (ML) techniques. Here we will present three clustering algorithms, K-Means, FarthestFirst and Canopy, based on flow statistic features of applications. The performance impact of the data set processed by the PCA dimension reduction algorithm on the above three algorithms will be an important topic for our discussion. Our results show that the classification accuracy and computational performance all have been significantly improved after dimension reduction.

Keywords: Clustering algorithms · Machine learning · Traffic clustering · Dimension reduction

1 Introduction

Network traffic classification is of fundamental importance for intrusion detection [16], Quality of Service and network migration trend or prediction [3]. We need efficient network traffic classification technology to implement network management [1,13], flow control, and security detection. Previous methods such as port-based or payload-based classification have their own drawbacks. There are many applications, such as P2P [15], which use random port (dynamic port) to make port-based method less accurate. Some applications transfer data using an unknown encryption protocol, so payload-based method cannot decrypt the data content and related features. In addition, payload-based method may cause data to be unsafe. And with the emergence of new applications, it needs to constantly analyze the application layer protocol, which will consume a lot of computer resources.

Many researchers began to use supervised machine learning algorithm based on flow statistic features. A set of manually classified and tagged data will be used to train a classifier through supervised algorithms, containing several attributes.

Supported by Graduate Innovation Capacity Development Funding Program of Guangzhou University (2018GDJC-M15).

J. K. Liu and X. Huang (Eds.): NSS 2019, LNCS 11928, pp. 443–455, 2019.
https://doi.org/10.1007/978-3-030-36938-5_27

Finally, the classifier determines the type of unknown data entered. However, the difficulty of above process is that it takes a lot of time to arrange the training data in advance. Today it is hard to analyze the flow data type by hand from the Internet, but cluster, which is unsupervised machine learning, can address above problems.

Cluster analysis is the process of dividing a set of unknown data objects into subsets. Each subset is a cluster, in which objects are similar to each other, but dissimilar to objects in other clusters. The clustering process is to generate a cluster set. We can mark the unknown data that has been grouped into several clusters. Then these training data can be used to train classifier, which can be applied in real-time traffic classification.

A lot of unsupervised machine learning algorithms are applied to network traffic classification [8,14], and the accuracy of many algorithms is already high. However, there are few studies on the impact of data dimensionality reduction on clustering. In order to reduce the impact of the inconsistency of the sample application types on the clustering results, we randomly extract ten samples from the original dataset, each of which has 6 application types of 1000 objects. Then PCA produces a subset of 30 new features. Finally, the accuracy and computational performance of the K-Means, Canopy and FarthestFirst algorithms before and after dimensionality reduction are compared. The accuracy is the mean of 10 samples. The main findings are:

- The computational performance of the algorithm has been greatly improved after data dimension reduction (feature attribute reduction).
- After the dimension is reduced, the over accuracy of the three algorithms has been significantly improved.
- For the first time, the Canopy algorithm is applied to network traffic clustering research. Although Canopy has been used as a coarse clustering algorithm for K-Means, its accuracy is almost the same as that of K-Means after dimensionality reduction.

The rest of this paper is structured as follows. Section 2 introduces the research on clustering of network traffic. Section 3 shows three clustering algorithms. Section 4 gives a brief introduction to the PCA dimensionality reduction algorithm. Section 5 analyzes the results of three algorithms from multi-aspects. Finally, Sect. 6 makes a conclusion and future work.

2   Related Work

Unsupervised learning has been developed in the application of traffic analysis area for a long time.

It is the first time that Erman et al. [2] applied K-Means algorithm to network traffic classification. The experiment result indicates that K-Means have an excellent clustering effect in contrast to the AutoClass and can converge more faster. On the other hand, though K-Means has a higher accuracy than DBSCAN, it can not produce a best cluster.

McCallum et al. [9] proposed canopy algorithm for large-scale high-dimensional data clustering, which uses the approximate distance to effectively divide the data into overlapping subsets. This method can be used with Greedy Agglomerative Clustering, Expectation-Maximization, K-means. Canopy not only reduces computation time but also increases clustering accuracy compared to previous clustering algorithms.

Wang et al. [18] proposed constrained clustering, which mainly includes some background information as the constraint condition in the observed traffic statistics. The research indicates that constrained clustering not only improves the quality of the traffic clustering, but also accelerates the convergence speed of the cluster analysis compared with the previous EM and K-Means algorithms.

Sharmila et al. [12] found that the FarthestFirst algorithm is very suitable for large data sets but is hard to generate a unified cluster. And by analyzing different samples, the algorithm is not affected by the initial value and the cluttered data sets.

Filho et al. [3] combined the PCA and K-Means algorithms to predict the level of short-term with origin-destination traffic data, the results with the real traffic data perform a acceptable error rate in the actual network.

Zhang et al. [20] proposed Robust Network Traffic Classification (RTC) method that combines supervised and unsupervised learning. It addresses zero-day application issues by extracting zero-day traffic samples from unlabeled network traffic and automatically optimizing RTC script parameters.

Williams et al. [19] Liu et al. compared five supervised machine learning algorithms in terms of classification accuracy and computational performance. Correlation-based and Consistencybased feature reduction algorithm were used to produce different feature subsets for clustering. The results show that the accuracy of each algorithm is roughly the same but the computation performance is significantly different that can distinguish classification algorithm.

Jamuna et al. [6] investigated a large number of algorithms, and machine learning can be well applied to network traffic classification. Many algorithms show high accuracy. The authors also point out that machine learning algorithms are still more dependent on offline analysis for grabbing traffic, and more and more research has begun to address real-time traffic classification.

3   Network Traffic Clustering Algorithm

This part is the core of this paper, which all experimental research is based on. Here we mainly introduce three hard clustering algorithms, that is K-Means, Canopy and FarthestFirst. They have a similar principle, all of them require to find cluster center though the method is very different, and an unanimous purpose that all objects in data set will be accurately assigned to a cluster, but some of objects cannot be correctly classified. So the accuracy (or purity) of the algorithm needs to be evaluated later.

3.1   K-Means

As a very popular clustering algorithm, K-Means has been used in various of areas. Hartigan et al. [4] have proposed an efficient version about this algorithm since 1979. Alphabet K shows the number of clustering we would like to. The key of K-Means is to define the centroid by calculating average of the distance from one point to the other's not only in one dimension but also in multi-dimension.

Euclidean distance [3] is considered as one of the most commonly approach for clustering. In fact, the distance is closely related to the similarity between entities, that is, small distance means higher similarity and large distance means lower similarity.

The mean value of each point in one cluster is considered as the centroid we have mentioned above. First of all, we will randomly select k of the objects in the data set as the initial centroid. After calculating the distance to the centroid by using the Euclidean distance, remaining point will be assigned to the nearest centroid group. The K-Means will compute new mean rather than a point such as the initial center using the object from each temporary group. Hence, the objects will be redistributed according to the new centroid. K-Means will repeat the progress iteratively until the assignment stay in stable. A formula can be intuitively represented the similarity as follow:

$$E = \sum_{i=1}^{k} \sum_{x \in G_i} dist(x, g_i)^2 \tag{1}$$

where $x \in G_i$, x is the object in one cluster; G_i represents the cluster; g_i is the centroid of cluster G_i. $dist(x, g_i)^2$ is the squared error between each x and g_i within a cluster; k is the number of clusters. So we can know E is the sum of squared error for all objects given in the data set. The smaller E is, the higher the compactness of cluster is.

However K-Means algorithm often converges to a local optimum rather than the global optimum due to the different initial centroid. In order to improve the clustering result, it is necessary to try more initial centroid or apply other algorithm, such as Canopy, to micro-clustering.

3.2   Canopy

The Canopy algorithm was first proposed in 2000 [9]. It is mainly used in two aspects: one is clustering analysis as a clustering algorithm alone, such as the traffic classification we mainly discuss here; the other is coarsely clustering before the K-Means algorithm, which can effectively and obviously help K-Means finding the centers and reducing the computation, which greatly speeds up the convergence of K-Means [7].

The Canopy algorithm mainly groups chaotic data into certain regular canopy by specifying two thresholds (represented by $T1$ and $T2$ respectively) to calculate the distance from the data to the center. Suppose there is a pile of

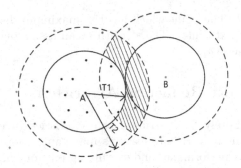

Fig. 1. A and B represent two canopies, and the shaded part indicates the overlap of the two canopies.

data scattered and placed in the set S and two distance thresholds $T1, T2$, where $T1 < T2$.

Select a point p from the set S as the center point, use the inverted index technique to calculate the distance dp between p and the remaining points in the list, and divide the point smaller than T2 into the canopy centered on p. Remove points less than T1 from set S, because these points are close enough to p and can no longer be the center point of the new canopy. Then select a point from the remaining S as the new center, and repeat until S is empty. Figure 1 shows the canopies after clustering.

It can be seen from the above algorithm that some points can be included by multiple canopy at the same time. Thus canopy may lead to the lower accuracy, but it is very simple and efficient. This paper will fully explore its effectiveness in network traffic clustering.

3.3   FarthestFirst

The core of FarthestFirst is the farthest-first traversal algorithm proposed by Hochbaum and Shmoys(1985) [5] whose purpose is to address k-center problem. In the condition of defined cost function and maximum clustering radius, farthest-first traversal algorithm can help to find the best center points for an optimal k-clustering. Fast and simple is the biggest advantage.

The procedure of FarthestFirst is similar to K-Means algorithm. Both of them will find a centroid for clustering and need to confirm k value for determining the number of clusters, but the method is extremely different. FartherFirst will select the point whose distance is farthest than points have been picked as the center point of a cluster, rather than using the mean of distance of all points from one iterative group in K-Means. After that the remaining points will be assigned to the nearest center. Now more detailed description about this algorithm will be given as follows.

Suppose S is the set of centers, $P_i(i \in \{1, 2, 3, ..., n\})$ represents non-central points, d_i represent the distance from $P_i(i \in \{1, 2, 3, ..., n\})$ to set S, thus $d_i =$

$min\{d(P_i, c), c \in S\}$. The point which has the maximum distance to set S will been chosen to the next center. The algorithm can assign one point to a cluster by evaluating the value d_i.

4   Dimensionality Reduction Algorithm

There are approximately 248 attribute characteristics in each object of the dataset we use. So many attribute features may cause some problems, such as the decline in cluster performance and overfitting phenomenon. As a result that it is necessary to use relevant measures to minimize the attributes that are most needed.

The following is a description about Principal Components Analysis (PCA), which is one of the most popular dimensionality reduction algorithms.

PCA is a linear transformation algorithm. For each object consisted of n attributes, the goal of PCA is to find m orthogonal vectors that can be applied to represent original data approximately. Different from feature selection algorithm, PCA reconstructs m-dimensional features based on the original n-dimensional features rather than selects a subset of the original attributes. These new features are mutually independent, so that fewer features can be used to represent the original feature information. The core of PCA is how to get the most different principal component direction. The following is the basic process of PCA implementation.

1. The input data needs to be standardized and zero-centered. The former maps data to a small data interval to reduce excessive differences among data. The latter can increase the orthogonality of the basis vectors during algorithm execution.
2. This algorithm looks for the orthogonal basis vector of the direction with the largest variance in the original data. This base vector is used as the principal component, the actual first coordinate axis. The next coordinate axis is selected to be orthogonal to the base vector and variance is the second largest. Similarly, the third coordinate selection is orthogonal to the first two axes. You can get m axes in turn, and then you can find that most of the variances are in the first m axes. Subsequent coordinate axises variance will approach 0.
3. The maximum variance of axises is in descending order, so we can reduce the number of features by eliminating components with smaller variance. Thus, the first m components that are more independent of each other can be approximated to represent the original data.

The advantages of PCA algorithm are significant. It measures the independence of data by variance. The calculation method is also relatively simple and easy to implement on a computer.

5   Dataset and Evaluate Methodology

Dataset. The dataset [11] used in this paper is collected, with the high-performance monitor, by Moore et al [10]. A full-duplex Gigabit Ethernet link with approximately 1000 hosts is connected to the research facility to obtain data whose number is more than 377,526 from 00:34:21 to 15:22:37 in August 20th, 2003. The data is divided into ten data sets and contains ten application data traffic, namely BULK, DATABASE, INTERACTIVE, MAIL, SERVICES, WWW, P2P, ATTACK, GAMES and MULITMEDIA as shown in Table 1. We randomly select 1000 flows for each application from above ten subsets to form a new single data set as shown in Table 2. There are a total of 6000 instances six applications in this reorganized dataset.

Table 1. The statistic of ten application classes in Moore's dataset

BULK	DB	INT	MAIL	SER	WWW	P2P	ATTACK	GAMES	MULTI	TOTAL
11539	2648	110	28567	2099	328092	2094	1793	8	576	377526

Table 2. Each reorganized dataset contains 6 applications with 1000 objects from Moore's trace

Classification	Application
DB	postgres, sqlneet oracle, ingres
MAIL	smtp, imap, pop2/3
SER	X11, dns, ident, ldap, ntp
WWW	www
P2P	KaZaA, BitTorrent, GnuTella
ATTACK	Internet worm, virus attacks

It is well known whether an object should be assigned to a class, some specific parameters are required. These parameters can be used to distinguish different applications. We can call them features or attributes. Each flow in the dataset contains many features, such as flow duration, TCP port, packet arrival interval, payload size, entropy-based effective bandwidth, fourier transform of packet arrival interval, etc.

Evaluate Methodology. The operational environment for the test is Intel Pentium 6200 series, clocked at 2.13Ghz, and 4GB utility memory. Our experimental process is mainly divided into two groups, and the first group is linearly transformed by PCA algorithm. This transformation process extracts the first 30 vectors with the largest variance. In other words, there are 30 features in each object. The second group uses the original dataset which contains 248 attributes in each object. In order to ensure the ground truth for the experiment, the overall accuracy of each cluster number is the average of the above 10 reorganized datasets. For all clustering algorithms, we use the number of clusters as input parameters p. Each p (from $5, 10, 15...$ to 200) corresponds to a cluster accuracy.

The key to measure clustering result is to calculate overall accuracy, which is the ratio of the number of correctly classified data objects to the total number of data objects. Suppose that M is the number of clusters. In each cluster $j \in (1, M)$, labeling cluster j with the an application A that having majority of flows. True positives (TP_j) represent the number of application A. Then the overall accuracy is the sum of TP divided by the total number of objects (N) [17].

$$Overall Accuracy = \frac{\sum_{j=1}^{M} TP_j}{N} \qquad (2)$$

6   Experimental Results

In this part, the accuracy and convergence speed of each algorithm in the same dimension will be compared firstly. Then we will discuss the effect of dimensional reducing.

6.1   Comparison of Three Algorithms

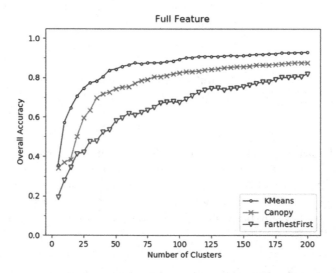

Fig. 2. Clustering performance of the original data set with full feature.

Figure 2 shows that the overall accuracy of three algorithms grows as the number of clusters increases. K-Means is obviously better than the first two algorithms. When the number of clusters exceeds 75, the accuracy has already been more

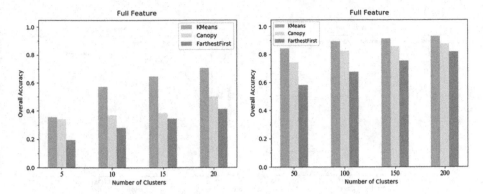

Fig. 3. The left of figure shows the change in overall accuracy when the number of clusters ranges from 5 to 20. The right shows the clustering performance from a macro perspective about Full Feature.

than 90%, compared to the other two algorithms whose accuracy is still below 80%. The FarthestFirst algorithm performs poorly with a small growth rate and the slowest convergence to higher accuracy. In the PCA section of Fig. 4, K-Means and Canopy algorithms are still excellent, which tend to converge above 98% accuracy. Although the over accuracy of FarthestFirst is still the worst, it has increased a lot after the dimension reduction compared to K-Means. The fastest calculation speed is the biggest advantage of Canopy. In order to display the overall situation more intuitively, a histogram analysis is performed on overall accuracy. Firstly, four nodes with cluster number 5, 10, 15 and 20 are selected from micro aspect, mainly to evaluate the performance of each algorithm when the number of clusters is small. Then select the cluster number 50, 100, 150 and 200 from a macro perspective. As can be seen from Fig. 3, the accuracy of each algorithm gradually increased. And the three algorithms will not converge to a certain value until the number of clusters is large enough.

6.2   The Impact of Dimensional Reducing

In many previous network traffic clustering studies, an algorithm was evaluated only for the evaluation of computational efficiency and accuracy. Few of which reduce the dimension of sample sets directly. The discussion here is to do some research on the impact of clustering accuracy after data reduction. Figure 4 illustrates that clustering accuracy has been greatly improved after PCA preprocessing, and the trend of K-Means and Canopy in PCA is almost the same. When the number of clusters is only 5, the accuracy rate of K-Means and Canopy has reached about 70% in Fig. 5 compared to 35% of full feature in Fig. 3. The three algorithms in PCA have begun to converge, the accuracy is as high as 99.8%, as the number of clusters is 25. In full feature, even if the number of clusters is 200 or more, it cannot converge to high accuracy. It is mentioned in Sect. 4.1 that the accuracy rate of FarthestFirst in full feature is relatively flat,

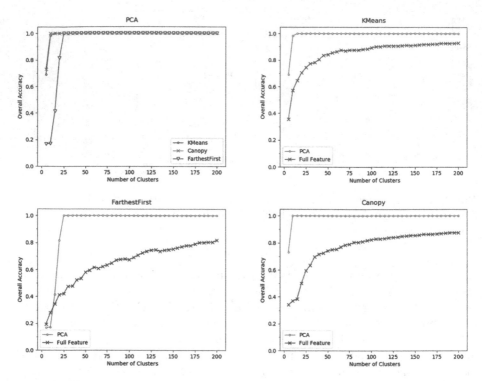

Fig. 4. Top left is the accuracy of the three clustering algorithms that the dataset is reduced to 30 dimensions with the PCA linear transformation. The rest of this figure is overall accuracy comparison of the three algorithms between PCA dimensionality reduction and full features

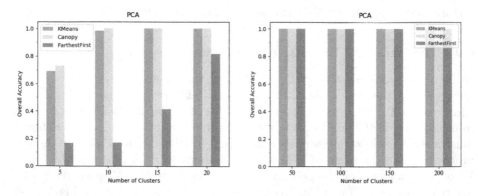

Fig. 5. The left shows the change in overall accuracy when the number of clusters ranges from 5 to 20. The right shows the clustering performance from a macro perspective about PCA.

but its performance rises rapidly after PCA pre-processing. Hence it is especially important to reduce the dimension of the sample set before clustering.

6.3   Computational Performance

Running time is a very important index for evaluating the pros and cons of clustering algorithms. Even if an algorithm has extremely high accuracy, it takes a lot of time in actual classification. As can be seen from Table 3, the PCA feature subset has a great improvement in runtime compared to the full feature subset. In the worst case, FarthestFirst increased by 86.3% while K-Means improved by 81.7% and Canopy rose by 74.7%. Thanks to the high efficiency of the approximate distance [9], Canopy showed the best computational performance, with an average maximum of 1.32 s in the full feature set, compared to K-Means taking nearly 90 times the time to get results.

Table 3. Running time for three algorithms (The number of clusters is from 5, 10, 15... to 200) under full and PCA feature set.

Clustering Algorithm	PCA	Full Feature
K-Means	$0.65s \sim 16.36s$	$4.38s \sim 89.5s$
Canopy	$0.19s \sim 0.27s$	$0.75s \sim 1.32s$
FarthestFirst	$0.1s \sim 2.62s$	$2.73s \sim 20.91s$

7   Conclusion and Future Work

The original data set contains 248 feature attributes, and 30 are left after dimension reduction. The computational performance has been greatly improved, and the overall running time of the algorithm has been reduced significantly. After the dimension reduction, not only the sample data space is reduced but also the accuracy of the three clustering algorithms is significantly improved. The accuracy of the improvement is at least 10%, and the final accuracy converges to 100%. This is a major discovery in this paper. Secondly, although Canopy is used for the first time in network traffic classification, it also shows good accuracy. Especially after the data set is reduced by PCA, the accuracy is almost the same as that of K-Means. Therefore, it is especially important to reduce the dimension of the data set before using new clustering algorithm in traffic clustering.

In future work, we will choose more clustering algorithms and feature selection algorithms. In addition, the profound effects of different sample sizes on clustering effects will be studied.

References

1. Al-Saadi, M., Ghita, B.V., Shiaeles, S., Sarigiannidis, P.: A novel approach for performance-based clustering and management of network traffic flows. In: 2019 15th International Wireless Communications Mobile Computing Conference (IWCMC), pp. 2025–2030, June 2019. https://doi.org/10.1109/IWCMC.2019.8766728

2. Erman, J., Arlitt, M., Mahanti, A.: Traffic classification using clustering algorithms. In: Proceedings of the 2006 SIGCOMM Workshop on Mining Network Data, MineNet 2006, pp. 281–286. ACM, New York (2006). https://doi.org/10.1145/1162678.1162679

3. Filho, R.H., Maia, J.E.B.: Network traffic prediction using pca and k-means. In: 2010 IEEE Network Operations and Management Symposium - NOMS 2010, pp. 938–941, April 2010. https://doi.org/10.1109/NOMS.2010.5488338

4. Hartigan, J.A., Wong, M.A.: Algorithm as 136: a k-means clustering algorithm. J. R. Stat. Soc. Seri. C (Appl. Stat.) (1), 100–108. http://www.jstor.org/stable/2346830

5. Hochbaum, D.S., Shmoys, D.B.: A best possible heuristic for the k-center problem. Math. Oper. Res. **10**(2), 180–184 (1985). http://www.jstor.org/stable/3689371

6. Jamuna, A., Ewards, V.: Survey of traffic classification using machine learning. Int. J. Adv. Res. Comput. Sci. **4**(4) (2013)

7. Kumar, A., Ingle, Y.S., Pande, A., Dhule, P.: Canopy clustering: a review on pre-clustering approach to k-means clustering. Int. J. Innov. Adv. Comput. Sci. (IJI-ACS) **3**(5), 22–29 (2014)

8. Liu, D., Wang, M., Shen, G.: A new combinatorial characteristic parameter for clustering-based traffic network partitioning. IEEE Access **7**, 40175–40182 (2019). https://doi.org/10.1109/ACCESS.2019.2905618

9. McCallum, A., Nigam, K., Ungar, L.H.: Efficient clustering of high-dimensional data sets with application to reference matching. In: Proceedings of the Sixth ACM SIGKDD International Conference on Knowledge Discovery and Data Mining, KDD 2000. pp. 169–178. ACM, New York (2000). https://doi.org/10.1145/347090.347123

10. Moore, A., Hall, J., Kreibich, C., Harris, E., Pratt, I.: Architecture of a network monitor. In: Passive & Active Measurement Workshop, vol. 2003 (2003)

11. Moore, A., Zuev, D., Crogan, M.: Discriminators for use in flow-based classification (2005)

12. Sharmila, K.M.: An optimized farthest first clustering algorithm. In: 2013 Nirma University International Conference on Engineering (NUiCONE), pp. 1–5, November 2013. https://doi.org/10.1109/NUiCONE.2013.6780070

13. Shim, K., Goo, Y., Lee, M., Hasanova, H., Kim, M.: The method of clustering network traffic classifications for extracting payload signature by function. In: 2018 International Conference on Information and Communication Technology Convergence (ICTC), pp. 1335–1337, October 2018. https://doi.org/10.1109/ICTC.2018.8539623

14. Takyi, K., Bagga, A., Goopta, P.: Clustering techniques for traffic classification: a comprehensive review. In: 2018 7th International Conference on Reliability, Infocom Technologies and Optimization (Trends and Future Directions) (ICRITO), pp. 224–230, August 2018. https://doi.org/10.1109/ICRITO.2018.8748772

15. Tapaswi, S., Gupta, A.S.: Flow-based p2p network traffic classification using machine learning. In: 2013 International Conference on Cyber-Enabled Distributed Computing and Knowledge Discovery, pp. 402–406, October 2013. https://doi.org/10.1109/CyberC.2013.75
16. Velea, R., Ciobanu, C., Margarit, L., Bica, I.: Network traffic anomaly detection using shallow packet inspection and parallel k-means data clustering. Stud. Inform. Control 26(4), 387–396 (2017)
17. Wang, Y., Xiang, Y., Zhang, J., Yu, S.: A novel semi-supervised approach for network traffic clustering. In: 2011 5th International Conference on Network and System Security, pp. 169–175, September 2011. https://doi.org/10.1109/ICNSS.2011.6059997
18. Wang, Y., Xiang, Y., Zhang, J., Zhou, W., Wei, G., Yang, L.T.: Internet traffic classification using constrained clustering. IEEE Trans. Parallel Distrib. Syst. 25(11), 2932–2943 (2014). https://doi.org/10.1109/TPDS.2013.307
19. Williams, N., Zander, S., Armitage, G.: A preliminary performance comparison of five machine learning algorithms for practical ip traffic flow classification. SIGCOMM Comput. Commun. Rev. 36(5), 5–16 (2006). https://doi.org/10.1145/1163593.1163596
20. Zhang, J., Chen, X., Xiang, Y., Zhou, W., Wu, J.: Robust network traffic classification. IEEE/ACM Trans. Netw. 23(4), 1257–1270 (2015). https://doi.org/10.1109/TNET.2014.2320577

Tell Them from Me: An Encrypted Application Profiler

Mohammad Mamun[1](✉), Rongxing Lu[2], and Manon Gaudet[1]

[1] National Research Council Canada, Ottawa, Canada
{mohammad.mamun,manon.gaudet}@nrc-cnrc.gc.ca
[2] University of New Brunswick, Fredericton, NB, Canada
rlu1@unb.ca

Abstract. Profiling internet users associated with encrypted applications has been a long-standing challenging issue that helps to identify targeted users' interests. This paper proposes a machine-learning based solution for creating encrypted application signatures without relying on any certain assumptions on the underlying network infrastructure such as IP address, port number, network flow characteristics. These applications signatures can later be used with passive network monitoring for profiling targeted users in terms of selected application usage such as Facebook, Tor. We propose a proof of concept (PoC) framework with effective features to identify (i) encrypted payloads from any network traffic, and (ii) targeted applications such as ToR, Skype for what the model is trained for. Our study shows that using classical Shannon's entropy alone can help recognize encrypted payload, but may not help identify particular application payloads. We design features based on standard encoding e.g., UTF-8, entropy e.g., Shannon entropy, BiEntropy, and payload size, so that machine learning algorithms can be used to identify encrypted applications.

Keywords: Encrypted application · User profiling · Machine learning · Cybersecurity

1 Introduction

Insider threat remains a top priority challenging issue for organization in the last decade. Combating insider threats is less about security of the devices, but about understanding users, e.g., employee behind the devices. Therefore, fighting inside attacker requires proper understanding the behaviour of the users. For example, users conferring abnormal profile or user-profile conferring new applications may be flagged as *malicious*. Besides that, profiling users may also help provide better Quality of Service (QoS) to the clients.

Conventionally, encrypted network traffic data seem to be a meaningless way to actually profile users or group them based on common interest. Collecting user data through extension or mobile app is a nightmare with the advent of privacy

© Her Majesty the Queen in Right of Canada 2019
J. K. Liu and X. Huang (Eds.): NSS 2019, LNCS 11928, pp. 456–471, 2019.
https://doi.org/10.1007/978-3-030-36938-5_28

regulations such as PIPEDA (Personal Information Protection and Electronic Documents Act), GDPR (General Data Protection Regulation). Profiling users based on web browsing history, retrieved either by accessing DNS server data or custom-designed app, has been studied extensively in the literature [2]. However, one DNS privacy technology, called DNS over HTTPS (DoH), which has been supported by Google, Mozilla and Cloudflare, will make classic web surveillance conducted by ISPs, corporations much more difficult. Tracking web addresses based on DNS request such as xyz.com-normally sent in the clear would be impossible over DoH technology, as it encrypts the request.

To address the drawbacks of port-based classification, various techniques have been introduced [1]. Broadly speaking, these approaches can fall into two classes: those aiming to classify traffic based on payloads, and flow-based technique – often called network behavioural statistics that only take into account information found in the packet headers. Flow-based techniques [1,3,14,15,35] usually work on general properties of the network traffic flow such as inter arrival time (IAT), average number of packets, network latency jitter, flow cut-off time, packet loss, and fragmentation etc., aiming to identify application fingerprints based on network behaviour [35]. Detection accuracy of this kind of schemes usually depends on the testing environment. Therefore, detection accuracy evaluated in one environment may fail tremendously in another one. On the other hand, payload based traffic classification [18,21], often called Deep Packet Inspection (DPI) technique, inspect the actual payload of the packets regardless of the port number, IP address, or any network infrastructure properties. Although they offer better accuracy results, these techniques cannot be used in many deployment environments due to several reasons including legal restriction to organizational private data, inability to cope with *encrypted payload* such as https, *encrypted channel* such as Tor [31]. DPI has been mainly used for unencrypted traffic classification [12,13,17,18,36]. However, authors in [21] proposes a scheme for identifying encrypted traffic applications such as Dropbox, Twitter based on first-order homogeneous Markov chain and Secure Socket Layer (SSL) sessions. One of the limitations mentioned by the authors is its abrupt failure in the absence of strict RFC specifications. For example, using SSL for tunnelling only (e.g., Skype, Tor). In addition, the technique needs frequent update of its application fingerprints.

Feature selection is the main challenge for any effective machine learning algorithms. Our solution is based on combining three information theoretic properties of a payload such as entropy, encoding, compression. Features used for proposed classification algorithms are based on standard entropy such as Shannon entropy, BiEntropy-a special entropy computed from the approximate entropy of a finite binary string of arbitrary length, sliding-window entropy that measures the entropy of the substring, size of the payload, standard encoding such as UTF-8, HEX. Entropy, often called information density in information theory, is a method for measuring uncertainty in a series of bytes. Theoretically, an encrypted data generated by a good encryption algorithm should remove any kind of pattern to ensure pseudo-randomness in the ciphertext and present an entropy value close to 1. However, encryption is not only the candidate that shows high entropy, compressed (or zipped) data may also yield high entropy value. For instance, compressed HTTP data where original data are compressed before they are sent to the web server in order to expedite transfer speed and bandwidth utilization, show high entropy as well [34]. Network packets conveying a compressed file such as gzip show a high entropy value even if they are unencrypted [23]. One more candidate which evidently shows higher entropy is encoding. For example, converting ASCII encoded texts to HEX encoding increases entropy.

Entropy-based approach has been broadly used for identifying malicious traffic [24–26]. In [25], Olivian et al. identify an N-truncated entropy range for the non-malicious traffic. A real-time classifier based on the first packet's payload of a flow has been proposed for identifying Skype at [20]. However, there is no guarantee for the first payload to be fully encrypted, but partially encrypted [21]. In [22], authors analyze web pages (https) based on entropy using individual object sizes in a page to identify encrypted pages. Authors in [19] uses flow based cumulative entropy to detect bots. A binary entropy analysis tool called BiEntropy is used in [34] to identify encrypted spreadsheet from the unencrypted one.

In order to build a proof of concept framework, we choose applications from several domains such as HTTPS, P2P, SSH, Skype etc. Unlike aiming all the applications from a certain protocol e.g. HTTPS [10], we select eight type of web applications such as *facebook, hangouts* from web traffic over HTTPS, *BitTorrent* from applications over P2P protocol, *Tor* from encrypted applications enabling anonymous communication, *skype* from proprietary Internet telephony network applications, *ftps, sftp* from secure file transfer protocol. We rely on the dataset captured and collected in a restricted environment in the lab from a wireless network client or user. Using this dataset we perform a large scale study to determine a set of effective features to distinguish encrypted web traffic from unencrypted ones and to determine encrypted applications. After ablation study to understand the effectiveness of the features, we propose 12 features to identify certain encrypted applications, and evaluate the effectiveness of the features by applying several state-of-the art classification algorithms.

2   Background

2.1   Entropy Overview

In information theory, entropy is called a measure of *unpredictability*. For example, entropy of a fair coin flipping is maximum, if the probability of getting head or tail is same (prob = .5). Since the coin is fair, no one can predict the outcome ahead. A lossless compressed messages produces higher entropy. Although total information in the compressed messages remains the same, but the information per character is higher (because of less redundancy). We use three entropy measurement algorithms:

- Entire-string where entropy is measured for the entire string (e.g., [5])
- Sliding-window that measures entropy of the substring (n-length) of the original string
- Binary-derivative or BiEntropy test which is a weighted average of the entropy of the binary derivatives (e.g., [6,20]).

Shannon Entropy: It estimates the information contained in a message. In other words, it measures the average minimum number of bits needed to encode a message based on the alphabet size and the frequency of the symbols [4].

Let S be a binary string $S \equiv s_1, s_2, \ldots, s_n$ with probability $p_1, p_2, \ldots p_n$ such that $p_i \geq 0$, $\sum_{i=1}^{n} p_i = 1$. $h(p)$ be a function defined as the uncertainty associated with the event $S = s_i$, where $i = 1, 2, \ldots, n$ on the interval $(0, 1]$. Shannon entropy $H(S)$ is a function of the n variables $p_1, p_2, \ldots, p_n$ that can be interpreted as the average uncertainty associated with the event $\{S = s_i\}$, $i = 1, 2, \ldots, n$.

$$H(S) \equiv - \sum_{i=1}^{n} p_i \ \log_2 p_i \qquad (1)$$

BiEntropy: Shannon's entropy cannot handle the periodic nature of a string. For instance, Shannon's entropy of a perfectly ordered string (e.g., '1111' or '0000') is 0. However, it results 1 for '0101' when the string is apparently random (same number of 0 and 1, the probability of occurring 0 or 1 is same .5), neglecting completely the periodic nature (i.e., '01') of the string. In [20], authors concentrate on the tests and measurement of ordering, regularity with entropy and concludes upon finding a weighted average of Shannon's entropy of the last binary derivatives of a string. Calculating binary derivatives of any string can discover the existence of repetitive patterns. In a perfectly *periodic* binary string, the last derivative equals to 0. On the other hand, in a perfectly *aperiodic* binary string, the derivative is 1. In this paper, we calculate binary derivatives of the traffic payload to resolve the issue of the periodicity within the string. BiEntropy is the first $n - 2$ binary derivatives of the string using a simple power law. In other words, this is a weighted average of the Shannon binary entropy. BiEntropy is a function $\Phi(S))$ associated with the event $\{S = s_k\}$, $k = 1, 2, \ldots, n$ for $0 \leq k < n$.

$$\Phi(S) = \left(1/(2^{n-1}-1)\right)\left(\sum_{k=0}^{n-2}((-p(k)\log_2 p(k)-(1-p(k))\log_2(1-p(k))\,)2^k\right) \quad (2)$$

However, if the higher derivative of a binary string $D_{n-2}(s)$ is periodic, the whole sequence exhibits periodicity and BiEntropy fall behind. Therefore, a logarithmic version of BiEntropy called TBiEn (Φ') can be used to evaluate binary derivatives.

$$\varPhi'(S) = \Big(1/\sum_{k=0}^{n-2}\log_2(k+2)\Big)\Big(\sum_{k=0}^{n-2}(-p(k)\log_2 p(k) - (1-p(k))\log_2 \tag{3}$$
$$(1-p(k)))\log_2(k+2)\Big)$$

3 Identifying Encrypted Application Using Machine Learning

In this section, we present our machine learning based encrypted application detection algorithm. We first present the design of dataset generation and features and then discuss our choice of machine algorithms.

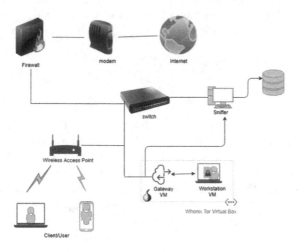

Fig. 1. Data collection model

3.1 Dataset and Preprocessing

Collecting a dataset and ensuring that it is of sufficient quality to reach experimental goals is really hard. Capturing application traffic data in a real life environment is challenging due to two main reasons: privacy concerns of the gathered data and noise such as unwanted network service packets. Typically, traffic is either collected from trusted sources or captured in a controlled environment. To address this challenge, our experimental dataset has been generated in a controlled testbed environment simulating real applications from a diverse set of application traces and background where ground truth was known.

For automating data collection, we run different encrypted and unencrypted applications at the end point such as workstation, mobile in various time frame and capture application packets by passive sniffing tools such as Wireshark [11], tcpdump [32]. Stored data captured by the sniffer later are filtered/sanitized to remove noises such as unwanted network data, packets with empty payload etc. For example, Internet or network service related applications such as DNS, NetBios are generated readily as a consequence of employing other applications. We labelled them as unencypted. For dataset generation, we discard any payloads smaller than 10 Bytes (considering noise).

The network digram for data collection is presented in Fig. 1. Our representative dataset consists of:

- encrypted payloads from eight different applications Facebook, Skype, Hangouts, Netflix, P2P (Bittorrent), FTP over SSL (FTPS), FTP over SSH (SFTP) and Tor.
- unencrypted payloads from six different applications unencrypted browsing, voip (Decphone), video streaming, DNS data, Mail service data, Network service data.

Note that for some applications such as Facebook, Skype, we combine data from several services e.g., text chatting, audio-streaming, video-streaming, file-transfer etc. together and give them a unique label. Since capturing and labelling Tor traffic is a challenging task for dataset generation, we use whonix Tor Virtual Environment (See Fig. 1) [8], an operating system based on the Tor anonymity network and security by isolation, for capturing tor application usage. It consists of two VMs, namely Whonix-Gateway and Whonix-Workstation connected by a virtual LAN. Whonix-Gateway is connected to Internet while Whonix-workstation needs to be securely connected to Whonix-Gateway by virtual LAN.

In our study we rely on user/client tagging as the ground truth. To validate that we filter specific application data flows with the help of nDPI [9], a deep packet inspection tool to recognize exact flows of the targeted data. With the help of flow information (source IP, destination IP, source port, destination port, protocol) and time period for any specific application runs, packets are recognized and labelled.

3.2 Payload and Feature Generation

As previously mentioned, design a set of effective features is the most challenging part of identifying encrypted application problem. Features that has been used in this work are listed in Table 2.

We observe that encoding the encrypted payload accelerates the entropy discrimination significantly that in turn helps distinguishing encrypted application. Along with entropy over entire payload, n-length word or sliding window entropy has also been considered for the feature set. Besides that BiEntropy is calculated only on *binary* payloads. We explain the feature details below.

1. Payload size: The actual data of a packet. Each packet consists of a payload appended to the header for transport.
   - Application layer payload size
   - Transport layer payload size
2. Entropy of the entire payload where conventional Shannon's entropy is used for computation.

- Binary payload: entropy is measured in bits where the symbol is either 0
  or 1.
- Entropy of the encoded payload
  - HEX-encoded payload
  - UTF-8 encoded payload
3. Entropy of n-length word or sliding-window technique where
   $n = \{4, 8, 16, 32, 64, 128, 256, 512, 1024\}$. It computes Shannon entropy over a
   sliding window of all the *word* tokens in a payload. For instance, measuring
   byte entropy over a sliding window (where *word* size or window size $n = 8$)
   provides entropy value for each byte.
   - Mean and Std. deviation of n-length word BiEntropy.
   - Mean and Std. deviation of n-length word TBiEn (logarithmic version of
     BiEntropy).

Table 1. AUC scores of different encrypted applications.

Model/Application	facebook	hangout	netflix	p2p	scp	sftp	skype	tor
Random forest	**0.994**	**0.981**	**0.965**	**0.999**	**1.0**	**0.998**	**0.979**	**0.96**
C5.0	0.958	0.933	0.855	0.993	0.999	0.989	0.935	0.931
Dtable	0.995	0.989	0.972	0.999	1.0	0.999	0.986	0.97

3.3   Machine Learning Models

In order to identify encrypted traffic and corresponding applications and validate
our data, we employ several state-of the-art machine learning algorithms: Random Forest [37], C5.0 [27], and Decision Table [29]. We evaluate each algorithm
with regard to their effectiveness to identifying applications. In the following, we
will discuss different models' performance, the effectiveness of different features
by an ablations analysis and the result after examining the features selected by
the best-performing model, random forest in our case.

Implementation Detail: We examine model performance by applying (1) 10-fold cross-validation, (2) train and test using data collected in different time
schedule, (3) train with one physical network and test on another. For Random
Forest [37], C5.0 [27], and Decision Table [29], we use their built-in implementation from R [30], XGBoost [7], and weka [28]. We conduct two consecutive
experiments as shown below for detecting encrypted applications. That is, result
of the first experiment (encrypted payloads) has been used as an input to the
second experiment.

- detecting encrypted payloads by employing a standard binary classification
  problem: classifying a payload either encrypted (1) or unencrypted (0) in the
  first step. Data from different encrypted applications such as Facebook, Hangouts, Netflix, P2P, FTPS, SFTP, Skype, Tor are labelled as 1 (encrypted) and
  data from different unencrypted applications such as HTTP, VOIP, Unencrypted video, DNS, SMTP, NetBioS are labelled as 0 (unencrypted).

Table 2. Feature category and list of selected features

Method	Selected Features
Binary classification (enc vs unenc)	s_Trans, s_Appl, e_ENC (HEX), e_BIN, 12_BIN, 16_ENC (UTF-8), 16_ENC (HEX) 256_$\widehat{BIN}$_s (log), 128_$\widehat{BIN}$_s (log), 512_$\widehat{BIN}$_s (log), 1024_$\widehat{BIN}$_s (log)
Multi-class classification (encrypted applications)	s_Trans, s_Appl, e_ENC (HEX), e_BIN, 16_ENC (HEX) , 16_ENC (UTF-8), 256_$\widehat{BIN}$_s, 512_$\widehat{BIN}$_m, 512_$\widehat{BIN}$_s, 128_$\widehat{BIN}$_m (log) , 128_$\widehat{BIN}$_s (log), 512_BIN_s (log)

Payload Size (in Bytes)	
Payload size in Transport layer (TCP or UDP)	s_Trans
Payload size in Application layer	s_Appl

Encoded payload	
Entire-payload entropy	e_ENC
n-length Word entropy	n_ENC

Binary payload	
Entire-payload entropy	e_BIN
Mean of n-length Word BiEntropy	n_BIN_m
n-length Word entropy	n_BIN
Std. Deviation of n-length Word BiEntropy	n_$\widehat{BIN}$_s

- detecting target applications if the output of the previous step is 1 (encrypted) by using multi-class classifier.

Our training and testing experiments are conducted on a workstation equipped with Intel(R)-Xeon(R) Gold 5118 CPU with 2 cores running at 2.29 GHz and 64 GB RAM. For all evaluations, 10-fold cross validation are conducted. While computing raw features from a payload takes less than 2 ms, prediction latency seems to be high (>20 ms) for the random forest model.

Effectiveness of the Features: Feature selection algorithms in data mining facilitates shorter training time, reduces data overfitting. Depending on how they combine the selection algorithm and the model building, feature selection algorithms are presented in two categories: filtering and wrapping methods. Filtering approach focuses on evaluation functions and the properties of the underlying data. On the other hand, wrapper approach recalls the use of classification algorithm repetitively with different sets of features to find the best set of features [16]. In our study we employ both the methods to analyse relative importance of the features and find the most effective subset of features to achieve the high classification accuracy.

A number of heuristic methods have been discussed in the literature for both the wrapper and filter method. A well-known procedure for feature selection is a 'step-wise selection' that adds (forward selection) or removes (backward elimination) features at each step. In our experiment, we analyse group inclusion and ablation analysis for forward selection and backward elimination respectively.

– Group Inclusion: To implement *forward selection* method, we categorized the features into three groups: payload Size, encoded payload, and binary Payload (see Table 2) for analysing each of the groups aiming to find a set of features in each group contributing the best. We choose Ranker, that ranks features individually as a *search method* and Infogain, that computes the information gain on a class as *evaluator*.
– Ablation analysis: To develop Backward Elimination method, we use ClassfierSubsetEval, that evaluates attribute subsets based on a classifier to estimate the merit of a set of attributes as *search method* and Ranker as *evaluator*. We examine several classifiers: random forest, c5.0, and decision table. Our aim is to remove features (in the best performing features of all the groups) one by one that contributes the least into the overall accuracy. In each iteration, we exclude one feature to observe its effect to the final detection rate. This process continues until we reach the maximum detection rate (greater than the first/base detection rate)

Let $(G = \{g_1, g_2, g_3\})$ be the set of groups and $F_i = \{f_{1,i}, \ldots, f_{k,i}\}$ be the set of features corresponding to the group g_i. *Group Inclusion* step outputs a set of features $F = \{f_{j,i} \mid 1 \le i \le 3, 1 \le j \le k\}$ produced from all the three groups. *Feature exclusion* step takes F as input and ends up with the best features in F described in Table 2.

We found features on payload size (Transport layer and Application layer) to be effective for both classifiers. In case of entire payload entropy, out of several encoding schemes such as UTF-8, UTF-32, HEX, ASCII, HEX encoded payload is elected eventually. It was challenging to choose the boundary value of n for n-length word related features. Note that, studying all possible values of n for a large dataset would burden a significant computational cost. To reduce the computational and memory overhead, we consider Geometric Sequence, where each term is calculated by multiplying the previous term by a constant using

$$\{a, ar, ar^2, ar^3, \ldots\} \tag{4}$$

where a is the first term and r is the factor between the terms. Let $a = 1$ and $r = 2$, the Geometric sequence will be: $\{1, 2, 4, 8, 16, 32, \ldots\}$. We consider the value of n between 4 and 1024 in all the experiment. Considering the value of n below 4 and above 1024 causes the detection rate dropped sharply.

Among the features, TriEntropy exhibits promising results surpassing the rest. Features consisting of higher Word-size (512-bit, 1024 bit) outperforms that of smaller one. AUC scores from the model outputs were low for any set of features such as payload size. We observe top-12 selected features in Table 2 are the most frequently used features in the decision trees of random forest model.

```
f2 <= 1337
|  f3 <= 0.769729
|  |  f1 > 1338
|  |  |  f8 <= 0.074194
|  |  |  |  f1 <= 2063
|  |  |  |  |  f4 <= 0.825462: scp (6.0/1.0)
|  |  |  |  |  f4 > 0.825462: p2p (25.0)
|  |  |  |  f1 > 2063: tor (64.0)
|  |  |  f8 > 0.074194: skype (36395.0)
```

Fig. 2. A sample tree from C5.0 where f1: $= s\text{-Trans}$, f2: $= s\text{-Appl}$, f3: $= e\text{-ENC}$ (HEX), f4: $= e\text{-BIN}$, f8: $= 512\widehat{\text{-BIN}}\text{-}m$

3.4 Evaluation and Validation

We focus several metrics for the evaluation and performance measurement. One is Area Under The Curve (AUC) score and Receiver Operating Characteristics (ROC) curve, oftern called AUROC (Area Under the Receiver Operating Characteristics). AUC represents degree of separability and ROC is a probability curve that presents the capability of the models to distinguish among classes. The larger area under the curve (AUC), the better performance is addressed (see Table 1).

We evaluate the trained model with testing data from different physical network and time schedule to observe if the model can be generalized over networks. By conducting this experiment, we try to prove that our application finger-printing solution does not rely on underlying network infrastructure such

Table 3. Binary classifier: accuracy & precision metrics for Random Forest (RF), C5.0, Decision Table (DTable)

		Encrypted	Unencrypted
Accuracy	RF	**0.998**	**0.997**
	C5.0	0.947	0.992
	DTable	0.997	0.99
Precision	RF	0.998	0.996
	C5.0	0.995	0.906
	DTable	0.995	0.995
F-Measure	RF	0.998	0.997
	C5.0	0.97	0.947
	DTable	0.996	0.992

Table 4. Multi-class classifier: accuracy & precision metrics for Random Forest (RF), C5.0, Decision Table (DTable)

		facebook	hangout	netflix	p2p	scp	sftp	skype	tor
Accuracy	**RF**	**0.974**	**0.902**	**0.907**	**0.999**	**1.000**	**0.991**	**0.908**	**0.934**
	C5.0	0.969	0.904	0.801	0.996	0.998	0.990	0.898	0.824
	DTable	0.944	0.845	0.791	0.972	0.996	0.986	0.85	0.817
Precision	RF	0.937	0.945	0.935	0.996	1.000	0.989	0.910	0.912
	C5.0	0.935	0.933	0.816	0.995	0.999	0.985	0.911	0.808
	DTable	0.877	0.928	0.811	0.981	0.999	0.987	0.849	0.805
F-Measure	RF	0.955	0.923	0.921	0.997	1.000	0.99	0.909	0.923
	C5.0	0.952	0.918	0.806	0.995	0.999	0.988	0.905	0.816
	DTable	0.909	0.884	0.801	0.977	0.997	0.986	0.849	0.811

as network latency, flow cut-off time etc. Our results from the experiments are uniform across the network.

We use Precision, known as positive prediction value, and F-Measure, known as Harmonic mean of Precision and Recall as accuracy metric for evaluating the effectiveness of the selected features and performance of the classifiers. Obtained results are presented in Table 3 for Binary classifier and Table 4 for Multi-class classifier.

For encrypted applications, we observe that the file transfer applications FTPS, SFTP (like Filezilla) outperform any other applications ($\approx$ 99.99%). Random Forest does well for all the experiments. Fluctuated detection rate can be better explained by

- common feature selection for several classes.
- nature of the type of data, e.g., secure file transfer applications show high accuracy because of the payloads they could generate. It is obvious that payloads generated by FTP application would be symmetric and stable in compare to Facebook or Skype data packets where payloads are generated from different type of activities e.g., chat, audio streaming, or video conversation etc.
- lack of diverse dataset since our dataset is partly biased containing payloads from limited number of applications. It can be extended to get in-depth; For instance, discovering application type in detail chat-Facebook, audio-Facebook, video-Facebook. However, as a *proof of concept* the result is worth promising.

Confidence interval of a prediction, also known as *prediction interval*, is a well-defined concept in statistical inference that estimates the prediction interval based on member decision tree scores. Random Forest produces a *hard decision* based on the maximum votes of the individual trees for a class to get elected at the time of prediction, and a *soft prediction* from the individual trees' voting which provides a confidence score for the prediction [37]. However, this confidence score can be used for *hard decision* once it exceeds a threshold value. For this experiment, we train a regression-type random forest model. For binary classifier (enc vs unenc), encrypted application is labelled as 0 and unencrypted as 1.

Table 5. Soft prediction based on SD

Filters									
Yellow		Green		Orchid		Blue		Red	
UnEnc	Enc	UnEnc	Enc	UnEnc	Enc	UnEnc	Enc	UnEnc	Enc
5815	18648	1980	1920	4449	8067	1169	799	305	491

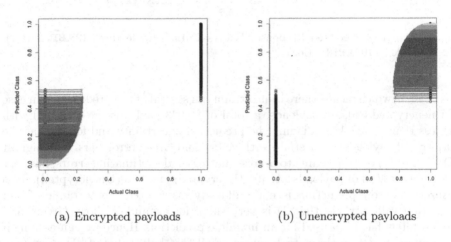

(a) Encrypted payloads   (b) Unencrypted payloads

Fig. 3. Scatter plot of prediction interval (see Table 5) (Color figure online)

The scatter plot of experiment ("Actual class" versus "Predicted class") are given in the Fig. 3 that depicts the data points overlaid with error bars. The error bars corresponding to a *soft prediction* is represented by a Standard Deviation (SD) of uncertainty for a certain class. Due to the large number of data points and to achieve a holistic view of data, we filter the result in five intervals:

- Yellow-filter: $.1 \leq SD > 0$
- green-filter: $.2 \leq SD > .1$
- Orchid-filter: $.3 \leq SD > .2$
- Blue-filter: $.4 \leq SD > .3$
- Red-filter: $SD > .4$

Results of binary classifier with filters is presented in Table 5. Lifted SD indicates considerable fluctuating among member decision tree scores. Higher lifting can be realized with prospective statistical outliers. Most of the payloads are grouped into the closest range of its respective class (0 or 1). For instance, a total of 1,026,266 encrypted payloads out of 1,069,907 observed in extremity of the range (aligned with average) while 43,641 payloads have a soft prediction of

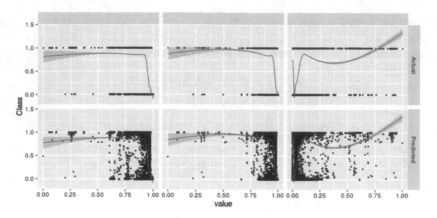

Fig. 4. Actual vs Predicted Response (Enc vs UnEnc) for features 128_$\widehat{\text{BIN}}$_s (log), 512_$\widehat{\text{BIN}}$_s (log), 1024_$\widehat{\text{BIN}}$_s (log)

less than .5, which means there is uncertainty in several of the predictions. In case of Unencrypted 640,448 payloads, a total of 29,923 payloads are observed with SD less than .5. We keep digging the prediction uncertainty and found that the majority of payloads are overlaid with yellow and Green error bars. The highest SD (Red filter) corresponding to overestimating/underestimating errors, has very few of either kind of payloads s.t. 491 (Encrypted) and 305 (Unencrypted). This ensures that soft prediction is not uniformly distributed. Some range of *soft prediction* values where the SD is very small for example Yellow, Green, and Orchid filters has been used for an infallible prediction. Hence we can assume if the soft prediction is closer to 1 with a small threshold value of SD score (e.g. up to Orchid filter), the payload is Unencrypted. In the opposite way, if the soft prediction value is close to 0 with a small SD score, the payload is Encrypted.

Furthermore, we examine predicted responses vs actual responses for the selected features after normalizing the values to [0,1]. Figure 4) presents a snapshot for some features. Similar experiments have been conducted on the multiclass classifier. Due to the space limitation, we defer the details to the extended version.

3.5   Profiling User

A user profile is a digital representation of the identity of the user describing her interest, preference, interactive behaviours [33]. Our aim for this work is to profile a user based on encrypted web applications that a user runs and interact with where the profiler can passively monitor the clients and provide a reliable details on the usage of targeted encrypted applications. As mentioned in the previous sections, eight encrypted applications are considered for analysis. Figure 5 presents a user's application usage in a day based on the binary and multi-classifiers we propose.

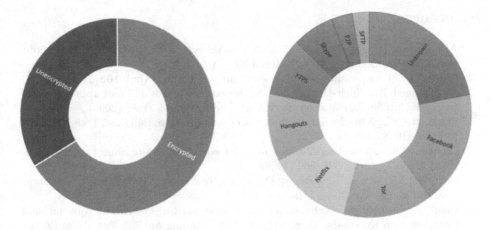

Fig. 5. User profiling based on Online Application behaviour

Nonetheless, payloads to be identified can be of any applications except eight applications we choose. Therefore, we add a new class named *unknown* for the unknown applications to the multi-class classifier. Labelling unknown payloads, where we label payloads obtained from arbitrary applications except the targeted applications such as Tor, is a bit tricky. Because the unknown class is, by definition, any applications in the web but the selected eight applications. In practice, we may not be able to capture representative dataset where we expect samples from every possible applications to train the model. One of the limitations of our work is that it cannot effectively handle new unknown application. Novelty or outlier detection may help mitigating this issue. This could be an important research direction for the project.

4   Conclusion

An efficient and effective user profiling is of great importance to cybersecurity, network resource management, and personalized service area. Fingerprinting user behaviour in terms of application usage can also be successfully used in an automated cyber-defence mechanisms. Our motivation is to identify encrypted applications used by clients connected to a network. We investigate several promising characteristics of application payloads related to encoding, *n-length* word, and observe the aftermath effect on entropy measurement and payload size.

Among the shortcomings, we consider only *eight* application protocols for experiment as a *proof of concept* and unintended noises in the training dataset. As a future work, we aim to investigate our proposed model on a wider range of applications with activity details (video, audio, chat, file transfer etc.). We also aim at analysing application signature from entropy and cross-validate its consistency with clustering algorithms.

References

1. Alshammari, R., Zincir-Heywood, A.N.: Can encrypted traffic be identified without port numbers. Comput. Netw. **55**(6), 1326–1350 (2011)
2. Cufoglu, A.: User profiling-a short review. Int. J. Comput. Appl. **108**(3), 1–9 (2014)
3. Alshammari, R., Zincir-Heywood, A.N.: Investigating two different approaches for encrypted traffic classification. In: Privacy, Security and Trust (2008)
4. Shannon, C.E.: A mathematical theory of communication. Bell Syst. Tech. J. **27**(3), 379–423 (1948)
5. Chaitin, G.J.: On the length of programs for computing finite binary sequences. J. ACM (JACM) **13**(4), 547–569 (1966)
6. Carroll, J.M., Sun, Y.: The Binary Derivative Test for the Appearance of Randomness and its use as a Noise Filter (1998)
7. Chen, T., Guestrin, C.: Xgboost: a scalable tree boosting system. In: International Conference on Knowledge Discovery and Data Mining, pp. 785–794. ACM (2016)
8. Whonix: A High Security Method of Surfing the Internet. https://www.whonix.org/
9. nDPI, Open and Extensible LGPLv3 Deep Packet Inspection Library. http://www.ntop.orgproductsndpi/
10. Dyer, K.P., et al.: Peek-a-boo, i still see you: why efficient traffic analysis countermeasures fail. In: IEEE Security and Privacy, pp. 332–346 (2012)
11. Wireshark sample captures. http://wiki.wireshark.org/SampleCaptures
12. Karagiannis, T., et al.: BLINK: multilevel traffic classification in the dark. In: SIGCOMM 2005, Philadelphia, USA, 21–26 August 2005
13. Moore, A.W., Zuev, D.: Internet traffic classification using Bayesian analysis techniques. In: SIGMETRIC 2005, Banff, Canada, 6–10 June 2005
14. Sen, S., Spatscheck, O., Wang, D.: Accurate, scalable in-network identification of P2P traffic using application signatures. In: WWW 2005, USA (2004)
15. Zander, S., Nguyen, T., Armitage, G.: Automated traffic classification and application identification using machine learning. In: LCN 2005, Australia (2005)
16. Guyon, I., Elisseeff, A.: An introduction to variable and feature selection. J. Mach. Learn. Res. **3**, 1157–1182 (2003)
17. Bonfiglio, D., et al.: Revealing Skype traffic: when randomness plays with you. In: ACM SIGCOMM 2007, pp. 37–48. ACM Press, USA (2007)
18. Smith, R., et al.: Deflating the big bang: fast and scalable deep packet inspection. In: ACM SIGCOMM 2008, pp. 207–218. ACM Press, USA (2008)
19. Zhang, H., Papadopoulos, C., Massey, D.: Detecting encrypted botnet traffic. In: INFOCOM Workshop. IEEE (2013)
20. Dorfinger, P., et al.: Entropy-based traffic filtering to support real-time Skype detection. In: ACM Wireless Communications and Mobile Computing (2010)
21. Korczynski, M., Duda, A.: Markov chain fingerprinting to classify encrypted traffic. In: INFOCOM, 2014 Proceedings IEEE. IEEE (2014)
22. Sun, Q., et al.: Statistical identification of encrypted web browsing traffic. In: Proceedings 2002 IEEE Symposium on Security and Privacy. IEEE (2002)
23. Weber, M., et al.: A toolkit for detecting and analyzing malicious software. In: Proceedings of the 18th Annual Computer Security Applications Conference. IEEE (2002)
24. Lyda, R., Hamrock, J.: Using entropy analysis to find encrypted and packed malware. In: IEEE Security & Privacy, pp. 40–45 (2007)

25. Olivain, J., Goubault-Larrecq, J.: Detecting subverted cryptographic protocols by entropy checking. Laboratoire Specification et Verification, ENS Cachan, France, Research Report LSV-06-13 (2006)
26. Wagner, A., Plattner, B.: Entropy based worm and anomaly detection in fast IP networks. In: WETICE 2005: Proceedings of the 14th IEEE International Workshops on Enabling Technologies: Infrastructure for Collaborative Enterprise, pp. 172–177. IEEE Computer Society, Washington, DC (2005)
27. Quinlan, J.R.: C4.5: Programs for Machine Learning. Morgan Kaufmann Publishers (1993). ISBN 1-55860-238-0
28. Hall, M., et al.: The WEKA data mining software: an update. ACM SIGKDD Explor. Newsl. **11**(1), 10–18 (2009)
29. Kohavi, R.: The power of decision tables. In: Lavrac, N., Wrobel, S. (eds.) ECML 1995. LNCS, vol. 912, pp. 174–189. Springer, Heidelberg (1995). https://doi.org/10.1007/3-540-59286-5_57
30. RStudio, an integrated development environment (IDE)for R. http://www.rstudio.com/
31. Sicker, D.C., Ohm, P., Grunwald, D.: Legal issues surrounding monitoring during network research. In: Proceedings of the 7th ACM SIGCOMM Conference on Internet Measurement, ser. IMC 2007, pp. 141–148. ACM, New York (2007)
32. Tcpdump packet analizer. http://www.tcpdump.org/
33. Poo, D., Chng, B., Goh, J.-M.: A hybrid approach for user profiling. In: Proceedings of the 36th Annual Hawaii International Conference on System Sciences, pp. 9–13. IEEE (2003)
34. Croll, G.J.: BiEntropy-The Approximate Entropy of a Finite Binary String. arXiv preprint arXiv:1305.0954 (2013)
35. Draper-Gil, G., et al.: Characterization of encrypted and VPN traffic using time-related features. In: Proceedings of the International Conference on Information Systems Security and Privacy (ICISSP 2016), Rome, Italy, pp. 407–414 (2016)
36. Mamun, M.S.I., Ghorbani, A.A., Stakhanova, N.: An entropy based encrypted traffic classifier. In: Qing, S., Okamoto, E., Kim, K., Liu, D. (eds.) ICICS 2015. LNCS, vol. 9543, pp. 282–294. Springer, Cham (2016). https://doi.org/10.1007/978-3-319-29814-6_23
37. Breiman, L.: Random forests. Mach. Learn. **45**(1), 5–32 (2001)

Indoor Security Localization Algorithm Based on Location Discrimination Ability of AP

Juan Luo$^{(\boxtimes)}$, Lei Yang, Chun Wang, and Huan Zhao

School of Information Science and Engineering, Hunan University, Changsha 410012, China
juanluo@hnu.edu.cn

Abstract. Indoor localization algorithm based on WIFI has attracted much attention due to its high localization accuracy, universal applicability and no need for additional equipment. However, when the indoor environment changes dynamically, the environment has different degrees of influence on access points (APs) communication in different regions. The traditional fingerprint localization algorithm cannot take into account the situation of abnormal received signal strength indication (RSSI) in different areas. This paper proposes an indoor security localization algorithm based on location discrimination ability of AP (SLABLDA), which is robust to indoor complex abrupt environments. In the offline detection phase, the AP location discrimination ability detection model is proposed to detect the location discrimination ability of AP in different regions in indoor complex abrupt environment. In the online phase, a fingerprint distance adjustment algorithm based on the minimum difference of RSSI is proposed to eliminate the abnormal RSSI interference caused by the regional dynamic environment. Through experiments we demonstrate the proposed method can effectively filter the influence of abnormal RSSI in indoor complex abrupt environment and can improve the localization accuracy effectively compared with the existing fingerprint localization algorithm.

Keywords: Indoor localization · Fingerprint · Security · Location discrimination ability

1 Introduction

With the rapid development of mobile Internet and the popularity of smart mobile terminals, mobile users are increasingly demanding real-time and accurate location information [1]. At present, in the outdoor environment, the universally applicable Global Positioning System (GPS) [2] has been widely used in military, economic, production and life fields [3]. However, in an indoor environment, due to obstacles such as buildings, the attenuated GPS signal cannot achieve line-of-sight communication and thus cannot meet the application requirements of indoor positioning [4]. Therefore, how to use the existing network infrastructure and mobile terminals to achieve high-precision positioning in complex indoor environment at low cost has become a hot topic and focus of domestic and foreign research.

© Springer Nature Switzerland AG 2019
J. K. Liu and X. Huang (Eds.): NSS 2019, LNCS 11928, pp. 472–487, 2019.
https://doi.org/10.1007/978-3-030-36938-5_29

In recent years, the development of positioning technology has become more and more mature, more and more positioning technologies are suitable for indoor environment. At present, traditional indoor positioning systems include: ZigBee positioning [5], Bluetooth (BT) positioning [6], Radio Frequency Identification (RFID) positioning [7], Ultrasonic (US) positioning and Ultra Wide Band (UWB) positioning [8], etc. The advantages of these positioning techniques are high precision, mostly up to the centimeter level. However, traditional indoor positioning systems also have disadvantages. For example, additional hardware deployment is required, which is greatly disturbed by noise signals and is not easy to integrate into mobile devices. The emergence of WIFI [9] based on the IEEE802.11 communication protocol enables the indoor positioning system to utilize the widely deployed wireless network to measure the RSSI through user equipment such as mobile phones, and has the advantages of low cost, easy deployment, wide coverage, and no need for any other hardware [10]. At present, the fingerprint positioning technology based on WIFI signal has became the mainstream technology for indoor localization.

However, WIFI signals may be affected by many factors [11]. The existing fingerprint localization algorithms have no resistance to abnormal RSSI [12, 13]. For example, accidental environmental changes, AP attacks, indoor personnel movements, or other sources of interference can cause RSSI data to be abnormal. In addition, the hardware performance of APs will also have a serious impact on RSSI, resulting in instability of the indoor positioning system.

For example, when a large indoor multi-floor shopping mall fired partially, the indoor environment changed badly due to heavy smoke and high temperature. Figure 1 depicts the scenario of using abnormal RSSI to locate when indoor mall fire occurs. The severity of fire and the number of evacuees is different in different regions. Therefore, AP communication in different regions is affected differently by fire. Continuing to use the abnormal RSSI for positioning will cause serious positioning errors, which will bring great difficulties to the rescue.

Fig. 1. Problem scenario.

In view of the above problems, this paper analyzes the known WIFI fingerprinting methods for indoor localization. We have studied the influence of dynamic environment on positioning accuracy, including the distribution of affected areas, the number of affected APs and the degree of different environmental interference. Through a large number of experiments and analysis of results, we have found a way to select the most discriminating AP and reduce the impact of abnormal RSSI in complex environment.

The rest of this article is organized as follows. Section 2 reviews the related work on reducing localization errors. Section 3 analyzes characteristics of indoor dynamic environment and influence of distribution of affected area on localization. Section 4 introduces the research content proposed in this paper. Section 5 shows the experimental analysis and the experimental results of the proposed work. Section 6 gives the conclusions drawn from this work.

2 Related Work

Indoor signal strength is easily influenced by environment, multipath refraction and human disturbance. In order to mitigate the interference of abnormal RSSI, Liu et al. [14] proposed an anti-interference indoor localization algorithm. The RSSI perturbation of long distance is filtered by setting threshold. Luo et al. [15] developed an adaptive wireless indoor localization system (ILS) for dynamic environments.

In the WIFI-based fingerprint localization algorithm, many scholars have done a lot of research on the distance calculation between the measurement signal and the fingerprint in the fingerprint database. Jian [16] proposed a Multi-dimensional Dynamic Time Warping (MDTW) to calculate the distance between the measured signals and the fingerprint in the database. He et al. [17] proposed an algorithm based on Hierarchical Edit Distance (HED) function to realize calibrations-free fingerprint comparison of heterogeneous devices.

Many scholars have done a lot of research on the selection of appropriate AP for location. Luo J proposed an algorithm for indoor localization based on Received Signal Strength (RSSI) [18]. The AP selection algorithm is reviewed and improved based on the stability of signals to remove useless AP. Zhang et al. [19] designed two attack-resistant algorithms to assure the efficiency and validity of the localization information under signal strength attacks. Zhang et al. [20] presented a novel algorithm which selects appropriate APs for positioning to make the calculated amount as less as possible.

In order to ensure that fingerprints with higher reliability weigh more in the positioning process, Juan [21] proposed a trust factor extraction mechanism based on the voting algorithm. APs are voted through the test of RSSI based on reference nodes (RN). Yao [22] proposed a fingerprint localization algorithm based on trusted value of reference point, the algorithm establishes different fingerprint databases for different environments, and updates the data in the fingerprint database periodically.

This paper presents an indoor security localization algorithm based on location discrimination ability of AP. The algorithm can accurately calculate the location discrimination ability of AP in different regions in complex mutation indoor environment, eliminate the interference of regional abnormal RSSI, and incorporate the weight of AP location discrimination ability into position estimation, which significantly improves the location accuracy. The main contributions of this paper are as follows:

1. An AP location discrimination ability detection model based on anomalous RSSI is proposed. The inter-class dispersion of each reference point is determined by

calculating the most valuable RSSI value among the RSSI sample data received at each reference node (RN), thereby determining the location discrimination ability of AP. According to the location discrimination ability of the AP, the untrusted AP can be checked to reduce the impact of the damaged AP on the positioning.

2. We propose a fingerprint distance adjustment algorithm based on RSSI minimum difference. Calculating the distance between the reference node and the target node (TN) with the minimum RSSI difference can alleviate the interference of the abnormal RSSI and reduce the influence of the untrusted fingerprint on the localization algorithm.

3. We designed a fingerprint matching algorithm based on weight distribution. The location discrimination ability of AP is numerically converted into a fingerprint weight, and the distance based on the minimum RSSI difference is matched to improve the localization accuracy.

3   System Security Model

WIFI fingerprinting is a well-known indoor localization solution, which relies on a fundamental assumption: the WIFI signals measured in the environment have a unique signature that comprises the WIFI fingerprint at a given position. The system architecture proposed in this paper is shown in Fig. 2.

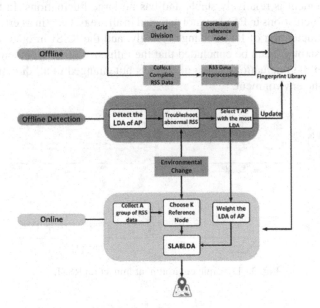

Fig. 2. System architecture.

The algorithm proposed in this paper is to maintain the stability of the positioning system when the indoor environment changes dynamically. In the positioning process, if the indoor environment changes dramatically, the proposed algorithm can select AP with strong location discrimination ability, and locate the target with secure and reliable fingerprint data. The proposed algorithm incorporates a fingerprint distance adjustment algorithm based on RSSI minimum difference, which improves the robustness of the positioning system.

3.1 Fingerprinting Localization

The traditional fingerprint-based localization process is usually divided into two phases: the first phase is the offline sampling phase. The main work of this phase is to collect the RSSI values of all reference nodes in the positioning area to form an offline fingerprint database. Each piece of information corresponds to a specific location. The second phase is the online positioning phase, which determines the actual location of the user by measuring the real-time RSSI value of the user location and then using the online matching algorithm to find the most matching data in the fingerprint database.

3.2 Analysis of Indoor Dynamic Environment

In order to verify that the impact of indoor dynamic environment on RSSI is regional. As shown in the Fig. 3, we collected RSSI in two different environmental conditions from four different directions. RSSI is recorded every 5 s for a total duration of 30 min. It can be seen from Fig. 3 that the RSSI measured from four different directions in a normal environment is relatively stable and has no large fluctuations. In the dynamic environment, fluctuations in RSSI are not detected in all areas. Only in a certain direction, the degree of fluctuation of RSSI changes greatly, and the RSSI in other directions is still relatively stable. It can be concluded that the influence of environmental factors is regional. When the fluctuation degree of RSSI is not changed in all directions, the AP is affected by the environment.

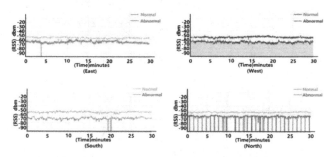

Fig. 3. Dynamic environment impact on RSSI.

3.3 Distribution of Affected Areas

Figure 4 shows the problem of the positioning system when the distribution of the affected area is different. Figure 4a shows the positioning error obtained by the positioning system when the target node is in the affected area and the AP is not in the affected area. When the target node is in the affected area, the RSSI received from all APs will be affected. Figure 4b shows the positioning error when the AP is in the affected area and the target node is not in the affected area. When only AP is in the affected area, only the RSSI of that AP is affected. Figure 4c shows the positioning error when AP and the target node are both in the affected area.

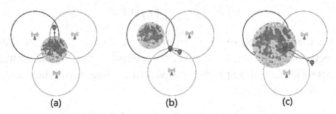

(a)   (b)   (c)

Fig. 4. Positioning error analysis when the affected area is distributed at different positions.

Based on the above analysis, as long as there is an environmental impact in the location area, no matter how the distribution area is distributed, it will have a serious impact on the positioning accuracy.

4 Indoor Security Localization Algorithm

The process of the indoor security localization algorithm based on location discrimination ability of AP is divided into three steps: The first is the offline preprocessing phase, in which continuously collect RSSI information at each reference node for a period of time and save the sampled data to the initial fingerprint database after preprocess. The second is offline detection phase, in which the location discrimination ability of the AP is calculated by collecting the RSSI of the same AP at the reference node, and T APs are selected for positioning and filtering the damaged AP. The third phase is online phase, in which continuously collect multiple RSSI values for a period of time when determining the user location, and calculate the distance between the measurement signal and the RSSI in the fingerprint database by the fingerprint distance adjustment algorithm based on the RSSI minimum difference, and then obtain the similarity between the reference node and the target node. Finally, the location discrimination ability of AP is weighted into the position estimation to obtain the final location.

4.1 Offline Preprocessing Phase

Collect Offline RSSI. In order to build an offline fingerprint database, we need to collect RSSI in the localization area. We divide the indoor network coverage area into $N = n \times n$ square grids; N is the total number of meshes; and the grid is encoded in coordinates. We consider each grid as a reference node. The offline fingerprint database is a set of all reference node fingerprints. We set the communication radius of an AP as r, when the range of the number of meshes N_{grid} is $\left(2S_{region}/r^2\right) \le N_{grid} \le \left[S_{region}/\left(10^{(\lg(I_{min})-\wedge)/\alpha}\right)\right]$, the acquisition cost of the offline stage is low [21]. When collecting fingerprints, we set the size of the grid to 0.5 m × 0.5 m.

In order to calculate average of RSSI from APi received at grid j, we place a reference anchor node at grid j to receive the RSSI sent by APi. Assuming that the total number of RSSI samples received by the reference anchor node is q, then the average RSSI received by the reference anchor node placed in grid j can be calculated as follows:

$$\phi_{i,j} = \sum_{\tau=1}^{q} \phi_{i,j}(\tau)/q \tag{1}$$

where $\phi_{i,j}(\tau)$ is the τ-th RSSI received from APi in the grid j. The number of APs is L. In order to better preserve the AP signal characteristics, the q signal values collected in different periods in the offline phase are saved in the fingerprint database. The initial database matrix Ψ is as follows:

$$\Psi = \left\{ \begin{matrix} RP1,1 & RP1,2 & \cdots & RP1,N \\ RP2,1 & RP2,2 & \cdots & RP2,N \\ \vdots & \vdots & \ddots & \vdots \\ RPL,1 & RPL,2 & \cdots & RPL,N \end{matrix} \right\} \tag{2}$$

$RP_{i,j} = \left[\phi_{i,j}(1), \phi_{i,j}(2), \ldots, \phi_{i,j}(q) \right]$ denotes a matrix containing q RSSI that the grid j receives from the APi.

RSSI Preprocessing. In order to establish an accurate and reliable fingerprint database, it is necessary to pre-process the RSSI sampled data before extracting the feature of the signal to remove the data with large deviation. The 3σ criterion is simple to use, it does not need to look up the table and is suitable for sampling values with a large number of sampling times. Therefore, it is suitable to use the 3σ criterion to eliminate coarse errors in the offline phase.

The information sample value received from the APi at the grid j is $RP_{i,j} = \left[\phi_{i,j}(1), \phi_{i,j}(2), \ldots, \phi_{i,j}(q) \right]$, and the average signal value of these RSSI sample values is $\phi i, j$. Then define the residual as: $x_t = \phi_{i,j}(t) - \phi_{i,j}$. The root mean square error of the sampled value is calculated from the residual by the Bessel formula:

$$\sigma = \sqrt{\frac{1}{q-1} \sum_{t=1}^{q} x_t^2} \tag{3}$$

Then the coarse error is removed according to criterion 3σ: if $|x_t| > 3\sigma$, then the sample value $\phi_{i,j}(t)$ corresponding to $x_t = \phi_{i,j}(t) - \phi_{i,j}$ should be considered as containing a coarse error and rejected.

Build the Offline Database. The offline fingerprint database includes the coordinate of each anchor node, the RSSI of each reference node in the offline phase, the distance between the grids and the location discrimination ability (LDA) matrix W. The initial value of LDA matrix is one. As shown in Eq. (4):

$$(X, Y; x, y; \Psi; D; W) \tag{4}$$

where (X, Y) is the coordinate of the AP and (x, y) is the grid coordinate. At the same time, we need to establish the distance matrix D between the grids to update the fingerprint database.

4.2 Offline Detection Phase

Due to the regional characteristics of the dynamic environment, if we do not detect the location discrimination ability of the AP, the affected AP will have a greater impact on the positioning result. Therefore, in offline detection phase proposes an AP location discrimination ability detection model based on abnormal RSSI to determine the position discrimination ability of APs.

LDA Detection of AP. The location discrimination ability of each AP in the location area is determined by judging the degree of data dispersion between the RSSI information matrices received from the same AP at different reference nodes.

For the APi, q RSSI signals $RP_{i,j} = [\phi_{i,j}(1), \phi_{i,j}(2), \ldots, \phi_{i,j}(q)]$ from different time periods of the APi will be collected at reference node j. The q RSSI signals collected by each reference node are used as a type of RSSI sample data, and then the location discrimination ability of the AP is calculated according to the N types of RSSI sample data collected at the N reference nodes. We define the position discrimination ability of the AP by calculating the inter-class dispersion between the N-type sample data. The greater the inter-class dispersion of such sample data, the greater the difference between the sampled values of the RSSI signals received from the reference nodes, and the stronger the distinguishing ability of the RSSI signals for the position. For each AP, a location discrimination ability value can be obtained.

Assuming that each AP is independent of each other and does not affect each other, the location discrimination ability value of the i-th AP is calculated as shown in the formula:

$$LDA_i = \frac{1}{N} \sum_{j=1}^{N} \left(\phi_{i,j} - \frac{1}{N} \sum_{j=1}^{N} \phi_{i,j}\right)^2 \tag{5}$$

N is the total number of samples, which is the number of reference nodes. q is the number of RSSI collected from the different time periods of the APi at the reference node j. $\phi_{i,j}$ is the average RSSI information of the APi received by the j-th grid.

We arrange the location discrimination ability of APs in descending order, and select T APs with strong location discrimination ability for positioning. Therefore, we can filter damaged APs and improve the efficiency of the positioning system. At the same time, updating the initial AP location discrimination ability matrix in the fingerprint database is beneficial to improve the positioning accuracy in the current environment.

Exclude Abnormal RSSI. However, due to the interference of regional environmental impacts, RSSI in different regions will produce different deviations. The average value of each type of RSSI sample data cannot accurately represent the characteristics of such data. If the average of each type of sample data is used as the eigenvalue of the data to calculate the inter-class dispersion, a large error will occur. Therefore, we need to rule out the impact of abnormal RSSI on AP location discrimination ability calculation.

We can eliminate the abnormal RSSI data caused by regional environmental interference by calculating the class representative value which best represents each kind of sample data. The formula for calculating the class representative value for each type of sample data is:

$$Minimize \sum_{t=1}^{q} (\phi_{i,j}(t) - \mu_j)^2 \quad Where \quad \mu_j = \{\phi_{i,j}(t) \mid \phi_{i,j}(t) \in RP_{i,j}\} \quad (6)$$

Each RSSI data in each type of sample data has the potential to be a representative value of such sample data. We need to calculate the distance between each RSSI data and such sample data. The RSSI with the smallest distance from the sample data is the class representative value μ_j of such sample data. Therefore, our function to calculate the position discrimination ability is as shown in the formula:

$$LDA_i = \frac{1}{N} \sum_{j=1}^{N} (\mu_j - \frac{1}{N} \sum_{j=1}^{N} \mu_j)^2 \quad (7)$$

4.3 Online Phase

The algorithm SLABLDA proposed in this paper redefines the distance calculation method between the reference node and the target node in the online phase, which mitigates the interference of abnormal RSSI. After weighting the position discrimination ability of AP in different regions into localization estimation, the positioning error is significantly reduced in the harsh dynamic indoor environment.

Calculate the Distance Between RN and TN. The regional environmental impacts may cause skipping mutations in real-time measured RSSI during the online phase. Therefore, in order to eliminate the interference of the mutated RSSI, q RSSI signals from the APi are continuously collected at the target node during online real-time positioning. Then the RSSI signal at the target node is: $TP = [TP_1, TP_2, \cdots, TP_L]$, $TP_i = [RSSI_1, RSSI_2, \cdots, RSSI_q](i = 1, 2, \cdots, L)$ represents q RSSI received from APi at the target node. Because the q RSSI are collected during the real-time positioning process, these signals can better indicate the characteristics of the AP, and have better robustness than collecting only one RSSI to match the fingerprint database in a dynamic environment. TPi is matched to each value in the $RP_{i,j}$ in the fingerprint library, the distance between the j-th reference node and the target node respectively receiving the RSSI at the APi can be expressed as:

$$MD_{i,j} = min|RSSI_t - \phi_{i,j}(t)|t = 1, 2 \ldots q \quad (8)$$

Then the distance between the reference node j and the target node can be expressed as:

$$D_j = \sqrt{\sum_{i=1}^{L} MD_{i,j}^2} \quad (9)$$

Incorporate LDA of AP into Location Estimation. According to the AP location discrimination ability function, the weight information of each AP is calculated by formula:

$$w_i = \frac{LDA_i}{\sum_{i=1}^{L} LDA_i} \tag{10}$$

The distance between the reference node j and the target node can be expressed as:

$$D_j = \sqrt{\sum_{i=1}^{L} \left(w_i MD_{i,j}^2 \right)} \tag{11}$$

According to this formula, Dj is calculated, and the smaller the value, the higher the similarity of the fingerprints in the online phase and the offline phase. According to this principle, we perform the ascending order of Dj, select K fingerprints with higher matching degree, and obtain the weight information of the reference node. The weight calculation formula is as follows:

$$w'_j = \frac{\frac{1}{D_j}}{\sum_{j=1}^{K} \frac{1}{D_j}} \tag{12}$$

Finally, the target node coordinates are calculated as follows:

$$\left(\hat{x}, \hat{y} \right) = \sum_{j=1}^{K} w'_j (x_j, y_j) \tag{13}$$

Where (x_j, y_j) represents the position coordinate of the reference node j, w'_j represents the weight of the reference node j, and $\left(\hat{x}, \hat{y} \right)$ represents the position coordinate of the point to be located obtained by the final positioning.

5   Evaluation

5.1   Experiments Settings

The positioning scene is shown in Fig. 5 We experimented in the square area divided by the laboratory. We divided the localization area into 100 grids, each grid representing a reference node. The number of APs is 6, and due to irregularities in the experimental environment in the mine, APs are placed irregularly. The experiments in this paper are carried out in an indoor dynamic environment. In the experimental environment, staffs are constantly holding electronic interference devices to interfere with the AP. We use mobile phone to collect RSSI of APs in different time periods to build fingerprint database. When collecting RSSI fingerprints, we control the acquisition height of 1 m from the ground position, and the AP is placed 2 m away from the ground position [21].

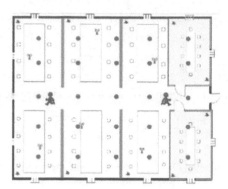

Fig. 5. Experiments settings.

5.2 Distribution Analysis of Affected Areas

In the indoor dynamic environment, the environmental impact has regional character-istics, so whether the location point and AP are located in the affected area has a great impact on the location results. The three situations of the distribution of the affected area are as follows: 1. Only AP is located in the affected area; 2. Only the locating point is located in the affected area; 3. AP and the locating point are located in the affected area at the same time. We simulate the environmental impact with the personnel of hand-held electronic jamming equipment, and do experiments in three situations respectively.

In the experiment, we set up two AP in the affected area in situation 1, and there were disturbing activities around the AP; in situation 2, there were disturbing activities around the locating point; and in situation 3, there were disturbing activities around the AP and the locating point; The experimental data are analyzed by the proposed algorithm (SLABLDA) and the traditional fingerprint localization algorithm (FL) in the three situation of the distribution of the affected areas. The experimental results are shown in Fig. 6. In Fig. 6, the solid line indicates the data obtained by the experiment with SLABLDA, and the broken line indicates the data obtained by the experiment with FL.

Figure 6a represents 10 positioning at the same position, Fig. 6b shows the average localization error results for 100 positioning at 10 points. As can be seen from Fig. 6, the localization error of FL is obviously larger, and the results of the same position are quite different. The positioning result of SLABLDA has obvious advantages, and the positioning result at the same point is more stable.

5.3 Quantitative Analysis of Affected AP

There may be multiple APs affected by the dynamic environment, so we analyzed the impact on the positioning system when the number of affected APs gradually increased. In the experiment, we set up to gradually increase the number of APs affected, and then perform 100 positioning in each case to calculate the probability distribution of the positioning error. Data analysis of the proposed algorithms SLABLDA and FL is carried out. The experimental results are shown in Fig. 7.

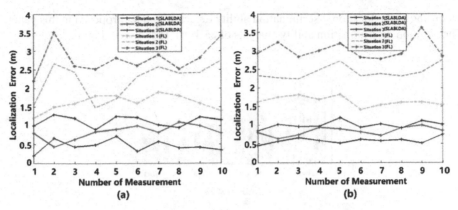

Fig. 6. Location error analysis of different distribution in affected areas.

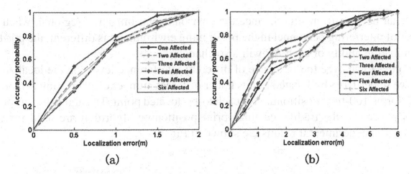

Fig. 7. Analysis of positioning errors with different affected AP numbers.

Figure 7a represents the positioning results of the algorithm SLABLDA proposed in this paper. Figure 7b represents the positioning result of the traditional fingerprint localization algorithm (FL). As can be seen from Fig. 7, as the number of affected APs increases, the localization errors of the two algorithms will increase. No matter how the number of affected APs increases, with the increase of localization error, the positioning accuracy of SLABLDA is much higher than FL.

5.4   Impact of Different Interference Degree

Due to the complex and variable positioning environment, we are unable to determine the degree of interference from the dynamic environment to RSSI. Therefore, firstly we analyze the impact on the positioning system when the degree of interference to the RSSI is gradually increased.

Figure 8 is mainly used to observe the influence of the number of different interference personnel on the AP location discrimination ability. In order to analyze the influence of different interference levels on the position discrimination ability of APs, we collect the RSSI of the APs for 5 min at each reference node under the condition that the number of interfering personnel H is different. Then calculate the LDA of AP according to the location discrimination ability detection model proposed in this paper. The location discrimination ability analysis of each AP is shown in Fig. 8.

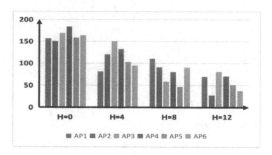

Fig. 8. AP location discrimination ability calculation.

As can be seen from Fig. 8, since the environmental impact is regional, when the number of interfering personnel in the positioning environment is different, the position discrimination ability of each AP will also change.

In order to analyze the influence of different interference levels on the localization error, we select 10 to-be-located points under different number of interfering personnel, and performs 100-time positioning for each to-be-located point. The algorithm proposed by this paper and the traditional fingerprint positioning algorithm are used for data analysis. The experimental results are shown in Fig. 9.

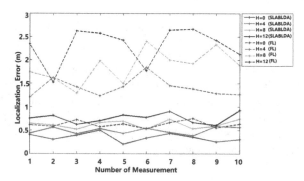

Fig. 9. Analysis of positioning error with different disturbance degree.

From Fig. 9 we can see that when the number of interfering personnel in the positioning environment increases, the localization error of the algorithm SLABLDA is always less than FL.

5.5 Location Accuracy Analysis

In the above experiments, SLABLDA is only compared with the FL, the analysis results are not representative of the performance of the entire positioning system. Therefore, we have analyzed and compared different localization algorithms. Figure 10 shows the localization accuracy obtained by performing different localization algorithms in the same experimental environment. In this experiment, we let 4 disturbers constantly move indoors randomly and then performed the proposed algorithm (SLABLDA), the traditional fingerprint localization algorithm (FL), the AP filtering algorithm based on exclusion method (FBE), the secure localization algorithm based on extracting trusted fingerprint (SFL). In this experiment, 100 positions were located and their localization errors were calculated.

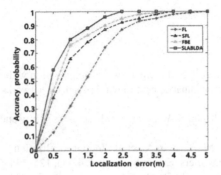

Fig. 10. Location accuracy analysis.

As shown in Fig. 10, when there is dynamic environmental interference in the positioning environment, the traditional fingerprint localization algorithm has a poor positioning effect, and only 31% of the positioning errors are within 1 m. The AP filtering algorithm based on the exclusion method and the secure localization algorithm based on extracting trusted fingerprint are superior to the traditional fingerprint localization algorithm, and the probability of the positioning error within 1 m is above 65%. The algorithm proposed in this paper can generally achieve better positioning effect, and more than 80% of the positioning error can be controlled within 1 m. Therefore, the proposed algorithm is robust to complex and variable dynamic positioning environments.

6 Conclusion

We studied the impact of dynamic environment on RSSI, proved that there are regional characteristics of environmental impact, and analyzed the interference of three kinds of affected area distribution to the positioning system. When the environmental impact leads to the instability or damage of AP, the RSSI of online and offline phases is quite different, which leads to the increase of positioning error.

Aiming at the existing problems, this paper proposes an AP location discrimination ability detection method. The method uses the RSSI received by the fixed reference node to perform the AP location discrimination ability detection, and the fixed reference node can reduce the interference factor when collecting the training data. In addition, a fingerprint distance calculation method based on minimum RSSI difference is proposed, which can eliminate the influence of different external factors on RSSI. In the experiment, we analysed the influence of the distribution of affected areas, the number of affected AP and the degree of environmental interference on the positioning system.

In future work, we will conduct various studies by detecting abnormal RSSI. For example, different levels of risk warnings are issued by judging the interference degree of RSSI and the distribution of affected areas. A reasonable escape route will be planned for the indoor escaper in the event of a fire to avoid unnecessary casualties.

Acknowledgments. This work was supported by the National Defense Basic Research Plan (JCKY2018110C145), National Natural Science Foundation of China (61672220).

References

1. Gumaida, B.F., Luo, J.: A hybrid particle swarm optimization with a variable neighborhood search for the localization enhancement in wireless sensor networks. Appl. Intell. **49**, 3539–3557 (2019)
2. Barre, P., Kasmi, C., Shehhi, E.A.: Spy the little spies - security and privacy issues of smart GPS trackers (2019)
3. Calderoni, L., Ferrara, M., Franco, A., et al.: Indoor localization in a hospital environment using random forest classifiers. Expert Syst. Appl. **42**(1), 125–134 (2015)
4. Hu, J., Luo, J., Zheng, Y., et al.: Graphene-grid deployment in energy harvesting cooperative wireless sensor networks for green IoT. IEEE Trans. Industr. Inf. **15**, 1820–1829 (2018)
5. Shue, S., Johnson, L.E., Conrad, J.M.: Utilization of XBee ZigBee modules and MATLAB for RSSI localization applications. In: SoutheastCon 2017. IEEE (2017)
6. Akeila, E., Salcic, Z., Swain, A., et al.: Bluetooth-based indoor positioning with fuzzy based dynamic calibration. In: Tencon IEEE Region 10 Conference. IEEE (2011)
7. Seco, F., Jiménez, A.R.: Smartphone-based cooperative indoor localization with RFID technology. Sensors **18**(1), 266 (2018)
8. Tiemann, J., Schweikowski, F., Wietfeld, C.: Design of an UWB indoor-positioning system for UAV navigation in GNSS-denied environments. In: 2015 International Conference on Indoor Positioning and Indoor Navigation (IPIN). IEEE (2015)
9. Yang, C., Shao, H.R.: WiFi-based indoor positioning. IEEE Commun. Mag. **53**(3), 150–157 (2015)
10. Zhang, W., Hua, X., Yu, K., et al.: Radius based domain clustering for WiFi indoor positioning. Sens. Rev. **37**(1), 54–60 (2017)
11. Zheng, H., Gao, M., Chen, Z., et al.: An adaptive sampling scheme via approximate volume sampling for fingerprint-based indoor localization. IEEE Internet Things J. **6**, 2338–2353 (2019)
12. Baoding, Z., Qingquan, L., Qingzhou, M., et al.: A robust crowdsourcing-based indoor localization system. Sensors **17**(4), 864 (2017)
13. Wang, C., Luo, J., Zheng, Y.: Optimal target tracking based on dynamic fingerprint in indoor wireless network. IEEE Access **6**, 77226–77239 (2018)
14. Liu, W., Zhang, J., Huang, G., Wang, G., Zhang, Z.: The indoor localization algorithm for combination of signal strength and anti-disturbance. In: Sun, J., Yang, C., Guo, S. (eds.) CSNC 2018. LNEE, vol. 497, pp. 341–353. Springer, Singapore (2018). https://doi.org/10. 1007/978-981-13-0005-9_28
15. Luo, R.C., Hsiao, T.J.: Dynamic wireless indoor localization incorporate with autonomous mobile robot based on adaptive signal model fingerprinting approach. IEEE Trans. Industr. Electron. **66**, 1940–1951 (2018)

16. Jian, C., Gang, O., Ao, P., et al.: An INS/WIFI indoor localization system based on the weighted least squares. Sensors **18**(5), 1458 (2018)
17. He, F., Wu, C., Zhou, X., et al.: Robust and fast similarity search for fingerprint calibrations-free indoor localization. In: 2017 3rd International Conference on Big Data Computing and Communications (BIGCOM). IEEE (2017)
18. Luo, J., Fu, L.: A smartphone indoor localization algorithm based on WLAN location fingerprinting with feature extraction and clustering. Sensors **17**(6), 1339 (2017)
19. Zhang, C., Luo, H., Li, Z., et al.: A robust fingerprinting localization algorithm against signal strength attacks. In: Liu, C. (ed.) Principle and Application Progress in Location-Based Services. LNGC, pp. 47–57. Springer, Cham (2014). https://doi.org/10.1007/978-3-319-04028-8_4
20. Zhang, X., Ma, L., Tan, X.Z., et al.: A novel algorithm based on clustering and access points selection for indoor fingerprint localization. Adv. Mater. Res. **756–759**, 3527–3531 (2013)
21. Juan, L., Xixi, Y., Yanliu, Z., et al.: Secure indoor localization based on extracting trusted fingerprint. Sensors **18**(2), 469 (2018)
22. Yao, J., Fan, Q., Zhang, E., et al.: Research on fingerprint location technology for indoor scene of power communication operation and maintenance. In: IEEE Information Technology, Networking, Electronic & Automation Control Conference. IEEE (2018)

Gnocchi: Multiplexed Payment Channels
for Cryptocurrencies

Chen Pan, Shuyang Tang$^{(\boxtimes)}$, Zhonghui Ge, Zhiqiang Liu$^{(\boxtimes)}$, Yu Long$^{(\boxtimes)}$, Zhen Liu$^{(\boxtimes)}$, and Dawu Gu$^{(\boxtimes)}$

Department of Computer Science and Engineering,
Shanghai Jiao Tong University, Shanghai, China
{htftsy,ilu_zq,longyu,liuzhen,dwgu}@sjtu.edu.cn

Abstract. As the underlying technology of mainstream cryptocurrencies such as Bitcoin and Ethereum, blockchain builds a decentralized payment system. However, the security and consistency of such system derive from the wide replication of transaction data and expensive distributed consensus mechanism, which makes current cryptocurrencies suffer great scalability gap from meeting commercial demand. To date, several solutions have been proposed to solve the scalability bottleneck of blockchain systems such as Bitcoin-NG, sharding mechanism and off-chain payment network. The off-chain payment network is one of the most promising approaches since it could significantly extend the throughput of the system and provide cheap instant micro-payment. In this work, we introduce Gnocchi, a multiplexed off-channel payment channel scheme that offers a novel method to construct an off-channel payment system to allow multi-party payment in one channel. We formally model our payment network and analyze network connectivity of our scheme to show that this newly proposed scheme significantly reduces the routing cost and transfer fee for cross-channel payment in contrast to existing off-chain payment scheme such as Lightning Network. This improves the efficiency of off-chain payment system further. We introduce transaction supervisor in a channel while maintaining the decentralization feature of the system by elaborately designing a fraud proof contract to restrain any adversary in the channel.

Keywords: Blockchain · Scalability · Off-chain · Bidirectional payment channel · Multiplexed payment channel

1 Introduction

Since Bitcoin [18] was first introduced in 2008, blockchain, the fundamental technology of Bitcoin, has shown great promise of decentralized payment infrastructure or other commercial application scenarios. Blockchain provides a novel

The research is supported by the National Natural Science Foundation of China (Grant No. 61672347).

trust model in an open network without relying on any trusted third party. In general, blockchains achieve their decentralization and security by wide replication of transaction data. All nodes in the system share the ledger and participate in the distributed consensus to modify the ledger database.

Despite its great potential, one of the main costs of the decentralization is performance. For instance, Bitcoin can only process up to 7 transactions per second [8], while the practical payment systems such as VISA are reported to process 2000 transactions/sec on average, with the peak rate of 56000 transactions/sec [3]. Simple approaches to improve the throughput of the system include adjusting key blockchain parameters such as block interval and block size. However, it has been shown that in this way the system cannot deal with more than 100 transactions per second [2]. Currently, effective blockchain scaling solutions can be roughly divided into three categories: (i) designing alternative underlying consensus mechanisms to support more transactions [5,26], (ii) introducing off-chain payment channels which process most transactions off-chain and reduce the blockchain load [1,20,21] or (iii) developing sharding mechanism to divide all nodes into several shards and process the transactions in parallel [7,14].

Off-chain payment network allows theoretically unlimited instant payments conducted simultaneously, providing almost infinite throughput for the system. Existing payment channel solutions consist of two components: bidirectional payment channel protocol and cross-channel payment protocol. In the bidirectional channel, to establish an off-chain channel, a pair of users generate a funding transaction and publish it to the blockchain to lock their fund as a deposit. The off-chain payment can be viewed as the local update of the new distribution of the balance in the channel. Then, the user wishing to withdraw his deposit needs to publish the final state of deposit balance to the blockchain. Importantly, to prevent users from publishing the previous state, the withdraw request would open a dispute time window for the counterparty to ratify the balance distribution and cause a penalty to user's misbehavior if necessary. Since the opening of bidirectional payment channel needs a deposit to lock in the channel, it's expensive to maintain excessive channels at the same time for common users. By the cross-channel payment protocol, channel users could borrow others' channels to complete indirect off-chain payments. The cross-channel payment relies on the hash pre-image to synchronize the payment result in the payment path to ensure the fund security of the channel provider. However, existing two-party payment channel schemes have the following drawbacks: (1) A high cost to maintain enough channels to ensure the success ratio of cross-channel payment, (2) A complicated routing algorithm to search for a payment path, (3) Expensive transaction fees during cross-channel payments in case of long payment routes.

In this work, we present Gnocchi, a multiplexed payment channel that supports multiplexed payment in one channel under a decentralized setting and outperforms the existing payment channel scheme such as *Lightning Network* and *Raiden Network*, in terms of cost to maintain the payment network connectivity and expense on cross-channel payments including transaction fees and payment route searching. In Gnocchi, several users could request to establish a multiplexed channel with the cooperation of a transaction supervisor. The supervisor is introduced to improve the efficiency of updating the state in the channel during off-chain delivery. However, by an elaborately designed fraud proof mechanism, the supervisor is not able to modify the balance of any user without the user's authentication for its own interests.

1.1 Paper Organization

The remainder of the paper is organized as follows. Section 2 overviews the related work on payment channel. In Sect. 4, we present our construction of Gnocchi, a multiplexed payment channel scheme. Then we analyze the security and connectivity of this scheme in Sect. 5.

2   Related Work

Alternative consensus protocols are proposed to improve the scalability of blockchains. For example, Bitcoin-NG [5] and AB-Chain [24] aim to improve the throughput or confirmation time by novel chain structures. Committee-based consensus schemes (see [12,13,19,25,27]) significantly improve both throughput and confirmation time by leveraging a permissioned consensus within a dynamically rotating committee of leaders. However, this paper mainly focuses on improvements from off-chain payment channels.

Two-Party Payment Channel. Payment channel was first proposed for instant micro-payment because of the expensive transaction fee and long confirmation period in Bitcoin. The protocol can be divided into two steps: *Establishment* and *Payment* [16]. In the establishment step, customer needs to deposit fund to a multi-signature contract address. To complete an off-chain payment, the customer needs to sign a newly update transaction to modify the current state of balance in the channel and send it to the merchant. Since only the merchant is allowed to close the channel by publishing the update transaction to the blockchain, it could only satisfy the scenario that customer sends incremental payments to the merchant. Payment channel shows great potential to scale the blockchain since it could support payment without the on-chain consensus. Generally, a payment network scheme includes two components: bidirectional payment protocol and cross-channel payment protocol. In the bidirectional payment channel, the payment protocol needs to prevent the involved user from publishing the previous state such as penalty mechanism in Lightning Network and invalidation tree structure in Duplex Channel [4]. Two-party bidirectional payment channel can be seen as the process to maintain a private ledger. The security of the payment channel is guaranteed by a dispute mechanism to affirm the current channel state during a fixed time window on the blockchain. Such a dispute mechanism can be divided into two categories. The first category relies on the penalty mechanism. One instance of such a payment channel is Lightning Network. The malicious attacker would lose all his deposit in the channel once publishing the previous balance distribution. Raiden Network also adopts such a penalty mechanism by introducing a round number i in update transactions to sort the update transactions. The second category relies on invalidation tree structure to invalidate the previous state. The invalidation tree is based on descending time lock on update transaction to ensure the update transaction with less time lock to be written in the blockchain. Other payment channel schemes were also proposed to improve the efficiency [10,22,23,28] or privacy [9,15] on payment channel. Sprites [17] introduced a global pre-image for parallel synchronization of the payment result to reduce the lock time of deposit in hashed timelock contract. Multi-hop HTLC [15] was introduced to keep the sender and receiver privacy during cross-channel payment since the hash locks are different in each hop.

Multiparty Payment Channel. NOCUST [11] introduces a commitment scheme to store the private ledger of the channel to provide N-party off-chain payment. Compared with the above off-chain solutions, it reduces the cost of channel setup and routing. However, the introduction of financial intermediary without any punishment for its misbehavior may cause complex malicious acts. In NOCUST, intermediary needs to publish the commitment of balance state periodically, which would expand the online ledger. Additionally, to prevent malicious withdrawal, customers could arise a challenge to ask the intermediary to open the current on-chain commitment. Once the challenge fails, to keep fund security, all transactions after the generation of fail-opened commitment would be reverted, which means the off-chain payment in NOCUST is not confirmed immediately in contrast to other off-chain schemes.

3 Notations and Building Blocks

3.1 Notations

$\mathcal{X}$ is the space of all public keys (i.e. pseudo identities) of our utilized signature schemes. H is a cryptographic hash function. For list $S_a = (a_1, a_2, \ldots, a_k)$ and $S_b = (b_1, b_2, \ldots, b_k)$, $(S_a, S_b) \oplus (a', b')$ denotes $((a_1, a_2, \ldots, a_k, a'), (b_1, b_2, \ldots, b_k, b'))$. $[M]$ stands for $\{1, 2, \ldots, M\}$. $A := B$ deterministically assigns B to A. $A \leftarrow B$ (probably randomly) assigns a value from a distribution or a protocol B to A.

3.2 Blockchain and Smart Contracts

In our scheme, we consider a blockchain as the existing platform serving as the trusted root of the system, which stores and maintains the global information of the transaction data and balance of each address (account) in the system. All parties in the system could manipulate their possessions with their respective private keys as certificates on the global blockchain. Besides, our construction requires a Turing-complete smart contract platform which could store the state and result of the contract execution, such that provided by Ethereum [6]. We assume that all participants in the multiplexed hub need to communicate by an extra underlying network, such as TCP connections.

3.3   Aggregate Signature

In this paper, we leverage an aggregate signature scheme to reduce the script cost of ledgers. The primitive description varies in different papers in the cryptographic literature, we adopt only (a simplified version of) one of them. An aggregate scheme $\mathsf{AS} = (\mathsf{Gen}, \mathsf{Sig}, \mathsf{Ag}, \mathsf{Vrf})$ consists of four protocols.

- $\mathsf{AS.Gen}(1^\kappa) \to (\mathsf{pk}_i, \mathsf{sk}_i)$. The generation protocol takes as input the security parameter and outputs a public key pk_i and its corresponding secret key sk_i.
- $\mathsf{AS.Sig}(\mathsf{sk}_i, m) \to \tau_i$. The signature protocol takes as input a secret key sk_i, the message to sign m and output a signature τ_i.
- $\mathsf{AS.Ag}((\mathsf{pk}_1, \mathsf{pk}_2, \ldots, \mathsf{pk}_k), k, (\tau_1, \tau_2, \ldots, \tau_k), m) \to \sigma$. The aggregate protocol takes k public keys $(\mathsf{pk}_1, \mathsf{pk}_2, \ldots, \mathsf{pk}_k)$ along with their corresponding signatures $(\tau_1, \tau_2, \ldots, \tau_k)$ on the same message m, and outputs a relatively short aggregation of k signatures as σ.
- $\mathsf{AS.Vrf}((\mathsf{pk}_1, \mathsf{pk}_2, \ldots, \mathsf{pk}_k), k, \sigma, m) \to \{0, 1\}$. The verification of an aggregated signature takes k public keys $(\mathsf{pk}_1, \mathsf{pk}_2, \ldots, \mathsf{pk}_k)$, the aggregated signature σ corresponding to these public keys and the message m. It returns 1 if and only if σ is a valid aggregation of signatures on message m from $(\mathsf{pk}_1, \mathsf{pk}_2, \ldots, \mathsf{pk}_k)$ and returns 0 otherwise.

Note that in the cryptocurrency literature, (pseudo)identities are essentially public keys so notations in the form of $P_1, P_2, \ldots$ stand for (pseudo)identities or public keys interchangeably. Specifically, for a pseudo-identity P, both pk_P and P stand for its public key and sk_P stands for its secret key. In the following context, the generation protocol is not explicitly described but we assume that each pseudo-identity of public key pk holds its corresponding secret key sk generated from $\mathsf{AS.Gen}(1^\kappa)$.

4   The Gnocchi Scheme

The payment channel scheme consists of two components: intra-channel payment and cross-channel payment technology. The intra-channel payment provides direct instant off-chain payment among all users in the channel, while cross-channel payment allows indirect payment in the payment network as other existing payment network scheme. With the intra-channel payment scheme, we are allowed to reuse the existing technology of the lightning network and build the cross-channel scheme with the same technology, specifically, utilize hash preimages to interconnect several multiplexed payment channels to establish a synchronized payment path. The detailed description of the intra-channel payment channel is presented in the following section while the cross-channel scheme is not described since it is a simple reusing of the same technology in the lightning network.

To support a multiplexed off-chain payment, a trivial solution is to simply adjust the two-party (the existing lightning network) payment channel scheme by introducing a mechanism that all the participants in the hub involve the update process of the state (balance of each party) during each off-chain payment delivery. However, such mechanism causes a high cost of interaction between all participants in one update and the online requirement for all the parties in the channel. Once some party in the channel is offline, any off-chain delivery cannot utilize this channel, which will reduce the usability of the off-chain payment channel. Therefore, we consider the intra-channel payment as a protocol similar to a permissioned consensus among channel members (considering the supervisor as a leader). All the off-chain payments happened in a multi-party channel form a sequential subchain of the global transaction history while a transaction supervisor S is introduced to take charge for the transaction linearization and verification. In this way, we do not require all member being online except the S and counterparty of payment. We introduced the role of supervisor only for the efficiency while the security of our scheme does not rely on the honesty of it. To this end, we elaborately design a fraud proof scheme to monitor the misbehavior of supervisors to prevent malicious supervisors and guarantee that each member receives a sufficient amount of refund even in the worst case.

4.1 Payment Channel Formalization

We describe a payment channel as a tuple conf $= (C, S, D_0)$ where C is the set of all members of the channel, $S \in C$ is the supervisor of the channel, and $D_0 : C \to \mathbb{R}^+$ maps each member to its initial deposit in the channel. The state of each channel is described as a tuple $\text{state}_i = (i, C, S, D_i, \text{update}_i)$ where i is the order of the state (i.e., the *round number* to the channel), $D_i : C \to \mathbb{R}^+$ maps each member to its deposit for state i and update_i describes the transfer that updates state i from state $i-1$. As for the initial state, $\text{state}_0 = (C, S, D_0, \_)$. The *update* of a channel state is notated as $\text{update}_i = (i, P, Q, S, m)$ where P, Q are sender and receiver of a transfer with amount m. The record by step i is the pair of $\text{rec}_i = ((\text{state}_0, \text{state}_1, \ldots, \text{state}_i), (\sigma_1, \sigma_2, \ldots, \sigma_i))$ where σ_i is the aggregated signature of the supervisor, sender, and receiver of update_i that changes the channel state $i-1$ to state i.

4.2 Consistent Updating

The update of $\text{update}_i = (i, P, Q, S, m)$ from $\text{state}_{i-1} = (i', C', S', D_{i-1}, \text{update}_{i-1})$ to $\text{state}_i = (i, C, S, D_i, \text{update}_i)$ is consistent, denoted as $\text{state}_{i-1} \triangleright \text{state}_i$ if and only if following conditions are satisfied.

- $i' + 1 = i$, $C' = C$ and $S' = S$.
- The balance is consistent with the updating. Namely,

$$D_i(P) = D_{i-1}(P) - (1 + \epsilon)m,$$
$$D_i(Q) = D_{i-1}(Q) + m,$$
$$D_i(S) = D_{i-1}(S) + \epsilon m,$$

(where ϵm is the fee to the supervisor) and $D_i(\mathsf{pk}) = D_{i-1}(\mathsf{pk})$ for each $\mathsf{pk} \in C \setminus \{P, Q, S\}$.

We write $\mathsf{state}_A \vdash \mathsf{state}_B$ if there is a tuple of states ($\mathsf{state}_0 = \mathsf{state}_A, \mathsf{state}_1, \ldots,$ $\mathsf{state}_k = \mathsf{state}_B$) that $\mathsf{state}_{i-1} \triangleright \mathsf{state}_i$ for each $i \in [k]$. Moreover, we denote $\mathsf{state}_{i-1} \overset{\sigma_i}{\triangleright} \mathsf{state}_i$ if

$$\mathsf{state}_{i-1} \triangleright \mathsf{state}_i \wedge \mathsf{AS.Vrf}((P, Q, S), 3, \sigma_i, H(\mathsf{update}_i)) = 1.$$

Each state_i is *sound* if each update_j for $j \in [i]$ is consistent. A record $\mathsf{rec}_i = ((\mathsf{state}_0, \mathsf{state}_1, \ldots, \mathsf{state}_i), (\sigma_1, \sigma_2, \ldots, \sigma_i))$ is *sound* if each state_i is sound and each signature is valid, in another word, $\mathsf{state}_{j-1} \overset{\sigma_j}{\triangleright} \mathsf{state}_j$ for each $j \in [i]$.

4.3   The Smart Contract

We leverage smart contracts to realize functionalities regarding the set-up of payment channels and the balance withdrawing from a fraud proof. The smart contract consists of four functions: system setup, channel startup, channel closure, and the penalty. System setup is executed only once when the system is deployed. Afterwards, remained functions are executed every time they are triggered.

System Setup. A set $\mathsf{R} := \emptyset$ is initially set empty. A partial map $\mathsf{L} : \mathcal{X} \to \mathbb{R}_0^+$ is set to map every pseudo identity to 0.

Channel Startup. The channel startup function is triggered with a tuple

$$(\mathtt{startup}, \mathsf{conf} = (C, S, D_0), \sigma).$$

After parsing $C \to \{\mathsf{pk}_1, \mathsf{pk}_2, \ldots, \mathsf{pk}_\ell\}$, it aborts if $S \notin C$, or $\mathsf{L}(S) \neq 0$, or $\mathsf{AS.Vrf}((\mathsf{pk}_1, \mathsf{pk}_2, \ldots, \mathsf{pk}_\ell), \ell, \sigma, H(\mathsf{conf})) = 0$. Afterwards, amount of $D_0(\mathsf{pk}_i)$ is temporarily deducted from pk_i (for each $i \in [\ell]$) and amount of $\ell \times \sum_{i=1}^{\ell} D_0(\mathsf{pk}_i)$ is deducted from S as the security deposit. It updates $\mathsf{R} := \mathsf{R} \cup \{\mathsf{conf}\}$ and $\mathsf{L}(S) := \ell \times \sum_{i=1}^{\ell} D_0(\mathsf{pk}_i)$ (abort if any balance is to be deducted to negative numbers).

Channel Closure. The channel closure function is triggered with a tuple

$$(\mathtt{closure}, C, S, D_0, (\mathsf{state}_f, \sigma_f), P, \sigma_P)$$

where D_0 is the initial deposit of members of C and state_f is the final state of the channel, σ_f is the aggregate signature of S and two participants of the last updating. σ_P is the signature of one channel member $P \in C$. It verifies that $\mathsf{conf} = (C, S, D_0) \in \mathsf{R}$, and remove conf from R. It verifies that $P \in C$ and σ_P is the valid signature of P on $H(\mathsf{state}_f)$. Also, parse $\mathsf{state}_f \to (i, C, S, D_i, \mathsf{update}_i)$, $\mathsf{update}_i \to (i, P, Q, S, m)$ and verify that $\mathsf{AS.Vrf}((P, Q, S), 3, \sigma_f, H(\mathsf{update}_i)) = 1$.

Pend for Δ block generation periods (which can be realized by leveraging another function in the contract code). During this period, the channel closure information is displayed on the public ledger. In case that state_f is not the final state of the channel but a state beneficial to P, any newer state $\widetilde{\text{state}_f}$ ($\text{state}_f \vdash \widetilde{\text{state}_f}$) from any channel member with proper signature can trigger the smart contract to update state_f. Also, fraud proofs (including inconsistent balance or double states) are allowed in this period in which case the channel closure phase is terminated. After Δ block generations, return amount of $D_k(\text{pk})$ to pk for each $\text{pk} \in C$. Finally, return the amount of $\mathsf{L}(S)$ to S after another Δ block generations[1] during which the amount of $\mathsf{L}(S)$ may still be withdrawn from fraud proofs.

Penalty from Fraud Proofs. In case of a dishonest supervisor $S \in C$ generating inconsistent or invalid records, all of its deposits $\mathsf{L}(S) = |C| \cdot \sum_{P \in C} D_0(P)$ are shared by all members of C and the channel is closed. In detail, the penalty function is triggered with a tuple

$$(\mathbf{fraud}, C, S, \text{state}_A, \text{state}_B, \sigma_A, \sigma_B).$$

The contract parses $\text{state}_A \rightarrow (i, C, S, D_i, \text{update}_i)$ and $\text{state}_B \rightarrow (i', C', S', D_{i'}, \text{update}_{i'})$. Abort if $C \neq C'$, or $S \neq S'$. Parse $\text{update}_i \rightarrow (i, P, Q, S, m)$ and abort if $\mathsf{AS.Vrf}((P, Q, S), 3, \sigma_A, H(\text{update}_i)) = 0$. Also, parse $\text{update}_{i'} \rightarrow (i', P', Q', S, m')$ and abort if $\mathsf{AS.Vrf}((P', Q', S), 3, \sigma_B, H(\text{update}_{i'})) = 0$. Terminate the channel and share $\mathsf{L}(S)$ (and set $\mathsf{L}(S) := 0$) to all member of $C \setminus \{S\}$ if any of two following conditions is satisfied

Inconsistent Balance. $i' = i + 1$ but $\text{state}_A \not\vdash \text{state}_B$. From the definition of consistent updating, the balance is consistent in this case.

Double States. $i' = i$ but $D_i \neq D_{i'}$. In this case, the supervisor is attempting to create view split attacks (like double-spending or tampering an existing record).

4.4   The Payment Scheme

The cross-channel payment in our scheme could reuse the existing technology of the lightning network, which utilizes hash pre-image to interconnect several multiplexed payment channels to establish a synchronized payment path. Thereby, it suffices to describe the one-hop (intra-channel) payment scheme.

Channel Setup. For a group of participants $C = \{\text{pk}_1, \text{pk}_2, \ldots, \text{pk}_\ell\}$ with a supervisor candidate $S \in C$ to setup a Gnocchi payment channel, they interact with each other and cooperatively determine the tuple for the initial channel configuration $\text{conf} = (C, S, D_0)$ where D_0 maps each of them into an initial deposit in the channel. Afterwards, each pk_i of them generate its signature on $H(\text{conf})$ as τ_i and send it to the supervisor candidate S (if $\text{pk}_i \neq S$). Finally, S aggregates ℓ signature as $\sigma \leftarrow \mathsf{AS.Ag}((\text{pk}_1, \text{pk}_2, \ldots, \text{pk}_\ell), \ell, (\tau_1, \tau_2, \ldots, \tau_\ell), H(\text{conf}))$ and invokes the smart contract via the tuple $(\mathbf{startup}, \text{conf}, \sigma)$.

---

[1] The realization of the channel closure phase requires multiple contract functions due to the pending.

Intra-Channel Payment. The intra-channel payment protocol consists of four phases.

1. For $P, Q \in C$ to execute a intra-channel payment from P to Q with amount m, they individually send to S the payment request, i.e., $(\text{payer}, P, Q, m', \sigma_P)$ and $(\text{payee}, P, Q, m, \sigma_Q)$ along with their proper signatures on the request (σ_P and σ_Q).

2. The supervisor S checks signatures of two tuples and checks that $m = m' \wedge D_i(P) > (1 + \epsilon)m$ where i is the round number of the newest state. Afterwards, S sends to P and Q an update tuple $\text{update}_{i+1} = (i + 1, P, Q, S, m)$.

3. P, Q check the update tuple and generate respective signatures

$$\tau_P \leftarrow \text{AS.Sig}\left(\text{sk}_P, H(\text{update}_{i+1})\right),$$
$$\tau_Q \leftarrow \text{AS.Sig}\left(\text{sk}_Q, H(\text{update}_{i+1})\right)$$

on it. They send τ_P, τ_Q to S.

4. Finally, S receives τ_P, τ_Q and generates an aggregate signature

$$\sigma_{i+1} \leftarrow \text{AS.Ag}\left((P, Q, S), 3, (\tau_P, \tau_Q, \tau_S), H(\text{update}_{i+1})\right)$$

where $\tau_S \leftarrow \text{AS.Sig}\left(\text{sk}_S, H(\text{update}_{i+1})\right)$. It generates a new state $\text{state}_{i+1} = \left(i + 1, C, S, D_{i+1}, \text{update}_{i+1}\right)$ where $D_{i+1}(P) = D_i(P) - (1 + \epsilon)m$, $D_{i+1}(Q) = D_i(Q) + m$, and $D_{i+1}(S) = D_i(S) + \epsilon m$. It updates the record $\text{rec}_{i+1} := \text{rec}_i \oplus (\text{state}_{i+1}, \sigma_{i+1})$ and publicizes the updated record to all members of C.

Channel Closure. Any member P of a channel C can choose to close the channel by triggering the contract via a tuple $(\text{closure}, C, S, D_0, (\text{state}_f, \sigma_f), P, \sigma_P)$ where state_f is the final state, σ_P is the signature of P on $H(\text{state}_f)$. Pend for a period of Δ block generations after finding the closure information displayed on the public ledger. During this period, all other members of C are allowed to update the final state state_f in case that it is only a state beneficial to P.

Fraud Proofs. In case that the tunnel record rec has inconsistency in its balance transfers, pick up the first inconsistent updating from state_i to state_{i+1} and trigger the penalty contract via $(\text{fraud}, C, S, \text{state}_i, \text{state}_{i+1}, \sigma_i, \sigma_{i+1})$. In case that the supervisor attempts to tamper the existing record, two different states with the same round number occur like

$$\text{state}_A = (i, C, S, D_i, \text{update}), \quad \text{state}_B = (i, C, S, D_i', \text{update}')$$

with corresponding signatures for updating σ_A, σ_B. Trigger the contract via $(\text{fraud}, C, S, \text{state}_A, \text{state}_B, \sigma_A, \sigma_B)$.

4.5   Cross-Channel Payments

Provided with the intra-channel payment scheme presented above, we are allowed to build up the cross-channel scheme with existing techniques from the lightning network. The specific protocol is complicated but we can illustrate its key designs by an example. We consider two nodes, Alice and Charlie, who share no direct payment channel while both have payment channels with Bob. Alice can make payments with Charlie through Bob with a value lower than the amount from Alice to Bob and Bob to Charlie. To guarantee the value transferred securely from sender to receiver, Hashed Timelock Contract (HTLC) is utilized and set-tled down between adjacent nodes along the path, which takes a receiver gen-erated hash preimage and time limit as the requirements of value transfer. The redemption of value is in the direction from receiver to sender and starts after the receiver redeems his value from the predecessor disclosing the preimage. Then intermediate nodes redeem their value from predecessors sequentially, complet-ing the value transfer.

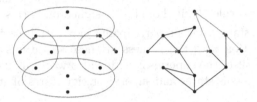

Fig. 1. Cross-channel payment for Gnocchi and the lightning network

5 Security and Efficiency Analysis

In this section, we will analyze the security and efficiency of Gnocchi. In the efficiency analysis, we compare our protocol with the lightning network to show that our network has a significantly better topology with the same script cost.

5.1 Security Analysis

The most basic safety properties of a distributed ledger are obviously satisfied. To begin with, the basic liveness of the network is guaranteed since any participant can terminate the channel (the channel closure) and hence redeem their deposits in case of the breaking down of participating nodes. Besides, in practice, this is unlikely to happen since no participant gains anything from an artificial mal-function unless a natural malfunction happens to the receiver or the supervisor. Anyway, states are not effective without valid signatures from the supervisor, senders, and receivers of all updates. Most importantly, our model is robust in the face of *inconsistent states* like transactions deducting excessive money from an address and account amounts not fitting the updating records. As long as an inconsistent state with the signature of the supervisor is broadcast to channel participants, a proof of misbehavior is formed and then other participants of the channel can trigger the smart contract of withdrawing (the penalty to the supervisor) via the proof and redeem their deposits (from the guarantee deposit $L(S)$ of the supervisor S).

In fact, despite the fact that participant can withdraw their deposit in case that the supervisor is an irrational adversary, we can show that the consistency of our scheme is incentive-compatible. Namely, any supervisor breaking the consistency is irrational. A rigorous definition of the incentive-compatibility is shown as follows. The incentive-compatibility consists of two parts. (1) A rational supervisor outputs a sound record $rec_r = rec_{r-1} \oplus (state_r, \sigma_r)$ for each update. (2) For each state $state_{r-1}$, a rational supervisor would not broadcast (and sign on) two sound states $state_r$ and $state_{r'}$ ($state_r \neq state_{r'}$) such that $(state_{r-1} \triangleright state_r) \wedge (state_{r-1} \triangleright state_{r'})$.

Demonstrating our defined incentive-compatibility of our system is equivalent to showing that any participant breaking rule (1) or rule (2) is irrational. This is easy to show since participants can withdraw their deposit if the supervisor is irrational and rule (1) or rule (2) is broken by the supervisor. Specifically, if the supervisor breaks rule (1), it should have signed on both $state_{r-1}$ and $state_r$ that $\neg(state_{r-1} \overset{\sigma_r}{\triangleright} state_r)$. Other participants can withdraw their money with a withdraw transaction with the witness of these signatures and states (from the guarantee deposit of the supervisor). This also works if rule (2) is broken in which case the witness is states and supervisor signatures of $state_r$ and $state_{r'}$.

5.2   Efficiency of Gnocchi Compared with the Lightning Network

We first define the connectivity property of off-chain payment network, with which we discuss the efficiency of Gnocchi in the following. A fine connectivity of nodes can be reached by any model of payment channels by covering the network with a sufficient amount of channels. However, in this way, a large cost of ledger storage (since payment channels are set-up by contracts which are essentially transactions with specialized scripts) is required to reach fine connectivity of the payment network. Therefore, it is crucial to estimate and compare the cost to reach the same network connectivity of the lightning network and our model. In fact, our model demands a smaller cost.

Since it is too ideal to ask for the full connectivity of all network nodes, we consider a network is well-connected if more than 90% of them are reachable to each other through existing channels. However, having nodes connected is far from claiming fine connectivity since the shortest path between two nodes is probably hundreds of tunnels in which case it is hard to build a "rapid" payment channel. Therefore, we define and estimate the *diameters* (the maximum number of least channels required to build a path between two nodes) of two well-connected networks to form a comparison of their connectivity.

We refer to the amount of information required to be recorded on the ledger to form the network of payment channels as the *script cost*. With the same script cost, our network has significantly better connectivity measured in graph diameter compared with the existing lightning network. Namely, less intermediate tunnels are required for one payment between two nodes in distant. For example, Fig. 1 shows a Gnocchi payment channel (on the left) and a lightning network (on the right) randomly set up with the same script cost, the Gnocchi payment channel has a diameter of 3 while the lightning network has a diameter of 5. To formally show this, we firstly provide a theoretical model based on which formal analyses are provided. Afterwards, we provide experimental simulations to show that our model matches the practice and that the difference in the connectivity of two networks is considerable.

5.2.1   Formal Model

Generally, our newly proposed multiplexed network is topologically equivalent to a *hypergraph* in the combinatorics literature where each (hyper-)edge is a set of nodes instead of two that represents for the multiplexed channel of our protocol. In contrast, the lightning network is topologically a classic graph connected by lightning channels.

We firstly show a certain script cost is sufficient to bring about a diameter of 3 of the multiplexed network. Afterwards, we show that the lightning network with the same amount of vertices and script cost has a greater diameter.

To describe a lightning network, we use a graph $G_{n',m'} = (V', E')$ (G for short) where V' of size $|V'| = n'$ is the set of all vertices where each one represents for a network node and E' of size m' in expectation is the set of all edges where each stands for a lightning channel. There is an edge between every two nodes with a probability of p (the density). Similarly, we use the notation $G_{n,m,\ell} = (V, E)$ to describe a multiplexed network where V of size $|V| = n$ is the set of all vertices, E of size $|E| = m$ is the set of all hyper-edges, each of which is a group of vertices $\{u_1, u_2, \ldots, u_{\ell'}\} \in E$ standing for a channel of our model and that the average size of all hyper-edges is ℓ. To each node, $\frac{m\ell}{n}$ hyper-edges it participates are randomly chosen from E. For a graph $G = (V, E)$ its diameter is defined as $\max_{u,v \in V}\{D(u,v)\}$ if well-connected where $D(u,v)$ is the minimum edges required to establish a path from u to v. If it is not well-connected, its diameter is defined as ∞. The diameter of hypergraph G is defined as same. Before arguing about the connectivity, we formalize the script cost.

Definition 1 (Script Cost). *The script cost is $\ell \times m$ to a hypergraph $G_{n,m,\ell}$, or $2 \times m'$ to a classical graph $G_{n',m'}$.*

In practice, the exact amount of information required to be stored on the ledger is $(\ell + \delta)m$ to the multiplexed network while $(2 + \delta)m'$ to the lightning network for some marginal cost δ for auxiliary information. However, this only strengthens our result since that given a multiplexed network of diameter 3 with script cost ℓm, if the lightning network with $m' = \frac{\ell m}{2}$ channels has a diameter greater than 3, it furthermore has a greater diameter with $\frac{(\ell + \delta)m}{2 + \delta} < \frac{\ell m}{2}$ edges.

Theorem 1 (Connectivity of Multiplexed Network). *Our multiplexed network $G_{n,m,\ell}$ almost surely has a diameter of 3 if $m = \frac{(1+\epsilon) \cdot n(2n \ln n)^{\frac{1}{3}}}{\ell^2}$, in which case its script cost is*

$$\frac{(1 + \epsilon) \cdot n(2n \ln n)^{\frac{1}{3}}}{\ell}. \tag{1}$$

Proof. When the graph is sparse and $\ell \ll n$, the event of two vertex pairs having two common hyper-edges are nearly independent. Due to this, we approximate the graph as a classical graph of n vertices and $m' = \binom{\ell}{2}m$ edges. Borrowing lemma. 1, this graph (hence $\mathcal{G}$) almost surely has a diameter of 3 if its density of edge $\frac{m'}{\binom{n}{2}} \approx \frac{\ell^2 m}{n^2} = \frac{(1+\epsilon)(2n \ln n)^{\frac{1}{3}}}{n}$, which leads to $m = \frac{(1+\epsilon)\cdot n(2n \ln n)^{\frac{1}{3}}}{\ell^2}$.

Theorem 2 (Connectivity of Lightning Network). *With the same vertex set* $|V'| = |V| = n$ *and the same script cost of formula (1), the existing lightning network* $G = (V', E')$ *can only reach a diameter of* $\lceil \frac{3 \ln(2n \ln n)}{\ln(2n \ln n) - 3 \ln \ell} \rceil > 3$.

Proof. With the same complexity of formula (1), we can build a graph of edges $m' = \frac{(1+\epsilon)\cdot n(2n \ln n)^{\frac{1}{3}}}{2\ell}$. This leads to a density $p' = \frac{m}{\binom{n}{2}} \approx \frac{(1+\epsilon)(2n \ln n)^{\frac{1}{3}}}{n\ell}$.

The threshold of the least diameter k it meets satisfies $\frac{(1+\epsilon')(2n \ln n)^{\frac{1}{k}}}{n} < p' \approx \frac{(1+\epsilon)(2n \ln n)^{\frac{1}{3}}}{n\ell}$. Rearrange the formula above, we have its diameter $k = \lceil \frac{3 \ln(2n \ln n)}{\ln(2n \ln n) - 3 \ln \ell} \rceil > 3$.

Lemma 1 (Threshold by Diameter). *The property of a connected graph* $G_{n,m}$ *of diameter k ($\ell \ll n$ and k is small) has a threshold at $p \gtrsim 2^{\frac{1}{k}} \cdot \frac{(\ln n)^{\frac{1}{k}}}{n^{\frac{k-1}{k}}}$. Namely, $G_{n,m}$ has a diameter no greater than k if $p \gtrsim 2^{\frac{1}{k}} \cdot \frac{(\ln n)^{\frac{1}{k}}}{n^{\frac{k-1}{k}}}$ except for a probability trends towards zero as n grows to infinity* $\lim_{n\to\infty} \Pr\left[diameter(G_{n,m}) > k\right] = 0$.

Proof. We call a movement from a vertex to an adjacent vertex as a hop. If G has a diameter greater than k, then there is a pair of nonadjacent vertices i, j such that i could not reach j in k hops. We call such a pair of vertices *bad*.

We introduce a set of indicator random variables $I_{i,j}$ for each $i < j$. $I_{i,j}$ is 1 iff (i, j) is a bad pair and 0 otherwise. Let $X = \sum_{i<j} I_{i,j}$ be the number of bad pairs. A graph has diameter at most k iff $X = 0$. Thus, $\lim_{n\to\infty} \Pr\left[diameter(G) > k\right] = \lim_{n\to\infty} \Pr[X \neq 0]$, $E[X] \cong \binom{n}{2} \cdot (1 - \mathsf{fes}_1^{n-2}) \cdot (1 - \mathsf{fes}_2^{n-2}) \cdots (1 - \mathsf{fes}_k^{n-2})$, where $\mathsf{fes}_k^{\bar{n}}$ ($\bar{n} = n-2$) is the probability that two given vertices are reachable in k hops passing through $\bar{n}$ other nodes. Thus,

$$\begin{cases} \mathsf{fes}_1^{\bar{n}} = p \\ \mathsf{fes}_k^{\bar{n}} = 1 - (1 - p + p(1 - \mathsf{fes}_{k-1}^{\bar{n}-1}))^{\bar{n}} \\ \quad\quad = 1 - (1 - p \cdot \mathsf{fes}_{k-1}^{\bar{n}-1})^{\bar{n}}. \end{cases}$$

Rearranging the formula, we find $1 - \mathsf{fes}_k^{\bar{n}} \cong (1 - \mathsf{fes}_{k-1}^{\bar{n}-1})^{p\bar{n}}$ where formulas on two sides of a "$\cong$" are almost equivalent for a sufficiently large n. By a simple induction, $1 - \mathsf{fes}_k^{\bar{n}} \cong (1 - p)^{p^{k-1}\cdot \bar{n}\cdot(\bar{n}-1)\cdots(\bar{n}-k+2)} \cong (1 - p)^{(p\bar{n})^{k-1}} \cong e^{-p^k \bar{n}^{k-1}}$.

Taking $\bar{n} = n-2$, $-\ln E[X] \cong -2 \ln n + p \cdot \sum_{i=0}^{k-1} p^i (n-2)^i = -2 \ln n + p^k \cdot n^{k-1}$. Setting $p = c \cdot \frac{(\ln n)^{\frac{1}{k}}}{n^{\frac{k-1}{k}}}$, $-\ln E[X] \cong -2 \ln n + c^k \ln n = (c^k - 2) \ln n$. To satisfy $\lim_{n\to\infty} -\ln E[X] = \infty$, we assign $c = (1 + \epsilon) \cdot 2^{\frac{1}{k}}$ with a small positive margin value ϵ. Therefore, with a density $p = \frac{(1+\epsilon)(2n \ln n)^{\frac{1}{k}}}{n} \gtrsim 2^{\frac{1}{k}} \cdot \frac{(\ln n)^{\frac{1}{k}}}{n^{\frac{k-1}{k}}}$, $E[X]$ goes to zero and thereby $\lim_{n\to\infty} \Pr\left[\text{diameter}(G) > k\right] = \lim_{n\to\infty} \Pr[X \neq 0] = 0$.

5.2.2 Simulations

To support our theoretical conclusion of better connectivity with the same script cost. We consider a lightning network G of $n' = 10^5$ total nodes and a multiplexed network $\mathcal{G}$ of expected group size $\ell = 25$ and total nodes of $n = n' = 10^5$. We randomly sample edges (hyper-edges) for G ($\mathcal{G}$) from the family of random graphs (hypergraphs) of 10^5 nodes with script cost varying from 0 to 2.0×10^6 (by 2500). Our results are shown in Fig. 2. Each triangle shows the diameter of a randomly sampled lightning network, while its corresponding dot on the same column shows the diameter of a randomly sampled multiplexed network. Obviously, hypergraph has significantly better connectivity especially when channels are distributed sparsely (manifesting as a low script cost).

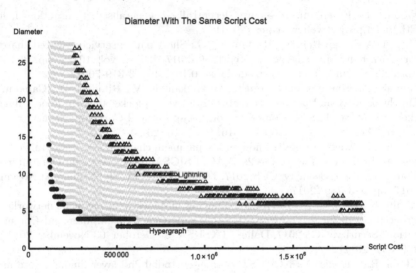

Fig. 2. Comparison on diameter

6   Conclusion

We presented Gnocchi, a multiplexed payment scheme, to address the drawbacks of current off-chain payment schemes. Gnocchi supports instant off-chain payment by introducing a fixed-member channel state consensus mechanism. While introducing a transaction supervisor in each channel, we maintained the decentralization of our scheme by elaborately designing the fraud proof contract to face malicious attacks. Security and efficiency analysis are presented.

References

1. Raiden network. http://raiden.networkwork/
2. Andresen, G.: BIP 101: increase maximum block size (2016). https://github.com/bitcoin/bips/blob/master/bip-0101.mediawiki
3. Croman, K., et al.: On scaling decentralized blockchains. In: Clark, J., Meiklejohn, S., Ryan, P.Y.A., Wallach, D., Brenner, M., Rohloff, K. (eds.) FC 2016. LNCS, vol. 9604, pp. 106–125. Springer, Heidelberg (2016). https://doi.org/10.1007/978-3-662-53357-4_8
4. Decker, C., Wattenhofer, R.: A fast and scalable payment network with bitcoin duplex micropayment channels. In: Pelc, A., Schwarzmann, A.A. (eds.) SSS 2015. LNCS, vol. 9212, pp. 3–18. Springer, Cham (2015). https://doi.org/10.1007/978-3-319-21741-3_1
5. Eyal, I., Gencer, A.E., Sirer, E.G., Van Renesse, R.: Bitcoin-NG: a scalable blockchain protocol. In: 13th USENIX Symposium on Networked Systems Design and Implementation, NSDI 2016, Santa Clara, CA, USA, 16–18 March 2016, pp. 45–59 (2016)
6. Wood, G.: Ethereum: a secure decentralised generalised transaction ledger. Ethereum project yellow paper (2014)
7. Gencer, A.E., van Renesse, R., Sirer, E.G.: Short paper: service-oriented sharding for blockchains. In: Kiayias, A. (ed.) FC 2017. LNCS, vol. 10322, pp. 393–401. Springer, Cham (2017). https://doi.org/10.1007/978-3-319-70972-7_22
8. Gervais, A., Karame, G.O., Wüst, K., Glykantzis, V., Ritzdorf, H., Capkun, S.: On the security and performance of proof of work blockchains. In: Proceedings of the 2016 ACM SIGSAC Conference on Computer and Communications Security, Vienna, Austria, 24–28 October 2016, pp. 3–16 (2016)
9. Green, M., Miers, I.: Bolt: anonymous payment channels for decentralized currencies. In: Proceedings of the 2017 ACM SIGSAC Conference on Computer and Communications Security, CCS 2017, Dallas, TX, USA, 30 October–03 November 2017, pp. 473–489 (2017)
10. Khalil, R., Gervais, A.: Revive: rebalancing off-blockchain payment networks. In: Proceedings of the 2017 ACM SIGSAC Conference on Computer and Communications Security, CCS 2017, Dallas, TX, USA, 30 October–03 November 2017, pp. 439–453 (2017)
11. Khalil, R., Gervais, A.: NOCUST - a non-custodial 2nd-layer financial intermediary. IACR Cryptol. ePrint Arch. **2018**, 642 (2018)
12. Kokoris-Kogias, E., Jovanovic, P., Gailly, N., Khoffi, I., Gasser, L., Ford, B.: Enhancing bitcoin security and performance with strong consistency via collective signing. In: 25th USENIX Security Symposium, USENIX Security 16, Austin, TX, USA, 10–12 August 2016, pp. 279–296 (2016)
13. Liu, Z., Tang, S., Chow, S.S.M., Liu, Z., Long, Y.: Fork-free hybrid consensus with flexible proof-of-activity. Future Gener. Comp. Syst. **96**, 515–524 (2019)
14. Luu, L., Narayanan, V., Zheng, C., Baweja, K., Gilbert, S., Saxena, P.: A secure sharding protocol for open blockchains. In: Proceedings of the 2016 ACM SIGSAC Conference on Computer and Communications Security, Vienna, Austria, 24–28 October 2016, pp. 17–30 (2016)
15. Malavolta, G., Moreno-Sanchez, P., Kate, A., Maffei, M., Ravi, S.: Concurrency and privacy with payment-channel networks. In: Proceedings of the 2017 ACM SIGSAC Conference on Computer and Communications Security, CCS 2017, Dallas, TX, USA, 30 October–03 November 2017, pp. 455–471 (2017)

16. McCorry, P., Möser, M., Shahandasti, S.F., Hao, F.: Towards bitcoin payment networks. In: Liu, J.K.K., Steinfeld, R. (eds.) ACISP 2016. LNCS, vol. 9722, pp. 57–76. Springer, Cham (2016). https://doi.org/10.1007/978-3-319-40253-6_4
17. Miller, A., Bentov, I., Kumaresan, R., McCorry, P.: Sprites: payment channels that go faster than lightning. CoRR, abs/1702.05812 (2017)
18. Nakamoto, S.: Bitcoin: a peer-to-peer electronic cash system (2008)
19. Pass, R., Shi, E.: Hybrid consensus: efficient consensus in the permissionless model. In: 31st International Symposium on Distributed Computing, DISC 2017, 16–20 October 2017, Vienna, Austria, pp. 39:1–39:16 (2017)
20. Poon, J., Buterin, V.: Plasma: scalable autonomous smart contracts (2017). https://www.plasma.io/plasma.pdf
21. Poon, J., Dryja, T.: The bitcoin lightning network: scalable off-chain instant payments (2016). https://lightning.network/lightning-network-paper.pdf
22. Prihodko, P., Zhigulin, S., Sahno, M., Ostrovskiy, A., Osuntokun, O.: Flare: an approach to routing in lightning network (2016). https://bitfury.com/content/downloads/whitepaper_flare_an_approach_to_routing_in_lightning_network_7_7_2016.pdf
23. Roos, S., Moreno-Sanchez, P., Kate, A., Goldberg, I.: Settling payments fast and private: efficient decentralized routing for path-based transactions. In: 25th Annual Network and Distributed System Security Symposium, NDSS 2018, San Diego, California, USA, 18–21 February 2018 (2018)
24. Tang, S., Chow, S.S.M., Liu, Z., Liu, J.K.: Fast-to-finalize Nakamoto-like consensus. In: Jang-Jaccard, J., Guo, F. (eds.) ACISP 2019. LNCS, vol. 11547, pp. 271–288. Springer, Cham (2019). https://doi.org/10.1007/978-3-030-21548-4_15
25. Vukolić, M.: The quest for scalable blockchain fabric: proof-of-work vs. BFT replication. In: Camenisch, J., Kesdoğan, D. (eds.) iNetSec 2015. LNCS, vol. 9591, pp. 112–125. Springer, Cham (2016). https://doi.org/10.1007/978-3-319-39028-4_9
26. Wan, C., et al.: Goshawk: a novel efficient, robust and flexible blockchain protocol. In: Guo, F., Huang, X., Yung, M. (eds.) Inscrypt 2018. LNCS, vol. 11449, pp. 49–69. Springer, Cham (2019). https://doi.org/10.1007/978-3-030-14234-6_3
27. Zamani, M., Movahedi, M., Raykova, M.: Rapidchain: scaling blockchain via full sharding. In: Proceedings of the 2018 ACM SIGSAC Conference on Computer and Communications Security, CCS 2018, Toronto, ON, Canada, 15–19 October 2018, pp. 931–948 (2018)
28. Zhong, L., Wang, H., Xie, J., Qin, B., Liu, J.K., Wu, Q.: A flexible instant payment system based on blockchain. In: Jang-Jaccard, J., Guo, F. (eds.) ACISP 2019. LNCS, vol. 11547, pp. 289–306. Springer, Cham (2019). https://doi.org/10.1007/978-3-030-21548-4_16

Difficulty of Decentralized Structure Due to Rational User Behavior on Blockchain

Mitsuyoshi Imamura[1,2(✉)] and Kazumasa Omote[1]

[1] University of Tsukuba, Tennodai 1-1-1, Tsukuba 305-8573, Japan
ic140tg528@gmail.com, omote@risk.tsukuba.ac.jp
[2] Nomura Asset Management Ltd., 1-11-1 Nihonbashi,
Chuo-ku, Tokyo 103-8260, Japan

Abstract. Blockchain is an autonomous decentralized system, the operation of which depends on the motivation of the users who provide the nodes for managing the accurate distributed ledger. For the management of an accurate ledger, a strong limitation exists that requires a large amount of storage, and it binds the node specifications to force users to perform rational management on the network. These are designed into the system as invisible rules that are not described in the program. Therefore, monitoring the dynamism of nodes on the network can aid in understanding the potential system mechanisms. In this study, by monitoring Bitcoin and Ethereum over a long comparative period of 455 days as a system based on the main blockchains actually used, we demonstrate that it is difficult to balance the distributed structure owing to the rational behavior of users. We empirically provide the following evidence: (1) the node density of a specific hosting region increases; and (2) a local hosting region with less than 1% of the total nodes closes. We conclude that this is a security risk problem that results in a weak network structure, and discuss possible solutions.

Keywords: Blockchain · Cryptocurrency · Security · Network monitoring

1 Introduction

Over 10 years have passed since Satoshi Nakamoto's original Bitcoin whitepaper [14] was published online for the first time. The blockchain concept presented in the original paper has attracted attention as a technology trend. Blockchain is an autonomous decentralized system that is maintained by users distributed in the network, and is of interest as a solution for systems in which centralized management costs are a problem [16].

The blockchain operates on the premise that the users distributed over the network manage all of the ledgers. However, a problem exists in that the storage for managing ledgers continually increases [3]. Therefore, the system continuation depends on the motivation of the user who provides the node for managing the accurate distributed ledger.

© Springer Nature Switzerland AG 2019
J. K. Liu and X. Huang (Eds.): NSS 2019, LNCS 11928, pp. 504–519, 2019.
https://doi.org/10.1007/978-3-030-36938-5_31

Considering its contribution to the system maintenance, the user cost is an important motivation. Following the original paper [14], only the user who conducted verification of the ledger received a reward for their work. If a user behaves rationally to receive more rewards, he or she attempts to search for a cheaper location to reduce working costs, such as electricity bills. Thus, a user who only has a full ledger and never receives rewards is more affected by the motivation to decrease costs. Owing to storage limitations relating to the maintenance of the distributed ledger, the user who has all ledgers also attempts to search for a cheaper server with large storage towards lower maintenance costs. It should be noted that user motivation follows implicit rules that are not described in the program.

Network node dynamism based on user motivation triggers extreme bias in limited environments, and occurs in various potential security risks that cannot be controlled by the program.

In this research, we investigated the potential security risks of network dynamism by observing Bitcoin and Ethereum over a period of 455 days as a system based on the main blockchains actually used. We empirically demonstrate the following: (1) the node density of a specific hosting region increases; and (2) a local hosting with less than 1% of the total node closes.

This means that, owing to the storage constraints associated with the distributed ledger management, the network distribution decreases when the user behaves reasonably, causing a specific regional bias. Small-scale network areas constituting a system are susceptible to fragmentation attacks, while large-scale network areas are less resistant to network failures. As this problem appears as a behavioral mechanism rather than a systematic defect, it is difficult to address by modifying the program.

The remainder of this paper is organized as follows: Sect. 2 presents the background of the technology and a review of related services, namely Bitcoin and Ethereum. Section 3 introduces related previous research, including network analysis and attack methods. Section 4 reports on the research of our method and analysis. Section 5 discusses the results. Finally, the conclusion is presented in Sect. 6.

2   Background

This section introduces the blockchain components and operation mechanism. We emphasize the cycle of roles on the blockchain network to demonstrate the user motivation and rational behavior mechanisms for the system continuity. Thereafter, we briefly review Bitcoin and Ethereum.

2.1   Overview of Blockchain

The key components of Blockchain are classified as the "Transaction" and "Block". "Transaction" consists of ledger data, records the contents of the transferred value, and is the smallest data structure unit in the blockchain. "Block"

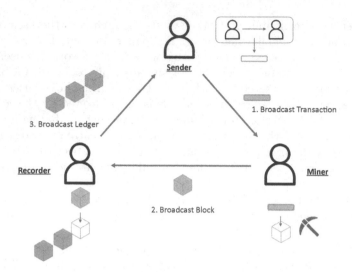

Fig. 1. Cycle of user roles in blockchain

contains a verified transaction and a hash value calculated from the previous block. Therefore, the blockchain data structure is characterized by the continuity of the block, and this characteristic structure contributes to the tamper-resistance feature of the blockchain. The data consistency in the network is supported by the distributed nodes with all blocks, and consistent storage is shared with users by connection to the network. Creating the transaction and storing the block are repeated in this blockchain network.

According to the original published paper [14], the role of the user who maintains this loop can be represented by the cycle illustrated in Fig. 1. The users on the blockchain network have three roles: "Sender" generates transactions, "Miner" verifies the transactions and stores them in blocks, and "Recorder" saves the latest blocks. It should be noted that the users may have duplicate roles. In the cycle presented in Fig. 1, the three roles function as follows:

1. "Sender" obtains the latest block from "Recorder", creates new transactions, and sends these to "Miner".
2. "Miner" collects new transactions to store into a block.
3. "Miner" works on finding a nonce of proof-of-work for its block to store the transaction.
4. When "Miner" finds a nonce, it broadcasts the block to "Recorder".
5. "Recorder" accepts the block only if all transactions therein are valid and not already spent.

We focus on the driving force of the cycle in which the blockchain network operates. If users exist who use the blockchain network, a user who plays the roles of "Miner" and "Recorder" is required. "Miner" receives a fee from "Sender" and a reward for the verification work, thereby providing "Miner" with motivation to play a role. However, "Recorder" can only use the correct data and will never receive any money for broadcasting the latest blocks on the network. Therefore, "Recorder" tries to work at a low cost to maintain the storage in the same behavior as "Miner" attempts to work at a low cost to receive more rewards. Consequently, we can understand the mechanism the users on the blockchain network tend to behave more rationally.

2.2 Bitcoin and Ethereum

Both Bitcoin and Ethereum are blockchain-based systems and have the same components. The main difference between the two is the type of data managed by the distributed nodes.

Bitcoin is a blockchain-based system that was initially defined as a cryptocurrency. The distributed nodes manage the value movements as data. Therefore, the node only performs a ledger function, and the network behaves as a single large ledger.

Ethereum is an extended blockchain that manages the operational processes as data in addition to the value movements. It is the first major blockchain that supports the smart contract describing the operation process using the Ethereum Virtual Machine (EVM). Therefore, the node performs the function of executing a unique opcode in addition to the ledger function, and the network behaves as a single large computer; that is, it functions as a distributed computing platform.

3 Related Work

The majority of research on blockchain security risks has reported on the implementation of smart contracts and system applications [9,15]. Previous studies have mainly discussed attacks on individuals using the network [2]. While, certain research has focused on the operations of the entire network composing the system, and the activities of distributed nodes in networks have been thoroughly investigated. These works are very important for understanding the potential security risks caused by the user behavior dynamism that is not described in the program.

This section introduces the research on the network topology of services based on the blockchains reported thus far, and attacks using the network system structure. In particular, it is necessary to emphasize the contradiction between the goal of making a system robust by distributing the ledger to the wide network and that of accelerating updates by rational management of the ledger on the closer network.

3.1 Network Topology

There are two topics of network topology and they are measurement method and monitoring.

The measurement method is a research on how to measure the entire network in a shorter time without effecting the nodes of the network. The previous work includes using the peering protocol function [10] and using two types of clients [4].

The monitoring is research analyzing the network characteristics including the node distribution, the geographical distribution and network latencies. This research is classified as a monitoring. In previous work, Bitcoin and Ethereum, which are the subjects of this study, have been demonstrated to exhibit the following network characteristics.

Feld et al. [5] reported on an initial study focusing on the regional distribution among autonomous systems (AS) in addition to anonymity analysis for Bitcoin, which formed the main research using IP addresses. This study explained that a bias exists in the network structure at the AS-level, and demonstrated that anonymity flaws and information propagation differ according to the network region.

Kim et al. [8] extended the survey of the Bitcoin network to the Ethereum network. According to this survey of the large-scale network, the network distribution of Ethereum exhibits a large regional bias, as with Bitcoin. Furthermore, the connections between Ethereum nodes are determined by random selection, and not by the geographical location and IP address information, as with Bitcoin. In this comparative experiment, it was noted that Ethereum is a random ad-hoc network with a wider distribution and higher delay than Bitcoin.

Park et al. [11] demonstrated the network structure growth by comparing the observed network state in previous studies with the current observed network state in the Bitcoin network. This study was based on the detailed properties of Bitcoin nodes, such as the IP addresses of the nodes, network size, power law in the geographical distribution, protocol, client versions, and network latencies. It proposed modifying the random connection (default) by the selection rule based on the geographical distribution of nodes for improved connectivity and faster data propagation.

Gencer et al. [6] show that the decentralization of Bitcoin and Ethereum using the Falcon Relay Network. And they reports that Bitcoin and Ethereum are less decentralized than previously thought.

3.2   Network Attack

Apostolaki et al. [1] reported on several attack methods that exploit the network structure. They discussed the partitioning attacks and delayed attacks that can be performed by AS-level attackers, and examined the issue from two perspectives: the small-scale network, such as the single node, and the large-scale network, such as the local network.

A partitioning attack means that several nodes are disconnected from the main network, and it is classified as a denial of service (DoS) attack. This attack triggers a vulnerability to double spends and the block fork which wastes mining power. A delayed attack means slowing down the propagation of new blocks between specific nodes on the network. This attack has the same effect as the partitioning attack, and it is more difficult to detect because the attack can occur without disconnecting from the target node.

The authors report that the node distribution bias at the AS-level is an important characteristic affecting AS-level attackers from an Internet routing perspective. When a specific AS exists with a biased node distribution, in the case of a delayed attack, the AS-level attacker inside the AS or routing route can easily gain an opportunity to intercept traffic, and if many mining pool gateways and nodes are attacked, the network will be more seriously affected. A partitioning attack has an impact on isolated ASes that are not major, which are not the ASes in which the nodes are concentrated.

4   Measurement

In this section, to gain insight into the potential security risks caused by user behavior in the blockchain, we collect the node information with the full ledger, and analyze the data using different measurement methods. Full nodes exhibit a bottleneck whereby the storage for managing the ledgers continues to increase on the Bitcoin and Ethereum networks.

Firstly, we confirm the data properties used in this research. To verify the data quality, we compared these data with those of previous research. Thereafter, we analyze the network characteristics in a node unit using IP address-level information to observe the trend of the dynamics at the network scale and the entire network. We perform analysis using AS-level information to observe the trend of the local network dynamics. Finally, we summarize the analyzed results.

4.1   Methodology

We collected full node data on the main networks of Bitcoin and Ethereum every hour from bitnodes.earn.com[1] and ethernodes.org[2], respectively, which have also been used in previous studies [4,8]. We aggregated the nodes that could be observed to exist even once in 12 scans during the day as daily data. Moreover, we cleansed the data collected from ethernodes.org to remove unnecessary parts and duplications. Our data-collection period was 455 days, from April 1, 2018 to June 30, 2019, with the exception of July 21, 2018, when a serious server failure occurred.

These collected data support three connection protocol types: Ipv4, IPv6, and TOR. We also converted the IP address-level information into AS-level information based on IP2Location[3].

This research was based on the assumption that full nodes are always connectable and open, so it did not include unconnectable nodes and light nodes that did not have all ledgers. Moreover, as the nodes hidden behind a firewall and network address translation (NAT), which are issues in network observation,

---

[1] https://bitnodes.earn.com/api/v1/snapshots.

[2] https://www.ethernodes.org/network/1/data?.

[3] https://www.ip2location.com/.

Table 1. Total number of nodes for each connection type during observation period from April 1, 2018 to June 30, 2019.

	Bitcoin	Ethereum
IPv4	188,502 (83.4%)	666,811 (99.99%)
IPv6	34,689 (15.3%)	34 (0.005%)
TOR	2,770 (1.2%)	0
Total	225,961	666,845

could not be reached completely, this approach exhibited the same potential limitations as those of previous research [8,11]. All of the analysis results described below are based on these collected data.

4.2   Data Quality

We confirm that our data quality is comparable to that of previous studies.

Park et al. [11] investigated the Bitcoin network in which the IP address version supported only IPv4 for 37 days, from January 16, 2018 to February 21, 2018. Researchers discovered a total of 1,099,322 unique IP addresses corresponding to machines running Bitcoin nodes, of which 23,725 were full nodes. According to this research, 8,500 full nodes exist every day on the Bitcoin network, and the number of newly discovered full nodes is approximately 1,000 to 300 per day.

As there was no overlap with this research, we measured only the IPv4 data for 37 days, from April 1 to May 7, 2018, the most recent date. As a result, we confirmed 28,964 unique IP addresses and observed an average of 8,972 nodes per day.

Kim et al. [8] investigated the Ethereum network for 82 days, from April 18, 2018 to July 8, 2018, and these data were compared with the observation data used in our research on April 23, 2018. However, the reported values (20,437 nodes) differed from our collected values (12,214 nodes). We confirmed similar values (22,690 nodes) before cleansing. As mentioned previously, the ethernodes.org data needs to consider the last confirmed data timing and duplication.

It was pointed out that the number of nodes that can actually be observed in the data of ethernodes.org (4,717 nodes) is less than the number of nodes observed in the experiment (15,454 nodes).

We could confirm that the observed value of the experiment (15,454 nodes) was near to the value after cleansing (12,214 nodes). Moreover, similarities with these reported results were identified, whereby the distribution of nodes is based in the United States and China, while the Ethereum network is an ad-hoc network with a larger delay than the Bitcoin network.

In summary, the data used in our research were of the same quality as those in previous research.

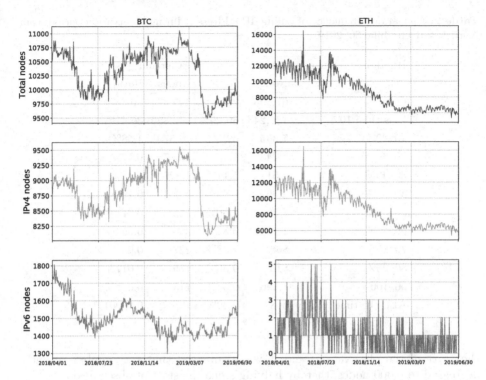

Fig. 2. Classification of networks and IP address versions for observation period from April 1, 2018 to June 30, 2019. The left figures indicate Bitcoin (BTC), while the right figures indicate Ethereum (ETH). The upper figures present the total numbers of nodes, namely IPv4 and IPv6. The middle figures indicate only IPv4, while the lower figures display only IPv6

4.3 IP Address-Level Analysis

Table 1 displays the quantities of all unique IP addresses acquired during the observation period to confirm the network scale. According to the observation results, approximately three times the number of nodes observed by Bitcoin were observed by Ethereum. Regarding node types, IPv6 and several TOR servers were observed in Bitcoin, but both Bitcoin and Ethereum were mostly running on IPv4. For this reason, the results of the previous research [11] using only IPv4 were regarded as being the same as when the connection type was considered.

To investigate the trend of the network dynamics during the observation period, we demonstrated the transition of the number of nodes in this period, as illustrated in Fig. 2 The figure displays the classification of the networks and IP address versions for the observation period from April 1, 2018 to June 30, 2019.

The average number of nodes in Bitcoin was approximately 10,000, which means that it was operated with approximately 10,000 nodes throughout the period. However, the number of Ethereum nodes decreased consistently from

Table 2. Appearance frequency of unique IP addresses during observation period from April 1, 2018 to June 30, 2019

IP address frequency	Bitcoin		Ethereum	
	Nodes	Ratio	Nodes	Ratio
Once	67,395	29.82%	405,374	60.78%
Less than 10%	136,243	60.29%	242,820	36.41%
10–20%	7,365	3.25%	10,570	1.58%
20–30%	4,243	1.87%	3,807	0.57%
30–40%	2,511	1.11%	1,920	0.28%
40–50%	2,092	0.92%	1,004	0.15%
50–60%	1,362	0.60%	516	0.077%
60–70%	1,205	0.53%	366	0.054%
70–80%	866	0.38%	227	0.034%
80–90%	815	0.36%	115	0.017%
90–100%	1,196	0.52%	115	0.017%
ALL the time	668	0.29%	13	0.00001%

the start of the observation, and it was confirmed that the number recently decreased to 6,000 nodes, thereby halving since the start of observation.

Regarding the number of nodes observed during the period, Ethereum had a large number of connections but was a network with large fluctuations, while Bitcoin maintained a stable network scale.

To investigate the network structure stability in further detail, we counted the number of days that a node was connected to the network. Table 2 summarizes the appearance distribution of unique IP addresses and ratio of connection counts over the 455 days. "Once" indicates the case where the connection was confirmed only once, while "All the time" indicates the case where the connection was confirmed every day during the observation period.

We focus on the number of nodes appearing within a short time. Comparing the connection characteristics of Bitcoin and Ethereum, many nodes on the Bitcoin network left the network within approximately one month, whereas many nodes on the Ethereum network connected only once. These phenomena are related to the network characteristics. The Ethereum network was connected by means of a random ad-hoc connection, as pointed out in previous research [8], compared to the Bitcoin network. In the Ethereum network, 60% of the connecting nodes were disconnected within one day, so the number of reconnections was more frequent than that in Bitcoin, resulting in an ad-hoc network. In terms of the entire network, almost 90% of the nodes left the network in less than one month in both Bitcoin and Ethereum.

In the IP address-level survey of Bitcoin and Ethereum, we confirmed the changes in the network scale during the observation period, and the differences in the building style of the network users. Although no significant difference was identified in the network scale at the start of observation, the Bitcoin network scale was stable throughout the period. However, Ethereum exhibited a wide network distribution range over the entire period, but numerous ad-hoc connections existed, and the network maintenance that was scaled down by nearly half was unstable.

It can be concluded from the observation results that the dynamism of the Bitcoin and Ethereum networks differed for the short-term nodes of less than 10%, as indicated in Table 2, which occupied the majority. Moreover, despite the short-lived nodes occupying the majority in the network, the network was maintained without stopping. These results provide insights regarding the minimum specification for maintaining the distributed network. Preventing a DoS attack by randomizing the IP addresses of nodes is certainly rational behavior. However, this is a countermeasure for general web services, and it is therefore not surprising that the same measures are applied to Bitcoin and Ethereum. Based on these results, we could not identify reasonable user behavior for the distributed ledger problem that requires large storage capacity using IP address-level information. Therefore, we present AS-level analysis in the following subsection.

4.4 AS-level Analysis

Important distributed network characteristics include the density, as well as the scale and dynamics of the entire network. Therefore, to measure the density bias in the network, we performed AS-level analysis, in which the IP addresses were grouped by the routing policy.

Figure 3 illustrates the node distributions on the Bitcoin and Ethereum networks on the observation start and end dates using AS-level information. The left figure indicates Bitcoin, while the right figure indicates Ethereum. The blue and red lines represent the cumulative distributions of nodes aggregated to the AS level on the observation start and end dates, respectively. The position of each vertical line indicates the number of ASes in which the cumulative node distribution was 100%.

In terms of the scale of ASes, we note that there were clearly fewer ASes in Ethereum than in Bitcoin. As illustrated in Fig. 3, both of the red line curves of the cumulative distribution for Bitcoin and Ethereum shifted to the outside of the blue line curves. This means that the cumulative node distribution increased in fewer AS regions. For the number of ASes with a cumulative distribution reaching 100%, the red vertical line shifted inside the blue vertical line for both Bitcoin and Ethereum. This indicates that the node distribution was concentrated in several areas and the density of the nodes increased in the local network.

As we confirmed the local network convergence for both Bitcoin and Ethereum, we explored the changes in detail for the density of the nodes. Figure 4 illustrates the changes in the number of ASes corresponding to the cumulative rate of the number of nodes during the observation period. The figures on the left indicate Bitcoin, while the figures on the right indicate Ethereum. The upper figures display the number of ASes when the cumulative node distribution

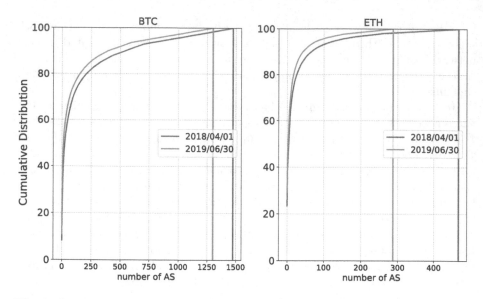

Fig. 3. Comparison of node distributions in ASes on April 1, 2018 and June 30, 2019

occupied 30%. Similarly, the middle figures indicate the number of ASes for 50%, while the lower figures present the number of ASes for 80%.

With the exception of the results in which 30% of the Ethereum nodes were covered by only two ASs, the number of ASs corresponding to a cumulative rate of less than 80% decreased from the first to final observations. Considering that the dynamics of the Bitcoin and Ethereum networks differed from those of the network-scale analysis, we can confirm the common rules in grouped networks. That is, regardless of the network scale or dynamism, an obviously tendency for accumulation in fewer regions was exhibited. In fact, 30% of the Bitcoin and Ethereum nodes were managed by cloud hosting providers during the observation period, such as Amazon, Alibaba, Contabo, DigitalOcean, OVH SAS, Hetzner, and Google. This finding emphasizes the rational behavior of users to maintain lower node maintenance costs.

This means that, if a rational decision is made to build nodes considering the storage cost, fewer options are available. The building node timing appears differently depending on the IP address-level information for Bitcoin and Ethereum; however, the AS in which the node is built appears only at a specific AS considering rationality.

Figure 5 illustrates the changes in the number of ASes with less than 100 nodes during the observation period. In contrast to the increased node density for the specific ASes, the number of local ASes with few nodes decreased. Almost 200 ASes disappeared on both Bitcoin and Ethereum from the first to final observations. This means that a small ASes is merged with a large ASse.

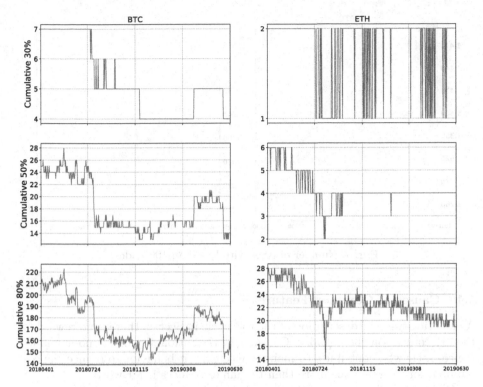

Fig. 4. Changes in number of ASes corresponding to cumulative rate of number of nodes during observation period from April 1, 2018 to June 30, 2019

4.5   Results

In this section, we summarize our observation results. Table 2 indicates that, in the IP address-level information analysis, approximately 90% of nodes existed only in the short term of less than one month. That is, during the observation period, both the Bitcoin and Ethereum networks had numerous nodes replaced every day. The AS-level information analysis confirmed the AS rules whereby the nodes are built under the condition that the building timing of these nodes is random. As illustrated in Fig. 4, the appearance positions converged, and Fig. 5 indicates that this was based on the fact that the local AS was closed and the node density of the major AS increased.

5   Discussion

According to the analysis results, the behavior of the nodes in the Bitcoin and Ethereum networks exhibited different dynamics; however, in the long term, we can confirm the common feature of clustering to a specific region.

In the following, based on the analysis results, we discuss the causes of the common features, security risks regarding these features, and countermeasures.

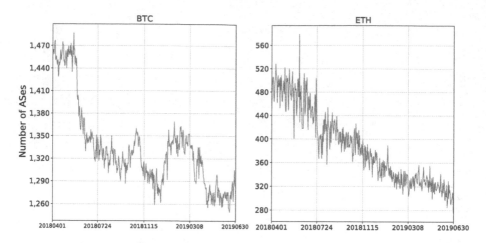

Fig. 5. Number of ASes with less than 100 nodes

5.1 Causes of Common Features

As mentioned in the description of the role cycle in Sect. 2, there is no reward for the "Recorder" on the network. Considering the rationality of the node maintenance, users who contribute to maintenance exhibit behavior to reduce the cost required for maintenance more than the miner reduces it for work.

Owing to the limitation of the blockchain, it is necessary to have all ledgers for verification, and users need storage that can manage the ever-increasing ledger capacity. If one attempts to satisfy all of these conditions, a limited range exists for selection.

From the perspective of continuous node maintenance, it is inevitable to use a cloud service without building nodes in residential areas. Moreover, Bitcoin and Ethereum require storage exceeding 100 GB, and cloud hosting providers that supply large-capacity storage are limited. Therefore, the node density increases at the AS level, where the cloud hosting providers build the nodes. In fact, in the AS-level survey, most users building Bitcoin and Ethereum nodes used cloud hosting providers such as Amazon, Alibaba, Contabo, DigitalOcean, OVH SAS, Hetzner, and Google. This trend is the same as that reported in previous studies.

Furthermore, the high integration of nodes is progressing, not only at the AS-level, but also at the application level. As additional research, Fig. 6 illustrates the transition of nodes where the IP addresses of Bitcoin and Ethereum overlapped during the observation period. Approximately 100 nodes managed multiple ledgers on a single server. This means that, in the most recent Bitcoin and Ethereum node distribution, approximately 1% of all nodes corresponded to duplicate nodes.

It is not surprising that duplicate nodes exist at the application level, because proposals are available for connecting blockchains, such as atomic swap [7]. However, it should be noted that additional large storage is required to maintain multiple applications.

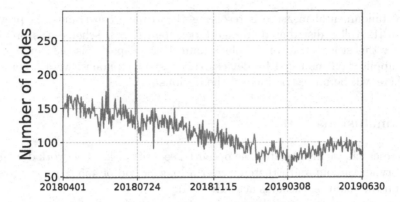

Fig. 6. Number of duplicated IP addresses for both Bitcoin and Ethereum during observation period from April 1, 2018 to June 30, 2019

To reiterate, the storage constraints in the blockchain appear as a common feature guiding users to behave more rationally.

5.2 Security Risks and Countermeasures

In Sect. 3, it was noted that, for AS-level attackers, a higher node density of a specific AS results in more attack opportunities. Considering the current distribution of nodes on the network, this is not a favorable situation. In particular, as the security risks that trigger the delay attack are considered, it is necessary to observe the node propagation status in the network by not only investigating the node distribution, but also building monitoring nodes in different ASes.

As a countermeasure to avoid this network structure, we consider two concepts: creating the motivation for users to distribute nodes, and solving the storage problem that is a limitation.

Focusing on the maintenance cost, an approach exists whereby maintenance fees are collected from users who require accurate data. If the block reward is abolished in the future, it will be reasonable to add the node maintenance cost to the transaction fee. According to blockchain.com, the average fee per transaction during the observation period was $1.05. If a node maintenance fee of 10% is added to the transaction fee, the average transaction amount included in one block will be 1,897.75, and the average reward of all nodes per day, calculated from the daily average block generation amount of 147.36 blocks, will be $30,406.65. This is sufficient to build a host that can cover the current capacity for one month.

The maintenance fees collected in this manner can be distributed by assigning specific gravity in units of AS and IP address prefixes. If we establish an incentive structure that can obtain a substantial amount of maintenance fees by building in an area with fewer connections, we believe that this will provide a distributed network structure using user motivation.

The fundamental measure is resolving the storage constraints. In previous research [12,13], a distributed storage blockchain (DSB) scheme was proposed to reduce this storage cost of the blockchain. If the capacity is the same as that of the application managed by devices such as smartphones, we are confident that there will be no restrictions on the options.

6 Conclusions

In this research, we investigated the potential security risks of network dynamism by observing Bitcoin and Ethereum over a long period of 455 days as a system based on the main blockchains actually used.

We reported on the natural expansion of network bias as a non-programmable security risk for blockchains, regardless of the daily changes in the number of nodes in each system. This means that, owing to the storage constraints associated with the management of the distributed ledger, the network distribution decreases when the users behave reasonably, causing a specific regional bias.

Our results provide two contributions: (1) the node density of a specific hosting region increases; and (2) a local hosting region that has less than 1% of the total node closes.

References

1. Apostolaki, M., Zohar, A., Vanbever, L.: Hijacking bitcoin: routing attacks on cryptocurrencies. In: 2017 IEEE Symposium on Security and Privacy (SP), pp. 375–392. IEEE (2017)
2. Conti, M., Kumar, E.S., Lal, C., Ruj, S.: A survey on security and privacy issues of bitcoin. IEEE Commun. Surv. Tutorials 20(4), 3416–3452 (2018)
3. Croman, K., et al.: On scaling decentralized blockchains. In: Clark, J., Meiklejohn, S., Ryan, P.Y.A., Wallach, D., Brenner, M., Rohloff, K. (eds.) FC 2016. LNCS, vol. 9604, pp. 106–125. Springer, Heidelberg (2016). https://doi.org/10.1007/978-3-662-53357-4_8
4. Deshpande, V., Badis, H., George, L.: BTCmap: mapping bitcoin peer-to-peer network topology. In: 2018 IFIP/IEEE International Conference on Performance Evaluation and Modeling in Wired and Wireless Networks (PEMWN), pp. 1–6. IEEE (2018)
5. Feld, S., Schönfeld, M., Werner, M.: Traversing bitcoin's P2P network: insights into the structure of a decentralised currency. Int. J. Comput. Sci. Eng. 13(2), 122–131 (2016)
6. Gencer, A.E., Basu, S., Eyal, I., Van Renesse, R., Sirer, E.G.: Decentralization in bitcoin and ethereum networks. In: Financial Cryptography and Data Security Conference 2018 (2018)
7. Herlihy, M.: Atomic cross-chain swaps. In: Proceedings of the 2018 ACM Symposium on Principles of Distributed Computing, pp. 245–254. ACM (2018)
8. Kim, S.K., Ma, Z., Murali, S., Mason, J., Miller, A., Bailey, M.: Measuring ethereum network peers. In: Proceedings of the Internet Measurement Conference 2018, pp. 91–104. ACM (2018)

9. Li, X., Jiang, P., Chen, T., Luo, X., Wen, Q.: A survey on the security of blockchain systems. Future Gener. Comput. Syst. (2017)
10. Miller, A., et al.: Discovering bitcoin's public topology and influential nodes (2015)
11. Park, S., Im, S., Seol, Y., Paek, J.: Nodes in the bitcoin network: comparative measurement study and survey. IEEE Access **7**, 57009–57022 (2019)
12. Raman, R.K., Varshney, L.R.: Distributed storage meets secret sharing on the blockchain. In: 2018 Information Theory and Applications Workshop (ITA), pp. 1–6. IEEE (2018)
13. Raman, R.K., Varshney, L.R.: Dynamic distributed storage for blockchains. In: 2018 IEEE International Symposium on Information Theory (ISIT), pp. 2619–2623. IEEE (2018)
14. Satoshi, N.: Bitcoin: a peer-to-peer electronic cash system (2008). http://www.bitcoin.org/bitcoin.pdf
15. Wohrer, M., Zdun, U.: Smart contracts: security patterns in the ethereum ecosystem and solidity. In: 2018 International Workshop on Blockchain Oriented Software Engineering (IWBOSE), pp. 2–8. IEEE (2018)
16. Yuan, Y., Wang, F.Y.: Towards blockchain-based intelligent transportation systems. In: 2016 IEEE 19th International Conference on Intelligent Transportation Systems (ITSC), pp. 2663–2668. IEEE (2016)

A DNS Tunneling Detection Method Based on Deep Learning Models to Prevent Data Exfiltration

Jiacheng Zhang[1,2], Li Yang[1(✉)], Shui Yu[3], and Jianfeng Ma[1]

[1] Xidian University, Xian, China
kulukami@gmail.com, yangli@xidian.edu.cn
[2] Science and Technology on Communication Networks Laboratory,
Shijiazhuang 050081, China
[3] School of Computer Science, University of Technology Sydney, Ultimo, Australia
Shui.yu@uts.edu.au

Abstract. DNS tunneling is a typical DNS attack that has been used for stealing information for many years. The stolen data is encoded and encapsulated into the DNS request to evade intrusion detection. The popular detection methods of machine learning use features, such as network traffic and DNS behavior. However, most features can only be extracted when data exfiltration occurs, like time-frequency related features. The key to prevent data exfiltration based on DNS tunneling is to detect the malicious query from single DNS request. Since we don't use the network traffic features and DNS behavior features, our method can detect DNS tunneling before data exfiltration.

In this paper, we propose a detection method based on deep learning models, which uses the DNS query payloads as predictive variables in the models. As the DNS tunneling data is a kind of text, our approach use word embedding as a part of fitting the neural networks, which is a feature extraction method in natural language processing (NLP). In order to achieve high performance, the detection decision is made by these common deep learning models, including dense neural network (DNN), one-dimensional convolutional neural network (1D-CNN) and recurrent neural network (RNN). We implement the DNS tunneling detection system in the real network environment. The results show that our approach achieves 99.90% accuracy and is more secure than existing methods.

Keywords: Data exfiltration · DNS tunneling · Anomaly detection · Deep learning models

1 Introduction

DNS (Domain Name System) is a hierarchical and decentralized naming system, which serves as a two-way mapping between domain names and IP addresses. As the perceived lack of security in the protocol, DNS has experienced DoS (Denial of Service) attacks [5], DNS cache poisoning [7], C&C (a command-and-control

© Springer Nature Switzerland AG 2019
J. K. Liu and X. Huang (Eds.): NSS 2019, LNCS 11928, pp. 520–535, 2019.
https://doi.org/10.1007/978-3-030-36938-5_32

channel for botnets) [15] and DNS tunneling [10]. DNS tunneling is a typical DNS attack that has been used for stealing information for many years. Since the current network security system does not check the DNS payload when the packet is in the normal DNS packet format, attackers use the DNS tunneling to transfer private data from compromised devices. The stolen data is encoded and encapsulated into the DNS request, which will not be blocked or detected by the existing security solutions.

Research on DNS tunneling detection begins with character frequency analysis [3] and N-Gram analysis [4]. In recent years, researchers working on covert channel detection propose many detecting methods based on MLTs (Machine Learning Techniques). Feature extraction is a vital step in tunnel detection based on MLTs. And most features are extracted from network traffic analysis [1] and DNS behavior analysis [2,10]. For example, unique query ratio, unique response ratio and average request length are extracted when many DNS packets passed [11]. In other words, the stolen data has been transmitted when extracting these features and calculating other time-frequency related features, such as the time interval of packet transmission, the time interval between the DNS request and response. To effectively defend against attackers, detecting a covert channel before data exfiltration is important. Detecting the malicious payloads from single DNS query is essential for DNS tunneling detection.

To address the issue above, we proposed a deep learning model based detection method. We use DNS query payloads as the predictive variable in the models. Then, We use word embedding as a part of fitting the common neural networks, including dense neural network (DNN), one-dimensional convolutional neural network (1D-CNN) and recurrent neural network (RNN). Accordingly, we build the one-model detection decision maker and the multi-model detection decision maker to make final decision.

We build the DNS tunneling detection system and validate the performance of our detection mechanism with real network environment, the detection accuracy can reach 99.90%. And we find McAfee's DNS tunnel data in the real network environment.

In summary, we make the following contributions:

* We propose a deep learning model based DNS tunneling detection mechanism which can identify the DNS tunneling from single dns request. Since we don't use the network traffic features and DNS behavior features, our approach can detect DNS tunneling before data exfiltration. In a sense, the network security system can immediately interrupt DNS tunneling.
* We build a DNS tunneling detection system and conduct experiments in a real network environment to evaluate the performance of our proposal. The results show that our approach can detect DNS tunneling accurately, and we find McAfee's DNS tunnel data in the real network environment.

The rest of this paper is organized as follows: Sect. 2 presents a description of the concepts that are used throughout the paper. Section 3 reviews the related work. Section 4 presents our solution to this problem, and Sect. 5 presents the experimental results. We conclude our work in Sect. 6.

2   Background

In this section, we present a description of the concepts that are used throughout the paper. In more detail, We describe the data exfiltration over DNS tunneling (Sect. 2.1), DNS tunneling architecture and tools (Sect. 2.2), and DNS tunneling data analysis (Sect. 2.3).

2.1   Data Exfiltration over DNS Tunneling

The compromised devices need to bypass intrusion detection to transmit information to attackers. Figure 1 shows a DNS tunneling scenario.

In this figure, the exfiltrated data is encoded into the sub-domain of the DNS requests. The compromised device sends the DNS requests for a malicious sub-domain (tunnel.server.example.com). However, the internal DNS server does not have the IP address of this domain, it forwards the request to the authoritative Name server, which is controlled by the attacker. The current network security systems do not check the DNS payload when the packet is in the normal DNS packet format. Therefore, the security systems do not intercept the packets. Finally, The attacker uses the server-side component to recover the data.

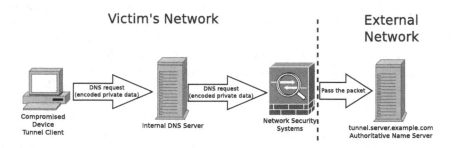

Fig. 1. DNS tunneling by sending a DNS query with encode exfiltrated data to a malicious sub-domain.

2.2   DNS Tunneling Architecture and Tools

There are various DNS tunneling tools available online, which can be used to generate DNS tunneling traffic. These DNS tunneling tools use similar core technologies, but there are differences on the encoding and other implementation details. Generally, to build a DNS tunnel, the following components are required:

* Domain or sub-domain controlled by the attacker
* Server-side component
* Client-side component
* Data encoding

These DNS tunneling tools use the Client-and-Server (C&S) architecture. The server-side component is named DNS tunnel server, which is an authoritative name server for the domain controlled by attacker. And the client-side component is named DNS tunnel client, which hosts the other end of the tunnel. The DNS tunnel could be used to communicate past the security systems and allow communication between the compromised device and an arbitrary host on the Internet. The DNS tunnel client initiates a DNS request for the DNS tunneling server which is the authoritative name server.

2.3 DNS Tunneling Data Analysis

When client needs to send data to a server, it will encode that data into the DNS payload. Figure 2 shows the DNS tunneling data from dns2tcp. For example, the client could send an 'A' record request where the data is encoded in the host name: su821DbsBA.tunnel.server.example.com. The server can respond with an answer as a CNAME response. In this way, any data can be transferred to the server.

```
DNS      508 Standard query response 0xc908 TXT su82zTblBA.a.tunnel.com TXT NS tunnel.com A 20.0.0.101
DNS       83 Standard query 0x49b8 TXT su820zbrBA.a.tunnel.com
DNS      508 Standard query response 0x4766 TXT su82zjbmBA.a.tunnel.com TXT NS tunnel.com A 20.0.0.101
DNS       83 Standard query 0xedae TXT su821DbsBA.a.tunnel.com
DNS      508 Standard query response 0x63a7 TXT su82zzbnBA.a.tunnel.com TXT NS tunnel.com A 20.0.0.101
DNS       83 Standard query 0x0d06 TXT su821TbtBA.a.tunnel.com
DNS      508 Standard query response 0x50f0 TXT su820DboBA.a.tunnel.com TXT NS tunnel.com A 20.0.0.101
DNS       83 Standard query 0x7461 TXT su821jbuBA.a.tunnel.com
DNS      508 Standard query response 0x1b62 TXT su820TbpBA.a.tunnel.com TXT NS tunnel.com A 20.0.0.101
DNS       83 Standard query 0xf616 TXT su821zbvBA.a.tunnel.com
DNS      508 Standard query response 0xfe24 TXT su820jbqBA.a.tunnel.com TXT NS tunnel.com A 20.0.0.101
DNS       83 Standard query 0x8c0a TXT su822DbwBA.a.tunnel.com
DNS      508 Standard query response 0x49b0 TXT su820zbrBA.a.tunnel.com TXT NS tunnel.com A 20.0.0.101
DNS       83 Standard query 0x7c8 TXT su822TbxBA.a.tunnel.com
```

Fig. 2. DNS tunneling data from dns2tcp.

However, there are limits. First, the data must be put into the domain name field. This field is split into labels and accepts up to 255 characters in total, including 63 character for each label. And each character can be a letter (case-insensitive), a number or a hyphen.

The encoding method including the DNS record type used is an area where tools are different. Some utilities use common record types such as 'A' records. Others use experimental types such as 'Null' records and EDNS to improve performance.

Base encoding of data is used in many situations to store or transfer data in environments that are restricted to ASCII data [9]. Base32 and Base64 are two of the most commonly used encodings for DNS tunneling. And there are some differences [13]:

* Base32 is a 5-bit encoding, it's generally used for requests from the client. Domain name characters can be letters (case-insensitive), which provide 26

characters. Additionally, numbers and the '-' character provide the other 11 characters. These are 37 unique characters. Then, attacker can generate data 5 bits at a time, this provides 32 possible values. These 32 values can fit within the total 37 available characters. Attacker can build malicious subdomains out of the encoded data.

* Base64 can be used for 'TXT' record responses. As the 'TXT' record is case-sensitive, it provides 52 characters. The numbers provide the other 10 characters. Addition, the '-' character and '+' character can be used, there are 64 unique characters which can be used for base 64 encoding. The response can be encoded 6 bits at a time using a 'TXT' response and sent back to the client.

As the encoding method is a part of DNS tunneling, character frequency analysis has great advantages for the detection research. And n-gram analysis is also one of the research points of the predecessors.

3 Literature Review and Related Work

Studys on DNS tunneling detection start with character frequency analysis [3] and N-Gram analysis [4]. In recent years, researchers focus on solving problems using machine learning methods.

Feature extraction is a vital step in tunnel detection based on MLTs. Predecessors' research about character frequency analysis can be used as a feature for reference. Domain names are usually human-readable, but DNS tunneling domains are obedient to random distribution. Extensive research has shown that N-gram character frequency is a good feature [2,10,12,13]. Aiello et al. [1] analyze second and third level DNS domains. They use statistical features of DNS queries-and-answers, and use the bayes classifier to build basic classifiers for DNS tunneling detection. Almusawi et al. [2] propose a multilabel support vector machine in order to detect and classify the DNS tunneling using byte frequencies, the length of packets and information entropy.

On the other hand, traffic based features and time-frequency related features can help improve the accuracy of the model. Liu et al. [10] use 4 kinds of features (totally, 18 features), including the time-interval features, request packet size features, domain entropy features and record type features for binary-classification.

These features mentioned above can help the model achieve good performance. Though, the stolen data has been transmitted when calculating time-frequency related features, such as the time interval of packet transmission, the time interval between the DNS request and response.

To effectively defend against attackers, detecting malicious queries from a single DNS request is critical for DNS tunneling detection.

We focus on detecting DNS tunneling using deep learning methods. As a part of machine learning techniques, deep learning can achieve good results in computer vision (CV) and natural language processing (NLP) related research [14]. Since the domain names are text type, deep learning models for text categorization can be used, such as 1D-CNN, RNN.

4   Method

4.1   Overview

The proposed method presents a constantly running process aimed at detecting DNS tunneling from single DNS request. Figure 3 shows the proposed solution. First, the network traffic is monitored by the Probe (a open source IDS, Zeek), which can generate logs for different protocols, including DNS log. After the data preprocessing and building deep learning models, we build the detection decision maker using these deep learning models. In the end, the security system can pass the legitimate DNS request and interrupt DNS tunneling request.

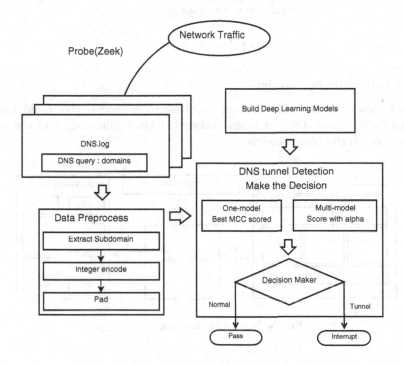

Fig. 3. Phases of the proposed solution.

In this section, we describe the solution in detail, including Data Preprocess (see Sect. 4.2), Build Deep learning models (see Sect. 4.3) and DNS tunneling detection decision maker (see Sect. 4.4).

4.2   Data Preprocess

Figure 4 shows the steps of the Data preparation. In DNS tunneling, TLD (Top-Level Domain) can be a malicious domain name controlled by attacker. In order to avoid the neural network learning useless features, we remove the top-level domain and extract the subdomain. Next, the characters need to be integer encoded and paded to fit the model input.

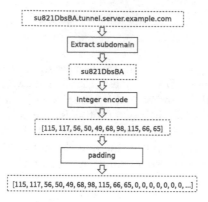

Fig. 4. Data preprocess.

4.3 Deep Learning Models

Figure 5 shows the steps of building Deep learning models. We build models with embedding and different neural networks. After split train and test data, we train and verify these models.

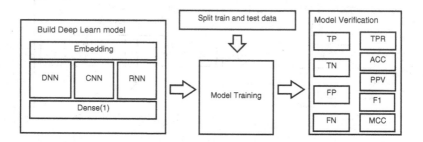

Fig. 5. Build deep learning models.

Word Embedding. Word embeddings provide a dense representation of words and their relative meanings. In our method, keras embedding layer is used as part of a deep learning model where the embedding is learning along with the model.

Neural Networks. We build 3 types of common deep learning models, including dense neural network, one-dimensional convolutional neural network and recurrent neural network.

* **Dense Neural Network.** The dense neural networks are the most commonly used model types in the deep learning neural networks. The dense neural networks have universality and can give solutions to many problems.

In the dense model, the layers are fully connected by the neurons in a network layer. After the embedding layer, the flatten layer collapses the spatial dimensions of the input into the channel dimension. Then, each neuron in a dense layer receives an input from all the neurons present in the previous layer. The dropout is a regularization layers for reducing overfitting in neural networks. At each training stage, the individual nodes are either dropped out of the net with probability $1 - P$ or kept with probability P. The deeper layer can learn high level hidden features. The last dense layer output 0 for false (legitimate request) and 1 for true (tunnel request) Table 1 presents the layers of the Dense model.

Table 1. Dense model

No.	Layer name
1	Embedding
2	Flatten
3	Dense
4	Dropout
5	Dense
6	Dropout
7	Dense
8	Dropout
9	Dense
10	Dropout
11	Dense

Table 2. 1D-CNN model

Num.	Layer name
1	Embedding
2	1D-Convolutional
3	1D-MaxPool
4	1D-Convolutional
5	1D-MaxPool
6	1D-Convolutional
7	1D-MaxPool
8	Flatten
9	Dropout
10	Dense

Table 3. RNN model

No.	Layer name
1	Embedding
2	LSTM or GRU
3	Dropout
4	Dense

* **One-Dimensional Convolutional Neural Network.** One-dimensional convolutional neural networks are often used in sequence models for natural language processing. Therefore, this type of neural network has an inherent advantage in detecting malicious payloads.

In the 1D-CNN model, the 1D-Convolutional layer allow the neural network to learn hidden features. The number of hidden features is defined by the number of filters. The max pooling layer is used after a convolutional layer for reduce the complexity of the output and prevent overfitting of the data. The flatten layer collapses the spatial dimensions of the input into the channel dimension. The purpose of using dropout layer and last dense layer is the same as that mentioned above. Table 2 presents the layers of the 1D-CNN model.

* **Recurrent Neural Network.** Recurrent neural network are often used in sequence models for classification and prediction of sequences. Thus, it can be used for detecting DNS tunneling requests.

We build two RNN models with LSTM (Long Short Term Memory) and GRU (Gated Recurrent Unit). Long Short Term Memory networks were introduced by Hochreiter & Schmidhuber [8]. They are a special kind of RNN, capable of learning long-term dependencies. Introduced by Cho, et al. [6] in

2014, GRU (Gated Recurrent Unit) aims to solve the vanishing gradient problem which comes with a standard recurrent neural network. GRU can also be considered as a variation on the LSTM because both are designed similarly. The purpose of using dropout layer and last dense layer is the same as that mentioned above. Table 3 presents the layers of the RNN model.

Model Verification. To evaluate the models, the results will be examined to determine the Sensitivity (TPR, true positive rate, recall), Accuracy (ACC), Precision (PPV, positive predictive value), F1 score and Matthews correlation coefficient (MCC) of each model.

Sensitivity (TPR) will measure the percentage of tunnel requests correctly predicted by the model. Accuracy (ACC) will measure the percentage of requests correctly predicted. Precision (PPV) will measure the percentage of predicted tunnel requests that were correct. F1 score is the harmonic mean of precision and sensitivity. Matthews correlation coefficient (MCC) is used in machine learning as a measure of the quality of binary (two-class) classifications. The MCC is in essence a correlation coefficient between the observed and predicted binary classifications; it returns a value between -1 and $+1$. A coefficient of $+1$ represents a perfect prediction, 0 no better than random prediction and -1 indicates total disagreement between prediction and observation.

The results will be calculated as follows:

$$TPR = \frac{TP}{TP + FN}$$

$$ACC = \frac{TP + TN}{TP + TN + FP + FN}$$

$$PPV = \frac{TP}{TP + FP}$$

$$F1_{score} = \frac{2 \times TP}{2 \times TP + FP + FN}$$

$$MCC = \frac{TP \times TN - FP \times FN}{\sqrt{(TP + FP)(TP + FN)(TN + FP)(TN + FN)}}$$

* TP (true positive) is the number of correctly predicted tunnel requests
* TN (true negative) is the number of correctly predicted legitimate requests
* FP (false positive) is the number of incorrectly predicted tunnel requests
* FN (false negative) is the number of incorrectly predicted legitimate requests

To calculate TP, TN, FP and FN, the results from the predictions from each model will be compared to the actual categories for all of the DNS requests in the test data.

4.4 DNS Tunneling Detection Decision Maker

Since each model can detect DNS tunnels, the detection decision is made using these models. First, the model with the best performance is chosen to be the one-model decision maker. Secondary, we build the multi-model detection decision maker using k models.

* **One-Model Detection Decision Maker.** The best MCC scored model is chosen to be the decision maker, while the other indicators also have good scores.
* **Multi-Model Detection Decision Maker.** In the case where many models perform well, the top k models can be chosen as the multi-model detection decision maker. As we have k models, the MCC scores of each model is represented as m_i, $i \in [1, k]$. For the DNS data d, the final detection decision of the multi-model detection decision maker is made by Algorithm 1.

Algorithm 1. The multi-model detection decision maker

Require:
    the MCC of the k models is represented as m_i, $i \in [1, k]$;
    the DNS query name data d;
    select the threshold α.
1: **for** each $i \in [1, k]$ **do**
2:      the detection decision of the ith model for data d is d_i, $i \in [1, k]$;
        $d_i \in \{0, 1\}$, $d_i = 1$ for tunnel , and $d_i = 0$ for legitimate;
3: **end for**
4: calculate the decision score : $Score = \frac{\sum_1^k (m_i * d_i)}{\sum_1^k m_i}$;
5: **if** $Score >= \alpha$ **then**
6:      **return** the data d is detected as tunnel requests.
7: **else**
8:      **return** the data d is detected as legitimate requests.
9: **end if**

The threshold α defines the probability of being judged as a DNS tunnel. By adjusting the value of α from 0 to 1, we can calculate multi-model detection decision maker's MCC and get the correspondence between the MCC and α. When the MCC reaches the maximum value, we select the α's value as the threshold.

5 Evaluations

5.1 Data Collection

We collect the Alexa-top-1-million websites and extract $772,311$ unique domain names as the legitimate data. As the DNS tunneling data is limited, we build the tunnel data collection architecture, and collect $333,311$ unique DNS tunneling request. Table 4 gives a summary of DNS tunneling tools used in the experiment.

Table 4. DNS tunneling tools

Year	Tunnel tool	Platform
2006	Iodine	Linux, Windows, Mac
2009	dns2tcp	Linux, Windows
2010	dnscat2	Linux, Windows
2015	DNS reverse shell	Linux, Windows

Figure 6 shows the tunnel data collection architecture. We build 4 types of DNS tunnel's clients and servers including iodine, dnscat2, dns2tcp and DNS reverse shell. And we setup a DNS server to resolve the IP addresses of these domains. In addition, we moniter the DNS traffic on the router using a probe. The probe extracts the DNS request and tags tunnel data by IP address.

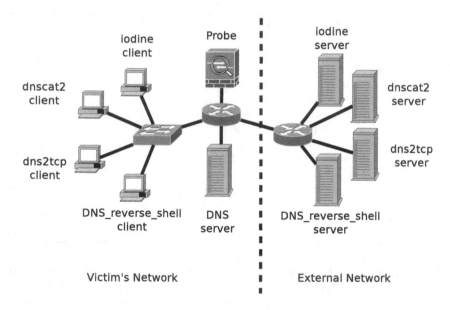

Fig. 6. DNS tunneling data collection architecture

5.2   Experiment

First, We divide the data into 80% training sets and 20% test sets, Fig. 7 shows the distributions of the datasets.

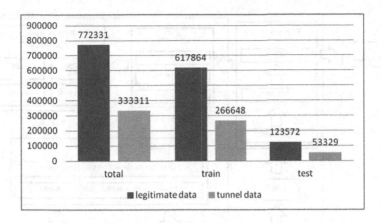

Fig. 7. The distributions of the datasets

These models, built with python and keras, are trained on a Xeon E5-2670 (2.60GHz, 8 cores, 16 threads) workstation. Each model is trained for 20 rounds, and verified with multiple indicators, including Sensitivity (TPR, true positive rate), Accuracy (ACC), Precision (PPV, positive predictive value), F1 score and Matthews correlation coefficient (MCC). In the model verification, each model has been tested for 5 times, and the average of each indicator has been calculated. In the end, we build the DNS tunneling detection system (Fig. 8) for experimental testing and real deployment.

DNS Tunneling Detection System. The system operates as part of a network security system that controls the network traffic. Considering the large volume of data in the real environment, the system is built with open source tools for big data processing.

First, the network traffic is monitored by the open source IDS, Zeek. Zeek can generate logs for different protocols, including the DNS log. Then, Kafka, a distributed streaming platform capable of handling trillions of events a day, is used to provide the log data to the ELK-stack. ELK-stack provides real-time search, analysis and visualization services. Next, the data will be preprocessed and then scored by the models. Afterwards, the Detection decision is made by these deep learning models. In the end, the system will pass the normal DNS request and interrupt tunnel request.

5.3 Results

Table 5 shows the performance of the 4 models, the results of DNN model are 93.04%, 92.04%, 94.04%, 92.54% and 0.9011 for sensitivity, precision, accuracy, F1 score and MCC. The results of 1D-CNN model are 98.36%, 98.63%, 99.88%, 98.01% and 0.9771 for sensitivity, precision, accuracy, F1 score and MCC. In addition, the results of RNN-LSTM model are 95.04%, 97.64%, 99.34%, 96.34%

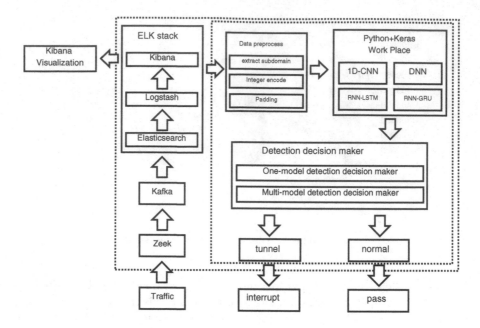

Fig. 8. Phases of the DNS tunneling detection system

and 0.9593 for sensitivity, precision, accuracy, F1 score and MCC. Finally, the results of RNN-GRU model are 94.92%, 97.57%, 99.33%, 96.23% and 0.9569 for sensitivity, precision, accuracy, F1 score and MCC.

Table 5. The performance of the models

Model	DNN	1D-CNN	RNN-LSTM	RNN-GRU
TPR	93.04%	98.36%	95.04%	94.92%
PPV	92.04%	98.63%	97.64%	97.57%
ACC	94.04%	99.88%	99.34%	99.33%
F1	92.54%	98.01%	96.34%	96.23%
MCC	0.9011	0.9771	0.9593	0.9569

As shown in Fig. 9, 4 deep learning models have good performance. In more detail, Fig. 10 shows that 1D-CNN model have the best performance on sensitivity, precision, accuracy, F1 score and MCC. Afterwards, the RNN-LSTM and RNN-GRU have littel differents on performance indecators. DNN model have the worst performance, but the MCC is still over 0.9.

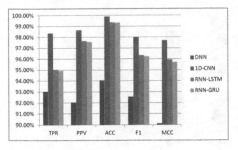

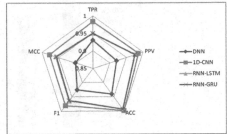

Fig. 9. Results of models: Histogram   **Fig. 10.** Results of models: Radar chart

Since the 1D-CNN model has the best performance among the 4 models, it is chosen to be the one-model decision maker. For the multi-model detection decision maker, we choose the top 3 models, including 1D-CNN, RNN-LSTM and RNN-GRU, then $k = 3$. After adjusting the value of α from 0 to 1, the correspondence between the MCC and α is shown as Fig. 11. When the value of α is around 0.5, the multi-model detection decision maker achieves the best results. It turns out that the value of α can be set to 0.5.

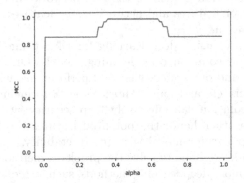

Fig. 11. The correspondence between the MCC and α.

Figure 12 shows the comparison with prior studies. The accuracy of one-model detection decision maker, multi-model detection decision maker, Behavior features based method [10] and Bigram based method [12] is 99.88%, 99.90%, 99.96% and 98.74%.

Comparing the results, we have the better accuracy than the method based on bigram [12]. Additionally, since we don't use the behavior features, we can effectively prevent data exfiltration, and our approach achieves the similar accuracy with the method based on behavior features [10].

In the end, it turns out that deep learning models can achieve good results by learning potential features. What's more, like Asaf Nadler's research [11], we also found McAfee's DNS tunneling data in the real network environment.

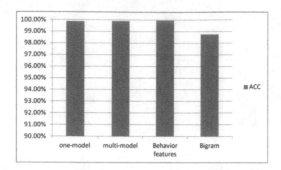

Fig. 12. Comparison with prior research

6   Conclusion

In this paper, we first illustrate the data exfiltration over DNS tunnel. Then, we explain that detecting the malicious payloads from single DNS query is essential for detecting a covert channel before data exfiltration. Accordingly, we propose a DNS tunneling detection method based on deep learning models, and we build a DNS tunneling detection system in the real network environment. Since we don't use the behavior features and network traffic features, we can effectively prevent data exfiltration.

For the first step of using deep learning for DNS tunneling detection, our approach is based on common deep learning models. On the one hand, our solution works well, and our system has good performance with. We can detect DNS tunneling accurately and found McAfee's DNS tunneling data in the real environment. Our solution can effectively help security systems prevent data exfiltration. On the other hand, the potential features are learned by neural networks, thus, deep learning model lacks interpretability.

In the future work, we hope to solve the problems mentioned above. What's more, we will study more deep learning methods, such as model fusion, ensemble learning, transfer learning, etc.

Acknowledgments. We would like to thank the reviewers for their comments. This work was founded by the National Natural Science Foundation of China (61671360, 61672415), the National Key Basic Research Program (2017YFB0801805), the Opening Project of Science and Technology on Communication Networks Laboratory (KX172600024).

References

1. Aiello, M., Mongelli, M., Papaleo, G.: Basic classifiers for DNS tunneling detection. In: 2013 IEEE Symposium on Computers and Communications, ISCC 2013, Split, Croatia, 7–10 July 2013, pp. 880–885 (2013)
2. Almusawi, A., Amintoosi, H.: DNS tunneling detection method based on multilabel support vector machine. Secur. Commun. Netw. **2018**, 6137098:1–6137098:9 (2018)

3. Born, K., Gustafson, D.: Detecting DNS tunnels using character frequency analysis. CoRR abs/1004.4358 (2010)
4. Born, K., Gustafson, D.: NgViz: detecting DNS tunnels through n-gram visualization and quantitative analysis. In: Proceedings of the 6th Cyber Security and Information Intelligence Research Workshop, CSIIRW 2010, Oak Ridge, TN, USA, 21–23 April 2010, p. 47 (2010)
5. Bushart, J., Rossow, C.: DNS unchained: amplified application-layer DoS attacks against DNS authoritatives. In: Bailey, M., Holz, T., Stamatogiannakis, M., Ioannidis, S. (eds.) RAID 2018. LNCS, vol. 11050, pp. 139–160. Springer, Cham (2018). https://doi.org/10.1007/978-3-030-00470-5_7
6. Cho, K., van Merrienboer, B., Bahdanau, D., Bengio, Y.: On the properties of neural machine translation: encoder-decoder approaches. In: Proceedings of SSST@EMNLP 2014, Eighth Workshop on Syntax, Semantics and Structure in Statistical Translation, Doha, Qatar, 25 October 2014, pp. 103–111 (2014)
7. Dagon, D., Antonakakis, M., Day, K., Luo, X., Lee, C.P., Lee, W.: Recursive DNS architectures and vulnerability implications. In: Proceedings of the Network and Distributed System Security Symposium, NDSS 2009, San Diego, California, USA, 8th February–11th February 2009 (2009)
8. Hochreiter, S., Schmidhuber, J.: Long short-term memory. Neural Comput. 9(8), 1735–1780 (1997)
9. Josefsson, S.: The base16, base32, and base64 data encodings. RFC 4648, 1–18 (2006)
10. Liu, J., Li, S., Zhang, Y., Xiao, J., Chang, P., Peng, C.: Detecting DNS tunnel through binary-classification based on behavior features. In: 2017 IEEE Trustcom/BigDataSE/ICESS, Sydney, Australia, 1–4 August 2017, pp. 339–346 (2017)
11. Nadler, A., Aminov, A., Shabtai, A.: Detection of malicious and low throughput data exfiltration over the DNS protocol. Comput. Secur. 80, 36–53 (2019)
12. Qi, C., Chen, X., Xu, C., Shi, J., Liu, P.: A bigram based real time DNS tunnel detection approach. In: Proceedings of the First International Conference on Information Technology and Quantitative Management, ITQM 2013, Dushu Lake Hotel, Sushou, China, 16–18 May 2013, pp. 852–860 (2013)
13. Shafieian, S., Smith, D., Zulkernine, M.: Detecting DNS tunneling using ensemble learning. In: Yan, Z., Molva, R., Mazurczyk, W., Kantola, R. (eds.) NSS 2017. LNCS, vol. 10394, pp. 112–127. Springer, Cham (2017). https://doi.org/10.1007/978-3-319-64701-2_9
14. Wiriyathammabhum, P., Summers-Stay, D., Fermüller, C., Aloimonos, Y.: Computer vision and natural language processing: recent approaches in multimedia and robotics. ACM Comput. Surv. 49(4), 71:1–71:44 (2017)
15. Zang, X., Gong, J., Mo, S., Jakalan, A., Ding, D.: Identifying fast-flux botnet with AGD names at the upper DNS hierarchy. IEEE Access 6, 69713–69727 (2018)

Cryptanalysis of Raindrop and FBC

Bingqing Ren[1,2], Jiageng Chen[1,2(✉)], Shihao Zhou[2], Xiushu Jin[1], Zhe Xia[3], and Kaitai Liang[4]

[1] School of Computer, Central China Normal University, Wuhan, China
chinkako@gmail.com
[2] Central China Normal University Wollongong Joint Institute, Wuhan, China
[3] School of Computer Science, Wuhan University of Technology, Wuhan, China
[4] Department of Computer Science, University of Surrey, Guildford, UK

Abstract. This paper introduces the results of several different security analysis of two new block ciphers: Raindrop and FBC, which are the two candidates of block cipher designs submitted to the Chinese Cryptographic Algorithms Design Competition in 2019. Raindrop applies two-branch Feistel structure, while FBC block cipher is based on the four-way dual Feistel structure design. We give detailed security evaluation on Raindrop and FBC, using differential, linear, impossible difference and boomerang cryptanalysis approaches. For Raindrop, we achieved the results as follows: differential attack on 12-round Raindrop based on the 11-round distinguisher with the computational complexity of $2^{62.41}$; linear attack on 13-round Raindrop based on 12-round distinguisher with the computational complexity of $2^{106.3}$; impossible differential attack on 18-round Raindrop based on 12-round distinguisher with the computational complexity of $2^{102.83}$; and boomerang attack on 15-round Raindrop based on 14-round distinguisher with the computational complexity of $2^{224.6}$. For FBC, results are as follows: differential attack on 12-round FBC based on 11-round distinguisher with the computational complexity of $2^{93.41}$; linear attack on 11-round FBC based on 10-round distinguisher with the computational complexity of $2^{112.54}$; impossible differential attack on 11-round FBC based on 7-round distinguisher with the computational complexity of $2^{94.54}$; and boomerang attack on 13-round FBC based on 12-round distinguisher with the computational complexity of $2^{247.67}$. At present, the best records achieved are 18-round impossible differential attack for Raindrop-128-128 and 13-round boomerang attack for FBC128-256. The statistical distinguishers we built are similar to the proposals but we provide the concrete key recovery attacks in this study.

Keywords: Raindrop · FBC · Differential cryptanalysis · Linear cryptanalysis · Impossible difference cryptanalysis · Boomerang cryptanalysis

1 Introduction

The Chinese Cryptographic Algorithms Design Competition is sponsored by the Chinese Association for Cryptologic Research CACR and directed by the Chinese

© Springer Nature Switzerland AG 2019
J. K. Liu and X. Huang (Eds.): NSS 2019, LNCS 11928, pp. 536–551, 2019.
https://doi.org/10.1007/978-3-030-36938-5_33

Cryptologic Administration. The project calls for various cryptographic designs including the block cipher algorithm designs and public key cipher algorithm designs. The purpose is to prosper the theory and application of cryptography in China; promote the design and implementation of the cryptographic algorithms as well as the growth of cryptographic talents. In total there are 60 proposals in 2019 which were submitted to the competition, including 22 proposals for block cipher algorithm design and 10 block cipher algorithm designs entered the second round of the competition. In this paper, we choose two ciphers Raindrop and FBC which are also two ciphers entered the second round of the competition to investigate their security in detail.

1.1   Raindrop

Raindrop [14] is a two-branch Feistel structure operating on the 128/256 bit length plaintext. Take the 128-bit version as an example, label the 128-bit plaintext from right to left, and the serial number from 0 to 127. 128-bit plaintext is divided into left and right branches in operation. 64–127 bits are the 64-bit state value of the left branch, and 0–63 bits are the 64-bit state value of the right branch, and 256-bit version are similar to 128-bit version. The overall structure of 128-bit block cipher algorithm is shown in Fig. 1 and 256-bit block cipher algorithm is shown in Fig. 2.

Raindrop block cipher contains three versions, Raindrop-128-128, Raindrop-128-256 and Raindrop-256-256. The main parameters can be referred to in Table 1.

Table 1. Parameters of Raindrop family

Version	Length of block	Length of key	Iteration rounds
Raindrop-128-128	128	128	60
Raindrop-128-256	128	256	80
Raindrop-256-256	256	256	100

Encryption Process. The round function RF_{64} of Raindrop-128-128 operates on the 64-bit state, which can be expressed as a 4×4 two-dimensional array, called the state matrix. Given a 64-bit state $p_0 p_2 ... p_{15}$, it can be mapped to a 4×4 state matrix in the following order

$$\begin{Bmatrix} p_0 & p_4 & p_8 & p_{12} \\ p_1 & p_5 & p_9 & p_{13} \\ p_2 & p_6 & p_{10} & p_{14} \\ p_3 & p_7 & p_{11} & p_{15} \end{Bmatrix}$$

For 128-bit version, the length of P_i is donated as $|P_i|$, which satisfies the condition that: when $i = 0, 4, 8, 12, 2, 6, 10, 14$, $|P_i| = 3$; in other cases, $|P_i| = 5$.

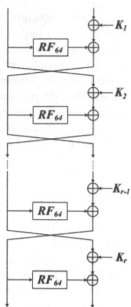

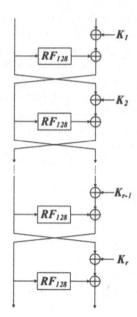

Fig. 1. Raindrop-128-128/256   **Fig. 2.** Raindrop-256-256

Each P_i is called a word, so that 64-bit state can be divided into 16 word combinations. Round function RF_{64} updates the state matrix by three operations in turn: S-box, MixRow and BitRot. The overall structure of the round function is similar to AES's 4×4 matrix encoding arrangement: the non-linear operation acts with each word unit through S-box, and then confuses and diffuses in rows and columns respectively. Similar designs also appear in Rectangle and other block ciphers. The difference is that Raindrop uses two different mixed designs of S-boxes, which was applied in MISTY [11] in a similar way.

1. S-box

   S-boxes are designed from Keccak's S-boxes, which are 3-bit and 5-bit S-boxes, respectively. For k-bit S-boxes, if the input is $(x_{k-1}, x_{k-2}, ..., x_1, x_0)$ and the output is $(y_{k-1}, y_{k-2}, ..., y_1, y_0)$. therefore, $y_i = x_i \oplus (\sim x_{(i-1) \bmod k}) \,\&\, x_{(i-2) \bmod k}$

2. MixRow

   Differential analysis shows that the row mixing operation provides strong diffusivity, and it is specific details as follows. The row mixing matrix is:

$$\begin{bmatrix} 0 & 0 & 1 & 1 \\ 1 & 0 & 0 & 1 \\ 0 & 1 & 0 & 0 \\ 1 & 1 & 0 & 0 \end{bmatrix}$$

Through this matrix right-multiply and state matrix, we can get the values of the mixed rows, which is

$$
\begin{Bmatrix} p_0 \ p_4 \ p_8 \ p_{12} \\ p_1 \ p_5 \ p_9 \ p_{13} \\ p_2 \ p_6 \ p_{10} \ p_{14} \\ p_3 \ p_7 \ p_{11} \ p_{15} \end{Bmatrix}
\times
\begin{bmatrix} 0 & 0 & 1 & 1 \\ 1 & 0 & 0 & 1 \\ 0 & 1 & 0 & 0 \\ 1 & 1 & 0 & 0 \end{bmatrix}
\Rightarrow
\begin{Bmatrix} p_4 \oplus p_{12} & p_8 \oplus p_{12} & p_8 & p_0 \oplus p_4 \\ p_5 \oplus p_{13} & p_9 \oplus p_{13} & p_9 & p_1 \oplus p_5 \\ p_6 \oplus p_{14} & p_{10} \oplus p_{14} & p_{10} & p_2 \oplus p_6 \\ p_7 \oplus p_{15} & p_{11} \oplus p_{15} & p_{11} & p_3 \oplus p_7 \end{Bmatrix}
$$

3. BitRot

The cascade value of column i of the state matrix is $Col_i = p_{4i} \| p_{4i+1} \| p_{4i+2} \|_{4i+3}$, where $0 < i < 3$. For each column, the bit level is cyclically shifted in the following way: Col_0 is unchanged, Col_1 is cyclically 6 bits to the left, Col_2 is cyclically 7 bits to the left, and Col_3 is cyclically 12 bits to the left.

1.2   FBC

FBC [5] is based on a dual Feistel architecture, which supports 128-bit and 256-bit plaintext blocks and 128-bit and 256-bit master keys. It consists of three versions: FBC128-128, FBC128-256 and FBC256-256. The different versions of the algorithm are named by the format $FBCn - m$, where n is the length of plaintext block and m is the length of master key. The states of different versions consist of four w-bit words. The relationship between the length of word w and the length of plaintext block n satisfies $w = n/4$. Let r be the number of iteration rounds. The main parameters can be referred to in Table 2.

Table 2. Parameters of FBC family

Version	Block size n	Master key size m	Word width w	Rounds r
FBC128-128	128	128	32	48
FBC128-256	128	256	32	64
FBC256-256	256	256	64	80

Encryption Process. Firstly, according to the key expansion algorithm, the primary key K is extended to the sub-key sequence $K_i, i = 0, 1, ...2r - 1$.

Secondly, The input plaintext block P is divided into four sub-blocks of w-bit length, namely $P = a_0 \| b_0 \| c_0 \| d_0$. Repeated execution of round function. The input of round function F consists of two w-bit words x and y, and the output is a w-bit word z, $z = F(x, y)$. The specific operation process is in Fig. 3.

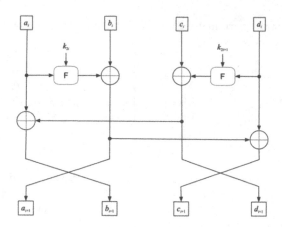

Fig. 3. FBC round function

1.3   Outline of the Paper

In this paper, we evaluate Raindrop and FBC based on four well established approaches. In Sect. 1, we give introductions to the structures of Raindrop and FBC, as well as the comparsions between our results and results of designers on Raindrop and FBC in Table 3. In Sects. 2 and 3, we give detailed security evaluation on Raindrop and FBC respectively: differential, linear, impossible difference and boomerang cryptanalysis. Finally, we present conclusions of our results of the cryptanalysis on Raindrop and FBC in which the best records achieved are 18-ROUND IMPOSSIBLE DIFFERENTIAL attack for Raindrop-128-128 and 12-round differential attack for FBC128-128.

2   Security Analysis of Raindrop

In this paper, we particularly evaluate the two ciphers by applying four well-established cryptanalysis methods, namely, differential attack, linear attack, impossible differential attack and boomerang attack. Differential and Linear cryptanalysis which are proposed by Biham, Shamir [1] and Matsui [8] in 1990s are two of the most widely used cryptanalysis methods. Many ciphers have been broken by these two approaches, and more importantly, they further led to the development of various related analyzing methods. Both approaches require building a statistical distinguisher, which should be significantly different from the uniform distribution. Branch and bound algorithm proposed by Matsui [10] is one of the popular approaches for searching the differential or linear characteristic. Many researches have been focusing on taking advantages of the multiple differential or linear characteristics such as [3] and [7]. As one of the variations of the differential cryptanalysis, impossible differentials was firstly introduced by Knudsen attacking the DEAL cipher in [9]. The idea is using differentials with probability 0 to retrieve the secrete key of block ciphers, and has been successfully applied to ciphers such as AES [4]. The idea of boomerang attack was first

Table 3. Comparsions on Raindrop and FBC

	Distinguisher				Key recovery			
	Raindrop-128-128		FBC128-128		Raindrop-128-128		FBC128-128	
	Ours	[14]	Ours	[6]	Ours	[14]	Ours	[6]
Differential	R:12 D:2^{104}	no valid 32-round or longer differential path	R:11 D:2^{122}	no valid 32-round or longer differential path	R:11+1 D:2^{80} C:$2^{62.41}$	/	R:11+1 D:2^{122} C:$2^{93.41}$	/
Linear	R:16 D:2^{116}	no valid 32-round or longer linear path	R:12 D:2^{120}	no valid 32-round or longer linear path	R:12+1 D:2^{86} C:$2^{106.3}$	/	R:10+1 D:2^{84} C:$2^{112.54}$	/
Impossible Differential	R:12 D:2^{35}	no 13 or more valid 1-1-word impossible differential round	R:7 D:2^{34}	R:7	R:3+12+3 D:2^{127} C:$2^{102.83}$	/	R:2+7+2 D:2^{127} C:$2^{94.54}$	/
Boomerang (Raindrop-128-256) (FBC128-256)	R:14 D:$2^{94.6}$	/	R:12 C:$2^{117.67}$	/	R:14+1 D:$2^{94.6}$ C:$2^{224.6}$	/	R:12+1 D:$2^{117.67}$ C:$2^{247.67}$	/

R: number of rounds, D: data complexity, C: computational complexity

proposed back in 1999 [13]. It is a differential-type attack, but differs from the original form, the cipher is divided into two parts to build the distinguisher. The core idea is that rather than searching for long differential path which is usually very hard, try to combine two short differential paths hoping to get a high probability distinguisher. The well known full round AES attack [2] was based on the boomerang framework. The above four methods are well established ones and have been proven to successfully analyzed many existed block ciphers, thus we select them for our investigation purpose in this paper.

2.1 Differential Cryptanalysis

Differential path searching for Raindrop is carried out by using branch and bound method and the 11 rounds of distinguisher is obtained.
The input difference is:
1 0 0 0 2 0 0 8 0 0 0 0 0 0 0 0 2 0 0 8 0 0 0 0 0 1 0 19 5 6 0 3
The output difference is:
6 4 0 9 0 8 1 0 0 0 0 17 4 22 2 3 0 4 0 2 0 0 0 1 0 4 1 0 4 4 0 0
The total difference probability is 2^{-80}. For key recovery attacks, we also need a set of counter T_δ, each δ corresponds to the value of the target part of the subkeys. In Raindrop's 11th round of ciphertext, there are 4 3-bit subkeys and 6 5-bit subkeys, $K_{11,16}$, $K_{11,17}$, $K_{11,18}$, $K_{11,19}$, $K_{11,20}$, $K_{11,25}$, $K_{11,26}$, $K_{11,28}$, $K_{11,30}$, $K_{11,31}$. Therefore, there are 2^{42} possible values for the target subkeys, and the counter number can be $0, 1, ..., 2^{42} - 1$. For all 2^{80} plaintext pairs ($2^{80} \times 2 = 2^{81}$ plaintext for a given input difference $\triangle m$) (m, c) and (m', c'), where $m \oplus m' = \triangle m$ and $c \oplus c' = \triangle c$, the steps are as follows:

1. If m and m' are found to be error pairs, they are discarded. For example, the 22-bit difference in ciphertext must be 0, and the remaining 42 bits can only take specific values. According to the cryptographic structure and differential distribution table:

The value(s) of $s(X_{11,31})$ can only be 1, 2, 5, 6; The value(s) of $s(X_{11,30})$ can only be 4, 12, 20, 28; The value(s) of $s(X_{11,28})$ can only be 8, 11, 12, 15, 24, 27, 28, 31; The value(s) of $s(X_{11,26})$ can only be 8, 9, 24, 25; The value(s) of $s(X_{11,25})$ can only be 1, 3, 5, 7; The value(s) of $s(X_{11,20})$ can only be 16, 17, 18, 19, 20, 21, 22, 23; The value(s) of $s(X_{11,19})$ can only be 4, 5, 6, 7; The value(s) of $s(X_{11,18})$ can only be 2, 4, 10, 12, 19, 21, 27, 29; The value(s) of $s(X_{11,17})$ can only be 2, 3, 6, 7; The value(s) of $s(X_{11,16})$ can only be 1, 3, 5, 7, 9, 11, 13, 15;

After filtering, there are around 2^{24} possible values of the output differences. Then, for the possible values of 2^{42} target subkeys, the 12th round of ciphertext is decrypted, and the 11th round of ciphertext c_{11} and c_{11}', with a time complexity of 2^{66}. If the differential p probability $c_{11} \oplus c_{11}' = \Delta m_{11}$, the counter with the corresponding subkey value is added one.

2. Determine the counter T_δ, for $0 < \delta < 2^{42} - 1$, with the expected value $N \times p$ (for all N intercepted text pairs (m, c) and (m, c)).

3. Guessing the value of the target partial subkey is δ.

The computation of signal-to-noise ratio SN [1] is as follows:

$SN = m \cdot p / (m \cdot \alpha \cdot \beta / 2^k) = 2^k \cdot p / (\alpha \cdot \beta)$, where m is the number of pairs, α is the average count per counted pair and β is the ratio of the counted to all pairs (i.e., counted and discarded), p is the characteristic's probability and k is the key bits. For Raindrop, $SN = 2^{42} \times 2^{-80} / (1 \times 2^{-64} \times (\frac{4}{16})^6 \times (\frac{8}{16})^4 \times (2^{-4})^{10}) = 2^{34}$.

Therefore, the data complexity of 12 rounds of differential attack based on 11 rounds of Raindrop is around 2^{80} (Data complexity is generally considered to be proportional to $1/p$. Here we estimate it with $1/p$) and the time complexity is around $2^{42} \times 2^{24} / 12 = 2^{66} / 12 = 2^{62.41}$.

2.2   Linear Cryptanalysis

Linear approximation search for Raindrop is carried out by using branch and bound method and the 12 rounds of distinguisher is obtained.

The input mask is:

1 1 0 4 0 0 0 0 0 0 0 0 0 0 0 0 0 0 0 0 0 0 0 0 0 0 5 3 0 16 3 3 0 16

The output mask is:

6 3 0 4 4 0 1 24 0 0 0 0 0 0 0 0 0 0 0 0 0 0 0 0 1 3 0 0 3 1 0 0

According to the piling-up lemma, the total bias is 2^{-43}. Therefore, the data complexity of linear attacks based on 12 rounds of Raindrop is around 2^{86}. For key recovery attacks, we also need a set of counter pairs $T_{0,0}$, ..., $T_{0,\delta-1}$, $T_{1,0}$, ..., $T_{1,\delta-1}$, subscript δ corresponds to the value of the target subkey K_r, and $T_{0,\delta} / T_{1,\delta}$ is its related counter pair. In the 12th round of Raindrop ciphertext, there are 3 3-bit subkeys and 3 5-bit subkey, $K_{12,24}$, $K_{12,25}$, $K_{12,27}$, $K_{12,28}$, $K_{12,30}$, $K_{12,31}$, so there are 2^{24} possible values for the target subkeys.

1. For all plaintext and ciphertext pairs (m, c):
For all possible target partial subkeys, the values are $0, 1, ..., \delta - 1$:
Compute $b = (m \cdot \alpha_0) \oplus (g^{-1}(c, \delta) \cdot \alpha_{r-1})$. If $b = 0$, $T_{0,\delta}$ is added one. Otherwise, $T_{1,\delta}$ is added one. (α_0, α_{r-1}) represents the linear hull of r-1 round and g^{-1} is the encryption algorithm.
2. Determine the maximum value of counter $T_{i,\delta}$ for $0 \leq t \leq \delta - 1$.
3. Guessing $K_r = t$.
Therefore, the data complexity of 13 rounds of linear attack based on 12-round distinguisher of Raindrop is about 2^{86}, and the time complexity is around $2^{86} \times 2^{24}/13 = 2^{106.3}$. Successful probability can be involved by applying the statistical approaches in [12].

2.3 Impossible Difference Cryptanalysis

12 rounds of the impossible differential path are discovered. Based on it, we extend 3 rounds forward and backward to launch the partial subkey recovery attack. In total 18 rounds of Raindrop-128-128 can be attacked.
The input difference is:
00000000000000000000000000000000000000000000000000000000000000000,
00000010000000000000000000000000000000000000000000000000000000000
The output difference is:
00000000000000000000000000000000000000000010000000000000000000000,
00000000000000000000000000000000000000000000000000000000000000000
The input difference of the forward direction is as follows:
R0: 00000000000000000000000000000000000000000000000000000000000000000
   00000010000000000000000000000000000000000000000000000000000000000
The output difference of the forward direction is as follows:
R6: **000********************
   000******************************00000*******0000***********0
The input difference of the backward direction is as follows:
R0: 0000000000000000000000000000000000000000000010000000000000000000000
   00000000000000000000000000000000000000000000000000000000000000000
The output difference of the backward direction is as follows:
R6: ***************************10*1********001*******************
   ****

3 rounds are added at the beginning and the end for the subkey recovery.
1. Choose a 2^{35} plaintext set
000, 00010, ***, 00000, 00*, *****, *10, 00000, 000, 00000, 000, 00000, 000,
00000, 000, 00000
1, ***, ***, 00000, 000, 00000, 000, 00000, 0**, *0000, 000, 00**0, 000,
0**1*, ***, ****0
Among them, 35 bits are non-deterministic, and the rest are deterministic.

Each of these structures can generate approximately 2^{69} plaintext pairs to satisfy the above input differential conditions. Choosing 2^{92} different structure sets can generate about 2^{161} candidate plaintext pairs.

2. After 18 rounds of encryption, for each corresponding ciphertext, the output differential conditions are chosen as follows:

000, 00**1, ***, ***1*, *1*, *****, **0, 0000*, ***, *0000, 000, 0**1*, 000, 0000*, *1*, ****0

000, **100, ***, 00000, 000, 00000, 000, 00000, 000, 00000, 000, 10000, 000, 0000*, *10, 0***0

After screening, it remains $2^{161} \times 2^{-87} = 2^{74}$ qualified candidate plaintext pairs.

3. For each possible guessed 23-bit subkey in the following location(bold):

000, **1**, ***, 00000, 000, **00000**, **000**, 00000, 000, 00000, 000, 100**, 000, 00**1, ***, ***1*

Round 18 is decrypted with the time complexity $T = 2^{97}$.

000, **100, ***, 00000, 000, 00000, 000, 00000, 000, 00000, 000, 10000, 000, 0000*, *10, 0***0

000, 00000, 000, 00000, 000, 00100, **0, 00000, 000, 00000, 000, 00000, 000, 00000, 000, 00000

After screening, it remains $2^{74} \times 2^{-18} = 2^{56}$ qualified candidate plaintext pairs.

4. For each possible guessed 7-bit subkey in the following location(bold):

000, 00000, 000, 00000, 000, **100, ***, 00000, 000, 00000, 000, 00**000**, 000, 00000, 000, 00000

Round 17 is decrypted with the time complexity $T = 2^{86}$.

000, 00000, 000, 00000, 000, 00100, **0, 00000, 000, 00000, 000, 00000, 000, 00000, 000, 00000

000, 00000, 000, 00000, 000, 00000, 000, 00000, 000, 00000, 000, 10000, 000, 00000, 000, 00000

After screening, it remains $2^{56} \times 2^{-5} = 2^{51}$ qualified candidate plaintext pairs.

5. For each possible guessed 2-bit subkey in the following location(bold):

000, 00000, 000, 00000, 000, 00000, 000, 00000, 000, 00000, 000, 100**, 000, 00000, 000, 00000

Round 16 is Encrypted with the time complexity $T = 2^{85}$.

000, 00000, 000, 00000, 000, 00000, 000, 00000, 000, 00000, 000, 10000, 000, 00000, 000, 00000

000, 00000, 000, 00000, 000, 00000, 000, 00000, 000, 00000, 000, 00000, 000, 00000, 000, 00000

After screening, it remains $2^{51} \times 2^{-2} = 2^{49}$ qualified candidate plaintext pairs.

6. For each possible guessed 22-bit subkey in the following location(bold):

000, 0**10, ***, 00000, **1, *****, ***, 00000, 000, 00000, 000, **00000**, 000, 00000, **000**, 00000

Round 1 is encrypted with the time complexity $T = 2^{103}$.

000, 00000, 000, 00000, 000, 00000, 000, 00000, 000, 00000, 000, 00**1, 000, 00000, **1, 00000

000, 00010, ***, 00000, 00*, *****, *10, 00000, 000, 00000, 000, 00000, 000, 00000, 000, 00000

After screening, it remains $2^{49} \times 2^{-15} = 2^{34}$ qualified candidate plaintext pairs.

7. For each possible guessed 9-bit subkey in the following location(bold):

000, 00**000**, 000, 00000, 000, 00000, 000, 00000, 000, 00000, 000, ****1, 000, 00000, ***, 00000

Round 2 is encrypted with the time complexity $T = 2^{97}$.

000, 00010, 000, 00000, 000, 00000, 000, 00000, 000, 00000, 000, 00000, 000, 00000, 000, 00000

000, 00000, 000, 00000, 000, 00000, 000, 00000, 000, 00000, 000, 00**1, 000, 00000, **1, 00000

After screening, it remains $2^{34} \times 2^{-7} = 2^{27}$ qualified candidate plaintext pairs.

8. For each possible guessed 2-bit subkey in the following location(bold):

000, 0******10, 000, 00000, 000, 00000, 000, 00000, 000, 00000, 000, 00000, 000, 00000, 000, 00000

Round 3 is encrypted with the time complexity $T = 2^{92}$.

000, 00000, 000, 00000, 000, 00000, 000, 00000, 000, 00000, 000, 00000, 000, 00000, 000, 00000

000, 00010, 000, 00000, 000, 00000, 000, 00000, 000, 00000, 000, 00000, 000, 00000, 000, 00000

9. If there is still no difference to satisfy plaintext pairs, then the 65-bits sub-key must have guessed incorrectly. Delete it from the candidate subkey table. If the candidate subkey table is not empty after analyzing all the remaining plaintext pairs, the remaining sub-key in the table is output as the correct subkeys.

For each possible candidate sub-key in step 8, the possibility of satisfying the filtering condition is 2^{-2}. Therefore, the probability of retaining the wrong subkey after step 7 is $(1 - 2^{-2})^{2^{27}}$. Next, we hope that after all the filtering conditions, the number of erroneous sub-keys is $2^{65} \times (1 - 2^{-2})^{2^{27}}$, which is far less than 1, and the only correct subkey will be output. Data and time complexity assessments for the attack is shown as follows. Firstly, 2^{92} structures are chosen, and the data complexity is $2^{92} \times 2^{35} = 2^{127}$ chosen plaintext. The time complexity is mainly composed of step 6, which requires 2^{103} S-boxes. Therefore, the time complexity of the attack is about $2 \times 2^{103} \times (1/16) \times (1/18) = 2^{102.83}$ of 18 rounds of Raindrop.

2.4 Boomerang Cryptanalysis

Boomerang Cryptanalysis is not effective for 128-bit key recovery attacks, so the following analysis focuses on the 256-bit key version. Based on the differential path analysis in differential analysis, we find that the active S-box of Raindrop-128-256 has a great improvement after 8 rounds (10 active S-boxes for 7 rounds of optimal path, 17 active S-boxes for 8 rounds). At present, the best specific differential path we get is 12 rounds. However, the path below 8 rounds can be optimized by the algorithm, so it can be inferred that dividing the differential path into two shorter paths can help to construct a more effective distinguisher than the single long path, and is superior to the differential analysis (non-theoretical security bound estimation) in specific case attacks. Here we use two paths to construct a distinguisher of 14 rounds (a combination of 7 rounds and 7 rounds):

Difference(input): 0 0 0 0 2 0 0 0 0 0 0 0 0 0 0 0 0 0 0 0 2 0 0 0 0 1 0 0 0 0 0 0

Difference(output): 0 0 0 0 2 0 0 0 0 0 0 0 0 0 0 0 0 0 0 0 2 0 0 0 0 1 0 0 0 0 0 0

In the 2 seven-round differential paths, 256 paths with 2^{-20} probability, 44288 paths with 2^{-24} probability are obtained. Suppose $\hat{p} = \sqrt{\sum_\beta Pr^2[\alpha \to \beta]}$ is the first phase probability and $\hat{q} = \sqrt{\sum_\gamma Pr^2[\gamma \to \delta]}$ is the second phase probability. Therefore, Effective distinguisher requires $(\hat{p} \cdot \hat{q})^2 > 2^{-128}$. From the above paths, we can get $(\hat{p} \cdot \hat{q}) = 2^{-61.2} > 2^{-128}$ and construct 14 rounds of specific distinguisher with better effect than differential attack. Data complexity is approximately $N = 2^{n/2}/pq = 2^{94.6}$.

The key recovery steps are as follows:

1. Guess the last round key K.

2. For all N-pair ciphertext (C_1, C_2), decrypt $D_k(C1) \oplus \delta$ and $D_k(C2) \oplus \delta$ and store it in a table (N rows in total), where D is one-round decryption algorithm.

3. For all N-pair ciphertext (C_3, C_4), decrypt $D_k(C3)$ and $D_k(C2)$ and find a match in the table in step 2.

4. If there is a match, the guessed key may be correct. The computational complexity of key recovery is around $N \times \#k \times 4 = 2^{94.6} \times 2^{128} \times 4 = 2^{224.6} < 2^{256}$.

3   Security Analysis for FBC

3.1   Differential Cryptanalysis

Differential path searching for FBC is carried out by using branch and bound method and the 11 rounds of distinguisher is obtained.

The input difference is:

0 0 0 0 0 0 0 0 0 0 0 0 0 0 0 0 4 1 0 0 2 0 0 0 0 0 0 0 2 0 0 0

The output difference is:

6 e a 4 3 5 2 0 0 5 9 8 5 0 0 2 8 c 2 0 0 6 2 0 2 2 9 2 3 2 8 6

The total difference probability is 2^{-122}. For key recovery attacks, we also need a set of counter T_δ, each δ corresponds to the value of the target part of the subkeys. In FBC's 11th round of ciphertext, there are 16 4-bit sub-keys, $K_{11,0}$, $K_{11,1}$, $K_{11,2}$, $K_{11,3}$, $K_{11,4}$, $K_{11,5}$, $K_{11,6}$, $K_{11,7}$, $K_{11,24}$, $K_{11,25}$, $K_{11,26}$, $K_{11,27}$, $K_{11,28}$, $K_{11,29}$, $K_{11,30}$, $K_{11,31}$. Therefore, there are 2^{64} possible values for the target subkeys, and the counter number can be $0, 1, ..., 2^{64} - 1$. For all 2^{122} plaintext pairs ($2^{122} \times 2 = 2^{123}$ plaintext for a given input difference $\triangle m$) (m, c) and (m', c'), where $m \oplus m' = \triangle m$ and $c \oplus c' = \triangle c$, the steps are as follows:

1. If m and m' are found to be error pairs, they are discarded; for example, according to the cryptographic structure and differential distribution table:

The value(s) of $s(X_{11,31})$ can only be 1, 4, c, d; The value(s) of $s(X_{11,30})$ can only be 3, 7, 8, 9, a, d; The value(s) of $s(X_{11,29})$ can only be 2, 4, 5, 7, 9, a, b, c; The value(s) of $s(X_{11,28})$ can only be 2, 6, a, e; The value(s) of $s(X_{11,27})$ can only be 3, 7, 8, 9, a, d; The value(s) of $s(X_{11,26})$ can only be 2, 3, 4, 5, 9, a, c, f; The value(s) of $s(X_{11,25})$ can only be 3, 7, 8, 9, a, d; The value(s) of $s(X_{11,24})$ can only be 2, 6, a, e; The value(s) of $s(X_{11,7})$ can only be 3, 4, 7, b, c, f; The value(s) of $s(X_{11,6})$ can only be 0; The value(s) of $s(X_{11,5})$ can only be 3, 7, 8, 9, d, e; The value(s) of $s(X_{11,4})$ can only be 2, 3, 6, 7, a, b, e, f; The value(s) of $s(X_{11,3})$ can only be 0; The value(s) of $s(X_{11,2})$ can only be 1, 3, 5, 7, b, f; The value(s) of $s(X_{11,1})$ can only be 2, 4, 5, 7, 9, a, b, c; The value(s) of $s(X_{11,0})$ can only be 0;

After filtering, there are around 2^{33} possible values of the output differences. Then, for the possible values of 2^{64} target subkeys, the 12th round of ciphertext is decrypted, and the 11th round of ciphertext c_{11} and c_{11}', with a time complexity of 2^{93}. If the differential p probability $c_{11} \oplus c_{11}' = \Delta m_{11}$, the counter with the corresponding subkey value is added one.

2. Determine the counter T_δ, for $0 < \delta < 2^{64} - 1$, with the expected value $N \times p$ (for all N intercepted text pairs (m,c) and (m,c)).

3. Guessing the value of the target partial subkey is δ.

The computation of signal-to-noise ratio SN [1] ia as follows:

$SN = 2^{64} \times 2^{-122} / (1 \times 2^{-64} \times (\frac{4}{16})^3 \times (\frac{6}{16})^6 \times (\frac{8}{16})^4 \times (\frac{1}{16})^3 \times (2^{-4})) = 2^{40.46}$

Therefore, the data complexity of 12 rounds of differential attack based on 11 rounds of FBC is around 2^{122}(Data complexity is generally considered to be proportional to $1/p$. Here we estimate it with $1/p$) and the time complexity is around $2^{64} \times 2^{33}/12 = 2^{97}/12 = 2^{93.41}$.

3.2 Linear Cryptanalysis

Linear approximation search for FBC is carried out by using branch and bound method and the 10 rounds of distinguisher is obtained.

The input mask is:

0 0 0 0 0 0 0 0 0 0 0 0 0 0 0 0 0 0 0 2 0 8 0 1 0 0 0 0 0 0 0 1

The output mask is:

0 0 2 0 8 0 1 0 0 1 0 1 1 0 0 1 8 2 2 8 e 0 1 4 0 1 0 1 5 0 1 5

According to the piling-up lemma, the total bias is 2^{-42}. Therefore, the data complexity of linear attacks based on 11 rounds of FBC is around 2^{84}. For key recovery attacks, we also need a set of counter pairs $T_{0,0}$, ..., $T_{0,\delta-1}$, $T_{1,0}$, ..., $T_{1,\delta-1}$, subscript δ corresponds to the value of the target subkey K_r, and $T_{0,\delta}/T_{1,\delta}$ is its related counter pair. In the 10th round of FBC ciphertext, there are eight 4-bit subkey, $K_{10,0}$, $K_{10,1}$, $K_{10,3}$, $K_{10,4}$, $K_{10,6}$, $K_{10,25}$, $K_{10,27}$, $K_{10,29}$, so there are 2^{32} possible values for the target subkeys.

1. For all plaintext and ciphertext pairs (m,c):

For all possible target partial subkeys, the values are $0, 1, ..., \delta - 1$:

Compute $b = (m \cdot \alpha_0) \oplus (g^{-1}(c,\delta) \cdot \alpha_{r-1})$ If $b = 0$, $T_{0,\delta}$ is added one. Otherwise, $T_{1,\delta}$ is added one. (α_0, α_{r-1}) represents the linear hull of $r - 1$ round and g^{-1} is the encryption algorithm.

2. Determine the maximum value of counter $T_{i,\delta}$ for $0 \le t \le \delta - 1$.

3. Guessing $K_r = t$.

Therefore, the data complexity of 11 rounds of linear attack based on 10-round distinguisher of FBC is about 2^{84}, and the time complexity is around $2^{84} \times 2^{32}/11 = 2^{112.54}$. Successful probability can be involved by applying the statistical approaches in [12].

3.3 Impossible Difference Cryptanalysis

7 rounds of the impossible differential path are discovered. Based on it, we extend 2 rounds forward and backward to lanch the partial subkey recovery attack. In total 11 rounds of FBC128-128 can be attacked.

The input difference is:

000000000000000000000000000000000000000000000000000000000000000000000000,
000000000010000000000000000000000000000000000000000000000000000000000000

The output difference is:

001000000000000000000000000000000000000000000000000000000000000000000000,
000000000000000000000000000000000000000000000000000000000000000000000000

The input difference of the forward direction is as follows:

R0: 000000000000000000000000000000000000000000000000000000000000000000000000
     000000000010000000000000000000000000000000000000000000000000000000000000

The output difference of the forward direction is as follows:

R4: *0000000*************000**
     *0000000*************000**

The input difference of of the backward direction is as follows:

R0: 001000000000000000000000000000000000000000000000000000000000000000000000
     000000000000000000000000000000000000000000000000000000000000000000000000

The output difference of the backward direction is as follows:

R4: *************000*********0000000************************************
     ****

2 rounds are added at the beginning and the end for the subkey recovery.

1. Choose a 2^{34} plaintext set

000000000010000000000000000000000000000000**10000000000000000****1
*0000000*************000********00000000**10000000000000000****1

Among them, 34 bits are non-deterministic (0/1), and the rest are deterministic.

Each of these structures can generate approximately 2^{67} plaintext pairs to satisfy the above input differential conditions. Choosing 2^{93} different structure sets can generate about 2^{160} candidate plaintext pairs.

2. After 10 rounds of encryption, for each corresponding ciphertext, the output differential conditions are chosen as follows:

*************000*********0000000**00000000000000000****000000000
*************000*********0000000**10000000000000000****100000000

After screening, it remains $2^{160} \times 2^{-71} = 2^{89}$ qualified candidate plaintext pairs.

3. For each possible guessed 12-bit subkey in the following location(bold):
S1: ****000000000000********00000000 S2: 0000000000000000000000000
00000000
Round 9 is decrypted with the time complexity $T = 2^{101}$.
10000000000000000**1000000000010000000000000000000000000000000
10000000000000000**10000000000000000000000000000000000000000000
After screening, it remains $2^{89} \times 2^{-12} = 2^{77}$ qualified candidate plaintext pairs.

4. For each possible guessed 2-bit subkey in the following location(bold):
S1: **10000000000000000000000000000000 S2: 0000000000000000000000000
00000000
Round 8 is decrypted with the time complexity $T = 2^{79}$.
0010000000000000000000000000000000000000000000000000000000000000000
0000000000000000000000000000000000000000000000000000000000000000000
After screening, it remains $2^{77} \times 2^{-2} = 2^{75}$ qualified candidate plaintext pairs.

5. For each possible guessed 14-bit subkey in the following location(bold):
S1:   00000000**1000000000000000000000   S2:   00000000****000000000
000********
Round 1 is encrypted with the time complexity $T = 2^{89}$.
0000000000000000000000000000000000000000000000000000000000000000000
00000000**1000000000000000****10000000000010000000000000000000000000
After screening, it remains $2^{75} \times 2^{-14} = 2^{61}$ qualified candidate plaintext pairs.

6. For each possible guessed 2-bit subkey in the following location(bold):
S1:
0000000000000000000000000000000000 S2: 00000000**1000000000000000000000
000
Round 2 is encrypted with the time complexity $T = 2^{63}$.
0000000000000000000000000000000000000000000000000000000000000000000
0000000000100000000000000000000000000000000000000000000000000000000
After screening, it remains $2^{63} \times 2^{-2} = 2^{61}$ qualified candidate plaintext pairs.

7. If there is still no difference to satisfy plaintext pairs, then the 30-bits sub-key must have guessed incorrectly. Delete it from the candidate subkey table. If the candidate subkey table is not empty after analyzing all the remaining plaintext pairs, the remaining sub-key in the table is output as the correct subkeys.

For each possible candidate sub-key in step 6, the possibility of satisfying the filtering condition is 2^{-2}. Therefore, the probability of retaining the wrong subkey after step 7 is $(1 - 2^{-2})^{2^{61}}$. Next, we hope that after all the filtering conditions, the number of erroneous sub-keys is $2^{30} \times (1 - 2^{-2})^{2^{61}}$, which is far less than 1, and the only correct subkey will be output. Data and time complexity assessments for the attack is shown as follows. Firstly, 2^{93} structures are chosen, and the data complexity is $2^{93} \times 2^{34} = 2^{127}$ chosen plaintext. The time complexity is mainly composed of step 3, which requires 2^{101} S-boxes. Therefore, the time complexity of the attack is about

$2 \times 2^{101} \times (1/16) \times (1/11) = 2^{94.54}$ of 11 rounds of FBC (16 is the number of one-round S-boxes).

3.4 Boomerang Cryptanalysis

Boomerang Cryptanalysis is not effective for 128-bit key recovery attacks, so the following analysis focuses on the 256-bit key version. Based on the differential path analysis, we find that the best specific differential path obtained by FBC128-256 is 10 rounds. The path below 5 rounds can be optimized by the algorithm, so it can be inferred that dividing the differential path into two shorter paths can help to construct a more effective distinguisher than the single long path, and is superior to differential analysis (non-theoretical security bound estimation) in specific case attacks. Here we use two paths to construct a distinguisher of 12 rounds (a combination of 6 rounds and 6 rounds):

Difference(input): 0 0 0 0 0 0 0 0 0 0 0 0 0 0 0 0 0 1 0 0 0 2 0 8 0 1 0 0 0 0 0 0

Difference(output): 0 0 0 0 0 0 0 0 0 0 0 0 0 0 0 0 0 1 0 0 0 2 0 8 0 1 0 0 0 0 0 0

In the 2 six-round differential paths, 4096 paths with 2^{-34} probability, 204800 paths with 2^{-36} probability and 966656 paths with 2^{-38} probability are obtained. Suppose $\hat{p} = \sqrt{\sum_\beta Pr^2[\alpha \to \beta]}$ is the first phase probability and $\hat{q} = \sqrt{\sum_\gamma Pr^2[\gamma \to \delta]}$ is the second phase probability. Therefore, Effective distinguisher requires $(\hat{p} \cdot \hat{q})^2 > 2^{-128}$ From the above paths, we can get $(\hat{p} \cdot \hat{q}) = 2^{-107.34} > 2^{-128}$ and construct 12 rounds of specific distinguisher with better effect than differential attack. Data complexity is approximately $N = 2^{n/2}/pq = 2^{117.67}$. The key recovery steps as follow:

1. Guess the last round key K.
2. For all N-pair ciphertext (c_1, c_2), decrypt $D_k(C1) \oplus \delta$ and $D_k(C2) \oplus \delta$ and store it in a table (N rows in total), where D is one-round decryption algorithm.
3. For all N-pair ciphertext (c_3, c_4), decrypt and find a match in the table in step 2.
4. If there is a match, the guessed key may be correct. The computational complexity of key recovery is around $N \times \#k \times 4 = 2^{117.67} \times 2^{128} \times 4 = 2^{247.67} < 2^{256}$.

4 Conclusion

Among the four classical attacks, we have found no design vulnerabilities of Raindrop. For 60 rounds of security parameters of Raindrop-128-128, the optimal number of rounds can be attacked at present is 18 rounds. Although there is room for optimization and improvement, it is still sufficient security margin. Due to the use of S-boxes with different structures, the efficiency of the algorithm has been greatly sacrificed, and the more conservative 60 rounds of security parameter settings make the algorithm less competitive in computing speed. Also, through a number of attack analysis, the best attack for FBC128-128 key version can achieve 12 rounds effectively based on 11-round distinguisher. For boomerang attacks, we analyze the 256-bit key version, and we can build 12-round distinguisher to attack 13 rounds effectively. Generally speaking, we have not found any loopholes in the design. For the security parameters given by the design, the best records achieved are 18-round impossible differential attack for Raindrop and 13-round boomerang attack for FBC which are more effective and concrete on more cryptanalysis methods comparing the results of designers. Although there is room for improvement, the security boundary is still sufficient.

Acknowledgement. This work has been partly supported by the National Natural Science Foundation of China under Grant No. 61702212 and the Fundamental Research Funds for the Central Universities under Grand No. CCNU19TS017.

References

1. Biham, E., Shamir, A.: Differential cryptanalysis of des-like cryptosystems. In: Conference on the Theory and Application of Cryptography (1990)
2. Biryukov, A., Khovratovich, D.: Related-key cryptanalysis of the full AES-192 and AES-256. In: Matsui, M. (ed.) ASIACRYPT 2009. LNCS, vol. 5912, pp. 1–18. Springer, Heidelberg (2009). https://doi.org/10.1007/978-3-642-10366-7_1
3. Blondeau, C., Gérard, B., Nyberg, K.: Multiple differential cryptanalysis using, and X^2 statistics. In: Visconti, I., De Prisco, R. (eds.) SCN 2012. LNCS, vol. 7485, pp. 343–360. Springer, Heidelberg (2012). https://doi.org/10.1007/978-3-642-32928-9_19
4. Cheon, J.H., Kim, M.J., Kim, K., Jung-Yeun, L., Kang, S.W.: Improved impossible differential cryptanalysis of rijndael and crypton. In: Kim, K. (ed.) ICISC 2001. LNCS, vol. 2288, pp. 39–49. Springer, Heidelberg (2002). https://doi.org/10.1007/3-540-45861-1_4
5. Feng, X., Zeng, X., Zhang, F., Zeng, G., Tang, D., Gan, G.: Block cipher algorithm FBC (2019)
6. Feng, X., Zeng, X., Zhang, F., Zeng, G., Tang, D., Gan, G.: The report of design and evaluation of block cipher algorithm FBC (2019)
7. Hermelin, M., Cho, J.Y., Nyberg, K.: Multidimensional linear cryptanalysis of reduced round serpent. In: Mu, Y., Susilo, W., Seberry, J. (eds.) ACISP 2008. LNCS, vol. 5107, pp. 203–215. Springer, Heidelberg (2008). https://doi.org/10.1007/978-3-540-70500-0_15
8. Howard, R.: Data encryption standard. Comput. Secur. **6**(3), 195–196 (1987)
9. Knudsen, L.: Deal-a 128-bit block cipher. Complexity **258**(2), 216 (1998)
10. Matsui, M.: On correlation between the order of S-boxes and the strength of DES. In: De Santis, A. (ed.) EUROCRYPT 1994. LNCS, vol. 950, pp. 366–375. Springer, Heidelberg (1995). https://doi.org/10.1007/BFb0053451
11. Ohta, H., Matsui, M.: A description of the MISTY1 encryption algorithm. RFC2994, November (2000)
12. Selçuk, A.A.: On probability of success in linear and differential cryptanalysis. J. Cryptology **21**(1), 131–147 (2008)
13. Wagner, D.: The boomerang attack. In: Knudsen, L. (ed.) FSE 1999. LNCS, vol. 1636, pp. 156–170. Springer, Heidelberg (1999). https://doi.org/10.1007/3-540-48519-8_12
14. Wang, M., Li, Y., Li, M., Fu, Y., Fan, Y., Huang, L.: Raindrop series block cipher algorithms design proposal (2019)

Attribute-Based Encryption with Publicly Verifiable Outsourced Decryption

Hui Zheng[1], Jun Shao[1(✉)], Guiyi Wei[1], Li Hu[2], Bianjing Pan[1], Kai Liu[1], and Xiaohang Mao[1]

[1] School of Computer and Information Engineering, Zhejiang Gongshang University, Hangzhou, China
zh312934@gmail.com, chn.junshao@gmail.com
[2] School of Computer Science and Cyber Engineering, Guangzhou University, Guangzhou, China

Abstract. Attribute-based encryption (ABE) is a useful cryptographic primitive for access control and fine-grained sharing on encrypted data. However, the main drawback of ABE is that the computational cost grows linearly with the complexity of the access policy. One of the promising solutions for the problem is to outsource computation securely. For example, the decryptor can outsource most of the decryption cost to others, while the underlying plaintext remains confidential. Nonetheless, the existing ABE with outsourced decryption cannot either outsource the decryption of existing ABE ciphertexts or support public verifiability. The first shortcoming demands that we need to design particular outsourced decryption for each ABE scheme. The second one hinders the use of ABE (with outsourced decryption) in the untrusted environment. To solve the above two problems, we propose a generic method to transform any ABE scheme (based on pairings) into an ABE scheme with publicly verifiable outsourced decryption. With the assumptions that the underlying ABE scheme is secure and that the one executing the outsourced decryption is rational, our proposal is secure.

Keywords: ABE · Outsourced decryption · Public verifiability · Game theory

1 Introduction

With the development of information technology, more and more data are generated each day, which intensively increases the difficulty for individuals to store these vast data locally. Among the solutions for this problem, the cloud storage is considered as the most economical and accessible one [38]. However, cloud servers are not always trusted. For example, they could be corrupted by attacks or mistakes [1]. Storing data in these cloud servers may lead the privacy and access control issues [33]. Encrypting the data before uploading them to the cloud could be a promising solution. Nevertheless, traditional encryption schemes are not

© Springer Nature Switzerland AG 2019
J. K. Liu and X. Huang (Eds.): NSS 2019, LNCS 11928, pp. 552–566, 2019.
https://doi.org/10.1007/978-3-030-36938-5_34

suitable for flexible data sharing or fine-grained access control. To address the above issue, a new cryptographic primitive named attribute-based encryption (ABE) was put forth by Sahai and Waters [35]. In such a scheme, only the one whose attribute set satisfies the access policy has the right key to decrypt the corresponding ciphertext. Since then, many ABE schemes with different properties have been proposed [9,14,18,22,23,26,27,36]. Usually speaking, ABE schemes can be categorized into ciphertext-policy ABE (CP-ABE) and key-policy ABE (KP-ABE) [11]. The former one associates the access policy directly with ciphertexts, while the latter one combines the access policy with the decryption key.

However, an unavoidable drawback of the traditional ABE schemes is their high computational cost. Specifically, ABE schemes usually employ a time-consuming operation named pairing, and its number of executions is in direct proportion to the complexity of access policy. This shortcoming hinders applications of ABE in resource-constrained devices such as mobile devices. To deal with this problem, Green et al. [13] proposed the concept of ABE with outsourced decryption (ABE-OD). In this kind of ABE, the decryptor delegates his/her partial decryption capability to a proxy (e.g., cloud server) with a transformation key. After the proxy's computation, the original decryptor will get a simple ElGamal-type ciphertext, which can be decrypted easily. The security of ABE-OD guarantees that the proxy cannot reveal the underlying plaintext during the whole transformation process. Following the idea of the transformation key, many new ABE-OD schemes with different security levels and efficiency levels have been proposed [21,24,25,30,32,34]. Nevertheless, the current ABE-OD schemes have the following weaknesses more or less.

- Some outsourced decryption algorithms are only designed for some specific ABE schemes, which requires new encryption algorithms. In this case, we have to design outsourced decryption algorithm for each ABE scheme; even worse, some of existing ABE ciphertexts cannot be outsourced for decryption.
- The existing ABE-OD schemes can only allow the original decryptor to check whether the third party returns the right transformed ciphertext. What is worse, once the dispute happens, the original decryptor should reveal his/her decryption key to the arbiter. Hence, the public verifiability is demanded in ABE-OD.

In this paper, we propose a generic construction for transforming any ABE scheme to an ABE-OD scheme with public verifiability by combining the transformation key and sampling techniques. As that in [13], the transformation key is used to realize the outsourced decryption. The sampling technique is applied to achieve public verifiability without changing the original encryption algorithm. In particular, the proxy will return a set of pairing results instead of an ElGamal-type ciphertext, and the verifier will randomly choose some pairing results to check. With the help of game theory, we can conclude that the rational proxy will always return the correct result if the related parameters are configured properly. A comparison between our proposal and some representative ABE-OD schemes in terms of efficiency and functionality is given in Table 1.

Table 1. The comparison between our proposal and previous schemes.

Scheme	Computational cost		Functionality	
	Proxy[a]	Original decryptor[b]	Public verifiability	Generic construction
GHW11 [13]	1	1	×	✓
LDG+13 [21]	≈2	≈2	×	×
LHL+14 [25]	≈2	≈1	×	×
QDL+15 [34]	≈1	≈1	×	×
LZM+15 [30]	≈1	≈1	×	×
MLM+16 [32]	≈1	≈1	×	✓
Our Proposal	≈1	≈1	✓	✓

[a]In terms of original decryption cost.
[b]In terms of ElGamal-type ciphertext decryption cost.

Organization: The remainder of this paper is organized as follows. In Sect. 2, we review the related works. Then, we give some preliminaries in Sect. 3, including the definition and the security model of ABE-OD schemes. In Sect. 4, we depict a generic construction of ABE-OD with public verifiability, then, we instantiate our construction, including a CP-ABE scheme and a KP-ABE scheme, and we give an analysis of the schemes. In Sect. 5, we have a short conclusion.

2   Related Work

Since ABE-OD can enhance the efficiency of ABE significantly, ABE-OD has received considerable attention from academia. As mentioned before, most of the current ABE-OD schemes [13,21,24,28,30,32,34,39] follow the idea of transformation key. There also exist other techniques for outsourced computation, such as replica-based [4–6], and blockchain-based [3,7,19,20,29]. However, none of them can be directly applied to constructing ABE-OD with public verifiability.

2.1   ABE-OD

At NDSS 2011, Green et al. [13] proposed the concept of ABE-OD to solve the efficiency problem of ABE. A generic method for transforming any ABE scheme into an ABE-OD scheme is also given. However, the resulting ABE-OD schemes can only support private verifiability. Almost at the same time, Zhou and Huang [40] also analyzed the outsourced decryption in ABE, but they did not consider the verifiability problem. Lai et al. [21] formally studied the verifiability in ABE-OD for the first time, but only the private verifiability is achieved. Furthermore, their scheme required a new encryption algorithm and two ElGame-type decryptions for the original decryptor. Following [21], Qin et al. [34] and Lin et al. [30] proposed two more efficient ABE-OD schemes while inheriting the first shortcomings of the scheme in [21]. Later on, Mao et al. [32]

proposed a generic method to transform any CPA-secure ABE-OD scheme into a CPA-secure or RCCA-secure construction with private verifiability. Xu et al. [39] proposed a publicly verifiable CP-ABE outsourced decryption scheme by using multi-linear pairing. However, Li et al. [24] pointed out that their scheme is not feasible and proposed a new public verifiable ABE-OD scheme. Unfortunately, the scheme is later broken by Liao et al. [28]. Zuo et al. [41] proposed the CCA security model for ABE-OD recently.

2.2 Replica-Based Outsourced Computation

The basic idea of the replica-based schemes is to outsource the computing task to two or more servers, and the verifiability is achieved by cross-checking the results returned from the servers. Based on refereed games [8], Canetti et al. [4] constructed an interactive verifiable computation scheme with multiple servers. Later on, they [5] proposed another protocol for any log-space uniform numerical control circuit with statistical soundness by extending the arithmetization techniques [10]. A more efficient protocol was proposed later in [6]. However, all the above schemes are feasible only with the assumption that the servers will not collude with each other.

2.3 Blockchain-Based Outsourced Computation

Blockchain is considered as such a system that allows mutual distrusted entities to build trust relationship among them. Hence, it is natural to use blockchain to realize the verifiability. By using Bitcoin, Kumaresan et al. [20] proposed a verifiable outsourced computation protocol with results timely delivery and fair payment. The main idea in this protocol is that each participant should firstly pay deposits that will be returned if the checking process passes. Campanelli et al. [3] defined zero-knowledge contingent service payment to realize service payment based on blockchains. However, their scheme lacks design details, and its efficiency needs to be improved. Based on game theory and smart contract, Dong et al. [7] proposed a very efficient verifiable outsourced computation protocol. However, two non-colluded servers are required in their solution. Huang et al. [16] proposed a blockchain-based outsourced computation solution based on commitment-based sampling, but it required a trusted third-party. Krol et al. [19] proposed an efficient and secure blockchain-based outsourced computation solution by using trusted hardware. Hu et al. [15] constructed a fair and searchable system with privacy protection by using the smart contract. Lin et al. [29] studied how to use blockchain to secure outsourcing bilinear pairings. However, none of the existing blockchain-based schemes could directly support ABE-OD.

3 Preliminaries

In this section, we briefly review the basic knowledge related to our proposal, including bilinear pairing, access structure and linear secret sharing schemes (LSSS).

3.1   Bilinear Maps

Let $\mathbb{G}_1$, $\mathbb{G}_2$, and $\mathbb{G}_T$ be cyclic groups of prime order p, and g_1 and g_2 be generators of $\mathbb{G}_1$ and $\mathbb{G}_2$, respectively. The bilinear map $e : \mathbb{G}_1 \times \mathbb{G}_2 = \mathbb{G}_T$ satisfies the following properties:

1. Bilinearity: For a, $b \in \mathbb{Z}_p$, we have $e(g_1^a, g_2^b) = e(g_1, g_2)^{ab}$.
2. Non-degeneracy: $e(g_1, g_2) \neq 1$.
3. Computability: There exists an efficient algorithm to compute $e(g_1, g_2)$.

3.2   Access Structure

Let $\{P_1, P_2, \cdots, P_n\}$ be a set of parties. If $\mathbb{A} \subseteq 2^{\{P_1, P_2, \cdots, P_n\}}$ and $\forall B, C$ satisfy if $B \in \mathbb{A}$ and $B \subseteq C$ then $C \in \mathbb{A}$, then we say $\mathbb{A}$ is monotone. An access structure is a collection of non-empty subsets of $\{P_1, P_2, \cdots, P_n\}$, i.e., $\mathbb{A} \subseteq 2^{\{P_1, P_2, \cdots, P_n\}} \setminus \{\emptyset\}$. Correspondingly, the unauthorized set is the one not in $\mathbb{A}$. In this paper, we assume that the role of the parties is determined by its attribute set. As a result, the access structure $\mathbb{A}$ is a collection of non-empty subset of attributes. For simplicity, we only consider the monotone access structure in this paper.

3.3   Linear Secexet Sharing Schemes (LSSS)

A secret sharing scheme [2] Π over a set of parties $\{P_1, P_2, \cdots, P_n\}$ is called linear (over $\mathbb{Z}_p$) if it satisfies the following two properties:

1. The shares of parties form a vector over $\mathbb{Z}_p$.
2. Assume M is a share-generating matrix for Π with ℓ rows and n columns, and for $i = 1, \cdots, \ell$, $\rho(i)$ maps the i-th row of M to an associated party. We denote $M\boldsymbol{v}$ as the vector of l shares of the secret s according to Π, where the column vector $\boldsymbol{v} = (s, r_2, \cdots, r_n)$, $(r_2, \cdots, r_n) \in \mathbb{Z}_p^{n-1}$ are randomly chosen, and $s \in \mathbb{Z}_p$ is the secret to be shared. Clearly, the share $(M\boldsymbol{v})_i$ belongs to the party $\rho(i)$.

Suppose that Π is an LSSS for an access structure $\mathbb{A}$, and $S \in \mathbb{A}$ is any authorized set. Let $I \subset \{1, 2, \cdots, \ell\}$ be defined as $I = \{i : \rho(i) \in S\}$. If λ_i are valid shares of any secret s according to Π, there exists constants $\{\omega_i \in \mathbb{Z}_p\}_{i \in I}$ such that $\Sigma_{i \in I} \omega_i \lambda_i = s$. Clearly, $\lambda_i = (M\boldsymbol{v})_i$.

3.4   ABE with Outsourced Decryption (ABE-OD)

Let S denote a set of attributes, and $\mathbb{A}$ is an access structure. We define the input of the encryption algorithm as (I_{enc}, I_{key}). In a CP-ABE scheme $(I_{enc}, I_{key}) = (\mathbb{A}, S)$, and in a KP-ABE scheme $(I_{enc}, I_{key}) = (S, \mathbb{A})$. We adopt Green et al.'s model [13] here. Formally, a CP-ABE (resp. KP-ABE) scheme with outsourced decryption in consists of the following five algorithms:

- $\mathtt{Setup}(1^\lambda, U)$: The setup algorithm takes the security parameter λ and an attribute description U as input. It outputs a public key $\mathtt{pk}$ and a master key $\mathtt{mk}$. This algorithm is usually performed by a trusted party named private key generator PKG.
- $\mathtt{Enc}(\mathtt{pk}, m, I_{enc})$: The encryption algorithm inputs the public key $\mathtt{pk}$, a message m, and an access structure (resp. attribute set) I_{enc}. It outputs the ciphertext $\mathtt{ct}$. This algorithm is performed by the encryptor.
- $\mathtt{KeyGen}(\mathtt{mk}, I_{key})$: The key generation algorithm inputs the master key $\mathtt{mk}$ and an attribute set (resp. access structure) I_{key}. It outputs the private key $\mathtt{sk}$ and the transformation key $\mathtt{tk}$. This algorithm is also performed by PKG.
- $\mathtt{Trans}(\mathtt{tk}, \mathtt{ct})$: The transformation algorithm inputs a transformation key $\mathtt{tk}$ for I_{key} and a ciphertext $\mathtt{ct}$ that associate with I_{enc}. If $S \in \mathbb{A}$, it outputs the partially decrypted ciphertext $\mathtt{ct}_{out}$. Otherwise, it outputs an error symbol $\perp$. This algorithm is usually performed by a proxy with the transformation key $\mathtt{tk}$ from the user holding the corresponding private key $\mathtt{sk}$.
- $\mathtt{Dec}(\mathtt{sk}, \mathtt{ct}_{out})$: The decryption algorithm inputs a private key $\mathtt{sk}$ for I_{key} and the partially decrypted ciphertext $\mathtt{ct}_{out}$ which was encrypted under I_{enc}. It outputs the error symbol $\perp$ if $S \notin \mathbb{A}$. Otherwise, it outputs the message m. This algorithm is performed by the user with the private key $\mathtt{sk}$.

Similar with ABE, the basic security requirement for ABE-OD is the confidentiality of plaintexts, namely indistinguishability under chosen-plaintext attacks (CPA security). Due to the space limitation, we omit the formal definition here. We refer readers to reference [13].

Remark 1. *It is easy to see that the above definition does not consider the case where the proxy may cheat the user by returning an invalid result. If the outsourced computation is a paid job, the user should be able to detect the proxy's misbehavior. In this paper, we would like to prevent the proxy from cheating by some publicly verifiable way.*

4   Generic Construction of ABE-OD with Public Verifiability

In this section, we present a generic construction to transfer a CPA-secure ABE-OD scheme to a CPA-secure ABE-OD scheme with public verifiability. Note that we only consider the pairing-based ABE-OD under the following scenario in this paper. The user outsources the ABE decryption task to a proxy with a reward promise. In particular, only the result returned from the proxy passed the verification could he/she get the reward. This could be realized by applying the smart contract in blockchain [7]. Of course, in this case, the proxy should also pay a deposit in the underlying smart contract to prevent him/her from cheating. We assume that the proxy in this scenario always adopts the best actions to obtain the highest revenue, i.e., he/she is rational. This assumption is in accordance with the real world where the one providing computing service is usually profit-driven.

As mentioned before, the main computational cost is due to the pairing operations. The transformation key technique [13] allows the proxy to execute all the pairings and return an ElGamal-style ciphertext to the user. While in our method, the proxy returns all the pairing results instead of the ElGamal-style ciphertext. Anyone can easily check whether the proxy execute pairings as promised by re-computing some of the results. Meanwhile, the user still does not need to perform the pairing operation. The details of our proposal can be found in next subsection.

4.1 Description of Our Proposal

With an ABE-OD scheme $\texttt{ABEOD} = (\texttt{Setup}, \texttt{KeyGen}, \texttt{Enc}, \texttt{Trans}, \texttt{Dec})$, we can have an ABE-OD with public verifiability scheme $\textsc{Abeodpv} = (\textsc{Setup}, \textsc{KeyGen}, \textsc{Enc}, \textsc{Trans}, \textsc{Verify}, \textsc{Dec})$ as follows. It is easy to see that algorithms $\textsc{Setup}, \textsc{KeyGen}, \textsc{Enc}$ are the same with that in $\texttt{ABEOD}$.

- $\textsc{Setup}(1^\lambda, U)$: It runs $\texttt{Setup}(1^\lambda, U)$ to get the system public key $\texttt{pk}$ and the corresponding master key $\texttt{mk}$.
- $\textsc{Enc}(\texttt{pk}, m, I_{enc})$: It runs $\texttt{Enc}(\texttt{pk}, m, I_{enc})$ to obtain the ciphertext $\texttt{ct}$.
- $\textsc{KeyGen}(\texttt{mk}, I_{key})$: It runs the $\texttt{KeyGen}(\texttt{mk}, I_{key})$ and outputs a private key $\texttt{sk}$ and the transformation key $\texttt{tk}$.
- $\textsc{Trans}(\texttt{tk}, \texttt{ct})$: The transformation algorithm inputs a transformation key $\texttt{tk}$ for I_{key} and a ciphertext $\texttt{ct}$ associating with I_{enc}. If $I_{key} \in I_{enc}$, it outputs the transformed ciphertext $\texttt{ct}_{out}$ which contains the vector of the pairing results $\boldsymbol{V}$. Otherwise, it outputs the error symbol $\bot$.
- $\textsc{Verify}(\texttt{ct}_{\texttt{tr}}, \texttt{ct}, \texttt{tk})$: The verifier could randomly choose some elements from $\texttt{ct}_{\texttt{tr}} = \boldsymbol{V}$, and recompute them by using $\texttt{ct}$ and $\texttt{tk}$. If all recomputed results are equal to that in $\boldsymbol{V}$, it outputs $\texttt{vr} = (\texttt{ct}, \texttt{ct}_{\texttt{tr}})$; $\texttt{vr} = \bot$ otherwise.
- $\textsc{Dec}(\texttt{sk}, \texttt{vr}, \texttt{ct})$: The decryption algorithm inputs a private key $\texttt{sk}$ for I_{key} and a verification result $\texttt{vr}$. If $\texttt{vr} = \bot$, it outputs the error symbol $\bot$; otherwise, it firstly obtains $\texttt{ct}_{out}$ from $\texttt{ct}_{\texttt{tr}}$ by combining the pairing results, and runs $\texttt{Dec}(\texttt{ct}_{out}, \texttt{sk})$ to obtain the resulting message.

4.2 Instantiation

For understanding our proposal easier, we would like to give some instantiations of our proposal. In particular, two concrete instantiations based on Green et al.'s schemes [13], including a CP-ABE scheme and a KP-ABE scheme. In order to show the differences among the original ABE scheme, the ABE-OD scheme, and the public-verifiable ABE-OD scheme, we put them together in the same figures. The CP-ABE scheme and KP-ABE scheme are given in Figs. 1 and 2, respectively. In these two figures, we denote $A \leftarrow_R B$ as that element A is chosen randomly from the set (group) B, and the security parameter is λ.

From Figs. 1 and 2, we can easily obtain the following observations.

- Algorithms SETUP and ENC are identical to that of the original ABE schemes. Note that we use the pairing $e : \mathbb{G}_1 \times \mathbb{G}_2 \to \mathbb{G}_T$ where $\mathbb{G}_1 \neq \mathbb{G}_2$ rather than the one satisfying $\mathbb{G}_1 = \mathbb{G}_2$ as described in [12,13,37]. It is mainly because that the pairing e with $\mathbb{G}_1 = \mathbb{G}_2$ is no longer secure due to Kiraz et al.'s work [17].
- Except the original ABE scheme, the algorithm KEYGEN in other two schemes will additionally output a transformation key tk. The transformation key is used for transforming the original ABE ciphertext to the ElGamal-type ciphertext, and all of the time-consuming pairing operations are executed during the transformation process as shown in the algorithm TRANS.
- Compared to the ABE-OD scheme, the algorithm TRANS does not combine the pairing results to generate the ElGamal-type ciphertext, while it outputs all the pairing results V instead. Anyone can check the validity of V by recomputing and comparing some elements from V as described in the algorithm VERIFY. Hence, the public verifiability is obtained. Note that this public verifiability cannot guarantee that the invalid result from the proxy can always be detected. However, if the proxy is rational, our public verifiability is sufficient enough as analyzed in the proof of Theorem 1.

4.3   Analysis of the Proposal

Recall the properties listed in Table 1, we would like to analyze computational cost, functionality, as well as the security properties in this part.

Computational Cost. It is easy to see that the CP-ABE instantiation and KP-ABE instantiation have the similar efficiency in terms of computational cost on the decryptor side. Hence, we only implemented the CP-ABE ones to show the effectiveness of our proposal. Specifically, the schemes are implemented by utilizing the Pairing-Based Cryptography [31], the underlying curve is d224. The execution environment is an Intel Core i7 processor with 8GB RAM running 32-bit Windows 10 operation system. From Fig. 3(a), we can see that the computational cost of the proxy in our scheme is almost the same as that of the decryptor in the original ABE scheme. Furthermore, Fig. 3(b) shows that the computational cost of the decryptor in our scheme is almost the same as that in the ABE-OD scheme. Hence, we have the numbers as shown in Table 1.

Functionality. It is easy to see that the correctness of the above construction can be easily obtained from that of the underlying ABE-OD scheme and sampling technique. Hence, the public verifiability holds in our proposal. As discussed in [13], the transformation key technique is suitable for any pairing-based ABE schemes. Hence, our proposal is also suitable for any pairing-based ABE schemes.

Security. From the description of our proposal, we can see that all the data potentially revealing the information of plaintexts can be generated in the underlying ABE-OD scheme. Hence, we can get the security proof of our proposal

	Original ABE [37]	ABE-OD [13]	Our proposal
Setup	Input: λ. Output: $(\mathsf{pk}, \mathsf{mk})$. where $\mathsf{pk} = (g_1, g_2, e(g_1,g_2)^\alpha, g_2{}^a,$ $F(\cdot))$, $\mathsf{mk} = g_1^\alpha$, $g_1 \leftarrow_R \mathbb{G}_1$, $g_2 \leftarrow_R \mathbb{G}_2$, and $a, \alpha \leftarrow_R \mathbb{Z}_p^*$.	Identical to that of the original ABE scheme.	Identical to that of the original ABE scheme.
Enc	Input: $(\mathsf{pk}, m, (M,\rho))$. Output: $(\mathsf{ct}, (M,\rho))$. where $\mathsf{ct} = (C, C', \{C_i, D_i\}_{i \in I})$, $C = m \cdot e(g_1,g_2)^{\alpha s}$, $C' = g_1^s$, $C_i = g_1^{a\lambda_i} \cdot F(\rho(i))^{-r_i}$, and $D_i = g_1^{r_i}$ (for $i \in I$).	Identical to that of the original ABE scheme.	Identical to that of the original ABE scheme.
KeyGen	Input: (mk, S). Output: sk. where $\mathsf{sk} = (K, L, \{K_x\}_{x \in S})$, $K = g_2^\alpha g_2^{a \cdot t}$, $L = g_2^t$, $\{K_x = F(x)^t\}_{x \in S}$, and $t \leftarrow_R \mathbb{Z}_p^*$.	Input: (mk, S). Output: $(\mathsf{sk}, \mathsf{tk})$. where $\mathsf{sk} = z$, $\mathsf{tk} = (\mathsf{pk}, K, L, \{K_x\}_{x \in S})$, $K = g_2^{\alpha/z} g_2^{a \cdot t/z}$, $L = g_2^{t/z}$, $\{K_x = F(x)^{t/z}\}_{x \in S}$, $t \leftarrow_R \mathbb{Z}_p^*$, and $z \leftarrow_R \mathbb{Z}_p^*$.	Identical to that of the ABE-OD scheme.
Trans	None	Input: $(\mathsf{tk}, \mathsf{ct})$. Output: $\mathsf{ct}_{\mathsf{tr}}$. where $\mathsf{ct}_{\mathsf{tr}} = (T_0, T_1)$, $T_0 = C$, and $T_1 =$ $\dfrac{e(C',K)}{\prod_{i \in I} e(C_i^{\omega_i}, L) \cdot e(D_i^{\omega_i}, K_{\rho(i)})}$.	Input: $(\mathsf{tk}, \mathsf{ct})$. Output: $\mathsf{ct}_{\mathsf{tr}}$. where $\mathsf{ct}_{\mathsf{tr}} = \boldsymbol{V} = (\overline{\mathsf{ct}}, \{V_i\}_{i \in I})$, $\overline{\mathsf{ct}} = e(C', K)$, and $V_i = e(C_i^{\omega_i}, L) \cdot e\left(D_i^{\omega_i}, K_{\rho(i)}\right)$.
Verify	None	None	Input: $(\mathsf{ct}, \mathsf{ct}_{\mathsf{tr}}, \mathsf{tk})$. Output: vr. Randomly select indexes i from $I \bigcup \{0\}$, and set it as I'. If $0 \in I'$, $\overline{\mathsf{ct}}' = e(C', K)$. For $i \in I$, $V_i' = e(C_i^{\omega_i}, L) \cdot e(D_i^{\omega_i}, K_{\rho(i)})$. If $\{\overline{\mathsf{ct}}', \{V_i'\}_{i \in I'/\{0\}}\} \subset \mathsf{ct}_{\mathsf{tr}}$, $\mathsf{vr} = (\mathsf{ct}, \mathsf{ct}_{\mathsf{tr}})$; $\mathsf{vr} = \perp$, otherwise.
Dec	Input: $(\mathsf{sk}, \mathsf{ct})$. Output: m. where $m = T_0/T_1$, $T_0 = C$, and $T_1 =$ $\dfrac{e(C',K)}{\prod_{i \in I} e(C_i^{\omega_i}, L) \cdot e(D_i^{\omega_i}, K_{\rho(i)})}$.	Input: $(\mathsf{sk}, \mathsf{ct})$. Output: m. where $m = T_0/T_1^z$.	Input: $(\mathsf{vr}, \mathsf{sk})$. Output: m where $m = T_0/T_1^z$, $T_0 = C$, and $T_1 = \dfrac{\overline{\mathsf{ct}}}{\prod_{i \in I} V_i}$.

Fig. 1. The CP-ABE scheme.

	Original ABE [12]	ABE-OD [13]	Our proposal
SETUP	Input: λ. Output : $(\mathrm{pk},\mathrm{mk})$. where $\mathrm{pk} = (g_1, g_2, g_1^{\alpha}, F(\cdot))$, $\mathrm{mk} = \alpha$, $g_1 \leftarrow_R \mathbb{G}_1$, $g_2 \leftarrow_R \mathbb{G}_2$, and $\alpha \leftarrow_R \mathbb{Z}_p^*$.	Identical to that of the original ABE scheme.	Identical to that of the original ABE scheme.
ENC	Input: $(\mathrm{pk}, m, (M, \rho))$. Output: $(\mathrm{ct}, (M, \rho))$ where $\mathrm{ct} = (S, C, C', \{C_x\}_{x \in S})$ $C = m \cdot e(g_1, g_2)^{\alpha s}$, $C' = g_1^s$ and $C_x = F(x)^s$.	Identical to that of the original ABE scheme.	Identical to that of the original ABE scheme.
KEYGEN	Input: (mk, S). Output: sk where $\mathrm{sk} = \{D_i, R_i\}_{i \in I}$, $D_i = g_2^{\lambda_i} \cdot F(\rho(i))^{r_i}$, and $R_i = g_1^{r_i}$.	Input: (mk, S). Output: $(\mathrm{sk}, \mathrm{tk})$ where $\mathrm{sk} = z, \mathrm{tk} = \{D_i, R_i\}_{i \in I}$, $D_i = h^{\lambda_i/z} \cdot F(\rho(i))^{r_i/z}$, $R_i = g^{r_i/z}$, and $z \leftarrow_R \mathbb{Z}_p^*$.	Identical to that of the ABE-OD scheme.
TRANS	None	Input: $(\mathrm{tk}, \mathrm{ct})$. Output: $\mathrm{ct}_{\mathrm{tr}}$. where $\mathrm{ct}_{\mathrm{tr}} = (T_0, T_1)$, $T_0 = C$, and $T_1 = \dfrac{e(C', \prod_{i \in I} D_i^{\omega_i})}{\prod_{i \in I} e(R_i, C_{\rho(i)}^{\omega_i})}$.	Input: $(\mathrm{tk}, \mathrm{ct})$. Output: $\mathrm{ct}_{\mathrm{tr}}$. where $\mathrm{ct}_{\mathrm{tr}} = \boldsymbol{V} = (\overline{\mathrm{ct}}, \{V_i\}_{i \in I})$, $\overline{\mathrm{ct}} = e(C', \prod_{i \in I} D_i^{\omega_i})$, and $V_i = e(R_i, C_{\rho(i)}^{\omega_i})$.
VERIFY	None	None	Input: $(\mathrm{ct}, \mathrm{ct}_{\mathrm{tr}}, \mathrm{tk})$. Output: vr. Randomly select indexes i from $I \bigcup \{0\}$, and set it as I'. If $0 \in I'$, $\overline{\mathrm{ct}}' = e(C', \prod_{i \in I} D_i^{\omega_i})$. For $i \in I$, $V_i' = e(R_i, C_{\rho(i)}^{\omega_i})$. If $\{\overline{\mathrm{ct}}', \{V_i'\}_{i \in I'/\{0\}}\} \subset \mathrm{ct}_{\mathrm{tr}}$, $\mathrm{vr} = (\mathrm{ct}, \mathrm{ct}_{\mathrm{tr}})$; $\mathrm{vr} = \bot$, otherwise.
DEC	Input: $(\mathrm{sk}, \mathrm{ct})$. Output : m. where $m = T_0/T_1$, $T_0 = C$, and $T_1 = \dfrac{e(C', \prod_{i \in I} D_i^{\omega_i})}{\prod_{i \in I} e(R_i, C_{\rho(i)}^{\omega_i})}$.	Input: $(\mathrm{sk}, \mathrm{ct})$. Output : m. where $m = T_0/T_1^z$.	Input: $(\mathrm{vr}, \mathrm{sk})$. Output : m where $m = T_0/T_1^z$, $T_0 = C$, and $T_1 = \dfrac{\overline{\mathrm{ct}}}{\prod_{i \in I} V_i}$.

Fig. 2. The KP-ABE scheme.

directly from that of the underlying ABE-OD scheme. The last thing we need to do is to prove that the proxy will always follow the proposal under the assumption that he/she is rational.

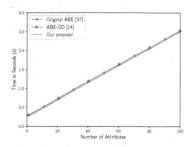 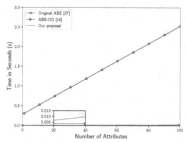

(a) The computational cost of the proxy in ABE-OD and ABE-OD with public verifiability, and the decryptor in the original ABE.

(b) The computational cost of the decryptor in the original ABE, ABE-OD and ABE-OD with public verifiability.

Fig. 3. Experiment results.

Theorem 1. *The proxy will always return the valid result when he/she is rational.*

Proof. We know that a rational proxy's action decision always depends on its expected revenue. According to the schemes in Sect. 4, the expected revenue of proxy Re_p is related to whether its transformed result can pass the verification. Specifically, for an outsourced ABE decryption task whose reward is c_{reward} and the deposit is $c_{deposit}$, the revenue Re_p can be calculated as follows:

$$Re_p = c_{reward} \cdot (1 - \Pr[F]) - c_p \cdot (n - n_{cheat}) - c_{deposit} \cdot \Pr[F],$$

where $\Pr[F]$ is the probability of verification failure, c_p is the cost of the proxy to execute each pairing operation, and n is the total number of pairings the proxy is expected to execute, and n_{cheat} is the number of pairings the proxy will cheat. According to Lemma 1, the revenue of proxy is

$$Re_p \leq \left(c_p - \frac{c_{reward} + c_{deposit}}{n} \right) \cdot n_{cheat} + c_{reward} - n \cdot c_p.$$

Note that the reward is usually larger than the execution cost on the proxy side in the outsourcing scenario, i.e., $n \cdot c_p < c_{reward}$. Hence, the proxy tends to choose the smallest n_{cheat}, i.e. $n_{cheat} = 0$, to get the highest reward.

As a result, the rational proxy will always execute the paring operations honestly if he/she always pursues the highest revenue. □

Lemma 1. *The probability of verification failure increases with the number of verified elements, and the minimum value is $\dfrac{n_{cheat}}{n}$.*

Proof. Suppose the verifier will select n_{verify} elements from the n elements. We only consider the scenario that $n_{cheat} + n_{verify} \leq n$ in this paper, since when

$n_{\text{cheat}} + n_{\text{verify}} > n$, at least one invalid pairing result will be verified. The probability of verification failure can be formulated as

$$\Pr[F] = 1 - \frac{n - n_{\text{cheat}}}{n} \cdot \frac{n - n_{\text{cheat}} - 1}{n - 1} \cdots \frac{n - n_{\text{cheat}} - n_{\text{verify}} - 1}{n - n_{\text{verify}} - 1}$$

$$= 1 - \frac{(n - n_{\text{cheat}})! \cdot (n - n_{\text{verify}})!}{(n - n_{\text{cheat}} - n_{\text{verify}})! \cdot n!}.$$

Let $f(n_{\text{verify}}) = \Pr[F] = 1 - \dfrac{(n - n_{\text{cheat}})! \cdot (n - n_{\text{verify}})!}{(n - n_{\text{cheat}} - n_{\text{verify}})! \cdot n!}$. We can have that

(1) when $n_{\text{cheat}} = 0$, $f(n_{\text{verify}}) = 1 - \dfrac{(n - n_{\text{cheat}})! \cdot (n - n_{\text{verify}})!}{(n - n_{\text{cheat}} - n_{\text{verify}})! \cdot n!} = 1$

(2) When $n_{\text{cheat}} > 0$, $f(n_{\text{verify}} + 1) = 1 - \dfrac{(n - n_{\text{cheat}})! \cdot (n - n_{\text{verify}} - 1)}{(n - n_{\text{cheat}} - n_{\text{verify}} - 1)! \cdot n!}$.

It's easy to obtain that $\dfrac{f(n_{\text{verify}} + 1)}{f(n_{\text{verify}})} = \dfrac{n - n_{\text{cheat}} - n_{\text{verify}}}{n - n_{\text{verify}}} < 1$, so we have $f(n_{\text{verify}} + 1) < f(n_{\text{verify}})$, and $f(n_{\text{verify}}) \leq f(1) = \dfrac{n - n_{\text{cheat}}}{n}$. Thus, $\Pr(F)$ increases with the number of verified elements, and the minimum value is $1 - f(1) = \dfrac{n_{\text{cheat}}}{n}$. Note that the cheating action cannot be detected when $n_{\text{verify}} < 1$, so n_{verify} must be 1 at least. $\qquad \square$

For the completeness, we also simulated the revenue of the proxy in Fig. 4, where we set $n = 100$, $c_{\text{deposit}} = n \cdot c_p$, and $c_{\text{reward}} = 3 \cdot n \cdot c_p$, and the color denotes the revenue of the proxy. From Fig. 4, the proxy will obtain the highest revenue when $n_{\text{verify}} = 0$. However, n_{verify} will never be 0. When $n_{\text{verify}} \neq 0$, the revenue in case of no-cheating is always higher than that in the case of cheating.

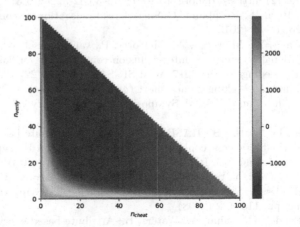

Fig. 4. The revenue of a proxy when $c_{\text{deposit}} = n \cdot c_p$, $c_{\text{reward}} = 3 \cdot n \cdot c_p$, and $n = 100$.

5   Conclusion

In this paper, we proposed a simple and generic method to convert any ABE-OD scheme to a public verifiable ABE-OD scheme, and the new scheme will have the same security level as the underlying scheme in terms of the confidentiality of the message. We also give two concrete ABE schemes based on Green et al.'s [13] construction by using our method. The game theoretical analysis shows that the rational proxy will always return the valid result.

The main method we used in this paper to enable public verifiability is combining the sampling technique and game theory. It seems that this method can be used in other kinds of verifiable outsourced computation. We leave it as the future work.

Acknowledgement. The authors would like to thank the anonymous reviewers for their invaluable comments. This work was supported in part by the Natural Science Foundation of Zhejiang under Grant LR18F020003 and the National Natural Science Foundation of China under Grant U1709217.

References

1. https://www.vice.com/en_us/article/ywanev
2. Beimel, A.: Secure schemes for secret sharing and key distribution (1996)
3. Campanelli, M., Gennaro, R., Goldfeder, S., Nizzardo, L.: Zero-knowledge contingent payments revisited: attacks and payments for services. In: Proceedings of the 2017 ACM SIGSAC, pp. 229–243 (2017)
4. Canetti, R., Riva, B., Rothblum, G.N.: Practical delegation of computation using multiple servers. In: Proceedings of the 18th ACM Conference on Computer and Communications Security, CCS, pp. 445–454 (2011)
5. Canetti, R., Riva, B., Rothblum, G.N.: Two protocols for delegation of computation. In: Smith, A. (ed.) ICITS 2012. LNCS, vol. 7412, pp. 37–61. Springer, Heidelberg (2012). https://doi.org/10.1007/978-3-642-32284-6_3
6. Canetti, R., Riva, B., Rothblum, G.N.: Refereed delegation of computation. Inf. Comput. **226**, 16–36 (2013)
7. Dong, C., Wang, Y., Aldweesh, A., McCorry, P., van Moorsel, A.: Betrayal, distrust, and rationality: smart counter-collusion contracts for verifiable cloud computing. In: Proceedings of the 2017 ACM SIGSAC, pp. 211–227 (2017)
8. Feige, U., Kilian, J.: Making games short (extended abstract). In: Proceedings of the Twenty-Ninth Annual ACM Symposium on the Theory of Computing, pp. 506–516 (1997)
9. Gokuldev, S., Leelavathi, S.: HASBE: a hierarchical attribute-based solution for flexible and scalable access control by separate encryption/decryption in cloud computing. Int. J. Eng. Sci. Innov. Technol. (IJESIT) **2**(3) (2013)
10. Goldwasser, S., Kalai, Y.T., Rothblum, G.N.: Delegating computation: interactive proofs for muggles. In: Proceedings of the 40th Annual ACM Symposium on Theory of Computing, pp. 113–122 (2008)
11. Goyal, V., Pandey, O., Sahai, A., Waters, B.: Attribute-based encryption for fine-grained access control of encrypted data. In: Proceedings of the 13th ACM Conference on Computer and Communications Security, pp. 89–98 (2006)

12. Goyal, V., Pandey, O., Sahai, A., Waters, B.: Attribute-based encryption for fine-grained access control of encrypted data. In: Proceedings of the 13th ACM Conference on Computer and Communications Security, pp. 89–98. ACM (2006)
13. Green, M., Hohenberger, S., Waters, B., et al.: Outsourcing the decryption of ABE ciphertexts. In: USENIX Security Symposium, vol. 2011 (2011)
14. Guo, F., Mu, Y., Susilo, W., Wong, D.S., Varadharajan, V.: CP-ABE with constant-size keys for lightweight devices. IEEE Trans. Inf. Forensics Secur. 9(5), 763–771 (2014)
15. Hu, S., Cai, C., Wang, Q., Wang, C., Luo, X., Ren, K.: Searching an encrypted cloud meets blockchain: a decentralized, reliable and fair realization. In: 2018 IEEE Conference on Computer Communications, INFOCOM, pp. 792–800 (2018)
16. Huang, H., Chen, X., Wu, Q., Huang, X., Shen, J.: Bitcoin-based fair payments for outsourcing computations of fog devices. Future Gener. Comput. Syst. 78, 850–858 (2018)
17. Kiraz, M.S., Uzunkol, O.: Still wrong use of pairings in cryptography. arXiv preprint arXiv:1603.02826 (2016)
18. Koppula, V., Waters, B.: Realizing chosen ciphertext security generically in attribute-based encryption and predicate encryption. In: Boldyreva, A., Micciancio, D. (eds.) CRYPTO 2019. LNCS, vol. 11693, pp. 671–700. Springer, Cham (2019). https://doi.org/10.1007/978-3-030-26951-7_23
19. Król, M., Psaras, I.: SPOC: secure payments for outsourced computations. CoRR abs/1807.06462 (2018)
20. Kumaresan, R., Bentov, I.: How to use bitcoin to incentivize correct computations. In: Proceedings of the 2014 ACM SIGSAC, pp. 30–41 (2014)
21. Lai, J., Deng, R.H., Guan, C., Weng, J.: Attribute-based encryption with verifiable outsourced decryption. IEEE Trans. Inf. Forensics Secur. 8(8), 1343–1354 (2013)
22. Lewko, A., Okamoto, T., Sahai, A., Takashima, K., Waters, B.: Fully secure functional encryption: attribute-based encryption and (hierarchical) inner product encryption. In: Gilbert, H. (ed.) EUROCRYPT 2010. LNCS, vol. 6110, pp. 62–91. Springer, Heidelberg (2010). https://doi.org/10.1007/978-3-642-13190-5_4
23. Li, J., Shi, Y., Zhang, Y.: Searchable ciphertext-policy attribute-based encryption with revocation in cloud storage. Int. J. Commun. Syst. 30(1), e2942 (2017)
24. Li, J., Wang, Y., Zhang, Y., Han, J.: Full verifiability for outsourced decryption in attribute based encryption. IEEE Trans. Serv. Comput. (2017, in press)
25. Li, J., Huang, X., Li, J., Chen, X., Xiang, Y.: Securely outsourcing attribute-based encryption with checkability. IEEE Trans. Parallel Distrib. Syst. 25(8), 2201–2210 (2013)
26. Li, J., Zhang, Y., Chen, X., Xiang, Y.: Secure attribute-based data sharing for resource-limited users in cloud computing. Comput. Secur. 72, 1–12 (2018)
27. Li, W., Xue, K., Xue, Y., Hong, J.: TMACS: a robust and verifiable threshold multi-authority access control system in public cloud storage. IEEE Trans. Parallel Distrib. Syst. 27(5), 1484–1496 (2015)
28. Liao, Y., He, Y., Li, F., Jiang, S., Zhou, S.: Analysis of an ABE scheme with verifiable outsourced decryption. Sensors 18(1), 176 (2018)
29. Lin, C., He, D., Huang, X., Xie, X., Choo, K.K.R.: Blockchain-based system for secure outsourcing of bilinear pairings. Inf. Sci. (2018, in press)
30. Lin, S., Zhang, R., Ma, H., Wang, M.: Revisiting attribute-based encryption with verifiable outsourced decryption. IEEE Trans. Inf. Forensics Secur. 10(10), 2119–2130 (2015)
31. Lynn, B., et al.: The pairing-based cryptography library. Internet: crypto. stanford. edu/pbc/[27 Mar. 2013] (2006)

32. Mao, X., Lai, J., Mei, Q., Chen, K., Weng, J.: Generic and efficient constructions of attribute-based encryption with verifiable outsourced decryption. IEEE Trans. Dependable Secur. Comput. **13**(5), 533–546 (2015)
33. Pasupuleti, S.K., Ramalingam, S., Buyya, R.: An efficient and secure privacy-preserving approach for outsourced data of resource constrained mobile devices in cloud computing. J. Netw. Comput. Appl. **64**, 12–22 (2016)
34. Qin, B., Deng, R.H., Liu, S., Ma, S.: Attribute-based encryption with efficient verifiable outsourced decryption. IEEE Trans. Inf. Forensics Secur. **10**(7), 1384–1393 (2015)
35. Sahai, A., Waters, B.: Fuzzy identity-based encryption. In: Cramer, R. (ed.) EURO-CRYPT 2005. LNCS, vol. 3494, pp. 457–473. Springer, Heidelberg (2005). https://doi.org/10.1007/11426639_27
36. Wang, S., Zhou, J., Liu, J.K., Yu, J., Chen, J., Xie, W.: An efficient file hierarchy attribute-based encryption scheme in cloud computing. IEEE Trans. Inf. Forensics Secur. **11**(6), 1265–1277 (2016)
37. Waters, B.: Ciphertext-policy attribute-based encryption: an expressive, efficient, and provably secure realization. In: Catalano, D., Fazio, N., Gennaro, R., Nicolosi, A. (eds.) PKC 2011. LNCS, vol. 6571, pp. 53–70. Springer, Heidelberg (2011). https://doi.org/10.1007/978-3-642-19379-8_4
38. Wu, J., Ping, L., Ge, X., Wang, Y., Fu, J.: Cloud storage as the infrastructure of cloud computing. In: 2010 International Conference on Intelligent Computing and Cognitive Informatics, pp. 380–383 (2010)
39. Xu, J., Wen, Q., Li, W., Jin, Z.: Circuit ciphertext-policy attribute-based hybrid encryption with verifiable delegation in cloud computing. IEEE Trans. Parallel Distrib. Syst. **27**(1), 119–129 (2015)
40. Zhou, Z., Huang, D.: Efficient and secure data storage operations for mobile cloud computing. In: 2012 8th International Conference on Network and Service Management (CNSM) and 2012 Workshop on Systems Virtualiztion Management (SVM), pp. 37–45 (2012)
41. Zuo, C., Shao, J., Wei, G., Xie, M., Ji, M.: CCA-secure ABE with outsourced decryption for fog computing. Future Gener. Comput. Syst. **78**, 730–738 (2018)

New Game-Theoretic Analysis of DDoS Attacks Against Bitcoin Mining Pools with Defence Cost

Rongxin Zheng[1], Cuiwen Ying[1], Jun Shao[1], Guiyi Wei[1(✉)], Hongyang Yan[2],
Jianmin Kong[1], Yekun Ren[1], Hang Zhang[1], and Weiguang Hou[1]

[1] School of Computer and Information Engineering, Zhejiang Gongshang University,
Hangzhou, China
weigy@zjgsu.edu.cn
[2] School of Computer Science and Cyber Engineering, Guangzhou University,
Guangzhou, China

Abstract. Since almost all new bitcoins nowadays are minted by mining pools, the security of mining pools is quite crucial to the health of the Bitcoin system. Among the attacks targeting at mining pools, the distributed denial-of-service (DDoS) attack is the notable one. Previous research shows that mining pools would launch DDoS attacks on others when the size is relatively large. However, no mining pools claimed responsibility to any DDoS attacks on mining pools till now. In this paper, we revise the previous game-theoretic analysis model by adding DDoS defense cost. With the assumption that the whole computing resource of any mining pool consists of mining, defense and attack, we obtain some interesting conclusions. (1) If the failure probability of DDoS attack is high, then mining pools would have a greater incentive to stay peacefully. (2) Increasing the computing resource in mining is always the primary choice for mining pools, no matter whether they are launching DDoS attacks or under DDoS attacks.

Keywords: Blockchain · Mining pool · DDoS · Game theory

1 Introduction

Due to the decentralized, crypto-protected, and transparent properties, Bitcoin [21] has gained considerable popularity during the past ten years. It has even become like a worldwide currency. One reason for this tremendous success is that everybody could be the minter of a new bitcoin. Only if he/she finds a solution to a specific cryptographic puzzle before others, he/she can own the new bitcoins. In other words, more computing resource, more bitcoins. This situation leads to two strategies to earn more bitcoins. One is to increase competitive computing resources, which results in a prosperous market for specialized hardware [6]. The other is to collaborate with some other miners to constitute a mining pool, which evolves to that almost all new bitcoins are minted/mined by mining pools currently [5].

© Springer Nature Switzerland AG 2019
J. K. Liu and X. Huang (Eds.): NSS 2019, LNCS 11928, pp. 567–580, 2019.
https://doi.org/10.1007/978-3-030-36938-5_35

Due to the importance of the mining pools in the Bitcoin system, many attacks targeting at mining pools have emerged. Among those, the distributed denial of service (DDoS) attack is the most famous one. The earliest reported DDoS attacks can even go back to 2011 [1], and one peak of DDoS incidents on mining pools happened in 2015 [2]. We also witnessed that several mining pools, such as Altcoin.pw [14] and GHash.io [3], shut down (partially) due to repeated DDoS attacks. Currently, anti-DDoS implementation is a crucial part of the standard configuration for mining pools [7]. However, DDoS attacks still happen from time to time [4]. It is believed that DDoS attacks come from two kinds of entities. One is the hackers whose goal is to hijack the attacked mining pool. The other is the competing mining pool who wants to increase the probability of winning the mining competition. Nonetheless, to the best of our knowledge, no mining pool claimed responsibility for any DDoS attack on mining pools till now. A natural question arises about whether the mining pools would really launch the DDoS attack on other mining pools.

Johnson et al. [14] responded to the above question by using the game theory. According to their analysis, the relative size of mining pools is a vital factor for the mining pool to choose the strategy between investing in computation and engaging in attack. In particular, large mining pools have a higher possibility to be attacked than small ones, and larger mining pools are more willing to attack compared to smaller ones. In other words, two relative large mining pools would like to launch DDoS attacks on each other. This analysis result is somewhat different from the reality where the large mining pools are living peacefully. In this paper, following Johnson et al.'s method, we would like to re-analyze the DDoS attacks happened between mining pools from game-theoretic point of view.

Our contributions in this paper can be summarized as follows.

– To reflect the fact that the current mining pools are usually equipped with an anti-DDoS system, we add DDoS defence cost into Johnson et al.'s model with the condition that the whole computing resource of any mining pool consists of mining, defense and attack. This modification makes the failure possibility of DDoS attacks dynamic and turns out some new game's equilibria.
– With the new analysis model, we obtain some interesting conclusions. (1) If the failure probability of DDoS attack is high, then mining pools would have a greater incentive to stay peacefully. (2) Increasing the computing resource in mining is always the primary choice for mining pools, no matter whether they are launching DDoS attacks or under DDoS attacks.

Our presentation proceeds as follows. In Sect. 2, we briefly discuss the related work. In Sect. 3, we modify Johnson et al.'s model by adding defense cost and operational cost, and carry out numerical and graph analysis with different failure probability of DDoS attacks. In Sect. 4, we further extend the analysis in Sect. 3 by restricting the whole computing resource, and obtaining the failure probability of DDoS attacks dynamically. In Sect. 5, we summarize this paper.

2   Related Work

Bitcoin's incentive mechanism encourages miners to mine and disseminate new blocks they have constructed to reap benefits. From the rational point of view, miners always pursuit higher profit even if they have to deviate from the standard mining strategy. This deviation strategy may even be a proactive attack on other miners or mining pools, such as DDoS attacks. It is natural to analyze the DDoS attacks and possible countermeasures from the economic point of view.

Many researchers have studied the problem by analyzing the characteristics of adversaries. Liu et al. [18] developed a game-theoretic AIOS (Attacker Intent, Objectives and Strategies) formalization to unify a large variety of attacker intents. Li et al. [17] studied the botnet-related attacks such as the DDoS attack. Their result showed that the profits of botnet masters and attacker can be maximized with the effective rental size and the optimal botnet size. Böhme et al. [8] believed that DDoS attacks seemed to be particularly effective and difficult to prevent in the Bitcoin system.

Analyzing the characteristics of the defense is another way to study the DDoS attack. Spyridopoulos et al. [23] modeled a DDoS attack as a one-shot, non-cooperative and zero-sum game, where the attacker can adaptively choose his/her strategy according to the defender's response. Their analysis result shows that only if the attacker is rational, the cost of the damages due to the DDoS attack can be minimized by a proper firewall configuration, no matter which strategy the attacker chooses for the next stage. Karami et al. [15] explored the facets of booters-based DDoS attacks by analyzing the leaked and scraped data from three major booters. They showed that the payment intervention could be a promising countermeasure to this kind of DDoS attacks.

The research on the incentive of adversarial behavior is one of our primary concerns. Schechter and Smith [22] took the advantages of the economic threat modeling to understand adversaries aiming at financial gain. Cremonini and Nizovtsev [10] used game theory to compare the strategies the attacker used to make decision in different scenarios. Clark and Konrad [9] proposed a game model where only one defender and one attacker exist. They showed that the defender would surrender if he/she needs to protect lots of nodes while the attacker only needs to win at only once. Fultz and Grossklags [12] solved the problem of strategy selection for attackers and cyber criminals. Grossklags et al. [13] modeled multiple attackers, and found that attackers and defenders had an impact on their inherent interdependence. Manshaei et al. [20] summarized the game theory research on network security and privacy.

Due to the economic nature of the Bitcoin system, it is natural to use game theory model to analyze the incentive of attacks. Vasek et al. [25] pointed out that the possibility of becoming an attacking target was related to the size of the mining pool. Accordingly, Johnson et al. [14] established a game theory model with two participants, big and small mining pools. The alternative strategy is investing in mining or launching DDoS attacks. They concluded that two relatively large mining pools are more likely to attack each other. Laszka et al. [16] established a model of two mining pools attacking each other and analyzed the long-term impact of DDoS attacks with the migration of miners. Tang et al. [24] argued that the win-or-nothing reward method may lead miners to behave maliciously.

Besides the DDoS attack, game theory is also applied to analyze the other attacks, such as block withholding attacks [11,19], in Bitcoin.

3 Modified Model from Johnson et al.'s Model

Before giving our proposed model for analyzing the DDoS attacks among mining pools, we would like to present a modified model original from [14]. In this model, we have two players, denoted as **B** and **S**, and we focus on the income of each player. It is worth mentioning that the rest mining pools in Bitcoin system are considered as an entity and denoted as **R**. We assume that the action of **R** will not effect on the income of player **B** and **S**. In other words, the whole computing resource of **R** is used for mining. If we denote B, S, and R as the computing resource as **B**, **S** and **R**, respectively. We have that $B + S + R = 1$.

3.1 Theoretical Analysis

Similar with Johnson et al.'s model [14], we assume that the whole computing resource in Bitcoin increases with a fixed rate ε over the game's time. The first option for each player in our model is to invest more computing resource to maintain the market equilibrium, and the second one is to launch a DDoS attack to decrease the other player's mining resource. We also assume that DDoS attacks will fail with a fixed probability σ. If one player launches a DDoS attack, the player's computing resource will no longer increase.

We would like to express the cost of mining, defense, and attack by using computing resource, especially the ratios to the whole computing resources. We denote γ, β, λ and η as the ratios of the cost of investment, mining, attack and defense to the whole computing resource, respectively. We also assume that the cost of attack is related to the computational power of the opponent, while the defense cost is related to the player's own resource.

- If player **B** chooses mining, then his/her investment cost, operational cost and defense cost are $\gamma \varepsilon B$, $\beta(1 + \varepsilon)B$ and $\eta(1 + \varepsilon)B$, respectively.
- If player **B** launches a DDoS attack on player **S** while player **S** invests in mining, then the operational cost, defense cost and attack cost of player **B** are βB, ηB, and $\lambda(1 + \varepsilon)S$, respectively.

For simplicity, we have that $\lambda < \gamma$. The payoffs for players **B** and **S** are summarized in Tables 1 and 2, respectively.

Best-Response Strategies. We denote $M_\mathbf{B}(i, j)$ (resp. $M_\mathbf{S}(i, j)$) as the value in the cell of the i-th column and the j-th row in Table 1 (resp. Table 2). For instance, we have that

$$M_\mathbf{B}(1,1) = \frac{B}{B + S + R} - \gamma \varepsilon B - \eta B(1 + \varepsilon) - \beta B(1 + \varepsilon)$$

Table 1. Payoff matrix for player **B**.

		B	
		Mining	DDoS
S	Mining	$\frac{B}{B+S+R} - \gamma\varepsilon B - \eta B(1+\varepsilon) - \beta B(1+\varepsilon)$	$\frac{B}{B+(\sigma S+R)(1+\varepsilon)} - \lambda S(1+\varepsilon) - \eta B - \beta B$
	DDoS	$\frac{\sigma B(1+\varepsilon)}{(\sigma B+R)(1+\varepsilon)+S} - \gamma\varepsilon B - \eta B(1+\varepsilon) - \beta B(1+\varepsilon)$	$\frac{\sigma B}{(\sigma B+\sigma S)+R(1+\varepsilon)} - \lambda S - \eta B - \beta B$

Table 2. Payoff matrix for player **S**.

		B	
		Mining	DDoS
S	Mining	$\frac{S}{B+S+R} - \gamma\varepsilon S - \eta S(1+\varepsilon) - \beta S(1+\varepsilon)$	$\frac{\sigma S(1+\varepsilon)}{B+(\sigma S+R)(1+\varepsilon)} - \gamma\varepsilon S - \eta S(1+\varepsilon) - \beta S(1+\varepsilon)$
	DDoS	$\frac{S}{(\sigma B+R)(1+\varepsilon)+S} - \lambda B(1+\varepsilon) - \eta S - \beta S$	$\frac{\sigma S}{(\sigma B+\sigma S)+R(1+\varepsilon)} - \lambda B - \eta S - \beta S$

$$(\text{resp. } M_{\mathbf{S}}(1,1) = \frac{S}{B+S+R} - \gamma\varepsilon S - \eta S(1+\varepsilon) - \beta S(1+\varepsilon)).$$

Hence, we have the following best response strategies for player **B**.

- Player **B** would invest in mining, if **S** also invest in mining and $M_{\mathbf{B}}(1,1) \geq M_{\mathbf{B}}(1,2)$, or player **S** chooses attack and $M_{\mathbf{B}}(2,1) \geq M_{\mathbf{B}}(2,2)$.
- Player **B** would launch the DDoS attack, if **S** invests in mining and $M_{\mathbf{B}}(1,1) \leq M_{\mathbf{B}}(1,2)$, or player **S** chooses attack and $M_{\mathbf{B}}(2,1) \leq M_{\mathbf{B}}(2,2)$.

Note that when the equalities hold, both of mining and attack are the best response strategies for player **B**. Similarly, we can get the best response strategies for player **S**.

Equilibria. With Tables 1 and 2, it is easy to see that there exist four Nash equilibria as follows.

- Both players launch DDoS attacks on each other, if $M_{\mathbf{B}}(2,2) \geq M_{\mathbf{B}}(2,1)$ and $M_{\mathbf{S}}(2,2) \geq M_{\mathbf{S}}(1,2)$.
- Both players invest in mining, if $M_{\mathbf{B}}(1,1) \geq M_{\mathbf{B}}(1,2)$ and $M_{\mathbf{S}}(1,1) \geq M_{\mathbf{S}}(2,1)$.
- Player **B** prefers attacks while player **S** invests in mining, if $M_{\mathbf{B}}(1,2) \geq M_{\mathbf{B}}(1,1)$ and $M_{\mathbf{S}}(1,2) \geq M_{\mathbf{S}}(2,2)$.
- Player **B** prefers mining while player **S** launches attacks, if $M_{\mathbf{B}}(2,1) \geq M_{\mathbf{B}}(2,2)$ and $M_{\mathbf{S}}(2,1) \geq M_{\mathbf{S}}(1,1)$.

3.2   Numerical Illustrations

For clarification, we give the numerical illustrations for the Nash equilibrium in this part. The values of ε, γ, λ, β and η are set as 0.1, 0.01, 0.001, 0.001 and 0.001, respectively.

Figures 1, 2, and 3 show the characteristics of the Nash equilibrium for different values of B and S and different attack failure probabilities. The first one demonstrates the equilibrium profiles of players **B** and **S** as a function of the values of B and S^1. The second one demonstrates the payoff of player **B** as a function of the values of B and S. If there exist multiple equilibria, the average value is applied. The last one demonstrates the payoffs of players **B** and **S** as a function of the values of B and a fixed value of S.

Clearly, these three figures conduct the results in [14]. In particular, large mining pools have a higher possibility to be attacked than small ones, and larger mining pools are more willing to attack compared to smaller ones. These figures also conduct that players are more willing to invest in mining when the attack failure probability increases.

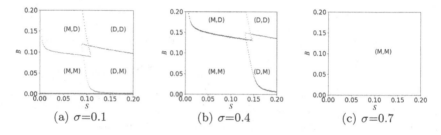

(a) $\sigma=0.1$ (b) $\sigma=0.4$ (c) $\sigma=0.7$

Fig. 1. Equilibrium strategy profiles for players **B** and **S**.

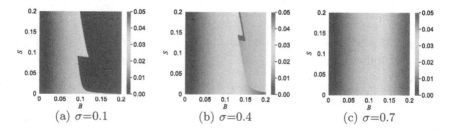

(a) $\sigma=0.1$ (b) $\sigma=0.4$ (c) $\sigma=0.7$

Fig. 2. The equilibrium payoff of player **B** (the red portions represent higher payoffs). If there exist multiple equilibria, then the average payoff is applied. (Color figure online)

---

[1] The pairs in figures denote the choices of players **B** and **S**, respectively. For example, (M, D) denotes that player **B** chooses mining while player **S** chooses DDoS attacks.

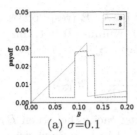 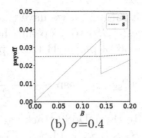 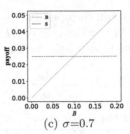

(a) $\sigma=0.1$ (b) $\sigma=0.4$ (c) $\sigma=0.7$

Fig. 3. Equilibrium payoffs of players **B** (solid) and **S** (dotted) as a function of B with $S = 0.1$.

4 Our Model with Limited Computing Resource

In the previous section, we re-analyzed the equilibrium distribution as a function of computing resource size with the operational cost and defense cost. However, we observe that the pool may need to allocate his/her computing resource for mining, defense or DDoS attack, when the whole computing resource is fixed. The strategy equilibrium of players will be accordingly affected by this allocation. In order to solve this problem, we will give a new model in this section.

The new model is almost the same as the previous model, except the following modifications.

- The Bitcoin mining market in this model would not increase computing resource over the game's time scale.
- Players **B** and **S** have the same computing resource, and we set that $B = S = C_{\text{BS}}$.
- The computing resources of players **B** and **S** contain three parts: mining, defense and attack. The attack part could be zero, which means that the player does not launch the DDoS attack on the other. While the defense part cannot be zero when he/she will launch the DDoS attack, and it is related to the mining part with the ratio α. If one player prefer mining to attack, the defense part could be zero.
- The attack failure probability σ is decided by the defense cost of the victim and the attack cost of the attacker. Specially, $\sigma = D/A$, where D and A are the defense cost of the victim and the attack cost of the attacker, respectively.

4.1 Theoretical Analysis

We use the subscripts m, d and a to denote the parts related to mining, defense and attack, respectively. Hence, we have that

$$B = B_m + B_d + B_a = (1+\alpha) \cdot B_m + B_a$$
$$= C_{\text{BS}} = S$$
$$= S_m + S_d + S_a = (1+\alpha) \cdot S_m + S_a.$$

Recall the operational cost ratio is β, we have that player **B** (resp. player **S**) should pay the cost of βB (resp. βS) to keep him/her running. If both players invest in mining, then the payoff of player **B** (resp. player **S**) is

$$\frac{B_m}{S_m + B_m + R} - \beta C_{BS} \qquad \left(\text{resp. } \frac{S_m}{S_m + B_m + R} - \beta C_{BS}\right).$$

If both play players initiate the DDoS attack against each other, then $B_d = \alpha B_m$, $B_a = C_{BS} - (1+\alpha)B_m$, $S_d = \alpha S_m$, and $S_a = C_{BS} - (1+\alpha)S_m$. Now, we have that the attack failure probability of player **B** (resp. player **S**) is $\frac{\alpha S_m}{C_{BS}-(1+\alpha)B_m}$ (resp. $\frac{\alpha B_m}{C_{BS}-(1+\alpha)S_m}$), and the payoff of player **B** (resp. player **S**) is

$$\frac{\frac{\alpha B_m}{C_{BS}-(1+\alpha)S_m}B_m}{\frac{\alpha S_m}{C_{BS}-(1+\alpha)B_m}S_m + \frac{\alpha B_m}{C_{BS}-(1+\alpha)S_m}B_m + R} - \beta C_{BS}$$

$$\left(\text{resp. } \frac{\frac{\alpha S_m}{C_{BS}-(1+\alpha)B_m}S_m}{\frac{\alpha S_m}{C_{BS}-(1+\alpha)B_m}S_m + \frac{\alpha B_m}{C_{BS}-(1+\alpha)S_m}B_m + R} - \beta C_{BS}\right).$$

If player **B** initiates a DDoS attack against player **S** who invests in mining, then $B_d = \alpha B_m$, $B_a = C_{BS} - (1+\alpha)B_m$, $S_d = C_{BS} - S_m$, and $S_a = 0$. Now, we have that the attack failure probability of player **B** is $\frac{C_{BS}-S_m}{C_{BS}-(1+\alpha)B_m}$, and the payoff of player **B** (resp. player **S**) is

$$\frac{B_m}{\frac{C_{BS}-S_m}{C_{BS}-(1+\alpha)B_m}S_m + B_m + R} - \beta C_{BS}$$

$$\left(\text{resp. } \frac{\frac{C_{BS}-S_m}{C_{BS}-(1+\alpha)B_m}S_m}{\frac{C_{BS}-S_m}{C_{BS}-(1+\alpha)B_m}S_m + B_m + R} - \beta C_{BS}\right).$$

If player **B** invests in mining while player **S** initiates a DDoS attack against him/her, then $B_d = C_{BS} - B_m$, $B_a = 0$, $S_d = \alpha S_m$, and $S_a = C_{BS} - (1+\alpha)S_m$. Now, we have that the attack failure probability of player **B** is $\frac{C_{BS}-S_m}{C_{BS}-(1+\alpha)B_m}$, and the payoff of player **B** (resp. player **S**) is

$$\frac{\frac{C_{BS}-B_m}{C_{BS}-(1+\alpha)S_m}B_m}{\frac{C_{BS}-B_m}{C_{BS}-(1+\alpha)S_m}B_m + S_m + R} - \beta C_{BS}$$

$$\left(\text{resp. } \frac{S_m}{\frac{C_{BS}-B_m}{C_{BS}-(1+\alpha)S_m}B_m + S_m + R} - \beta C_{BS}\right).$$

Best-Response Strategies and Equilibria. Similar with that in Sect. 3, we can conduct the best response strategies for players **B** and **S**, and four Nash equilibria from Tables 3 and 4.

Table 3. Payoff matrix for player **B** with limited computing resource.

		B	
		Mining	DDoS
S	Mining	$\dfrac{B_m}{S_m+B_m+R} - \beta C_{BS}$	$\dfrac{B_m}{\frac{C_{BS}-S_m}{C_{BS}-(1+\alpha)S_m}S_m+B_m+R} - \beta C_{BS}$
	DDoS	$\dfrac{\frac{C_{BS}-B_m}{C_{BS}-(1+\alpha)S_m}B_m}{\frac{C_{BS}-B_m}{C_{BS}-(1+\alpha)S_m}B_m+S_m+R} - \beta C_{BS}$	$\dfrac{\frac{\alpha B_m}{C_{BS}-(1+\alpha)S_m}B_m}{\frac{\alpha S_m}{C_{BS}-(1+\alpha)B_m}S_m+\frac{\alpha B_m}{C_{BS}-(1+\alpha)S_m}B_m+R} - \beta C_{BS}$

Table 4. Payoff matrix for player **S** with limited computing resource.

		B	
		Mining	DDoS
S	Mining	$\dfrac{S_m}{S_m+B_m+R} - \beta C_{BS}$	$\dfrac{\frac{C_{BS}-S_m}{C_{BS}-(1+\alpha)B_m}S_m}{\frac{C_{BS}-S_m}{C_{BS}-(1+\alpha)B_m}S_m+B_m+R} - \beta C_{BS}$
	DDoS	$\dfrac{S_m}{\frac{C_{BS}-B_m}{C_{BS}-(1+\alpha)S_m}B_m+S_m+R} - \beta C_{BS}$	$\dfrac{\frac{\alpha S_m}{C_{BS}-(1+\alpha)B_m}S_m}{\frac{\alpha S_m}{C_{BS}-(1+\alpha)B_m}S_m+\frac{\alpha B_m}{C_{BS}-(1+\alpha)S_m}B_m+R} - \beta C_{BS}$

4.2 Numerical Illustrations

The players **B** and **S** are, in essence, the same in the game. Hence, in this subsection, we only show the numerical illustrations of player **B**'s payoff. As that in Sect. 3, the red portions in the figures in this subsection represent higher payoff. The white parts in Figs. 4, 5 and 6 demonstrate that there is no Nash equilibria for the underlying strategies. For example, from the point $(0.05, 0.15)$ in Fig. 4(a), we conduct that there is no Nash equilibria when both players **B** and **S** invest in mining with $B_m = 0.05$ and $S_m = 0.15$. However, if we combine the four sub-figures in each figure together, there would be no white region left. The parameters of Figs. 4, 5 and 6 are almost the same, except with different α. It is easy to see that when α increases, the colorful region corresponding to strategies (mining, mining) and (attack, attack) enlarges. In Figs. 4, 5 and 6, if the probability of attack failure is larger than 1, we set it as 1.

Figures 4(a), 5(a) and 6(a) show the equilibrium payoff of player **B** when both players **B** and **S** invest in mining. The colorful region in these figures only exists when the values of B_m and S_m are similar. Furthermore, the payoff of player **B** increases when B_m and S_m increase, which means that B_m and S_m are willing to increase their computing resource in mining when they both invest in mining.

Figures 4(b), 5(b) and 6(b) show the equilibrium payoff of player **B** when both players **B** and **S** launch DDoS attacks on each other. The size of the colorful region in these figures is much smaller than that in other figures. Especially, there exists only one tiny colorful area in Fig. 4(b). It is quite interesting that the colorful region in these figures only exists when B_m and S_m are of similar values and relatively large, and the larger the values, the more playoffs. This means that even if both players **B** and **S** launch DDoS attacks on each other,

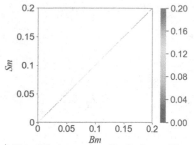

(a) Equilibrium payoff of player **B** with that both players **B** and **S** invest in mining.

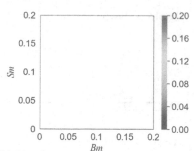

(b) Equilibrium payoff of player **B** with that both players **B** and **S** launch DDoS attacks.

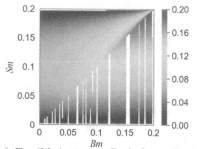

(c) Equilibrium payoff of player **B** with that player **B** invests in mining while player **S** launches the DDoS attack.

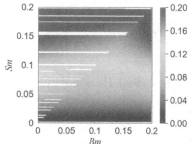

(d) Equilibrium payoff of player **B** with that player **B** launches the DDoS attack while player **S** invests in mining.

Fig. 4. Equilibrium for various values of B_m and S_m with $B = S = C_{BS} = 0.2$, $\beta = 0.001$ and $\alpha = 0.001$. (Color figure onine)

they are still willing to invest the computing resource in mining as much as possible.

We have the following observations from Figs. 4(c), 5(c) and 6(c).

Observation 1. When S_m is smaller than some threshold value, the payoff of player **B** won't change no matter how B_m changes.

Observation 2. When S_m is higher than some threshold value, the payoff of player **B** increases proportionally with $B_m (\leq S_m)$.

Furthermore, we have the following observations from Figs. 4(d), 5(d) and 6(d).

Observation 3. If S_m is fixed, then the payoff of player **B** is almost fixed no matter how B_m changes.

Observation 4. If S_m increases, then the payoff of player **B** increases no matter how B_m changes.

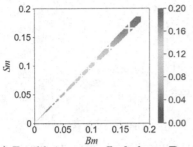

(a) Equilibrium payoff of player **B** with that both players **B** and **S** invest in mining.

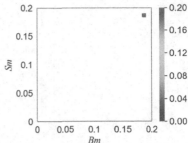

(b) Equilibrium payoff of player **B** with that both players **B** and **S** launch DDoS attacks.

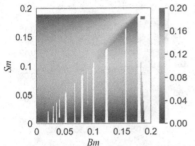

(c) Equilibrium payoff of player **B** with that player **B** invests in mining while player **S** launches the DDoS attack.

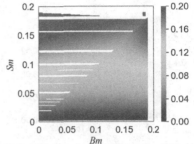

(d) Equilibrium payoff of player **B** with that player **B** launches the DDoS attack while player **S** invests in mining.

Fig. 5. Equilibrium for various values of B_m and S_m with $B - S = C_{BS} = 0.2$, $\beta = 0.001$ and $\alpha = 0.01$. (Color figure onine)

Now, we analyze the actions of players **B** and **S** if only one of them launches the DDoS attack. Without loss of generality, we assume that player **B** is the attacker. According to Observation 3 and Observation 4, the only way to increase the payoff of player **B** is to increase S_m. However, player **S** increases S_m only if B_m is large enough according to Observation 1 and Observation 2. As a result, both players **B** and **S** are willing to invest computing resource in mining as much as possible, when only one of them launches the DDoS attack.

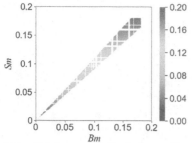

(a) Equilibrium payoff of player **B** with that both players **B** and **S** invest in mining.

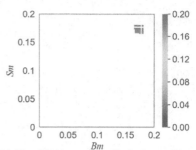

(b) Equilibrium payoff of player **B** with that both players **B** and **S** launch DDoS attacks.

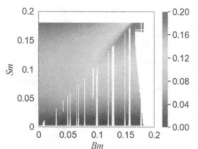

(c) Equilibrium payoff of player **B** with that player **B** invests in mining while player **S** launches the DDoS attack.

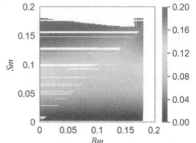

(d) Equilibrium payoff of player **B** with that player **B** launches the DDoS attack while player **S** invests in mining.

Fig. 6. Equilibrium for various values of B_m and S_m with $B = S = C_{BS} = 0.2$, $\beta = 0.001$ and $\alpha = 0.1$. (Color figure onine)

5   Conclusion

It is a folklore that mining pools would launch DDoS attacks to other mining pools. The previous research (e.g., [14]) also shows that relative large mining pools are willing to attack each other by a game-theoretic analysis. In this paper, we further extended the result by adding defence cost into the previous game-theoretic model. Our analysis conducts some interesting results: (1) The probability of launching DDoS attacks is related to the failure possibility of DDoS attacks. (2) Increasing the computing resource in mining is always the primary choice for mining pools, no matter whether they are launching attacks or under attacks.

In reality, the computing resources of mining pools increase gradually; however, it remains the same in our proposed model. This situation could be analyzed by the evolutionary game theory. We leave it as the future work.

Acknowledgement. The authors would like to thank the anonymous reviewers for their invaluable comments. This work was supported in part by the Natural Science Foundation of Zhejiang under Grant LR18F020003 and the National Natural Science Foundation of China under Grant U1709217.

References

1. https://defuse.ca/bitcoin-pool-ddos.htm, June 2011
2. https://www.coindesk.com/bitcoin-mining-pools-ddos-attacks, March 2015
3. https://news.8btc.com/a-brief-history-of-bitcoin-mining-pools-over-17-mining-pools-choose-to-shut-down, November 2018
4. https://www.cbronline.com/news/cryptocurrency-verge-attack, May 2018
5. https://www.blockchain.com/explorer, August 2019
6. https://www.buybitcoinworldwide.com/mining/hardware, July 2019
7. https://www.investopedia.com/tech/how-choose-cryptocurrency-mining-pool/, June 2019
8. Böhme, R., Christin, N., Edelman, B., Moore, T.: Bitcoin: economics, technology, and governance. J. Econ. Perspect. **29**(2), 213–38 (2015)
9. Clark, D.J., Konrad, K.A.: Asymmetric conflict: weakest link against best shot. J. Conflict Resolut. **51**(3), 457–469 (2007)
10. Cremonini, M., Nizovtsev, D.: Understanding and influencing attackers' decisions: implications for security investment strategies. In: 5th Annual Workshop on the Economics of Information Security, WEIS 2006, Robinson College, University of Cambridge, England, UK, 26–28 June 2006 (2006)
11. Eyal, I.: The miner's dilemma. In: 2015 IEEE Symposium on Security and Privacy, SP 2015, San Jose, CA, USA, 17–21 May 2015, pp. 89–103 (2015). https://doi.org/10.1109/SP.2015.13
12. Fultz, N., Grossklags, J.: Blue versus red: towards a model of distributed security attacks. In: Dingledine, R., Golle, P. (eds.) FC 2009. LNCS, vol. 5628, pp. 167–183. Springer, Heidelberg (2009). https://doi.org/10.1007/978-3-642-03549-4_10
13. Grossklags, J., Johnson, B., Christin, N.: When information improves information security. In: Sion, R. (ed.) FC 2010. LNCS, vol. 6052, pp. 416–423. Springer, Heidelberg (2010). https://doi.org/10.1007/978-3-642-14577-3_37
14. Johnson, B., Laszka, A., Grossklags, J., Vasek, M., Moore, T.: Game-theoretic analysis of ddos attacks against bitcoin mining pools. In: Böhme, R., Brenner, M., Moore, T., Smith, M. (eds.) FC 2014. LNCS, vol. 8438, pp. 72–86. Springer, Heidelberg (2014). https://doi.org/10.1007/978-3-662-44774-1_6
15. Karami, M., Park, Y., McCoy, D.: Stress testing the booters: understanding and undermining the business of DDoS services. In: Proceedings of the 25th International Conference on World Wide Web, pp. 1033–1043. International World Wide Web Conferences Steering Committee (2016)
16. Laszka, A., Johnson, B., Grossklags, J.: When bitcoin mining pools run dry - a game-theoretic analysis of the long-term impact of attacks between mining pools. In: Financial Cryptography and Data Security - FC 2015 International Workshops, BITCOIN, WAHC, and Wearable, San Juan, Puerto Rico, 30 January 2015, Revised Selected Papers, pp. 63–77 (2015)
17. Li, Z., Liao, Q., Striegel, A.: Botnet economics: uncertainty matters. In: Johnson, M.E. (ed.) Managing Information Risk and the Economics of Security, pp. 245–267. Springer, Boston (2009). https://doi.org/10.1007/978-0-387-09762-6_12

18. Liu, P., Zang, W., Yu, M.: Incentive-based modeling and inference of attacker intent, objectives, and strategies. ACM Trans. Inf. Syst. Secur. **8**(1), 78–118 (2005)
19. Luu, L., Saha, R., Parameshwaran, I., Saxena, P., Hobor, A.: On power splitting games in distributed computation: the case of Bitcoin pooled mining. In: IEEE 28th Computer Security Foundations Symposium, CSF 2015, Verona, Italy, 13–17 July 2015, pp. 397–411 (2015). https://doi.org/10.1109/CSF.2015.34
20. Manshaei, M.H., Zhu, Q., Alpcan, T., Basar, T., Hubaux, J.: Game theory meets network security and privacy. ACM Comput. Surv. **45**(3), 25:1–25:39 (2013)
21. Nakamoto, S.: Bitcoin: A peer-to-peer electronic cash system (2009). http://www.bitcoin.org/bitcoin.pdf
22. Schechter, S.E., Smith, M.D.: How much security is enough to stop a thief? In: Wright, R.N. (ed.) FC 2003. LNCS, vol. 2742, pp. 122–137. Springer, Heidelberg (2003). https://doi.org/10.1007/978-3-540-45126-6_9
23. Spyridopoulos, T., Karanikas, G., Tryfonas, T., Oikonomou, G.: A game theoretic defence framework against dos/ddos cyber attacks. Comput. Secur. **38**, 39–50 (2013)
24. Tang, C., Wu, L., Wen, G., Zheng, Z.: Incentivizing honest mining in blockchain networks: A reputation approach. IEEE Trans. Circuits Syst. II: Express Briefs (2019, in press)
25. Vasek, M., Thornton, M., Moore, T.: Empirical analysis of denial-of-service attacks in the bitcoin ecosystem. In: Financial Cryptography and Data Security - FC 2014 Workshops, BITCOIN and WAHC 2014, Christ Church, Barbados, 7 March 2014, Revised Selected Papers, pp. 57–71 (2014). https://doi.org/10.1007/978-3-662-44774-1_5

Lattice Based Verifiably Encrypted Double Authentication Preventing Signatures

Jinhui Liu and Yong Yu[✉]

School of Computer Science, Shaanxi Normal University, Xi'an 710062, China
yuyong@snnu.edu.cn

Abstract. Verifiably encrypted signatures (VES) have been widely used in various applications, such as signing contract, fair exchange and so on. However, most of them do not provide deterable function and with the development of quantum computers, they face new challenges. Verifiably encrypted double authentication preventing signatures (VEDAPS) with deterable function, have a property of punishing misbehavior parties by extracting their secret keys. In this paper, we propose a concrete VEDAPS based on Ring-SIS problem and Ring-LWE problem. Security analysis shows that our proposed scheme satisfies security properties including completeness, opacity, unforgeability and punishability in the random oracle model. Theory and parameter analyses demonstrate that our construction has reasonable efficiency for real applications.

Keywords: Verifiably encrypted signatures · Double authentication preventing signatures · Zero knowledge proof · Lattice · Punishability

1 Introduction

Currently, with the rapid development of e-commence transactions, such as financial transactions (online shopping transactions, online stock trading, and a large number of businesses), medical data transactions, software transactions and so on, an important issue is how to make those transactions between two or more potentially parties in a fair manner. Fair exchange protocol is a central problem in the process of e-commence transactions. It allows two or more mistrusted participants to exchange digital items so that either each participant gets the other's desired item or none of them gets anything [1–9]. Verifiable encrypted signatures are most practical paradigm for building fair exchange protocols. Until now, numerous efforts have been devoted to the study of the verifiably encrypted signatures.

A verifiably encrypted signature (VES), which includes a signature scheme and an encryption scheme [10, 11], allows a signer to encrypt his or her signatures under public keys of a trusted third party (TTP) and to convince a verifier that his or her ciphertext is a encryption of a signature on a given message. In 2003,

© Springer Nature Switzerland AG 2019
J. K. Liu and X. Huang (Eds.): NSS 2019, LNCS 11928, pp. 581–595, 2019.
https://doi.org/10.1007/978-3-030-36938-5_36

Boneh et al. proposed the first VES by using an aggregate signature [12]. Gu et al. and Zhang et al. proposed an identity-based VES scheme in random oracle model [13] and in the standard model [14] respectively. However, the Gu's schemes is not secure [15] and there exists a weak version of Zhang et al.'s scheme [16]. In 2017, Wang et al. proposed a group signature based VES scheme in random oracle model [17]. All above VESs can not provide punishment function for misbehavior participants. So we have to use another technique called double authentication preventing signature to solve this problem.

Double authentication preventing signatures (DAPS) whose secret keys are extractable if there are two signatures on colliding messages (m_0, p_1) and (m_0, p_1), can deter unfair problems. The formal definition and theory analysis of DAPS was first proposed by Pottering et al. in 2014 [19,20]. After that Bellare et al. proposed how to construct some DAPS by FS transform, Swap transform and H2 transform etc. and analyze security of those schemes security [21]. Boneh generalized DAPS by defining some predicates, muti-signer, muti-authorization center to propose some new syntaxs and formal definitions of generalized DAPS [22]. Based on ECDSA scheme, Derler et al. proposed a concrete DAPS by combing secret sharing, non-interactive zero knowledge proof and encryption scheme and generalize NAPS by using (n, n) threshold secret sharing scheme [23]. Poettering et al. proposed a shorter DAPS to decrease size of signature, size of signature key and size of verification key by analyzing the ECDSA scheme [24]. In ProvSec18, Deter et al. overcome the drawback that there is a linear relationship between bounded polynomial signature address space and size of public/private keys [25]. Liu et al. proposed a lattice based double authentication preventing ring signatures (DAPRS) [26]. Most designed DAPS are based on classic mathematical hard problem, due to the Shor algorithm, quantum computers pose a serious threat to these schemes [27], post quantum computational attack DAPS has important research value.

Motivated by above works, we first formalized a new verifiably encrypted signature called a verifiably encrypted double authentication preventing signatures (VEDAPS), which is derived from a double authentication preventing signature (DAPS) and a verifiably encrypted signature (VES). VEDAPS has similar natures with both VES and DAPS. VEDAPS can be deterable or punishable by extracting signer's secret keys of a signature on colliding messages if there exists a dispute. The procedure of our proposed VEDAPS is given in Fig. 1. Thus VEDAPS can be used to design fair exchange protocol which can be deterable when there exists dispute. For example, a buyer wants to buy a software (or a ticket) using money, however in our daily life there exists many fake softwares (or tickets) which have some same contents with the true software (or ticket). When there make a exchange where the seller sends a true verifiably encrypted signature on (m_0, p_1) to a trusted third party (TTP). If the seller sends a verifiably encrypted signature on (m_0, p_2) to the buyer, after asking for resolution of the TTP, the buyer can obtain signature secret keys of seller by DAPS which can be as a punishment for the seller.

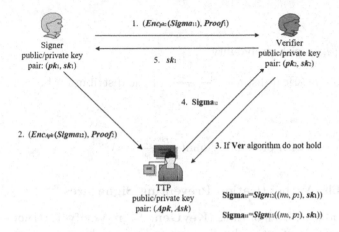

Fig. 1. The general procedure of our proposed VEDAPS

In this paper, we propose a new lattice-based verifiably encrypted double authentication preventing signature. First, we introduce the notion of verifiably encrypted double authentication preventing signatures (VEDAPS) and present a formal definition. Second, we present a concrete lattice-based VEDAPS construction with completeness, unforgeability against chosen message attack, opacity and extractability. Finally, we analyze our VEDAPS construction from both security and parameter perspectives.

2 Preliminaries

2.1 Mathematical Symbols

For a set $\mathcal{S}$, $a \leftarrow \mathcal{S}$ means that a is chosen randomly from the set $\mathcal{S}$.

Ring $\mathcal{R} = \mathbb{Z}[x]/(x^n + 1)$.

Column vector $\mathbf{a} = \begin{pmatrix} a_1 \\ \vdots \\ a_k \end{pmatrix}$ can be written as $[a_1; \ldots; a_k]$.

$\|a\|_1 = \sum_{i=0}^{n-1} |a_i|$, $\|a\| = \sqrt{\sum_{i=0}^{n-1} a_i^2}$, $\|a\|_\infty = \max_i |a_i|$.

For a full rank integer lattice $\bigwedge$, the discrete distribution

$$D_{\bigwedge, \mathbf{c}, \sigma} = \frac{e^{\frac{-\|\mathbf{v}-\mathbf{c}\|^2}{2\sigma^2}}}{\sum_{\mathbf{w} \in \bigwedge} \frac{-\|\mathbf{v}-\mathbf{c}\|^2}{2\sigma^2}}.$$

Rejection sampling lemma [28] are given as follows:

Suppose that $V \subseteq \mathbb{Z}^m$, $h : V \rightarrow \mathbb{R}$ is a distribution. If $\sigma = \omega(T\sqrt{log m})$, there exists a constant M such that the distribution below

- $v \leftarrow h$
- $z \leftarrow D_\sigma^m$
- Output (z, v) with probability $\frac{1}{M}$

is within statistical distance $\frac{2^{-\omega(logm)}}{M}$ of the distribution below:

- $v \leftarrow h$
- $z \leftarrow D_{\mathbf{v},\sigma}^m$
- Output (z, v) with probability $\min(\frac{D_\sigma^m(\mathbf{z})}{MD_{\mathbf{v},\sigma}^m(\mathbf{z})}, 1)$

2.2 Double Authentication Preventing Signatures

A DAPS is four PPT algorithms (**KeyGen, Sign, Verify, Extract**) as follows:

KeyGen(1^λ) outputs public keys pk and private keys sk on inputting security parameter λ.

Sign(sk, a, p) outputs a signature π on inputting private keys sk and subject/message pair $(a, p) \in \{0, 1\}^*$.

Verify(pk, a, p) outputs either 0 for rejection or 1 for acceptance on inputting pk, $(a, p) \in \{0, 1\}^*$ and π.

Extract$(pk, a_1, p_1, a_2, p_2, \pi_1, \pi_2)$ outputs the private key sk on inputting pk, $(a_1, p_1), (a_2, p_2) \in \{0, 1\}^*, (a_1 = a_2, p_1 \neq p_2)$ and π_1, π_2.

A DAPS needs to satisfy EUF-CMA (existentially unforgeable under chosen message attack) and DSE (double signature extractability) [24].

2.3 Ring-LWE Encryption Scheme

Secret key: $s_1 \leftarrow S_1$

Public key: $a \leftarrow R_q$ and $t \leftarrow as_1 + s_2$

Encryption: Given a message $m \leftarrow R_p$, encryptor randomly chooses $r, e, e' \leftarrow S_1$ and computes $v \leftarrow p(ar + e)$ and $w \leftarrow p(tr + e') + m$.

Decryption: Compute

$$(w - vs_1) \bmod q \bmod p = p(rs_2 + e' - es_1) + m \bmod p = m$$

while $\| p(rs_2 + +e' - es_1) \|_\infty < q/2$.

From the Ring LWE encryption scheme, we can transform it to the vector relation below:

$$\begin{pmatrix} v \\ w \end{pmatrix} = \begin{pmatrix} pa & p & 0 & 0 \\ pt & 0 & p & 1 \end{pmatrix} \begin{pmatrix} cr \\ e \\ e' \\ m \end{pmatrix} \bmod q.$$

Furthermore, we can obtain the following relation about the encryption of k messages $m_1, \cdots, m_k$ under the known information $a, t, w_1, \cdots, w_k, v_1, \cdots, v_k$ and unknown information $r_1, \cdots, r_k, e_1, \cdots, e_k, e'_1, \cdots, e'_k$.

$$
\begin{pmatrix}
pa & & & p & & & \\
 & \ddots & & & \ddots & & \\
 & & pa & & & p & \\
pt & & & p & & & 1 \\
 & \ddots & & & \ddots & & \ddots \\
 & & pt & & & p & & 1
\end{pmatrix}
\begin{pmatrix}
r_1 \\ \vdots \\ r_k \\ e_1 \\ \vdots \\ e_k \\ e'_1 \\ \vdots \\ e'_k \\ m_1 \\ \vdots \\ m_k
\end{pmatrix}
=
\begin{pmatrix}
v_1 \\ \vdots \\ v_k \\ w_1 \\ \vdots \\ w_k
\end{pmatrix}
\mod q.
$$

So we can transform the equation of encryption procedure as follows:

$$
\begin{pmatrix}
pa\mathbf{I}_k & p\mathbf{I}_k & \mathbf{0}^{k \times k} & \mathbf{0}^{k \times k} \\
pt\mathbf{I}_k & \mathbf{0}^{k \times k} & p\mathbf{I}_k & \mathbf{I}_k
\end{pmatrix}
\begin{pmatrix}
\mathbf{r} \\ \mathbf{e} \\ \mathbf{e}' \\ \mathbf{m}
\end{pmatrix}
=
\begin{pmatrix}
\mathbf{v} \\ \mathbf{w}
\end{pmatrix}
\mod q.
$$

The decryption procedure can be written as follows:

$$
\mathbf{m} = \mathbf{w} - \mathbf{v}\mathbf{s}_1 \bmod q \bmod p.
$$

2.4 Proofs of Knowledge of Linear Relations

Given $\mathbf{s} \in R^k$ satisfying the relation $\mathbf{As} = \mathbf{t} \mod q$, it needs to prove the knowledge of low norm $\bar{\mathbf{s}}$ and $\bar{c}$ which satisfy that

$$
\mathbf{A}\bar{\mathbf{s}} = \bar{c}\mathbf{t} \bmod q
$$

Consider a language L of linear relations R_L over short vectors and its extended language $\overline{L}$ with relation $R_{\overline{L}}$, where

$$
R_L = \{((\mathbf{A},\mathbf{t}),(\mathbf{s},1)) \in (R_p^{l \times k} \times R_p^l) \times (R_p^k \times R_p) : \mathbf{As} = \mathbf{t} \bmod p \wedge \mathbf{s} \in S_\gamma^k\}
$$

$$
R_{\overline{L}} = \{((\mathbf{A},\mathbf{t}),(\bar{\mathbf{s}},\bar{c})) \in (R_p^{l \times k} \times R_p^l) \times (R_p^k \times R_p) : \mathbf{A}\bar{\mathbf{s}} = \bar{c}\mathbf{t} \bmod p \wedge \|\bar{\mathbf{s}}\|_\infty < 12\sigma \bigwedge \bar{c} \in \overline{C}\}
$$

The proof of knowledge of linear relations is introduced as follows:

Let $\mathbf{A} \in R^{l \times k}, \mathbf{t} \in R^l, \mathbf{q} \in Z^l$ and a vector $\mathbf{s} \in S \subset R^k$ such that $\mathbf{As} = \mathbf{t} \bmod q$. Cryptographic hash function $H : \{0,1\}^* \to C$, where $C \subset R$, standard deviation $\sigma \in R^+$ and $\sigma \geq 11 \cdot max_{s \in S, c \in C}\|sc\|$.

1. Prover picks $\mathbf{y} \leftarrow D_{R^k, 0, \sigma}$, and sends $\mathbf{Ay}$ to Verifier.
2. Verifier samples $c \leftarrow H(\mathbf{A},\mathbf{t},\mathbf{Ay} \bmod \mathbf{q})$ and sends it to the Prover.
3. Prover computes $\mathbf{z} \leftarrow \mathbf{s}c + \mathbf{y}$. Depending on sampling, either sends it to Verifier or abort as follows:
   If $\|\mathbf{z}\|_\infty > 6\sigma$, goto (1); else output $(c,\mathbf{z})$ with probability $1 - D_{R^k, 0, \sigma}(\mathbf{z})/$ $D_{R^k, \mathbf{s}c, \sigma}(\mathbf{z})$.
4. If $\|\mathbf{z}\|_\infty > 6\sigma$ or $c \neq H(\mathbf{A},\mathbf{t},\mathbf{Ay} \bmod \mathbf{q})$, the verifier rejects; else accepts.

3   Security Definitions

In this section, we will define a syntax and security requirements of VEDAPS.

Define 3.1 (Verifiably encrypted double authentication preventing signatures) An VEDAPS scheme consists of eight probabilistic polynomial time (PPT) algorithms in the following:

AKeyGen(Param): On inputting **Param**, the algorithm outputs a public-private key pair (APK, ASK) and auxiliary information τ of an arbitrator.

KeyGen(Param, APK, τ): On inputting **Param** and the arbitrator's public key APK with τ, the algorithm outputs a public-private key pair (PK, SK) for a seller, where public keys form a list **L**.

DAPSig$((m_0, p_1), (m_0, p_2), \mathbf{L}, SK)$: On inputting colliding message pair $(m_0, p_1), (m_0, p_2)$, a public key list **L** and private key SK, the algorithm outputs a double authentication preventing signatures pair (σ_1, σ_2).

DAPVer$((m_0, p_1), (m_0, p_2), \mathbf{L}, \sigma_1, \sigma_2, PK_i, APK)$: On inputting colliding message pair $(m_0, p_1), (m_0, p_2)$, a public key list **L** and a signature pair (σ_1, σ_2), the algorithm outputs 0 which means reject or 1 which means accept.

VEDAPSig$((m_0, p_1), (m_0, p_2), \mathbf{L}, \sigma_1, \sigma_2, SK, ASK)$: On inputting colliding message pair $(m_0, p_1), (m_0, p_2)$, the seller's public key SK, a public key list **L** and the arbitrator's public key APK, the algorithm outputs a pair of verifiably encrypted double authentication preventing signatures δ_1, δ_2 on (m_0, p_1) and (m_0, p_2) respectively.

VEDAPVer$((m_0, p_1), (m_0, p_2), \mathbf{L}, \delta_1, \delta_2, PK, APK)$: On inputting colliding message pair $(m_0, p_1), (m_0, p_2)$, a public key list **L**, (δ_1, δ_2), the seller's public key PK and the arbitrator's public key APK, the algorithm outputs 0 which means reject or 1 which means accept.

Adjudication$((m_0, p_1), (m_0, p_2), \mathbf{L}, \delta_1, \delta_2, SK, ASK)$: On inputting colliding message pair $(m_0, p_1), (m_0, p_2)$, a public key list **L**, (δ_1, δ_2), the seller's secret key SK and the arbitrator's secret key ASK, the algorithm outputs the seller's a pair of signatures $(\overline{\sigma}_1, \overline{\sigma}_2)$ respectively.

Extract$((m_0, p_1), (m_0, p_2), \mathbf{L}, \overline{\sigma}_1, \overline{\sigma}_2)$: On inputting colliding message pair $(m_0, p_1), (m_0, p_2)$, a public key list **L** and a valid signature pair $(\overline{\sigma_1}, \overline{\sigma_2})$, the algorithm extracts the seller's secret key SK.

If the VEDAPS scheme above is Correctness, Unforgeability, Opacity and Extractability (or punishability), we consider it is secure.

Correctness means that any honestly computed VEDAPS can be verified and the arbiter can extract a valid signature secret key.

Define 3.2 (Correctness) A VEDAPS is correctness if for any $\kappa > 0$, $(APK, ASK) \leftarrow$ **AKeyGen(1^κ)**, $(PK, SK) \leftarrow$ **KeyGen(1^κ)** and $(m_0, p_i) \in \mathcal{M}$, for $\delta_1 \leftarrow$ **VEDAPSig$((m_0, p_1), \mathbf{L}, \sigma_1, ASK)$**, $\delta_2 \leftarrow$ **VEDAPSig$((m_0, p_2), \mathbf{L}, \sigma_2, SK)$** it holds that

$$Pr[\textbf{VEDAPVer}((m_0, p_1), \mathbf{L}, \delta_1, APK) = 1] = 1,$$

$$Pr[\textbf{VEDAPVer}((m_0, p_2), \mathbf{L}, \delta_2, PK) = 1] = 1,$$

$$Pr[\mathbf{DAPVer}((m_0, p_1), \mathbf{L}, \sigma_1, APK) = 1] = 1,$$

and

$$Pr[\mathbf{DAPVer}((m_0, p_2), \mathbf{L}, \sigma_2, PK) = 1] = 1.$$

Unforgeability means that it is infeasible to produce a valid signature for an adversary who do not know signer's secret key.

Define 3.3 (Unforgeability) A VEDAPS is unforgeability under the chosen message attack if for any PPT adversary $\mathcal{A}$ having access to oracles

$$\mathcal{O}_1 \leftarrow \left\{ \begin{array}{c} (a, p_1) \leftarrow m \\ a \notin R, \sigma_1 \leftarrow \mathbf{DAPSign}(ASK, m) \\ Q \leftarrow Q \cup \{m\}, R \leftarrow R \cup \{a\} \\ \mathbf{VEDAPSig}(\cdot, \sigma_1, ASK) \\ \mathbf{Adjudication}((\cdot, \delta_1, ASK) \end{array} \right\},$$

and

$$\mathcal{O}_2 \leftarrow \left\{ \begin{array}{c} (a, p_2) \leftarrow m \\ a \notin R, \sigma_2 \leftarrow \mathbf{DAPSign}(SK, m) \\ Q \leftarrow Q \cup \{m\}, R \leftarrow R \cup \{a\} \\ \mathbf{VEDAPSig}(\cdot, \sigma_2, SK) \\ \mathbf{Adjudication}((\cdot, \delta_2, SK) \end{array} \right\},$$

there exists a negligible function $\varepsilon(\kappa)$ such that the following equation holds:

$$Pr \left[\begin{array}{ll} (APK, ASK) \leftarrow \mathbf{AKeyGen}(1^\kappa), & (a, p^*) \notin Q \wedge \\ (PK, SK) \leftarrow \mathbf{KeyGen}(1^\kappa), & : \mathbf{VEDAPVer}(\cdot, \delta_1, APK) = 1 \\ (a, p^*, \sigma_1^*, \sigma_2^*) \leftarrow \mathcal{A}^{\mathcal{O}_1, \mathcal{O}_2}(PK, APK) & \wedge \mathbf{VEDAPVer}(\cdot, \delta_2, PK) = 1 \end{array} \right] \leq \varepsilon(\kappa).$$

Opacity means that only the ones who have secret keys are able to compute the underlying signature.

Define 3.4 (Opacity) A VEDAPS is opacity if for any PPT adversary $\mathcal{A}$ having access to oracles

$$\mathcal{O}_1 \leftarrow \left\{ \begin{array}{c} (a, p_1) \leftarrow m \\ a \notin R, \sigma_1 \leftarrow \mathbf{DAPSign}(ASK, m) \\ Q \leftarrow Q \cup \{m\}, R \leftarrow R \cup \{a\} \\ \mathbf{VEDAPSig}(\cdot, \sigma_1, ASK) \\ \mathbf{Adjudication}((\cdot, \delta_1, ASK) \end{array} \right\},$$

and

$$\mathcal{O}_2 \leftarrow \left\{ \begin{array}{c} (a, p_2) \leftarrow m \\ a \notin R, \sigma_2 \leftarrow \mathbf{DAPSign}(SK, m) \\ Q \leftarrow Q \cup \{m\}, R \leftarrow R \cup \{a\} \\ \mathbf{VEDAPSig}(\cdot, \sigma_2, SK) \\ \mathbf{Adjudication}((\cdot, \delta_2, SK) \end{array} \right\},$$

there exists a negligible function $\varepsilon(\cdot)$ such that the following equation holds:

$$Pr\begin{bmatrix} (APK, ASK) \leftarrow \mathbf{AKeyGen}(1^\kappa), & (a, p^*) \notin Q \wedge \\ (PK, SK) \leftarrow \mathbf{KeyGen}(1^\kappa), & : \mathbf{VEDAPVer}(\cdot, \delta_1, \delta_2, APK) = 1 \\ (a, p_1^*, p_2^*, \delta_1^*, \delta_2^*) \leftarrow \mathcal{A}^{\mathcal{O}_1, \mathcal{O}_2}(PK, APK) & \wedge \mathbf{VEDAPVer}(\cdot, \delta_1, \delta_2, PK) = 1 \end{bmatrix} \leq \varepsilon(\cdot).$$

Extractability (or punishability) means that the buyer is indeed able to extract seller's secret keys if there exists a dispute between the buyer and the seller.

Define 3.5 (Punishability) A VEDAPS provides punishability, if there exists a negligible function $\varepsilon(\kappa)$ for any PPT adversaries $\mathcal{A}$ having access to oracles $\mathcal{O}_1 \leftarrow \mathbf{Adjudication}(\cdot, \delta_1, ASK)$ and $\mathcal{O}_2 \leftarrow \mathbf{Adjudication}(\cdot, \delta_2, SK)$ such that the following probability is negligible:

$$Pr$$

$$\begin{bmatrix} & p_1 \neq p_2 \wedge p_1 \neq 0, p_2 \neq 0 \wedge \\ (ASK, APK) \leftarrow \mathbf{AKeyGen}(1^\kappa) & SK' \leftarrow \mathbf{Extract}(m_0, p_1, p_2, \overline{\sigma}_1, \overline{\sigma}_2, ASK) \\ (SK, PK) \leftarrow \mathbf{KeyGen}(1^\kappa) & \wedge \mathbf{VEDAPVer}(m_0, p_1, \delta_1, APK) = 1 \\ (m_0, p_1, p_2, \overline{\sigma}_1, \overline{\sigma}_2) \leftarrow \mathcal{A}^{\mathcal{O}_1, \mathcal{O}_2}(PK, APK) & : & \wedge \mathbf{VEDAPVer}(m_0, p_2, \delta_2, PK) = 1 \\ SK' \neq SK & \wedge \mathbf{DAPVer}(m_0, p_1, \overline{\sigma}_1, APK) = 1 \\ & \wedge \mathbf{DAPVer}(m_0, p_2, \overline{\sigma}_2, PK) = 1 \end{bmatrix}.$$

4   A Concrete VEDAPS Based on Lattice

Based on relaxed non-interactive zero-knowledge proofs over lattice, we propose a concrete non-relaxed lattice based VEDAPS [29–31].

AKeyGen: Choose $s_1, s_2 \leftarrow \mathcal{S}_1, \mathbf{B} \leftarrow \mathcal{R}^{l \times k}, \mathbf{t} \leftarrow \mathcal{R}^l, \mathbf{s} \leftarrow \mathcal{R}^k$ and $a \leftarrow \mathcal{R}$ such that $t_1 \leftarrow as_1 + s_2$ and $\mathbf{Bs} = \mathbf{t}$. The algorithm outputs a public-private key pair $((a, t_1, \mathbf{B}, \mathbf{t}), (s_1, \mathbf{s}))$ and auxiliary information $(\alpha, k, n, \gamma, \sigma)$ of an arbitrator.

KeyGen: On inputting **Param** and the arbitrator's public key $(\mathbf{B}, \mathbf{t})$ with auxiliary information, a signer chooses $\overline{s}_1, \overline{s}_1' \leftarrow \mathcal{S}_1, \overline{\mathbf{t}} \leftarrow \mathcal{R}^l$ and $\overline{\mathbf{s}} \leftarrow \mathcal{R}^k$ such that $\overline{t}_1 \leftarrow a\overline{s}_1 + \overline{s}_2$. The algorithm outputs a public-private key pair $((\overline{\mathbf{t}}, \overline{t}_1), (\overline{s}_1, \overline{\mathbf{s}}))$ such that $\mathbf{B}\overline{\mathbf{s}} = \overline{\mathbf{t}}$.

DAPSig: On inputting colliding message pair $(m_0, p_1), (m_0, p_2)$, the signer computes a signature pair (σ_1, σ_2) in the following:

1. $\mathbf{r}, \mathbf{e}, \mathbf{e}' \xleftarrow{} \mathcal{S}_1^k$

2. $\begin{pmatrix} \mathbf{v} \\ \mathbf{w} \\ \mathbf{t} \end{pmatrix} = \begin{pmatrix} pa\mathbf{I}_k & p\mathbf{I}_k & \mathbf{0}^{k \times k} & \mathbf{0}^{k \times k} \\ pt_1\mathbf{I}_k & \mathbf{0}^{k \times k} & p\mathbf{I}_k & \mathbf{I}_k \\ \mathbf{0}^{l \times k} & \mathbf{0}^{k \times k} & \mathbf{0}^{l \times k} & \mathbf{B} \end{pmatrix} \begin{pmatrix} \mathbf{r} \\ \mathbf{e} \\ \mathbf{e}' \\ \mathbf{s} \end{pmatrix} \begin{matrix} \bmod q \\ \bmod q \\ \bmod p \end{matrix}.$

3. $\mathbf{y} \leftarrow \begin{pmatrix} \mathbf{y_r} \\ \mathbf{y_e} \\ \mathbf{y_{e'}} \\ \mathbf{y_s} \end{pmatrix} \leftarrow \mathcal{D}_{\mathcal{R}, 0, \sigma}$

4. $c_1 \leftarrow H(\begin{pmatrix} pa\mathbf{I}_k & p\mathbf{I}_k & \mathbf{0}^{k\times k} & \mathbf{0}^{k\times k} \\ pt_1\mathbf{I}_k & \mathbf{0}^{k\times k} & p\mathbf{I}_k & \mathbf{I}_k \\ \mathbf{0}^{l\times k} & \mathbf{0}^{k\times k} & \mathbf{0}^{l\times k} & \mathbf{B} \end{pmatrix}, \begin{pmatrix} \mathbf{v} \\ \mathbf{w} \\ \mathbf{t} \end{pmatrix}$,

$\begin{pmatrix} pa\mathbf{I}_k & p\mathbf{I}_k & \mathbf{0}^{k\times k} & \mathbf{0}^{k\times k} \\ pt_1\mathbf{I}_k & \mathbf{0}^{k\times k} & p\mathbf{I}_k & \mathbf{I}_k \\ \mathbf{0}^{l\times k} & \mathbf{0}^{k\times k} & \mathbf{0}^{l\times k} & \mathbf{B} \end{pmatrix} \begin{pmatrix} \mathbf{y_r} \\ \mathbf{y_e} \\ \mathbf{y_{e'}} \\ \mathbf{y_s} \end{pmatrix} \begin{matrix} \bmod q \\ \bmod q, p_1). \\ \bmod p \end{matrix}$

5. $\mathbf{z}_1 \leftarrow \bar{\mathbf{s}}c_1 + m_0\mathbf{y}$
6. Depending on sampling, either keeps $\sigma_1 = (c_1, \mathbf{z}_1)$ or abort as follows:
If $\|\mathbf{z}_1\|_\infty > 6\sigma$, goto (1); else output $(c_1, \mathbf{z}_1)$ with probability

$$\left(1 - D_{R^k,0,\sigma_1}(\mathbf{z}_1)/D_{R^k,\mathbf{s}c_1,\sigma}(\mathbf{z}_1)\right)^2.$$

Using similar way, the signer computes a signature σ_2 on message (m_0, p_2) as follows:

1. $\bar{\mathbf{r}}, \bar{\mathbf{e}}, \bar{\mathbf{e}}' \longleftarrow \mathcal{S}_1^k$

2. $\begin{pmatrix} \bar{\mathbf{v}} \\ \bar{\mathbf{w}} \\ \bar{\mathbf{t}} \end{pmatrix} = \begin{pmatrix} pa\mathbf{I}_k & p\mathbf{I}_k & \mathbf{0}^{k\times k} & \mathbf{0}^{k\times k} \\ p\bar{t}_1\mathbf{I}_k & \mathbf{0}^{k\times k} & p\mathbf{I}_k & \mathbf{I}_k \\ \mathbf{0}^{l\times k} & \mathbf{0}^{k\times k} & \mathbf{0}^{l\times k} & \mathbf{B} \end{pmatrix} \begin{pmatrix} \bar{\mathbf{r}} \\ \bar{\mathbf{e}} \\ \bar{\mathbf{e}}' \\ \bar{\mathbf{s}} \end{pmatrix} \begin{matrix} \bmod q \\ \bmod q. \\ \bmod p \end{matrix}$

3. $\mathbf{y} \leftarrow \begin{pmatrix} \mathbf{y_{\bar{r}}} \\ \mathbf{y_{\bar{e}}} \\ \mathbf{y_{\bar{e}'}} \\ \mathbf{y_{\bar{s}}} \end{pmatrix} \leftarrow \mathcal{D}_{\mathcal{R},0,\sigma}$

4. $c_2 \leftarrow H(\begin{pmatrix} pa\mathbf{I}_k & p\mathbf{I}_k & \mathbf{0}^{k\times k} & \mathbf{0}^{k\times k} \\ p\bar{t}_1\mathbf{I}_k & \mathbf{0}^{k\times k} & p\mathbf{I}_k & \mathbf{I}_k \\ \mathbf{0}^{l\times k} & \mathbf{0}^{k\times k} & \mathbf{0}^{l\times k} & \mathbf{B} \end{pmatrix}, \begin{pmatrix} \bar{\mathbf{v}} \\ \mathbf{w} \\ \mathbf{t} \end{pmatrix}$,

$\begin{pmatrix} pa\mathbf{I}_k & p\mathbf{I}_k & \mathbf{0}^{k\times k} & \mathbf{0}^{k\times k} \\ p\bar{t}_1\mathbf{I}_k & \mathbf{0}^{k\times k} & p\mathbf{I}_k & \mathbf{I}_k \\ \mathbf{0}^{l\times k} & \mathbf{0}^{k\times k} & \mathbf{0}^{l\times k} & \mathbf{B} \end{pmatrix} \begin{pmatrix} \mathbf{y_{\bar{r}}} \\ \mathbf{y_{\bar{e}}} \\ \mathbf{y_{\bar{e}'}} \\ \mathbf{y_{\bar{s}}} \end{pmatrix} \begin{matrix} \bmod q \\ \bmod q, p_2). \\ \bmod p \end{matrix}$

5. $\mathbf{z}_2 \leftarrow \bar{\mathbf{s}}c_2 + m_0\mathbf{y}$
6. Depending on sampling, either keeps $\sigma_2 = (c_2, \mathbf{z}_2)$ or abort as follows:
If $\|\mathbf{z}_2\|_\infty > 6\sigma$, goto (1); else output $(c_2, \mathbf{z}_2)$ with probability

$$\left(1 - D_{R^k,0,\sigma}(\mathbf{z})/D_{R^k,\bar{\mathbf{s}}c_2,\sigma_2}(\mathbf{z}_2)\right)^2.$$

VEDAPSig: The signer computes verifiable encryption signatures of $\mathbf{z}_1$ and $\mathbf{z}_2$ in the following:

- The signer computes verifiable encryption signatures δ_1 on $\mathbf{z}_1$ using the public key of Arbitrator and sends it to the Arbitrator.
- At the same time, the signer also computes verifiable encryption signatures δ_2 on $\mathbf{z}_2$ using the public key of verifier and sends it to the verifier.

1. $\mathbf{r}_1, \mathbf{e}_1, \mathbf{e}_1' \longleftarrow \mathcal{S}_1^k$
2. Encrypt a witness $\omega_i = \sigma_i$ for language member $x = (\mathbf{B}, \mathbf{u}_i)$ such that $\mathbf{B}\sigma_i = \mathbf{u}_i$ for $i = 1, 2$.

3.
$$\begin{pmatrix} \mathbf{v}_1 \\ \mathbf{w}_1 \\ \mathbf{u}_1 \end{pmatrix} = \begin{pmatrix} pa\mathbf{I}_k & p\mathbf{I}_k & \mathbf{0}^{k\times k} & \mathbf{0}^{k\times k} \\ pt_1\mathbf{I}_k & \mathbf{0}^{k\times k} & p\mathbf{I}_k & \mathbf{I}_k \\ \mathbf{0}^{l\times k} & \mathbf{0}^{k\times k} & \mathbf{0}^{l\times k} & \mathbf{B} \end{pmatrix} \begin{pmatrix} \mathbf{r}_1 \\ \mathbf{e}_1 \\ \mathbf{e}_1' \\ \sigma_1 \end{pmatrix} \begin{matrix} \bmod q \\ \bmod q \\ \bmod p \end{matrix}$$

4.
$$\begin{pmatrix} \overline{\mathbf{v}}_1 \\ \overline{\mathbf{w}}_1 \\ \mathbf{u}_2 \end{pmatrix} = \begin{pmatrix} pa\mathbf{I}_k & p\mathbf{I}_k & \mathbf{0}^{k\times k} & \mathbf{0}^{k\times k} \\ p\overline{t}_1\mathbf{I}_k & \mathbf{0}^{k\times k} & p\mathbf{I}_k & \mathbf{I}_k \\ \mathbf{0}^{l\times k} & \mathbf{0}^{k\times k} & \mathbf{0}^{l\times k} & \mathbf{B} \end{pmatrix} \begin{pmatrix} \mathbf{r}_1 \\ \mathbf{e}_1 \\ \mathbf{e}_1' \\ \sigma_2 \end{pmatrix} \begin{matrix} \bmod q \\ \bmod q \\ \bmod p \end{matrix}$$

5. $\mathbf{y} \leftarrow \begin{pmatrix} \mathbf{y}_{r_1} \\ \mathbf{y}_{e_1} \\ \mathbf{y}_{e_1'} \\ \mathbf{y}_\sigma \end{pmatrix} \leftarrow \mathcal{D}_{\mathcal{R},0,\sigma}$

6. $\xi_1 \leftarrow$
$$H\left(\begin{pmatrix} pa\mathbf{I}_k & p\mathbf{I}_k & \mathbf{0}^{k\times k} & \mathbf{0}^{k\times k} \\ pt_1\mathbf{I}_k & \mathbf{0}^{k\times k} & p\mathbf{I}_k & \mathbf{I}_k \\ \mathbf{0}^{l\times k} & \mathbf{0}^{k\times k} & \mathbf{0}^{l\times k} & \mathbf{B} \end{pmatrix}, \begin{pmatrix} \mathbf{v}_1 \\ \mathbf{w}_1 \\ \mathbf{u}_1 \end{pmatrix}, \begin{pmatrix} pa\mathbf{I}_k & p\mathbf{I}_k & \mathbf{0}^{k\times k} & \mathbf{0}^{k\times k} \\ pt_1\mathbf{I}_k & \mathbf{0}^{k\times k} & p\mathbf{I}_k & \mathbf{I}_k \\ \mathbf{0}^{l\times k} & \mathbf{0}^{k\times k} & \mathbf{0}^{l\times k} & \mathbf{B} \end{pmatrix} \begin{matrix} \bmod q \\ \mathbf{y} \bmod q, p_1) \\ \bmod p \end{matrix} \right.$$

7. $\xi_2 \leftarrow$
$$H\left(\begin{pmatrix} pa\mathbf{I}_k & p\mathbf{I}_k & \mathbf{0}^{k\times k} & \mathbf{0}^{k\times k} \\ p\overline{t}_1\mathbf{I}_k & \mathbf{0}^{k\times k} & p\mathbf{I}_k & \mathbf{I}_k \\ \mathbf{0}^{l\times k} & \mathbf{0}^{k\times k} & \mathbf{0}^{l\times k} & \mathbf{B} \end{pmatrix}, \begin{pmatrix} \overline{\mathbf{v}}_1 \\ \overline{\mathbf{w}}_1 \\ \mathbf{u}_2 \end{pmatrix}, \begin{pmatrix} pa\mathbf{I}_k & p\mathbf{I}_k & \mathbf{0}^{k\times k} & \mathbf{0}^{k\times k} \\ p\overline{t}_1\mathbf{I}_k & \mathbf{0}^{k\times k} & p\mathbf{I}_k & \mathbf{I}_k \\ \mathbf{0}^{l\times k} & \mathbf{0}^{k\times k} & \mathbf{0}^{l\times k} & \mathbf{B} \end{pmatrix} \begin{matrix} \bmod q \\ \cdot \mathbf{y} \bmod q, p_2) \\ \bmod p \end{matrix} \right.$$

8. $\zeta_1 \leftarrow \overline{\mathbf{s}}\xi_1 + m_0\mathbf{y}$
9. Depending on sampling, either keeps $\delta_1 = (\xi_1, \zeta_1)$ to signer or abort as follows:
   If $\|\zeta_1\|_\infty > 6\sigma_1$, goto (1); else output (ξ_1, ζ_1) with probability

$$\left(1 - D_{R^k,0,\delta}(\zeta_1)/D_{R^k,\overline{\mathbf{s}}\xi_1,\delta_1}(\zeta_1) \right)^2 .$$

10. The signer sends ciphertext $ch_1 = (\mathbf{v}_1, \mathbf{w}_1, \xi_1, \zeta_1)$ to the arbitrator.
11. In similar way, the signer sends ciphertext $ch_2 = (\overline{\mathbf{v}}_1, \overline{\mathbf{w}}_1, \xi_2, \zeta_2)$ to the verifier.

VESDAPVer:

- If $\|\zeta_i\|_\infty > 6\sigma$ or $\xi_i \neq H(\cdot, \cdot, \cdot, p_i)$ for $i = 1, 2$, the verifier rejects; else accepts.

Adjudication:

- The arbitrator inputs secret key s_1, language member $(\mathbf{B}, \mathbf{u}_1)$, ciphertext and constant $C = max_{c,c'} \|c - c'\|_1$.

  1. $\mathbf{z}' \leftarrow [\mathbf{z}_1; \ldots; \mathbf{z}_{3k}; \mathbf{z}_{6k+1}; \ldots; \mathbf{z}_{6k+l}]$
  2. $c' \leftarrow C$
  3. $\overline{c} \leftarrow c - c'$
  4. $\overline{\sigma}_1 \leftarrow (\mathbf{w}_1 - \mathbf{v}_1 s_1)\overline{c} \bmod q$
     loop
  5. $c' \leftarrow C$

6. $\overline{c}' \leftarrow c - c'$
7. $\overline{\sigma}'_1 \leftarrow \overline{c}' \cdot \overline{\sigma}_1 / \overline{c} \bmod p$
8. If $\|\overline{\sigma}'_1\|_\infty \leqslant q/2C$ and $\|\overline{\sigma}'_1 \bmod p\|_\infty \leqslant 12\sigma$, then return

$$(\overline{\sigma}'_1 \bmod p, \overline{c}'_1) := (\overline{\mathbf{z}}_1, \overline{c}_1)$$

and sends it to the signer.
- The signer inputs his secret key $\overline{s}_1$, language member $(\mathbf{B}, \mathbf{u}_2)$, ciphertext ch_2 and constant $C = max_{\overline{c}, \overline{c}'}\|\overline{c} - \overline{c}'\|_1$. By similar method above, the signer obtains

$$(\overline{\sigma}'_2 \bmod p, \overline{c}'_2) := (\overline{\mathbf{z}}_2, \overline{c}_2)$$

and keeps it.

DAPVer:

- If $\|\overline{\mathbf{z}}_i\|_\infty > 6\sigma$ or $\overline{c}_i \neq H(\cdot, \cdot, \cdot, p_i)$ for $i = 1, 2$, the verifier rejects; else accepts.

Extract: Due to a valid signature pair $(\overline{\mathbf{z}}_1, \overline{c}_1)$ and $(\overline{\mathbf{z}}_2, \overline{c}_2)$, the signer computes

1. $\overline{\mathbf{z}}_1 \leftarrow \overline{s}\overline{c}_1 + m_0\mathbf{y}$ and $\overline{\mathbf{z}}_2 \leftarrow \overline{s}\overline{c}_2 + m_0\mathbf{y}$
2. $\overline{s} \leftarrow (\overline{\mathbf{z}}_1 - \overline{\mathbf{z}}_2)/(\overline{c}_1 - \overline{c}_2)$

5 Security Analysis and Concrete Parameters Analysis

5.1 Security Analysis

Theorem 1. *The proposed VEDAPS scheme is correct.*

Proof. According to the concrete scheme, it is easy to verify that these equations of **Define 3.2** hold. Therefore, the proposed lattice based VEDAPS scheme is correct.

Theorem 2. *The proposed VEDAPS scheme is unforgeability against chosen message attack under the hardness of the Ring-SIS.*

Proof. Unforgeability of the proposed VEDAPS scheme requires that a ciphertext with a valid proof for $(\mathbf{B}, \mathbf{u}_1, \mathbf{u}_2) \in L$ can be decrypted to a valid witness $\overline{\sigma}_1, \overline{\sigma}_2$ satisfying $\mathbf{B}\overline{\sigma}_1 = \mathbf{u}_1$ and $\mathbf{B}\overline{\sigma}_2 = \mathbf{u}_2$ with overwhelming probability. That is to say, the following probability is negligible:

$$Pr\left[\begin{array}{c} b = 1 \wedge \\ (\mathbf{B}, \mathbf{u}_1, \mathbf{u}_2, \overline{\sigma}_1, \overline{\sigma}_2) \notin \mathcal{R}_{\overline{L}} \end{array} : \begin{array}{c} ((a, t_1, \mathbf{B}, \mathbf{t}), (s_1, \mathbf{s})) \leftarrow \mathbf{AKeyGen}(1^\kappa) \\ ((a, \overline{t}_1, \mathbf{B}, \overline{\mathbf{t}}), (\overline{s}_1, \overline{\mathbf{s}})) \leftarrow \mathbf{KeyGen}(1^\kappa) \\ (\mathbf{B}, \mathbf{u}_1, ch_1) \leftarrow \mathcal{A}^{\mathcal{O}_1, \mathcal{O}_2}(APK, ASK) \\ (\mathbf{B}, \mathbf{u}_2, ch_2) \leftarrow \mathcal{A}^{\mathcal{O}_1, \mathcal{O}_2}(PK, SK) \\ b \leftarrow \mathbf{VEDAPVer}(APK, \mathbf{B}, \mathbf{u}_1, ch_1) \\ b \leftarrow \mathbf{VEDAPVer}(PK, \mathbf{B}, \mathbf{u}_2, , ch_2) \\ \overline{\sigma}_1 \leftarrow \mathbf{Adjudication}(ASK, \mathbf{B}, \mathbf{u}_1, ch_1) \\ \overline{\sigma}_2 \leftarrow \mathbf{Adjudication}(SK, \mathbf{B}, \mathbf{u}_2, ch_2) \end{array}\right]$$

From the lattice based VEDAPS scheme, we can see that $(\overline{\sigma}_1, \overline{\sigma}_2)$ is hard to solve under the hardness of the Ring-SIS. Therefore, the proposed VEDAPS scheme is unforgeability against chosen message attack.

Theorem 3. *The proposed VEDAPS scheme is opacity under IND-CPA security of Ring-LWE encryption.*

Proof. The opacity of our proposed VEDAPS scheme requires that there exists a simulator **Sim** such that any adversary $\mathcal{A}$ can not distinguish real ciphertexts from simulated ciphertexts. That is to say, there exists a negligible $\varepsilon(\kappa)$ such that the following equation holds:

$$
\left| Pr \left[b' = b : \begin{array}{c} b \leftarrow \{0,1\}, \\ ((a, t_1, \mathbf{B}, \mathbf{t}), (s_1, \mathbf{s})) \leftarrow \mathbf{AKeyGen}(1^\kappa) \\ ((a, \overline{t}_1, \mathbf{B}, \overline{\mathbf{t}}), (\overline{s}_1, \overline{\mathbf{s}})) \leftarrow \mathbf{KeyGen}(1^\kappa) \\ (st, \mathbf{B}, \mathbf{u}_1, \mathbf{u}_2, \sigma_1, \sigma_2) \leftarrow \mathcal{A}^{\mathcal{O}_1, \mathcal{O}_2}(APK) \\ \overline{\delta}_0 \leftarrow \mathbf{VEDAPSig}(APK, PK, \mathbf{B}, \mathbf{u}_1, \sigma_1, \mathbf{u}_2, \sigma_2) \\ \overline{\delta}_1 \leftarrow \mathbf{Sim}(APK, PK, \mathbf{B}, \mathbf{u}_1, \mathbf{u}_2) \\ b' \leftarrow \mathcal{A}^{\mathbf{Adjudication}(SK, ASK, \cdot)}(\cdot, \overline{\delta}_b) \end{array} \right] - 1/2 \right| \leq \varepsilon(\kappa),
$$

where $\mathcal{A}$ is not allowed to query its **Adjudication** oracle on the challenge ciphertext $\overline{\delta}_b$. From the probability above we can see that if Ring-LWE encryption is secure, the advantage of $\mathcal{A}$ is negligible. Therefore, the proposed VEDAPS scheme is opacity.

Theorem 4. *The proposed VEDAPS scheme is extractability.*

Proof. On the basis of **Theorem 1**, it is easy to verify the extractability from the algorithm **Extract**.

5.2 Concrete Parameters Analysis

In our VEDAPS scheme, the security in terms of the "gamma factor" is from [18]. Its values of less than 1.005 are believed to require more than 2^{128} time for quantum computers. Secret and error parameters of Ring-LWE is from the set $\{-1, 0, 1\}$, when constructing Ring-LWE encryption schemes with smaller errors there have not found any weakness. According to the hardness of solving Ring-LWE problem and SIS problem, we give some concrete parameters in Table 1.

From the Table 1, we can see that our constructed VEDAPS has reasonable efficiency for real applications.

Table 1. Sample parameter sets for our VEDAPS scheme

n	1024	2048	2048
k	1	2	2
p	13	2^{15}	2^{30}
$\|\sigma_i\|_\infty$	1	1	2^{18}
σ	50688	101376	$\approx 2^{24.6}$
q	$\approx 2^{34}$	$\approx 2^{47}$	$\approx 2^{70}$
Gamma factor	1.0046	≈ 1.0033	≈ 1.0052
Proof size	18 KB	76 KB	108 KB
Ciphertext size	18 KB	96 KB	142 KB

6   Conclusions and Future Work

In this paper, we formalized the concept of VEDAPS which is derived from verifiably encrypted signatures and double authentication preventing signatures. Then we presented the first lattice-based VEDAPS. Security analysis shows that our scheme satisfies our defined security properties including correctness, opacity, unforgeability and extractability. We also proved our VEDAPS scheme is secure in the random oracle model according to these definitions. Parameter analyses demonstrate that our construction has reasonable efficiency for real applications. In future work, we will focus on applications of lattice-based verifiable encrypted double authentication preventing signatures.

Acknowledgement. This work was supported by National Key R&D Program of China (2017YFB0802000), National Natural Science Foundation of China (61872229, 61802239), NSFC Research Fund for International Young Scientists (61750110528), National Cryptography Development Fund during the 13th Five-year Plan Period (MMJJ20170216), Natural Science Basic Research Plan in Shaanxi Province of China (Program No. 2019JQ-667), China Postdoctoral Science Foundation (2018M631121) and Fundamental Research Funds for the Central Universities(GK201702004, 2018CBLY006).

References

1. Asokan, N., Shoup, V., Waidner, M.: Optimistic fair exchange of digital signatures. In: Nyberg, K. (ed.) EUROCRYPT 1998. LNCS, vol. 1403, pp. 591–606. Springer, Heidelberg (1998). https://doi.org/10.1007/BFb0054156
2. Asokan, N., Shoup, V., Waidner, M.: Optimistic fair exchange of digital signatures. IEEE J. Sel. Areas Commun. **18**(4), 593–610 (2000)
3. Park, J.M., Chong, E.K.P., Siegel, H.J.: Constructing fair-exchange protocols for E-commerce via distributed computation of RSA signatures. In: Proceedings of the Twenty-Second Annual Symposium on Principles of Distributed Computing, pp. 172–181. ACM (2003)

4. Dodis, Y., Reyzin, L.: Breaking and repairing optimistic fair exchange from PODC 2003. In: Proceedings of the 3rd ACM Workshop on Digital Rights Management, pp. 47–54. ACM (2003)
5. Dodis, Y., Lee, P.J., Yum, D.H.: Optimistic fair exchange in a multi-user setting. In: Okamoto, T., Wang, X. (eds.) PKC 2007. LNCS, vol. 4450, pp. 118–133. Springer, Heidelberg (2007). https://doi.org/10.1007/978-3-540-71677-8_9
6. Zhang, Z., Feng, D., Xu, J., Zhou, Y.: Efficient ID-based optimistic fair exchange with provable security. In: Qing, S., Mao, W., López, J., Wang, G. (eds.) ICICS 2005. LNCS, vol. 3783, pp. 14–26. Springer, Heidelberg (2005). https://doi.org/10.1007/11602897_2
7. Huang, Q., Wong, D.S., Susilo, W.: The construction of ambiguous optimistic fair exchange from designated confirmer signature without random oracles. Inf. Sci. **228**, 222–238 (2013)
8. Wang, Y., Wu, Q., Wong, D.S., et al.: Provably secure robust optimistic fair exchange of distributed signatures. Future Gener. Comput. Syst. **62**, 29–39 (2016)
9. Seo, J.H., Emura, K., Xagawa, K., et al.: Accumulable optimistic fair exchange from verifiably encrypted homomorphic signatures. Int. J. Inf. Secur. **17**(2), 193–220 (2018)
10. Rückert, M., Schröder, D.: Security of verifiably encrypted signatures and a construction without random oracles. In: Shacham, H., Waters, B. (eds.) Pairing 2009. LNCS, vol. 5671, pp. 17–34. Springer, Heidelberg (2009). https://doi.org/10.1007/978-3-642-03298-1_2
11. Lu, S., Ostrovsky, R., Sahai, A., et al.: Sequential aggregate signatures, multisignatures, and verifiably encrypted signatures without random oracles. J. Cryptol. **26**(2), 340–373 (2013)
12. Boneh, D., Gentry, C., Lynn, B., Shacham, H.: Aggregate and verifiably encrypted signatures from bilinear maps. In: Biham, E. (ed.) EUROCRYPT 2003. LNCS, vol. 2656, pp. 416–432. Springer, Heidelberg (2003). https://doi.org/10.1007/3-540-39200-9_26
13. Gu, C., Zhu, Y.: An ID-Based verifiable encrypted signature scheme based on Hess's scheme. In: Feng, D., Lin, D., Yung, M. (eds.) CISC 2005. LNCS, vol. 3822, pp. 42–52. Springer, Heidelberg (2005). https://doi.org/10.1007/11599548_4
14. Zhang, L., Wu, Q., Qin, B.: Identity-based verifiably encrypted signatures without random oracles. In: Pieprzyk, J., Zhang, F. (eds.) ProvSec 2009. LNCS, vol. 5848, pp. 76–89. Springer, Heidelberg (2009). https://doi.org/10.1007/978-3-642-04642-1_8
15. Zhenfeng, Z.: Cryptanalysis of an identity-based verifiably encrypted signature scheme. Chin. J. Comput. **29**(9), P1688–1693 (2006)
16. Galindo, D., Herranz, J., Kiltz, E.: On the generic construction of identity-based signatures with additional properties. In: Lai, X., Chen, K. (eds.) ASIACRYPT 2006. LNCS, vol. 4284, pp. 178–193. Springer, Heidelberg (2006). https://doi.org/10.1007/11935230_12
17. Wang, Z., Luo, X., Wu, Q.: Verifiably encrypted group signatures. In: Okamoto, T., Yu, Y., Au, M.H., Li, Y. (eds.) ProvSec 2017. LNCS, vol. 10592, pp. 107–126. Springer, Cham (2017). https://doi.org/10.1007/978-3-319-68637-0_7
18. Gama, N., Nguyen, P.Q.: Predicting lattice reduction. In: Smart, N. (ed.) EUROCRYPT 2008. LNCS, vol. 4965, pp. 31–51. Springer, Heidelberg (2008). https://doi.org/10.1007/978-3-540-78967-3_3
19. Poettering, B., Stebila, D.: Double authentication preventing signatures. Int. J. Inf. Secur. **16**(1), 1–22 (2014)

20. Poettering, B., Stebila, D.: Double-authentication-preventing signatures. In: Kutyłowski, M., Vaidya, J. (eds.) ESORICS 2014. LNCS, vol. 8712, pp. 436–453. Springer, Cham (2014). https://doi.org/10.1007/978-3-319-11203-9_25

21. Bellare, M., Poettering, B., Stebila, D.: Deterring certificate subversion: efficient double-authentication-preventing signatures. In: Fehr, S. (ed.) PKC 2017. LNCS, vol. 10175, pp. 121–151. Springer, Heidelberg (2017). https://doi.org/10.1007/978-3-662-54388-7_5

22. Boneh, D., Kim, S.: Nikolaenko, V.: Self- enforcement in signature schemes. In: ACNS, Lattice-Based DAPS and Generalizations, pp. 457–477 (2017)

23. Derler, D., Ramacher, S., Slamanig, D.: Short double and N times authentication preventing signatures from ECDSA and more. In: IEEE EuroS&P 2018, pp. 273–287 (2018)

24. Poettering, B.: Shorter double-authentication preventing signatures for small address spaces. In: Joux, A., Nitaj, A., Rachidi, T. (eds.) AFRICACRYPT 2018. LNCS, vol. 10831, pp. 344–361. Springer, Cham (2018). https://doi.org/10.1007/978-3-319-89339-6_19

25. Derler, D., Ramacher, S., Slamanig, D.: Generic double-authentication preventing signatures and a post-quantum instantiation. In: Baek, J., Susilo, W., Kim, J. (eds.) ProvSec 2018. LNCS, vol. 11192, pp. 258–276. Springer, Cham (2018). https://doi.org/10.1007/978-3-030-01446-9_15

26. Liu, J., Yu, Y., Jia, J., Wang, S., Wang, H.: Lattice based double authentication preventing ring signature for security and privacy in vehicular ad-hoc networks. Tsinghua Sci. Technol. 24, 575–584 (2019)

27. Shor, P.W.: Polynomial-time algorithms for prime factorization and discrete logarithms on a quantum computer. SIAM Rev. 41(2), 303–332 (1999)

28. Gentry, C., Peikert, C., Vaikuntanathan, V.: Trapdoors for hard lattices and new cryptographic constructions. In: Proceedings of the 40th Annual ACM Symposium on Theory of Computing, Victoria, British Columbia, Canada, 17–20 May 2008. ACM (2008)

29. Boschini, C., Camenisch, J., Neven, G.: Relaxed lattice-based signatures with short zero-knowledge proofs. In: Chen, L., Manulis, M., Schneider, S. (eds.) ISC 2018. LNCS, vol. 11060, pp. 3–22. Springer, Cham (2018). https://doi.org/10.1007/978-3-319-99136-8_1

30. Chaidos, P., Couteau, G.: Efficient designated-verifier non-interactive zero-knowledge proofs of knowledge. In: Nielsen, J.B., Rijmen, V. (eds.) EUROCRYPT 2018. LNCS, vol. 10822, pp. 193–221. Springer, Cham (2018). https://doi.org/10.1007/978-3-319-78372-7_7

31. Lyubashevsky, V., Neven, G.: One-shot verifiable encryption from lattices. In: Coron, J.-S., Nielsen, J.B. (eds.) EUROCRYPT 2017. LNCS, vol. 10210, pp. 293–323. Springer, Cham (2017). https://doi.org/10.1007/978-3-319-56620-7_11

Privacy-Preserving Sequential Data Publishing

Huili Wang[1,2], Wenping Ma[1], Haibin Zheng[3(✉)], Zhi Liang[3],
and Qianhong Wu[4]

[1] State Key Laboratory of Integrated Services Networks, Xidian University,
Xi'an 710071, People's Republic of China
wpma@mail.xidian.edu.cn
[2] China Electronics Standardization Institute, Beijing, China
wanghuili@cesi.cn
[3] School of Electronic and Information Engineering, Beihang University,
Beijing, China
zhenghaibin29@buaa.edu.cn, seaeory@126.com
[4] School of Cyber Science and Technology, Beihang University, Beijing, China
qianhong.wu@buaa.edu.cn

Abstract. Machine learning in artificial intelligence relies on legitimate big data, where the process of data publishing involves a large number of privacy issues. m-Invariance is a fundamental privacy-preserving notion in microdata republication. Unfortunately, if for big data release, the existing generalization based m-Invariance requiring to modify the origin microdata incurs the problems of data utility loss and poor aggregate querying performance. Furthermore, due to the high dimension of quasi-identifiers in big data, unaffordable generalization operations makes it difficult to be practical. In this paper, we remedy the drawbacks above to achieve m-Invariance in big data release. We first propose a new anatomy based m-Invariance definition and framework, where the anatomy approach tries to achieve privacy by breaking the correlations between the sensitive attributes and non-sensitive identifiers. We next establish a series of criteria for anatomy to cope with republication due to the data dynamics. We then develop an algorithm to realize the above ideas. Theoretical and experimental analysis confirm the advantages of our anatomy based m-Invariance approach in the terms of data utility, aggregate querying accuracy and capacity to process high dimension of quasi-identifiers in big data release.

Keywords: Artificial intelligence · Big data · Microdata disclosure · Privacy · m-Invariance · Anatomy

1 Introduction

With the development of big data and cloud computing technology, artificial intelligence (AI) has been one of the most popular Internet applications. Big

J. K. Liu and X. Huang (Eds.): NSS 2019, LNCS 11928, pp. 596–614, 2019.
https://doi.org/10.1007/978-3-030-36938-5_37

data has become an important driver for artificial intelligence, because many algorithms of artificial intelligence depend on big data, such as machine learning and deep learning [1]. Legitimate big data collection comes from everyone in our daily lives, which makes data security and privacy protection become more urgent during the process of data publishing [2]. At present, most work on big data focuses on information processing, such as data mining and analysis. However, since big data contains much sensitive information of users, the privacy concerns of users must be addressed for such applications based on big data. This motivates us to investigate practical privacy-preserving technologies in big data release.

A lot of privacy-preserving methods have been proposed to ensure the privacy during data publications. The well-known approaches include k-anonymity [3], ℓ-diversity [4], t-closeness [5], δ-presence [6], and differential privacy [7]. The corresponding algorithms have also been developed [8,9]. However, such requirements focused on "one-time" publication privacy. For big data, due to its high dynamic, there is a great demand of republication to meet updated data sets. The above technologies fail to cope with the privacy requirements in such a scenario.

m-Invariance [10] is a fundamental concept to achieve privacy in republication of data sets. It requires that every tuple's hosting quasi-identifier group has the same sensitive attributes sets on *each publication*, so that the attacker can not figure out the correct sensitive values from the different publications. However, the existing m-Invariance employs *generalization* of the attributes, which incurs information loss of the original data and decreases the accuracy of aggregate queries. Furthermore, when the dimension of quasi-identifier gets very high, numerous *generalization* operations are required to meet the m-Invariance requirement. All these pitfalls hinders the m-Invariance employing *generalization* technique to be deployed for privacy protection in big data release.

Anatomy has been proposed to achieve ℓ-diversity notion in microdata disclosure. In *anatomy* [9], the original data set is split into two tables of quasi-identifiers and sensitive attributes, where the data tuples' mapping relations between two tables are confused to achieve privacy. Compared with the *generalization* approach, there is no original data to be generalized in *anatomy* which means data loss, while released data can satisfy the same privacy level, as shown in [9]. Although *anatomy* has better properties than *generalization*, the existing *anatomy* approach doesn't support republication of data sets due to data updates, and thus cannot be deployed for big data release.

1.1 Motivation

We observe the deficiency of *anatomy* when dealing with data publications. Consider the scenario of a medical data disclosure where sensitive medical big data is released and shared by medical staffs, scientific researchers, the medical officials and the public for various applications. Table 1 shows the original microdata. The original microdata is anatomized into Tables 3 and 4. The microdata of the second publication is presented in Table 2, in which the tuples regarding Alice, Andy, Helen, Ken, and Steve have been deleted from the Table 1, and five new tuples about Ray, Emily, Vince, Tom, and Mary are inserted. Similarly, anato-mized relations of Table 2 are presented in Tables 5 and 6, respectively. Tuple's insertion and deletion stands for the practical conditions when the patient is admitted and discharged from the hospital.

Table 1. Microdata $T(1)$

Name	Age	Zip.	Disease
Alice	36	27000	Gastritis
Andy	24	18000	Flu
Bob	56	34000	Gastritis
David	21	12000	Dyspepsia
Gary	23	25000	Gastritis
Helen	52	33000	Dyspepsia
Jane	41	20000	Flu
Ken	22	14000	Bronchitis
Linda	37	33000	Dyspepsia
Paul	43	26000	Gastritis
Steve	40	35000	Flu

Table 2. Microdata $T(2)$

Name	Age	Zip.	Disease
Emily	25	21000	Gastritis
Mary	46	30000	Flu
Bob	56	34000	Gastritis
David	21	12000	Dyspepsia
Gary	23	25000	Gastritis
Ray	54	31000	Dyspepsia
Jane	41	20000	Flu
Vince	65	36000	Gatritis
Linda	37	33000	Dyspepsia
Paul	43	26000	Gastritis
Tom	60	44000	Flu

One may note that both publications are 2-diverse. However, by comparing the published tables, if an adversary has the background knowledge of Jane's age and Zipcode and knows that Jane has a record in both quarter's tables, then the adversary can conclude that Jane's sensitive value, her disease, is *flu*. Specifically, according to Tables 3 and 4, the adversary can conclude that Jane has caught flu or bronchitis; from Tables 5 and 6, the adversary knows that Jane

Table 3. The quasi-identifier table $T_{QI}^*(1)$

Name	Age	Zip.	Group ID
Alice	36	27000	1
Andy	24	18000	1
Bob	56	34000	2
David	21	12000	2
Gary	23	25000	3
Helen	52	33000	3
Jane	41	20000	4
Ken	22	14000	4
Linda	37	33000	5
Paul	43	26000	5
Steve	40	35000	5

Table 4. The sensitive table $T_{SA}^*(1)$

Group ID	Disease	Count
1	Gastritis	1
1	Flu	1
2	Gastritis	1
2	Dyspepsia	1
3	Gastritis	1
3	Dyspepsia	1
4	Flu	1
4	Bronchitis	1
5	Dyspepsia	1
5	Gastritis	1
5	Flu	1

has contacted flu or gastritis. Therefore, the adversary is sure that Jane has caught a flu, which implies the compromise of Jane's sensitive information. The background knowledge mentioned is not hard for the adversary to collect.

Table 5. The quasi-identifier table $T_{QI}^*(2)$ **Table 6.** The sensitive table $T_{SA}^*(2)$

Name	Age	Zip.	Group ID
Emily	25	21000	1
Mary	46	30000	1
Bob	56	34000	2
David	21	12000	2
Gary	23	25000	3
Ray	54	31000	3
Jane	41	20000	4
Vince	65	36000	4
Linda	37	33000	5
Paul	43	26000	5
Tom	60	44000	5

Group ID	Disease	Count
1	Gastritis	1
1	Flu	1
2	Gastritis	1
2	Dyspepsia	1
3	Gastritis	1
3	Dyspepsia	1
4	Flu	1
4	Gastritis	1
5	Dyspepsia	1
5	Gastritis	1
5	Flu	1

Due to the leaked correlations between two publications, the *anatomy* approach can not be directly employed to protect privacy in big data release. However, as an privacy-preserving technique in data disclosure, the *anatomy* approach has its advantages in computation efficiency, low data distortion, aggregate query accuracy and independence of non-sensitive identifiers. A natural arising problem is whether we can improve the *anatomy* approach without losing its advantages. To the best of our knowledge, there is no research work on this problem in the public literatures.

1.2   Our Contribution

Our main idea is to incorporate the *anatomy* approach into the privacy concept of m-Invariance for big data release. Concretely, our main contributions include the following aspects. First, we adapt the classic *generalization* based m-Invariance implementation mechanism, and propose a new *anatomy* based m-Invariance definition and framework. Second, we develop a series of criteria to stipulate performances for anatomy to cope with the subtleties incurred by republication. Third, we instantiate the *anatomy* based m-Invariance framework. In addition, extensive theoretical and experimental analysis are also conducted.

Now we briefly illustrate our *anatomy* based m-Invariance approach using the above example. For this purpose, let us see Tables 7, 8 and 9. Table 7 is the anatomized quasi-identifier table of the original microdata in Table 2 using our algorithm, together with two counterfeit tuples c_1 and c_2. Here, the age and

Zipcode messages are substituted with the mathematical symbol $\emptyset$. Table 8 shows the number of the sensitive attributes in each quasi-identifier group. Table 9 indicates that two counterfeits are placed in QI groups 4 and 5, respectively. Assume that the adversary has the age and Zipcode information about Jane and knows that Jane is in the published tables in the two sequential publications. From Tables 3, 4, 7, 8, the QI group which Jane is in has the same sensitive values *dyspepsia, bronchitis*. Therefore, the adversary can not decide the exact disease Jane has caught. This illustrates that our *anatomy* based m-Invariance approach does not leak information about the correlations among released tables.

Table 7. $T^*_{QI}(2)$ with counterfeits

Name	Age	Zip.	Group ID
Emily	25	21000	1
Mary	46	30000	1
Bob	56	34000	2
David	21	12000	2
Gary	23	25000	3
Ray	54	31000	3
Jane	41	20000	4
c_1	$\emptyset$	$\emptyset$	4
Linda	37	33000	5
Paul	43	26000	5
c_2	$\emptyset$	$\emptyset$	5
Vince	65	36000	6
Tom	60	44000	6

Table 8. $T^*_{SA}(2)$ with counterfeits

Group ID	Disease	Count
1	Gastritis	1
1	Flu	1
2	Gastritis	1
2	Dyspepsia	1
3	Gastritis	1
3	Dyspepsia	1
4	Flu	1
4	Bronchitis	1
5	Dyspepsia	1
5	Ggastritis	1
5	Flu	1
6	Gastritis	1
6	Flu	1

Table 9. Published counterfeits statistics

Group ID	Count
4	1
5	1

1.3 Related Work

Privacy in big data release has received great attentions recent years. k-anonymity [3] and ℓ-diversity [4] are popular privacy requirements. k-anonymity requires that each QI group should have k identical quasi-attributes so the adversary can not conclude sensitive value with possibility beyond $1/k$. ℓ-diversity proposes two new type of attacks called homogeneity attack and background knowledge attack, which k-anonymity can not resist, so ℓ-diversity demands that each QI group should have at least 1 distinct sensitive values. Many algorithms (e.g., [8,9,11–13]) have been proposed to implement these two privacy requirements in various practice scenarios. Traditional anonymity methods are generalization and suppression. Two methods may be used together or separately. Though Meyerson et al. [14] pointed that an optimal anonymity algorithm is a NP-hard problem, Bayardo et al. [15] proposed an approach to find optimal k anonymity algorithm. Other popular anonymity methods include *anatomy* [9], *permutation* [16], and *perturbation* [17].

Since the well-knwon *k*-anonymity were proposed, more requirements have been recognized to protect privacy on certain conditions. *t*-closeness [5] requires that the distribution of the sensitive values in QI group should have the differences below a threshold t with the distribution of the total table. Soria et al. [18] recently proposed and shows how to use microaggregation to generate t -close data sets. δ-presence [6] was proposed to require that the possibility a target tuple is in a table should have the min and max bounds of $(\delta_{min}, \delta_{max})$ in order to resist table linkage attacks. Differential privacy [7] requires the results of certain queries should not change no matter whether one record is in the dataset or not. The related research about differential privacy includes [19–21]. However, all the requirements and algorithms focus on "one-time" publication, while in practice the table may be published more than one time through inserting or deleting tuples.

m-Invariance [10] has been introduced to handle the issue in the republication scenarios. Before *m*-Invariance was proposed, people focused on maintaining anonymity for incremental datasets. In [22], the paper proposed an algorithm which applies the conventional Mondrian method to incremental republication and achieves good efficiency. Byun et al. [23] analyzed various inference channels that exist in multiple republication tables and proposed to store unqualified tuples. Aiming at conditions where the sensitive values may change each publication time, [24] proposed an approach called HD-composition to solve the problem. There are also literatures achieving microdata disclosure privacy by tools of cluster [25,26], concerning collaborative data [27], and in the scenarios of artificial intelligence [28,29].

2   Fundamental Definitions and New Anatomy Based *m*-Invariance Framework

In this section, we extend the fundamental notions related to *anatomy* and *m*-Invariance so that they can be employed in our new *anatomy* based *m*-Invariance framework.

Let T be a microdata table maintained by the publisher. We classify the columns of T into several parts: (i) an identifier attribute A^{id}, which is the primary key of each tuple of the table, (ii) d quasi-identifier attributes, $A_1^{qi}, ..., A_d^{qi}$, which represent the insensitive attributes but indicate the personal information such as age, Zipcode, and etc, (iii) a sensitive attribute A^s. Each time when T is updated, the tuples of T may be inserted or deleted. We denote $T(j)$ as the snapshot of T at time j, $T_{QI}^*(j)$ as the quasi-identifier attributes table with counterfeits of T at time j, $T_{SA}^*(j)$ as the sensitive attributes table at the j-th time, and finally, $R(j)$ as the table recording the counterfeits statistics. The publisher releases a set of relation tables $\{T_{QI}^*(j), T_{SA}^*(j), R(j)\}$ each time.

To capture *anatomy* based m-Invariance, inspired by the corresponding definitions mentioned in [9,10], we clarify the following basic notions.

Definition 1 (Partition/QI group). *For a microdata table $T(j)$, a **partition** consists several subsets of $T(j)$, such that each tuple in T belongs to one subset. A **QI group** is a subset of the tuples after partition, and we denote them as $QI_1, QI_2, ...QI_m$, where each QI group is assigned an unique ID.*

In addition, for a tuple $t \in T(j)$, we denote $t.QI(j)$ as the hosting group of t in $T_{QI}^*(j)$. Compared with conventional definition in *anatomy*, we no longer require that each QI group is not overlapped.

Definition 2 (Counterfeit substitution). *For each QI group QI_k of $T_{QI}^*(j)$, QI_k may have some **counterfeit tuples** t_c. For t_c in the quasi-identifier table of $T_{QI}^*(j)$ which has $d + 1$ columns, t_c has the schema as follows:*

$$(\emptyset, \emptyset, ..., \emptyset, k)$$

where there are d number of $\emptyset$ in the quasi-identifier table filling all quasi-attributes columns of one counterfeit tuple.

The symbol $\emptyset$ represents null. We can consider the counterfeit tuple as an infilling of the missing rows. In fact, the adversary can get nothing from the counterfeit tuples. The counterfeit tuple is employed here to keep consistency of the distribution of the original QI group.

Definition 3 (Auxiliary relation). *The **auxiliary relation** $R(j)$ accompanying $T_{QI}^*(j)$ has two columns "Group-ID" and "count". For each QI-group QI^* in $T_{QI}^*(j)$ that contains at least a counterfeit, there is a row $\langle g, c \rangle$, where g represents the group ID of the counterfeit tuple and c represents the number of counterfeits in this QI-group.*

The counterfeit tuples are necessary for privacy in m-Invariance requirement to deal with the deletion when the table is updated. The counterfeit tuples doesn't disturb the origin microdata but hold the privacy through projection relations by *anatomy*. Now we refine the *anatomy* definition to satisfy m-Invariance notion.

Definition 4 (Anatomy). *Given an m-Invariance partition with d QI-groups, for the jth time republication $T(j)$, anatomy produces a quasi-identifier table $T_{QI}^*(j)$, a sensitive table $T_{SA}^*(j)$ and an auxiliary relation table $R(j)$ as follows. The $T_{QI}^*(j)$ has the schema:*

$$(A_1^{qi}, A_2^{qi} ..., A_d^{qi}, groupID)$$

For each QI-group $QI_k(1 \leq k \leq d)$, and each tuple $t \in QI_k$, $T_{QI}^*(j)$ has a tuple of form:

$$(t[1], t[2], ..., t[d], k)$$

The $T_{SA}^*(j)$ has the schema:

$$(groupID, A^s, count_s)$$

Then auxiliary relation $R(j)$ has the schema:

$$(groupID, count_c)$$

Here, $count_s$ represents the number of each sensitive attributes in a certain QI group; $count_c$ represents the number of counterfeits in a certain QI group. Thus when one applies *anatomy* to the m-Invariance concept, one will get three tables as feedback: the quasi-identifier table representing the relation between the quasi-attributes and the QI groups with possible counterfeit tuples, the sensitive table indicating the number of the sensitive values in each separated QI group, and the auxiliary relation table denoting the number of the counterfeit tuples in each QI group.

The classic m-Invariance mechanism was proposed based on the *generalization* tables. The mechanism requires that (i) each QI group of $T^*(j)$ has m unique sensitive values, similarly to the definition of ℓ-diversity, and (ii) for each republication, the tuple t_i within its lifespan should have the same hosting group. Unlike the conventional *generalization* approach which releases only one table, the *anatomy* approach releases three tables. To achieve the same privacy goal of the m-Invariance in a single publication, we incorporate the *anatomy* technique and extend the m-Invariance to a sequential microdata disclosure setting.

Definition 5 (Anatomy based m-Invariance). *Suppose a set of tables*

$$\{T_{QI}^*(j), T_{SA}^*(j), R(j)\}(1 \leq j \leq n).$$

We say that the released tables satisfies m-Invariance if the following conditions hold:

1. *In $T_{SA}^*(j)(1 \leq j \leq n)$, each group has at least m tuples, and all the tuples in group have different sensitive values.*
2. *For every tuple t in $T_{QI}^*(j)(1 \leq j \leq n)$, with its lifespan between x and y, $t.QI(x), t.QI(x+1), ..., t.QI(y)$ have the same signature, where $t.QI(j)$ is the sensitive hosting group.*

where the signature means the corresponding set of the distinct sensitive values in the QI group $T_{SA}^*(j)$ for $t \in T_{SA}^*(j)$. The tuple's lifespan between x and y means that tuple t exists from the x-th publication to the y-th publication tables.

The first rule implies ℓ-diversity privacy, where each group contains at least m distinct sensitive attributes values. This means that, for each group in $T_Q^*I(j)$

and $T^*_{SA}(j)$, the sensitive attributes satisfy m-diversity. To further protect the privacy between the tables, the second rule ensures that, the hosting group of the tuple should have the same sensitive distribution in the sequential publications. To understand the rules, let tuple t be Gary in Table 7. When Table 3 was published, Gary lay in group 3. We check group 3 in Table 4 and can find that group 3 includes the sensitive attribute set $\{gastritis, dyspepsia\}$. When Table 7 was published, although the tuple Helen was substituted for Ray, the sensitive values in group 3 remained the same. All the groups in Tables 7 and 8 still have at least 2 distinct sensitive values. Therefore, Tables 7, 8 and 9 satisfy the m-Invariance. From the analysis above, we can conclude that the m-Invariance privacy covers the ℓ-diversity privacy. As shown in [10], when $\{T^*_{QI}(j), T^*_{SA}(j), R(j)\}(1 \leq j \leq n)$ satisfy m-Invariance, the risk that privacy disclosure is no more than $1/m$.

Finally, we introduce the definition of re-construction error (RCE) mentioned in [9] to measure the error to be made when data is recovered from the tables anatomized by *anatomy*. We hope the RCE to be small, which indicates less information loss.

Definition 6 (Re-construction error). *Taking all tuples $t \in T$ into consideration, the re-construction error (RCE) is defined by the sum of each tuple's error Err_t, where Err_t is defined as follows:*

$$Err_t = \int_{x \in DS} (\tilde{\mathcal{G}}_t(x) - \mathcal{G}_t(x))^2 \tag{1}$$

where $\mathcal{G}_t(x)$ is represented for probability density function of a certain tuple t, $\tilde{\mathcal{G}}_t(x)$ is denoted as the probability density function of the tuple $t's$ QI hosting group in $T^*_{SA}(j)$. The definition is as follows:

Definition 7 (Probability density function). *Probability density function reveals the distribution of a tuple in the anonymized tables, $\tilde{\mathcal{G}}_t(x)$ and $\mathcal{G}_t(x)$ have the definitions below:*

$$\mathcal{G}_t(x) = \begin{cases} 1 & if\ x = (t[1], ...t[d]) \\ 0 & otherwise \end{cases} \tag{2}$$

$$\tilde{\mathcal{G}}_t(x) = \begin{cases} num(v_1)/|QI| & if\ x = (t[1], ...t[d], v_1) \\ num(v_2)/|QI| & if\ x = (t[1], ...t[d], v_2) \\ ... \\ num(v_k)/|QI| & if\ x = (t[1], ...t[d], v_k) \\ 0 & otherwise \end{cases} \tag{3}$$

where $|QI|$ means the total number of the tuples in the hosting QI group of tuple t, $num(v_i)(1 \leq i \leq k)$ represents the count of tuples whose sensitive value equals v_i in QI group. We can find that the RCE reflects the difference between the distributions of one tuple and its hosting group. If the distribution of the hosting group is similar to the distribution of the tuple itself, to recover the original information is easier. The smaller the RCE is, the less information anonymity operation contributes. Therefore, one can use RCE to measure the loss of information.

3   The Algorithm

To apply the requirement to *anatomy*, we first provide the m-Invariance requirement for *anatomy* in Sect. 2. Based on the design thought of m-Invariance, we aim at achieving two goals in the algorithm when the privacy is guaranteed.

Assume that an adversary holds all the past time publication of microdata, $T(1), T(2), ..., T(n)$ and the target man's all quasi-identifier attributes (e.g. in Tables 1 and 2, the adversary knows the age and Zipcode of Jane). To illustrate the algorithm conveniently, we introduce two symbols: $S_\cap = T(n) \cap T(n-1)$ and $S_- = T(n) - T(n-1)$, where $S_\cap$ indicates the mutual tuples between contiguous tables, and S_- represents the tuples that $T(n)$ contains but $T(n-1)$ does not have. Thanks to Lemma 1, we can produce published tables on dependence of last published tables. Therefore, the rules in Definition 5 can be translated into the following form:

1. For any tuple $t \in S_\cap$, its anonymized hosting groups $t.QI(n-1)$ and $t.QI(n)$ in $T^*_{SA}(n-1)$ and $T^*_{SA}(n)$ have the same signature.
2. For any tuple $t \in S_-$, the anonymized tuple t in $T^*_{QI}(n)$ is in the group of $T^*_{SA}(n)$ which has at least m tuples and all the tuples have distinct values.

From the statements above we can conclude the basic idea is that the hosting group of the remaining tuples should maintain the same signature, and the new inserted tuples which is different from previous ones should be filled into new created hosting group to satisfy m-diversity. In the view of making the results simplified and efficient, we should also try to meet more requirements. First, the number of counterfeit tuples should be minimized, for the reason that a counterfeit tuple responds to no actual record in the microdata. Too many counterfeits may lead to the accumulation of useless information decreasing validity. Second, the algorithm should minimize the re-construction error (RCE) mentioned. The smaller RCE is, the less the information of the microdata loses. Therefore the algorithm produces $\{T^*_{QI}(n), T^*_{SA}(n), R(n)\}$ in four phase: *division, balancing, assignment, populate*. The corresponding pseudocode of the algorithm *m-Anatomize* is presented in Algorithm 1. To make our algorithm more comprehensible, we will illustrate the algorithm by introducing generations of the Tables mentioned above, where $m = 2, n = 2$, and Tables 1, 2, 3, 4, 7, 8, 9.

Division. (Lines 1–5) We partition the $S_\cap$ into several groups, each group has certain sensitive values which counts at least m. We call such group the *bucket*, such that each *bucket* contains only the tuples with the same signature.

In the running example, $S_\cap$ contains the tuples of Bob, David, Gary, Jane, Linda, Paul, and there are four buckets containing the residual tuples. Figure 1a shows the contents of the buckets after division. For example, the bucket BUC_3 has the signature of two sensitive attributes $\{flu, bronchitis\}$, while the bucket holds only Jane because Alice is deleted from Table 2. Also, the buckets can contain nothing (such as BUC_1) or tuples more than the number of the sensitive values (such as BUC_2), caused by different *delete* selections. The division phase

(a) Bucket contents after the division phase   (b) Bucket contents after the balancing phase

(c) Bucket contents after the assignment phase

Fig. 1. Illustration of algorithm

mainly deals with the tuples in $S_\cap$, filling the bucket with the residual tuples in $S_\cap$.

Balancing. (Lines 6–27) After filling the $S_\cap$ tuples in the buckets, we aim at balancing the buckets using new inserted tuples in S_- and counterfeit tuples. We say that the bucket is balanced if every sensitive value in its signature is owned by the same number of tuples in BUC or its multiple [10]. The number of the tuples is needed to balance the bucket. To balance the buckets in Fig. 1a, the balancing phase takes the following steps:

1. We sort the tuples in S_- by the descending order of count of sensitive values, we get a set of tuples $s_1, s_2, ..., s_q$, s_1 represents the set of tuples which has the same sensitive value, and count of this sensitive value is larger than any other sensitive value.
2. We sort the buckets in the descending order of the number of tuples that is needed to balance the bucket.
3. Then we begin with the iteration. We randomly choose one tuple in s_1 to fill in the unbalanced bucket which lacks the same sensitive value as s_1, and the tuple is inserted into priority to the BUC ranked at front in step 2. Each time when a filling operation is taken, s_1 and the bucket are updated by steps 1 and 2. The iteration breaks when (i) no tuple in S_- carries the sensitive values which the unbalanced buckets lack, or (ii) s_1 is no more than $1/m$ of the sum of the number of the residual tuples in S_- if one more tuple is removed:

$$s_1 \leq \frac{s_1 + s_2 + ... + s_q}{m} \tag{4}$$

4. For each buckets whose blank is not zero, we fill the counterfeit tuples $c_1, c_2, ...c_w$ into the blank.

In our running example, we first sort the tuples in S_-. By a descending order, we get the sensitive value set $\{gastritis, flu, dyspepsia\}$ with their counts $\{2, 2, 1\}$. Then we sort the buckets first by blanks, then count of signature, then we get $\{BUC_1, BUC_2, BUC_3, BUC_4\}$. We randomly select tuple Emily in the max count of sensitive value $gastritis$, and insert Emily into BUC_1. Then the max count of sensitive value is 2, that is flu. We also randomly select a tuple Mary in flu and insert tuple into BUC_1 as the size of signature is less than

BUC_4 even though both buckets lack one *flu* to balance the bucket. Now we get sensitive value sets $\{gastritis, flu, dyspepsia\}$ with their counts $\{1, 1, 1\}$, we randomly select the tuple in *dyspepsia* and insert it into BUC_2. We find the remaining sensitive set $\{gastritis, flu\}$ with corresponding tuple $\{Vince, Tom\}$. If any tuple is removed from the sensitive set $\{gastritis, flu\}$, the sensitive set will not satisfy the inequality 4. Hence, we stop the iteration and insert the counterfeit tuples c_1, c_2 respectively into BUC_3 and BUC_4.

Algorithm 1. m-**Anatomize**

Input: Microtables $T(n-1)$ and $T(n)$, released tables $\{T_{QI}^*(n-1), T_{SA}^*(n-1), R(n-1)\}$ on the $(n-1)$th time, and security parameter m

Output: A set of relation tables $\{T_{QI}^*(n), T_{SA}^*(n), R(n)\}$ on the nth time

1:   $S_\cap = T(n) \cap T(n-1)$, $S_- = T(n) - T(n-1)$
2:   extract existing buckets from tuples in $S_\cap$
3:   $cnt = $ the number of the existing buckets
4:   $q = $ the number of the distinct sensitive values in S_-
5:   $ucnt = $ the number of the unbalanced buckets
6:   **while** S_- is not empty **do**
7:      sort the tuples in S_- by the descending order of the count of sensitive values and get tuple sets $s_1, s_2, ..., s_q$
8:      sort the unbalanced buckets by the descending order of the count of blanks and get $ucnt$ buckets
9:      **if** $s_1 \leq \frac{s_1+s_2+s_3+...+s_q}{m}$ or no tuple in S_- carries the sensitive values which the unbalanced buckets lack **then**
10:         **break**
11:     **else**
12:        **for** $j = 1$ to q **do**
13:           $v = $ the sensitive value in s_j
14:           **for** $k = 1$ to $ucnt$ **do**
15:              **if** there is a blank in BUC_k equals v **then**
16:                 remove v from the set s_j
17:                 insert v into BUC_k
18:                 update q, $ucnt$
19:                 **Continue**
20:              **end if**
21:           **end for**
22:        **end for**
23:     **end if**
24:   **end while**
25:   **for** each non-empty bucket **do**
26:     fill the blank with the counterfeits
27:   **end for**
28:   **for** each balanced bucket **do**
29:     **if** tuples' signature in S_- is identical to one bucket **then**
30:        fill all the tuples into the bucket
31:     **end if**
32:   **end for**
33:   **if** the count of distinct sensitive values in $S_- < m$ **then**
34:     $S = $ the set of m largest tuple sets

35:    create a new bucket BUC_c
36:    **for** each tuple sets in S **do**
37:        remove an arbitrary tuple from the tuple set
38:        insert the tuple to BUC_c
39:    **end for**
40:    $cnt++$
41: **end if**
42: split buckets which has a multiple of the volume and update cnt
43: **for** each tuple t in S_- **do**
44:    BUC_i = the bucket which doesn't contains t
45:    insert tuple t to BUC_i
46: **end for**
47: **for** group ID $i = 1$ to cnt **do**
48:    **for** each tuple in BUC_i **do**
49:        insert tuple $(t[1], ..., t[d], i)$ into $T^*_{QI}(n)$
50:    **end for**
51:    **for** each distinct A^s value v **do**
52:        $num_i(v)$ = the number of v in $group_i$
53:        insert $(i, v, num_i(v))$ into $T^*_{SA}(n)$
54:    **end for**
55:    **for** distinct counterfeit tuple c **do**
56:        $num_i(c)$ = the number of counterfeits in $group_i$
57:        insert $(i, num_i(c))$ into $R(n)$
58:    **end for**
59: **end for**
60: **return** $\{T^*_{QI}(n), T^*_{SA}(n), R(n)\}$

Assignment. (Lines 28–46) In this phase, we assign remaining tuples in S_- into buckets. The assignment phase takes the following steps:

1. If all tuples' signature in S_- is identical to one existing bucket, then we fill tuples into the bucket.
2. Else we begin an iteration. We create a new bucket whose size is m, then we remove a random tuple into the new bucket from each tuple set of m most frequent sensitive values of the remaining tuples until no more than m distinct sensitive values in S_-.
3. We now split buckets which have a multiple of the bucket volume tuples into several buckets, where each bucket has just the same number of tuples as the bucket volume.
4. Then for each residual tuple t in S_-, we choose an existing bucket which does not have the same sensitive values as t, and fill t into this bucket and extend the volume of the bucket by one. As long as S_- satisfies inequality 4, all tuples in S_- can be assigned to the balanced buckets, as noted in [10].

Following the rules shown in the Assignment phase, one may notice that the remaining tuples in S_- have just the same signature with BUC_1, so we fill the tuples $\{Vince, Tom\}$ into BUC_1. Now we have the buckets in as illustrated in Fig. 1c. We observe that in BUC_1 and BUC_2, the tuples are twice of the signature of the buckets. So we respectively split BUC_1 and BUC_2 into two buckets each of which contains tuples of $\{Vince, Tom\}$, $\{Emily, Mary\}$, $\{Gary, Ray\}$, $\{Bob, David\}$. Notice that there is no tuple remaining in S_-, so we finish the assignment phase.

Contrarily, in the *generalization* algorithm of m-Invariance, splitting the buckets into smaller buckets is necessary, which can decrease the information loss of generalization. However, in our algorithm, splitting buckets aims at inserting residual tuples after step 2 into buckets in the case of breaking m-Invariance. As for information loss, according to Eqs. 1, 2, and 3, it's easy to prove that splitting the buckets does not change the original RCE. Let us consider two cases. In the first case we do not split the $BUC2$ which contains the sensitive sets $\{gastritis, gastritis, flu, flu\}$ with corresponding tuples $\{Gary, Bob, Ray, David\}$. In the second case we split the $BUC2$ into two buckets, which has the same signature of $\{gastritis, flu\}$, respectively with corresponding tuples $\{Gary, Ray\}$ and $\{Bob, David\}$. We take the tuple Bob as an example to calculate the ERR_t. For Bob, the $\mathcal{G}_t(x)$ is as follows:

$$\mathcal{G}_t(x) = \begin{cases} 1 & if\ x = (age = 21, Zip = 21000) \\ 0 & otherwise \end{cases} \tag{5}$$

In both cases, $\tilde{\mathcal{G}}_t(x)$ is the same according to Eq. 3, which is defined as follows:

$$\tilde{\mathcal{G}}_t(x) = \begin{cases} 1/2 & if\ x = (age = 21, Zip = 12000, gastritis) \\ 1/2 & if\ x = (age = 21, Zip = 12000, flu) \\ 0 & otherwise \end{cases} \tag{6}$$

In the first case, $ERR_{Bob} = (1 - 1/2)^2 + (0 - 1/2)^2 = 0.5$. The result is the same for other tuples in the group. This implies $RCE = 0.5 \times 4 = 2$. In the second case, ERR_{Bob} is 0.5 as well, which is the same for another tuple David in the group, so $ERR_{David} = 0.5$. We notice that the bucket $\{Gary, Ray\}$ has the same distribution with $\{Bob, David\}$. So the total $RCE = 0.5 \times 2 \times 2 = 2$. Splitting does not change the distribution of splitted buckets and the total RCE is the same.

Populate. (Lines 47–60) As the Definition 4 indicates, to satisfy the m-Invariance, *anatomy* needs to release three tables for the n-th publication, $\{T_{QI}^*(n), T_{SA}^*(n), R(n)\}$. The phase operates as follows:

1. For each tuple in $BUC_1, BUC_2, ..., BUC_cnt$, insert tuple $(t[1], ..., t[d], i)$ into $T_{QI}^*(n)$, with the group ID from $1 \leq i \leq cnt$.
2. For each distinct A^s value v, count $num_i(v)$, the number of sensitive value v in $group_i$ and insert $(i, v, num_i(v))$ into $T_{SA}^*(n)$.
3. For each distinct counterfeit tuple c, count $num_i(c)$, the number of counterfeits in $group_i$ and insert $(i, num_i(c))$ into $R(n)$.

With three steps noted above, we can populate the tuples in the buckets as shown in Fig. 1c, and then we get the published anatomized tables, as depicted in Tables 7, 8, 9. Now all tuples have m distinct sensitive values in each group and the tuples in both publications have the same sensitive values distribution, which satisfies the requirement of m-Invariance. We can conclude the property that our algorithm can produce the n-th anatomized table which satisfies m-Invariance. It is easy to prove the property, because in each group-creation steps, we maintain that every QI-group has m-distinct sensitive values, and the tuples in publications at consecutive times have the same sensitive value distribution. Therefore, our final results also meet the m-Invariance rules.

Finally, we analyze the information loss during the *anatomy* operation on certain datasets. We will measure the loss by re-construction error (RCE) mentioned in the earlier paragraph. We prove that our algorithm has the same RCE as *anatomy*. We have the theorem as follows.

Theorem 1. *If the j-th microdata $T(j)$ has n records, where n is the multiple of m, then the RCE of the anatomized tables at the j-th publication is $n(1 - \frac{1}{m})$; otherwise, RCE increases by a multiple factor at most $1 + \frac{r}{n(m-1)}$.*

Proof. In the first case, we assume that the total number of records on j-th microdata $T(j)$ is the multiple of m, thus there are $\frac{n}{m}$ QI groups and each group has m tuples with distinct sensitive values. According to Eqs. 2 and 3, we can calculate the RCE for a tuple t at random QI group is as below.

$$Err_t = (1 - \frac{1}{m})^2 + (0 - \frac{1}{m})^2 \times (m - 1) = 1 - \frac{1}{m} \tag{7}$$

Since the distribution is the same for other tuples in anatomized tables, so RCE is the same for other $(n - 1)$ tuples. So the $RCE = n(1 - \frac{1}{m})$.

In the second case, we assume that there are totally k QI groups, and each group has at least m tuples with distinct sensitive values. We define $r = \sum_{i=1}^{k}(|QI_i| - m)$ where $|QI|$ is the number of tuples in QI_i group, so $(n - r)$ is multiple of m. For the convenience of explanation, we assume that the $(n - r)$ tuples are all in the groups with m distinct sensitive values, and the other r tuples are inserted into existing groups as step 4 in the assignment phase. For the $(n - r)$ tuples, their RCE is $(n - r)(1 - \frac{1}{m})$ according to Eq. 7. For the other r tuples, we first consider one QI group of β tuples, when a new tuple is inserted into this QI group following step 4, the group has $\beta + 1$ tuples. The RCE difference between the *insert* operation is

$$(\beta + 1)(1 - \frac{1}{\beta + 1}) - \beta(1 - \frac{1}{\beta}) = 1 \tag{8}$$

Therefore, there are totally r tuples to be inserted, each time one tuple is inserted into a QI group, and then RCE will increase by 1. Hence the total RCE is presented as follows,

$$(n - r)(1 - \frac{1}{m}) + r = n(1 - \frac{1}{m})(1 + \frac{r}{n(m - 1)}) \tag{9}$$

where r is determined by the time of the *insert* operation in the assignment phase in and before j-th publication. In this case, RCE increases by a multiple factor at most $1 + \frac{r}{n(m-1)}$. We complete the proof.

4   Experiments

We deployed the database downloaded from http://archive.ics.uci.edu/ml/
datasets/Adult, and chose the *Adult* database from Census of America. A
tuple of the database includes 14 numerical and categorical attributes including
*age, workclass, finalweight, education, education-num, marital-status, occupa-
tion, relationship, race, sex, capital gain, capital loss, hours-per-week, native-
country*. We chose *occupation* as the sensitive attribute, and other attributes as
quasi-identifier attributes. The attribute domain size of *occupation* is 14, which
means that there are 14 various optional values in the column of *occupation*.

As for the number of the counterfeit tuples, they are illustrated in Figs. 2
and 3. From the results one can conclude that our algorithm has the similar
number of counterfeits. Figure 3a plots the average number of counterfeits with
as a various m. When m increases, the number of counterfeits also increases. This
is as expected because a larger m means more optional sensitive values, leading
to a higher possibility of unbalanced buckets. Figure 3b illustrates the number
of counterfeits related to update volume r. When r increases, the number of
counterfeits decreases. A larger r means that there are more tuples to fill the
buckets, having more opportunities to balance the buckets.

We also tested the aggregate querying accuracy of the released table.
Figure 4a shows the median relative error with respect to m, where the error
increases with the increasing m. Because a larger m means a more uniform distribution of the sensitive values and a higher privacy level. Figure 4b plots the

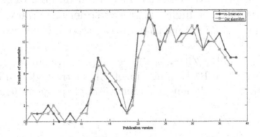

Fig. 2. Number of counterfeits vs. publication version j (m = 2, r = 1k)

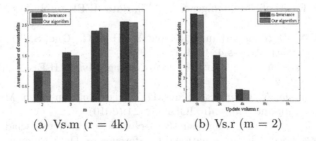

(a) Vs.m (r = 4k)   (b) Vs.r (m = 2)

Fig. 3. Average number of counterfeits vs. m and r

error related to r, where r almost has no influence on the results. This is also as expected because the update volume does not directly affect the distribution of the sensitive values.

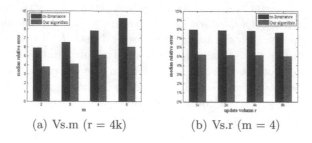

(a) Vs.m (r = 4k)   (b) Vs.r (m = 4)

Fig. 4. Query accuracy vs. m and r

5   Conclusion

In this paper, we proposed to achieve m-Invariance requirement with *anatomy* aiming at improving the usability in big data release. We adapted the existing m-Invariance requirement to adapt *anatomy* and presented a new *anatomy* based m-Invariance definitions and framework. We then established a series of criteria for *anatomy* based m-Invariance and developed a new algorithm according to new definition and criteria. We achieved the similar number of generated counterfeits with *generalization* but a higher aggregate query accuracy. The experiments also confirm the analysis and show that our approach is secure and practical.

Acknowledgements. Haibin Zheng is the corresponding author. This paper is supported by the National Key R&D Program of China through project H1943050901, by the Natural Science Foundation of China through projects 61972019, 61932011, 61772538.

References

1. O'Leary, D.E.: Artificial intelligence and big data. IEEE Intell. Syst. **28**(2), 96–99 (2013)
2. Mehmood, A., Natgunanathan, I., Xiang, Y., Hua, G., Guo, S.: Protection of big data privacy. IEEE Access **4**, 1821–1834 (2016)
3. Sweeney, L.: k-anonymity: a model for protecting privacy. IEEE Secur. Priv. Mag. **10**(5), 1–14 (2002)
4. Machanavajjhala, A., Gehrke, J., Kifer, D., Venkitasubramaniam, M.: L-diversity: privacy beyond k-anonymity. In: ICDE, p. 24 (2010)
5. Li, N., Li, T., Venkatasubramanian, S.: t-closeness: Privacy beyond k-anonymity and l-diversity. In: IEEE International Conference on Data Engineering, pp. 106–115 (2007)

6. Nergiz, M.E., Atzori, M., Clifton, C.: Hiding the presence of individuals from shared databases. In: ACM SIGMOD International Conference on Management of Data, pp. 665–676, Beijing, China, June 2007
7. Dwork, C.: Differential privacy: a survey of results. In: Proceedings of International Conference on Theory and Applications of MODELS of Computation, Tamc 2008, Xi'an, China, 25–29 April 2008, pp. 1–19 (2008)
8. Lefevre, K., Dewitt, D.J., Ramakrishnan, R.: Mondrian multidimensional k-anonymity. In: International Conference on Data Engineering, pp. 25–25 (2006)
9. Xiao, X., Tao, Y.: Anatomy: simple and effective privacy preservation. In: International Conference on Very Large Data Bases, pp. 139–150, Korea, September, Seoul (2006)
10. Xiao, X., Tiao, Y.: M-invariance: towards privacy preserving re-publication of dynamic datasets. In: ACM SIGMOD International Conference on Management of Data, Beijing, China, June 2007, pp. 689–700 (2007)
11. Liu, X., Xie, Q., Wang, L.: Personalized extended (α, k)-anonymity model for privacy-preserving data publishing. Concurr. Comput. Pract. Exp. **29**(6), e3886 (2017)
12. Wang, P., Wang, J.: L-diversity algorithm for incremental data release. Appl. Math. Inf. **7**(5), 2055–2060 (2013)
13. Pramanik, M.I., Lau, R.Y.K., Zhang, W.: K-anonymity through the enhanced clustering method. In: IEEE International Conference on E-Business Engineering, pp. 85–91 (2016)
14. Meyerson, A., Williams, R.: On the complexity of optimal k-anonymity. In: ACM Sigact-Sigmod-Sigart Symposium on Principles of Database Systems, 14–16 June 2004, Paris, France, 2004, pp. 223–228 (2004)
15. Bayardo, R.J., Agrawal, R.: Data privacy through optimal k-anonymization. In: ICDE, pp. 217–228 (2005)
16. Zhang, Q., Koudas, N., Srivastava, D., Yu, T.: Aggregate query answering on anonymized tables. In: IEEE International Conference on Data Engineering, pp. 116–125 (2007)
17. Agrawal, R., Srikant, R.: Privacy-preserving data mining. Decis. Eng. **2**(3), 86–92 (2008)
18. Soria-Comas, J., Domingo-Ferrer, J., Snchez, D.: t-closeness through microaggregation: strict privacy with enhanced utility preservation. In: IEEE Transactions on Knowledge and Data Engineering, vol. 27, no. 11, pp. 3098–3110 (2015)
19. Clifton, C., Tassa, T.: On syntactic anonymity and differential privacy. In: IEEE International Conference on Data Engineering Workshops, pp. 88–93 (2013)
20. Zhao, J., Jung, T., Wang, Y., Li, X.: Achieving differential privacy of data disclosure in the smart grid. In: 2014 Proceedings IEEE INFOCOM, pp. 504–512 (2014)
21. Ji, Z., Elkan, C.: Differential privacy based on importance weighting. Mach. Lear. **93**(1), 163 (2013)
22. Pei, J., Xu, J., Wang, Z., Wang, W., Wang, K.: Maintaining k-anonymity against incremental updates. In: International Conference on Scientific and Statistical Database Management, pp. 5 (2007)
23. Byun, J.-W., Sohn, Y., Bertino, E., Li, N.: Secure anonymization for incremental datasets. In: Jonker, W., Petković, M. (eds.) SDM 2006. LNCS, vol. 4165, pp. 48–63. Springer, Heidelberg (2006). https://doi.org/10.1007/11844662_4
24. Bu, Y., Fu, A.W.C., Wong, R.C.W., Chen, L., Li, J.: Privacy preserving serial data publishing by role composition. Proc. VLDB Endow. **1**(1), 845–856 (2008)

25. Merugu, S., Ghosh, J.: Privacy-preserving distributed clustering using generative models. In: IEEE International Conference on Data Mining, pp. 211–218 (2003)
26. Fung, B.C.M., Wang, K., Wang, L., Hung, P.C.K.: Privacy-preserving data publishing for cluster analysis. Data Knowl. Eng. **68**(6), 552–575 (2009)
27. Goryczka, S., Li, X., Fung, B.C.M.: m-privacy for collaborative data publishing. In: International Conference on Collaborative Computing: Networking, Applications and Worksharing, pp. 1–10 (2011)
28. Horvitz, E., Mulligan, D.: Data, privacy, and the greater good. Science **349**(6245), 253–255 (2015)
29. Leenen, L., Meyer, T.: Artificial intelligence and big data analytics in support of cyber defense. In: Developments in Information Security and Cybernetic Wars, pp. 42–63 (2019)

A Secure and Efficient Privacy-Preserving Authentication Scheme for Vehicular Networks with Batch Verification Using Cuckoo Filter

Kang Li[1,2], Wang Fat Lau[2], and Man Ho Au[2(✉)]

[1] Research Institute for Sustainable Urban Development,
The Hong Kong Polytechnic University, Kowloon, Hong Kong
kang.li@connect.polyu.hk
[2] Department of Computing, The Hong Kong Polytechnic University,
Kowloon, Hong Kong
{franky.wf.lau,man-ho-allen.au}@polyu.edu.hk

Abstract. The wireless nature of vehicular networks causes serious security and privacy issues that need to be addressed. To satisfy the security and privacy requirements in vehicular networks, a number of certificateless signature based authentication schemes have been proposed as it not only avoid certificate management issue in PKI-based solutions but also solves the key escrow problem in solutions that depends on ID-based signatures. However, many schemes are inefficient due to the use of computationally intensive bilinear pairing operation and map-to-point hash function. To further improve efficiency, schemes supporting batch verification is highly desirable. In this paper, based on a pairing free online/offline certificateless signature scheme, we propose a secure and efficient privacy-preserving authentication scheme for vehicular networks by specifically improving the batch verification efficiency using cuckoo filter. The signature scheme does not use the expensive pairing operations or map-to-point hash functions, thus has a higher computation efficiency. More importantly, by using the cuckoo filters, the roadside units can generate a notification message for vehicles about the validity of the signatures in the batch verification to assist the message authentication of vehicles. Moreover, the binary search method is used in the batch verification process to avoid dropping the whole batch in case an invalid signature exists. Our proposed scheme is secure, efficient and it satisfies all the security and privacy requirements of vehicular networks.

1 Introduction

Due to the rapid advancement of wireless technologies, the vehicular network is introduced to build a safe and intelligent transportation system in metropolitan cities. In general, a vehicular network is a novel class of wireless network which allows vehicles to share real-time traffic-related information with each. Hence, drivers can get a better awareness of their driving environment and can take

© Springer Nature Switzerland AG 2019
J. K. Liu and X. Huang (Eds.): NSS 2019, LNCS 11928, pp. 615–631, 2019.
https://doi.org/10.1007/978-3-030-36938-5_38

early action to respond to an emergent situation to avoid any possible damage or to follow a better route by circumventing traffic bottleneck. However, the transmitted message, which is critical to driver's safety, in wireless protocol could be easily monitored, altered and forged by an adversary, thus greatly undermines driving safety. Hence, it is crucial to ensure message security and privacy before the vehicular network can be deployed successfully. For message security, the receiver should validate the legitimacy and integrity of the received message before taking further action. In terms of the privacy issue, anonymity must be provided to prevent the adversaries from extracting private information, such as the real identity, from the transmitted messages. However, privacy protection should be conditional, which means that the trusted authorities should be able to reveal the real identity of a malicious or a misbehaving vehicle and revoke its membership when it is necessary.

In recent years, due to its advantages of avoiding the certificate management issue of the PKI-based scheme and solving the key escrow problem of the ID-based signature scheme, many authentication schemes using certificateless signatures have been proposed to tackle the security and privacy problems in vehicular network [6,13,16,20]. However, many certificateless signature schemes require computationally expensive bilinear pairings or the map-to-point hash functions, which decreases the computation efficiency. In vehicular networks, the onboard unit, which is the communication device of vehicles, only has limited computation capacity to handle large amount of messages authentication. Another problem is that due to the high speed and possible high density of vehicles, the scheme should be able to handle the authentication of large amount of messages very efficiently. Hence, for the certificateless signature scheme to be used in vehicular networks in practice, the efficiency of signature generation and verification should be improved.

In order to reduce the computation cost in certificateless signature based approach, several directions have been explored, including online/offline signature generation, and batch verification. The former approach splits signature generation into two phase, namely, offline phase and online phase. In the offline phase, some heavy computations are executed and the intermediate results are stored in resource-constrained devices. Then in the online phase, upon receiving the message to be signed, the device can very efficiently compute a signature using the intermediate result from the offline phase. Batch verification technique, as its name suggested, allows multiple signatures to be verified in batch so that the amortised cost is lower than the verification of an individual signature. The scheme proposed in [18] adopts both approaches for improved efficiency. It also has the added advantage of not requiring the expansive pairing operations or map-to-point hash functions. Another commonly employed technique to reduce message overhead and improve success rate of batch verification is through the use of Bloom filer, a space-efficient data structure that is used to check the membership of an item. This approach has been adopted in [3,4,17,22].

Recently, a data structure supporting set-membership test, known as Cuckoo filter [9], has been proposed. Unlike Bloom filter, it supports dynamically adding and removing items and at the same time offers better lookup performance in terms of time and space complexity. Recognising the potential of Cuckoo filter, [7] proposed a new privacy-preserving authentication scheme with cuckoo filter to improve batch verification efficiency. However, due to the use of ID-based signature, this scheme was not fully immune from the key escrow problem as pointed out in [19].

The goal of this paper is, therefore, to propose a new authentication scheme for vehicular networks with desirable features from various schemes in the literature, including simplified certificate management, immune against key escrow problem, support online/offline (signature) generation, support efficient batch verification, support RSU-assisted signature verification, does not rely on expansive operations such as pairing and map-to-point hash function. Looking ahead, our scheme is based on the recent proposal of [18], with enhanced features and RSU-assisted verification though the use of Cuckoo filter.

1.1 Related Works

The first certificateless signature scheme was proposed by Al-Riyami and Paterson in [1]. After that, many certificateless signature schemes were proposed. Yum and Lee [24] described a general method to construct a CL-PKS scheme from any ID-based signature scheme. Au et al. [2] presented a new security model for CL-PKS schemes, in which a malicious KGC attack is considered. More recently, Yeh et al. [23] proposed a CL-PKS scheme for IoT deployment. However, Jia et al. [15] pointed out that it has security flaws, as any malicious KGC can impersonate the KGC and it cannot resist a public key replacement attack. The first online/offline signature scheme was introduced by Even, Goldreich and Micali [8]. Liu et al. [21] proposed an efficient identity based online/offline signature scheme, but it has the key escrow problem.

The first batch cryptography based on RSA was introduced by Fiat [11]. Due to its advantage of allowing a verifier to efficiently verify multiple signatures at one time instead of verifying it one by one, batch verification has been used in many authentication schemes for vehicular networks, such as [6,12,14,25]. In order to further improve the verification efficiency, some works proposed to apply the space-efficient data structure bloom filter to reduce the overhead and improve the success rate of the batch verification, such as [3,4,17,22]. For instance, in [22], two bloom filters were used to check the MAC address the pseudonyms of the incoming messages. In 2014, a new data structure called cuckoo filter was proposed in [10] to replace bloom filter. Comparing to bloom filter, cuckoo filter supports adding and removing items dynamically with a better performance. Recently, cuckoo filter was used in the batch verification of some authentication schemes for vehicular networks, such as [7]. However, in [19], the authors point out that [7] suffers from key escrow problem.

1.2   Our Contributions

The contributions of this paper are described as follows. Firstly, based on scheme proposed in [18], we develop an efficient privacy-preserving authentication scheme for vehicular networks. This paper improves [18] in terms of the efficiency of message verification process through road side units assisted verification. Specifically, after the batch verification, the road side units can generate a notification message about the validity of signatures using the cuckoo filter, to assist the message authentication of vehicles. This improves the overall authentication efficiency, as the vehicles do not need to verify the individual signature one by one and can authenticate the message using the notification message. Secondly, we employ the binary search technique to extract the valid signatures from the batch, thus avoiding the problem of dropping the whole batch due to the invalid signatures. Thirdly, we demonstrate that the proposed scheme meets all the security and privacy requirements of vehicular networks. Finally, we analyze the cuckoo filter approach in terms of its advantages over bloom filter method, its false positive rate and computation overhead. We show that the probability of the case 3, in which a re-confirmation is needed in the verification process, is very low. Furthermore, we perform an experiment on the computation cost of the basic operations of cuckoo filter and the result shows that the computation overhead of cuckoo filter is negligible.

2   Background and Preliminaries

2.1   System Model

A typical vehicular network consists of three main components, namely, the trusted authorities (TAs), such as the key generation center, the onboard unit (OBU) installed on every vehicle, and the roadside unit (RSU) located at critical points of the roads. TAs are responsible for vehicle registration and communication with other entities using a secure channel. OBU and RSU are used to send, receive and forward messages in V2V (Vehicle-to-Vehicle) communication, V2I (Vehicle-to-Infrastructure) communication and V2X (Vehicle-to-Everything) communication in vehicular networks. The wireless communication is realized using technology based on the Dedicated Short Range Communication (DSRC) protocol. Typically, a two-layer network model is suitable for vehicular networks, as presented in Fig. 1. The lower layer composed of vehicles and roadside units located at critical points along the road. Each vehicle is equipped with an OBU, which enables vehicles to communicate with other network participants. Each vehicle has a real identity, a number of pseudo identities, public/private key pairs.

The upper layer of vehicular networks consists of an application server (traffic control and analysis center), trace authority (TRA) and key generation center (KGC). The TRA is responsible for RSU and vehicle registration by generating

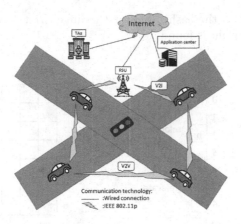

Fig. 1. A typical architecture of vehicular networks

pseudo identities for them and is able to extract the real identity of a vehicle from its signed message. The KGC is also in charge of generating partial private keys and update time keys for RSU and vehicles. Besides, we assume the following assumptions hold:

1. The TRA and KGC are always trusted and cannot be comprised. The TAs have sufficient computation power and storage capacity. During the registration phase, the TAs communicate with the vehicles and RSUs securely using wired networks and secure protocols, such as Transport Layer Security protocol.
2. The RSU is also a trusted entity. The communication range of RSU to the vehicle is at least twice of the inter-vehicle communication range so that if an RSU receives a message, all vehicles receiving the same message can receive the notification from the RSU. RSUs has higher computation capability than OBUs to handle batch verification of many signatures.

2.2 Cuckoo Filter

In order to handle massive data efficiently, various index data structures with low memory usage and fast access speed, have been developed. One popular data structure was the bloom filter created in 1970 by Burton Howard Bloom. However, bloom filter does not support item deletion. Cuckoo filter [9] is a new data structure for high-speed approximate set-membership tests. Compared with the conventional bloom filter, it not only supports dynamic item addition and deletion, but also achieves higher lookup performance and better space efficiency. A cuckoo filter is a compact variant of a cuckoo hash table that stores only fingerprints, that is, a bit string derived from the item using a hash function, for each item inserted, instead of key-value pairs [10]. A set membership query for item x simply searches the hash table for the fingerprint of x and returns true if an identical fingerprint is found.

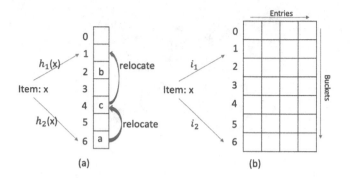

Fig. 2. (a) Insertion operation of cuckoo hash table; (b) A cuckoo filter with four entries per bucket

A basic hash table consists of an array of buckets where each item has two candidate buckets determined by two hash functions (see Fig. 2(a)). In order to insert an item, firstly we check both buckets to see whether either contains the item. If either of the two buckets is empty, we insert a new item into this empty bucket. If neither is empty, it selects another candidate bucket (e.g., bucket 6), kicks out the existing item ("a"), and re-inserts this existing item to its own alternate bucket (e.g, bucket 4). This re-insert process may require kicking out another item ("c"), so it may repeat until a vacant bucket is found. A typical cuckoo filter with four entries per bucket is given in Fig. 2(b). In order to support dynamic insertion, cuckoo filter uses the partial-key cuckoo hashing to derive an item's alternate location using only its fingerprint. For each item x, the cuckoo filter calculates the indexes of the candidate buckets i_1 and i_2 as follows:

$$i_1 = hash(x) mod\ M$$

$$i_2 = (i_1 \oplus hash(Fingerprint(x))) mod\ M$$

where M is the number of buckets in the cuckoo filter. The cuckoo filter algorithm includes three basic functions: query, insert and delete. The query and insert functions are depicted in Algorithm 1 and Algorithm 2. In this paper, cuckoo filter will be used in the batch verification process to generate a notification message to assist the message authentication of vehicles and enhance the overall efficiency.

Algorithm 1. Insert(x)

1: $f = Fingerprint(x)$;
2: i_1=hash(x) mod M;
3: i_2=($i_1 \oplus$hash(f)) mod M;
4: **if** bucket[i_1] or bucket[i_2] has an empty entry **then**;
5:     add f to that bucket;
6:     return done
7: **else**
8:     i= randomly pick i_1 or i_2;
9:     **for** $n = 0; n < MaxNumKicks; n{+}{+}$ **do**
10:         randomly select an entry e from bucket[i];
11:         swap f and the fingerprint stored in ehtry e;
12:             $i{=}i \oplus hash(f)$
13:         **if** bucket[i] has an empty entry **then**
14:             add f to bucket[i]
15:             return done
16:         **end if**
17:     **end for**
18:     return failure
19: **end if**

Algorithm 2. Query(x)

1: $f = Fingerprint(x)$
2: i_1=hash(x) mod M
3: i_2=($i_1 \oplus$hash(f)) mod M
4: **if** bucket[i_1] or bucket[i_2] has f **then**
5:     return true
6: **else**
7:     return false
8: **end if**

2.3   Security and Privacy Requirement

The proposed authentication scheme should satisfy the following security and privacy requirements.

1. **Identity Privacy Preserving**: RSUs, vehicles and any third participants cannot extract a vehicle's real identity from its pseudo identity and the transmitted message.
2. **Message Authentication and Integrity**: RSUs and vehicles should be able to check the validity of the signed message, and verify that the message is not modified during transmission.
3. **Traceability**: The TRA can reveal the vehicle's real identity from its pseudo identity and revoke its membership from vehicular networks in some cases. For example, TRA needs to reveal a malicious vehicle which sends a false message to mislead other vehicles.
4. **Unlinkability**: The adversaries are not able to link the pseudo identities or two messages sent by the same vehicle.
5. **Resistance to Various Attacks**: The proposed authentication scheme can resist various possible attacks, such as the impersonation attack, modification attack, replay attack.

3   The Proposed Authentication Scheme

In this section, we present our authentication scheme in details. The system parameter setup, pseudo identity generation, private key generation, vehicle key generation, message signing mainly follows the scheme in [18], described using our notations listed in Table 1. In other words, our authentication scheme make use of the same certificateless digital signature scheme as a way to authenticate messages. The main difference lies in how these signatures are verified, in which we propose to speed up through an RSU-assisted verification procedure. Specifically, after describing the scheme of [18], we present the enhanced message verification process, which includes the individual signature verification, batch verification and message verification using a notification message from the RSUs.

3.1   System Parameter Setup

- The TAs chooses two large primes p and q, and will choose a non-singular elliptic curve E, which is defined by the equation $y^2 = x^3 + ax + b$, where $p > 3$, $a, b \in F_p$. The TAs will choose a generator P of the additive group G with the order of q. The TRA randomly chooses number $\beta \in Z_q^*$ as its master private key, and computes its public key as $T_{pub} = \beta \cdot P$. Also, the KGC selects a random number $\alpha \in Z_q^*$ as its master private key, and compute its public key as $P_{pub} = \alpha \cdot P$. The TAs also choose three secure hash functions which are $H_1\colon G \times \{0,1\}^* \times \{0,1\}^* \to Z_q^*$, $H_2\colon \{0,1\}^* \times G \to Z_q^*$, $H_3\colon \{0,1\}^* \times G \times G \times \{0,1\}^* \to Z_q^*$.
- Then, TAs publish $params = \{P, p, q, E, G, H_1, H_2, H_3, P_{pub}, T_{pub}\}$ as the public parameters. Finally, each vehicle pre-loads the public parameters into its temper-proof device and RSU stores $params$ into its local storage.

3.2   Pseudo Identity Generation and Partial Private Key Generation

In this registration phase, the vehicle obtains its pseudonyms and partial private key from the TAs.

1. In this phase, the vehicle interacts with the TRA to get its pseudo-identity. Firstly, the vehicle chooses a random value $k_i \in Z_q^*$, computes $PID_{i,1} = k_i P$, and sends its real identity RID_i with $PID_{i,1}$ to the TRA in a secure way. Then, after checking the validity of RID_i, the TRA computes $PID_{i,2} = RID_i \oplus H_1((\beta \cdot PID_{i,1}) \| T_i \| T_{pub})$ and sends the $PID_{i,2}$ to the vehicle. Hence, the vehicle obtains its pseudo-identity as $PID_i = (PID_{i,1}, PID_{i,2}, T_i)$ where T_i is the valid period of the pseudo identity.
2. In this phase, the vehicle interacts with the KGC to get the partial private key, which will be used to sign messages. The vehicle sends the PID_i to the KGC. Then, the KGC selects a random number $d_i \in Z_q^*$, calculates $Q_{ID_i} = d_i P$, and computes the partial private key as $psk_{ID_i} = d_i + H_2(PID_i \| Q_{ID_i}) \cdot \alpha \pmod{q}$. Finally, the KGC transmits psk_{ID_i} to the vehicle via a secure channel. Note that the value Q_{ID_i} should be public.

Table 1. Notations and Descriptions

Notation	Description
V_i	The i-th vehicle
psk_i	A partial private key of vehicle V_i
x_{ID_i}	A secret key of vehicle V_i
vpk_{ID_i}	A public key of vehicle V_i
(P_{pub}, α)	The public/private key pair of KGC
(T_{pub}, β)	The public/private key pair of TRA
RID_i	The real identity of a vehicle V_i
PID_i	The pseudo identity of a vehicle V_i
H_1, H_2, H_3	Secure hash functions
T_i	A valid period of the pseudo identity
t_i	A current timestamp
m_i	A traffic-related message
$\oplus$	The exclusive **OR** operation
$\|$	The message concatenation operation

3.3 Vehicle Key Generation

In this phase, the vehicle chooses a random number $x_{ID_i} \in Z_q^*$ as its secret value and compute $vpk_{ID_i} = x_{ID_i} \cdot P$ as its public key. The vehicle computes $sk_i = x_{ID_i} + psk_{ID_i}$ as the full private key.

3.4 Message Signing

3.4.1 Offline-Sign

When the vehicle is idle or the network density is not high, the vehicle can offline pre-computes some tuples, which will be used directly to generate online signatures. Note that, generating the offline tuples does not require the messages, so the vehicle can offline pre-computes many tuples for future use.

1. V_i randomly selects a number $r_i \in Z_q^*$
2. V_i computes $R_i = r_i \cdot P$
3. V_i stores the offline $\phi_i = (r_i, R_i)$ locally

3.4.2 Online-Sign

In this phase, the vehicle online signs the message and broadcast the signatures with the messages over the network.

1. V_i obtains a fresh offline signature tuple $\phi_i = (r_i, R_i)$ from its storage.
2. V_i computes $h_{3i} = H_3(m_i \| PID_i \| vpk_{ID_i} \| R_i \| t_i)$.
3. V_i computes $s_i = h_{3i} \cdot r_i + sk_i \ (mod q)$
4. V_i outputs the signature as $\sigma_i = (R_i, s_i)$. Finally, the broadcast message including the signature is the $\{m_i, PID_i, \sigma_i, t_i, vpk_{ID_i}, Q_{ID_i}\}$.

3.5   Message-Verification

This phase consists of the individual signature verification and the batch verification of multiple signatures.

3.5.1   Individual-Verify

This phase corresponds to the case that a vehicle needs to authenticate by verifying the signature. Actually, a vehicle could authenticate the message by using the notification message from the RSUs, of which the process is described in the following subsection. On receiving the message $\{m_i, PID_i, \sigma_i, t_i, vpk_{ID_i}, Q_{ID_i}\}$, the verifier accepts or rejects the message after verifying the validity of the signature as follows.

1. The verifier will check the freshness of the timestamp t_i. If it is not fresh, then the verifier reject the message and stop the verifying process.
2. The verifier calculates $h_{3i} = H_3(m_i \| PID_i \| vpk_{ID_i} \| R_i \| t_i)$ and $h_{2i} = H_2(PID_i \| Q_{ID_i})$.
3. The verifier checks whether the equation $s_i \cdot P = h_{3i} \cdot R_i + vpk_{ID_i} + Q_{ID_i} + h_{2i} \cdot P_{pub}$ holds or not. If this equation holds, then the verifier accepts this message, otherwise reject.

3.5.2   Batch Verification

In this phase, we consider the scenario where the RSUs verify a batch of signatures and then generate a notification message about the validity of the signatures using the cuckoo filter and broadcast it within the communication range to aid the message authentication of the vehicles. Batch verification allows the RSUs to verify many signatures at one time instead of verifying them one by one, thus greatly improves the overall authentication efficiency of vehicular networks, especially when the message density is very high. Furthermore, by using the notification message, the message authentication efficiency of vehicles can be improved, as they do not need to verify every signature anymore. We will firstly show the procedure of verifying the multiple messages and signature pairs at the same time. Then we show how to apply the cuckoo filter to generate a notification message to reduce the message overhead. We also consider the situation where there exist invalid signatures in the batch. Normally, once an invalid signature is found, the whole batch signature is dropped by the RSU. However, this approach is inefficient in the sense that most of the signatures in the batch are actually valid and can be used. Hence, in order to tackle this problem, we construct a binary search algorithm to extract valid signatures from the batch.

3.5.2.1   Batch Verification Procedure

On receiving multiple messages $\{m_i, PID_i, \sigma_i, t_i, vpk_{ID_i}, Q_{ID_i}\}$ where $i = 1, 2, 3, ...n$, the verifier checks the signature validity as follows.

1. Firstly, the verifier will check the freshness of the timestamp t_i, for $i = 1, 2, 3, ...n$. If it is not fresh, then the verifier rejects the message.

2. To ensure the non-repudiation of signatures using batch verification, the verifier randomly choose a vector $v = \{v_1, v_2, v_3, ..., v_n\}$, where v_i is a small random integer in $[1, 2^t]$ and t is a small integer that incurs very little computation head.

3. The verifier checks whether the following equation holds, if it holds, it accepts the messages, otherwise rejects the messages.

$(\sum_{i=1}^{n} s_i \cdot v_i) \cdot P = \sum_{i=1}^{n}(h_{3i} \cdot R_i \cdot v_i) + \sum_{i=1}^{n}(vpk_{ID_i} \cdot v_i) + \sum_{i=1}^{n}(Q_{ID_i} \cdot v_i) + (\sum_{i=1}^{n} h_{2i} \cdot v_i) \cdot P_{pub}$

3.5.2.2 Generating Notification Message

Before generating the notification message about verification result to the vehicles within the communication range, the RSU should extract the valid signatures in case some invalid signatures exist in the batch, which will lead to the failure of batch verification. Hence, we adopt the similar binary search algorithm in [4, 6, 7], to extract the valid signatures contained in the batch. Suppose there are n signatures in the batch, we first arrange them into a list as $List = \{\sigma_1, \sigma_2, \sigma_3, ..., \sigma_n\}$, and set an empty list $List1$ for storing invalid signatures. Here, we denote the algorithm of the batch verification of the signatures from the first one to the $i - th$ signature in the $List$ as $batchVerity(List, 1, i)$. It output strue, if all signatures are valid, otherwise, it outputs false. During the verification process, the RSUs perform the algorithm $signatureExtract(List, List1, 1, n)$, where $signatureExtract(List, List1, low, high)$ is defined as Algorithm 3, to get the list of valid signatures in the batch.

Algorithm 3. $signatureExtract(List, List1, low, high)$

1: **if** $batchVerity(List, low, high) == true$ **then**
2:     **return** $List - List1$
3: **else**
4:     **if** $low == high$ **then**
5:         $List1.append(List[low])$
6:         **return** $List - List1$
7:     **else**
8:         $mid = (low + high)/2$
9:         $signatureExtract(List, List1, low, mid)$
10:         $signatureExtract(List, List1, mid + 1, high)$
11:         **return** $List - List1$
12:     **end if**
13: **end if**

Algorithm 4. The RSU generates notification message

1: **for** $PID_i \in validList(V_i)$ **do**
2:     $x_i \leftarrow (PID_i \| t_i \| m_i)$
3:     $posFilter.Insert(x_i)$
4: **end for**
5: **for** $PID_i \in invalidList(V_i)$ **do**
6:     $x_i \leftarrow (PID_i \| t_i \| m_i)$
7:     $negFilter.Insert(x_i)$
8: **end for**
9: **return** $\{posFilter,$ $negFilter,$ $SIG_{sk_{RSU}}(posFilter, negFilter)\}$

After obtaining the verification results of the signatures in the batch, the RSU creates two pseudo identity lists, i.e, $validList_{V_i}$, which corresponds to valid signatures in the batch, and $invalidList_{V_i}$, which corresponds to the invalid signatures in the batch. Then, the RSU initializes two cuckoo filters, i.e, the positive filter $posFilter$, which is used to store the hash value of pseudo identity and messages of vehicles whose signatures are valid, and the negative filter $negFilter$, which is used to store the hash value of pseudo identity and messages of signatures are invalid. More specifically, the RSU calculates the fingerprint $f_i = Fingerprint(PID_i||t_i||m_i)$ corresponding to every element in $validList_{V_i}$ and store the fingerprint into the $posFilter$ by executing the insert function of cuckoo filter. Also the RSU computes the fingerprint $f_i = Fingerprint(PID_i||t_i||m_i)$ corresponding to the every element in $invalidList_{V_i}$ and store it into the $negFilter$ by performing the insert function of cuckoo filter. Finally, the RSU broadcasts the positive filter $posFilter$ and the negative filter $negFilter$ and the corresponding signature $SIG_{sk_{RSU}}(posFilter, negFilter)$ as the notification message to the vehicles within this communication range. The algorithm of generating the notification message is given in Algorithm 4.

3.6   Message Verification Using Cuckoo Filters

In this phase, we consider the scenario where a vehicle V_i wants to verify the validity of the messages from vehicle V_j. Instead of verifying the corresponding signatures, we show that V_i could achieve message authentication using the cuckoo filters. The verifier firstly compute the fingerprint $f_j = Fingerprint(x_j)$, where $x_j = (PID_j||t_j||m_j)$. Then it calculates the two location index values $i_1 = \text{hash}(x_j) \bmod M$, $i_2 = (i_1 \oplus \text{hash}(Fingerprint(x_j))) \bmod M$. From the notification messages broadcasted by the nearby RSUs, the vehicle V_i checks if the item corresponding to the fingerprint value exists in either one of the two locations in the two cuckoo filters by executing the query function of cuckoo filter. The verification process using cuckoo filter is described in Algorithm 5. Due to the existence of false positive rate, there are four possible cases of the query results, as given in Table 2.

Table 2. Possible query results and their implications

Cases	Positive filter	Negative filter	Implications
1	Ture	False	σ_j is valid
2	False	True	σ_j is invalid
3	True	True	False positive happens
4	False	False	σ_j has not been verified

If the result is the first two cases, then the validity of the signature can be confirmed. If it is the third case, there exists a false positive in either filter and vehicle V_i needs to resend σ_j to the RSU for confirmation. The last case indicates that the signature has not been verified by the RSU, so the vehicle needs to wait for the next notification message from the RSU. In order to handle case 3, we require the RSU to store the valid signatures that it has verified with the pseudo identity of the sender for at least one more batch verification period after the signature is requested. Hence, on receiving the signature σ_j from

---

Algorithm 5. V_i verifies σ_j of V_j

1:    $x_j \leftarrow (PID_j \| t_j \| m_j)$
2:    **while** t_j is fresh **do**
3:       V_i queries $posFilter, negFilter$ on f_j
4:       **if** $posFilter.Query(x_j) == true$ **then**
5:         **if** $negFilter.Query(x_j) == false$ **then**
6:           V_i accepts the validity of σ_j; break;
7:         **else**
8:           **if** $negFilter.Query(x_j) == true$ **then**
9:             V_i resends σ_j to the RSU or V_i verifies the σ_j by itself; break;
10:           **end if**
11:         **end if**
12:       **else**
13:         **if** $negFilter.Query(x_j) == true$ **then**
14:           V_i rejects the validity of σ_j; break;
15:         **end if**
16:         **if** $negFilter.Query(x_j) == false$ **then**
17:           V_i waits for next notification broadcast or V_i verifies the σ_j by itself;break;
18:         **end if**
19:       **end if**
20: **end while**

---

the vehicle, the RSU will query its verification table, which stores the verified signatures. If σ_j can be found, the RSU adds the fingerprint value corresponds to the signature into the positive filter by executing the insert function. Otherwise, it inserts the fingerprint value into the negative filter. Finally, the RSU embeds the re-confirmation result in the next notification message and broadcasts it to the nearby vehicles. Actually, as will be discussed in the last section, the probability of case 3 is very small and could be reduced to be negligible by selecting appropriate cuckoo filter parameters. For the third and fourth cases, vehicle V_i could choose to verify the signature σ_j by itself.

4 Security Analysis

In this section, we present the security analysis and prove that our proposed scheme satisfies all the security and privacy requirements in vehicular networks.

1. **Identity Privacy Preserving**: Vehicles use the pseudo identities, which are computed by the TRA using its private key, to communicate with other network participants. And the only way for an adversary to extract the real identity from the pseudo identity is to compute $RID_i = PID_{i,2} \oplus H_1((\beta \cdot PID_{i,1}), T_i, T_{pub})$ using β. However, it is impossible for an adversary to extract the private key β from the public key $T_{pub} = \beta \cdot P$. Hence, the requirement of identity privacy preserving is ensured.
2. **Message Authentication and Integrity**: In the proposed scheme, a secure certificateless signature scheme in [18] is used to guarantee the message authentication and integrity. And due to the hardness of the discrete logarithm problem, there is no polynomial-time adversary can forge a valid signature. Moreover, any modification of the signature will cause the failure of

the signature verification. Hence, if the equation $s_i \cdot P = h_{3i} \cdot R_i + vpk_{ID_i} + Q_{ID_i} + h_{2i} \cdot P_{pub}$ is verified to be true, the verifier is sure that the message is signed by a legitimate user and is not modified during transmission. Therefore, the proposed scheme ensures the message authentication and integrity.

3. **Nonrepudiation**: This requirement is ensured by the property of the signature scheme, as only the user who has the private key is able to generate a valid signature. Once the signature is generated and verified using the corresponding public key, the signer cannot deny having signed the message. Hence the requirement of nonrepudiation is guaranteed.

4. **Traceability**: The pseudo identity used for communication is generated by the TRA using its own private key. When it is necessary, the TRA can reveal the real identity from the pseudo identity by computing $RID_i = PID_{i,2} \oplus H_1((\beta \cdot PID_{i,1}), T_i, T_{pub})$ using its private key β.

5. **Unlinkability**: In the process of pseudo identity generation, a random value k_i is selected by the vehicle to ensure the randomness of the pseudo identity. And, each time the vehicle signs a message, it chooses a random value r_i to compute the signature. Due to the randomness of k_i and r_i used in generating the pseudo identity and the signature, the adversary cannot link two pseudo identities or signatures generated by the same vehicle. Hence, the requirement of unlinkability is also guaranteed by our scheme.

6. **Resistance to Various Attacks**:
   - **Reply Attack**: In the transmitted message, there exist a timestamp t_i that is used resist reply attack. On receiving the message, the verifier will check the freshness of the timestamp t_i before verifying the validity of the signature. If the timestamp is not fresh, the message will be rejected. Hence, reply attack is avoided by adding a timestamp to the transmitted message.
   - **Message Modification Attact**: In order to ensure message security, each message is signed by a legitimate sender before being broadcasted to others and the receiver will verify the validity of the signature before accepting the message. Any message modification will lead to the failure of signature verification, thus the modified message will be rejected by the receiver. Hence, the message modification attack is not possible in the proposed authentication scheme.
   - **Impersonation Attack:** In order to launch a successful impersonation attack, the adversary has to forge a valid signature to pass the signature verification process. However, the ability to forge a valid signature implies the ability to solve the discrete logarithm problem, which is believed to be hard. Hence the impersonation attack is impossible for our scheme.

5 Analysis on Cuckoo Filter

In this section, we analyze the cuckoo filter used in our scheme, including its advantages over bloom filter, computation cost of its basic operations.

1. Comparing with the bloom filter, cuckoo filter has several advantages. Cuckoo filter supports adding and removing items dynamically, which is impossible for conventional bloom filter. This function is necessary for message authentication in vanet scenario, where the RSU can update the signature validity information timely by adding and removing items into the two filters. For example, if the timestamp of a signature is not fresh, the RSU will remove its signature validity information timely. Moreover, cuckoo filter provides higher lookup performance than the traditional bloom filters.

2. The false positive rate is a critical metric for probabilistic data structures, and it corresponds to the case 3 of the message authentication process using cuckoo filters. The upper bound of the total probability of a false fingerprint collision is $1 - (1 - 1/2^f)^{2b} \approx 2b/2^f$, where f is the fingerprint length in bits and b is the number of entries per bucket. According to [10], we set $b = 4$ to achieve the best or close-to-best space efficiency for false positive rates that most practical applications may be interested in. If we set f to be 12 bits, the false positive rate is 0.00195, which indicates that less than 2 out of 1000 signatures will be affected by the false positive rate. Hence, the probability of case 3, where a re-confirmation process is needed, in the verification phase is very low. Since the false positive rate decreases exponentially as f increases linearly, we can easily achieve very low false positive rate while still keeping the fingerprint length relatively small.

3. In order to analyze the computation overhead incurred by the cuckoo filters, we performed an experiment to obtain the execution time of the basic query, insert and delete operations by running the C++ library implemented in the original paper [10]. We adopt similar cuckoo filter parameters in [5], as given in Table 3, to perform our experiment. The experiment is performed on a MacBook Pro notebook, which consists of an Intel i5 processor with 3.1 GHz clock frequency and 16 gigabytes memory, and macOS operating system. The result shows that the time of executing 1million times query, insert and delete operations are 56 ms, 75 ms and 67 ms respectively, which are negligible compared to the time of signature generation and verification. Hence, the computation overhead incurred by cuckoo filters can be neglected.

Table 3. Cuckoo filter parameters setting

Parameter	Setting
Number of entries per bucket(b)	4
Fingerprint length in bits	12
Load factor	95.36%
Filter capacity	1000000
False positive rate	0.0944%
Number of operations	1000000

6   Conclusions

In this paper, we propose a secure and efficient privacy-preserving authentication scheme for vehicular networks using pairing-free certificateless online/offline signature with efficient batch verification. Our scheme is an enhancement of [18] regarding verification three the use of cuckoo filter. Specifically, the notification messages generated by the RSUs in the batch verification phase using cuckoo filters can assist the message authentication of the vehicles, thus enhancing the overall authentication efficiency, as the vehicles do not need to verify the individual signature one by one. The proposed authentication scheme is secure, efficient and it meets all the security and privacy requirements of vehicular networks.

References

1. Al-Riyami, S.S., Paterson, K.G.: Certificateless public key cryptography. In: Laih, C.-S. (ed.) ASIACRYPT 2003. LNCS, vol. 2894, pp. 452–473. Springer, Heidelberg (2003). https://doi.org/10.1007/978-3-540-40061-5_29
2. Au, M.H., Mu, Y., Chen, J., Wong, D.S., Liu, J.K., Yang, G.: Malicious KGC attacks in certificateless cryptography. In: Proceedings of the 2nd ACM Symposium on Information, Computer and Communications Security, pp. 302–311. ACM (2007)
3. Biswas, S., Mišić, J.: Relevance-based verification of vanet safety messages. In: 2012 IEEE International Conference on Communications (ICC), pp. 5124–5128. IEEE (2012)
4. Chim, T.W., Yiu, S.-M., Hui, L.C., Li, V.O.: Specs: secure and privacy enhancing communications schemes for vanets. Ad Hoc Netw. 9(2), 189–203 (2011)
5. Cui, J., Wei, L., Zhang, J., Xu, Y., Zhong, H.: An efficient message-authentication scheme based on edge computing for vehicular ad hoc networks. IEEE Trans. Intell. Transp. Syst. 20(5), 1621–1632 (2019)
6. Cui, J., Zhang, J., Zhong, H., Shi, R., Xu, Y.: An efficient certificateless aggregate signature without pairings for vehicular ad hoc networks. Inf. Sci. 451, 1–15 (2018)
7. Cui, J., Zhang, J., Zhong, H., Xu, Y.: SPACF: a secure privacy-preserving authentication scheme for vanet with cuckoo filter. IEEE Trans. Veh. Technol. 66(11), 10283–10295 (2017)
8. Even, S., Goldreich, O., Micali, S.: On-line/off-line digital signatures. In: Brassard, G. (ed.) CRYPTO 1989. LNCS, vol. 435, pp. 263–275. Springer, New York (1990). https://doi.org/10.1007/0-387-34805-0_24
9. Fan, B., Andersen, D.G., Kaminsky, M., Mitzenmacher, M.: Cuckoo filter: practically better than bloom. In: Seneviratne, A., Diot, C., Kurose, J., Chaintreau, A., Rizzo, L. (eds.) Proceedings of the 10th ACM International on Conference on Emerging Networking Experiments and Technologies, CoNEXT 2014, Sydney, Australia, 2–5 December 2014, pp. 75–88. ACM (2014)
10. Fan, B., Andersen, D.G., Kaminsky, M., Mitzenmacher, M.D.: Cuckoo filter: practically better than bloom. In: Proceedings of the 10th ACM International on Conference on Emerging Networking Experiments and Technologies, pp. 75–88. ACM (2014)
11. Fiat, A.: Batch RSA. In: Brassard, G. (ed.) CRYPTO 1989. LNCS, vol. 435, pp. 175–185. Springer, New York (1990). https://doi.org/10.1007/0-387-34805-0_17

12. He, D., Zeadally, S., Xu, B., Huang, X.: An efficient identity-based conditional privacy-preserving authentication scheme for vehicular ad hoc networks. IEEE Trans. Inf. Forensics Secur. **10**(12), 2681–2691 (2015)
13. Horng, S.-J., Tzeng, S.-F., Huang, P.-H., Wang, X., Li, T., Khan, M.K.: An efficient certificateless aggregate signature with conditional privacy-preserving for vehicular sensor networks. Inf. Sci. **317**, 48–66 (2015)
14. Horng, S.-J., et al.: b-specs+: batch verification for secure pseudonymous authentication in vanet. IEEE Trans. Inf. Forensics Secur. **8**(11), 1860–1875 (2013)
15. Jia, X., He, D., Liu, Q., Choo, K.-K.R.: An efficient provably-secure certificateless signature scheme for internet-of-things deployment. Ad Hoc Netw. **71**, 78–87 (2018)
16. Kamil, I.A., Ogundoyin, S.O.: An improved certificateless aggregate signature scheme without bilinear pairings for vehicular ad hoc networks. J. Inf. Secur. Appl. **44**, 184–200 (2019)
17. Kim, S.-H., Lee, I.-Y.: A secure and efficient vehicle-to-vehicle communication scheme using bloom filter in vanets. Int. J. Secur. Appl. **8**(2), 9–24 (2014)
18. Li, K., Au, M.H., Ho, W.H., Wang, Y.L.: An efficient conditional privacy-preserving authentication scheme for vehicular ad hoc networks using online/offline certificateless aggregate signature. In: Steinfeld, R., Yuen, T.H. (eds.) ProvSec 2019. LNCS, vol. 11821, pp. 59–76. Springer, Cham (2019). https://doi.org/10.1007/978-3-030-31919-9_4
19. Limbasiya, T., Das, D.: Secure message confirmation scheme based on batch verification in vehicular cloud computing. Phys. Commun. **34**, 310–320 (2019)
20. Liu, D., Shi, R.-H., Zhang, S., Zhong, H.: Efficient anonymous roaming authentication scheme using certificateless aggregate signature in wireless network. J. Commun. **37**(7), 182–192 (2016)
21. Liu, J.K., Baek, J., Zhou, J., Yang, Y., Wong, J.W.: Efficient online/offline identity-based signature for wireless sensor network. Int. J. Inf. Secur. **9**(4), 287–296 (2010)
22. Malhi, A., Batra, S.: Privacy-preserving authentication framework using bloom filter for secure vehicular communications. Int. J. Inf. Secur. **15**(4), 433–453 (2016)
23. Yeh, K.-H., Su, C., Choo, K.-K.R., Chiu, W.: A novel certificateless signature scheme for smart objects in the internet-of-things. Sensors **17**(5), 1001 (2017)
24. Yum, D.H., Lee, P.J.: Generic construction of certificateless signature. In: Wang, H., Pieprzyk, J., Varadharajan, V. (eds.) ACISP 2004. LNCS, vol. 3108, pp. 200–211. Springer, Heidelberg (2004). https://doi.org/10.1007/978-3-540-27800-9_18
25. Zhang, C., Lu, R., Lin, X., Ho, P.-H., Shen, X.: An efficient identity-based batch verification scheme for vehicular sensor networks. In: IEEE INFOCOM 2008-The 27th Conference on Computer Communications, pp. 246–250. IEEE (2008)

Keyed Non-parametric Hypothesis Tests
Protecting Machine Learning from Poisoning Attacks

Yao Cheng[1], Cheng-Kang Chu[1(✉)], Hsiao-Ying Lin[1],
Marius Lombard-Platet[2,3], and David Naccache[2]

[1] Huawei International, Singapore, Singapore
{chengyao101,chu.cheng.kang,lin.hsiao.ying}@huawei.com
[2] DIENS, École normale supérieure, CNRS, PSL Research University, Paris, France
{marius.lombard-platet,david.naccache}@ens.fr
[3] Be-studys, Geneva, Switzerland

Abstract. The recent popularity of machine learning calls for a deeper understanding of AI security. Amongst the numerous AI threats published so far, poisoning attacks currently attract considerable attention. In a poisoning attack the opponent partially tampers the dataset used for learning to mislead the classifier during the testing phase. This paper proposes a new protection strategy against poisoning attacks. The technique relies on a new primitive called *keyed non-parametric hypothesis tests* allowing to evaluate *under adversarial conditions* the training input's conformance with a previously learned distribution $\mathfrak{D}$. To do so we use a secret key κ unknown to the opponent. Keyed non-parametric hypothesis tests differs from classical tests in that the secrecy of κ prevents the opponent from misleading the keyed test into concluding that a (significantly) tampered dataset belongs to $\mathfrak{D}$.

Keywords: Poisoning · Machine learning security · Hypothesis tests

1 Introduction and Formalism

The recent popularity of machine learning calls for a deeper understanding of AI security. Amongst the numerous AI threats published so far, poisoning attacks currently attract considerable attention.

An ML algorithm $\mathcal{A}$ is a state machine with a two-phase life-cycle: during the first phase, called *training*, $\mathcal{A}$ builds a *model* (captured by a state variable σ_i) based on sample data D, called "training data":

$$D = \{d_1, \ldots, d_k\} \text{ where } d_i = \{\text{data}_i, \text{label}_i\}$$

Learning is hence defined by:

$$\sigma_i \leftarrow \mathcal{A}(\text{learn}, \sigma_{i-1}, d_i)$$

e.g. data$_i$ can be human face images and the label$_i \in \{♂, ♀\}$.

© Springer Nature Switzerland AG 2019
J. K. Liu and X. Huang (Eds.): NSS 2019, LNCS 11928, pp. 632–645, 2019.
https://doi.org/10.1007/978-3-030-36938-5_39

During the second phase, called *testing*[1], $\mathcal{A}$ is given an unlabelled data. $\mathcal{A}$'s goal is to predict as accurately as possible the corresponding label given the distribution $\mathfrak{D}$ inferred from D.

$$\underline{\text{label}} = \mathcal{A}(\text{test}, \sigma_k, \text{data})$$

We denote by T the dataset $\{\text{data}_i, \text{label}_i\}$ used during testing where label_i is the correct label (solution) corresponding to data_i and $\underline{\text{label}}_i$ is the label predicted by $\mathcal{A}(\text{test}, \sigma_k, \text{data}_i)$[2].

In a poisoning attack the opponent partially tampers D to influence σ_k and mislead $\mathcal{A}$ during testing. Formally, letting $\overline{d} = \{\overline{\text{data}}, \overline{\text{label}}\}$, the attacker generates a *poison* dataset

$$\tilde{D} = \{\tilde{d}_1, \ldots, \tilde{d}_k\}$$

resulting in a corrupted model $\tilde{\sigma}_k$ such that

$$\overline{\text{label}} \neq \underline{\text{label}} = \mathcal{A}(\text{test}, \tilde{\sigma}_k, \overline{\text{data}})$$

Poisoning attacks were successfully implemented by tampering both incremental and periodic training models. In the *incremental training model*[3], whenever a new d_i is seen during testing, $\mathcal{A}$'s performance on d_i is evaluated and σ is updated. In the *periodic retraining model*, data is stored in a buffer. When $\mathcal{A}$ falls below a performance threshold (or after a fixed number of queries) the buffer's data is used to retrain $\mathcal{A}$ anew. Retraining is either done using the buffer alone (resulting in a totally new σ) or by merging the buffer with previous information (updating σ).

Protections against poisoning attacks can be categorized into two types: *robustification* and *sanitizing*:

Robustification (built-in resistance) modifies $\mathcal{A}$ so that it takes into account the poison but tolerates its effect. Note that $\mathcal{A}$ does not need to identify the poisoned data as such but the effect of poisonous data must be diminished, dampened or nullified up to a point fit for purpose.

The two main robustification techniques discussed in the literature are:

Feature squeezing [26,32] is a model hardening technique that reduces data complexity so that adversarial perturbations disappear because of low sensitivity. Usually the quality of the incoming data is degraded by encoding colors with fewer values or by using a smoothing filter over the images. This maps several inputs onto one "characteristic" or "canonical input" and reduces the perturbations introduced by the attacker. While useful in practice, those techniques inevitably degrade the $\mathcal{A}$'s accuracy.

Defense-GANs [25] use Generative Adversarial Networks [10] to reduce the poison's efficiency. Informally, the GAN builds a model of the learned data and projects the input onto it.

---

[1] Or *inference*.
[2] i.e. if $\mathcal{A}$ is perfect then $\underline{\text{label}}$=label.
[3] Also called the *incremental update model*.

Sanitizing detects (by various methods e.g. [8,17]) and discards poisoned d_is. Note that sanitizing necessarily decreases $\mathcal{A}$'s ability to learn.

This work prevents poisoning by sanitizing.

Figure 1 shows a generic abstraction of sanitizing. $\mathcal{A}$ takes D (periodically or incrementally) and outputs a σ for the testing phase. But d_is go through the poisoning detection module Det before entering $\mathcal{A}$. If Det decides that the probability that some d_i is poisoned is too high, the suspicious d_i is trashed to avoid corrupting σ.

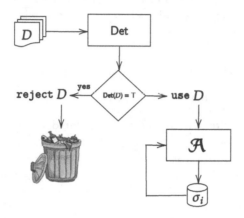

Fig. 1. Before entering $\mathcal{A}$, D is given to the poison detection module Det. If Det decides that D is poisoned, D is trashed. Otherwise D is fed into $\mathcal{A}$ who updates σ.

Because under normal circumstances D and T are drawn from the same distribution $\mathfrak{D}$ it is natural to implement Det using standard algorithms allowing to test the hypothesis $D \in \mathfrak{D}$.

The most natural tool allowing one to do so is *nonparametric hypothesis tests* (NPHTs, hereafter denoted by G). Let A, B be two datasets. $G(A, B) \in \{\mathsf{T}, \mathsf{F}\}$ allows to judge how compatible is a difference observed between A and B with the hypothesis that A, B were drawn from the same distribution $\mathfrak{D}$.

It is important to underline that G is nonparametric, i.e. G makes no assumptions on $\mathfrak{D}$.

The above makes NPHTs natural candidates for detecting poison. However, whilst NPHTs are very good for natural hypothesis testing, they succumb spectacularly in adversarial scenarios where the attacker has full knowledge of the target's specification [13]. Indeed, Sect. 3.1 illustrates such a collapse.

To regain a head-up over the attacker, our strategy will consist in mapping A and B into a *secret* space unpredictable by the adversary where G can work confidentially. This mapping is defined by a key κ making it hard for the adversary to design $A \in \mathfrak{D}$ and $B \in \mathfrak{D}'$ such that

$$G(A, B) = \mathsf{T} \text{ and } \mathfrak{D} \neq \mathfrak{D}'$$

2   A Brief Overview of Poisoning Attacks

Barreno et al. [2] were the first to coin the term "poisoning attacks". Follow-up works such as Kearns et al. [12] sophisticated and theorized this approach.

Classical references introducing poisoning are [4,7,15,18,20–24,30,31]. At times (e.g. [15]) the opponent does not create or modify d_i's but rather adds legitimate but carefully chosen d_i's to D to bias learning. Those inputs are usually computed using gradient descent. This was later generalized by [25].

During a poisoning attack, data modifications can either concern data or labels. [3] showed that a random flip of 40% of labels suffices to seriously affect SVMs. [14] showed that inserting malicious points into D could gradually shift the decision boundary of an anomaly detection classifier. Poisoning points were obtained by solving a linear programming problem maximizing the mean of the displacement of the mass center of D. For a more complete overview we recommend [5].

Adversarial Goals. Poisoning may seek to influence the classifier's decision when presented with a later target query or to leak information about D or σ.

The attacker's goals always apply to the testing phase and may be:

- *Confidence Reduction*: Have $\mathcal{A}$ make more errors. In many cases, "less confidence" can clear suspicious instances at the benefit of doubt (*in dubio pro reo*).
- *Mis-classification attacks*: are defined by replacing adj_1, adj_2 in the definition:

  "Make $\mathcal{A}$ conclude that a adj_1 $data_i$ belongs to a adj_2 wrong label."

Attack	adj_1	adj_2
Mis-classification[a]	random	random
Targeted Mis-classification	chosen	random
Source-Target Mis-classification	chosen	chosen

[a]This is useful if any mistake may serve the opponent's interests e.g. any navigation error would crash a drone with high probability.

Adversarial Capabilities. Designate the degree of knowledge that the attacker has on the target system. Bibliography distinguishes between *training phase capabilities* and *testing phase capabilities*. Poisoning assumes training phase capabilities.

The attacker's capabilities may be:

- *Data Injection*: Add new data to D.
- *Data Modification*: Modify D before training.
- *Logic Corruption*: Modify the code (behavior) of $\mathcal{A}$[4].

---

[4] This is the equivalent of fault attacks in cryptography.

3   Keyed Anti-poisoning

To illustrate our strategy, we use Mann-Whitney's U-test and Stouffer's method that we recall in the appendix.

We assume that when training starts, we are given a safe subset of D denoted D_s (where the subscript s stands for "safe"). Our goal is to assess the safety of the upcoming subset of D denoted D_u (where the subscript u stands for "unknown").

We assume that D_s and T come from the same distribution $\mathfrak{D}$. As mentioned before, the idea is to map D_s and D_u to a space $f_\kappa(\mathfrak{D})$ hidden from the opponent. f is keyed to prevent the attacker from predicting how to create adversarial input fooling $\mathcal{A}$.

Figure 2 shows the details of the Det plugin added to $\mathcal{A}$ in Fig. 1. Det takes a key κ, reads D_s, D_u, performs the keyed transformation, calls G on $f_\kappa(D_u), f_\kappa(D_s)$ and outputs a decision.

G can be Mann-Whitney's test (illustrated in this paper) or any other NPHT e.g. the location test, the paired T test, Siegel-Turkey's test, the variance test, or multidimensional tests such as deep gaussianization [29].

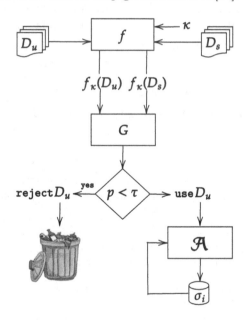

Fig. 2. Implementing Det using keying. Red: unknown to the opponent. Orange: known by the opponent. Blue: controlled by the opponent. (Color figure online)

3.1   Trivial Mann-Whitney Poisoning

Let G be Mann-Whitney's U-Test returning a p-value:

$$p = G(A, B) = G(\{a_0, \ldots, a_{n_1-1}\}, \{b_0, \ldots, b_{n_2-1}\})$$

G is, between others, susceptible to poisoning as follows: assume that A is sampled from a Gaussian distribution $A \in_R \mathcal{N}(\mu_A, \sigma_A)$ and that B is sampled from $\{-q, q\}$ where $\mu_A \ll q$ (Fig. 3). While A and B are totally different, G will be misled.

For instance, after picking 10^6 samples $A \in_R \mathcal{N}(0, 3)$ and 10^6 samples $B \in_R$ $\{-15, 15\}$ (i.e. we took $q = 15$), we get a p-value of 0.99. From Mann-Whitney's perspective, A, B come from the same parent distribution with a very high degree of confidence while, in all evidence, they do not.

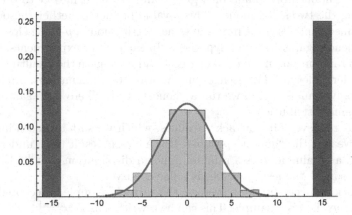

Fig. 3. Trivial Mann-Whitney poisoning. Samples drawn from the blue distribution are Mann-Whitney-indistinguishable from samples drawn from the orange one. (Color figure online)

3.2   Keyed Mann-Whitney

We instantiate f_κ by secret random polynomials i.e. polynomials $R(x)$ whose coefficients are randomly and secretly refreshed before each invocation of G. Instead of returning $G(A, B)$, Det returns $G(R(A), R(B))$ where:

$$R(A) = \left\{ R(a_0), \ldots, R(a_{n_1 - 1}) \right\} \quad \text{and} \quad R(B) = \left\{ R(b_0), \ldots, R(b_{n_2 - 1}) \right\}$$

The rationale is that R will map the attacker's input to an unpredictable location in which the Mann-Whitney is very likely to be safe.

ℓ random polynomials $R_1(x), \ldots, R_\ell(x)$ are selected as keys and Det calls G for each polynomial. To aggregate all resulting p-values, Det computes:

$$\Delta = \text{Stouffer}\left(G\left(R_1(A), R_1(B) \right), \ldots, G\left(R_\ell(A), R_\ell(B) \right) \right)$$

If $\Delta \approx 0$, the sample is rejected as poisonous with very high probability.

Note that any smooth function can be used as R, e.g. B-splines. The criterion on R is that the random selection process must yield significantly different functions.

3.3 Experiments

We illustrate the above by protecting $\mathcal{N}(0,1)$. The good thing about $\mathcal{N}(0,1)$ is that random polynomials tend to diverge when $x = 1$ but adapt well to the central interval in which the Gaussian is not negligible.

We attack $\mathcal{N}(0,1)$ by poisoning with $\{-q, q\}$, where q is set to 3, 2, 1, and 0.5, respectively. For each value of q, two sets of 50 samples are drawn from the two distributions. Those samples are then transformed into other sets by applying a random polynomial of degree 4 and then fed into G to obtain a p-value (using the two-sided mode). This p-value predicts whether these two sets of transformed samples come from the same distribution: a p-value close to 0 is a strong evidence against the null hypothesis. In each of our experiments, we apply nine secret random polynomials of degree 4 and aggregate the resulting p-values using Stouffer's method. For each setting, we run 1000 simulations. Similarly, for the same polynomials and q, we run a "honest" test, where both samples come from the same distribution.

We thus retrieve 1000 "attack" p-values, which we sort by ascending order. Similarly, we sort the "honest" p-values. It is a classic result that, under the null hypothesis, a p-value follows a random uniform distribution over $[0, 1]$, hence a plot of the sorted "honest" p-values is a linear curve.

An attack is successful if, on average, the "attack" sample is accepted as least as often as the "honest" sample. This can be rewritten as $\mathrm{E}(p^{\text{attack}}) \geq \mathrm{E}(p^{\text{honest}})$, with E the acceptations expected value. Hence, a sufficient condition for the validity is that the curve of sorted attack p-values (solid lines in our figures) is above the curve of sorted honest p-values (dashed lines).

Experimental results are summarized in Figs. 4, 5, 6 and 7.

The first quadrant illustrates the polynomials used in the simulation and two bars for $\{-q, q\}$. The same random polynomials were used for each experiment. For simplicity, the coefficients of the polynomials were uniformly selected from $\{-1, 0, 1\}$, and (useless) polynomials of degree lower than 2 were excluded from the random selection. Then, we also added the identity polynomial (poly0), as a witness of what happens when there is no protection.

The following nine quadrants give the distribution of p-values for each polynomial, over 1000 simulations, sorted in increasing order. The dotted distribution corresponds to what an honest user would obtain, whereas the plain line simulation is based on poisoned datasets.

The last quadrant contains the sorted distribution of the aggregated p-values using Stouffer. Experimental results show that for poisoned datasets, the aggregated p-values remain close to zero, while a honest dataset does not appear to be significantly affected. In other words, with very high probability, keyed testing detects poisoning.

3.4 Discussion

We observe a saturation when q is too far from μ_A, this is due to the fact that even after passing through R the attack samples remain at the extremes. Hence

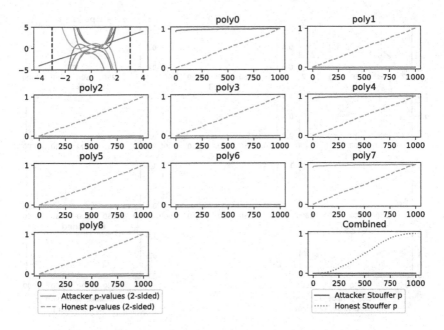

Fig. 4. Attack with $q = 3$. Defense with polynomials of degree 4.

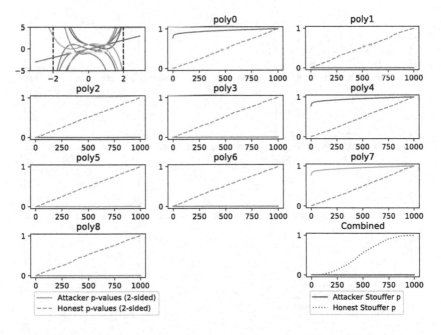

Fig. 5. Attack with $q = 2$. Defense with polynomials of degree 4.

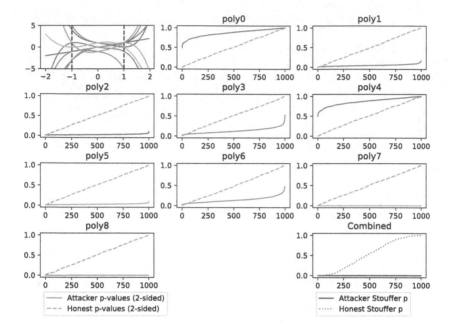

Fig. 6. Attack with $q = 1$. Defense with polynomials of degree 4.

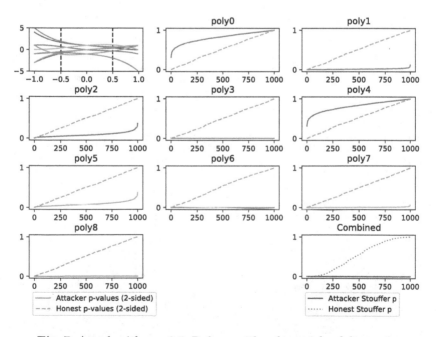

Fig. 7. Attack with $q = 0.5$. Defense with polynomials of degree 4.

if R is of odd degree, nothing changes. If the degree of R is even then the two extremes are projected to the same side and Mann-Whitney detects 100% of the poisonings. It follows that at saturation a keyed Mann-Whitney gives either very high or very low p-value. This means that polynomials or B-splines must be carefully chosen to make keying effective.

The advantage of combining the p-values with Stouffer's method is that the weak p-values are very penalizing (by opposition to Pearson's method whose combined p-value degrades much slower). A more conservative aggregation would be using Fisher's method.

All in all, experimental results reveal that keying managed to endow the test with a significant level of immunity.

Interestingly, Det can be implemented independently of $\mathcal{A}$.

A cautionary note: Our scenario assumes that testing does not start before learning is complete. If the opponent can alternate learning and testing then he may infer that a poisonous sample was taken into account (if σ was updated and $\mathcal{A}$'s behavior was modified). This may open the door to attacks on $\mathcal{A}$.

4 Notes and Further Research

This paper opens perspectives beyond the specific poisoning problem. e.g. cryptographers frequently use randomness tests $\mathcal{R}$ to assess the quality of random number generators. In a strong attack model where the attacker knows $\mathcal{R}$ and controls the random source it becomes possible to trick many $\mathcal{R}$s into declaring flagrantly non random data as random. Hence, the authors believe that developing keyed randomness tests $\mathcal{R}_\kappa$ is important and useful as such.

For instance, in the original minimum distance test 8000 points (a set S) sampled from the tested randomness source S are placed in a 10000×10000 square. Let δ be the minimum distance between the pairs. If S is random then δ^2 is exponentially distributed with mean 0.995. To key the test a secret permutation R_κ of the plan can be generated and the test can be applied to $R_\kappa(S)$.

To the best of our knowledge such primitives were not proposed yet.

We note, however, that keyed protections to different (non cryptographic!) decision problems in very diverse areas do emerge independently e.g. [1,9,19,28].

A   Mann-Whitney's U-Test

Let $\mathfrak{D}$ be an arbitrary distribution.

Mann-Whitney's U-test is a non-parametric hypothesis test. The test assumes that the two compared sample sets X_0, X_1 are independent and that a total order exists on their elements (which is the case for real-valued data such as ML feature vectors).

Assuming that $X_0 \in_R \mathfrak{D}$:

- The null hypothesis H_0 is that $X_1 \in_R \mathfrak{D}$.
- The alternative hypothesis H_1 is that $X_1 \in_R \mathfrak{D}'$ for $\mathfrak{D} \neq \mathfrak{D}'$.

The test is consistent[5] when, under H_1, $P(X_0 > X_1) \neq P(X_1 > X_0)$.

The test computes a statistic called U, which distribution under H_0 is known. When $\#X_0$ and $\#X_1$ are large enough, the distribution of U under H_0 is approximated by a normal distribution of known mean and variance.

U is computed as follows:

1. Merge the elements of X_0 and X_1. Sort the resulting list by ascending order.
2. Assign a rank to each element of the merged list. Equal elements get as rank the midpoint of their adjusted rankings[6].
3. Sum the ranks for each set. Let R_i be this sum for X_i. Note that if $n_i = \#X_i$ then $R_{1-i} = n(n+1)/2 - R_i$, with $n = n_0 + n_1$.
4. Let $U_i = R_i - \frac{n_i(n_i+1)}{2}$ and $U = \min(U_0, U_1)$.

When the $\#X_i$ are large enough (> 20 elements) U approximately follows a normal distribution.

Hence, one can check if the value

$$z = \frac{U - \lambda_U}{\sigma_U}$$

follows a standard normal distribution under H_0, with λ_U being the mean of U, and σ_U its standard deviation under H_0:

$$\lambda_U = \frac{n_0 n_1}{2} \text{ and } \sigma_U = \sqrt{\frac{n_0 n_1 (n+1)}{12}}$$

However, the previous formulae are only valid when there are no tied ranks. For tied ranks, the following formula is to be used:

$$\sigma_U = \sqrt{\frac{n_0 n_1}{12}\left((n+1) - \sum_{i=1}^{k} \frac{t_i^3 - t_i}{n(n-1)}\right)}$$

Because under H_0, z follows a normal distribution, we can estimate the likelihood that the observed values comes from a standard normal distribution, hence getting a related p-value from the standard normal table.

B   Stouffer's p-Value Aggregation Method

p values can be aggregated in different ways [11]. Stouffer [27] observes that the z-value defined by $z = \Phi^{-1}(p)$ is a standard normal variable under H_0 where Φ is the standard normal CDF. Hence when $\{p_1, \ldots, p_\ell\}$ are translated into $\{z_1, \ldots, z_\ell\}$, we get a collection of independent and identically distributed standard normal variables under H_0. To combine the effect of all tests we sum all

---

[5] i.e., its power increases with $\#X_0$ and $\#X_1$.
[6] e.g., in the list $1, 4, 4, 4, 4, 6$, the fours all get the rank 3.5.

the z_i which follows a normal distribution under H_0 with mean 0 and variance ℓ. The global test statistic

$$Z = \frac{1}{\ell} \sum_{i=1}^{\ell} z(p_i)$$

is hence standard normal under H_0 and can thus be reconverted into a p-value in the standard normal table.

Note that in theory, combining p-values using Stouffer's method requires that the tests are independent. Other methods can be used for combining p-values from non-independent tests, e.g. [6,16]. However, these calculations imply that the underlying joint distribution is known, and the derivation of the combination statistics percentiles requires a numerical approximation.

References

1. Albrecht, M.R., Massimo, J., Paterson, K.G., Somorovsky, J.: Prime and prejudice: primality testing under adversarial conditions. Cryptology ePrint Archive, Report 2018/749 (2018). https://eprint.iacr.org/2018/749
2. Barreno, M., Nelson, B., Joseph, A.D., Tygar, J.: The security of machine learning. Mach. Learn. **81**(2), 121–148 (2010)
3. Biggio, B., Nelson, B., Laskov, P.: Support vector machines under adversarial label noise. In: Hsu, C.N., Lee, W.S. (eds.) Proceedings of the Asian Conference on Machine Learning. Proceedings of Machine Learning Research, PMLR, Taoyuan, 14–15 November 2011, vol. 20, pp. 97–112 (2011)
4. Biggio, B., Nelson, B., Laskov, P.: Poisoning attacks against support vector machines. In: Proceedings of the 29th International Conference on Machine Learning, ICML 2012, Omnipress, Madison, pp. 1467–1474 (2012)
5. Biggio, B., Roli, F.: Wild patterns: ten years after the rise of adversarial machine learning. Pattern Recogn. **84**, 317–331 (2018)
6. Brown, M.: A method for combining non-independent, one-sided tests of significance. Biometrics **31**(4), 987–992 (1975)
7. Burkard, C., Lagesse, B.: Analysis of causative attacks against SVMs learning from data streams. In: Proceedings of the 3rd ACM on International Workshop on Security and Privacy Analytics, IWSPA 2017, pp. 31–36. ACM, New York (2017)
8. Cretu, G.F., Stavrou, A., Locasto, M.E., Stolfo, S.J., Keromytis, A.D.: Casting out demons: sanitizing training data for anomaly sensors. In: 2008 IEEE Symposium on Security and Privacy (SP 2008), pp. 81–95, May 2008
9. Géraud, R., Lombard-Platet, M., Naccache, D.: Quotient hash tables - efficiently detecting duplicates in streaming data. CoRR abs/1901.04358 (2019)
10. Goodfellow, I., et al.: Generative adversarial nets. In: Advances in Neural Information Processing Systems, pp. 2672–2680 (2014)
11. Heard, N.A., Rubin-Delanchy, P.: Choosing between methods of combining-values. Biometrika **105**(1), 239–246 (2018)
12. Kearns, M., Li, M.: Learning in the presence of malicious errors. In: Proceedings of the Twentieth Annual ACM Symposium on Theory of Computing, STOC 1988, pp. 267–280. ACM, New York (1988)
13. Kerckhoffs, A.: La cryptographie militaire. J. Sci. Mil. **IX**, 5–38 (1883)

14. Kloft, M., Laskov, P.: Online anomaly detection under adversarial impact. In: Teh, Y.W., Titterington, M. (eds.) Proceedings of the Thirteenth International Conference on Artificial Intelligence and Statistics. Proceedings of Machine Learning Research, PMLR, Sardinia, 13–15 May 2010, vol. 9, pp. 405–412 (2010)

15. Koh, P.W., Liang, P.: Understanding black-box predictions via influence functions. In: Proceedings of the 34th International Conference on Machine Learning, ICML 2017, vol. 70, pp. 1885–1894. JMLR.org (2017)

16. Kost, J.T., McDermott, M.P.: Combining dependent p-values. Stat. Probab. Lett. **60**(2), 183–190 (2002)

17. Laishram, R., Phoha, V.V.: Curie: a method for protecting SVM classifier from poisoning attack. arXiv abs/1606.01584 (2016)

18. Mei, S., Zhu, X.: Using machine teaching to identify optimal training-set attacks on machine learners. In: Proceedings of the Twenty-Ninth AAAI Conference on Artificial Intelligence, AAAI 2015, pp. 2871–2877. AAAI Press (2015)

19. Naor, M., Yogev, E.: Bloom filters in adversarial environments. CoRR abs/1412.8356 (2014)

20. Nelson, B., et al.: Exploiting machine learning to subvert your spam filter. In: Proceedings of the 1st USENIX Workshop on Large-Scale Exploits and Emergent Threats, LEET 2008, pp. 7:1–7:9. USENIX Association, Berkeley (2008)

21. Newell, A., Potharaju, R., Xiang, L., Nita-Rotaru, C.: On the practicality of integrity attacks on document-level sentiment analysis. In: Proceedings of the 2014 Workshop on Artificial Intelligent and Security Workshop, AISec 2014, pp. 83–93. ACM, New York (2014)

22. Newsome, J., Karp, B., Song, D.: Paragraph: thwarting signature learning by training maliciously. In: Zamboni, D., Kruegel, C. (eds.) RAID 2006. LNCS, vol. 4219, pp. 81–105. Springer, Heidelberg (2006). https://doi.org/10.1007/11856214_5

23. Perdisci, R., Dagon, D., Lee, W., Fogla, P., Sharif, M.: Misleading worm signature generators using deliberate noise injection. In: 2006 IEEE Symposium on Security and Privacy (S&P 2006), pp. 15–31, May 2006

24. Rubinstein, B.I., et al.: ANTIDOTE: understanding and defending against poisoning of anomaly detectors. In: Proceedings of the 9th ACM SIGCOMM Conference on Internet Measurement, IMC 2009, pp. 1–14. ACM, New York (2009)

25. Samangouei, P., Kabkab, M., Chellappa, R.: Defense-GAN: protecting classifiers against adversarial attacks using generative models. arXiv preprint arXiv:1805.06605 (2018)

26. Shaham, U., et al.: Defending against adversarial images using basis functions transformations. arXiv abs/1803.10840 (2018)

27. Stouffer, S., Suchman, E., DeVinney, L., Star, S., Williams, R.J.: The American Soldier. Adjustment During Army Life, vol. 1 (1949)

28. Taran, O., Rezaeifar, S., Voloshynovskiy, S.: Bridging machine learning and cryptography in defence against adversarial attacks. In: Leal-Taixé, L., Roth, S. (eds.) ECCV 2018. LNCS, vol. 11130, pp. 267–279. Springer, Cham (2019). https://doi.org/10.1007/978-3-030-11012-3_23

29. Tolpin, D.: Population anomaly detection through deep gaussianization. In: Proceedings of the 34th ACM/SIGAPP Symposium on Applied Computing, SAC 2019, pp. 1330–1336. ACM, New York (2019). https://doi.org/10.1145/3297280.3297414

30. Xiao, H., Xiao, H., Eckert, C.: Adversarial label flips attack on support vector machines. In: Proceedings of the 20th European Conference on Artificial Intelligence, ECAI 2012, pp. 870–875. IOS Press, Amsterdam (2012)

31. Xiao, H., Biggio, B., Brown, G., Fumera, G., Eckert, C., Roli, F.: Is feature selection secure against training data poisoning? In: International Conference on Machine Learning, pp. 1689–1698 (2015)
32. Xu, W., Evans, D., Qi, Y.: Feature squeezing: detecting adversarial examples in deep neural networks. In: Proceedings of the 25th Annual Network and Distributed System Security Symposium (NDSS) (2017)

SparkDA: RDD-Based High-Performance Data Anonymization Technique for Spark Platform

Sibghat Ullah Bazai[✉][iD] and Julian Jang-Jaccard[iD]

Massey University, Auckland, New Zealand
{s.bazai,j.jang-jaccard}@massey.ac.nz

Abstract. Recent proposals in data anonymization have mostly been focused around MapReduce, though the advantages of Spark have been well documented. To address this concern, we propose a new novel data anonymization technique for Apache Spark. SparkDA, our proposal, takes the full advantages of innovative Spark features, such as better partition control, in-memory process, and cache management for iterative operations, while providing high data utility with privacy. These are achieved by proposing data anonymization algorithms through Spark's Resilient Distributed Dataset (RDD). Our data anonymization algorithms are implemented at two main data processing RDD transformations, FlatMapRDD and ReduceByKeyRDD, respectively. Our experimental results show that our proposed approach provides required data privacy and utility levels while providing scalability with high-performance that are essential to many large datasets.

Keywords: High-performance · Data anonymization · Spark · Big data mining · Privacy and utility

1 Introduction

With the popularity of Big Data, distributed parallel processing platforms have emerged with the features required for processing large amount of data for example high capacity storage, processing units, and execution memory, etc. Many traditional data anonymization techniques have been adapted to work along with such distributed parallel processing platforms, such as MapReduce, to take the advantages of many scalability features offered by them [7–9]. However, existing MapReduce-based data anonymization approaches would often suffer performance issues due to inherent MapReduce architectural design, which requires data (and their by-products such as intermediate data) to travel to disks frequently [17], the lack of mechanisms which can share data across multiple nodes or run iterative tasks more efficiently [10].

Spark [16] has been emerged as the next generation big data processing platform offering new advanced features that were limited in MapReduce [12]. With

© Springer Nature Switzerland AG 2019
J. K. Liu and X. Huang (Eds.): NSS 2019, LNCS 11928, pp. 646–662, 2019.
https://doi.org/10.1007/978-3-030-36938-5_40

the popularity of Spark in recent years, the proposals for data anonymization techniques to run on Spark platform also has emerged [2,3,13]. However, these proposals are often two sketchy to understand neither the details of the data anonymization strategies nor provide benchmark figures for privacy, scalability and performance. We present a novel data anonymization approach named SparkDA that implements data anonymization algorithms while taking the full advantages of Spark's advanced features. Our SparkDA provides the following capabilities.

- The main data anonymization algorithms are offered through Resilient Distributed Dataset (RDD) transformation, by designing FlatMapRDD and ReduceByKeyRDD transformations, respectively.
- By utilizing RDDS, our data anonymization algorithms are run in memory (instead of disk as done in MapReduce). This reduces the overheads of having to travel to expensive disk I/O – especially for intermediary results which are often used by subsequent executions.
- Iterative operations, such as generalization and suppression algorithm, in SparkDA are cached then re-used which results in high-performance.
- Our experimental results illustrate the feasibility of our proposal by showing that data utility is still high when compared with its counterpart in standalone operation (i.e., data utility is not destroyed as the results of taking advantage of high-performance).
- Results show the scalability of SparkDA while maintaining high-performance.

The rest of this paper is organized as follows: Sect. 2 provides the background that is related to this paper. Section 3 explains the details of our proposed method SparkDA and two data anonymization RDD transformation algorithms. Section 4 discusses our experimental setup, results and key findings in details. Section 5 provides the conclusion along with future work.

2   Background

This section provides the background materials to better understand our proposal. The section starts with the main architectural ideas behind MapReduce and Spark, their similarities and differences. An illustration of the main idea behind a data anonymization technique based on Datafly [14] is presented.

2.1   MapReduce vs Spark

The Hadoop MapReduce [9] has been a popular big data processing platform for the last decade. The MapReduce programming paradigm is based on Map and Reduce. MapReduce starts with multiple mappers on various nodes based on data locality to process the mappers in parallel at each node. The input data, typically large, is split into mappers of multiple nodes. The data in a mapper, which is a collection of records either structured or unstructured, is assigned with key-value combinations. The mapper writes key-value pairs in the local disk at each data node. The reduce function is designed to collect mappers' results. The reducer reads these key-value pairs from local disk and exchanges the relevant keys to the respective reducers. Figure 1 illustrates the execution cycle of a MapReduce job to highlight data movement from an input to an output. However, some performance degradation in the current MapReduce paradigm can occur in the following places.

- Problem (1): When splitting the input data, the size and the number of splits decide the number of mappers at each node – often with no knowledge of the capability of mappers. One such allocation is done, there is no movement of mappers across nodes. This creates several performance issues. For example, it can create a long execution queue if a node contains too many mappers as MapReduce only use the memory of each node for processing the mapper at the local node. Any subsequent mappers have to wait until the memory is freed even though other nodes could be idle. Subsequently, it also creates delay in the reducer as it needs to wait until this busy node with many mappers finishes all processing even though the mappers in other nodes have already finished much earlier. This problem is illustrated as "Problem 1" in Fig. 1.
- Problem (2): Mappers create intermediate values which are written in the local disks at each node in MapReduce. This creates a several trips to the expensive disk I/O as the number of intermediate results increases. This problem is illustrated as "Problem 2" in Fig. 1.
- Problem (3): The reducer produces the final results. All intermediate results across multiple nodes require to be transferred to the reducer which could often locate in another node in the network. The transmissions of intermediate results across multiple nodes and the reducer can also create performance degrade. This problem is illustrated as "Problem 3" in Fig. 1.

These problems results in a tremendous performance bottleneck with iterative operations. In the current MapReduce architecture, a severe execution queue is created with iterative operations which require a series of sequential MapReduce jobs, where each iteration to be waited and executed one by one until all iterations are done.

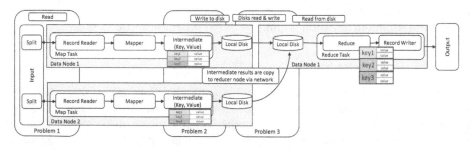

Fig. 1. Components and data flow in the MapReduce execution cycle

To address the performance concern of MapReduce, Spark has emerged as a high-performance distributed processing platform for big data. Spark uses Resilient Distributed Datasets (RDDs), which are immutable collection of records partitioned in a parallel manner. Input data is read from the disk as a split block as it was done in MapReduce environment, however, the blocks are further split into several partitions. An input RDD is created which contains all the partitions. The input RDD understands the memory capability at each worker's node, and by taking this account, assigns the optimal number of partitions to each node. This can effectively reduce the issue we discussed in the earlier problem (1). Once partitions are done, more RDDs are created to transform the original data. The intermediate values at each RDD transformation are written in the memory rather than the disk. This architecture can effectively remove the performance degradation mentioned in the problem (2).

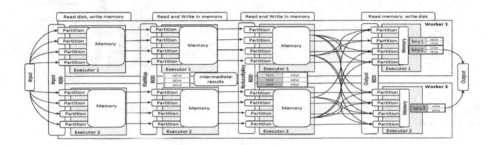

Fig. 2. Components and data flow in Spark execution cycle

In MapReduce, each node is executed as a separate unit where the intermediate values are not shared but being hold at its respective node. The intermediate results across different nodes occur at the reducer as a result of transferring data. This is not necessary in the Spark model as each RDD has the global knowledge of the previous stages and their intermediate results. We illustrate the execution flow of Spark in Fig. 2 which reads the input data in the memory, pre-process it, and then transform it through RDDs.

2.2 Data Anonymization

Data anonymization involves transforming an original data into an anonymized data in such a way where individually identifiable attributes or tuples in the original data are changed to a set of indistinguishable attributes or tuples. The transformation typically utilizes two techniques; generalization and suppression, respectively.

- Generalization refers to a process where the value of an attribute is replaced with a less specific value. In general, generalization is based on a Domain Generalization Hierarchy (DGH) associated to that attribute. A DGH specify a Generalization Level (GL) for each attribute. DGH is usually provided by a domain expert based on the attribute characteristics.

- Suppression replaces the attribute with the one that do not release any information about the attribute at all.

Figure 3 illustrates the general generalization approach that applies generalization levels (*GLs*) defined in a *DGH*. *GL*5 in "Date of Birth" represents an example of suppression with "*". Among many variations of data anonymization exists, our approach follows the basic idea from Datafly [14].

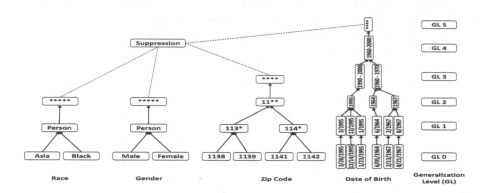

Fig. 3. Examples of Generalization and Domain Generalization Hierarchies including suppression

The data anonymization in this approach starts by counting the frequency over the Quasi Identifiers Attributes (*QID*). Then, it generalizes the attribute having the most distinct values until *k*-anonymity [15] is satisfied. The *QID* refers to a set of attributes that can be used to uniquely identify an individual (e.g. data of birth, age, and address).

Table 1 illustrates how the original data, depicted in Table 1(a), can be anonymized. To start the transformation, the algorithm first computes the frequency of each tuple and the distinct values of each attributes. These frequency counts is written as illustrated in Table 1(b). In the next step, the algorithm uses a *DGH* (such as one seen in Fig. 3) to perform a generalization step to satisfy *k*-anonymity rules from the attribute having the most number of distinct values. For example, "Date of Birth" is first generalized as it has the most number of distinct attributes values followed by "Zip Code". One or multiple levels of generalizations are applied from the generalization hierarchy until it satisfies *k*-anonymity – see Table 1(c).

Table 1(d) shows the effect of the full generalization/suppression with respect to the frequency list update. For example, for *k* = 2 anonymity, "Date of Birth" is generalized to level = 5, "Zip Code" to level = 3, followed by "Gender" and "Race" up to level = 2. Table 1(d) represents *k* = 2 anonymization as final result.

Table 1. Data anonymization steps

(a) Original Data

Date of Birth	Gender	Zip Code	Race	Disease
3/20/1995	Female	2141	Asian	Fever
12/14/1995	Female	2141	Asian	Back Pain
1/23/1995	Male	2138	Asian	Chest Pain
6/05/1964	Female	2139	Black	Brocken Hand
2/13/1967	Male	2138	Black	Asthma
8/21/1967	Male	2138	Black	Heart Attack

(b) Frequency counts

Date of Birth	Gender	Zip Code	Race	Frequency	Tuple
3/20/1995	Female	2141	Asian	1	T1
12/14/1995	Female	2141	Asian	1	T2
1/23/1995	Male	2138	Asian	1	T3
6/05/1964	Female	2139	Black	1	T4
2/13/1967	Male	2138	Black	1	T5
8/21/1967	Male	2138	Black	1	T6
6	**2**	**3**	**2**		

(c) Partially Anonymized Data

Date of Birth	Gender	Zip Code	Race	Frequency	Tuple
1995	Female	2141	Asian	2	T1, T2
1995	Male	2138	Asian	1	T3
1964	Female	2139	Black	1	T4
1967	Male	2138	Black	2	T5,T6
3	**2**	**3**	**2**		

(d) Fully Anonymized Data

Date of Birth	Gender	Zip Code	Race	Disease
1995	Female	2141	Asian	Fever
1995	Male	2138	Asian	Back Pain
1964	Female	2139	Black	Asthma
1967	Male	2138	Black	Heart Attack

3   SparkDA

We first outline the basic symbols and notations in Table 2 to clearly define the elements of data across different scopes in a dataset. Figure 4 illustrates a

Table 2. Basic symbol and notations

Symbol	Definition
PT	A table (dataset) that contains records
$RECORD$	A record contains a number of attributes, $RECORD \in PT$ and $RECORD = \{qid_1, qid_2, \ldots, qid_{attr}, sa\}$, where $qid_i, 1 \leq i \leq attr$, is the qid attribute and sa sensitive attribute
$attr$	Indicates a quasi-identifiable attribute
qid	A quasi-identifier attribute
QID	A set of attributes that belongs to the same qid
sa	Indicates a sensitive attribute
SA	Contains a set of attributes that belongs to the same sa
qid_{tuple}	Contains all qid(s) within a record $qid_{tuple} = \{qid_1, qid_2, \ldots, qid_{attr}\}$
QID_{Tuple}	Contains a set of qid_{tuple}, $QID_{Tuple} = \{qid_{tuple_1}, \ldots, qid_{tuple_{attr}}\}$
$freq(qid_{tuple})$	A set that contains a frequency associated to a qid_{tuple} for all qid_{tuple}(s) within a QID_{Tuple}
$freqSet$	A set that contains $freq(qid_{tuple})$ associated to a qid_{tuple}, $FreqSet = \{(qid_{tuple_1}, freq(qid_{tuple})_1), \ldots, (qid_{tuple_{attr}}, freq(qid_{tuple})_{attr})\}$
$dint_{qid}\text{-}cnt$	A number of occurrences for a distinct QID(s)in qid
$dint_{qid}\text{-}cntSet$	A set that contains $dint_{qid}\text{-}cnt$ a associated to a QID for all qid(s) within a QID_{Tuple}, $dint_{qid}\text{-}cntSet = \{dint_{qid}\text{-}cnt_1, \ldots, dint_{qid}\text{-}cnt_{attr}\}$
DGH	A Domain Generalization Hierarchy
GL	Generalization Level of $QID \in DGH$
K	K defines the level of k-anonymization
EC	Finds the number of the same qid(s) within a QID for a given group based on K

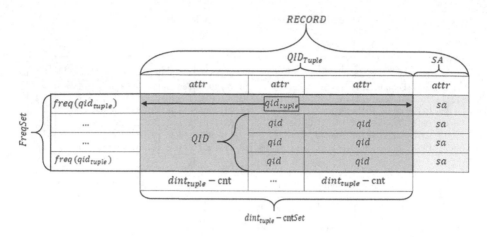

Fig. 4. Notations representation for any given table

diagram as how our notations can be mapped into a relational database table. In the followed sections, we describe the details of two main RDD transformations where the main idea of our anonymization techniques is applied – FlatMapRDD and RedueByKeyRDD followed by the description of our proposed approach SparkDA.

3.1 RDD-Based Data Anonymization

We have implemented new data anonymization supports in two Spark RDD transformations, FlatMapRDD and ReduceByKeyRDD, respectively.

FlatMap Transformation (FlatMapRDD): The FlatMapRDD runs an algorithm to get the frequency counts for distinct tuples that contains all quasi-identifiable attributes as well as for the distinct variations within each quasi-identifiable attribute. The details of the FlatMapRDD algorithm are shown in Algorithm 1.

The start of the FlatMapRDD algorithm, it requires QID_{Tuple} as an input. In the initial stage, the QID_{Tuple} contains the original quasi-identifiable attributes. The first part of the algorithm, from step 2–11, is used to get the frequency count for distinct set of quasi-identifiable attributes. This is done by first measuring the size of QID_{Tuple} to identify the total number of qid_{tuple} it contains (in step 3). Then, the current qid_{tuple} is compared with the subsequent qid_{tuple}. If there is a match between $qid_{tuple}(s)$, a frequency count is updated by adding the number 1. This is done for each qid_{tuple} within the QID_{Tuple}. By step 10, $FreqSet$ for all $qid_{tuple}(s)$ is updated with the frequency counts for each unique tuple.

Algorithm 1. FlatMapRDD

Input: QID_{Tuple}
Output: $FreqSet$, $dint_{qid}\text{-}cntSet$
1 **begin**
2   $freq(qid_{tuple}) = 1$
3   **for** i in $Size(QID_{Tuple})$ **do**
4   **if** $qid_{tuple_i} = qid_{tuple_{i+1}}$ **then**
5 | $freq(qid_{tuple}) + +$
6   **end**
7   **else**
8 | $freq(qid_{tuple})$
9   **end**
10 | $FreqSet + = (qid_{tuple}, freq(qid_{tuple}))$
11 **end**
12 $dint_{qid}\text{-}cnt = 0$
13 **for** i in $Size(QID_{Tuple})$ **do**
14   **for** j in $Size(qid_{tuple})$ **do**
15 | $QID_j = qid_{tuple(i)(j)}$
16   **end**
17 **end**
18 **for** i in $Size(QID)$ **do**
19   **if** $qid_i = qid_{(i+1)}$ **then**
20 | $dint_{qid}\text{-}cnt_{(i)}$
21   **end**
22   **else**
23 | $dint_{qid}\text{-}cnt_{(i)} + +$
24   **end**
25    $dint_{qid}\text{-}cntSet += dint_{qid}\text{-}cnt_{(i)}$
26 **end**
27 return $(FreqSet, dint_{qid}\text{-}cntSet)$
28 **end**

ReduceByKey Transformation (ReduceByKeyRDD): The main purpose of ReduceByKeyRDD is to run an iteration of (anonymization) transformation from the given $FreqSet$ and $dint_{qid}\text{-}cntSet$. Here, the transformation refers to the change such as taking place in Table 1(a) and (b), and from Table 1(b) and (c), and so on until reaches Table 1(d). It utilizes an "anonymization statue $(anonymization_s)$" to identify whether a given QID_{Tuple} is fully anonymized or if it further needs to run more transformations. Algorithm 2 describes the ReduceByKeyRDD.

The algorithm starts by receiving the (DGH, K) which was sent via a broadcast mechanism from Spark driver node, which runs the main SparkDA algorithms. (DGH, K), as notation implies, contains both the Domain Generalization Hierarchies (DGH) and the size of K-group (K). Once received, DGH is further processed to extract the generalization level (GL) for each quasi-identifiable attribute as seen in step 3 and 4.

Algorithm 2. ReduceByKeyRDD

  Input: $FreqSet, dint_{qid}\text{-}cntSet$
  Output: $QID_{Tuple}, anonymization_s$
 1 **begin**
 2 | $(DGH, K) \leftarrow broadcast(DGH, K)$
 3 | $GL_{qid} \leftarrow (DGH, K)$
 4 | $K \leftarrow (DGH, K)$
 5 | $anonymization_s = false$
 6 | **for** i **in** $Size(FreqSet)$ **do**
 7 | | **if** $dint_{qid}\text{-}cnt < K$ **then**
 8 | | | **for** $j = 0$ **in** $Size(dint_{qid}\text{-}cntSet)$ **do**
 9 | | | | **if** $MAX(dint_{qid}\text{-}cnt_j) < MAX(GL_{qid})$ **then**
10 | | | | | UPDATE $qid_{(i)(j)}$ with value of $GL_{qid_j} + 1$
11 | | | | **end**
12 | | | | **else**
13 | | | | | $qid_{(i)(j)}$
14 | | | | **end**
15 | | | | $qid_{tuple} += qid_{(i)(j)}$
16 | | | **end**
17 | | | $QID_{Tuple} += qid_{tuple}$
18 | | | $anonymization_s \leftarrow false$
19 | | **end**
20 | | **else**
21 | | | **for** j **in** $Size(qid_{tuple})$ **do**
22 | | | | UPDATE $qid_{(i)(j)}$ with "*"
23 | | | | $qid_{tuple} += qid_{(i)(j)}$
24 | | | **end**
25 | | | $QID_{Tuple} += qid_{tuple}$
26 | | | $anonymization_s \leftarrow true$
27 | | **end**
28 | **end**
29 | return $(QID_{Tuple}, anonymization_s)$
30 **end**

The first part of the algorithm, the steps 6–18, is to generalize attributes up to a single generalization level for all quasi-identifiable attribute sets. This is done if the frequency counts ($freq(qid_{tuple})$) has not exceed the size of K (k-anonymization) and while the maximum generalization level ($MAX(GL_{qid})$) has not met. The single generalization level is done in the order of the attributes with the highest distinct attribute counts ($MAX(dint_{qid}\text{-}cntt)$) to lower. The anonymization status is set to false as there is more transformation to be done.

The second part of the algorithm, the steps 20–26, is to suppress all attributes for a given tuple that have violated k-anonymity rules – that is, there exist no indistinguishable tuples. At this stage, all transformation is done including the suppression. The anonymization status is set to true as there is no more transformation to be done. The anonymized results (either or both being generalized/suppressed) are sent back to FlatMapRDD along with the anonymization status (as seen in step 29). FlatMapRDD will re-calculate the frequency counts for tuples and attributes when anonymization status is false.

3.2 Overall SparkDA Scheme

This part describes the overall process of our SparkDA that are associated not only with the data anonymization but also other parts that assist the data anonymization process.

To run the SparkDA, it first needs an input dataset (i.e., the original data) along with other user defined information such as the size of K and the definition for DGH. The user defined information is used as global variables that can be shard across all Spark worker nodes that process RDDs (such as Reduce-ByKeyRDD). The global variables can be sent via the use of broadcast mechanism in Spark.

Algorithm 3 illustrates the overall pseudo-code. The algorithm starts by reading the file from HDFS as an input dataset which are subsequently stored by the InputRDD. The InputRDD processes the input data in a way that is easier for other RDDs to progress. For example, it splits the input data into two separate sets, one set containing all quasi-identifiable attributes (QID_{Tuple}-RDD) while the other set containing all sensitive attributes (SA-RDD) – seen in step 5.

Algorithm 3. SparkDA

Input: Dataset, K, DGH
Output: $Anonymized(RDD)$

1 **begin**
2    $InputRDD \leftarrow textFile(Dataset)$
3    $broadcast(DGH, K) \leftarrow broadcast(DGH)$
4    $broadcast(DGH, K) \leftarrow broadcast(K)$
5    $anonymization_s = false$
6    $SA\text{-}RDD, QID_{Tuple}\text{-}RDD \leftarrow InputRDD.filter(qid_{tuple}, sa)$
7    $SA\text{-}RDD_c \leftarrow SA\text{-}RDD.cache$
8    $QID_{Tuple_c} \leftarrow QID_{Tuple}\text{-}RDD.cache$
9   **while** $anonymization_s = false$ **do**
10      $Result\text{-}RDD(QID_{Tuple}, anonymization_s) \leftarrow$
        $QID_{Tuple}.\text{FlatMapRDD}(QID_{Tuple})$
        $.\text{ReduceByKeyRDD}(dint_{qid}\text{-}cntSet, FreqSet)$
11      $QID_{Tuple}\text{-}RDD.cache \leftarrow filter.Result\text{-}RDD(QID_{Tuple},$
        $anonymization_s)$
12      $QID_{Tuple_c} \leftarrow QID_{Tuple}\text{-}RDD.cache$
13      $anonymization_s \leftarrow filter.Result\text{-}RDD(QID_{Tuple}, anonymization_s)$
14   **end**
15    $Anonymized_{Tuple} \leftarrow filter.Result\text{-}RDD(QID_{Tuple}, anonymization_s)$
16    $Anonymized(RDD) \leftarrow Anonymized_{Tuple}.join(SA\text{-}RDD_c)$
17   **return** $Anonymized(RDD)$
18 **end**

Both SA-RDD and QID_{Tuple}-RDD are cached in memory for further processing. The cached QID_{Tuple_c} is used by FlatMapRDD and ReduceByKeyRDD for data anonymization as described in the above section. The anonymization status at this stage is set to false to execute FlatMapRDD and Reduce-ByKeyRDD to signal the start of the anonymization process. If anonymization is finished, which fully QID_{Tuple} is returned from ReduceByKeyRDD, then the anonymization status is set to true. At this stage, QID_{Tuple} only contains the distinct qid_{tuple} but are not joined with the sensitive value. The joining between QID_{Tuple} and SA-RDD only happens in step 19.

4 Experimental Results

In this section, we first explain our experimental setups that include the details of the dataset and the system environment (hardware/software) configurations. This is followed by the description of data utility metrics we used and the results we obtained to understand the information loss as the results of our data anonymization. In addition, we also provide the results of scalability and performance.

4.1 Datasets

We used two datasets in our study: US Census dataset (often described as Adult dataset) [4] and Irish Census dataset [1]. We downloaded the original Adult dataset, then synthesized it to create a set of larger datasets for the experiments. Similarly, we downloaded already synthesized Irish dataset and further created more data from it. The synthesized datasets are generated by using Java opensource tool "Benerator" [5]. We followed the guideline from [6] to increase the number of records. Table 3 illustrates the quasi-identifiable attributes (QID) we used in our experiments, and generalization level (GL) of each QID obtained from the domain generalization hierarchy (DGH) for both the datasets. The "Salary" in Adult dataset and the "Field of Study" in Irish dataset are set as sensitive attributes.

Table 3. Datasets

(a) Adult dataset

QID	Distinct Value	GL
Age	74	4
Work Class	8	2
Education	16	4
Marital Status	7	3
Occupation	14	2
Gender	2	1

(b) Irish dataset

QID	Distinct Value	GL
Age	70	4
Economic Status	9	2
Education	10	4
Marital Status	7	3
Industrial Group	22	2
Gender	2	1

4.2   System Environment Configurations

We ran two types of experiments, first one with distributed processing platform using Spark and the other with standalone desktop. The standalone desktop environment was used to understand the comparability of data utility results – this should stay the same though our data anonymization technique takes advantage of scalability and high-performance features of Spark. For Spark, as a distributed processing platform, we configured Yarn and Hadoop Distributed File System (HDFS) using Apache Ambari. HDFS distributes data in a NameNode (worked as a master node), a secondary NameNode and six DataNodes (worked as worker nodes). We configured 3 GB memory for Yarn NodeManager while 1 GB memory was allocated to ResourceManager, Driver, and Executor memories each. We used Spark version 2.1 along with Yarn as a cluster manager. Table 4(a) illustrate the Spark and Hadoop Parameters. Table 4(b) depicts the details of the spark cluster and standalone computer and their respective CPU, Memory, Disk, and Network speed (Gbit/s). Note that we used a Windows 10 as a standalone desktop. We ran our experiments 10 times and the average was used to ensure the reliability and consistency of the results.

Table 4. Hardware and cluster configuration

(a) Spark and Hadoop Parameters

Spark		Hadoop	
ResourceManager Memory	1 GB	NameNode	1
Driver Memory	1GB	DataNode	6
Executor Memory	1 GB	Block Replication	3
Driver Cores	1	Block Size	128MB
Executor Cores	1	HDFS Disk	18 TB

(b) Hardware Configuration

Configuration	Cluster Node		Standalone
	Master	Worker	Desktop
CPU (Cores)	32	8	12
Memory (GB)	64	32	32
Disk (TB)	24	8	4
Network (Gbit/s)	10	10	10

4.3   Privacy and Utility Trade-Offs

We used the following four privacy and utility metrics to validate and understand the rate of information loss between the original data and the anonymized datasets produced as the results of running our SparkDA algorithms.

Average Equivalence Class Size Metric (C_{AVG}): C_{AVG} is used to measure data utility based on attributes of the average size of the equivalence class. The increase in the number of equivalence sizes result in the higher data utility as it is more difficult to identify an attribute among many identical attributes. In k-anonymized dataset, the size of the equivalence classes is greater than or equal to K. As a result, the quality of the data is lower if the size of all or part of the equivalence classes greatly exceeds the value K. The score of C_{AVG} sensitive to the K group size [11]. C_{AVG} for AnonymizedRDD is calculated as following.

$$C_{AVG} = \frac{|\ AnonymizedRDD\ |}{|\ EC\ |}/K \qquad (1)$$

| $AnonymizedRDD$ | represents the total number of records of $Anonymized$ RDD, whereas | EC | represents the total number of equivalence classes.

Precision Metric (PM): PM [14] is used to choose the least distorted records (i.e., both from attributes and tuple perspective) from the set containing all anonymized records. PM is sensitive to the GL. Following equation defines PM_{score} for AnonymizedRDD.

$$PM_{score} = 1 - \frac{\sum_{qid=1}^{qid_{tuple}} \sum_{qid_{tuple}=1}^{QID_{Tuple}} \frac{GL}{|DGH_{qid_{tuple}}|}}{qid_{tuple}.QID_{Tuple}} \qquad (2)$$

Where GL defines a generalization level (defined in DGH) including suppression. Attributes with higher generalization level typically maintains a rate of precision better when compared to attributes with lower generalization levels.

Table 5. Experimental configurations for data utility

#	Utility metrics	Anonymization parameters	Dataset size	Platform
1	C_{AVG}, PM	K-value $\in$ {2, 5, 10, 25, 50, 75, 100}, $|QID| = 5^a$	Adult = 30K	Spark, standalone
		K-value $\in$ {2, 5, 10, 25, 50, 75, 100}, $|QID| = 5^a$	Irish = 30K	Spark, standalone

[a] Indicates the total number of attributes, we use 5 attributes in the experiment

To understand the privacy and utility trade-offs, we varied the K group sizes in our experiment. This implies that the increased in the K group size would obviously make data utility reduced - which would results in the increase in data privacy. What it means is that as there are more data made indistinguishable, it is harder to identify an individual. Note that $K2$ depicts that two tuples to become indistinguishable while $K5$ to have five tuples to be same so on. The experimental setup for privacy vs. utility is shown in Table 5. We ran two experiments; one on Spark platform and the other on the standalone desktop against two different datasets.

The results of data utility metrics for SparkDA and standalone are illustrated, first with the Adult dataset Fig. 5(a)–(b) then for Irish dataset Fig. 5(c)–(d).

We first discuss the data utility results of Adult dataset. C_{AVG} measure data utility based on the equivalence class. The data utility decreases with the increase in the size of K group as there are more distinct attributes for matching. As there are more data matching between two equivalent classes, it implies the data privacy is high but data utility is low. However, the average penalty remains the same because at some point, approximately around $K = 10$, data is no longer either generalized or suppressed in an equivalence class hence no changes in the penalty value. Thus, the average penalty of an equivalent class decreases as the number of K group size increases which is seen in Fig. 5(a).

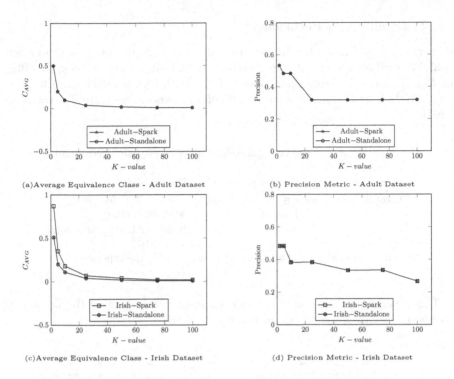

(a)Average Equivalence Class - Adult Dataset

(b) Precision Metric - Adult Dataset

(c)Average Equivalence Class - Irish Dataset

(d) Precision Metric - Irish Dataset

Fig. 5. Data utility vs Adult dataset and Irish dataset on Spark and standalone

Precision Metric (PM), in Fig. 5(b), demonstrates the level of distortion at the record level (i.e., the combination of tuples and attributes). It is expected that PM score will be higher as the number of K group size increases as there are more records that have lost its original values. The PM score is highly sensitive to GL for each qid. This is shown in Fig. 5(d) where the PM score increases as the number of K group size increases for both Spark and standalone. This is because the level of GL applied in each qid is increased to its highest as the size of K group increases. We observe that at $K = 25$ and onward, the qid are appeared to have been generalized to its highest level as the PM score stays the same.

The data privacy and utility results for Irish dataset shows slightly differ-ent data utility scores. We observe that in overall, Irish dataset contains the records that are more distinct from each other. The data utility increases with the increase in the size of K group where there are more distinct quasi-identifiable attributes; this is shown in C_{AVG} score in Fig. 5(c). The PM scores in Fig. 5(d), are same for Spark and standalone environment ensuring that the data privacy and utility were not affected between two implementations.

4.4   Scalability and Performance

We perform experiments to understand scalability and performance of our proposal. We used the increasing size of records and measure the execution for different K group size. The execution time includes both FlatMapRDD and ReduceByKeyRDD transformation. The details of the experiments are illustrated in Table 6.

Table 6. Experimental configurations for scalability and performance

#	Experiment	Anonymization parameters	Dataset size
1	Records size	K-$value \in \{10, 20, 25, 50, 75, 100\}$, $\mid QID \mid = 5^a$	Adult $= (5M, 10M, 20M, 30M, 40M, 50M)$
			Irish $= (5M, 10M, 20M, 30M, 40M, 50M)$

[a]It indicates the number of attributes that were used in the experiments

The experiments are aimed at understanding the impact of the number of records on various K-group size in Fig. 6(a) and (b).

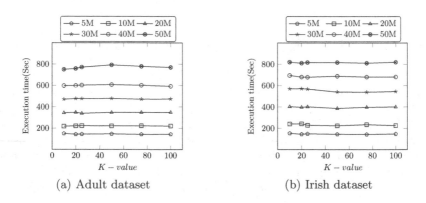

(a) Adult dataset   (b) Irish dataset

Fig. 6. Efficiency of SparkDA for varied record size

We first only increased the size of K-group on a fixed number of records to understand the relationship between the execution time and the size of K-group. Results show that the execution time appears not to be affected by increasing K group size. The number of iterations from the original data to fully anonymized dataset is decided based on the frequency of distinct tuples. The number of K group size would increase the number of tuples. With the fixed number of $QIDs$, the number of tuples that are increased doesn't necessarily are distinct. This means the frequency count stays the same. With the frequency count remaining the same, the same number of operations are done irrespective to the increasing number of K-size thus the execution time stays the same.

This appears that some operations (e.g., involved in QID generalization) are cached in memory then re-used and this does not affect too much on execution time. However, this changes as soon as the number of records is increased. The execution time linearly increases as the number of records increase Fig. 6(a) and (b) in both datasets.

5   Conclusion and Future Work

We proposed a novel data anonymization approach name SparkDA for Spark platform. Our data anonymization algorithms are implemented in FlatMapRDD and ReduceByKeyRDD to take the full advantages of many innovations in Spark which includes; better partition control, in-memory processing, and cache management. Our experimental results show high data utility scores compared to a standalone version meaning that the level of privacy is preserved while taking advantage of Spark features. Our experimental results also illustrate the linear grows of the execution time in line with the increasing number of QID(s) and the number of records. The linear grows, without any visible peaks and anomalies, validates that our proposed approach is feasible by supporting scalability with performance.

In future, we plan to extend our study in the number of areas. First, we plan to validate the cache performance on different storage levels and its effectiveness. Secondly, we plan to better understand Spark's support for shuffle and sort operations and their impacts. We also plan to add a number of privacy metrics. Furthermore, we also plan to extend our current study to work with multidimensional attributes.

References

1. Central Statistics Office (Internet) (2011). http://www.cso.ie/en/databases/. Accessed 16 Aug 2019
2. Al-Zobbi, M., Shahrestani, S., Ruan, C.: Sensitivity-based anonymization of big data. In: IEEE 41st Conference on Local Computer Networks Workshops (LCN Workshops), pp. 58–64. IEEE (2016)
3. Antonatos, S., Braghin, S., Holohan, N., Gkoufas, Y., Mac Aonghusa, P.: Prima: an end-to-end framework for privacy at scale. In: IEEE 34th International Conference on Data Engineering (ICDE), pp. 1531–1542. IEEE (2018)
4. Asuncion, A., Newman, D.: UCI machine learning repository (2007). http://archive.ics.uci.edu/ml. Accessed 16 July 2019
5. Ayala-Rivera, V., McDonagh, P., Cerqueus, T., Murphy, L.: Synthetic data generation using benerator tool. arXiv preprint arXiv:1311.3312 (2013)
6. Ayala-Rivera, V., McDonagh, P., Cerqueus, T., Murphy, L., et al.: A systematic comparison and evaluation of k-anonymization algorithms for practitioners. Trans. Data Priv. **7**(3), 337–370 (2014)
7. Bazai, S.U., Jang-Jaccard, J., Wang, R.: Anonymizing k-NN classification on MapReduce. In: Hu, J., Khalil, I., Tari, Z., Wen, S. (eds.) MONAMI 2017. LNICST, vol. 235, pp. 364–377. Springer, Cham (2018). https://doi.org/10.1007/978-3-319-90775-8_29

8. Bazai, S.U., Jang-Jaccard, J., Zhang, X.: A privacy preserving platform for MapReduce. In: Batten, L., Kim, D.S., Zhang, X., Li, G. (eds.) ATIS 2017. CCIS, vol. 719, pp. 88–99. Springer, Singapore (2017). https://doi.org/10.1007/978-981-10-5421-1_8

9. Dean, J., Ghemawat, S.: MapReduce: simplified data processing on large clusters. Commun. ACM 51(1), 107–113 (2008)

10. Grolinger, K., Hayes, M., Higashino, W.A., L'Heureux, A., Allison, D.S., Capretz, M.A.: Challenges for MapReduce in big data. In: IEEE World Congress on Services, pp. 182–189. IEEE (2014)

11. LeFevre, K., DeWitt, D.J., Ramakrishnan, R., et al.: Mondrian multidimensional k-anonymity. In: ICDE, vol. 6, p. 25 (2006)

12. Shi, J., et al.: Clash of the titans: MapReduce vs. spark for large scale data analytics. Proc. VLDB Endow. 8(13), 2110–2121 (2015)

13. Sopaoglu, U., Abul, O.: A top-down k-anonymization implementation for apache Spark. In: IEEE International Conference on Big Data (Big Data), pp. 4513–4521. IEEE (2017)

14. Sweeney, L.: Achieving k-anonymity privacy protection using generalization and suppression. Int. J. Uncertain. Fuzziness Knowl. Based Syst. 10(05), 571–588 (2002)

15. Sweeney, L.: k-anonymity: a model for protecting privacy. Int. J. Uncertain. Fuzziness Knowl. Based Syst. 10(05), 557–570 (2002)

16. Zaharia, M., Chowdhury, M., Franklin, M.J., Shenker, S., Stoica, I.: Spark: cluster computing with working sets. HotCloud 10(10–10), 95 (2010)

17. Zhang, X., Liu, C., Nepal, S., Yang, C., Dou, W., Chen, J.: Combining top-down and bottom-up: scalable sub-tree anonymization over big data using MapReduce on cloud. In: 12th IEEE International Conference on Trust, Security and Privacy in Computing and Communications, pp. 501–508. IEEE (2013)

Short Papers

An Efficient Leakage-Resilient Authenticated Group Key Exchange Protocol

Ou Ruan, Yang Yang, and Mingwu Zhang[✉]

School of Computer Science, Hubei University of Technology, Wuhan 430068, China
mzzhang@mail.hbut.edu.cn

Abstract. Leakage-resilient (LR) cryptography including LR authenticated key exchange has been extensively studied in recent years. However, there is few literature to model and construct LR authenticated group key exchange (AGKE) protocol, which is the most practical cryptographic primitive for the group communication applications. In this paper, we first introduce an λ-bounded after-the-fact LR (λ-BAFLR) CK security model to assess the security of AGKE protocols in the leakage environments. Then by appropriately combining Diffie-Hellman (DH) group key exchange protocol and public key encryption with the security against adaptively chosen plaintext after-the-fact leakage attacks, we propose the first LR AGKE protocol, and show a formal proof of the λ-BAFLR CK security in the standard model based on the game simulation techniques. Our result shows that the proposed AGKE protocol attains the property of LR without incurring additional communication and computation cost by comparing with the related non-LR schemes.

Keywords: Leakage-resilience · Authenticated key exchange · Group setting · Provable security

1 Introduction

With the development of the Internet of things, the mobile Internet, the Industrial Internet and the cloud computing, there are more and more group communication applications such as audio or video conference, collaborative computing, group chatting, online teaching, and so on. In these distributed group computing applications, how to establish a security context becomes a key problem, where messages sent among parties are encrypted and authenticated. A cryptographic technique to solve this problem is authenticated group key exchange (AGKE) scheme, which is used to generate a shared secure session key in the public networks among all group members by using their secret keys. The original works on AGKEs were studied by Ingemarsson et al. [1], Burmester et al. [2], and Steiner et al. [3]. Then, many scholars have studied AGKE protocols for security models [4–7], efficiency [5, 8–10], and dynamicity [11–13].

© Springer Nature Switzerland AG 2019
J. K. Liu and X. Huang (Eds.): NSS 2019, LNCS 11928, pp. 665–674, 2019.
https://doi.org/10.1007/978-3-030-36938-5_41

All above AGKE protocols were only secure in the traditional security model that assumed the adversary couldn't obtain any information of the secret key. During the past two decades, many researches showed that an adversary could obtain some information about the secret key by the side-channel attacks [14], this partial information is called leakage. By this kind of attacks, an adversary could obtain the internal state of the system by observing the physical properties of the devices, such as running time, power consumption, electromagnetic effect, and so on. For example, in Internet of things, Mobile Internet or Ad Hoc network, the side-channel attacks may threaten the security of nodes which are exploded in the public environments. Thus, traditional AGKEs are completely insecure in the leakage environments. However, there is no prior work for designing AGKEs that are secure against leakage attacks. In the paper, we propose a bounded leakage-resilient (LR) security model for AGKEs that is secure against the leakage attacks on the secret keys. Then, we present a LR AGKE protocol based on the Diffie-Hellman (DH) group key exchange (GKE) protocol [2] and the public key encryption (PKE) that is secure against adaptively chosen plaintext after-the-fact leakage attacks (CPLA2). Finally, we present a formal security proof in the standard model according to the new bounded LR security model.

In a nutshell, the contributions of this paper are threefold:

- First, we provide a provable-security framework to assess the security of AGKE protocols in the leakage environments by extending the CK security framework properly. The framework formalizes the leakage attacks as leakage functions, captures the adversary's capabilities as queries to the oracles that are players in the session instance, and defines the security via the notion of semantic security. In the framework, the leakages are bounded by the system leakage parameter λ and may occur at any stage of the security game, thus we call it λ-bounded after-the-fact LR (λ-BAFLR) CK security model for AGKEs.
- Second, we first propose a LR AGKE protocol by combining the DH GKE protocol and the CPLA2-secure PKE scheme appropriately. Moreover, we evaluate the performance and demonstrate that it achieves the property of LR without incurring additional communication and computation cost by comparing with the related non-LR schemes.
- Third, we further formally prove the λ-BAFLR security in the standard model based on the game simulation techniques. Remarkably, the resistance to the leakage attacks is defined in a formal way for the first time.

The paper is organized as follows. In Sect. 2, we review the related works. In Sect. 3, we define an λ-BAFLR security model for AGKEs. In Sect. 4, we describe the new protocol. Finally, in Sect. 5, we show the conclusion.

2   Related Works

During the last decade, the LR cryptography was studied by numerous scholars [15–20], which provided secure solutions against the leakage attacks. In 2011, the first LR AKE protocol was proposed by Moriyama and Okamoto (MO) [21] based on hash proof system, in which they first defined a formal security model for LR AKE, called the MO model. The shortcoming of the MO model is that the leakage attacks were not permitted after the challenge was given. After-the-fact (AF) leakages are leakage attacks that happen after the challenger has sent his chosen challenge. In 2014, Alawatugoda et al. [22] first presented a continuous LR AKE protocol that was secure against AF leakage attacks. Their model was based on the CK AKE security model [23], called continuous AFLR (CAFLR) security model. But this model was vulnerable to key compromise impersonation (KCI) attack. To resist KCI attack, Alawatugoda et al. [24] first defined AFLR AKE eCK security model based on the eCK AKE security model [25]. Then, [24] and [26] showed two AKE protocols respectively under the bounded AFLR (BAFLR) eCK security model and the CAFLR eCK security model. In 2016, Chen et al. [27,28] first introduced a new AFLR eCK security model for AKEs, where leakage attacks may happen not only on the private keys and but also on the ephemeral secret randomnesses. Then, they proposed a BAFLR AKE protocol, and Wu et al. [29] gave a CAFLR AKE protocol under this strong model. In 2017, Ruan et al. [30] gave the first password-based CAFLR AKE protocol; and, Chakraborty et al. [31] presented a generic compiler that can transfer a PKE scheme with security against adaptively chosen ciphertext after-the-fact leakage attacks(CCLA2) to an AFLR AKE protocol with the BAFLR-eCK security. In 2018, Ruan et al. [32] first showed an ID-based BAFLR AKE protocol. Recently, Ruan et al. [33] first designed an AFLR eCK-security model for three-party password-based AKE (3PAKE) and presented an LR 3PAKE protocol; Chakraborty et al. [34] first proposed an LR non-interactive AKE protocol under the continuous-memory leakage model, which could be used to construct LR PKE schemes, interactive AKE and low-latency AKE protocols.

3   The λ-BAFLR Security Model for AGKE

By following the only computation leakage (OCL) model and the CK security model, we formally define an λ-BAFLR security model for AGKEs. The new model assumes that leakages only occur in the calculations associated with the secret key. In the λ-BAFLR security model, an adversary A could adaptively select any PPT leakage functions $f = (f_1, \cdots, f_n)$ to obtain the leakages of the secret key, and we require that the whole leakages are bounded by a leakage parameter λ, i.e., $\sum_1^n(f_i) \leq \lambda$.

3.1   System Framework

In the typical system model of AGKE protocols, each party $U_i(1 \leq i \leq n, n = poly(\kappa))$ has a public/private key pair (sk_i, pk_i) and seeks to establish a shared group key k_G.

Notations in the system framework are shown as follows:

- Principal: is a party involved into a protocol instance.
- Session: represents a protocol instance with principals.
- Oracle: $\Pi_{U_i}^t$ denotes the principal U_i interacting with the intended principals in the tth session.
- Session ID: Each session at a principal is identified by a unique ID. The session ID of $\Pi_{U_i}^t$ is denoted by $sid_{U_i}^t$.
- partner ID: The partner ID $pid_{U_i}^t$ of $\Pi_{U_i}^t$, is a set of identities of the principals with whom U_i wishes to generate a secure group key. Note that, the partner ID includes the identity of U_i itself, i.e., $pid_{U_i}^t = \{\Pi_{U_1}^t, \cdots, \Pi_{U_n}^t\}$.

The interactions between an adversary A and the protocol principals are modelled via the following queried oracles:

- Send($\Pi_{U_i}^t, m, f$): Upon receiving Send query with (m, f), $\Pi_{U_i}^t$ of the tth session will generate and send $(m', f(sk_i))$ to A, where m is a protocol message, m' is the normal response message to m, f is a leakage function, and sk_i is the private key. A new protocol instance can be activated by Send($\Pi_{U_i}^t, (start), ()$) to the initiator principal.
- RevealSessionKey($\Pi_{U_i}^t$): Upon receiving this query, $\Pi_{U_i}^t$ sends his t^{th} session key to A if he has generated the session key k_G^t; otherwise, he gives $\perp$ to A.
- RevealEphemeralKey($\Pi_{U_i}^t$): Upon receiving this query, $\Pi_{U_i}^t$ sends his t^{th} random ephemeral keys to A if he has; otherwise, he gives $\perp$ to A.
- Corrupt($\Pi_{U_i}^t$): After receiving this query, $\Pi_{U_i}^t$ gives his private key sk_i to A.
- Test(sid^t): After receiving this query, the challenger picks a bit b at random, gives the actual t^{th} session key to A if $b = 1$, otherwise sends a random key to A.

3.2   λ-BAFLR Security Model

In the λ-BAFLR security model, the whole leakage amount of the private key sk_i are bounded by the leakage parameter λ, i.e., $\sum_{j=1}^n f_j(sk_i) \leq \lambda$.

Definition 1. *Partners in the λ–BAFLR security model*
Two oracles $\Pi_{U_i}^t$ and $\Pi_{U_j}^{t'}$ are called partners if the followings satisfy:

(1) Two oracles $\Pi_{U_i}^t$ and $\Pi_{U_j}^{t'}$ have produced a common group session key;
(2) $sid_{U_i}^t = sid_{U_j}^{t'}$;
(3) $pid_{U_i}^t = pid_{U_j}^{t'}$.

Definition 2. *λ-BAFLR-freshness*
Suppose $f = (f_1, \cdots, f_n)$ be n arbitrary PPT leakage functions for a session picked by A. An oracle $\Pi_{U_i}^t$ is λ-BAFLR-fresh if the followings satisfy:

(1) The oracle $\Pi_{U_i}^t$ or any of its partners has not been queried a RevealSessionKey().

(2) If the partners exist, A could not query any of the following combinations:

    (a) Corrupt() and RevealEphemeralKey() to anyone of the principals.

    (b) RevealEphemeralKey() to all principals.

(3) If none of its partners exists, A could not query any of the following combinations:

    (a) Corrupt($\Pi_{U_i}^t$) and RevealEphemeralKey($\Pi_{U_i}^t$).

    (b) RevealEphemeralKey() to all principals.

    (c) Corrupt($\Pi_{U_j}^t$) where $j \neq i$.

(4) For all Send($\cdots, \Pi_{U_j}^t, \cdots, \cdots, f_k, \cdots$) queries to any principal $\Pi_{U_j}^t$, there has $\sum_{k=1}^{n} f_k(sk_j) \leq \lambda$.

Definition 3. λ-BAFLR security game

λ-BAFLR security game is defined by the following:

(1) A queries any of Send, RevealSessionKey, RevealEphemeralKey and Corrupt to any oracle;

(2) A picks an λ-BAFLR-fresh oracle as Test oracle and queries a Test. Then, A gets back the challenger's response;

(3) A repeats the queries as it does in Step (1). However, the λ-BAFLR-freshness of Test oracle should be obeyed;

(4) A wins the game if his output bit b' is equal to b.

Definition 4. λ-BAFLR security

λ-BAFLR security means that:

$$\mathrm{Adv}_{AGKE}^{\lambda-\mathrm{BAFLR}}(\mathcal{A}) = |\Pr[b = b'] - 1/2| = \epsilon(\cdot),$$

where $\mathrm{Adv}_{AGKE}^{\lambda-\mathrm{BAFLR}}(\mathcal{A})$ denotes the advantage A winning the λ-BAFLR security game in Definition 3 and $\epsilon(\cdot)$ is a negligible function.

4   A New λ-BAFLR AGKE Secure Protocol

In the section, we propose our λ-BAFLR AGKE protocol based on CPLA2-secure PKE scheme [35] and pseudo-random function (PRF) [36], then show its provably secure in the standard model, finally compare its security features and performance with other related schemes.

4.1   The Proposed Protocol

Suppose $U_1, \cdots, U_n(n = poly(\kappa))$, be a group of parties who seek to establish a session key. Each party U_i generates his public/private key pair (sk_i, pk_i), keeps the private key sk_i secretly and broadcasts the public key pk_i.

    Figure 1 shows the proposed protocol, in which G is a cyclic multiplicative group that has a large prime order p and a random generator g, and the used PKE is CPLA2-secure and PRF is secure. The new protocol includes the following steps:

1. Each party $U_i(1 \leq i \leq n)$ chooses a value $r_i \leftarrow Z_p^*$ at random, computes $z_i = g^{r_i}$ and $c_{i,j} = Enc(pk_j, z_i)$ for each $j(1 \leq j \leq n \wedge j \neq i)$, and broadcasts $(U_i, c_{i,j}(1 \leq j \leq n \wedge j \neq i))$;
2. Each party $U_i(1 \leq i \leq n)$ computes $z_{i+1} = Dec(sk_i, c_{i+1,i})$, $z_{i-1} = Dec(sk_i, c_{i-1,i})$ and $X_i = (z_{i+1}/z_{i-1})^{r_i}$, and broadcasts (U_i, X_i), where the indices are taken in a cycle;
3. Each party $U_i(1 \leq i \leq n)$ calculates $K_i = (z_{i-1})^{nr_i} \cdot (X_i)^{n-1} \cdot (X_{i+1})^{n-2} \cdots$ $(X_{i-3})^2 \cdot (X_{i-2})^1$ and $k_G = PRF_{K_i}(U_1\| \cdots \|U_n)$ is the session key.

User U_i

$$(sk_i, pk_i) = KG(1^k)$$

$r_i \xleftarrow{\$} Z_p^*, z_i = g^{r_i}$ $(U_i, c_{i,j}(1 \leq j \leq n \wedge j \neq i))$

For each $1 \leq j \leq n \wedge j \neq i$, $\xrightarrow{\hspace{2cm}}$

$c_{i,j} = Enc(pk_j, z_i)$

$z_{i+1} = Dec(sk_i, c_{i+1,i})$ (U_i, X_i)

$z_{i-1} = Dec(sk_i, c_{i-1,i})$ $\xrightarrow{\hspace{2cm}}$

$X_i = (z_{i+1} / z_{i-1})^{r_i}$

$K_i = (z_{i-1})^{nr_i} \cdot (X_i)^{n-1} \cdot (X_{i+1})^{n-2}$

$\quad \cdots \cdot (X_{i-3})^2 \cdot (X_{i-2})^1$

$k_G = KDF(U_1 \| \cdots \| U_n, K_i)$

Fig. 1. The LR AGKE protocol

4.2   Security Proof

Theorem 1. Suppose $\mathcal{P}$ be the new proposed AGKE protocol. If the used PKE scheme of $\mathcal{P}$ is λ-CPLA2-secure, the PDDH assumption holds, and PRF is secure, $\mathcal{P}$ is λ-BAFLR secure, i.e.,

$$\text{Adv}_{AGKE}^{\lambda-\text{BAFLR}}(\mathcal{A}) \leq 1/(c_{N_p}^n \cdot c_{N_s}^2)(\text{Adv}_{PDDH} + \text{Adv}_{KDF} + \text{Adv}_{PKE}^{\text{CPLA2}})$$

where $\text{Adv}_{AGKE}^{\lambda-\text{BAFLR}}$ is the advantage of an adversary $\mathcal{A}$ in winning the λ-BAFLR security game of the proposed protocol $\mathcal{P}$, Adv_{PDDH}, Adv_{PRF}, $\text{Adv}_{PKE}^{\text{CPLA2}}$ represent advantages of $\mathcal{A}$ in winning the security game of PDDH, PRF and λ-CPLA2-secure PKE, respectively, and N_p denotes the number of protocol principals, N_s is the number of sessions on a principal, $c_{N_p}^n$ is the number of choosing n elements from a set of N_p elements.

The proof is based on the game hopping technique, which has a series of hybrid games, starting with the original λ-BAFLR security game and ending in a game where $\mathcal{A}$'s advantage is 0, and any two consecutive games are computationally indistinguishable for $\mathcal{A}$. The details could be found in the full paper.

4.3 Security and Performance Analysis

The security and performance are analyzed and compared with other representative AGKE protocols. The results are shown in Table 1, in which we could get that our proposed protocol enjoys three advantages: (1) our protocol is the first LR AGKE protocol; (2) the proposed protocol attains the property of LR without incurring additional communication and computation cost by comparing with the related non-LR schemes; (3) its security is formally proven in the standard model.

Table 1. Security and performance comparison among relevant AGKE schemes

	Rounds	P2P	Bc	Computation overload	Security model	Provable security	Leakage resilience
[2]	2	0	n	$(n+2) \cdot Ex$		×	×
[8]	2	0	n	$1 \cdot S + (n-1) \cdot V + 3 \cdot Ex$	RO	✓	×
[9]	1	0	n	$2 \cdot Ex + (2n-1) \cdot Pa$	$Standard$	✓	×
[37]	1	0	n	$1 \cdot S + (n-1) \cdot V + 2 \cdot Ex + (2n-1) \cdot Ml$	$Standard$	✓	×
[4]	$n/2$	$n-2$	$n/2+1$	$n/2 \cdot S + n^2/2 \cdot V + 3n/2 \cdot Ex + 5n/2 \cdot Pa$	$Standard$	✓	×
Ours	2	0	n	$(n+2) \cdot Ex + (n+1) \cdot Enc$	$Standard$	✓	✓

* Let n denote the maximum group members; Suppose $P2P$ represent point-to-point communication and Bc represent multi-cast broadcast; Assume Ex be exponentiation, Enc be encryptions, Pa be pairing operation, ML be multilinear operation, S be signature signing operation, V be the signature verifying operation

5 Conclusion

In this paper, we first introduced an λ-BAFLR CK security model to assess the security of AGKE protocols in the leakage environments. Then, we proposed the first LR AGKE protocol by combining DH GKE protocol and the CPLA2-secure PKE scheme appropriately. The comparison results showed that the proposed protocol attains the property of LR without incurring additional communication and computation cost by comparing with the related non-LR schemes.

Acknowledgment. This work is supported by the National Natural Science Foundation of China under grants 61672010, 61702168 and 61701173, the Hubei Natural Science Foundation (2017CFB596), the HBUT Green Industry Technology Leading Project (ZZTS2017006), and the fund of Hubei Key Laboratory of Transportation Internet of Things (WHUTIOT-2017B001).

References

1. Ingemarsson, I., Tang, D., Wong, C.K.: A conference key distribution system. IEEE Trans. Inf. Theory **28**(5), 714–719 (1982)
2. Burmester, M., Desmedt, Y.: A secure and efficient conference key distribution system. In: De Santis, A. (ed.) EUROCRYPT 1994. LNCS, vol. 950, pp. 275–286. Springer, Heidelberg (1995). https://doi.org/10.1007/BFb0053443
3. Steiner, M., Tsudik, G., Waidner, M.: Diffie-hellman key distribution extended to group communication. In: Proceedings ACM CCS 1996, pp. 31–37. ACM (1996)
4. Yang, Z., Liu, C., Liu, W., Zhang, D., Luo, S.: A new strong security model for stateful authenticated group key exchange. Int. J. Inf. Secur. **2017**(2), 1–18 (2017)
5. Boyd, C., Nieto, J.M.G.: Round-optimal contributory conference key agreement. In: Desmedt, Y.G. (ed.) PKC 2003. LNCS, vol. 2567, pp. 161–174. Springer, Heidelberg (2003). https://doi.org/10.1007/3-540-36288-6_12
6. Bresson, E., Chevassut, O., Pointcheval, D.: Provably authenticated group Diffie-Hellman key exchange—the dynamic case. In: Boyd, C. (ed.) ASIACRYPT 2001. LNCS, vol. 2248, pp. 290–309. Springer, Heidelberg (2001). https://doi.org/10.1007/3-540-45682-1_18
7. Zhu, L., Guo, C., Zhang, Z., Fu, W., Xu, R.: A novel contributory cross-domain group password-based authenticated key exchange protocol with adaptive security. In: Proceedings of Second International Conference on Data Science in Cyberspace, pp. 213–222. IEEE (2017)
8. Kim, H.J., Lee, S.M., Lee, D.H.: Constant-round authenticated group key exchange for dynamic groups. In: Lee, P.J. (ed.) ASIACRYPT 2004. LNCS, vol. 3329, pp. 245–259. Springer, Heidelberg (2004). https://doi.org/10.1007/978-3-540-30539-2_18
9. Gorantla, M.C., Boyd, C., González Nieto, J.M.: Modeling key compromise impersonation attacks on group key exchange protocols. In: Jarecki, S., Tsudik, G. (eds.) PKC 2009. LNCS, vol. 5443, pp. 105–123. Springer, Heidelberg (2009). https://doi.org/10.1007/978-3-642-00468-1_7
10. Halford, T.R., Courtade, T.A., Chugg, K.M., Li, X., Thatte, G.: Energy efficient group key agreement for wireless networks. IEEE Trans. Wireless Commun. **14**(10), 5552–5564 (2015)
11. Katz, J., Yung, M.: Scalable protocols for authenticated group key exchange. In: Boneh, D. (ed.) CRYPTO 2003. LNCS, vol. 2729, pp. 110–125. Springer, Heidelberg (2003). https://doi.org/10.1007/978-3-540-45146-4_7
12. Wu, S., Zhu, Y.: Efficient hybrid password-based authenticated group key exchange. In: Li, Q., Feng, L., Pei, J., Wang, S.X., Zhou, X., Zhu, Q.M. (eds.) APWeb/WAIM 2009. LNCS, vol. 5446, pp. 562–567. Springer, Heidelberg (2009). https://doi.org/10.1007/978-3-642-00672-2_52
13. Teng, J., Wu, C.: Efficient group key agreement for wireless mobile networks. In: Proceedings IET-WSN2010, pp. 323–330. IET (2010)
14. Yu, Q., Li, J., Zhang, Y.: Leakage resilient certificate based encryption. Secur. Commun. Netw. **8**(18), 3346–3355 (2016)
15. Zhou, Y., Yang, B.: Leakage-resilient CCA2-secure certificateless public-key encryption scheme without bilinear pairing. Inf. Process. Lett. **130**(2), 16–24 (2018)
16. Aggarwal, D., et al.: Stronger leakage-resilient and non-malleable secret sharing schemes for general access structures. In: Boldyreva, A., Micciancio, D. (eds.) CRYPTO 2019. LNCS, vol. 11693, pp. 510–539. Springer, Cham (2019). https://doi.org/10.1007/978-3-030-26951-7_18

17. Boyle, E., Segev, G., Wichs, D.: Fully leakage-resilient signatures revisited. J. Theor. Comput. Sci. **660**(C), 23–56 (2017)
18. Bogdanov, A., Ishai, Y., Srinivasan, A.: Unconditionally secure computation against low-complexity leakage. In: Boldyreva, A., Micciancio, D. (eds.) CRYPTO 2019. LNCS, vol. 11693, pp. 387–416. Springer, Cham (2019). https://doi.org/10.1007/978-3-030-26951-7_14
19. Srinivasan, A., Vasudevan, P.N.: Leakage resilient secret sharing and applications. In: Boldyreva, A., Micciancio, D. (eds.) CRYPTO 2019. LNCS, vol. 11693, pp. 480–509. Springer, Cham (2019). https://doi.org/10.1007/978-3-030-26951-7_17
20. Wei, C., Zheng, C., Wen, C.C., Alawatugoda, J.: Review on leakage resilient key exchange security models. Int. J. Commun. Netw. Inf. Secur. **11**(1), 119–127 (2019)
21. Moriyama, D., Okamoto, T.: Leakage resilient eCK-secure key exchange protocol without random oracles. In: Proceedings ACM CCS 2011, pp. 441–447. ACM (2011)
22. Alawatugoda, J., Boyd, C., Stebila, D.: Continuous after-the-fact leakage-resilient key exchange. In: Susilo, W., Mu, Y. (eds.) ACISP 2014. LNCS, vol. 8544, pp. 258–273. Springer, Cham (2014). https://doi.org/10.1007/978-3-319-08344-5_17
23. Canetti, R., Krawczyk, H.: Analysis of key-exchange protocols and their use for building secure channels. In: Pfitzmann, B. (ed.) EUROCRYPT 2001. LNCS, vol. 2045, pp. 453–474. Springer, Heidelberg (2001). https://doi.org/10.1007/3-540-44987-6_28
24. Alawatugoda, J., Stebila, D., Boyd, C.: Modelling after-the-fact leakage for key exchange. In: Proceedings ASIACCS 2014, pp. 207–216. ACM (2014)
25. LaMacchia, B., Lauter, K., Mityagin, A.: Stronger security of authenticated key exchange. In: Susilo, W., Liu, J.K., Mu, Y. (eds.) ProvSec 2007. LNCS, vol. 4784, pp. 1–16. Springer, Heidelberg (2007). https://doi.org/10.1007/978-3-540-75670-5_1
26. Alawatugoda, J., Stebila, D., Boyd, C.: Continuous after-the-fact leakage-resilient eCK-secure key exchange. In: Groth, J. (ed.) IMACC 2015. LNCS, vol. 9496, pp. 277–294. Springer, Cham (2015). https://doi.org/10.1007/978-3-319-27239-9_17
27. Chen, R., Mu, Y., Yang, G., Susilo, W., Guo, F.: Strong authenticated key exchange with auxiliary inputs. Des. Codes Crypt. **85**(1), 145–173 (2017)
28. Chen, R., Mu, Y., Yang, G., Susilo, W., Guo, F., Zheng, Y.: A note on the strong authenticated key exchange with auxiliary inputs. Des. Codes Crypt. **85**(1), 175–178 (2017)
29. Wu, J.D., Tseng, Y.M., Huang, S.S.: Efficient leakage-resilient authenticated key agreement protocol in the continual leakage eCK model. IEEE Access **6**(1), 17130–17142 (2018)
30. Ruan, O., Chen, J., Zhang, M.W.: Provably leakage-resilient password-based authenticated key exchange in the standard model. IEEE Access **5**(99), 26832–26841 (2017)
31. Chakraborty, S., Paul, G., Rangan, C.P.: Efficient compilers for after-the-fact leakage: from CPA to CCA-2 secure PKE to AKE. In: Pieprzyk, J., Suriadi, S. (eds.) ACISP 2017. LNCS, vol. 10342, pp. 343–362. Springer, Cham (2017). https://doi.org/10.1007/978-3-319-60055-0_18
32. Ruan, O., Zhang, Y., Zhang, M., Zhou, J., Harn, L.: After-the-fact leak-age-resilient identity-based authenticated key exchange. IEEE Syst. J. **12**(2), 2017–2026 (2018)
33. Ruan, O., Wang, Q., Wang, Z.: Provably leakage-resilient three-party password-based authenticated key exchange. J. Ambient Intell. Humaniz. Comput. **10**(1), 163–173 (2019)

34. Chakraborty, S., Alawatugoda, J., Pandu Rangan, C.: Leakage-resilient non-interactive key exchange in the continuous-memory leakage setting. In: Okamoto, T., Yu, Y., Au, M.H., Li, Y. (eds.) ProvSec 2017. LNCS, vol. 10592, pp. 167–187. Springer, Cham (2017). https://doi.org/10.1007/978-3-319-68637-0_10
35. Halevi, S., Lin, H.: After-the-fact leakage in public-key encryption. In: Ishai, Y. (ed.) TCC 2011. LNCS, vol. 6597, pp. 107–124. Springer, Heidelberg (2011). https://doi.org/10.1007/978-3-642-19571-6_8
36. Bellare, M., Kilian, J., Rogaway, P.: The security of the cipher block chaining message authentication code. J. Comput. Syst. Sci. **61**(3), 362–399 (2000)
37. Yang, Z., Zhang, D.: Towards modelling perfect forward secrecy for one-round group key exchange. Int. J. Netw. Secur. **18**(2), 304–315 (2016)

Traceable and Fully Anonymous Attribute Based Group Signature Scheme with Verifier Local Revocation from Lattices

Maharage Nisansala Sevwandi Perera[✉], Toru Nakamura, Masayuki Hashimoto, and Hiroyuki Yokoyama

Adaptive Communications Research Laboratories, Advanced Telecommunications Research Institute International (ATR), Kyoto, Japan
{perera.nisansala,tr-nakamura,masayuki.hashimoto,hr-yokoyama}@atr.jp

Abstract. Efficient user and attribute tracing is desirable in Attribute-Based Group Signatures (ABGS). Tracing cost is high in ABGS schemes with verifier-local revocation (VLR) as it requires to scan almost all the users and all the attributes of the identified user. Thus we propose a new lattice-based VLR-ABGS scheme that supports efficient user and attribute tracing.

Keywords: Attribute-Based Group Signatures · Verifier-local revocation · Traceability · Full anonymity · Lattice-based cryptography

1 Introduction

Attribute-Based Group Signature (ABGS) schemes allow any member of the group who possesses the attributes required by the policy to sign on behalf of the group without revealing his identity or attributes. On the other hand, the group manager can cancel the anonymity of the signature, especially in case of a dispute. ABGS schemes are a subgroup of Group Signature schemes.

Group Signature (GS) schemes, first introduced by Chaum and van Heyst [5] in 1991, permit any group member to produce signatures representing the group. Group signature schemes have two features called *Anonymity* and *Traceability*. *Anonymity* hides the identity of the signer, while *Traceability* guarantees that the third party authority can recognize the signer.

Bellare et al. [1] (BMW03 model) presented two strong security notions *full-anonymity* and *full-traceability*. The full-anonymity allows an outsider to see all the secret keys of the members, and still, he cannot identify the signer of a given signature. The full-traceability guarantees that the colluded members or an outsider cannot produce a signature that the group manager cannot identify or direct to an innocent member who did not sign. The BMW03 model was presented for static groups, where the group members and their properties are fixed at the setup. Thus applying the BMW03 model for dynamic groups showed

J. K. Liu and X. Huang (Eds.): NSS 2019, LNCS 11928, pp. 675–684, 2019.
https://doi.org/10.1007/978-3-030-36938-5_42

some technical difficulties. For instance, traditional GS schemes with Verifier-local revocation (VLR) could not achieve full-anonymity; they satisfy a weaker security notion called *selfless-anonymity*. The selfless-anonymity assumes that any group member's secret key is not being corrupted.

Verifier-local revocation (VLR) was first suggested by Brickell [4]. Later, Boneh et al. [2] formalized VLR in their GS scheme. VLR-GS schemes employ a token system. VLR requires only the verifiers to have up-to-date revocation list with revoked users' tokens. Thus he accepts signatures generated by an unrevoked member.

1.1 Related Work

In 2007, Dalia Khader introduced the first Attribute-Based Group Signature (ABGS) scheme [9] and subsequently presented a VLR-ABGS scheme [8]. However, since both of the schemes are constructed using bilinear mappings, those schemes are not quantum resist. Kuchta et al. [10] proposed the first quantum resist ABGS scheme from lattices with member and attribute registration. Later, in 2018, Zhang et al. [14] presented a VLR-ABGS scheme. Thus as general VLR-GS schemes, the security of their scheme [14] achieves the selfless-anonymity. The selfless-anonymity is much weaker than the full-anonymity [1]. The full-anonymity ensures the privacy of the signer, even if the attacker knows all the users' secret signing keys. The selfless-anonymity applies when the secret signing keys cannot be revealed to the outsiders. In VLR schemes, tokens are part of the secret signing keys. Thus, an outsider can retrieve the tokens from the possessing secret signing keys and identify whether the token owner is the signer of the given signature. In the case of ABGS schemes, he can identify whether the attributes related to the tokens are used to generate the given signature. In other words, revealing tokens results in the corruption of the anonymity of the scheme. Recently, a new VLR-ABGS scheme [12] was proposed to achieve the full-anonymity. They separated the tokens from the secret signing keys. To prevent forging tokens, they proposed a new underlying argument system.

The existing VLR-ABGS schemes [12,14] employ the implicit tracing algorithm to trace the signer and his attributes. The implicit tracing algorithm executes the verification algorithm for each user until the signer is traced and then executes the verification algorithm for all the signer's attributes to track the attributes that he used to sign. Without any doubt, we can see that using the implicit tracing algorithm in ABGS schemes is very inefficient.

1.2 Contribution

This paper proposes a new VLR-ABGS scheme with an efficient tracing mechanism. We use the explicit-tracing algorithm used in the static group signature scheme [11] to trace the signer and his attributes used for signing in our scheme. The explicit-tracing algorithm uses the group manager's public key to encrypt the identity of the signer and his attributes. Thus only the group manager can identify the signer and attributes of the signer. We employ the VLR-ABGS scheme given in [12], which achieved full-anonymity, as the base scheme, and extend that scheme to serve the explicit tracing algorithm.

2 Preliminary

2.1 Notation

We denote matrices by upper-case bold letters and vectors by lower-case bold letters. For any integer $k \geq 1$, a set of integers $\{1, 2, \ldots, k\}$ is denoted by $[k]$. If S is a finite set, $|S|$ is its size. $S(k)$ indicates its permutations of k elements and $b \hookleftarrow D$ denotes that b is sampled from a uniformly random distribution D.

2.2 Average Case Lattice Problems and Lattice Related Algorithms

Definition 1 (Learning With Errors (LWE)). *For integers $n, m \geq 1$, and $q \geq 2$, a vector $s \in \mathbb{Z}_q^n$, and the Gaussian error distribution χ, the distribution $A_{s,\chi}$ is obtained by sampling $a \in \mathbb{Z}_q^n$ and $e \leftarrow \chi$, and outputting the pair $(a, a^T \cdot s + e)$. LWE problem (decision-LWE problem) requires to distinguish LWE samples from truly random samples $\leftarrow \mathbb{Z}_q^n \times \mathbb{Z}_q$.*

For a prime power q, $b \geq \sqrt{n}\omega(\log n)$, and distribution χ, solving $LWE_{n,q,\chi}$ problem is at least as hard as solving $SIVP_\gamma$ (*Shortest Independent Vector Problem*), where $\gamma = \tilde{\mathcal{O}}(nq/b)$ [6,13].

Definition 2 (Small Integer Solution (SIS)). *Given uniformly random matrix $A \in \mathbb{Z}_q^{n \times m}$, find non-zero vector $x \in \mathbb{Z}^m$, such that $A \cdot x = 0 \mod q$ and $\|x\|_\infty \leq \beta$.*

For any m, $\beta = \mathsf{poly}(n)$, and $q > \sqrt{n}\beta$, solving $SIS_{n,m,q,\beta}$ problem with non-negligible probability is at least as hard as solving $SIVP_\gamma$ problem, for some $\gamma = \beta \cdot \tilde{\mathcal{O}}(\sqrt{nm})$ [6,11].

We now recall two lattice related algorithms.

– GenTrap(n, m, q) takes integers $n \geq 1, q \geq 2$, and sufficiently large $m = O(n \log q)$, and outputs a matrix $A \in \mathbb{Z}_q^{n \times m}$ and a trapdoor matrix $\mathbf{R}$. The distribution of the output A is $\mathsf{negl}(n)$-far from the uniform distribution.
– SampleD$(\mathbf{R}, A, u, \sigma)$ takes as inputs a vector u in the image of A, a trapdoor $\mathbf{R}$, and $\sigma = \omega(\sqrt{n \log q \log n})$, and outputs $x \in \mathbb{Z}^m$ sampled from the distribution $D_{\mathbb{Z}^m, \sigma}$, such that $A \cdot x = u \mod q$.

3 The Proposed Scheme

Our new scheme provides an explicit tracing mechanism that supports the group manager to identify the signer and the attributes that the signer used to generate the given signature. We require the signer to encrypt his id and his attributes' ids with the group manager's public key at the time of signing. Accordingly, only the group manager can decrypt and identify the signer and the signer's attributes. To achieve CCA-anonymity, we rely on the combination of the one-time signature (OTS) scheme and the identity-based encryption (IBE) scheme. We construct our scheme based on the modified Boyen's Signature scheme [3] given in [11].

3.1   Construction of the New Scheme

Let λ be the security parameter and $N = 2^\ell = poly(\lambda)$ be the maximum number of members in a group. OGen, OSig, and OVer are algorithms of OTS for key-generation, signing and verification.

- Setup(1^λ): On input λ, set the public parameters $param$ as below.
  Let integer $n = poly(\lambda)$, the modulus $q = \mathcal{O}(\ell n^2)$, and the dimension $m = \lceil 2n \log q \rceil$. Gaussian parameter $\sigma = \omega(\log m)$. The infinity norm bound for signature is $\beta = \tilde{\mathcal{O}}(\sqrt{\ell n})$. Let $k = \lfloor \log \beta \rfloor$ and the sequence of integers $\beta_1, \ldots, \beta_k$ be as $\beta_1 = \lceil \beta/2 \rceil; \beta_2 = \lceil (\beta - \beta_1)/2 \rceil; \beta_3 = \lceil (\beta - \beta_1 - \beta_2)/2 \rceil; \ldots; \beta_k = 1$. The norm bound for LWE noises is integer b such that $q/b = \ell\tilde{\mathcal{O}}(n)$. Let $\bar{k} = \lfloor \log b \rfloor + 1$, $k_1 = m + \ell$ and $k_2 = n + m + \ell$.
  Then the attribute authority proceeds as below.
  1. Define the universal set of attributes $Att = \{\mathbf{u}_1, \mathbf{u}_2, \ldots, \mathbf{u}_u\}$, where vectors $\{\mathbf{u}_i\}_{i \in \{1,2,\ldots,u\}} \in \mathbb{Z}_q^n$ is uniform random and $|Att| = u$.
  2. Let ℓ_u be the bit length of the index of an attribute such as $u = 2^{\ell_u}$.
  3. Then assign an index a, where the bit length is ℓ_u, for each attribute. Thus, each attribute att_i is associated to a uniform random vector $\mathbf{u}_i$ and an index a_i via a list $attList = \{(att_i, \mathbf{u}_i, a_i)\}_{i \in \{1,2,\ldots,u\}}$.
  4. Let the hash function $\mathcal{H}_1 : \{0,1\}^* \to \mathbb{Z}^{n \times \ell}$, $\mathcal{H}_2 : \{0,1\}^* \to \{1,2,3\}^t$ and $\mathcal{G} : \{0,1\}^* \to \mathbb{Z}_q^{n \times m}$ to be random oracles, where $t = \omega(\log n)$.
  5. Output the public parameters $PP = (param, Att, attList, \mathcal{H}_1, \mathcal{H}_2, \mathcal{G})$.
- KeyGen(PP, N): On inputs the public parameters PP and $N = 2^\ell$, this randomized algorithm KeyGen proceeds as bellow.
  1. Run GenTrap(n, m, q) to obtain $\mathbf{A} \in \mathbb{Z}^{n \times m}$ and trapdoor $\mathbf{T_A} \in \mathbb{Z}^{m \times m}$.
  2. Sample $\mathbf{A}_0, \ldots, \mathbf{A}_\ell \xleftarrow{\$} \mathbb{Z}_q^{n \times m}$.
  3. Generate encryption and decryption key pair ($\mathbf{F} \in \mathbb{Z}_q^{n \times m}, \mathbf{T_F} \in \mathbb{Z}^{m \times m}$) for GPV-IBE scheme [6] using GenTrap algorithm.
  4. For a group user with an index $d \in \{0, 1, \ldots, N-1\}$ and a set of attributes $S_d = \{\mathbf{u}_{d_1}, \mathbf{u}_{d_2}, \ldots, \mathbf{u}_{d_s}\} \subseteq Att$ ($|S_d| = s$), let $d[i] \ldots d[\ell] \in \{0,1\}^\ell$ be the binary representation of d and execute the following steps.
     (a) Compute $\mathbf{A}_d = [\mathbf{A} \mid \mathbf{A}_0 + \sum_{i=1}^\ell d[i] \cdot \mathbf{A}_i] \in \mathbb{Z}^{n \times 2m}$.
     (b) For all the possessing attributes $j \in \{1, 2, \ldots, s\}$ sample $\mathbf{z}_{d,j} \in \mathbb{Z}^{2m}$ as the secret key for an attribute $\mathbf{u}_{d_j}$, such that $\mathbf{A}_d \cdot \mathbf{z}_{d,j} = \mathbf{u}_{d_j}$ and $\|\mathbf{z}_{d,j}\| \leq \beta$.
     (c) For the universal attributes $u - s$, that the user does not possess, sample fake credentials $\mathbf{z}_{d,j} \hookleftarrow D_{\mathbb{Z}^{2m}, \sigma}$, such that $\mathbf{A}_d \cdot \mathbf{z}_{d,j} = \mathbf{u}_j$ and $\|\mathbf{z}_{d,j}\| \nleq \beta$.

(d) Get $\mathbf{A}'_d = [0 \in \mathbb{Z}_q^{n \times m} \mid 0 \in \mathbb{Z}_q^{n \times m} + \sum_{i=1}^{\ell} d[i] \cdot \mathbf{A}_i]$ by replacing $\mathbf{A}$ and $\mathbf{A}_0$ with zero matrices in the step (a).

(e) For all the universal attributes, compute $\mathbf{v}_{d_j} = \mathbf{A}'_d \cdot \mathbf{z}_{d_j} \in \mathbb{Z}^n$ and run $\mathsf{SampleD}(\mathbf{T_A}, \mathbf{A}, \mathbf{u}_j - \mathbf{v}_{d_j}, \sigma)$ to obtain $\mathbf{t}_{d_j} \in \mathbb{Z}^m$.

(f) Let the secret signing key of d be $\mathbf{gsk}[d] = \{\mathbf{z}_{d_j}, \mathbf{u}_j\}_{j \in [u]}$ and the revocation token be $\mathbf{grt}[d] = \{\mathbf{r}_{d_j} = \mathbf{A} \cdot \mathbf{t}_{d_j}\}_{j \in [u]}$.

5. Output the group public key $\mathbf{gpk} = (\mathbf{A}, \mathbf{A}_0, \mathbf{A}_1, \ldots, \mathbf{A}_\ell, \mathbf{u}_1, \mathbf{u}_2, \ldots, \mathbf{u}_u, \mathbf{F})$, the group manager's secret key $\mathbf{gmsk} = \mathbf{T_F}$, the vector of group users' private keys $\mathbf{gsk} = (\mathbf{gsk}[0], \mathbf{gsk}[1], \ldots, \mathbf{gsk}[N-1])$, and the vector of group users' revocation tokens $\mathbf{grt} = (\mathbf{grt}[0], \mathbf{grt}[1], \ldots, \mathbf{grt}[N-1])$.

- $\mathsf{Sign}(PP, \Gamma, \mathbf{gpk}, \mathbf{gsk}[d], \mathbf{grt}[d], S_d, M)$: On input $\mathbf{gpk}$, a message M, user secret signing key $\mathbf{gsk}[d]$, and revocation token $\mathbf{grt}[d]$, and a set of user possessing attributes $S_d \subseteq \mathsf{Att}$, generates a signature as below for the threshold predicate $\Gamma = (t, S = \{\mathbf{u}_1, \mathbf{u}_2, \ldots, \mathbf{u}_p\} \subseteq \mathsf{Att})$, where $1 \le t \le |S| = p$.

1. Generate a key pair $(\mathbf{ovk}, \mathbf{osk}) \leftarrow \mathsf{OGen}(1^n)$.

2. Let $S_m \subseteq (S \cap S_d) \subseteq \mathsf{Att}$ be the matching attributes that the user d possesses, where $|S_m| = t$.

3. For the attributes $S \setminus S_m$ the user d has the fake credentials.

4. Let $\mathbf{G} = \mathcal{H}_1(\mathbf{ovk}) \in \mathbb{Z}_q^{n \times \ell}$.

5. Encrypt signer id $= d$;
   (a) Sample $\mathbf{s} \hookleftarrow \chi^n$, $\mathbf{e}_1 \hookleftarrow \chi^m$, $\mathbf{e}_2 \hookleftarrow \chi^\ell$.
   (b) Compute ciphertext $\mathbf{c} = (\mathbf{c}_1, \mathbf{c}_2) \in \mathbb{Z}_q^m \times \mathbb{Z}_q^\ell$ as below.

$$\mathbf{c}_1 = \mathbf{F}^\mathbf{T}\mathbf{s} + \mathbf{e}_1, \quad \mathbf{c}_2 = \mathbf{G}^\mathbf{T}\mathbf{s} + \mathbf{e}_2 + \lfloor q/2 \rfloor d.$$

6. Encrypt attribute ids $= \{a_i\}$; For all the attributes $i \in [p]$,
   (a) Sample $\mathbf{s}_i \hookleftarrow \chi^n$, $\mathbf{e}_{i_1} \hookleftarrow \chi^m$, $\mathbf{e}_{i_2} \hookleftarrow \chi^\ell$.
   (b) Compute ciphertext $\mathbf{c}_i = (\mathbf{c}_{i_1}, \mathbf{c}_{i_2}) \in \mathbb{Z}_q^m \times \mathbb{Z}_q^\ell$ as below.

$$\mathbf{c}_{i_1} = \mathbf{F}^\mathbf{T}\mathbf{s}_i + \mathbf{e}_{i_1}, \quad \mathbf{c}_{i_2} = \mathbf{G}^\mathbf{T}\mathbf{s}_i + \mathbf{e}_{i_2} + \lfloor q/2 \rfloor a_i.$$

7. Encrypt attributes' tokens. For all the attributes $i \in [p]$,
   (a) Sample $\rho_i \xleftarrow{\$} \{0, 1\}^n$, let $\mathbf{B}_i = \mathcal{G}(\bar{\mathbf{A}}, \mathbf{u}_i, \mathbf{F}, M, \rho_i) \in \mathbb{Z}_q^{n \times m}$, where $\bar{\mathbf{A}} = [\mathbf{A} | \mathbf{A}_0 | \mathbf{A}_1 | \ldots | \mathbf{A}_\ell] \in \mathbb{Z}^{n \times (\ell+2)m}$.
   (b) Sample $\bar{\mathbf{e}} \hookleftarrow \chi^m$ ($\|\bar{\mathbf{e}}_i\|_\infty \le \beta$ with overwhelming probability).
   (c) Compute $\mathbf{b}_i = \mathbf{B}_i \cdot (\mathbf{A} \cdot \mathbf{t}_{d_i}) + \bar{\mathbf{e}}_i \mod q$.

8. Generate a non-interactive zero-knowledge argument of knowledge Π as below to prove that the prover d is indeed a valid group member possessing at least non-revoked t attributes among $S \subseteq \mathsf{Att}$, the attributes he used for signature generations are true, and ids (his id and attribute ids) are correctly encrypted.
   (a) Form,

$$\mathbf{P} = \left(\frac{\mathbf{F}^T}{\mathbf{G}^T} \middle| \mathbf{I}_{m+\ell} \right) \in \mathbb{Z}_q^{k_1 \times k_2}; \tag{1}$$

$$c = \begin{pmatrix} \mathbf{c}_1 \\ \mathbf{c}_2 \end{pmatrix} \in \mathbb{Z}^{k_1}; \mathbf{e} = \begin{pmatrix} \mathbf{s} \\ \mathbf{e}_1 \\ \mathbf{e}_2 \end{pmatrix} \in \mathbb{Z}^{k_2} \tag{2}$$

$$\text{For } i \in [p]\, \mathbf{c}_i = \begin{pmatrix} \mathbf{c}_{i_1} \\ \mathbf{c}_{i_2} \end{pmatrix} \in \mathbb{Z}^{k_1}; \mathbf{e}_i = \begin{pmatrix} \mathbf{s}_i \\ \mathbf{e}_{i_1} \\ \mathbf{e}_{i_2} \end{pmatrix} \in \mathbb{Z}^{k_2} \tag{3}$$

(b) Using LWE we can define a relationship of $\mathbf{P} \in \mathbb{Z}_q^{k_1 \times k_2}$, $\mathbf{c} \in \mathbb{Z}_q^{k_1}$ and $\mathbf{e} \in \mathbb{Z}^{k_2}$ satisfying $\|\mathbf{e}\|_\infty \leq b$ as below [11].

$$\mathbf{Pe} + (0^{k_1-\ell} \| \lfloor q/2 \rfloor d) = \mathbf{c} \mod q.$$

Applying LWE to the related set of attributes we get,

$$\{\mathbf{Pe}_i + (0^{k_1-\ell} \| \lfloor q/2 \rfloor a_i) = \mathbf{c}_i \mod q\}_{i \in [p]}.$$

(c) Then repeat the underlying interactive protocol given in Sect. 3.2, $t = \omega(\log n)$ times with public inputs $pin = (\mathbf{A}, \{\mathbf{A}_i\}_{i=0}^\ell, \{\mathbf{u}_i\}_{i \in [p]}, \{\mathbf{B}_i\}_{i \in [p]}, \{\mathbf{b}_i\}_{i \in [p]}, \mathbf{P}, \mathbf{c}, \{\mathbf{c}_i\}_{i \in [p]})$ and witness parameters $(d, \{a_i\}_{i=1}^p, \{\mathbf{z}_i\}_{i \in [p]}, \{\bar{\mathbf{e}}_i\}_{i \in [p]}, \mathbf{e}, \{\mathbf{e}_i\}_{i \in [p]})$, then making it non-interactive via the Fiat-Shamir heuristic as a triple $\Pi = (\{\text{CMT}^{(k)}\}_{k=1}^t, \text{CH}, \{\text{RSP}^{(k)}\}_{k=1}^t)$, where $\text{CH} = (\{Ch^{(k)}\}_{k=1}^t) = \mathcal{H}_2(M, pin, \{\text{CMT}^{(k)}\}_{k=1}^t)$.

9. Compute $\mathcal{OTS}$; $sig = \text{OSig}(osk, (\mathbf{c}, \{\mathbf{c}_i\}_{i \in [p]}, \Pi))$.
10. Output a signature $\Sigma = (\mathbf{ovk}, \mathbf{c}, \{\mathbf{c}_i\}_{i=1}^p, \Pi, sig, M, \{\rho_i\}_{i=1}^p, \{\mathbf{b}_i\}_{i=1}^p)$.

– Verify($PP, \Gamma, \mathbf{gpk}, RL, M, \Sigma$): This deterministic algorithm takes as inputs $\mathbf{gpk}$, a threshold predicate $\Gamma = (t, S = \{\mathbf{u}_1, \mathbf{u}_2, \ldots, \mathbf{u}_p\} \subseteq \text{Att})$, a signature Σ on a message M, and a list of revocation tokens $RL = \{\mathbf{r}_i = (\mathbf{r}_{i_1}, \mathbf{r}_{i_2}, \ldots, \mathbf{r}_{i_a})\}_{i \leq N} \subseteq \mathbf{grt}$, where $a \leq u$, and verifies as below.

1. Pares the signature Σ as $(\mathbf{ovk}, \mathbf{c}, \{\mathbf{c}_i\}_{i=1}^p, \Pi, sig, M, \{\rho_i\}_{i=1}^p, \{\mathbf{b}_i\}_{i=1}^p)$.
2. If $\text{OVer}(\mathbf{ovk}, sig, (\mathbf{c}, \{\mathbf{c}_i\}_{i \in [p]}, \Pi)) = 0$ then return 0.
3. Get $\{\mathbf{B}_i = \mathcal{G}(\bar{\mathbf{A}}, \mathbf{u}_i, \mathbf{F}, M, \rho_i) \in \mathbb{Z}_q^{n \times m}\}_{i \in [p]}$.
4. Pares Π as $(\{\text{CMT}^{(k)}\}_{k=1}^t, \{Ch^{(k)}\}_{k=1}^t, \{\text{RSP}^{(k)}\}_{k=1}^t)$.
5. Form $\mathbf{P}, \mathbf{c}$, and $\{\mathbf{c}_i\}_{i=1}^p$ (as in functions 1, 2, and 3 respectively).
6. Return 0, if $(Ch_1, \ldots Ch_t) \neq \mathcal{H}_2(M, \mathbf{A}, \{\mathbf{A}_i\}_{i=0}^\ell, \{\mathbf{u}_i\}_{i=1}^p, \{\mathbf{B}_i\}_{i=1}^p, \{\mathbf{b}_i\}_{i=1}^p, \mathbf{P}, \mathbf{c}, \{\mathbf{c}_i\}_{i=1}^p, \{\text{CMT}^{(k)}\}_{k=1}^t)$.
7. For $i = 0$ to t, run the verification steps of the protocol given in Sect. 3.2 with the public inputs to validate $\text{RSP}^{(k)}$ with respect to $\text{CMT}^{(k)}$ and $Ch^{(k)}$. If any of the conditions fails then return 0.
8. For each $\mathbf{r}_{i_x}$ in the given revocation list RL, where $x \leq u$ and $i \leq N$ compute $\mathbf{e}'_i = \mathbf{b}_i - \mathbf{B}_i \cdot \mathbf{r}_{i_x} \mod q$ to check whether there exists an index i such that $\|\mathbf{e}'_i\|_\infty \leq \beta$. If so return 0.
9. Return 1.

- Open(**gpk**,**gmsk**, M, Σ): On input **gpk**, the group manager's secret key **gmsk** $=$ $\mathbf{T_F}$, and valid message signature pair $(M, \Sigma =$ $(\mathbf{ovk}, \mathbf{c}, \{\mathbf{c}_i\}_{i=1}^p, \Pi, sig, M, \{\rho_i\}_{i=1}^p, \{\mathbf{b}_i\}_{i=1}^p))$, this algorithm decrypts the ciphertexts $\mathbf{c} = (\mathbf{c}_1, \mathbf{c}_2)$ and $\{\mathbf{c}_i\}_{i=1}^p = (\{\mathbf{c}_{i_1}\}_{i=1}^p, \{\mathbf{c}_{i_2}\}_{i=1}^p)$ as follows.
  1. Let $\mathbf{G} = \mathcal{H}_1(\mathbf{ovk})$.
  2. Let $\mathbf{Y} = [\mathbf{y}_1 | \ldots | \mathbf{y}_\ell] \in \mathbb{Z}^{m \times \ell}$, where $\mathbf{F} \cdot \mathbf{Y} = \mathbf{G}$.
  3. Compute $d' = (d'_1, \ldots, d'_\ell) = \mathbf{c}_2 - \mathbf{Y}^T \cdot \mathbf{c}_1 \in \mathbb{Z}_q^\ell$.
  4. For each $i \in [\ell]$, if d'_1 is closer to 0 than to $\lfloor q/2 \rfloor$ modulos q, then let $d_i = 0$. Otherwise, let $d_i = 1$.
  5. Create $d = (d'_1, \ldots, d_\ell) \in \{0,1\}^\ell$.
  6. For $i \in [p]$
     (a) Compute $a'_i = (a'_{i_1}, \ldots, a'_{i_{\ell_u}}) = \mathbf{c}_{i_2} - \mathbf{Y}^T \cdot \mathbf{c}_{i_1} \in \mathbb{Z}_q^{\ell_u}$.
     (b) For each $j \in [\ell_u]$, if a'_{i_1} is closer to 0 than to $\lfloor q/2 \rfloor$ modulus q, then let $a_{i_j} = 0$. Otherwise, let $a_{i_j} = 1$.
     (c) Create $a_i = (a'_{i_1}, \ldots, a'_{i_{\ell_u}}) \in \{0,1\}^{\ell_u}$.
  7. Return d and $\{a_i\}_{i=1}^p$.
- Revoke(PP, **gpk**, **gmsk**, RL, d, S_r): On input **gpk**, the revocation list RL, and revoking attribute set S_r the group manager with **gmsk**, do the followings.
  1. For each $\mathbf{u}_{d_x}^t \in S_r : RL = RL \cup \mathbf{u}_{d_x}^t$.
  2. Return RL.

3.2 Underlying Interactive Protocol

This section provides a general description of zero-knowledge argument system that we use in our scheme.

Let COM be the statistically hiding and computationally binding commitment scheme described in [7]. We use matrices $\mathbf{A}, \{\mathbf{A}_i\}_{i=0}^\ell, \{\mathbf{B}_i\}_{i=1}^p, \mathbf{P}$, vectors $\{\mathbf{u}_i\}_{i=1}^p, \{\mathbf{b}_i\}_{i=1}^p, \mathbf{c}, \{\mathbf{c}_i\}_{i=1}^p$, and a threshold predicate $\Gamma = (t, S)$ as public parameters. The prover's witness consists of d, $\{a_i\}_{i=1}^p$, $\{\mathbf{z}_i\}_{i=1}^t$, $\{\mathbf{z}_i\}_{i=1}^{[p-t]}$, $\{\mathbf{t}_i\}_{i=1}^p, \{\mathbf{e}'_i\}_{i=1}^p, \mathbf{e}$, and $\{\mathbf{e}_i\}_{i=1}^p$.

The prover's goal is to convince the verifier in zero-knowledge that,

- for $i \in [t]$, $\mathbf{A}_d \mathbf{z}_i = \mathbf{u}_i \mod q$ and $\|\mathbf{z}_i\|_\infty \le \beta$, where $\mathbf{A}_d = \mathbf{A} \mid \mathbf{A}_0 + \sum_{i=1}^\ell d[i] \cdot \mathbf{A}_i]$,
- for $i \in [p - t]$, $\mathbf{A}_d \mathbf{z}_i = \mathbf{u}_i \mod q$ and $\|\mathbf{z}_i\|_\infty \not\le \beta$,
- for $i \in [t]$, $\|\bar{\mathbf{e}}_i\| \le \beta$ and $\mathbf{B}_i \cdot (\mathbf{A} \cdot \mathbf{t}_i) + \bar{\mathbf{e}}_i = \mathbf{b}_i \mod q$,
- for $i \in [t]$, $(\mathbf{A} \cdot \mathbf{t}_i) + (\mathbf{A}'_d \cdot \mathbf{z}_i) = \mathbf{u}_i \mod q$, where $\mathbf{A}'_d = 0 \mid 0 + \sum_{i=1}^\ell d[i] \cdot \mathbf{A}_i]$,
- $\mathbf{Pe} + (0^{k_1 - \ell} \| \lfloor q/2 \rfloor d) = \mathbf{c} \mod q$, and
- for $i \in [p]$, $\mathbf{Pe}_i + (0^{k_1 - \ell} \| \lfloor q/2 \rfloor a_i) = \mathbf{c}_i \mod q$.

In the full version of this paper we provide the detailed underlying zero-knowledge argument system with the analysis.

4 Security Proof of the Proposed Scheme

We prove the security of the proposed scheme in the random oracle model under the hardness of lattice problems LWE and SIS.

4.1   Proof of Anonymity

Theorem 1. *The proposed VLR-ABGS scheme is full-anonymous under the hardness of the LWE problem, strong unforgeability of the one-time signature (OTS) scheme, and the simulation soundness and zero-knowledge properties of the underlying interactive protocol.*

Proof. We prove that the proposed VLR-ABGS scheme is fully anonymous for users and attributes using a sequence of games between an adversary $\mathcal{A}$ and a challenger $\mathcal{C}$ as follows.

Game 1. In this game, the challenger $\mathcal{C}$ sets everything honestly. First, $\mathcal{C}$ produces all the keys and gives the group public key and all the secret signing keys of the users to the adversary $\mathcal{A}$. The challenger $\mathcal{C}$ answers all the opening queries that the adversary makes. Thus it returns $d, \{a_i\}_{i=1}^p \leftarrow$ Open($\mathbf{gpk}, \mathbf{gmsk}, M, \Sigma$). Finally, $\mathcal{C}$ produces a signature Σ^* with the honest identities $(i_0, i_1, S_0, S_1, \Gamma^*, M^*)$ that $\mathcal{A}$ sent, and forwards Σ^* to $\mathcal{A}$. The adversary wins the game if he can identify the index of the signer i_b correctly.

Game 2. In this game, $\mathcal{C}$ generates the OTS key pair $(\mathbf{ovk}^*, \mathbf{osk}^*)$ at the start of the game, not at the signature generation. During this game, if $\mathcal{A}$ requested for a opening of a valid signature $\Sigma = (\mathbf{ovk}, \mathbf{c}, \{\mathbf{c}_i\}_{i=1}^p, \Pi, sig, M, \{\rho_i\}_{i=1}^p, \{\mathbf{b}_i\}_{i=1}^p)$, where $\mathbf{ovk} = \mathbf{ovk}^*$, then $\mathcal{C}$ outputs a random bit and aborts the game. However, due to the strong unforgeability of OTS scheme, this is unlikely to happen. On the other hand, since $\mathbf{ovk}^*$ is independent of $\mathcal{A}$'s view, $\mathcal{A}$ comes up with a signature with $\mathbf{ovk}^*$ is negligible. Furthermore, after the challenging phase, if $\mathcal{A}$ comes up with a valid signature $\Sigma = (\mathbf{ovk}^*, \mathbf{c}, \{\mathbf{c}_i\}_{i=1}^p, \Pi, sig, M, \{\rho_i\}_{i=1}^p, \{\mathbf{b}_i\}_{i=1}^p)$, then sig must be forged one-time signature, which defeats the strong unforgeability of OTS scheme. Without loss of generality for upcoming games, we assume that $\mathcal{A}$ does not request for the opening of valid signatures that include $\mathbf{ovk}^*$.

Game 3. At the beginning of this game, $\mathcal{C}$ samples uniformly random $\mathbf{F}^* \in \mathbb{Z}_q^{n \times m}$ and $\mathbf{G}^* \in \mathbb{Z}_q^{n \times \ell}$. The distribution of $(\mathbf{F}^*, \mathbf{G}^*)$ is statistically close to $(\mathbf{F}, \mathbf{G})$ in the real game [6]. As for answering the opening queries, $\mathcal{C}$ samples a decrypting matrix $\mathbf{Y} \hookleftarrow D_{\mathbb{Z}^m, \sigma}^\ell$ and programs the oracle to have $\mathcal{H}_1(\mathbf{ovk}) = \mathbf{F}^*\mathbf{Y}$. The chosen $\mathbf{Y}$ is recorded to answer future queries. In the challenge phase, $\mathcal{C}$ programs $\mathcal{H}_1(\mathbf{ovk}^*) = \mathbf{G}^*$ and generates Σ^*. Since the distribution of $(\mathbf{F}^*, \mathbf{G}^*)$ is statistically close to that of Game 2, the two games are statistically indistinguishable.

Game 4. In this game, $\mathcal{C}$ simulates the zero-knowledge argument Π^* for the challenging signature Σ^* instead of generating an honest non-interactive zero-knowledge argument Π. Since the underlying argument system is statistically zero-knowledge, the distribution of simulated Π^* is statistically close to that of the legitimate Π. Thus, Game 3 and Game 4 are indistinguishable.

Game 5: In this game, $\mathcal{C}$ modifies the generation of ciphertexts $\mathbf{c} = (\mathbf{c}_1^*, \mathbf{c}_2^*)$ and $\mathbf{c}_i = (\mathbf{c}_{i_1}^*, \mathbf{c}_{i_2}^*)$ of the challenging signature. Let $\mathbf{c}_1^* = \mathbf{z}_1$ and $\mathbf{c}_2^* = \mathbf{z}_2 + \lfloor q/2 \rfloor d_b$, where $\mathbf{z}_1 \in \mathbb{Z}^m$ and $\mathbf{z}_2 \in \mathbb{Z}^{2m}$ are uniformly random and d_b is the index of $\mathcal{A}$'s challenging bit. Let $\mathbf{c}_{i_1}^* = \mathbf{z}_{i_1}$ and $\mathbf{c}_{i_2}^* = \mathbf{z}_{i_2} + \lfloor q/2 \rfloor a_{b_i}$, where $\mathbf{z}_{i_1} \in \mathbb{Z}^m$ and $\mathbf{z}_{i_2} \in \mathbb{Z}^{2m}$ are uniformly random and a_{b_i} are the indices of the related attribute set. Game 4 and Game 5 are indistinguishable under the assumption of the hardness of $LWE_{n,q,\chi}$. Indeed, if $\mathcal{A}$ can distinguish two games, then he can also solve Decision-LWE problem.

Game 6: In this game, $\mathcal{C}$ makes Σ^* totally independent of the bit b. $\mathcal{C}$ samples two vectors $\mathbf{z}'_1 \in \mathbb{Z}_q^m$ and $\mathbf{z}'_2 \in \mathbb{Z}_q^{2m}$ uniformly random and assigns $\mathbf{c}_1^* = \mathbf{z}'_1$ and $\mathbf{c}_2^* = \mathbf{z}'_2$. Then again samples two set of vectors $\mathbf{z}'_{i_1} \in \mathbb{Z}_q^m$ and $\mathbf{z}'_{i_2} \in \mathbb{Z}_q^{2m}$ uniformly random and assigns $\{\mathbf{c}_{i_1}^* = \mathbf{z}'_{i_1}, \mathbf{c}_{i_2}^* = \mathbf{z}'_{i_2}\}_{i \in [p]}$. Thus, Game 5 and Game 6 are statistically indistinguishable. Since this game is totally independent from the challenging bit b, the advantage of $\mathcal{A}$ in this game is zero.

The above sequence of games proves that the proposed scheme is full anonymous for users and attributes.

4.2   Traceability

Theorem 2. *The proposed VLR-ABGS scheme is fully traceable under the assumption that the SIS problem is hard.*

Proof. Our proof can be seen as an extension of the proof given in [11] to attributes. Even the scheme of [11] is for static groups since we do not allow to corrupt the tokens of the attribute in our scheme, which is an additional property of our scheme, we can extend the proof given in [11].

We assume their exists a PPT adversary $\mathcal{A}$ with noticeable advantage ε. Thus the adversary $\mathcal{A}$ can produce a valid message signature pair (M^*, Σ^*) with a predicate (Γ^*) which opens to $\perp$ or a user (not controlled by the adversary) who did not sign (M^*). Then we construct a reduction PPT forgery $\mathcal{B}$ that uses $\mathcal{A}$ to produce a forgery Boyen's signature with advantage polynomially smaller than ε. Since the Boyen signature is unforgeable based on the hardness of SIS problem, we prove that our scheme is traceable.

The verification key $(\mathbf{A}, \mathbf{A}_0, \mathbf{A}_1, \dots, \mathbf{A}_\ell, \mathbf{u}_1, \mathbf{u}_2, \dots, \mathbf{u}_u)$ for Boyen's signature scheme is given to the forgery $\mathcal{B}$. Then $\mathcal{B}$ produces a key-pair $(\mathbf{F}, \mathbf{T_F})$ for GPV-IBE encryption scheme and interacts with $\mathcal{A}$ by giving gpk=$(\mathbf{A}, \mathbf{A}_0, \mathbf{A}_1, \dots, \mathbf{A}_\ell, \mathbf{u}_1, \mathbf{u}_2, \dots, \mathbf{u}_u, \mathbf{F})$ and $\mathbf{T_F}$. The adversary $\mathcal{A}$ is allowed to do *Random Oracle*, *Secret Signing Key*, and *Signing* queries. Finally, $\mathcal{A}$ outputs a message M^*, a forgery signature Σ^*, a revocation list RL^*, and a threshold predicate Γ^*, which satisfies the requirements of the traceability game, where $\Sigma^* = (\mathbf{ovk}, \mathbf{c}, \{\mathbf{c}_i\}_{i=1}^p, (\{\text{CMT}^{(k)}\}_{k=1}^t, \text{CH}, \{\text{RSP}^{(k)}\}_{k=1}^t), sig, M, \{\rho_i\}_{i=1}^p, \{\mathbf{b}_i\}_{i=1}^p)$ and passes the signature verification.

Using the knowledge extractor of the underlying argument system $\mathcal{B}$ can obtain $(d^*, \mathbf{z}^* = \{\mathbf{z}_i^*\}_{i \in [t]}, \{\bar{\mathbf{e}}^*_i\}_{i \in [t]}, \mathbf{e}^*, \{\mathbf{e}_i^*\}_{i \in [t]})$, such that $\mathbf{z}^*$ is the Boyen's signature for the message d^*. To succeed $\mathcal{A}$ should not have used d^* in *Secret Signing Key*. Finally, we observe that if $\mathcal{A}$ has non-negligible success probability and runs in polynomial time, then same applies for $\mathcal{B}$.

5   Conclusion

This paper provided a new VLR-ABGS scheme which serves efficient tracing mechanism using the explicit-tracing mechanism. Moreover, the proposed scheme achieved strong security under the hardness of the lattice problems and statistical ZK property of the proposed argument system. The proposed scheme satisfied the full anonymity for users and attributes and full traceability.

References

1. Bellare, M., Micciancio, D., Warinschi, B.: Foundations of group signatures: formal definitions, simplified requirements, and a construction based on general assumptions. In: Biham, E. (ed.) EUROCRYPT 2003. LNCS, vol. 2656, pp. 614–629. Springer, Heidelberg (2003). https://doi.org/10.1007/3-540-39200-9_38
2. Boneh, D., Shacham, H.: Group signatures with verifier-local revocation. In: ACM-CCS 2004, pp. 168–177. ACM (2004)
3. Boyen, X.: Lattice mixing and vanishing trapdoors: a framework for fully secure short signatures and more. In: Nguyen, P.Q., Pointcheval, D. (eds.) PKC 2010. LNCS, vol. 6056, pp. 499–517. Springer, Heidelberg (2010). https://doi.org/10.1007/978-3-642-13013-7_29
4. Brickell, E.: An efficient protocol for anonymously providing assurance of the container of the private key. Submitted to the Trusted Comp. Group, April 2003
5. Chaum, D., van Heyst, E.: Group signatures. In: Davies, D.W. (ed.) EUROCRYPT 1991. LNCS, vol. 547, pp. 257–265. Springer, Heidelberg (1991). https://doi.org/10.1007/3-540-46416-6_22
6. Gentry, C., Peikert, C., Vaikuntanathan, V.: Trapdoors for hard lattices and new cryptographic constructions. In: ACM 2008, pp. 197–206. ACM (2008)
7. Kawachi, A., Tanaka, K., Xagawa, K.: Concurrently secure identification schemes based on the worst-case hardness of lattice problems. In: Pieprzyk, J. (ed.) ASIACRYPT 2008. LNCS, vol. 5350, pp. 372–389. Springer, Heidelberg (2008). https://doi.org/10.1007/978-3-540-89255-7_23
8. Khader, D.: Attribute based group signature with revocation. IACR Cryptol. ePrint Arch. **2007**, 241 (2007)
9. Khader, D.: Attribute based group signatures. IACR Cryptol. ePrint Arch. **2007**, 159 (2007)
10. Kuchta, V., Sahu, R.A., Sharma, G., Markowitch, O.: On new zero-knowledge arguments for attribute-based group signatures from lattices. In: Kim, H., Kim, D.-C. (eds.) ICISC 2017. LNCS, vol. 10779, pp. 284–309. Springer, Cham (2018). https://doi.org/10.1007/978-3-319-78556-1_16
11. Ling, S., Nguyen, K., Wang, H.: Group signatures from lattices: simpler, tighter, shorter, ring-based. In: Katz, J. (ed.) PKC 2015. LNCS, vol. 9020, pp. 427–449. Springer, Heidelberg (2015). https://doi.org/10.1007/978-3-662-46447-2_19
12. Perera, M.N.S., Nakamura, T., Hashimoto, M., Yokoyama, H.: Zero-knowledge proof system for fully anonymous attribute based group signatures from lattices with VLR. In: WISA 2019, LNCS (2019, to appear)
13. Regev, O.: On lattices, learning with errors, random linear codes, and cryptography. In: In STOC, pp. 84–93. ACM Press (2005)
14. Zhang, Y., Gan, Y., Yin, Y., Jia, H.: Attribute-based VLR group signature scheme from lattices. In: Vaidya, J., Li, J. (eds.) ICA3PP 2018. LNCS, vol. 11337, pp. 600–610. Springer, Cham (2018). https://doi.org/10.1007/978-3-030-05063-4_46

Privacy-Preserving *k*-means Clustering: an Application to Driving Style Recognition

Othmane El Omri[1], Aymen Boudguiga[1,2(✉)], Malika Izabachene[2], and Witold Klaudel[1,3]

[1] IRT SystemX, 91120 Palaiseau, France
{othmane.omri,aymen.boudguiga,witold.klaudel}@irt-systemx.fr
[2] CEA-LIST, 91191 Gif-sur-Yvette, France
{aymen.boudguiga,malika.izabachene}@cea.fr
[3] Renault, 1 Avenue du Golf, 78288 Guyancourt, France
witold.klaudel@renault.com

Abstract. With the advent of connected vehicles, drivers will communicate personal information describing their driving style to their vehicles manufacturers, stakeholders or insurers. These information will serve to evaluate remotely vehicle state via an e-diagnostics service, to provide over-the-air update of vehicles controllers and to offer new third parties services targeting profiled drivers. An inherent problem to all the previous services is privacy. Indeed, the providers of these services will need access to sensitive data in order to propose in return an adequate service.

In this paper, we propose a privacy-preserving *k*-means clustering for drivers subscribed to the *pay how you drive* service, where vehicles insurance fees are adjusted according to driving behavior. Our proposal relies on secure multi-party computation and additive homomorphic encryption schemes to ensure the confidentiality of drivers data during clustering and classification.

Keywords: Pay how you drive · Privacy · Mutli-party computation

1 Introduction

When drivers of connected vehicles subscribe to a *pay how you drive* service (PHYD), their vehicles communicate information about their position, speed, acceleration and braking frequencies to the insurer. The insurer uses this information to classify drivers and to adjust their insurance fees with respect to their driving behaviors.

The problem with PHYD is that the collected data can be used by a malicious adversary to deduce information about drivers such as their home address or workplace, their travelling habits, their speed infractions, etc. Consequently, it is compulsory to provide a privacy-preserving drivers clustering and classification algorithm.

© Springer Nature Switzerland AG 2019
J. K. Liu and X. Huang (Eds.): NSS 2019, LNCS 11928, pp. 685–696, 2019.
https://doi.org/10.1007/978-3-030-36938-5_43

Contribution–In this work, we propose to rely on an unsupervised machine learning algorithm for drivers' clustering as insurers keep confidential their clustering algorithms due to IP and business reasons. Among the unsupervised learning techniques, we choose, the simple k-*means* algorithm. We consider three types of drivers (i.e. $k = 3$): aggressive, normal, and cautious; as proposed by the driving simulator SCANeR Studio[1].

We use secure multi-party computation techniques and an additive homomorphic encryption algorithm to make k-means ensure the privacy of drivers' data. That is, drivers' features are not exposed neither during k-means model training nor during classification[2]. We make use of Yao garbled circuits protocol [1] for Squared Euclidien Distances computation and Paillier [2] cryptosystem for means computation.

Paper Organization–In Sect. 2, we present the state of the art regarding the private processing of vehicles' data. In Sect. 3, we present the background concepts used in these paper such as the k-means algorithm, the secure multiparty computation and the homomorphic encryption. In Sect. 4, we specify our privacy-preserving extension to k-means when applied to drivers clustering. In Sect. 5, we discuss our proposed protocol security and performance. Finally, Sect. 6 concludes the paper and provides future research directions.

2   State of the Art on Private Processing of Vehicles Data

In 2011, Troncoso et al. [3] proposed to install a secure hardware, i.e. a black box, in vehicles to compute the insurance fees locally. The obtained fees are transmitted later to insurances for billing. As such, vehicles' private data are kept secret from insurances. They also specified an auditing mechanism to check that neither the insurance nor the owner of the vehicle cheated of fees. Indeed, they store the data needed for calculating insurance costs on an auxiliary storage. The data are encrypted using a split key between the vehicle owner and the insurance. In case of a dispute, the vehicle owner and the insurance combine their split key to decrypt the auxiliary storage and check how the insurance fee has been computed.

In 2013, Kargl et al. [4] used differential privacy techniques to protect Floating Car Data (FCD). Differential privacy provides mathematical privacy guarantees. However, it allows only to make a limited number of queries, such as computing the sum, the minimum/maximum and the average. It is not well fitted for private k-means calculus.

In 2015, Rizzo et al. [5] proposed a technique to train a decision tree to classify drivers behavior (as aggressive or defensive), while preserving the privacy of collected data and the confidentiality of the decision tree computed by the insurance company. They used a secure version of the ID3 algorithm to build the decision tree using the homomorphic properties of Paillier cryptosystem [2].

---

[1] http://www.oktal.fr/en/automotive/range-of-simulators/range-of-simulators.

[2] Note that our protocol is not only limited to drivers clustering and can be easily generalized to cover all use-cases using k-means for clustering.

3   Background

In this section, we review the key concepts used in this paper.

3.1 k-means Clustering Algorithm

k-means algorithm [6] produces automatically k clusters ($\{c_1, \ldots, c_k\}$) from a collection of data sets ($\{d_1, \ldots, d_n\}$) in a simple way. k-means relies on distance and mean computation for data clustering as presented in Algorithm 1. First, we select k random cluster centers ($\{\mu_1, \mu_2, \ldots, \mu_k\}$). Then, we iterate the algorithm until converging to the best choice of clusters' centers or reaching a preselected number of iterations.

---

input : n data vectors and the number of clusters k
output: k clusters

1 Select k cluster centers $\{\mu_1, \mu_2, ..., \mu_k\}$;
2 **repeat**
3   Assign each data vector $d_{j,j \in [\![1,n]\!]}$ to the closest cluster $c_{i,i \in [\![1,k]\!]}$ whom center is $\mu_{i,i \in [\![1,k]\!]}$ (i.e., the distance between μ_i and d_j is minimum);
4   Replace each cluster center μ_i by the mean of elements d_j belonging to the cluster c_i;
5 **until** *cluster centers do not vary significantly or the number of iterations is reached*;

Algorithm 1. k-means clustering

3.2   Yao Garbled Circuit

Yao's garbled circuit [1] allows two parties to evaluate a boolean circuit C without revealing their respective inputs. The circuit *generator* creates a garbled circuit GC by obfuscating the inputs to C wires. Indeed, for each wire w_i of the circuit, the *generator* chooses randomly two secret values w_i^0 and w_i^1. w_i^0 and w_i^1 are the garbled values corresponding to 0 and 1, respectively. Finally, she creates a garbled table GT_i for each gate G_i. Each line of GT_i contains two garbled inputs $w_{i,1}^j$ and $w_{i,2}^j$ (where $j \in \{0,1\}$) and their corresponding output $E(H(w_{i,1}^j, w_{i,2}^j), w_{i,o}^j)$ where E is an encryption algorithm and H a key generation function. After decryption, GT_i allows to get the garbled value of the output $w_{i,o}^j$.

The circuit generator transmits GC, i.e. all the garbled tables, to the circuit *evaluator*. In addition, the generator provides the evaluator with her garbled inputs $w_{i,g}^j$ for all input gates $G_i \in GC$. Finally, the evaluator recovers her own garbled inputs $w_{i,e}^j$ to the same input gates $GT_i \in GC$ using oblivious transfers [7,8]. At this point, the evaluator can compute all the garbled gates of GC. She starts with the decryption of the *input* gates with the keys $E(H(w_{i,g}^j, w_{i,e}^j), w_{i,o}^j)$, and continues until reaching the final output of the boolean circuit C.

3.3   Additive Homomorphic Public Key Encryption

A public key encryption (PKE) consists of 3 algorithms: KG which given a security parameter λ generates a public key pk and a secret key sk. One produces an encryption of a message m using pk and a randomness. We denote $E_{pk}(m)$ the obtained ciphertext. To decrypt a ciphertext c, one uses the secret key sk and outputs either a message or $\perp$. We denote $D_{sk}(c)$ this output.

We say that a PKE scheme is correct if for $(pk, sk) \leftarrow KG$ and $c \leftarrow E_p k(m)$, we have that $D_{sk}(c) = m$ holds with high probability. The PKE encryption function is assumed to be additively homomorphic i.e. $E_{pk}(m_1 \oplus m_2) = E_{pk}(m_1) \circledast E_{pk}(m_2)$, where $\oplus$ and $\circledast$ are the group laws over the message space and the ciphertext space, respectively. Example of such cryptosystems is Paillier scheme [2].

4   Privacy-Preserving k-means Clustering of Drivers

In this section, we detail our proposed protocol for running k-means while keeping drivers' features private. We denote by N the total number of vehicles (or drivers), V_i is the driver identifier for $i \in [\![1, N]\!]$ and $X_i = (x_{i1}, \ldots, x_{im})$ is the vector of features of V_i. k is a fixed integer and denotes the number of clusters ($k = 3$). S is the model provider. In our application, S refers to the insurer server. $C(V_i)$ is the label of the cluster containing X_i.

4.1   Assumptions

Clustering. During clustering, each driver inputs his driving data to the k-means algorithm. These driving data are private and must not be shared or analyzed in plaintext. The k-means algorithm returns to a driver the *index* of the cluster to which he belongs. Meanwhile, the insurer receives the *centers* of all created clusters. The centers of clusters are insurer's private data, and must not be shared with drivers.

Classification. During classification, we assume that each driver inputs his data to the k-means algorithm. In return, the insurer and the driver only obtain the index of the cluster to which the driver belongs.

Communication Model. We assume no communications between vehicles. We only consider direct communications between a vehicle and the insurer. We do not have real-time constraints as driver insurance fees are paid once per month. So, the upcoming computation can be done in background by an insurance application installed in one of the trusted electronic control units of the vehicle.

---

input : n data entities and the number of clusters k
output: k clusters

1   S randomly selects k cluster centers $\{\mu_1, \mu_2, ..., \mu_k\}$;
2   **repeat**
3   **for** $i = 1..N$ **do**
4   V_i and S engage in a secure two-party cluster attribution protocol;
5   V_i gets $C(V_i)$, S gets no information;
6          $S, V_1, \ldots, V_n$ engage in a secure multi-party mean computation protocol to update cluster centers;
7   **end**
8   **until** *cluster centers do not vary significantly or the number of iterations is reached;*

Algorithm 2. Privacy-preserving k-means clustering

Attacker Model. In this work, we consider a honest-but-curious model. Each of the N players (e.g. vehicles) possesses private features. The model provider S (e.g. the insurer) has no access to these features. One player V_1 is chosen as the dealer player in the honest but curious model; V_1 is the only one who knows the private key sk_1. Each player sends his encrypted features under public key pk_1 to S. We assume that S and V_1 act as honest players. Also, we assume that no collusion between players is possible.

4.2 Proposed Protocol for Privacy-Preserving k-means

We enhance k-means clustering with secure multi-party computation (as presented in Algorithm 2). First, we propose a *secure two-party protocol for the closest cluster computation* (i.e. for drivers attribution to clusters). Then, we define a protocol for *secure multi-party mean computation*. The computed mean serves to privately update the centers of clusters.

Secure Computation of the Closest Cluster. We use a secure two-party protocol between a vehicle (V_i) and the insurer (S) to compute the closest cluster to V_i. To meet our requirement of keeping the centers of clusters private, we use an unfair version of Yao's protocol, where only the driver (V_i) obtains the result of the computation, the insurer gets no information.

For our protocol, we propose the circuit of Fig. 1a. If the insurer is the *evaluator* of the circuit, she sends the output labels to the vehicle. If the insurer is the *generator* of the circuit, she sends the table mapping each label to its value. In our circuit, we compute the Squared Euclidean Distance (SED) and then returns the index of the lowest distance, i.e. the closest cluster. SED is computed with respect to the 3 current cluster centers.

First, we use the circuit of Fig. 1b to compute the Squared Euclidean Distance (SED) between two n-dimensional vectors $X = (x_1, \ldots, x_m)$ and $Y = (y_1, \ldots, y_m)$. It computes $\|X - Y\|_2^2 = \sum_{i=1}^{m}(x_i - y_i)^2 = \sum_{i=1}^{m} x_i^2 - 2\sum_{i=1}^{m} x_i.y_i + \sum_{i=1}^{m} y_i^2$.

The second circuit computes the minimal distance to a cluster center. We use the min circuit described in [9] to compare 2 distances d_1 and d_2. The min circuit returns the smallest distance between d_1 and d_2 with its respective index

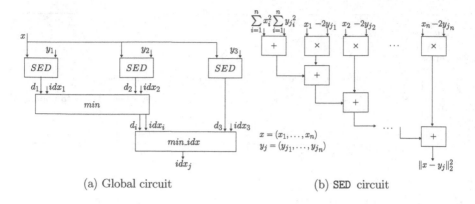

(a) Global circuit   (b) SED circuit

Fig. 1. Circuit for closest cluster index calculus

(i.e. 1 or 2). The `min` circuit is composed of a comparison ($>$) gate and two multiplexer gates (`MUX`). The comparison gate takes two inputs x, y and outputs 1 if $x > y$ and 0 otherwise. The `MUX` gate takes 3 inputs x, y and a bit b. If $b = 1$, `MUX` outputs x, otherwise it outputs y. Finally, we remove one `MUX` gate from the `min` circuit to get the `min_idx` circuit (Fig. 2b). The latter outputs the *index* of the minimum distance and *not* the value of the minimum.

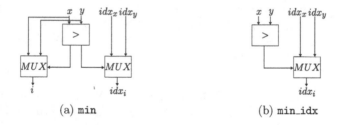

(a) `min`   (b) `min_idx`

Fig. 2. `min` and `min_idx` circuits

Secure Computation of Clusters' New Centers. The second k-means computation updates the centers of clusters. The new centers are simply the *mean* of driving data that belong to drivers from the same cluster. Our protocol requires a semantic secure and homomorphic additive cryptosystem. Semantic security ensures that encrypting twice the same driving data returns two different ciphertexts. Meanwhile, the homomorphic addition sums encrypted data of drivers belonging to the same cluster. Example of such cryptosystems is Paillier scheme [2].

Our protocol contains 3 phases: an initialization, a secure sum computation and a secure mean computation. First, the insurer S nominates a vehicle as V_1 to initiate the protocol as depicted in Algorithm 3. We assume w.l.o.g that V_1 belongs to the first cluster (i.e. $C(V_1) = 1$). V_1 picks 6 random values

---

1   S nominates a vehicle as V_1;
2   V_1 picks 6 random values $r_{f1}^1, r_{f2}^1, r_{f3}^1, r_{n1}^1, r_{n2}^1, r_{n3}^1$;
3   V_1 computes:
4   $c_{f1}^1 = E_{pk_1}(x_1 + r_{f1}^1)$ $c_{n1}^1 = E_{pk_1}(1 + r_{n1}^1)$;
5   $c_{f2}^1 = E_{pk_1}(r_{f2}^1)$ $c_{n2}^1 = E_{pk_1}(r_{n2}^1)$;
6   $c_{f3}^1 = E_{pk_1}(r_{f3}^1)$ $c_{n3}^1 = E_{pk_1}(r_{n3}^1)$;
7   V_1 sends to S: $c_{f1}^1, c_{f2}^1, c_{f3}^1, c_{n1}^1, c_{n2}^1, c_{n3}^1$;
8   S initializes:
9   $S_{f1} \leftarrow c_{f1}^1$ $S_{n1} \leftarrow c_{n1}^1$;
10 $S_{f2} \leftarrow c_{f2}^1$ $S_{n2} \leftarrow c_{n2}^1$;
11 $S_{f3} \leftarrow c_{f3}^1$ $S_{n3} \leftarrow c_{n3}^1$;

Algorithm 3. Secure multi-party mean computation protocol: initialization phase

---

1   for $i = 2..N$ do
2   $\quad$ Let j be V_i's cluster label, $j = C(V_i)$. V_i computes $c_{fi}^j = E_{pk_1}(x_i)$ and $c_{ni}^j = E_{pk_1}(1)$;
3   $\quad$ For $k \in \{1, 2, 3\} \setminus \{j\}$, V_i computes $c_{fk}^i = E_{pk_1}(0)$ and $c_{nk}^i = E_{pk_1}(0)$;
4   $\quad$ V_i sends to S: $c_{f1}^i, c_{f2}^i, c_{f3}^i, c_{n1}^i, c_{n2}^i, c_{n3}^i$;
5   $\quad$ S computes:
6   $\qquad$ $S_{f1} \leftarrow S_{f1} * c_{f1}^i$ $S_{n1} \leftarrow S_{n1} * c_{n1}^i$;
7   $\qquad$ $S_{f2} \leftarrow S_{f2} * c_{f2}^i$ $S_{n2} \leftarrow S_{n2} * c_{n2}^i$;
8   $\qquad$ $S_{f3} \leftarrow S_{f3} * c_{f3}^i$ $S_{n3} \leftarrow S_{n3} * c_{n3}^i$;
9   end

Algorithm 4. Secure multi-party mean computation protocol: sum calculus

---

$(r_{f1}^1, r_{f2}^1, r_{f3}^1, r_{n1}^1, r_{n2}^1, r_{n3}^1)$ and encrypts them with his own public key pk_1 to obtain 6 ciphertexts $(c_{f1}^1, c_{f2}^1, c_{f3}^1, c_{n1}^1, c_{n2}^1, c_{n3}^1)$. c_f contains encrypted features of vehicles. For example, V_1 belongs to the cluster 1, so V_1 encrypts her features x_1 as $c_{f1}^1 = E_{pk_1}(x_1 + r_{f1}^1)$, while c_{f2} and c_{f3} encrypt r_{f2}^1 and r_{f3}^1, respectively. Meanwhile, c_n indicates whether a vehicle belongs to a cluster or not. For V_1, c_{n1} encrypts $r_{n1}^1 + 1$ while c_{n2} and c_{n3} encrypt r_{n2}^1 and r_{n3}^1, respectively. The encryption results $(c_{f1}^1, c_{f2}^1, c_{f3}^1, c_{n1}^1, c_{n2}^1, c_{n3}^1)$ are transmitted to S which uses them to initialize the sum values $(S_{f1}, S_{f2}, S_{f3}, S_{n1}, S_{n2}, S_{n3})$.

Second, the insurer S requests from each vehicle $V_{i,i \neq 1}$ to provide its encrypted feature. To do so, each vehicle generates 6 ciphertexts $(c_{f1}^i, c_{f2}^i, c_{f3}^i, c_{n1}^i, c_{n2}^i, c_{n3}^i)$ as explained in Algorithm 4. V_i encrypts in c_{fj}^i her features when her cluster label $C(V_i)$ equals j, or 0 otherwise. In the same way, V_i encrypts in c_{nj}^i 1 when her cluster label $C(V_i)$ equals j, or 0 otherwise.

Finally, S picks 6 random values $(r_{f1}^S, r_{f2}^S, r_{f3}^S, r_{n1}^S, r_{n2}^S, r_{n3}^S)$, encrypts them with pk_1 and adds them to $(S_{f1}, S_{f2}, S_{f3}, S_{n1}, S_{n2}, S_{n3})$, respectively. Then, S transmits the obtained results to V_1 as presented in Algorithm 5. V_1 deciphers $(S_{f1}, S_{f2}, S_{f3}, S_{n1}, S_{n2}, S_{n3})$ and substracts $(r_{f1}^S, r_{f2}^S, r_{f3}^S, r_{n1}^S, r_{n2}^S, r_{n3}^S)$ to obtain $(f_1, f_2, f_3, n_1, n_2, n_3)$ which are retransmitted to S. S computes $f_i = f_i - r_{fi}^S$, $n_i = n_i - r_{ni}^S$ and the new clusters' means as: $\mu_i = f_i / n_i$.

Note that for simplicity concerns, we described the previous algorithm while considering that each vehicle V_i is transmitting one feature x_i. If vehicles are transmitting t features, each $c_{fj}^i, j \in \{1, 2, 3\}$ will be a vector of encrypted features or 0, namely $c_{fj}^i = (E_{pk_1}(x_1^i), ..., E_{pk_1}(x_t^i))$ or $(E_{pk_1}(0), ..., E_{pk_1}(0))$. In this case,

---

1   S picks 6 random values $r_{f_1}^S, r_{f_2}^S, r_{f_3}^S, r_{n_1}^S, r_{n_2}^S, r_{n_3}^S$;
2   S computes for $i \in \{1, 2, 3\}$:
3   $S_{f_i} \leftarrow S_{f_i} * E_{pk_1}(r_{f_i}^S)$ $S_{n_i} \leftarrow S_{n_i} * E_{pk_1}(r_{n_i}^S)$;
4   S sends to V_1: $S_{f_1}, S_{f_2}, S_{f_3}, S_{n_1}, S_{n_2}, S_{n_3}$;
5   V_1 computes for $i \in \{1, 2, 3\}$:
6   $f_i = D_{sk_1}(S_{f_i}) - r_{f_i}^1$ $n_i = D_{sk_1}(S_{n_i}) - r_{n_i}^1$;
7   V_1 sends to S: $f_1, f_2, f_3, n_1, n_2, n_3$;
8   S computes for $i \in \{1, 2, 3\}$:
9   $f_i \leftarrow f_i - r_{f_i}^S$ $n_i \leftarrow n_i - r_{f_i}^S$;
10 S finally computes the new cluster means for $i \in \{1, 2, 3\}$: $\mu_i = f_i / n_i$;

Algorithm 5. Secure multi-party mean computation protocol: mean calculus

V_1 would compute in the initialization phase the following c_f values: $c_{f_1}^1 = (E_{pk_1}(x_1^1 + r_{f_1}^1), ..., E_{pk_1}(x_t^i + r_{f_1}^1))$, $c_{f_2}^1 = (E_{pk_1}(r_{f_2}^1), ..., E_{pk_1}(r_{f_2}^1))$ and $c_{f_3}^1 = (E_{pk_1}(r_{f_3}^1), ..., E_{pk_1}(r_{f_3}^1))$.

4.3 k-means Classification of New Drivers

Once the clusters are properly defined, it becomes easy to privately classify a new driver. The driver and the insurer will engage in the *secure two-party cluster attribution protocol* defined previously. However, the result of this computation is revealed to both parties. The driver cluster will determine the category of the driver and therefore his insurance fee.

5   Protocol Evaluation

In this section, we discuss the correctness and complexity of our proposed scheme.

5.1   Correctness

Correctness of the secure two-party cluster attribution protocol is trivial since the circuits are constructed to compute the correct value. We therefore focus on correctness of the secure multi-party mean computation protocol. When all the vehicles have sent their encrypted features, S computes:

$$S_{f_1} = \prod_{i=1..N} c_{f_1}^i \qquad\qquad S_{n_1} = \prod_{i=1..N} c_{n_1}^i$$

$$S_{f_2} = \prod_{i=1..N} c_{f_2}^i \qquad\qquad S_{n_2} = \prod_{i=1..N} c_{n_2}^i$$

$$S_{f_3} = \prod_{i=1..N} c_{f_3}^i \qquad\qquad S_{n_3} = \prod_{i=1..N} c_{n_3}^i$$

Which is equivalent to[3]:

$$S_{f1} = c_{f1}^1 * \prod_{C(V_i)=1} c_{f1}^i * \prod_{C(V_i)\neq1} c_{f1}^i$$

$$S_{n1} = c_{n1}^1 * \prod_{C(V_i)=1} c_{n1}^i * \prod_{C(V_i)\neq1} c_{n1}^i$$

We keep considering w.l.o.g that V_1 is in the first cluster. So, $c_{f1}^1 = E_{pk_1}(x_1 + r_{f1}^1)$ and $c_{n1}^1 = E_{pk_1}(1 + r_{n1}^1)$. Moreover, for i s.t. $C(V_i) = 1$, we have $c_{f1}^i = E_{pk_1}(x_i)$ and $c_{n1}^i = E_{pk_1}(1)$, while for i s.t. $C(V_i) \neq 1$ we have $c_{f1}^i = E_{pk_1}(0)$ and $c_{n1}^i = E_{pk_1}(0)$. Therefore, we obtain:

$$S_{f1} = E_{pk_1}(x_1 + r_{f1}^1) * \prod_{C(V_i)=1} E_{pk_1}(x_i) * \prod_{C(V_i)\neq1} E_{pk_1}(0)$$

$$S_{n1} = E_{pk_1}(1 + r_{n1}^1) * \prod_{C(V_i)=1} E_{pk_1}(1) * \prod_{C(V_i)\neq1} E_{pk_1}(0)$$

Thanks to the homomorphic property, we rewrite:

$$S_{f1} = E_{pk_1}(r_{f1}^1 + \sum_{C(V_i)=1} x_i)$$

$$S_{n1} = E_{pk_1}(r_{n1}^1 + \sum_{C(V_i)=1} 1) = E_{pk_1}(r_{n1}^1 + card\{V_i/C(V_i) = 1\})$$

In the last exchange between V_1 and S, S hides the real values from V_1 by homomorphically adding $r_{f_i}^S$ and $r_{n_i}^S$, for $i \in \{1, 2, 3\}$. V_1 decrypts S_{f_i} and S_{n_i} and removes his random values $r_{f_i}^1$ and $r_{n_i}^1$, for $i \subset \{1, 2, 3\}$. Finally, S obtains the sums $f_j = \sum_{C(V_i)=j} x_i$ and the cardinal of each cluster $n_j = card\{V_i/C(V_i) = 1\}$ for $j \in \{1, 2, 3\}$. S is then able to compute the cluster means $\mu_j = f_j/n_j$.

5.2   Privacy

We check that our protocol fulfills the following requirements in the semi-honest model: (1) the inputs x_i and the closest cluster label $C(V_i)$ should be kept private for each vehicle V_i, (2) the clusters' means μ_i should be kept private for S.

The *secure two-party cluster attribution protocol* is proven in the literature [10] to compute privately the cluster attribution in the presence of semi-honest adversaries.

We therefore focus more on the *secure multi-party mean computation protocol*. In the first part of the protocol, S receives $c_{f_j}^i, c_{n_j}^i$ from each V_i for $i \in [1, N]$ and $j \in \{1, 2, 3\}$. These values do not reveal information about the vehicles inputs since the Paillier cryptosystem provides indistinguishablity under chosen plaintext (IND-CPA). S cannot distinguish $c_{f_j}^i = E_{pk_1}(0)$ from $c_{f_j}^i = E_{pk_1}(x_i)$ and $c_{n_j}^i = E_{pk_1}(0)$ from $c_{n_j}^i = E_{pk_1}(1)$. Therefore, S cannot obtain any information

---

[3] we rewrite only S_{f1} and S_{n1} for the sake of clarity.

about a vehicle's features nor its intermediary cluster label. The second part of the protocol is the final exchange between S and V_1. S adds homomorphically to the encrypted sums S_{f_j} and S_{nj} the random values $r_{f_j}^S$ and r_{nj}^S, for $j \in \{1, 2, 3\}$ to hide the sums from V_1.

Upon reception of the (S_{f_j}, S_{nj}), V_1 decrypts them with his private key and substracts his initial random values $r_{f_j}^1$ and r_{nj}^1, for $j \in \{1, 2, 3\}$. The values obtained do not reveal any information since they are still masked by the random values of S. S is finally able to obtain the sums by substracting his random values $r_{f_j}^S$ and r_{nj}^S from f_j and n_j, for $j \in \{1, 2, 3\}$. In this second part of the protocol, each computed value does not reveal any sensitive information to the concerned party in the semi-honest model. However, when we consider that V_1 and S are malicious, they can collude and recover all the information regarding the other vehicles.

5.3   Complexity

Our protocol relies on Yao garbled circuit for the closest cluster computation. Indeed, once the distances to clusters' centers are computed with SED circuit, we compare them and return the index of the closest cluster using the min and min_idx circuits. In the sequel, we assume that the number of features per vehicle is n and that each feature is l-bit long.

We use the information from Table 1 [11,12] to estimate the number of gates of the closest cluster index calculus circuit (of Fig. 1a). The *size* of a circuit refers to the number of AND gates. Meanwhile, the multiplicative *depth* of a circuit refers to the maximum number of AND gates on any path of the circuit. Let us denote by $S()$ the function that returns a circuit size and by $D()$ the function that returns a circuit depth. The size and depth of the circuit for the closest cluster computation are $3S(SED) + S(min) + S(min\_idx)$ and $3D(SED) + D(min) + D(min\_idx)$, respectively.

Table 1. Number of gates of elementary circuits

Operand	Method	Depth	Size
+ [11]	ripple-carry	$l - 1$	$l - 1$
	Sklansky	$\lceil log(l) \rceil + 1$	$l \lceil log(l) \rceil$
× [11]	standard	$2l - 1$	$l^2 - l$
	Wallace	$2\lceil log(l) \rceil + 3$	$2l^2 + l\lceil log(l) \rceil$
MUX [13]	Kolesnikov and Schneider	1	l
> [12]	Kolesnikov et al. [9]	l	l
	Garay et al. [14]	$\lceil log(l) \rceil + 1$	$3l - \lceil log(l) \rceil - 2$

Using inputs from Table 1, we obtain the results presented in Table 2 when we lower the size of our circuit for closest cluster index calculus to the maximum.

That is, if we consider a garbling method compatible with free-XOR [13], we will have to manage at most 4 ciphertexts per AND gate, for a total of $3nl^2 + 5l - 3n$ AND gates. In addition, we will engage in $3(n + 1)l$ oblivious transfers between the circuit generator and verifier. It is clear that it is important to reduce at maximum the number n of features to improve the circuit computation time and to reduce bandwidth consumption during oblivious transfers.

Table 2. Number of gates of the closest cluster index calculus circuit

Circuit	Size
SED	$n(l^2 - 1)$
min	$3l$
min_idx	$2l$
Closest cluster index circuit	$3nl^2 + 5l - 3n$

The secure computation of new cluster centers relies on a homomorphic additive cryptosystem (as presented in Algorithms 3, 4 and 5). Each vehicle $V_{i,i \in [\![1,N]\!]}$ encrypts $3n + 3$ plaintexts, i.e. a plaintext per feature and per cluster, using the public key of V_1. Then, it transmits them to the insurer S. S sums the received ciphertexts to obtain 3 vectors of encrypted features $S_{f_{i,i \in \{1,2,3\}}}$ and 3 sums of the total number of vehicles in a cluster $S_{n_{i,i \in \{1,2,3\}}}$. Finally, V_1 decrypts these sums for S. That is, V_1 decrypts $3n + 3$ ciphertexts. Note that the good choice of the homomorphic additive cryptosystem is of a great importance to reduce the bandwidth consumption during ciphertexts exchange. Indeed, as the number of exchanged ciphertexts $(3n + 3)$ depends on the number of vehicles features (n), vehicles may have to transmit large bulks of data due to the size of ciphertext.

Note that for the PHYD use-case, we do not have real-time constraints as insurance fees are paid once a month and drivers may delay their payments by one month. That is, drivers clustering and then classification will be updated monthly. In practice, it is up to the insurer to fix the number of vehicles and to delimit the geographical area used for drivers clustering.

6   Conclusion

We presented in this work a privacy preserving k-means clustering and then classification for driving profiles. The proposed protocol avoids disclosing drivers personal data to semi-honest insurers. It relies on Yao's garbled circuit for the computation of distances to clusters' centers. In addition, it uses a homomorphic additive and semantic secure encryption scheme for the computation of clusters new centers. Our future work will consist in implementing a proof of concept of the proposed solution and providing a complete security proof for the protocol.

References

1. Yao, A.C.C.: How to generate and exchange secrets. In: 27th Annual Symposium on Foundations of Computer Science, pp. 162–167. IEEE (1986)
2. Paillier, P.: Public-key cryptosystems based on composite degree residuosity classes. In: Stern, J. (ed.) EUROCRYPT 1999. LNCS, vol. 1592, pp. 223–238. Springer, Heidelberg (1999). https://doi.org/10.1007/3-540-48910-X_16
3. Troncoso, C., Danezis, G., Kosta, E., Balasch, J., Preneel, B.: PriPAYD: privacy-friendly pay-as-you-drive insurance. IEEE Trans. Dependable Secure Comput. 8(5), 742–755 (2011)
4. Kargl, F., Friedman, A., Boreli, R.: Differential privacy in intelligent transportation systems. In: Proceedings of the Sixth ACM Conference on Security and Privacy in Wireless and Mobile Networks, pp. 107–112. ACM (2013)
5. Rizzo, N., Sprissler, E., Hong, Y., Goel, S.: Privacy preserving driving style recognition. In: 2015 International Conference on Connected Vehicles and Expo (ICCVE), pp. 232–237. IEEE (2015)
6. MacQueen, J., et al.: Some methods for classification and analysis of multivariate observations. In: Proceedings of the Fifth Berkeley Symposium on Mathematical Statistics and Probability, Oakland, CA, USA, vol. 1, pp. 281–297 (1967)
7. Even, S., Goldreich, O., Lempel, A.: A randomized protocol for signing contracts. In: Chaum, D., Rivest, R.L., Sherman, A.T. (eds.) Advances in Cryptology, pp. 205–210. Springer, Boston, MA (1983). https://doi.org/10.1007/978-1-4757-0602-4_19
8. Naor, M., Pinkas, B., Pinkas, B.: Efficient oblivious transfer protocols. In: Proceedings of the Twelfth Annual ACM-SIAM Symposium on Discrete Algorithms SODA 2001, Philadelphia, PA, USA, Society for Industrial and Applied Mathematics, pp. 448–457 (2001)
9. Kolesnikov, V., Sadeghi, A.-R., Schneider, T.: Improved garbled circuit building blocks and applications to auctions and computing minima. In: Garay, J.A., Miyaji, A., Otsuka, A. (eds.) CANS 2009. LNCS, vol. 5888, pp. 1–20. Springer, Heidelberg (2009). https://doi.org/10.1007/978-3-642-10433-6_1
10. Lindell, Y., Pinkas, B.: A proof of security of yao's protocol for two-party computation. J. Cryptology 22(2), 161–188 (2009)
11. Buescher, N., Holzer, A., Weber, A., Katzenbeisser, S.: Compiling low depth circuits for practical secure computation. In: Askoxylakis, I., Ioannidis, S., Katsikas, S., Meadows, C. (eds.) ESORICS 2016. LNCS, vol. 9879, pp. 80–98. Springer, Cham (2016). https://doi.org/10.1007/978-3-319-45741-3_5
12. Schneider, T., Zohner, M.: GMW vs. Yao? Efficient secure two-party computation with low depth circuits. In: Sadeghi, A.-R. (ed.) FC 2013. LNCS, vol. 7859, pp. 275–292. Springer, Heidelberg (2013). https://doi.org/10.1007/978-3-642-39884-1_23
13. Kolesnikov, V., Schneider, T.: Improved garbled circuit: free XOR gates and applications. In: Aceto, L., Damgård, I., Goldberg, L.A., Halldórsson, M.M., Ingólfsdóttir, A., Walukiewicz, I. (eds.) ICALP 2008. LNCS, vol. 5126, pp. 486–498. Springer, Heidelberg (2008). https://doi.org/10.1007/978-3-540-70583-3_40
14. Garay, J., Schoenmakers, B., Villegas, J.: Practical and secure solutions for integer comparison. In: Okamoto, T., Wang, X. (eds.) PKC 2007. LNCS, vol. 4450, pp. 330–342. Springer, Heidelberg (2007). https://doi.org/10.1007/978-3-540-71677-8_22

Derandomized PACE with Mutual Authentication

Adam Bobowski$^{(\boxtimes)}$ and Mirosław Kutyłowski

Department of Computer Science, Wrocław University of Science and Technology,
Wrocław, Poland
adam.bobowski@pwr.edu.pl, miroslaw.kutylowski@pwr.wroc.pl

Abstract. We present a derandomized version of the ICAO protocol
PACE – a PAKE protocol (password authenticated key exchange) used
for identity documents including biometric passports and future European personal ID documents. The modification aims to remove necessity
of implementing random number generator and thereby reduce the cost
of the chip and its certification, while maintaining the level of security.
As a side effect we achieve better verifiability properties as well as chip
and terminal authentication.

Keywords: PAKE · PACE · Chip and terminal authentication ·
Derandomization

1 Introduction

Electronic identification is one of fundamental tasks when developing ubiquitous
systems. For the sake of personal identity documents a number of cryptographic
protocols has been developed by the ICAO organization [2]. They have been
deployed on biometric passports around the world and on some national ID cards.
A recent decision European Union authorities is to follow the ICAO specification
on all national ID cards issued by the member states.

One of the core schemes in the ICAO specification is PACE developed for
German identity documents by the German IT security authority BSI [1]. PACE
enables to establish a session (and its session keys) provided that both the chip
and the reader are using the same password. The goal of PACE is to prevent
activation of the chip without the consent of it holder. – in case of wireless
communication it might be particularly easy (skimming ID documents). PACE
is resistant to offline and online attacks aiming to derive the password used – the
only attack vector is to guess the password at random and check if the protocol
execution terminates successfully.

Current widespread adoption of PACE for the classical identity documents
suggests to adapt and reuse it in other areas, such as the IoT.

This research has been initiated in project OPUS 2014/15/B/ST6/02837 funded by
Polish National Science Centre, later supported by grant 049U/0044/19 at Wrocław
University of Science and Technology.

J. K. Liu and X. Huang (Eds.): NSS 2019, LNCS 11928, pp. 697–705, 2019.
https://doi.org/10.1007/978-3-030-36938-5_44

Moreover, due to its specific and proven features regarding (un)traceability, PACE is particularly attractive when high standards of personal data protection apply.

The PACE protocol (and the proposed extension) are presented on Fig. 1.

Implementation Issues. Selection of random elements, like in most cryptographic schemes, plays a crucial role in security of standard PACE protocol. Convenient assumption of having access to source of truly random elements solves many issues. On the other hand, in real world this theoretical assumption is almost practically unobtainable.

The problems might be diverse. First, a physical source of randomness might be affected by aging problems and start to provide biased and predictable output – in this case the whole security argumentation collapses. Second, if we apply solutions based on PRNG, then it is hard to guarantee that nobody knows the seed. Finally, verifying that a device is following the protocol and there is neither trapdoor utilizing randomness nor implementation errors is difficult. This increases substantially the costs of certification process and well as reduces the trust level.

Our Goals. Let us summarize our design approach:

derandomization: While there are cryptographic methods for constructing verifiable randomness, any solution to be deployed in practice must be extremely simple and effective. We follow a different strategy – we eliminate random elements and replace them by unpredictable elements.

backwards compatibility: The devices running our protocol should interact smoothly with the devices running the regular PACE (or PACE CAM).

indistinguishability: It should be infeasible for an observer to distinguish which version of the protocol is run. Therefore, many security and privacy properties of the regular PACE should be inherited.

deniability: Moreover, even a party executing the protocol should be unable to convince a third party that a presented protocol transcript has not been forged.

authentication: The protocol should enable strong authentication of communicating parties.

reuse: We wish to reuse the old designs and therefore the number of changes in the original protocol should be small. This reduces the effort in adjusting the old software to the new protocols.

password as a context: We concern the password not only as a guard against an illegitimate device activation. It should provide a context – only the devices with the same context should establish a session.

2   Deterministic PACE with Mutual Authentication

The protocol consists of 4 phases depicted on Fig. 1.

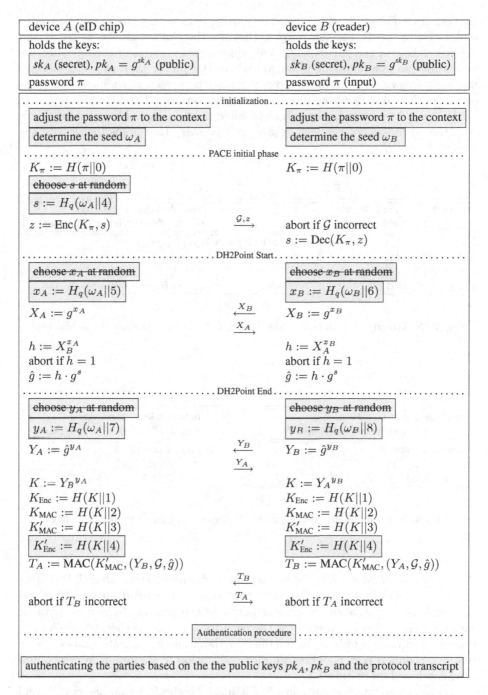

Fig. 1. A deterministic version of the PACE protocol with mutual authentication. Changes to the original PACE are marked in gray boxes (with the original version striked out.)

Initialization Phase. In this phase the participants adjust the shared password and derive the seeds. For this purpose they use the *context* Δ (see Sect. 2.1) and the secret keys of the participants. We propose two versions of the initialization procedure: an non-anonymous version where the public keys pk_A and pk_B are mutually known, and an anonymous version where each participant uses only own keys. The details of the proposal are given on Figs. 2 and 3.

We intend to simplify as much as possible the first case. The price for this is that the scheme is not resilient against an adversary that holds the private key of, say, device B.

device A	device B
holds the keys: sk_A (secret)	holds the keys: sk_B (secret)
$pk_A = g^{sk_A}$ (public), π' (password)	$pk_B = g^{sk_B}$ (public), π' (password)
A and B exchange their public keys pk_A, pk_B	
$\theta := pk_B^{sk_A}, \quad$ acquire context Δ	$\theta := pk_A^{sk_B}, \quad$ acquire context Δ
$\pi := H(\theta\|\Delta\|1\|\pi')$	$\pi := H(\theta\|\Delta\|1\|\pi')$
$\omega_A := H_G(\theta\|\Delta\|2)$	$\omega_B := H_G(\theta\|\Delta\|2)$

Fig. 2. Non-anonymous initialization - the devices must exchange the public keys

device A	device B
holds the keys: sk_A (secret)	holds the keys: sk_B (secret)
$pk_A = g^{sk_A}$ (public), π' (password)	$pk_B = g^{sk_B}$ (public), π' (password)
acquire context Δ	acquire context Δ
$\pi := H(\Delta\|1\|\pi')$	$\pi := H(\Delta\|1\|\pi')$
$\zeta := H_G(\Delta\|2), \quad \omega_A := \zeta^{sk_A}$	$\zeta := H_G(\Delta\|2), \quad \omega_B := \zeta^{sk_B}$

Fig. 3. Anonymous initialization: the devices do not show their public keys

Authentication Phase. This phase is executed immediately after PACE (see Fig. 4). It consists of a common part that does not depend on the initialization and the initialization dependent parts. In the case of the non-anonymous case no extra action is required (as the equality $\omega_A = \omega_B$ is checked implicitly). Figure 5 contains details corresponding to the anonymous initialization. Note that the common part may contain also verification of the public keys pk_B and pk_A, e.g. based on certificates.

In case of anonymous initialization it must be checked that $\omega_A = \zeta^{sk_A}$ and $\omega_B = \zeta^{sk_B}$. In fact, the authentication proof is based on the KEA1 assumption: as the discrete logarithm of ζ is unknown, nobody but the holder of sk_A can compute ζ^{sk_A} (resp., only the holder of sk_B can compute ζ^{sk_B}). So we deal with

device A	device B
.... retrieval and verification of seeds	
procedure dependent on initialization	
.... verification of the execution transcript	
abort if $X_B \neq g^{H_q(\omega_B \| 6)}$	abort if $X_A \neq g^{H_q(\omega_A \| 5)}$
abort if $Y_B \neq \hat{g}^{H_q(\omega_B \| 8)}$	abort if $Y_A \neq \hat{g}^{H_q(\omega_A \| 7)}$
	abort if $s \neq H_q(\omega_A \| 4)$
verify pk_B	verify pk_A
.... authentication of seeds	
procedure dependant on initialization	

Fig. 4. Common part of authentication.

the problem of equality of discrete logarithms for the tuples $(g, pk_A, \zeta, \omega_A)$ and $(g, pk_B, \zeta, \omega_B)$. A solution based on Schnorr signatures may be the simplest, but it requires random numbers and leaves an undeniable proof of interaction.

In Fig. 5 we instantiate the authentication process with a textbook procedure.

Note that it starts with a choice of random elements. Hence it may appear that we need a source of strong randomness - just violating our assumptions. However, here we only need that these numbers are to some degree unpredictable for the other side of the protocol. Unlike in the case of Schnorr signatures, it does not endanger the secret keys – it only makes the proof of equality of discrete logarithms weaker.

2.1 Comments on Design Approach

Complexity. In practice, for devices like smart cards or sensors a small storage capacity is one of the key limitations. For this reason reusing the same code or adding just a few lines of code might be crucial for implementability of a scheme. For similar reasons, the communication volume and the number of messages exchanged should be minimized.

Modularity. Depending on the application case, there might be different requirements for the strength of authentication. Sometimes the pure password authentication is enough and any kind of strong authentication of a protocol participant would violate the *data minimality* principle. So we follow the approach where authentication comes as a plug-and-play component that can be injected into the original code. Our scheme can be modified easily and enable to authenticate either both communicating parties or only one of them or none of them. Note that in the ICAO specification contains the PACE CAM protocol with strong authentication of the ID document. However, it needs a secure PRNG - otherwise the secret key may leak.

Context. The parameter Δ from the protocol description may have different origins and play different roles. For example, in case of VANET, sometimes only

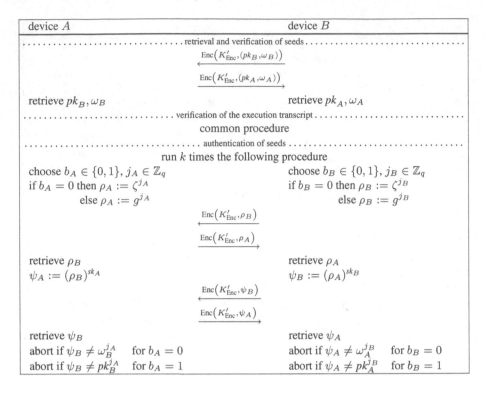

Fig. 5. Details of authentication in case of anonymous initialization.

the vehicles in a close proximity should establish communication. In order to enforce this, Δ may contain an (approximate) GPS location or a string broadcasted locally by a Road Side Unit. Another option is an optical channel. Δ may be encoded in a QR code exposed to the communicating devices (like in case of the WeChat and Alipay systems). Finally, Δ might follow from the past events – e.g. contain a nonce from the previous interaction.

3　Security Discussion

A detailed security proof even for the standard PACE turns out to be quite long and tedious, if we take into account active adversaries and privacy issues (see [4] for a draft!). Therefore in this paper we provide only some comments on the crucial issues.

Privacy Features of PACE. Privacy protection was apparently one of the main goals for the designers of PACE. However, it is hard to express exactly what privacy protection means and to present the relevant models. Fortunately, one can allude the problem by determining situations where there are no concerns about privacy protection.

Similarly to the Abdalla model and the left-or-right games we can attempt to show that given access to a protocol execution an adversary cannot distinguish whether it has been executed with the keys attributed to a given participant or situation (when the password is derived from e.g. location), or with ad hoc keys selected at random. In this situation any kind of conclusion regarding the device's identity is impossible.

For PACE one can show that even if an adversary knows a password, then he cannot distinguish between a protocol execution with this password and a protocol execution with a random password - the only exception is when the adversary executes the protocol himself [4]. This property follows from the KEA1 assumption: deriving the shared key in the Diffie-Hellmann protocol by the adversary indicates that they knows at least one of the exponents used. However, this might be an Achilles heel of PACE for weak devices: if a source of randomness is corrupted on one side, then the argument fails.

Full Key Compromise. Now let us consider our schemes. First note that if an adversary knows the key sk_A or sk_B and Δ, then he can easily check whether a given communication transcript corresponds to these keys and derive the session keys. Simply, the adversary mimics the deterministic computation of A or B. If Δ is unknown but has low entropy, then the same attack applies – it suffices to recompute X_A (resp., X_B) and compare with the value transmitted.

The attack described above cannot be prevented as long as the computation is deterministic. Unfortunately, for the regular PACE the situation need not to be better as the protocol might be based on a PRNG with a secret seed. The seed might be compromised or replaced after subverting the device. Detecting or preventing this attack requires nontrivial countermeasures (such as watchdogs).

Reduction Arguments. Security of our schemes is based on the fact that an adversary cannot distinguish between executions of our protocols and the cases where the key steps are randomized again to meet the original specification. So we can argue that certain properties are the same as for the original PACE.

From now on we assume that the adversary knows neither sk_A nor sk_B. However, we admit that the adversary may guess Δ.

Non-anonymous Initialization Case. The first observation is that due to difficulty of the DDH Problem, the adversary should not see any difference in the protocol execution when we replace θ by a random element. Then to proceed we need the Correlated Input Hash Assumption (CIHA) [4]:

One cannot distinguish between the tuples $H(C_1(r)), \ldots, H(C_n(r))$ and the random tuples of the same length and from the same domain provided that the circuits $C_1, \ldots, C_n$ are in some sense independent and min-entropy of their output is sufficiently large.

It is impossible to use directly CIHA for π and ω_A, since different hash functions H and H_G are used. However, one can define H_G as a composition: $H_G(x) = F(H(x))$. Thus, we can assume that the adversary would not see any difference if we replace π and ω_A by random values. Then in the same way we may replace the derivation for s, x_A, x_B, y_A, y_B by the random choice.

As the initialization and authentication phases are executed without any interaction, this finalizes the argument in this case.

Anonymous Initialization Case. In this case the adversary can derive π and ζ, as he knows Δ. However, due to the DDH Assumption, the adversary cannot distinguish the original computation from the computation where ω_A and ω_B are chosen independently at random. The next step is to replace the derivation for s, x_A, x_B, y_A, y_B by the random choice and argue that due to CIHA the adversary cannot see any difference.

After the changes, the main part of the protocol is exactly the original PACE (apart from computing additional key K'_{Enc}). However, there is still the authentication part presented on Fig. 5. Now we can replace the computation of ψ_A and ψ_B by random values and skip the tests from the last two lines in Fig. 5. (Effectively, we can simply replace the last four ciphertexts with random values.) Again, the adversary cannot detect the manipulation, even when given an oracle for decryption of the last 4 messages. The only remaining part dependent on the participants' keys are the ciphertexts exchanged in the first part of the authentication phase. These key are unrelated now to the rest of the computation, so we are now in the situation of the original PACE, where the session key is used for encrypting some data. One can provide an argument based on the security of PACE that the plaintexts can be replaced by random elements. (Note that the key K'_{Enc} has been introduced only for the sake of a formal proof at this point.)

Active Adversary. In general, an active adversary acting as man-in-the-middle is the most interesting and complicated case for any protocol. The difficulty comes from the fact that the number of possible attack scenarios is enormous. However, in our case we can follow [4] showing protocol's fragility: it means that if an adversary manipulates any message, then the protocol execution will change the behavior of the protocol parties always in the same way. We postpone the details to the full version of the paper.

Deniability. A dishonest protocol participant, say A, might create a proof of interaction with B, and offer it to third parties. In case of PACE this is doable due to the extensive use of randomness enabling malicious cryptography. Derandomization applied to our protocols helps here a lot: in case of the non-anonymous initialization the responses of B can be created by A himself. In case of anonymous initialization the issue is slightly more complicated: A cannot create ω_B, but on the other hand if the proof is created by A before presenting the data for sale, then A can present any value as ω_B together with a fake proof from the authentication phase.

Authentication. In the non-anonymous case party A can compute the values x_B and y_B to be used by B. On the other hand, x_A and x_B are computed as hash values, so A may assume that B knows the arguments used to compute these hash values (this feature is captured by the Extractable Hash Function property – cf. [3]). Hence B must know ω_B and then in turn must know θ. However, by the KEA1 Assumption, if B can compute θ given the keys pk_A and pk_B, then B knows either sk_A or sk_B. If A is sure about secrecy of its key sk_A, then the other party is either B (holding sk_B) or a party that has got either sk_B or θ from B. The same argument applies for authentication of B against A.

The price to be paid for protocol simplicity is twofold. First, A can be cheated if sk_A is compromised. Second, B can delegate its ability to talk with A by presenting θ to a third party. If this is unacceptable for an application scenario, then anonymous initialization should be used.

In the case of anonymous initialization the situation is less complicated. A accepts B, if B presents ω_B which, due to the interactive proof in the last phase, equals to ζ^{sk_B} with a high probability. As the discrete logarithm of ζ is unknown (recall that ζ has been computed as a hash value), by KEA1 we can conclude that B must have known sk_B. The same argument concerns authenticating A against B.

References

1. BSI: Technical guideline TR-03110 v2.21 - advanced security mechanisms for machine readable travel documents and eIDAS token (2016)
2. ICAO: machine readable travel documents - part 11: security mechanism for MRTDs. Doc 9303 (2015)
3. Kiayias, A., Liu, F., Tselekounis, Y.: Practical non-malleable codes from l-more extractable hash functions. In: Weippl, E.R., Katzenbeisser, S., Kruegel, C., Myers, A.C., Halevi, S. (eds.) Proceedings of ACM CCS 2016, pp. 1317–1328. ACM (2016)
4. Kubiak, P., Kutyłowski, M.: Privacy and security analysis of PACE GM protocol. In: TrustCom/BigData 2019 Proceedings, pp. 763–768 (2019)

A Multi-attributes-Based Trust Model of Internet of Vehicle

Wei Ou[1]($\boxtimes$), Entao Luo[1], Zhiyuan Tan[2], Lihong Xiang[1], Qin Yi[1], and Chen Tian[1]

[1] Hunan University of Science and Engineering, Yongzhou, China
ouwei1978430@163.com
[2] School of Computing, Edinburgh Napier University, Edinburgh, UK

Abstract. Internet of Vehicle (IoV) is an open network and it changes in constant, where there are large number of entities. Effective way to keep security of data in IoV is to establish a trustworthy mechanism. Through transmission and dissemination of trust, credibility of the entity of IoV is calculated and measured. In this paper a multi-attributes-based trust model is proposed. When the trust relationship between nodes is evaluated, overall experiences of the evaluator are considered as the main reference content, which have a significant restraining effect on malicious behaviors of bad nodes. Moreover, this model combines heuristic algorithm and takes the previous trust evaluation as an important reference content. Thus accuracy of evaluation of trust relationship is improved and sensitivity of this algorithm on behaviors of nodes is enhanced.

Keywords: Internet of Vehicle · Multidimensional attributes · Direct trust · Recommendation trust · Trust evaluation

1 Introduction

Internet of Vehicle (IoV) refers to the realization of all-round network connection in vehicles, vehicles and persons, vehicles and vehicles, vehicles and roads, vehicles and service platforms with help of new generation of information and communication technologies. It improves the level of intelligent vehicles and automatic driving ability and constructs new business form of automobile and traffic services. It improves traffic efficiency and driving experiences, and provide users with intelligent, comfortable, safe, energy-saving and efficient comprehensive services [1]. Internet of Vehicle is centered on "both ends – cloud", supplemented by roadbed facilities, including intelligent networked cars, mobile intelligent terminals, car networking service platforms and other objects. It involves five communication scenarios: vehicle-cloud communication, vehicle-vehicle communication, vehicle-to-person communication, vehicle-road communication, and in-vehicle communication [2]. As shown in Fig. 1.

Internet of Vehicle is an open network that is constantly changing. There are a large number of entities, such as floating cars and various types of drive test equipment. The effective way to ensure data security in network is to establish a trust mechanism, through the transmission and dissemination of trust. Calculating and measuring the credibility

© Springer Nature Switzerland AG 2019
J. K. Liu and X. Huang (Eds.): NSS 2019, LNCS 11928, pp. 706–713, 2019.
https://doi.org/10.1007/978-3-030-36938-5_45

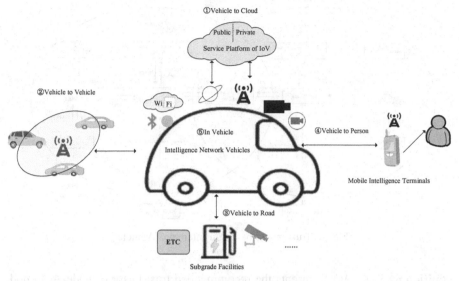

Fig. 1. Application scene of IoV

of the target entity, and selecting the data provided by the reliable entity as the object of processing is to ensure that the result is more accurate and close to the real data. At present, the trust model of Internet of Vehicle mainly has four problems: ① Lack of trust model to consider multi-application scenarios. ② Lack of trust calculation method to support dynamic update. ③ Lack of ability to adapt to a dynamic trust decision-making mechanism. ④ Lack of consideration for future communication environments.

2 Description of Trust Model

2.1 Basic Definitions

The multi-attributes-based trust model based on IoV [3, 4] is shown in Fig. 2.

Definition 1. Multidimensional vector A: $\overline{A} = [A_1, A_2, \cdots, A_i], i \in N$. A_i represents the transaction trust of node A of IoV in terms of i.

Definition 2. If node A_i in domain A is not the first transaction with node B_j in domain B, $hdtv_{B_j}^{A_i}$ represents the last historical direct trust between A_i and B_j. $dtv_{B_j}^{A_i}$ represents the direct trust between A_i and B_j.

Definition 3. $dt_{A_j}^{TA}$ represents the direct trust of domain agent to node A_j.

Definition 4. $rtv_{A_i}^A$ represents the recommended trust of domain A to node A_i.

Definition 5. The recommended trust of domain A to domain B is defined as rtv_B^A. $rtv_{B_j}^{A_i}$ represents the recommended trust of node A_i and node B_j.

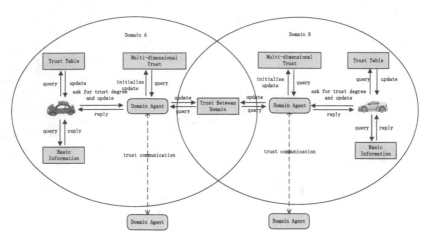

Fig. 2. Trust model based on Internet of Vehicle

Definition 6. $R(A_i, A_k)$ represents the recommended trust factor of node A_i to node A_k. Range of the value is [0, 1].

Definition 7. Domain maintains two tables, one is the trust table in the domain. Each node in the domain maintains a value of trust, which is used to describe performance of nodes in services. It is defined as f_{A-A_i}. It represents the trust value of the node A_i granted by the admin domain A.

Definition 8. The number of successful transactions between nodes are defined as S.

Definition 9. The number of unsuccessful transactions between nodes are defined as f.

2.2 Calculation of Trust

(1) **Initialization of Trust**

For newly registered nodes, each domain agent is obliged to give them an appropriate initial trust value. If the trust value is too low, it will not meet the conditions of transactions between nodes. If the trust value is too high, some malicious nodes will use the method of rc-registering node to improve their trust value, which will damage the programs of other nodes. Reference [5] sets the initial trust value of the newly joined node to 0.5, and then improves or reduces trust of the node according to its performance.

(2) **Calculation of Direct Trust**

Direct trust refers to the direct transaction between two nodes in the past. Thus a direct trust relationship is established. The source of trust value is based on the transaction between two nodes.

Calculation of direct trust has the following two situations:

- Node A_i and node B_j have ever traded. For both parties, current trust can be calculated by direct trust of the latest history. Considering the time decay factor, direct trust of current two nodes is as shown in the following formula:

$$dtv_{B_j}^{A_i} = hdtv_{B_j}^{A_i} * T(\Delta t, \sigma) \tag{1}$$

In formula (1), $T(\Delta t, \sigma)$ is time decay function, Δt is time difference between current time and the latest transaction, σ is type of transaction and it represents some kind of scientific calculation, data storage and file download. Time decay function is as follows:

$$T(\Delta t, \sigma) = \frac{1}{\Delta t + 1} \tag{2}$$

- When transaction between two nodes is completed, current trust between them needs to be calculated. Trust of a single service is shown in the following formula:

$$dtv_{B_j}^{A_i} = f(\sigma, \omega) = \sum_{k=1}^{n} \gamma_k \omega_k \tag{3}$$

In formula (3) ω represents dimension of service trust and γ_k represents the Kth dimension coefficient which satisfies the expression $\sum_{k=1}^{n} \gamma_k \omega_k$. This expression is suitable for any case regardless of whether there has been a transaction between two nodes.

(3) Calculation of Recommendation Trust in Domain

Recommendation trust in domain, that is indirect trust in domain, refers to the fact that there has never been a direct transaction between two nodes in same domain. Source of trust value is based on recommendation and evaluation of other nodes. Calculation of recommendation trust in domain can be divided into the following two cases:

- Node A_i in domain needs to evaluate trust of another node A_j in another domain. Firstly, neighbors of node A_i are asked whether they have had direct transactions with node A_j. If so, recommended trust between nodes is shown in the following formula:

$$rtv_{A_j}^{A_i} = \frac{\sum_{k-1}^{n} rtv_{A_k}^{A_i} * R(A_i, A_k) * dtv_{A_j}^{A_k}}{\sum_{k-1}^{n} rtv_{A_k}^{A_i} * R(A_i, A_k)} \tag{4}$$

- If two transaction nodes belong to the same domain, they can directly ask domain agent TA (Trust Agent) of that domain. Nodes can trust domain agent completely, as shown in the following formula:

$$rtv_{A_j}^{A_i} = dt_{A_j}^{TA} \tag{5}$$

(4) Calculation of Recommendation Trust Between Domains

Recommendation trust between domains refers to trust recommendation between trust agents when two nodes that do not belong to the same domain judge each other's trust. If the neighbor node has a direct transaction with the target node, then the formula (4) and formula (5) can be used to calculate the trust. In contrary, if the neighbor node has no direct transaction with the target node (service provider), then the domain agent must find a recommended trust path. Here, we can abstract the trust relationship between domains into a directed graph. Each domain is represented by each node in the graph. The trust relationship between domains is represented by the edge of the graph. It is recorded as a directed graph G = (V, E). Nodes (service applicants) need to send requests of trust recommendation and basic information of target nodes to domain agents. Trust agent needs to find a recommendation path and calculate trust of target node. As shown in Fig. 3.

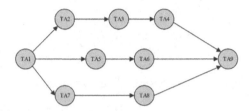

Fig. 3. Recommendation trust between domains

Describe the above situation as G = (V, E). Here we use the method *the shortest path maximum trust value* to select the most suitable path. As shown in Fig. 3, there are three paths: TA2-TA3-TA4, TA5-TA6 and TA7-TA8. Firstly the shortest path is selected. We can see that TA5-TA6 and TA7-TA8 are the shortest path. Then we select the maximum value of trust from the two paths. The method of calculating trust value is as follows:

$$
\text{rtv}_{B_j}^{A_i} = \text{dt}_{B_j}^{TA} * \prod_{k=m}^{n-1} \text{rtv}_{TA_{k+1}}^{TA_k} \tag{6}
$$

2.3   Trust Updating

(1) Trust Update of Nodes

After using services provided by node B_j, node A_i needs to update its own direct trust table to reflect changes of trust relationship between them. If node A_i is satisfied with the service of node B_j, it needs to improve the trust of node B_j. In contrary it needs to reduce its trust. As shown in the following:

$$
\text{hdtv}_{B_j}^{A_i} = \text{dtv}_{B_j}^{A_i} = f(\sigma, \omega) = \sum_{k=1}^{n} \gamma_k \omega_k \tag{7}
$$

Formula (7) is also applicable to the case that two nodes belong to the same domain.

(2) Updating of Trust in Domain

Trust tables in domain agents need to be updated after the transaction between two nodes. If the transaction is successful, trust value of corresponding nodes will increase. On the contrary it decreases. As shown in the following:

$$\begin{cases} f_{A-A_i} = H + \mu \times \varphi(s) & Transaction\ Successed \\ f_{A-A_i} = H - \mu \times \varphi(f) & Transaction\ Failed \\ \varphi(x) = e^{-1/x} \end{cases} \tag{8}$$

In formula (8) $\mu(0 < \mu < 1)$ represents updating coefficient, H represents the trust value before updating, s and f represent the number of success and failure respectively. Referring to Beth model, we define $\varphi(x) = e^{-1/x}$ and make $\varphi(x)$ increases with increases of x. Because of $\mu(0 < \mu < 1)$, it can be concluded that the more number of success is, the faster trust value increases. On the contrary the faster trust value decreases. When total trust value of a node is reduced to certain value, if it is less than zero, the domain agent will kick the node out.

For updating coefficient, the data in reference [6] is used as the updating coefficient of success transaction when $\mu_1 = 0.01$. And when $\mu_2 = 0.1$ it is used as the updating coefficient for failure transaction. The purpose is to reduce the trust value of malicious nodes when they provide services that harm other nodes.

(3) Updating of Trust Between Domains

Assuming that two nodes from different domains trade with each other, if the transaction succeeds, the trust value between domains involved in the recommendation increases and on the contrary decreases. For the specific value of increase or decrease, it should be based on the number of success or failure transactions between nodes. As shown in the following:

$$\begin{cases} rtv_B^A = H + \mu \times \varphi(s) & Transaction\ Successed \\ rtv_B^A = H - \mu \times \varphi(f) & Transaction\ Failed \\ \varphi(x) = e^{-1/x} \end{cases} \tag{9}$$

3 Experiments

We demonstrate security and effectiveness of our algorithm through simulation experiments. The main verification contents are sensitivity and accuracy of our algorithm in describing the trust relationship between nodes of IoV.

The service providers of this experiment were randomly selected. The steps to provide the service are as follows: Firstly, we ensure that the first 30 services are of high quality, then provide 20 low quality services, at last provide 50 quality services. It can be known from experiments (as shown in Fig. 4) that through use of our calculation methods, the results of the experimental objects will change accordingly due to the quality of the service. Moreover, although the quality of service has risen to the previous level and the quantity provided has far exceeded the original level, its trust value cannot be

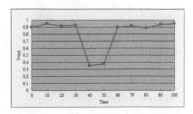

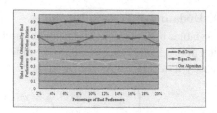

Fig. 4. Sensitivity and accuracy   **Fig. 5.** Containment of bad nodes

restored to its original level. It can be seen that the algorithm can make rapid feedback on the situation of degraded service quality, thus effectively curbing the cheating trend of malicious nodes.

After completing the above experiment, 20% of the nodes were randomly selected as bad nodes, and 60% of them were normal nodes to provide good quality of service. In this experiment, the results calculated by model PathTrust show that the interest ratio between the normal node and the malicious node is almost the same (as shown in Fig. 5). It can be seen that the Path Trust algorithm has poor ability to constrain bad nodes, and the algorithm incorporates a penalty mechanism to control the benefits of bad nodes below 60%. Compared with the Path Trust algorithm, bad nodes have a higher cost in our algorithm.

4   Conclusion

In this paper the trust model of Internet of Vehicle is studied and analyzed. From aspects of trust initialization, trust calculation and trust updating, we propose a trust model for Internet of Vehicle. When evaluating the trust relationship between nodes, overall experiences of the evaluator are considered as the main reference content, which have a significant restraining effect on malicious behaviors of bad nodes. Moreover, our model combines heuristic algorithm and takes the previous trust evaluation as an important reference content. Thus accuracy of evaluation of trust relationship is improved and sensitivity of our algorithm on behaviors of nodes is enhanced.

Acknowledgements. This work was supported by the construct program of applied characteristic discipline in Hunan University of Science and Engineering.

References

1. Security of Internet of Vehicle. China Information and Communication Research Institute (2017)
2. Zhang, Z.: Study on grid multidimensional trust model based on fuzzy comprehensive evaluation. Qufu Normal University (2014)
3. Wang, L., Yang, S.: A trust model in the grid environment. Comput. Eng. Appl. **40**(23), 50–53 (2004)

4. Richardson, M., Agrawal, R., Domingos, P.: Trust management for the semantic web. In: Fensel, D., Sycara, K., Mylopoulos, J. (eds.) ISWC 2003. LNCS, vol. 2870, pp. 351–368. Springer, Heidelberg (2003). https://doi.org/10.1007/978-3-540-39718-2_23
5. Ahn, J., Sui, X.: Identifying beneficial teammates using multi-dimensional trust. In: Proceedings of the 7th International Joint Conference on Autonomous Agents and Multiagent Systems, pp. 1469–1472 (2008)
6. Li, K., Jiang, H.: A trust model with classification decision attributes. Comput. Technol. Dev. **20**(03), 36–39+43 (2010)

Using Sparse Composite Document Vectors to Classify VBA Macros

Mamoru Mimura[✉]

National Defense Academy, Yokosuka, Japan
mim@nda.ac.jp

Abstract. To detect new macro malware, NLP-based detection methods have been proposed. These methods mainly use a Doc2vec model to represent the source code, which provides a vector space to classify malicious macros and benign ones. Recently, more sophisticated models outperform Doc2vec in performance and time complexity. However, there is no study to compare these language models for macro malware detection. In this paper, we focus on Sparse Composite Document Vectors (SCDV), which is a simple feature construction algorithm. To evaluate the performance for malware detection, we compare SCDV and other language models: Bag-of Words, Latent Semantic Indexing (LSI), Doc2vec. The experimental result with actual macro malware shows the most suitable language model for macro malware detection.

Keywords: VBA macro · SVM · NLP · Bag-of-Words · LSI · Doc2vec · SCDV

1 Introduction

Visual Basic for Applications (VBA) is an implementation of Microsoft's programming language, which enables building user-defined functions, automating processes and accessing Windows API and other low-level functionality through dynamic-link libraries. VBA macros can be created with malicious intent such as infecting target computers. To detect new macro malware, NLP-based detection methods have been proposed [4,5]. The idea is applying Natural Language Processing (NLP) techniques to the source code. These methods mainly use a language model to represent the source code, which provides a vector space to classify malicious VBA macros and benign ones. Recently, more sophisticated models outperform Doc2vec in performance and time complexity. However, there is no study to compare these language models for malicious macro detection. Hence, the most suitable language model for macro malware detection is still open to discussion. In this paper, we focus on the language model. No previous study focused on the differences among language models in the cyber security field. Our goal is revealing the most suitable language model for macro malware detection. In particular, our detection model uses Sparse Composite Document Vectors (SCDV) for malware detection, which is a simple feature construction

© Springer Nature Switzerland AG 2019
J. K. Liu and X. Huang (Eds.): NSS 2019, LNCS 11928, pp. 714–720, 2019.
https://doi.org/10.1007/978-3-030-36938-5_46

algorithm [3]. To evaluate the performance of our method, thousands of actual VBA macros are obtained from Virus Total[1]. Moreover, we compare the SCDV model and other language models: BoW, LSI, and Doc2vec.

To the best of our knowledge, this is the first attempt to apply SCDV to malware detection. This study is also the first attempt to compare comprehensive language models for malware detection. The main contributions of this paper are summarized as follows.

- Apply SCDV to macro malware detection.
- Compare the SCDV model and other language models comprehensively.
- The performance will maintain at least 2 years.
- Updating the training models improve the performance significantly.

2 Related Work

There are several methods to detect malicious VBA macros. Bearden et al. proposed a method to classify MS Office files contain VBA macros as malicious or benign with the K-Nearest Neighbors algorithm [1]. Kim et al. proposed an obfuscated macro code detection method with machine learning classifiers [2]. These methods are not evaluated with the time series datasets. We proposed a method to detect malicious VBA macros with Doc2vec [4] and LSI [5]. These methods extract words from the source code, and constructs a language model to represent VBA macros for classifiers. Based on this method, our detection model uses various language models to represent VBA macros.

3 SCDV

To apply machine learning techniques to documents, the documents have to be converted into vectors. This section provides SCDV a method to convert documents into vectors. SCDV combines syntax and semantics learnt by word embedding models together with a latent topic model which could handle different senses of words. The topic space is learnt efficiently using a clustering technique over embeddings and the final document vectors are converted sparsely. Figure 1 shows the outline.

The feature formation algorithm can be divided into three steps. First, word embeddings in the vocabulary are divided into clusters. The number of clusters K to be formed is a parameter of the SCDV model. Second, this model creates different word cluster vectors by weighing the word embedding with its probability distribution in the cluster. Thereafter, this model concatenates all word cluster vectors into a hundreds dimensional embedding, and weigh it with inverse document frequency of a word to form a word topics vector. Finally, for all words appearing in a document, this model sums their word topic vectors to obtain the document vector.

---

[1] https://www.virustotal.com/.

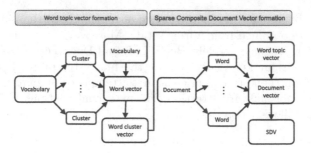

Fig. 1. Word topics vector and Sparse Composite Document Vector formation.

4   Experimental Model

4.1   Outline

To evaluate the performance of SCDV model, we developed our experimental model with 4 language models. Figure 2 shows the outline of the experimental model.

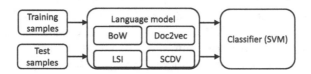

Fig. 2. Outline of the experimental model.

First, our experimental model extracts words from training VBA macros, and constructs language models. For the sake of comparison, our experimental model uses 4 language models: BoW, LSI, Doc2vec, and SCDV. Subsequently, the labeled feature vectors are extracted from training VBA macros by the language models, and trains the SVM classifier.

In the test phase, feature vectors are extracted from test VBA macros by the trained language models. Thereafter, the trained SVM classifier predicts the labels from the feature vectors.

4.2   Environment

Our experimental model is written in the Python language. The experiments are conducted on the computer with Windows 10, Core i9-7900X 3.3 GHz CPU, 128 GB DDR4 memory, and GeForce GTX1080/11G. To implement each language model and a classifier, our experimental model uses gensim and scikit-learn. These are popular libraries to provide various language models or machine learning models. To implement the SCDV model, our experimental model uses the Word2vec model.

5   Evaluation

5.1   Dataset

To evaluate our experimental model, the datasets are constructed from actual VBA macros. These samples are obtained from VirusTotal, which is a popular virus sample distribution site. Table 1 shows the number of VBA macros.

Table 1. The number of VBA macros obtained from virus total

Label	2015	2016	2017	Total
Benign	622	1,200	2,220	4,042
Malicious	870	1,150	1,083	3,103

Malicious samples are VBA macros which are judged as malicious by more than 50% of security vendors. Malware in targeted attacks is not always shared by all security vendors. Moreover, these vendors require enough time to add the correct label. Hence, we chose enough-old samples which had been completely analyzed. Benign samples are judged as benign all security vendors. The datasets are organized in chronological order to evaluate the persistence of the detection model, according to the first upload date.

5.2   Methodology

First, we conduct 5-fold cross-validation with 2015's dataset to evaluate the generalized performance. Next, we use 2015's samples as the training data, and 2016's samples as the test data. In the time series analysis, we repeat 5 times to remove the training bias. Moreover, we vary the number of clusters in the SCDV model to derive the optimum value. Furthermore, we conduct additional experiments to evaluate the long-term performance and how update improves the performance. To evaluate the long-term performance, we use 2017's samples as the test data. Finally, we renew the training data and confirm how this improves the performance.

5.3   Result

Figure 3 shows the result of the 5-fold cross-validation and average scores of the time series analysis.

The vertical axis indicates each performance. In the cross-validation, LSI and SCDV produced slightly better performance than other language models. All metrics achieved almost perfect. As we expected, BoW is less than other language models even in cross-validation. In the time series analysis, the performance is generally reduced due to the realistic restriction. Regarding to accuracy and f1 score, Doc2vec produced the best performance than other language models.

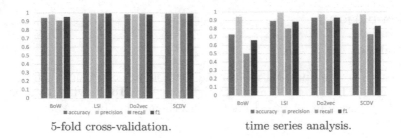

5-fold cross-validation.   time series analysis.

Fig. 3. Result of the 5-fold cross-validation and time series analysis

The best f1 score achieves 0.93. LSI provides the second best performance. Contrary to expectations, SCDV does not produce better performance. The SCDV is, however, decent and better than BoW.

Table 2 shows the average required time of the time series analysis.

Table 2. Average required time of the time series analysis.

	BoW	LSI	Doc2vec	SCDV
Construction	-	3.8 s	21.3 s	1.5 s
Training	1.1 s	0.2 s	0.1 s	0.3 s
Detection	0.1 s	0.1 s	0.1 s	0.1 s

The construction indicates the time for the language model construction. In the SCDV model, the construction includes the entire process such as cluster formation and document vector formation. The training and detection indicate the time for the SVM classifier. Doc2vec requires more time than other language models for training which includes construction time. All language models could inspect 2,350 samples within 0.1 s.

Next, we varied the number of clusters in the SCDV model. Figure 4 shows the performance in each cluster number.

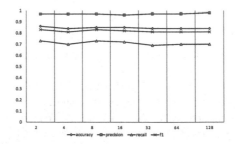

Fig. 4. Performance in each cluster number.

The vertical axis indicates each performance, and horizontal axis indicates the number of clusters. Regardless of the clusters, the performance remains almost flat. Hence, the number of clusters will be set to 2 for binary classification in the following experiments.

Thereafter, we replaced 2016's datasets with 2017's as the test data, and replaced 2015's datasets with 2016's as the training data to renew the training model. Figure 5 shows the long-term performance and improved performance.

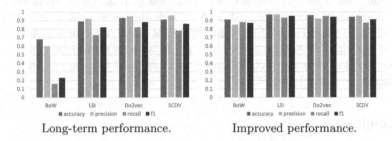

Long-term performance.   Improved performance.

Fig. 5. Long-term performance of the detection model and the improved performance by updating the training model.

The vertical axis indicates each performance. Even though the training model is constructed over a year ago, the LSI, Doc2vec, and SCDV models maintain decent performance. The best f1 score achieves 0.88 in the Doc2vec model. In contrast, the BoW model could no longer classify VBA macros. After updating the training model, all models improved the performance significantly. The best f1 score achieves 0.95 in the LSI model. The Doc2vec and SCDV model also achieves more than 0.9. Thus, time aging slightly reduces the performance in the LSI, Doc2vec, and SCDV models. This can be improved by updating the training models. In the BoW model, time aging dramatically reduces the performance.

6 Discussion

In the cross-validation, LSI and SCDV produced better performance than other language models. In the time series analysis, Doc2vec produced the best performance than other language models. Hence, we conclude that LSI and SCDV are effective to classify known VBA macros. According to the experimental result, Doc2vec is the most effective language model to classify unknown VBA macros. Despite the training model is constructed over a year ago, the LSI, Doc2vec, and SCDV models maintain the performance. According to the result, the performance will maintain at least 2 years. Hence, we conclude the LSI, Doc2vec, and SCDV models are persistent. In particular, Doc2vec is the most persistent language model to classify unknown VBA macros.

These language models require time for training. In this experiment, these language models with 1,492 samples were constructed in seconds or tens of seconds. Hence, we could update the language models within practical time. Updating the training models improve the performance significantly. The large scale of samples might increase the training time. The detection model, however, could construct the language models in advance. All language models could inspect 2,350 samples within 0.1 s. Hence, we conclude the detection model could detect malicious VBA macros within practical time.

According to the study [3], SCDV outperforms previous methods in multi-class and multi-label classification tasks. The performance is evaluated by 5-fold cross-validation of 20 news groups on an almost balanced dataset with SVM. In our study, the result of 5-fold cross-validation of binary classification on an almost balanced dataset was almost perfect. This suggests our dataset for binary classification is easier. Hence, SCDV might be not suitable for such a simple task. To reveal the suitable task, more complicated datasets should be generated by huge samples. Perhaps more complicated tasks such as malware family classification might be suitable for SCDV.

7   Conclusion

In this paper, we focus on Sparse Composite Document Vectors (SCDV), which is a simple feature construction algorithm. To evaluate the performance for malware detection, we compare the BoW, LSI, Doc2vec, and SCDV models comprehensively. The experimental result with actual macro malware shows that LSI, Doc2vec, and SCDV models are effective to detect macro malware. The performance will maintain at least 2 years. Updating the training models improve the performance significantly. However, the experimental result also shows the possibility that SCDV is suitable for more complicated tasks.

References

1. Bearden, R., Lo, D.C.T.: Automated Microsoft office macro malware detection using machine learning. In: Nie, J.Y., et al. (eds.) IEEE International Conference on Big Data, BigData 2017, Boston, MA, USA, 11–14 December 2017, pp. 4448–4452. IEEE (2017). http://ieeexplore.ieee.org/xpl/mostRecentIssue.jsp?punumber=8241556
2. Kim, S., Hong, S., Oh, J., Lee, H.: Obfuscated VBA macro detection using machine learning. In: DSN, pp. 490–501. IEEE Computer Society (2018). http://ieeexplore.ieee.org/xpl/mostRecentIssue.jsp?punumber=8415926
3. Mekala, D., Gupta, V., Paranjape, B., Karnick, H.: SCDV: sparse composite document vectors using soft clustering over distributional representations. In: Palmer, M., Hwa, R., Riedel, S. (eds.) Proceedings of the 2017 Conference on Empirical Methods in Natural Language Processing, EMNLP 2017, Copenhagen, Denmark, 9–11 September 2017, pp. 659–669. Association for Computational Linguistics (2017). http://aclweb.org/anthology/D17-1
4. Mimura, M., Miura, H.: Detecting unseen malicious VBA macros with NLP techniques. JIP **27**, 555–563 (2019). https://doi.org/10.2197/ipsjjip.27.555
5. Mimura, M., Ohminami, T.: Towards efficient detection of malicious VBA macros with LSI. In: Attrapadung, N., Yagi, T. (eds.) IWSEC 2019. LNCS, vol. 11689, pp. 168–185. Springer, Cham (2019). https://doi.org/10.1007/978-3-030-26834-3_10

A High-Performance Hybrid Blockchain System for Traceable IoT Applications

Xu Wang[1,2]([✉]), Ping Yu[1,3], Guangsheng Yu[1,2], Xuan Zha[1,4], Wei Ni[5],
Ren Ping Liu[1,2], and Y. Jay Guo[1]

[1] Global Big Data Technologies Centre, University of Technology Sydney,
Sydney, Australia
{Xu.Wang-1,Guangsheng.Yu,RenPing.Liu,Jay.Guo}@uts.edu.au
{Ping.Yu-2,Xuan.Zha}@student.uts.edu.au
[2] Food Agility CRC Ltd., 81 Broadway, Ultimo, NSW 2007, Australia
[3] State Key Laboratory of Networking and Switch Technology,
Beijing University of Posts and Telecommunications, Beijing, China
[4] China Academy of Information and Communications Technology, Beijing, China
[5] Data61, CSIRO, Sydney, Australia
Wei.Ni@data61.csiro.au

Abstract. Blockchain, as an immutable distributed ledger, can be the
key to realize secure and trustworthy IoT applications. However, existing blockchains can hardly achieve high-performance and high-security
for large-scale IoT applications simultaneously. In this paper, we propose a hyper blockchain architecture combining the security of public
blockchains with the efficiency of private blockchains. An IoT anchoring smart contract is proposed to anchor private IoT blockchains into
a public blockchain. An IoT device management smart contract is also
designed to trace sensory data. A comprehensive analysis reveals that
the proposed hybrid blockchain system can achieve the performance of
private blockchains and resist tampering.

Keywords: Blockchain · Internet of Things · Smart contract

1 Introduction

The Internet-of-Things (IoT) technology has been digitizing the physical world
with ubiquitous smart devices [1]. The IoT data in centralized IoT systems are
exposed to various threats, e.g., natural disasters and cyber-attacks. Meanwhile,
the centralized IoT system cannot guarantee data transparency and therefore,
goes against IoT data sharing among multiple parties. By storing data in blocks
with their hash values chained in a peer-to-peer network, the blockchain technology is able to provide immutable, transparent and trustworthy ledger services
for IoT applications [1]. The blockchain technology has been employed in IoT as
the root of trust, e.g., access control [2] and data securing [3].

A significant challenge of applying the blockchain technology into IoT applications is the trade-off between performance and security [4]. To be specific,

© Springer Nature Switzerland AG 2019
J. K. Liu and X. Huang (Eds.): NSS 2019, LNCS 11928, pp. 721–728, 2019.
https://doi.org/10.1007/978-3-030-36938-5_47

blockchains can be divided into private (consortium) blockchains, e.g., Hyperledger Fabric [5], and public blockchains, e.g., Ethereum [6]. Running in small-scale networks, private blockchains are able to provide high capacity and low latency services but can only tolerate limited failures or attacks. For example, Fabric can achieve 3,500 transactions per second with a latency of less than one second [5]. Public blockchains, on the contrary, can tolerate large-scale failures but can only provide low capacity and long delay. For example, Bitcoin can only accept seven transactions per second and needs a confirmation time of 10 min [1].

In this paper, we propose a hybrid blockchain system combining the advantages of public blockchains and private blockchains. The proposed hybrid blockchain system is able to achieve the capacity of thousands of transactions per second with a latency of seconds based on the private blockchain technology. The hybrid blockchain system can achieve tamper-proof of existing blocks and stop a limited number of victim nodes from creating forged blocks and fake anchoring proof. An IoT device registration and revocation smart contract is developed to ensure the traceability of IoT sensory data and prevent forged IoT data. We carry out a comprehensive analysis of the performance and security of the hybrid blockchain system. Our analysis indicates that the hybrid blockchain system can achieve the performance of private blockchains and resist tampering even all the IoT blockchain miners are compromised.

The rest of the paper is organized as follows. In Sect. 2, the related works are surveyed, followed by the proposed hybrid blockchain system in Sect. 3. A comprehensive analysis of the hybrid blockchain system is carried out in Sect. 4, followed by the conclusions in Sect. 5.

2   Related Work

As pieces of computer code running on top of blockchain, smart contract translates various assets, such as IoT devices and digital assets, into virtual identities in blockchain, and enables them to interact with other assets [7]. Smart contract technology plays an important role in providing authentication rules, managing and securing IoT data [8] in an automatic manner.

Blockchain has been introduced into IoT applications for access control [2], data securing [3], etc. A smart contract was developed in [2]. The smart contract allowed managers to define access control policy for IoT data. In [3], a secured IoT data storage system was presented over a blockchain. Specifically, the data was stored in Distributed Hash Tables (DHTs) while the pointer to the DHT storage address was secured in a blockchain. The blockchain also took charge of the access control of the IoT data.

The combination of public blockchains and private blockchains can achieve the security of the public blockchain with the efficiency and confidentiality of the private blockchain [9–11]. In [9], the private blockchain was introduced to verify the accuracy of IoT data and broadcast transactions, while the public blockchain was used to verify consistency and store data. A hybrid blockchain system combining a public blockchain and private blockchains was developed in [10]. The public blockchain was introduced as external monitors to store public information, e.g., geolocation information from trucks. The private blockchains were used for sensitive information, e.g., shipment information.

By utilizing the immutability of public blockchains, data can be anchored to a public blockchain to create a timestamp proof [12]. The anchoring technology was further extended to IoT applications [2,3,13,14]. For example, IoT devices were clustered into groups where the header nodes signed the IoT data centrally and attached the data to the public blockchain directly [14].

3 Hybrid Blockchain System

3.1 Overview

The proposed hybrid blockchain system consists of a public blockchain and multiple IoT blockchains, as shown in Fig. 1. The hybrid blockchain system provides a trusted and reliable IoT data storage service that only the sensory data from registered IoT devices can be recorded and verified.

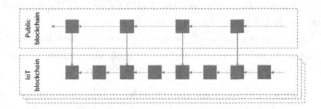

Fig. 1. The proposed hybrid blockchain system.

The public blockchain is considered to be trustworthy and used as the root of trust for IoT blockchains. This is a practical assumption because popular Proof-of-Work (PoW) blockchains can resist attacks with less 25% of the total computing power [15]. The public blockchain takes in charge of low-frequent functions, e.g., IoT blockchain initialization and IoT blockchain anchoring, by running smart contracts. As a public popular blockchain platform, Ethereum can be a good choice for the public blockchain, which has been widely adopted in researches [6,16].

IoT blockchains can be private blockchains and run at high speeds for high-capacity and low-latency IoT services. IoT blockchains adopt consortium consensus protocols, e.g., Practical Byzantine Fault-Tolerant (PBFT) [17]. Each IoT blockchain, consisting of miners and IoT devices, can be set up and maintained by a consortium. The IoT devices collect and send sensory data to the IoT blockchain in the form of transactions. The miners are requested to be registered in the public blockchain and managed by participators of the IoT blockchain. The miners validate IoT transactions and generate blocks in IoT blockchain.

All the nodes, including IoT blockchain miners and IoT devices, have their unique public/private keys and can be identified by their corresponding public keys (or the equivalent blockchain addresses). The private keys, with the assumption of absolute security, are the foundation of blockchain security and prevent identity forging attacks [16]. Note that, miners of an IoT blockchain use the same pairs of public/private keys across the public blockchain and IoT blockchain.

The IoT blockchain blocks are anchored to the public blockchain periodically with a predefined interval of t to improve data integrity. This is achieved by calculating the hash values of the anchoring blocks in the IoT blockchain and then registering the hash values on the public blockchain. In order to stop attackers from forging and/or stopping the blockchain anchoring, a vote-based consensus protocol is proposed over smart contracts.

3.2 Steps to Run an IoT Blockchain

IoT Blockchain Registration. Let m denote the number of IoT blockchain miners. An IoT blockchain is registered on the public blockchain first before starting the IoT blockchain. This is realized by a smart contract on the public blockchain. The smart contract stores the IoT blockchain ID, hash of the genesis block, and a list of IoT blockchain miners.

The IoT blockchain registration needs to be confirmed by all the miners of the IoT blockchain. In other words, the IoT registration smart contract needs m different confirmations and cannot tolerate any failure.

IoT Devices Registration and Revocation. IoT devices need to be registered on the IoT blockchain before sending sensory data. The devices are identified by their blockchain addresses/public keys. The public keys of IoT devices are registered by the IoT blockchain miners for the verification of IoT transactions. The IoT revocation also needs to be confirmed by IoT blockchain miners. The private keys of IoT devices can only be seen by the IoT devices, which suppresses forged transactions.

Suppose that the IoT device registration/revocation can tolerate τ_m failures and needs at least $(m - \tau_m)$ confirmations. The threshold τ_m can be defined by the IoT consortium to trade off between security and failure tolerance. The registration and revocation of IoT devices can be realized by an IoT management smart contract on the IoT blockchain. The smart contract storing IoT blockchain miners and registered IoT devices can only be called by IoT blockchain miners.

IoT Transaction Generation. The IoT devices generate transactions by embedding sensory data in the data field of the transactions, sign the transactions with their private keys and send the signed transactions to IoT blockchain miners.

IoT Blockchain Growing. The IoT blockchain miners collect IoT transactions and then verify the senders by checking whether the senders are registered in the IoT management smart contract. If the transactions are from registered IoT devices, the transactions are kept for further mining. Otherwise, the transactions will be dropped by the miners.

The IoT blockchain miners then run consensus protocols to mine transactions into blocks. The miners also anchor the IoT blockchain into the public blockchain by sending the hash values of check blocks with a predefined interval to the smart contract in the public blockchain. The hash of the check block in the IoT blockchain must be consistent with the registered block in the public blockchain. The verification process can be adopted as a part of the block consensus protocol.

Suppose that the IoT blockchain anchoring can tolerate τ_r malicious miners and needs at least $(m - \tau_r)$ different confirmations. The threshold τ_r is defined by IoT blockchain miners to trade off between integrity and failure tolerance.

IoT Sensory Data Verification. The proposed hybrid blockchain system realizes a chain of trust where the trust is passed from the public blockchain to IoT transactions through the IoT blockchain anchoring contract, IoT blockchain miners, and the IoT device management contract.

To verify an IoT transaction, the examiner first verifies the latest check block and the IoT blockchain miners with the help of the IoT anchoring smart contract on the public blockchain. The examiner then checks the identity of the sender of the IoT transaction with the IoT device management contract on the IoT blockchain at the height of the IoT transaction. The examiner lastly checks the signature of the IoT transaction. The IoT transaction is trustworthy if all the above steps are verified successfully.

3.3 Smart Contracts

We propose an IoT blockchain anchoring contract on the public blockchain to connect the public blockchain and IoT blockchain and an IoT device management contract on the IoT blockchain for IoT device registration and revocation.

IoT Blockchain Anchoring Contract. This contract provides blockchain registration and anchoring service for a single IoT blockchain. An IoT blockchain can be registered with its IoT blockchain ID, the hash value of the genesis block and miners. The contract needs to be deployed on the public blockchain by one of the miners. The IoT blockchain ID, the hash value of the genesis block and miner list can be hard-coded into the smart contract. In this way, the other IoT blockchain miners only need to give approval to the contract rather than pass all the data to the contract for registration.

Functions in the IoT blockchain anchoring contract can be given as follows.

1. *IoT blockchain confirmation function:* This function manages the state of the IoT blockchain. The smart contract sets the state of the IoT blockchain as "pending" by default. The contract keeps a list of predefined IoT blockchain miners and their states. When all the miners have confirmed the IoT blockchain, the contract marks the IoT blockchain as "running".
2. *IoT block anchoring function:* This function implements the block anchoring service. The smart contract stores an object, including a block index, a block

state, callers and the block hash values from the callers, for an anchored block. After the smart contract has received $(m - \tau_r)$ confirmations from different miners with the same block index, block hash value, the block state is updated to be "registered".

IoT Device Management Contract. This smart contract manages IoT devices with their blockchain address. This contract is deployed in the genesis block of the IoT blockchain by one of the miners. The contract provides IoT device registration and revocation services by two functions. This smart contract only accepts function calls from IoT blockchain miners. We assume that these two functions are independent and can tolerate τ_m failures. In other words, both IoT registration and revocation need $(m - \tau_m)$ approvals from different IoT blockchain miners.

1. *IoT device registration function:* This function collects verification about IoT devices from IoT blockchain miners and then registers the IoT devices into the IoT blockchain. In the first time that an IoT device uploads IoT data to the IoT blockchain, it notifies its IoT blockchain address to all the IoT miners. The IoT miners call the IoT device registration function and pass the IoT blockchain address of the IoT device to the smart contract for the registration of the IoT device.

   If this function is called with a new IoT blockchain address, the contract creates a new IoT object containing the blockchain address, the default "unconfirmed" state, and the caller address. If this function is called with an existing IoT blockchain address, the contract first adds the caller into the corresponding IoT object. If the address is confirmed by $(m - \tau_m)$ different miners, the state of the IoT blockchain address is updated as "registered".

2. *IoT device revocation function:* This function collects IoT device revocation requests from IoT blockchain miners and updates the states of IoT devices. The IoT blockchain miners should reach consensus to revoke an IoT device. The IoT miners then call the IoT device revocation function and pass the IoT blockchain address of the IoT device to the smart contract.

   In the case that this function is called with an unknown IoT blockchain address, the smart contract just ignores the function call. In the case that this function is called with a registered IoT blockchain address for the first time, the smart contract adds a "pending" state and the caller address to the corresponding IoT object in the smart contract. In the case that the function is called to update a "pending" address, the smart contract adds the caller to the IoT object. If the revocation request for an IoT blockchain address is confirmed by $(m - \tau_m)$ different miners, the smart contract removes the IoT object of the IoT blockchain address.

4   System Analysis

4.1   Performance Analysis

The performance of IoT blockchain is upper bounded by the performance of its consensus protocol. Between block anchoring, the IoT blockchain can achieve the performance of the consensus protocol. For example, the IoT blockchain can use the consensus protocol realized in the FastFabric blockchain with the capacity of up to 20,000 transactions per second [18].

When a block is anchored to the public blockchain, the IoT blockchain needs to temporarily synchronize with the public blockchain. Thus, the performance of the IoT blockchain is reduced around check blocks. However, long block anchoring intervals can have a negative impact on the IoT blockchain security, as will be analyzed in Sect. 4.2.

4.2   Security Analysis

We assume that the public blockchain is trustworthy and cannot be tampered. The IoT blockchain has been confirmed by all the IoT blockchain miners. Attackers can temporarily control v IoT blockchain miners at the same time. In this paper, we analyze the case that IoT device registration and block registration follow the same failure tolerance of the consensus protocol, i.e., $\tau = \tau_c = \tau_m = \tau_r$. Other cases can be similarly analyzed.

Stopping Services. We first analyze the attack that victim miners stop working. We can have the following conclusions. (a) When $v \leq \tau$, the IoT blockchain can tolerate the failure and keep on growing and anchoring blocks into the public chain, and IoT devices can register in or revoke from the IoT blockchain; (b) When $v > \tau$, the IoT blockchain cannot grow, and IoT device cannot register in or revoke from the IoT blockchain.

Tampering Existing Transactions and Blocks. The attackers cannot tamper existing IoT transactions in the name of registered IoT devices. This is because the IoT transactions are signed with the private keys of IoT devices, and the private keys are kept by their owners. The tampered transactions, if any, cannot pass the signature verification. When $v < (m - \tau)$, attackers cannot tamper any existing block in the IoT blockchain. When $(m - \tau) \leq v \leq m$, attackers can tamper existing blocks after the last check block, e.g., forking the IoT chain and dropping transactions in existing blocks. The attackers cannot tamper any block before the last check block because the blocks are secured in the public blockchain by the anchoring.

IoT Devices Registration and Revocation. (a) When $v < (m - \tau)$, attackers cannot register any IoT device nor revoke IoT devices. (b) When $(m - \tau) \leq v \leq m$, attackers are able to register their own IoT devices and revoke any registered IoT devices.

Forging Transactions and Blocks. (a) When $v < (m - \tau)$, attackers cannot create forged transactions nor blocks. (b) When $(m - \tau) \leq v \leq m$, attackers can register their IoT devices and then create forged new transactions and blocks.

5   Conclusion

In this paper, we designed a hybrid blockchain system which anchors private IoT blockchains to a public blockchain. The proposed hybrid blockchain system is able to provide high capacity and low latency services for IoT application while preserving data integrity with the help of public blockchains. An IoT device management smart contract on IoT blockchain was also proposed for IoT device registration and revocation to improve traceability.

Acknowledgement. This project was partially supported by funding from Food Agility CRC Ltd., funded under the Commonwealth Government CRC Program. The CRC Program supports industry-led collaborations between industry, researchers and the community.

References

1. Wang, X., Zha, X., Ni, W., et al.: Survey on blockchain for Internet of Things. Comput. Commun. **136**, 10–29 (2019)
2. Novo, O.: Blockchain meets IoT: an architecture for scalable access management in IoT. IEEE Internet Things J. **5**(2), 1184–1195 (2018)
3. Li, R., Song, T., et al.: Blockchain for large-scale internet of things data storage and protection. IEEE Trans. Serv. Comput. **12**(5), 762–771 (2019)
4. Wang, X., Guangsheng, Y., et al.: Capacity of blockchain based internet-of-things: testbed and analysis. Internet Things **8**, 100109 (2019)
5. IBM: Behind the architecture of hyperledger fabric. https://www.ibm.com/blogs/research/2018/02/architecture-hyperledger-fabric/
6. Wood, G., et al.: Ethereum: a secure decentralised generalised transaction ledger. Ethereum project yellow paper, vol. 151, pp. 1–32 (2014)
7. Christidis, K., Devetsikiotis, M.: Blockchains and smart contracts for the internet of things. IEEE Access **4**, 2292–2303 (2016)
8. Khan, M.A., Salah, K.: IoT security: review, blockchain solutions, and open challenges. Futur. Gener. Comput. Syst. **82**, 395–411 (2018)
9. Wu, L., Meng, K., et al.: Democratic centralism: a hybrid blockchain architecture and its applications in energy internet. In: 2017 IEEE International Conference on Energy Internet (ICEI), pp. 176–181, April 2017
10. Li, Z., Wu, H., et al.: A hybrid blockchain ledger for supply chain visibility. In: International Symposium on Parallel and Distributed Computing, June 2018
11. Yu, J., Kozhaya, D., et al.: RepuCoin: your reputation is your power. IEEE Trans. Comput. **68**(8), 1225–1237 (2019)
12. Chainpoint. https://chainpoint.org
13. Faizod: Faizod.anchoring. https://faizod.com
14. Dorri, A., Kanhere, S.S., et al.: Towards an optimized blockchain for IoT. In: Proceedings of the 2nd International Conference on IoT Design and Implementation, pp. 173–178. ACM (2017)
15. Natoli, C., Yu, J., et al.: Deconstructing blockchains: a comprehensive survey on consensus, membership and structure (2019)
16. Wang, X., Zha, X., et al.: Attack and defence of ethereum remote APIs. In: 2018 IEEE Globecom Workshops (GC Wkshps), pp. 1–6, December 2018
17. Yu, G., et al.: An optimized round-robin scheduling of speakers for peers-to-peers-based byzantine faulty tolerance. In: 2018 IEEE GC Wkshps, December 2018
18. Gorenflo, C., Lee, S., et al.: Fastfabric: scaling hyperledger fabric to 20, 000 transactions per second. CoRR, abs/1901.00910 (2019)

Author Index

Printed in the United States
By Bookmasters